ENGLISH
DICTIONARY

ENGLISH DICTIONARY

GALLEY PRESS

Published in this edition by Galley Press, an imprint of
W. H. Smith Limited, Registered No. 237811 England.
Trading as W. H. Smith Distributors, St John's House
East Street, Leicester, LE1 6NE.

ISBN 0 86136 041 9

Production services by
Book Production Consultants, Cambridge

Printed and bound in Great Britain by
Richard Clay Ltd, Bungay, Suffolk

A

A, a, *n.* the first letter of the English alphabet.

A, a, *n.* an abbreviation.

A, *n.* a Roman numeral denoting 50 or 500 ; with a bar (Ā), 5,000.

A (unstressed), *indef. art.* one ; any ; some ; each ; used before consonants ; becomes *an* before vowels and *h* mute.

A, *prep.* to, in, at, on, upon, etc., with various significations, as motion, position, state, condition, time ; implying movement.

A- a common English prefix, having various values.

A FLAT (flat), a musical tone half a step below A.

A FLAT MAJOR (ma′jer), a major scale having a signature of four flats.

A MAJOR, a major scale having a signature of three sharps.

A MINOR (mi′ner), a minor key relative to the natural or normal scale and having neither flats nor sharps in its signature.

A1 (a′wun), *adj.* superior ; of the highest class.

AARDVARK (ard′vark), *n.* an African mammal with a long, protrusile, slimy tongue.

AARDWOLF (ard′woolf), *n.* a nocturnal carnivorous mammal of South Africa.

AB (ab), *n.* the fifth month of the Jewish year.

ABACK (a-back′), *adv.* backward ; against the mast ; said of sails ; by surprise.

ABACUS (ab′a-kus), *n.* beads or balls strung upon rods or wires ; used for computation.

ABAFT (a-baft′), *adv. & prep.* toward, or in the direction of, the stern of a ship ; astern.

ABANDON (a-ban′dun), *n.* surrender of one's self to a feeling ; a giving up to natural impulses : *v.t.* to desert ; forsake utterly.

ABANDONED (a-ban′dund), *adj.* given up entirely.

ABANDONMENT (a-ban′dun-ment), *n.* the act of abandoning ; the state of being abandoned.

A-BAS (a-ba′), [Fr.] down with.

ABASE (a-bas′), *v.t.* to humble or degrade ; dishonour.

ABASH (a-bash′), *v.t.* to put to confusion ; confound or make ashamed.

ABATE (a-bat′), *v.t.* to lessen ; suppress : *v.i.* to decrease ; moderate ; subside.

ABATEMENT (a-bat′ment), *n.* the act of abating.

ABATTOIR (a-bat-twar′), *n.* a public slaughter-house.

ABB (ab), *n.* the yarn of the warp in weaving.

ABBE (a-ba′), *n.* a R.C. ecclesiastic ; a curate.

ABBESS (ab′es), *n.* the lady-superior of a convent or nunnery.

ABBEY (ab′i), *n.* an establishment for religious devotees.

ABBREVIATE (ab-bre′vi-at), *v.t.* to shorten, as by contraction of a word, or the omission of words.

ABBREVIATION (ab-bre′vi-a′shun), *n.* the act of shortening ; the state of being abbreviated.

ABBREVIATOR (ab-bre′vi-a-ter), *n.* one who shortens or abbreviates.

ABBREVIATURE (ab-bre′vi-a′tur), *n.* the sign used for contraction.

ABDICATE (ab′di-kat), *v.t.* to give up or withdraw from.

ABDICATION (ab-di-ka′shun), *n.* the act of relinquishment or resignation.

ABDICATOR (ab′di-ka-ter), *n.* one who abdicates or resigns.

ABDOMEN (ab-do′men), *n.* the cavity containing the digestive apparatus or viscera.

ABDOMINAL (ab-dom′i-nal), *adj.* pertaining to the abdomen.

ABDUCE (ab-dus′), *v.t.* to draw away by persuasion or argument.

ABDUCT (ab-dukt′), *v.t.* to carry off by stealth or force ; kidnap.

ABDUCTION (ab-duk'shun), *n.* the act of abducting or kidnapping.

ABDUCTOR (ab-duk'ter), *n.* one who, or that which, abducts.

ABEAM (a-bem'), *adv.* at right angles to the keel of a ship.

ABERRANT (ab-er'ant), *adj.* departing from the usual path, type, or standard.

ABERRATION (ab'er-ra-shun), *n.* the act of departing from the usual path ; mental derangement ; the unequal refraction of rays of light from a lens.

ABET (a-bet'), *v.t.* to encourage ; to aid or assist in the performance of an act.

ABETMENT (a-bet'ment), *n.* the act of abetting.

ABETTOR (a-bet'er), *n.* one who aids or abets.

ABEYANCE (a-ba'ans), *n.* held or kept back.

ABHOR (ab-hor'), *v.t.* to hate ; loathe ; abominate.

ABHORRENCE (ab-hor'ens), *n.* detestation ; extreme hatred.

ABHORRENT (ab-hor'rent), *adj.* detestable ; hateful ; repulsive.

ABIDE (a-bid'), *v.t.* to await ; endure ; withstand ; tolerate : *v.i.* to dwell ; reside.

ABIDING (-ing), *p.adj.* remaining ; steadfast in purpose.

ABILITY (a-bil'i-ti), *n.* power to perform ; skill to achieve ; capability for carrying out ; capacity to devise, receive, retain, or make use of.

ABIOLOGY (ab-i-ol'o-ji), *n.* the study of non-living things.

ABJECT (ab'jekt), *adj.* worthless ; mean.

ABJECTEDNESS (ab-jek'ted-ness), *n.* the act of being cast down.

ABJECTION (ab-jek'shun), *n.* cast away ; degradation.

ABJURATION (ab-ju-ra'shun), *n.* an oath of renunciation, as of allegiance.

ABJURE (ab-jur'), *v.t.* to renounce upon oath.

ABLATION (ab-la'shun), *n.* the act of removal ; a wasting away, as of rock.

ABLAZE (a-blaz'), *adv.* or *adj.* on fire ; well alight ; in a blaze.

ABLE (a'bl), *adj.* possessed of power, means or ability ; qualified ; competent.

ABLE-BODIED (bod'id), *adj.* possessed of physical strength.

ABLEGATE (ab'le-gat), *n.* the envoy sent by the Pope.

ABLOOM (a-bloom'), *adv.* & *adj.* in bloom.

ABLUENT (ab'lu-ent), *adj.* cleansing : *n.* that which cleanses.

ABLUTION (ab-lu'shun), *n.* a washing or cleansing of the body by water.

ABLUTIONARY (ab-lu'shun-a-ri), *adj.* pertaining to cleansing.

ABNEGATE (ab'ne-gat), *v.t.* to refuse ; deny ; reject ; abjure.

ABNEGATION (ab-ne-ga'shun), *n.* an act of self-denial.

ABNEURAL (ab-nu'ral), *adj.* relating to the side of the body farthest from the neural or nervous axis.

ABNORMAL (ab-nor'mal), *adj.* irregular ; deformed ; unnatural.

ABNORMALITY (ab-nor-mal'i-ti), *n.* the state or condition of being abnormal.

ABNORMITY (ab-nor'mi-ti), *n.* deformity ; irregularity.

ABOARD (a-bord'), *adv.* on or within a vessel.

ABODE (a-bod'), *n.* a place of continued residence.

ABOLISH (a-bol'ish), *v.t.* to efface ; do away with ; put an end to.

ABOLITION (ab-o-lish'un), *n.* the act of abolishing.

ABOLITIONISM (ab-o-lish'un-izm), *n.* the doctrine or principles of those advocating the abolition of certain laws or customs.

ABOLITIONIST (ab-o-lish'un-ist), *n.* one who is in favour of the repeal or abolition of some existing law or custom.

ABOMINABLE (a-bom'i-na-bl), *adj.* hateful ; odious ; offensive.

ABOMINATE (a-bom'i-nat), *v.t.* to abhor.

ABOMINATION (a-bom-i-na'shun), *n.* excessive hatred ; the thing abominated.

ABORIGINAL (ab-o-rij'i-nal), *n.* the species of animals or plants presumed to have originated within a given area.

ABORIGINES (ab-o-rij'i-nez), *n. pl.* the first or primitive inhabitants of a country.

ABORTION (a-bor'shun), *n.* untimely birth.

ABORTIONIST (a-bor'shun-ist), *n.* one who is guilty of the crime of procuring a criminal abortion.

ABORTIVE (a-bor'tiv), *adj.* born imperfect; arrested in development; without issue or result.

ABOUND (a-bound'), *v.i.* to have in plenty or abundance.

ABOUT (a-bout'), *adv.* around; on every side.

ABOVE (a-buv'), *adv.* in a higher place; overhead; in heaven; before; besides.

ABOVEBOARD (a-buv'bord), *adj.* & *adv.* in open sight.

ABRACADABRA (ab-ra-ka-da'bra), *n.* a mystical combination of letters in the form of a triangle.

ABRADANT (ab-ra'dant), *n.* substance for abrading or scouring.

ABRADE (ab-rad'), *v.t.* to wear or rub away.

ABRASION (ab-ra'zhun), *n.* the act of wearing or rubbing away; a chafe.

ABREAST (a-brest'), *adv.* side by side; in line with; opposite to; at the same level.

ABRIDGE (a-brij'), *v.t.* to curtail; shorten.

ABRIDGMENT (a-brij'ment), *n.* the state of being contracted or curtailed.

ABROACH (a-broch'), *adv.* & *adj.* letting out; placed in position for yielding the contents.

ABROAD (a-brawd'), *adv.* widely; expansively.

ABROGATE (ab'ro-gat), *v.t.* to abolish, annul, or repeal.

ABROGATION (ab-ro-ga'shun), *n.* the act of abrogating.

ABROGATOR (ab'ro-ga-ter), *n.* one who repeals by authority.

ABRUPT (a-rupt'), *adj.* broken; terminating suddenly; steep; precipitous; rough; unceremonious.

ABRUPTED (ab-rupt'ed), *p.adj.* broken off with suddenness.

ABRUPTION (ab-rup'shun), *n.* a separation with violence; a sudden or abrupt termination.

ABRUPTLY (ab-rupt'ly), *adv.* in an abrupt or sudden manner.

ABSCESS (ab'ses), *n.* a collection of morbid matter or pus in the tissues.

ABSCISSION (ab-sizh'un), *n.* the act of severance.

ABSCOND (ab-skond'), *v.i.* to flee or retire in haste.

ABSENCE (ab'sens), *n.* the state of being absent; the period of being absent.

ABSENT (ab'sent), *adj.* not present; away.

ABSENT (ab-sent'), *v.t.* to retire or keep away from.

ABSENTEE (ab-sen-te'), *n.* one who is absent.

ABSENTLY (ab'sent-li), *adv.* in an abstracted manner.

ABSINTHE (ab'sinth), *n.* wormwood; a bitter liqueur.

ABSOLUTE (ab'so-lut), *adj.* free as to condition; perfect in itself; unlimited in power.

ABSOLUTION (ab-so-lu'shun), *n.* the act of absolving.

ABSOLUTISM (ab'so-lu-tizm), *n.* the state of being absolute.

ABSOLUTIST (ab'so-lut-ist), *n.* a supporter or advocate of absolute government.

ABSOLUTORY (ab-sol'u-to-ri), *adj.* absolving; capable of absolving.

ABSOLVATORY (ab-sol'va-to-ri), *adj.* containing or conferring absolution.

ABSOLVE (ab-solv'), *v.t.* to release or set free.

ABSONANT (ab'so-nant), *adj.* discordant; harsh; unmusical.

ABSORB (ab-sorb'), *v.t.* to drink in; imbibe.

ABSORBABILITY (ab-sorb-a-bil'i-ti), *n.* the state or quality of being absorbable.

ABSORBABLE (ab-sorb'a-bl), *adj.* capable of being absorbed.

ABSORBEFACIENT (ab'sor-be-fa'-shent), *adj.* tending to bring about absorption : *n.* that which causes absorption.

ABSORBENCY (ab-sorb′en-si), *n.* capacity for absorbing.

ABSORBENT (ab-sorb′ent), *adj.* absorbing : *n.* anything which absorbs or takes in nutritive matter.

ABSORBER (er), *n.* that which absorbs ; device for absorbing the shock of a machine in motion.

ABSORPTIOMETER (ab-sorp-shi-om′e-ter), *n.* an instrument to show the amount of gas absorbed by a unit volume of a fluid.

ABSORPTION (ab-sorp′shun), *n.* the process or act of absorbing.

ABSORPTIVE (ab-sorp′tiv), *adj.* having power or capacity for absorption.

ABSORPTIVITY (ab-sorp-tiv′i-ti), *n.* the power of absorption.

ABSTAIN (ab-stan′), *v.t.* to forbear ; refrain ; hold aloof ; keep away from.

ABSTAINER (ab-stan′er), *n.* one who abstains, especially from intoxicants.

ABSTEMIOUS (ab-ste′mi-us), *adj.* moderate and sparing in the use of food and drink.

ABSTENTION (ab-sten′shun), *n.* the act of holding off or abstaining.

ABSTENTIONIST (ab-sten′shun-ist), *n.* one who favours or practises abstention.

ABSTENTIOUS (ab-sten′shus), *adj.* characterized by abstention.

ABSTERGENT (ab-ster′jent), *adj.* possessing cleansing or purging properties.

ABSTERSION (ab-ster′shun), *n.* the act of wiping clean ; the act of cleansing by the use of abstergents.

ABSTERSIVE (ab-ster′siv), *adj.* cleansing ; of the nature or quality of an abstergent.

ABSTINENCE (ab′sti-nens), *n.* the act or practice of abstaining ; self-denial.

ABSTINENT (ab′sti-nent), *adj.* refraining from over-indulgence.

ABSTRACT (ab-strakt′), *v.t.* to take or draw away ; separate ; purloin or steal.

ABSTRACT (ab′strakt), *n.* an epitome ; a summary : *adj.* considered

or conceived apart from its concrete or material nature.

ABSTRACT NOUN (noun), the quality of a noun considered apart from the object to which it belongs.

ABSTRACTED (ab-strakt′ed), *p.adj.* separated ; disjoined ; mentally absent.

ABSTRACTION (ab-strak′shun), *n.* the act of separating or drawing away.

ABSTRACTIONAL (ab-strak′shun-al), *adj.* pertaining to abstraction.

ABSTRACTIONIST (ab-strak′shun-ist), *n.* one who deals with abstractions ; an idealist.

ABSTRACTIVE (ab-strak′tiv), *adj.* having the quality or power of abstraction.

ABSTRUSE (ab-stroos′), *adj.* obscure ; hidden ; difficult of comprehension.

ABSURD (ab-serd′), *adj.* contrary to reason.

ABSURDITY (ab-serd′i-ti), *n.* the state of being absurd ; that which is absurd.

ABUNDANCE (a-bun′dans), *n.* in great plenty.

ABUNDANT (a-bun′dant), *adj.* plentiful.

ABUSE (a-buz′), *v.t.* to use ill ; treat rudely or wrongfully.

ABUSE (a-bus′), *n.* ill-treatment ; the excessive or injudicious use of anything.

ABUSIVE (a-bu′siv), *adj.* practising abuse.

ABUT (a-but′), *v.i.* to border upon ; touch at one end ; terminate.

ABUTILON (ab-u′ti-lon), *n.* a genus of plants of the mallow family.

ABUTMENT (a-but′ment), *n.* that which borders upon something else ; the solid structure which supports the extremity of a bridge or arch.

ABYSM (a-bizm′), *n.* an abyss, a gulf.

ABYSMAL (a-biz′mal), *adj.* pertaining to an abyss ; bottomless.

ABYSS (a-bis′), *n.* a bottomless gulf ; that which is unfathomable ; hell.

ACACIA (a-ka′shi-a), *n.* a genus of flowering trees and shrubs.

ACADEMIC (ak-a-dem′ik), **ACADEMICAL** (-al), *adj.* belonging or appertaining to a college or university.

ACADEMICALLY (-li), *adv.* in an academical manner.

ACADEMICIAN (ak-a-de-mish'an), *n.* a member of an academy or society.

ACADEMY (a-kad'e-mi), *n.* a private school or seminary for the teaching of the higher branches of education.

ACANACEOUS (ak'a-na'shus), *adj.* prickly ; pointed ; sharp ; rough.

ACANTHACEÆ (ak-an-tha'se-e), *n.pl.* a large family of trees and shrubs.

ACANTHACEOUS (-shus), *adj.* of the family Acanthaceæ.

ACANTHINE (a-kan'thin), *adj.* pertaining to the plant acanthus.

ACANTHOID (-thoid), *adj.* spiny ; formed like a spine.

ACANTHUS (a-kan'thus), *n.* a plant having sharp-toothed leaves ; ornamentation adopted in the capitals of the Corinthian and Composite orders of architecture.

ACARID (ak'a-rid), *n.* one of the Acarida.

ACARIDA (a-kar'i-da), *n.pl.* an order which includes mites and ticks and other minute parasites.

ACARUS (ak'a-rus), *n.* [*pl.* acari (ri)], a genus which includes many species of mites.

ACATALEPSY (-si), *n.* the state of not being able to comprehend.

ACATASTASIA (ak'a-tas-ta'zhia), *n.* condition of not being normal.

ACAUDAL (a-kaw'dal), *adj.* without a tail.

ACCEDE (ak-sed'), *v.i.* to come or attain to ; to agree or yield to.

ACCELERANDO (ak-chel-e-ran'do), *adv.* a musical term indicating faster tempo.

ACCELERATE (ak-sel'er-at), *v.t.* to hasten ; to cause to move or progress faster.

ACCELERATION (ak-sel-er-a'shun), *n.* the act of accelerating.

ACCELERATIVE (ak-sel'er-a-tiv), *adj.* hastening ; tending to increase velocity.

ACCELERATOR (ak-sel'er-a-ter), *n.* that which quickens or accelerates.

ACCELERATORY (ak-sel'er-a-to-ri),

adj. accelerating or tending to accelerate.

ACCENT (ak'sent), *n.* the stress laid by the voice upon a particular syllable or word so as to render it more prominent than the rest ; the mark or character used in writing and printing to express the manner of pronouncing of a word.

ACCENTUAL (ak-sen'tu-al), *adj.* belonging to accent ; rhythmical.

ACCENTUATE (ak-sen'tu-at), *v.t.* to speak, pronounce or mark with an accent.

ACCENTUATION (ak-sen-tu-a'shun), *n.* the act of accentuating by stress or accent.

ACCEPT (ak-sept'), *v.t.* to take or receive with approbation.

ACCEPTABILITY (ak-sep'ta-bil'i-ti), **ACCEPTABLENESS** (ak-sep'ta-bl-nes), *n.* the quality of being acceptable or agreeable.

ACCEPTABLE (ak-sep'ta-bl), *adj.* capable of giving pleasure.

ACCEPTANCE (ak-sep'tans), *n.* the act of accepting ; the subscription to a bill of exchange.

ACCEPTANT (-tant), *n.* one who accepts.

ACCEPTATION (ak-sep-ta'-shun), *n.* the act of accepting, or state of being accepted or acceptable.

ACCEPTER, ACCEPTOR (ak-sep'-ter), *n.* one who accepts.

ACCESS (ak'ses), *n.* admittance or approach to a person or place.

ACCESSARY (ak-ses'a-ri), *n.* a person who aids in a subordinate manner.

ACCESSIBILITY (ak-ses-i-bil'i-ti), *n.* the condition of being accessible.

ACCESSIBLE (ak-ses'i-bl), *adj.* capable of being approached ; easy of access.

ACCESSION (ak-sesh'un), *n.* a coming to, as by succession or by right ; entrance or attainment.

ACCESSIONAL (ak-sesh'un-al), *adj.* additional ; pertaining to an accession.

ACCESSORIAL (ak-ses-o'ri-al), *adj.* pertaining to an accessory.

ACCESSORY (ak-ses'o-ri), *adj.* aiding ; contributing to result or effect :

n. one who aids in the commission of a felony.

ACCIDENCE (ak'si-dens), *n.* the portion of grammar which deals with the inflections of words.

ACCIDENT (ak'si-dent), *n.* an event which is unexpected, or the cause of which was unforeseen.

ACCIDENT INSURANCE (in-shur'-ans), *n.* an insurance which indemnifies the policy holder in case of accident.

ACCIDENTAL (ak-si-den'tal), *adj.* happening by chance or unexpectedly ; fortuitous ; non-essential.

ACCIDENTALLY (-li), *adv.* in an accidental manner.

ACCLAIM (a-klam'), *v.i.* to shout applause : *n.* a shout of joy or praise.

ACCLAMATION (ak-kla-ma'shun), *n.* a shout of applause ; an outburst of joy, or praise ; the adoption of a resolution *viva voce.*

ACCLAMATORY (a-klam'a-to-ri), *adj.* expressing joy or applause by acclamation.

ACCLIMATE (a-kli'mat), *v.t.* to accustom a person to a foreign climate.

ACCLIMATION (ak-kli-ma'shun), *n.* the process of acclimatizing, or the state of being inured to a foreign climate.

ACCLIMATIZE (a-kli'ma-tiz), *v.t.* & *v.i.* to accustom or become accustomed to a foreign climate.

ACCLIVITY (a-kliv'i-ti), *n.* an ascent or upward slope of the earth.

ACCLIVOUS (a-kli'vus), *adj.* rising or sloping, as a hillside.

ACCOLADE (ak'o-lad), *n.* an embrace on the conferring of knighthood.

ACCOLATED (ak'ko-la-ted), *p.adj.* displaying two or more profile heads.

ACCOMMODATE (a-kom'mo-dat), *v.t.* to adapt or make fit or suitable ; adjust ; settle ; supply or furnish ; do a favour to.

ACCOMMODATING (-da-ting), *p.adj.* obliging ; adapting one's self to the desires of others.

ACCOMMODATION (-da'shun), *n.* the act of accommodating ; or the state of being accommodated.

ACCOMPANIMENT (a-kum'pa-ni-

ment), *n.* something which is added to, or attends the original or principal thing by way of ornament.

ACCOMPANIST (a-kum'pa-nist), *n.* one who plays an accompaniment.

ACCOMPANY (a-kum'pa-ni), *v.t.* to keep company with ; escort ; join in movement or action.

ACCOMPLICE (a-kom'plis), *n.* an associate in crime.

ACCOMPLISH (a-kom'plish), *v.t.* to bring to completion, or to an issue.

ACCOMPLISHED (a-kom'plisht), *p.adj.* finished ; perfected ; possessed of complete qualifications.

ACCOMPLISHMENT (a-kom'-plish-ment), *n.* the completion of an act or undertaking ; an acquirement or qualification in art or manners.

ACCORD (a-kord'), *v.t.* & *v.i.* to be in agreement with ; reconcile ; agree ; give ; grant.

ACCORDANCE (a-kord'ans), *n.* the state of being in harmony or accord.

ACCORDANT (a-kord'ant), *adj.* corresponding ; of the same mind.

ACCORDING (a-kord'ing), *p.adj.* agreeing ; harmonious : *adv.* in accordance (*with*) or agreeably (*to*).

ACCORDION (a-kord'i-un), *n.* a small wind instrument.

ACCOST (a-kost'), *v.t.* to draw near, or come face to face with ; speak to ; salute.

ACCOUCHEMENT (a-koosh'mang), *n.* delivery in childbed.

ACCOUCHEUR (a-koo-sher'), *n.* a medical man who attends confinement cases.

ACCOUCHEUSE (a-koo-shuz'), *n.* a midwife ; a female obstetrician.

ACCOUNT (a-kount'), *v.t.* compute ; count : *v.i.* to assign an explanation [with *for*] ; take into consideration ; relate : *n.* a financial statement or memorandum ; a narrative.

ACCOUNT CURRENT (kur'ent), *n.* the statement of account between two or more persons.

ACCOUNT RENDERED (ren'der'd), *n.* an account presented by a creditor to a debtor.

ACCOUNTABILITY (a-kount-a-bil'-

i-ti), *n.* the state of being liable or accountable.

ACCOUNTABLE (a-kount'a-bl), *adj.* answerable; responsible; liable to be called to account.

ACCOUNTABLY (-bli), *adv.* in an accountable manner.

ACCOUNTANCY (a-koun'tan-si), *n.* the practice of an accountant.

ACCOUNTANT (a-koun'tant), *n.* one skilled in the keeping or examination of accounts: *adj.* giving account; responsible.

ACCOUTREMENTS (a-koo'ter-ments), *n.pl.* equipage; dress; military equipments.

ACCREDIT (ak-kred'it), *v.t.* to give credit to; have confidence in; authorize.

ACCRESCENT (a-kres'ent), *adj.* increasing; growing.

ACCRETE (a-kret'), *v.i.* to adhere; be added: *v.t.* to cause to grow or unite.

ACCRETION (a-kre'shun), *n.* increase by natural growth; the addition of external parts.

ACCRETIVE (a-kre'tiv), *adj.* adding to or increasing by growth.

ACCROACHMENT (a-kroch'ment), *n.* the act of accroaching; usurpation.

ACCRUE (a-kroo'), *v.i.* to happen or to result naturally as an increment, as of profit or loss.

ACCUMBENT (a-kum'bent), *adj.* reclining or recumbent.

ACCUMULATE (a-ku'mu-lat), *v.t.* to collect or bring together; amass; heap up: *v.i.* to increase in size, number, or quantity.

ACCUMULATION (a-ku-mu-la'-shun), *n.* the act of accumulating or amassing; the addition of interest to principal; the mass accumulated.

ACCUMULATIVE (a-ku'mu-la-tiv), *adj.* tending to accumulate.

ACCUMULATOR (a-ku'mu-la-ter), *n.* one who or that which accumulates; an apparatus for equalising pressure; an electric storage battery.

ACCURACY (ak'ku-ra-si), *n.* the quality of being accurate; exactness or correctness.

ACCURATE (ak'ku-rat), *adj.* in exact conformity with the truth; free from error.

ACCURSED (a-ker'sed), **ACCURST** (a-kerst'), *p.adj.* under or subject to a curse; doomed to destruction; detestable.

ACCUSABLE (a-kuz'a-bl), *adj.* liable to be censured or accused.

ACCUSATION (ak-ku-za'shun), *n.* a charge or imputation of wrongdoing.

ACCUSATIVE (a-ku'za-tiv), *adj.* accusing: *n.* the fourth case in Latin and Greek nouns denoting the object of a transitive verb.

ACCUSATORY (a-ku'za-to-ri), **ACCUSATORIAL** (-to'ri-al), *adj.* accusing, or containing an accusation.

ACCUSATORIALLY (-li), *adv.* in an accusatorial manner.

ACCUSE (a-kuz'), *v.t.* to charge with guilt or blame.

ACCUSER (a-kuz'er), *n.* one who accuses.

ACCUSTOM (a-kus'tum), *v.t.* to habituate or familiarize by custom or use.

ACCUSTOMED (a-kus'tumd), *p.adj.* frequent; usual; often practised.

ACE (as), *n.* a unit; in playing cards and dice, a card or die marked with a single pip; an aviator destroying five enemy airplanes.

ACENTRIC (a-sen'trik), *adj.* away from the centre; having no centre.

ACEPHALA (a-sef'a-la), *n.pl.* a class of Mollusca which includes all ordinary bi-valves, as the oyster, having no distinct head.

ACEPHALOUS (a-sef'a-lus), *adj.* headless; without a leader; an ovary of a plant that has its style springing from the base instead of the apex.

ACER (ah-ser), *n.* a genus of trees of which the maple is the type.

ACERACEÆ (as-e-ra'se-e), *n.pl.* the maple family of trees.

ACERBITY (a-ser'bi-ti), *n.* sourness; sharpness; harshness or severity of temper or expression.

ACERVATE (a-ser'vat), *adj.* formed in heaps; growing in clusters.

ACESCENCE (a-ses'ens), *n.* a state of sourness or acidity.

ACESCENT (-ent), *adj.* turning sour ; becoming acid.

ACETATE (as'e-tat), *n.* a salt of acetic acid.

ACETATED (as'e-tat-ed), *p.adj.* combined with acetic acid.

ACETIC (a-se'tik), *adj.* pertaining to vinegar; sour.

ACETIC ACID (a-se'tik & a-set'ik as'id), *n.* a clear liquid, with a strong acid taste and peculiar sharp smell ; present in a dilute form in vinegar.

ACETIFY (a-set'i-fi), *v.t.* to turn into vinegar ; make acetous.

ACETIMETER (as-e-tim'e-ter), *n.* an instrument for gauging the strength or purity of vinegar or acetic acid.

ACETIN (as'e-tin), *n.* a combination of acetic acid with glycerine.

ACETONE (as'e-ton), *n.* a clear volatile liquid, composed of carbon, hydrogen, and oxygen.

ACETOUS (a-se'tus), *adj.* of the quality of acid ; sour ; producing vinegar.

ACETUM (a-se'tum), *n.* vinegar ; a drug prepared from acetic acid.

ACETYLENE (a-set'i-len), *n.* a brilliant illuminating gas, produced by subjecting calcium carbide to the action of water.

ACHE (ak), *n.* pain, more or less continuous : *v.i.* to suffer, or be in pain.

ACHIEVABLE (a-che'va-bl), *adj.* possible to achieve ; capable of being performed.

ACHIEVE (a-chev'), *v.t.* to perform, carry out, accomplish ; to gain or bring to a successful issue by an effort ; *v.i.* to bring about a desired result.

ACHIEVEMENT (a-chev'ment), *n.* the act of achieving ; accomplishment.

ACHILLES TENDON (a-kil'ez ten'-dun), the powerful tendon placed in, and moving, the heel.

ACHING (ak'ing), *p.adj.* enduring or causing pain ; painful: *adv.* with aching ; painfully.

ACHROMATIC (ak-ro-mat'ik), *adj.* free from colouration ; transmitting light without decomposition.

ACHROMATIC LENS (lenz), a lens free from chromatic aberration.

ACHROMATIZE (a-kro'ma-tiz), *v.t.* to deprive of the power of transmitting colour ; to render achromatic.

ACID (as'id), *adj.* sour and sharp or biting to the taste, as vinegar : *n.* the name applied to a large number of compounds.

ACIDITY (a-sid'i-ti), *n.* the quality of being acid or sour.

ACIDOSIS (as-i-do'sis), *n.* an excess of acid in the system.

ACID TEST, a thorough test to determine true value, as of gold.

ACIDULATE (a-sid'u-lat), *v.t.* to render slightly acid.

ACIDULENT (a-sid'u-lent), *adj.* somewhat acid ; tart ; peevish.

ACIDULOUS (a-sid'u-lus), *adj.* slightly sour ; subacid ; sharp-tempered.

ACIFORM (as'i-form), *adj.* needle-shaped.

ACINUS (as'i-nus), *n.* one of a cluster ; a berry ; a grapeseed.

ACKNOWLEDGE (ak-nol'ej), *v.t.* to admit or own to be true ; recognize ; confess ; admit the receipt of.

ACKNOWLEDGMENT (ak-nol'ej-ment), *n.* the act of acknowledging ; the admission or recognition of a truth ; confession ; the expression of appreciation of a favour or benefit conferred ; a receipt.

ACLINIC (a-klin'ik), *adj.* without inclination.

ACLINIC-LINE (-lin), *n.* the imaginary point near the equator where the magnetic needle has no dip.

ACME (ak'me), *n.* the highest point ; the utmost reach ; the crisis of a disease.

ACNE (ak'ne), *n.* a pustular eruption of the body, chiefly confined to the face, shoulders and chest.

ACOLYTE (ak'o-lit), *n.* the highest of the minor orders in the R.C. Church.

ACOMIA (a-ko'mi-a), *n.* absence of hair, usually due to skin disease.

ACONITE (ak'o-nit), *n.* monk's-hood ; the drug prepared from the plant.

ACORN (a'korn), *n.* the fruit of the

oak ; a conical piece of wood affixed to the spindle above a vane at the masthead.

ACOUMETER (a-kou'me-ter), *n.* an instrument to test the power of hearing.

ACOUSTIC (a-kous'tik), *adj.* belonging to the science of sound.

ACOUSTICS (a-kous'tiks), *n.* the science of sound.

ACOUSTOMETER (ak-ous-tom'e-ter), *n.* an apparatus for testing the acoustic properties of an auditorium.

ACQUAINT (a-kwant'), *v.t.* to familiarize or make one's self conversant with ; furnish information.

ACQUAINTANCE (a-kwant'ans), *n.* the state of being acquainted with a person or subject ; a person with whom one is acquainted.

ACQUAINTED (a-kwan'ted), *p.adj.* having personal knowledge.

ACQUIESCE (ak-wi-es'), *v.i.* to agree ; comply passively.

ACQUIESCENCE (ak-wi-es'ens), *n.* the act of submitting ; silent assent.

ACQUIRABLE (a-kwir'a-bl), *adj.* capable of being acquired.

ACQUIRE (a-kwir'), *v.t.* to gain or obtain possession of by one's own physical or intellectual exertions.

ACQUISITION (ak-kwi-zish'un), *n.* the act of acquiring ; the object acquired.

ACQUISITIVE (ak-wiz'i-tiv), *adj.* having a propensity to acquire ; greedily disposed.

ACQUISITIVENESS (-nes), *n.* the propensity to acquire.

ACQUIT (a-kwit'), *v.t.* to release ; set free ; discharge ; to pronounce not guilty.

ACQUITTAL (a-kwit'al), *n.* the act of releasing or acquitting.

ACQUITTANCE (a-kwit'ans), *n.* a discharge or release from debt or other liability.

ACRE (a'ker), *n.* a superficial measure of land containing 4,840 sq. yds.

ACREAGE (a'ker-aj), *n.* the number of acres in a tract of land.

ACRE-FOOT (a'ker-foot), *n.* the amount of water necessary to cover one acre to the depth of one foot.

ACRID (ak'rid), *adj.* sharp or biting to the taste.

ACRIMONIOUS (ak-ri-mo'ni-us), *adj.* bitter ; caustic ; stinging.

ACRIMONY (ak'ri-mo-ni), *n.* sharpness of temper ; bitterness of expression.

ACROBAT (ak'ro-bat), *n.* a performer on the tight-rope ; one who practises tumbling, vaulting, trapezing, etc.

ACROPOLIS (a-krop'o-lis), *n.* the highest part or citadel of a Grecian city, as that of Athens ; hence, a citadel.

ACROSS (a-kros'), *adv.* & *prep.* from side to side ; transversely ; adversely ; athwart ; intersecting at an angle.

ACROSTIC (a-kros'tik), *n.* a composition, usually in verse, in which the first or last letters of the lines, or other letters, taken in order, form a name, or word.

ACT (akt), *n.* an action ; process of doing ; a decree, edict, or enactment ; a formal writing, as one of the principal divisions of a drama ; a thesis : *v.t.* to do ; perform : *v.i.* to exert force or energy.

ACTING (akt'ing), *p.adj.* performing services.

ACTINIC RAYS (raz), *n.* the rays at the violet end of the spectrum.

ACTINISM (ak'tin-izm), *n.* that property of the sun's rays which produces chemical action.

ACTINOLOGY (ak-ti-nol'o-ji), *n.* the science that treats of the chemical action of light.

ACTION (ak'shun), *n.* the state of being active, as opposed to rest ; the effect of one body upon another (*used in sing.*) ; an act or thing done (*used in pl.*) ; a suit instituted by one party against another ; the performance of a function ; effective motion, as of machinery.

ACTIONABLE (ak'shun-a-bl), *adj.* giving grounds for an action at law.

ACTIVE (ak'tiv), *adj.* endowed with or exercising the power or quality of action.

ACTIVITY (ak-tiv'i-ti), *n.* energy ; the state of action.

ACTOR (ak'ter), *n.* one who acts or performs.

ACTRESS (ak'tres), *n.* a female actor.

ACTUAL (ak'tu-al), *adj.* real ; existing.

ACTUALITY (ak-tu-al'i-ti), *n.* the state of being real.

ACTUALIZATION (ak'tu-al-i-za'-shun), *n.* making actual.

ACTUALIZE (ak'tu-al-iz), *v.t.* to make actual.

ACTUALLY (ak'tu-al-li), *adv.* as an existing fact.

ACTUARY (ak'tu-a-ri), *n.* a registrar ; one skilled in life assurance.

ACTUATE (ak'tu-at), *v.t.* to move or incite to action.

ACTUATION (ak-tu-a'shun), *n.* the state of being actuated.

ACUMEN (a-ku'men), *n.* quickness of perception ; insight.

ACUMINATE (a-ku'min-at), *adj.* ending in a sharp point.

ACUTE (a-kut'), *adj.* sharp-pointed ; intellectually sharp.

ACUTE ACCENT (ak'sent), *n.* stress of voice on a syllable.

ACUTE ANGLE (ang'gl), *n.* an angle smaller than a right angle.

ADAGE (ad'aj), *n.* an ancient proverb.

ADAGIO (a-da'jo), *adv.* in music, a somewhat slower tempo.

ADAM'S ALE (ad'amz al), *n.* water.

ADAM'S APPLE (ap'l), *n.* the prominence in the throat.

ADAMANT (ad'a-mant), *n.* a substance of extreme hardness.

ADAMANTINE (ad-a-man'-tin), *adj.* made of adamant ; impenetrable.

ADAMITE (ad'am-it), *n.* a descendant of Adam ; [a-], an arsenate of zinc.

ADAPT (a-dapt'), *v.t.* to make to correspond ; fit by alteration.

ADAPTABILITY (a-dap-ta-bil'i-ti), *n.* the quality of being adaptable.

ADAPTATION (ad-ap-ta'-shun), *n.* the act of adjusting.

ADAR (a-dar'), *n.* the sixth month of the Jewish year.

ADD (ad), *v.t.* to join ; unite ; sum up.

ADDAX (ad'aks), *n.* an African antelope.

ADDEND (ad'end), *n.* a member or quantity.

ADDENDUM (a-den'dum), *n.* [*pl.* addenda (-da)], an appendix.

ADDER (ad'er), *n.* the common viper.

ADDICT (a-dikt'), *v.t.* to devote or give one's self up to.

ADDICTED (-ed), *p.adj.* habituated.

ADDICTION (a-dik'shun), *n.* state of being addicted.

ADDITION (a-dish'un), *n.* the act of adding together ; increase.

ADDITIONAL (a-dish'un-al), *adj.* added ; supplementary.

ADDITIONALLY (-li), *adv.* in addition to.

ADDITIVE (ad'i-tiv), *adj.* that may be added.

ADDLE (ad'l) *adj.* rotten, as eggs that are putrid.

ADDLE-HEADED (-hed'ed), **ADDLE-PATED** (-pa'ted), *adj.* stupid ; weak-brained ; muddled.

ADDRESS (a-dres'), *v.t.* to direct, speak or write to : *n.* manners and bearing.

ADDRESSEE (ad-dres-e'), *n.* one who is addressed.

ADDRESSOGRAPH (-dres'o-graf), *n.* a machine for printing addresses.

ADDUCE (a-dus'), *v.t.* to bring forward or cite.

ADDUCENT (-du'sent), *adj.* bringing forward or together.

ADDUCIBLE (-du'si-bl), *adj.* capable of being adduced.

ADDUCT (a-dukt'), *v.t.* to draw the muscles toward the axis of the body.

ADDUCTIVE (a-duk'tiv), *adj.* bringing forward.

ADDUCTOR (a-duk'ter), *n.* one who draws to.

ADENOID (ad'e-noid), *n.* a swelling of the tissue in the roof of the pharynx.

ADEPT (a-dept'), *adj.* well skilled.

ADEQUACY (ad'e-kwa-si), *n.* sufficiency.

ADEQUATE (ad'e-kwat), *adj.* equal to requirement.

ADHERE (ad-her'), *v.i.* to stick fast.

ADHERENCE (ad-her'ens), *n.* the act or state of adhering.

ADHERENT (ad-her'ent), *adj.* adhering ; sticking : *n.* one who adheres.

ADHESION (ad-he'shun), *n.* the state or act of adhering.

ADHESIVE (ad-he'siv), *adj.* holding fast ; gummed for use.

ADHIBIT (ad-hib'it), *v.t.* to admit.

ADIAPHOROUS (ad-i-af'o-rus), *adj.* neutral.

ADIEU (a-du'), *n.* a farewell ; good wishes.

ADIPOMA (ad-i-po'ma), *n.* any mass of internal fat.

ADIPOMATOUS (ad-i-pom'a-tus), *adj.* composed of adipose tissue.

ADIPOSE (ad'i-pos), *adj.* pertaining to fat.

ADIT (ad'it), *n.* an entrance or passage.

ADJACENCY (a-ja'sen-si), *n.* the state of being close.

ADJACENT (a-ja'sent), *adj.* near ; close to.

ADJECTIVE (aj'ek-tiv), *n.* a word used with a substantive or noun to express the quality or attribute of the thing named.

ADJOIN (a-join'), *v.t.* to unite or join : *v.i.* to lie next to.

ADJOURN (a-jern'), *v.t.* to put off.

ADJOURNMENT (a-jern'-ment), *n.* the act of adjourning.

ADJUDGE (a-juj'), *v.t.* to determine in a controversy.

ADJUDGED (a-jujd'), *adj.* determined.

ADJUDGMENT (a-juj'ment), *n.* the act of judging.

ADJUDICATE (a-joo'di-kat), *v.t.* to determine a case as a court.

ADJUDICATION ('di-ka'shun), *n.* the act of determining judicially.

ADJUDICATOR ('di-ka-ter), *n.* one who adjudicates.

ADJUNCT (aj'ungkt), *n.* something added to another thing.

ADJUNCTIVE (-jungk'tiv), *adj.* having the quality of uniting.

ADJUNCTLY (-jungkt-li), *adv.* in connection with.

ADJURATION (aj-oo-ra'shun), *n.* the solemn charging on oath.

ADJURE (a-joor'), *v.t.* to command on oath under pain of penalty.

ADJUST (a-just'), *v.t.* to fit, or make exact.

ADJUSTER (a-jus'ter), *n.* one who regulates or adjusts.

ADJUSTMENT (a-just'ment), *n.* the act of adjusting.

ADJUTANCY (aj'oo-tan-si), *n.* the office of an adjutant.

ADJUTANT (-tant), *n.* a regimental staff-officer.

ADJUTANT-GENERAL (-gen'er-al), [*pl.* adjutants-general], the chief staff-officer of an army.

ADJUVANT (aj'oo-vant), *adj.* helping ; auxiliary ; assistant.

ADMEASURE (ad-mezh'ur), *v.t.* to measure dimensions.

ADMEASUREMENT (ad-mezh'ur-ment), *n.* measurement by a rule.

ADMINISTER (ad-min'is-ter), *v.t.* to manage as chief agent.

ADMINISTERIAL (ad-min-is-te'ri-al), *adj.* pertaining to administration.

ADMINISTRABLE (ad-min'is-tra-bl), *adj.* capable of being adminis-tered.

ADMINISTRATION (ad-min-is-tra'-shun), *n.* the act of administering, as government.

ADMINISTRATIVE (ad-min'is-tra-tiv), *adj.* pertaining to administration.

ADMINISTRATOR (ad-min-is-tra'-ter), *n.* one who administers affairs.

ADMINISTRATRIX (-tra'triks), *n.* a female administrator.

ADMIRABLE (ad'mi-ra-bl), *adj.* worthy of admiration.

ADMIRAL (ad'mi-ral), *n.* a naval officer of the highest rank.

ADMIRATION (ad-mi-ra'shun), *n.* wonder excited by excellence.

ADMIRE (ad-mir'), *v.t.* to regard with approval.

ADMISSIBLE (ad-mis'-i-bl), *adj.* worthy of being admitted.

ADMISSION (ad-mish'un), *n.* the power or permission to enter.

ADMIT (ad-mit'), *v.t.* to permit to enter ; allow in argument ; receive.

ADMITTANCE (ad-mit'ans), *n.* the act of admitting ; permission to enter ; entrance.

ADMIX (ad-miks'), *v.t.* to mix with something else.

ADMIXTURE (ad-miks'tur), *n.* a compound of substances.

ADMONISH (ad-mon'ish), *v.t.* to reprove.

ADMONITION (ad-mo-nish'un), *n.* friendly reproof.

ADMONITORY (ad-mon'i-to-ri), *adj.* conveying reproof.

ADNASCENT (ad-nas'ent), *adj.* growing upon something else.

ADNATE (ad'nat), *adj.* with organic cohesion of unlike parts.

ADO (a-doo'), *n.* bustle ; trouble.

ADOBE (a-do'ba), *n.* brick dried in the sun.

ADOLESCENCE (ad-o-les'ens), *n.* youth.

ADOLESCENT (ad-o-les'ent), *adj.* growing to maturity.

ADON (a-don'), *n.* a combination of lenses.

ADOPT (a-dopt'), *v.t.* to choose or take.

ADOPTION (a-dop'shun), *n.* the act of adopting.

ADOPTIVE (a-dop'tiv), *adj.* constituted by adoption.

ADORABLE (a-dor'a-bl), *adj.* worthy of worship.

ADORATION (ad-or-ra'shun), *n.* the act of worship.

ADORE (a-dor'), *v.t.* to pay divine honours to ; honour highly.

ADORN (a-dorn'), *v.t.* to beautify ; dignify.

ADORNMENT (a-dorn'ment), *n.* ornament.

ADOSCULATION (ad-os-ku-la'shun), *n.* fertilization of flowers by drifting pollen.

ADOWN (a-doun'), *adv. & prep.* downward.

ADRIFT (a-drift'), *adj. & adv.* floating at random.

ADROIT (a-droit'), *adj.* exhibiting skill ; dextrous.

ADULATE (ad'u-lat), *v.t.* to flatter.

ADULATION (ad-u-la'shun), *n.* interested praise.

ADULATOR (ad'u-la-ter), *n.* a flatterer.

ADULATORY (ad'u-la-to-ri), *adj.* flattering.

ADULT (a-dult'), *adj.* grown up to full age.

ADULTERATE (a-dul'ter-at), *v.t.* to corrupt by baser admixture.

ADULTERATION (a-dul'ter-a'shun), *n.* the debasing by admixture ; deterioration.

ADULTERATOR (a-dul'ter-a-ter), *n.* one who adulterates.

ADULTERER (a-dul'ter-er), *n.* a man who commits adultery.

ADULTERESS (-es), *n.* a woman who commits adultery.

ADULTERY (a-dul'ter-i), *n.* violation of the marriage bed.

ADUMBRAL (ad-um'bral), *adj.* shady ; in shadow.

ADUMBRANT (ad-um'brant), *adj.* shadowing forth.

ADUMBRATE (ad-um'brat), *v.t.* to shadow forth.

ADUMBRATION (ad-um-bra'shun), *n.* something that shadows forth.

ADVANCE (ad-vans'), *v.i.* to go forward ; payment before hand.

ADVANCEMENT (ad-vans'ment), *n.* progress ; promotion.

ADVANTAGE (ad-van'taj), *n.* a state of advance or forwardness ; a benefit.

ADVANTAGEOUS (ad-van-ta'jus), *adj.* of advantage ; beneficial.

ADVENT (ad'vent), *n.* the period including the four Sundays before Christmas ; [a-], arrival ; approach.

ADVENTIST (-ist), *n.* one of a religious sect which stresses Christ's second coming.

ADVENTITIOUS (ad-ven-tish'us), *adj.* happening by chance ; casual.

ADVENTUAL (ad-ven'tu-al), *adj.* relating to Advent.

ADVENTURE (ad-ven'tur), *n.* an event determined by chance.

ADVENTURER (ad-ven'tur-er), *n.* one who undertakes adventures.

ADVENTURESOME (ad-ven'tur-sum), **ADVENTUROUS** ('tur-us), *adj.* inclined to incur risk.

ADVENTURESS ('tur-es), *n.* a female adventurer.

ADVERB (ad'verb), *n.* a word used to modify the sense of a verb or adjective.

ADVERBIAL (ad-ver'bi-al), *adj.* of the nature of an adverb.

ADVERBIALLY (-li), *adv.* with the force of an adverb.

ADVERSARY (ad'ver-sar-i), *n.* an opponent.

ADVERSATIVE (ad-ver'sa-tiv), *adj.* expressing opposition.

ADVERSE (ad'vers), *adj.* opposed to ; contrary.

ADVERSITY (ad-ver'si-ti), *n.* the reverse of prosperity.

ADVERT (ad-vert'), *v.i.* to turn one's attention to.

ADVERTENCE (ad-ver'tens), *n.* attention.

ADVERTENCY (ad-ver'ten-si), *n.* the habit of being attentive.

ADVERTENT (ad-ver'tent), *adj.* attentive.

ADVERTENTLY (-li), *adv.* in an intentional manner.

ADVERTISE (ad'ver-tiz), *v.t.* announce ; publish.

ADVERTISEMENT (ad-ver'tiz-ment), *n.* a notice in print.

ADVICE (ad-vis'), *n.* an opinion given ; counsel.

ADVISABILITY (ad-viz-a-bil'i-ti), *n.* the quality of being advisable.

ADVISABLE (ad-vi'za-bl), *adj.* fit to be advised ; prudent.

ADVISE (ad-viz'), *v.t.* to offer an opinion to ; counsel ; inform.

ADVISED (ad-vizd'), *p.adj.* acting with caution.

ADVISEDLY (ad-vi'zed-li), *adv.* with advice.

ADVISORY (ad-vi'zo-ri), *adj.* having power to advise.

ADVOCACY (ad'vo-ka-si), *n.* the act of pleading for.

ADVOCATE (ad'vo-kat), *n.* one who pleads the cause of another.

ADVOLUTION (ad-vo-lu'shun), *n.* evolution philosophically considered.

ADYTUM (ad'i-tum), *n.* any secret place.

ADZE, ADZ (adz), *n.* a cutting tool.

ADZE-PLANE (-plan), *n.* a tool for moulding.

ÆON, EON (e'on), *n.* a period of immense duration.

AERATE (a'er-at), *v.t.* to combine or charge with carbonic-acid gas, or air.

AERATION (a-er-a'shun), *n.* the act of aerating.

AERIAL (a-e'ri-al), *adj.* belonging to the air ; *n.* n antenna, as used in radio.

AERIALLY (-li), *adv.* like the air.

AERIE (e'er-i), *n.* nest of an eagle.

AERIFICATION (a-er-if-i-ka'shun), *n.* the state of being aeriform.

AERIFEROUS (a-er-if'er-us), *adj.* containing air.

AERIFORM (a'er-i-form), *adj.* having the form of air ; gaseous.

AERIFY (a'er-i-fi), *v.t.* to combine with air.

AERO (a'er-o), *n.* an air-carrier.

AERO-, a combining form from the Greek *aer,* air, denoting *relation to air.*

AERODROME (a'er-o-drom), *n.* a place for flying machines.

AERODYNAMICS (a-er-o-di-nam'-iks), *n.* the science which treats of air in motion.

AEROGRAM (a'er-o-gram), *n.* a wireless message.

AEROLITE (a'er-o-lit), *n.* a meteorite.

AEROLOGY (a-er-ol'o-ji), *n.* the science that treats of the atmosphere.

AEROMANCY (a'er-o-man'si), *n.* forecasting weather from atmospheric changes.

AEROMETER (a-er-om'e-ter), *n.* an instrument for weighing the air.

AERONAUT (a'er-o-nawt), *n.* a balloonist.

AERONAUTIC (a-er-o-naw'tik), **AERONAUTICAL** (-al), *adj.* pertaining to aeronautics.

AERONAUTICS (a-e-ro-naw'tiks), *n.* aerial navigation.

AEROPHONE (a'er-o-fon), *n.* an instrument for increasing the intensity of sound.

AEROPLANE (a'er-o-plan), *n.* a flying machine, as distinguished from an airship or balloon.

AEROSTATICS (a-er-o-stat'iks), *n.* the science which treats of the equilibrium of bodies sustained in air.

AEROVIEW (a′er-o-vu), *n.* a view from an aeroplane.

AERY (a′er-i), *adj.* high ; lofty.

ÆSTHETIC, ESTHETIC (es-thet′-ik), *adj.* pertaining to æsthetics.

ÆSTHETICISM (es-thet′i-sizm), *n.* love for, or devotion to, the beautiful.

ÆSTHETICS, ESTHETICS (es-thet′iks), *n.* the science or theory of the beautiful, in taste and art.

ÆTHER, see ether.

AFAR (a-far′), *adv.* at, to, or from, a distance.

AFFABILITY (af-a-bil′i-ti), *n.* the quality of being affable.

AFFABLE (af′a-bl), *adj.* easy to be addressed ; courteous.

AFFAIR (af-ar′), *n.* that which is done, or is to be done ; business.

AFFECT (a-fekt′), *v.t.* to produce an effect upon ; seek by natural affinity.

AFFECTATION (af-ek-ta′shun), *n.* the assuming a manner which is not one's own.

AFFECTED (-ed), *p.adj.* not natural ; false.

AFFECTING (af-ek′ting), *p.adj.* pathetic.

AFFECTION (a-fek′shun), *n.* inclination ; attachment ; fondness ; disease.

AFFECTIONAL (-fek′shun-al), *adj.* relating to the affections.

AFFECTIONATE (-fek′shun-at), *adj.* having affection.

AFFERENT (af′er-ent), *adj.* conveying inwards or to a part.

AFFIANCE (a-fi′ans), *n.* trust ; marriage-contract : *v.t.* to betroth.

AFFIDAVIT (af-i-da′vit), *n.* a sworn statement in writing.

AFFILIABLE (a-fil′a-bl), *adj.* capable of being affiliated.

AFFILIATE (a-fil′i-at), *v.t.* to adopt ; *v.i.* to be intimately connected with.

AFFILIATION (a-fil-i-a′shun), *n.* relationship ; connection.

AFFINITY (a-fin′i-ti), *n.* nearness of kin ; mutual attraction.

AFFIRM (a-ferm′), *v.t.* to assert.

AFFIRMANCE (-fer′mans), *n.* confirmation.

AFFIRMANT (-fer′mant), *n.* one who affirms.

AFFIRMATION (-fer-ma′shun), *n.* an averment.

AFFIRMATIVE (-fer′ma-tiv), *n.* that which affirms.

AFFIX (a-fiks′), *v.t.* to fix to ; attach.

AFFLICT (a-flikt′), *v.t.* to cause pain ; distress.

AFFLICTION (-flik′shun), *n.* prolonged pain of body or mind.

AFFLICTIVE (-flik′tiv), *adj.* causing pain.

AFFLUENCE (af′loo-ens), *n.* an abundant supply.

AFFLUENT (-ent), *n.* a tributary stream : *adj.* abundant.

AFFLUX (af′luks), *n.* an increase ; an influx.

AFFORD (a-ford′), *v.t.* to supply ; be capable of bearing expense of.

AFFOREST (a-for′est), *v.t.* to convert into a forest.

AFFORESTATION (-es-ta′shun), *n.* the act of turning into forest.

AFFRANCHISE (a-fran′chiz), *v.t.* to make free ; enfranchise.

AFFRAY (a-fra′), *n.* the fighting of persons in a public place.

AFFRIGHT (a-frit′), *v.t.* to frighten.

AFFRONT (a-frunt′), *v.t.* to confront ; insult designedly.

AFFUSION (a-fu′zhun), *n.* the act of pouring upon.

AFGHAN (af′gan), *adj.* pertaining to Afghanistan : *n.* a native of Afghanistan.

AFGHAN (af′gan), *n.* a crocheted or knitted soft wool blanket.

AFIELD (a-feld′), *adv.* to, in, or on, the field.

AFLAME (a-flam′), *adj.* & *adv.* in flames.

AFLOAT (a-flot′), *adj.* & *adv.* floating ; in circulation.

AFOOT (a-foot′), *adv.* on foot ; astir.

AFOUL (a-foul′), *adj.* & *adv.* in entanglement ; enmeshed ; entangled.

AFRAID (a-frad′), *adj.* frightened.

AFRESH (a-fresh′), *adv.* again ; anew.

AFRICAN (af′ri-kan), *adj.* pertaining to Africa : *n.* a native of Africa.

AFT (aft), *adj.* & *adv.* towards the stern.

AFTER (af′ter), *adj.* next ; subsequent ; later.

AFTERMATH (-math), *n.* a second mowing in a season.

AFTERNOON (-noon'), *n.* the part of the day between noon and evening.

AFTERWARD (-werd), **AFTERWARDS** (-werdz), *adv.* at a later time ; subsequently.

AGAIN (a-gen'), *adv.* a second time ; in return ; further ; anew.

AGAINST (a-genst'), *prep.* opposite to ; in opposition to.

AGAPE (a-gap'), *adj. & adv.* gaping.

AGATE (ag'at), *n.* a precious stone.

AGAVE (a-ga've), *n.* a genus of plants.

AGE (aj), *n.* a particular period of time in life or in history ; time : *v.i.* to grow old.

AGENCY (a'jen-si), *n.* operation ; action ; an establishment for the purpose of doing business for another.

AGENDUM (a-jen'dum), *n.* a programme of business to be carried out.

AGENT (a'jent), *n.* one who acts for another ; an active power or cause.

AGGLOMERATE (ag-glom'er-at), *v.t.* to gather into a heap ; accumulate.

AGGLOMERATION (ag-glom-er-a'shun), *n.* a heap.

AGGLOMERATIVE (ag-glom'-er-a-tiv), *adj.* tending to gather together.

AGGLUTINANT (a-glu'ti-nant), *adj.* uniting.

AGGLUTINATE (a-glu'ti-nat), *v.t.* to glue together.

AGGRANDIZE (ag'gran-diz), *v.t.* to make greater.

AGGRANDIZEMENT (a-gran'diz-ment), *n.* exaltation ; advancement.

AGGRAVATE (ag'ra-vat), *v.t.* to add to a load ; be troublesome.

AGGRAVATING (ag'ra-va-ting), *p.adj.* making worse.

AGGRAVATION (ag-gra-va'-shun), *n.* the act of making worse.

AGGREGATE (ag're-gat), *v.t.* to gather into a mass or body ; accumulate : *n.* total ; mass.

AGGREGATION (ag're-ga'shun), *n.* a collection of particulars.

AGGREGATIVE (ag'gre-ga-tiv), *adj.* collective ; social.

AGGRESS (a-gres'), *v.i.* to attack ; begin a quarrel or controversy.

AGGRESSION (-gresh'un), *n.* unprovoked attack.

AGGRESSIVE (-gres'iv), *adj.* unjustly attacking.

AGGRESSOR (-gres'er), *n.* one who attacks.

AGGRIEVE (a-grev'), *v.t.* to bear heavily upon.

AGHAST (a-gast'), *adj.* struck with astonishment.

AGILE (aj'il), *adj.* easily driven about ; active ; nimble.

AGILITY (a-jil'i-ti), *n.* nimbleness.

AGIST (a-jist'), *v.t.* to feed or pasture cattle for a fixed sum.

AGISTMENT (-ment), *n.* the process of feeding or grazing cattle.

AGITABLE (aj'i-ta-bl), *adj.* capable of being moved, or debated ; debatable.

AGITATE (aj'i-tat), *v.t.* to stir violently.

AGITATION (aj-i-ta'shun), *n.* the act of agitating.

AGITATIVE (aj'i-ta-tiv), *adj.* tending to agitate.

AGITATOR (aj'i-ta-ter), *n.* one who starts or keeps up an agitation.

AGLOW (a-glo'), *adj. & adv.* in a glow ; glowing.

AGLUTITION (ag-lu-tish'un), *n.* inability to swallow.

AGNOMEN (ag-no'men), *n.* an additional name or epithet, as Milton, the poet.

AGNOSTIC (ag-nos'tik), *n.* one who denies any knowledge of the ultimate nature of things : *adj.* expressing ignorance.

AGNOSTICISM (ag-nos'ti-sizm), *n.* the doctrines of the agnostics.

AGO (a-go'), *adj.* gone ; past : *adv.* in past time.

AGOG (a-gog'), *adj. & adv.* in agitation or expectation ; eager.

AGOING (a-go'ing), *adv.* on the going ; in motion.

AGONISTICS (ag-o-nis'tiks), *n.* the science of athletic contests.

AGONIZE (ag'o-niz), *v.i.* to suffer anguish : *v.t.* to torture.

AGONIZINGLY (ag'o-ni-zing-li), *adv.* with anguish or struggles.

AGONY (ag'o-ni), *n.* extreme pain; anguish.

AGOUTI (a-goo'ti), *n.* a rodent found in the West Indies and South America.

AGRARIAN (a-gra'ri-an), *adj.* relating to land, or to land-tenure.

AGRARIANISM (-izm), *n.* the principle of a uniform division of land.

AGREE (a-gre'), *v.i.* to harmonize; to accord.

AGREEABILITY (a-gre-a-bil'i-ti), *n.* agreeableness.

AGREEABLE (a-gre'a-bl), *adj.* pleasing.

AGREEMENT (a-gre'ment), *n.* harmony of opinions; a contract.

AGRICULTURAL (ag-ri-kul'tu-ral), *adj.* pertaining to tillage.

AGRICULTURE (ag'ri-kul-tur), *n.* the science and art of cultivating fields.

AGRICULTURIST (ag-ri-kul'tur-ist), *n.* one engaged in farming.

AGRONOMY (a-gron'o-mi), *n.* scientific agriculture.

AGROUND (a-ground'), *adj. & adv.* on the ground.

AGUE (a'gu), *n.* an intermittent fever.

AGUE TREE (tre), the sassafras.

AGUISH (a'gu-ish), *adj.* producing ague; intermittent.

AH (a), *interj.* an exclamatory expression of surprise.

AHA (a-ha'), *interj.* an exclamation expressive of satisfaction or irony.

AHEAD (a-hed'), *adv.* in the front; forward.

AHOY (a-hoi'), *interj.* a term used in hailing a vessel.

AID (ad), *v.t.* to assist; support: *n.* help; assistance.

AIDE-DE-CAMP (ad'de-kong), *n.* [*pl.* aides-de-camp], an officer who assists a general.

AIGRET, AIGRETTE (a-gret'), *n.* the small white heron.

AIL (al), *v.t.* to give or cause pain: *v.i.* to feel pain.

AILERON (al'er-on), *n.* a small deflecting plane, between the upper and lower planes, to steady an airplane.

AILMENT (al'ment), *n.* a disorder of the body; sickness.

AIM (am), *v.i.* direct at something: *n.* a purpose.

AIR (ar), *v.t.* to expose to the air: *n.* the fluid which we breathe; the atmosphere.

AIR BRAKE (brak), an automatic brake.

AIREDALE (ar'dal), *n.* a dog of the terrier type.

AIR-GAS (-gas), *n.* an illuminating gas made from air charged with the vapour of petroleum, naphtha, etc.

AIR-GUN (-gun), *n.* a gun discharged by the elastic force of compressed air.

AIRILY (ar'i-li), *adv.* in an airy manner; gaily.

AIRINESS (ar'i-ness), *n.* the state of being airy; gaiety.

AIRING (ar'ing), *n.* a walk, ride, or drive in the open air; exposure to the air or fire.

AIR-LINE (-lin), *n.* a straight line; bee-line.

AIR-MINDED (ar-min-ded), *adj.* tending to think in terms of aviation.

AIRPLANE (ar-plan), *n.* same as aeroplane.

AIR-PLANT (-plant), *n.* a plant which derives its nourishment from the air.

AIR-PUMP (-pump), *n.* a machine for exhausting the air from a receiver.

AIRSHIP (ar'ship), *n.* a steerable balloon.

AIR-TIGHT (-tit), *adj.* impenetrable by, or impermeable to, air.

AIRY (ar'i), *adj.* breezy; unsubstantial; gay.

AISLE (il), *n.* a passageway between rows of seats.

AJAR (a-jar'), *adj. & adv.* slightly turned or opened, as a door.

AJOG (a-jog'), *adv.* on the jog; jogging.

AKIMBO (a-kim'bo), *adv.* with the hands on the hips.

AKIN (a-kin'), *adj. & adv.* of kin; related by blood; allied by nature.

ALABASTER (al'a-bas-ter), *n.* a white marble-like mineral.

A LA CARTE (a la kart'), [French], in accordance with the bill of fare.

ALACK (a-lak'), *interj.* an exclamation expressive of blame, sorrow, or surprise.

ALACRITY (a-lak'ri-ti), *n.* eager readiness ; joyous activity ; briskness.

ALAMO (a'la-mo), the poplar ; [A-], a mission.

ALAMODE (a-la-mod'), *adv.* in the fashion ; *adj.* fashionable.

ALAR (a'lar), *adj.* pertaining to or having wings ; wing-shaped.

ALARM (a-larm'), *v.t.* arouse to a sense of danger : *n.* a call to arms.

ALARMING (a-larm'ing), *adj.* exciting apprehension ; ominous.

ALARY (a'la-ri), *adj.* of or pertaining to wings ; wing-shaped.

ALAS (a-las'), *interj.* an exclamation expressive of disappointment or sorrow.

ALATE (a'lat), *adj.* winged.

ALB (alb), *n.* a priestly vestment.

ALBACORE (al'ba-kor), *n.* a fish of the mackerel family.

ALBATROSS (al'ba-tros), *n.* a sea-bird allied to the petrel.

ALBEIT (awl-be'it), *conj.* although ; even though ; notwithstanding.

ALBINO (al-bi'no), *n.* white skin and hair and pinkish eyes.

ALBUGINEOUS (al-bu-jin'e-us), *adj.* albuminous ; pertaining to the white of the eye or the white of eggs.

ALBUM (al'bum), *n.* a blank book for autographs, photographs, etc.

ALBUMEN (al-bu'men), *n.* the white of an egg.

ALBUMIN (-min), *n.* any of a class of proteids.

ALBUMINOUS (al-bu'mi-nus), *adj.* like, or containing albumin.

ALCALDE (al-kal'da), *n.* a magistrate in Spain or Portugal.

ALCAZAR (al-ka'zar), *n.* a Spanish castle.

ALCHEMIST (al'ke-mist), *n.* one who studies alchemy.

ALCHEMY (al'ke-mi), *n.* the chemistry of the Middle Ages.

ALCOHOL (al'ko-hol), *n.* pure or rectified spirits of wine ; compounds of the same type as spirits of wine.

ALCOHOLIC (al-ko-hol'ik), *adj.* containing, or pertaining to, alcohol.

ALCOHOLISM (al'ko-hol-izm), *n.* a diseased condition produced by alcohol.

ALCOHOLIZE (al'ko-hol-iz), *v.t.* to subject to the influence of alcohol ; to rectify (spirits of wine).

ALCOVE (al-kov'), *n.* a recess in a room or a garden ; a bower.

ALDER (awl'der), *n.* a small tree of the oak family.

ALDERMAN (awl'der-man), *n.* a member of a city-governing body.

ALE (al), *n.* a liquor made from an infusion of malt by fermentation.

ALEE (a-le'), *adv. & adj.* on the lee or sheltered side of the ship.

ALERT (a-lert'), *adj.* on the watch ; active : *n.* an alarm ; a sudden attack.

ALEWIFE (al-wif'), *n.* a fish of the herring family.

ALFALFA (al-fal'fa), *n.* lucerne, a clover-like plant.

ALFRESCO (al-fres'ko), *adv.* in the open air.

ALGÆ (al'je), *n.pl.* one of the great divisions of cryptogamic plants.

ALGEBRA (al'je-bra), *n.* the science of calculation by symbols.

ALIAS (a'li-as), *adv.* otherwise (named) : *n.* an assumed name.

ALIBI (al'i-bi), *n.* the plea of having been elsewhere when the alleged act was committed.

ALIEN (al'yen), *adj.* belonging to another : *n.* a foreign-born resident of a country in which he is not naturalized.

ALIENABILITY (a-li-en-a-bil'i-ti), *n.* the quality of being alienable.

ALIENABLE (a'li-en-a-bl), *adj.* saleable. (As real estate.)

ALIENAGE (-aj), *n.* the legal status of an alien.

ALIENATE (-at), *v.t.* to estrange ; transfer to another.

ALIENATION (-a'shun), *n.* estrangement ; transference.

ALIENISM (al'yen-izm), *n.* the position of being an alien ; the study and treatment of mental diseases.

ALIENIST (-ist), *n.* a doctor who specializes in mental diseases.

ALIGHT (a-lit'), *v.i.* to dismount; to descend and settle.

ALIGN (a-lin'), *v.t.* to lay out or adjust by line.

ALIGNMENT, ALINEMENT (a-lin'ment), *n.* laying out by a line.

ALIKE (a-lik'), *adj.* like one another: *adv.* similar.

ALIMENT (al'i-ment), *n.* food; the necessaries of life generally.

ALIMENTARY (al-i-men'ta-ri), *adj.* pertaining to food; nutritious.

ALIMENTARY CANAL (ka-nal'), *n.* the great duct which conveys food to the stomach and carries off waste matter.

ALIMENTATION (al-i-men-ta'shun), *n.* the act of giving nourishment.

ALIMONY (al'i-mon-i), *n.* an allowance made by court to a wife on separation, or pending action for same.

ALINEMENT (a-lin'ment), *n.* the act of laying out by a line.

ALIQUANT (al'i-kwant), *adj.* being a part of a number which does not divide it without a remainder.

ALIQUOT (al'i-kwot), *adj.* being part of a number which will divide it without remainder, as 8 of 24.

ALIVE (a-liv'), *adj.* having life; in a state of action.

ALKALI (al'ka-li & -li), *n.* one of a class of caustic bases, as soda.

ALKALINE (al'ka-lin & -lin), *adj.* pertaining to, or having the properties of an alkali.

ALKALOID (al'ka-loid), *n.* a body or substance containing alkaline properties.

ALL (awl), *adj.* the whole quantity of, as substance, duration, extent, degree or amount.

ALLAH (al'la), *n.* the Arabic name for the Supreme Being.

ALLAY (a-la'), *v.t.* to quiet or calm; assuage.

ALLEGATION (al-e-ga'shun), *n.* assertion; excuse or justification.

ALLEGE (a-lej'), *v.t.* to affirm; declare; assert.

ALLEGEABLE (al-lej'a-bl), *adj.* that may be alleged or affirmed.

ALLEGIANCE (a-le'jans), *n.* fealty; fidelity to a cause or person.

ALLEGORIC (al-e-gor'ik), **ALLEGORICAL** (al-e-gor'i-kal), *adj.* in the nature of allegory; figurative.

ALLEGORICALLY (-li), *adv.* figuratively; in an allegorical manner.

ALLEGORIZE (al'e-go-riz), *v.t.* to turn into allegory; to treat allegorically.

ALLEGORY (al'e-go-ri), *n.* a figurative manner of treating a subject.

ALLEVIATE (al-le'vi-at), *v.t.* to lighten; lessen; make easier.

ALLEVIATION (-vi-a'shun), *n.* the act of alleviating.

ALLEVIATIVE (-le'vi-a-tiv), *adj.* tending to alleviate.

ALLEVIATOR (-le'vi-a-ter), *n.* one who or that which alleviates.

ALLEY (al'i), *n.* a passage; a lane.

ALLHALLOWE'EN (awl-hal-o-en'), *n.* evening before All Saints' Day.

ALLIANCE (a-li'ans), *n.* relation or connection by birth or marriage; union between nations.

ALLIED (a-lid'), *p.a.* united; attached; leagued together.

ALLIGATION (al-i-ga'shun), *n.* a rule for ascertaining the value or price of a compound.

ALLIGATOR (al'i-ga-ter), *n.* the American crocodile.

ALLITERATE (a-lit'er-at), *v.t.* to make alliterative: *v.i.* to use alliteration.

ALLITERATION (-a'shun), *n.* the repetition of the same initial letter in succeeding words.

ALLITERATIVE (-lit'er-a-tiv), *adj.* characterized by alliteration.

ALLOCATE (al'o-kat), *v.t.* to assign or allot.

ALLOCATION (al-o-ka'shun), *n.* the act of allotting, allocating, or assigning.

ALLOCATUR (al'o-ka-tur), *n.* the judicial endorsement of a writ.

ALLOCUTION (al-o-ku'shun), *n.* an address of a formal nature.

ALLODIUM (a-lo'di-um), *n.* [*pl.* allodia (-a)], freehold estate.

ALLOGAMY (a-log′a-mi), *n.* fertilization of a flower by the pollen of another of the same kind.

ALLOGRAPH (al′o-graf), *n.* a signature by one person in behalf of another ; opposed to *autograph.*

ALLOPATH (al′o-path), *n.* an allopathist.

ALLOPATHY (-lop′a-thi), *n.* a method of treating disease by inducing an action opposite to the disease it is sought to cure ; opposed to *homœopathy.*

ALLOQUIALISM (a-lo′kwi-al-izm), *n.* a phrase used in addressing.

ALLOT (a-lot′), *v.t.* to distribute or divide, as by lot ; apportion, as shares.

ALLOTMENT (a-lot′ment), *n.* the act of allotting.

ALLOTROPIC (al-o-trop′ik), *adj.* pertaining to or characterized by allotropy.

ALLOTROPISM (a-lot′ro-pizm), *n.* diversity of molecular arrangement.

ALLOTROPY (a-lot′ro-pi), *n.* the capability shown by certain chemical elements to assume different forms.

ALLOW (a-lou′), *v.t.* to grant ; yield ; admit ; deduct ; permit.

ALLOWABLE (a-lou′a-bl), *adj.* that may be allowed.

ALLOWANCE (a-lou′ans), *n.* admission ; concession ; a definite sum granted ; sanction or approval.

ALLOY (a-loi′), *v.t.* to combine ; debase : *n.* a fusion of metals.

ALLSPICE (awl′spis), *n.* the fruit or berry of the pimento.

ALLUDE (a-lud′), *v.t.* to compare : *v.i.* refer or make an allusion indirectly (with *to*).

ALLURE (a-lur′), *v.t.* to entice ; attract.

ALLUREMENT (a-lur′ment), *n.* the act of alluring.

ALLUSION (a-lu′zhun), *n.* a casual reference.

ALLUSIVE (a-lu′siv), *adj.* having reference to something not definitely expressed.

ALLUSORY (a-lu′so-ri), *adj.* allusive.

ALLUVIAL (a-lu′vi-al), *adj.* pertaining to alluvium.

ALLUVION (a-lu′vi-on), *n.* land added to a shore or river-bank by action of water.

ALLUVIUM (a-lu′vi-um), *n.* [*pl.* alluvia (-a)], a deposit of mingled sand and clay (mud).

ALLY (a-li′), *v.t.* to unite by marriage, treaty, league or confederacy : *n.* one united, related, or associated by these means ; a confederate.

ALMA MATER (al′ma ma′ter), the college or institution in which one has been educated.

ALMANAC (awl′ma-nak), *n.* a year-book or calendar.

ALMIGHTY (awl-mi′ti), *adj.* possessing all power ; omnipotent.

ALMIGHTY (awl-mi′ti), *n.* the omnipotent God.

ALMOND (a′mund, al′mund), *n.* a small tree of the peach family.

ALMONER (al′mun-er), *n.* one who dispenses or distributes alms.

ALMOST (awl′most), *adv.* nearly ; very nearly.

ALMS (amz), *n. sing. & pl.* a gift or gifts to relieve the poor.

ALMSHOUSE (-hous), *n.* a poor-house.

ALOES (al′oz), *n.* a drug.

ALOFT (a-loft′), *adv.* on high ; at the mast-head.

ALONE (a-lon′), *adj. & adv.* apart from another.

ALONG (a-long′), *prep. & adv.* in a line parallel with the length ; onward.

ALONGSHOREMAN (-shor′man), *n.* a labourer employed at docks.

ALONGSIDE (-sid), *adv.* by the side.

ALOOF (a-loof′), *adv.* at a moderate distance but within sight.

ALOUD (a-loud′), *adv.* with raised voice ; loudly.

ALPACA (al-pak′a), *n.* the fabric constructed from the wool of the llama.

ALPEN-HORN (al′pen-horn), *n.* a long horn used by mountaineers.

ALPEN-STOCK (-stok), *n.* a stout staff, with an iron spike.

ALPHA (al′fa), *n.* the beginning ; first letter of Greek alphabet.

ALPHABET (al'fa-bet), *n.* the letters of a language.

ALPHABETIC (al-fa-bet'ik), **ALPHABETICAL** ('i-kal), *adj.* pertaining to an alphabet.

ALPHABETICALLY (-li), *adv.* in an alphabetical order.

ALPHABETIZE (al'fa-bet-iz), *v.t.* to arrange in alphabetical order.

ALPHA RAYS (raz), *n.pl.* rays emitted by radium.

ALREADY (awl-red'i), *adv.* prior to some specified time; previously.

ALSO (awl'so), *adv.* & *conj.* wholly so; in like manner.

ALTAR (awl'ter), *n.* a place of worship.

ALTAZIMUTH (alt-az'i-muth), *n.* an instrument to determine the altitudes of heavenly bodies.

ALTER (awl'ter), *v.t.* to effect some change in; modify.

ALTERABLE (awl'ter-a-bl), *adj.* capable of being changed.

ALTERANT (awl'ter-ant), *adj.* producing or effecting change.

ALTERATION (awl-ter-a'shun), *n.* the act of altering.

ALTERATIVE (awl'ter-a-tiv), *adj.* producing change; the power to alter.

ALTERCATE (awl'ter-kat), *v.i.* to contend in words; wrangle.

ALTERCATION (awl-ter-ka'shun), *n.* the act of wrangling.

ALTER EGO (e'go), a second self.

ALTERNANT (al-ter'nant), *adj.* composed of alternate layers.

ALTERNATE (al'ter-nat), *v.t.* to perform by turns.

ALTERNATING CURRENT (cur'rent), *n.* one which periodically changes its direction.

ALTERNATION (al-ter-na'shun), *n.* the act of alternating.

ALTERNATIVE (al-ter'na-tiv), *adj.* giving the choice of two things.

ALTERNATOR (al'ter-na-ter), *n.* an alternating current dynamo.

ALTHOUGH (awl-*tho*'), *conj.* granting that; notwithstanding.

ALTIMETER (al-tim'e-ter), *n.* an instrument for measuring altitudes trigonometrically.

ALTIMETRY (al-tim'e-tri), *n.* the art of measuring altitudes.

ALTISCOPE (al'ti-skop), *n.* an instrument by means of which an object is brought to the view notwithstanding intervening obstacles.

ALTITUDE (al'ti-tud), *n.* space extended upward; height.

ALTITUDINAL (al-ti-tu'di-nal), *adj.* of or pertaining to height.

ALTO (al'to), *adj.* high: *n.* the contralto; the tenor violin or viola.

ALTOGETHER (awl-too-ge*th*'er), *adv.* wholly; completely.

ALTROPATHY (al-trop'a-thi), *n.* sympathy for others.

ALTRUISM (al'troo-izm), *n.* the principles involving the sacrifice of self in the interests of others; opposed to *egoism*.

ALTRUIST (al'troo-ist), *n.* one who advocates or practises altruism.

ALTRUISTIC (al-troo-is'tik), *adj.* pertaining to altruism.

ALTRUISTICALLY (-al-li), *adv.* in an altruistic manner.

ALUM (al'um), *n.* a double sulphate formed of aluminium and some other element.

ALUMINA (a-lu'mi-na), *n.* the single oxide of aluminium.

ALUMINATE ('mi-nat), *n.* a salt formed by the action of hydroxyl on aluminium.

ALUMINITE (a-lu'mi-nit), *n.* the hydrous sulphate of aluminium.

ALUMINOUS (a-lu'mi-nus), *adj.* pertaining to, or containing, alum or alumina.

ALUMINUM (a-lu'mi-num), **ALUMINIUM** (al-u-min'i-um), *n.* a light, malleable metal.

ALUMNA (a-lum'na), *n.* [*pl.* alumnæ (-ne)], a female graduate of a university or college.

ALUMNUS (a-lum'nus), *n.* [*pl.* alumni (-ni)], one educated at a school, college, or university.

ALUM-ROOT (-root), *n.* a popular name given to certain roots of an astringent nature.

ALWAYS (awl-waz), *adv.* constantly; ever.

AMAIN (a-man'), *adv.* with force or violence.

AMALGAM (a-mal'gam), *n.* any metallic mixture.

AMALGAMATE (a-mal'ga-mat), *v.t.* to alloy mercury with another metal.

AMALGAMATION (a-mal-ga-ma'-shun), *n.* the blending or mixing of different elements or things.

AMALGAMATOR (a-mal'ga-ma-ter), *n.* one who or that which amalgamates.

AMANUENSIS (a-man-u-en'sis), *n.* [*pl.* amanuenses (-sez)], one who is employed to write at the dictation of another.

AMARANTH (am'a-ranth), *n.* a plant of the genus Amaranthus.

AMARANTHINE (am-a-ran'thin), *adj.* pertaining to the amaranth.

AMARANTHUS (am-a-ran'thus), *n.* a widely distributed genus of plants.

AMARYLLIS (am-a-ril'is), *n.* a genus of bulbous plants.

AMASS (a-mas'), *v.t.* to collect into a heap ; accumulate.

AMASSMENT (a-mas'ment), *n.* the act of amassing.

AMATEUR (am'a-tur), *n.* one who cultivates an art or pursues a study from love without reference to gain.

AMATEURISH (-ish), *adj.* like the work of an amateur.

AMATI (a-ma'te), *n.* a violin.

AMATIVE (am'a-tiv), *adj.* amorous ; full of love.

AMATIVENESS (am'a-tiv-nes), *n.* tendency to love.

AMATORIAL (am-a-tor'i-al), *adj.* pertaining to love ; amatory.

AMATORY (am'a-to-ri), *adj.* relating to or expressive of love.

AMAUROSIS (am-aw-ro'sis), *n.* loss or decay of sight due to paralysis of the optic nerve.

AMAZE (a-maz'), *v.t.* to confound or astonish : *n.* astonishment ; perplexity.

AMAZEMENT (a-maz'ment), *n.* the state of being amazed.

AMBASSADOR (am-bas'a-der), *n.* an accredited representative of a state at the court of another.

AMBASSADOR EXTRAORDINARY (eks-tra-or'din-a-ri), an ambassador sent on a special mission.

AMBASSADOR PLENIPOTENTIARY (plen-i-po-ten'shi-a-ri), an ambassador sent with full powers to make a treaty.

AMBASSADORIAL (am-bas-a-do'ri-al), *adj.* belonging to an ambassador, or to his office.

AMBER (am'ber), *n.* a yellowish fossil resin.

AMBERGRIS (am'ber-gres), *n.* a secretion from the sperm-whale ; used in perfumery.

AMBIDEXTER (am-bi-deks'ter), *n.* a person of unusual dexterity.

AMBIDEXTROUS (am-bi-deks'trus), *adj.* able to use both hands alike.

AMBIENT (am'bi-ent), *adj.* surrounding ; investing.

AMBIGUITY (am-bi-gu'i-ti), *n.* dubious signification ; vagueness.

AMBIGUOUS (am-big'u-us), *adj.* doubtful ; equivocal.

AMBIT (am'bit), *n.* a circuit or compass ; the perimeter.

AMBITION (am-bish'un), *n.* a seeking for preferment.

AMBITIOUS (am-bish'us), *adj.* having ambition ; aspiring.

AMBLE (am'bl), *v.i.* to move with a peculiar pace, as a horse.

AMBLYOPIA (am'bli-o-pi-a), **AMBLYOPY** (-pi), *n.* dimness of vision.

AMBROSIA (am-bro'zhi-a), *n.* anything exquisitely pleasing to taste or smell.

AMBROSIAL (am-bro'zhi-al), *adj.* delicious ; fragrant.

AMBULANCE (am'bu-lans), *n.* a wagon or auto for conveyance of sick and wounded.

AMBULANT (am'bu-lant), *adj.* walking ; moving about.

AMBULATION (am-bu-la'shun), *n.* the act of walking about.

AMBULATOR (am'bu-la-ter), *n.* a walker ; a pedometer.

AMBULATORY (am'bu-la-to-ri), *adj.* of or pertaining to walking.

AMBUSCADE (am-bus-kad'), *n.* a disposition of troops in ambush.

AMBUSH (am′boosh), *n.* a lying in wait to attack by surprise.

AMEER (a-mer′), *n.* a prince ; governor.

AMELIORABLE (a-me′li-or-a-bl), *adj.* capable of improvement.

AMELIORATE (a-me′li-or-at), *v.t.* to make better : *v.i.* to improve.

AMELIORATION (a-me-li-or-a′shun), *n.* improvement.

AMELIORATIVE (a-me′li-or-a-tiv), *adj.* producing amendment ; improving.

AMELIORATOR (a-me′li-or-a-ter), *n.* one who amends.

AMEN (a-men′, a′men′), *adv.* verily ; *interj.* so be it.

AMENABILITY (a-me-na-bil′i-ti), **AMENABLENESS** (a-me′na-bl-nes), *n.* liability to answer (to a charge, etc.) ; tractableness.

AMENABLE (a-me′na-bl), *adj.* submissive ; liable.

AMEND (a-mend′), *v.t.* to free from fault ; improve.

AMENDATORY (a-men′da-to-ri), *adj.* tending to amend.

AMENDMENT (a-mend′-ment), *n.* the alteration of a bill.

AMENDS (a-mendz′), *n.pl.* compensation for loss ; reparation.

AMENITY (a-men′i-ti), *n.* pleasantness ; geniality.

AMENTIA (a-men′shi-a), *n.* want of reason ; mental imbecility.

AMERCE (a-mers′), *v.t.* to punish by an arbitrary fine.

AMERCEMENT (a-mers′ment), *n.* an arbitrary fine.

AMERICAN (a-mer′i-kan), *adj.* belonging to, or characteristic of, America : *n.* a citizen of the United States.

AMERICANA (-kan′a), *n.* a collection of things American, as literary and scientific papers.

AMERICANISM (a-mer′i-kan-ism), *n.* a form of expression peculiar to the U.S.

AMERICANIZE (a-mer′i-kan-iz), *v.t.* assimilate to the political institutions of the U.S.

AMERICAN LEGION (a-mer′i-kan le′jun), see Legion.

AMETHYST (am′e-thist), *n.* a violet-purple quartz or rock-crystal.

AMIABILITY (a-mi-a-bil′i-ti), *n.* amiableness ; excellence of disposition.

AMIABLE (a′mi-a-bl), *adj.* friendly ; lovable.

AMICABLE (am′i-ka-bl), *adj.* friendly ; peaceable.

AMID (a-mid′), **AMIDST** (′st), *prep.* in the middle of ; among.

AMIDSHIPS (a-mid′ships), *adv.* in the middle of a ship.

AMISS (a-mis′), *adj.* wrong ; faulty.

AMITY (am′i-ti), *n.* friendly relations ; friendship.

AMMETER (am′me-ter), *n.* instrument for measuring currents in amperes in a circuit.

AMMONIA (a-mo′ni-a), *n.* spirits of hartshorn.

AMMONIAC (a-mo′ni-ak), *n.* chloride of ammonium.

AMMONITE (am′on-it), *n.* a fossil shell.

AMMONIUM CHLORIDE (klo′rid), a white crystalline compound.

AMMONIUM NITRATE (ni′trat), crystalline salt.

AMMONIUM SULPHATE (sul′fat), a crystalline salt formed by sulphuric acid and ammonia.

AMMONOL (am′o-nol), *n.* a drug used for relieving pain.

AMMUNITION (am-u-nish′un), *n.* powder, balls, etc., used in charging firearms of all kinds.

AMNESIA (am-ne′si-a), *n.* loss of memory.

AMNESTY (am′nes-ti), *n.* a general pardon ; *v.t.* to grant pardon to.

AMOEBA (a-me′ba), *n.* a form of microscopic organisms.

AMONG (a-mung′), **AMONGST** (′st), *prep. & adv.* mixed with ; amidst.

AMOROUS (am′o-rus), *adj.* loving.

AMORPHISM (a-mor′fizm), *n.* want of regular form.

AMORPHOUS (a-mor′fus), *adj.* formless ; unorganized.

AMORTIZE (a-mor′tiz), *v.t.* to extinguish a debt by a sinking fund.

AMOUNT (a-mount′), *v.i.* to mount up to : *n.* the totality sum.

AMOUR (a-moor'), *n.* a love-intrigue.

AMPELOPSIS (am-pe-lop'sis), *n.* a genus of plants of the vine family.

AMPERE (am-par'), *n.* the unit of measurement of the strength of an electrical current.

AMPHIBIA (am-fib'i-a), *n.pl.* the fourth division of vertebrates.

AMPHIBIAN (am-fib'i-an), *n.* an airplane to arise from or alight on either land or water.

AMPHIBIOUS (am-fib'i-us), *adj.* living both on land and in water.

AMPHITHEATRE (am-fi-the'a-ter), *n.* a theatre with seats all round the arena; a circus.

AMPHITYPE (am'fi-tip), *n.* a photographic process which simultaneously produces negatives and positives.

AMPLE (am'pl), *adj.* full; large; abundant.

AMPLECTANT (am-plek'tant), *adj.* in botany, clasping a support.

AMPLIATION (am-pli-a'shun), *n.* a legal term for postponement of decision.

AMPLIATIVE (am'pli-a-tiv), *adj.* enlarging; synthetic.

AMPLIFICATION (am-pli-fi-ka'-shun), *n.* the act of amplifying.

AMPLIFIER (-li-fi'er), *n.* one who amplifies; a negative lens put behind objective to enlarge the field of vision.

AMPLIFY (am'pli-fi), *v.t.* to make large : *v.i.* to expand.

AMPLITUDE (am'pli-tud), *n.* largeness; fullness; scope.

AMPLY (-li), *adv.* in an ample manner; liberally.

AMPUTATE (am'pu-tat), *v.t.* to lop off in pruning; to cut off a limb.

AMPUTATION (am-pu-ta'shun), *n.* the operation of cutting off a limb.

AMUCK (a-muk'), *adj.* or *adv.* (used only in the phrase, *to run amuck*, running about, attacking all who come in the way.

AMULET (am'u-let), *n.* a charm; a talisman.

AMUSE (a-muz'), *v.t.* to occupy the attention pleasantly; entertain.

AMUSEMENT (a-muz'ment), *n.* that which amuses; a pastime.

AMYGDALACEÆ (-la'se-e), *n.pl.*

the almond or plum family of trees and shrubs.

AMYL (am'il), *n.* the hypothetical alcohol radical of many chemical compounds.

AMYLENE (am'i-len), *n.* a hydrocarbon obtained by the removal of water from amyl alcohol.

AMYLIC (a-mil'ik), *adj.* of or pertaining to amyl.

AN (an), *indef. art.* any; each; one.

ANA (a'na), *n.pl.* a collection of notable sayings, literary gossip, anecdotes, etc., as Shakesperi*ana*.

ANACHRONISM (an-ak'ron-izm), *n.* an error in the order of time.

ANACHRONISTIC (an-ak-ron-is'-tik), *adj.* out of date.

ANACONDA (an-a-kon'da), *n.* a large South American snake.

ANADROMOUS (an-ad'ro-mus), *adj.* ascending from sea to freshwater rivers to spawn, as the salmon.

ANÆMIA, ANEMIA (a-ne'mi-a), *n.* deficiency or low condition of the blood.

ANÆSTHESIA, ANESTHESIA (an-es-the'si-a), *n.* a condition of insensibility to pain, combined with loss of the sense of touch.

ANÆSTHETIC, see anesthetic.

ANAGLYPH (an'a-glif), *n.* a work of art carved in relief, as distinguished from intaglio.

ANAGRAM (an'a-gram), *n.* a word, or a sentence, constructed out of another by the transposition of the letters contained in the second; a word obtained by reading the letters of another word backwards.

ANAGRAMMATIC (an-a-gra-mat'-ik), **ANAGRAMMATICAL** ('i-kal), *adj.* relating to, or forming an anagram.

ANALECT (an'a-lekt), *n.* a passage or extract from a published work.

ANALECTIC (an-a-lek'tik), *adj.* pertaining to, or composed of, selections from other works.

ANALGESIA (an-al-je'si-a), *n.* the insensibility to pain in any part of the body.

ANALGESIC (an-al-jes'ik), *adj.* designating that which allays pain : *n.* an anodyne.

ANALGETIC (an-al-jet'ik), *adj.* pertaining to analgesia.

ANALOGICAL (an-a-loj'i-kal), *adj.* bearing reference ; having relation or resemblance.

ANALOGISM (a-nal'o-jism), *n.* a reasoning from the cause to the effect.

ANALOGIST (a-nal'o-jist), *n.* one who reasons from the standpoint of analogy.

ANALOGIZE (a-nal'o-jiz), *v.t.* to reason or expound by reference to analogy.

ANALOGOUS (a-nal'o-gus), *adj.* possessing points of analogy ; linked by resemblance ; similar.

ANALOGUE (an'a-log), *n.* an object which bears analogy to something else.

ANALOGY (a-nal'o-ji), *n.* agreement, resemblance, or correspondence in relations between different objects.

ANALYSIS (a-nal'i-sis), *n.* [*pl.* analyses (-sez)], the resolution of a compound into its constituent parts.

ANALYST (an'a-list), *n.* one who is skilled in analysis.

ANALYTIC (an-a-lit'ik), **ANALYTICAL** (-i-kal), *adj.* relating to, or characterized by, the method of analysis.

ANALYTICALLY (-al-li), *adv.* in the manner or by means of analysis.

ANALYTICS (an-a-lit'iks), *n.pl.* the science of analysis.

ANALYZABLE (an'a-li-za-bl), *adj.* capable of being resolved by analysis.

ANALYZE (an'a-liz), *v.t.* to separate or resolve.

ANAPLASTY (an-a-plas'ti), *n.* the repairing of wounds by the transplantation of adjacent healthy tissue.

ANARCH (an'ark), *n.* an instigator or abettor of anarchy.

ANARCHIC (an-ar'kik), **ANARCHICAL** (-al), *adj.* of or pertaining to anarchy.

ANARCHISM (an'ar-kizm), *n.* the doctrines of the anarchists.

ANARCHIST (an'ar-kist), *n.* one who supports or promotes a scheme for anarchy.

ANARCHY (an'ar-ki), *n.* a lawless condition of society ; the theory of individual liberty.

ANARTHROUS (an-ar'thrus), *adj.* without the article, in Greek grammar ; destitute of joints.

ANASTIGMAT (an-as'tig-mat), *n.* a combination of lenses used in photography.

ANASTIGMATIC (-mat'ik), *adj.* free from astigmatism ; in reference to a lens.

ANASTOMOSIS (-to-mo'sis), *n.* a running together, as of two streams.

ANATHEMA (a-nath'e-ma), *n.* an imprecation ; the thing or person held to be accursed.

ANATHEMATIZE (a-nath'e-ma-tiz), *v.t.* to pronounce a decree of excommunication against : *v.i.* to curse.

ANATOMICAL (an-a-tom'i-kal), *adj.* relating to, or according to, the laws of anatomy.

ANATOMISM (a-nat'o-mizm), *n.* the application of the principles of anatomy.

ANATOMIST (a-nat'o-mist), *n.* one possessing a knowledge of anatomy.

ANATOMIZE (a-nat'o-miz), *v.t.* to separate by dissection.

ANATOMY (a-nat'o-mi), *n.* separation by dissection of the various parts of a body.

ANATRIPSIS (an-a-trip'sis), *n.* massage.

ANCESTOR (an'ses-ter), *n.* a forefather or progenitor.

ANCESTRAL (an-ses'tral), *adj.* belonging to, or connected with, ancestors.

ANCESTRY (an'ses-tri), *n.* the line of one's descent.

ANCHOR (ang'ker), *n.* an iron weight, with flukes and attached to a cable, used for holding ships.

ANCHORAGE (ang'ker-aj), *n.* a suitable place for the anchoring of vessels.

ANCHORET (ang'ko-ret), **ANCHORITE** (-rit), *n.* one who voluntarily secludes himself from society.

ANCHOR-ICE (ang'ker-is), *n.* ground-ice.

ANCHOVY (an-cho'vi), *n.* a diminutive fish.

ANCIENT (an'shent), *adj*. of or pertaining to the early history of the world.

ANCILLARY (an'sil-ar-i), *adj*. attendant upon ; accessory ; subservient.

ANCIPITAL (an-sip'i-tal), *adj*. double-faced ; two-edged.

ANCON (ang'kon), *n*. the upper extremity of the forearm or ulna ; the elbow.

AND (and), *conj*. a copulative joining words and sentences.

ANDESINE (an'de-sin), *n*. a triclinic feldspar.

ANDESITE (an'de-sit), *n*. a silicate of alumina, soda, and lime.

ANDIRONS (and'i-ernz), *n.pl*. metal standards used for open fires.

ANDRADITE (an'dra-dit), *n*. a garnet of a dark green colour.

ANDROCEPHALOUS (an-dro-sef'a-lus), *adj*. having a human head on an animal body, as a sphinx.

ANDROGENOUS (an-droj'e-nus), *adj*. producing males.

ANDROID (an'droid), *adj*. resembling a man.

ANDROSPHINX (an'dro-sfingks), *n*. a sphinx with a body of a lion and the head of a man.

ANECDOTAL (an'ek-dot-al), *adj*. relating to, or consisting of, anecdotes.

ANECDOTE (an'ek-dot), *n*. a brief narrative of an entertaining character.

ANECDOTIC (an-ek-dot'ik), **ANEC-DOTICAL** ('i-kal), *adj*. relating to anecdotes.

ANELECTRIC (an-e-lek'trik), *adj*. without the properties of electricity ; non-electric : *n*. a non-electric substance.

ANELECTRODE (an-e-lek'trod), *n*. the positive pole of a galvanic battery.

ANEMIA, see anæmia.

ANEMOGRAPH (a-nem'o-graf), *n*. an instrument for registering the force or direction of the wind.

ANEMOMETER (an-e-mom'e-ter), *n*. an instrument which indicates the pressure of the wind.

ANEMOMETRY (-mom'e-tri), *n*. process of determining force of the wind.

ANEMONE (a-nem'o-ne), *n*. the wind-flower ; marine zoophyte.

ANEMOSCOPE (a-nem'o-skop), *n*. an apparatus for exhibiting the direction of the wind.

ANEROID (an'e-roid), *n*. a barometer with action depending on the varying pressure of the atmosphere.

ANESTHESIA, see anæsthesia.

ANESTHETIC, ANÆSTHETIC (an-es-thet'ik), *adj*. pertaining to loss of the sense of feeling : *n*. a drug which produces insensibility.

ANESTHETIZE, ANÆSTHETIZE (an-es'the-tiz), *v.t*. to bring under the influence of an anæsthetic ; render insensible to pain.

ANEURISM (an'u-rizm), *n*. a local swelling or dilation of an artery at a point where the coat is thinned or weakened by disease.

ANEW (a-nu'), *adv*. afresh ; over again.

ANGARIA (an-gar'ia), *n*. seizure in war.

ANGEL (an'jel), *n*. a messenger of God ; one of an order of spiritual attendants.

ANGEL-FISH (-fish), *n*. a species of shark.

ANGELIC (an-jel'ik), **ANGELICAL** ('i-kal), *adj*. belonging to or resembling an angel.

ANGELUS (an'je-lus), *n*. an R.C. devotional exercise.

ANGER (ang'ger), *n*. excessive emotion or passion.

ANGINA (an-ji'na, an'ji-na), *n*. an inflamed condition of the throat.

ANGINA PECTORIS (pek'to-ris), *n*. muscular spasm of the chest.

ANGLE (ang'gl), *n*. the inclination of two lines which meet at a point ; the vertex.

ANGLE (ang'gl), *v.i*. to fish : *v.t*. to fish for.

ANGLER (ang'gler), *n*. one who fishes with rod and line.

ANGLE-WORM (-werm), *n*. an earth-worm.

ANGLICAN (ang'gli-kan), *adj*. pertaining to England as a nation ; pertaining to the Church of England.

ANGLICANISM (ang'gli-kan-izm), *n*.

the principles of the Anglican Church.

ANGLICE (ang'gli-se), *adv.* according to the English language or manner.

ANGLICISM (ang'gli-sizm), *n.* a form of speech ; a principle or mannerism peculiar to England.

ANGLICIZE (ang'gli-siz), *v.t.* to make or to render into English.

ANGLING (ang'gling), *n.* the act of fishing.

ANGLO-AMERICAN (ang'glo-a-mer'i-kan), *adj.* pertaining to England and the U.S.

ANGLOMANIA (ang'glo-ma'ni-a), *n.* a predilection carried to excess for everything that is English.

ANGLOPHILE (-fil), *n.* one who favours or loves England.

ANGLOPHOBE (-fob), *n.* one affected with Anglophobia.

ANGLOPHOBIA (-fo'bi-a), *n.* an aversion for everything English.

ANGLO-SAXON (-saks'un), *adj.* pertaining to the Saxon settlers in England prior to the Conquest.

ANGORA (ang-go'ra), *n.* cloth made from Angora wool.

ANGORA CAT (kat), a cat with long handsome hair.

ANGORA GOAT (got), one of a breed of goats native to the province of Angora, Asia Minor.

ANGORA WOOL (wool), the coat of the Angora goat.

ANGOSTURA BARK (ang-gos-tu'ra bark), a bitter aromatic bark used as a tonic.

ANGRILY ('gri-li), *adv.* in an angry manner.

ANGRY (ang'gri), *adj.* inflamed with anger ; wrathful.

ANGUINE (an'gwin), *adj.* like a serpent.

ANGUISH (ang'gwish), *n.* intense pain or grief.

ANGULAR (ang'gu-lar), *adj.* possessing an angle or angles.

ANGULARITY (ang-gu-lar'i-ti), *n.* the quality of being angular.

ANGULATE (ang'gu-lat), *adj.* in botany, having the form of an angle.

ANGUSTATE (ang-gus'tat), *adj.* narrow at base and expanded at top.

ANHYDRIDE (an-hi'drid), *n.* an oxygen compound.

ANHYDRITE (an-hi'drit), *n.* anhydrous sulphate of lime.

ANHYDROUS (an-hi'drus), *adj.* without water.

ANIL (an'il), *n.* the indigo plant; indigo dye.

ANILINE (an'i-lin), *n.* a base used in the formation of many rich dyes.

ANILISM (an'il-izm), *n.* aniline poisoning.

ANIMADVERSION (an-i-mad-ver'-shun), *n.* capacity for perception; censure.

ANIMADVERSIVE (an-i-mad-ver'-siv), *adj.* attentive ; observing.

ANIMADVERT (an-i-mad-vert'), *v.i.* to give the mind to ; pass comment on.

ANIMAL (an'i-mal), *n.* an organized living body.

ANIMALCULAR (an-i-mal'ku-lar), **ANIMALCULINE** (-lin), *adj.* of or relating to animalcules.

ANIMALCULE (an-i-mal'kul), *n.* one of a class of minute or microscopic organisms.

ANIMAL HEAT (het), natural heat in the body of a living animal or being.

ANIMALISM (an'i-mal-izm), *n.* the state of being animal, or actuated by animal instincts or appetites.

ANIMALITY (an-i-mal'i-ti), *n.* possessing animal characteristics.

ANIMALIZE (an'i-mal-iz), *v.t.* to make animal.

ANIMAL MAGNETISM (mag'net-izm), mesmerism ; hypnotism.

ANIMATE (an'i-mat), *v.t.* to impart life to.

ANIMATION (an-i-ma'shun), *n.* the act of giving life or spirit.

ANIMATIVE (an'i-ma-tiv), *adj.* denoting power to impart life or spirit.

ANIMOSITY (an-i-mos'i-ti), *n.* hostility ; hatred ; enmity.

ANIMUS (an'i-mus), *n.* intention, temper, spirit or purpose ; hostility.

ANISE (an'is), *n.* a plant yielding the aniseed of commerce.

ANKLE (ang'kl), *n.* the joint connecting the foot with the leg.

ANKLET (ang'klet), *n.* an ornament or support for the ankle.

ANKUS (ang'kus), *n.* a spiked staff for goading an elephant.

ANNAL (an'al), *n.* the record of a year.

ANNALIST (an'a-list), *n.* a compiler of annals.

ANNALS (an'alz), *n.pl.* a description, history or chronicle issued from time to time.

ANNEAL (a-nel'), *v.t.* to heat or fix by heat.

ANNEALING (-ing), *n.* the process of tempering.

ANNEX (a-neks'), *v.t.* to add or affix at the end : *n.* (an-neks', an'neks), that which is added.

ANNEXATION (an-eks-a'shun), *n.* the act of annexing.

ANNIHILATE (a-ni'hi-lat), *v.t.* to reduce to nothing.

ANNIHILATION (a-ni-hi-la'shun), *n.* the act of annihilating.

ANNIVERSARY (an-i-ver'sa-ri), *n.* the recurrence in each year of the date of an event.

ANNOTATE (an'o-tat), *v.t.* to mark or note by way of explanation.

ANNOTATION (an-o-ta'shun), *n.* the act of noting or commenting upon.

ANNOTATOR (an'o-ta-ter), *n.* one who annotates.

ANNOUNCE (a-nouns'), *v.t.* to proclaim or make known.

ANNOUNCEMENT (a-nouns'ment), *n.* that which is announced ; a proclamation.

ANNOY (a-noi'), *v.t.* to vex or trouble by repeated acts.

ANNOYANCE (an-noi'ans), *n.* the act of annoying ; the thing or act which annoys.

ANNUAL (an'u-al), *adj.* once in twelve months ; yearly : *n.* a plant which completes its growth in a year.

ANNUALLY (-li), *adv.* happening, returning, year by year.

ANNUITANT (a-nu'i-tant), *n.* one who is in receipt of an annuity.

ANNUITY (a-nu'i-ti), *n.* the payment of a sum of money by yearly instalments.

ANNUL (a-nul'), *v.t.* to make void, abolish.

ANNULAR (an'u-lar), *adj.* ring-like ; in the form of a ring.

ANNULATE (an'u-lat), *adj.* ringed ; having ring-like bands.

ANNULATION (an-u-la'shun), *n.* a ring-like formation.

ANNULET (an'u-let), *n.* a little ring.

ANNULMENT (a-nul'ment), *n.* act of reducing to nothing ; invalidation.

ANNULOSE (an'u-los), *adj.* composed of a succession of rings.

ANNULUS (an'u-lus), *n.* the space between two concentric circles.

ANNUNCIATE (a-nun'shi-at), *v.t.* to make known officially or publicly.

ANNUNCIATION (a-nun-shi-a'-shun), *n.* the act of annunciating.

ANNUNCIATION LILY (lil'i), the common white lily.

ANNUNCIATOR (a-nun'shi-a-ter), *n.* a signalling apparatus.

ANODE (an'od), *n.* the path of the electric current from the positive to the negative.

ANODYNE (an'o-din), *adj.* assuaging pain : *n.* a drug which relieves pain.

ANOINT (a-noint'), *v.t.* to pour oil upon.

ANOMALISTIC (a-nom-a-lis'tik), *adj.* pertaining to the anomaly or angular distance of a planet from its perihelion.

ANOMALOUS (a-nom'a-lus), *adj.* deviating from the common order ; abnormal.

ANOMALY (a-nom'a-li), *n.* deviation from the natural order ; the angular distance of a planet from its perihelion.

ANON (a-non'), *adv.* soon ; presently ; again.

ANONYM (an'o-nim), *n.* a person who remains nameless ; a pseudonym.

ANONYMITY (an-o-nim'i-ti), *n.* the state of being anonymous.

ANONYMOUS (a-non'i-mus), *adj.* bearing no author's name ; nameless.

ANOPHELES (a-nof'e-lez), *n.* a genus of the mosquito family.

ANOREXIA (an-o-rek'si-a), *n.* loss of appetite.

ANORTHOPIA (an-or-tho'pi-a), *n.* distorted vision which sees straight lines as crooked.

ANORTHOSCOPE (an-or'tho-skop), *n.* an optical instrument through which distorted figures appear normal.

ANOSMIA (an-os'mi-a), *n.* loss of the sense of smelling.

ANOTHER (a-nuth'er), *adj. & pron.* one more ; not the same ; any other ; any or some one else.

ANSER (an'ser), *n.* the genus consisting of the geese.

ANSERINE (an'ser-in), *adj.* relating to or resembling a goose.

ANSWER (an'ser), *v.t.* to swear in opposition to ; to reply to a charge ; make a counter-statement : *n.* a response ; a solution.

ANSWERABLE ('ser-a-bl), *adj.* liable to give answer ; responsible.

ANT (ant), *n.* a small active insect.

ANTACID (ant-as'id), *adj.* counteracting acidity.

ANTAGONISM (an-tag'o-nizm), *n.* the active opposition of opposing forces ; hostility.

ANTAGONIST (an-tag'o-nist), *n.* a competitor in any sphere of action.

ANTAGONISTIC (an-tag-o-nis'tik), *adj.* acting in opposition ; opposed.

ANTAGONISTICALLY (-al-li), *adv.* in rivalry or opposition.

ANTAGONIZE (an-tag'o-niz), *v.t.* to oppose ; hinder ; counteract.

ANTARCTIC (ant-ark'tik), *adj.* pertaining to the south-polar regions.

ANT-BEAR (ant-bar), *n.* the great anteater.

ANT-BIRD (-berd), *n.* a large black and white passerine bird.

ANTEATER ('e-ter), *n.* one of a group of quadrupeds which feed upon ants.

ANTECEDE (an-te-sed'), *v.t.* to precede or go before in time or space.

ANTECEDENCE (an-te-se'-dens), **ANTECEDENCY** ('den-si), *n.* precedence ; the act or state of going before ; priority.

ANTECEDENT (an-te-se'dent), *adj.* preceding : *n.* the substantive or noun to which a relative or other pronoun refers.

ANTECENDENTLY (-li), *adv.* at a time preceding.

ANTECESSOR (an-te-ses'er), *n.* one who goes before (in office).

ANTECHAMBER (an'te-cham'ber), *n.* an apartment next the principal room ; an outer room.

ANTEDATE (an'te-dat), *v.t.* to carry back to an earlier period.

ANTEDILUVIAN (an-te-di-lu'vi-an), *adj.* of or pertaining to the world before the Flood ; belonging to very ancient times.

ANTELOPE (an'te-lop), *n.* one of numerous species of deer-like ruminants.

ANTEMERIDIAN (an-te-me-rid'i-an), *adj.* preceding noon.

ANTEMUNDANE (an-te-mun'dan), *adj.* before the creation of the world.

ANTENATAL (an-te-na'tal), *adj.* before birth.

ANTENNA (an-ten'a), *n.* [*pl.* antennæ ('e)], feelers upon the heads of insects ; an upraised aerial wire for transmitting and receiving electric waves.

ANTENUPTIAL (an-te-nup'shal), *adj.* before marriage.

ANTEPASCHAL (an-te-pas'kal), *adj.* before Easter.

ANTEPENDIUM (-pen'di-um), *n.* the screen in front of an altar.

ANTEPENULT (an-te-pe-nult'), **ANTEPENULTIMA** (an-te-pe-nul'ti-ma), *n.* the last syllable but two of a word.

ANTEPENULTIMATE (an-te-pe-nul'ti-mat), *adj.* pertaining to the last but two.

ANTEPOSITION (an-te-po-zish'un), *n.* the place of a word before another which it usually follows.

ANTEPRANDIAL (an-te-pran'di-al), *adj.* before dinner.

ANTERIOR (an-te'ri-er), *adj.* more to the front ; former.

ANTERIORITY (-te-ri-or'i-ti), *n.* the quality of being anterior.

ANTEROOM (an'te-room), *n.* a room before another ; an antechamber.

ANTETEMPLE (an'te-tem-pl), *n.* the portico of an ancient temple.

ANTETYPE (-tip), *n.* a prototype.

ANTHEM (an'them), *n.* a composition set to sacred music ; a hymn.

ANTHER (an'ther), *n.* the summit of the stamen of a flower containing the pollen or fertilizing dust.

ANTHEROID (an'ther-oid), *adj.* having the form of an anther.

ANTHESIS (an-the'sis), *n.* full bloom ; a state of complete expansion in a flower.

ANTHOGRAPHY (an-thog'ra-fi), *n.* the scientific description of flowers.

ANTHOID (an'thoid), *adj.* like a flower.

ANTHOLOGICAL (an-tho-loj'i-kal), *adj.* consisting of beautiful extracts, more especially of those from the poets.

ANTHOLOGIST (an-thol'o-jist), *n.* one who compiles an anthology.

ANTHOLOGY (an-thol'o-ji), *n.* a collection of choice poems, epigrams, and fugitive pieces by various authors ; a hymnal.

ANTHRACENE (an'thra-sen), *n.* a complex hydrocarbon obtained from coal-tar.

ANTHRACITE (an'thra-sit), *n.* non-bituminous coal which burns without smoke.

ANTHRACITIC (an-thra-sit'ik), *adj.* resembling, or of the nature of anthracite.

ANTHRACOSIS (an-thra-ko'sis), *n.* a lung disease, peculiar to miners who inhale coal dust.

ANTHRAX (an'thraks), *n.* [*pl.* anthraces (-sez)], a carbuncle, or malignant boil ; the splenic fever of sheep and cattle.

ANTHROPOID (an'thro-poid), *adj.* resembling man : *n.* one of the higher apes.

ANTHROPOLOGICAL (an-thro-po-loj'i-kal), *adj.* relating to anthropology.

ANTHROPOLOGIST (an-thro-pol'o-jist), *n.* a student of anthropology.

ANTHROPOLOGY (an-thro-pol'o-ji), *n.* the science of man, considered zoölogically or ethnographically.

ANTHROPOMETRY (an-thro-pom'e-tri), *n.* the measurement of the human body.

ANTHROPOMORPHIC (an-thro-po-mor'fik), *adj.* resembling man ; having human shape.

ANTHROPOZOIC (an'thro-po-zo'-ik), *a.* pertaining to the time during which man has existed on the earth.

ANTIC (an'tik), *adj.* grotesque : *n.* a clown ; a trick.

ANTICHRIST (an'ti-krist), *n.* an opponent of Christ, especially the great personal opponent expected to appear before the end of the world.

ANTICIPANT (an-tis'i-pant), *adj.* denoting that which operates before-hand : *n.* one who looks forward.

ANTICIPATE (an-tis'i-pat), *v.t.* to take beforehand ; use in advance ; look for as certain.

ANTICIPATION (an-tis-i-pa'shun), *n.* the act of taking beforehand ; expectation ; hope ; preconception.

ANTICIPATIVE (an-tis'i-pa-tiv), **ANTICIPATORY** (-to-ri), *adj.* taking beforehand ; anticipating.

ANTICLERICAL (-kler'i-kal), *adj.* opposed to the clergy.

ANTICLIMAX (an'ti-kli-maks), *n.* a ludicrous descent in thought and expression.

ANTICLINAL (-kli'nal), *adj.* bent or curved, with the convex side up.

ANTICYCLONE (an'ti-si-klon), *n.* a meteorological condition in which the ordinary features of a cyclone are reversed.

ANTIDOTAL (an'ti-dot-al), *adj.* of the nature or quality of an antidote.

ANTIDOTE (an'ti-dot), *n.* a sub-stance which acts medicinally as a counter-active to the effects of poison or disease.

ANTIFAT (an'ti-fat), *adj.* for pre-venting or reducing fatness.

ANTIFEBRILE (an-ti-feb'ril), *adj.* capable of allaying fever : *n.* a fever medicine or antipyretic.

ANTI-IMPERIALISM (-im-pe'ri-al-izm), *n.* opposition to imperialism.

ANTIMACASSAR (-ma-kas'-ar), *n.* a cover for a chair or sofa.

ANTIMONY (an'ti-mo-ni), *n.* a white lustrous metal, entering largely into medicinal preparations and various alloys.

ANTINOMY (an-tin'o-mi), *n.* the

opposition of one law, or part of a law, to another.

ANTIPARALLEL (an-ti-par'a-lel), *adj.* running parallel, but in an opposite direction.

ANTIPATHETIC (an-ti-pa-thet'ik), **ANTIPATHETICAL** ('i-kal), *adj.* possessing a natural antipathy or aversion [with *to*].

ANTIPATHIC (an-ti-path'ik), *adj.* pertaining to antipathy ; adverse ; opposite.

ANTIPATHY (an-tip'a-thi), *n.* natural aversion ; an instinctive dislike ; the object of aversion (followed by *to*, *against*, *between*, *for*).

ANTIPERIODIC (an-ti-pe-ri-od'ik), *adj.* preventive of return in periodic or intermittent diseases.

ANTIPHLOGISTIC (an-ti-flo-jis'-tik), *adj.* efficacious in counteracting fever or inflammation.

ANTIPHON (an'ti-fon), **ANTIPHONE** (-fon), *n.* chant or hymn rendered alternately by two choirs.

ANTIPHONAL (an-tif'o-nal), *adj.* characterized by antiphony or responsive singing.

ANTIPHONARY (an-tif'o-na-ri), *n.* a book of responses used in church services.

ANTIPHONETIC (an-ti-fo-net'ik), *adj.* similar in sound.

ANTIPHONY (an-tif'o-ni), *n.* the alternate or responsive rendering of psalms or chants by a dual choir.

ANTIPHRASIS (an-tif'ra-sis), *n.* the employment of a word, or words, in a sense contrary to its, or their, true meaning.

ANTIPODAL (an-tip'o-dal), *adj.* pertaining to the antipodes ; opposite or extreme.

ANTIPODE (an'ti-pod), *n.* that which is directly opposite to another.

ANTIPODEAN (an-tip-o-de'an), *adj.* belonging to the antipodes.

ANTIPODES (an-tip'o-dez), *n.pl.* those who reside at opposite sides of the globe ; the two portions of the earth's surface which are exactly opposite to each other.

ANTIPYRETIC (an-ti-pi-ret'ik), *adj.*

preventive of, or remedial to, fever : *n.* a remedy of such nature.

ANTIPYRIN (an-ti-pi'rin), *n.* a drug obtained from coal-tar, employed for the relief of neuralgia, nervous headaches, and reduction of heat in fevers.

ANTIQUARIAN (an-ti-kwar'i-an), *adj.* pertaining to antiquaries or to antiquity : *n.* an antiquary.

ANTIQUARIANISM (an-ti-kwar'i-an-izm), *n.* attachment to what is old or antiquated.

ANTIQUARY (an'ti-kwa-ri), *n.* one who is attached to ancient things, and is learned in their history.

ANTIQUATED (an'ti-kwated), *p.adj.* grown old ; obsolete.

ANTIQUE (an-tek'), *adj.* of or belonging to a former age ; ancient.

ANTIQUENESS (-nes), *n.* the quality of being ancient.

ANTIQUITY (an-tik'wi-ti), *n.* great age ; ancientness ; early ages ; people or races of ancient times.

ANTI-SEMITE (an-ti-sem'it), *n.* one who favours the social and political persecution of Jews.

ANTI-SEMITIC (an-ti-sem-it'ik), *adj.* pertaining to, or characterized by, anti-Semitism.

ANTI-SEMITISM (an-ti-sem'it-izm), *n.* antagonism to the Jewish race.

ANTISEPSIS (an-ti-sep'sis), *n.* the exclusion of bacteria from wounds, etc., by the use of antiseptics.

ANTISEPTIC (an-ti-sep'tik), *adj.* destructive to the germs of disease or putrefaction: *n.* a substance that acts as a preventive to putrefaction.

ANTISLAVERY (an-ti-slav'er-i), *adj.* opposed to slavery : *n.* opposition to slavery.

ANTITHERMIC (an-ti-ther'mik), *adj.* tending to reduce the bodily temperature.

ANTITHESIS (an-tith'e-sis), *n.* [*pl.* antitheses (-sez)] opposition ; contrast.

ANTITHETIC (an-ti-thet'ik), **ANTITHETICAL** (-al), *adj.* pertaining to antithesis.

ANTITOXIN (an-ti-toks'in), *n.* a

serum used hypodermically as a preventive of, or cure for, certain diseases.

ANTI-TRUST (an′ti-trust), *adj.* antagonistic to trusts formed to control trade.

ANTITYPE (an′ti-tip), *n.* that which preceded the type.

ANTLER (ant′ler), *n.* the individual branches of a stag's horns.

ANTONYM (an′to-nim), *n.* a word meaning the opposite of some other word, as, unhappy is the *antonym* of happy.

ANVIL (an′vil), *n.* an iron block used for the hammering and shaping of metals.

ANXIETY (ang-zi′e-ti), *n.* condition of mental uneasiness arising from fear or solicitude.

ANXIOUS (ang′shus), *adj.* deeply concerned; very solicitous; apprehensive.

ANY (en′i), *adj. & pron.* one indeterminately, or unlimited; some; an indefinite number, quantity, or degree : *adj.* one indefinitely; (*pl.*) some : *pron.* one; anyone; (*pl.*) some ; *adv.* to any extent.

ANYBODY (-bod-i), *n.* any person; some one of importance as opposed to nobody.

ANYHOW (-hou), *adv.* in any way or manner; in any case; at any rate.

ANYTHING (-thing), *n.* any object as distinguished from a person.

ANYWAY (-wa), *adv.* in any manner.

ANYWHERE (-hwar), *adv.* in any place.

AORIST (a′o-rist), *n.* one of the tenses of a Greek verb, denoting past indefinite time.

AORTA (a-or′ta), *n.* [*pl.* aortæ (-te)], the chief artery or main trunk of the arterial system, opening from the left ventricle of the heart.

APACE (a-pas′), *adv.* quickly; at a quick pace; speedily.

APACHE (a-pa′cha), *n.* an American Indian; [a-] (a-pash′), a Parisian ruffian.

APART (a-part′), *adv.* separately; aside; asunder.

APARTMENT (a-part′ment), *n.* a room or part of a divided building.

APATHETIC (ap-a-thet′ik), **APATHETICAL** (-al), *adj.* devoid of, or insensible to, feeling or emotion.

APATHETICALLY (-li), *adv.* in an apathetical manner.

APATHY (ap′a-thi), *n.* lack of feeling ; indifference.

APE (ap), *n.* a tailless monkey.

APEAK (a-pek′), *adv.* nearly vertical in position.

APERIENT (a-pe′ri-ent), *adj.* gently laxative ; opening the bowels.

APERIODIC (a-pe-ri-od′ik), *adj.* without periodicity.

APERITIVE (a-per′i-tiv), same as aperient.

APERTURE (ap′er-tur), *n.* an opening ; a perforation or passage.

APETALOUS (a-pet′al-us), *adj.* without petals or corolla.

APEX (a′peks), *n.* [*pl.* apices (ap′i-sez), apexes (a′pek-sez)], the point, tip, or summit of anything.

APHAGIA (a-fa′ji-a), *n.* inability to swallow.

APHASIA (a-fa′zhi-a), *n.* loss of the power of speech, or the appropriate use of words, due to disease or injury of the brain.

APHELION (a-fe′li-on), *n.* [*pl.* aphelia (-a)], that point in the orbit of a planet farthest from the sun.

APHID (af′id), *n.* a plant louse.

APHIDIAN (a-fid′i-an), *n.* an aphid.

APHIS (a′fis), *n.* [*pl.* Aphides (af′i-dez)], the genus of plant lice.

APHLOGISTIC (af-lo-jis′tik), *adj.* flameless ; without flame.

APHONIA (a-fo′ni-a), *n.* loss of voice ; an affection of the vocal cords.

APHORISM (af′o-rizm), *n.* a concise and pithy statement.

APHOTIC (a-fo′tik), *adj.* without light.

APHRASIA (a-fra′zhi-a), *n.* a disorder of speech preventing utterance of intelligible words.

APHTHONG (af′thong), *n.* a letter or letters not sounded in a word.

APHYLLOUS (a-fil′us), *adj.* without leaves ; leafless.

APIACEÆ (a-pi-a′se-e), *n.* a

family of plants, including parsley, celery and carrot.

APIARIAN (-a'ri-an), *adj.* relating to beekeeping.

APIARY (a'pi-a-ri), *n.* a place where bees are kept; a bee-house.

APICULTURE (-kul'tur), *n.* beekeeping.

APICULUS (a-pik'u-lus), *n.* the point of a leaf.

APIECE (a-pes'), *adv.* to or for each; each severally.

APISH (ap'ish), *adj.* resembling an ape in manners; foppish; foolish.

APLOMB (a-plong'), *n.* [French], self-possession; assurance.

APOCALYPSE (a-pok'a-lips), *n.* the last book of the New Testament.

APOCALYPTIC (a-pok-a-lip'tik), **APOCALYPTICAL** (ti-kal), *adj.* pertaining to or containing the Apocalypse.

APOCOPE (a-pok'o-pe), *n.* the cutting off or deletion of the last letter or syllable of a word.

APOCRYPHA (a-pok'ri-fa), *n.pl.* a writing or something of doubtful authorship; [-A] certain writings found in the Septuagint version of the Old Testament accepted as canonical by the R.C. Church, but rejected by Protestants.

APOCRYPHAL (a-pok'ri-fal), *adj.* of doubtful authority; uncanonical; of or pertaining to the Apocrypha.

APODICTIC (ap-o-dik'tik), *adj.* absolute certainty.

APOGEE (ap'o-je), *n.* that point in the orbit of a planet which is most distant from the earth.

APOLOGETIC (a-pol-o-jet'ik), **APOLOGETICAL** (i-kal), *adj.* in the way of defence or apology.

APOLOGETICS (a-pol-o-jet'iks), *n.* the branch of theology which defends Christian doctrine on the grounds of reason.

APOLOGIA (ap-o-lo'ji-a), *n.* an argument in defence of principles.

APOLOGIST (a-pol'o-jist), **APOLOGIZER** (-jiz-er), *n.* one who apologizes; one who pleads in defence of another.

APOLOGIZE (a-pol'o-jiz), *v.i.* to make an apology; to express regret.

APOLOGUE (ap'o-log), *n.* a moral fable.

APOLOGY (a-pol'o-ji), *n.* a vindication; something spoken, written, or offered in defence.

APOPLECTIC (ap-o-plek'tik), **APOPLECTICAL** ('ti-kal), *adj.* pertaining to, or of the nature of, apoplexy.

APOPLEXY (ap'o-plek-si), *n.* the sudden loss of consciousness and motive power, resulting from cerebral rupture.

APORT (a-port'), *adv.* on or towards the port or left side of a ship.

APOSTASY (a-pos'ta-si), *n.* the forsaking of what one has hitherto professed or adhered to.

APOSTATE (a-pos'tat) *n.* one who has forsaken or apostatized his faith or party.

APOSTATIZE (a-pos'ta-tiz), *v.i.* to abandon one's faith, church, or party.

A POSTERIORI (a pos-te-ri-o'ri), characterizing reasoning founded on observation of facts, effects, or consequences, by means of which the causes are reached.

APOSTLE (a-pos'l), *n.* one charged with a high mission; one of the twelve persons specially selected by Christ to propagate His gospel.

APOSTLES' CREED (kred), *n.* the confession of faith accepted by all professing Christians.

APOSTOLATE (a-pos'to-lat), *n.* apostleship; now restricted to the dignity or office of the Pope.

APOSTOLIC (ap-os-tol'ik), **APOSTOLICAL** ('i-kal), *adj.* of or pertaining to an apostle.

APOSTROPHE (a-pos'tro-fe), *n.* a breaking off in a speech to address directly a person or persons who may or may not be present; the omission from a word of one or more letters.

APOSTROPHIZE (a-pos'tro-fiz), *v.t.* to address by apostrophe; omit a letter or letters.

APOTHECARY (a-poth'e-ka-ri), *n.* one who prepares and dispenses medicines and drugs for profit; a pharmacist.

APOTHECARIES' WEIGHT (wat), the weight used for dispensing drugs, and comprising the pound (12 oz.), the ounce (8 drachms), the drachm (3 scruples), the scruple (20 grs.), and the grain.

APOTHEGM (ap'o-them), *n.* a pithy saying, embodying a wholesome truth or precept.

APOTHEOSIS (ap-o-the'o-sis), *n.* [*pl.* ap-o-the'o-ses (-sez)], deification.

APOTHEOSIZE (ap-o-the'o-siz), *v.t.* to exalt to the rank of a god; deify.

APPAL, APPALL (a-pawl'), *v.t.* to fright; dismay; terrify.

APPALLING (a-paw'ling), *p.adj.* inspiring horror or dismay.

APPARATUS (ap-a-ra'tus), *n. sing. & pl.* an outfit of tools, instruments adapted to the accomplishment of any branch of work.

APPAREL (a-par'el), *n.* clothing.

APPARENT (a-par'ent), *adj.* open to view; capable of being readily perceived; evident.

APPARITION (ap-a-rish'un), *n.* a visible object; an appearance of something not real or tangible.

APPEAL (a-pel'), *v.t.* to transfer or refer to a superior court or judge, to another person or tribunal; entreat.

APPEAR (a-per'), *v.i.* to become visible; seem.

APPEARANCE (a-per'ans), *n.* the act of becoming visible; the object seen; a phenomenon; an apparition.

APPEASABLE (a-pez'za-bl), *adj.* capable of being appeased.

APPEASE (a-pez'), *v.t.* to allay; assuage; quiet; satisfy; pacify.

APPEASEMENT (ap-pez'ment), *n.* the act of appeasing; the state of being appeased.

APPELLANT (a-pel'ant), *n.* one who appeals to a judge, or to any tribunal.

APPELLATE (a-pel'at), *adj.* pertaining to appeals.

APPELLATION (ap-e-la'shun), *n.* the name, title, or designation by which a person or thing is called.

APPELLATIVE (a-pel'a-tiv), *adj.* serving to distinguish, as a name or denomination of a group or class.

APPELLEE (ap-e-le'), *n.* the person appealed against; the defendant in an appeal.

APPEND (a-pend'), *v.t.* to attach, hang or suspend; annex; subjoin or add to as a necessary part.

APPENDAGE (a-pen'daj), *n.* something attached as a part of; something added as an adjunct.

APPENDANT (a-pen'dant), **APPENDENT** ('dent), *adj.* attached or annexed.

APPENDICITIS (a-pen-di-si'tis), *n.* inflammation of the vermiform appendix of the caecum.

APPENDIX (a-pen'diks), *n.* [*pl.* appendixes ('dik-sez), appendices ('di-sez)], that which is added as supplemental.

APPERCEPTION (ap-er-sep'shun), *n.* perception involving self-consciousness; the relation of new ideas to old ideas.

APPERTAIN (ap-er-tan'), *v.i.* to belong or pertain to.

APPETITE (ap'e-tit), *n.* the desire for gratification of some want, craving.

APPETIZER (ap'e-ti-zer), *n.* something that excites or whets the appetite.

APPLAUD (a-plawd'), *v.t.* to praise.

APPLAUSE (a-plawz'), *n.* the expression of approval; approbation openly shown.

APPLE (ap'l), *n.* a round fleshy fruit; the tree bearing such fruit.

APPLE-JACK (jak'), [U.S.], apple brandy.

APPLIANCE (a-pli'ans), *n.* the act of applying; that which is used with, or as a part of, something else.

APPLICABILITY (ap-li-ka-bil'i-ti), *n.* the quality of being applicable.

APPLICABLE (ap'li-ka-bl), *adj.* capable of being, or fit to be, applied.

APPLICANT (ap'li-kant), *n.* one who applies.

APPLICATION (ap-li-ka'shun), *n.* the act of applying; the thing applied; the practical demonstration of a principle.

APPLIED (ap-plid'), *p.adj.* practical.

APPLIQUE (ap-li-ka'), *adj.* [French], applied or put on; said of patterns put on textiles.

APPLY (a-pli'), *v.t.* to place one to another; lay on; put into practice.

APPOINT (a-point'), *v.t.* to fix; settle; found; make fast; establish.

APPOINTEE (a-poin-te'), *n.* one in whose favour an appointment is made.

APPOINTMENT (a-point'ment), *n.* the act of appointing; the assigning to an office or trust; the state of being appointed; the position or office assigned or held; a stipulation.

APPORTION (a-por'shun), *v.t.* to assign by equal or proportionate division.

APPORTIONMENT (a-por'shunment), *n.* the act of apportioning or dividing into just shares.

APPOSITE (ap'o-zit), *adj.* proper; fit, pertinent.

APPOSITION (ap-o-zish'un), *n.* the act of adding; addition by application.

APPOSITIONAL (ap-o-zish'un-al), *adj.* belonging to apposition.

APPRAISAL (a-praz'al), *n.* the act of appraising, or putting a price upon with a view to sale.

APPRAISE (a-praz'), *v.t.* to set a price upon; value.

APPRAISEMENT (a-praz'ment), *n.* the act of valuing; an authorized valuation.

APPRAISER (a-praz'er), *n.* one who appraises; person licensed and sworn to estimate the value of goods or estates.

APPRECIABLE (a-pre'shi-a-bl), *adj.* capable of being appreciated.

APPRECIATE (a-pre'shi-at), *v.t.* to value; estimate the worth of; esteem highly; prize; raise in value.

APPRECIATION (a-pre-shi-a'shun), *n.* the just valuation; a rise in value.

APPRECIATIVE (a-pre'shi-a-tiv), *adj.* exhibiting appreciation.

APPRECIATORY (ap-pre'shi-a-to-ri), *adj.* expressive of admiration.

APPREHEND (ap-re-hend'), *v.t.* to take or lay hold of; seize; arrest.

APPREHENSIBLE (ap-re-hen'si-bl), *adj.* capable of being apprehended or conceived.

APPREHENSION (ap-re-hen'shun), *n.* the act of seizure or laying hold of; arrest; the act of conceiving; perception; fear or distrust of the future.

APPREHENSIVE (ap-re-hen'siv), *adj.* capable of apprehending; quick to learn, or grasp; fearful of evil; anxious for the future.

APPRENTICE (a-pren'tis), *n.* one bound or articled by indenture to serve a certain number of years to learn some trade.

APPRIZE (a-priz'), *v.t.* to give notice to; inform.

APPROACH (a-proch'), *v.i.* to draw or grow near.

APPROBATE (ap'ro-bat), *v.t.* to express approval of; license or sanction.

APPROBATION (ap-ro-ba'shun), *n.* the act of approving.

APPROBATIVE (ap'ro-ba-tiv), *adj.* approving; expressing approbation.

APPROPRIABLE (a-pro'pri-a-bl), *adj.* capable of appropriation.

APPROPRIATE (a-pro'pri-at), *v.t.* to take to one's self, in exclusion of others: *adj.* peculiar; fit; apt.

APPROPRIATION (a-pro-pri-a'shun), *n.* the act of assigning to one's self, or to a particular use or person.

APPROPRIATOR (ap-pro'pri-a-ter), *n.* one who appropriates.

APPROVABLE (a-proo'va-bl), *adj.* deserving of approval.

APPROVAL (-proov'al), *n.* approbation; sanction; consent.

APPROVE (-proov'), *v.t.* to prove; demonstrate; ratify.

APPROVER (-proo'ver), *n.* one who approves.

APPROVINGLY (-proo'ving-li), *adv.* in a commendatory manner.

APPROXIMATE (a-prok'si-mat), *v.t.* to bring or carry near.

APPROXIMATELY (a-prok'si-mat-li), *adv.* very nearly but not absolutely.

APPROXIMATION (a-prok-si-ma'-shun), *n.* the act of approximating ; approach to any thing as a standard.

APPURTENANCE (a-per'te-nans), *n.* that which belongs or relates to something else.

APPURTENANT (a-per'te-nant), *adj.* belonging or pertaining to ; accessory.

APRICOT (a'pri-kot, ap'ri-kot), *n.* the fruit of a tree, allied to the plum.

APRIL (a'pril), *n.* the fourth month of the year.

APRIL FOOL (fool), one who is imposed upon or deceived in a jocular manner on April 1st, All Fools' Day.

A PRIORI (a pri-o'ri), [Latin], from something prior ; proceeding from antecedent to consequent.

APRON (a'prun), *n.* a portion of cloth, leather, or other material, worn as a protective or ornamental covering to the front of the person.

APROPOS (ap-ro-po'), *adv.* to the purpose ; to the point; opportunely.

APROSEXIA (ap-ro-sek'si-a), *n.* inability to concentrate the mind.

APSE (aps), *n.* a polygonal or semicircular recess terminating the choir or other portion of a church ; a reliquary for relics.

APSIDAL (ap'si-dal), *adj.* pertaining to the apse of a church, or to the apsis of an orbit.

APSIS (ap'sis), *n.* [*pl.* apsides (si-dez)], one of two points in the orbit of a planet situated at the farthest or the least distance from the central body or sun ; the imaginary line connecting these points.

APT (apt), *adj.* suitable ; pertinent.

APTEROUS (ap'ter-us), *adj.* destitute of wings.

APTERYX (ap'ter-iks), *n.* a wingless and tailless bird peculiar to New Zealand.

APTITUDE (ap'ti-tud), *n.* capacity for anything.

APTNESS (-nes), *n.* quality of being apt.

AQUA (a'kwa), *n.* water ; a term much used in pharmacy in the abbre-viated form of Aq. and denoting the addition of water.

AQUA AMMONIÆ (a-mo'ni-e), water containing an infusion of ammonia-gas.

AQUA FORTIS (for'tis), strong water ; impure nitric acid.

AQUAMARINE (a-kwa-ma-ren'), *n.* a pale bluish-green variety of beryl.

AQUAPLANE (-plan), *n.* a surf-board which skims the water behind a power boat.

AQUA REGIA (a'kwa re'ji-a), a mixture of nitric and hydrochloric acids capable of dissolving gold.

AQUARIUM (a-kwa'ri-um), *n.* [*pl.* aquaria (-a) & accuariums (-umz)], a tank or globe for the keeping and cultivation of aquatic plants and fish.

AQUATIC (a-kwat'ik), *adj.* pertaining to water.

AQUATINT (a'kwa-tint), *n.* a species of etching resembling a water-colour drawing in India ink or in sepia.

AQUA VITÆ (a'kwa vi'te), water of life ; unrectified alcohol and other ardent spirits.

AQUEDUCT (ak'we-dukt), *n.* a structure in the form of conduit or artificial channel for conducting water from a source, as for the supply of a large city.

AQUEOUS (a'kwe-us), *adj.* of the nature of, or abounding in, water.

AQUIFORM (a'kwi-form), *adj.* having the form of water ; liquid.

AQUILA (ak'wi-la), *n.* a genus of birds which includes the eagle and allied species ; a constellation of the Milky Way.

AQUILINE (ak'wi-lin & -lin), *adj.* belonging to or resembling an eagle ; curved, as the beak of an eagle.

ARAB (ar'ab), *n.* a native of Arabia.

ARABESQUE (ar-a-besk'), *n.* the style of Arabic decorative art.

ARABIC (ar'a-bik), *adj.* pertaining to Arabia.

ARABIC NUMERALS (num'er-alz), the figures 0, 1, 2, 3, etc., of Indian origin, used by the Arabs and introduced into Europe in the 12th century.

ARABLE (ar'a-bl), *adj.* fit for the plough.

ARACHNIDA (a-rak'ni-da), *n.pl.* a class of arthropods which includes spiders and scorpions.

ARBITER (ar'bi-ter), *n.* an umpire or judge ; an arbitrator.

ARBITRAMENT (ar-bit'ra-ment), *n.* the decision of arbitrators ; an award.

ARBITRARILY (-li), *adv.* in a capricious manner ; imperiously.

ARBITRARY (ar'bi-trar-i), *adj.* depending on will, discretionary ; capricious.

ARBITRATE (ar'bi-trat), *v.i.* to act as arbiter ; to settle a dispute.

ARBITRATION (ar-bi-tra'shun), *n.* the settlement of a dispute.

ARBITRATOR (ar'bi-tra-ter), *n.* one chosen by the parties in a dispute to settle it ; an umpire.

ARBOR (ar'ber), *n.* a shaded nook or walk.

ARBORACEOUS (ar-bo-ra'shus), *adj.* pertaining to, or of the nature of, tree or trees ; living on or among trees.

ARBOR DAY (ar'ber da), a day legally set apart in certain states for planting trees.

ARBOREOUS (ar-bo're-us), **AR-BOREAL** (-al), *adj.* pertaining to trees.

ARBORESCENCE (ar-bo-res'ens), *n.* something having the shape of a tree, as certain crystals.

ARBORESCENT (ar-bo-res'ent), *adj.* tree-like.

ARBORETUM (ar-bo-re'tum), *n.* [*pl.* arboreta, (-ta) & arboretums (-tumz)], a place in which rare trees are cultivated.

ARBORICULTURE (ar-bo-ri-kul'-tur), *n.* the cultivation of trees.

ARBOR VITÆ (ar'ber vi'te), an evergreen tree of the pine family.

ARBUSCLE (ar'bus'l), *n.* a dwarf tree.

ARBUTUS (ar-bu'tus), *n.* a genus of evergreen shrubs.

ARC (ark), *n.* a curved line or any part of a curve forming the segment of a circle.

ARCADE (ar-kad'), *n.* a series of arches supported by pillars ; an arched gallery, or promenade.

ARCADIA (ar-ka'di-a), *n.* a place or region of rural peace and simplicity.

ARCADIAN (ar-ka'di-an), *adj.* rurally simple.

ARCANUM (ar-ka'num), *n.* [*pl.* arcana ('na)], a secret ; a mystery.

ARCH (arch), *n.* structure of brick or masonry, the component wedge-shaped parts of which follow a curved line.

ARCHÆOLOGIC (ar-ke-o-loj'ik), **ARCHÆOLOGICAL** ('i-kal), *adj.* pertaining to the study of antiquities.

ARCHÆOLOGIST, ARCHEOLO-GIST (ar-ke-ol'o-jist), *n.* one versed in the study of ancient things.

ARCHÆOLOGY, ARCHEOLOGY (ar-ke-ol'o-ji), *n.* the science of antiquities.

ARCHAIC (ar-ka'ik), **ARCHAI-CAL** ('i-kal), *adj.* pertaining to a remote period ; antiquated.

ARCHAISM (ar'ka-izm), *n.* antiquity of style or use.

ARCHANGEL (ark-an'jel), *n.* an angel of the highest order.

ARCHBISHOP (arch-bish'up), *n.* the chief bishop.

ARCHBISHOPRIC (arch-bish'up-rik), *n.* the jurisdiction, office, or see of an archbishop.

ARCHDEACON (arch-de'kn), *n.* a dignitary ranking next below a bishop.

ARCHDEACONATE (-at), *n.* office of archdeacon.

ARCHDEACONRY (arch-de'kn-ri), *n.* the office, rank, jurisdiction, or residence of an archdeacon.

ARCHDIOCESE (-di'o-sis), *n.* the jurisdiction of an archbishop.

ARCHDUCAL (arch-du'kal), *adj.* pertaining to an archduke.

ARCHDUCHESS (arch-duch'es), *n.* the wife of an archduke.

ARCHDUCHY (arch-duch'i), *n.* the territory or rank of an archduke or archduchess.

ARCHDUKE (arch-duk'), *n.* a prince of the former imperial house of Austria.

ARCHDUKEDOM (arch-duk'dom), *n.* the dignity or territory of an arch-duke.

ARCHENEMY (arch-en'e-mi), *n.* a principal enemy; Satan.

ARCHER (ar'cher), *n.* a bowman.

ARCHER-FISH (-fish), *n.* a fish of Java, which catches insects by darting drops of water upon them.

ARCHERY (ar'cher-i), *n.* the art, practice, or skill of one who uses the bow and arrow.

ARCHETYPE (ar'ke-tip), *n.* the original type or pattern upon or after which a thing is made; a model.

ARCHING (ar'ching), *adj.* curving like an arch: *n.* arched work.

ARCHIPELAGIC (ar-ki-pe-laj'ik), *adj.* pertaining to a collection of islands with the sea dividing them.

ARCHIPELAGO (ar-ki-pel'a-go), *n.* any sea or body of salt water interspersed with numerous islands.

ARCHITECT (ar'ki-tekt), *n.* one versed in the art of building and the various styles of architecture.

ARCHITECTIVE (ar'ki-tek-tiv), *adj.* used in building; proper for building.

ARCHITECTONICS (ar-ki-tek-ton'iks), *n.pl.* the science of architecture.

ARCHITECTURAL (ar-ki-tek'tu-ral), *adj.* pertaining to the art of building.

ARCHITECTURALLY (-li), *adv.* with regard to the principles of the building art.

ARCHITECTURE (ar'ki-tek-tur), *n.* the science or art of building.

ARCHITRAVE (ar'ki-trav), *n.* the lowest division of an entablature.

ARCHIVAL (ar'ki-val), *adj.* pertaining to, or included in, state records.

ARCHIVE (ar'kiv), *n.* a record preserved as evidence; *pl.* the place where public or state records are kept.

ARCHLY (-li), *adv.* roguishly; waggishly.

ARCHNESS (-nes), *n.* shyness; coyness.

ARCHPRIEST (arch'prest), *n.* a chief priest; a rural dean.

ARCHWAY (arch'wa), *n.* an opening or passage beneath an arched or vaulted roof.

ARCTIC (ark'tik), *adj.* pertaining to the region of the north pole.

ARCTIC CIRCLE (ser'kl), an imaginary circle parallel to the equator and distant 23° 28′ from the north pole.

ARCUATE (ar'ku-at), *adj.* arched; shaped like an arch.

ARCUATION (ar-ku-a'shon), *n.* the act of bending; condition of being bent.

ARDENT (ar'dent), *adj.* hot; burning; fiery; warm; glowing.

ARDENT SPIRITS (spir'itz), alcoholic beverages.

ARDOUR (ar'der), *n.* eager desire; zeal.

ARDUOUS (ar'du-us), *adj.* steep; hard to climb; difficult.

ARE (ar), *pres. tense pl.* of the verb to be.

ARE (ar), *n.* the unit of French superficial or square measure containing 100 sq. metres or 1,076.44 English sq. ft.

AREA (a're-a), *n.* any plane surface having bounds.

ARECA (ar'e-ka), *n.* a genus of palms.

ARENA (a-re'na), *n.* the central enclosed space for exhibitions of any kind.

ARENACEOUS (ar-e-na'shus), *adj.* sandy.

AREOLOGY (a-re-ol'o-ji), *n.* a study of the physical features of Mars.

AREOMETER (ar-e-om'e-ter), *n.* an instrument for measuring the specific gravity of liquids.

ARGALI (ar'ga-li), *n.* an Asiatic sheep, remarkable for large horns.

ARGENT (ar'jent), *n.* the silver of a coat of arms, represented in drawing or engraving by a plain white surface.

ARGENTINE (ar'jen-tin), *n.* silver; plate metal; a small fish with silvery scales.

ARGENTITE (ar'jen-tit), *n.* sulphide of silver of a lead-grey colour.

ARGENTOUS (ar-jen'tus), adj. pertaining to, or containing, silver.

ARGIL (ar'jil), n. potters' clay or earth.

ARGILLACEOUS (ar-ji-la'shus), adj. of the nature of, or containing, clay; clayey.

ARGILLITE (ar'ji-lit), n. clay-slate.

ARGON (ar'gon), n. an element associated with nitrogen, and forming one of the constituents of the air.

ARGONAUT (ar'go-nawt), n. a cephalopod commonly known as the paper-nautilus; [A-], one of the gold seekers who went to California in 1849.

ARGOSY (ar'go-si), n. a large richly-freighted merchant-vessel.

ARGOT (ar'go), n. [French], slang; thieves' jargon.

ARGUABLE (ar'gu-a-bl), adj. capable of being disputed or discussed.

ARGUE (ar'gu), v.i. to show or offer reasons in support of, or in opposition to, a proposition, opinion, or measure; to reason, dispute, discuss.

ARGUMENT (ar'gu-ment), n. that which is advanced in support or proof with a view to persuade or convince the mind; a discussion, controversy, or debate.

ARGUMENTAL (ar-gu-men'tal), adj. pertaining to reasoning.

ARGUMENTATION (ar-gu-men-ta'shun), n. the act of arguing; discussion.

ARGUMENTATIVE (ar-gu-men'ta-tiv), adj. consisting of or exhibiting a process of reasoning.

ARGUS-EYED (ar'gus-id), adj. watchful; vigilant; extremely observant.

ARIA (ar'ri-a), n. an air; a melody or tune.

ARID (ar'id), adj. dry; barren.

ARIDITY (a-rid'i-ty), **ARIDNESS** (ar'id-nes), n. dryness; want of life or interest.

ARIETTA (a-ri-et'ta), n. a short song or air.

ARIGHT (a-rit'), adv. rightly; in a right way or form.

ARISE (a-riz'), v.i. to mount up or ascend; to come into view.

ARISTOCRACY (ar-is-tok'ra-si), n. government by persons of the highest rank in a state; the nobility or chief persons in a state.

ARISTOCRAT (ar'is-to-krat), n. a personage of rank and noble birth.

ARISTOCRATIC (ar-is-to-krat'ik), **ARISTOCRATICAL** (-i-kal), adj. pertaining to, or consisting in, a government of the nobles.

ARISTOCRATICALLY (-li), adv. in an aristocratic manner.

ARITHMETIC (a-rith'me-tik), n. the science of numbers; the art of computation by figures.

ARITHMETICAL (a-rith-met'i-kal), adj. of or pertaining to arithmetic.

ARITHMETICIAN (a-rith-me-tish'-an), n. one skilled in the science of numbers.

ARK (ark), n. the repository of the Covenant, or tables of the Law, in the Jewish Tabernacle, subsequently placed in the Temples of Solomon; the vessel in which Noah and his family were preserved during the Deluge.

ARM (arm), n. the limb of the human body which extends from the shoulder to the hand; might; power; support.

ARM (arm), n. a weapon; a branch of the military service: v.t. to furnish or equip with weapons.

ARMADA (ar-ma'da), n. fleet of war vessels; especially, the Spanish fleet destroyed by England in 1588.

ARMADILLO (ar-ma-dil'o), n. a South American quadruped, armed with a bony shell divided into belts consisting of numerous small plates, and resembling a coat of mail.

ARMAGEDDON (ar-ma-ged'on), n. the place of a mighty battle against evil, to be fought on " the great day of God "; used symbolically.

ARMAMENT (ar'ma-ment), n. a body of forces equipped for war, either military or naval.

ARMATURE (ar'ma-tur), n. armour; that which serves as a means of defence; a piece of soft iron connecting the poles of a magnet, or electro-magnet.

ARM-CHAIR (arm'char), *n.* a chair furnished with supports for the elbows.

ARMFUL (arm'fool), *n.* as much as can be compassed by the arms.

ARMISTICE (ar'mis-tis), *n.* a temporary cessation of hostilities; a truce.

ARMISTICE DAY (da), November 11; the Allies and Central Powers in the World War I ceased hostilities on this day in 1918.

ARMLET (arm'let), *n.* a small arm of the sea; a band for the arm used for ornament or for protection.

ARMOIRE (ar-mwar'), *n.* [French], a movable cupboard with doors.

ARMOUR (ar'mer), *n.* defensive arms; protective covering for the body in battle; the steel plating of a warship.

ARMOUR-CLAD (-klad), *adj.* iron-clad; *n.* a war vessel protected by steel plating.

ARMOUR-GRATING (-grat'ing), *n.* deep iron gratings.

ARMOUR-PLATE (-plat), *n.* a plate of iron or steel intended to be affixed to the side of a ship as part of a casing for protection against shell fire.

ARMOURER (ar'mer-er), *n.* the custodian of the arms of a troop or battleship.

ARMOURY (ar'mer-i), *n.* a place for arms or the assembly of soldiers; a manufactory of arms.

ARM-PIT (arm'pit), *n.* cavity beneath shoulder; the axilla.

ARMS (arms), *n.pl.* weapons of offence or defence; the military service.

ARMY (ar'mi), *n.* a body of men trained and equipped for war, and organized in regiments, brigades, or similar divisions.

ARMY CORPS (kor), two or more divisions of an army.

ARMY-WORM (-werm), *n.* the larva of a moth which devastates grain and other crops.

ARNICA (ar'ni-ka), *n.* a genus of perennial herbs of the aster family.

AROMA (a-ro'ma), *n.* the odour exhaled by plants or other substances; perfume.

AROMATIC (ar-o-mat'ik), **AROMATICAL** ('i-kal), *adj.* giving out aroma; fragrant; spicy.

AROMATIC VINEGAR (vin'e-gar), a powerful perfume composed of strong acetic acid.

AROUND (a-round'), *adv.* in a circle; on every side.

AROUSAL (a-rouz'al), *n.* the act of awakening; being awakened.

AROUSE (a-rouz'), *v.t.* to excite or stir to action; animate.

ARPEGGIO (ar-ped'jo), *n.* the playing of chords in quick succession.

ARRAIGN (a-ran'), *v.t.* censure publicly; impeach; indict.

ARRAIGNMENT (a-ran'ment), *n.* an accusation; an impeachment.

ARRANGE (a-ranj'), *v.t.* to put in proper order or sequence.

ARRANGEMENT (a-ranj'ment), *n.* a preparatory measure; preparation; settlement.

ARRANT (ar'ant), *adj.* notorious; unmitigated; shameless.

ARRAS (ar'as), *n.* hangings made of rich figured fabric.

ARRASENE, ARASENE (ar-a-sen'), *n.* a kind of mixed thread of wool and silk used in raised embroidery.

ARRAY (a-ra'), *n.* order; an orderly collection or series of things imposingly displayed; dress arranged on the person; apparel: *v.t.* marshal; deck or dress.

ARRAYAL (a-ra'al), *n.* the process of arraying.

ARREAR (a-rer'), *n.* that which is not done, is outstanding, or unpaid.

ARREARAGE (a-rer'aj), *n.* the state or condition of being in arrears.

ARREST (a-rest'), *v.t.* to stop or stay; check or hinder the action or motion of; seize, take, or apprehend by legal authority.

ARRIVAL (a-riv'al), *n.* reaching a destination from a distance; attainment of any object.

ARRIVE (a-riv'), *v.i.* to come to or

reach, as a destination; reach a point or stage; attain to a state or result [with *at*].

ARROGANCE (ar'o-gans), *n.* an undue degree of self-importance; a lordly contempt of others.

ARROGANT (ar'o-gant), *adj.* making exorbitant claims to dignity; overbearingly haughty.

ARROGATE (ar'o-gat), *v.t.* to assume or lay claim to unduly.

ARROGATION (ar-o-ga'shun), *n.* the act of arrogating.

ARROW (ar'o), *n.* a pointed missile weapon, made to be shot from a bow.

ARROW-HEAD (-hed), *n.* the head or barb of an arrow; an aquatic plant.

ARROWROOT (-root), *n.* a starch obtained from the rootstocks of several species of West Indian plants.

ARROYO (a-roi'o), *n.* a watercourse or rivulet; the dry bed of a small stream.

ARSENAL (ar'se-nal), *n.* a magazine for the storage of arms and military stores, or their manufacture.

ARSENIC (ar'se-nik), *n.* a very poisonous element of steel-grey colour and brilliant lustre.

ARSENIC (ar-sen'ik), **ARSENICAL** ('i-kal), *adj.* pertaining to or containing arsenic.

ARSENIOUS (ar-se'ni-us), *adj.* pertaining to or containing arsenic.

ARSENITE (ar'sen-it), *n.* a salt of arsenious acid.

ARSON (ar'son), *n.* the malicious firing of any building, produce, etc.

ART (art), *n.* the employment of means to the accomplishment of some end; the skilful adaptation and application to some purpose or use of knowledge or power acquired from nature; a system of rules and established methods to facilitate the performance of certain actions; one of the fine arts: *pl.* the branches of learning included in academic study.

ARTERIAL (ar-te'ri-al), *adj.* pertaining to an artery.

ARTERIALIZATION (ar-te-ri-al-i-za'shun), *n.* the process of converting venous blood into arterial blood.

ARTERIALIZE (ar-te'ri-al-iz), *v.t.* to convert venous blood into arterial blood by exposure to oxygen in the lungs.

ARTERIOLOGY (ar-te'ri-ol'o-ji), *n.* that branch of anatomy which treats of the arteries.

ARTERIOSCLEROSIS (ar-te'ri-o-skle-ro'sis), *n.* thickening of the walls of the arteries.

ARTERIOTOMY (ar-te-ri-ot'o-mi), *n.* the opening of an artery.

ARTERITIS (ar-te-ri'tis), *n.* inflammation of an artery.

ARTERY (ar'ter-i), *n.* one of a system of tubes or vessels which convey the blood from the heart to all parts of the body.

ARTESIAN WELL (ar-te'zhan wel), a well formed by boring, often to great depth, when water rises by pressure in the tube and overflows at the surface.

ARTFUL (art'fool), *adj.* cunning; crafty.

ARTFULLY (-li), *adv.* in a cunning or crafty manner.

ARTHRAGRA (ar-thrag'ra), *n.* gout.

ARTHRALGIA (ar-thral'ji-a), *n.* neuralgic pain in a joint.

ARTHRITIS (ar-thri'tis), *n.* any inflammation of the joints; the gout.

ARTHROPOD (ar'thro-pod), *n.* member of a sub-kingdom of animals, which includes invertebrates with articulated bodies and jointed legs, as spiders, crabs, etc.; an arachnid.

ARTICHOKE (ar'ti-chok), *n.* a plant with thistle-like foliage, and bearing large terminal flower-heads, the lower portion of which is used as food.

ARTICLE (ar'ti-kl), *n.* a distinct portion or member; a single clause, item, or particular, as in a formal agreement or treaty; a concise statement; in Grammar, one of the words, *a*, *an*, or *the*, placed before nouns to limit their application; *v.t.* to bind by articles of covenant.

ARTICULAR (ar-tik′u-lar), *adj.* pertaining to the joints.

ARTICULATE (ar-tik′u-lat), *v.t.* to joint; unite by means of a joint; to form words; utter in distinct syllables.

ARTICULATION (ar-tik-u-la′shun), *n.* the act of joining; the act of speaking distinctly; a distinct utterance.

ARTICULATOR (ar-tik′u-la-ter), *n.* one who pronounces distinctly; one who mounts skeletons.

ARTIFICE (ar′ti-fis), *n.* an ingenious expedient; a trick.

ARTIFICER (ar-tif′i-ser), *n.* a skilled worker; a mechanic.

ARTIFICIAL (ar-ti-fish′al), *adj.* made or contrived by art; unreal.

ARTIFICIALITY (-fish-i-al′i-ti), **ARTIFICIALNESS** (-nes), *n.* the quality of being unreal or unnatural.

ARTIFICIALLY (-li), *adv.* by human skill or contrivance.

ARTILLERY (ar-til′er-i), *n.* cannon; great guns; ordnance of all kinds.

ARTISAN (ar′ti-zan), *n.* one skilled in any art or trade.

ARTIST (ar′tist), *n.* one skilled in any branch of art; *fem. artiste.*

ARTISTIC (ar-tis′tik), **ARTISTICAL** (′ti-kal), *adj.* pertaining to art or to artists.

ARTISTICALLY (-kal-li), *adv.* conformable to the rules and principles of art.

ARTISTRY (ar′tis-tri), *n.* the qualities peculiar to an artist.

ARTLESS (art′les), *adj.* lacking art; unskilful.

ARYAN (ar′yan), *n.* a member of the Caucasian race.

AS (az), *conj., adv.* like; comparable or proportionate to.

ASAFETIDA, ASAFŒTIDA (as-a-fet′i-da), *n.* a fetid sap obtained from the roots of several large umbelliferous plants.

ASBESTINE (as-bes′tin), *adj.* pertaining to or of the nature of asbestos.

ASBESTOS (as-bes′tos), **ASBESTUS** (′tus), *n.* a fibrous variety of

hornblende, separable into flexible filaments and possessing the property of being incombustible.

ASCEND (a-send′), *v.i.* to take an upward direction.

ASCENDABLE (as-sen′da-bl), or **ASCENDIBLE** (′di-bl), *adj.* capable of being climbed or navigated.

ASCENDANCY (a-sen′dan-si), **ASCENDENCY** (′den-si), *n.* a governing or controlling power or influence.

ASCENDANT (a-sen′dant), **ASCENDENT** (′dent), *adj.* rising; superior; above the horizon.

ASCENDING (-ing), *adj.* rising upward.

ASCENSION (a-sen′shun), *n.* the act of moving upward.

ASCENSION DAY (da), *n.* a movable feast to commemorate Christ's ascension, celebrated on the Thursday which falls on the fortieth day after Easter.

ASCENT (a-sent′), *n.* the act of rising; an upward movement.

ASCERTAIN (as-er-tan′), *v.t.* to make certain; find out or determine.

ASCERTAINMENT (as-er-tan′ment), *n.* the act of ascertaining.

ASCETIC (a-set′ik), *adj.* exceedingly rigid in the exercise of religious duties.

ASCETICALLY (-kal-li), *adv.* in an ascetical manner.

ASCETUM (a-se′tum), *n.* vinegar; a drug prepared with acetic acid.

ASCIDIAN (a-sid′i-an), *n.* a sea squirt; one of a class of marine animals having a tough sac.

ASCRIBABLE (a-skri′ba-bl), *adj.* capable of being attributed or imputed.

ASCRIBE (as-krib′), *v.t.* to attribute, impute, or refer.

ASCRIPTION (as-krip′shun), *n.* the act of attributing or imputing.

ASEPTIC (a-sep′tik), *adj.* free from the germs of disease or putrefaction.

ASEXUAL (a-sek′shu-al), *adj.* not sexual.

ASH (ash), *n.* a common timber and shade tree of the olive family.

ASH (ash), *n.* the residue of plant or animal substance remaining after burning.

ASH WEDNESDAY (-wenz'da), the first day of Lent.

ASHAMED (a-shamd'), *p.adj.* affected or touched by shame.

ASHEN (ash'n), *adj.* pertaining to the ash-tree ; made of ash ; pale.

ASHORE (a-shor'), *adv.* on shore ; to the shore.

ASIDE (a-sid'), *adv.* on or to one side ; out of a given direction ; apart.

ASININE (as'i-nin), *adj.* pertaining to the ass ; stupid.

ASININITY (as-i-nin'i-ti), *n.* the quality of being asinine.

ASK (ask), *v.t.* to request ; seek to obtain by words.

ASKANCE (a-skans'), **ASKANT** (a-skant'), *adv.* sideways ; obliquely ; disdainfully.

ASKEW (a-sku'), *adv.* obliquely ; awry.

ASLANT (a-slant'), *adv.* not at right angles.

ASLEEP (a-slep'), *adj. & adv.* sleeping ; dormant.

ASP (asp), *n.* a small venomous snake.

ASPARAGUS (as-par'a-gus), *n.* a plant having edible shoots.

ASPECT (as'pekt), *n.* visual or mental appearance ; look ; mien.

ASPEN (as'pen), *n.* a species of poplar.

ASPER (as'per), *adj.* rugged.

ASPERATE ('per-at), *adj.* rough to the touch.

ASPERITY (as-per'i-ti), *n.* roughness of surface ; bitterness of taste.

ASPERMOUS (a-sper'mus), *adj.* without seed ; not producing seed.

ASPERSE (as-pers'), *v.t.* injure by calumny ; slander.

ASPERSION (as-per'shun), *n.* injury by calumnious charges ; slander.

ASPHALT (as'falt), *n.* a compact, brittle variety of bitumen.

ASPHODEL (as'fo-del), *n.* a plant of the lily family.

ASPHYXIA (as-fik'si-a), **AS-**

PHYXY ('si), *n.* suspension of respiration ; suffocation.

ASPHYXIATE (as-fik'si-at), *v.t.* to suffocate.

ASPIC (as'pik), *n.* a venomous asp.

ASPIRANT (as-pir'ant), *adj.* aspiring ; ambitious : *n.* one who seeks a high object.

ASPIRATE (as'pi-rat), *v.t.* to pronounce with a full breathing ; to prefix the sound of the letter *h*.

ASPIRATION (as-pi-ra'shun), *n.* the act of aspirating ; the yearning for something higher and better.

ASPIRATORY (as-pir'a-to-ri), *adj.* pertaining to breathing.

ASPIRE (as-pir'), *v.i.* to seek after or desire.

ASPORTATION (as-por-ta'shun), *n.* felonious removal.

ASQUINT (a-skwint'), *adv.* with a squint ; obliquely.

ASS (as), *n.* a quadruped, allied to the horse.

ASSAFŒTIDA, see asafetida.

ASSAGAI, ASSEGAI (as'a-gi), *n.* a spear.

ASSAGAI TREE (tre), a tree of the dogwood family.

ASSAIL (a-sal'), *v.t.* to attack with vehemence.

ASSAILANT (a-sa'lant), *n.* one who, or that which, assails.

ASSASSIN (a-sas'sin), *n.* one who slays treacherously.

ASSASSINATE (a-sas'si-nat), *v.t.* slay suddenly or unawares ; murder.

ASSASSINATION (a-sas-si-na'shun), *n.* the act of slaying.

ASSAULT (a-sawlt'), *n.* an attack with violence by physical means.

ASSAY (a-sa'), *n.* the chemical analysis of a metal, ore, or alloy to determine its ingredients and their proportion.

ASSAYER (a-sa'er), *n.* one who assays.

ASSEMBLAGE (a-sem'blaj), *n.* a group or collection of persons or particular things ; the fitting together of parts or pieces, as of machinery.

ASSEMBLE (a-sem'bl), *v.t.* to

collect or gather together in one place or body.

ASSEMBLY (a-sem'bli), *n.* a collection or company of persons brought together; a meeting; a congregation; the second house of the legislature in some States.

ASSEMBLYMAN (-man), *n.* a member of a legislative assembly.

ASSENT (a-sent'), *v.i.* to admit as true; concede.

ASSENTATION (as-sen-ta'shun), *n.* compliance with the opinion of another.

ASSENTIENT (a-sen'shi-ent), *adj.* assenting : *n.* one who assents.

ASSERT (a-sert'), *v.t.* to maintain; declare positively, or with assurance.

ASSERTION (a-ser'shun), *n.* the act of asserting.

ASSERTIVE (a-ser'tiv), *adj.* positive; dogmatical.

ASSERTOR (as-ser'ter), *n.* one who asserts.

ASSESS (a-ses'), *v.t.* to fix or determine, as damages; fix, rate, or set a certain charge upon, as a tax.

ASSESSED TAXES (taks'ez), taxes levied on income, houses, and property.

ASSESSMENT (a-ses'ment), *n.* the specific tax, or sum assessed for damages.

ASSESSOR (a-ses'er), *n.* one appointed to assess.

ASSESSORIAL (as-ses-so'ri-al), *adj.* pertaining to an assessor.

ASSETS (as'ets), *n.pl.* the property of a deceased person which is subject to the discharge of his debts and legacies; the property or effects of an insolvent debtor; the entire property of a business.

ASSEVERATE (a-sev'er-a⁺), *v.t.* to affirm or aver.

ASSEVERATION (a-sev-er-a'shun), *n.* a solemn affirmation or declaration.

ASSIBILATE (a-sib'i-lat), *v.t.* to pronounce with a hissing sound.

ASSIBILATION (a-sib-i-la'shun), *n.* pronunciation with a hissing sound.

ASSIDUITY (as-i-du'i-ti), *n.* close application; diligence.

ASSIDUOUS (a-sid'u-us), *adj.* constant in application.

ASSIGN (a-sin'), *v.t.* to appoint, mark out, apportion, make over; fix; designate for a specific purpose; point out exactly; to transfer or make over to another.

ASSIGNATION (as-ig-na'shun), *n.* the act of assigning; an appointment to meet; the transfer of title, or the deed of transferment.

ASSIGNEE (as-i-ne'), *n.* one to whom an assignment of anything is made.

ASSIGNMENT (a-sin'ment), *n.* allotment, or appointment to some particular person; transfer of title or interest.

ASSIGNOR (as-i-nor'), *n.* one who assigns.

ASSIMILABLE (as-sim'i-la-bl), *adj.* capable of being assimilated.

ASSIMILATE (a-sim'i-lat), *v.t.* to bring to conformity or agreement with something else.

ASSIMILATION (a-sim-i-la'shun), *n.* the act or process of assimilating.

ASSIMILATIVE (a-sim'i-la-tiv), *adj.* having the power of assimilating.

ASSIST (a-sist'), *v.t.* to help; aid.

ASSISTANCE (a-sis'tans), *n.* help; furtherance; aid; succour; support.

ASSISTANT (a-sis'tant), *adj.* helping; lending aid : *n.* one who assists; a helper.

ASSIZE (a-siz'), *n.* a court or session of justice for the trial by jury of civil or criminal cases; the sessions held periodically in each county of England by circuit judges; the time or place of holding the assize; generally in *pl.*

ASSIZEMENT (a-siz'ment), *n.* an inspection of weights and measures.

ASSOCIATE (a-so'shi-at), *v.t.* to unite; join with; connect; accompany, as a companion, friend, or confederate.

ASSOCIATION (a-so-shi-a'shun), *n.* the act of associating or state of being associated; union; conjunction; an associate body of persons formed for a common object.

ASSONANCE (as'o-nans), *n.* resemblance of sound ; a species of rhyme which consists in the use of the same vowel-sound in the last syllable of words having different consonants.

ASSONANT (as'o-nant), *adj.* having resemblance of sound.

ASSORT (a-sort'), *v.t.* to divide or separate.

ASSORTMENT (a-sort'ment), *n.* a classified collection of articles of a varied character.

ASSUADE (as-wad'), *v.t.* to present, as advice ; urge.

ASSUAGE (a-swaj'), *v.t.* to soften, mitigate, allay.

ASSUAGEMENT (a-swaj'ment), *n.* mitigation.

ASSUME (a-sum'), *v.t.* to take to ; take for granted ; take upon one's self.

ASSUMPSIT (a-sump'sit), *n.* a verbal or unsealed contract based on a consideration.

ASSUMPTION (a-sump'shun), *n.* the act of assuming or taking to or upon one's self ; taking for granted.

ASSUMPTIVE (as-sump'tiv), *adj.* characterized by assumption ; arrogant.

ASSURABLE (a-shur'a-bl), *adj.* capable of being assured or insured.

ASSURANCE (a-shoor'ans), *n.* the act of assuring ; testimony intended to inspire confidence ; certain expectation ; confidence ; self-possession ; self-reliance ; impudence.

ASSURE (a-shoor'), *v.t.* to make sure or certain ; to inspire confidence.

ASSURED (a-shoord'), *p.adj.* made certain ; guaranteed : *n.* a person insured.

ASSUREDLY (-li), *adv.* certainly ; with assurance.

ASSUREDNESS (-nes), *n.* certainty ; full confidence.

ASSYRIAN (a-sir'i-an), *adj.* pertaining to Assyria or to its inhabitants.

ASSYRIOLOGY (a-sir-i-ol'o-ji), *n.* the science or study of the language and antiquities of Assyria.

ASTATIC (a-stat-ik), *adj.* lacking, tendency to take a definite position or direction ; without polarity.

ASTATICISM (a-stat'i-sizm), *n.* the state of being astatic.

ASTEISM (as'te-izm), *n.* veiled irony ; genteel derision.

ASTER (as'ter), *n.* genus of flowering plants.

ASTERIAL (as-te'ri-al), *adj.* connected with, related to stars.

ASTERIATED (as-te'ri-at-ed), *adj.* radiated ; having the form of a star.

ASTERISK (as'ter-isk), *n.* the mark (*) used in printing as a reference to a marginal passage or footnote appended to the text, or to indicate letters or words omitted (***) : *v.t.* to mark with an asterisk.

ASTERN (a-stern'), *adj.* & *adv.* at or toward the hinder part of a ship.

ASTERNAL (a-ster'nal), *adj.* not joined to the sternum or breast-bone ; said of ribs.

ASTEROID (as'ter-oid), *adj.* star-like ; resembling a star-fish : *n.* one of the small planets.

ASTHENIA (as-the-ni'a), *n.* debility.

ASTHENIC (as-then'ik), *adj.* characterized by asthenia ; feeble.

ASTHMA (as'ma), *n.* a respiratory disease.

ASTHMATIC (as-mat'ik), **ASTHMATICAL** ('i-kal), *adj.* pertaining to asthma.

ASTIGMATIC (as-tig-mat'ik), *adj.* pertaining to, affected with, or curing, astigmatism.

ASTIGMATISM (a-stig'ma-tizm), **ASTIGMISM** ('mizm), *n.* a defect in the structure of the eye causing variation of the focus of the crystalline lens.

ASTIR (a-ster'), *adv.* or *adj.* on the move ; active ; stirring.

ASTONISH (as-ton'ish), *v.t.* to strike with sudden wonder ; surprise.

ASTONISHMENT (as-ton'ish-ment), *n.* the state of being astonished.

ASTOUND (as-tound'), *v.t.* to strike with amazement ; shock ; stun.

ASTRADDLE (a-strad'l), *adv.* with one leg on each side of something ; astride.

ASTRAGAL (as'tra-gal), *n.* a small

moulding or bead of semicircular form.

ASTRAGALUS (as-trag'a-lus), *n.* [*pl.* astragali (-li)], the ball of the ankle-joint.

ASTRAKHAN (as'tra-kan), *n.* the skins of lambs with curly wool, from Astrakhan, Russia ; an imitation resembling this fur.

ASTRAL (as'tral), *adj.* pertaining to the stars.

ASTRAL BODY (bod'i), a kind of ethereal body.

ASTRAY (a-stra'), *adv.* out of the right way ; wandering.

ASTRIDE (a-strid'), *adv.* with the legs wide apart ; astraddle.

ASTRINGENCY (as-trin'jen-si), *n.* the quality of being astringent.

ASTRINGENT (as-trin'jent), *adj.* binding ; contracting ; opposed to *laxative.*

ASTROLABE (as'tro-lab), *n.* an instrument formerly employed for taking the altitude of the sun or stars.

ASTROLOGER (as-trol'o-jer), *n.* one who professes to forecast events by means of the stars.

ASTROLOGICAL (as-tro-loj'i-kal), *adj.* pertaining to astrology.

ASTROLOGY (as-trol'o-ji), *n.* predestination by the stars ; the art anciently pursued of foretelling or forecasting the future.

ASTRONOMER (as-tron'o-mer), *n.* one who studies, or is versed in, astronomy.

ASTRONOMICAL CLOCK (klok), a clock which keeps sidereal time.

ASTRONOMICAL SIGNS (sinz), the signs of the zodiac.

ASTRONOMICAL YEAR (yer), the period required by the earth to make a complete revolution around the sun.

ASTRONOMY (as-tron'o-mi), *n.* the study of the heavenly bodies.

ASTROPHOTOGRAPHY (as-tro-fo-tog'ra-fi), *n.* photography applied to heavenly bodies.

ASTROPHYSICAL (as-tro-fiz'i-kal), *adj.* pertaining to the physical structure of the stars.

ASTUTE (as-tut'), *adj.* shrewd ; keenly penetrating ; sagacious ; cunning ; crafty.

ASUNDER (a-sun'der), *adv.* separately ; apart ; into parts.

ASYLUM (a-si'lum), *n.* an institution for the care of the aged, destitute, or afflicted.

ASYNDETON (a-sin'de-ton), *n.* a figure of speech which omits connectives, as "I came, I saw, I conquered."

AT (at), *prep.* on the point of ; on the coming of : of time ; on ; upon ; near ; within : of space ; up to ; to the extent of : of degree ; to ; toward ; after ; through : of motion ; in response to : of occasion or cause ; in ; engaged in ; dependent on : of relations in general.

ATARAXIA (at-a-rak'si-a), *n.* complete peace of mind ; contentment.

ATAVISM (at'a-vizm), *n.* the reversion, or tendency to revert, to the ancestral type of a species.

ATAVISTIC (at-a-vis'tik), *adj.* pertaining to atavism.

ATAXIA (a-tak'si-a), **ATAXY** ('si), *n.* irregularities in the functions of the body.

ATAXIC (a-tak'sik), *adj.* pertaining to ataxy.

ATAXIC FEVER (fe'ver), typhus fever of a malignant type.

ATE (et & at), *v.t.* to eat.

ATELIER (a'te-lya), *n.* [French], the studio of a painter or sculptor.

ATHANASIA (ath'a-na'zhi-a), **ATHANASY** (-than'a-si), *n.* immortality ; deathlessness.

ATHEISM (a'the-izm), *n.* disbelief in the existence of a God.

ATHEIST (a'the-ist), *n.* one who disbelieves or denies the existence of a God.

ATHEISTIC (a-the-is'tik), **ATHEISTICAL** ('ti-kal), *adj.* pertaining to, or implying, atheism.

ATHENEUM, ATHENÆUM (ath-e-ne'um), *n.* an institution, club, or building devoted to the purposes or study of literature, science and art.

ATHERMANCY (a-ther'man-si), *n.* impermeability to radiant heat.

ATHERMANOUS ('ma-nus), *adj.* impervious to radiant heat.

ATHIRST (a-therst'), *adj.* thirsty.

ATHLETE (ath'let), *n.* a competitor for a prize in public games.

ATHLETIC (ath-let'ik), *adj.* pertaining to athletes.

ATHLETICALLY ('i-kal-li), *adv.* in an athletic manner.

ATHLETICISM (ath-let'i-sizm), *n.* the practice of athletic games.

ATHLETICS (ath-let'iks), *n.* any system of athletic training.

AT HOME (hom), a more or less formal reception.

ATHWART (a-thwawrt'), *prep.* across; from side to side: *adv.* cross-wise; obliquely.

ATHWARTSHIPS (-ships), *adv.* across a ship.

ATILT (a-tilt'), *adv. & adj.* in the position, or with the action, of a person making a thrust; tilted.

A-TIPTOE (a-tip'to), *adv.* on tiptoe; keenly expecting.

ATLAS (at'las), *n.* a collection of maps in a volume.

ATLEE (at'le), *n.* the tamarisk salt tree.

ATMOLOGY (at-mol'o-ji), *n.* the science of aqueous vapour.

ATMOSPHERE (at'mos-fer), *n.* the entire mass of air and other gases surrounding the earth.

ATMOSPHERIC (at-mos-fer'ik), **ATMOSPHERICAL** ('i-kal), *adj.* pertaining to atmosphere.

ATMOSPHERIC PRESSURE (presh'ur), the pressure exerted in every direction upon a body by the atmosphere : equivalent to 14⅔ lbs. on the sq. in.

ATOLL (a-tol'), *n.* a coral island.

ATOM (at'um), *n.* a unit of the matter of which the material universe is composed ; formerly considered indivisible, now known to consist of a nucleus bearing a positive charge of electricity, surrounded by a number of electrons, which revolve round the nucleus like the planets round the sun.

ATOMIC (a-tom'ik), **ATOMICAL** ('i-kal), *adj.* pertaining to, or consisting of, atoms.

ATOMIC BOMB (a-tom'ik), a bomb containing a quantity of a certain type of uranium known as U-235, the atoms of which are, at a pre-arranged moment, subjected to bombardment by neutrons which split the nuclei of the atoms, thereby releasing vast stores of energy : the resulting explosion is more destructive than that of any other known agency. First tried out in New Mexico on July 16, 1945 : first used in war on August 6, 1945, when a bomb was dropped by an American plane on Hiroshima, Japan.

ATOMICITY (at-o-mis'i-ti), *n.* equivalence ; the number of atoms in a molecule.

ATOMIC WEIGHT (a-tom'ik wat), the weight of the atom of any element as compared with another.

ATOMIZE (at'um-iz), *v.t.* to reduce to atoms.

ATOMIZER (at'um-i-zer), *n.* an instrument constructed to reduce a liquid to spray ; a sprayer.

ATONABLE (a-ton'a-bl), *adj.* capable of being atoned for.

AT ONE, in agreement with.

ATONE (a-ton'), *v.i.* to make reparation.

ATONEMENT (a-ton'ment), *n.* reparation or satisfaction offered or made in return for injury.

ATONIC (a-ton'ik), *adj.* wanting tone.

ATRABILIOUS (at'ra-bil'yus), **ATRABILARIOUS** (-bi-la'ri-us), *adj.* melancholy ; morose.

ATRAMENTAL (at'ra-men'tal), *adj.* like ink.

ATRIUM (a'tri-um), *n.* [*pl.* atria (-a)], a hall or entrance-court ; a portico.

ATROCIOUS (a-tro'shus), *adj.* wicked in the highest degree.

ATROCITY (a-tros'i-ti), *n.* an atrocious deed.

ATROPHY (at'ro-fi), *n.* a wasting, or diminution in bulk, of the body.

ATROPIN (at'ro-pin), **ATROPINE** (-pin), *n.* a crystalline alkaloid of very poisonous nature.

ATROPISM (at'ro-pizm), *n.* poisoning by atropin or belladonna.

ATROUS (a'trous), *adj.* intensely black.

ATTABOY (at'a-boi), *interj.* [Slang], a compound exclamation denoting approval.

ATTACH (a-tach'), *v.t.* to fasten, or fix, to or on; bind; connect; appoint to; connect by ties of affection; to take, or seize, by legal authority : *v.i.* to adhere.

ATTACHE (a-ta-sha'), *n.* one of a staff, as of an embassy or legation.

ATTACHMENT (a-tach'ment), *n.* the act of attaching; taking into custody by legal process.

ATTACK (a-tak'), *v.t.* to assault.

ATTAIN (a-tan'), *v.t.* to achieve; gain.

ATTAINABLE (at-ta'na-bl), *adj.* capable of being attained.

ATTAINMENT (a-tan'ment), *n.* the act of attaining; an acquisition.

ATTAINT (a-tant'), *v.t.* to taint; corrupt.

ATTAR OF ROSES (at'ar), *n.* an essential oil.

ATTEMPER (a-tem'per), *v.t.* to reduce, modify, or moderate by mixture.

ATTEMPT (a-tempt'), *v.t.* to make an effort to accomplish.

ATTEND (a-tend'), *v.t.* to wait upon.

ATTENDANCE (a-ten'dans), *n.* the act of attending.

ATTENDANT (a-ten'dant), *n.* one who attends or accompanies in service or train of another.

ATTENTION (a-ten'shun), *n.* the act of applying the mind to anything.

ATTENTIVE (a-ten'tiv), *adj.* heedful; regardful of the wishes of others.

ATTENUANT (a-ten'u-ant), *adj.* making thin.

ATTENUATE (a-ten'u-at), *v.t.* to make thin.

ATTENUATION (a-ten-u-a'shun), *n.* the act or process of making slender.

ATTEST (a-test'), *v.t.* to bear witness to.

ATTESTATION (a-tes-ta'shun), *n.* the act of attesting.

ATTESTOR (at-tes'ter), *n.* one who attests.

ATTIC (at'ik), *n.* an uppermost room in a house.

ATTIC (at'ik), *adj.* pertaining to Attica, in Greece; classical; elegant.

ATTICISM (at'i-sizm), *n.* a peculiarity of style or idiom characterizing the Attic rendering of the Greek language.

ATTIRE (a-tir'), *n.* dress; clothes.

ATTITUDE (at'i-tud), *n.* the bearing assumed by a person indicative of feeling, opinion, etc.

ATTITUDINAL (at-i-tu'di-nal), *adj.* pertaining to attitude.

ATTITUDINARIAN (at-i-tu-di-na'ri-an), *n.* one who affects attitudes.

ATTITUDINIZE (at-i-tu'di-niz), *v.i.* to pose for effect.

ATTORNEY (a-ter'ni), *n.* one legally qualified to act for another.

ATTORNEY-GENERAL (-jen'er-al), *n.* the chief law officer appointed to act for the government; the chief law officer of a state.

ATTRACT (a-trakt'), *v.t.* to draw to or toward.

ATTRACTABILITY (a-trak'ta-bil'i-ti), *n.* the quality of being attractable.

ATTRACTION (a-trak'shun), *n.* the power or act of attracting.

ATTRACTIVE (a-trak'tiv), *adj.* having the power or tendency to attract.

ATTRIBUTABLE (a-trib'u-ta-bl), *adj.* capable of being attributed.

ATTRIBUTE (a-trib'ut), *v.t.* to ascribe : *n.* (at'ri-but), that which is attributed.

ATTRIBUTION (at-ri-bu'shun), *n.* the act of attributing.

ATTRIBUTIVE (a-trib'u-tiv), *adj.* pertaining to an attribute : *n.* a word denoting an attribute.

ATTRITE (a-trit'), *adj.* worn by friction.

ATTRITION (a-trish'un), *n.* the act of wearing by rubbing; abrasion.

ATTUNE (a-tun'), *v.t.* to put in tune.

ATYPIC (a-tip'ik), **ATYPICAL** ('i-kal), *adj.* without definite typical character.

AUBURN (aw'burn), *adj.* reddish-brown.

AUCTION (awk'shun), *n.* a public sale of property : *v.t.* to sell by auction.

AUCTION BRIDGE (brij), a variation of bridge in card-playing.

AUCTIONEER (awk-shun-er'), *n.* one licensed to sell by auction.

AUCTION POOL (pool), a guessing contest held on ship-board.

AUDACIOUS (aw-da'shus), *adj.* bold ; daring ; spirited.

AUDACITY (aw-das'i-ti), *n.* boldness ; daring.

AUDIBLE (aw'di-bl), *adj.* capable of being heard.

AUDIENCE (aw'di-ens), *n.* the act of hearing ; an assembly of hearers.

AUDIENT (aw'di-ent), *adj.* hearing ; listening.

AUDIO-FREQUENCY (aw'di-o-fre'-kwen-si), *n.* in radio, the frequency of electrical waves.

AUDIOMETER (aw-di-om'e-ter), *n.* an instrument for gauging the power of hearing.

AUDION (aw'di-on), *n.* a vacuum tube used in *Radio*.

AUDIPHONE (aw'di-fon), *n.* an instrument to assist the deaf.

AUDIT (aw'dit), *n.* official examination and verification of claims or accounts.

AUDITOR (aw'di-ter), *n.* a listener ; a person appointed to verify accounts.

AUDITORIUM (aw-di-to'ri-um), *n.* [*pl.* auditoria (-a)], the space assigned to the audience.

AUDITORY (aw'di-to-ri), *adj.* pertaining to hearing.

AUDITORY CANAL (ka-nal'), a passage from the middle ear to the outside.

AUDITORY NERVE (nerv), the nerve that carries to the brain the impulse which causes hearing.

AUGEND (aw'jend), *n.* a number or quantity to which another is to be added.

AUGER (aw'ger), *n.* a tool for boring holes.

AUGHT (awt), *n.* anything ; any part : *adv.* in any way ; at all.

AUGITE (aw'jit), *n.* an aluminous pyroxene.

AUGMENT (awg-ment'), *v.t.* to increase : *v.i.* to grow larger : *n.* increase.

AUGMENTATION (awg men-ta'-shun), *n.* increase ; the increase in time-value of the notes of a theme.

AUGMENTATIVE (awg-men'ta-tiv), *adj.* having the quality or power of augmenting : *n.* a word or affix which expresses with greater force the idea conveyed by the term from which it is derived.

AUGUR (aw'ger), *n.* one who professes to foretell events : *v.t.* to predict.

AUGURY (aw'gu-ri), *n.* the practice of foretelling events.

AUGUST (aw-gust'), *adj.* grand ; majestic ; of a nature to inspire awe and reverence.

AUGUST (aw'gust), *n.* the eighth month of the year.

AUK (awk), *n.* a web-footed bird of the Arctic : the **GREAT AUK** is now extinct.

AULD LANG SYNE (lang sin), old times ; long since.

AUNT (ant), *n.* the sister of one's father or mother.

AURA (aw'ra), *n.* a subtle, vaporous streaming, or exhalation, supposed to emanate from a living body.

AURAL (aw'ral), *adj.* pertaining to the air or to an aura ; pertaining to the ear, or to the sense of hearing.

AURAMINE (aw-ram'in), *n.* a yellow dye.

AURATE (aw'rat), *n.* a salt of auric acid.

AURATED (aw'rat-ed), *adj.* gilded ; like gold ; having ears.

AUREATE (aw're-at), *adj.* golden ; gilded ; golden-yellow.

AURELIA (aw-re'lya), *n.* the pupa or chrysalis of an insect ; [A-], a genus of jelly fishes.

AUREOLA (aw-re'o-la), **AUREOLE** (aw're-ol), *n.* a halo, encircling the figures of Christ, the Virgin, and the saints as represented by painters.

AUREOUS (aw're-us), *adj.* golden ; gilded.

AU REVOIR (o re-vwar') [French], until we meet again.

AURIC (aw'rik), *adj.* pertaining to gold.

AURIC ACID (as'id), a weak solution of hydrated auric oxide which combines with bases to form aurates.

AURICLE (aw'ri-kl), *n.* the external ear; one of two chambers of the heart.

AURIC OXIDE (ok'sid), a compound from the action of nitric acid on magnesium aurate.

AURICULA (-rik'u-la), *n.* an Alpine primrose.

AURICULAR (aw-rik'u-lar), *adj.* pertaining to the ear: 1. a feather overlying the ear of birds.

AURICULAR FINGER (fing'ger), the little finger.

AURICULAR METHOD (meth'od), a method of teaching the almost deaf.

AURICULATE (aw-rik'u-lat), **AURICULATED** (-ed), *adj.* ear-shaped.

AURIFEROUS (aw-rif'er-us), *adj.* gold-bearing.

AURIFORM (aw'ri-form), *adj.* ear-shaped.

AURISCOPE (aw'ri-skop), *n.* an instrument for examining the ear.

AURIST (aw'rist), *n.* one skilled in the treatment of ear disorders.

AUROCHS (aw'roks), *n.* the European bison, now nearly extinct.

AURORA (aw-ro'ra), *n.* the rising light of the morning.

AURORA AUSTRALIS (aw-stra'lis), the aurora, as seen in southern latitudes.

AURORA BOREALIS (bo-re-a'lis), the northern lights.

AURORAL (-ro'ral), *adj.* pertaining to the dawn; roseate.

AUROUS (aw'rus), *adj.* pertaining to gold.

AUSCULTATE (aws'kul-tat), *v.t.* to examine by auscultation.

AUSCULTATION (aws-kul-ta'shun), *n.* a method of detecting chest disease.

AUSCULTATOR (aws'kul-ta-ter), *n.* one who practises auscultation.

AUSCULTATORY (aws-kul'ta-to-ri), *adj.* pertaining to auscultation.

AUSPICE (aws'pis), *n.* a prediction as to the future.

AUSPICIOUS (aws-pish'us), *adj.* having promise of success or happiness.

AUSTERE (aws-ter'), *adj.* sour; harsh; rough to the taste; severe.

AUSTERITY (aws-ter'i-ti), *n.* severity of manner or life.

AUSTRAL (aws'tral), *adj.* southern; torrid.

AUTHENTIC (aw-then'tik), **AUTHENTICAL** ('ti-kal), *adj.* genuine; original.

AUTHENTICALLY (-li), *adj.* in an authentic manner.

AUTHENTICATE (aw-then'ti-kat), *v.t.* to make authentic.

AUTHENTICATION (aw-then-ti-ka'shun), *n.* the act of authenticating.

AUTHENTICITY (aw-then-tis'i-ti), *n.* the quality of being authentic.

AUTHOR (aw'ther), *n.* the beginner or prime mover of anything; the writer of a book or other literary production.

AUTHORESS (aw'ther-es), *n.* a female author.

AUTHORITATIVE (aw-thor'i-ta-tiv), *adj.* having due authority.

AUTHORITY (aw-thor'i-ti), *n.* power or right to act or command.

AUTHORIZATION (aw-ther-i-za'shun), *n.* act of authorizing.

AUTHORIZE (aw'ther-iz), *v.t.* to vest with authority.

AUTHORIZED VERSION (ver'shun), known as *King James's Version of the Bible*.

AUTHORIZER (-iz'er), *n.* one who authorizes.

AUTHORSHIP (-ship), *n.* quality or function of an author.

AUTO (aw'to), *n.* an abbreviation for automobile: *v.i.* to ride in an automobile.

AUTO-, a combining form from the Greek *autos*, self.

AUTOBIOGRAPHICAL (aw-to-bi-o-graf'i-kal *adj.* pertaining to autobiography.

AUTOBIOGRAPHY (aw-to-bi-og'ra-fi), *n.* character-sketch of a person written by himself.

AUTOBUS (aw'to-bus), *n.* an automobile omnibus.

AUTOCAR (-kar), *n.* a carriage containing within itself the machinery necessary for its own propulsion.

AUTOCEPHALOUS (-sef'a-lus), *adj.* self-governing.

AUTOCLAVE (-klav), *n.* a stewpan with tight lid.

AUTOCRACY (aw-tok'ra-si), *n.* government by one invested with absolute authority.

AUTOCRAT (aw'to-krat), *n.* one who rules without restriction.

AUTOCRATIC (aw-to-krat'ik), **AUTOCRATICAL** ('i-kal), *adj.* pertaining to autocracy.

AUTOCYCLE (aw'to-si-kl), *n.* a motor bicycle.

AUTODYNAMIC (aw-to-di-nam'ik), *adj.* operating by its own force.

AUTOGRAPH (aw'to-graf), *adj.* self-written ; in one's own handwriting : *n.* a person's own handwriting.

AUTOGRAPHIC (aw-to-graf'ik), **AUTOGRAPHICAL** ('i-kal), *adj.* pertaining to an autograph.

AUTOGRAPHY (aw-tog'ra-fi), *n.* the science or study of autographs.

AUTOHARP (-harp), *n.* a musical instrument.

AUTOHYPNOTIC (aw-to-hip-not'-ik), *adj.* producing in one's self a hypnotic state.

AUTO-INFECTION (-in-fek'shun), *n.* poisoning of the system through chemical changes within the body itself.

AUTO-INTOXICATION (-in-tok-si-ka'shun), *n.* a form of auto-infection usually due to imperfect digestion of food.

AUTOIST (aw'to-ist), *n.* one who runs or rides in an automobile.

AUTOLATRY (aw-tol'a-tri), *n.* self-worship.

AUTOLOGY (aw-tol'o-ji), *n.* the scientific study of one's self.

AUTOMANUAL (-man'u-al), *adj.* designating or referring to a system of block signals.

AUTOMAT (aw-to-mat'), *n.* a camera shutter operated by a pneumatic bulb ; an apparatus for serving foods automatically.

AUTOMATIC (aw-to-mat'ik), **AUTOMATICAL** ('i-kal), *adj.* having the power of self-motion or self-action.

AUTOMATICALLY (-li), *adv.* in an automatic manner.

AUTOMATISM (aw-tom'a-tizm), *n.* the doctrine which assigns all animal functions to physical laws.

AUTOMATON (aw-tom'a-ton), *n.* [*pl.* automata (-ta)], that which possesses the power of spontaneous movement without consciousness ; a self-acting machine.

AUTOMOBILE (aw-to-mo'bil), *adj.* self-moving.

AUTOMOBILE (aw-to-mo-bel', -mo'bil), *n.* a motor-driven vehicle.

AUTOMOBILIST (aw-to-mo'bil-ist), *n.* one who rides in and manages an automobile.

AUTOMORPHISM (aw-to-mor'-fizm), *n.* the judgment of others by analogy from the knowledge of one's self.

AUTOMOTIVE (aw-to-mo'tiv), *adj.* pertaining to self-propelling machines.

AUTOMOTOR (aw-to-mo'ter), *n.* an automobile.

AUTONOMIC (aw-to-nom'ik), **AUTONOMOUS** (-ton'o-mus), *adj.* pertaining to autonomy ; self-governing.

AUTONOMIST (aw-ton'o-mist), *n.* a supporter of autonomy.

AUTONOMY (aw-ton'o-mi), *n.* the power or right of self-government.

AUTONYM (aw'to-nim), *n.* one's own name : opposed to *pseudonym*.

AUTOPHON (aw'to-fon), *n.* a barrel-organ.

AUTOPHONY (-i), *n.* sound of the examiner's own voice in testing the chest of a patient by ear.

AUTOPLASTY (aw'to-plas-ti), *n.* the process of repairing lesions by application of tissue removed from another part.

AUTOPSY (aw'top-si), *n.* a post-mortem examination.

AUTOSUGGESTION (aw-to-sug-jes'chun), *n.* self-suggestion.

AUTOTOXIC (aw-to-tok'sik), *adj.* self-poisoning.

AUTOTOXIN ('sin), *n.* a toxin produced by changes in tissues of the body.

AUTOTRUCK (aw'to-truk), *n.* a motor-driven truck.

AUTOTYPE (aw'to-tip), *n.* a facsimile; photogelatine process of producing pictures.

AUTUMN (aw'tum), *n.* the season between summer and winter.

AUTUMNAL (aw-tum'nal), *adj.* belonging to autumn.

AUTUMNAL EQUINOX (e'kwi-noks), the time of the sun's passage across the equator.

AUXANOMETER (awk-sa-nom'e-ter), *n.* an instrument for measuring plants.

AUXESIS (awk-se'sis), *n.* a figure of speech in which a high-sounding word is used for a common one.

AUXILIARY (awg-zil'ya-ri), *adj.* helping; aiding; assisting; subsidiary: *n.* a helper; an assistant; a verb which helps to form the moods and tenses of other verbs.

AVAIL (a-val'), *v.i.* to be of use, value, or service; give profit: *pl.* proceeds or profits.

AVAILABILITY (a-va'la-bil-i-ti), *n.* the state of being available.

AVALANCHE (av'a-lanch), *n.* the sudden descent of a mass of snow or ice from the higher parts of a mountain; a fall of rocks or earth; anything that overwhelms.

AVANT- (a-vant'), a prefix signifying *before.*

AVANT-COURIER (-koo'ri-er), *n.* a person detailed to go in advance; a scout.

AVARICE (av'a-ris), *n.* covetousness; cupidity; greediness.

AVARICIOUS (av-a-rish'us), *adj.* impelled by avarice.

AVAST (a-vast'), *interj.* stop! cease! hold!

AVAUNT (a-vawnt', a-vant'), *interj.* begone! depart!

AVE (a've, a've), *interj.* hail! farewell! *n.* a prayer to the Virgin.

AVENACEOUS (av-e-na'shus), *adj.* belonging to or resembling oats.

AVENGE (a-venj'), *v.t.* to exact punishment for wrong: *v.i.* to execute vengeance.

AVENUE (av'e-nu), *n.* a way or means of approach to a place; a broad street planted with trees.

AVER (a-ver'), *v.t.* to affirm positively.

AVERAGE (av'er-aj), *n.* an equal proportion; a mean sum or amount: *v.t.* to find the mean, as of unequal sums.

AVERSE (a-vers'), *adj.* unwilling; unfavourable.

AVERSION (a-ver'shun), *n.* opposition or repugnance of mind; antipathy.

AVERT (a-vert'), *v.t.* to turn aside or away.

AVERTIBLE (a-vert'i-bl), *adj.* capable of being warded off.

AVES (a'vez), *n.pl.* the class of warm-blooded vertebrates consisting of birds.

AVIAN (a'vi-an), *adj.* pertaining to birds.

AVIARY (a'vi-a-ri), *n.* enclosure for the keeping and rearing of birds.

AVIATION (a-vi-a'shun), *n.* the art of flying.

AVIATOR (a'vi-a-ter), *n.* one who operates a flying machine.

AVIATRESS (-a'tres), **AVIATRIX** (-a'triks), *n.* a female aviator.

AVICULA (a-vik'u-la), *n.* a genus of marine bivalves, allied to the pearl oysters.

AVICULTURE (a'vi-kul-tur), *n.* the breeding and rearing of birds.

AVID (av'id), *adj.* eager; greedy.

AVIDITY (a-vid'i-ti), *n.* greediness; eagerness; strong appetite.

AVIFAUNA (-faw'na), *n.* all the birds of any given region considered collectively.

AVOCADO (a-vo-ka'do), *n.* the pulpy fruit of a West Indian tree; the alligator-pear.

AVOCATION (av-o-ka'shun), *n.* a calling away; a distraction; customary employment.

AVOCET (av'o-set), *n.* a shore bird with long legs and webbed feet.

AVOID (a-void'), *v.t.* to keep away, shunning.

AVOIDANCE (a-voi′dans), *n.* the act of annulling or making void.

AVOIRDUPOIS (av-er-du-poiz′), *n.* a system of weights in which one pound contains 16 ounces.

AVOUCH (a-vouch′), *v.t.* to affirm openly ; vouch for.

AVOW (a-vou′), *v.t.* to declare openly.

AVOWAL (a-vou′al), *n.* an open declaration ; a confession.

AVULSION (a-vul′shun), *n.* a separation ; a tearing away ; the cutting off, as by water.

AVUNCULAR (a-vung′ku-lar), *adj.* pertaining to or like an uncle.

AWAIT (a-wat′), *v.t.* to wait for ; be ready for.

AWAKE (a-wak′), *v.t.* to arouse from sleep ; put into action : *v.i.* to cease to sleep : *adj.* roused from sleep ; in a state of vigilance.

AWAKENING (a-wak′ning), *n.* the act of rousing from sleep : *adj.* rousing ; exciting ; alarming.

AWARD (a-wawrd′), *v.t.* to adjudge ; assign by judicial sentence ; bestow in consideration of merit : *n.* a judgment ; a decision.

AWARE (a-war′), *adj.* on guard ; vigilant ; watchful.

AWASH (a-wosh′), *adj. & adv.* on a level with the waves.

AWAY (a-wa′), *adv.* absent ; at a distance ; out of.

AWE (aw), *n.* reverential fear ; the feeling or emotion inspired by the contemplation of something sublime : *v.t.* to strike or inspire with feelings of reverential respect or fear.

AWESOME (aw′sum), *adj.* inspiring terror ; appalling.

AWFUL (aw′ful), *adj.* inspiring or impressing with profound fear or reverence.

AWFULLY (-li), *adv.* in an awful manner ; excessively.

AWHILE (a-hwil′), *adv.* for a period of time.

AWKWARD (awk′werd), *adj.* wanting dexterity ; clumsy.

AWL (awl), *n.* a pointed instrument for piercing.

AWN (awn), *n.* appendage of the glume of wheat, barley and numerous grasses.

AWNING (awn′ing), *n.* a covering of canvas used as a shelter from wind or sun.

A.W.O.L., abbreviation for absent without official leave.

AWRY (a-ri′), *adj.* or *adv.* turned or twisted toward one side.

AXE, AX (aks), *n.* a tool, with a steeled edge, used for hewing timber and chopping wood.

AXIAL (aks′i-al), *adj.* pertaining to an axis in any sense of the word.

AXIFEROUS (ak-sif′e-rus), *adj.* consisting of stem or axis alone without leaves.

AXIFORM (ak′si-form), *adj.* in the form of an axis.

AXIL (ak′sil), *n.* the angle formed by the upper side of an organ or branch with the stem or trunk to which it is attached.

AXILLA (ak-sil′a), [*pl.* axillæ (′e)], *n.* the armpit, or cavity in the junction of the arm and shoulder.

AXILLAR (ak′si-lar), **AXILLARY** (-la-ri), *adj.* pertaining to the armpit ; pertaining to the axil.

AXIOM (ak′si-um), *n.* an indisputable self-evident truth.

AXIOMATIC (ak-si-o-mat′ik), **AXIO-MATICAL** (′i-kal), *adj.* of the nature of an axiom.

AXIOMATICALLY (-li), *adv.* in the manner, or by use, of accepted truth.

AXIS (ak′sis), *n.* [*pl.* axes (sez)], the straight line, real or imaginary, passing through a body, upon or around which such body revolves.

AXIS (ak-sis), *n.* the hog-deer of India.

AXLE (ak-sel), *n.* the spindle, or portion of the axle-tree, which is inserted in the hub of the wheel, and on which the wheel revolves.

AXLE-BOX (-boks), *n.* a bushing in the hub of a wheel.

AXLE-TREE (-tre), *n.* a bar connecting the opposite wheels of a carriage, on the rounded ends of which the wheels revolve.

AY, AYE (a), *adv.* always ; for ever.

AYE, AY (a or i), *adv.* or *interj.* yes ;

yea; even so; indeed: *n.pl.* the affirmative votes.

AYE-AYE (i'i), *n.* a nocturnal quadruped of Madagascar.

AYRSHIRE (ar'shir), *n.* a fine breed of cattle which originated in the county of Ayr, Scotland, noted for their rich milk.

AZALEA (a-za'le-a), *n.* a genus of plants.

AZARINE (az'a-rin), *n.* a bright red dye.

AZIMUTH (az'i-muth), *n.* an arc of the horizon intercepted between the meridian of a place and the vertical circle passing through the centre of a celestial body.

AZOIC (a-zo'ik), *adj.* without life; antedating life on the earth.

AZOTEMIA (az-o-te'mi-a), *n.* a disease of the horse characterized by profuse sweating.

AZRAEL (az'ra-el), *n.* name given by the Mohammedans to the Angel of Death.

AZTEC (az'tek), *adj.* pertaining to the Aztecs: *n.* one of the race in Mexico when Cortez invaded that country in 1519.

AZURE (ash'ur, a'zhur), *adj.* like the blue of the sky; cerulean: *n.* any pigment of this colour.

AZURE-STONE (-ston), *n.* the lapis lazuli, from which genuine ultramarine is made.

AZURINE (azh'ur-in), *n.* a greyish-blue colour.

AZURITE (azh'u-rit), *n.* blue carbonate of copper.

B

B, b (be), *n.* a letter; the second letter in the English alphabet.

B, b (be), *n.* an abbreviation.

B (be), *n.* a Roman numeral representing 300; with a bar (B̄), 3,000.

B FLAT (flat), a tone half a step below B.

B FLAT MAJOR (ma'jer), a major scale having a signature of two flats.

B FLAT MINOR (min'er), a minor scale having a signature of five flats.

B MAJOR, a major scale having a signature of five sharps.

B MINOR, a minor scale having a signature of two sharps.

BAAL (ba'al), *n.* the sun-god of the ancient Semitic races.

BAALISM (ba'al-izm), *n.* the worship of Baal; gross idolatry.

BABBITT METAL (bab'it met'al), an anti-friction alloy of copper, tin, and zinc.

BABBLE (bab'bl), *v.i.* to utter indistinct or imperfect sounds; prattle; talk childishly.

BABBLER (bab'ler), *n.* one who babbles.

BABE (bab), *n.* an infant or young child.

BABIROUSSA, BABIRUSSA (bab-i-roo'sa), *n.* the wild hog of Eastern Asia.

BABOON (ba-boon'), *n.* one of a large division of monkeys.

BABY (ba'bi), *n.* an infant of either sex.

BABYHOOD (ba'bi-hood), *n.* the stage of infancy.

BACCALAUREATE (bak-a-law're-at), *n.* the degree of Bachelor of Arts, Science, etc.: *adj.* pertaining to the degree of Bachelor.

BACCALAUREATE SERMON (-ser'mun), a sermon or lecture delivered on Commencement Day.

BACCARAT (bak-a-ra'), *n.* a French card game.

BACCATE (bak'at), **BACCATED** (-ed), *adj.* having many berries.

BACCHANAL (bak'a-nal), **BACCHANALIAN** (bak-a-na'li-an), *adj.* indulging in or characterized by drunken revelry.

BACCHANT (bak'ant), *n.* a devotee of Bacchus.

BACCHANTE (ba-kant'), *n.* female votary of Bacchus.

BACCHANTIC (ba-kan'tik), *adj.* of or resembling a bacchanal; noisy; jovial.

BACCHIC (bak'ik), **BACCHICAL**

('i-kal), *adj.* pertaining to Bacchus.

BACHELOR (bach'el-er), *n.* one who has taken the lowest university degree in any faculty ; an unmarried man.

BACHELOR GIRL (gerl), a modern young woman who enjoys bachelor-like independence.

BACHELORHOOD (bach'el-er-hood), *n.* a state of an unmarried man.

BACHELOR'S BUTTON (bach'el-erz but'n), one of several flowering plants.

BACHELOR'S HALL (hawl), a home where the wife is absent.

BACILLARIALES (bas-i-la-ri-a'lez), *n.pl.* an order of microscopic diatoms.

BACILLARY (bas'i-la-ri), *adj.* rod-shaped ; consisting of rod-like bodies.

BACILLIAN (ba-sil'i-an), *adj.* pertaining to, or of the nature of, a bacillus.

BACILLICIDE (ba-sil'i-sid), *n.* an agent employed for destroying bacilli.

BACILLICULTURE (ba-sil'i-kul-tur), *n.* the culture of bacilli.

BACILLUS (ba-sil'us), *n.* [*pl.* bacilli ('i)], a genus of microscopic vegetable organisms commonly known as bacteria.

BACK, BAC (bak), *n.* a large cistern or vat.

BACK (bak), *n.* the hinder part of the body in man, or in other animals the upper portion ; that which is opposed to the front ; the rear or hinder part of anything.

BACKBITE (bak'bit), *v.t.* to slander.

BACKBONE ('bon), *n.* the vertebral column in man or in animals.

BACK DOOR, a door in the back part of a house or building.

BACKER (bak'er), *n.* one who sustains or abets another.

BACKFIRE (bak'fir), *v.i.* to fight forest or prairie fires by starting local fires that can be controlled or extinguished.

BACK-FIRING (bak-fir'ing), *n.* premature ignition of the gas and air in the cylinder of an internal combustion engine.

BACKGAMMON (bak-gam'un), *n.* a game played by two persons upon a table or board.

BACKGROUND (bak'ground), *n.* the distant portion of a landscape.

BACKHAND (bak'hand), *n.* writing which slopes backward.

BACKHANDED (bak'han-ded), *adj.* unfair ; indirect ; ambiguous.

BACKING (bak'ing), *n.* aid or support given to a person or cause.

BACK-RENT ('rent), *n.* arrears of rent.

BACK-REST (bak'rest), *n.* a guide, attached to the slide-rest of a lathe.

BACKSET (-set), *n.* an obstacle or check to progress ; relapse.

BACK-SETTLEMENT (bak-set'l-ment), *n.* an outlying portion of a country.

BACKSETTLER (-set'ler), *n.* one living in back-settlements.

BACKSLIDE (bak-slid'), *v.i.* to fall off or away from.

BACKSTAIR (bak'star), **BACKSTAIRS** ('starz), *n.* stairs in the back part of a house.

BACKSTAYS (bak'staz), *n.pl.* ropes extending from the masthead to the side of the ship, slanting a little aft, to assist in supporting the mast.

BACKSWEPT ('swept), *adj.* having the front edge of an airplane tilted backward.

BACKSWORD (bak'sord), *n.* a sword with one sharp edge.

BACKWARD (bak'werd), **BACKWARDS** ('werdz), *adv.* toward past times or events ; from a better to a worse state : *adj.* reluctant ; hesitating ; slow ; behind in learning or progress.

BACKWASH (-wosh), *n.* water thrown back as from a paddle wheel ; wash of a receding wave.

BACKWOODSMAN (bak-woodz'-man), *n.* a dweller in forests ; one who lives remote from villages or towns.

BACON (ba'kn), *n.* hog's flesh salted, or pickled and dried, usually in smoke.

BACTERIA (bak-te'ri-a), *n.pl.* a widely distributed group of vegetable micro-organisms.

BACTERIOLOGICAL (bak-te-ri-o-loj'i-kal), *adj.* of or pertaining to bacteriology.

BACTERIOLOGIST (bak-te-ri-ol'o-jist), *n.* a student of bacteriology.

BACTERIOLOGY (bak-te-ri-ol'o-ji), *n.* the scientific investigation or study of bacteria.

BACTERIUM (bak-te'ri-um), *n.* [*pl.* bacteria (-a)], a large genus of the bacteria : distinguished from the *Bacillus* by the absence of cilia.

BACULIFORM (ba-ku'li-form), *adj.* shaped like a rod.

BAD (bad), *adj.* the opposite of good.

BAD BLOOD (blud), bitterness ; hostility.

BAD FORM (form), that which is bad ; not refined.

BADGE (baj), *n.* a mark, sign, or token, or cognizance.

BADGER (baj'er), *n.* a plantigrade carnivorous mammal : *v.t.* to worry or annoy.

BADGER DOG (dog), the dachshund.

BADINAGE (bad'i-naj, ba-de-nazh'), *n.* light or playful raillery or banter.

BAD LANDS (landz), barren regions.

BADMINTON (bad'min-tun), *n.* game played with net, rackets, and shuttle-cocks.

BAFFLE (baf'l), *v.t.* to elude or circumvent.

BAG (bag), *n.* a sack ; a pouch ; a wallet ; a receptacle for holding anything.

BAGASSE (ba-gas'), *n.* sugar-cane refuse.

BAGATELLE (bag-a-tel'), *n.* a trifle ; a game played on a nine-holed board.

BAGGAGE (bag'aj), *n.* the trunks, bags, and other impedimenta of a traveller.

BAGGAGE-MASTER (bag'aj-mas'-ter), *n.* person in charge of receiving and forwarding baggage.

BAGGING (bag'ing), *n.* the act of putting into bags ; coarse cloth or other material used for bags.

BAGGY (bag'i), *adj.* having a loose or flabby appearance.

BAGPIPE (bag'pip), *n.* a musical instrument, consisting of a leathern wind-bag from which air is forced

by the performer's elbow into pipes.

BAH (ba), *interj.* an exclamation expressing incredulous contempt.

BAIL (bal), *v.t.* to set free or liberate from arrest on security for reappearance : *n.* the person or persons who become surety for the released ; the security tendered or accepted.

BAIL (bal), *v.i.* to free from water by dipping.

BAILIE (ba'li), *n.* [Scotch], a magistrate ; a municipal officer.

BAILIFF (ba'lif), *n.* a sheriff's officer who serves processes, etc.

BAILIWICK (ba'li-wik), *n.* the district within which a bailiff has jurisdiction.

BAILMENT (bal'ment), *n.* a delivery of goods in trust to another ; the action of becoming surety for one in custody.

BAILOR (ba'ler) or **BAILER** (ba'ler), *n.* one who delivers goods to another in bailment.

BAIRN (barn), *n.* [Scotch], a child.

BAIT (bat), *v.t.* to harass or provoke ; worry ; torment : *n.* any substance used to allure fish or other animals with a view to capture.

BAIZE (baz), *n.* a coarse woollen stuff.

BAKE (bak), *v.t.* to cook or prepare food by subjection to dry heat in a closed place, as an oven ; to dry and harden by heat.

BAKELITE (ba'ke-lit), *n.* a substance derived from phenols and formaldehyde, of strong chemical resistance.

BAKER (ba'ker), *n.* one whose business is to make bread, biscuits, etc.

BAKER'S DOZEN (duz'n), thirteen.

BAKERY (ba'ker-i), *n.* a place used for bread-making ; a baker's shop.

BAKING (bak'ing), *n.* the quantity of anything that is baked at the same time ; a batch.

BALANCE (bal'ans), *n.* an instrument for determining the weight of bodies ; a pair of scales ; equilibrium ; equipoise ; equality : *v.t.* to weigh ; compare ; bring to a state of equipoise ; equal or make equal ; counterbalance ; adjust or settle ; to examine and compare accounts.

BALANCE OF POWER (pou'er), a

theory in diplomacy that there should be a balance among nations, so that no single power should be over-whelmingly dominant.

BALANCE OF TRADE (trad), the difference between the imports and exports of a country.

BALANCE-SHEET (-shet), *n.* a statement of the assets and liabilities of a business.

BALANCE-WHEEL (hwel), *n.* a wheel in a watch or chronometer which regulates the beats.

BALBRIGGAN (bal-brig'an), *n.* a cotton fabric, used for underwear and hosiery.

BALCONY (bal'ko-ni), *n.* a platform or gallery projecting from the wall of a building, enclosed by a balustrade or parapet.

BALD (bawld), *adj.* destitute of hair; unadorned; bare.

BALD EAGLE (e'gl), the common eagle of North America.

BALDERDASH (bawl'der-dash), *n.* a nonsensical jumble of words; silly talk or writing; a worthless mixture.

BALE (bal), *n.* a bundle or package of goods : *v.t.* to make up into a bale or bales; to bale out, as water.

BALE (bal), *n.* calamity; sorrow.

BALEEN (ba-len'), *n.* the horny elastic material fringing the jaws of certain whales; whalebone.

BALE-FIRE (bal'fir), *n.* a beacon or signal-fire; a bonfire.

BALEFUL (bal'fool), *adj.* replete with deadly influence.

BALINE (ba-len'), *n.* coarse woollen stuff used in packing.

BALISE or **BALIZE** (ba-lez), *n.* a sea-mark or beacon.

BALK (bawk), *n.* a strip or ridge of land left unploughed; a thick heavy piece of timber; a barrier or check; frustration or disappointment : *v.t.* to thwart, check.

BALL (bawl), *n.* a round body; any mass resembling a sphere; a spherical body used for play; a bullet.

BALL (bawl), *n.* a dance; a social assembly of persons for the purpose of dancing.

BALL BEARING (bar'ing), *n.* a bear-

ing in which the revolving part turns upon loose steel balls which roll freely.

BALLAD (bal'ad), *n.* a short narrative poem.

BALLAST (bal'ast), *n.* weighty material carried by a ship to ensure stability; sand carried in the car of a balloon to steady it; gravel or rubble filling the space between the sleepers of a railway.

BALLAST-TANK (bal'ast-tank), *n.* one of a series of tanks in a ship.

BALLET (bal'a), *n.* a theatrical representation in which a story is told, accompanied by music and dancing.

BALLISTIC (bal-lis'tik), *adj.* pertaining to the scientific construction and use of projectiles.

BALLISTICS (bal-is'tiks), *n.* the science of the motion of projectiles.

BALLOON (ba-loon'), *n.* a large bag of prepared silk or other material, which, when inflated by gas, ascends and floats in the atmosphere.

BALLOONIST (ba-loon'ist), *n.* one who makes or ascends in a balloon; an aeronaut.

BALLOON JIB (jib) *n.*, a triangular sail used by yachts in a light breeze.

BALLOT (bal'ot), *n.* a ball, ticket, or paper by which a vote is registered; also the total number of votes cast or recorded : *v.i.* to vote or decide by secret vote.

BALLOT-BOX (-boks), *n.* a receptacle for the deposit of ballots.

BALLROOM (-room), *n.* a large hall for balls and dancing.

BALM (bam), *n.* the oily aromatic exudation of certain trees or shrubs.

BALM OF GILEAD (gil'e-ad), *n.* an oriental evergreen tree; the American balsam-fir.

BALMINESS (-nes), *n.* the state or quality of being soothing.

BALMORAL (bal-mor'al), *n.* a heavy woollen petticoat; a high-top laced boot.

BALMY (bam'i), *adj.* having the qualities of balm; soft; fragrant; refreshing.

BALSAM (bawl'sam), *n.* an oily, aromatic, resinous substance obtained from certain trees or shrubs, and used medicinally or in perfumery.

BALSAM FIR (fer), a valuable variety of pine which grows in northern United States and Canada.

BALSAMIC (bawl-sam'ik), **BALSAMICAL** ('i-kal), *adj.* having the qualities of, or yielding, balsam; soft; soothing; healing.

BALSA WOOD (wood), the wood of a small tree of Central and South America: it is lighter than cork.

BALTIMORE ORIOLE (bawl'ti-mor o'ri-ol), an American oriole with black and orange plumage.

BALUSTER (bal'us-ter), *n.* a small column or pilaster to support the rail of a parapet or balustrade.

BALUSTRADE (bal-us-trad'), *n.* a series of small columns or pilasters, surmounted by a top-rail or coping, serving as a parapet or protective railing, staircase, etc.

BALZARINE (bal-za-ren'), *n.* a dress fabric of wool and cotton.

BAMBINO (bam-be'no), *n.* [*pl.* bambini ('ne)], a child or baby.

BAMBOO (bam-boo'), *n.* the name of certain tropical grasses having thick-jointed stems of exceeding hardness.

BAMBOOZLE (bam-boo'zl), *v.t.* to hoax; deceive by trickery.

BAN (ban), *n.* an edict of proscription or interdiction; prohibition; excommunication: *v.t.* to place under a ban.

BAN (ban), *n.* a kind of fine muslin.

BANANA (ba-na'na), *n.* a tropical herbaceous plant, closely allied to the plantain; its soft, luscious fruit.

BAND (band), *n.* that which binds together; that which connects; tie; shackle or fetter; collar; ligature; a driving belt; a company of persons united by a common object: *v.i.* to unite for a common purpose.

BANDAGE (ban'daj), *n.* a roller of cotton or other material used in dressing and binding up wounds, etc.: *v.t.* to dress or bind with a bandage.

BANDALA (ban-da'la), *n.* manila white rope.

BANDANA, BANDANNA (ban-dan'a), *n.* a large silk or cotton handkerchief, dyed red, blue, or yellow, with white or yellow spots; a style of calico printing in imitation of the bandana.

BANDBOX (band'boks), *n.* a light box of pasteboard, etc.

BANDEAU (ban-do'), *n.* [*pl.* bandeaux (-doz')], a ribbon worn over the forehead to confine the hair.

BANDED (ban'ded), *p.adj.* allied; confederated; having bands; marked by stripes of different colour or material.

BANDEROLE (ban'de-rol), **BANDEROL** (-rol), *n.* a small flag carried at the head of a lance or mast.

BANDICOOT (ban'di-koot), *n.* a large rat, native of India and Ceylon.

BANDIT (ban'dit), *n.* [*pl.* bandits, ('its) & banditti (-dit'i)], an outlaw; a brigand; a robber.

BANDLET (band'let), *n.* a small band.

BANDOG (ban'dog), *n.* a large fierce kind of dog; a mastiff.

BANDOLEER (ban-do-ler'), *n.* a broad leather belt, for holding ammunition.

BANDORE (ban'dor), *n.* an ancient stringed instrument resembling a guitar.

BANDSAW (band'saw), *n.* an endless steel saw running on pulleys.

BANDY (ban'di), *v.t.* to throw or beat to and fro, as a ball in play.

BANE (ban), *n.* that which causes death, ruin, or destruction; a disease (rot) in sheep.

BANEFUL (ban'fool), *adj.* poisonous; pernicious.

BANG (bang), *v.t.* to beat, as with a club or cudgel; thump; handle roughly.

BANG (bang), *n.* [*pl.* bangz], hair cut straight across the forehead.

BANGLE (bang'gl), *n.* an ornamental ring.

BANGTAIL (bang'tal), *n.* a horse with a docked tail.

BANIAN, BANYAN (ban'yan), *n.* a Hindu trader or merchant.

BANISH (ban'ish), *v.t.* to condemn to exile.

BANISHMENT (ban'ish-ment), *n.* the act of expelling or driving away.

BANISTER, BANNISTER (ban'is-ter), *n.* corrupt forms of baluster.

BANJO (ban'jo), *n.* a musical instrument.

BANK (bangk), *n.* a heap, mound, or ridge of earth ; any steep acclivity ; an elevation or rising ground beneath the sea or at the mouth of a river, forming a shoal or shallow : *v.t.* to enclose, defend, or fortify with a bank ; pile or heap up.

BANK (bangk), *n.* an establishment for the custody, loan, exchange, or issue of money : *v.t.* to deposit money in a bank : *v.i.* to have an account with a banker.

BANK (bangk), *n.* the lateral inclination of an airplane rounding a curve : *v.i.* to incline an airplane in a lateral direction when rounding a curve.

BANK-BILL (bangk'bil), *n.* a note or a bill of exchange of a bank payable on demand or at a future specified time.

BANK-BOOK (bangk-book), *n.* the pass-book kept by a depositor.

BANK CREDIT (kred'it), the amount a person, on giving proper security, is allowed to draw upon a bank.

BANKER (bangk'er), *n.* one who keeps a bank ; a vessel employed in cod-fishing.

BANKING (bangk'ing), *n.* the act of raising a mound or bank ; fishing on the banks of Newfoundland.

BANK-NOTE (bangk-not), *n.* a promissory note issued by a legally authorized bank, payable on demand.

BANKRUPT (bangk'rupt), *n.* a person legally declared to be unable to discharge his liabilities.

BANKRUPTCY (bangk'rupt-si), *n.* [*pl.* bankruptcies (-siz)], the state of being legally insolvent.

BANNER (ban'er), *n.* a piece of cloth or silk attached to a pole or staff ; an ensign, standard, or flag.

BANNOCK (ban'uk), *n.* a thick cake made of oatmeal, barley-meal, or pease-meal.

BANNS (banz), *n.pl.* the proclamation in church of an intended marriage.

BANQUET (bang'kwet), *n.* a sumptuous entertainment or feast.

BANSHEE (ban'she), **BENSHIE** (ben'she), *n.* a female fairy.

BANTAM (ban'tam), *n.* a diminutive breed of domestic fowl.

BANTER (ban'ter), *v.t.* to rail at good-humouredly : *n.* humorous raillery.

BANTLING (bant'ling), *n.* a young child.

BANYAN, see banian.

BANZAI (ban'za'e), *interj.* [lit. ten thousand years] the Japanese battle-cry ; hurrah.

BAOBAB (ba'o-bab), *n.* an African tree of huge size.

BAPTISM (bap'tizm), *n.* the application of water by an authorized administrator, in the name of the Holy Trinity.

BAPTISMAL (bap-tiz'mal), *adj.* pertaining to the ceremonial or initiatory rite of the Christian Church.

BAPTIST (bap'tist), *n.* one of a Christian denomination.

BAPTISTERY (bap'tis-ter-i), **BAPTISTRY** (-tri), *n.* a building or portion of a building in which the rite of baptism is administered.

BAPTIZE (bap-tiz'), *v.t.* to administer the rite of baptism to ; admit to the Christian Church by the ceremonial application of water ; christen.

BAR (bar), *n.* a piece of wood, metal, or other solid matter, long in proportion to its thickness ; a bank of sand, gravel, etc., obstructing navigation at the entrance to a harbour or mouth of a river ; the place in court where prisoners are stationed for trial, or sentence ; the members of the legal profession collectively : *v.t.* to hinder ; obstruct ; exclude : *prep.* save ; except.

BARB (barb), *n.* the sharp point projecting backwards from the extremity of an arrow, fish-hook, etc.

BARB (barb), *n.* a horse of the Barbary breed ; a short-beaked pigeon of a breed originally brought from Barbary.

BARBARIAN (bar-ba'ri-an), *n.* a man in a rude, savage state.

BARBARIC (bar-bar'ik), *adj.* pertaining to or characteristic of savage or uncivilized people.

BARBARISM (bar'ba-rizm), *n.* an offence against purity of style or language; a cruel or barbarous action; an outrage.

BARBARITY (bar-bar'i-ti), *n.* the state of being uncivilized.

BARBAROUS (bar'ba-rus), *adj.* uncivilized; rude and ignorant; contrary to pure idiom; savage; cruel.

BARBATE (bar'bat), **BARBATED** ('bat-ed), *adj.* bearded; furnished with long stiff hairs.

BARBECUE (bar'be-ku), *n.* a frame on which many kinds of meat or fish are roasted or smoke-dried; the carcass of an ox, hog, etc., roasted whole; a social or political entertainment at which animals are roasted whole.

BARBEL (bar'bel), *n.* a slender vermiform process appended to the lips of certain fishes; a European fresh-water fish, having its upper jaw furnished with four barbels.

BARBER (bar'ber), *n.* one whose occupation is to shave the beard and cut and dress the hair.

BARBERRY (bar'ber-i), *n.* a shrub with yellow flowers and crimson berries.

BARBET (bar'bet), *n.* a South American puff-bird; a woolly-haired dog of the poodle type.

BARBETTE (bar-bet'), *n.* the platform or breastwork of a fortification.

BARBETTE TURRET (tur'et), the rotary protected mechanism in which the heavy guns of modern battleships are commonly mounted.

BARBOTINE (bar'bo-tin), *n.* kaolin clay, thinly mixed, used for ornamenting pottery.

BARBULE (bar'bul), *n.* a very minute barb.

BARCAROLE, **BARCAROLLE** (bar'ka-rol), *n.* a simple song or melody sung by Venetian gondoliers; a piece of music in imitation of such a song.

BARD (bard), *n.* a poet and singer.

BARDIC (bar'dik), *adj.* pertaining to bards or to their poetry.

BARE (bar), *adj.* naked; unconcealed; simple; unfurnished.

BAREFACED (bar'fast), *adj.* with the face uncovered; undisguised; shameless.

BAREGE (ba-razh'), *n.* thin gauze-like fabric, usually of silk and worsted.

BARGAIN (bar'gen), *n.* an agreement or contract between two or more parties with reference to the sale or transfer of property; a compact or pledge mutually agreed upon; the thing purchased or stipulated for; that which is acquired or sold at a low price: *v.i.* to make a contract or agreement: *v.t.* to sell or transfer for a consideration.

BARGE (barj), *n.* a flat-bottomed vessel.

BARGE MASTER (mas'ter), the manager of a barge.

BARILLA (bar-ril'a), *n.* an impure carbonate and sulphate of soda.

BARILLET (bar'il-let), *n.* the cylindrical case containing the mainspring of a watch.

BARITONE, see barytone.

BARIUM (ba'ri-um), *n.* a non-volatile, malleable element of the alkaline earth group.

BARK (bark), *v.i.* to utter a sharp, short sound, as the cry of a dog.

BARK (bark), *n.* the exterior layer or rind of woody stems or trunks.

BARK, BARQUE (bark), *n.* a three-masted vessel having the fore- and main-mast square-rigged, and the mizzen-mast fore-and-aft-rigged.

BARKANTINE, **BARKENTINE** (bar'ken-ten), *n.* a three-masted vessel having the fore-mast square-rigged, and the main- and mizzen-mast fore-and-aft-, or schooner-rigged.

BARKER (bark'er), *n.* a person who stands outside of a side-show or place of amusement to attract attention of passers-by.

BARKER (bark'er), *n.* one who strips trees of their bark.

BARKING (bark'ing), *n.* a sharp

sound like that of a dog: *n*. the process of stripping bark from trees.

BARK LOUSE (lous), *n*. a scale insect found beneath the bark of trees and plants.

BARLEY (bar'li), *n*. the grain grown and used chiefly for malting; the plant which yields the grain.

BARLEY-CORN (bar'li-korn), *n*. a grain of barley; formerly a measure of length equal to the third part of an inch.

BARM (barm), *n*. the foam rising upon beer or other malt liquors when fermenting, and used as leaven in bread-making; yeast.

BARMY (barm'i), *adj*. containing or consisting of yeast; frothy.

BARN (barn), *n*. a covered building for the storage of grain or other farm produce.

BARNACLE (bar'na-kl), *n*. a wild goose; a shell-fish which attaches itself to rocks, ship-bottoms, etc.

BARN OWL (barn oul), *n*. the white or screech owl.

BAROGRAM (bar'o-gram), *n*. the record traced by the barograph.

BAROGRAPH (bar'o-graf), *n*. an instrument recording automatically variations in atmospheric pressure.

BAROLOGY (ba-rol'o-gi), *n*. the science of weight or gravity.

BAROMETER (ba-rom'e-ter), *n*. an instrument for measuring the weight or pressure of the atmosphere: used for indicating the various changes of weather, or to determine the altitude of a particular place.

BAROMETRIC (bar-o-met'rik), **BAROMETRICAL** ('ri-kal), *adj*. pertaining to, or indicated by, a barometer.

BAROMETRIC PRESSURE (presh'ur), weight of the atmosphere at a given point in terms of the height of a column of mercury.

BAROMETRY (ba-rom'e-tri), *n*. the art of making barometric measurements.

BARON (bar'un), *n*. the title of an English peer of the lowest rank, next below a viscount.

BARONAGE (bar'un-aj), *n*. the whole body of barons; the dignity or rank of a baron.

BARONESS (bar'un-es), *n*. a baron's wife; a lady holding a baronial title in her own right.

BARONET (bar'un-et), *n*. a title of hereditary rank or degree of honour next below a baron and above a knight.

BARONETAGE (bar'un-et-aj), *n*. the collective body of baronets; the dignity or rank of a baronet.

BARONETCY (bar'un-et-si), *n*. the title and dignity of a baronet.

BARONIAL (ba-ro'ni-al), *adj*. the domain or lordship of a barony.

BARONY (bar'un-i), *n*. the domain or lordship of a rank or dignity of a baron.

BAROQUE (ba-rok'), *adj*. grotesque; fantastic in design or style: *n*. an ornament or object in baroque style.

BAROSCOPE (bar'o-skop), *n*. an instrument for indicating variations in the pressure of the atmosphere without actual measurement of its weight; a storm or weather glass.

BAROUCHE (ba-roosh'), *n*. a four-wheeled carriage with a folding top.

BARQUE, see bark.

BARRACAN (bar'a-kan), *n*. a thick strong stuff made of camel's hair.

BARRACK (bar'ak), *n*. a large building, or series of buildings, for the lodgment of soldiers.

BARRACUDA (bar'a-ku-da), *n*. a voracious fish, like a pike.

BARRAGE (bar-razh'), *n*. a barrier; curtain; an attack by a line of shell-fire prior to a drive against the enemy.

BARRATRY (bar'a-tri), *n*. the practice of vexatiously inciting and encouraging to law-suits or litigation.

BARRED (bard), *p.adj*. furnished with bars; obstructed; secured; striped.

BARREL (bar'el), *n*. a vessel or cask, cylindrical in form.

BARREL ORGAN (or'gan), *n*. a hand organ in which a revolving cylinder, studded with spikes, is acted upon by air coming from a bellows through a series of pipes.

BARREL ROLL (rol), a manœuvre by an airplane in flight, in which a complete revolution about the longitudinal axis is made.

BARREN (bar'en), *adj.* incapable of producing its kind ; unproductive ; sterile.

BARRICADE (bar-ri-kad'), *n.* a fortification constructed in haste, and which will serve to obstruct the progress or attack of an enemy ; any bar or obstruction : *v.t.* to obstruct or stop up.

BARRIER (bar'i-er), *n.* anything which hinders or obstructs.

BARRIER-REEF (-ref), *n.* a reef of coral encircling an island.

BARRING (bar'ing), *p.pr.* as *prep.* excepting ; leaving out of account.

BARRISTER (bar'is-ter), *n.* in Great Britain, a counsel who pleads cases in the superior courts, as distinguished from a *solicitor*, who instructs him, that is, prepares the cases. In the U.S. an attorney does the duties of both.

BARROW (bar'o), *n.* an open box furnished with handles and set on wheels ; a wheel-barrow.

BARROW (bar'o), *n.* a mound ; a small hill.

BARTER (bar'ter), *v.i.* to traffic or trade.

BARTIZAN (bar'ti-zan), *n.* a small overhanging turret.

BARWOOD (bar'wood), *n.* a red dye wood.

BARYTA (ba-ri'ta), *n.* the oxide of barium.

BARYTES (ba-ri'tez), *n.* the native sulphate of barium.

BARYTONE, BARITONE (bar'i-ton), *n. & adj.* denoting a male voice intermediate between bass and tenor.

BARYTONE CLEF (klef), the F clef on the middle line of the bass staff.

BASAL (bas'al), *adj.* fundamental.

BASALT (ba-sawlt', bas'awlt), *n.* an igneous rock of greenish black colour.

BASANITE (baz'a-nit), *n.* a black siliceous rock or jasper ; touchstone.

BASCULE (bas'kul), *n.* a mechanical arrangement on the see-saw principle by which the lowering of one end raises the other.

BASE (bas), *adj.* worthless ; spurious ; of mean spirit.

BASE (bas), *n.* the part of a thing on which it rests ; a foundation or groundwork ; that which combines with an acid to form a salt ; a starting place : *v.t.* to lay a foundation.

BASEBALL (bas'bawl), *n.* a game of ball played by nine on a side ; ball used in playing baseball.

BASEMAN (bas'man), *n.* a player placed at baseball at the first, second, and third bases, respectively.

BASEMENT (bas'ment), *n.* the lowest part of a structure.

BASH (bash), *v.t.* to strike heavily : *n.* a smashing blow.

BASHAW (ba-shaw'), *n.* a pasha ; a magnate or grandee ; a bigwig.

BASHFUL (bash'fool), *adj.* easily disconcerted ; modest to excess.

BASIC (bas'ik), *adj.* pertaining to a base ; fundamental ; performing the office of a base in a salt.

BASIL (baz'il), *n.* a sheepskin tanned with bark.

BASIL (baz'il), *n.* the angle to which the cutting edge of a tool is ground : *v.t.* to grind or form the edge of an angle.

BASILAR (bas'i-lar), **BASILARY** (-la-ri), *adj.* pertaining to, or situated at, the base.

BASILIC (ba-zil'ik), **BASILICAL** ('i-kal), *adj.* kingly ; royal ; pertaining to a basilica : *n.* the middle vein of the arm.

BASILICA (ba-sil'i-ka), *n.* in ancient Rome, a public hall of rectangular shape.

BASIN (ba'sin), *n.* a circular vessel for holding water or other liquid ; a pond, or dock ; the area drained by a river.

BASINET (bas'i-net), *n.* a light, tight-fitting steel helmet.

BASIS (ba'sis), *n.* [*pl.* bases ('sez)], a foundation ; the groundwork or fundamental principle of anything.

BASK (bask), *v.i.* to lie in warmth ; be exposed to genial heat.

BASKET (bas'ket), *n.* a framework

covered with rods, rushes, or other flexible material, plaited or interwoven.

BASKET-BALL (bas'ket-bawl), *n.* an indoor or open-air game.

BASKETFUL (bas'ket-fool), *n.* as much as a basket will hold.

BASKET STITCH (stich), in embroidery, a stitch worked over a cord to give the resemblance of basket-work.

BASKET-WORK (-werk), *n.* osiers interwoven ; plaited twigs.

BASKING-SHARK (bas'king-shark), *n.* one of the largest of the sharks inhabiting the northern seas.

BASQUE (bask), *adj.* of, or pertaining to, the Basque race or language.

BASQUE (bask), *n.* a woman's jacket with a short skirt.

BAS-RELIEF (ba-re-lef'), *n.* [French], low relief ; a form of relief in which the figures stand out.

BASS, BASSE (bas), *n.* one of various edible fishes allied to the perch.

BASS (bas), *n.* the American lime-tree.

BASS (bas), *adj.* low ; deep ; grave : *n.* the lowest part in the harmony of a musical composition ; the lowest male voice, ranging from D below the bass staff to D or E above it ; one who sings bass.

BASS-BAR (bas'bar), *n.* a piece of wood placed lengthwise inside stringed instruments to resist the pressure of the bridge.

BASS CLEF (klef), *n.* the character placed at the beginning of the bass staff.

BASS DRUM (drum), the largest kind of drum.

BASSET (bas'et), *v.i.* to crop out at the surface.

BASSET (bas'et), *n.* a small hound.

BASSET-HORN (bas'et-horn), *n.* an instrument resembling a clarionet.

BASS HORN (horn), a modified form of a clarionet.

BASSINET (bas'i-net), *n.* a wicker basket with a hood.

BASSO (bas'o), *adj.* [Italian], denoting a bass voice : *n.* one who sings bass.

BASSO-PROFUNDO (-pro-fun'do),

n. the lowest bass voice ; a singer having such a voice.

BASSOON (ba-soon'), *n.* a musical wind instrument of the reed kind.

BASS STAFF (staf), *n.* the staff on which the notes of the bass of a harmonized composition are written.

BASS VIOL (vi'ol), *n.* a large stringed instrument of the violin class for playing bass.

BASSWOOD (bas'wood), *n.* the linden-tree.

BAST (bast), *n.* the tough inner fibrous bark of various trees, especially of the lime.

BASTARD (bas'tard), *n.* born out of wedlock ; a kind of hawk formerly used in falconry.

BASTE (bast), *v.t.* to beat ; to pour fat or butter on meat while roasting ; to sew slightly, or fasten with long stitches.

BASTILE, BASTILLE (bas-tel'), *n.* an old castle in Paris used as a state prison, demolished by the populace in 1789.

BASTINADO (bas-ti-na'do), *n.* an Oriental mode of punishment.

BASTION (bas'chun), *n.* an earthwork faced with brick or stone.

BAT (bat), *n.* a heavy stick or club ; a batsman ; a part of a brick ; a plate of flexible gelatine used to print impressions on glaze ; bituminous shale : *v.t.* to hit or strike : *v.i.* to use or wield a bat.

BAT (bat), *n.* an insectivorous mammal furnished with wings.

BATCH (bach), *n.* the quantity of bread baked at one time ; a quantity of anything produced at one operation.

BATE (bat), *v.t.* to lessen or reduce ; deduct.

BATEAU, BATTEAU (ba-to'), *n.* [*pl.* bateaux, batteaux (-toz)], a light boat ; a pontoon of a floating bridge.

BATEAU-BRIDGE (-brij), *n.* a floating bridge constructed on boats.

BATH (bath), *n.* the act of washing or immersing the body in water ; vessel holding water for bathing ; a building fitted up for bathing purposes.

BATH BRICK (brik), *n.* a composition, in the shape of a brick, used for scouring.

BATH HOUSE (hous), *n.* a building or structure for the convenience of bathers.

BATHE (ba*th*), *v.t.* to subject to a bath ; to suffuse or moisten with a liquid : *v.i.* to take a bath.

BATHOMETER (ba-thom´e-ter), *n.* an apparatus for measuring depths.

BATHOS (ba´thos), *n.* commonplace in writing or speech.

BATIK (ba´tik), *n.* a process of putting designs in colour on textile fabrics.

BATISTE (ba-test´), *n.* a kind of cambric ; cotton muslin.

BATON (bat´un), *n.* a staff used as a weapon, or as a mark or badge of office ; the wand of an orchestral conductor : *v.t.* to strike with a baton.

BATRACHIAN (ba-tra´ki-an), *adj.* pertaining to the Batrachia : *n.* one of that order.

BATRACHOID (bat´ra-koid), *adj.* having the form of a frog.

BATSMAN (bats´man), *n.* the man wielding the bat in baseball or cricket.

BATTALION (ba-tal´yun), *n.* a body of infantry.

BATTEN (bat´n), *v.t.* to make fat by plenteous living ; fertilize or enrich : *v.i.* to grow or become fat.

BATTEN (bat´n), *n.* a narrow strip of wood used to fasten a tarpaulin over a hatchway.

BATTER (bat´er), *v.t.* strike with heavy, repeated blows : *v.i.* to make an attack by heavy blows.

BATTER (bat´er), *n.* a mixture of several ingredients, used in cookery.

BATTERING-RAM (bat´er-ing-ram), *n.* a military engine anciently used to beat down the walls of besieged places.

BATTERY (bat´er-i), *n.* the act of battering or beating ; a body of cannon, with its complement of officers, men, and equipments, for field operations ; an apparatus for generating electricity.

BATTERY (bat´er-i), *n.* a celebrated

park at the extreme southern end of Manhattan Island, New York City.

BATTLE (bat´l), *n.* a fight or encounter between opposing forces.

BATTLE-AX, BATTLE-AXE (-aks), *n.* a broad flat axe, formerly used in battle.

BATTLE CRUISER (krooz´er), a warship of the size of a dreadnaught and of the highest speed and heaviest battery.

BATTLEDORE (bat´l-dor), *n.* a kind of light racket used for playing battledore.

BATTLEMENT (bat´l-ment), *n.* an indented parapet.

BATTLE PIECE (pes), a painting, poem or writing descriptive of a battle.

BATTLE ROYAL (roi´al), a match in which more than two are engaged ; a mêlée.

BATTLESHIP (bat´l-ship), *n.* a heavily-armoured warship, classed just below a modern dreadnaught.

BATULE (bat´ul), *n.* a springboard.

BAUBLE (baw´bl), *n.* a trifling piece of finery.

BAWL (bawl), *v.i.* to cry out with a loud, full, and sustained sound ; vociferate : *v.t.* to proclaim loudly.

BAY (ba), *v.i.* to bark as a dog ; *v.t.* to bark at ; to pursue with barking so as to bring to bay.

BAY (ba), *adj.* red or reddish, approaching to chestnut ; applied to horses.

BAY (ba), *n.* a recess in the shore of a sea or lake ; the expanse of water between two capes or headlands ; a recess or opening in walls ; the fore part of a ship between decks ; the laurel-tree.

BAYA (ba´ya), *n.* the weaverbird of the East Indies.

BAYBERRY (ba´ber-i), *n.* the fruit of the bay tree or laurel ; a tree of the myrtle family.

BAY BIRD (berd), *n.* one of a numerous species, including curlews, snipes and plovers.

BAY LEAF (lef), the aromatic leaf of the bay tree ; used in cookery.

BAY RUM (rum), *n.* a fragrant preparation made from the oil of bay-berry.

BAY-SALT (ba'sawlt), n. salt resulting from the evaporation of seawater.

BAY-WINDOW (ba'win'do), n. a window forming a bay or recess in a room.

BAYONET (ba'o-net), n. a short dagger-like instrument constructed to fix on to the barrel of a rifle.

BAYOU (bi'oo), n. in southern U.S., the outlet of a lake, or one of the delta streams of a river; a sluggish watercourse.

BAZAAR, BAZAR (ba-zar'), n. in the East, a market-place or exchange; a sale of fancy articles in aid of some charity.

BDELLIUM (del'yum), n. an aromatic gum-resin, used medicinally and as a perfume.

BE (be), v.i. to exist; have existence in fact, physical or mental; include or involve as a result; produce; come about; become; remain; signify; answer to.

BEACH (bech), n. the portion of the shore of the sea or of a lake which is washed by the waves; the strand.

BEACH-COMBER (bech'komer), n. a long curling wave rolling in from the ocean; one on the look-out for wreckage.

BEACHY (bech'i-), adj. having a beach; covered with shingle.

BEACON (be'kn), n. a signal of warning or guidance, on sea or land.

BEAD (bed), n. a little perforated ball of any suitable material, intended to be strung with others and worn as an ornament; a small knob of metal at the end of a gun-barrel used as a sight; a narrow rounded moulding; an astragal.

BEADY (bed'i), adj. covered with, resembling, or characterized, by beads.

BEAGLE (be'gl), n. a small hound; a constable; a small shark.

BEAK (bek), n. the bill of a bird; the horny jaws or mandibles of other animals.

BEAKER (bek'er), n. a large drinking cup or vessel with a wide mouth.

BEAM (bem), n. a long piece of timber or iron used horizontally or vertically to support the rafters of a building; the extreme breadth of a ship; the oscillating lever which transmits motion in a steam-engine; the bar of a balance which suspends the scales; a collection of parallel rays of light emitted from the sun or other luminous body: v.t. to send forth, as rays of light: v.i. to shine.

BEAMY (be'mi), adj. emitting rays of light; joyous; having much breadth of beam.

BEAN (ben), n. the smooth kidney-shaped seed of many leguminous plants.

BEAR (bar), v.t. to support, hold up; carry or convey; suffer or endure; be answerable for; possess, wear, or use; have in or on; contain; cherish; carry in the mind; bring forth or produce; to endeavour to lower or depress the price of stock: v.i. to be capable of supporting; be fruitful; to bear, press, or weigh upon or against; tend; relate; take effect; be situated.

BEAR (bar), n. a plantigrade carnivorous mammal, belonging to the genus Ursus; [B-], either of two constellations in the northern heavens, called the Great Bear and the Little Bear.

BEARD (berd), n. the hair that grows on the chin, lips, and adjacent parts of the human face; anything which resembles a beard; the awn of barley and other grains: v.t. to take by the beard; oppose to the face; set at defiance.

BEARING (bar'ing), n. the act of enduring with patience; carriage; behaviour; mutual relation of the parts of a whole; the part of a machine that bears the friction; the direction or point of the compass in which an object is seen.

BEARISH (bar'ish), adj. resembling a bear in qualities; rude; surly.

BEAST (best), n. any four-footed animal, as distinguished from birds, insects, fishes, and man.

BEASTLY (best'li), *adj.* like a beast.

BEAT (bet), *v.t.* to strike with repeated blows; thrash; knock; dash or strike against, as water or wind: *v.i.* to strike repeatedly; signal or summon by beat of a drum; sound, as a drum, when struck; *n.* a recurring stroke; a pulsation; a throb; a footfall.

BEAT (bet), *p.adj.* exhausted by mental or bodily fatigue.

BEATEN (be'tn), *p.adj.* worn by use.

BEATIFIC (be-a-tif'ik), *adj.* having power to bless or render perfectly happy.

BEATIFICATION (be-at-i-fi-ka'-shun), *n.* the act of blessing or the state of being blessed.

BEATIFIC VISION (vizh'un), the direct vision of God, regarded as the bliss of the angels and saints.

BEATIFY (be-at'i-fi), *v.t.* to make happy; bless with the completion of celestial enjoyment.

BEATING (be'ting), *n.* the act of striking; a flogging; tacking against the wind.

BEATITUDE (be-at'i-tud), *n.* felicity of the highest kind.

BEAU (bo), *n.* [*pl.* beaus, beaux (boz)], a suitor.

BEAU BRUMMELL (brum'l), George Bryan Brummell (1778-1840), he set the fashions for the London society of his time.

BEAU IDEAL (boi -de'al), *n.* ideal excellence.

BEAU MONDE (bo-mongd'), *n.* the fashionable world.

BEAUTEOUS (bu'te-us), *adj.* possessing beauty.

BEAUTIFUL (bu'ti-ful), *adj.* possessing qualities which charm and delight the senses; lovely.

BEAUTIFY (bu'ti-fi), *v.t.* to make or render beautiful; embellish: *v.i.* to grow beautiful.

BEAUTY (bu'ti), *n.* an assemblage of graces or properties which command the approbation of the senses.

BEAVER (be'ver), *n.* a rodent quadruped of amphibious habits, and valued for its fur.

BEAVERTEEN (be'ver-ten), *n.* a fustian of coarse, twilled cotton.

BEAVER TREE (tre), *n.* the sweet-bay, common in the U.S.

BECALM (be-kam'), *v.t.* to make calm or still.

BECAUSE (be-kawz'), *conj.* by reason of; on account of the fact.

BECK (bek), *n.* a nod, or other significant gesture.

BECK (bek), *n.* a small brook, or valley.

BECKET (bek'et), *n.* a contrivance to confine loose ropes, etc.

BECKON (bek'n), *v.i.* to make a signal to another: *v.t.* summon or signal by signs.

BECOME (be-kum'), *v.i.* to pass from one state to another; come or grow to be: *v.t.* to suit, or be suitable to.

BECOMING (be-kum'ing), *p.adj.* fit; suitable; proper; appropriate.

BECQUEREL RAYS (bek-rel'raz), radiations emitted by a radioactive substance, as radium.

BED (bed), *n.* an article of domestic furniture; a portion of a garden prepared and set apart for plants; the bottom of a river or other stream; a layer or stratum of rock: *v.t.* to furnish with a bed; plant, as flowers; lay in a stratum; lay flat, or in order: *v.i.* to go to bed.

BEDDING (bed'ing), *n.* a bed and its furniture; the materials of a bed, whether for man or beast; stratification; occurrence in layers.

BEDEVIL (be-dev'l), *v.t.* to throw into disorder or confusion.

BEDEVILMENT (be-dev'l-ment), *n.* the state of being vexatiously and bewilderingly disordered or confused.

BEDEW (be-du'), *v.t.* to moisten with dew.

BEDIZEN (be-diz'n), *v.t.* to deck or adorn.

BEDLAM (bed'lam), *n.* an asylum or hospital for lunatics.

BEDOUIN (bed'oo-in), *n.* a nomadic Arab.

BEDPAN (bed'pan), *n.* a warming-pan; a utensil for the use of those confined to bed.

BEDRID (bed'rid), **BEDRIDDEN** ('rid'n), *adj.* confined to bed by age or infirmity.

BEDROCK (-rok), *n.* the solid rock underneath the surface.

BEDTICK (bed'tik), *n.* a bag of strong cotton for containing the materials of a bed.

BEE (be), *n.* a hymenopterous insect; a social meeting; a contest, as a spelling bee.

BEE-BREAD (be'bred), *n.* the pollen of flowers collected and stored by bees as food for their young.

BEECH (bech), *n.* a tree of the oak family.

BEEF (bef), *n.* the flesh of an ox, bull, or cow, when killed.

BEEHIVE (be'hiv), *n.* a box or other covering for a swarm of bees.

BEE-LINE (be'lin), *n.* the straight course pursued by a bee returning laden to the hive.

BEER (ber), *n.* a fermented liquor made from any farinaceous grain.

BEESWAX (bez'waks), *n.* the wax secreted by bees : *v.t.* to smear with beeswax.

BEET (bet), *n.* a plant, cultivated for its edible succulent root ; a different species grown for fodder and making sugar.

BEETLE (be'tl), *n.* a heavy wooden mallet ; a club for beating linen, etc., in washing.

BEETLE (be'tl), *n.* any insect belonging to the order of Coleoptera.

BEETLE (be'tl), *v.i.* to be prominent ; jut out ; overhang, as a cliff.

BEETLING (bet'ling), *adj.* standing out ; overhanging.

BEFALL, BEFAL (be-fawl'), *v.t.* to happen or occur to ; *v.i.* come to pass.

BEFIT (be-fit'), *v.t.* to suit ; become.

BEFORE (be-for'), *prep.* in front of ; preceding in space, time, or rank ; in presence or sight of ; rather than ; earlier than : *adv.* in front ; in advance ; previously ; formerly ; already.

BEFOREHAND (be-for'hand), *adv.* in advance.

BEFOUL (be-foul'), *v.t.* to soil ; make foul.

BEFRIEND (be-frend'), *v.t.* to act as a friend.

BEFUDDLE (be-fud'l), *v.t.* to confuse ; mix up.

BEG (beg), *v.t.* & *v.i.* to ask for earnestly ; beseech ; entreat with humility ; ask as a favour.

BEGET (be-get'), *v.t.* to procreate ; generate ; produce ; cause to exist.

BEGGAR (beg'er), *n.* one who entreats or supplicates ; one who makes it his business to beg or ask for alms : *v.t.* to exhaust the resources of ; outdo.

BEGGARLINESS (-li-nes), *n.* extreme poverty ; meanness.

BEGGARLY (beg'er-li), *adj.* like, or in the condition of, a beggar.

BEGGARY (beg'er-i), *n.* the state of a beggar ; extreme poverty.

BEGIN (be-gin'), *v.i.* to commence ; to take the initiatory step ; make a start.

BEGINNER (be-gin'er), *n.* one who begins or originates ; a novice.

BEGINNING (be-gin'ing), *n.* the first cause ; origin.

BEGONE (be-gon') *interj.* go away ! depart !

BEGONIA (be-go'ni-a), *n.* a genus of tropical plants.

BEGRUDGE, see grudge.

BEGUILE (be-gil'), *v.t.* to impose upon or delude by guile ; divert or entertain.

BEGUILEMENT (be-gil'ment), *n.* the act of beguiling.

BEHALF (be-haf'), *n.* advantage ; favour ; support ; defence [governed always by the preposition *in, on,* or *upon*].

BEHAVE (be-hav'), *v.t.* to conduct, comport, demean, or acquit : *v.i.* to act ; conduct one's self in a proper manner.

BEHAVIOUR (be-hav'yer), *n.* manner of behaving, whether good or bad.

BEHEAD (be-hed'), *v.t.* to cut off the head of.

BEHELD (be-held'), *p.t.* & *p.p.* of behold.

BEHEMOTH (be-he′moth), *n.* an animal described in *Job xl*, 15-24.

BEHEST (be-hest′), *n.* a command; precept.

BEHIND (be-hind′), *prep.* at the back of; in the rear of; remaining after; inferior to.

BEHINDHAND (be-hind′hand), *adv.* or *adj.* in a state of backwardness.

BEHOLD (be-hold′), *v.t.* to fix the eyes upon; have in sight; look at.

BEHOLDEN (be-hol′dn), *p.adj.* indebted; obliged; bound in gratitude.

BEHOOF (be-hoof′), *n.* advantage; interest; profit; use; behalf.

BEHOOVE, BEHOVE (be-hoov′), *v.t.* to be meet, necessary, or fit for.

BEIGE (bazh), *adj.* having its natural colour, as a fabric of undyed wool; *n.* a soft woollen fabric.

BEING (be′ing), *n.* existence, as opposed to non-existence.

BEJEWEL (be-ju′el), *v.t.* to ornament with jewels.

BELABOUR (be-la′ber), *v.t.* to beat soundly.

BELATE (be-lat′), *v.t.* to make late, or retard.

BELATED (be-lat′ed), *p.adj.* delayed; too late; overtaken by darkness.

BELAY (be-la′), *v.t.* make fast, as a rope.

BELAYING PIN (be-la′ing), *n.* a pin on which to fasten a rope.

BELCH (belch), *v.t.* to eject with force or violence : *v.i.* to eject wind from the stomach.

BELDAM (bel′dam), **BELDAME** (′dam), *n.* a grandmother.

BELEAGUER (be-le′ger), *v.t.* to besiege; blockade.

BELEMNITE (bel′em-nit), *n.* the fossil of an extinct family of cuttle-fishes.

BELFRY (bel′fri), *n.* a bell tower; that part of a steeple or tower in which a bell is hung.

BELGIAN HARE (bel′ji-an har), a kind of domestic rabbit.

BELGIAN MARBLE (mar′bl), a brick-red marble with blue and white markings.

BELIE (be-li′), *v.t.* to calumniate; show to be false.

BELIEF (be-lef′), *n.* faith; a creed; a conviction.

BELIEVABLE (be-le′va-bl), *adj.* capable of being accepted as truth; credible.

BELIEVE (be-lev′), *v.t.* to place credence in and accept as true, upon the ground of authority, testimony, or logical inference apart from personal knowledge; place confidence in; expect or hope : *v.i.* to have faith; be more or less firmly persuaded of the truth of anything; think or suppose.

BELIEVER (be-le′ver), *n.* one who accepts as truth something not actually demonstrated.

BELIKE (be-lik′), *adv.* probably.

BELITTLE (be-lit′l), *v.t.* to lower or depreciate.

BELL (bel), *n.* a hollow metallic vessel, giving a ringing sound when struck; anything in the form of a bell; *pl.* the divisions of daily time marked each half-hour on shipboard by strokes on a bell.

BELLADONNA (bel-a-don′a), *n.* a poisonous plant used as medicine.

BELL-BIRD (bel′berd), *n.* an American bird whose note resembles a bell.

BELLE (bel), *n.* a reigning beauty.

BELLES-LETTRES (bel-let′r), *n.pl.* polite or elegant literature.

BELLICOSE (bel′i-kos), *adj.* pugnacious; contentious; warlike.

BELLIED (bel′id), *adj.* having a belly; swelled out in the middle.

BELLIFEROUS (be-lif′er-us), *adj.* bringing war.

BELLIGERENCE (be-lij′er-ens), **BELLIGERENCY** (-en-si), *n.* the act or state of warfare.

BELLIGERENT (be-lij′er-ent), *adj.* waging war; pertaining to war or warfare : *n.* a power recognized as carrying on war; a person engaged in fighting.

BELLITE (bel′it), *n.* an explosive compound formed of ammonium nitrate and other substances.

BELL-METAL (bel-met′al), *n.* an alloy of copper and tin.

BELLOW (bel′o), *v.i.* to utter a full

resonant sound, as a bull; bawl or vociferate

BELLOWS (bel'oz), *n. sing.* & *pl.* an instrument for producing a current of air, and used for various purposes, as blowing fires, or filling the pipes of an organ.

BELL-PUNCH (bel'punch), *n.* a punch with a signal bell.

BELLWETHER (bel-weth'er), *n.* a wether which leads the flock with a bell on his neck.

BELLY (bel'i), *n.* the abdomen; the part of anything that swells out into a larger capacity: *v.i.* to swell and become protuberant; bulge out: *v.t.* to cause to swell out, as sails.

BELLYBAND (bel'i-band), *n.* a band that encircles the belly of a horse; a saddle-girth.

BELONG (be-long'), *v.i.* to be the property (of); be a part (of).

BELONGING (be-long'ing), *n.* that which belongs to one; qualities; endowments; property; possessions; appendages.

BELOVED (be-luvd', -luv'ed), *p.adj.* greatly loved: *n.* one who is greatly loved.

BELOW (be-lo'), *prep.* under in place; beneath; not so high: *adv.* in a lower place; on the earth.

BELT (belt), *n.* a girdle or band used to encircle the waist; a strip; a band; one of the rings surrounding the planet Jupiter; a band connecting two wheels and transmitting motion from one to the other.

BELTANE (bel'tan), *n.* the first day of May.

BELTING (bel'ting), *n.* belts collectively.

BELUGA (be-lu'ga), *n.* the large white sturgeon; the white whale of the Northern Seas.

BELVEDERE (bel-ve-der'), *n.* a pavilion or structure raised upon the top of a house; a summer house.

BEMIRE (be-mir'), *v.t.* to soil by passing through mire.

BEMOAN (be-mon'), *v.t.* to lament; sympathize with.

BENCH (bench), *n.* a long seat; a strong table on which mechanics do their work; the seat where judges sit in court; the persons who sit as judges; the court.

BENCH SHOW (sho), an exhibition of animals, especially dogs.

BENCH WARRANT (wor'ant), a warrant issued by a court or judge.

BEND (bend), *v.t.* to curve or make crooked; move or deflect out of a straight line.

BENDAY or **BEN DAY**, *n.* a process used in plate engraving.

BENDS (bendz), *n.* a disease incident to caisson work.

BENEATH (be-neth'), *prep.* lower in place; under the pressure of; unworthy of: *adv.* in a lower place; below.

BENEDICT (ben'e-dikt), *n.* a newly-married man.

BENEDICTION (ben-e-dik'shun), *n.* the act of blessing.

BENEDICTIVE (ben-e-dik'tiv), **BENEDICTORY** ('to-ri), *adj.* tending to bless; conveying or expressing good wishes.

BENEFACTION (ben-e-fak'shun), *n.* the act of conferring a benefit.

BENEFACTOR (ben-e-fak'ter), *n.* a male who confers a benefit.

BENEFACTRESS (-fak'tres), *n.* a female who confers a benefit.

BENEFICE (ben'e-fis), *n.* a fief, or estate in lands; an ecclesiastical living; a church endowed.

BENEFICENCE (be-nef'i-sens), *n.* active goodness; a benefaction.

BENEFICENT (be-nef'i-sent), *adj.* characterized by benevolence.

BENEFICIAL (ben-e-fish'al), *adj.* contributing to a valuable end; helpful; profitable.

BENEFICIALLY (li–), *adv.* in an advantageous manner.

BENEFICIARY (ben-e-fis'i-a-ri), *adj.* holding office under another; freely bestowed: *n.* the person to whom an insurance policy is payable.

BENEFIT (ben'e-fit), *n.* an act of kindness; a favour conferred: *v.t.* to do good to; be of service to: *v.i.* to gain advantage.

BENEVOLENCE (be-nev'o-lens), *n.*

the disposition to do good ; philanthropy.

BENEVOLENT (be-nev'o-lent), *adj.* kind ; charitable ; philanthropic.

BENGALINE (beng'ga-len), *n.* a soft, silk fabric, resembling poplin.

BENGAL LIGHT (ben-gawl' lit), *n.* a firework, used also for signalling.

BENGAL TIGER (ti'ger), *n.* a large ferocious cat-like beast.

BENIGHT (be-nit'), *v.t.* to enshroud in darkness.

BENIGN (be-nin'), *adj.* of a kind or gentle disposition ; favourable.

BENIGNANT (be-nig'nant), *adj.* kind ; gracious.

BENIGNITY (be-nig'ni-ti), *n.* kindness of nature ; gentleness ; mildness.

BENISON (ben'i-zn), *n.* a blessing.

BENITIER (ba-ne-tya'), *n.* [French], a font for holy water.

BENT (bent), *adj.* curved ; crooked : *n.* a stiff or wiry grass.

BENTHOS (ben'thos), *n.* the fauna and flora at bottom of the sea.

BENUMB (be-num'), *v.t.* to deprive of sensation ; stupefy.

BENUMBED (-numd'), *adj.* stupefied ; deadened.

BENUMBMENT (be-num'ment), *n.* act of stupefying ; torpidity.

BENZENE (ben'zen), *n.* a volatile, highly inflammable liquid.

BENZINE (ben-zen'), *n.* a liquid compounded of the volatile hydrocarbons of petroleum.

BENZOATE (ben'zo-at), *n.* a salt of benzoic acid.

BENZOIC (ben-zo'ik), *adj.* pertaining to benzoin.

BENZOIC ACID (as'id), *n.* an acid which crystallizes in the form of white flakes.

BENZOIN (ben-zo'in), *n.* the resinous juice of a tree of Java and Sumatra.

BENZOL (ben'zol), *n.* a coal-tar derivative.

BEQUEATH (be-kweth'), *v.t.* to give or leave by will.

BEQUEST (be-kwest'), *n.* the act of leaving by will.

BERBERINE (ber'ber-in), *n.* an alkaloid used in dyeing.

BERCEUSE (ber-suz'), *n.* a cradle song.

BEREA GRIT (be-re'a grit), a sandstone, used for grindstones.

BEREAVE (be-rev'), *v.t.* to deprive ; make destitute.

BEREAVEMENT (be-rev'ment), *n.* the loss of a relative or friend by death.

BERG (berg), *n.* a large floating mass of ice.

BERGAMOT (ber'ga-mot), *n.* variety of lemon, the rind of which yields a volatile oil.

BERI-BERI (ber'i-ber'i), *n.* a malignant Oriental disease.

BERMUDA GRASS (ber-mu'da gras'), *n.* a valuable variety of pasture grass.

BERMUDA LILY (ber-mu'da lil'i), a large white lily extensively grown in Bermuda.

BERRY (ber'i), *n.* any small pulpy or succulent fruit, as the strawberry, etc.

BERTH (berth), *n.* a station which a ship occupies at anchorage or port ; a sleeping place for a passenger in a ship or railway carriage ; a situation or appointment : *v.t.* to allot an anchorage to ; give space to lie in ; allot a sleeping place to.

BERTHAGE (ber'thaj), *n.* dues levied upon vessels ; the space for mooring vessels in harbour or dock.

BERTILLON-SYSTEM (ber-te-yong' sis'tem), *n.* a system of personal identification by recording the dimensions of the human body.

BERYL (ber'il), *n.* a mineral of varying colours.

BESEECH (be-sech'), *v.t.* to entreat ; implore ; beg eagerly for.

BESEEM (be-sem'), *v.i. & v.t.* to be suitable or seemly ; to become ; to seem.

BESET (be-set'), *v.t.* to set or stud ; surround ; besiege ; press hard on.

BESETTING (be-set'ing), *adj.* habitually attacking or coming upon.

BESHREW (be-shroo), *v.t.* to wish a curse to ; execrate.

BESIDE (be-sid'), *prep.* at the side

of ; near ; apart from ; not connected with.

BESIDES (be-sidz'), *adv.* more than that ; in addition ; as well : *prep.* over and above ; separate or distinct from.

BESIEGE (be-sej'), *v.t.* to encompass with armed forces ; lay siege to ; beset or harass.

BESIEGEMENT (be-sej'ment), *n.* the act of besetting.

BESLAVER (be-slav'er), *v.t.* to besmear with spittle ; cover with fulsome praise ; a broom.

BESLOBBER (be-slob'er), *v.t.* kiss effusively all over the mouth ; to flatter fulsomely.

BESMIRCH (be-smerch'), *v.t.* to soil ; discolour.

BESOM (be'zum), *n.* a brush of twigs for sweeping ; a broom.

BESOT (be-sot'), *v.t.* to bestialize, as with drink.

BESOTMENT (be-sot'ment), *n.* the act or state of being besotted.

BESOTTED (-ed), *adj.* muddled, as with liquor ; stupefied ; senseless.

BESPANGLE (be-spang'gl), *v.t.* to adorn with spangles.

BESPATTER (be-spat'er), *v.t.* to soil by spattering.

BESPEAK (be-spek'), *v.t.* to speak beforehand.

BESSEMER STEEL (bes'em-er stel), *n.* steel made by a process of forcing air into cast iron while in a molten state.

BEST (best), *adj.* having the highest degree of goodness or excellence ; *n.* the highest state of excellence : *adv.* in the highest degree : *v.t.* to get the better of.

BESTIAL (bes'chal), *adj.* belonging to a beast ; having the qualities of a beast ; brutal.

BESTIALIZE (bes'chal-iz), *v.t.* to make like a beast.

BESTIALITY (bes-chi-al'i-ti), *n.* the qualities or nature of a beast.

BESTIALLY (bes'chal-li), *adv.* in a beast-like manner.

BESTIR (be-ster'), *v.t.* to put into brisk or vigorous action.

BEST-MAN (best'man), *n.* the

groomsman at the wedding ceremony.

BESTOW (be-sto'), *v.t.* deposit in safe keeping ; use or apply ; give or confer [followed by *on* or *upon*].

BESTOWMENT (be-sto'ment), **BESTOWAL** ('al), *n.* the act of giving or conferring.

BESTRADDLE (be-strad'l), *v.t.* to bestride.

BESTREW (be-stroo'), **BESTROW** (-stro'), *v.t.* to strew or scatter over.

BESTRIDE (be-strid'), *v.t.* to stand or sit on with legs astride.

BET (bet), *v.t.* to stake or pledge on the event of a future contingency.

BETAKE (be-tak'), *v.t.* to have recourse to.

BETA-RAYS (ba'ta-raz), *n.pl.* one of the three principal forms of rays given out by radio-active substances.

BETEL (be'tl), *n.* a species of pepper, native of the East Indies.

BETEL-NUT (-nut), *n.* the nut-seed of the East Indian areca-palm.

BETE NOIRE (bat nwar), [French, lit. black beast], a bugbear ; especially repellent.

BETHEL (beth'el), *n.* a hallowed spot ; a dissenting chapel.

BETHINK (be-think'), *v.t. & v.i.* to call to mind ; consider.

BETIDE (be-tid'), *v.t.* to happen to ; befall.

BETIMES (be-timz'), *adv.* in good season or time ; early ; soon.

BETOKEN (be-to'kn), *v.t.* to indicate by signs ; serve as a sign.

BETON (ba-tong'), *n.* a concrete used for submarine structures.

BETONY (bet'o-ni), *n.* a woodland plant, with purple flowers.

BETRAY (be-tra'), *v.t.* to deliver into the hands of an enemy by treachery.

BETRAYAL (be-tra'al), *n.* the act of betraying.

BETROTH (be-troth'), *v.t.* to contract to give any one in marriage.

BETROTHAL (be-troth'al), **BETROTHMENT** ('ment), *n.* the act of engaging to marry ; an engagement to marry.

BETTER (bet'er), *adj.* having good

qualities in a greater degree than another ; preferable or more suitable : *adv.* in a more excellent manner.

BETTERMENT (bet'er-ment), *n.* the improvement of land or houses.

BETTING (bet'ing), *n.* the act of making bets.

BETWEEN (be-twen'), *prep.* in the space or interval which separates.

BETWIXT (be-twikst'), *prep.* between ; in the space which separates.

BEVEL (bev'el), *v.t.* to cut to a bevel-angle : *v.i.* an instrument used for drawing angles : *adj.* having the form of a bevel ; aslant.

BEVEL GEAR (ger), a kind of wheel-work in which the axis or shaft of the driving-wheel forms an angle with the shaft of the wheel driven.

BEVEL WHEEL (hwel), a cog-wheel with its working face oblique to the axis.

BEVERAGE (bev'er-aj), *n.* drink of any description.

BEVY (bev'i), *n.* a company of persons ; a flock of quails, etc.

BEWAIL (be-wal'), *v.t.* to mourn or weep for ; lament.

BEWAILMENT (be-wal'ment), *n.* the act of lamenting.

BEWARE (be-war'), *v.i.* to be on one's guard.

BEWILDER (be-wil'der), *v.t.* to lead into perplexity or confusion ; puzzle.

BEWILDERMENT (be-wil'der-ment), *n.* the state of being greatly perplexed.

BEWITCH (be-wich'), *v.t.* charm beyond the power of resistance ; fascinate.

BEWITCHERY (be-wich'er-i), *n.* witchery ; fascination ; charm.

BEWITCHING (be-wich'ing), *adj.* having power to fascinate.

BEWITCHMENT (be-wich'ment), *n.* fascination ; charm.

BEWRAY (be-ra'), *v.t.* to expose ; reveal.

BEY (ba), *n.* a governor in the Turkish dominions.

BEYLIK (ba'lik), *n.* the territory ruled by a bey.

BEYOND (be-yond'), *prep.* on the further side of ; before ; past :

adv. further away ; yonder : *n.* that state of existence which is beyond our present experience.

BEZEL (bez'el), *n.* the slope at the edge of a cutting tool ; the groove in which the glass of a watch is fitted.

BEZETTA (be-zet'ta), *n.* a dye obtained by immersing coarse rags in a coloured solution.

BEZIQUE (be-zek'), *n.* a modern game of cards.

BIANNUAL (bi-an'u-al), *adj.* occurring twice in a year.

BIANNUALLY (-li), *adv.* twice a year.

BIARTICULATE (bi-ar-tik'u-lat), *adj.* having two joints.

BIAS (bi'as), *n.* a seam formed by uniting the edges of two pieces of cloth cut obliquely to the texture ; prepossession or undue propensity for ; prejudice.

BIAURICULATE (bi-aw-rik'u-lat), *adj.* having two auricles ; having two ear-like projections at the base, as a leaf.

BIAXIAL (bi-aks'i-al), **BI-AXAL** ('al), *adj.* having two axes.

BIB (bib), *n.* a piece of cloth placed under an infant's chin.

BIBASIC (bi-bas'ik), *adj.* a term applied to acids which combine with two equivalents of a base.

BIBBER (bib'er), *n.* a tippler.

BIBLE (bi'bl), *n.* the Book ; the writings of the Old and New Testament, whether in the original tongue or translated.

BIBLICAL (bib'li-kal), *adj.* of or pertaining to the Bible ; scriptural.

BIBLIOGRAPHER (bib-li-og'ra-fer), *n.* one who is versed in the making of books, or writes a history of their production.

BIBLIOGRAPHY (bib-li-og'ra-fi), *n.* the science or description of books ; a list of authorities on any subject.

BIBLIOKLEPT (bib'li-o-klept), *n.* a book thief.

BIBLIOLATER (bib-li-ol'a-ter), **BIBLIOLATRIST** (-trist), *n.* a book worshipper ; one addicted to bibliolatry.

BIBLIOLATRY (bib-li-ol'a-tri), *n.* book worship.

BIBLIOLOGICAL (bib-li-o-loj'i-kal), *adj.* pertaining to bibliology.

BIBLIOLOGY (bib-li-ol'o-ji), *n.* an account of books ; Biblical literature or doctrine.

BIBLIOMANIA (bib-li-o-ma'ni-a), *n.* mania for acquiring rare and curious books.

BIBLIOMANIAC (bib-li-o-ma'ni-ak), *n.* one who has a mania for acquiring books.

BIBLIOPEGY (bib-li-o-pe'ji), *n.* art of bookbinding.

BIBLIOPHILE (bib'li-o-fil), *n.* a lover of books.

BIBLIOPHILISM (bib-li-of'i-lizm), *n.* love of books.

BIBLIOPOLE (bib'li-o-pol), *n.* a bookseller, especially one who deals in rare works.

BIBLIOTHECA (bib-li-o-the'ka), *n.* a library.

BIBLUS (bib'lus), *n.* the papyrus.

BIBULOUS (bib'u-lus), *adj.* readily absorbing or imbibing fluids ; spongy; addicted to drink.

BICARBONATE (bi-kar'bon-at), *n.* a carbonate or salt containing two equivalents of carbonic acid to one of a base.

BICARINATE (bi-kar'i-nat), *adj.* having two keel-like projections.

BICAUDATE (bi-kaw'dat), *adj.* furnished with or ending in two tails.

BICE (bis), *n.* a blue pigment obtained from carbonate of copper.

BICENTENARY (bi-sen'te-na-ri), *n.* the two hundredth anniversary of any event.

BICENTENNIAL (bi-sen-ten'i-al), *adj.* comprising two hundred years ; *n.* the two hundredth anniversary.

BICEPHALOUS (bi-sef'a-lus), *adj.* having two heads.

BICEPS (bi'seps), *n.* muscle having two heads ; the large flexor muscle of the arm and thigh.

BICHIR (be-sher'), *n.* a food fish of the Nile.

BICHLORIDE (bi-klo'rid, 'rid), *n.* a compound of two or more atoms of chlorine combined with a base.

BICHORD (bi'kord), *adj.* having two chords in unison for each note, as in a mandolin.

BICHROMATE (bi-kro'mat), *n.* a salt having two parts of chromic acid to one of the base.

BICIPITAL (bi-sip'it-al), *adj.* having two heads ; pertaining to a biceps muscle.

BICKER (bik'er), *v.i.* to engage in petty altercation.

BICONCAVE (bi-kon'kav), *adj.* hollow on both sides.

BICONJUGATE (bi-kon'ju-gat), *adj.* twice paired.

BICONVEX (bi-kon'veks), *adj.* rounded on both sides.

BICORN (bi'korn), *adj.* having two horns.

BICORPORAL (bi-kor'po-ral), *adj.* having two bodies.

BICUSPID (bi-kus'pid), **BICUSPIDATE** (-at), *adj.* having two points or prominences.

BICYCLE (bi'si-kl), *n.* a vehicular machine of various forms.

BICYCLIST (bi-sik-list), *n.* one who rides a bicycle ; a cyclist.

BID (bid), *v.t.* to make an offer of ; propose as a price ; offer for : *n.* a price offered at auction.

BIDDABLE (bid'a-bl), *adj.* docile; obedient.

BIDDER (bid'er), *n.* one who bids or offers a price.

BIDDING (bid'ing), *n.* an order ; the act of offering a price at auction.

BIDE (bid), *v.i.* inhabit ; reside : *v.t.* to endure.

BIDENT (bi'dent), *n.* a two-pronged instrument ; a two-year-old sheep.

BIDENTAL (bi-den'tal), *adj.* having two teeth.

BIDET (bi-det'), *n.* a portable bath ; a small pack horse.

BIDUOUS (bid'u-us), *adj.* remaining open for two days, as some flowers.

BIENNIAL (bi-en'ni-al), *adj.* happening once in two years : *n.* a plant which produces roots and leaves in the first year, and in the second flowers, fruit, and seed, afterward perishing.

BIENNIALLY (-li), *adv.* once in two years.

BIER (ber), *n.* a frame or carriage on which a corpse is placed.

BIFACIAL (bi-fa'shi-al), *adj.* having two similar faces or the opposite surfaces alike.

BIFARIOUS (bi-fa'ri-us), *adj.* two-fold ; pointing in two ways.

BIFEROUS (bif'er-us), *adj.* bearing flowers or fruit twice a year.

BIFID (bi'fid), *adj.* partially divided into two.

BIFILAR (bi-fi'lar), *adj.* two-threaded ; fitted with two threads.

BIFOCAL (bi-fo'kal), *adj.* having two foci : *n.* a bifocal glass.

BIFOLD (bi'fold), *adj.* two-fold ; double.

BIFOLIATE (bi-fo'li-at), *adj.* having two leaves.

BIFURCATE (bi-fer'kat), *adj.* two-pronged : *v.i.* to divide in two directions or branches.

BIFURCATE (bi-fer'kat), **BIFUR-CATED** (-ed), *adj.* divided into two branches.

BIFURCATION (bi-fer-ka'shun), *n.* a forking or division into two branches.

BIG (big), *adj.* of great bulk or magnitude ; grown up.

BIGAMY (big'a-mi), *n.* the offence or contracting a second marriage during the existence of former marriage.

BIGAMIST (big'a-mist), *n.* one guilty of bigamy.

BIGAMOUS (big'a-mus), *adj.* pertaining to, or involving, bigamy.

BIG GAME (gam), a hunter's name for large animals.

BIGHORN (-horn), *n.* the wild sheep of the Rocky Mountains.

BIGHT (bit), *n.* a loop or bend of a rope, in distinction from the ends ; a bend in a coast-line.

BIGNONIA (big-no'ni-a), *n.* a large genus of American tropical climbing plants.

BIGOT (big'ot), *n.* one who is unreasonably and blindly attached to a particular creed, church, or party ; a fanatic.

BIGOTED (big'ot-ed), *adj.* characterized by bigotry.

BIGOTRY (big'ot-ri), *n.* the state or condition of a narrow-minded, intolerant person.

BIGWIG (big'wig), *n.* a person of importance ; usually used ironically.

BIJOU (be-zhoo'), *n.* [*pl.* bijoux (shooz')], a jewel ; any small and elegantly finished article.

BIJOUTERIE be-zhoo'tre), *n.* jewelry or other small articles of vertu.

BIKE (bik), *n.* a bicycle : *v.i.* to ride a bicycle.

BILABIATE (bi-la'bi-at), *adj.* having two lips.

BILATERAL (bi-lat'er-al), *adj.* pertaining to, or having two sides.

BILATERALLY (-li), *adv.* in a two-sided manner ; on both sides.

BILBERRY (bil'ber-ri), *n.* the whortle-berry.

BILBO (bil'bo), *n.* a rapier or sword.

BILE (bil), *n.* a yellow bitter fluid secreted by the liver from venous blood.

BILE-STONE (-ston), *n.* a gall-stone.

BILGE (bilj), *n.* the bulging part of a bottom, on which a ship rests when aground.

BILGE-KEEL (kel), *n.* a piece of timber secured edgewise under a vessel to prevent heavy rolling.

BILGE-WATER (-waw-ter), *n.* water which accumulates in the bilge of a ship.

BILGE-WAYS (-waz), *n.pl.* the timber supporting the cradle of a vessel.

BILIARY (bil'i-a-ri), *adj.* pertaining to the bile ; conveying the bile.

BILINEAR (bi-lin'e-ar), *adj.* pertaining to, or enclosed by, two lines.

BILINGUAL (bi'ling'gwal), *adj.* written or expressed in two languages.

BILIOUS (bil'yus), *adj.* pertaining to the bile ; having the system disordered by derangement of the biliary function ; choleric.

BILIOUSNESS (-nes), *n.* the state of being bilious.

BILITERAL (bi-lit'er-al), *adj.* consisting of two letters : *n.* a word, root, or syllable consisting of two letters.

BILK (bilk), *v.t.* to deceive ; defraud.

BILKER (bilk'er), *n.* a swindler.

BILL (bil), *n.* the beak of a bird.

BILL (bil), *n.* a kind of hatchet with a blade hook-shaped toward the point.

BILL (bil), *n.* an account for goods sold, services rendered, or work done ; a draft of a proposed statute presented to a legislature : *v.t.* to present a bill or account ; to advertise by bills.

BILL-BOARD (bill'bord), *n.* a level surface on which advertisements are pasted.

BILL-BOOK (-book), *n.* a book for bills payable, bills receivable, etc.

BILLET (bil'et), *n.* a small paper in writing ; ticket directing soldiers at what house to lodge.

BILLET (bil'et), *n.* a small stick or log of wood.

BILLET-DOUX (bil-e-doo′), *n.* [*pl.* billets-doux (bil-e-dooz′)], a love letter.

BILLFISH (bil'fish), *n.* the freshwater garfish.

BILL FOLD (fold), a pocket-book for bank notes.

BILLHOOK (bil'hook), *n.* a small kind of hatchet.

BILLIARDS (bil'yardz), *n* a game played on a rectangular, cloth-covered slate table, with ivory balls and a cue.

BILLIKEN (bil'i-ken), *n.* grotesque image ; symbol of good cheer.

BILL OF ENTRY (en'tri), a written account of goods entered at the custom house.

BILL OF EXCHANGE (eks-chanj′), a written order to pay to the person designated a certain sum at a fixed time.

BILL OF HEALTH (-helth), a certificate given to the master of a vessel, specifying the state of the health of a ship's company or passengers.

BILL OF LADING (lad'ing), a document specifying the goods shipped on board a vessel or railroad.

BILL OF MORTALITY (mor-tal'i-ti), the official return of the deaths (also births) occurring in a particular district within a certain period.

BILL OF RIGHTS (ritz), a statement of certain rights and privileges claimed by the people.

BILL OF SALE (sal), an instrument for the conveyance or transfer of goods, property, chattels, etc.

BILLINGSGATE (bil'ingz-gat), *n.* coarse or profane language. Supposed to be used in Billingsgate, a London fish market.

BILLION (bil'yun), *n.* in the U.S. one thousand millions (1,000,000,000) ; in England a million millions (1,000,000,000,000).

BILLON (bil'on), *n.* an alloy of gold and silver, with a large proportion of copper.

BILLOT (bil'ot), *n.* bullion in the mass or bar.

BILLOW (bil'o), *n.* a great wave of the sea.

BILLY (bil'i), *n.* a roving machine, in the carding of wool ; a policeman's club ; a male goat ; a hard, grey quartzite.

BILOBATE (bi-lo'bat), *adj.* divided into two lobes.

BIMANOUS (bim'a-nus), *adj.* having two hands.

BIMANUAL (bi-man'u-al), *adj.* done with two hands.

BIMETALLISM (bi-met'al-izm), *n.* the legalized adoption of two metals (as gold and silver) in the currency of a country, at a fixed ratio.

BIMONTHLY (bi-munth'li), *adj.* occurring once in two months ; sometimes incorrectly employed to designate *semi-monthly* periodicals.

BIN (bin), *n.* a receptacle for any commodity.

BINARY (bi'na-ri), *adj.* consisting of two things or parts ; twofold.

BINARYSTAR (star), a double star or sun whose members revolve round their common centre of gravity.

BINATE (bi'nat), *adj.* growing in couples.

BIND (bind), *v.t.* to confine or make fast ; unite by bonds of affection, loyalty, or duty ; hinder or restrain ; fasten together ; cause to cohere.

BINDER (-er), *n.* a device on reaping

machines; anything that binds; a cover for holding loose papers.

BINDERY ('er-i), *n.* a place where books are bound.

BINDING (bind'ing), *n.* the act of making fast; a bandage; the cover of a book.

BINDWEED (-wed), *n.* a common name for plants belonging to the genus Convolvulus.

BINE (bin), *n.* the slender stem of a twining plant.

BING (bing), *n.* a heap or pile.

BINGLE (bin'gle), *n.* a base hit in baseball.

BINNACLE (bin'a-kl), *n.* a box containing a ship's compass.

BINOCLE (bin'o-kl), *n.* a field or opera glass with two eyetubes for the use of both eyes at once.

BINOCULAR (bin-ok'u-lar), *adj.* having two eyes; pertaining to, or suited to, the use of both eyes.

BINOMIAL (bi-no'mi-al), *n.* an expression or quantity consisting of two terms connected by the sign plus or minus.

BIODYNAMICS (bi-o-di-nam'iks), *n.* the doctrine of vital force or energy.

BIOGENESIS (bi-o-jen'e-sis), **BIOGENY** (-oj'e-ni), *n.* the doctrine that living organisms can proceed only from, or be generated by, living parents or germs.

BIOGEOGRAPHY (bi-o-je-og'ra-fi), *n.* the science which treats of the distribution of animals and plants.

BIOGRAPH (bi'o-graf), *n.* a device for projecting animated pictures on to a screen.

BIOGRAPHER (bi-og'ra-fer), *n.* one who writes the history of a particular person's life.

BIOGRAPHY (bi-og'ra-fi), *n.* the history of the life of a particular person.

BIOLOGIC bi-o-loj'ik), **BIOLOGICAL** ('i-kal), *adj.* pertaining to the science of life.

BIOLOGIST (bi-ol'o-jist), *n.* one who studies, or is skilled in, the science of living forms.

BIOLOGY (bi-ol'o-ji), *n.* the science which deals with the origin and life-history of plants and animals.

BIONOMY (bi-on'o-mi), *n.* the science which treats of living functions.

BIOPLASM (bi'o-plazm), *n.* living germinal matter or protoplasm.

BIOPLAST (bi'o-plast), *n.* a minute mass of protoplasm.

BIOSTATICS (-stat'iks), *n.* that part of biology which deals with the structure and potentiality of organisms.

BIOTAXY (bi'o-tak-si), *n.* the classification of living organisms.

BIPAROUS (bip'a-rus), *adj.* bringing forth two at a birth.

BIPARTITE (bi-par'tit), *adj.* divided into two similar parts.

BIPED (bi'ped), *adj.* having two feet : *n.* a two-footed animal.

BIPEDAL (bi'pe-dal), *adj.* pertaining to a biped; two-footed.

BIPENNATE (bi-pen'at), **BIPENNATED** (-ed), *adj.* having two wings.

BIPINNATE (bi-pin'at), *adj.* doubly pinnate, as a leaf.

BIPLANAR (bi-pla'nar), *adj.* lying in two planes.

BIPLANE (bi'plan), *n.* an aeroplane with two planes.

BIPLICATE (bi'pli-kat), *adj.* doubly folded.

BIQUADRATE (bi-kwod'rat), *n.* the fourth power, arising from the multiplication of a square number or quantity by itself.

BIRAMOUS (bi-ra'mus), *adj.* having two branches.

BIRCH (berch), *n.* a tree or shrub belonging to the genus Betula.

BIRD (berd), *n.* a warm-blooded feathered vertebrate, furnished with wings, and belonging to the class Aves.

BIRDLIME (berd'lim), *n.* a viscous substance prepared from holly-bark and used for entangling small birds.

BIRDMEN (berd'men), *n.* aviators.

BIRD'S-EYE (berdz'i), *adj.* seen from above, or at a glance, as by a flying bird; hence, general, not minute or detailed : *n.* a kind of primrose.

BIRD'S EYE MAPLE (ma'pl), the wood of a variety of maple.

BIRETTA (bi-ret'a), *n.* a square ecclesiastical cap.

BIROSTRATE (bi-ros'trat), *adj.* having a double beak, or beak-like process.

BIRTH (berth), *n.* the act of coming into life ; lineage ; descent ; origin.

BIRTH-RATE ('rat), *n.* the increase of population as shown by the percentage of registered births.

BIRTHRIGHT ('rit), *n.* any right or privilege to which a person is entitled by birth.

BISCUIT (bis'kit), *n.* a kind of unraised bread, baked hard and dry ; pottery after the first baking.

BISECT (bi-sekt'), *v.t.* to cut or divide into two equal parts.

BISECTION (bi-sek'shun), *n.* division into two equal parts.

BISECTOR (bi-sek'ter), *n.* one who or that which, bisects ; a straight line which bisects an angle.

BISHOP (bish'up), *n.* one of the highest orders in Christian Churches ; the spiritual head or ruler of a diocese ; one of the pieces used in playing chess.

BISHOPRIC (bish'up-rik), *n.* the office of a bishop ; diocese.

BISHOP'S STAFF (staf), *n.* a crosier.

BISK (bisk), *n.* soup composed of meat or fish boiled together.

BISMUTH (bis', biz'muth), *n.* a light reddish-coloured metal of brittle texture.

BISON (bi'son), *n.* a large, bovine quadruped, of western U.S. inaccurately termed the buffalo.

BISQUE (bisk), *n.* an unglazed white porcelain, used for statuettes, etc.

BISSEXTILE (bi-seks'til), *n.* leap-year : *adj.* pertaining to leap-year.

BISULPHATE (bi-sul'fat), *n.* a salt of sulphuric acid.

BISULPHITE (bi-sul'fit), *n.* a salt of sulphurous acid.

BISYMMETRY (bi-sim'e-tri), *n.* correspondence of the right and left parts of anything.

BIT (bit), *n.* a tool for boring ; the metal mouthpiece of a bridle ; a small piece or fragment of anything.

BITCH (bich), *n.* the female of the dog, or of other canine animals.

BITE (bit), *v.t.* to seize with the teeth ; sting, as an insect ; cut ; pinch, as with intense cold ; blight or blast ; to corrode or eat into.

BITER (-er), *n.* one that bites.

BITINGLY (-ing-li), *adv.* in a sarcastic manner.

BITT (bit), *n.* a post of wood or iron to which cables are made fast.

BITTER (bit'er), *adj.* having a sharp or harsh taste ; acrid ; piercing ; painful.

BITTER-CUP (-kup), *n.* a cup made of quassia wood, which imparts a bitter taste to liquids.

BITTER END (end), the last extremity.

BITTER ENDER (-er), one who holds out to the bitter end.

BITTERISH (ish), *adj.* somewhat bitter.

BITTERN (bit'ern), *n.* a bird of streaked and speckled plumage, of the heron family ; a bitter native liquor remaining in salt works after the salt has crystallized, from which is obtained sodium sulphate, magnesium chloride, bromides, and iodides.

BITTER-NUT (-nut), *n.* a species of hickory of eastern U.S.

BITTER-ROOT (-root), *n.* a plant with fleshy, farinaceous root and pink flowers.

BITTERS (bit'erz), *n. pl.* liquor in which herbs or roots are steeped.

BITTER-SWEET (-swet), *n.* the woody nightshade.

BITUMEN (bi-tu'men), *n.* mineral pitch.

BITUMINOUS (bi-tu'min-us), *adj.* having the qualities of, or containing, bitumen.

BIVALENT (bi'va-, biv'a-lent), *n.* an element, one of the atoms of which can replace two atoms of hydrogen.

BIVALVE (bi'valv), *adj.* having two valves or shells united by a ligament : *n.* a mollusk.

BIVOUAC (biv'oo-ak), *n.* an encampment of soldiers.

BIWEEKLY (bi-wek'li), *adj.* occurring or appearing every two weeks; fortnightly.

BIZARRE (bi-zar'), *adj.* odd in manner of appearance; fanciful; grotesque.

BLAB (blab), *v.t.* to tell thoughtlessly : *v.i.* to talk indiscreetly.

BLACK (blak), *adj.* destitute of light; of the darkest hue; opposed to white.

BLACK ALDER (awl'der), the alder buckthorn.

BLACKAMOOR (blak'a-moor), *n.* a negro.

BLACK ANTIMONY (an'ti-mo-ni), *n.* the black sulphide of antimony.

BLACK ART (art), necromancy; magic.

BLACKBALL (blak'bawl), *v.t.* to reject or exclude (as a candidate).

BLACKBERRY (blak'ber-ri), *n.* the fruit of several species of bramble.

BLACKBIRD (blak'berd), *n.* a song bird, a species of thrush; a crow-like bird of North America.

BLACKBOARD (blak'bord), *n.* a smooth surface painted black for use with chalk crayons.

BLACK CANKER (kangk'er), a disease in root crops.

BLACKCAP (blak'kap), *n.* one of several black-crested birds; the black raspberry.

BLACK CURRANT (kur'ent), the well-known garden bush, and its fruit.

BLACKEN (blak'n), *v.i* to grow black or dark : *v.t.* to make black; defame.

BLACK-EYED SUSAN (blak'-id su'-san), yellow daisy.

BLACKFISH (-fish), *n.* a common name for several species of English and American fish.

BLACK FLY (fli), a black plant-louse; a minute beetle injurious to turnips.

BLACK FRIAR (fri'er), a friar of the Dominican order.

BLACK FRIDAY (fri'da), any Friday upon which a disaster has occurred.

BLACK FROST (frost), an intense frost.

BLACKGUARD (blag'ard), *n.* a man of low character; a scoundrel.

BLACKING (blak'ing), *n.* a black polish for shoes.

BLACKISH (blak'ish), *adj.* somewhat black.

BLACK-JACK (-jak), *n.* the ensign of a pirate; dwarf oak; a bludgeon with flexible handle.

BLACKLEAD (blak'led), *v.t.* to cover with blacklead or plumbago.

BLACKLEG (blak'leg), *n.* one who endeavours to obtain money by cheating at races or cards; a crook; disease affecting sheep and cattle.

BLACK-LETTER (blak'let-er), *n.* the old English or Gothic letter.

BLACKLIST (blak'list), *n.* a list of persons who are deemed to be deserving of punishment.

BLACKMAIL (blak'mal), *n.* extortion by means of intimidation.

BLACK MAPLE (ma'pl), the sugar maple.

BLACK SHEEP (shep), a member of a family who disgraces the other members.

BLACKSMITH (blak'smith), *n.* a smith who works in iron and makes horseshoes, etc.

BLACKTHORN (blak'thorn), *n.* the sloe; a stick cut from the stem of the sloe.

BLADDER (blad'er), *n.* a thin elastic membranous bag in animals, in which a fluid is collected.

BLADE (blad), *n.* the leaf of a grass; the young stalk or spire of a grass; the cutting part of an instrument.

BLADE-BONE (blad'bon), *n.* the scapula or shoulder-blade.

BLAIN (blan), *n.* a pustule or blister.

BLAMABLE, BLAMEABLE (blam'-a-bl), *adj.* deserving of censure.

BLAME (blam), *v.t.* to censure; reproach.

BLAMEFUL (blam'fool), *adj.* meriting blame.

BLAMEWORTHY (-wer'thi), *adj.* meriting blame.

BLANCH (blanch), *v.t.* to take the colour out; to remove the covering of : *v.i.* turn pale.

BLAND (bland), *adj.* mild ; soft ; gentle ; affable ; soothing.

BLANDISHMENT (blan'dish-ment), *n.* winning expressions or actions.

BLANK (blangk), *adj.* confounded ; confused ; dejected ; empty ; free from writing or printing ; disk of metal prior to stamping.

BLANKET (blang'ket), *n.* a soft, woven woollen cloth for a covering : *v.t.* pass to windward ; to cover, as with a blanket.

BLANKETING (blang'ket-ing), *n.* coarse cloth for blankets.

BLANKITE (blangk'it), *n.* an unstable salt, used as a bleaching agent in the preparation of sugar cane ; hydrosulphite.

BLANK VERSE (vers), poetry without rhyme.

BLARE (blar), *v.i.* to bellow ; to give forth a loud sound like a trumpet.

BLARNEY (blar'ni), *n.* soft, wheedling speech ; flattery.

BLARNEY STONE (ston), a stone in the wall of Blarney Castle, Cork.

BLASE (bla-za'), *adj.* exhausted by excess of pleasure.

BLASPHEME (blas-fem'), *v.t.* to speak irreverently of ; mock ; revile.

BLASPHEMOUS (blas'fe-mus), *adj.* uttering, containing, or exhibiting blasphemy.

BLASPHEMY (blas'fe-mi), *n.* impious, profane, or mocking speech concerning God or sacred things.

BLAST (blast), *n.* a violent or sudden gust of wind ; the explosion of gunpowder, dynamite, etc.

BLASTEMA (blas-te'ma), *n.* [*pl.* blastemata (-ma-ta)], the point of growth of an organ as yet unformed, from which it is developed.

BLAST FURNACE (fer'nas), a furnace for the smelting of ores.

BLASTO-, a combining form from the Greek *blastos*, a sprout, and denoting relation to a germ or bud.

BLASTODERM (blas'to-derm), *n.* the germinal spot in an ovum, from which the embryo is developed.

BLASTOGENESIS (blas-to-jen'e-sis), *n.* reproduction by gemmation or budding.

BLAST PIPE (pip), *n.* the exhaust pipe of a steam engine.

BLATANT (bla'tant), *adj.* bawling ; noisy.

BLATHER (blath'er), *n.* foolish chatter : *v.i.* to talk foolishly.

BLATHERSKITE (blath'er-skit), *n.* a foolish chatterer.

BLAZE (blaz), *n.* a body of flame ; a white spot on the face of a horse or other quadruped ; a mark cut on a tree, to serve as a guide.

BLAZER (blaz'er), *n.* that which shines ; a bright coloured striped jacket.

BLAZON (bla'zn), *n.* a coat of arms ; ostentatious display.

BLAZONRY (bla'zn-ri), *n.* heraldic device ; decoration, as with heraldic devices.

BLEACH (blech), *v.t.* to make white by removing colour or dirt by the action of the sun's rays, or by chemical process : *v.i.* to grow or become white.

BLEACHERY (blech'er-i), *n.* a place where bleaching is done.

BLEACHING POWDER (-pou'der), *n.* chloride of lime.

BLEAK (blek), *adj.* exposed to wind and cold ; desolate.

BLEAK (blek), *n.* a small river fish.

BLEAR (bler), *adj.* sore or dim from a watery discharge : said of the eyes : *v.t.* to dim or obscure.

BLEAT (blet), *v.i.* to cry as, or like, a sheep.

BLEB (bleb), *n.* a blister.

BLEED (bled), *v.i.* to emit, or lose blood : *v.t.* to take blood from ; take money, etc., from.

BLEEDING (-ing), *p.adj.* emitting blood, or sap.

BLEEDING-HEART (-hart), *n.* a pink-coloured flower.

BLEMISH (blem'ish), *v.t.* to injure ; mar ; tarnish : *n.* a defect or flaw.

BLENCH (blench), *v.i.* to start back ; flinch.

BLEND (blend), *v.t.* to mix together : *v.i.* to mingle : *n.* a mixture as of colours, liquids, tobaccos, teas, etc.

BLENDE (blend), *n.* native sulphide of zinc.

BLENNY (blen'i), *n.* a small marine fish.

BLERIOT MONOPLANE (ble-re-o' mon'o-plan), a French make of aeroplane : after Louis Bleriot who was the first to cross the English Channel in this kind of machine, in 1909.

BLESBOK (bles'bok), *n.* a large South African antelope.

BLESS (bles), *v.t.* to consecrate ; invoke a blessing upon.

BLESSEDNESS (bles'ed-nes), *n.* the state of being blessed.

BLESSING (bles'ing), *n.* an invocation of happiness on another ; a benediction.

BLET (blet), *n.* a decayed spot in fruit.

BLEWITS (bloo'its), *n.* the edible purple mushroom.

BLIGHT (blit), *n.* a disease in plants, which causes them to wither partly or wholly ; smut ; mildew ; anything which checks, nips, or destroys.

BLIGHTY (blit'i), *n.* [Slang], home, England, to the British soldier.

BLIMP (blimp), *n.* a small airship propelled by an engine.

BLIND (blind), *adj.* destitute of the sense of sight : *n.* a window-screen ; a blinker : *v.t.* to deprive of sight.

BLIND COAL (kol), a flameless anthracite.

BLINDFISH (-fish), *n.* a diminutive fish inhabiting the water of Mammoth Cave, Kentucky.

BLINDFOLD (-fold), *adj.* having the eyes covered : *v.t.* to cover the eyes of, as with a bandage ; hinder from seeing.

BLINDMAN (-man), *n.* a man who is blind.

BLINDMAN'S BUFF (buf), *n.* a game in which one of the players is blindfolded.

BLINDNESS (-nes), *n.* want of sight ; want of discernment ; ignorance.

BLIND SHELL (shel), a shell which falls without exploding.

BLIND SIDE (sid), the weaker side.

BLIND SPOT (spot), that point in the retina where the optic nerve enters the eye, but is not sensitive to the light.

BLINK (blink), *v.i.* to wink with the eye ; twinkle : *v.t.* to evade or shut one's eyes to ; shirk.

BLINKER (bling'ker), *n.* one who blinks ; a leather flap placed one on each side of a horse's bridle.

BLISS (blis), *n.* highest degree of happiness.

BLISSFULLY (-fool-li), *adv.* in a blissful manner.

BLISTER (blis'ter), *n.* a vesicle or pustule on the skin ; an application to the skin to produce a blister.

BLITHE (blith), *adj.* gay ; joyous ; glad.

BLITHESOME (blith'sum), *adj.* gay ; merry.

BLIZZARD (bliz'ard), *n.* a furious hurricane of wind with blinding snow.

BLOAT (blot), *v.t.* to cure or dry in smoke ; to cause to swell.

BLOATER (blot'er), *n.* a herring smoked and partially dried.

BLOB (blob), *n.* a blister ; a bubble.

BLOCK (blok), *n.* any unshaped solid mass of matter, as of wood, stone, etc. ; a log or log-like table ; the piece of hard wood to which an electrotype, etc., is secured ; a row of buildings ; a square or portion of a city enclosed by streets : *v.i.* to obstruct so as to hinder the passage of persons or things.

BLOCKADE (blok-ad'), *n.* the shutting up of a place, as port, by hostile ships or troops.

BLOCKAGE (blok'aj), *n.* an obstruction.

BLOCKHEAD (blok'hed), *n.* stupid fellow.

BLOCKHOUSE (blok'hous), *n.* an edifice constructed of heavy timber, and finished with loopholes for musketry.

BLOCK SIGNAL (sig'nal), a safety device on railroads.

BLOCK SYSTEM (sis'tem), a system of working railway traffic by which the line is divided into short sections, no train being allowed to leave a section until the next section is signalled clear.

BLOND, BLONDE (blond), *adj.* of a fair colour ; light coloured : *n.* a person of very fair complexion and light hair, especially a girl.

BLONDE-LACE ('las), *n.* a silk lace.

BLOOD (blud), *n.* the fluid which circulates in the arteries and veins of an animal; kinship; consanguinity; lineage.

BLOODED (-ed), *adj.* of the best stock or breed.

BLOOD-HEAT (blud'het), *n.* the normal heat of the human blood: in health 98° F.

BLOOD-HORSE (blud'hors), *n.* a horse of pure breed or pedigree.

BLOODHOUND (blud'hound), *n.* one of a breed of large dogs remarkable for their acuteness of smell.

BLOODILY (blud'i-li), *adv.* in a bloody manner.

BLOODINESS (-nes), *n.* the state of being bloody.

BLOOD-MONEY (blud-mun'i), *n.* money obtained at the cost of another's life.

BLOOD PRESSURE (presh'ur), the stress or tension of the blood on the walls of the blood vessels.

BLOODSHED (-shed), *n.* the shedding of blood; slaughter.

BLOODSHOT (-shot), *adj.* red; inflamed; suffused with blood.

BLOODSTONE (blud'ston), *n.* a dark green variety of quartz spotted with red jasper.

BLOODSUCKER (-suk'er), *n.* one, or that, which sucks blood.

BLOODTHIRSTY (-therst'i), *adj.* eager to shed blood; extremely cruel.

BLOODWOOD (-wood), *n.* one of the redwoods of Australia, the logwoods of the West Indies, or the crape myrtles of the East Indies.

BLOODY (blud'i), *adj.* pertaining to, containing, or resembling blood.

BLOOM (bloom), *n.* a blossom; the flower of a plant; the blossoming of flowers; the blue colour upon certain newly-gathered fruits.

BLOOMERY (bloom'er-i), **BLOOMARY** ('a-ri), *n.* a forge in which wrought iron is made.

BLOSSOM (blos'um), *n.* the flower of a plant; the state of flowering; bloom.

BLOT (blot), *n.* a spot or stain; a blemish; disgrace.

BLOTCH (bloch), *n.* a clumsy daub; an eruption, or pustule.

BLOUSE (blouz), *n.* a light, loose over-garment.

BLOW (blo), *n.* a mass of blossoms; the state or condition of flowering.

BLOW (blo), *n.* a stroke with the hand or with a weapon; a knock; a sudden shock or calamity.

BLOW (blo), *v.i.* to form or make a current of air; pant; breathe quickly; sound by being blown; spou: water: *v.t.* to drive a current of air upon; to melt, as a fuse; impel by a current of air; sound a wind instrument by forcing air through it: *n.* a blowing; a blast; a gale of wind; an egg deposited by a fly; the spouting of a whale; a braggart.

BLOWFLY (blo'fli), *n.* any species of fly which deposits its eggs upon flesh.

BLOWHOLE (-hol), *n.* a hole for air or gas to escape; the nostril of a whale; a defect in a casting.

BLOWING-MOLD (blo'ing-mold), *n.* a metal mold in which bottles and other hollow glass objects are blown.

BLOWN (blon), *p.adj.* swollen; inflated; out of breath; covered with the eggs and larva of flies.

BLOW-OUT (blo'out), *n.* the act of blowing out something; the explosive destruction of a fuse; the bursting of a pneumatic tyre from air pressure within; the cleaning of a boiler-flue by a steam blast.

BLOWPIPE (blo'pip), *n.* a tube through which a current of air or gas is driven upon a flame so as to concentrate its heat upon a substance to fuse it.

BLOWY (blo'i), *adj.* windy; breezy.

BLOWZED (blouzd), **BLOWZY** (blou'zi), *adj.* ruddy-faced.

BLUBBER (blub'er), *v.i.* to weep violently: *n.* the fat of whales and other cetaceans, from which oil is prepared.

BLUCHER (blooch'er), *n.* a strong boot.

BLUDGEON (bluj'un), *n.* a short, heavy stick.

BLUE (blu), *adj.* of the colour of the clear sky; azure; low-spirited: *n.* colour of the clear sky; one of the primary colours; azure; a dye or pigment of this colour; pale without glare, as a flame.

BLUEBELL ('bel), *n.* the wild hyacinth.

BLUE BLOOD (blud), aristocratic lineage.

BLUEBOOK ('book), *n.* a governmental official report, etc.

BLUEBOTTLE ('bot-l), *n.* a common field flower; a large flesh-fly.

BLUEBUCK ('buk), *n.* a small antelope of South America.

BLUECOAT (-kot), *n.* a sailor; a policeman.

BLUE-DEVILS ('dev-ilz), *n.pl.* low spirits; mental depression; [B- D-], a company of French soldiers who distinguished themselves in the World War.

BLUEFISH (-fish), *n.* a very voracious, edible fish.

BLUE-GRASS ('gras), *n.* a rich pasture grass.

BLUE-GUM ('gum), *n.* a lofty tree of Australia.

BLUEJACKET (blu'jak-et), *n.* a sailor.

BLUE JAY (ja), the common, blue-coloured jay of eastern U.S.

BLUELIGHT (-lit), *n.* a pyrotechnic composition.

BLUEMOLD (-mold), *n.* a minute fungus which attacks bread and other foodstuffs.

BLUE-PENCIL (-pen'sil), *v.t.* to edit with a blue pencil; hence, to censor; to disapprove.

BLUE-PETER (-pe'ter), *n.* a small blue flag with a white square in the centre, used as a signal for sailing, etc.

BLUE-POINT (-point), *n.* an oyster.

BLUE-PRINT (-print), *n.* a positive print obtained by a ferricyanic process from a transparent negative.

BLUE RIBBON (rib'un), a prized distinction; mark of success.

BLUE-SPAR (-spar), *n.* lazulite.

BLUESTOCKING (blu'stok-ing), *n.* a woman of literary tastes or occupation.

BLUESTONE (-ston), *n.* sulphate of copper.

BLUE-SKY LAW (-ski law), in the U.S., a law to prevent the issue of fraudulent securities.

BLUE VITRIOL, same as bluestone.

BLUING (blu'ing), *n.* the process of imparting a blue tint; the indigo, etc., used in the washing of white goods.

BLUFF (bluf), *adj.* having a broad, flattened front; rising steeply or boldly; rough and hearty; surly; gruff: *n.* a high steep bank; a cliff or headland: *v.t.* to deceive, or gain an advantage.

BLUFFER (bluf'er), *n.* one who tries to frighten another by a pretension to power or strength.

BLUFFY (bluf'i), *adj.* having bold, steep banks, or headlands.

BLUISH (blu'ish), *adj.* somewhat blue.

BLUNDER (blun'der), *v.i.* to make a gross mistake: *n.* a gross or stupid mistake.

BLUNDERHEAD (-hed), *n.* a stupid, ignorant fellow.

BLUNDERINGLY (blun'der-ing-li), *adv.* in a blundering manner.

BLUNT (blunt), *adj.* having a thick or rounded edge or point; not sharp; dull in understanding; abrupt in address; plain-spoken.

BLUNTISH (blunt'ish), *adj.* somewhat blunt.

BLUR (bler), *v.t.* to dim; sully; stain.

BLURT (blert), *v.t.* to speak inadvertently; divulge unadvisedly [usually with *out*].

BLUSH (blush), *v.i.* to become red in the face, as from shame or confusion.

BLUSHFUL (blush'fool), *adj.* full of blushes.

BLUSTER (blus'ter), *v.i.* to be windy and boisterous, as the weather; talk in a noisy, swaggering style.

BLUSTERER (-er), *n.* a noisy swaggerer.

BLUSTEROUS (blus'ter-us), **BLUS-**

TROUS ('trus), **BLUSTERY** ('ter-i), *adj.* noisy ; tumultous ; rough.

BOA (bo'a), *n.* a huge serpent of South America ; a long fur tippet.

BOA-CONSTRICTOR (-kon-strik'-ter), *n.* a reptile remarkable for its length and power of destroying its prey by constriction.

BOAR (bor), *n.* the male of swine.

BOARD (bord), *n.* a piece of timber sawed thin ; a table for food ; a council or court ; a number of persons elected to the management of some public or private office or trust ; a thick stiff kind of paper ; one of the two stiff covers of a book : *v.t.* to cover with boards ; place at a board ; furnish with food, for a compensation ; go on board of ; enter a ship by force.

BOARD FOOT (foot), the volume of a board 1 foot square and 1 inch thick.

BOARDING (bord'ing), *n.* light timber collectively ; a covering of boards ; the act of supplying, or state of being supplied with, food and lodging ; the act of entering a ship.

BOARD OF TRADE (trad), a body for the regulation and promotion of business interests in a community.

BOARD WALK (wawk), a promenade made of planking.

BOARHOUND (-hound), *n.* a dog for hunting wild boars ; the great Dane.

BOARISH (bor'ish), *adj.* swinish ; brutal.

BOAST (bost), *v.i.* to brag ; vaunt ; exult : *v.t.* to brag of : *n.* proud, vainglorious speech.

BOAST (bost), *v.t.* to dress (stone) with a broad chisel and mallet.

BOASTFUL (bost'fool), *adj.* given to boasting.

BOAT (bot), *n.* a small open vessel usually moved by oars but often by a sail ; a ship.

BOATSWAIN (bot'swan, bo'sn), *n.* a petty officer of a ship.

BOB (bob), *v.t.* to impart a short jerking motion to ; to cut short : *n.* any small round object playing loosely at the end of a cord, chain, etc.

BOBBIN (bob'in), *n.* one of the pins or small cylinders of wood used to carry threads ; a spool or reel with a head at one or both ends, used for spinning, weaving, or sewing ; a machine-made cotton netting or lace.

BOBBINET ('i-net), *n.* a machine netting of cotton.

BOBOLINK (bob'o-lingk), *n.* an American song-bird.

BOBSTAY (bob'sta), *n.* one of two or more ropes or chains to hold the bowsprit down toward the stem.

BOBTAIL (bob'tal), *n.* a short tail : *adj.* having the tail cut short.

BOB VEAL (vel), the flesh of a newly-born calf.

BODE (bod), *v.t.* to portend ; be an omen of : *v.i.* to augur ; presage.

BODICE (bod'is), *n.* the close-fitting waist or body of a woman's dress.

BODILY (bod'i-li), *adj.* not mental ; corporeal : *adv.* corporeally ; entirely.

BODING (bod'ing), *n.* an omen ; presentiment : *adj.* foreboding ; ominous.

BODKIN (bod'kin), *n.* a pointed instrument for piercing holes ; an awl-like printer's tool.

BODY (bod'i), *n.* the material, organized substance of an animal, as distinguished from the soul, spirit, or vital principle ; the main or principal part of anything ; a person ; a number of individuals united by some common tie ; any solid geometrical figure ; a material thing ; a certain consistency or density ; substance, etc. : *v.t.* to furnish with a body ; embody ; produce in definite shape.

BODY POLITIC (pol'i-tik), the collective body of people living under an organized government.

BOER (boor), *n.* a Dutch colonist of South Africa.

BOG (bog), *v.t.* to sink, or submerge in a bog or quagmire : *n.* a tract of wet, spongy ground, composed of decayed vegetable matter ; a quagmire.

BOGY (bo'gi), *n.* a hobgoblin ; a spectre.

BOGGLE (bog'gl), *v.i.* to hesitate ; waver ; bungle.

BOGGY (bog'i), *adj.* full of bogs; marshy.

BOGUS (bo'gus), *adj.* counterfeit; spurious.

BOHEMIAN (bo-he'mi-an), *n.* a person who disregards social conventionalities.

BOHEMIAN GLASS (glas), *n.* a glass made in Bohemia, Austria, noted for its beautiful ornamentation and hardness.

BOHEMIANISM (bo-he'mi-an-izm), *n.* the life or habits of a person who leads a free and easy, unconventional existence.

BOIL (boil), *v.i.* to be in a state of ebullition through the action of heat ; seethe ; be agitated or excited by passion or anger : *v.t.* to heat to the boiling point.

BOIL (boil), *n.* an inflamed and painful suppurating tumour.

BOILER (boil'er), *n.* one who boils ; a vessel in which anything is boiled ; a strong metallic vessel, in which steam is generated for driving engines or for other purposes.

BOILING (-ing), *n.* a state of ebullition ; that which is boiled, or is to be boiled ; a batch : *adj.* heated to the point of bubbling.

BOILING POINT (point), the temperature (212° F.), at which water boils.

BOISTEROUS (bois'ter-us), *adj.* violent ; rough ; stormy ; turbulent.

BOLAR (bo'lar), *adj.* pertaining to soft clay.

BOLAS (bo'las), *n. sing.* or *pl.* a hunting implement consisting of two or more balls of iron or stone attached to the ends of a leather cord.

BOLD (bold), *adj.* courageous ; venturesome ; planned or excuted with courage ; forward ; rude ; impudent ; over-stepping conventional rules ; striking to the eye ; steep ; abrupt ; prominent.

BOLE (bol), *n.* the trunk or stem of a tree ; a general term for friable clayey shale or clay, usually coloured by oxide of iron.

BOLERO (bo-ler'o), *n.* a lively Spanish dance ; the music accompanying such

a dance ; a short jacket without sleeves.

BOLL (bol), *n.* the pod or capsule of a plant.

BOLLARD (bol'ard), *n.* a strong post of wood or iron for securing hawsers.

BOLL WEEVIL (we'vl), an insect which infests the cotton plant.

BOLO (bo'lo), *n.* a large knife, used in the Philippines.

BOLOGNA SAUSAGE (bo-lo'nya saw'saj), a sausage of mixed meats, highly seasoned.

BOLOMETER (bo-lom'e-ter), *n.* an instrument for measuring minute quantities of radiant heat.

BOLSHEVIKI (bol-she-ve-ke', ve'ki), *n.pl.* the radical or extreme branch of the Social Democratic Party who became dominant in Russia in 1917.

BOLSTER (bol'ster), *n.* a long pillow or cushion used to support the head ; a pad to ease pressure ; a compress : *v.t.* to support with a pillow or cushion ; prop ; maintain ; or support [usually with *up*].

BOLT (bolt), *n.* a thunderbolt ; a stout metallic pin or rod used for holding objects together ; the portion of a lock shot or withdrawn by the key ; a roll or length of certain textile fabrics ; a refusal to support a nomination made by one's party, or withdrawal from one's party : *v.t.* to shoot ; discharge ; start or spring ; fasten or secure with a bolt ; swallow hurriedly or without chewing : *v.i.* depart with suddenness ; start and run off.

BOLT (bolt), *v.t.* to sift or separate the coarser from the finer particles.

BOLT-ROPE (bolt'rop), *n.* a rope to which the edges of sails are sewed.

BOLUS (bo'lus), *n.* a medicine in the form of a soft rounded mass, larger than an ordinary pill, to be swallowed at once.

BOMB (bom, bum), *n.* a hollow iron ball or shell filled with an explosive material.

BOMBARD (bom-bard'), *v.t.* to attack with cannon ; assail hotly ; fire questions at.

BOMBARDMENT (bom-bard'ment),

n. a continuous attack with shot and shell.

BOMBARDON (bom-bar′don), **BOMBARDONE** (-do′ne), *n.* a large-sized musical instrument of the trumpet class.

BOMBAST (bom′bast), *n.* cotton or other soft material used for stuffing garments; hence, high-sounding words; inflated language or style.

BOMBASTIC (-bas′tik), **BOMBASTICAL** (ti-kal), *adj.* inflated; high-sounding.

BOMBAZINE (bom-, bum-ba-zen′), *n.* a twilled fabric.

BOMBSHELL, same as bomb.

BONA FIDE (bo′na fi′de), genuine; in good faith.

BONA FIDES (fi′dez), good faith; honourable dealing.

BONANZA (bo-nan′za), *n.* a rich vein of ore.

BONBON (bong′bong), *n.* a sugar-plum; a Christmas cracker.

BONBONNIERE (bong-bo-nyar′), *n.* a small fancy dish for holding bonbons.

BOND (bond), *n.* anything that binds, fastens, or confines; a ligament : *pl.* fetters; imprisonment; duty; obligation; an instrument under seal by which a person binds himself, his heirs, etc., to do, or abstain from doing, a certain act; a promise to pay a certain sum on or before a specified date; a certificate, bearing interest, issued by a government, a corporation, or company, for the purpose of borrowing money; a unit of combining power equivalent to one atom of hydrogen : *v.t.* to put in bond or into a bonded warehouse, as dutiable goods; to bind together : *v.i.* to hold together, as by a bond.

BONDAGE (bond′aj), *n.* slavery; subjection.

BONE (bon), *n.* the ossified tissue forming the skeleton of most vertebrate animals; one of the parts or pieces of an animal skeleton.

BONE-BLACK (bon′blak), *n.* animal charcoal.

BONE-DRY (bon-dri), *n.* to signify non-use of intoxicants.

BONFIRE (bon′fir), *n.* any fire made in the open air to celebrate an event.

BONHOMIE (bon-o-me′), *n.* [French], good-heartedness.

BONIFACE (bon′i-fas), *n.* an inn-keeper.

BON MARCHE (bong marsha′), good market.

BON MOT (bong-mo′), *n.* [French], a witty saying.

BONNE (bon), *n.* a French nurse.

BONNET (bon′et), *n.* a woman's head-covering, varying according to fashion.

BONNIE, BONNY (bon′ni), *adj.* handsome; beautiful; pretty.

BON-TON (bong-tong′), *n.* the style of persons in high life.

BONUS (bo′nus), *n.* a sum given, or paid, over and above what is required; an additional dividend out of accumulated profits; a sum paid in addition to regular pay or wages.

BOO (boo), *interj.* an expression of aversion or contempt.

BOOBY (boo′bi), *n.* dunce; a stupid fellow.

BOODLE (bood′l), *n.* money paid for undue political influence; bribe money.

BOODLER (bood′ler), *n.* one who gives or accepts a bribe.

BOO-HOO (boo-hoo′), *v.i.* to cry noisily, like a baby.

BOOK (book), *n.* a collection of sheets of paper and other material, blank, written, or printed, bound together; a volume; a treatise; a division, section, or part of a literary composition; a register or record; the words of a play; the music of an opera; the Bible, or any of its divisions : *v.t.* to enter or register in a book; record; to secure or engage beforehand by registry or payment.

BOOKISH (book′ish), *adj.* given to reading.

BOOKKEEPER (-kep′er), *n.* one who keeps accounts.

BOOKKEEPING (book-kep-ing), *n.* the art of recording business transactions in a regular and systematic manner.

BOOKLET (book'let), *n.* a little book.

BOOKMAKER (book'mak-er), *n.* one who makes and publishes books; a compiler; one who bets against the success of a horse in a race, and enters his transactions in a book; a professional betting man.

BOOKMAN (book'man), *n.* a studious man; a scholar.

BOOKMUSLIN (book'muz-lin), *n.* a fine kind of transparent muslin.

BOOKWORM (book'werm), *n.* the larva or grub of various species of insects which infest and injure books; a person closely addicted to study.

BOOM (boom), *n.* a pole or spar run out to extend the foot of certain sails; a strong chain, cable, or line of spars bound together, extended across a river or harbour to exclude an enemy's ships; a deep, hollow sound; a rapid rise in price; a sudden burst of popular favour: *v.i.* to make a deep, hollow, reverberating sound; go off with a rush: *v.t.* to push with energy.

BOOMER (boom'er), *n.* one who starts or promotes a boom.

BOOMERANG (boom'er-ang), *n.* a missile weapon used by the Australian aborigines, consisting of a piece of flat, curved, hard wood, which, when thrown by the hand in a certain manner, describes a series of curves, and finally returns to the thrower; hence, any action which may recoil on its projector.

BOON (boon), *n.* prayer or petition; a benefit: *adj.* jovial; merry; convivial.

BOOR (boor), *n.* a rude, ill-mannered, clownish person.

BOORISH (boor'ish), *adj.* like a boor; clownish; awkward in manner; illiterate.

BOOST (boost), *v.t.* to lift by pushing from behind; to benefit: *v.i.* to be of avail: *n.* a lift.

BOOT (boot), *n.* a leather covering for the feet.

BOOTH (boo*th*), *n.* a temporary structure made of boards, canvas, etc.

BOOTJACK (-jak), *n.* a device for pulling off boots.

BOOTLEG (-leg), *v.t.* in the U.S. to sell intoxicating liquors in defiance of the law.

BOOTLEGGER (-er), *n.* one who bootlegs.

BOOTLESS ('les), *adv.* without advantage.

BOOT-TREE ('tre), *n.* a wooden form, placed in boots or shoes to keep their shape.

BOOTY (boo'ti), *n.pl.* spoil taken in war, plunder; pillage.

BOOZE, BOOSE (booz), *v.i.* to drink immoderately; tipple: *n.* liquor; drink; a carouse; spree.

BORACIC (bo-ras'ik), **BORIC** (bo'-rik), *adj.* pertaining to, or produced from, boron.

BORACIC ACID (as'id), *n.* a colourless, crystalline compound obtained by treating borax with an acid: also, called *boric acid.*

BORAX (bo'raks), *n.* a white, or colourless, crystalline salt.

BORDER (bor'der), *n.* the outer part or edge of anything; boundary; a narrow flower bed.

BORDERLAND (-land), *n.* land forming a border or frontier.

BORE (bor), *v.t.* to drill a hole in; form by piercing or drilling; weary by tedious repetition: *n.* the calibre or internal diameter of a hole; a person or thing that wearies by prolixity or dullness.

BOREAL (bo're-al), *adj.* northern; pertaining to the North.

BOREAS (bo're-as), *n.* the north wind.

BOREDOM (bor'dum), *n.* ennui; the realm of bores; bores collectively.

BORIDE (bo'rid), *n.* a compound of boron with a metallic base.

BORN (born), *p.adj.* innate; inherited.

BORON (bo'ron), *n.* a non-metallic element, occurring abundantly in borax.

BOROUGH (bur'o), *n.* a corporate town.

BORROW (bor'o), *v.t.* to obtain on loan; adopt; appropriate; copy.

BORT (bort), *n.* imperfect or inferior diamonds.

BOSCAGE, BOSKAGE (bos'kaj), *n.* ground covered with trees and shrubs.

BOSH (bosh), *n.* absurd or empty talk.

BOSKET (bos'ket), *n.* a grove; a thicket.

BOSKY (bos'ki), *adj.* woody; bushy.

BOSOM (boo'zum), *n.* the breast; something likened to a bosom, as a sustaining surface, inmost recess, etc.

BOSS (bos), *n.* a protuberant part; a stud or knob.

BOSS (bos), *n.* a foreman; leader; political dictator: *adj.* chief: *v.t.* to direct; manage.

BOTANIC (bo-tan'ik), **BOTANICAL** ('i-kal), *adj.* pertaining to botany.

BOTANIST (bot'a-nist), *n.* one who studies or is skilled in a knowledge of plants.

BOTANIZE (bot'a-niz), *v.i.* to seek after plants for the purpose of studying them.

BOTANY (bot'a-ni), *n.* the science which treats of plants.

BOT (bot), *n.* the larva of a botfly.

BOTCH (boch), *v.t.* to mend or patch in a clumsy manner.

BOTFLY (bot'fli), *n.* a dipterous insect.

BOTH (both), *adj. & pron.* the one and the other; the two; the pair without excepting either: *adv. & conj.* as well.

BOTHER (both'er), *v.t.* to annoy; tease; give trouble: *v.i.* to trouble one's self; be troublesome: *n.* worry; annoyance.

BOTHERATION (both-er-a'shun), *n.* the act of bothering.

BOTHERSOME (both'er-sum), *adj.* troublesome.

BOTTLE (bot'l), *n.* a hollow vessel, usually with a narrow neck, made of glass for holding liquids.

BOTTLE-NOSE (bot'l-noz), *n.* one of several species of cetaceans.

BOTTOM (bot'um), *n.* the deepest part of anything; the base; foundation.

BOTTOM LANDS (lanz), low lands, along river banks, formed by alluvial deposits.

BOUDOIR (boo'dwar), *n.* a small room, elegantly furnished.

BOUFFE (boof), *n.* opera-bouffe; comic opera.

BOUGH (bou), *n.* arm or branch of a tree.

BOUGHT, *p.t. & p.p.* of buy.

BOUILLON (bool-yong'), *n.* a clear soup produced from boiled meat.

BOULDER (bol'der), *n.* a large stone.

BOULEVARD (boo'le-vard), *n.* a broad street, planted with trees.

BOUNCE (bouns), *v.t.* to cause to bound; to eject summarily: *n.* a sudden bound or spring.

BOUND (bound), *n.* a limit; confine; extent; boundary: *pl.* territory within certain boundaries.

BOUND (bound), *v.i.* to jump or spring suddenly or in succession; leap; rebound: *n.* a leap; jump.

BOUND (bound), *adj.* ready to go; destined.

BOUND (bound), *p.adj.* made fast; confined; restrained; having a cover or binding.

BOUNDARY (boun'da-ri), *n.* the extent or limit of anything.

BOUNTEOUS (boun'te-us), *adj.* giving freely; liberal in gifts.

BOUNTIFUL (boun'ti-fool), *adj.* liberal in bestowing gifts; generous.

BOUNTY (boun'ti), *n.* liberality in bestowing gifts or favours.

BOUQUET (boo-ka'), *n.* a nosegay; a perfume or aroma.

BOURDON (boor'don), *n.* a baton; a cudgel.

BOURGEOIS (boor-zhwa'), *n.* a French citizen of the mercantile class; a shopkeeper; (ber-jois'), a size of type between long primer and brevier.

BOURN, BOURNE (born), *n.* a stream; destination; goal.

BOURSE (boors), *n.* a stock exchange for the transaction of business, especially the Bourse of Paris.

BOUT (bout), *n.* a turn or bend; as much as is performed at one time; a trial; round; contest.

BOUTONNIERE (boot-ton-nyar'), *n.* a bouquet worn in the buttonhole.

BOVINE (bo'vin), *adj.* of, or pertaining to, oxen.

BOW (bou), *n.* the forepart or prow of a ship.

BOW (bou), *v.t.* to bend; bend or incline, as the head or body in token of respect.

BOW (bo), *n.* a weapon for discharging arrows; an implement with which instruments of the violin kind are played: a looped ornamental knot of ribbon or other material.

BOWDLERIZE (bod'ler-iz), *v.t.* to expurgate, as an editor, everything deemed offensive or indelicate.

BOWEL (bou'el), *n.* one of the intestines of an animal.

BOWER (bou'er), *n.* a shelter of boughs; an arbor.

BOWER (bou'er), *n.* anchor carried at the bow of a ship; one of the two highest cards in euchre.

BOWERY (bou'er-i), *n.* a country retreat; farm.

BOWL (bol), *n.* a circular hollow vessel for holding liquids; an arena for games and contests.

BOWLINE (bo'lin), *n.* a rope fastened near the middle of a square-sail, to keep the ship near the wind.

BOWLING ALLEY (bo'ling al'i), *n.* a specially prepared court for the game of bowls.

BOWSE (bouz), *v.i.* to pull hard.

BOWSPRIT (bo'sprit), *n.* a large boom or spar running out from the stem of a ship or other vessel to carry its jib sails.

BOWSTRING (bo'string), *n.* string of a bow.

BOX (boks), *n.* an evergreen shrub or small tree, yielding a hard, close-grained wood.

BOX (boks), *n.* a case or receptacle for holding anything; a compartment in a theatre or other public place; a Christmas present; a small country house used by sportsmen.

BOX (boks), *n.* a blow on the head with the fist, or on the ear with the open hand.

BOXER (bok'ser), *n.* one who fights with his fists; one who puts things in boxes.

BOXING (-ing), *n.* an act of enclosing in a box; material used for boxes.

BOXING GLOVE (gluv), a padded glove.

BOX METAL (met'al), any alloy used for lining boxes in which pins, pivots, journals, etc., turn or revolve.

BOY (boi), *n.* a male child; a young lad.

BOYCOTT (boi'kot), *v.t.* to combine against a person, business or profession, as a means of punishment or intimidation.

BOYHOOD (boi'hood), *n.* state of being a boy.

BOYISH (boi'ish), *adj.* pertaining to a boy or boyhood.

BOY SCOUT (skout), one of a world-wide organization for the physical and moral development of boys.

BRACE (bras), *n.* a curved instrument for holding and turning boring tools; a rope reeved through a block, by which the yard is swung from the deck; a timber or scantling to strengthen the framework of a building.

BRACE-DRILL (bras'dril), *n.* a drill for boring metals.

BRACELET (bras'let), *n.* an ornamental band or ring for the wrist.

BRACHIAL (bra'ki-, brak'i-al), *adj.* pertaining to, or connected with, the arm.

BRACHIATE (bra'ki-, brak'i-at), *adj.* having branches in pairs.

BRACING (bras'ing), *p.adj.* imparting tone or vigour.

BRACKEN (brak'en), *n.* the brake fern.

BRACKET (brak'et), *n.* a supporting piece projecting from a wall; a single or jointed gas-pipe, burner, etc.; one of two marks [ ], used to enclose a word or note, or to indicate an interpolation; a brace.

BRACKISH (brak'ish), *adj.* saltish.

BRACT (brakt), *n.* a modified leaf growing from the flower stem, or enveloping a head of flowers.

BRACTEATE (brak'te-at), *adj.* furnished with bracts.

BRAD (brad), *n.* a slender, flat nail.

BRAE (bra), *n.* a hillside ; sloping ground.

BRAG (brag), *v.t.* to boast ; speak vaingloriously.

BRAGGADOCIO (brag-a-do′shi-o), *n.* empty boasting.

BRAGGART (brag′art), *n.* a boaster.

BRAGGER (brag′er), *n.* one who brags.

BRAHMA (bra′ma), *n.* one of useful variety of large domestic fowl.

BRAHMA (bra′ma), *n.* the chief god of the Hindu trinity.

BRAHMAN (bra′min), *n.* a member of the Hindu priestly caste.

BRAHMANISM, BRAHMINISM (bra′min-izm), *n.* the religion or doctrines of the Brahmans.

BRAHMANIST (bra′min-ist), *n.* an adherent of Brahmanism.

BRAID (brad), *v.t.* to weave or intertwine ; plait.

BRAIL (bral), *n.* a rope used to gather up the foot and leeches of a sail prior to furling.

BRAILLE (bral), *n.* a system of printing for the blind, by means of raised characters.

BRAIN (bran), *n.* the soft whitish convoluted mass occupying the cranium of a vertebrate ; intellectual power.

BRAIN FEVER (fe′ver), inflammation of the brain.

BRAIN STORM (storm), a temporary abnormal condition of the brain, presumably causing insanity while existing.

BRAINY (bran′i), *adj.* possessed of brain ; acute ; sharp-witted.

BRAISE (braz), *v.t.* to stew (as meat) in a covered vessel.

BRAIT (brat), *n.* a rough diamond.

BRAKE (brak), *n.* an instrument to break flax ; the handle of a pump ; a baker's kneading trough ; a sharp bit or snaffle ; a kind of wagonette ; a heavy harrow for breaking clods ; a mechanical device for checking the motion of a vehicle or machine.

BRAKE (brak), *n.* a place overgrown with bracken, brushwood, etc. ; the common fern.

BRAKE SHOE (shoo), that part of a brake which presses against the wheel.

BRAMBLE (bram′bl), *n.* the English blackberry ; any prickly bush or shrub.

BRAN (bran), *n.* husks of wheat, rye, etc., separated from the flour by bolting.

BRANCH (branch), *n.* a shoot or limb from a main bough ; an off-shoot ; any member or part of a body or system ; a department ; a section or subdivision : *v.i.* to ramify ; diverge ; spread diffusely [with *out*] : *v.t.* to divide.

BRANCHIÆ (brang′ki-e), *n.pl.* the respiratory organs of fishes ; gills.

BRANCHIAL (brang′ki-al), *adj.* pertaining to the branchiæ or gills.

BRAND (brand), *n.* a burning piece of wood ; any form of trade-mark.

BRANDISH (bran′dish), *v.t.* to move, wave, or shake, as a raised weapon.

BRAND-NEW (brand′nu), *adj.* quite new.

BRANDY (bran′di), *n.* an ardent alcoholic liquor.

BRANNY (bran′i), *adj.* having the appearance of bran.

BRANT-FOX (brant′foks), *n.* a variety of fox.

BRANT-GOOSE (brant′goos), *n.* the smallest species of the wild goose.

BRASH (brash), *adj.* brittle, as wood ; quick-tempered ; saucy.

BRASH (brash), *n.* broken, loose, and angular fragments of rock underlying alluvial deposits ; debris ; rubbish.

BRASH (brash), *n.* acidity of the stomach ; a short shower of rain.

BRASQUE (brask), *n.* a paste used for lining crucibles, etc.

BRASS (bras), *n.* an alloy of copper and zinc.

BRASSARD (bras′ard), *n.* an emblem denoting some particular distinction.

BRASSIE (bras′i), *n.* a stick or club used in the game of golf.

BRASSIERE (bras′er), *n.* a woman's under vest and support.

BRASSY (bras′i), *adj.* pertaining to,

or resembling, brass; impudent; brazen.

BRAVADO (bra-va'do), *n.* arrogant menace; defiance.

BRAVE (brav), *adj.* bold; courageous; intrepid; making a fine show: *n.* an Indian warrior.

BRAVERY (bra'ver-i), *n.* the quality of being brave.

BRAVO (bra'vo), *interj.* well done! good! *n.* a cheer.

BRAVURA (bra-voo'ra), *n.* an air of florid, brilliant style.

BRAWL (brawl), *v.i.* to quarrel noisily and outrageously.

BRAWN (brawn), *n.* boar's flesh; muscular strength.

BRAWNINESS (-nes), *n.* strength.

BRAWNY (brawn'ni), *adj.* muscular.

BRAXY (brak'si), *n.* a disease in sheep.

BRAY (bra), *v.t.* to pound or beat fine or small: *v.i.* to utter a loud, harsh cry, as the ass.

BRAZEN (bra'zn), *adj.* made of brass; pertaining to brass; impenetrable; impudent.

BRAZIER (bra'zher), *n.* an open pan for burning charcoal.

BRAZILIN (braz'i-lin), *n.* the colouring substance extracted from Brazil wood.

BRAZIL NUT (nut), the three-cornered seed of a palm.

BRAZIL WOOD (wood), a very heavy wood of a red colour from Brazil.

BREACH (brech), *n.* the act of breaking; the violation of a law, contract, or any other engagement; a gap; a difference; quarrel.

BREAD (bred), *n.* food made from ground grain.

BREADFRUIT (-froot), *n.* the fruit of a tree growing in the Pacific Islands.

BREADTH (bredth), *n.* the measure of any surface from side to side.

BREAK (brak), *v.t.* to separate; interrupt; fracture; weaken or destroy; disperse; violate.

BREAKAGE (brak'aj), *n.* the act of breaking.

BREAKDOWN (brak'doun), *n.* a collapse; failure; a noisy dance.

BREAKER (brak'er), *n.* one who, or

that which breaks; a wave broken against the shore, or a rock.

BREAKFAST (brek'fast), *n.* the first meal in the day.

BREAKNECK (brak'nek), *adj.* excessively speedy.

BREAKWATER ('waw-ter), *n.* any structure to break the force of the waves.

BREAST (brest), *n.* the fore part of the body between the neck and abdomen; the front of anything.

BREASTPLATE ('plat), *n.* armour covering the front of the body.

BREASTWORK ('werk), *n.* a hastily constructed work thrown up breast-high for defence.

BREATH (breth), *n.* the air inhaled and exhaled in respiration.

BREATHE (breth), *v.i.* to inhale air and expel it from the lungs.

BREATHING (bre'thing), *n.* respiration.

BREATHLESS (breth'les), *adj.* out of breath; panting.

BREECH (brech), *n.* the buttocks; the part of a cannon or other firearm behind the bore.

BREECHES (brich'ez), *n.pl.* trousers or pantaloons.

BREECHING (brich'ing), *n.* the harness which passes round a horse's breech.

BREED (bred), *v.t.* to procreate; hatch; produce; train; rear: *n.* progeny from the same stock.

BREEDING (-ing), *n.* training of the young; manners.

BREEZE (brez), *n.* a gadfly or horse-fly; a fresh soft wind.

BRENT (brent), *adj.* smooth; unwrinkled.

BRETHREN (breth'ren), *n.* brothers; members of a brotherhood.

BREVE (brev), *n.* a note of time equal to two semibreves or four minims; a mark (◡) used to indicate a short vowel.

BREVET (bre-vet'), *n.* a commission to an officer in the army conferring a higher rank; a patent; a warrant; a licence.

BREVIARY (bre'vi-a-ri), *n.* a book

containing the daily Roman Catholic offices and prayers.

BREVIER (bre-ver'), *n.* a size of type between bourgeois and minion.

BREVITY (brev'i-ti), *n.* shortness; conciseness.

BREW (broo), *v.t.* to make liquors from malt or other materials; plot.

BREWERY (broo'er-i), *n.* a brewhouse.

BREWING (-ing), *n.* the process of preparing malt, or fermented, liquors.

BRIAR (bri'er), *n.* a prickly bush of the rose family.

BRIAR-ROOT (-root), *n.* the root of the white heath.

BRIBE (brib), *n.* a gift in money given with the object of corrupting the conduct of the recipient.

BRIBERY (brib'er-i), *n.* the act or practice of bribing.

BRIC-A-BRAC (brik'a-brak), *n.* antique articles of vertu.

BRICK (brik), *n.* an oblong block of clay burned in a kiln.

BRICK-KILN (-kiln), *n.* a kiln or furnace in which bricks are baked.

BRIDAL (brid'al), *n.* a marriage.

BRIDE (brid), *n.* a woman newly-married, or about to be married.

BRIDEGROOM ('groom), *n.* a man newly-married, or about to be married.

BRIDESMAID (bridz'mad), *n.* a young un-married woman who attends on a bride.

BRIDEWELL (brid'wel), *n.* house of correction.

BRIDGE (brij), *n.* a structure of iron, stone, or wood, spanning a river, road, valley, etc.; an observation platform above the deck of a ship; the arch of the nose; a game of cards.

BRIDGING (brij'ing), *n.* a piece of wood between two beams.

BRIDLE (bri'dl), *n.* the headstall, bit, and reins by which a horse is controlled; a restraint: *v.t.* to control; guide.

BRIEF (bref), *adj.* short; concise; contracted; narrow: *n.* an epitome; an abridged statement of a case.

BRIER, same as briar.

BRIG (brig), *n.* a two-masted square-

rigged vessel; a place of confinement on a ship.

BRIGADE (bri-gad'), *n.* a subdivision of an army.

BRIGADIER (brig-a-der'), *n.* a general officer commanding a brigade, and ranking next below a major-general.

BRIGAND (brig'and), *n.* a robber; a bandit.

BRIGANDAGE (brig'an-daj), *n.* the practices of a brigand.

BRIGANTINE (brig'an-ten), *n.* a small two-masted vessel, square rigged like a brig.

BRIGHT (brit), *adj.* luminous; brilliant; shining; witty; clever; lively; alert.

BRIGHTEN (brit'n), *v.i.* to grow bright; clear up: *v.t.* to make gay or cheerful.

BRIGHT'S DISEASE (brits di-zez'), a form of kidney disease.

BRILLIANCY (bril'yan-si), *n.* splendour.

BRILLIANT (bril'yant), *adj.* sparkling; lustrous; glittering; distinguished: *n.* a cut diamond; the smallest size of type.

BRIM (brim), *n.* the edge of anything: *v.t.* to fill to the brim.

BRIMFUL (brim'fool), *adj.* overflowing.

BRIMSTONE (brim'ston), *n.* sulphur.

BRINDLE (brind'l), an animal of tawny colour.

BRINDLED ('d'ld), *adj.* tawny, with streaks or spots.

BRINE (brin), *n.* salt water; pickle; tears.

BRING (bring), *v.t.* to convey from another place; fetch; cause to come.

BRINK (bringk), *n.* the edge; verge.

BRINY (bri'ni), *adj.* very salt.

BRIOCHE (bri-osh'), *n.* a sweet roll made of eggs, flour and sugar, mixed with butter.

BRIOLETTE (bri-o-let'), *n.* a pear-shaped diamond.

BRIQUETTE (bri-ket'), *n.* coal-dust moulded into the shape of bricks.

BRISK (brisk), *adj.* lively; active.

BRISKET (bris'ket), *n.* that part of an animal's breast where the ribs join the breast-bone.

BRISTLE (bris'l), *n.* a short stiff, coarse hair, especially upon the back and sides of swine.

BRISTLY (bris'li), *adj.* covered with bristles.

BRISTOL BOARD (bris'tol bord), *n.* smooth, white pasteboard.

BRISTOL PAPER (pa'per), *n.* a kind of stout drawing paper.

BRISTOL STONE (ston), *n.* a transparent rock-crystal.

BRIT (brit), *n.* the young of the herring and sprat.

BRITANNIA METAL (bri-tan'i-a met'al), *n.* a white metal alloy of tin, copper, antimony, and bismuth.

BRITISH (brit'ish), *adj.* of, or pertaining to, Great Britain or its inhabitants.

BRITON (brit'un), *n.* a native of Great Britain.

BRITTLE (brit'l), *adj.* apt to break.

BROACH (broch), *n.* an awl ; spike : *v.t.* begin a discussion about.

BROAD (brawd), *adj.* wide ; ample ; vast ; liberal.

BROADCAST (-kast), *v.t.* in a radio, to send out from a central station ; communications to receivers located within range of the wave lengths.

BROADCLOTH ('kloth), *n.* a fine woollen cloth.

BROADEN (brawd'n), *v.t.* to grow broad.

BROADSIDE ('sid), *n.* the entire side of a ship ; a simultaneous volley from one side of a warship.

BROADSWORD ('sord), *n.* a cutting sword.

BROADTAIL (-tal), *n.* an Asiatic sheep.

BROCADE (bro-kad'), *n.* a silk stuff variegated with gold and silver flowers, etc.

BROCATEL, BROCATELLE (brok'a-tel), *n.* a beautifully variegated marble ; a figured fabric of silky texture.

BROCCOLI (brok'o-li), *n.* a variety of cabbage ; dwarf cauliflower.

BROCHURE (bro-shoor'), *n.* a pamphlet.

BROGUE (brog), *n.* a coarse, rough shoe ; a dialectic pronunciation.

BROIL (broil), *v.t.* to cook upon a gridiron : *n.* something broiled ; a noisy quarrel.

BROILER (-er), *n.* one who broils ; a device for broiling ; a chicken suitable for broiling.

BROKEN (bro'kn), *p.adj.* not entire ; in pieces.

BROKER (bro'ker), *n.* one who acts as agent for another.

BROKERAGE (bro'ker-aj), *n.* the business of a broker ; his fee or commission.

BROMA (bro'ma), *n.* ailment ; a light preparation of cocoa or chocolate.

BROMAL (bro'mal), *n.* a colourless, oily fluid obtained by the action of bromine on alcohol.

BROMATE (bro'mat), *n.* a salt of bromic acid.

BROMIC ACID (bro'mik as'id), a compound of bromine and oxygen.

BROMIDE (bro'mid, 'mid), *n.* a compound of bromine ; a sensitized paper used in photography.

BROMIDE OF POTASSIUM (po-tas'i-um), a compound of bromine.

BROMINE (bro'min, 'min), *n.* a non-metallic cement related to chlorine and iodine.

BROMIZE (bro'miz), *v.t.* to prepare or treat with a bromide.

BROMOGELATIN (bro-mo-jel'a-tin), *adj.* denoting a process of preparing dry plates with an emulsion of bromides, nitrate of silver, and gelatin.

BRONCHIA (brong'ki-a), *n.pl.* the bronchial tubes.

BRONCHITIC (brong-kit'ik), *adj.* of or pertaining to bronchitis.

BRONCHITIS (brong-ki'tis), *n.* an inflammation, acute or chronic, of the mucous lining of the bronchial tubes.

BRONCHUS (brong'kus), *n.* [*pl.* bronchi ('ki)], one of the two principal branches of the windpipe or trachea.

BRONCO (brong'ko), *n.* an unbroken horse of the south-western plains.

BRONCO-BUSTING (brong'ko-bus'ting), *n.* breaking broncos to the saddle.

BRONTOGRAPH (bron'to-graf), *n.* an apparatus to record sound waves.

BRONTOMETER (bron-tom'e-ter), *n.* an instrument for recording the effects of a thunderstorm.

BRONTOSAURUS (bron'to-saw'-rus), *n.* a huge prehistoric dinosaur.

BRONZE (bronz), *n.* an alloy of copper and tin, to which other metallic substances are sometimes added.

BRONZE AGE (aj), *n.* the age succeeding the Stone Age.

BRONZE-STEEL (bronz'stel), *n.* an alloy of copper, tin and iron.

BROOCH (broch), *n.* an ornamental dress-clasp.

BROOD (brood), *n.* offspring; a hatch: *v.i.* linger over sorrowfully (with *on* or *over*).

BROODER (-er), *n.* a room or enclosure, used for raising fowl.

BROOK (brook), *n.* a small stream.

BROOK (brook), *v.t.* to bear; put up with.

BROOM (broom), *n.* a shrub, bearing large yellow flowers; a brush.

BROTH (broth), *n.* a kind of soup.

BROTHER (bru*th*'er), *n.* a male having the same father and mother.

BROTHERHOOD (bru*th*'er-hood), *n.* state or quality of being a brother; a fraternity.

BROTHER-IN-LAW (-in-law), *n.* the brother of one's husband or wife.

BROTHER JONATHAN (jon'a-than), a personification of the people of the U.S. collectively.

BROTHERLY (bru*th*'er-li), *adj.* as becomes a brother; affectionate.

BROUGHAM (broo'am), *n.* a kind of closed carriage.

BROUGHT, *p.t.* & *p.p.* of bring.

BROW (brou), *n.* the arch of hair over the eye; the forehead; top of a hill.

BROWBEAT (brou'bet), *v.t.* to depress or bully.

BROWN (broun), *n.* a dark colour, inclined to red or yellow.

BROWNIE (brou'ni), *n.* [Scotch], a beneficent spirit supposed to haunt old farmhouses.

BROWSE (brouz), *n.* the shoots of shrubs and trees. *v.t.* pasture on; graze.

BRUIN (broo'in), *n.* the brown bear.

BRUISE (brooz), *n.* an injury caused by a blow.

BRUIT (broot), *n.* report; rumour.

BRUMAL (broo'mal), *adj.* pertaining to winter; foggy; misty.

BRUNETTE (broo-net'), *n.* a woman or girl with dark hair and eyes.

BRUNT (brunt), *n.* a violent shock.

BRUSH (brush), *n.* a thicket; an instrument composed of bristles, etc.; the tail of a fox; a slight encounter.

BRUSHWOOD (brush'wood), *n.* a thicket; small wood, suitable for the fire.

BRUSQUE (brusk), *adj.* abrupt in manner.

BRUSSELS CARPET (brus'elz kar'-pet), *n.* a strong kind of woollen carpet.

BRUSSELS LACE (las), various kinds of lace.

BRUSSELS SPROUTS (sproutz), *n. pl.* a variety of cabbage.

BRUT (broot), *adj.* raw; crude.

BRUTAL (broo'tal), *adj.* pertaining to a brute; savage; cruel.

BRUTALITY (broo-tal'i-ti), *n.* the quality of being brutal; pitiless cruelty.

BRUTALIZE (broo'tal-iz), *v.t.* to make brutal.

BRUTALLY (broo'tal-i), *adv.* in a brutal manner.

BRUTE (broot), *adj.* without reason or intelligence; rough; brutal: *n.* a beast.

BRUTISH (broot'ish), *adj.* pertaining to, or resembling, a brute.

BUBBLE (bub'l), *n.* a small bladder of fluid filled with air or gas; anything unreal or unsubstantial.

BUBO (bu'bo), *n.* an inflammatory swelling in the groin or armpit.

BUBONIC PLAGUE (bu-bon'ik plag), a malignant, infectious epidemic disease.

BUCCAL (buk'al), *adj.* pertaining to the cheek.

BUCCANEER (buk-a-ner'), *n.* a pirate; a sea-robber.

BUCCINATOR (buk'si-na-ter), *n.* a muscle of the cheek.

BUCK (buk), *n.* lye in which raw yarn is steeped for bleaching.

BUCK (buk), *n.* the male of the deer, hare, rabbit; also applied to the male of other animals.

BUCK (buk), *n.* the act of bucking, as of a bronco : *v.t.* to butt; to run against; to break up ores.

BUCK (buk), *n.* a frame on which to saw wood; a saw-buck.

BUCKBOARD (buk'boord), *n.* a light vehicle which has a long elastic board resting directly on the bolsters, and on which the seat is placed.

BUCKET (buk'et), *n.* a vessel for holding water.

BUCKET SHOP (shop), an office for gambling in stocks, etc.

BUCKEYE ('i), *n.* the American horse-chestnut.

BUCKEYE STATE (stat), Ohio.

BUCKHOUND ('hound), *n.* a stag-hound.

BUCKJUMPER ('jump'er), *n.* a vicious untrained horse.

BUCKLE (buk'l), *n.* a metal clasp; a bend or kink, as in a blade : *v.t.* to fasten with a buckle; twist; bend; confine.

BUCKLED (buk'ld), *adj.* warped; bent.

BUCKLER (buk'ler), *n.* a printing press device that turns back the edges of paper sheets.

BUCKRAM (buk'ram), *n.* coarse linen cloth stiffened with dressing.

BUCKSHOT ('shot), *n.* shot of a large size.

BUCKWHEAT ('hwet), *n.* a plant cultivated for its seeds, which are ground into meal.

BUCOLIC (bu-kol'ik), *adj.* pastoral : *n.* a pastoral poem.

BUD (bud), *v.t.* to graft : *v.i.* to put forth or produce buds; begin to grow : *n.* the rudimentary, undeveloped stage of a branch, leaf, or flower.

BUDDHA (bood'a), *n.* founder of the Buddhists.

BUDDHISM (bood'ism), *n.* the re-ligious system founded by Buddha in 6th century B.C.

BUDDHIST (bood'ist), *n.* one who accepts the doctrines of Buddhism.

BUDDY (bud'i), *n.* a chum; a U.S. soldier.

BUDGE (buj), *v.i.* to move from one's position : *v.t.* change the position of.

BUDGE (buj), *n.* lambskin dressed with the wool outwards.

BUDGET (buj'et), *n.* a stock or store; a statement showing the financial state of any governing body.

BUFF (buf), *n.* a thick leather prepared from the skin of the buffalo, ox, etc.; a wheel covered with leather or cloth, used in polishing; a light yellow : *adj.* buff-coloured : *v.t.* to polish with a buff; to colour or stain buff.

BUFFALO (buf'a-lo), *n.* ruminant mammal; the North American bison.

BUFFER (buf'er), *n.* any contrivance which serves to deaden concussion.

BUFFER (buf'er), *n.* one who polishes with a buff; a buffing wheel.

BUFFET (buf'et), *n.* a blow with the hand; violence of waves.

BUFFET (buf'et, boo-fa'), *n.* a side-board; a counter for refreshments.

BUFFING (buf'ing), *n.* the process of polishing with a buff.

BUFFOON (bu-foon'), *n.* one who amuses by jests, antics, odd gestures, etc.

BUFFOONERY ('er-i), *n.* the arts and practices of a buffoon.

BUFO (bu'fo), *n.* a genus of toads.

BUG (bug), *n.* any insect of the order Hemiptera.

BUGABOO (bug'a-boo), *n.* a bugbear.

BUGBEAR (bug'bar), *n.* a frightful object of the imagination.

BUGGY (bug'i), *n.* a light four-wheeled carriage.

BUGLE (bu'gl), *n.* hunting horn; a military wind-instrument.

BUHL (bool), *n.* decorative inlaying for cabinet work.

BUILD (bild), *v.t.* to construct; erect, as a house; form by art; raise any-thing on a support or foundation; establish.

BUILDING (bild'ing), *n.* the act of

constructing, raising, or establishing ; an edifice.

BULB (bulb), *n.* an onion-shaped root ; a kind of leaf bud ; a radio tube.

BULBOUS (bul'bus), *adj.* pertaining to or resembling a bulb.

BULGE (bulj), *n.* the widest part of a cask ; a bending outwards.

BULK (bulk), *n.* magnitude or size ; the main mass or body.

BULK-HEAD (-hed), *n.* a partition in a vessel which separates one part of it from another ; an embankment to hold back earth.

BULKY (bul'ki), *adj.* of great size or bulk.

BULL (bool), *n.* the male of any bovine mammal ; one who endeavours to raise the price of stock.

BULL (bool), *n.* Papal letter.

BULL (bool), *n.* a blunder in speech or writing.

BULLDOG ('dog), *n.* a variety of dog of strong muscular build.

BULLDOZE ('doz), *v.t.* to bully ; to attempt to intimidate.

BULLET ('et), *n.* a small projectile.

BULLETIN (bool'e-tin), *n.* an official report regarding some matter or event of public interest.

BULLFROG ('frog), *n.* a large North American species of frog.

BULLHEAD ('hed), *n.* see catfish.

BULLION (bool'yun), *n.* uncoined gold or silver ; foreign coin.

BULL MOOSE (moos), *n.* a follower of Theodore Roosevelt in the campaign of 1912.

BULLOCK (bool'ok), *n.* an ox ; a full-grown steer.

BULL'S-EYE (boolz'i), *n.* a boss of glass ; a lantern with a convex lens ; the centre of a target.

BULL TERRIER (ter'i-er), a cross breed of bulldog and terrier.

BULLY (bool'i), *n.* one who domineers by insolence or threats.

BULLY (bool'i), *adj.* good ; fine : *interj.* well done ! bravo !—an exclamation of satisfaction.

BULLYRAG (bool'i-rag), *v.t.* to intimidate by bluster and threat.

BULRUSH (bool'rush), *n.* a rush-like aquatic plant ; the cat-tail.

BULWARK (bool'werk), *n.* a rampart ; a fortification ; the boarding round the sides of a ship.

BUMBLEBEE (bum'bl-be), *n.* a large bee.

BUMBOAT (bum'bot), *n.* a boat used for the conveyance of provisions, fruit, etc., for sale to vessels.

BUMP (bump), *n.* a shock from a blow ; a swelling protuberance.

BUMPER (bum'per), *n.* something that bumps ; a buffer on a railroad car.

BUMPKIN (bump'kin), *n.* an awkward, clumsy rustic.

BUMPTIOUS (bump'shus), *adj.* self-assertive.

BUN (bun), *n.* a small light cake.

BUNCH (bunch), *n.* a cluster ; a collection of things of the same kind.

BUNCO (bung'ko), *n.* a confidence game.

BUNCOMBE or **BUNKUM** (bung'kum), *n.* idle or showy speech.

BUNCO-STEERER (-ster'er), *n.* one who entices the gullible or unwary into a swindle.

BUNDLE (bun'dl), *n.* a number of things bound together ; a roll or package.

BUNG (bung), *n.* a large cork for stopping a hole in a cask.

BUNGALOW (bung'ga-lo), *n.* a single-storeyed house.

BUNGLE (bung'gl), *v.i.* to botch ; manage awkwardly.

BUNION (bun'yun), *n.* a swelling on the foot.

BUNK (bungk), *n.* a box or recess serving for a sleeping-berth in a vessel, sleeping-car, etc. : *v.i.* to sleep in a bunk.

BUNK (bungk), *n.* [Slang], misleading speech ; humbug.

BUNKER (bung'ker), *n.* a large bin or receptacle ; a sandhole on golf links.

BUNKIE (bung'ki), *n.* a soldier who shares a shelter with another.

BUNNY (bun'i), *n.* a pet rabbit.

BUNSEN BURNER (bun'sen bern'er), a gas tube, with holes at the bottom to admit air : when lighted, the mixture of air and gas gives an intensely hot flame.

BUNT (bunt), *n*. a species of fungus.

BUNTING (bunt'ing), *n*. a bird; a woollen stuff used for making flags; flags collectively.

BUOY (boi), *n*. a floating body to indicate the position of channel or obstruction; a lifebuoy.

BUOYANCY (boi'an-si), *n*. relative lightness; elasticity of spirits.

BUOYANT (boi'ant), *adj*. having the quality of floating in a fluid; not easily depressed.

BUR, BURR (ber), *n*. the rough prickly seed-case of certain plants; the rough ridges of metal.

BURDEN (ber dn), *n*. that which is borne or carried; a load.

BURDOCK (ber'dok), *n*. a large wayside weed.

BUREAU (bu'ro), *n*. a desk or cabinet furnished with drawers; an office; a governmental department.

BUREAUCRACY (bu-ro'kra-si), *n*. the system of centralized government.

BUREAUCRAT (bu'ro-krat), *n*. an advocate or supporter of bureaucracy.

BURG (berg), *n*. a borough.

BURGEE (ber'je), *n*. a flag, used on yachts and vessels.

BURGEON (ber'jun), *v.i.* to put forth buds.

BURGESS (ber'jes), *n*. a citizen or freeman of a borough.

BURGHER (ber'ger), *n*. a citizen or freeman of a burg or borough.

BURGLAR (ber'gler), *n*. one who breaks into a house with intent to commit a felony.

BURGLARIOUS (ber-gla'ri-us), *adj*. pertaining to, or constituting, burglary.

BURGLARY (ber'gla-ri), *n*. the act or crime of breaking u.to a house with intent to commit a felony.

BURGUNDY (ber'gun-di), *n*. a wine.

BURGUNDY PITCH (-pitch), spruce-fir resin.

BURIAL (ber'i-al), *n*. the act of burying.

BURIN (bu'rin), *n*. a cutting tool.

BURL (berl), *n*. a small knot or lump in thread or cloth; a knot in wood.

BURLAP (ber'lap), *n*. a coarse fabric made of jute, hemp, etc.

BURLESQUE (ber-lesk'), *adj*. tending to excite laughter by extravagant contrast or caricature.

BURLETTA (ber-let'a), *n*. a comic opera; a musical farce.

BURLY (ber'li), *adj*. bulky; large; corpulent.

BURN (bern), *v.t.* to consume or injure with fire; reduce to ashes; scorch; affect with a burning sensation; cauterize: *v.i.* to be on fire.

BURN (bern), *n*. a rivulet; a brook.

BURNER (ber'ner), *n*. one who burns or sets fire to anything; the part of a lamp or gas fixture from which the flame issues.

BURNING (ber'ning), *p.adj*. fiery; hot; consuming.

BURNING GLASS (glas), a double convex lens used for concentrating sun-rays.

BURNISH (ber'nish), *v.t.* polish by friction: *n*. polish; gloss; brightness.

BURNT OFFERING (of'er-ing), something offered and burnt upon an altar as a sacrifice.

BURRO (bur'o), *n*. a small donkey used as a pack-animal.

BURROW (bur'o), *n*. a hole in the ground: *v.i.* to exacavate; work a way into or under something.

BURRY (bur'i), *adj*. full of burs.

BURSA (ber'sa), *n*. a sac or sack-like cavity.

BURSAR (ber'ser), *n*. the treasurer of a college.

BURSARY (ber'ser-i), *n*. the treasury of a college or monastery.

BURST (berst), *v.i.* to rend or break open with violence; yield to force or pressure; explode; give way under grief or pain.

BURSTING (berst'ing), *p.adj*. ready to burst; at the point of breaking out.

BURUCHA (boo-ruch'a), *n*. crude rubber; hardened sap of the rubber tree.

BURY (ber'i), *n*. a manor-house; a borough.

BURY (ber'i), *v.t.* to deposit and cover in a grave or tomb, or in any final resting-place; entomb; keep secret; hide.

BURYING (ber'i-ing), *n.* burial.

BUS (bus), *n.* a shortened form of omnibus.

BUS BOY (boi), a waiter's assistant.

BUSH (boosh), *n.* a thick shrub; a forest region.

BUSH (boosh), *n.* a lining or tube of hard metal inserted in an orifice, to reduce friction.

BUSHEL (boosh'el), *n.* a dry measure containing eight gallons or four pecks.

BUSH HARROW (har'o), a harrow formed of bushes tied to a frame.

BUSHINESS ('i-nes), *n.* the quality of being bushy.

BUSHMAN (boosh'man), *n.* one of a race of nomadic aborigines of South Africa.

BUSHRANGER (boosh'ranj-er), *n.* one who leads a predatory life in the bush country.

BUSHWHACKER (boosh'hwak-er), *n.* a backwoodsman.

BUSHY (boosh'i), *adj.* thick and spreading like a bush.

BUSILY (biz'i-li), *adv.* in a busy manner.

BUSINESS (biz'nes), *n.* employment; trade; profession; something to be transacted.

BUSKIN (bus'kin), *n.* kind of half-boot or high shoe.

BUSS (bus), *n.* a small two-masted vessel used in herring fishing.

BUST (bust), *n.* the chest or thorax; the head, shoulders, and breast of a person.

BUSTLE (bus'l), *v.i.* to be busy, with a certain amount of noise; move quickly.

BUSY (biz'i), *adj.* earnestly or closely employed; bustling; diligent.

BUSYBODY (biz'i-bod-i), *n.* a meddling, officious person.

BUT (but), *conj.* except; excluding the fact; on the contrary; nevertheless; however; though; notwithstanding; even if; that.

BUTCHER (booch'er), *n.* one who slaughters animals for food.

BUTCHERY (booch'er-i), *n.* the business of slaughtering cattle.

BUTLER (but'ler), *n.* a manservant.

BUTT (but), *n.* a push or thrust delivered by the head of an animal.

BUTT (but), *n.* a large cask.

BUTTE (but), *n.* an abrupt hill or ridge.

BUTTER (but'er), *n.* a smooth, oily substance obtained from cream or milk by churning.

BUTTERCUP (-kup), *n.* a plant bearing yellow cup-shaped flowers.

BUTTER-FISH (-fish), *n.* a food fish of eastern U.S.

BUTTERFLY (-fli), *n.* one of a species of diurnal lepidopterous insects.

BUTTERINE (-in), *n.* an imitation butter.

BUTTERMILK (-milk), *n.* whey separated from the cream in butter-making.

BUTTERNUT (-nut), *n.* the fruit of a North American tree.

BUTTER-SCOTCH (-skoch), *n.* a candy.

BUTTERY (but'er-i), *n.* an apartment in which provisions, etc., are kept.

BUTTING (but'ing), *n.* an abuttal; a boundary.

BUTTOCK (but'ok), *n.* the rump or protuberant hinder part of a man or animal.

BUTTON (but'n), *n.* any small rounded object used to secure different parts of a garment, etc.

BUTTONHOLE (but'n-hol), *n.* a slit to receive and hold a button.

BUTTRESS (but'res), *n.* masonry or brickwork built on a wall to afford support.

BUXOM (buk'som), *adj.* cheerful; jolly; robust; plump and comely.

BUY (bi), *v.t.* to acquire by paying a price; purchase.

BUYER'S OPTION (bi'erz op'shun), a purchaser's privilege of taking an agreed amount of stock within a certain period.

BUZZ (buz), *n.* a continuous humming noise, as of bees; a confused murmur, as of many voices.

BUZZARD (buz'ard), *n.* the name of several species of hawks.

BUZZER (buz'er), *n.* an electric push-button.

BUZZ-SAW (-saw), *n.* a circular saw.

BY (bi), *prep.* beside; near; close to; towards; along; over; through; in the course of; after; past; to the amount of.

BY ALL MEANS, assuredly.

BYE (bi), *adj.* aside, in reference to position, direction, or purpose; *interj.* a hushing or soothing word for infants.

BY-LAW (-law), *n.* a law or statute framed by a corporate body.

BY-PRODUCT (bi'prod-ukt), *n.* a secondary product resulting from the manufacture of the main product.

BYROAD (-rod), *n.* a side road.

BYSTANDER ('stan-der), *n.* one present but not taking part.

BYWORD (bi-werd), *n.* a proverb; nickname; an object of derision.

BYZANTINE (biz-an'tin), *adj.* of, or pertaining to Byzantium (Constantinople), the ancient capital of the Eastern Roman Empire.

C

C (se), *n.* the third letter of the English alphabet.

C, c, an abbreviation.

C, a Roman numeral denoting 100; with a bar (c̄), 100,000.

C MAJOR (ma'jer), the scale in music having C as the keynote.

C MINOR (mi'ner), the scale in music having a signature of three flats.

CAB (kab), *n.* a public carriage; the shelter for the driver of a locomotive.

CABAL (ka-bal'), *n.* a secret combination; an intrigue: *v.i.* to plot or intrigue.

CABALISM (kab'a-lizm), *n.* occult doctrine.

CABALLERO (ka-bal-ya'ro), *n.* a Spanish gentleman; a Spanish dance.

CABARET (kab'a-ret), *n.* a place of refreshment and dancing.

CABBAGE (kab'aj), *n.* a vegetable: *v.t.* to appropriate to one's own use.

CABIN (kab'in), *n.* a small hut, cottage, or room; a room in a ship for officers or passengers.

CABIN-BOY (kab'in-boi), *n.* a general utility boy on shipboard.

CABINET (kab'in-et), *n.* a piece of furniture to hold objects of vertu, etc.; a photograph; a body of advisers to the executive of a nation.

CABINET FINISH (fin'ish), in carpentry, a finish given to woods.

CABINETMAKER (-ma'ker), *n.* an artisan who turns out fine woodwork.

CABLE (ka'bl), *n.* large strong rope or chain; submarine telegraph line; measure of distance = 100 to 140 fathoms: *v.t.* to fasten with a cable; transmit by telegraph cable.

CABLEGRAM (ka'bl-gram), *n.* a message sent by a submarine cable.

CABOOSE (ka-boos'), *n.* a ship's galley or kitchen; the trainmen's car attached to a freight train.

CABRIOLET (kab-ri-o-la'), *n.* a covered carriage.

CACANTHRAX (ka-kan'thraks), *n.* a malignant disease that infects cattle.

CACAO (ka-ka'o), *n.* a small evergreen tree of tropical America, from the seeds of which cocoa and chocolate are prepared.

CACHALOT (kash'a-lot), *n.* the sperm whale.

CACHE (kash), *n.* a place of concealment for food for future use.

CACHINNATION (kak-i-na'shun), *n.* loud or unrestrained laughter.

CACHOLONG (kash'o-long), *n.* a greyish-white variety of opal.

CACHOU (ka-shoo'), *n.* a pill for sweetening the breath.

CACIQUE (ka-sek'), *n.* an oriole.

CACKLE (kak'l), *v.i.* to cry like a hen; giggle; prattle.

CACOGRAPHY (ka-kog'ra-fi), *n.* erroneous spelling; cramped, indistinct writing.

CACTUS (kak'tus), *n.* [*pl.* cacti ('ti)] a spiny, fleshy plant with showy flowers.

CAD (kad), *n.* a vulgar, ill-bred fellow.

CADAVER (ka-da'ver), *n.* a dead body.

CADAVEROUS (ka-dav'er-us), *adj.* pale ; ghastly.

CADDIE (kad'i), *n.* a lad who carries golf clubs.

CADDIS (kad'is), *n.* a kind of coarse woollen stuff.

CADDIS FLY (fli), an insect, the larvæ of which are called caddis worms.

CADDY (kad'i), *n.* a small box for tea.

CADENCE (ka'dens), *n.* modulation of the voice.

CADENZA (ka-den'za), *n.* a vocal or instrumental flourish.

CADET (ka-det'), *n.* a younger son ; student in a naval or military academy.

CADGE (kaj), *v.t.* & *v.i.* to hawk ; sponge on.

CADGER (-er), *n.* a hawker ; one who lives by trickery.

CADI (ka'di), *n.* a Mohammedan judge.

CADMEAN (kad-me'an), *adj.* of or belonging to Cadmus ; Theban.

CADMEAN VICTORY (vik'to-ri), a victory as fatal to those who win as to those who lose.

CADMIUM (kad'mi-um), *n.* a bluish-white ductile metal.

CADRE (ka'dr), *n.* a framework ; a skeleton.

CÆCUM (se'kum), *n.* [*pl.* cæca ('ka)], the blind gut.

CÆSARIAN (se-za're-an), *adj.* pertaining to Cæsar ; imperial.

CÆSARIAN OPERATION (op-er-a'shun), *n.* a delivery of a fœtus by cutting through the walls of the abdomen.

CÆSARISM (se'zar-izm), *n.* imperialism ; absolute rule of government.

CAFE (ka-fa'), *n.* a restaurant ; coffee.

CAFETERIA (kaf-e-te'ri-a), *n.* a cafe for self-service.

CAFFEINE (kaf'e-in), *n.* a bitter alkaloid extracted from coffee.

CAGE (kaj), *n.* a box or enclosure furnished with metal bars for confining birds or animals.

CAIRN (karn), *n.* a heap of stones erected as a monument.

CAIRNGORM (karn'gorm), *n.* a yellow or brown variety of quartz.

CAISSON (ka'sun), *n.* an ammunition-wagon or chest ; a water-tight box or casing used for building structures in water ; a structure for raising sunken vessels.

CAISSON DISEASE (di-zez'), a disease caused by high atmospheric pressure of a caisson called *the bends.*

CAITIFF (ka'tif), *n.* a despicable or cowardly wretch.

CAJOLE (ka-jol'), *v.t.* to coax or deceive.

CAKE (kak), *n.* a small mass of dough, sweetened and baked.

CAKEWALK (kak'wawk), *n.* a grotesque dance or parade.

CALABASH (kal'a-bash), *n.* the fruit of the calabash tree, used as a vessel for liquids, etc.

CALABASH TREE (tre), a tree of the bigonia family.

CALABOOSE (kal-a-boos'), *n.* a jail ; a lock-up.

CALAMITOUS (ka-lam'i-tus), *adj.* producing, or resulting from calamity.

CALAMITY (ka-lam'i-..), *n.* any cause that produces evil, disaster.

CALCAREOUS (kal-kar'e-us), *adj.* of the nature of, or containing, lime.

CALCIFEROUS (kal-sif'er-us), *adj.* yielding calcium carbonate.

CALCIFY (kal'si-fi), *v.t.* to convert into lime.

CALCIMINE (kal'si-min), *n.* white or tinted wash for walls or ceilings.

CALCINATION (kal-si-na'shun), *n.* the process of reducing to powder by heat.

CALCINE (kal-sin'), *v.t.* to reduce a substance to powder by heat.

CALCITE (kal'sit), *n.* crystallized carbonate of lime.

CALCIUM (kal'si-um), *n.* the metallic base of lime.

CALCIUM CARBIDE (kar'bid), a compound of quick-lime and carbon.

CALCIUM CARBONATE (kar'bon-at), a white amorphous powder.

CALCIUM LIGHT (lit), a very strong light.

CALCOGRAPHY (kal-kog'ra-fi), *n.* the art of drawing with coloured chalks.

CALCULARY (kal'ku-la-ri), *adj.* pertaining to, or of the nature of, calculi.

CALCULATE (kal'ku-lat), *v.t.* to compute; ascertain or determine by any process of reasoning.

CALCULATION (kal-ku-la'shun), *n.* the art of reckoning by numbers; something deduced by reasoning or inference.

CALCULATOR (kal'ku-la-ter), *n.* one who computes; a machine used for reckoning.

CALCULOUS (kal'ku-lus), *adj.* stony; gritty.

CALCULUS (kal'ku-lus), *n.* [*pl.* calculi (-li)], a stony concretion in the body; a method of computation by algebraic symbols.

CALDRON, CAULDRON (kol'drun), *n.* a large kettle or boiler.

CALENDAR (kal'en-dar), *n.* a register of the days, weeks and months of the year, etc.; a register or list; a list of causes arranged for trial.

CALENDAR MONTH (munth), *n.* a solar month reckoned according to the calendar.

CALENDER (kal'en-der), *n.* a machine consisting of heated rollers, used for smoothing and glazing paper or cloth.

CALENDS (kal'endz), *n.pl.* in the Old Roman calendar.

CALESCENT (ka-les'ent), *adj.* increasing in temperature.

CALF (kaf), *n.* a young bovine quadruped; the young of certain marine mammalia; leather made from the skin of a calf; the thick, fleshy part of the leg.

CALIBER, CALIBRE (kal'i-ber), *n.* the diameter of a cylindrical body; mental capacity.

CALIBRATE (kal'i-brat), *v.t.* to graduate a thermometer, etc.

CALICO (kal'i-ko), *n.* cotton print.

CALIPERS (kal'i-perz), *n.pl.* compasses or measuring diameters.

CALIPH, CALIF (ka'lif), *n.* a title of the successors of Mohammed.

CALISTHENIC (kal-is-then'ik), *adj.* pertaining to calisthenics.

CALISTHENICS, CALLISTHENICS (kal-is-then'iks), *n.pl.* the art of promoting health by physical exercise.

CALK, CAULK (kawk), *v.t.* to drive oakum into the seams of (a ship).

CALK (kawk), *n.* part of a horseshoe.

CALL (kawl), *v.t.* to summon from, or invite to, any place : *n.* a summons or invitation; a demand for payment due on shares.

CALLA (kal'a), *n.* a plant with a fleshy, yellowish spadix and producing a flower in the spathe; the calla-lily.

CALLIGRAPH (kal'i-graf), *n.* a specimen of elegant penmanship.

CALLIGRAPHER (kal-lig'ra-fer), **CALLIGRAPHIST** (-fist), *n.* one skilled in handwriting.

CALLING (kawl'ing), *n.* the act of summoning; a summons or invitation; a vocation.

CALLIOPE (kal-li'o-pe), *n.* an organ with steam-whistles.

CALLOSITY (kal-os'i-ti), *n.* the state or quality of being hardened; a callus.

CALLOUS (kal'us), *adj.* hardened; insensible.

CALLOW (kal'o), *adj.* unfledged; inexperienced.

CALLUS (kal'us), *n.* [*pl.* calli (-i)], the hardening of skin from pressure.

CALM (kam), *adj.* tranquil; still; undisturbed.

CALOMEL (kal'o-mel), *n.* mercurous chloride.

CALORIC (ka-lor'ik), *n.* the principle of heat.

CALORIE, CALORY (kal'o-ri), *n.* the unit of heat (metric system) to express the amount of heat required to raise one kilogram of water from 0° to 1° centigrade.

CALORIFIC (kal-o-rif'ik), *adj.* heating.

CALORIFICATION (ka-lor-i-fi-ka'shun), *n.* the production of heat.

CALORIFIC RAYS (raz), the invisible rays emanating from the sun and heated bodies.

CALORIMETER (kal-o-rim'e-ter), *n.* an apparatus for measuring heat.

CALOTTE (ka-lot'), *n.* a skull-cap.

CALUMET (kal'u-met), *n.* the tobacco-pipe of the North American

Indians, smoked as a symbol of peace, or to ratify treaties.

CALUMNIATE (ka-lum'ni-at), *v.t.* to accuse falsely.

CALUMNIOUS (ka-lum'ni-us), *adj.* slanderous ; defamatory.

CALUMNY (kal'um-ni), *n.* a false accusation ; a slander.

CALVARY (kal'va-ri), *n.* the place where Christ was crucified.

CALVINISM (kal'vin-izm), *n.* the doctrines of John Calvin 1509-64].

CALVINIST (kal'vin-ist), *n.* one who holds the doctrines of Calvin.

CALX (kalks), *n.* lime or chalk ; the residuum of a metal left after calcination.

CALYX (ka'liks), *n.* the whorl of a flower.

CAM (kam), *n.* a projecting part of a wheel or other moving piece of machinery for imparting an eccentric or alternating motion.

CAMARADERIE (ka-ma-ra-de-re'), *n.* [French], good fellowship.

CAMARILLA (kam-a-ril'a), *n.* a cabal ; a clique.

CAMBER (kam'ber), *n.* a convexity on an upper surface ; a piece of timber thus bent.

CAMBRIC (kam'brik), *n.* a very fine thin linen.

CAMBRIC MUSLIN (muz'lin), *n.* a fine cotton imitation of cambric.

CAMEL (kam'el), *n.* a large ruminant quadruped, of which there are two species, the Arabian camel or dromedary, with a single hump, and the Bactrian camel, with two humps.

CAMELLIA (ka-mel'i-a), *n.* a genus of Asiatic evergreen shrubs.

CAMELOPARD (ka-mel'o-pard), *n.* the giraffe ; [C-], a constellation.

CAMEMBERT CHEESE (ka-mangber'chez), *n.* a soft, unpressed cream cheese.

CAMEO (kam'e-o), *n.* a precious stone or shell on which figures are engraved.

CAMERA (kam'er-a), *n.* a box in which the image of an object is thrown upon a sensitized plate by a lens ; a room ; a judge's chamber.

CAM-GEAR (kam'ger), *n.* a gear not

centred on the shaft, used in many forms of machinery where discontinuous action is required.

CAMION (ka-mi-yong'), *n.* a military truck.

CAMOMILE (kam'o-mil), *n.* a plant of the aster family.

CAMORRA (ka-mor'a), *n.* an Italian secret society.

CAMOUFLAGE (ka-moo-flazh'), *n.* a covering of any kind to hide or deceive.

CAMP (kamp), *n.* the ground occupied by an army at rest, with tents, huts.

CAMPAIGN (kam-pan'), *n.* an open tract of land ; the period during which an army carries on active operations.

CAMPANILE (kam-pa-ne'le), *n.* a bell-tower detached from the body of a church.

CAMPANULATE (kam-pan'u-lat), *adj.* bell-shaped.

CAMPEACHY WOOD (kam-pech'i wood), *n.* logwood.

CAMPFIRE (-fir), *n.* a fire for an encampment.

CAMPFIRE GIRLS (gerlz), *n.* an organization, similar to the Boy Scouts.

CAMPHINE (kam-fen'), *n.* rectified oil of turpentine.

CAMPHOR (kam'fer), *n.* a volatile, aromatic, whitish substance, obtained from various trees and plants of Asia.

CAMPHORATE (kam'fer-at), *v.t.* to saturate or treat with camphor.

CAMPHOR TREE (tre), a species of laurel yielding camphor.

CAMP-MEETING (-met'ing), *n.* an outdoor religious gathering.

CAMP-STOOL (-stool), *n.* a folding stool.

CAMPUS (kam'pus), *n.* the grounds of a school or college.

CAMWOOD (kam'wood), *n.* a red dyewood.

CAN (kan), *v.i.* to be able ; possess power physically, morally, or mentally (used as an auxiliary verb).

CAN (kan), *n.* a tin vessel for holding liquids, etc.

CANADA BALSAM (kan'a-da bawl'-

sam), *n.* a resin obtained from a species of fir.

CANAILLE (ka-nal'), *n.* the rabble.

CANAL (ka-nal'), *n.* an artificial waterway ; a tube for the passage of fluids ; a channel or groove.

CANARD (ka-nard'), *n.* an absurd report ; a hoax.

CANARY (ka-na'ri), *n.* a small singing bird with yellow plumage.

CANCEL (kan'sel), *v.t.* to deface ; void ; annul ; strike out common factors : *n.* the part of a book deleted.

CANCELLATION (-la'shun), *n.* the act or process of cancelling.

CANCER (kan'ser), *n.* a genus of crustaceans ; one of the twelve zodiacal signs, the sign of the summer solstice ; [c-], a malignant tumour or growth.

CANCEROUS (kan'ser-us), *adj.* like a cancer.

CANDELABRUM (kan-de-la'brum), *n.* [*pl.* candelabra ('bra)], an ornamented branched candlestick.

CANDENT (kan'dent), *adj.* glowing with a white heat.

CANDESCENCE (kan-des'ens), *n.* a state of glowing.

CANDID (kan'did), *adj.* honest ; outspoken ; sincere.

CANDIDATE (kan'di-dat), *n.* one who offers himself, or is proposed by others, to fill some office.

CANDIDATURE (kan'di-dat-tur), *n.* the state of being a candidate.

CANDIED (kan'did), *p.adj.* preserved or incrusted with sugar.

CANDLE (kan'dl), *n.* a cylindrical body of tallow, wax, etc., enclosing a wick, and used to furnish light.

CANDLEMAS (kan'dl-mas), *n.* the feast of the Purification of the Virgin Mary (Feb. 2nd).

CANDLE-POWER (-pou'er), *n.* the illuminating power of a candle taken as a unit in determining the luminosity of any flame.

CANDOUR (kan'der), *n.* openness ; frankness.

CANDY (kan'di), *n.* confections of sugar, combined with flavouring or colouring substances : *v.t.* to conserve with sugar.

CANDYTUFT (kan'di-tuft), *n.* a plant grown in gardens.

CANE (kan), *n.* the stem of certain palms, grasses, and other plants, as the bamboo, sugar-cane, rattan, etc. ; a walking-stick.

CANE-BRAKE ('brak), *n.* a thicket of canes.

CANINE (ka-nin'), *adj.* pertaining to dogs.

CANINE TEETH (teth), two sharp-pointed teeth on each side of the upper and lower jaws of most mammals.

CANISTER (kan'is-ter), *n.* a metal box or case for tea, etc. ; a case containing shot.

CANKER (kang'ker), *n.* a cancerous or ulcerous disease ; anything that insidiously corrodes, corrupts or destroys.

CANKEROUS (kang'ker-us), *adj.* malignant ; ulcerous.

CANKER SORE (sor), *n.* an ulceration affecting mouth and lips.

CANKER WORM (werm), *n.* a caterpillar.

CANNED (kand), *adj.* preserved in tins.

CANNEL-COAL (kan'el-kol), *n.* a hard bituminous coal.

CANNERY (kan'e-ri), *n.* an establishment for preserving meat, fish, etc., in cans.

CANNIBAL (kan'i-bal), *n.* a human being who eats human flesh.

CANNIBALISM (-izm), *n.* the act or practice of a cannibal.

CANNON (kan'un), *n.* a large gun ; also used collectively.

CANNONADE (kan-un-ad'), *n.* the act of discharging cannon against a town, fort, etc.

CANNONEER (kan-un-er'), *n.* an artilleryman.

CANNY, CANNIE (kan'i), *adj.* shrewd ; knowing ; cautious ; wary ; artful.

CANOE (ka-noo'), *n.* a light boat of bark, hide, wood, canvas, etc.

CANOEIST (ka-noo'ist), *n.* one who paddles or sails a canoe.

CANON (kan'un), *n.* a law or rule in general ; the books of the Holy

Scriptures received as authoritative; a cathedral dignitary; one of a bishop's council.

CANON (kan'yun), *n.* a gorge; a valley between high hills.

CANONIST (kan'on-ist), *n.* one skilled in the study and in the practice of ecclesiastical law.

CANOPY (kan'o-pi), *n.* a covering fixed above a bed, or suspended over a throne; any similar covering.

CANOROUS (ka-no'rus), *adj.* tuneful; melodious; musical.

CANT (kant), *v.i.* to speak in a whining voice; make whining pretensions to goodness.

CANT (kant), *n.* an external angle; an inclination from the level; a sudden jerk producing a change in direction.

CANTALOUP (kan'ta-loop), *n.* a variety of muskmelon.

CANTANKEROUS (kan-tang'ker-us), *adj.* ill-tempered; contentious.

CANTATA (kan-ta'ta), *n.* a short choral composition.

CANTATRICE (kan-ta-tre'cha), *n.* a female singer.

CANTEEN (kan-ten'), *n.* a shop in barracks or camp where provisions are sold; a vessel used by soldiers for carrying water.

CANTER (kan'ter), *n.* an easy gallop.

CANT HOOK (hook), *n.* a lever with a movable iron hook, used in logging.

CANTICLE (kan'ti-kl), *n.* a song; one of the non-metrical hymns of the Bible arranged for chanting in church.

CANTILEVER (kan'ti-le-ver), *n.* a bracket or block projecting from the wall of a house, to support a balcony, cornice, etc.; one of two arms projecting from opposite banks serving to form a bridge.

CANTILLATE (kan'ti-lat), *v.t.* to recite; intone; chant.

CANTING (kan'ting), *p.adj.* affectedly pious; whining.

CANTO (kan'to), *n.* a part of a poem; the highest vocal part in concerted music.

CANTON (kan'ton), *n.* a district or division of a territory.

CANTONMENT ('ment), *n.* a part of a town or village allotted to troops.

CANTOR (kan'ter), *n.* a choirmaster; a precentor; an official in a Hebrew synagogue.

CANVAS (kan'vas), *n.* a coarse heavy cloth of hemp or flax, used for tents, sails, etc., and, also, for painting on; sails in general; a painting.

CANVAS-BACK (-bak), *n.* a North American duck.

CANVASS (kan'vas), *v.t.* to examine; sift; discuss; solicit votes or opinions, orders, etc.

CANYON (kan'yun), same as cañon.

CAOUTCHOUC (koo'chook), *n.* an elastic, gummy substance obtained from the milky juice of several tropical trees; india-rubber.

CAP (kap), *n.* a covering for the head; anything resembling a cap; a percussion cap; the top or summit.

CAPABILITY (ka-pa-bil'i-ti), *n.* the quality of being capable.

CAPABLE (ka'pa-bl), *adj.* receptive; susceptible; having power, skill, or capacity.

CAPACIOUS (ka-pa'shus), *adj.* roomy; spacious.

CAPACITATE (ka-pas'i-tat), *v.t.* to make capable; enable; qualify.

CAPACITIVE (ka-pas'i-tiv), *adj.* pertaining to electrical capacity.

CAPACITY (ka-pas'i-ti), *n.* the power of receiving or containing; cubic contents; intellectual ability.

CAP-A-PIE (kap-a-pe'), *adv.* from head to foot.

CAPARISON (ka-par'i-son), *n.* an ornamental covering; gay or rich clothing : *v.t.* to adorn with rich dress.

CAPE (kap), *n.* a covering for the shoulders; a headland.

CAPER (ka'per), *v.i.* to skip; jump : *n.* a prank.

CAPER (ka'per), *n.* a plant, the flower-buds of which are pickled and used as a condiment.

CAPFUL (kap'fool), *n.* as much as fills a cap; a small quantity; a passing gust.

CAPIAS (ka'pi-as), *n.* a writ authorizing the arrest of the person.

CAPILLARITY (kap-i-lar'i-ti), *n.* the state of being capillary.

CAPILLARY (kap'il-a-ri, ka-pil'a-ri), *adj.* resembling a hair; minute; slender; possessing a very small bore; pertaining to the capillary vessels of the body.

CAPILLARY ATTRACTION (a-trak'shun), the action which takes place when the molecules of a liquid are attracted by a solid.

CAPITAL (kap'i-tal), *adj.* affecting the head or life; punishable with death; chief; principal; good; excellent; first-rate: *n.* the chief city; a capital letter.

CAPITAL (kap'i-tal), *n.* the sum invested in any particular business.

CAPITALISM (kap'i-tal-izm), *n.* the possession of capital; the power of combined capital.

CAPITALIST (kap'i-tal-ist), *n.* one who possesses capital.

CAPITALIZE (kap'i-tal-iz), *v.t.* to convert into capital; print with a capital.

CAPITATE (kap'i-tat), *adj.* growing in a head; head-shaped.

CAPITATION (kap-i-ta'shun), *n.* a tax, fee, or grant per head.

CAPITOL (kap'i-tul), *n.* the building occupied by the U.S. Congress at Washington; the legislative building of a State.

CAPITULAR (ka-pit'u-lar), **CAPITULARY** (-la-ri), *adj.* pertaining to a chapter; growing in a head.

CAPITULATE (ka-pit'u-lat), *v.i.* to surrender on conditions agreed upon.

CAPITULATION (ka-pit-u-la'shun), *n.* the act of capitulating.

CAPLIN (kap-lin), *n.* a small fish.

CAPON (ka'pon), *n.* a cock-chicken castrated.

CAPRICE (ka-pres'), *n.* a whim; a freak.

CAPRICIOUS (ka-prish'us), *adj.* characterized by caprice; fickle.

CAPSICIN, CAPSICINE (kap'si-sin), *n.* an alkaloid extracted from capsicum.

CAPSICUM (kap'si-kum), *n.* a genus of South American plar..s.

CAPSIZE (kap-siz'), *v.i.* to be overturned; upset.

CAPSTAN (kap'stan), *n.* an upright drum revolving upon a spindle, and worked by levers.

CAPSULAR (kap'su-lar), *adj.* pertaining to, or of the nature of a capsule.

CAPSULE (kap'sul), *n.* a seal or cover for a bottle; a small envelope of gelatine enclosing a drug.

CAPTAIN (kap'tin), *n.* in the army, the commander of a company; in the navy, an officer commanding a ship of war; the master of a merchant vessel; the head of a team or side.

CAPTAINCY (kap'tan-si), *n.* the rank of a captain.

CAPTION (kap'shun), *n.* the title of, or introduction to, a legal document; a heading to a chapter or section.

CAPTIOUS (kap'shus), *adj.* ready to catch at faults; quibbling.

CAPTIVATE (kap'ti-vat), *v.t.* to charm or lure; fascinate.

CAPTIVATION (kap-ti-va'shun), *n.* the act of charming.

CAPTIVE (kap'tiv), *adj.* made prisoner: *n.* fascinated.

CAPTIVITY (kap-tiv'i-ti), *n.* the state of being held in confinement.

CAPTURE (kap'tur), *n.* the act of seizing or taking; arrest.

CAPUT (kap'ut), *n.* [*pl.* capita ('i-ta)], the head.

CAR (kar), *n.* a wheeled vehicle; a coach running upon rails; an automobile.

CARACOLE (kar'a-kol), *n.* a half turn which a horseman makes; a spiral staircase.

CARAFE (ka-raf'), *n.* a glass water bottle.

CARAMEL (kar'a-mel), *n.* burnt sugar, used for colouring; a candy.

CARAT (kar'at), *n.* the weight of 3.17 grains, used for weighing precious stones; a twenty-fourth part; a term used to express the fineness of gold.

CARAVAN (kar'a-van, kar-a-van'), *n.* a company of travellers, associated together for mutual security.

CARAVANSARY (kar-a-van'sa-ri), *n.* in the East, a kind of inn.

CARBIDE (kar′bid), *n.* a compound of carbon with a metal.

CARBINE (kar′bin), *n.* a short rifle.

CARBOLATED (kar′bo-lat-ed), *adj.* impregnated or treated with carbolic acid.

CARBOLIC (kar-bol′ik), *adj.* pertaining to, or derived from, carbon or coal-tar.

CARBOLIC ACID (as′id), *n.* an acid obtained from coal-tar.

CARBON (kar′bon), *n.* an elementary substance present in all organic compounds.

CARBONATE (kar′bon-at), *n.* a compound of carbonic acid with a base.

CARBONATED (-ed), *adj.* combined, or impregnated, with carbonic acid.

CARBON DIOXIDE (di′ok-sid), *n.* a heavy, colourless gas, commonly called *carbonic acid gas*.

CARBONIC ACID (as′id), *n.* a gaseous colourless compound of carbon and oxygen in the proportion of 12 parts of carbon to 32 of oxygen.

CARBONIFEROUS (kar-bon-if′er-us), *adj.* the containing or yielding of carbon or coal.

CARBON MONOXIDE (mon-ok′sid), a product of the incomplete combustion of carbon : this gas is odourless, as well as colourless, and is very poisonous.

CARBORUNDUM (kar-bo-run′-dum), *n.* an exceedingly hard compound made of silicon and carbon.

CARBOY (kar′boi), *n.* a large globular bottle of glass.

CARBUNCLE (kar′bung-kl), *n.* a beautiful gem of a deep red colour ; an inflammatory tumour, or ulcer.

CARBURETTER, CARBURET-TOR (kar-bu-ret′er), *n.* a device which mixes vaporized oil with air and feeds it to the cylinder of a gaseline engine.

CARCASE, CARCASS (kar′kas), *n.* a dead body.

CARD (kard), *n.* a printed piece of pasteboard ; the dial of a mariner's compass ; an instrument for combing the fibres of wool, etc., preparatory to spinning.

CARDAMOM (kar′da-mum), *n.* the capsule of several species of plants of the ginger family, with its aromatic seeds.

CARDIA (kar′di-a), *n.* the heart ; the upper or cardiac end of the stomach where the œsophagus or gullet enters it.

CARDIAC (kar′di-ak), *adj.* pertaining to the heart : *n.* a cordial ; stimulant.

CARDIALGIA (kar-di-al′ji-a), *n.* heartburn.

CARDIGAN (kar′di-gan), *n.* a knitted woollen jacket or waistcoat.

CARDINAL (kar′di-nal), *adj.* chief ; preeminent ; fundamental.

CARDINAL (kar′di-nal), *n.* a member of the Pope's council ; an American song bird.

CARDINAL NUMBERS (num′berz), the numbers *one, two, three,* etc., in distinction from *first, second, third,* etc., which are called *ordinal numbers.*

CARDINAL POINTS (pointz), the four principal points of the compass, N., S., E., W.

CARDINAL SIGNS (sinz), *n.pl.* Aries, Libra, Cancer, and Capricorn.

CARDINAL VIRTUES (ver′tuz), virtues of primary importance, as justice, prudence, temperance and fortitude.

CARDINAL-WINDS (windz), *n.pl.* winds which blow due N., S., E., or W.

CARDITIS (kar-di′tis), *n.* inflammation of the muscular tissue of the heart.

CARE (kar), *n.* concern ; solicitude ; anxiety ; a burdensome responsibility; caution.

CAREEN (ka-ren′), *v.t.* to bring (a ship) on one side for the purpose of calking, cleansing, or repairing : *v.i.* to incline on one side, as a ship under press of sail.

CAREER (ka-rer′), *n.* a run at full speed ; an occupation or calling.

CAREFUL (kar′fool), *adj.* full of care ; anxious ; attentive.

CAREFULLY (-li), *adv.* in a careful manner.

CARELESS (kar′les), *adj.* wanting in care or interest ; neglectful.

CARESS (ka-res'), *n.* any act or expression of affection.

CARET (ka'ret, kar'et), *n.* a mark (∧) used in writing, or in correcting proofs.

CARGO (kar'go), *n.* the lading or freight of a ship.

CARIBOU, CARIBOO (kar'i-boo), *n.* the North American reindeer.

CARICATURE (kar'i-ka-tur), *n.* a pictorial or descriptive representation of a person or thing, in which the defects or peculiarities are exaggerated so as to produce a ludicrous effect ; parody.

CARICATURIST (-ist), *n.* one who represents in caricature.

CARIES (ka'ri-ez), *n.* decay of bones, teeth, or vegetable tissue.

CARILLON (kar'i-lon), *n.* a chime of bells diatonically tuned.

CARK (kark), *v.i.* to be anxious or concerned : *v.t.* to vex.

CARMINATIVE (kar-min'a-tiv), *n.* a medicine which expels wind and relieves colic and flatulence.

CARMINE (kar'min), *n.* the essential colouring principle of cochineal ; a rich crimson pigment.

CARNAGE (kar'naj), *n.* slaughter ; massacre.

CARNAL (kar'nal), *adj.* pertaining to the body, its passions and its appetites ; animal ; sensual.

CARNATION (kar-na'shun), *n.* a plant of the pink family ; the clove pink ; a light rose-pink.

CARNIVAL (kar'ni-val), *n.* the season of rejoicing before Lent.

CARNIVOROUS (kar-niv'o-rus), *adj.* eating or feeding on flesh.

CAROL (kar'ul), *n.* a song of joy or praise, especially one in honour of the Nativity.

CAROM (kar'um), *n.* the impact of a billiard ball against two other balls : *v.i.* to rebound after striking.

CAROTID (ka-rot'id), *n.* one of the two principal arteries, which convey the blood from the aorta to the head.

CAROUSAL (ka-rouz'al), *n.* a noisy revel.

CAROUSEL (kar-oo-zel'), *n.* a merry-go-round.

CARP (karp), *v.i.* to cavil or find fault.

CARP (karp), *n.* a fresh-water fish.

CARPAL (kar'pal), *adj.* pertaining to the carpus or wrist.

CARPENTER (kar'pen-ter), *n.* an artificer who works in timber.

CARPENTRY (kar'pen-tri), *n.* the art of cutting, framing, and joining timber.

CARPET (kar'pet), *n.* a thick woven or felted fabric used for covering floors or stairs : *v.t.* bring under consideration ; reprimand.

CARPET-BAGGER (-bag'er), *n.* a political adventurer.

CARPETING (kar'pet-ing), *n.* cloth for carpets ; carpets in general.

CARRIAGE (kar'ij), *n.* the act of carrying or transporting ; cost of conveyance ; behaviour ; deportment ; a wheeled vehicle.

CARRIER (kar'i-er), *n.* one who, or that which, carries or conveys.

CARRIER-PIGEON (-pij'un), *n.* a variety of pigeon trained to convey letters, etc.

CARRION (kar'i-on), *n.* dead or putrefying flesh ; filth ; garbage.

CARROT (kar'ot), *n.* the well-known field and garden-plant of the celery family ; the edible root of this plant.

CARRY (kar'i), *v.t.* to convey from one point to another ; convey by force ; transfer ; accomplish.

CARRY ON (kar'i-on), *v.* to persist ; endure.

CART (kart), *n.* a carriage for the conveyance of goods.

CARTAGE (kart'aj), *n.* the charge made for conveyance by a cart ; the act of carting.

CARTE (kart), *n.* a bill of fare.

CARTE BLANCHE (kart blangsh), a blank paper ; unlimited power to decide.

CARTEL (kar'tel), *n.* an agreement between hostile states regarding the exchange of prisoners.

CARTILAGE (kar'ti-laj), *n.* elastic animal tissue, forming bone ; gristle.

CARTOGRAPHER (kar-tog'ra-fer), *n.* one who makes charts or maps.

CARTOGRAPHY (kar-tog'ra-fi), *n.* the art or business of making maps.

CARTON (kar'ton), *n.* a pasteboard box.

CARTOON (kar-toon'), *n.* a pictorial sketch dealing with a political or social subject ; a caricature.

CARTRIDGE (kar'trij), *n.* a case containing the charge of a firearm.

CARVE (karv), *v.t.* to form a design ; shape by cutting ; cut into slices.

CASABA MELON (ka-sa'ba mel'un), a kind of melon.

CASCADE (kas-kad'), *n.* a fall of water.

CASCARA (kas'ka-ra), *n.* the bark of the buckthorn.

CASCARILLA (kas-ka-ril'a), *n.* the bark of a West Indian shrub.

CASE (kas), *n.* a receptacle ; a sheath ; a box ; a frame or casing ; a divided tray for types.

CASE (kas), *n.* that which happens or befalls ; the matters involved in a question under discussion or investigation ; a suit or action at law ; one of the forms or inflections in the declension of a noun, pronoun, or adjective, which indicates its relation to other words.

CASEHARDEN (kas-har'dn), *v.t.* to harden iron into steel ; to make one impervious to good advice or influence.

CASEIN (ka'se-in), *n.* the curd-matter of milk, forming the main part of cheese.

CASEMENT (kas'ment), *n.* a hinged window-frame made to open outward.

CASH (kash), *n.* money ; ready money : *v.t.* to turn into, or exchange for, money.

CASH-AND-CARRY (-kar'i), *n.* a store system where goods are paid for and carried away.

CASH-BOOK (-book), *n.* a book in which a register is kept of money received or paid out.

CASHIER (kash-er'), *n.* one who has charge of the money : *v.t.* to dismiss from service or place of trust ; discharge.

CASHMERE (kash'mer), *n.* a soft woollen fabric for shawls, etc.

CASH-REGISTER (-rej'is-ter), *n.* a machine for registering cash receipts.

CASING (kas'ing), *n.* the act of covering with or placing in a case ; a covering.

CASINO (ka-se'no), *n.* a public room or building used for social meetings, dancing, gaming, etc. ; a game of cards.

CASK (kask), *n.* a vessel composed of wooden staves, bound by iron hoops.

CASKET (kas'ket), *n.* a small chest or box for jewels, etc. ; a coffin.

CASQUE (kask), *n.* a helmet.

CASSATION (kas-a'shun), *n.* abrogation ; annulment.

CASSAVA (ka-sa'va), *n.* a plant of tropical America and Africa.

CASSEROLE (kas'er-ol), *n.* an earthenware vessel in which meat, etc., is cooked and served.

CASSIMERE (kas'i-mer), *n.* a thin twilled woollen cloth.

CASSINO (ka-se'no), see casino.

CASSOCK (kas'uk), *n.* a long close-fitting vestment worn by clergymen, choristers, etc.

CASSOWARY (kas'o-wa-ri), *n.* a large bird resembling the ostrich.

CAST (kast), *v.t.* throw ; hurl ; throw down ; calculate ; assign to various actors ; receive form or shape in a mould : *n.* the act of casting ; the company of actors to whom the parts of a play are assigned.

CASTANETS (kas'ta-nets), *n. pl.* small spoon-shaped shells of hard wood or ivory, fastened loosely at the top, a pair of which is fastened to each thumb and shaken with the fingers to beat time.

CASTAWAY (kast'a-wa), *n.* a person or vessel wrecked on an unfrequented coast ; an outcast.

CASTE (kast), *n.* one of the artificial or hereditary divisions into which Hindus are restricted by Brahman religious law.

CASTER (kas'ter), *n.* a computer ; a cruet or small vessel for holding condiments at table ; a small swivelled wheel.

CASTIGATE (kas'ti-gat), *v.t.* to correct ; chastise ; punish.

CASTILIAN (kas-til'ian), *adj.* of, or pertaining to, Castile.

CASTING (kast'ing), *n.* the action of the verb to cast ; the act or process of founding or moulding.

CAST IRON (i-ern), iron produced in a blast-furnace and cast into moulds.

CASTLE (kas'l), *n.* a fortified residence ; a fortress ; a strong and imposing mansion ; one of the pieces at chess.

CASTOR OIL (kas'ter oil), cathartic oil from the seeds of the castor-oil plant.

CASTOR-OIL PLANT (plant), an herbaceous, palmate Asiatic plant.

CASTRATE (kas'trat), *v.t.* to emasculate ; geld ; expurgate ; a eunuch.

CASUAL (kazh'u-al), *adj.* happening by chance ; accidental ; occasional.

CASUALTY (kazh'u-al-ti), *n.* an accident.

CASUIST (kazh'u-ist) *n.* one who studies cases of conscience.

CASUISTRY (kazh'u-ist-ri), *n.* the science or doctrine which deals with cases of conscience as determined by theological dogmas or ethical rules.

CAT (kat), *n.* a carnivorous animal which has been long domesticated as a household pet.

CATACLYSM (kat'a-klizm), *n.* a deluge ; flood.

CATACOMB (kat'a-kom), *n.* a subterraneous burial place.

CATACOUSTICS (kat-a-kous'tiks), *n.* that part of the science of acoustics which treats of reflected sounds.

CATAFALQUE (kat'a-falk), *n.* a structure erected to support the coffin of a distinguished person on the occasion of a ceremonious funeral.

CATALEPSY (kat'a-lep-si), *n.* a sudden suspension of voluntary sensation.

CATALOGUE (kat'a-log), *n.* an arranged list : *v.t.* to enter in, or make, a catalogue of.

CATALPA (ka-tal'pa), *n.* a genus of trees of China, Japan, and North America.

CATAMARAN (kat-a-ma-ran'), *n.* a raft or float propelled by sails or paddles.

CATAMOUNT (kat'a-mount), *n.* the wild cat ; the puma, cougar, or mountain lion.

CATAPULT (kat'a-pult), *n.* an ancient military engine for hurling darts and stones.

CATARACT (kat'a-rakt), *n.* a large waterfall ; a furious rush or downpour of water ; a disease of the eye.

CATARRH (ka-tar'), *n.* an inflammatory affection of any mucous membrane.

CATARRHAL (ka-tar'al), *adj.* pertaining to, or produced by catarrh.

CATASTROPHE (ka-tas'tro-fe), *n.* a great calamity or disaster.

CATAWBA (ka-taw'ba), *n.* a light-red variety of American grape.

CATBIRD (-berd), *n.* an American song bird.

CAT BOAT (bot), a small boat with one sail on a mast near the bow.

CATCALL (kat'kawl), *n.* a sound like that made by a cat : *v.t.* to express disapproval of by a catcall.

CATCH (kach), *v.t.* to seize or grasp ; take by contagion ; attack, or communicate to, as a fire.

CATCHING (-ing), *adj.* charming ; attractive ; contagious.

CATCHPENNY (kach'pen-i), *n.* an article of little value to effect a quick sale.

CATCHUP (kach'up), *n.* a sauce made from mushrooms, tomatoes, walnuts, etc. ; ketchup.

CATECHISM (kat'e-kizm), *n.* an elementary manual of instruction in the form of question and answer.

CATECHIZE (kat'e-kiz), *v.t.* to instruct by means of questions and answers ; interrogate.

CATEGORICAL (kat-e-gor'i-kal), *adj.* pertaining to a category ; absolute.

CATEGORICALLY (-li), *adv.* in a categorical manner.

CATEGORY (kat'e-go-ri), *n.* one of the highest classes to which the objects of knowledge or thought can be reduced, and by which they may be arranged into a system.

CATER (ka'ter), *v.i.* to supply food, amusement, etc. [with *for* and *to*].

CATERPILLAR (kat'ter-pil'er), *n.* the hairy worm-like larva of a butterfly or lepidopterous insect.

CATERPILLAR TRACTOR (trak'-ter), a tractor which travels on two endless belts.

CATERWAUL (-wawl), *n.* the cry of a cat.

CATFISH (kat'fish), *n.* a fish; bullhead; pout.

CATGUT (kat'gut), *n.* a kind of cord made from the intestines of animals, usually sheep, and used as strings for musical instruments and some other purposes.

CATHARTIC (ka-thar'tik), *adj.* purgative: *n.* a purgative medicine.

CATHEDRAL (ka-the'dral), *n.* the chief church in a diocese in which is the throne of a bishop.

CATHETER (kath'e-ter), *n.* a tubular instrument to withdraw urine from the bladder.

CATHODE (kath'od), *n.* the negative pole of a current; opposed to *anode*.

CATHODE RAY (kath'od-ra), the stream of electrons in an electric bulb which generates the X-ray.

CATHOLIC (kath'o-lik), *adj.* universal; general; embracing all; liberal; large-hearted; free from prejudice; including all mankind.

CATHOLIC (kath'o-lik), *adj.* pertaining to the Church of Rome.

CATHOLICISM (ka-thol'i-sizm), *n.* the belief of, or adherence to the Roman Catholic Church.

CATKIN (kat'kin), *n.* the pendulous inflorescence of the willow, birch, etc.

CATMINT (kat'mint), **CATNIP** (kat'nip), *n.* a strong-scented perennial herb.

CATOPTRIC LIGHT (ka-top'trik lit), form of light, used in lighthouses.

CATOPTRICS (ka-top'triks), *n.* that branch of optics which treats of the principles of reflected light.

CAT'S-EYE (kats-i), *n.* a variety of quartz or chalcedony.

CAT'S PAW (-paw), *n.* a dupe; one used as a tool to accomplish a purpose.

CATTLE (kat'l), *n.pl.* live stock-especially oxen, bulls and cows.

CATTLE-PLAGUE (-plag), *n.* a popular name for the rinderpest.

CAUCASIAN (kaw-ka'shi-an), *n.* a member of the white division of mankind.

CAUCUS (kaw'kus), *n.* a preliminary meeting of representatives of a political party to decide upon a line of policy.

CAUDAL (kaw'dal), *adj.* pertaining to a tail.

CAUDATE (kaw'dat), *adj.* having a tail.

CAUGHT, *p.t.* & *p.p.* of catch.

CAUL (kawl), *n.* a membrane, sometimes enclosing a child's head at birth.

CAULDRON, *see Caldron.*

CAULIFLOWER (kawl'li-flou-er), *n.* a garden variety of cabbage.

CAULK, see calk.

CAUMA (kaw'ma), *n.* excess of bodily heat; fever heat.

CAUSAL (kaw'zal), *adj.* relating to or expressing cause; creative.

CAUSALITY (kaw-zal'i-ti), *n.* the relation of cause to effect.

CAUSATION (kaw-za'shun), *n.* relation between cause and effect.

CAUSE (kawz), *n.* that which produces or contributes to a result; a reason; motive; principle; subject in debate; a side or party; a suit or action.

CAUSEWAY (kawz'wa), **CAUSEY** ('zi), *n.* a pathway raised and paved with stone; a highway.

CAUSTIC (kaws'tik), *adj.* corrosive; sarcastic; cutting.

CAUSTIC POTASH (pot'ash), potassium as a powerful cautery.

CAUSTIC SODA (so'da), sodium hydrate.

CAUTERIZE (kaw'ter-iz), *v.t.* to burn or sear with a hot iron, or with cauterants.

CAUTERY (kaw'ter-i), *n.* a burning or searing.

CAUTION (kaw'shun), *n.* heedfulness ; watchfulness ; an admonition : *v.t.* to warn.

CAUTIOUS (kaw'shus), *adj.* exercising caution ; wary ; vigilant.

CAVALCADE (kav-al-kad'), *n.* a train or procession of persons, chiefly on horseback.

CAVALIER (kav-a-ler'), *n.* a gallant ; a gay military man ; a beau or attendant upon a lady.

CAVALIERLY (li), *adv.* in a haughty or supercilious manner.

CAVALRY (kav'al-ri), *n.* horse soldiers.

CAVATINA (kav-a-te'na), *n.* a short simple melody.

CAVE (kav), *n.* a hollow place in the earth ; a den.

CAVEAT (ka've-at), *n.* a notice filed to stop procedure until the party giving such notice is heard.

CAVE BEAR (bar), *n.* fossil bear of the Quaternary epoch.

CAVE MAN (man), *n.* a man belonging to the prehistoric race who inhabited caves.

CAVERN (kav'ern), *n.* a large natural hollow under the earth ; a den ; cave.

CAVERNOUS (kav'er-nus), *adj.* hollow like a cavern, filled with small cavities.

CAVIARE (kav-i-ar'), **CAVIAR** (-i-ar'), *n.* the roes of certain large fish, especially the sturgeon, salted and dried.

CAVIL (kav'il), *v.i.* to raise captious or frivolous objections ; carp [followed by *at*].

CAVITY (kav'i-ti), *n.* a hollow place or part.

CAVORT (ka-vort'), *v.i.* to prance about.

CAVY (ka'vi), *n.* a rough-haired, short-tailed rodent of South America ; a guinea pig.

CAW (kaw), *v.i.* to cry like a crow.

CAYENNE (ki-en', ka-en'), *n.* a kind of pepper made from capsicum.

CAYMAN (ka'man), *n.* a large alligator of tropical America.

CAYUSE (ki-us'), *n.* a broncho ; an Indian pony.

CEASE (ses), *v.i.* to come to an end ; stop ; desist [followed by *from* before a noun] : *v.t.* to put a stop to ; end.

CEDAR (se'der), *n.* the name of several evergreen trees.

CEDE (sed), *v.t.* to give up or surrender.

CEDILLA (se-dil'a), *n.* a mark placed under *c* to indicate the sound of *s*, as in French *leçon*.

CEIL (sel), *v.t.* to overlay or cover the inner surface of a roof.

CEILING (se'ling), *n.* the inner roof of an apartment.

CELEBRANT (sel'e-brant), *n.* one who celebrates.

CELEBRATE (sel'e-brat), *v.t.* to praise, extol, or honour.

CELEBRATED (-ed), *adj.* distinguished ; famous.

CELEBRATION (sel-e-bra'shun), *n.* an observance or ceremony to celebrate anything.

CELEBRITY (se-leb'ri-ti), *n.* fame ; renown ; distinction ; a renowned person.

CELERITY (se-ler'i-ti), *n.* rapidity ; swiftness.

CELERY (sel'e-ri), *n.* a plant cultivated for a salad and vegetable.

CELESTE (se-lest'), *n.* sky-blue.

CELESTIAL (se-les'chal), *adj.* of, or pertaining to the sky or heavens ; [C-] a native of China.

CELIBACY (sel'i-ba-si), *n.* the state of being unmarried ; single life, especially that of a bachelor.

CELIBATE (sel'i-bat), *n.* one who is unmarried or practises celibacy : *adj.* unmarried.

CELL (sel), *n.* a small room in a prison ; a small cavity ; a minute mass of contractile protoplasm forming the structural unit of every organized body ; a single element of a galvanic battery ; a receptacle for generating electricity.

CELLAR (sel'er), *n.* a vault for storing provisions.

CELLO (chel'o), *n.* a violoncello.

CELLULAR (sel'u-lar), *adj.* formed of cells.

CELLULOID (sel'u-loid), *n.* a compound of camphor and gun-cotton, resembling ivory.

CELLULOSE (sel'u-los), **CELLULIN** (-lin), *n.* the substance resembling and allied to starch which forms cellular plant tissue.

CELT (selt), **KELT** (kelt), *n.* one of that branch of the Aryan family.

CELTIC (sel'tik), **KELTIC** (kel'-), *adj.* pertaining to the Celts or Kelts.

CEMENT (se-ment'), *n.* any adhesive substance which makes two bodies cohere.

CEMENTATION (sem-en-ta'shun), *n.* the act of cementing.

CEMETERY (sem'e-ter-i), *n.* a public burial ground.

CENOTAPH (sen'o-taf), *n.* an empty tomb, or a monument erected in honour of persons buried elsewhere.

CENSOR (sen'ser), *n.* an official appointed to examine books, manuscripts, plays, etc., prior to publication or performance to ascertain if there is anything immoral or offensive in them ; one who censures or blames ; a critic.

CENSORIOUS (sen-so'ri-us), *adj.* addicted to censure ; carping ; critical.

CENSURABLE (sen'shur-a-bl), *adj.* blamable.

CENSURE (sen'shur), *n.* blame ; reproof ; the act of finding fault.

CENSUS (sen'sus), *n.* an official enumeration of the inhabitants of a country, with details of sex, age, occupation, etc.

CENT (sent), *n.* the 1-100th part of a dollar ; a coin of this value.

CENTAL (sen'tal), *adj.* pertaining to or consisting of a hundred : *n.* a weight for corn = 100 lb. avoirdupois.

CENTARE (sang-tar'), *n.* in the metric system, one hundredth part of an are ; one square metre.

CENTAUR (sen'tawr), *n.* a fabulous being, half man and half horse.

CENTENARIAN (sen-te-na'ri-an), *adj.* of, or pertaining to, a centenary or to a person a hundred years old.

CENTENARY (sen'te-na-ri), *n.* the space of a hundred years ; the commemoration of the hundredth anniversary of an event.

CENTENNIAL (sen-ten'i-al), *adj.* consisting of, or enduring, a hundred

years : *n.* the commemoration of a 100th anniversary.

CENTESIMAL (sen-tes'i-mal), *adj.* hundredth : *n.* a hundredth part.

CENTIARE (sen'ti-ar), *n.* a centare.

CENTIGRADE (sen'ti-grad), *adj.* graduated or divided into a hundred degrees.

CENTIGRADE THERMOMETER (ther-mom'e-ter), a thermometer the scale of which is divided into 100 equal parts or degrees.

CENTIGRAM, CENTIGRAMME (sen'ti-gram), *n.* a measure of weight = 100th of a gramme (.15432 of a grain troy).

CENTILITRE (sen'ti-le-tr), *n.* a measure of capacity = the hundredth part of a litre (.6102 of a cubic inch).

CENTIME (sang-tem'), *n.* a small French coin = the hundredth part of a franc.

CENTIMETRE (sen'ti-me-tr), *n.* a measure of length = 100th of a metre (.3937 inch).

CENTIPEDE (sen'ti-ped), *n.* an articulated insect, with two legs to each joint.

CENTRAL (sen'tral), *adj.* relating to, or situated in, the centre.

CENTRALIZATION (sen-tral-i-za'shun), *n.* the act of bringing all local administrations under one central government.

CENTRALIZE (sen'tral-iz), *v.t.* to draw or bring to a centre ; bring all administrations under one central government.

CENTRE (sen'ter), *n.* the middle point of anything.

CENTRE-BIT (-bit), *n.* a carpenter's tool.

CENTRE OF GRAVITY (grav'i-ti), that point of a body through which the resultant of all the forces, acting upon it in consequence of the earth's attraction, will pass.

CENTRIFUGAL (sen-trif'u-gal), *adj.* tending or causing to fly off from the centre.

CENTRIFUGALLY (-li), *adv.* from the centre.

CENTRING (sen'ter-ing), *n.* the timber framing by which vaulted work is supported during construction.

CENTRIPETAL (sen-trip'e-tal), adj. tending, or causing, to approach the centre.

CENTURION (sen-tu'ri-un), n. a Roman officer commanding a hundred men.

CENTURY (sen'tu-ri), n. a hundred; a hundred years.

CENTURY PLANT (plant), a name of the American aloe.

CEPHALALGIA (sef-a-lal'ji-a), n. bilious headache.

CERAMIC (se-ram'ik), KERAMIC (ke-), adj. of or pertaining to pottery.

CEREAL (se're-al), adj. pertaining to, or producing, wheat or edible grain : n. edible grain.

CEREBELLUM (ser-e-bel'um), n. [pl. cerebella ('a)], the hinder and lower part of the brain in vertebrate animals.

CEREBRAL HEMISPHERE (hem'-is-sfer), n. one of the two lateral halves of the cerebrum.

CEREBRATION (ser-e-bra'shun), n. the conscious or unconscious action of the brain.

CEREMENT (ser'ment), n. a grave-cloth or shroud.

CEREMONIAL (ser-e-mo'ni-al), adj. relating to, or performed with, external rites or ceremonies.

CEREMONIOUS (ser-e-mo'ni-us), adj. full of ceremony.

CEREMONY (ser'e-mo-ni), n. a sacred rite or observance ; behaviour regulated by the laws of strict etiquette.

CERIPH (ser'if), n. one of the fine lines of a printing type, especially a stroke at the bottom or top of a letter.

CERISE (se-rez'), adj. colour of a red cherry : n. a dyestuff.

CEROGRAPHY (se-rog'ra-fi), n. the art of writing or engraving on wax.

CERTAIN (ser'tin), adj. sure ; beyond a doubt.

CERTAINLY (ser'tin-li), adv. surely ; without any doubt.

CERTAINTY (ser'tin-ti), n. full assurance.

CERTES (ser'tez), adv. certainly ; assuredly.

CERTIFICATE (ser-tif'i-kat), n. written testimony to the truth of any fact ; a testimonial as to character or ability.

CERTIFICATION (ser-ti-fi-ka'shun), n. the act of certifying.

CERTIFY (ser'ti-fi), v.t. to testify ; assure.

CERTIORARI (ser-shi-o-ra'ri), n. a writ issuing from a superior court calling for the records of an inferior court.

CERTITUDE (ser'ti-tud), adj. certainty ; freedom from doubt ; assurance.

CERULEAN (se-roo'le-an), adj. sky-coloured.

CERULIN (se'roo-lin), n. an olive-green dye.

CERUMEN (se-roo'men), n. wax secreted in the ear-tube.

CERVICAL (ser'vi-kal), adj. of or pertaining to the neck.

CESSATION (se-sa'shun), n. the act of ceasing.

CESSION (sesh'un), n. a yielding up, as of territory, property, or rights.

CESSPOOL (ses'pool), n. a hole in the ground, or the well of a drain, for the reception of filth.

CETACEA (se-ta'she-a), n.pl. an order of marine mammals, including whales, dolphins, and porpoises.

CETACEAN (se-ta'shun), adj. pertaining to the Cetacea.

CETIC ACID (se'tik as'id), n. an acid obtained from spermaceti.

CHAFE (chaf), v.t. to make warm by friction ; irritate ; annoy.

CHAFER (cha'fer), n. the cockchafer.

CHAFF (chaf), n. the husk of grain.

CHAFF (chaf), v.t. to banter.

CHAFFER (chaf'er), v.i. to haggle about a purchase.

CHAFFINCH (chaf'inch), n. a common British bird of the finch family.

CHAFING DISH (chaf'ing dish), a vessel for cooking at table, and for keeping foods hot.

CHAGRIN (sha-grin', -gren'), n. vexation due to disappointment; ill-humour; mortification.

CHAIN (chan), *n.* a connected series of links; a bond; a measure of 100 links = 66 ft. : *v.t.* to fasten, secure.

CHAIN GANG (gang), a gang of convicts working in chains.

CHAIN STORE (stor), one of a number of retail stores under the same control.

CHAIR (char), *n.* a movable seat; an official seat; a professorship; the presiding officer of an assembly.

CHAIR CAR (kar), a parlour car or a car with reclining or adjustable chairs.

CHAIRMAN (char'man), *n.* the president of an assembly, meeting, public company, etc.

CHAISE (shaz), *n.* a light two-wheeled carriage.

CHALCEDONY (kal'se-do-ni), *n.* a cryptocrystalline variety of quartz.

CHALCEDONYX (kal'sed-o-niks), *n.* a variety of agate.

CHALDRON (chawl'dron), *n.* a measure for coal and coke : in the U.S., from 2,500 to 2,900 lb.

CHALET (sha-la'), *n.* a Swiss cottage.

CHALICE (chal'is), *n.* a Eucharist cup.

CHALK (chawk), *n.* a soft limestone rock composed of carbonate of lime.

CHALLENGE (chal'enj), *n.* an invitation to a contest; a summons to fight; a duel; an objection taken to a voter or juror; the demand of a soldier on sentry.

CHALLIS (shal'i), *n.* a light all-wool fabric.

CHALYBEATE (ka-lib'e-at), *adj.* impregnated with iron.

CHAMBER (cham'ber), *n.* a private room; a political or commercial body; a cavity; that part of a gun, etc., which contains the charge : *pl.* a judge's private room.

CHAMBERLAIN (cham'ber-lin), *n.* the treasurer of a city or corporation.

CHAMBRAY (sham'bra), *n.* gingham with a linen finish.

CHAMELEON (ka-me'le-un), *n.* an insectivorous, lizard-like reptile.

CHAMFER (cham'fer), *n.* a small furrow cut in wood or metal.

CHAMOIS (sham'i), *n.* a soft, pliant leather, formerly of the skin of the chamois, but now prepared from the skin of the sheep.

CHAMP (champ), *v.t.* to bite with the teeth repeatedly and impatiently.

CHAMPAGNE (sham-pan'), *n.* light, sparkling wine.

CHAMPAIGN (sham-pan'), *n.* flat, open country.

CHAMPION (cham'pi-un), *n.* anyone who defends the cause of another; a successful competitor against all rivals.

CHAMPS ELYSEES (shang za-le-za'), the fashionable promenade and drive of Paris.

CHANCE (chans), *n.* an unforeseen event; an accident; a possibility; an opportunity.

CHANCEL (chan'sel), *n.* that part in a church where the altar stands; the sanctuary.

CHANCELLERY (chan'sel-er-i), *n.* an embassy and its officials.

CHANCELLOR (chan'sel-er), *n.* a judge of a court of equity or chancery; the president or highest official of a university.

CHANCERY (chan'ser-i), *n.* a Court of Equity.

CHANDELIER (shan-de-ler'), *n.* a hanging frame with branches for lights.

CHANGE (chanj), *v.t.* to alter; substitute; exchange or give an equivalent for.

CHANGEABLE (chanj'a-bl), *adj.* fickle.

CHANGELING (chanj'ling), *n.* a child left in place of another.

CHANNEL (chan'el), *n.* the bed of a stream; the deepest part of a strait, bay, harbour, etc.; a groove; a medium of conveyance.

CHANT (chant), *v.t.* to sing; intone.

CHANTEY (chan'ti), *n.* a song sung by sailors at work.

CHANTICLEER (chan'ti-kler), *n.* a cock.

CHANTRY (chan'tri), *n.* a side chapel.

CHAOS (ka'os), *n.* the confused matter out of which the universe was formed; confusion.

CHAP (chap), *v.t.* to cause to crack :

v.i. to have the skin crack : *n.* a young fellow.

CHAPARRAL (chap-a-ral'), *n.* a dense thicket.

CHAP-BOOK (chap'book), *n.* a small book, usually of fairy tales, romances, etc.

CHAPE (chap), *n.* any piece of metal or leather, used for attaching.

CHAPEAU (sha'po), *n.* [*pl.* chapeaux (-poz)], a hat or head covering.

CHAPEL (chap'el), *n.* a subordinate place of public worship ; an association of journeymen in a printing house.

CHAPERON (shap'er-on), *n.* a lady who accompanies young ladies in public.

CHAPFALLEN (chap'faw-len), *adj.* dejected.

CHAPITER (chap'i-ter), *n.* the upper part or capital of a pillar.

CHAPLAIN (chap'lin), *n.* a clergyman who performs service in the army, navy, a public institution.

CHAPLET (chap'let), *n.* a wreath or garland encircling the head.

CHAPPIE (chap'i), *n.* familiar for chap.

CHAPTER (chap'ter), *n.* a division of a book ; a meeting of certain organized societies or orders.

CHAR (char), *n.* work by the day ; a single job ; a chore.

CHAR (char), *v.t.* burn or reduce to charcoal ; burn partially.

CHARACTER (kar'ak-ter), *n.* a letter, sign, or figure ; distinctive qualities or traits ; moral excellence.

CHARACTERISTIC (kar-ak-ter-is'-tik), *adj.* pertaining to or indicating the character.

CHARACTERIZE (kar'ak-ter-iz), *v.t.* describe by peculiar qualities.

CHARADE (sha-rad'), *n.* an acted enigma ; a word to be determined from a pictorial description of it.

CHARCOAL (char'kol), *n.* burnt wood ; impure carbon.

CHARD (chard), *n.* a variety of beet with large leaves and succulent stalk.

CHARGE (charj), *v.t.* to rush on or attack ; load; fill up ; impose ; com-mand or enjoin ; instruct ; accuse ; place on the debit side.

CHARGEABLE (char'ja-ble), *adj.* liable to be charged ; rateable.

CHARGE D'AFFAIRES (shar-zha'-da-far'), *n.* a government official who acts for an ambassador.

CHARGER (charj'er), *n.* a cavalry horse ; a large dish.

CHARIOT (char'i-ot), *n.* an ancient two-wheeled car.

CHARIOTEER (er'), *n.* one who drives a chariot.

CHARITABLE (char'i-ta-bl), *adj.* benevolent in disposition ; kind and liberal.

CHARITY (char'i-ti), *n.* the disposition to think well of others ; liberality ; alms.

CHARIVARI (shar-i-va'ri), *n.* a mock serenade of discordant music.

CHARLATAN (shar'la-tan), *n.* a quack.

CHARLOTTE (shar'lot), *n.* fruit and cream enclosed in a cake.

CHARLOTTE RUSSE (shar'lut rus), whipped cream enclosed in sponge-cake.

CHARM (charm), *n.* a spell or enchantment ; a trinket : *v.t.* subdue or fascinate.

CHARMER (char'mer), *n.* one who charms.

CHARMEUSE (shar'moos), *n.* a soft, clinging satin.

CHARNEL (char'nel), *adj.* containing dead bodies ; sepulchral.

CHART (chart), *n.* a map of any part of the sea, river, etc. ; the representation of a ship's course.

CHARTER (char'ter), *n.* a document bestowing certain rights ; an act of incorporation.

CHARTOGRAPHY (kar-tog'ra-fi), *n.* the art or business of drawing charts or maps.

CHARY (char'i), *adj.* cautious ; sparing.

CHASE (chas), *v.t.* to pursue ; capture or kill ; hunt ; drive away.

CHASE (chas), *n.* a groove ; an iron frame for securing types : *v.t.* to engrave or emboss metals.

CHASER (chas'er), *n.* one who chases.

CHASING, *n.* ornamental work on metal.

CHASM (kazm), *n.* a deep gap or opening in the earth ; a void space.

CHASSEUR (sha-ser'), *n.* a French light-armed foot or cavalry soldier.

CHASSIS (sha'se), *n.* a framework ; the frame, with the mechanical parts of an automobile.

CHASTE (chast), *adj.* morally pure ; modest ; refined.

CHASTEN (chas'n), *v.t.* to punish ; purify ; refine.

CHASTISE (chas-tiz'), *v.t.* to correct by punishment.

CHASTISEMENT (chas'tiz-ment), *n.* punishment.

CHASTITY (chas'ti-ti), *n.* moral and sexual purity.

CHAT (chat), *v.i.* to talk in an easy familiar manner.

CHATEAU (sha-to'), *n.* [*pl.* chateaux (-toz')], a castle ; a manor house or country seat.

CHATELAINE (shat'e-lan), *n.* a bunch of chains to which are attached trinkets.

CHATTEL (chat'l), *n.* personal property except freehold ; usually in *pl.*

CHATTER (chat'er), *v.i.* to utter sounds rapidly ; rattle the teeth, as in shivering ; talk idly.

CHATTERBOX (chat'er-boks), *n.* an incessant talker.

CHATTY (chat'i), *adj.* talkative, unconventional.

CHAUFFEUR (sho-fer'), *n.* an operator of an automobile.

CHAUTAUQUA SYSTEM (sha-tok'wa sis'tem), a system of education and home study.

CHAUVINISM (sho'vin-izm), *n.* blind and unreasoning attachment to a fallen cause.

CHAUVINIST (Sho'vin-ist), *n.* an extravagant patriot.

CHEAP (chep), *adj.* purchasable for a low price ; common.

CHEAPEN (chep'en), *v.t.* to lessen the price of.

CHEAT (chet), *n.* a fraud or deception : *v.t.* to deceive or defraud.

CHECK (chek), *n.* a restraint ; a reproof ; a pass, ticket, or token ; a term in chess ; cloth in squares of alternate patterns.

CHECKER (chek'er), *n.* piece with which to play checkers : *pl.* game played on a checker-board ; draughts: *v.t.* variegate.

CHECKER-BOARD (-bord), *n.* board for the game of checkers.

CHECKMATE (chek'mat), *n.* the winning move at chess ; a complete defeat.

CHECKREIN (-ran), *n.* short rein from bridle to saddle.

CHEEK (chek), *n.* the side of the face beneath either eye.

CHEEKY (-i), *adj.* impudent ; brazen.

CHEEP (chep), *n.* a shrill noise, as that of a young chicken.

CHEER (cher), *n.* a state of gladness or joy ; a shout of applause ; tidings.

CHEERFUL (cher'fool), *adj.* full of good spirits or joy.

CHEERFULLY (-li), *adv.* in a cheerful manner.

CHEERILY (cher'i-li), *adv.* heartily.

CHEERINESS (cher'i-ness), *n.* the state of being cheery.

CHEERY (cher'i), *adj.* cheerful ; gay.

CHEESE (chez), *n.* curd or casein of milk coagulated, pressed and allowed to dry in a mould.

CHEESE-CAKE ('kak), *n.* a cake containing soft curds, butter, and sugar.

CHEESE-PARING (-par'ing), *adj.* niggardly ; mean.

CHEF (shef), *n.* a head or professional cook ; a chief ; a director.

CHEF-D'ŒUVRE (sha-de'vr), *n.* [*pl.* chefs-d'œuvre (sha-de'vr)] [French], a master-piece.

CHEMICAL (kem'i-kal), *adj.* pertaining to chemistry : *n.* a chemical substance.

CHEMISE (she-mez'), *n.* a woman's undergarment.

CHEMIST (kem'ist), *n.* one skilled in chemistry.

CHEMISTRY (kem'is-tri), *n.* the

science which treats of the properties of elementary and compound substances and the laws which govern their molecular and atomic relations.

CHENILLE (she-nel'), *n.* silk or worsted cord.

CHEQUE (chek), *n.* an order or draft on a bank.

CHERISH (cher'ish), *v.t.* to hold or esteem dear; treat with tenderness.

CHEROOT (she-root'), *n.* a kind of cigar.

CHERRY (cher'i), *n.* the fruit of a tree allied to the plum.

CHERUB (cher'ub), *n.* an angel next to a seraphim in rank; a beautiful child.

CHESS (ches), *n.* a game played by two persons with 16 pieces each on a checkered board.

CHEST (chest), *n.* a large box; the breast or thorax.

CHESTNUT (ches'nut), *n.* the nut or seed of a tree of the beech family; a reddish-brown colour; a horse of such colour.

CHESTY (ches'ti), *adj.* conceited.

CHEVAL GLASS (she-val' glas), *n.* a large swing looking-glass.

CHEVALIER (shev-a-ler'), *n.* a knight; a gallant.

CHEVIOT (chev'i-ot), *n.* a sheep bred on the Cheviot Hills; [c-], a cloth made from its wool.

CHEVRON (shev'ron), *n.* the badge on the coat sleeve of a non-commissioned officer.

CHEVY (chev'i), **CHIVY** (chiv'i), *n.* hunt; pursuit; chase.

CHEW (choo), *v.t.* to crush and grind with the teeth; masticate; meditate upon.

CHIC (shek), *adj.* stylish: *n.* Parisian elegance in dress.

CHICANE (shi-kan'), *n.* mean or unfair artifices; sophistry; trickery.

CHICANERY (-kan'er-i), *n.* trickery; artifice.

CHICK (chik), *n.* the young of a bird.

CHICKADEE (chik'a-de), *n.* the American black-cap tit-mouse.

CHICKEN (chik'en), *n.* the young of a fowl, especially the domestic fowl.

CHICKEN-HEARTED (-hart'ed), *adj.* timid.

CHICKEN-POX (-poks), *n.* a mild eruptive disease of children.

CHICKWEED (chik'wed), *n.* a common wild plant.

CHICLE (chik'l), *n.* a plastic substance obtained from the bully tree and sapodilla.

CHICORY (chik'o-ri), *n.* a perennial plant with a tapering root, which, when roasted and ground, is sometimes used to mix with coffee.

CHIDE (chid), *v.t.* to find fault with; scold.

CHIEF (chef), *n.* a commander or leader; the most important part.

CHIEFTAIN (chef'tin), *n.* the head of a class or tribe.

CHIFFON (shif'un), *n.* a thin gauze fabric.

CHIFFONIER (shif-o-ner'), *n.* a piece of furniture.

CHIGNON (she-nyong'), *n.* a roll of hair worn by women over a pad at the back of the head.

CHIGOE (chig'o), *n.* a species of West Indian and South American flea which burrows beneath the skin of the feet, and produces ulcers.

CHILBLAIN (chil'blan), *n.* a sore on the hands or feet, caused by frost or cold.

CHILD (child), *n.* a son or daughter; a very young person.

CHILDBIRTH ('berth), *n.* the act or time of bringing forth a child.

CHILDHOOD ('hood), *n.* the period from infancy to puberty.

CHILE CON CARNE (kon kar'na), a Mexican dish of minced red peppers and meats.

CHILI (chil'i), *n.* the dried pod of a capsicum; red peppers.

CHILL (chil), *n.* a sudden coldness: *adj.* depressing; discourteous.

CHIME (chim), *n.* the musical harmony produced by striking a set of bells with hammers; a set of bells tuned to the musical scale: usually in *pl.*: *v.i.* join in.

CHIMERA (ki-me'ra), *n.* an incongruous conception of the fancy.

CHIMERICAL (ki-mer'ik-al), *adj.* merely imaginary ; fantastic.

CHIMNEY (chim'ni), *n.* the flue, vent, or passage through which smoke or heated air, etc., escapes ; a glass tube for a lamp.

CHIMPANZEE (chim-pan'ze), *n.* large anthropoid ape of Africa.

CHIN (chin), *n.* the part of the face below the underlip.

CHINA (chi'na), *n.* a fine porcelain.

CHINCH (chinch), *n.* a fetid insect destructive to corn crops.

CHINCHILLA (chin-chil'a), *n.* a small South American rodent with a soft fine fur.

CHINE (chin), *n.* the backbone or spine of an animal.

CHINESE (chi-nez'), *adj.* of or pertaining to, China.

CHINK (chingk), *n.* a small fissure ; a narrow aperture.

CHINKAPIN, CHINQUAPIN (ching'ka-pin), *n.* the dwarf chestnut of the U.S.

CHINSE (chins), *v.t.* to force oakum in the seams of a ship.

CHINTZ (chints), *n.* cotton cloth, printed in various colours.

CHIP (chip), *v.t.* to cut into small pieces : *v.i.* break or fly off into small pieces : *n.* a small piece of stone, wood, etc., cut or broken off.

CHIPMUNK (chip'mungk), *n.* a small squirrel, having dark and light stripes on its back.

CHIPPENDALE (chip'en-dal), *adj.* denoting a kind of furniture of the 18th century.

CHIPPER (chip'er), *adj.* active.

CHIROGRAPHY (ki-rog'ra-fi), *n.* the art of writing or engrossing.

CHIROMANCY (ki'ro-man-si), *n.* palmistry.

CHIROPODIST (ki-rop'o-dist), *n.* one who removes corns, bunions, etc.

CHIROPRACTIC (ki-ro-prak'tik), *n.* a treatment to cure disease by manipulation of the spine.

CHIROPRACTOR (-'ter), *n.* one who practises chiropractic.

CHIROSOPHY (ki-ros'o-fi), *n.* science of the hand ; chiromancy.

CHIRP (cherp), *n.* a short, shrill, cheerful note.

CHISEL (chiz'el), *n.* an edged tool of steel for cutting wood : *v.t.* to cut, pare, gouge, or engrave.

CHIT-CHAT (-chat), *n.* familiar talk.

CHIVALROUS (shiv'al-rus), *adj.* relating to chivalry ; gallant.

CHIVALRY (shiv'al-ri), *n.* the qualifications of a knight, as bravery, nobleness, courtesy, etc.

CHIVE (shiv), *n.* a garden plant.

CHLORAL (klo'ral), *n.* an oily, colourless narcotic.

CHLORIDE OF LIME (klo'rid lim), a powder obtained by treating slaked lime with chlorine : used for disinfecting and bleaching.

CHLORINE (klo'rin), *n.* a greenish-yellow, heavy, poisonous gas.

CHLOROFORM (klo'roform), *n.* a liquid compound : used as an anæsthetic.

CHLOROPHYLL (klo'ro-fil), *n.* the green colouring matter in plants.

CHLOROSIS (klo-ro'sis), *n.* a disease affecting young women, characterized by anæmia.

CHOCOLATE (chok'o-lat), *n.* a paste made from the roasted kernels of the cacao-nut.

CHOICE (chois), *n.* the act of choosing ; option ; thing chosen : *adj.* select.

CHOIR (kwir), *n.* a band of singers in a church.

CHOKE (chok), *v.t.* to suffocate by obstructing the windpipe ; block up.

CHOKE-DAMP (-damp), *n.* carbonic acid generated in mines.

CHOLER (kol'er), *n.* bile ; irascibility.

CHOLERA (kol'er-a), *n.* a disease with violent vomiting and purging.

CHOLERIC (kol'er-ik), *adj.* quick-tempered ; prone to anger.

CHOOSE (chooz), *v.t.* to take by preference ; select.

CHOP (chop), *v.t.* to cut with blows ; hew ; mince.

CHOPPER (-er), *n.* one who chops ; tool for chopping.

CHOPSTICK (-stik), *n.* two pieces of wood, used by Chinese as eating-forks.

CHOP SUEY (soo′i), a Chinese dish made up of a medley of meats, rice, etc.

CHORAL (ko′ral), *adj.* of, or pertaining to, a choir ; chanted or sung by a choir.

CHORD (kord), *n.* the string of a musical instrument ; notes in harmony : *v.t.* to string, as a musical instrument.

CHORES (chorz), *n.pl.* the daily light work of a farmyard.

CHORISTER (kor′is-ter), *n.* a choir member.

CHORTLE (chort′l), *v.* to chuckle.

CHORUS (ko′rus), *n.* a number singing in concert.

CHOSEN (cho′zn), *adj.* selected ; choice.

CHOW (chou), *n.* one of a breed of dogs.

CHOW-CHOW (chou′chou), *adj.* a mixed pickle.

CHOWDER (chou′der), *n.* a dish of fish ; clams, stewed together with pork and biscuits, etc.

CHRISM (krizm), *n.* consecrated oil.

CHRIST (krist), *n.* the Messiah ; the Lord's Anointed ; Jesus, the Saviour ; perfect humanity, as typified by Jesus.

CHRISTEN (kris′n), *v.t.* to baptize ; give a Christian name to.

CHRISTENDOM (kris′n-dum), *n.* countries whose inhabitants profess the Christian faith ; Christians collectively.

CHRISTIAN (kris′chan), *n.* a professor of the religion of Christ.

CHRISTIAN ERA (e′ra), *n.* the present era reckoned from the birth of Christ.

CHRISTIANITY (kris-chi-an′i-ti), *n.* the precepts and doctrines taught by Christ.

CHRISTIAN SCIENCE (si′ens), *n.* a religious system founded by Mary Baker Eddy in 1866, taking as its fundamental doctrine the Scriptures and teachings of Jesus.

CHRISTMAS (kris′mas), *n.* the festival (Dec. 25) celebrating the birth of Christ.

CHRISTMASTIDE (-tid), *n.* Christmas Eve (Dec. 24) to Epiphany (Jan. 6).

CHRISTMAS TREE (tre), *n.* an evergreen, as fir, set up at Christmastide for the children, and hung with gifts, ornaments, and lights.

CHROMATE (kro′mat), *n.* a salt of chromic acid.

CHROMATIC (kro-mat′ik), *adj.* relating to colours.

CHROMO (kro′mo), *n.* a chromolithograph or picture produced by lithography.

CHROMOGEN (kro′mo-jen), *n.* the colouring matter of plants.

CHRONIC (kron′ik), *adj.* continuing a long time, or recurring : said of a disease.

CHRONICLE (kron′i-kl), *n.* an historical record according to date ; a register of facts or events.

CHRONICLER (′i-kler), *n.* a writer of a chronicle ; a recorder of events.

CHRONOGRAPH (kron′o-graf), *n.* an instrument for recording the exact time of an event.

CHRONOLOGICAL (kron-o-loj′i-kal), *adj.* relating to, or containing an account of past events in the order of time.

CHRONOLOGIST (kro-nol′o-jist), *n.* one versed in chronology.

CHRONOLOGY (′o-ji), *n.* the science that treats of events and arranges their dates in proper sequence.

CHRONOMETER (kro-nom′e-ter), *n.* an instrument for measuring time with extreme accuracy.

CHRYSALIS (kris′a-lis), *n.* the final stage through which a lepidopterous insect, or butterfly, passes prior to its winged state.

CHRYSANTHEMUM (kris-an′the-mum), *n.* a large genus of plants of the aster family.

CHUB (chub), *n.* a fresh-water fish.

CHUBBINESS (chub′i-nes), *n.* plumpness.

CHUBBY (chub′i), *adj.* plump ; fat and round.

CHUCK (chuk), *v.t.* to pat in a playful manner : *n.* a light blow under the chin ; a short toss ; an appendage to a lathe ; the part of beef around the neck and shoulder blade.

CHUCKLE (chuk'l), *n.* a quiet, suppressed laugh.

CHUM (chum), *n.* one who lodges in the same apartment ; an old or intimate friend.

CHUNK (chungk), *n.* a short, thick piece.

CHUNKY (chungk'i), *adj.* short and thick.

CHURCH (cherch), *n.* a building consecrated for divine worship ; the collective body of Christians.

CHURCHMAN ('man), *n.* a church member ; an ecclesiastic.

CHURCHWARDEN ('wawr-dn), *n.* in the Anglican Church, one of two officers chosen at Easter in every parish to attend to the secular affairs of the church.

CHURCHYARD ('yard), *n.* the yard or enclosure around a church ; a burial ground.

CHURL (cherl), *n.* a surly, ill-bred person ; a niggard.

CHURLISH ('ish), *adj.* ill-bred.

CHURN (chern), *n.* a vessel in which milk or cream is agitated to form butter.

CHUTE (shoot), *n.* an inclined trough for sending articles down ; a riverfall over which timber is floated.

CHUTNEY (chut'ni), *n.* a relish made up of fruits and spices.

CHYLE (kil), *n.* a milk-like fluid separated from digested matter in the stomach, absorbed by the lacteal vessels, and assimilated into blood.

CHYME (kim), *n.* the pulpy mass of digested food prior to the separation of the chyle.

CICATRIX (sik'a-triks), *n.* the scar remaining after a wound has healed.

CICERONE (sis-e-ro'ne), *n.* a guide who explains the antiquities and chief features of a place.

CID (sid), *n.* a chief or commander ; the name of a Spanish epic.

CIDER (si'der), *n.* the juice of apples fermented ; a beverage.

CIGAR (si-gar'), *n.* a small roll of tobacco and leaf for smoking.

CIGARETTE (sig-a-ret'), *n.* tobacco rolled in thin paper, or leaf.

CIMEX (si'meks), *n.* a genus of bugs.

CINCH (sinch), *n.* a saddle girth firmly fastened in place ; a sure grip or hold : [Slang] a sure thing ; something easy.

CINCHONA (sin-ko'na), *n.* a South American tree.

CINCINSIS (sin-sin'sis), *n.* a valuable variety of pear.

CINCTURE (singk'tur), *n.* a belt or girdle worn round the waist ; a raised or carved ring at the bottom and top of a pillar.

CINDER (sin'der), *n.* any piece of a body thoroughly burnt but not reduced to ashes.

CINEMA (sin'e-ma), *n.* a motion picture show.

CINEMATOGRAPH (sin-e-mat'o-graf), *n.* a French device similar to the biograph.

CINERARY (sin'e-ra-ri), *adj.* pertaining to, or containing, ashes.

CINNABAR (sin'a-bar), *n.* red sulphide of mercury.

CINNAMON (sin'a-mun), *n.* the inner aromatic bark of an East Indian tree.

CINQUEFOIL (singk'foil), *n.* a plant ; an architectural design of five cusps.

CIPHER (si'fer), *n.* the symbol o ; a monogram ; a secret manner of writing ; a code.

CIRCASSIAN (ser-kash'an), *n.* a light cashmere ; a twilled fabric of wool and cotton.

CIRCLE (ser'kl), *n.* a round body ; a plane figure bounded by a single curved line, circumference, every part of which is equally distant from the centre.

CIRCLET (ser'klet), *n.* a small circle.

CIRCUIT (ser'ket), *n.* the act of going round anything ; the journey of a judge from one place to another to hold assizes ; the arrangement by which an electrical current is kept up between the two poles of a battery or machine ; the path of the electric current.

CIRCUITOUS (ser-ku'i-tus), *adj.* roundabout.

CIRCULAR (ser'ku-lar), *adj.* round

like a circle; ending in itself; intended for circulation : *n*. a printed letter or notice.

CIRCULARIZE (-iz), *v.t.* to make circular; send circulars to.

CIRCULATE (ser'ku-lat), *v.t.* to cause to pass from point to point or from one person to another : *v.i.* move round and return to the same point; pass from hand to hand; to be diffused or distributed; to travel.

CIRCULATION (-la'shun), *n.* the act of moving round; the movement of the blood in the veins and arteries; the extent to which a thing is circulated; currency of money.

CIRCUM- (ser'kum), a prefix signifying *about, around, on all sides.*

CIRCUMFERENCE (ser-kum'fer-ens), *n.* the line that bounds a circle; a periphery.

CIRCUMFLECT (ser-kum-flekt'), *v.t.* to bend around.

CIRCUMFLEX (ser'kum-fleks), *n.* a mark over vowel or syllable to denote accent or contraction.

CIRCUMFUSE (ser-kum-fuz'), *v.t.* to pour or spread around.

CIRCUMJACENT (ser-kum-ja'sent), *adj.* lying around; bordering on every side.

CIRCUMLOCUTION (ser-kum-lo-ku'shun), *n.* a roundabout way of speaking; an indirect mode of statement.

CIRCUMNAVIGATE (ser-kum-nav'i-gat), *v.t.* to sail round : usually the globe.

CIRCUMNAVIGATOR (ser-kum-nav'i-ga-ter), *n.* one who circumnavigates.

CIRCUMSCRIBE (ser-kum-skrib'), *v.t.* to enclose within certain lines or boundaries; restrict.

CIRCUMSCRIPTION (-skrip'-shun), *n.* the act of circumscribing.

CIRCUMSCRIPTIVE (-skrip'tiv), *adj.* limiting.

CIRCUMSPECT (ser'kum-spekt), *adj.* cautious; prudent; watchful.

CIRCUMSPECTION (ser-kum-spek'shun), *n.* caution; watchfulness; prudence.

CIRCUMSTANCE (ser'kum-stans),

n. something relative or appendant to a fact; an event.

CIRCUMSTANTIAL (ser-kum-stan'-shal), *n.* something incidental and subordinate to the main subject.

CIRCUMSTANTIAL EVIDENCE (ev'i-dens), evidence which gives ground for belief as to fact, or the guilt or innocence of a person accused.

CIRCUMSTANTIALLY (-li), *adv.* incidentally; not essentially; minutely; exactly.

CIRCUMVENT (ser-kum-vent'), *n.* to gain an advantage over by deception; to pass around.

CIRCUMVENTION (-ven'shun), *n.* the act of circumventing; a stratagem.

CIRCUMVENTIVE ('tiv), *adj.* deceiving by artifice.

CIRCUMVOLUTION (-vo-lu'shun), *n.* the act of rolling round; the state of being rolled round; circumlocution.

CIRCUS (ser'kus), *n.* a large level oblong space for feats of horsemanship, trained animals, balancing, tumbling, etc.

CIS-, a prefix signifying *on this side.*

CISATLANTIC (sis-at-lan'tik), *adj.* on this side of the Atlantic Ocean.

CISTERN (cis'tern), *n.* a receptacle for storing water; a reservoir.

CITABLE (sit'a-bl), *adj.* capable of being cited.

CITADEL (sit'a-del), *n.* a fortress.

CITATION (si-ta'shun), *n.* an official summons to appear before a court; a quotation.

CITE (sit), *v.t.* to summon to appear in court; quote.

CITIZEN (sit'i-zen), *n.* a native or inhabitant of a town or city, and who enjoys political rights.

CITRATE (sit'rat), *n.* a salt of citric acid.

CITRIC ACID (sit'rik as'id), an acid found in the lemon and orange.

CITRON (sit'run), *n.* a tree with a fruit like the lemon.

CITRUS (sit'rus), *n.* a genus of trees, shrubs, and herbs of the rue family, including oranges and lemons.

CITY (sit'i), *n.* corporate town governed

by a mayor and other elected and appointed officials.

CIVET CAT (siv'et kat), *n.* a carnivore of northern Africa.

CIVIC (siv'ik), *adj.* pertaining to a city.

CIVIL (siv'il), *adj.* relating to the affairs of a city or government; complaisant; well-bred.

CIVILIAN (si-vil'yan), *n.* one engaged in the pursuits of civil life.

CIVILITY (si-vil'i-ti), *n.* good breeding; courtesy.

CIVILIZATION (siv-i-li-za'shun), *n.* the act or state of being civilized; culture; refinement.

CIVILIZE (siv'i-liz), *v.t.* to reclaim from a savage state.

CIVIL SERVICE (ser'vis), paid service of the State, not exclusively naval or military.

CLAIM (klam), *v.t.* to demand as a right, or by authority : *n.* a demand; a right or title to anything.

CLAIMANT (kla'mant), *n.* one who demands anything as his right.

CLAIRVOYANCE (klar-voi'ans), *n.* the power attributed to persons in a mesmeric state of seeing objects not usually perceptible; intuition.

CLAIRVOYANT ('ant), *n.* one who professes to have the power of clairvoyance.

CLAM (klam), *v.t.* to dig for clams : *n.* one of various edible, bivalve molluscs.

CLAMANT (kla-mant), *adj.* crying out; noisy.

CLAMBAKE (-bak), *n.* a picnic at which baked clams form the chief dish.

CLAMBER (klam'ber), *v.t.* to ascend or climb with difficulty.

CLAMMY (klam'i), *adj.* soft and sticky.

CLAMOROUS (klam'er-us), *adj.* vociferous.

CLAMOUR (klam'er), *n.* a loud and continued noise.

CLAMP (klamp), *n.* anything that fastens or binds.

CLAN (klan), *n.* a tribe or association of families.

CLANDESTINE (-des'tin), *adj.* secret; private.

CLANG (klang), *n.* a loud, sharp, ringing, metallic sound.

CLANGOUR ('ger), *n.* a sharp clang.

CLANK (klangk), *n.* a sharp, hard, metallic sound.

CLANNISH (klan'ish), *adj.* pertaining to a clan; closely adherent.

CLAP (klap), *v.t. & v.i.* to strike one thing against another with a quick, sharp noise.

CLAPBOARD (klap'bord), *n.* a thin board, used for the covering of frame houses.

CLAPPER ('er), *n.* one who, or that which, claps; the tongue of a bell.

CLAQUE (klak), *n.* an organized body who applaud or express disapproval.

CLARET (klar'et), *n.* a dark-red table-wine : *adj.* of a dark-red colour.

CLARIFICATION (klar-i-fi-ka'shun), *n.* the act of clarifying.

CLARIFY (klar'i-fi), *v.t.* to make clear from impurities.

CLARINET (klar'i-net), *n.* a keyed reed instrument of the oboe class.

CLARION (klar'ri-un), *n.* a kind of trumpet; a sound as of a trumpet.

CLARITY (klar'i-ti), *n.* clearness.

CLASH (klash), *v.t.* to strike violently together : *n.* the noise so produced.

CLASP (klasp), *v.t.* to shut or fasten together with, or as with, a clasp : *n.* a hook to hold anything close; a close embrace.

CLASP-KNIFE (-nif), *n.* a large pocket-knife.

CLASS (clas), *n.* a rank or order of persons or things; a number of students of the same status.

CLASSIC (klas'ik), **CLASSICAL** ('si-kal), *adj.* of, or relating to, the highest class or rank in literature or art; pure; refined; clear-cut : *n.* an author of the first rank whose works serve as a standard.

CLASSIFICATION (klas-i-fi-ka'shun), *n.* the art of forming or dividing into classes.

CLASSIFIER (klas'i-fi-er), *n.* one who classifies.

CLASSIFY (klas'i-fi), *v.t.* to arrange in classes; systematize.

CLASSMATE ('mat), *n.* a member of

the same class at school or college.

CLATTER (klat′er), *v.i.* talk idly and noisily : *n.* a continuous or confused noise ; idle gossip.

CLAUSE (klawz), *n.* a separate part of a composition, or a sentence ; a special proviso in a document.

CLAVICLE (klav′i-kl), *n.* the collarbone.

CLAW (klaw), *n.* a sharp hooked nail in the foot of an animal ; the whole foot of a bird ; anything resembling a claw : *v.t.* to tear or scratch with claws.

CLAW-HAMMER COAT (-ham′er kot), a swallow-tail coat for full dress.

CLAY (kla), *n.* soft plastic earth ; the bodily or earthly nature of man.

CLAY PIGEON (pij′un), a flying target of baked clay.

CLEAN (klen), *adj.* free from dirt or extraneous matter.

CLEAN-CUT (-kut), *adj.* clear-cut ; well-shaped.

CLEANLINESS (klen′li-nes), *n.* the state of being clean.

CLEANLY (klen′li), *adj.* neat ; pure.

CLEANNESS (klen′nes), *n.* moral or physical purity ; neatness.

CLEANSE (klenz), *v.t.* to make clean.

CLEAR (kler), *adj.* bright ; pure ; undimmed ; unobstructed ; audible : *v.i.* leave a port.

CLEARANCE (kler′ans), *n.* the act of clearing.

CLEAR-CUT (kut), *adj.* having a sharp, clearly defined outline.

CLEARING (kler′ing), *n.* the act of making clear ; land cleared of timber.

CLEARING-HOUSE (-hous), *n.* an institution by which banks adjust their balances.

CLEAT (klet), *n.* a thin piece of iron worn on boots to make more durable ; a piece of wood or iron to keep ropes from slipping ; a strip of wood nailed across a board.

CLEAVABLE (kle′va-bl), *adj.* divisible.

CLEAVAGE (kle′vaj), *n.* the act of splitting.

CLEAVE (klev), *v.i.* to adhere to ; be attached strongly to.

CLEAVE (klev), *v.t.* to divide with violence.

CLEAVER (kle′ver), *n.* a butcher's heavy hatchet.

CLEF (klef), *n.* a figure at the beginning of each staff in music.

CLEFT (kleft), *n.* a crack ; crevice.

CLEMATIS (klem′a-tis), *n.* a perennial vine.

CLEMENCY (klem′en-si), *n.* compassion ; remission.

CLENCH (klench), *v.t.* to grip tightly : *n.* a firm grip.

CLERGY (kler′ji), *n.* a body of men set apart by ordination for the service of God.

CLERGYMAN (-man), *n.* a minister of a church.

CLERIC (kler′ik), *n.* a clerk in holy orders.

CLERICAL (kler′i-kal), *adj.* pertaining to the clergy ; pertaining to a clerk, writer, or copyist.

CLERICAL ERROR (er′er), an error in copying.

CLERK (klerk), *n.* one engaged to conduct correspondence, or transact business generally ; an assistant salesman.

CLEVER (klev′er), *adj.* possessing skill or ability ; expert.

CLEW (kloo), *n.* a ball of thread ; something that leads to a solution as a *clew* to crime ; one of the corners of a sail.

CLICK (klik), *v.i.* to make a short sharp noise.

CLIENT (kli′ent), *n.* one who employs a lawyer.

CLIENTELE (kli-en-tel′), *n.* clients collectively.

CLIFF (klif), *n.* high steep rock or bank.

CLIMACTERIC (kli-mak′ter-ik), *n.* any critical period.

CLIMATE (kli′mat), *n.* the temperature and meteorological conditions of a country.

CLIMATIC (kli-mat′ik), *adj.* relating to climate.

CLIMATIZE (kli′ma-tiz), *v.t.* to accustom to a new climate.

CLIMAX (kli′maks), *n.* the summit ; acme.

CLIMB (klim), *v.i.* to mount or ascend.

CLIME (klim), *n.* a country, region, or tract.

CLINCH (klinch), *v.t.* to rivet; fix firmly by folding over; double up tightly, as the fingers.

CLING (kling), *v.i.* to adhere closely.

CLINIC (klin'ik), *n.* a medical lecture; a dispensary.

CLINK (klingk), *v.i.* to strike so as to make a slight sharp sound.

CLINKER ('er), *n.* a mass of partly vitrified brick; slag.

CLIP (klip), *v.t.* to cut with scissors; cut off: *v.i.* move quickly.

CLIPPER ('er), *n.* one who, or that which, clips; an instrument for cutting the hair; a sailing vessel.

CLIQUE (klek), *n.* a group of persons united for some common purpose; a coterie; a ring.

CLOAK (klok), *n.* a sleeveless, loose garment; a pretext; disguise: *v.t.* cover up or conceal.

CLOCK (klok), *n.* a machine for telling time.

CLOCKWISE ('wiz), *adv.* in the direction of the rotation of the hands of a clock.

CLOD (klod), *n.* a lump of earth, turf, or clay; a dull, stupid fellow.

CLOG (klog), *v.t.* to load with anything that may impede motion; wooden shoe.

CLOISTER (klois'ter), *n.* a place of religious retirement; an arched way or covered walk.

CLOSE (kloz), *v.t.* to shut; surround closely; unite; consolidate; end: *adj.* without ventilation; oppressive.

CLOSEFISTED (-fist'ed), *adj.* miserly.

CLOSEHAULED (-hawld), *adj.* kept as near to the wind as possible when sailing.

CLOSE SEASON (se'zun), certain months in the year in which it is illegal to kill game.

CLOSET (kloz'et), *n.* a small room for privacy or retirement; a place for storing clothing, etc.

CLOSE-UP (klos'up), *n.* in moving pictures, a scene or character taken nearer to the camera than others.

CLOSURE (klo'zhur), *n.* the act of shutting up; that which closes; the end; the closing of a debate by the vote of the majority (the clôture).

CLOT (klot), *v.i.* to coagulate: *n.* concrete or coagulate mass of soft or fluid matter.

CLOTH (kloth), *n.* a woven fabric.

CLOTHE (kloth), *v.t.* to put raiment on.

CLOTHES (klothz), *n.pl.* covering for the body; dress; bedclothes.

CLOTHIER (kloth'yer), *n.* one who manufactures or sells clothes.

CLOTHING (kloth'ing), *n.* garments in general.

CLOTURE, see closure.

CLOUD (kloud), *n.* a mass of visible vapour floating in the atmosphere.

CLOUD-BURST (-berst), *n.* a violent downpour of rain.

CLOUDY ('i), *adj.* overcast; dark; gloomy; confused.

CLOUT (klout), *n.* a piece of cloth or leather for patching; a blow with the hand.

CLOVE (klov), *n.* a pungent, aromatic spice.

CLOVEN (klo'ven), *p.adj.* divided into two parts.

CLOVER (klo'ver), *n.* one of a species of plants of the genus Tritolium.

CLOWN (kloun), *n.* a professional jester or buffoon.

CLOY (kloi), *v.t.* to fill to repletion; surfeit.

CLUB (klub), *n.* a heavy stick; one of the suits of cards; persons associated for a common purpose or mutual benefit.

CLUBFOOT ('foot), *n.* a deformed foot.

CLUE (kloo), *n.* a hint; a clew.

CLUMP (klump), *n.* a thick cluster; a dull sound.

CLUMSILY (klum'zi-li), *adv.* awkwardly; heavily.

CLUMSY (klum'zi), *adj.* awkward; heavy.

CLUNG, *p.t.* of cling.

CLUSTER (klus'ter), *n.* a bunch: *v.i.* congregate.

CLUTCH (kluch), *v.t.* to grasp, seize, or grip strongly : *n.* a machine coupling ; a brake.

CO- (ko), a prefix, signifying *with*, *together*, entering into the composition of many words, the sense of which is generally self-evident, as *co*-trustee, a joint trustee.

COACH (koch), *n.* a large covered four-wheeled carriage ; a tutor who especially prepares another for an examination or an athletic contest.

COAGULANT (ko-ag'u-lant), *n.* a substance that produces coagulation.

COAGULATE (ko-ag'u-lat), *v.t.* to clot or curdle.

COAGULATION (-u-la'shun), *n.* the act of coagulating ; the state of being coagulated.

COAGULIN (co-ag'u-lin), *n.* a drug which coagulates the blood.

COAL (kol), *n.* mineralized vegetable matter, used in its hardened form as fuel ; a piece of this matter.

COALESCE (ko-a-les'), *v.t.* to grow together ; combine ; unite.

COALESCENCE ('ens), *n.* the act of coalescing.

COALITION (ko-a-lish'un), *n.* union in a body or mass ; a combination of persons.

COAL-OIL ('oil), *n.* petroleum.

COAL-TAR ('tar), *n.* a thick, opaque liquid distilled from bituminous coal, and from which many dye colours are obtained.

COARSE (kors), *adj.* large in texture or size ; not refined ; rough ; rude ; indelicate.

COARSE-GRAINED ('grand), *adj.* having a coarse grain ; ill-tempered.

COARSELY (kors'li), *adv.* in a coarse manner.

COARSENESS ('nes), *n.* quality of being coarse.

COAST (kost), *n.* the margin of the land next the sea : *v.i.* to sail near or along the coast.

COASTER ('er), *n.* a home-trading vessel ; one who coasts on a sled.

COASTGUARD ('gard), *n.* a member of the service for watching the sea, to check smuggling.

COASTING-TRADE ('ing-trad), the trade carried on from port to port of the same country.

COASTWISE ('wiz), *adv.* by, or along, the coast.

COAT (kot), *n.* an outer garment covering the upper part of the body ; an external covering, as fur, etc. ; a thin layer.

COAT OF ARMS (armz), the emblazonment of armorial bearings on an escutcheon.

COAX (koks), *v.t.* to wheedle ; cajole.

COAXIAL (ko-ak'si-al), *adj.* having a common axis.

COB (kob), *n.* a roundish piece of anything ; the spike of corn ; a strong, thick-set pony.

COBALT (ko'bawlt), *n.* a steel-grey metal.

COBBLE (kob'l), *n.* a pebble ; a stone for paving : *v.i.* work clumsily.

COBBLER ('ler), *n.* one who mends boots and shoes.

COBRA (ko'bra), **COBRA-DE-CAPELLO** (-de-ka-pel'o), *n.* a large venomous hooded snake of India.

COBWEB (kob'web), *n.* a spider's web.

COCA (ko'ka), *n.* the dried leaf of a small South American shrub.

COCAINE (ko'ka-in), *n.* a powerful alkaloid : usually pronounced ko-kan'.

COCHINEAL (koch'i-nel), *n.* a scarlet dye obtained from the dried body of an insect.

COCHLEA (kok'le-a), *n.* [*pl.* cochleæ (-e)], the spiral-shaped cavity of the inner ear.

COCK (kok), *n.* the male of birds ; a turn-valve for regulating the flow of a liquid or gas ; a heap of hay.

COCKADE (-ad'), *n.* a badge or ribbon worn on the hat.

COCKATOO (-a-too'), *n.* a crested bird of the parrot family.

COCKCHAFER ('cha-fer), *n.* the May-bug ; a destructive beetle.

COCKEREL ('er-el), *n.* a young cock.

COCK-EYED ('id), *adj.* having squinting eyes.

COCKFIGHT (-fit), *n.* a contest between game cocks.

COCKPIT (kok'pit), *n.* an open space

in an airplane or open sail boat for the pilot and passengers.

COCKROACH ('roch), *n.* a black beetle.

COCKTAIL (kok'tal), *n.* a mixed alcoholic drink.

COCOA (ko'ko), *n.* a palm which produces the cocoanut.

COCOA (ko'ko), *n.* the ground seeds of the cacao or chocolate tree; the beverage made from it.

COCOANUT (-nut), *n.* the fruit of the cocoa palm.

COCOON (ko-koon'), *n.* the silky oblong case covering the larvæ of many spinning insects.

COD (kod), *n.* a large edible fish.

CODDLE (kod'l), *v.t.* to make effeminate by pampering; treat tenderly.

CODE (ked), *n.* a body of classified laws; a system of signals.

CODEX (ko'deks), *n.* [*pl.* codices ('di-sez)], a volume of statutes; a manuscript volume, especially of the sacred Scriptures.

CODGER (koj'er), *n.* a miser.

CODICIL (kod'i-sil), *n.* an appendix to a will.

CODIFY (ko'di-, kod'i-fi), *v.t.* to reduce to a code or digest.

CODLING MOTH (moth), a moth whose larvæ feed on apples.

COEFFICIENT (ko-e-fish'ent), *adj.* co-operating: *n.* that which co-operates with another; a number or known quantity prefixed in algebra as a multiplier to a variable or an unknown quantity.

COERCE (ko-ers'), *v.t.* to restrain or constrain by force.

COERCION ('shun), *n.* the act of coercing.

COERCIVE ('siv), *adj.* having power to coerce.

COEVAL (ko-e'val), *adj.* contemporaneous.

COEXTENSIVE (ko-eks-ten'siv), *adj.* equally extensive.

COFFEE (kof'e), *n.* the seeds of a small tropical tree or shrub: a decoction of these seeds, when roasted and ground.

COFFER (kof'er), *n.* a chest; a kind of caisson or floating dock: *pl.* a treasury.

COFFER-DAM (-dam), *n.* a temporary enclosure in water to enable workmen to lay foundations for piers, etc.

COFFIN ('in), *n.* a case or box for the dead.

COG (kog), *n.* the tooth of a wheel.

COGENT (ko'jent), *adj.* forcible; not easily resisted.

COGITATE (koj'i-tat), *v.i.* to meditate: *v.t.* to devise or plan.

COGITATION (-ta'shun), *n.* act of cogitating.

COGITATIVE (-ta-tiv), *adj.* meditative.

COGNATE (kog'nat), *adj.* allied by blood; of the same stock, nature, or quality.

COGNITION (kog-nish'un), *n.* knowledge.

COGNITIVE (kog'ni-tiv), *adj.* having power of mental apprehension.

COGNIZANCE (kon'i-zans), *n.* judicial knowledge or notice; perception.

COGNIZANT (kon'i-zant), *adj.* having knowledge of anything.

COGNOMEN (kog-no'men), *n.* a surname.

COHABIT (ko-hab'it), *v.i.* to dwell together as husband and wife.

COHERE (ko-her'), *v.i.* to stick together.

COHERENCE ('ens), *n.* the state or quality of cohering.

COHERENT ('ent), *adj.* cohering together; consistent; logical.

COHERER (ko-her'er), *n.* a device for detecting electro-magnetic waves.

COHESION (ko-he'zhun), *n.* the force that unites molecules of the same material; coherence.

COHESIVE ('siv), *n.* causing to cohere.

COHORT (ko'hort), *n.* any band or company of individuals.

COIFFEUR (kwa'fer), *n.* [French] a hairdresser.

COIFFURE (koif'ur), *n.* style of arranging the hair.

COIGN (koin), *n.* corner; projecting stone.

COIL (koil), *n.* a rope gathered into a ring; anything resembling it.

COIN (koin), *n.* money stamped with a legal impression.

COINAGE ('aj), *n.* the process of coining.

COINCIDE (ko-in-sid'), *v.i.* to correspond exactly; occur at the same time.

COINCIDENCE (ko-in'si-dens), *n.* the act of coinciding.

COINCIDENT (ko-in'si-dent), *adj.* coinciding.

COKE (kok), *n.* the residue of coal after the gas, etc., has been expelled.

COLANDER (kul'an-der), *n.* a vessel with a perforated bottom.

COLA NUT (ko'la nut), *n.* the large bitter seed of an African tree.

COLD (kold), *adj.* without heat or warmth; frigid; indifferent; insensible; blue in tone : *n.* a catarrh.

COLD-BLOODED (-blud'ed), *adj.* having the blood below 90° Fahr. in temperature; heartless; brutal.

COLE (kol), *n.* rape; cabbage plants in general.

COLESLAW ('slaw), *n.* cabbage salad.

COLIC (kol'ik), *n.* acute spasmodic pain in the abdomen or bowels.

COLISEUM, see colosseum.

COLLABORATE (ko-lab'o-rat), *v.i.* to work jointly, especially in literary or scientific work.

COLLABORATION (-o-ra'shun), *n.* united labour.

COLLABORATOR (-lab'o-ra-ter), *n.* one who assists another, especially in literary or scientific work.

COLLAPSE (ko-laps'), *n.* a falling in or together; sudden and complete failure.

COLLAPSIBLE (-lap'si-bl), *adj.* capable of collapsing.

COLLAR (kol'ar), *n.* anything encircling the neck.

COLLARETTE (-et), *n.* a fichu of lace, etc.

COLLATE (ko-lat'), *v.t.* to compare critically, text of books.

COLLATERAL (ko-lat'er-al), *adj.* side by side; auxiliary; concurrent.

COLLATERAL SECURITY (se-kur'i-ti), money or property pledged as security.

COLLATION (ko-la'shun), *n.* comparison; a light repast; a conference.

COLLATOR ('ter), *n.* one who collates.

COLLEAGUE (kol'eg), *n.* an associate.

COLLECT (kol'ekt), *n.* a short comprehensive prayer.

COLLECT (ko-lekt'), *v.t.* gather together; assemble; obtain payment.

COLLECTED ('ed), *adj.* self-possessed.

COLLECTION (ko-lek'shun), *n.* a mass; a crowd; an assemblage of works of art, etc.; a contribution.

COLLECTIVE ('tiv), *adj.* accumulative.

COLLECTIVISM (-izm), *n.* the socialistic theory that land and capital should be owned by society collectively.

COLLECTIVIST (-ist), *n.* an advocate of collectivism.

COLLECTOR (ko-lek'ter), *n.* one who collects.

COLLEGE (kol'ej), *n.* a place to receive instruction in the higher branches of learning.

COLLEGIAN (ko-le'ji-an), *n.* a member of a college.

COLLEGIATE (-at), *adj.* pertaining to, or containing, a college.

COLLIDE (ko-lid'), *v.i.* to come into collision.

COLLIE (kol'i), *n.* a Scotch sheep-dog.

COLLIER (kol'yer), *n.* a coal-digger; a vessel in the coal trade.

COLLIERY (-i), *n.* a coal mine.

COLLISION (ko-lizh'un), *n.* the act of striking two bodies violently together; concussion.

COLLODION (ko-lo'di-un), *n.* a preparation of soluble gun-cotton with ether.

COLLOQUIAL (ko-lo'kwi-al), *adj.* used in ordinary conversation.

COLLOQUIALISM (-izm), *n.* a colloquial form of speech.

COLLOQUY (kol'o-kwi), *n.* a conversation; a dialogue.

COLLUSION (ko-lu'zhun), *n.* a secret

agreement for a fraudulent or evil purpose.

COLLUSIVE ('siv), *adj.* fraudulently concerted.

COLOGNE WATER (ko-lon' waw'-ter), *n.* eau-de-cologne.

COLON (ko'lon), *n.* a mark of punctuation [:]; the largest of the intestines.

COLONEL (ker'nel), *n.* the chief officer of a regiment.

COLONIAL (ko-lo'ni-al), *adj.* pertaining to a colony : *n.* an inhabitant of a colony.

COLONIST (kol'o-nist), *n.* inhabitant of a colony.

COLONIZATION (kol'o-ni-za'shun), *n.* act of colonizing or state of being colonized.

COLONIZE (kol'o-niz), *v.t.* to settle or establish a colony.

COLONNADE (kol-o-nad'), *n.* a series of columns.

COLONY (kol'o-ni), *n.* a body of people from their native country who settle in another land, under the jurisdiction of the parent country.

COLORADO BEETLE (kol-o-ra'do be'tl), *n.* a yellowish beetle, destructive to potato crops.

COLOSSAL (ko-los'al), *adj.* like a colossus ; gigantic.

COLOSSEUM (kol-o-se'um), *n.* the Flavian amphitheatre at ancient Rome, which seated 87,000.

COLOSSUS (ko-los'us), *n.* [*pl.* colossi (-i)], anything huge or marvellously great.

COLOUR (kul'er), *n.* the hue or appearance that a body presents to the eye ; a pigment or paint ; complexion.

COLOUR BLIND (kul'er blind), *n.* having a defect in one's vision, which renders one unable to differentiate one colour from another.

COLPORTAGE (kol'por-taj), *n.* a system of distributing Bibles, religious books, etc.

COLPORTEUR (-ter), *n.* one engaged in colportage.

COLT (kolt), *n.* a young horse.

COLTISH ('ish), *adj.* like a colt ; frisky.

COLUMBIAN (ko-lum'bi-an), *adj.* pertaining to the U.S. or to Christopher Columbus.

COLUMBINE (kol'um-bin), *n.* a plant with flowers of five petals.

COLUMBUS DAY (da), October 12.

COLUMN (kol'umn), *n.* a round pillar to support a building ; a division of the page of a book, etc. ; a formation of troops.

COLUMNAR (ko-lum'nar), *adj.* having the form or shape of a column.

COMA (ko'ma), *n.* insensibility ; stupor.

COMATOSE (kom'a-tos), *adj.* torpid ; lethargic.

COMB (kom), *n.* a toothed instrument to separate and adjust the hair ; the crest of a cock ; the crest of a wave ; a honeycomb.

COMBAT (kom'bat), *v.i.* to fight ; act in opposition.

COMBATANT (-ant), *n.* one who combats.

COMBATIVE (-iv), *adj.* pugnacious.

COMBINATION (kom-bi-na'shun), *n.* the union of bodies or qualities ; an association of persons for a common object.

COMBINE (kom'bin), *v.t.* to unite or join ; link closely together : *n.* a combination.

COMBUSTIBLE (kom-bus'ti-bl), *adj.* inflammable.

COMBUSTION (-bust'yun), *n.* the union of an inflammable substance with oxygen, etc.

COME (kum), *v.i.* to move toward ; draw near ; reach.

COMEDIAN (ko-me'di-an), *n.* an actor or player in comedy.

COMEDIENNE (ko-me-di-en'), *n.* an actress who plays in comedies.

COMEDY (kom'e-di), *n.* dramatic representation of the humorous side of life.

COMELINESS (kum'li-nes), *n.* grace ; beauty.

COMELY (kum'li), *adj.* graceful ; handsome.

COMESTIBLE (ko-mes'ti-bl), *adj.* suitable for eating.

COMET (kom'et), *n.* a luminous celestial body.

COMFIT (kum'fit), *n.* a dry sweet-meat.

COMFORT (kum'fert), *v.t.* to console; strengthen; inspirit.

COMFORTABLE ('fer-ta-bl), *adj.* imparting or enjoying comfort: *n.* bed quilt.

COMFORTER (kum'fer-ter), *n.* one who comforts; a long woollen scarf.

COMIC (kom'ik), **COMICAL** ('-kal), *adj.* exciting mirth.

COMING (kum'ing), *n.* an arrival: *adj.* expected; future.

COMITY (kom'i-ti), *n.* civility; politeness; acts of international courtesy.

COMMA (kom'a), *n.* a punctuation point [,].

COMMAND (ko-mand'), *v.t.* control; exercise supreme authority over; lead: *v.i.* act as a commander: *n.* authority; an order or mandate.

COMMANDANT (kom-an-dant'), *n.* [French], an officer in command of a fortified place or a body of troops.

COMMANDEER (kom-man-der'), *v.t.* to seize for the benefit of military needs.

COMMANDER (ko-man'der), *n.* one who commands.

COMMANDMENT (ko-mand'ment), *n.* a command; a precept; a law, especially any one of the Decalogue.

COMMEMORATE (ko-mem'o-rat), *v.t.* to call to remembrance by a solemn act.

COMMENCE (ko-mens'), *v.i.* to come into existence; begin.

COMMENCEMENT ('ment), *n.* beginning; origin; the annual festival when degrees, etc., are conferred at colleges.

COMMEND (ko-mend'), *v.t.* recommend as worthy of notice; praise.

COMMENDATION (kom-en-da'shun), *n.* the act of commending.

COMMENDATORY ('da-to-ri), *adj.* serving to commend.

COMMENSURABLE (ko-men'shoo-ra-bl), *adj.* having, or reducible to, a common measure.

COMMENSURATE ('shoo-rat), *adj.* reducible to a common measure; equal.

COMMENT (kom'ent), *n.* a spoken or written remark, especially a written note by way of explanation, etc.; criticism.

COMMENTARY (kom'en-ta-ri), *n.* a series of explanatory notes.

COMMENTATOR ('en-ta-ter), *n.* one who writes notes to explain an author.

COMMERCE (kom'ers), *n.* interchange of merchandise between nations or individuals; intercourse.

COMMERCIAL (ko-mer'shal), *adj.* pertaining to trade or commerce.

COMMERCIALISM (-izm), *n.* commercial habits, methods, or principles.

COMMERCIALLY (-li), *adv.* in a commercial manner.

COMMINGLE (ko-ming'gl), *v.t.* & *v.i.* to mix; blend.

COMMISERATE (ko-miz'er-at), *v.t.* feel pity for; sympathize.

COMMISERATION (-er-a'shun), *n.* pity.

COMMISERATOR ('er-a-ter), *n.* one who pities.

COMMISSARIAT (kom-i-sa'ri-at), *n.* the department of an army concerned with the supply of transports, provisions, etc.

COMMISSARY ('i-sa-ri), *n.* one to whom some charge is committed by a superior; a delegate.

COMMISSION (ko-mish'un), *n.* a delegation of business to any one; one or more persons appointed to perform certain specified duties; brokerage.

COMMISSIONER (-mish'un-er), *n.* a person empowered by a commission.

COMMISSION GOVERNMENT (guv'ern-ment), a form of municipal government by a board of experts.

COMMIT (ko-mit'), *v.t.* to give in charge or trust; surrender; consign; perpetrate.

COMMITMENT (-mit'ment), *n.* the act of committing.

COMMITTEE (-mit'e), *n.* persons appointed to consider or manage any matter.

COMMODE (ko-mod'), *n.* a chest of drawers.

COMMODIOUS (mo'di-us), *adj.* useful; convenient; roomy.

COMMODITY (-mod'i-ti), *n.* that which is useful; an article of commerce.

COMMODORE (kom'o-dor), *n.* the senior captain of a line of vessels.

COMMON (kom'un), *adj.* belonging equally to more than one; public; usual; frequent; inferior; applied to nouns that are both masculine and feminine.

COMMON LAW (law), the unwritten law of England based on immemorial usage.

COMMONLY (-li), *adv.* usually; meanly.

COMMONPLACE (-plas), *n.* an obvious remark; anything ordinary.

COMMONS ('unz), *n.pl.* the Lower House of the English Parliament.

COMMON-SENSE (-sens), *adj.* characterized by sound, practical judgment.

COMMONWEAL (-wel), *n.* the public good.

COMMONWEALTH (-welth), *n.* the whole body of people in a state; a republic.

COMMOTION (ko-mo'shun), *n.* violent agitation.

COMMUNAL (kom'u-nal), *adj.* pertaining to a commune.

COMMUNE (ko-mun'), *v.t.* to converse together; impart; take counsel.

COMMUNICABLE (-u'ni-ka-bl), *adj.* impartible.

COMMUNICANT (ko-mu'ni-kant), *adj.* communicating: *n.* a partaker.

COMMUNICATE (-kat), *v.t.* to impart; reveal: *v.i.* to share.

COMMUNICATION (-ka'shun), *n.* the act of communicating; means of passing from one place to another; news.

COMMUNION (-mun'yun), *n.* intercourse; fellowship; a religious body.

COMMUNISM (kom'u-nizm), *n.* the doctrine of having property in common.

COMMUNITY (-mu'ni-ti), *n.* a body of persons having common rights, interests, and privileges; a corporation.

COMMUTABLE (-muta-bl), *adj.* interchangeable.

COMMUTATION (kom-u-ta'shun), *n.* the substitution of a less for a greater.

COMMUTATION TICKET (tik'et), a ticket issued to a frequent passenger.

COMMUTATOR (kom'u-ta-ter), *n.* an electrical device for making an alternating current continue or discontinue.

COMMUTE (ko-mut'), *v.t.* to exchange; reduce the severity of: *v.i.* travel at commutation rates.

COMMUTER (ko-mut'er), *n.* one who commutes.

COMPACT (kom'pakt), *n.* an agreement or covenant: *v.t.* (kom-pakt'), to press or pack closely.

COMPANION (kom-pan'yun), *n.* a comrade.

COMPANIONSHIP (-ship), *n.* fellowship.

COMPANION-WAY (-way), *n.* the entrance and stairway from deck to deck on a ship or vessel.

COMPANY (kum'pa-ni), *n.* an assemblage; a body of persons associated together; a number of guests; society; fellowship; a firm; a ship's crew; a subdivision of a regiment.

COMPARABLE (kom'par-a-ble), *adj.* capable of being compared.

COMPARATIVE (-par'a-tiv), *adj.* estimated by comparison.

COMPARE (-par), *v.t.* to make one thing the measure of another.

COMPARISON (-par'i-sun), *n.* the act of comparing.

COMPARTMENT (-part'ment), *n.* a division by a partition.

COMPASS (kum'pas), *v.t.* to encircle; besiege: *n.* an instrument indicating the magnetic meridian: *pl.* a mathematical instrument.

COMPASSION (kom-pash'un), *n.* sorrow for the sufferings of others.

COMPASSIONATE (-at), *v.t.* to have compassion for: *adj.* sympathetic.

COMPATIBILITY (kom-pat-i-bil'i-ti), *n.* the quality of being compatible; congruity.

COMPATIBLE ('i-bl), *adj.* congruous; suitable.

COMPATRIOT (-pa'tri-ot), *n.* a fellow countryman.

COMPEER (kom-per'), *n.* an equal.

COMPEL (kom-pel'), *v.t.* to urge irresistibly; force.

COMPEND (kom'pend), *n.* an abridgment.

COMPENDIOUS (-pen'di-us), *adj.* succinct; concise; abridged.

COMPENDIUM ('di-um), *n.* an abridgment.

COMPENSATE (kom'pen-, kom-pen'sat), *v.t.* to recompense.

COMPENSATION (-sa'sun), *n.* recompense; a set-off.

COMPETE (kom-pet'), *v.i.* contend in emulation with another.

COMPETENCE (kom'pe-tens), **COMPETENCY** (-ten-si), *n.* the state of being competent; sufficiency.

COMPETENT (-tent), *adj.* fit; able; suitable.

COMPETITION (-tish'un), *n.* rivalry.

COMPETITIVE (kom-pet'i-tiv), *adj.* pertaining to competition; emulous.

COMPETITOR ('i-ter), *n.* a rival.

COMPILATION (-pi-la'shun), *n.* the thing compiled.

COMPILE (kom-pil'), *v.t.* to put together in fresh form existing materials; to arrange and edit material for a book.

COMPLACENCE (kom-pla'sens), **COMPLACENCY** ('sens-si), *n.* inward satisfaction.

COMPLACENT ('sent), *adj.* affable.

COMPLAIN (kom-plan'), *v.i.* to express grief, pain, or resentment; charge formally.

COMPLAINANT ('ant), *n.* a plaintiff.

COMPLAINT (-plant'), *n.* an accusation; an expression of grief or pain; ailment.

COMPLAISANCE (-pla'zans), *n.* courtesy.

COMPLAISANT (-zant), *adj.* courteous.

COMPLEMENT ('ple-ment), *n.* full number or quantity; a complete set.

COMPLEMENTAL ('al), *adj.* completing.

COMPLEMENTARY (-ta-ri), *adj.* helping to supply a want.

COMPLETE (kom-plet'), *adj.* free from deficiency; entire; absolute; finished.

COMPLETELY ('li), *adv.* in a complete manner.

COMPLETION (-ple'shun), *n.* accomplishment.

COMPLEX (kom'pleks), *adj.* composite; intricate.

COMPLEXION (-plek'shun), *n.* the colour of the skin, especially the face; aspect.

COMPLEXITY ('-ti), *n.* the state of being complex.

COMPLIABLE (kom-pli'a-bl), *adj.* compliant.

COMPLIANCE ('ans), *n.* acquiescence.

COMPLIANT ('ant), *adj.* yielding.

COMPLICATE ('pli-kat), *v.t.* to make intricate; involve.

COMPLICATION (-ka'shun), *n.* the state of being complicated.

COMPLICITY (-plis'i-ti), *n.* partnership in crime.

COMPLIMENT ('pli-ment), *v.t.* to flatter; congratulate; praise.

COMPLIMENTARY ('ta-ri), *adj.* conveying a compliment.

COMPLY (kom-pli'), *v.i.* to yield assent; agree to.

COMPONENT (kom-po'nent), *adj.* constituent : *n.* elementary part of a compound.

COMPORT (-port'), *v.i.* to agree : *v.t.* to behave.

COMPORTMENT ('ment), *n.* bearing; behaviour.

COMPOSE (-poz'), *v.t.* to form by combination; write, as an author; calm.

COMPOSED (-pozd'), *adj.* tranquil; quiet.

COMPOSER (-poz'er), *n.* one who composes; a musical author.

COMPOSITE (kom'po-zit), *adj.* compound; made up of separate elements.

COMPOSITION (-po-zish'un), *n.* a mass formed by mingling various ingredients; mutual settlement or agreement; a musical or literary work; typesetting.

COMPOSITOR (-poz'i-ter), *n.* one who sets type.

COMPOST ('post), *n.* a mixture for fertilizing the ground.

COMPOSURE (-po'zhur), *n.* tranquillity.

COMPOTE ('pot), *n.* stewed fruit.

COMPOUND (-pound'), *v.t.* to mix or combine together: *adj.* (kom'-pound), composed of two or more elements.

COMPOUND INTEREST (in'terest), interest that accrues from the addition of principal and interest.

COMPREHEND (kom-pre-hend'), *v.t.* to include or comprise; grasp with the mind.

COMPREHENSIBLE (-hen'si-bl), *adj.* intelligible.

COMPREHENSION (-hen'shun), *n.* the act of comprehending; understanding.

COMPREHENSIVE (-hen'siv), *adj.* including much; full.

COMPRESS (kom-pres'), *v.t.* to press together; condense: *n.* (kom'-pres), a soft pad used in surgery.

COMPRESSED AIR (ar), air under pressure.

COMPRESSIBLE (-pres'i-bl), *n.* condensable.

COMPRESSION (-presh'un), *n.* state of being compressed.

COMPRISAL (kom-priz'al), *n.* the act of comprising.

COMPRISE (-priz'), *v.t.* to comprehend; include.

COMPROMISE (kom'pro-miz), *n.* a settlement by mutual concessions.

COMPTROLLER (kon-trol'er), see controller.

COMPULSION (kom-pul-shun), *n.* the act of compelling; force.

COMPULSORY (-pul'so-ri), *adj.* exercising compulsion.

COMPUNCTION (-pungk'shun), *n.* contrition; self-reproach.

COMPUTABLE (kom-put'a-bl), *adj.* that may be computed.

COMPUTATION (-pu-ta'shun), *n.* the act or process of computing; estimate.

COMPUTE (-put'), *v.t.* to number; reckon.

COMRADE (kom'rad), *n.* a companion.

CON (kon), *v.t.* to peruse carefully.

CONCAVE (kon'kav), *adj.* hollow and curved.

CONCAVE LENS (lenz), a lens one side of which is flat and the other slightly concave.

CONCEAL (kon-sel), *v.t.* to hide; keep secret; disguise.

CONCEALMENT ('ment), *n.* a place of hiding; shelter.

CONCEDE (-sed'), *v.t.* to yield; admit.

CONCEIT (-set'), *n.* an idea; an overestimate of one's own abilities; a quaint fancy.

CONCEIVABLE (-sev'a-bl), *adj.* imaginable.

CONCEIVE (-sev'), *v.t.* imagine; understand: *v.i.* to think; become pregnant.

CONCENTRATE (kon'sen-trat), *v.t.* to bring to one point or common centre; condense.

CONCENTRATION (-sen-tra'shun), *n.* the state of being concentrated.

CONCENTRATOR (kon'sen-tra-ter), *n.* an apparatus for separating dry ores.

CONCENTRIC (-sen'trik), *adj.* having a common centre.

CONCEPT (kon'sept), *n.* an abstract general notion or conception.

CONCEPTION (-sep'shun), *n.* the impregnation of the ovum; the act or power of conceiving in the mind.

CONCEPTIVE (-sep'tiv), *adj.* capable of conceiving mentally or physically.

CONCERN (kon-sern'), *v.t.* to relate or belong to: *n.* anxiety; a firm.

CONCERNMENT ('ment), *n.* solicitude; affair; participation.

CONCERT (kon-sert'), *v.t.* to contrive or devise together; adjust or arrange mutually: *n.* (kon'sert), a musical entertainment.

CONCERTED ('ed), *adj.* mutually planned.

CONCERTINA (-ser-te'na), *n.* a musical instrument.

CONCERTINO (-te′no), *n.* a small concerto.

CONCERTO (-ser′to), *n.* a musical composition for a solo instrument.

CONCESSION (kon-sesh′un), *n.* the act of conceding; privileges, etc., granted.

CONCESSIONAIRE (-un′ar′), *n.* a person holding a concession.

CONCH (kongk), *n.* a marine shell.

CONCILIATE (kon-sil′i-at), *v.t.* to reconcile; win or gain the affections of.

CONCILIATOR (-a-ter), *n.* one who conciliates.

CONCILIATORY (-to-ri), *adj.* tending to conciliate or reconcile.

CONCISE (kon-sis′), *adj.* condensed; terse.

CONCISELY (′li), *adv.* tersely; briefly.

CONCISENESS (′nes), *n.* brevity.

CONCLAVE (kon′klav), *n.* a private meeting, as of cardinals for the election of a Pope.

CONCLUDE (kon-klud′), *v.t.* to infer; determine; settle; end.

CONCLUSION (-klu′zhun), *n.* a final determination; result; end.

CONCLUSIVE (-klu′siv), *adj.* decisive; final.

CONCOCT (kon-kokt′), *v.t.* to digest; cook; assimilate mentally; plot.

CONCOCTION (-kok′shun), *n.* the act of concocting; a compound of various ingredients.

CONCOMITANCE (-kom′i-tans), *n.* the state of being concomitant.

CONCOMITANT (′i-tant), *n.* an attendant circumstance.

CONCORD (kong′, kon′kord), *n.* harmony; union.

CONCORDANCE (kon-kor′dans), *n.* agreement; a dictionary of words or passages, with references to the places where they occur; especially in the Bible.

CONCORDANT (′dant), *adj.* harmonious.

CONCOURSE (kong′kors), *n.* arriving together; an assembly; a place for assembly.

CONCRETE (kon′kret), *adj.* united in growth; coalesced: *n.* a compact mass of lime, sand, gravel, mortar, etc., used for building.

CONCRETION (kon-kre′shun), *n.* the act of concreting.

CONCRETIVE (′tiv), *adj.* producing concretes.

CONCUR (kon-ker′), *v.i.* to agree or unite in action.

CONCURRENCE (-kur′ens), *n.* the act of concurring; agreement.

CONCURRENT (-kur′ent), *adj.* acting in union or conjunction.

CONCUSSION (-kush′un), *n.* the shock caused by two bodies coming violently together.

CONDEMN (kon-dem′), *v.t.* to pronounce or judge guilty; blame; censure.

CONDEMNATION (-dem-na′shun), *n.* the act of condemning.

CONDENSABLE (-den′sa-bl), *adj.* capable of condensation.

CONDENSATION (-den-sa′shun), *n.* compression.

CONDENSE (-dens′), *v.t.* to compress: *v.i.* to grow dense.

CONDENSER (′er), *n.* an apparatus for reducing gases or vapours to a liquid or solid form; a device for storing or regulating electricity.

CONDESCEND (kon-de-send′), *v.i.* to stoop; descend; yield.

CONDESCENSION (de-sen′shun), *n.* the act of condescending.

CONDIGN (-din′), *adj.* well-deserved; suitable.

CONDIMENT (kon′di-ment), *n.* a seasoning.

CONDITION (kon-dish′un), *n.* state; quality; external circumstances.

CONDITIONALLY (-al-li), *adv.* with certain limitations.

CONDOLE (kon-dol′), *v.t.* to lament: *v.i.* to express sympathy.

CONDOLENCE (′ens), *n.* sympathy.

CONDONATION (-do-na′shun), *n.* the act of pardoning a wrong act.

CONDONE (kon-don′), *v.t.* to pardon.

CONDUCE (-dus′), *v.i.* to tend to; contribute.

CONDUCIVE (-du′siv), *adj.* having the quality or power of conducing [with *to*].

CONDUCT (kon-dukt′), *v.t.* to guide;

direct ; manage ; behave : n. (kon'-dukt), personal behaviour.

CONDUCTANCE (kon-duk'tans), n. power of or capacity for conducting electricity.

CONDUCTIBILITY (kon-duk-ti-bil'i-ti), n. the capability of being conducted ; the transmission of electricity, heat, or sound.

CONDUCTOR (duk'ter), n. a leader or guide ; one who has charge of a car or train ; a substance which conducts or transmits certain forces, as electricity.

CONDUIT (kon'dit), n. a canal or pipe for the conveyance of water, etc.

CONE (kon), n. a geometrical figure broad, round, and broad at the bottom, and lessening the circumference toward the top ; the fruit of the fir, pine, etc.

CONE FLOWER (-flou'er), n. a plant of the aster family.

CONEY (ko'ni), n. the European rabbit.

CONFAB (kon'fab), v.i. to chat.

CONFECTION (-fek'shun), n. a sweetmeat.

CONFECTIONER (-er), n. one who prepares and sells sweetmeats, etc.

CONFECTIONERY (-i), n. sweetmeats, cakes, preserves, etc.

CONFEDERACY (-fed'er-a-si), n. persons, states, or nations united in a league.

CONFEDERATE ('er-at), n. an ally ; an accomplice.

CONFEDERATION (-er-a'shun), n. an alliance of states.

CONFER (kon-fer'), v.t. to give or bestow : v.i. to consult.

CONFERENCE ('fer-ens), n. the act of consulting together formally.

CONFESS (kon-fes'), v.t. to admit or acknowledge ; avow ; grant.

CONFESSION (-fesh'un), n. act of confessing.

CONFESSIONAL (-al), n. cabinet in which a priest sits to hear confessions.

CONFESSOR (kon', kon-fes'er), n. a priest who hears confessions.

CONFETTI (kon-fet'ti), n.pl. minute pieces of coloured paper thrown

and scattered at weddings, carnivals, etc.

CONFIDANT ('fi-dant), n. a confidential friend.

CONFIDANTE (kon-fi-dant'), n. a woman to whom secrets are confided.

CONFIDE (kon-fid'), v.i. have confidence in : v.t. to trust fully [with to].

CONFIDENCE (kon'fi-dens), n. trust ; reliance.

CONFIDENT (-dent), adj. full of confidence.

CONFIDENTIAL (-den'shal), adj. spoken or written in confidence.

CONFIDENTIALLY (-li), adv. in a confidential manner.

CONFINE (kon'fin), n. a boundary, border, or limit ; a frontier ; usually pl. : v.t. (kon-fin'), imprison.

CONFINEMENT (kon-fin'ment), n. the act of confining ; childbirth.

CONFIRM (kon-ferm'), v.t. to strengthen ; ratify.

CONFIRMATION (-fer-ma'shun), n. the act of confirming ; verification ; evidence.

CONFISCATE (kon-fis', kon'fis-kat), v.t. to adjudge to be forfeited to the public treasury ; seize.

CONFISCATION (-ka'shun), n. the act of confiscating.

CONFISCATOR ('fis-ka-ter), n. one who confiscates.

CONFISCATORY (-fis'ka-to-ri), adj. characterized by, or attended with confiscation.

CONFLAGRATION (-fla-gra'shun), n. a great fire.

CONFLICT (kon-flikt'), v.i. contend ; fight : n. (kon'flikt), a fight or struggle for the mastery.

CONFLICTING ('ing), adj. opposing.

CONFLUENCE (kon'floo-ens), n. the junction of two or more streams ; an assembly.

CONFLUENT (-ent), adj. flowing or running together.

CONFLUX ('fluks), n. the meeting of two or more streams ; a crowd.

CONFORM (kon-form'), v.t. to make like ; bring into harmony [usually with to] : v.i. to be in harmony with ; comply with.

CONFORMABLE ('a-bl), adj. like ;

corresponding ; compliant ; in parallel order.

CONFORMATION (-for-ma'shun), *n.* structure ; arrangement ; shape.

CONFORMITY ('i-ti), *n.* compliance with established forms ; resemblance.

CONFOUND (kon-found'), *v.t.* to mingle ; astonish ; confuse.

CONFRERE (kon-frar'), *n.* an associate.

CONFRONT (kon-frunt'), *v.t.* to stand face to face [with *with*].

CONFUSE (kon-fuz'), *v.t.* to mingle ; render indistinct.

CONFUSION (-fu'zhun), *n.* perplexity ; disorder ; tumult.

CONFUTE (kon-fut'), *v.t.* to prove to be false or invalid.

CONGE (kong-zha'), *n.* leave-taking.

CONGEAL (kon-jel'), *v.t.* to freeze.

CONGELATION (-je-la'shun), *n.* the act of congealing.

CONGENIAL (-jen'yal), *adj.* pleasant and sympathetic.

CONGENIALITY (-je-ni-al'i-ti), *n.* the state or quality of being congenial.

CONGER (kong'ger), *n.* a large sea eel.

CONGERIES (kon-je'ri-ez), *n. sing. & pl.* a collection of particles into one mass.

CONGEST (kon-jest'), *v.t.* to accumulate ; to surcharge with blood.

CONGESTED ('ed), *p.adj.* unduly crowded.

CONGESTION (-jes'chun), *n.* an overcrowded condition.

CONGESTIVE ('tiv), *adj.* implying congestion.

CONGLOMERATE (-glom'er-at), *adj.* collected or clustered together.

CONGLOMERATION (-er-a'shun), *n.* a miscellaneous collection.

CONGRATULATE (kon-grat'u-lat), *v.t.* to felicitate [with *on* or *upon*].

CONGRATULATION (-grat-u-la'-shun), *n.* the act of congratulating.

CONGRATULATORY (-to-ri), *adj.* expressing congratulations.

CONGREGATE (kong'gre-gat), *v.t.* to assemble.

CONGREGATION (-ga'shun), *n.* an assembly.

CONGREGATIONAL (-al), *adj.* pertaining to a congregation.

CONGRESS (kong'gres), *n.* a conference.

CONGRESS (kong'gres), *n.* the national legislature of the U.S.

CONGRESSIONAL (kon-gresh'un-al), *adj.* pertaining to Congress.

CONGRESSMAN (-man), *n.* a member of Congress.

CONGRESSWOMAN (-woom'an), *n.* a woman member of the House of Representatives.

CONGRUENCE (kong'groo-ens), *n.* suitability ; consistency.

CONGRUITY ('i-ti), *n.* agreement ; fitness.

CONGRUOUS ('groo-us), *adj.* accordant ; fit.

CONIC (kon'ik), *adj.* pertaining to, or shaped like a cone.

CONIFEROUS (ko-nif'er-us), *adj.* bearing cones.

CONJECTURAL (kon-jek'tur-al), *adj.* doubtful.

CONJECTURALLY (-li), *adv.* doubtfully.

CONJECTURE ('tur), *n.* a probable inference : *v.t.* to imagine ; surmise.

CONJOIN (kon-join'), *v.t.* to join together : *v.i.* to unite.

CONJOINT (-joint'), *adj.* united ; co-operating.

CONJUGAL ('joo-gal), *adj.* of, or pertaining to, marriage ; connubial.

CONJUGATE (kon'ju-gat), *v.t.* to inflect (verbs) : *adj.* combined in pairs ; kindred in meaning.

CONJUGATION (-ga'shun), *n.* the act of conjugating ; the inflection of a verb.

CONJUNCTION (-jungk'shun), *n.* union ; association ; connection.

CONJUNCTIVE MOOD (mood), *n.* the mood which expresses contingency or condition.

CONJURE (kon-jur'), *v.t.* to summon in a sacred name ; enjoin with the highest solemnity : (kun'jer), influence by magic.

CONJURER (kun'jer-er), *n.* one who performs tricks.

CONJUROR (kun-jer'er), *n.* one bound by an oath with others.

CONNATE (kon'nat), *adj.* united at the base ; innate.

CONNECT (ko-nekt'), *v.t.* to bind or fasten together ; unite.

CONNECTED ('ed), *adj.* linked together.

CONNECTION, CONNEXION (-nek'shun), *n.* the state of being connected ; cohesion ; relation by marriage or blood.

CONNING-TOWER (-tou'er), *n.* the low pilot-house of an armoured vessel.

CONNIVANCE (ko-ni'vans), *n.* the act of conniving ; collusion.

CONNIVE (ko-niv'), *v.i.* be in secret complicity [with *at*].

CONNOISSEUR (kon-i-ser'), *n.* a critical judge.

CONNOTE (ko-not'), *v.t.* to designate by implication.

CONNUBIAL (ko-nu'bi-al), *adj.* of, or pertaining to, the marriage state.

CONQUER (kong'ker), *v.t.* overcome ; subdue.

CONQUEROR (-er), *n.* a victor.

CONQUEST ('kwest), *n.* subjugation ; victory.

CONSANGUINEOUS (kon-sang-gwin'e-us), *adj.* denoting relationship by blood.

CONSCIENCE (kon'shens), *n.* the moral sense which determines right and wrong.

CONSCIENTIOUS (-shi-en'shus), *adj.* influenced by conscience.

CONSCIOUS ('shus), *adj.* aware of one's thoughts and actions.

CONSCIOUSNESS (-nes), *n.* the knowledge of that which passes in one's own mind.

CONSCRIPT (kon-skript'), *v.t.* to enrol for compulsory military or naval service.

CONSCRIPTION (-skrip'shun), *n.* compulsory military or naval service.

CONSECRATE (kon'se-krat), *v.t.* to set apart as sacred.

CONSECUTIVE (-sek'u-tiv), *adj.* successive.

CONSENSUS (-sen'sus), *n.* general agreement ; accord.

CONSENT (kon-sent'), *n.* acquiescence : *v.i.* to comply.

CONSEQUENCE (kon'se-kwens), *n.* inference ; result ; significance.

CONSEQUENT (-kwent), *adj.* following as a result.

CONSEQUENTIAL (-kwen'shəl), *adj.* following as the effect ; self-important.

CONSERVABLE (-ser'-va-bl), *adj.* that may be preserved.

CONSERVATIVE ('va-tiv), *adj.* having the tendency to preserve.

CONSERVATOR (kon'ser-va-ter), *n.* one who preserves.

CONSERVATORY (-ser'va-to-ri), *adj.* tending to preserve : *n.* a greenhouse.

CONSERVE (kon-serv'), *v.t.* to preserve from injury or destruction ; preserve with sugar.

CONSIDER (kon-sid'er), *v.t.* contemplate : *v.i.* to deliberate.

CONSIDERABLE (-a-bl), *adj.* important ; more than a little.

CONSIDERATE (-at), *adj.* having regard for others ; prudent.

CONSIDERATION (-a'shun), *n.* claim to notice ; mature thought ; an equivalent.

CONSIGN (kon-sin'), *v.t.* to deliver in a formal manner ; to send goods.

CONSIGNEE (kon-si-ne'), *n.* the person to whom goods are sent.

CONSIGNMENT (-sin'ment), *n.* the thing consigned.

CONSIGNOR ('er), *n.* the person who consigns goods.

CONSIST (kon-sist), *v.i.* to be composed of, co-exist.

CONSISTENCE (-sis'tens), **CONSISTENCY** (-ten-si), *n.* degree of density or firmness.

CONSISTENT ('tent), *adj.* solid ; not contradictory.

CONSOLABLE (kon-sol'a-bl), *adj.* admitting of consolation.

CONSOLATION (-so-la'shun), *n.* alleviation of mental or physical distress ; solace.

CONSOLE (kon-sol'), *v.t.* to give comfort to.

CONSOLE SET (kon'sol set), a fruit-bowl and two candlesticks.

CONSOLIDATE (-sol'i-dat), *v.t.* to make solid ; harden ; condense.

CONSOLIDATION (-da'shun), *n.* the act of consolidating.

CONSOMME (kon-so-ma'), *n.* a strong clear soup or bouillon.

CONSONANCE (kon'so-nans), *n.* agreement of sounds ; harmony.

CONSONANT (-nant), *adj.* harmonious : *n.* a letter other than a vowel.

CONSORT (kon'sort), *n.* a companion ; a husband or wife.

CONSPICUOUS (-spik'u-us), *adj.* mentality or physically visible ; distinguished.

CONSPIRACY (-spir'a-si), *n.* a plot.

CONSPIRATOR ('a-ter), *n.* one who conspires.

CONSPIRE (kon-spir'), *v.i.* to combine for an unlawful purpose.

CONSTABLE (kun'sta-bl), *n.* a policeman.

CONSTANCY (kon'stan-si), *n.* firmness ; fidelity.

CONSTANT ('stant), *adj.* steadfast ; firm ; continuous.

CONSTELLATION (-stel-a'shun), *n.* a group or cluster of fixed stars.

CONSTERNATION (-ster-na'shun), *n.* excessive terror, or surprise.

CONSTIPATION (-pa'shun), *n.* costiveness.

CONSTITUENCY (-stit'u-en-si), *n.* the body of electors ; the district represented.

CONSTITUENT ('u-ent), *adj.* necessary or essential : *n.* an elector.

CONSTITUTE ('sti-tut), *v.t.* to compose or make up ; appoint.

CONSTITUTION (-tu'shun), *n.* bodily strength ; mental or physical temperament ; the system of fundamental laws of a nation, state or society.

CONSTITUTIONAL (-al), *adj.* inherent in the constitution ; fundamental.

CONSTRAIN (kon-stran'), *v.t.* to keep back by force ; restrain.

CONSTRAINT (-strant'), *n.* compulsion.

CONSTRICT (-strikt'), *v.t.* to bind ; cramp.

CONSTRICTION (-strik'shun), *n.* compression ; contraction.

CONSTRUCT (kon-strukt'), *v.t.* to build ; form ; compose.

CONSTRUCTION (-struk'shun), *n.* the act of building ; that which is constructed ; an edifice ; interpretation.

CONSTRUE (kon'stroo), *v.t.* to put into proper order by syntactical rules ; interpret.

CONSUBSTANTIAL (sub-stan'shal), *adj.* having the same substance, essence, or nature.

CONSUL (kon'sul), *n.* an officer commissioned by a government to reside in a foreign country.

CONSULATE ('su-lat), *n.* the office and residence of a consul.

CONSULT (kon-sult'), *v.t.* to ask advice of : *v.i.* to take counsel together.

CONSULTATION (-sul-ta'shun), *n.* the act of consulting.

CONSUME (kon-sum'), *v.t.* to destroy ; waste.

CONSUMMATE (kon'sum-at), *v.t.* to complete ; finish.

CONSUMMATION (-a'shun), *n.* completion.

CONSUMPTION (-sump'shun), *n.* a gradual wasting away ; phthisis.

CONSUMPTIVE ('tiv), *adj.* affected with phthisis.

CONTACT (kon'takt), *n.* touch ; close union.

CONTAGION (kon-ta'jun), *n.* transmission of disease by contact.

CONTAGIOUS ('jus), *adj.* transmitted by contact.

CONTAIN (kon-tan'), *v.t.* to hold, as a vessel ; enclose.

CONTAMINATE (-tam'i-nat), *v.t.* to pollute.

CONTAMINATION (-na'shun), *n.* pollution.

CONTAMINATIVE ('i-na-tiv), *adj.* tending to contaminate.

CONTEMN (kon-tem'), *v.t.* to despise.

CONTEMPLATE ('plat), *v.t.* to consider with continued attention ; meditate.

CONTEMPLATION (-pla'shun), *n.* the act of contemplating.

CONTEMPLATIVE ('pla-tiv), *adj.* thoughtful.

CONTEMPORANEOUS (-po-ra'ne-us), *adj.* contemporary.

CONTEMPORARY ('po-ra-ri), *adj.* existing or occurring at the same time : *n.* one living at the same time as another.

CONTEMPT (kon-tempt'), *n.* disdain ; scorn.

CONTEMPTIBLE ('i-bl), *adj.* meriting scorn.

CONTEMPTUOUS (-temp'tu-us), *adj.* disdainful.

CONTEND (kon-tend'), *v.i.* to strive in opposition ; vie [with *with* or *against*].

CONTENT (kon-tent'), *adj.* satisfied : *v.t.* to satisfy : *n.* (kon'tent), that which is comprised in anything.

CONTENTION (-ten'shun), *n.* contest ; debate.

CONTENTIOUS (-ten'shus), *adj.* causing contention ; litigious.

CONTEST (kon-test'), *v.t.* to dispute ; oppose ; litigate.

CONTESTANT (-tes'tant), *n.* one who contests.

CONTEXT (kon'tekst), *n.* the parts in a book immediately adjoining a word, phrase, or sentence quoted.

CONTIGUITY (-ti-gu'i-ti), *n.* contact.

CONTIGUOUS (-tig'u-us), *adj.* adjacent.

CONTINENCE (kon'ti-nens), *n.* chastity ; self-restraint.

CONTINENT ('ti-nent), *adj.* chaste : *n.* a large extent of land forming a geographical division.

CONTINENTAL ('al), *adj.* pertaining to a continent.

CONTINGENCE (kon-tin'jens), **CONTINGENCY** (-jen-si), *n.* a possible occurrence.

CONTINGENT ('jent), *adj.* accidental : *n.* quota of troops.

CONTINUAL ('u-al), *adj.* proceeding without interruption.

CONTINUANCE ('u-ans), *n.* permanence ; uninterrupted succession.

CONTINUE (kon-tin'u), *v.t.* to carry on without interruption.

CONTINUITY (-ti-nu'i-ti), *n.* uninterrupted connection ; a scenario.

CONTINUOUS (-tin'u-us), *adj.* uninterrupted.

CONTORTION (-tor'shun), *n.* a twist.

CONTORTIONIST (-ist), *n.* an acrobat who contorts his body.

CONTOUR (kon-toor'), *n.* an outline : *v.t.* to make an outline of.

CONTRABAND (kon'tra-band), *adj.* prohibited from importation ; illegal.

CONTRACT (kon-trakt'), *v.t.* draw closer together ; condense : *v.i.* bargain ; agree upon : *n.* (kon'trakt), a written agreement.

CONTRACTION (-trak'shun), *n.* the act of contracting ; abbreviation.

CONTRACTOR (-trak'ter), *n.* one who contracts to supply or construct for a stipulated sum.

CONTRADICT (kon-tra-dikt'), *v.t.* assert the contrary or opposite of ; deny.

CONTRADICTION (-dik'shun), *n.* the act of contradicting ; denial.

CONTRALTO (kon-tral'to), *n.* the part sung by the highest male (*counter-tenor*) or the lowest female voice (*alto*) ; one who sings contralto.

CONTRARIETY (-tra-ri'e-ti), *n.* opposition.

CONTRARILY ('tra-ri-li), *adv.* in a contrary manner.

CONTRARIWISE ('tra-ri-wiz), *adv.* conversely.

CONTRARY ('tra-ri), *adj.* opposite ; perverse.

CONTRAST (kon-trast'), *v.t.* to place in contrast ; compare : *n.* (kon'trast), dissimilitude.

CONTRAVENE (kon-tra-ven'), *v.t.* to obstruct ; violate.

CONTRIBUTE (kon-trib'ut), *v.t.* to furnish as a share.

CONTRIBUTION (-tri-bu'shun), *n.* the act of contributing ; a subscription ; a writing furnished to a periodical.

CONTRIBUTIVE (-trib'u-tiv), *adj.* contributing.

CONTRIBUTOR ('u-ter), *n.* one who contributes.

CONTRIBUTORY ('u-to-ri), *adj.* promoting the same end.

CONTRITE (kon'trit), *adj.* penitent.

CONTRITION (-trish′un), *n.* sorrow for sin.

CONTRIVANCE (-tri′vans), *n.* a device ; scheme ; plan.

CONTRIVE (kon-triv′), *v.t.* to devise ; invent ; plan ; scheme.

CONTROL (kon-trol′), *n.* a check ; restraint ; authority ; a repair station for aircraft.

CONTROLLABLE (′a-bl), *adj.* subject to control.

CONTROLLER (′er), *n.* one who controls ; one who has charge of the expenditures of a city, or corporation.

CONTROVERSIAL (-tro-ver′shal), *adj.* polemical.

CONTROVERSY (′tro-ver-si), *n.* agitation of contrary opinions ; debate.

CONTROVERT (-tro-vert′), *v.t.* to contend against ; refute.

CONTROVERTIBLE (-ver′ti-bl) *adj.* capable of being disputed.

CONTUMACIOUS (-tu-ma′shus), *adj.* perverse ; obstinate.

CONTUMACY (′tu-ma-si), *n.* obstinate or perverse.

CONTUMELIOUS (-tu-me′li-us), *adj.* contemptuous ; supercilious.

CONTUMELY (′tu-me-li), *n.* contemptuous ; rudeness ; scornful insolence.

CONTUSION (-tu′shun), *n.* the act of contusing ; a bruise.

CONUNDRUM (ko-nun′drum), *n.* a riddle.

CONVALESCE (kon-va-les′), *v.i.* to recover strength and health.

CONVALESCENCE (′ens), *n.* gradual recovery after illness.

CONVENE (kon-ven′), *v.i.* to meet together : *v.t.* cause to assemble.

CONVENIENCE (-ven′yens), *n.* fitness ; accommodation.

CONVENIENT (′yent), *adj.* suitable ; appropriate.

CONVENT (kon′vent), *n.* a community of religious recluses ; a nunnery.

CONVENTION (-ven′shun), *n.* an assembly ; a diplomatic agreement.

CONVENTIONAL (-al), *adj.* sanctioned by custom.

CONVENTIONALITY (-al′i-ti), *n.* adherence to conventional rules.

CONVERGE (kon-verj′), *v.i.* tend to one point.

CONVERGENCE (-ver′jens), *n.* tendency to one point.

CONVERSABLE (kon-vers′a-bl), *a.* social ; inclined to converse.

CONVERSANT (kon′ver-sant), *adj.* acquainted or familiar with ; proficient.

CONVERSATION (-sa′shun), *n.* informal or familiar talk.

CONVERSATIONAL (-al), *adj.* pertaining to conversation.

CONVERSATIONIST (-ist), **CONVERSATIONALIST** (-al-ist), *n.* one who excels in conversation.

CONVERSE (kon-vers′), *v.i.* to interchange thoughts : *adj.* & *n.* (kon′vers), reversed in order or relation.

CONVERSION (-ver′shun), *n.* change from one state to another.

CONVERT (kon-vert′), *v.t.* to transmute ; apply to any use : *n.* (kon′vert), one who changes from one religion to another.

CONVERTER (′er), *n.* one who converts ; a retort for converting pig iron into steel ; a kind of electrical induction coil.

CONVEX (kon′veks), *adj.* curved on the exterior surface ; opposed to concave : *n.* a convex body.

CONVEXITY (-vek′si-ti), *n.* roundness.

CONVEY (kon-va′), *v.t.* to transport ; impart ; communicate ; transfer title.

CONVEYANCE (′ans), *n.* the act of conveying ; a document transferring title.

CONVICT (kon-vikt′), *v.t.* to prove or pronounce guilty of a crime : *n.* (kon′vikt), one found guilty of crime.

CONVICTION (-vik′shun), *n.* the act of convicting ; strong belief.

CONVINCE (kon-vins′), *v.t.* to satisfy by evidence or argument ; persuade.

CONVIVIAL (kon-viv′i-al), *adj.* festive.

CONVOCATION (kon-vo-ka′shun), *n.* the act of convoking an assembly.

CONVOKE (kon-vok′), *v.t.* to call or summon together ; convene.

CONVOLUTE (kon′vo-lut), *adj.* rolled upon itself ; twisted.

CONVOY (kon-voi'), *v.t.* to accompany for protection : *n.* (kon'voi), a protecting force.

CONVULSE (kon-vuls'), *v.t.* to agitate violently ; shake.

CONVULSION (-vul'shun), *n.* an agitation ; a violent contraction of the muscles.

COOK (kook), *v.t.* to prepare food by boiling, baking, or roasting : *n.* one who prepares food.

COOKIE ('i), a small cake.

COOL (kool), *adj.* moderately cold ; calm ; deliberate.

COOP (koop), *n.* a cage ; pen.

COOPER ('er), *n.* a maker of barrels, casks, etc.

CO-OPERATE (ko-op'er-at), *v.i.* to act or work jointly.

CO-ORDINATE (-or'di-nat), *v.t.* to place in the same order, class, etc.

COPE (kop), *v.i.* to strive or contend [with *with*].

COPIOUS (pi-us), *adj.* abundant ; diffusive.

COPPER (kop'er), *n.* a red, ductile, malleable, tenacious metal ; a penny ; a cent.

COPPERHEAD (-hed), *n.* a poisonous snake.

COPPERPLATE (-plat), *n.* a polished copper plate for printing.

COPSE (kops), *n.* a thicket.

COPULA (kop'u-la), *n.* a word which joins the subject and predicate in a sentence or proposition.

COPY (kop'i), *n.* an imitation ; a transcript ; an original work.

COPYIST (-ist), *n.* one who copies.

COPYRIGHT (-rit), *n.* the exclusive right of an author in his literary or artistic work for a prescribed number of years.

COQUET (ko-ket'), *v.i.* to flirt.

COQUETRY (ko'ket-ri), *n.* flirtation.

COQUETTE (ko-ket'), *n.* a vain woman who seeks to gain men's attention and admiration.

CORAL (kor'al), *n.* the hard, calcareous skeleton of certain marine polyps.

CORD (kord), *n.* a string ; a measure of wood.

CORDAGE ('aj), *n.* ropes and rigging collectively.

CORDIAL (kor'jal), *adj.* hearty ; sincere : *n.* an aromatic spirit.

CORDIALITY ('i-ti), *n.* sincerity ; heartiness.

CORDON (kor'don), *n.* a ribbon worn as the badge of an order ; a band.

CORDUROY ('du-roi), *n.* a stout ribbed or corded cotton.

CORDUROY ROAD (rod), *n.* a roadway formed of logs.

CORE (kor), *n.* the innermost part of anything, especially of fruit.

CORESPONDENT (ko-re-spond'-ent), *n.* a joint respondent in a divorce suit.

CORK (kork), *n.* the bark of a cork tree ; a stopper for a bottle.

CORMORANT (kor'mo-rant), *n.* a diving bird.

CORN (korn), *n.* maize ; bread-stuff.

CORN (korn), *v.t.* to preserve meats.

CORNEA (kor'ne-a), *n.* the horny circular transparent membrane which forms the anterior portion of the eyeball.

CORNED (kornd), *p.adj.* pickled.

CORNER (kor'ner), *n.* an angle ; a retired place.

CORNET ('net), a kind of trumpet.

CORNICE ('nis), *n.* the highest projection or border on a wall.

CORNSTARCH (korn'starch), *n.* starch made from meal of corn.

CORNUCOPIA (kor-nu-ko'pi-a), *n.* [*pl.* cornucopiæ (-e)], the horn of plenty.

COROLLA (ko-rol'a), *n.* the inner envelope of a flower composed of two or more petals.

COROLLARY (kor'o-la-ri, ko-rol'a-ri), *n.* an additional deduction or inference drawn from a demonstrated proposition.

CORONA (ko-ro'na), *n.* [*pl.* coronæ ('ne)], a crown ; a halo.

CORONATION (kor-o-na'shun), *n.* the act or ceremony of crowning a sovereign.

CORONER (kor'o-ner), *n.* officer who inquires into cases of sudden or accidental death.

CORPORAL (kor'po-ral), *adj.* relating

to the body : *n.* a non-commissioned officer.

CORPORATE (-rat), *adj.* united in a body or community by legal enactment.

CORPORATION (-ra'shun), *n.* a body politic legally authorized to act as one individual.

CORPOREAL (-po're-al), *adj.* having a material body ; physical.

CORPS (kor), *n.* [*pl.* corps (korz)], a body of troops.

CORPSE (korps), *n.* a dead body.

CORPULENCE (kor'pu-lens), *n.* excessive fatness of body.

CORPUS CHRISTI ('pus kris'ti), (Latin, the body of Christ), a festival of the R.C. Church.

CORPUSCLE ('pus-l), *n.* a minute particle.

CORRAL (ko-ral'), *n.* a pen for live stock : *v.t.* to drive into a corral ; corner.

CORRECT (ko-rekt'), *v.t.* to set straight ; rectify : *adj.* exact ; accurate.

CORRECTION ('shun), *n.* the act of correcting.

CORRELATE (kor'e-lat), *v.i.* to be reciprocally related.

CORRELATION (-la'shun), *n.* reciprocal relation ; similarity or parallelism of relation or law.

CORRESPOND (kor-e-spond'), *v.i.* to agree ; suit ; answer ; communicate by letters.

CORRESPONDENCE ('ens), *n.* communication by letters ; mutual adaptation.

CORRESPONDENT ('ent), *adj.* agreeing with ; similar : *n.* one with whom intercourse is maintained by letters.

CORRIDOR (kor'i-dor), *n.* a gallery or open passage in a building.

CORROBORATE ('o-rat), *v.t.* confirm ; strengthen ; establish ; verify.

CORROBORATION (-ra'shun), *n.* verification.

CORRODE (ko-rod'), *v.t.* to eat away ; consume ; disintegrate.

CORROSIVE (ko-ro'siv), *adj.* capable of producing corrosion.

CORRUGATE (kor'oo-gat), *v.t.* to draw, or shape, into wrinkles or folds.

CORRUPT (ko-rupt'), *v.t.* to make impure ; seduce ; bribe.

CORRUPTIBLE (-rup'ti-bl), *adj.* capable of being corrupted ; subject to decay.

CORRUPTION (-rup'shun), *n.* physical dissolution ; an evil influence.

CORSAGE (kor'saj), *n.* a bodice ; waist.

CORSAIR ('sar), *n.* a pirate.

CORSE (kors), *n.* poetic for corpse.

CORSET ('set), *n.pl.* a pair of stays.

CORTEGE (kor-tazh'), *n.* a train of attendants ; retinue ; procession.

CORTEX (kor'teks), *n.* [*pl.* cortices ('ti-sez)], outer bark or covering.

CORUSCATE (ko-rus', kor'us-kat), *v.i.* to sparkle ; flash.

CORUNDUM (ko-run'dum), *n.* native aluminium oxide.

CORUSCANT (ko-rus'kant), *adj.* glittering.

COSILY (ko'zi-li), *adv.* snugly.

COSMETIC (koz-met'ik), *adj.* imparting or improving beauty.

COSMIC (koz'mik), *adj.* pertaining to the universe.

COSMOGONY (-mog'o-ni), *n.* a theory on the world's origin.

COSMOLOGY (-mol'o-ji), *n.* the science which investigates the origin of the world.

COSMOPOLITAN (-mo-pol'i-tan), *n.* a citizen of the world.

COSMOS (koz'mos), *n.* the world or universe as an orderly system : opposed to *chaos*.

COST (kost), *n.* charge ; a price ; expense ; labour : *pl.* law charges.

COSTAL ('tal), *adj.* pertaining to a rib.

COSTERMONGER ('ter-mung-ger), *n.* a hawker of fruit, vegetables, fish, etc.

COSTUME (kos'tum), *n.* dress in general ; style of dress : *v.t.* (kostum') to provide with costumes.

COT (kot), *n.* a small bed.

COTEMPORARY, same as contemporary.

COTERIE (ko'te-ry), *n.* an association or set of persons united for social or other intercourse ; a clique.

COTILLION, COTILLON (ko-til'-

yun), *n.* a lively dance for eight or more persons.

COTTAGE (kot'aj), *n.* a small dwelling.

COTTON (kot'n), *n.* a white substance around the seeds of the cotton-plant.

COTTON-GIN (-jin), *n.* a machine for separating the seeds from cotton fibre.

COUCH (kouch), *n.* a bed; sofa.

COUGAR (koo'gar), *n.* the puma.

COUGH (kof), *v.i.* to expel air from the lungs by a violent effort.

COULOMB (koo-lom'), *n.* the electrical current of one ampere per second.

COUNCIL (koun'sil), *n.* an assembly of persons in consultation; a convocation; a municipal body.

COUNCILLOR (-er), *n.* a member of a common council.

COUNSEL ('sel), *n.* advice; consultation; a barrister: *v.t.* to give advice to.

COUNSELLOR (-er), *n.* one who gives advice, especially legal advice.

COUNT (kount), *n.* a title of nobility: *v.t.* to reckon or sum up.

COUNTENANCE (koun'te-nans), *n.* the whole form of the face; appearance; support: *v.t.* encourage; favour.

COUNTER (koun'ter), *n.* one who, or that which, counts; a shop table: *adv.* contrary; adverse.

COUNTERACT (-akt'), *v.t.* to act in opposition; neutralize.

COUNTERFEIT (koun'ter-fit), *v.t.* forge; imitate: *v.i.* to carry on deception: *adj.* feigned; spurious; forged: *n.* an imitation; a forgery.

COUNTERMAND (-mand), *v.t.* to revoke or annul, as an order or command.

COUNTERPANE (-pan), *n.* a bed coverlet.

COUNTERPART (-part), *n.* a duplicate.

COUNTERPOINT (-point), *n.* the science of harmony.

COUNTERSIGN (-sin), *v.t.* to authenticate by an additional signature: *n.* a military watchword.

COUNTESS (koun'tes), *n.* the wife of an earl or count.

COUNTRY (kun'tri), *n.* region; rural parts; one's native land.

COUNTY (koun'ti), *n.* a definite district of a state.

COUNTY COURT (kort), a court having jurisdiction in the county.

COUP (koo), *n.* [French], a sudden, telling blow; a master-stroke.

COUPE (koo-pa'), *n.* a certain kind of carriage or automobile.

COUPLE (kup'l), *n.* two of anything.

COUPLET (kup'let), *n.* two successive lines of verse which rhyme.

COUPON (koo'pon), *n.* a certificate attached to transferable bonds; a section of a ticket.

COURAGE (kur'aj), *n.* fortitude; valour.

COURAGEOUS (-a'jus), *adj.* brave; bold.

COURIER (koo'ri-er), *n.* a travelling attendant who makes arrangements.

COURSE (kors), *n.* a race; a path or track; career; the portion of a meal served at one time; conduct.

COURT (kort), *n.* an enclosed space; a royal palace; the retinue of a sovereign; a hall of justice; the judges, etc.: *v.t.* to woo; flatter.

COURTEOUS (ker'te-us), *adj.* polite; obliging.

COURTESY ('te-si), *n.* politeness combined with kindness; civility.

COURTLINESS ('li-nes), *n.* elegance of manners.

COURTLY ('li), *adj.* refined; elegant.

COURT-MARTIAL (-mar'shal), *n.* a court of justice composed of naval or military officers.

COURT-PLASTER ('plas-ter), *n.* a kind of sticking-plaster.

COURTSHIP ('ship), *n.* the act of wooing.

COURTYARD ('yard), *n.* an enclosed space adjoining a house.

COUSIN (kuz'n), *n.* the son or daughter of an uncle or aunt; a kinsman.

COVE (kov), *n.* a small sheltered inlet or creek; a retired nook.

COVENANT (kuv'e-nant), *n.* a written agreement; deed; bargain: *v.i.* to enter into a formal agreement.

COVER (kuv'er), *v.t.* to overspread.

as the top of anything, with something else ; hide.

COVERLET (-let), *n.* a bed quilt.

COVERT (kuv'ert), *adj.* concealed ; covered ; disguised ; insidious.

COVERTURE ('er-tur), *n.* the status of a married woman.

COVET (kuv'et), *v.t.* to desire earnestly.

COVETOUS (-tus), *adj.* inordinately desirous, avaricious.

COVEY (kuv'i), *n.* a hatch or brood of birds.

COW (kou), *n.* the female of cattle, or of various other animals : *v.t.* to depress with fear.

COWARD ('ard, 'erd), *n.* one without courage ; a dastard ; poltroon.

COWARDICE ('er-dis), *n.* dishonourable fear.

COWBOY ('boi), *n.* rider employed by a rancher.

COWER (kou'er), *v.i.* to crouch or sink down through fear.

COWL (koul), *n.* a monk's hood.

COWLICK ('lik), *n.* a tuft of hair turned up on the forehead.

COWPOX ('poks), *n.* a disease of cows.

COWSLIP ('slip), *n.* a species of primrose.

COXCOMB (koks'kom), *n.* a vain fellow : a fop.

COXSWAIN (kok'swan), *n.* the steersman of a boat.

COY (koi), *adj.* modest ; bashful ; demure.

COYOTE (ki'ot, ki-o'te), *n.* the small prairie wolf.

COZY (ko'zi), *adj.* warm and comfortable ; snug.

CRAB (krab), *n.* a short-tailed, ten-footed crustacean.

CRAB APPLE (ap'l), *n.* a variety of small apple.

CRABBED ('ed), *adj.* morose.

CRACK (krak), *n.* a chink or fissure ; a fracture ; a sharp sound ; a sharp blow.

CRACKED (krakt), *adj.* split ; blemished ; broken.

CRACKER (krak'er), *n.* a biscuit ; a firework ; a kind of bonbon.

CRACKLE (krak'l), *v.i.* to make a slight, sharp explosive noise.

CRACKSMAN (kraks'man), *n.* [Slang] a burglar.

CRADLE (kra'dl), *n.* a baby's crib ; infancy ; a frame of timbers placed under a ship for launching it.

CRAFT (kraft), *n.* manual skill ; a trade ; cunning ; vessels and aircraft collectively.

CRAFTILY ('i-li), *adv.* cunningly.

CRAFTSMAN (krafts'man), *n.* a skilled artisan.

CRAFTY (kraf'ti), *adj.* cunning.

CRAG (krag), *n.* a steep, rugged rock.

CRAM (kram), *v.t.* fill beyond satiety : *v.i.* qualify speedily for examination.

CRAMP (kramp), *n.* a spasmodic muscular contraction of the muscles : *v.t.* to confine.

CRANBERRY (kran'ber-ri), *n.* the marsh whortleberry.

CRANE (kran), *n.* a large wading bird ; a machine for raising heavy weights.

CRANIAL (kra'ni-al), *adj.* pertaining to the skull.

CRANIUM ('ni-um), *n.* the skull.

CRANK (krangk), *n.* a device for causing the rotation of an axis or for converting rotary into reciprocal motion, or the contrary ; an iron brace ; a twist or turn ; a crotchety or impracticable person.

CRANKY ('i), *adj.* full of crotchets ; liable to be upset.

CRANNIED (kran'id), *adj.* full of chinks.

CRAPE (krap), *n.* a thin gauze of raw silk and gummed.

CRASH (krash), *v.t.* to damage an airplane in landing : *n.* a loud, sudden, confused noise ; a coarse, linen fabric.

CRASS (kras), *adj.* gross ; dense ; obtuse.

CRATE (krat), *n.* a hamper : *v.t.* to put in a crate.

CRATER (kra'ter), *n.* the cup-shaped cavity of a volcano.

CRAVAT (kra-vat'), *n.* a necktie.

CRAVE (krav), *v.t.* beg earnestly ; long for eagerly.

CRAVEN (kra'vn), *adj.* cowardly ; base : *n.* a coward.

CRAVENETTE (cra-ven-ette'), *n.* a waterproof cloth.

CRAVING ('ving), n. a strong desire.

CRAW (kraw), n. a bird's crop.

CRAWFISH (kraw'fish), **CRAYFISH** (kra'), n. a fresh-water lobster-like crustacean.

CRAWL (krawl), v.i. move slowly and with difficulty; creep.

CRAYON (kra'un), n. a kind of chalk pencil; a drawing done with crayons.

CRAZE (kraz), v.i. to become demented; open in slight cracks.

CRAZILY (-li), adv. in a crazy manner.

CRAZY (kra'zi), adj. insane; dilapidated; foolishly eager.

CREAK (krek), v.i. to make a sharp, harsh, grating sound.

CREAM (krem), n. the rich part of milk; hence, the choicest part of anything.

CREAMERY ('er-i), n. a place where butter and cheese are made.

CREAM-LAID ('lad), adj. denoting a paper of a creamy-white colour.

CREASE (kres), n. a mark made by folding or doubling anything.

CREATE (kre-at'), v.t. to cause to come into existence: v.i. to originate.

CREATION (-a'shun), n. the act of creating: the universe.

CREATOR (-ter), n. the Supreme Being; [c-], one who creates.

CREATURE (kre'tur), n. anything created; a living being.

CRECHE (kresh), n. [French], a public nursery.

CREDENCE (kre'dens), n. belief; trust.

CREDENTIAL (kre-den'shal), n. [pl.] letters given to a person to show he has a right to confidence.

CREDIBLE (kred'i-bl), adj. worthy of credit; probable.

CREDIT (kred'it), v.t. to believe; trust: n. belief; honour.

CREDITOR (-er), n. one to whom another is indebted for money or goods.

CREDULITY (-du'li-ti), n. ready belief.

CREDULOUS (kred'u-lus), adj. easily imposed upon.

CREED (kred), n. a brief statement of belief.

CREEK (krek), n. a small bay; cove.

CREEP (krep), v.i. to move slowly along the ground.

CREEPER ('er), n. a plant which clings to some support.

CREEPY ('i), adj. shivering.

CREMATE (kre'mat), v.t. to reduce to ashes.

CREMATORY (krem'a-to-ri), adj. pertaining to cremation: n. place for burning the dead.

CREOLE (kre'ol), n. a native of Spanish America or the West Indies, descended from European (originally Spanish) ancestors.

CREOSOTE ('o-sot), n. a heavy, oily liquid, prepared from wood-tar.

CREPT, p.t. & p.p. of creep.

CRESCENT (kres'ent), adj. growing: n. an increasing moon; [C-], the Moslem power.

CRESS (kres), n. a name for various cruciferous plants.

CREST (krest), n. a plume of feathers on the head of a bird, etc.; coat of arms; the ridge of a wave; summit of a hill.

CRESTFALLEN ('fawl-'n), adj. dejected.

CRETONNE (kre-ton'), n. a glazed or an unglazed cotton fabric printed on one side.

CREVASSE (kre-vas'), n. a fissure in a glacier ice; a breach in a levee.

CREVICE (krev'is), n. a crack; fissure.

CREW (kroo), n. a ship or boat's company.

CRIB (krib), n. a rack or manger; a child's bed; a plagiarism: v.t. to steal; plagiarize.

CRIBBAGE ('aj), n. a card game.

CRICKET (krik'et), n. the well-known game played with wickets, bats, and a ball; an insect.

CRIER (kri'er), n. a court officer.

CRIME (krim), n. a violation of the law; wrong-doing.

CRIMINAL (krim'i-nal), n. one guilty of a crime.

CRIMINALITY ('i-ti), n. guilt.

CRIMP (krimp), v.t. to bend or twist in regular undulations.

CRIMSON (krim'z'n), n. a deep red colour.

CRINGE (krinj), *v.i.* to crouch from fear or with servility.

CRINKLE (kring'kl), *v.t.* to wrinkle.

CRINOLINE (krin'o-lin), *n.* a hoop-skirt.

CRIPPLE (krip'l), *v.t.* disable : *n.* one who is lame or disabled.

CRISIS (kri'sis), *n.* [*pl.* crises (-sez)], a turning point ; a critical turn in a disease.

CRISP (krisp), *adj.* wavy ; curled ; brittle ; cheerful ; sparkling.

CRISS-CROSS ('kros), *n.* a mark made as a signature by a person unable to write.

CRITERION (kri-te'ri-on), *n.* [*pl.* criteria (-a)], a standard, or rule by which a correct judgment can be formed.

CRITIC (krit'ik), *n.* one skilled in criticism.

CRITICAL (-al), *adj.* nicely exact ; skilled in criticism ; censorious.

CRITICISE (krit'i-siz), *v.t.* to examine or judge as a critic ; censure.

CRITICISM ('i-sizm), *n.* the art of judging and defining the merits of a literary or artistic work ; censure.

CROAK (krok), *v.i.* to make a sound like a raven or frog ; grumble.

CROCHET (kro-sha'), *n.* a kind of knitting with a hooked needle.

CROCK (krok), *n.* an earthenware pot or vessel ; soot ; smut.

CROCODILE ('o-dil, -dil), *n.* a large lizard-like amphibian reptile.

CROCUS (kro'kus), *n.* a plant of the iris family.

CROIX DE GUERRE (krwa de gar), a French war decoration.

CRONY (kro'ni), *n.* a familiar friend.

CROOK (krook), *n.* a bend ; a shepherd's staff ; a swindler.

CROP (krop), *n.* the produce of the ground, as corn, etc. ; a bird's craw.

CROPPER (krop'er), *n.* a fall : usually from a horse.

CROQUET (kro-ka'), *n.* a lawn game.

CROQUETTE (-ket'), *n.* ball of mince-meat, fish, or fowl, seasoned and fried brown.

CROSIER, CROZIER (kro'zher), *n.* a bishop's staff.

CROSS (kros), *n.* wood formed of an upright and a cross piece : now the emblem of the Christian faith : *v.i.* to cancel ; pass ; thwart : *adj.* fretful ; perverse.

CROSS-BILL ('bil), *n.* bill brought by a defendant against a plaintiff praying for relief.

CROSS-EXAMINATION (-eg-zam-i-na'shun), *n.* the questioning of a witness by his own, or the opposing, counsel.

CROSSLY ('li), *adv.* athwart ; peevishly.

CROTCH (kroch), *n.* a hook or fork.

CROTCHET ('et), *n.* a musical note = ¼th a semibreve ; a bracket ; a whim or fancy.

CROTON OIL (kro'tun oil), a viscid vegetable oil.

CROUCH (krouch), *v.i.* to stoop low.

CROUP (kroop), *n.* inflammation of the trachea and larynx.

CROW (kro), *v.i.* to make a shrill sound like a cock ; boast in triumph : *n.* a familiar bird.

CROWBAR ('bar), *n.* an iron hand lever.

CROWD (kroud), *n.* a number of persons or things collected closely together.

CROWN (kroun), *n.* a royal headdress ; regal power ; a wreath ; the top ; an English silver coin (5s.) ; the corona of a flower ; upper part of a tooth.

CRUCIAL (kroo'shal), *adj.* cruciform ; intersecting ; severe ; extremely critical.

CRUCIBLE ('si-bl), *n.* a melting-pot.

CRUCIFIX ('si-fiks), *n.* a cross with the sculptured figure of Christ.

CRUCIFIXION (-si-fik'shun), *n.* the act of crucifying, especially the crucifixion of Christ upon the cross.

CRUCIFORM ('si-form), *adj.* cross-shaped.

CRUCIFY ('si-fi), *v.t.* to put to death by nailing the hands and feet to a cross.

CRUDE (krood), *adj.* in a natural state ; unripe ; raw.

CRUDITY ('i-ti), *n.* the state or condition of being crude.

CRUEL (kroo'el), *adj.* disposed to give

pain to others; merciless; unrelenting.

CRUELTY ('el-ti), *n.* inhumanity; savageness.

CRUET ('et), *n.* a small glass vial.

CRUISE (krooz), *v.i.* to sail to and fro : *n.* a voyage from place to place.

CRUISER ('er), *n.* a person, or ship, that cruises; fast warship.

CRUMB (krum), *n.* a fragment of bread; little piece.

CRUMBLE ('bl), *v.t.* to break into crumbs.

CRUMPLE ('pl), *v.t.* to press into wrinkles; rumple.

CRUNCH (krunch), *v.t.* to crush with the teeth; grind violently.

CRUPPER (krup'er), *n.* the leather band passing under a horse's tail.

CRUSADE (kroo-sad'), *n.* vigorous concerted action for the defence of some cause, or the advancement of some idea.

CRUSE (kroos), *n.* an earthen pot or dish.

CRUSH (krush), *v.t.* to press between two opposite bodies; squeeze.

CRUST (krust), *n.* a hard external coating or rind.

CRUTCH (kruch), *n.* a support for cripples.

CRUX (kruks), *n.* a cross; anything difficult; a perplexing problem.

CRY (kri), *v.i.* to call aloud; proclaim; exclaim vehemently.

CRYPT (kript), *n.* a subterranean cell or vault.

CRYPTIC (krip'tik), *adj.* hidden; secret.

CRYPTOGRAM ('to-gram), *n.* a writing, or a system of writing, in cipher.

CRYSTAL (kris'tal), *n.* an inorganic body having a definite geometrical form : *adj.* clear; transparent.

CRYSTALLIZE ('tal-iz), *v.t.* to cause to form crystals or a crystalline structure.

CUBBY-HOLE (kub'i-hol), *n.* a snug place.

CUBE (kub), *n.* a regular solid body with six equal square sides or faces; the products obtained by multiplying the square of a quantity by the quantity itself.

CUBE ROOT ('root), the first power of a cube—as 5 of 125.

CUBEB (ku'beb), *n.* the berry of a species of pepper.

CUBIC ('bik), *adj.* having the form or properties of a cube.

CUBIST (ku'bist), *n.* one of a new school of painters, which holds that art shall be nothing but an expression of the individual.

CUBIT ('bit), *n.* an ancient measure of about 18 inches; the forearm from the elbow to the wrist.

CUCKOO (kook'oo), *n.* a passerine bird.

CUCUMBER (ku'kum-ber), *n.* a creeping plant.

CUD (kud), *n.* food brought from the first stomach of a ruminating animal back into the mouth and chewed again.

CUDDLE (kud'l), *v.t.* to embrace closely : *v.i.* to lie close or snug.

CUDGEL (kuj'el), *n.* a short thick stick : *v.t.* to beat with a cudgel.

CUE (ku), *n.* the tail or end of a thing; a queue; a hit; the last word of an actor's speech; the tapering rod used in billiards.

CUISINE (kwe-zen'), *n.* the kitchen of a hotel, etc.

CUL-DE-SAC (kul-de-sak'), *n.* [French], a passage open only at one end.

CULINARY (ku'li-na-ri), *adj.* pertaining to the art of cooking.

CULL (kul), *v.t.* to pick out; select.

CULMINATE ('mi-nat), *v.i.* to reach the highest point.

CULPABLE ('pa-bl), *adj.* deserving censure; blameworthy.

CULPRIT ('prit), *n.* one accused of a crime or fault.

CULT (kult), *n.* a particular ritual or system of worship.

CULTIVATE (kul'ti-vat), *v.t.* to till; improve by care, labour, or study.

CULTIVATOR ('ti-va-ter), *n.* a farmer; an agricultural implement.

CULTURE ('tur), *n.* tillage; the training or refining of the moral or intellectual faculties.

CULVERT ('vert), *n.* a drain or water-way of masonry.

CUMBER (kum'ber), *v.t.* to hinder; embarrass; oppress; perplex.

CUMBERSOME (-sum), *adj.* unwieldy.

CUMBROUS ('brus), *adj.* troublesome; heavy.

CUMULATIVE (ku'mu-la-tiv), *adj.* increasing by successive additions.

CUNEIFORM (ku'ne-i-form), *adj.* having the form of a wedge.

CUNNING (kun'ing), *adj.* crafty; sly; designing : *n.* deceit.

CUP (kup), *n.* a small drinking vessel.

CUPBOARD (kub'erd), *n.* a closet for holding cups, plates, etc.

CUPFUL (kup'fool), *n.* as much as a cup will contain; a half-pint.

CUPIDITY (ku-pid'i-ti), *n.* covetousness.

CUPOLA ('po-la), *n.* a spherical cup-shaped roof.

CUR (ker), *n.* a mongrel dog.

CURABLE (kur'a-bl), *adj.* remediable.

CURATE (ku'rat), *n.* a clergyman who assists a vicar or incumbent.

CURATIVE (kur'a-tiv), *n.* that which cures or serves to cure.

CURATOR (ku-ra'ter), *n.* the superintendent of a museum, art gallery, etc.

CURB (kerb), *v.t.* restrain : *n.* that which checks, restrains, or subdues; a part of a horse's bridle.

CURBING (kerb'ing), *n.* curbstones collectively.

CURBSTONE ('ston), *n.* the stone-edge of a path or street.

CURD (kerd), *n.* the coagulated part of milk : *v.t.* to cause to curdle.

CURDLE (ker'dl), *v.t.* to thicken into curd : *v.i.* to coagulate.

CURE (kur), *n.* restoration to health : *v.t.* to heal; preserve by salting.

CURE (ku-ra'), *n.* in France, an R.C. parish priest.

CURFEW (ker'fu), *n.* a bell originally rung at 8 p.m. as an intimation that fires and lights were to be extinguished.

CURIO ('ri-o), *n.* bric-a-brac; a curiosity.

CURIOSITY (-os'i-ti), *n.* the quality of being curious; something strange or rare.

CURIOUS ('ri-us), *adj.* inquisitive; scrutinizing; exact; extraordinary.

CURL (kerl), *n.* a ringlet of hair : *v.t.* to twist into ringlets.

CURLING ('ling), *n.* a popular Scottish game played on the ice.

CURLY ('li), *adj.* having curls; wavy.

CURMUDGEON (-mud'jun), *n.* a grasping, churlish fellow.

CURRANT ('ant), *n.* the well-known shrub and its berry.

CURRENCY ('ens-i), *n.* a continual passing from hand to hand; the circulating monetary medium of a nation.

CURRENT ('ent), *adj.* widely circulated; generally accepted or credited; prevalent; common : *n.* a flow or passing : said of fluids and electricity.

CURRICULUM (-ik'u-lum), *n.* [*pl.* curricula (-a)], a prescribed course of study in a university, school, etc.

CURRY (kur'i), *v.t.* to dress (leather); beat; flatter; clean (a horse): *n.* an Indian sauce.

CURRY-COMB (-kom), *n.* a comb used in grooming horses.

CURSE (kers), *n.* an imprecation of evil; a profane oath.

CURSORILY ('so-ri-li), *adv.* hastily.

CURSORY ('so-ri), *adj.* hasty; superficial.

CURST, *p.p.* of curse.

CURT (kert), *adj.* abrupt.

CURTAIL (ker-tal'), *v.t.* to cut short; reduce.

CURTAIN ('tin), *n.* a textile hanging screen : *v.t.* to enclose with curtains.

CURTSY (kert'si), *n.* a salutation made by bending the knees.

CURVATURE ('va-tur), *n.* a bending.

CURVE (kerv), *adj.* bent without angles.

CUSHION (koosh'un), *n.* a pillow or soft pad; anything to deaden an impact.

CUSP (kusp), *n.* a sharp rigid point.

CUSPIDAL (kus'pi-dal), *adj.* ending in a point.

CUSPIDOR ('pi-dor), *n.* a spittoon.

CUSTARD ('terd), *n.* a composition of eggs and milk, etc., baked or boiled.

CUSTODIAN (-to'di-an), *n.* one who has the care of anything.

CUSTODY ('to-di), *n.* guardianship ; imprisonment.

CUSTOM ('tum), *n.* established usage ; business support ; unwritten law ; duties on goods.

CUSTOMARY (-a-ri), *adj.* habitual ; conventional ; common.

CUSTOMER (-er), *n.* a purchaser.

CUSTOM-HOUSE (-hous), *n.* a building where duties are paid, and vessels are entered and cleared.

CUT (kut), *v.t.* separate with a sharp instrument ; make an incision in ; divide ; diminish ; wound deeply: *n.* the fashion of a garment ; shape.

CUTAWAY (kut'a-wa), *adj.* cut back from the waist : *n.* a coat.

CUTE (kut), *adj.* sharp : clever.

CUT-GLASS (kut'glas), *n.* flint glass cut into facets or figures.

CUTICLE (kut'i-kl), *n.* the scarf-skin.

CUTLASS (kut'las), *n.* a broad cutting sword.

CUTLER ('ler), *n.* one who makes or sells cutting instruments.

CUTLERY (-i), *n.* edged or cutting instruments.

CUTLET ('let), *n.* a chop or slice of meat.

CUTTER ('er), *n.* one who cuts or hews ; one who cuts out and shapes garments ; a light sledge ; a small fast-sailing vessel ; a man-of-war's boat.

CUTTLEFISH (kut'l-fish), *n.* a cephalopod.

CUTWATER ('waw-ter), *n.* the fore part of a ship's prow.

CUTWORM ('werm), *n.* a destructive larval moth.

CYCLE (si'kl), *n.* a revolution of a certain period of time ; an imaginary circle in the heavens : *v.i.* to occur, or recur, in cycles.

CYCLOMETER (si-klom'e-ter), *n.* an instrument for registering the revolutions of a wheel.

CYCLONAL ('klo-nal), *adj.* pertaining to a cyclone. Also cyclonic.

CYCLONE ('klon), *n.* a violent storm.

CYCLOPÆDIA or **CYCLOPEDIA** (si-klo-pe'di-a), *n.* abbreviation of encyclopædia.

CYCLORAMA (-klo-ra'ma), *n.* a series of related pictures extended circularly so as to appear in natural perspective to the spectator standing in the centre.

CYGNET (sig'net), *n.* a young swan.

CYLINDER (sil'in-der), *n.* a long circular body, solid or hollow, of uniform diameter ; a hollow roller for printing.

CYLINDRIC ('drik), **CYLINDRICAL** ('dri-kal), *adj.* having the form, or properties, of a cylinder.

CYMBAL (sim'bal), *n.* one of a pair of circular disc-shaped brass plates, which, when struck, produce a clashing sound.

CYNIC (sin'ik), *n.* a morose, surly, or sarcastic person.

CYNICAL ('i-kal), *adj.* like a cynic.

CYNICISM ('i-sizm), *n.* the temper and practice of a cynic.

CYNOSURE (si'no-, sin'o-shoor), *n.* an object of general attraction.

CYPRESS (si'pres), *n.* a coniferous tree.

CYST (sist), *n.* a bladder ; pouch.

CZAR (zar), *n.* a despot : title of the former Emperors of Russia.

CZECH (chek), *n.* a member of the most westerly branches of the Slavonic family, including Bohemians, Moravians and Slovaks.

CZECHOSLOVAKIAN ('o-slo-vak'-ki-an), *adj.* pertaining to Republic of Czechoslovakia.

D

D, d (de), *n.* the fourth letter in the English alphabet.

D, d (de), *n.* an abbreviation.

D (de), *n.* a numeral : 500 in Roman notation ; with a bar (D̄), 500,000.

D FLAT (flat), in music, the tone half a step below D.

D FLAT MAJOR (ma'jer), a major scale having the signature of five flats.

D MAJOR, a major scale having the signature of two sharps.

D MINOR (mi'ner), a minor scale relative to F major and having the signature of one flat.

D SHARP (sharp), the tone half a step above D.

D SHARP MINOR, a minor scale relative to F sharp major and having the signature of six sharps.

DAB (dab), *v.t.* to strike or touch lightly : *n.* a small soft lump ; a gentle blow.

DABBLE (dab'l), *v.t.* to dip slightly : *v.i.* to play in water ; do anything in a superficial manner.

DA CAPO (da ka'po), a term in music meaning to repeat from the beginning.

DACTYL (dak'til), *n.* a poetical foot of three syllables, one long and two short.

DADDLE (dad'l), *v.i.* waddle ; trifle.

DADO (da'do), *n.* the solid block forming the body of a pedestal ; an ornamental border.

DAFFODIL (daf'o-dil), *n.* the narcissus.

DAFFY (daf'i), *adj.* crazy ; like a person of unsound mind.

DAFT (daft), *adj.* foolish ; idiotic.

DAGGER (dag'er), *n.* a short edged weapon ; a reference mark in printing (†).

DAGUERREOTYPE (da-ger'o-tip), *n.* a picture produced on a silvered plate.

DAHLIA (dal'ya), *n.* a genus of plants, with large tube roots.

DAIL EIREANN (dal' ar'in), the legislative republican assembly of Ireland.

DAILY (da'li), *n.* a newspaper or periodical published each week-day : *adj.* diurnal : *adv.* day by day.

DAINTINESS (dan'ti-nes), *n.* the quality of being dainty.

DAINTY (dan'ti), *n.* something choice or delicious.

DAIRY (da'ri), *n.* a place where milk is kept and converted into butter and cheese, etc.

DAIS (da'is), *n.* a raised platform.

DALE (dal), *n.* a vale ; glen.

DALLIANCE (dal'i-ans), *n.* the act of dallying.

DALLY (dal'i), *v.i.* to trifle away time ; loiter ; procrastinate.

DAM (dam), *n.* a barrier across a water-course : *v.t.* to restrain (usual with *in* or *up*).

DAMAGE ('aj), *n.* injury or harm : *pl.* money recovered for loss suffered.

DAMASK ('ask), *n.* a rich fabric ; a fine twilled table-linen.

DAME (dam), *n.* a title formerly used instead of mistress ; the wife of a knight ; a lady.

DAMN (dam), *v.t.* to sentence to punishment judicially ; consign to a certain fate.

DAMNATION (-na'shun), *n.* the state of being damned.

DAMNIFY (dam'ni-fi), *v.t.* [*p.t.* & *p.p.* damnified, *p.pr.* damnifying], to cause loss to.

DAMOSEL ('o-zel), *n.* see damsel.

DAMP (damp), *adj.* moist ; foggy ; humid.

DAMPER ('er), *n.* something which depresses or discourages ; a valve in a flue to regulate the draft.

DAMSEL (dam'zel), *n.* a maiden.

DAMSON (dam'zn), *n.* a small plum.

DANCE (dans), *n.* a regulated movement of the feet to a rhythmical musical accompaniment ; a dancing party.

DANDELION (dan'de-li-un), *n.* a biennial composite plant.

DANDER ('der), *n.* dandruff ; anger.

DANDLE (dan'dl), *v.t.* to move up and down on the knee or in the arms in affectionate play ; fondle.

DANDRUFF ('druf), *n.* scurf on the scalp.

DANDY ('di), *n.* a fop ; something very neat.

DANGER ('jer), *n.* hazard ; peril.

DANGEROUS (-us), *adj.* involving, or beset with, danger ; perilous ; hazardous.

DANGLE (dang'gl), *v.i.* to hang or swing loosely ; follow.

DANK (dangk), *adj.* humid ; damp.

DAPPER (dap'er), *adj.* small and active ; trim and neat.

DAPPLE (dap'l), *adj.* spotted ; variegated.

DARE (dar), *v.i.* to have courage ; attempt.

DARE-DEVIL ('dev-il), *adj.* characteristic of a reckless man.

DARING (dar'ing), *n.* intrepidity : *adj.* fearless.

DARK (dark), *adj.* destitute of light ; obscure : *n.* darkness.

DARKEN ('en), *v.t.* to make dark ; obscure.

DARKLY ('li), *adv.* with imperfect light ; not clearly ; mysteriously.

DARKNESS ('nes), *n.* absence of light ; obscurity ; gloom.

DARKY ('i), *n.* something dark ; [Slang], a negro.

DARLING (dar'ling), *n.* a favourite ; pet.

DARN (darn), *v.t.* to mend (a rent) : *n.* a patch made by darning.

DART (dart), *n.* a small spear : *v.i.* move swiftly ; start suddenly.

DASH (dash), *v.t.* to throw violently or hastily ; hurl ; suffuse ; depress ; sketch rapidly : *n.* a collision ; ostentatious parade ; mark (—) in writing or printing.

DASTARD (das'tard), *n.* a coward.

DATA, *pl.* of datum (q.v.).

DATE (dat), *n.* the time of an epoch or transaction ; duration ; the edible fruit of the date-palm.

DATIVE (da'tiv), *adj.* denoting the case of a noun, pronoun, or adjective which expresses the remoter object.

DATUM ('tum), *n.* [*pl.* data ('ta)], something assumed, known, or conceded for the basis of an argument or inference.

DAUB (dawb), *v.t.* to cover or smear with adhesive matter ; paint coarsely ; plaster.

DAUBING ('ing), *n.* the application of rough mortar to a wall to imitate stone.

DAUGHTER (daw'ter), *n.* the female offspring of a man or woman.

DAUGHTER-IN-LAW (-in-law), *n.* a son's wife.

DAUNT (dant), *v.t.* to intimidate ; dishearten.

DAUNTLESS ('les), *adj.* fearless.

DAVENPORT (dav'en-port), *n.* a high backed lounge.

DAVIT (dav'it), *n.* one of a pair of f-shaped uprights projecting over the side of a vessel for suspending or lowering a boat.

DAW (daw), *n.* a jackdaw.

DAWDLE (daw'dl), *v.i.* to waste time ; loiter : *n.* a dawdler.

DAWN (dawn), *v.i.* to begin to grow light ; break as the day.

DAWNING ('ing), *n.* daybreak.

DAY (da), *n.* the period of light between sunrise and sunset ; the space of twenty-four hours.

DAYDREAM ('drem), *n.* a visionary fancy.

DAYS OF GRACE (gras), a period, usually three days, allowed in some states for payment of certain commercial paper after maturity.

DAZE (daz), *v.t.* to stupefy : *n.* state of being dazed.

DAZZLE (daz'l), *v.t.* to overpower by a glare of light ; overpower by splendour.

DEACON (de'kn), *n.* a layman appointed to assist the minister of a church.

DEAD (ded), *adj.* destitute of life ; inactive ; monotonous ; flat ; useless : *n.* dead persons individually or collectively.

DEAD-BEAT ('bet), *adj.* thoroughly exhausted : *n.* a dead-beat escapement ; a loafer.

DEADEN (ded'n), *v.t.* retard ; blunt ; render non-conductive.

DEADHEAD ('hed), *n.* a person who had a free pass.

DEAD LETTER (let'er), *n.* an unclaimed letter; that which has lost its authority.

DEAD-LIFT ('lift), *n.* a heavy weight.

DEADLOCK ('lok), *n.* a situation in which progress is impossible.

DEADLY ('li), *adj.* causing death; fatal.

DEAD-RECKONING (-rek'un-ing), *n.* the calculation of a ship's place at sea by the log and the compass courses.

DEAD-SET ('set), *n.* a determined effort or attack.

DEAD-WEIGHT ('wat), *n.* freight charged for by weight instead of by bulk.

DEAF (def), *adj.* deprived of hearing.

DEAFEN (def'n), *v.t.* to make deaf.

DEAL (del), *n.* an indefinite quantity, degree or extent; a division of cards to the players; a mercantile combination : *v.t.* to distribute, apportion, or divide.

DEALER ('er), *n.* one who deals; a trader.

DEAN (den), *n.* the presiding dignitary in cathedral and collegiate churches; the president of a faculty in a college.

DEAR (der), *adj.* expensive; costly; beloved; precious.

DEARTH (derth), *n.* want; scarcity.

DEARY (der'i), *n.* a darling.

DEATH (deth), *n.* extinction of life or feeling; the state of the dead; decay; destruction.

DEATH-RATE ('rat), *n.* the percentage of deaths, usually reckoned per thousand, for a given period.

DEATH'S-HEAD (deths'hed), *n.* a skull, or representation of a skull, emblematic of death.

DEATH-WATCH ('woch), *n.* a vigil beside a dying person; a guard set over a criminal prior to his execution.

DEBACLE (de-bak'l), *n.* a violent flood carrying with it debris in great masses; a dispersion; a rout; a stampede.

DEBAR (de-bar'), *v.t.* to shut out; exclude.

DEBARK (de-bark'), *v.i.* to disembark.

DEBASE (de-bas'), *v.t.* to reduce from a higher to a lower state.

DEBASEMENT ('ment), *n.* act of debasing.

DEBATABLE (de-ba'ta-bl), *adj.* admitting of question or debate.

DEBATE (de-bat'), *v.t.* to contend for in words or arguments; meditate upon.

DEBAUCH (de-bawch'), *v.t.* to corrupt in morals or principles; seduce; pollute.

DEBAUCHEE (deb-aw-she'), *n.* a drunkard; a libertine.

DEBAUCHERY (de-baw'cher-i), *n.* excessive intemperance; corruption of fidelity.

DEBENTURE (de-ben'tur), *n.* a government voucher of indebtedness.

DEBILITY (-bil'i-ti), *n.* abnormal functional weakness; languor.

DEBIT (deb'it), *n.* that which is owing : *v.t.* to charge with debt.

DEBOUCH (de-boosh'), *v.i.* to march out of a confined space into open ground.

DEBRIS (da-bre'), *n.* fragments : broken rubbish; loose pieces of rock, etc.

DEBT (det), *n.* that which is due from one person to another; obligation.

DEBTOR ('er), *n.* one who owes something to another; one who is in debt.

DEBUT (da-boo'), *n.* [French], a first appearance.

DEBUTANT (-boo-tang'), *n.* [French], one who makes début.

DEBUTANTE (-boo-tangt'), *n.* [French], young girl on making first appearance in society.

DECADE (dek'ad), *n.* a group of ten; ten consecutive years.

DECADENCE (de-ka'dens), **DECADENCY** (-den-si), *n.* a state of decay; retrogression.

DECADENT ('dent), *adj.* deteriorating.

DECAGRAMME (dek'a-gram), *n.* a weight of ten grammes.

DECALITRE (dek'a-le-tr), *n.* a measure of capacity containing 10 litres = 2 1-5 imperial gallons.

DECALOGUE ('a-log), *n.* the Ten Commandments; the moral law.

DECAMETRE ('a-me-tr), *n.* a measure of length of 10 metres = 32.8 feet.

DECAMP (de-kamp'), *v.t.* to depart speedily.

DECANT (de-kant'), *v.t.* to pour off gently.

DECANTER (-kan'ter), *n.* an ornamental glass bottle.

DECAPITATE (de-kap'i-tat), *v.t.* to behead.

DECARE (dek-ar'), *n.* a superficial measure of 1,000 sq. metres.

DECARNATE (de-kar'nat), *adj.* divested of flesh.

DECAY (de-ka), *v.i.* rot; decline or fall: *n.* deterioration; rottenness; corruption.

DECEASE (de-ses'), *v.i.* to die: *n.* death.

DECEDENT (de-se'dent), *adj.* departing: *n.* a deceased person.

DECEIT (de-set'), *n.* deception.

DECEIVABLE (-sev'a-bl), *adj.* capable of being, or liable to be, deceived.

DECEIVE (-sev'), *v.t.* to mislead or cause to err; delude.

DECEMBER (de-sem'ber), *n.* the twelfth month of the year.

DECEMVIRATE ('vi-rat), *n.* a body of ten men in authority.

DECENCY (de'sen-si), *n.* the state of being decent.

DECENNIAL ('-al), *adj.* lasting for or occurring every ten years.

DECENT ('sent), *adj.* decorous; respectable; modest.

DECEPTION (-sep'shun), *n.* the act of deceiving; fraud.

DECEPTIVE ('tiv), *adj.* tending to deceive.

DECIDABLE (de-sid'a-bl), *adj.* capable of being decided.

DECIDE (de-sid'), *v.t.* to bring to an issue or conclusion; resolve.

DECIDUOUS (-sid'u-us), *adj.* falling off at maturity, or in season.

DECIGRAMME (des'i-gram), *n.* a metric weight, 1-10th of a gramme.

DECILITRE ('i-le-tr), *n.* a measure of capacity, 1-10th of a litre.

DECILLION (de-sil'yun), *n.* in France and the U.S. a unit followed by 33 ciphers; in England, a unit followed by 60 ciphers.

DECIMAL ('-imal), *adj.* pertaining to, or based upon, the number 10.

DECIMAL POINT (point), a dot placed before or at the left of a decimal fraction.

DECIMAL SYSTEM (sis'tem), a system of reckoning or measuring by 10, or powers of 10.

DECIMATE (des'i-mat), *v.t.* to put to death, or punish; destroy a large proportion of.

DECIMATION (-ma'shun), *n.* the act of decimating.

DECIMETRE ('i-me-tr), *n.* a measure of length, 1-10th of a metre=3.937 inches.

DECIPHER (de-si'fer), *v.t.* to read (secret writing); discover or make out the meaning of; solve; unravel.

DECISION (-sizh'un), *n.* the act of deciding; determination; judgment; settlement.

DECISIVE (-sis'iv), *adj.* final; conclusive.

DECK (dek), *v.t.* to array in finery or ornaments; adorn: *n.* the flooring of a ship; a pack of playing cards.

DECKLE-EDGED (dek'l-ejd), *adj.* having the edges rough and uncut as of paper.

DECLAIM (de-klam'), *v.t.* to speak in a rhetorical style; harangue.

DECLAMATION (dek-la-ma'shun), *n.* the art of declaiming; impassioned oratory.

DECLAMATORY (de-klam'a-to-ri), *adj.* pertaining to, or characterized by, declamation.

DECLARATION (dek-la-ra'shun), *n.* an assertion; publication; a statement reduced to writing.

DECLARATION OF INDEPENDENCE (in-de-pen'dens), the public act, passed July 4, 1776, by which the Second Continental Congress declared the thirteen North American colonies free states.

DECLARATORY ('a-to-ri), *adj.* affirmative.

DECLARE (de-klar'), *v.t.* to make known; tell openly or publicly; make a full statement as to goods, etc.

DECLENSION (-klen'shun), *n.* decline; a falling off; the inflection of nouns, pronouns, and adjectives.

DECLINABLE (-klin'a-bl), *adj.* capable of being declined.

DECLINATION (dek-li-na'shun), *n.* the act or state of bending or moving, downward; deterioration; decay; the angular distance of a heavenly body N. or S. of the celestial equator.

DECLINE (de-klin'), *v.i.* to incline from a right line: *v.t.* to refuse; bend downward; depress: *n.* diminution; decay; deterioration.

DECLIVITOUS (de-kliv'i-tus), *adj.* moderately steep.

DECLIVITY (-kliv'i-ti), *n.* a gradual descent.

DECOCT (de-kokt'), *v.t.* extract the essence of by boiling.

DECOCTION (-kok'shun), *n.* an extract obtained by boiling.

DECODE (de-kod'), *v.t.* to translate a message into ordinary language from a cipher.

DECOLLATE (-kol'at), *v.t.* to behead.

DECOLLETE (da-kol-e-ta'), *adj.* [French], cut low in the neck: said of a dress.

DECOMPOSE (de-com-poz'), *v.t.* to resolve into constituent elements; cause to decay.

DECOMPOSITION (-po-zish'un), *n.* the act of resolving into constituent elements.

DECORATE (dek'o-rat), *v.t.* to ornament, embellish, or beautify; confer an honour upon.

DECORATION (-ra'shun), *n.* the art of decorating; an ornament or embellishment; a badge of honour.

DECORATIVE ('o-ra-tiv), *adj.* tending to decoration.

DECORATOR (-ter), *n.* one who decorates.

DECOROUS (de-ko', dek'er-us), *adj.* marked by propriety; fit; proper.

DECORUM (de-ko'rum), *n.* propriety and decency of words, dress, and conduct.

DECOY (de-koi'), *v.t.* to lead or allure into danger by artifice: *n.* a deceptive stratagem; a lure.

DECREASE (de-kres'), *v.i.* to become less; diminish; abate.

DECREE (de-kre'), *n.* an ordinance, law, or edict; a judicial decision.

DECREPIT (de-krep'it), *adj.* enfeebled by age, or infirmity; wasted.

DECREPITUDE ('i-tud), *n.* physical infirmity caused by old age.

DECRESCENT (-kres'ent), *adj.* growing less.

DECRIAL (de-kri'al), *n.* clamorous censure.

DECRY (de-kri'), *v.t.* to blame clamorously; cry down; disparage.

DECUMBENT (-kum'bent), *adj.* lying down; prostrate; reclining.

DECURSIVE (-kur'siv), *adj.* running down.

DEDICATE (ded'i-kat), *v.t.* to set apart by a solemn act; inscribe, as a literary work.

DEDICATION (-i-ka'shun), *n.* the act of dedicating; an inscription or address.

DEDICATORY (ded'i-ka-to-ri), *adj.* pertaining to a dedication.

DEDUCE (de-dus'), *v.t.* to gather by reasoning; infer; derive [with *from* or *out of*].

DEDUCT (de-dukt'), *v.t.* to take away.

DEDUCTION (-duk'shun), *n.* the act or process of deducting; subtraction.

DEED (ded), *n.* an act; an illustrious achievement; a written instrument for the transfer of real estate.

DEEM (dem), *v.t.* to think; determine.

DEEP (dep), *adj.* extending far down; penetrating; sagacious; profound; absorbed; grave in tone, or low in pitch.

DEEPEN ('n), *v.t.* to make deep; make darker; make sad.

DEER (der), *n. sing. & pl.* a general

name for ruminants, the males of which have branching horns.

DEFACE (de-fas'), *v.t.* to mar; disfigure; impair the legibility of; spoil.

DE FACTO (de fak'to), in fact; actually.

DEFALCATION (-fal-ka'shun), *n.* embezzlement; diminution.

DEFAMATION (def-a-ma'shun), *n.* the act of injuring another's reputation without justification.

DEFAMATORY (de-fam'a-to-ri), *adj.* injurious to the character or reputation.

DEFAME (de-fam'), *v.t.* accuse falsely; asperse; vilify.

DEFAULT (de-fawlt'), *n.* failure or omission to do any act.

DEFAULTER ('er), *n.* one who makes a default.

DEFEASANCE (de-fez'ans), *n.* the annulment of a contract.

DEFEAT (de-fet'), *v.t.* to overcome or vanquish; frustrate; blame.

DEFECATE (def'e-kat), *v.t.* to free from impurities; to clarify sugar.

DEFECT (de-fekt'), *n.* an imperfection; fault; error.

DEFECTION (-fek'shun), *n.* a falling away from duty or allegiance; desertion.

DEFECTIVE ('tiv), *adj.* having a defect or flaw of any kind.

DEFENCE (de-fens'), *n.* protection; vindication by force or argument; a defendant's plea or answer.

DEFEND (de-fend'), *v.t.* to guard or protect; maintain.

DEFENDANT (-fen'dant), *n.* a person sued or accused in a civil or criminal court.

DEFENSIBLE ('si-bl), *adj.* capable of being defended.

DEFENSIVE (-fen'siv), *adj.* serving to defend or protect.

DEFER (de-fer'), *v.t.* to put off to a future time; delay.

DEFERENCE (def'er-ens), *n.* a yielding to the opinions or wishes of another; regard.

DEFERENTIAL (-er-en'shal), *adj.* characterized by, or expressing, deference.

DEFERMENT (de-fer'ment), *n.* delay.

DEFIANCE (-fi'ans), *n.* contemptuous disregard; a challenge.

DEFIANT ('ant), *adj.* characterized by defiance.

DEFICIENCY (-fish'en-si), *n.* the state of being deficient; incompleteness.

DEFICIENT ('ent), *adj* wanting; incomplete.

DEFICIT (def'i-sit), *n.* falling off, especially of receipts.

DEFILE (de-fil'), *v.t.* to make foul or impure: *v.i.* to march off in a file.

DEFILEMENT ('ment), *n.* moral or physical pollution.

DEFINABLE (-fin'a-bl), *adj.* capable of being defined.

DEFINE (de-fin'), *v.t.* to determine the limits of; describe the nature or properties of.

DEFINITE (def'i-nit), *adj.* having fixed or distinct limits; certain.

DEFINITELY (-li), *adv.* distinctly.

DEFINITION (-nish'un), *n.* a brief description of the precise meaning of a term, word, phrase, etc.

DEFINITIVE (de-fin'i-tiv), *adj.* determining; conclusive: *n.* a word used in grammar to define the signification of a noun.

DEFLECT (de-flekt'), *v.t.* to bend from a straight line.

DEFLECTION (-flek'shun), *n.* a bending.

DEFLECTIVE ('tiv), *adj.* causing deflection.

DEFLOWER (de-flou'er), *v.t.* to deprive of flowers or bloom.

DEFOREST (de-for'est), *v.t.* to clear of forest.

DEFORM (-form), *v.t.* to render unshapely; disfigure; mar.

DEFORMITY (-for'mi-ti), *n.* physical malformation; disfigurement.

DEFRAUD (-frawd)', *v.t.* to deprive of some right or interest by deception; cheat.

DEFRAY (de-fra'), *v.t.* to discharge (the expenses of anything); pay; settle.

DEFRAYAL ('al), *n.* the act of defraying.

DEFT (deft), *adj.* dexterous; handy; clever.

DEFUNCT (de-fungkt'), *adj.* dead; extinct: *n.* a dead person, or persons.

DEFY (-fī'), *v.t.* to challenge or provoke to strife; set at defiance.

DEGENERACY (de-jen'er-a-si), *n.* the state of being degenerate.

DEGENERATE ('er-at), *v.i.* to become inferior in goodness or quality; deteriorate.

DEGENERATION (-a'shun), *n.* the act, state, or process of growing worse; decline.

DEGRADATION (deg-ra-da'shun), *n.* the act of degrading.

DEGRADE (de-grad'), *v.t.* to reduce in rank; deprive of honours; diminish; wear away.

DEGREE (de-gre'), *n.* a step or grade; rank or station; rank conferred; the 360th part of the circumference of a circle; 60 geographical miles.

DEHORN (-horn'), *v.t.* to deprive of horns.

DEHYPNOTIZE (-hip'mo-tiz), *v.t.* to awaken from hypnotism.

DEIFICATION (de-i-fi-ka'snun), *n.* the act of deifying; apotheosis.

DEIFY ('i-fi), *v.t.* to make, or exalt to the rank of, a deity.

DEIGN (dan), *v.i.* to condescend; vouchsafe: *v.t.* to permit.

DEISM (de'izm), *n.* the creed of a deist.

DEIST ('ist), *n.* one who believes in the existence of a personal God, but not in revealed religion.

DEITY ('ti), *n.* a god, goddess, or person worshipped as a divine being.

DEITY ('ti), *n.* God; Jehovah; the Godhead.

DEJECT (de-jekt'), *v.t.* to depress; sadden.

DEJECTION (-jek'shun), *n.* lowness of spirits; melancholy; depression.

DELAY (de-la'), *v.t.* to postpone; hinder for a time.

DELE (de'le), *v.t.* to take out (a letter, etc.), in proof-reading.

DELECTABILITY (de-lek-ta-bil'i-ti), *n.* the quality of being delectable.

DELECTABLY (-bli), *adv.* delightfully.

DELECTATION (-ta'shun), *n.* delight; pleasure.

DELEGATE (del'e-gat), *v.t.* entrust; commit: *n.* one sent to represent and act for others.

DELEGATION (-ga'shun), *n.* a person or body of persons chosen to act for others.

DELETE (de-let'), *v.t.* to blot out; erase.

DELETERIOUS (-ter'i-us), *adj.* harmful; poisonous.

DELF (delf), *n.* glazed earthenware.

DELIBERATE (de-lib'er-at), *v.t.* to think upon or consider; ponder.

DELIBERATION (-er-a'shun), *n.* calm and careful consideration.

DELICACY (del'i-ka-si), *n.* grace; sensitiveness; refinement; sensibility; consideration for the feelings of others.

DELICATE (del'i-kat), *adj.* frail; easily injured; fine in texture; refined; dainty.

DELICATESSEN (-ka-tes'en), *n.pl.* table delicacies.

DELICIOUS (de-lish'us), *adj.* highly pleasing to taste, or mind; exquisite.

DELIGHT (de-lit'), *v.t.* to gratify or please greatly; charm: *n.* high satisfaction; joy.

DELIMIT (-lim'it), *v.t.* to mark out or fix the limits of.

DELINEATE (-lin'e-at), *v.t.* to mark out with lines; sketch; portray.

DELINEATION (e-a'shun), *n.* the act or art of delineating.

DELINEATOR ('e-a-ter), *n.* one who delineates.

DELINQUENCY (-ling'kwen-si), *n.* neglect of, or failure in, duty; a misdeed; fault.

DELINQUENT ('kwent), *adj.* falling short of duty: *n.* an offender.

DELIRIOUS (de-lir'i-us), *adj.* lighthearted; insane.

DELIRIUM ('i-um), *n.* excitement and aberration of the mind.

DELIRIUM TREMENS (tre'mens), a disease of the brain caused by the excessive use of intoxicating liquors.

DELIVER (de-liv'er), *v.t.* to set free; save; yield possession or control of.

DELIVERANCE ('er-ans), *n.* the act of delivering ; rescue.

DELIVERY ('er-i), *n.* a setting free ; a surrender ; transfer ; manner of utterance.

DELL (del), *n.* a small, secluded valley.

DELTA (del'ta), *n.* an alluvial deposit formed at the mouth of a river ; any triangular surface.

DELUDE (de-lud'), *v.t.* to impose upon ; beguile ; deceive.

DELUGE (del'uj), *n.* an inundation ; a great overflowing of the land by water, especially that of the time of Noah.

DELUSION (-lu'zhun), *n.* the act of deluding ; deceit ; illusion.

DELUSIVE (-lu'siv), *adj.* tending to delude or deceive ; deceptive.

DE LUXE (looks), [French], of superior quality or finish.

DELVE (delv), *v.t.* to open with a spade ; fathom ; penetrate.

DEMAGNETIZE (de-mag'net-iz), *v.t.* to deprive of magnetic properties.

DEMAGOGISM (dem'a-gog-izm), *n.* the principles or practice of a demagogue.

DEMAGOGUE ('a-gog), *n.* a factious orator, one who inveighs against constituted authority.

DEMAND (de-mand'), *v.t.* to claim as by right or authority ; ask in a peremptory manner ; summon.

DEMANDANT ('ant), *n.* a plaintiff.

DEMARCATION (-mar-ka'shun), *n.* the act of defining, or marking, the bounds of separation.

DEMEAN (de-men'), *v.t.* to debase, lower, or degrade.

DEMEANOUR ('er), *n.* behaviour ; deportment.

DEMENTIA (-men'shi-a), *n.* insanity.

DEMI- (dem'i), a prefix signifying *half.*

DEMIGOD (dem'i-god), *n.* the offspring of a god and a human being ; a deified hero.

DEMIJOHN (-jon), *n.* a large glass bottle.

DEMISE (de-miz'), *n.* death ; the conveyance of an estate by will : *v.i.* to pass by bequest.

DEMIT (de-mit'), *v.i.* to relinquish an office : *n.* a paper certifying a person has demitted, as from a lodge.

DEMI-TASSE (dem'i-tas), *n.* a small cup of, or for, black coffee.

DEMOBILIZE (-mo'bi-liz), *v.t.* to disband or dismiss (troops that have been mobilized).

DEMOCRACY (-mok'ra-si), *n.* government by the people collectively as by elected representatives.

DEMOCRAT (dem'o-krat), *n.* one who advocates and upholds the principles of democracy.

DEMOCRATIC (-krat'ik), **DEMOCRATICAL** ('i-kal). *adj.* pertaining to democracy.

DEMOLISH (de-mol'ish), *v.t.* to throw down ; reduce to ruins ; destroy.

DEMOLITION (dem-o-lish'un), *n.* the act or process of demolishing ; destruction.

DEMOLOGY (de-mol'o-ji), *n.* the statistical study of populations and social conditions.

DEMON (de'mon), *n.* an evil spirit ; devil.

DEMONETIZE (-mon'e-tiz), *v.t.* to deprive of standard value, as currency.

DEMONIAC (-mo'ni-ak), *n.* one possessed by a demon.

DEMONSTRABLE (de-mon'stra-bl), *adj.* capable of being demonstrated.

DEMONSTRATE (de-mon'strat), *v.t.* to prove beyond the possibility of a doubt ; teach by examples.

DEMONSTRATION (dem-on-stra'-shun), *n.* manifestation ; a public exhibition of sympathy with some political or social movement.

DEMONSTRATIVE ('stra-tiv), *adj.* conclusive ; manifesting the feelings openly and strongly : *n.* a demonstrative pronoun.

DEMORALIZE (-mor'al-iz), *v.t.* to corrupt ; deprive of spirit or energy ; throw into confusion.

DEMOTE (de-mot'), *v.t.* to reduce to a lower grade.

DEMOUNTABLE (de-mount'a-bl), *adj.* capable of being taken off.

DEMUR (de-mur'), *v.i.* to hesitate; raise objections.

DEMURE (-mur'), *adj.* sober; modest or grave.

DEMURRAGE (-mur'aj), *n.* the compensation paid by the freighter for the detention of a vessel in port beyond the stipulated time.

DEMURRER ('er), *n.* in law, a pleading that admits the facts, but contends that they do not constitute a good cause of action or defence.

DEN (den), *n.* the cave of a beast; lair.

DENATIONALIZE (de-nash'un-al-iz), *v.t.* to deprive of national rights or character; render local.

DENATURALIZE (-nat'u-ral-iz), *v.t.* to make unnatural; divest of the acquired rights of citizenship in a foreign country.

DENATURE (de-na'tur), *v.t.* to deprive of natural qualities; change; alter as alcohol.

DENIAL (de-ni'al), *n.* the act of denying; refusal; contradiction.

DENIM (den'im), *n.* a twilled cotton fabric.

DENIZEN (den'i-zen), *n.* an inhabitant; citizen.

DENOMINATE (de-nom'i-nat), *v.t.* to designate; name: *adj.* made up of units of a specified kind.

DENOMINATION (i-na'shun), *n.* the act of designating; a sect, class, or division.

DENOMINATIVE ('i-na-tiv), *adj.* giving a name: *n.* a verb formed from a substantive or adjectival stem.

DENOMINATOR ('i-na-ter), *n.* one who, or that which, denominates; expression of a fraction which, when placed below the line, gives the name or value to the unit.

DENOTATIVE (-not'a-tiv), *adj.* having the power to denote or point out; significant.

DENOTE (de-not'), *v.t.* to signify or identify by a visible sign; indicate.

DENOUEMENT (da-noo-mang'), *n.* [French], the act of solving a plot; outcome.

DENOUNCE (de-nouns'), *v.t.* to threaten or accuse publicly; censure; stigmatize.

DENSE (dens), *adj.* thick; compact; intense.

DENSITY (den'si-ti), *n.* compactness; mass of matter per unit of volume.

DENT (dent), *n.* a slight depression caused by a blow; a tooth-like indentation or notch.

DENTAL (den'tal), *adj.* pertaining to the teeth.

DENTATE ('tat), *adj.* toothed.

DENTIFRICE ('tis-fris), *n.* tooth-powder.

DENTIL ('til), *n.* one of the small square projections in cornices.

DENTINE (den'tin), *n.* the hard, dense, calcified tissue of a tooth.

DENTIPHONE ('ti-fon), *n.* an audiphone.

DENTIST ('tist), *n.* a dental surgeon.

DENTISTRY ('tis-tri), *n.* dental surgery.

DENTITION (-tish'un), *n.* the process, or period, of cutting the teeth.

DENTOID ('toid), *adj.* tooth-shaped.

DENUDATE (de-nud'at), *adj.* laid bare; naked: *v.t.* (den'u-dat), to lay bare.

DENUDATION (de-nu, den-u-da'-shun), *n.* the act of stripping or making bare.

DENUDE (de-nud'), *v.t.* to make bare or naked.

DENUNCIATION (-nun-si-a'shun), *n.* a threat; menace.

DENUNCIATORY (-to-ri), *adj.* pertaining to, or containing, a denunciation.

DENY (de-ni'), *v.t.* to refuse to believe or admit; contradict.

DEODORANT (-o'der-ant), *n.* a disinfectant.

DEODORIZE ('der-iz), *v.t.* to disinfect.

DEPART (de-part'), *v.i.* to go or move away; leave; die; desist.

DEPARTMENT ('ment), *n.* a separate office for business; a branch of business, study, or science.

DEPARTMENT STORE (de-part'-ment stor), a store having many departments for different lines of business.

DEPARTURE (de-par'tur), *n.* a going away ; deviation ; death.

DEPEND (de-pend'), *v.i.* to rely for support ; trust ; hang down.

DEPENDENCE ('dens), *n.* the state of being dependent ; connection ; reliance ; trust.

DEPENDENCY (de-pen'den-si), *n.* a tributary state ; colony.

DEPENDENT ('dent), *adj.* hanging down ; conditional ; subordinate : *n.* one dependent upon another.

DEPICT (de-pikt'), *v.t.* to paint or portray ; represent vividly.

DEPILATORY (de-pil'a-to-ri), *adj.* having the power of removing hair.

DEPLETION (-ple'shun), *n.* the act of emptying or exhausting.

DEPLORABLE (-plor'a-bl), *adj.* sad ; calamitous ; grievous.

DEPLORE (-plor'), *v.t.* to lament ; grieve for.

DEPLOY (-ploi'), *v.t.* & *v.i.* to open out ; extend in line so as to present a wider front.

DEPONENT (-pon'ent), *n.* a witness who makes an affidavit to a statement of fact.

DEPOPULATE (-pop'u-lat), *v.t.* to deprive of inhabitants ; devastate ; lay waste.

DEPORT (-port'), *v.t.* banish ; behave (one's self).

DEPORTMENT ('ment), *n.* conduct ; behaviour.

DEPOSE (-poz'), *v.t.* deprive of office : *v.i.* testify on oath.

DEPOSIT (-poz'it), *v.t.* to put or set down ; place ; in trust to another for security.

DEPOSITARY ('i-ta-ri), *n.* one with whom something is intrusted ; a guardian.

DEPOSITION (dep-o-zish'un), *n.* the act of depositing or deposing ; an affidavit.

DEPOSITOR (de-poz'i-ter), *n.* one who deposits.

DEPOSITORY ('i-to-ri), *n.* the place where anything is deposited for security.

DEPOT (de'po, dep'o), *n.* a warehouse ; a railway station ; the headquarters of a regiment.

DEPRAVATION (dep-ra-va'shun), *n.* the act of depraving.

DEPRAVE (de-prav'), *v.t.* to make bad.

DEPRAVED (-pravd'), *p.adj.* morally debased ; corrupt.

DEPRAVITY (-prav'i-ti), *n.* the state of being depraved ; wickedness.

DEPRECATE ('re-kat), *v.t.* to pray against ; disapprove strongly.

DEPRECATION (-ka'shun), *n.* the act of deprecating.

DEPRECIATE (de-pre'sjhi-at), *v.t.* to lower the value, or rate, of ; disparage.

DEPRECIATION (-a'shun), *n.* fall in value.

DEPREDATE (dep're-dat), *v.t.* to pillage ; rob ; prey upon.

DEPREDATOR (dep're-da-ter), *n.* a plunderer.

DEPRESS (de-pres'), *v.t.* to press or thrust down ; humble : dispirit.

DEPRESSED (-prest'), *p.adj.* cast down.

DEPRESSION (-presh'un), *n.* the act of depressing ; abasement ; dejection.

DEPRIVATION (dep-ri-va'shun), *n.* the act of taking away ; destitution.

DEPRIVE (de-priv'), *v.t.* to take from ; dispossess ; debar ; depose from office.

DEPTH (depth), *n.* the state or degree of being deep ; profoundness.

DEPTH BOMB (bom), **DEPTH CHARGE** (charj), *n.* a container filled with a powerful explosive, to be lowered from a vessel ; at a regulated depth it explodes with terrific force, shattering everything above it.

DEPUTATION (dep-u-ta'shun), *n.* the act of deputing ; the persons deputed.

DEPUTE (de-put'), *v.t.* to appoint as an agent or deputy.

DEPUTIZE (dep'u-tiz), *v.t.* to appoint as a deputy.

DEPUTY ('u-ti), *n.* one appointed to act for another ; a delegate.

DERAIL (de-ral'), *v.i.* to run off the rails.

DERANGE (-ranj'), *v.t.* to throw into confusion ; displace.

DERANGEMENT ('ment), *n.* the act of deranging ; insanity.

DERBY (dar'bi), *n.* a race for three-year-old horses, run annually (since 1780), near London.

DERBY (der'bi), *n.* a kind of stiff felt hat.

DERELICT (der'e-likt), *adj.* abandoned ; adrift ; neglectful : *n.* a ship abandoned at sea.

DERIDE (-rid'), *v.t.* to mock : *v.i.* scorn, or ridicule.

DERISION (-rizh'un), *n.* the act of deriding ; ridicule ; scorn ; contempt.

DERISIVE (-ri'siv), *adj.* expressing derision.

DERIVABLE (-riv'a-bl), *adj.* capable of being derived.

DERIVATION (der-i-va'shun), *n.* the process of tracing a word from its original source ; evolution ; deduction.

DERIVATIVE (de-riv'a-tiv), *adj.* derived or taken from another ; deducible.

DERIVE (-riv'), *v.t.* to draw from an original source ; deduce ; infer.

DERMAL (dur'mal), *adj.* pertaining to, consisting of, skin.

DERMATOLOGY (-ma-tol'o-ji), *n.* the science which treats of the skin and its diseases.

DEROGATE (der'o-gat), *v.t.* to take away ; annul partially : *v.i.* detract (with *from*).

DEROGATION (-ga'shun), *n.* the act of derogating ; detraction ; depreciation.

DEROGATORY (de-rog'a-to-ri), *adj.* tending to derogate from honour, or value (with *to*, *from*).

DERRICK (der'ik), *n.* an apparatus for hoisting heavy weights.

DERVISH (dur'vish), *n.* a Mohammedan monk or friar.

DESCANT (des'kant), *n.* a varied song or melody ; a disquisition or comment.

DESCEND (de-send'), *v.i.* to pass from a higher to a lower position.

DESCENDANT ('dant), *n.* offspring.

DESCENDENT ('dent), *adj.* descending.

DESCENSION (-sen'shun), *n.* the act of descending ; declension ; moving downwards.

DESCENT (-sent'), *n.* change from a higher to a lower place ; moral or social declension ; derivation from a common ancestor ; birth.

DESCRIBE (-skrib'), *v.t.* to delineate ; narrate ; set forth.

DESCRIBABLE (de-skrib'a-bl), *adj.* capable of description.

DESCRIPTION (-skrip'shun), *n.* delineation by marks or signs ; an account of anything.

DESCRIPTIVE ('tiv), *adj.* serving to describe ; containing description.

DESCRY (de-skri'), *v.t.* to discover a distant or obscure object.

DESECRATE (des'e-krat), *v.t.* to divert from a sacred to a secular use ; profane.

DESECRATION (-kra'shun), *n.* profanation.

DESERT (de-zert'), *v.t.* to forsake ; abandon.

DESERT (dez'ert), *n.* a barren tract ; a solitude.

DESERTER (de-zer'ter), *n.* one who forsakes a duty.

DESERVE (-zerv'), *v.t.* to earn by service ; merit : *v.i.* to be worthy or deserving (usual with *well* or *ill*).

DESERVEDLY ('ed-li), *adv.* justly.

DESERVING (de-zer'ving), *adj.* meritorious ; worthy.

DESICCATE (des'i-kat), *v.t.* to dry thoroughly.

DESICCATION (-ka'shun), *n.* the act of drying.

DESIDERATE (de-sid'er-at), *v.t.* to feel want or need of.

DESIDERATIVE (-a-tiv), *adj.* having desire.

DESIDERATUM (-a'tum), *n.* [*pl.* desiderata ('ta)], anything desired.

DESIGN (-zin'), *v.i.* to formulate designs or execute original work : *n.* an outline, plan, or drawing ; project ; intention.

DESIGNATE (des'ig-nat), *v.t.* to indicate by marks, lines, or a description the limits of ; point out ; distinguish ; name : *adj.* designated ; selected.

DESIGNATION (-na'shun), *n.* the

act of designating; nomination; appointment.

DESIGNEDLY (de-zin'ed'li), *adv*. intentionally.

DESIGNING (-zin'ing), *adj*. scheming; artful; cunning; insidious; wily.

DESIRABILITY (-zir-a-bil'i-ti), *n*. the state or quality of being desirable.

DESIRABLE ('a-bl), *adj*. pleasing; agreeable.

DESIRE (-zir'), *v.t*. to wish earnestly for; crave : *v.i*. be in a state of desire : *n*. a longing for the possession of some object; a petition or prayer; natural or sensual tendency; the object longed for.

DESIST (-sist'), *v.i*. to cease from.

DESK (desk), *n*. a sloping frame or table for reading or writing upon; a clerk's position.

DESOLATE (des'o-lat), *v.t*. to lay waste; overwhelm with sorrow : *adj*. solitary; abandoned; miserable.

DESOLATION (-la'shun), *n*. a solitude; ruin; destruction; affliction; misery.

DESPAIR (de-spar'), *v.i*. to abandon all hope, or expectation : *n*. hopelessness; desperation.

DESPATCH (de-pach'), **DISPATCH** (dis-), *v.t*. to send off; expedite; put to death; finish quickly.

DESPERADO (-per-a'do), *n*. a man reckless of danger; a ruffian.

DESPERATE ('per-at), *adj*. reckless; hopeless.

DESPICABLE ('pi-ka-bl), *adj*. contemptible.

DESPISE (de-spiz'), *v.t*. to look down upon with scorn or contempt; disdain.

DESPITE (-spit'), *n*. extreme contempt; scorn; hatred : *prep*. notwithstanding.

DESPOIL (-spoil'), *v.t*. to rob; deprive.

DESPOND (-spond'), *v.i*. to give way to despondency.

DESPONDENCE (-spon'dens), **DESPONDENCY** ('den-si), *n*. absence of hope or courage; deep mental depression.

DESPONDENT ('dent), *adj*. cast down; dejected.

DESPOT (des'pot), *n*. an autocrat; tyrant.

DESPOTIC (-pot'ik), **DESPOTICAL** ('i-kal), *adj*. autocratic; irresponsible; tyrannical.

DESPOTISM ('pot-izm), *n*. absolute power or government; tyranny.

DESSERT (de-zert'), *n*. a course of fruits, sweets, etc.

DESTINATION (des-ti-na'shun), *n*. ultimate design; goal.

DESTINE (des'tin), *v.t*. fix unalterably; doom.

DESTINY ('ti-ni), *n*. fate; inevitable necessity.

DESTITUTE ('ti-tut), *adj*. forsaken; poor; penniless.

DESTITUTION (-tu'shun), *n*. poverty; want.

DESTROY (de-stroi'), *v.t*. to pull down; overturn; lay waste; kill.

DESTRUCTIBLE (-struk'ti-bl), *adj*. that may be destroyed.

DESTRUCTION (struk'shun), *n*. subversion; overthrow; ruin; death.

DESUETUDE (des'we-tud), *n*. disuse.

DESULTORY (des'ul-to-ri), *adj*. cursory; erratic.

DETACH (de-tach'), *v.t*. to disconnect; detail for a specific purpose.

DETAIL (de-tal'), *v.t*. to relate minutely; enumerate; tell off for a given duty.

DETAIN (de-tan'), *v.t*. to hold back; restrain.

DETECT (de-tekt'), *v.t*. to discover; bring to light; expose.

DETECTION ('shun), *n*. the act of detecting or its result; discovery.

DETECTIVE ('tiv), *n*. one whose business it is to trace wrong-doers.

DETECTOR ('ter), *n*. one who, or that which, detects; in radio, a device for regulating the high frequency electrical oscillations.

DETENTION (-ten'shun), *n*. restraint; delay.

DETER (de-ter), *v.t*. to discourage or hinder.

DETERIORATE (-te'ri-o-rat), *v.t*. to impair : *v.i*. to grow worse.

DETERMINABLE (-ter'mi-na-bl),

adj. defined with clearness; terminable.

DETERMINATE ('mi-nat), *adj.* having definite or fixed limits; specific.

DETERMINATION (-na'shun), *n.* purpose; resolution.

DETERMINATIVE ('min-a-tiv), *adj.* determining, limiting, or defining.

DETERMINE (de-ter'min), *v.i.* to decide; end : *v.t.* to restrict.

DETERRENT (-ter'ent), *adj.* serving to deter : *n.* that which deters.

DETEST (-test'), *v.t.* to hate intensely.

DETESTATION (de-tes-, det-es-ta'shun), *n.* extreme dislike; loathing.

DETHRONE (-thron'), *v.t.* to remove from a throne; deprive of authority.

DETINUE (det'i-nu), *n.* a writ for the recovery of chattels.

DETONATE (det'o-nat), *v.i.* to explode loudly and suddenly.

DETONATOR ('o-na-ter), *n.* a substance that detonates; a percussion-cap.

DETOUR (de-toor'), *n.* a circuitous way.

DETRACT (-trakt'), *v.t.* to draw or take away (with *from*) : *v.i.* take away the reputation.

DETRACTION (-trak'shun), *n.* depreciation; defamation; slander.

DETRAIN (de-tran'), *v.t.* to remove from a train, as troops.

DETRIMENT (det'ri-ment), *n.* that which injures, reduces in value, or causes damage.

DETRIMENTAL ('tal), *adj.* injurious.

DE TROP (de tro'), [French], out of place; not wanted.

DEUCE (dus), *n.* the devil; a card or dice with two spots; a term used in scoring at lawn tennis.

DEVAPORATION (de-vap-o-ra'shun), *n.* the change of vapour into water.

DEVASTATE (dev'as-tat), *v.t.* to lay waste; plunder.

DEVELOP (de-vel'op), *v.t.* to unfold gradually; complete.

DEVEST (de-vest'), *v.t.* to alienate or annul, as right or title.

DEVIATE (de'vi-at), *v.i.* to turn aside from a certain course; diverge; err.

DEVIATION (-a'shun), *n.* digression; wandering; error.

DEVICE (de-vis'), *n.* a contrivance; invention; a stratagem.

DEVIL (dev'l), *n.* the Evil Spirit.

DEVILISH (-sh), *adj.* diabolical.

DEVILRY (-ri), **DEVILTRY** (tri), *n.* malicious mischief; diabolical.

DEVIOUS (de'vi-us), *adj.* rambling; circuitous.

DEVISABLE (-viz'a-bl), *adj.* capable of being imagined or bequeathed.

DEVISE (-viz'), *v.t.* to imagine; scheme; contrive; concoct; bequeath by will.

DEVISEE (dev-i-ze'), *n.* the person to whom a bequest has been made.

DEVISER (de-viz'er), *n.* one who devises or invents.

DEVISOR (-vi'zor), *n.* one who bequeaths by will.

DEVOID (-void'), *adj.* destitute of.

DEVOIR (de-war'), *n.* [French], a service or duty owed.

DEVOLVE (-volv'), *v.t.* to transfer from one to another; transmit.

DEVOTE (de-vot'), *v.t.* to dedicate or consecrate; apply (one's self).

DEVOTEE (dev-o-te'), *n.* a votary; enthusiast.

DEVOTION (de-vo'shun), *n.* strong affection; ardent love; religious worship : *pl.* prayers.

DEVOUR (de-vour'), *v.t.* to swallow greedily or ravenously.

DEVOUT (-vout'), *adj.* devoted to religion; heartfelt.

DEW (du), *n.* aqueous vapour condensed; moisture in little drops.

DEXTER (deks'ter), *adj.* right; opposed to *left*.

DEXTERITY ('i-ti), *n.* manual skill; adroitness; cleverness.

DEXTEROUS (deks'ter-us), *adj.* quick, mentally or physically; adroit; clever.

DIABETES (di'a-be'tez), *n.* a disease characterized by excessive discharge of urine.

DIABOLIC (di-a-bol'ik), **DIABOLICAL** ('i-kal), *adj.* devilish; outrageously wicked.

DIACOUSTICS (di-a-koos'tiks), *n.*

the science of refracted sounds; diaphonics.

DIACRITICAL (-krit′i-kal), *adj.* serving to separate or distinguish.

DIACRITICAL MARK (mark), a mark employed to distinguish letters or sounds which resemble each other, and to indicate their true pronunciation.

DIADEM (′a-dem), *n.* a crown; tiara.

DIÆRESIS, same as dieresis.

DIAGNOSE (-ag-nos′), *v.t.* to ascertain as a disease, by its general symptoms.

DIAGNOSIS (-no′sis), *n.* [*pl.* diagnoses (′sez)], the recognition of a disease by its symptoms.

DIAGONAL (-ag′o-nal), *n.* a straight oblique line dividing a rectangular figure into equal parts.

DIAGRAM (′a-gram), *n.* a mechanical plan; an outline, drawing, or figure.

DIAL (di′al), *n.* an instrument for showing the time by the sun′s shadow; the face of a timepiece; any plate on which an index finger marks revolutions, pressure, etc.

DIALECT (′a-lekt), *n.* idiom; a subdivision of a language.

DIALECTIC (′ik), *adj.* pertaining to a dialect, or to logic.

DIALOGUE (′a-log), *n.* a conversation between two or more persons.

DIAMETER (di-am′e-ter), *n.* the length of a line passing through the centre of any object from one side to the other.

DIAMETRICAL (-a-met′ri-kal), *adj.* pertaining to a diameter; directly adverse or opposite.

DIAMOND (di′a-mund), *n.* a gem of extreme hardness and refractive power; a glass cutter′s tool.

DIAMOND WEDDING (wed′ing), 60 years of married life.

DIAPASON (-a-pa′zon), *n.* the entire compass of a voice or instrument.

DIAPER (′a-per), *n.* linen cloth woven in geometric patterns; an infant′s napkin.

DIAPHANOUS (-af′a-nus), *adj.* transparent.

DIAPHRAGM (′a-fram), *n.* the midriff, which divides the chest from the abdomen; any substance that intercepts or divides.

DIARIST (′a-rist), *n.* one who keeps a diary.

DIARRHŒA (di-a-re′a), *n.* a morbidly persistent purging of the bowels.

DIARY (′a-ri), *n.* a register of daily occurrences.

DIASCOPE (di′a-skop), *n.* machine for showing motion pictures in daylight.

DIASTOLE (-as′to-le), *n.* the rhythmical expansion and dilation of the heart and arteries in beating; the lengthening of a syllable naturally short.

DIATRIBE (′a-trib), *n.* a continued discourse or disputation; bitter criticism.

DICE (dis), *n.pl.* small cubes marked on the sides with one to six spots: *v.t.* cut into cubes.

DICKER (′er), *v.i.* to barter or trade.

DICTATE (dik′tat), *v.t.* declare with authority: *n.* an injunction; command.

DICTATION (-ta′shun), *n.* the act of dictating; the thing dictated.

DICTATOR (′ter), *n.* one who dictates; one invested with absolute powers of government.

DICTATORIAL (-to′ri-al), *adj.* absolute; imperious.

DICTION (dik′shun), *n.* manner of speaking or expression; choice of words; style.

DICTIONARY (-a-ri), *n.* a book containing all, or the principal, words in a language, with their meanings, etc.; lexicon; vocabulary.

DICTOGRAPH (dik′to-graf), *n.* a telephonic instrument with a device for magnifying sound.

DICTUM (′tum), *n.* [*pl.* dicta (′ta)], a dogmatic assertion.

DIDACTIC (di-dak′tik), *adj.* teaching; instructing; explanatory.

DIDO (di′do), *n.* a caper.

DIDYMOUS (did′i-mus), *adj.* growing in pairs; paired or double.

DIE (di), *v.i.* to cease to live; expire; perish.

DIE (di), *n.* a small cube; a device for

coining money, medals, etc. : *v.t.* to mould, stamp, cut with a die.

DIELECTRIC (di-e-lek'trik), *n.* any medium, as glass, etc., that transmits electric force by induction.

DIERESIS (-er'e-sis), *n.* a sign (``) placed over the second of two separate vowels to show that each has a separate sound in pronunciation, as aërated.

DIET (di'et), *n.* solid or liquid food ; a deliberative convention.

DIETARY (di'e-ta-ri), *n.* a certain fixed allowance of food ; system of diet.

DIETETIC (di-e-tet'ik), *n.pl.* that branch of hygiene which relates to rules of diet.

DIFFERENCE ('er-ens), *n.* disparity ; distinction ; controversy ; quarrel.

DIFFERENT ('er-ent), *adj.* unlike ; distinct.

DIFFERENTIA (-en'shi-a), *n.* [*pl.* differentiæ (-e)], that which distinguishes one species from another of the same genus.

DIFFERENTIAL ('shal), *adj.* indicating a difference ; having different velocities : *n.* in mathematics, an infinitesimal difference between two values.

DIFFERENTIAL CALCULUS (kal'-ku-lus), the method of finding an infinitely small quantity which shall equal a given quantity when taken infinite times.

DIFFERENTIATE (-en'shi-at), *v.t.* to constitute a difference between : *v.i.* to acquire a distinctive and separate character.

DIFFICULT ('i-kult), *adj.* not easy ; arduous.

DIFFICULTY (-kul-ti), *n.* something that requires labour or skill to overcome ; scruple ; objection ; controversy.

DIFFIDENCE ('i-dens), *n.* lack of self-reliance ; modest reserve.

DIFFIDENT ('i-dent), *adj.* shy ; modest.

DIFFUSE (di-fuz'), *v.t.* to pour out and spread all around ; scatter ; *adj.* (di-fus'), verbose ; redundant.

DIFFUSION (-fu'zhun), *n.* a spreading abroad ; the passing by osmosis through animal membranes.

DIFFUSIVE (-fu'siv), *adj.* capable of diffusing ; spreading every way ; widely reaching.

DIG (dig), *v.i.* to work with a spade ; study hard : *v.t.* to excavate.

DIGEST (di'jest), *n.* any compilation, abridgment, or summary of laws ; a synopsis : *v.t.* (di-jest'), to arrange methodically ; classify ; dissolve in the stomach : *v.i.* to be digested.

DIGESTIBILITY (-jes-ti-bil'i-ti), *n.* the quality of being digestible.

DIGESTIBLE ('ti-bl), *adj.* capable of being digested.

DIGESTION (-jes'chun), *n.* the act of digesting ; mental or physical assimilation.

DIGESTIVE ('tiv), *adj.* pertaining to digestion.

DIGGER (dig'er), *n.* one who or that which digs.

DIGIT (dij'it), *n.* a finger or toe ; a measure ($\frac{3}{4}$ inch) ; 1-12th the diameter of sun or moon ; any one of the Arabic numerals.

DIGNIFIED (dig'ni-fid), *adj.* with dignity ; noble.

DIGNIFY ('ni-fi), *v.t.* confer honour upon ; elevate ; ennoble.

DIGNITARY (-ta-ri), *n.* one who holds a position of dignity or honour.

DIGNITY ('ni-ti), *n.* elevation of rank ; degree of excellence ; moral worth.

DIGRESS (di-, di-gres'), *v.i.* to turn aside ; deviate ; wander.

DIGRESSION (-gresh'un), *n.* deviation from moral rectitude ; divergence.

DIKE, DYKE, (dik), *n.* embankment of earth.

DILAPIDATE (di-lap'i-dat), *v.t.* to bring into partial ruin by neglect or misuse.

DILAPIDATION ('i-da'shun), *n.* a state of partial ruin.

DILATE (-lat'), *v.t.* to enlarge or expand ; distend : *v.i.* speak fully and copiously.

DILATORY (dil'a-to-ri), *adj.* causing, or tending to cause, delay ; slow.

DILEMMA (di-, di-lem'a), *n.* an awkward or vexatious situation.

DILETTANTE (dil-e-tan'te), n. [pl. dilettanti (-ti)], an amateur.

DILIGENCE ('i-jens), n. careful attention; assiduity; industry.

DILL (dil), n. an herb.

DILUTE (di-, di-lut'), v.t. to thin or weaken : v.i. to become thinner.

DILUTION (-lu'shun), n. a weak liquid.

DILUVIAL (-lu'vi-al), adj. pertaining to a deluge.

DIM (dim), adj. hazy; obscure; ill-defined.

DIME (dim), n. a silver coin worth ten cents.

DIMENSION (di-men'shun), n. the size of a body; cubic capacity : pl. magnitude or importance.

DIMENSIONAL (-al), adj. pertaining to dimension.

DIMINISH (di-min'ish), v.t. to make less : v.i. to lessen; dwindle.

DIMINUTION (dim-i-nu'shun), n. reduction; lessening.

DIMINUTIVE (di-min'u-tiv), adj. below the average size, little.

DIMITY ('i-ti), n. a cotton cloth.

DIMPLE (dim'pl), n. a small depression or hollow in the cheek or chin.

DIN (din), n. a continued and violent noise.

DINE (din), v.t. to give or provide a dinner for; feed.

DINGHY (ding'gi), n. a small boat used as a tender.

DINGLE (ding'gl), n. a narrow hollow between hills : v.t. & v.i. to tinkle.

DINGO (ding'go), n. the Australian wild dog.

DINGY (din'ji), adj. dark-coloured; worn.

DINNER ('er), n. the chief meal of the day; a public banquet.

DINT (dint), n. a mark left by a blow; force or power (with of).

DIOCESE ('o-ses), n. a bishop's see; a bishopric.

DIP (dip), v.t. to plunge for a short time into a fluid; lower and raise quickly.

DIPHTHERIA (dif-, dip-the'ri-a), n. a contagious throat disease.

DIPHTHONG ('thong), n. the union of two vowel sounds pronounced in one syllable.

DIPLOMA (di-plo'ma), n. a writing on parchment or paper under sign and seal, conferring some honour, authority, etc.

DIPLOMACY ('ma-si, -plom'a-si), n. the art of conducting negotiations between two states or nations.

DIPLOMAT (dip'lo-mat), n. a diplomatist.

DIPLOMATIC (-mat'ik), adj. pertaining to diplomacy.

DIPLOMATIST (di-plo'ma-tist), n. one who is skilled in diplomacy.

DIPPER (dip'er), n. a small utensil; [D-], the group of 7 stars in the constellation of Ursa Major.

DIPSOMANIA (so-ma'ni-a), n. a morbid and uncontrollable craving for alcoholic drinks.

DIPSOMANIAC ('ni-ak), n. one who suffers from dipsomania.

DIRE (dir), adj. dreadful; mournful.

DIRECT (di-rekt'), adj. straight; open; plain; straightforward : v.t. guide or show : v.i. to act as a guide.

DIRECTION (-rek'shun), n. relative position; a command; order; guidance.

DIRECTOR ('ter), n. one who directs; one appointed to transact the affairs of a company, etc.

DIRECTORATE ('to-rat), n. a board of directors.

DIRECTORY ('to-ri), n. a book containing the names, addresses, and occupations of the residents of a place; a body of directors.

DIRECT PRIMARY (di-rekt' pri'ma-ri), method of making nominations for political elective offices.

DIREFUL (dir'fool), adj. dreadful; dismal.

DIRGE (derj), n. a funeral hymn.

DIRIGIBLE (dir'i-ji-ble), n. an airship.

DIRK (derk), n. a dagger.

DIRT (dert), n. any foul substance; garden earth.

DIRTILY (der'ti-li), adv. filthily; meanly.

DIS-, a prefix signifying separation, privation, negation.

DISABILITY (dis-a-bil'i-ti), *n.* lack of physical, intellectual, or social fitness.

DISABLE (-a'bl), *v.t.* to deprive of power; incapacitate.

DISABUSE (dis-a-buz'), *v.t.* to clear from mistakes; set right.

DISAFFECT (-a-fekt'), *v.t.* to fill with discontent.

DISAFFECTION (-fek'shun), *n.* alienation of affection.

DISAGREEABLE (a-gre'a-bl), *adj.* displeasing or unsatisfactory.

DISAPPEAR (-a-per'), *v.i.* to pass away; vanish.

DISAPPEARANCE ('ans), *n.* removal from sight.

DISAPPOINT (-point'), *v.t.* to thwart or frustrate the hopes of.

DISARM (-arm'), *v.t.* to deprive of arms; reduce to a peace footing; render harmless.

DISARMAMENT (-arm'a-ment), *n.* reduction to a peace footing.

DISARRAY (a-ra'), *v.t.* throw into disorder; undress: *n.* confusion.

DISASTER (-as'ter), *n.* a sudden or unexpected misfortune.

DISASTROUS ('trus), *adj.* unfortunate; calamitous.

DISAVOW (dis-a-vou'), *v.t.* to deny; to repudiate.

DISBAND (-band'), *v.t.* to dismiss from military service; break up.

DISBAR (-bar'), *v.t.* to deprive a lawyer of his right to practice.

DISBURDEN (-ber'dn), *v.t.* to remove a burden from.

DISBURSE (-bers'), *v.t.* to expend.

DISBURSEMENT ('ment), *n.* money expended.

DISC, DISK (disk), *n.* an ancient quoit; a flat, circular plate.

DISCARD (-kard), *v.t.* to cast off as useless; reject as useless.

DISCERN (di-zern'), *v.t.* to distinguish mentally, or with the eye.

DISCERNIBLE ('ni-bl), *adj.* perceptible.

DISCHARGE (dis-charj'), *v.t.* unload; disembark; free from any burden, impediment, or obligation; perform (a trust or duty).

DISCIPLE (di-si'pl), *n.* one who

receives the teaching of another.

DISCIPLINARIAN (dis-i-plin-a'ri-an), *n.* one who advocates, or enforces, strict discipline.

DISCIPLINARY ('i-plin-a-ri), *adj.* pertaining to discipline.

DISCIPLINE ('i-plin), *n.* mental or moral training; education; chastisement.

DISCLAIM (-klam'), *v.t.* to repudiate.

DISCLOSE (-kloz'), *v.t.* to uncover; reveal.

DISCLOSURE (-klo'zhur), *n.* discovery; uncovering; a telling.

DISCOLOUR (-kul'er), *v.t.* to change from the natural colour; stain.

DISCOMFIT (-kum'fit), *v.t.* to defeat; rout; frustrate; thwart.

DISCOMFITURE ('fi-tur), *n.* defeat; disappointment.

DISCOMMODE (-ko-mod'), *v.t.* to inconvenience.

DISCOMPOSE (-kom-poz'), *v.t.* disarrange; vex; ruffle.

DISCONCERT (-kon-sert'), *v.t.* to disturb the composure or self-possession of; frustrate.

DISCONSOLATE ('so-lat), *adj.* hopeless; sad.

DISCORD ('kord), *n.* disagreement; a confused noise.

DISCOUNT (dis'kount), *n.* a sum deducted for prompt payment of an account; a deduction made according to the current rate of interest: *v.t.* (dis-kount'), to allow a discount on; make a deduction from.

DISCOURAGE (-kur'aj), *v.t.* to deprive or lessen the courage of; dishearten; deter.

DISCOURSE (-kors'), *n.* conversation; a treatise or sermon: *v.t.* & *v.i.* to talk or converse; communicate ideas orally.

DISCOVER (dis-kuv'er), *v.t.* to bring to light; reveal.

DISCOVERY (-i), *n.* a bringing to light or making known; disclosure.

DISCREDIT (-kred'it), *v.t.* to disbelieve; injure in credit or reputation.

DISCREET (-kret'), *adj.* prudent; circumspect.

DISCREPANCY (-krep'an-si), *n.* inconsistency; difference.

DISCREPANT ('ant), *adj.* disagreeing ; different.

DISCRETE (-kret'), *adj.* separate from others ; not continuous.

DISCRETION (-kresh'un), *n.* prudence ; judgment ; sagacity.

DISCRIMINATE (-krim'i-nat), *v.t.* to observe or mark the differences between ; select.

DISCRIMINATION (-i-na'shun), *n.* faculty of nice discernment.

DISCURSIVE (-ker'siv), *adj.* desultory.

DISCUSS (dis-kus'), *v.t.* to debate ; reason upon.

DISCUSSION (-kush'un), *n.* argument ; debate.

DISDAIN (-dan'), *v.t.* to think unworthy : *n.* contempt.

DISEASE (di-zez'), *n.* any mental, moral, or physical disorder ; malady ; illness.

DISFIGURE (dis-fig'ur), *v.t.* to injure form, or beauty of ; deform.

DISFRANCHISE (-fran'chiz), *v.t.* to deprive of electoral or municipal privileges.

DISGORGE (-gorj'), *v.t.* to force out of the mouth or stomach with violence ; surrender what has been unlawfully obtained.

DISGRACE (-gras'), *n.* ignominy ; shame ; dishonour.

DISGUISE (-giz'), *v.t.* to counterfeit ; conceal : *n.* false pretence.

DISGUST (-gust'), *n.* strong aversion or repugnance.

DISHABILLE (dis-a-bil'), *n.* negligent attire.

DISHEARTEN (-har'tn), *v.t.* to discourage.

DISHEVEL (dis-hev'el), *v.t.* to disorder : *v.i.* to be spread in disorder.

DISHONEST (dis-on'est), *adj.* lacking in honesty.

DISHONOUR (-on'er), *v.t.* to deprive of honour ; violate the chastity of : *n.* disgrace ; ignominy ; shame.

DISINFECT (dis-in-fekt'), *v.t.* to purify ; free from contagious matter.

DISINFECTANT (-fek'tant), *n.* a cleanser ; a purifer.

DISINGENUOUS (dis-in-jen'u-us), *adj.* wanting in sincerity.

DISINTEGRATE (-in'te-grat), *v.t.* to break up into component parts.

DISINTEGRATION (-gra'shun), *n.* the act of disintegrating ; separation.

DISJUNCTIVE (-jungk'tiv), *n.* a disjunctive conjunction which connects grammatically two words or clauses disjoined in meaning.

DISK-PLOUGH (disk'plou), *n.* a plough the action of which depends upon revolving disks, instead of ploughshares.

DISLIKE (dis-lik'), *n.* a strong feeling of repugnance or aversion ; antipathy.

DISLOCATE ('lo-kat), *v.t.* to put out of joint.

DISLODGE (-loj'), *v.t.* to remove or drive out from a place of lodgment.

DISLOYAL (dis-loi'al), *adj.* untrue to one's obligations.

DISMAL (diz'mal), *adj.* gloomy ; depressing ; dark.

DISMANTLE (dis-man't'l), *v.t.* to strip or divest ; raze ; demolish.

DISMAY (-ma'), *v.t.* to terrify ; dispirit ; discourage : *n.* a condition of terror.

DISMEMBER (-mem'ber), *v.t.* sever into parts and distribute ; dislocate ; divide.

DISMISS (-mis'), *v.t.* to send away ; discharge from employment.

DISMISSAL ('al), *n.* the act of dismissing.

DISMOUNT (dis-mount'), *v.i.* to get down.

DISOBEDIENCE (dis-o-be'di-ens), *n.* refusal to obey.

DISORDER (-or'der), *n.* want of order or arrangement ; mental or physical disease.

DISORGANIZE (dis-or'gan-iz), *v.t.* to disarrange ; to throw into confusion.

DISOWN (dis-on'), *v.t.* to deny relationship ; to cast off.

DISPARAGE (-par'aj), *v.t.* treat with contempt ; belittle.

DISPARITY (-par'i-ti), *n.* inequality ; disproportion.

DISPASSIONATE (-pash'un-at), *adj.* calm ; unprejudiced ; impartial.

DISPASSIONATELY (-li), *adv.* in a dispassionate manner.

DISPATCH, same as despatch.

DISPEL (dis-pel'), *v.t.* to drive away by scattering ; disperse ; dissipate.

DISPENSABLE (-pen'sa-bl), *adj.* that for which a dispensation may be granted.

DISPENSARY ('sa-ri), *n.* a place where medicines are kept and made up.

DISPENSATION (-sa'shun), *n.* the act of dispensing ; distribution.

DISPENSE (dis-pens'), *v.t.* to deal out ; distribute ; excuse.

DISPERSE (dis-pers'), *v.t.* to scatter ; diffuse ; spread ; cause to vanish.

DISPERSION (-per'shun), *n.* the act of dispersing.

DISPIRIT (-pir'it), *v.t.* to depress ; dishearten.

DISPLACE (-plas'), *v.t.* to put out of place ; depose from office or dignity.

DISPLACEMENT ('ment), *n.* the act of displacing ; substitution ; the weight of water displaced by a solid body.

DISPLAY (-pla'), *v.t.* to spread out ; unfold ; exhibit : *v.i.* to make a display.

DISPLEASURE (dis-plezh'ur), *n.* annoyance ; vexation ; distaste.

DISPORT (-port'), *v.t.* to amuse or divert.

DISPOSABLE (-poz'a-bl), *adj.* subject to disposal.

DISPOSAL ('al), *n.* arrangement ; order ; control.

DISPOSE (-poz'), *v.t.* to place ; arrange ; order ; distribute.

DISPOSITION (-po-zish'un), *n.* the act of disposing ; tendency ; natural temperament.

DISPOSSESS (dis-po-zes'), *v.t.* to deprive of possession ; eject.

DISPUTABLE ('pu-ta-bl), *adj.* liable to be disputed.

DISPUTATIOUS ('shus), *adj.* contentious.

DISPUTE (dis-put'), *v.i.* to debate ; argue : *v.t.* controvert : *n.* a controversy.

DISQUISITION (-kwi-zish'un), *n.* a systematic investigation or discussion.

DISRATE (-rat'), *v.t.* to degrade or lower.

DISRUPTION (-rup'shun), *n.* forcible separation ; breach.

DISSATISFACTION (-sat-is-fak'-shun), *n.* state of being discontented.

DISSATISFY ('is-fi), *v.t.* to render discontented.

DISSECT (di-sekt'), *v.t.* anatomize ; divide and examine minutely.

DISSECTION (-sek'shun), *n.* the act of dissecting for examination.

DISSEIZE (-sez'), *v.t.* to dispossess unlawfully.

DISSEMBLE (-sem'bl), *v.t.* to hide under a false appearance.

DISSEMINATE (-sem'i-nat), *v.t.* to scatter abroad ; propagate ; diffuse.

DISSENSION (di-sen'shun), *n.* strife ; disagreement.

DISSENT (-sent'), *v.i.* to disagree in opinion (with *from*).

DISSENTER (-sen'ter), *n.* an objector.

DISSERTATION (-er-ta'shun), *n.* a formal discourse ; essay ; thesis.

DISSERVICE (dis-ser'vis), *n.* injurious help.

DISSEVER (di-sev'er), *v.t.* to cut in two ; disjoin ; divide.

DISSIDENCE (dis'i-dens), *n.* disagreement.

DISSIMULATE (-sim'u-lat), *v.i. & v.t.* to dissemble ; feign ; disguise.

DISSIPATE (dis'i-pat), *v.t.* to scatter completely ; squander.

DISSOCIATE (-so'shi-at), *v.t.* to separate.

DISSOLUBLE ('o-lu-bl), *adj.* capable of being disintegrated.

DISSOLUTE ('o-lut), *adj.* given to vice or dissipation.

DISSOLUTION (-lu'shun), *n.* separation of component parts ; separation of the soul from the body ; death.

DISSOLVABLE (di-zol'va-bl), *adj.* that may be dissolved.

DISSOLVE (-zolv'), *v.t.* to melt ; terminate ; annul : *v.i.* to become liquefied ; separate.

DISSUADE (di-swad'), *v.t.* to advise or counsel against.

DISSUASION (-swa'zhun), *n.* the act of dissuading.

DISSYLLABLE (-sil′a-bl), *n.* a word of two syllables.

DISTAFF (dis′taf), *n.* the staff from which flax is drawn in spinning.

DISTANCE (′tans), *n.* the space or interval between two objects or points.

DISTEMPER (-tem′per), *n.* a catarrhal disease affecting dogs.

DISTEND (-tend′), *v.t.* to stretch out ; expand : *v.i.* to swell.

DISTENTION (-ten′shun), *n.* a swelling out.

DISTIL (-til′), *v.i.* to fall in drops ; flow gently ; rectify : *v.t.* to let fall in drops.

DISTILLATION (-a′shun), *n.* the process of distilling.

DISTINCT (-tingkt′), *adj.* separate ; different ; clear ; plain.

DISTINCTION (-tingk′shun), *n.* mark of difference or superiority.

DISTINGUISH (-ting′gwish), *v.t.* to separate from others by some mark of honour or preference.

DISTORT (-tort′), *v.t.* to twist or turn from the natural shape or figure ; twist ; misrepresent.

DISTORTION (-tor′shun), *n.* perversion ; a deformity.

DISTRACT (-trakt′), *v.t.* to perplex ; harass ; confuse the mind.

DISTRACTION (-trak′shun), *n.* perplexity ; embarrassment.

DISTRAUGHT (dis-trawt′), *adj.* bewildered or harassed.

DISTRESS (dis-tres′), *v.t.* to inflict pain or suffering upon ; grieve ; harass ; perplex.

DISTRIBUTE (-trib′ut), *v.t.* to deal out ; allot ; apportion ; arrange according to classification.

DISTRIBUTION (-tri-bu′shun), *n.* apportionment ; arrangement ; classification.

DISTRICT (′trikt), *n.* a territorial division ; circuit.

DISTRUST (-trust′), *n.* want of confidence ; suspicion ; discredit.

DISTURB (-terb′), *v.t.* to trouble ; vex ; agitate ; displace.

DISTURBANCE (′bans), *n.* uproar ; mental agitation.

DITCH (dich), *n.* a trench cut in the earth.

DITTO (dit′o), *n.* that which has been said ; a duplicate.

DITTY (′i), *n.* a little song.

DIURETIC (di-u-ret′ik), *adj.* promoting the secretion and flow of urine.

DIURNAL (-er′nal), *adj.* pertaining to a day ; daily.

DIURNALLY (-li), *adv.* daily.

DIVA (de′va), *n.* a prima donna.

DIVAN (di-van′), *n.* a court of justice ; a council-hall ; a smoking-room ; couch.

DIVE (div), *v.i.* to plunge head foremost : *v.t.* to explore by diving.

DIVE (div), *n.* a low resort.

DIVERGE (di-verj′), *v.i.* to spread out from one point.

DIVERGENCE (-ver′jens), *n.* a receding from each other ; a tending apart.

DIVERS (di′verz), *adj.* various ; sundry.

DIVERSE (di-vers′), *adj.* essentially different ; dissimilar.

DIVERSIFY (di-ver′si-fi), *v.t.* to make different from another ; give variety to.

DIVERSION (′shun), *n.* variation ; alteration ; pastime.

DIVERT (di-vert′), *v.t.* to draw away from ; entertain.

DIVERTISEMENT (di-ver′tiz-ment), *n.* diversion ; amusement.

DIVEST (di-vest′), *v.t.* to strip or deprive of anything ; make bare.

DIVIDE (di-vid′), *v.t.* to cut into two or more parts ; separate ; keep apart ; disunite by discord ; distribute.

DIVIDEND (div′i-dend), *n.* a share of the profits of a public company or business.

DIVINATION (-i-na′shun), *n.* the pretended art of foreseeing future events.

DIVINE (di-vῑn), *adj.* excellent in the

highest degree; godlike; sacred; holy; clergyman.

DIVING (div'ing), *n.* the act of plunging head first into water.

DIVING-BELL (-bel), *n.* a hollow apparatus supplied with air, used in work below the suface of the water.

DIVINITY (di-vin'i-ti), *n.* the state or quality of being divine; Godhead.

DIVISION (-vizh'un), *n.* separation; a partition; discord; difference; two or more brigades; a section of a fleet; the process of finding how many times one number is contained in another.

DIVISOR (di-vi'zer), *n.* the number by which another (the dividend) is divided.

DIVORCE (-vors'), *n.* a dissolution of the marriage contract by legal authority; disunion.

DIVORCEMENT ('ment), *n.* the act or process of divorcing.

DIVULGE (di-vulj'), *v.t.* to make known; disclose.

DIZEN (di'zn), *v.t.* to deck out.

DIZZINESS (diz'i-nes), *n.* giddiness.

DIZZY (diz'i), *adj.* giddy.

DO (doo), *v.t.* to perform; achieve; cause to bring about.

DOCILE (dos'il, do'sil), *adj.* easy to teach; tractable.

DOCILITY (do-sil'i-ti), *n.* the quality of being docile.

DOCK (dok), *n.* a place for constructing and laying up ships; the place where a prisoner stands in a court; a coarse weed: *v.t.* to cut off; deduct from; diminish.

DOCKAGE ('aj), *n.* reduction; provision for docking vessels.

DOCKET ('et), *v.t.* to mark the contents or titles of papers; indorse: *n.* a digest.

DOCKYARD ('yard) *n.* a place where ships are built.

DOCTOR ('ter), *n.* an academical degree denoting the highest proficiency in a faculty of a university; a medical practitioner.

DOCTRINE ('trin), *n.* the principles, belief or dogma of any church sect, or party.

DOCUMENT ('u-ment), *n.* a paper relied upon to establish some fact or assertion.

DOCUMENTARY (-men'ta-ri), *adj.* pertaining to documents.

DODGE (doj), *v.i.* evade by craft; avoid.

DOE (do), *n.* the female of deer, or rabbit.

DOFF (dof), *v.t.* to take or put off.

DOG (dog), *n.* a canine animal.

DOG DAYS (daz), *n.pl.* a period in July and August when the dog star or Sirius rises and sets with the sun.

DOGGED ('ed), *adj.* stubborn; pertinacious.

DOGMA ('ma), *n.* [*pl.* dogmata ('ma-ta)], a decree or opinion of principle, tenet, or doctrine.

DOGMATIC (-mat'ik), *adj.* pertaining to dogma.

DOGMATIZE ('ma-tiz), *v.i.* to make dogmatic assertions; utter positive assertions without adducing proof.

DOG-STAR (dog'-star), *n.* brightest of the stars; known as Sirius.

DOG-WATCH ('woch), *n.* one of two watches on board ship of two hours each, between 4 and 8 p.m.

DOGWOOD ('wood), *n.* a flowering tree of the U.S.

DOILY (doi'li), *n.* a small mat or napkin.

DOLDRUMS (dol'drums), *n.pl.* a sailor's term for the tropical zones of calms and variable winds; depression of spirits.

DOLE (dol), *n.* that which is dealt out sparingly.

DOLESOME (dol'sum), *adj.* melancholy.

DOLL (dol), *n.* a girl's toy-baby.

DOLLAR ('er), *n.* monetary unit of the U.S. and other countries equal to 100 cents.

DOLT (dolt), *n.* a stupid fellow.

DOMAIN (do-man'), *n.* lordship; authority; empire; range; scope.

DOME (dom), *n.* a hemispherical roof; any circular top.

DOMESTIC (do-mes'tik), *adj.* pertaining to household affairs; home-made: *n.* a household servant.

DOMESTICATE ('ti-kat), *v.t.* to make domestic.

DOMESTIC ECONOMY (e-kon'o-mi), the art of managing household affairs.

DOMESTICITY (-tis'i-ti), *n.* the state of being domestic.

DOMICILE (dom'i-sil), *n.* a permanent residence or place of abode ; home.

DOMINANT ('i-nant), *adj.* exercising chief authority ; ruling.

DOMINATION (-na'shun), *n.* the act of dominating ; power.

DOMINEER (-i-ner'), *v.i.* to exercise authority arrogantly ; bluster.

DOMINICAL (do-min'i-kal), *adj.* pertaining to Christ as Lord, or to Sunday.

DOMINION (do-min'yun), *n.* supreme authority ; sovereignty.

DOMINO (dom'i-no), *n.* a large loose silk cloak : *pl.* a game.

DON (don), *v.t.* to put on ; invest with ; assume : *n.* [D-], in Spain, corresponding to Sir, or Mr. : *fem.* Dona.

DONATE (do'nat), *v.t.* to contribute.

DONATION (-na'shun), *n.* a charitable gift.

DONATOR (do-na'ter), *n.* a giver.

DONE (dun), *p.adj.* completed ; cooked sufficiently.

DONEE (do-ne'), *n.* one to whom property is given.

DONKEY (dong'ki), *n.* an ass ; a stupid fellow.

DONOR (do'ner), *n.* a giver.

DOOM (doom), *n.* irrevocable destiny ; fate ; ruin.

DOOMSDAY (doomz'da), *n.* the day of final and universal judgment.

DOOR (dor), *n.* a gate or entrance ; means of access.

DORIC ORDER (dor'ik or'der), the oldest and simplest of the three orders of Greek architecture.

DORMANT ('mant), *adj.* sleeping ; quiet ; in abeyance.

DORMER ('mer), *n.* a bedroom ; a window set vertically in the side of a roof-gable.

DORMITORY ('mi-to-ri), *n.* a large sleeping apartment holding several beds.

DORSAL ('sal), *adj.* pertaining to, or situated near, the back.

DORY (do'ri), *n.* the pike-perch ; flat-bottomed skiff.

DOSE (dos), *n.* quantity of medicine to be taken at one time.

DOTAGE (dot'aj), *n.* imbecility of mind.

DOTARD (do'tard), *n.* one whose intellect is impaired by age.

DOTE (dot), *v.i.* to exhibit the weakness of age ; bestow excessive love.

DOUBLE (dub'l), *adj.* twice as much ; insincere : *n.* a duplicate.

DOUBLE-BASS (-bas), *n.* the largest violin.

DOUBLE-DAGGER (-dag'er), *n.* a reference mark (‡).

DOUBLE-DEALING (-del'ing), *n.* duplicity.

DOUBLET (dub'let), *n.* a duplicate ; a close-fitting man's garment.

DOUBLING (dub'ling), *n.* a turning ; a lining, as in a garment, or book-binding.

DOUBT (dout), *v.i.* to waver in opinion ; hesitate ; be in suspense : *v.t.* to suspect ; distrust ; question : *n.* suspense ; scruple ; perplexity ; fear ; disbelief.

DOUBTFUL ('fool), *adj.* of uncertain issue ; questionable.

DOUBTLESS ('les), *adv.* assuredly.

DOUCEUR (doo-ser'), *n.* [French], a small gift ; tip.

DOUCHE (doosh), *n.* [French], a jet of water directed upon some part of the body ; a shower bath.

DOUGH (do), *n.* a soft mass of moistened flour yet unbaked.

DOUGHBOY (do'boi), *n.* an American infantryman.

DOUGHNUT (do'nut), *n.* a small cake cooked in hot lard.

DOUGHTY (dou'ti), *adj.* valiant ; strong.

DOUGHY (do'i), *adj.* soft like dough.

DOUSE (dous), *v.t.* to plunge suddenly into a liquid ; drench ; extinguish.

DOVE (duv), *n.* a pigeon.

DOVECOTE ('kot), *n.* a small house for pigeons.

DOVETAIL ('tal), *v.t.* to join by

interlocking joints; fit closely and exactly.

DOWAGER (dou'a-jer), *n.* the widow of a person of rank.

DOWDINESS ('di-nes), *n.* the state of being dowdy.

DOWDY ('di), *adj.* slovenly or ill-dressed; shabby.

DOWER ('er), *n.* that part of a husband's property which his widow enjoys during her life; jointure.

DOWNCAST (doun'kast), *adj.* dejected; sad.

DOWNFALL ('fawl), *n.* sudden fall from rank or reputation; ruin.

DOWNGRADE ('grad), *n.* a downward movement; reverse of fortune.

DOWNRIGHT ('rit), *adj.* straight to the point; blunt : *adv.* completely; thoroughly.

DOWNWARD ('werd), *adj.* moving from a higher to a lower place, grade, or direction; descending.

DOWNY ('i), *adj.* covered with, or made of, down; soft; restful.

DOXOLOGY (dok-sol'o-ji), *n.* an ascription or short hymn of praise to God.

DOZE (doz), *v.i.* to sleep lightly.

DOZEN (duz'n), *n.* twelve units.

DRAB (drab), *n.* a kind of thick dull brown or yellowish-grey colour; dull.

DRABBLE ('l), *v.t.* to make wet or dirty by dragging through mud or water.

DRAFT, DRAUGHT (draft), *n.* a sketch or outline; bill of exchange; an order for money; detachment of soldiers; the act of drinking or the amount drunk at once; the depth of water a vessel draws; a current of air : *v.t.* select by a draft for military service.

DRAG (drag), *v.t.* to pull or draw along by force; haul; tug.

DRAGGLE (drag'l), *v.t.* to wet or soil by dragging in the mud.

DRAGOMAN (drag'o-man), *n.* in the East, an interpreter, guide.

DRAGON ('un), *n.* a fabulous animal.

DRAGOON (dra-goon'), *n.* a cavalryman in the British army.

DRAIN (dran), *v.t.* to draw off; exhaust : *n.* a sewer.

DRAINAGE ('aj), *n.* the means of draining; that which is drained off.

DRAKE (drak), *n.* a male duck.

DRAM (dram), *n.* ⅛th of an ounce troy, and 1/16 of an ounce avoirdupois; a small quantity of liquor.

DRAMA (dra'ma), *n.* a composition depicting a story of human life in character, etc., on the stage.

DRAMATIC (dra-mat'ik), *adj.* pertaining to the drama.

DRAMATIS PERSONÆ (dram'a-tis per-so'ne), [Latin], the characters in a play or drama.

DRAMATIZE (dram'a-tiz), *v.t.* to compose or adapt for stage representation.

DRAPE (drap), *v.t.* to cover with cloth; arrange in folds or hangings.

DRAPER (dra'per), *n.* a dealer in woollen or cotton cloth, etc.

DRAPERY (-i), *n.* textile cloths or fabrics used for garments or hangings.

DRASTIC (dras'tik), *adj.* powerful; vigorous; extreme.

DRAUGHTS (drafts), *n.pl.* game of checkers.

DRAW (draw), *v.t.* to pull or haul; sketch; draft; require a certain depth to float in; entice or allure; induce; receive; write out; leave undecided.

DRAWBACK ('bak), *n.* loss of advantage; a discouragement; money paid back.

DRAWBRIDGE ('brij), *n.* a bridge which may be lifted up or drawn aside.

DRAWEE (-e'), *n.* one on whom an order, bill of exchange, or a draft is drawn.

DRAWER ('er), *n.* a draftsman; a sliding box-like arrangement for holding clothes, etc.; one who draws a bill of exchange, or an order for the payment of money : *pl.* underclothing.

DRAWING ('ing), *n.* delineation.

DRAWING-ROOM (-room), *n.* a room for the reception of company.

DRAWL (drawl), *v.t.* to utter in a slow, lazy tone.

DRAWN (drawn), *p.adj.* left undecided; contracted.

DRAY (dra), *n.* a low, stoutly-built cart used for heavy loads.

DREAD (dred), *v.t.* to fear greatly; venerate : *adj.* awful ; solemn.

DREADFUL ('fool), *adj.* inspiring dread.

DREADFULLY (-li), *adv.* in a dreadful manner.

DREADNOUGHT (dred'nawt), *n.* a type of battleship; a person who fears nothing.

DREAM (drem), *n.* a train of thoughts or images passing through the mind during sleep ; an idle fancy.

DREAMY ('i), *adj.* indistinct ; visionary.

DREAR (drer), *adj.* dismal ; sorrowful.

DREARY ('i), *adj.* cheerless ; gloomy.

DREDGE (drej), *n.* a drag for sweeping the bottoms of water-ways ; a scoop ; a dredging-machine.

DREDGER (-er), *n.* one who dredges ; a boat used for dredging.

DREGS (dregz), *n.pl.* the sediment of liquor ; worthless matter.

DRENCH (drench), *v.t.* to wet thoroughly ; steep in moisture.

DRESDEN (dres'den), *n.* a fine kind of decorated porcelain.

DRESS (dres), *v.t.* adorn ; deck out ; embellish ; prepare or make ready ; cook ; curry or rub down ; prune or trim : *n.* a robe ; elegant clothing, or fashionable attire ; clothing.

DRESS CIRCLE (ser'kl), the first gallery in a theatre.

DRESSER ('er), *n.* one who regulates or adjusts dress ; mirror and bureau.

DRESSING ('ing), *n.* the act of putting on clothes ; material used in sizing, etc. ; the smoothing of stone ; sauce or stuffing used in cooking ; reprimand ; an external application to a wound.

DRESSY (dres'i), *adj.* fond of dress ; stylish.

DRIBBLE (drib'l), *v.i.* to fall in small drops ; drip : *n.* a drizzling shower.

DRIBLET (drib'let), *n.* a small drop, piece, part, or sum.

DRIER (dri'er), *n.* one who, or that which, dries ; a substance added to paint, etc.

DRIFT (drift), *n.* the direction in which anything is driven ; an accumulation heaped up by sea or wind ; tendency ; leeway made.

DRIFTWOOD (-wood), *n.* pieces of timber cast ashore by the sea ; wreckage.

DRILL (dril), *v.t.* to pierce with a drill ; bore ; perforate ; instruct thoroughly in the rudiments of any business, etc. ; train ; sow : *n.* a tool for boring.

DRINK (dringk), *v.i.* to swallow a liquid : *n.* any beverage swallowed to quench thirst.

DRIP (drip), *v.i.* to fall in drops : *n.* that which falls in drops ; a projecting moulding.

DRIVE (driv), *v.t.* to impel by force ; propel ; communicate motion to ; compel : *v.i.* to press, or be impelled forward with violence ; travel in a carriage : *n.* a strong blow ; a road prepared for driving ; activity to secure funds, as a drive for charity.

DRIVEL (driv'el), *v.i.* to slaver ; be weak or foolish : *n.* senseless talk.

DRIZZLE (driz'l), *n.* a fine misty rain.

DROIT (droit, drwa), *n.* equity ; right of ownership.

DROLE (drol'), *n.* an artful person.

DROLL (drol'), *adj.* comical ; funny.

DROLLERY ('er-i), *n.* the quality of being droll ; buffoonery.

DROMEDARY (drum'e-da-ri), *n.* one of a breed of camels, with one hump.

DRONE (dron), *v.i.* to utter in a monotonous tone or sound : *n.* a dull, monotonous tone ; the male of the honey-bee which produces no honey ; a lazy fellow.

DRONY (dro'ni), *adj.* like a drone.

DROOL (drool), *v.i.* to drip saliva like a baby ; to drivel.

DROOP (droop), *v.i.* to sink or hang down ; languish.

DROP (drop), *v.i.* to fall in drops ; distil ; sink to a lower position ; visit informally (with *in*) : *v.t.* to let fall ; discontinue : *n.* a globule of moisture ; a small quantity of a liquid ; a falling trap-door ; the curtain of a theatre (drop-scene).

DROPSICAL ('si-kal), *adj.* affected with dropsy.

DROPSY ('si), *n.* an unnatural accumulation of serous fluid in any cavity of the body.

DROSS (dros), *n.* the scum or slag of melted metal ; refuse.

DROUGHT (drout), *n.* continued absence of rain ; dryness.

DROVE (drov), *n.* a collection of cattle, etc., driven in a body ; a mason's chisel.

DROWN (droun), *v.i.* to perish by suffocation in water ; overwhelm ; deluge.

DROWSE (drouz), *v.i.* to be heavy with sleepiness.

DROWSINESS ('zi-nes), *n.* sleepiness.

DROWSY ('zi), *adj.* sleepy ; sluggish.

DRUB (drub), *v.t.* to beat vigorously : *n.* a thump.

DRUDGE (druj), *v.i.* to labour hard at mean or uncongenial tasks.

DRUDGERY ('er-i), *n.* mean servile labour.

DRUG (drug), *n.* an ingredient used in medicine ; a narcotic.

DRUGGIST ('ist), *n.* a dealer in drugs.

DRUM (drum), *n.* an instrument consisting of a hollow cylinder with skin or vellum at the ends, and beaten with sticks (drumsticks) ; the tympanum of the ear ; a cylinder or revolving shaft.

DRUMMER ('er), *n.* one who plays a drum ; a commercial traveller.

DRUNK (drungk), *n.* a drunken person : *adj.* intoxicated.

DRUNKARD ('ard), *n.* one habitually drunk.

DRUNKEN ('en), *p.adj.* habitually intemperate.

DRY (dri), *adj.* free from moisture ; devoid of interest ; unintentionally humorous or quaint.

DRY BATTERY (dri bat'er-i), a battery for generating electricity by means of dry chemicals.

DRY-DOCK (dri'dok), *n.* a repair dock for ships.

DRYLY ('li), *adv.* without moisture ; coldly ; sarcastically.

DRYNURSE ('ners), *v.t.* to rear without the breast.

DRY-POINT (-point), *n.* a fine, hard needle, used on copperplate ; a line, or work, thus engraved.

DUAL (du'al), *adj.* expressing, or composed of, the number 2 : *n.* the form of the noun or verb connoting two persons or things.

DUAL ALLIANCE (a-li'ans), *n.* the compact between Austria-Hungary and Germany in the European war of 1914.

DUB (dub), *v.t.* to confer any rank ; rub, dress, or smooth : *n.* a tap or blow.

DUBIOUS (du'bi-us), *adj.* doubtful.

DUCAL ('kal), *adj.* pertaining to a duke.

DUCHESS (duch'es), *n.* the consort or widow of a duke.

DUCHY ('i), *n.* the territory, dominions, or jurisdiction of a duke.

DUCK (duk), *n.* the common domestic water-fowl.

DUCKING ('ing), *n.* the act of putting under water ; sport of shooting wild ducks.

DUCKLING ('ling), *n.* a young duck.

DUCT (dukt), *n.* a passage, tube, or canal by which a fluid is conveyed.

DUCTILE ('til), *adj.* capable of being drawn out into threads or wire ; tractable.

DUCTILITY ('i-ti), *n.* flexibility.

DUCTLESS GLANDS (dukt'les glandz), glands that discharge their secretion into the blood stream.

DUD, *n.* shell that failed to explode.

DUDE (dud), *n.* a kind of dandy.

DUDGEON (duj'un), *n.* sullen anger ; resentment ; ill-will.

DUDS (dudz), *n.pl.* clothes ; belongings.

DUE (du), *adj.* owed or owing ; payable ; proper : *adv.* exactly ; directly : *n.* a custom, toll, tribute, or fee.

DUEL ('el), *n.* a combat between two persons with deadly weapons.

DUET (du-et'), *n.* a vocal or instrumental composition for two performers.

DUFFER (duf'er), *n.* a dull, stupid, inefficient person.

DUFFING ('ing), *adj.* worthless.

DUGONG (du'gong), *n.* the sea-cow.

DUGOUT (dug'out), *n.* a canoe hollowed out from a log ; a rough kind of shelter excavated in the side of a hill or bank for protection from gunfire, shells, etc.

DUKE (duk), *n.* a person of the highest order of English nobility.

DULCET (dul'set), *adj.* sweet or pleasant to the ear; harmonious.

DULCIMER ('si-mer), *n.* an instrument with wire strings and played with padded hammers.

DULL (dul), *adj.* slow of apprehension or action; stupid; sluggish; not bright; blunt.

DULLARD ('ard), *n.* a stupid person.

DULNESS, DULLNESS ('nes), *n.* the state of being dull.

DULY (du'li), *adv.* in a fit and becoming manner; regularly.

DUMB (dum), *adj.* incapable of speech.

DUMB-BELL ('bel), *n.* weights used for muscular exercise.

DUMB-SHOW ('sho), *n.* gesture without speech.

DUMB-WAITER (-wa'ter), *n.* a movable framework for lifting light articles.

DUMMY (dum'i), *n.* that which imitates a reality.

DUMP (dump), *n.* a thud or heavy sound; a place to discharge rubbish in: *pl.* low spirits.

DUMPLING (dump'ling), *n.* dough cooked in gravy.

DUMPY ('pi), *adj.* short and thick; discontented; sulky.

DUN (dun), *adj.* of a dull brown colour: *n.* an urgent request for payment of a debt.

DUNCE (duns), *n.* a dull, ignorant person.

DUNDERHEAD ('der-hed), *n.* a dolt.

DUNE (dun), *n.* a heap of drifted sand piled up by the wind.

DUNGEON ('jun), *n.* a dark underground cell; a prison.

DUNNAGE ('aj), *n.* baggage; personal effects.

DUNNITE (dun'nit), *n.* a high explosive.

DUODECIMAL (du-o-des'i-mal), *adj.* consisting of, or computing by twelves or any power of 12.

DUODECIMO ('i-mo), *n.* a sheet folded into 12 leaves (12mo): said of a book.

DUPABLE (dup'a-bl), *adj.* capable of being duped.

DUPE (dup), *n.* one who is, or can be, easily tricked; a credulous person.

DUPLEX (du'pleks), *adj.* double; compound; in machinery having two parts that operate in the same way.

DUPLICATE ('pli-kat), *v.t.* to make or render double; two-fold; double: *n.* facsimile; an exact copy.

DUPLICATION (-ka'shun), *n.* the act of duplicating.

DUPLICITY (-plis'i-ti), *n.* deceit; hypocrisy.

DURABILITY (du-ra-bil'i-ti), *n.* endurance.

DURABLE ('ra-bl), *adj.* not perishing; stable; lasting.

DURALUMIN (du'ra-lu'min), *n.* an alloy of aluminium.

DURA MATER ('ra ma'ter), the tough covering which envelops the brain and spinal cord.

DURANCE ('rans), *n.* imprisonment.

DURATION (-ra'shun), *n.* continuance in time; permanency.

DURESS (du-res', du'res), *n.* restraint by fear or force; imprisonment.

DURING (dur'ing), *prep.* in the time of; at some period of.

DURST (durst), *p.t.* of dare.

DUSK (dusk), *adj.* tending to darkness; twilight.

DUSKILY ('i-li), *adv.* with a tendency to darkness or blackness.

DUSKY (dus'ki), *adj.* somewhat dark; swarthy.

DUST (dust), *n.* fine dry particles of matter.

DUSTY (dus'ti), *adj.* covered with dust.

DUTEOUS ('te-us), *adj.* fulfilling duty; obedient.

DUTIABLE (du'ti-a-bl), *adj.* subject to duty.

DUTIFUL (-fool), *adj.* respectful; obedient.

DUTY ('ti), *n.* obligatory service; tax, or toll levied by a Government.

DUVETINE, DUVETYN (doo-ve-ten'), *n.* any fabrics with a nap like plush.

DWARF (dwarf), *n.* below the average height: *v.i.* become stunted; grow smaller.

DWELL (dwel), *v.i.* to reside for a length of time; have a fixed abode.

DWELLING ('ing), *n.* a house.

DWINDLE (dwin'dl), *v.i.* to become gradually less; diminish.

DYE (di), *v.t.* to stain or colour: *n.* a colouring liquid or stain.

DYING ('ing), *p.adj.* the passing away from life.

DYNAMIC (-nam'ik), *adj.* pertaining to mechanical forces not in equilibrium; effective: *n.pl.* that branch of mechanics which treats of the effects of force in producing motion; kinetics.

DYNAMITE ('na-mit), *n.* a highly explosive compound of nitroglycerine, etc.: *v.t.* to destroy by dynamite.

DYNAMO ('na-mo), *n.* machine for converting mechanical into electric energy.

DYNASTY ('nas-ti), *n.* a line or succession of sovereigns of a particular family.

DYNE (din), *n.* the force which, acting upon a gramme per second, generates a velocity of 1 centimetre.

DYSENTERY (dis'en-ter-i), *n.* a tropical disease akin to diarrhœa.

DYSOPIA (-o'pi-a), **DYSOPSIA** (-op'si-a), *n.* impaired vision.

DYSPEPSIA (-pep'si-a), *n.* indigestion.

DYSPEPTIC ('tik), *n.* a person having dyspepsia.

E

E, e (e), *n.* the fifth letter of the English alphabet.

E, e (e), *n.* an abbreviation.

E (e), *n.* a number in Roman notation representing 250.

E FLAT (flat), a tone half a step below E.

E FLAT MAJOR (ma'jer), a major scale indicated by three flats.

E FLAT MINOR (mi'ner), a minor scale indicated by six flats.

E MAJOR, a major scale indicated by four sharps.

E MINOR, a minor scale indicated by one sharp.

EACH (ech), *adj. & pron.*, one of two; every one.

EAGER (e'ger), *adj.* impetuous; vehement; earnest; keen; enthusiastic.

EAGLE ('gl), *n.* a bird of prey; a gold coin of the U.S. = 10 dollars.

EAGLET ('glet), *n.* a young eagle.

EAR (er), *n.* the organ of hearing.

EARL (erl), *n.* nobleman next in rank below a marquis.

EARLY (er'li), *adj.* before the usual time: *adv.* soon; seasonably.

EARMARK (er'mark), *n.* a mark for identification.

EAR-MINDED (er'min-ded), *adj.* tending to learn and remember and think in terms of auditory images.

EAR-MUFF (er'muf), *n.* a covering to protect the ears.

EARN (ern), *v.t.* to gain for one's labour, service, etc.; merit.

EARNEST ('nest), *adj.* in serious reality; ardent; zealous; eager.

EARNINGS ('ningz), *n.pl.* wages; reward.

EARRING (er'ring), *n.* an ear ornament.

EAR-SPLITTING (er'split-ing), *a.* deafening; overpoweringly noisy.

EARTH (erth), *n.* the inhabited terraqueous globe; the solid materials which compose the globe; soil.

EARTHENWARE (war), *n.* vessels or objects made of clay.

EARTH INDUCTOR COMPASS (in-duk'ter kum'pas), an instrument used in long-distance air navigation, consisting of a generator in the tail-end of the plane which acts upon a compass dial on the instrument board in which a needle indicates the true course to steer: invented by Maurice Titterington, and used by Col. Chas. A. Lindbergh on his non-stop flight of 33½ hours from New York to Paris, May 21, 1927.

EARTHLY (-li), *adj.* pertaining to the earth; worldly; coarse.

EARTHQUAKE ('kwak), *n.* a shaking or trembling of the earth produced by subterranean volcanic forces.

EARTHWORK ('werk), *n.* an offensive or defensive fortification.

EARTHWORM ('werm), *n.* a burrowing worm.

EARTHY ('i), *adj.* pertaining to the earth; dull; coarse.

EARWAX (er'waks), *n.* cerumen.

EARWIG (er'wig), *n.* an insect : *v.t.* to gain the ear of and influence by whispered or covert statements.

EASE (ez), *n.* quiet; repose; facility : *v.t.* give rest or relief.

EASEL (e'zl), *n.* a frame for supporting a canvas, blackboard, etc.

EASEMENT (ez'ment), *n.* a right of accommodation in another's land, or a right of passage.

EAST (est), *n.* that part of the heavens where the sun rises; one of the four cardinal points.

EAST (est), *n.* the Orient; eastern part of any country.

EASTER (es'ter), *n.* a festival of the Christian Church to commemorate the resurrection of Jesus Christ.

EASTERLY (-li), *adv.* in the direction of the east.

EASTERN (est'ern), *adj.* situated toward, or lying in, the east.

EASTERN CHURCH (cherch), *n.* the Orthodox Oriental or Greek Church.

EASTWARD (est'werd), *adv.* toward, or in the direction of, the east.

EASY (ez'i), *adj.* free from pain, disturbance, etc.; moderate; well-to-do; yielding; gentle.

EAT (et), *v.t.* to chew and swallow, as food; devour; consume; corrode.

EAU (o), *n.* [*pl.* eaux (oz), (French)], water, especially as applied to perfumes, cordials.

EAU DE COLOGNE (de ko-lon'), *n.* a perfumed liquid for the toilet.

EAVES (evz), *n.pl.* the edges of a roof.

EAVESDROP ('drop), *v.i.* to listen to the private conversation of others.

EBB (eb), *n.* the flowing back of the tide; decline.

EBONITE ('un-it), *n.* a variety of vulcanite.

EBONIZE (-iz), *v.t.* to stain like ebony.

EBONY ('un-i), *n.* a hard, durable, black wood.

EBULLITION (eb-u-lish'un), *n.* effervescence; a sudden outburst of feeling.

EBURNATED (e-ber'na-ted), *adj.* like ivory or bone.

EBURNATION (e-ber-na'shun), *n.* a turning into bone.

ECCENTRIC (ek-sen'trik), *adj.* not situated in, or deviating from the centre; peculiar in manner; erratic : *n.* a mechanical device for converting continuous circular motion into reciprocating rectilinear motion.

ECCENTRICITY (-tris'i-ti), *n.* peculiarity of manner or character; idiosyncrasy.

ECCLESIASTIC (e-kle-zl-as'tik), *n.* a person in holy orders.

ECHO (ek'o), *n.* the repetition of a sound caused by reflection; the repetition of the words or opinions of others.

ECLAIR (a-klar'), *n.* a small oblong cake containing flavoured cream, etc., covered on the top with sugar or chocolate.

ECLAT (a-klaht'), *n.* a bursting forth, as of applause; striking effect.

ECLECTIC (ek-lek'tik), *adj.* selecting or choosing from different systems, doctrines, or sources.

ECLIPSE (e-klips'), *n.* the total or partial obscuration of the light of a heavenly body caused by its entering the shadow of another body; hence, diminution; obscuration; temporary failure.

ECONOMIC (ek-o-, e-ko-nom'ik), **ECONOMICAL** ('i-kal), *adj.* frugal; saving : *n.pl.* political economy.

ECONOMIST (-kon'o-mist), *n.* one prudent in expenditure; a student of political economy.

ECONOMIZE ('o-miz), *v.i.* to be careful in outlay.

ECONOMY ('o-mi), *n.* the regulation

of household affairs; frugality in expenditure.

ECRU (a-kroo'), *n.* goods of un-bleached linen.

ECSTASY (ek'sta-si), *n.* the state of being beside one's self; excessive joy.

ECSTATIC (-stat'ik), *adj.* overpower-ing; entrancing.

ECUMENIC, ŒCUMENIC (ek-u-men'ik), **ECUMENICAL, ŒCU-MENICAL** ('i-kal), *adj.* general; universal.

ECZEMA ('ze-ma), *n.* an inflam-matory disease of the skin.

EDDY (ed'i), *n.* a contrary current of air or water causing a circular motion; whirl.

EDEN (e'dn), *n.* Paradise.

EDGE (ej), *n.* the sharp or cutting part of an instrument; extreme border; brink; margin; keenness; mental acuteness.

EDGED (ejd), *p.adj.* furnished with an edge.

EDGE-TOOL (ej-tool), *n.* any sharp tool.

EDGING ('ing), *n.* that which forms an edge or border.

EDIBLE (ed'i-bl), *adj.* fit to be eaten as food.

EDICT (e'dikt), *n.* a public proclama-tion or decree.

EDIFICATION (ed-i-fi-ka'shun), *n.* a building up in a moral or religious sense; instruction.

EDIFY ('i-fi), *v.t.* to strengthen; impart instruction to.

EDIT ('it), *v.t.* to revise and prepare for publication; direct, select, and adapt literary matter.

EDITION (e-dish'un), *n.* the pub-lished form of a literary work; the number of copies printed.

EDITION DE LUXE (de looks), a superior edition of a book.

EDITOR (ed'i-ter), *n.* one who super-intends, revises, or prepares a literary work for publication.

EDITORIAL (-to'ri-al), *adj.* pertain-ing to an editor, or his duties: *n.* a leading article.

EDUCATE ('u-kat), *v.t.* to impart knowledge to; cultivate the moral or intellectual faculties of; instruct.

EDUCATION (-ka'shun), *n.* the sys-tematic training of the moral and intellectual faculties.

EDUCATOR (-ka'ter), *n.* one who, or that which, educates; a tutor.

EDUCE (e-dus'), *v.t.* to draw out; evolve.

EDUCTIVE (-duk'tiv), *adj.* drawing out.

EEL (el), *n.* an elongated fish.

EERIE (e'ri), *adj.* lonely; weird; gloomy.

EFFACE (e-fas'), *v.t.* to obliterate; destroy.

EFFACEABLE ('a-bl), *adj.* capable of being effaced.

EFFACEMENT ('ment), *n.* oblitera-tion.

EFFECT (e-fekt'), *n.* result; purpose; realization; efficiency; purport: *pl.* goods; personal estate.

EFFECTIVE (-fek'tiv), *adj.* having the power to effect; operative; efficient; powerful.

EFFECTUAL (fek'tu-al), *adj.* com-pletely operative; efficient.

EFFEMINACY (-fem'i-na-si), *n.* womanish softness or delicacy.

EFFEMINATE ('i-nat), *v.i.* become womanish: *adj.* delicate or unmanly.

EFFENDI (e-fen'di), *n.* a Turkish title of respect.

EFFERVESCE (ef-er-ves'), *v.i.* to be in a state of natural ebullition; bubble or hiss.

EFFERVESCENT ('ent), *adj.* gently bubbling and hissing.

EFFETE (-fet'), *adj.* worn out; barren; exhausted.

EFFICACIOUS (-i-ka'shus), *adj.* capa-ble of producing a desired effect.

EFFICACY (ef'i-ka-si), *n.* power to produce results or effects; ability.

EFFICIENCY (-fish'en-si), *n.* effec-tual agency or power.

EFFICIENT ('ent), *adj.* powerful; ready: *n.* an agent or cause.

EFFIGY (ef'i-ji), *n.* an image; a likeness.

EFFLUENCE (ef'loo-ens), *n.* an issu-ing out.

EFFLUENT (-ent), *n.* a stream which flows out of another.

EFFLUVIUM ('vi-um), *n.* [*pl.* effluvia

(-a)], an invisible, subtle emanation.

EFFLUX (ef'luks), *n.* the act of flowing out ; effluence ; emanation.

EFFORT (ef'ert), *n.* strenuous exertion ; attempt.

EFFRONTERY (e-frun'ter-i), *n.* impudence ; presumption ; boldness.

EFFULGENCE (-ful'jens), *n.* a great lustre, brightness or splendour.

EFFUSION (-fu'zhun), *n.* the act of pouring out, or shedding forth ; an outpouring of thought or sentiment.

EFFUSIVE ('siv), *adj.* pouring forth freely or widely.

EGG (eg), *n.* the oval body laid by birds and certain animals.

EGGING ('ing), *n.* incitement.

EGGPLANT ('plant), *n.* a vegetable.

EGO (e'go), *n.* self ; personality.

EGOISM (-izm), *n.* regarding self as the centre of everything.

EGOIST (-ist), *n.* one given to thought of self alone.

EGO-MANIAC (ma'ni-ak), *n.* one whose self-love is so excessive as to become a disease.

EGOTISM (e'go-, eg'o-tizm), *n.* self-exaltation in thought, speech, or writing ; vanity.

EGOTIST (-tist), *n.* one characterized by egotism.

EGREGIOUS (e-gre'jus), *adj.* extraordinary ; flagrant ; gross.

EGRESS ('gres), *n.* departure ; a place of exit.

EGRET (e'gret), *n.* a species of heron ; a heron's plume.

EIDER (i'der), *n.* a large marine duck.

EIGHT (at), *adj.* one more than 7 ; a cardinal numeral : *n.* a symbol, VIII, representing 8 units.

EIGHTEEN (a'ten), *adj.* one more than 17 ; a cardinal number.

EIGHTEENMO (-mo), *n.* a book whose sheets are folded into 18 leaves.

EIGHTEENTH ('tenth), *adj.* next in order after 17th ; an ordinal numeral.

EIGHTH (ath), *adj.* next after seventh ; an ordinal numeral.

EIGHTIETH (a'ti-eth), *adj.* next to 79th.

EIGHTY ('ti), *adj.* 8 times 10.

EISEGESIS (i-se-je'sis), *n.* interpretation of a text according to one's own idea, as of a Biblical passage.

EITHER (e', i'ther), *adj.* one or the other of two ; both : *pron.* one of two : *conj.* the correlative to *or.*

EJACULATE (e-jak'u-lat), *v.t.* to utter suddenly.

EJACULATION (-la'shun), *n.* an exclamation.

EJACULATORY ('u-la-to-ri), *adj.* uttered suddenly.

EJECT (e-jekt'), *v.t.* to cast forth ; dismiss from office ; evict.

EJECTION (-jek'shun), *n.* expulsion.

EJECTMENT ('ment), *n.* the act of ejecting.

EJECTOR ('ter), *n.* one who, or that which, ejects ; a mechanism in a breech-loading firearm.

EKE (ek), *v.t.* to extend or lengthen (with *out*) : *adv.* also ; likewise.

ELABORATE (e-lab'o-rat), *v.t.* improve or refine with study or labour : *adj.* highly-finished.

ELABORATELY ('li), *adv.* in an elaborate manner.

ELABORATOR (-ra-ter), *n.* one who, or that which, elaborates.

ELAN (a-lang'), *n.* [French], dash ; ardour ; spirit.

ELAND (e'land), *n.* a large South African antelope.

ELAPSE (e-laps'), *v.i.* to slip or glide away ; run out without notice.

ELASTIC (-las'tik), *adj.* springing back ; rebounding ; springy ; capable of extension.

ELASTICITY (-tis'i-ti), *n.* the quality of being elastic.

ELATE (-lat'), *v.t.* to raise the spirits of ; excite.

ELATION (e-la'shun), *n.* the state of being elated.

ELBOW (el'bo), *n.* the joint or bend of the arm : *v.i.* push rudely.

ELDER ('der), *adj.* older : *n.* one of a body of laymen, in certain churches ; a shrub or tree.

ELDERLY ('li), *adj.* somewhat old.

ELDEST ('est), *adj.* oldest ; firstborn.

EL DORADO (do-ra'do), *n.* an imaginary country in South America, fabled to be very rich in gold.

ELECT (e-lekt'), *v.t.* to choose for

any office or use ; choose by ballot.

ELECTION (-lek'shun), *n.* the act of choosing a person for some office ; one of the five points of Calvinism.

ELECTIONEER (-shun-er'), *v.i.* to employ means for influencing result of an election.

ELECTIONEERING ('ing), *n.* the act of canvassing for votes.

ELECTIVE (-lek'tiv), *adj.* regulated by choice ; exerting the power of choice ; opposed to *hereditary*.

ELECTOR ('ter), *n.* one legally qualified to vote ; a member of a U.S. electoral college.

ELECTORAL COLLEGE (kol'ej), body of representatives elected by the voters of the several states to choose a president of the U.S.

ELECTORATE ('to-rat), *n.* the whole body of persons entitled to vote.

ELECTRIC ('trik), **ELECTRICAL** (-kal), *adj.* pertaining to, containing, generated by, or produced by electricity.

ELECTRICIAN (-trish'an), *n.* one who is skilled in the science of electricity.

ELECTRICITY (-tris'i-ti), *n.* an imponderable and invisible agent producing light, heat, chemical decomposition, and other physical phenomena.

ELECTRIFY ('tri-fi), *v.t.* to charge with, or act upon, by electricity ; arouse or excite suddenly.

ELECTRO-, a combining form denoting *electric*.

ELECTROCAUTERY (-kaw'ter-i), *n.* cauterizing by a platinum wire heated by electricity.

ELECTROCULTURE (-kul'tur), *n.* the use of electric light to promote the growth of plants.

ELECTROCUTE ('tro-kut), *v.t.* to put to death by an electric current.

ELECTROCUTION (ku'shun), *n.* the act of electrocuting.

ELECTRODE (e-lek'trod), *n.* either of the terminals of an electric source ; anode or cathode.

ELECTRODYNAMICS (-di-nam'-iks), *n.* that branch of physics which treats of electric currents.

ELECTRODYNAMOMETER (-na-mom'e-ter), *n.* an instrument for measuring the strength of an electric current.

ELECTROLIER (-tro-ler'), *n.* an ornamental bracket for electric lamps.

ELECTROMAGNET (-mag'net), *n.* a coil of soft iron rendered magnetic by the passage of an electric current through it.

ELECTROMAGNETISM (-mag'net-izm), *n.* the science which deals with the relations between electricity and magnetism.

ELECTROMETALLURGY (-met'-al-er-ji), *n.* the art of precipitating certain metals from their solutions, or of separating metals from their ores, etc., by electric current.

ELECTRON (e-lek'tron), *n.* an electrical unit ; a component of the hydrogen atom, estimated as $1/1700$ of its mass.

ELECTROPLATE ('tro-plat), *v.t.* to cover or give a coating of metal to by means of a current of electricity.

ELECTROSCOPE (-skop), *n.* an electrometer.

ELECTROTYPE ('tro-tip), *n.* a facsimile in metal of any object made by covering a mould, plate, etc., with a coating of copper.

ELEEMOSYNARY (el-e-mos'i-na-ri), *adj.* devoted to charitable purposes.

ELEGANCE ('e-gans), *n.* polish ; refinement.

ELEGY (el'e-ji), *n.* a funeral song or ode, dirge.

ELEMENT (el'e-ment), *n.* a first or constituent principle ; a component or essential part ; natural environment.

ELEMENTAL ('tal), *adj.* fundamental.

ELEMENTARY ('ta-ri), *adj.* simple.

ELEPHANT ('e-fant), *n.* a large mammal of Asia and Africa.

ELEPHANTINE ('tin), *adj.* huge ; unwieldy.

ELEVATE (el'e-vat), *v.t.* to ennoble, animate ; inspire ; raise.

ELEVATOR (-ter), *n.* that which raises up or exalts ; a hoisting machine or lift ; a warehouse for the storage of grain.

ELEVEN (e-lev'n), *adj.* 10 with 1 added.

ELF (elf), *n.* a sprite; dwarf; fairy.

ELFIN ('fin), *n.* an inhabitant of fairyland, a sportive child.

ELF-FIRE (elf'fir), *n.* will-o'-the-wisp.

ELFLOCK ('lok), *n.* a knot of hair twisted in an intricate manner.

ELICIT (e-lis'it), *v.t.* to draw out.

ELIDE (-lid'), *v.t.* to slur over, or cut off, as a final vowel.

ELIGIBILITY (el-i-ji-bil'i-ti), *n.* the quality of being eligible.

ELIGIBLE (el'i-ji-bl), *adj.* capable of being, or fit to be, chosen; qualified.

ELIMINATE (e-lim'i-nat), *v.t.* to leave out of consideration, or cast aside.

ELISION (e-lizh'un), *n.* the cutting off of a vowel or syllable for the sake of euphony, as o'er for over.

ELITE (a-let'), *n.* the choicest part, as of society, a profession, etc.

ELIXIR (e-lik'ser), *n.* an imaginary liquid of the alchemists, supposed to be capable of prolonging life indefinitely, and of changing baser metals into gold; a tincture, essence.

ELK (elk), *n.* the moose-deer.

ELLIPSE (e-lips'), *n.* one of the sections of a cone; the elliptical orbit of a planet.

ELM (elm), *n.* a large leafy tree.

ELOCUTION (el-o-ku'shun), *n.* the art, manner, or style of speaking in public.

ELOCUTIONIST (-ist), *n.* one skilled in, or a teacher of, elocution.

ELONGATE (e-long'gat), *v.t.* to stretch out; extend; lengthen.

ELOPE (e-lop'), *v.i.* to escape privately; run away.

ELOQUENCE (el'o-kwens), *n.* the art of speaking with fluency and elegance.

ELOQUENT (-kwent), *adj.* having the power of fluent and elegant oratory.

ELSE (els), *adv.* besides; otherwise.

ELSEWHERE ('hwar), *adv.* in another place.

ELUCIDATE (e-lus'i-dat), *v.t.* to make clear; render intelligible.

ELUDE (e-lud'), *v.t.* to avoid by artifice; escape.

ELUSION (-lu'zhun), *n.* evasion; artifice.

ELUSIVE (-siv), *adj.* deceptive, fallacious.

ELUSORY ('so-ri), *adj.* evasive, deceptive.

ELYSIUM (e-lizh'i-um), *n.* the Greek paradise or residence of the blessed after death.

EM (em), *n.* the square body of any size of type, serving as a unit of measurement.

EMACIATE (e-ma'shi-at), *v.i.* to lose flesh gradually; pine away.

EMANATE (em'a-nat), *v.i.* to flow out, issue, or proceed, as from a source.

EMANCIPATE (e-man'si-pat), *v.t.* to liberate; set free; enfranchise.

EMANCIPATOR (-pa-ter), *n.* a liberator.

EMARGINATE (-mar'jin-at), *adj.* indented at the edges.

EMASCULATE (-mas'ku-lat), *v.t.* deprive of virility; weaken by expurgation.

EMBALM (em-bahm'), *v.t.* to preserve from decay.

EMBANK (-bangk'), *v.t.* to enclose with a bank; protect by a bank.

EMBANKMENT ('ment), *n.* a bank of earth, stones, etc.

EMBARGO (-bar'go), *n.* an order by authority prohibiting the departure of vessels from a port.

EMBARK (-bark'), *v.i.* to go on board a vessel; engage in any affairs.

EMBARRASS (-bar'as), *v.t.* to hinder; perplex; distress.

EMBASSY ('ba-si), *n.* the public function, mission, or official residence of an ambassador; a legation.

EMBED (-bed'), *v.t.* to lay in, or as in, a bed.

EMBELLISH (-bel'ish), *v.t.* to make beautiful; set off by ornamentation.

EMBER ('ber), *n.* a small live coal.

EMBEZZLE (-bez'l), *v.t.* to appropriate fraudulently.

EMBITTER (-bit'er), *v.t.* to make bitter; exasperate.

EMBLAZON (-bla'zn), *v.t.* to adorn with heraldic figures; decorate.

EMBLEM ('blem), *n.* a symbolical figure or design.

EMBLEMATIC (-blem-at'ik), *adj.* pertaining to an emblem.

EMBODIMENT ('i-ment), *n.* the act of embodying, or uniting in a whole.

EMBODY (-bod'i), *v.t.* to collect into one mass or united whole; to incorporate.

EMBOLDEN (em-bol'd'n), *v.t.* to encourage.

EMBONPOINT (ang-bong-pwang'), *n.* [French], plumpness of figure.

EMBOSOM (em-booz'um), *v.t.* to hold in the bosom; enclose in the midst.

EMBOSS (-bos'), *v.t.* raise in relief from the surface.

EMBRACE (-bras'), *v.t.* to take in close, or press to the bosom with affection; include.

EMBROCATE ('bro-kat), *v.t.* to moisten and rub.

EMBROIDER (-broid'er), *v.t.* to decorate with needlework.

EMBROIL (-broil'), *v.t.* to throw into confusion; involve in contention.

EMBRYO ('bri-o), *n.* the first germ or rudiment of an organism.

EMENDATION (e-men-da'shun), *n.* the alteration or correction of a text.

EMERALD (em'e-rald), *n.* a precious stone.

EMERALD ISLE (il), Ireland.

EMERGE (e-merj'), *v.i.* to rise up, or come forth.

EMERGENCY (-mer'jen-si), *n.* a sudden occasion; pressing necessity; crisis.

EMERITUS (-mer'i-tus), *adj.* retired from service with honour.

EMERY (em'er-i), *n.* a very hard variety of corundum.

EMETIC (e-met'ik), *adj.* inducing vomiting.

EMIGRANT (em'i-grant), *n.* one who quits his own country to settle in another.

EMIGRATE ('i-grat), *v.i.* to leave one's country to settle in another.

EMINENCE (em'i-nens), *n.* that which is lofty; elevation; height; exalted rank.

EMINENT (-nent), *adj.* high in office, rank, or reputation.

EMISSARY (em'i-sa-ri), *n.* a person, or agent, sent on a mission.

EMISSION (e-mish'un), *n.* the act of sending out.

EMIT (-mit'), *v.t.* to send or give forth; issue.

EMOTION (-mo'shun), *n.* mental agitation; excited feeling.

EMOTIVE (-mo'tiv), *adj.* producing emotion.

EMPEROR (em'per-er), *n.* the sovereign of an empire.

EMPHASIS ('fa-sis), *n.* a particular stress of the voice on a word or words in reading or speaking.

EMPHASIZE ('fa-siz), *v.t.* to pronounce and bring out clearly and distinctly.

EMPHATIC (-fat'ik), *adj.* uttered with emphasis; forcibly significant.

EMPIRE ('pir), *n.* supreme power or dominion; imperial rule or sovereignty.

EMPIRIC (-pir'ik), *adj.* pertaining to experience: *n.* one who relies on practical experience to guide his actions.

EMPIRICISM ('i-sizm), *n.* observation, or practical experience apart from scientific knowledge.

EMPLOY (-ploi'), *v.t.* to give occupation to; keep busy.

EMPLOYE, EMPLOYEE (a', e'), *n.* one who works for another.

EMPORIUM (-po'ri-um), *n.* a centre or place of trade.

EMPOWER (-pou'er), *v.t.* to authorize; enable.

EMPRESS ('pres), *n.* a woman invested with sovereign sway over an empire.

EMPTINESS (emp'ti-nes), *n.* the state of being empty.

EMPTY ('ti), *adj.* containing nothing; vague; vacant.

EMU (e'mu), *n.* a large Australian ostrich-like bird.

EMULATE (em'u-lat), *v.t.* to strive to equal or excel.

EMULATOR (-la-ter), *n.* a rival; competitor.

EMULSION (e-mul'shun), *n.* a liquid preparation resembling milk.

ENABLE (en-a'bl), *v.t.* to make able; empower.

ENACT (-akt'), *v.t.* to decree.

ENACTING CLAUSE (klawz), the introductory clause of a bill or act, usually commencing, "Be it enacted."

ENACTMENT ('ment), *n.* a statute; the passing of a bill into law.

ENAMEL (-am'el), *n.* any substance used in coating the surface of metals or porcelain, and afterwards fired; anything enamelled; the dense white substance of the teeth.

ENAMOUR (-am'er), *v.t.* to captivate.

ENCAMP (-kamp'), *v.i.* to form a camp; halt on the march.

ENCHAIN (en-chan'), *v.t.* to hold fast with, or as with, a chain.

ENCHANT (-chant'), *v.t.* to charm or subdue; bewitch; fill with delight.

ENCIRCLE (-ser'kl), *v.t.* to form, or enclose, in a circle; embrace.

ENCOMIUM ('mi-um), *n.* formal praise; eulogy.

ENCOMPASS (-kum'pas), *v.t.* to surround.

ENCORE (ang-kor'), *adv.* [French], once more : *n.* a repetition in response to a call by an audience.

ENCOUNTER (en-koun'ter), *v.t.* meet face to face : *v.i.* to come into collision.

ENCOURAGE (-kur'aj), *v.t.* to give, or inspire with, courage; stimulate.

ENCROACH (-kroch'), *v.i.* infringe; intrude (usually with *on* or *upon*).

ENCUMBER (-kum'ber), *v.t.* to impede; retard; clog; obstruct.

ENCUMBRANCE ('brans), *n.* a lien or liability attached to real property.

ENCYCLOPÆDIA, ENCYCLOPEDIA (-si-klo-pe'di-a), *n.* the circle of the arts and sciences and literature; a cyclopædia.

ENCYST (-sist'), *v.t. & v.i.* to enclose, or become enclosed, in a cyst or vesicle.

END (end), *n.* the extreme limit; logical outcome; death : *v.t.* to finish; terminate; destroy.

ENDANGER (en-dan'jer), *v.t.* expose to, or bring into, danger.

ENDEAR (-der'), *v.t.* to make dear or beloved.

ENDEARMENT ('ment), *n.* affection.

ENDEAVOUR (-dev'er), *v.i.* to strive for the attainment of some object; attempt.

ENDEMIC (-dem'ik), *adj.* peculiar to a nation, people, or locality; applied to a disease.

ENDOW (-dou'), *v.t.* to furnish, as with some gift or quality (with *with*).

ENDOWMENT ('ment), *n.* that which is bestowed, settled, or appropriated to any object : *pl.* natural gifts.

ENDUE (-du'), *v.t.* to clothe; invest; assume.

ENDURABLE (-dur'a-bl), *adj.* bearable.

ENDURANCE (-dur'ans), *n.* the capacity to endure; continuance; fortitude.

ENDURE (-dur'), *v.t.* to support without breaking or yielding.

ENEMA (en'e-ma), *n.* an injection as a medicine.

ENEMY ('e-mi), *n.* foe; antagonist; a hostile army.

ENERGETIC (-er-jet'ik), *adj.* possessing, or displaying, energy; vigorous in action; forcible.

ENERGIZE ('er-jiz), *v.t.* to endow with energy.

ENERGY ('er-ji), *n.* internal or inherent power; capacity for performing work.

ENERVATE (en'er-vat, e-ner'vat), *v.t.* to deprive of nerve, force, or vigour; to render effeminate.

ENFEEBLE (en-fe'bl), *v.t.* to weaken; relax.

ENFILADE (-fi-lad'), *n.* a straight line or passage : *v.t.* to pierce or rake with shot in a straight line.

ENFORCE (-fors'), *v.t.* to compel; make clear or intelligible.

ENGAGE (en-gaj'), *v.t.* to pledge or bind by oath or contract; encounter in battle; interlock.

ENGAGEMENT (-gaj'ment), *n.* the

act of engaging ; the state or condition of being engaged ; betrothal.

ENGENDER (-jen′der), *v.t.* to beget : *v.i.* to come into existence.

ENGINE (′jin), *n.* anything used to effect a purpose ; a machine by which power is applied for the performance of work.

ENGINEER (-ji-ner′), *n.* one who has charge of and manages an engine ; one who carries through a scheme or undertaking by skill or astuteness.

ENGINEERING (′ing), *n.* the art and science by which natural forces and materials are utilized in structures or machines.

ENGLISH (ing′glish), *adj.* belonging to, characteristic of, or pertaining to, the language or the people of England, or those descended from them.

ENGRAVE (en-grav′), *v.t.* to cut or carve in sunken patterns.

ENGRAVING (′ing), *n.* the art of producing designs, etc., on metal, stone, or hard wood.

ENGROSS (-gros′), *v.t.* to monopolize ; write in a large distinct round hand.

ENHANCE (-hans′), *v.t.* to raise in esteem ; advance in price or value.

ENIGMA (e-nig′ma), *n.* a riddle.

ENIGMATIC (-mat′ik), *adj.* obscure or puzzling.

ENJOIN (-join′), *v.t.* to enforce ; prohibit or restrain by an injunction.

ENJOY (-joi′), *v.t.* to feel or perceive with pleasure.

ENKINDLE (-kin′dl), *v.t.* to set on fire.

ENLARGE (-larj′), *v.t.* to make larger.

ENLIGHTEN (-lit′n), *v.t.* to illuminate ; make clear.

ENLIST (-list′), *v.t.* to enroll ; register ; gain over.

ENLIVEN (-liv′n), *v.t.* to make vigorous, active, or vivacious.

EN MASSE (ang mas′), [French], collectively ; altogether.

ENMITY (en′mi-ti), *n.* animosity ; hostility ; ill-will.

ENNOBLE (-no′bl), *v.t.* to dignify ; exalt.

ENNUI (ang-we′), *n.* [French], languor of mind ; listlessness.

ENORMITY (e-nor′mi-ti), *n.* something outrageous ; an atrocity.

ENORMOUS (′mus), *adj.* excessive ; very great ; immense ; huge.

ENOUGH (e-nuf′), *adj.* sufficient : *n.* a sufficiency : *interj.* stop !

EN PASSANT (ang pas-sang), [French], in passing ; by the way.

ENQUIRE, same as inquire.

ENRAGE (en-raj′), *v.t.* to throw into a rage.

ENRAIL (-ral′), *v.t.* to place a car upon rails.

EN RAPPORT (ang ra-por′), [French], in sympathy with (with *with*).

ENRAPT (-rapt′), *adj.* enraptured.

ENRAPTURE (-rap′tur), *v.t.* to transport with delight ; please intensely.

ENRICH (en-rich′), *v.t.* to make rich ; fertilize ; store ; adorn.

ENROBE (-rob′), *v.t.* to clothe ; invest.

ENROLL (-rol′), *v.t.* to insert in a register ; enlist ; record.

EN ROUTE (ang root′), [French], on the way.

ENS (enz), *n.* [*pl.* entia (en′shi-a)], an entity ; existence ; being.

ENSANGUINE (en-sang′gwin), *v.t.* smear or cover with blood.

ENSEMBLE (ang-sang′bl), *n.* [French], the whole ; united musical performance of voices or instruments.

ENSHRINE (en-shrin′), *v.t.* to place in a shrine ; keep sacred.

ENSHROUD (-shroud′), *v.t.* to cover with, or as with, a shroud ; conceal.

ENSIGN (′sin), *n.* a flag ; badge ; the flag which indicates nationality ; a sign or token.

ENSILAGE (′si-laj), *n.* fodder or vegetable produce stored in a silo.

ENSLAVE (-slav′), *v.t.* to bring into, or reduce to, slavery ; enthrall.

ENSNARE (-snar′), *v.t.* to take by craft ; allure.

ENSUE (-su′), *v.i.* to follow as a consequence ; succeed.

EN SUITE (ang swet′), [French], in a series.

ENTAIL (en-tal'), *v.t.* to involve; necessitate.

ENTANGLE (-tang'gl), *v.t.* to involve; perplex.

ENTENTE (an-tangt'), *n.* [French], an understanding, politically, between nations.

ENTER ('ter), *v.t.* to go or come into; penetrate; set down in writing.

ENTERPRISE ('ter-priz), *n.* an undertaking of importance or risk.

ENTERTAIN (-tan'), *v.t.* to receive and treat hospitably; take into consideration.

ENTHRALL (-thrawl'), *v.t.* to enslave.

ENTHRONE (-thron'), *v.t.* to invest with sovereign power.

ENTHUSE (-thuz'), *v.t.* to render enthusiastic: *v.i.* manifest enthusiasm.

ENTHUSIASM (-thu'zi-azm), *n.* elevation of fancy; fervent zeal.

ENTHUSIAST ('zi-ast), *n.* one who is filled with enthusiasm.

ENTICE (-tis'), *v.t.* attract or allure.

ENTIRE (-tir'), *adj.* complete in all parts; whole.

ENTITLE (en-ti'tl), *v.t.* to give a title, name, or designation to; give a right to.

ENTITY ('ti-ti), *n.* anything that exists; being.

ENTO-, ENT-, a combining form denoting *within*.

ENTOMB (en-toom'), *v.t.* to place in a tomb.

ENTOMOLOGIST ('to-mol'o-jist), *n.* a student of entomology.

ENTOMOLOGY (-to-mol'o-ji), *n.* that branch of zoology which treats of insects and their habits.

ENTR'ACTE (ang'trakt), *n.* [French], the interval between the acts of a play or opera.

ENTRAILS ('tralz), *n.pl.* the intestines.

ENTRAIN (-tran'), *v.t.* to dispatch (troops), by train.

ENTRANCE ('trans), *n.* the act of entering; a passage; avenue.

ENTRAP (-trap'), *v.t.* to inveigle; ensnare.

ENTREAT (-tret'), *v.t.* to importune; beseech.

ENTREATY (-tret'i), *n.* an earnest petition or request.

ENTREE (ang-tra'), *n.* [French], entrance; admission; a subordinate dish.

ENTRENCH, same as intrench.

ENTRE NOUS (ang'tr noo), [French], confidentially.

ENTRUST, same as intrust.

ENTRY (en'tri), *n.* an entrance; passage; the act of taking rightful possession of property, or feloniously entering another's premises.

ENTWINE (-twin'), *v.t.* to twine around; twist together.

ENUMERATE (e-nu'mer-at), *v.t.* to reckon or name singly; count.

ENUMERATION (-a'shun), *n.* the act of numbering; counting up.

ENUNCIATE ('shi-at), *v.t.* to declare or proclaim; utter; speak.

ENUNCIATION (-a'shun), *n.* definite or declaratory statement; articulation.

ENUNCIATOR (shi-a-ter), *n.* one who enunciates or declares.

ENVELOP (-vel'up), *v.t.* to surround with, or as with, a wrapper; covered.

ENVELOPE (en'vel-op), *n.* a case or wrapper; covering; an integument.

ENVELOPMENT (-vel'up-ment), *n.* the act of enveloping.

ENVENOM (-ven'um), *v.t.* make poisonous; embitter.

ENVIABLE ('vi-a-bl), *adj.* capable of awakening the desire to possess.

ENVIOUS ('vi-us), *adj.* feeling, or characterized by, envy.

ENVIRON (-vi'run), *v.t.* to surround : *n.pl.* suburbs.

ENVIRONMENT (-ment), *n.* that which surrounds.

ENVOY ('voi), *n.* a diplomatic representative sent on a special mission.

ENVY ('vi), *v.t.* to grudge; covet : *n.* malice; ill-will.

ENWRAP (-rap'), *v.t.* to wrap up.

EPAULET (ep'aw-let), *n.* a badge worn on the shoulder by naval and military officers.

EPHEMERAL (e-fem'er-al), *adj.* existing only for a day; short-lived.

EPIC (ep'ik), *n.* a narrative poem of some heroic deed or event.

EPICURE ('i-kur), *n.* one devoted to luxury.

EPICUREAN (-ku-re'an), *n.* a gormand ; epicure.

EPIDEMIC (-i-dem'ik), *adj.* attacking many at the same time ; said of a disease.

EPIDERMIS ('mis), *n.* the cuticle or scarf skin.

EPIGRAM ('i-gram), *n.* a verse or phrase ending in some ingenious or witty turn.

EPIGRAMMATIC (-mat'ik), *adj.* pertaining to, or of the nature of, an epigram ; pointed.

EPILEPSY ('i-lep-si), *n.* a chronic nervous disease.

EPILOGUE ('i-log), *n.* a poem or speech at the conclusion of a play.

EPIPHANY (e-pif'a-ni), *n.* a Church festival (Jan. 6) to commemorate the visit of the Magi to Bethlehem, and the manifestation of Christ to the Gentiles.

EPISCOPACY (e-pis'ko-pa-si), *n.* church government by bishops ; prelacy.

EPISCOPALIAN (-pa'li-an), *adj.* pertaining to the Protestant Episcopal Church.

EPISODE (ep'i-sod), *n.* an incident ; a digression, or incidental narrative.

EPISTLE (e-pis'l), *n.* a letter.

EPISTOLARY ('to-la-ri), *adj.* pertaining to letters.

EPITAPH (ep'i-taf), *n.* a memorial inscription on a tomb or monument.

EPITHET ('i-thet), *n.* an adjective denoting any quality either good or bad ; appellation.

EPITOME (e-pit'o-me), *n.* a summary ; abridgment.

EPITOMIZE ('o-miz), *v.t.* to describe briefly ; condense.

EPOCH (e'pok), *n.* a point of time from which succeeding years are reckoned ; era ; date.

EPODE (ep'od), *n.* the last part of an ode.

EPSOM SALTS ('sum sawltz), sulphate of magnesia.

EQUABILITY (e-kwa-bil'i-ti), *adj.* evenness.

EQUABLE ('kwa-bl), *adj.* uniform ; equal.

EQUAL ('kwal), *adj.* of the same extent, or magnitude ; adequate ; of the same rank, degree, or value.

EQUALITY (-kwal'i-ti), *n.* the state of being equal ; uniformity.

EQUALIZE ('kwal-iz), *v.t.* to make equal.

EQUANIMITY (-kwa-nim'i-ti), *n.* evenness of temper or mind ; calmness.

EQUATE (-kwat'), *v.t.* to reduce to an average.

EQUATION (-kwa'shun), *n.* in mathematics, a proposition expressing the equality of two quantities, the sign = being placed between them.

EQUATOR (-kwa'ter), *n.* the imaginary circle which passes round the middle of the earth.

EQUATORIAL (-to'ri-al), *adj.* pertaining to the equator.

EQUESTRIAN (e-kwes'tri-an), *adj.* pertaining to horses or horsemanship.

EQUESTRIENNE (-kwes-tri-en'), *n.* a skillful horsewoman.

EQUI-, a prefix meaning *equal, equally, same,* found in many words, the sense of which is usually self-evident, as *equi*-angular, *equi*distant, etc.

EQUILATERAL (e-kwi-lat'er-al), *adj.* having all the sides equal.

EQUILIBRATOR (e-kwi-li'bra-ter), *n.* that which conduces to equilibrium.

EQUILIBRIUM (-lib'ri-um), *n.* equality of weight, power, force, etc. ; equipoise.

EQUINE (e'kwin), *adj.* pertaining to or resembling, a horse.

EQUINOCTIAL (-kwi-nok'shal), *adj.* pertaining to the equinoxes.

EQUINOX ('kwi-noks), *n.* the time the sun enters one of the two equinoctial points when the days and nights are of equal duration.

EQUIP (e-kwip'), *v.t.* to furnish or fit ; accoutre.

EQUIPMENT (e-kwip'ment), *n.* articles or supplies necessary for any particular service.

EQUIPOISE (e'kwi-poiz), *n.* equilibrium ; equality of weight.

EQUITABLE (ek'wi-ta-bl), *adj.* impartial ; just.

EQUITY ('wi-ti), *n.* justice ; just regard to right or claim ; impartiality.

EQUIVALENCE (e-kwiv'a-lens), *n.* equality of value or power.

EQUIVALENT ('a-lent), *adj.* equal in value or power.

EQUIVOCAL ('o-kal), *adj.* of a doubtful or double significance ; ambiguous.

EQUIVOCATE ('o-kat), *v.i.* to use words of double meaning ; prevaricate.

ERA (e'ra), *n.* the point of time from which a series of years is reckoned ; period.

ERADICATE (e-rad'i-kat), *v.t.* to destroy thoroughly ; exterminate.

ERASE (-ras'), *v.t.* to obliterate ; expunge.

ERASER (-ra'ser), *n.* a knife or india-rubber for rubbing out marks, etc.

ERASURE ('zhur), *n.* the act of erasing.

ERE (ar), *conj. & prep.* before ; sooner than.

ERECT (e-rekt'), *v.t.* to raise upright ; construct ; build ; raise ; establish.

ERECTION ('shun), *n.* the act of constructing or raising edifices.

ERECTOR ('ter), *n.* one who erects.

ERGO (er'go), *adv.* therefore.

ERIN (e'rin), *n.* Ireland.

ERMINE (er'min), *n.* a weasel-like animal, much valued for its fur.

ERODE (e-rod'), *v.t.* to wear away ; corrode.

EROSION (-ro'zhun), *n.* the act of eroding.

EROTIC (-rot'ik), *adj.* pertaining to love ; amorous.

ERR (er), *v.i.* to commit an error or mistake ; wander.

ERRAND (er'and), *n.* a message ; commission.

ERRANT ('ant), *adj.* roving ; wandering.

ERRATIC (e-rat'ik), *adj.* wandering ; irregular ; eccentric.

ERRONEOUS (-ro'ne-us), *adj.* incorrect ; mistaken ; wrong.

ERROR (er'er), *n.* deviation from the truth ; mistake ; blunder.

ERST (erst), *adv.* formerly.

ERUCTATION (e-ruk-ta'shun), *n.* the act of throwing off wind from the stomach.

ERUDITE (er'u-dit), *adj.* learned.

ERUDITION (-dish'un), *n.* learning.

ERUPTED (e-rupt'ed), *p.adj.* violently ejected.

ERYSIPELAS (er-i-sip'e-las), *n.* an inflammation of the skin.

ESCADRILLE (es-ka-dril'), *n.* [French], a group of aeroplanes.

ESCALATOR (es'ka-la-ter), *n.* a moving stairway.

ESCAPADE (-pad'), *n.* a breach of propriety ; misdeed.

ESCAPE (-kap'), *v.t.* to flee from ; get out of the way of ; avoid.

ESCAPEMENT ('ment), *n.* a mechanical device for securing regularity of movement.

ESCHEAT (-chet'), *v.t.* to forfeit through failure of heirs.

ESCHEW (-choo'), *v.t.* to shun ; avoid.

ESCORT (es'kort), *n.* a body of armed men acting as a guard ; a retinue.

ESCROW (es-kro'), *n.* in law, a deed or bond delivered to a third person, who is to turn it over to the grantee upon the fulfilment of certain conditions.

ESCULENT ('ku-lent), *adj.* eatable.

ESCUTCHEON (-kuch'un), *n.* a shield on which the heraldic arms of a family are emblazoned.

ESKIMO ('ki-mo), *adj.* pertaining to a tribe inhabiting Greenland and other arctic regions ; also *Eskimau*.

ESOPHAGUS, ŒSOPHAGUS (e-sof'a-gus), *n.* the gullet or canal through which food and drink pass to the stomach.

ESOTERIC (es-o-ter'ik), *adj.* pertaining to secret doctrines taught privately.

ESPECIAL (-pesh'al), *adj.* particular ; chief.

ESPERANTO (es-per-an'to), *n.* an artificial language, based on root-words from several languages.

ESPIONAGE ('pi-o-naj), *n.* the act or practice of spying.

ESPLANADE (-pla-nad'), *n.* a level walk or drive, especially by the seaside ; a lawn ; glacis.

ESPOUSAL (-pouz'al), *n.* the act of espousing or betrothing.

ESPOUSE (-pouz'), *v.t.* to promise in marriage ; wed ; adopt.

ESPRIT DE CORPS (-pre'de kor'), [French], a spirit of common devotion, honour, interest, binding together persons of the same profession.

ESPY (-pi'), *v.t.* to see at a distance ; see unexpectedly.

ESQUIRE (-kwir'), *n.* a title applied to professional men, and often used instead of Mr. in the address of a letter.

ESSAY ('sa), *n.* a short written composition or treatise ; an attempt ; experiment.

ESSENCE ('ens), *n.* the concentrated preparation of any substance.

ESSENTIAL (-sen'shal), *adj.* indispensable ; pure ; volatile ; highly rectified.

ESTABLISH (-tab'lish), *v.t.* to fix firmly ; settle ; prove legally.

ESTABLISHMENT (-ment), *n.* ratification ; settlement ; a place of residence or business.

ESTATE (-tat'), *n.* rank, position, or quality ; the title or interest one has in lands or tenements ; property in general.

ESTEEM (-tem'), *v.t.* to set a high value upon : *n.* favourable opinion ; estimation ; respect ; reverence.

ESTIMABLE ('ti-ma-bl), *adj.* worthy of regard, esteem, or honour ; calculable.

ESTIMATE ('ti-mat), *v.t.* to compute ; determine the value or cost of ; appraisement.

ESTIMATION (-ma'shun), *n.* calculation ; appraisement ; honour, respect.

ESTOPPEL (-top'el), *n.* a legal prohibition.

ESTRANGE (-tranj'), *v.t.* to alienate ; keep at a distance.

ESTUARY ('tu-a-ri), *n.* the mouth of a tidal river.

ET CÆTERA (et set'er-a), [Latin], and others of the same kind ; and so forth ; usually abbreviated, etc.

ETCH (ech), *v.t.* to engrave by biting out with an acid the design previously drawn with an etching needle.

ETERNAL (e-ter'nal), *adj.* without beginning or end ; everlasting.

ETERNAL, *n.* an appellation of God (with *the*).

ETERNITY ('ni-ti), *n.* infinite duration ; unending existence.

ETHER (e'ther), *n.* an extremely fine fluid, lighter than air, supposed to pervade all space beyond the atmosphere of the earth ; a volatile liquid produced by the distillation of alcohol with sulphuric acid.

ETHEREAL (-the're-al), *adj.* pertaining to, or formed of, ether ; airy ; exquisite.

ETHICAL (eth'i-kal), *adj.* pertaining to ethics ; moral.

ETHICS ('iks), *n.pl.* the science that treats of the principles of human morality and duty ; moral philosophy.

ETHIOPIAN (-thi-o'pi-an), *adj.* pertaining to Ethiopia.

ETHNOLOGY (eth-nol'o-ji), *n.* the science that treats of the origin of mankind.

ETIQUETTE (et'i-ket), *n.* the conventional rules or ceremonial observed in polite society.

ETYMOLOGICAL (et-i-mo-loj'i-kal), *adj.* pertaining to etymology.

ETYMOLOGY ('o-ji), *n.* that branch of philology which treats of the origin and derivation of words ; that part of grammar which treats of the parts of speech and their inflections.

EUCALYPTUS (u-ka-lip'tus), *n.* [*pl.* Eucalypti ('ti)], a genus of Australian evergreen trees.

EUCHARIST (u'ka-rist), *n.* the sacrament of the Lord's Supper ; the elements, bread and wine, used in that sacrament.

EUCHRE ('ker), *n.* a game of cards.

EUCLID (u'klid), *n.* in general, the science of geometry.

EUGENICS (u-jen'iks), *n.* the science relating to the betterment of the human race by improving conditions as to birth, etc.

EULOGIST ('lo-jist), *n.* one who eulogizes.

EULOGIZE ('lo-jiz), *v.t.* to praise highly ; commend.

EULOGY (-ji), *n.* the praise of anyone spoken or written.

EUPHEMISM ('fe-mizm), *n.* the substitution of a delicate or pleasing expression in place of that which is offensive or indelicate.

EUPHONIC (-fon'ik), *adj.* sounding pleasantly to the ear.

EUPHONIUM (-fo'ni-um), *n.* a bass brass instrument.

EUPHONY ('fo-ni), *n.* an agreeable sound, or pronunciation.

EURASIAN (u-ra'zhan), *adj.* pertaining to a person whose parentage is partly European and partly Asiatic.

EUREKA (u-re'ka), *interj.* an exclamation of triumph meaning " I have found it."

EUROPEAN (-ro-pe'an), *adj.* pertaining to Europe : *n.* a native of Europe.

EUSTACHIAN (-sta'ki-an), *adj.* denoting a tube which leads from the cavity of the tympanum of the ear to the pharynx.

EVACUATE (e-vak'u-at), *v.t.* to make void or empty ; abandon.

EVADABLE ('a-bl), **EVADIBLE** ('i-bl), *adj.* capable of being evaded.

EVADE (-vad'), *v.t.* to elude by stratagem, or sophistry.

EVANESCENT (ev-a-nes'ent), *adj.* disappearing gradually from sight ; vanishing.

EVANGELICAL (e-van-jel'i-kal), *adj.* pertaining to the Gospel, or four Gospels ; maintaining fundamental doctrines of the Protestant faith.

EVANGELISM ('jel-izm), *n.* the doctrine and preaching of evangelical principles.

EVANGELIST (-ist), *n.* one of the four writers of the Gospel ; an itinerant preacher.

EVANGELIZE ('jel-iz), *v.t.* to instruct in the Gospel ; convert to Christianity.

EVAPORATE (-vap'o-rat), *v.i.* to disperse in vapour.

EVAPORATION (-ra'shun), *n.* the slow conversion of a fluid into vapour.

EVASION (-va'zhun), *n.* an excuse ; equivocation ; subterfuge.

EVASIVE (-va'siv), *adj.* tending to evade.

EVE (ev), *n.* the first woman.

EVE (ev), *n.* the period immediately preceding some important event ; evening.

EVEN (e'ven), *adj.* level ; smooth ; equal ; calm ; whole : *n.* evening.

EVENING (-ning), *n.* the close of the day and beginning of the night.

EVENLY (-li), *adv.* smoothly ; uniformly.

EVENT (e-vent'), *n.* an occurrence.

EVENTIDE ('vn-tid), *n.* evening.

EVENTUAL (-ven'tu-al), *adj.* happening as a result ; ultimate.

EVENTUALITY (al'i-ti), *n.* a possible occurrence.

EVENTUATE ('tu-at), *v.i.* to happen ; terminate ; result.

EVER (ev'er), *adv.* always ; without end ; in any degree.

EVERGLADE (-glad), *n.* a low, swampy tract of land.

EVERGREEN (-gren), *n.* a tree or plant which retains its foliage throughout the year.

EVERLASTING (-las'ting), *adj.* perpetual : *n.* eternity.

EVERMORE (-mor), *adv.* eternally.

EVERT (e-vert'), *v.t.* to destroy ; overthrow.

EVERY (ev'ri, ev'er-i), *adj.* the whole, taken one at a time ; each.

EVICT (e-vikt'), *v.t.* to expel or dispossess.

EVICTION (-vik'shun), *n.* the act of evicting.

EVIDENCE (ev'i-dens), *n.* indubitable certainty ; proof ; testimony.

EVIDENT (-dent), *adj.* plain ; obvious.

EVIL (e'vil), *adj.* wicked ; sinful ; disastrous : *n.* moral depravity.

EVINCE (e-vins'), *v.t.* to manifest ; demonstrate.

EVINCIBLE (-vin′si-bl), *adj.* capable of proof or demonstration.

EVISCERATE (-vis′er-at), *v.t.* to disembowel.

EVOKE (e-vok′), *v.t.* to call forth.

EVOLUTION (ev-o-lu′shun), *n.* development or growth ; the gradual development or descent of forms of life from simple or low organized types.

EVOLVE (e-volv′), *v.t.* to develop ; unfold.

EWE (u), *n.* a female sheep.

EWER (′er), *n.* a large water jug.

EX (eks), *prep.* out of ; from ; without.

EX-, a prefix signifying *out of, away from, beyond, completely.*

EXACT (egz-akt′), *adj.* very correct or accurate ; precise.

EXACTING (′ing), *p.adj.* oppressive ; severe ; arduous.

EXACTION (-ak′shun), *n.* extortion.

EXACTLY (′li), *adv.* accurately ; precisely.

EXAGGERATE (egz-aj′er-at), *v.t.* to enlarge or heighten by overstatement.

EXALT (-awlt′), *v.t.* to elevate in rank, glorify, or extol.

EXAMINE (-am′in), *v.t.* to scrutinize or investigate carefully.

EXAMPLE (-am′pl), *n.* a pattern ; model or copy ; sample.

EXASPERATE (egz-as′per-at), *v.t.* to irritate exceedingly.

EX CATHEDRA (eks ka-the′dra), [Latin, from the chair], with official authority.

EXCAVATE (eks′ka-vat), *v.t.* to dig or hollow out.

EXCAVATION (-va′shun), *n.* a hollow cavity formed by cutting or digging out earth.

EXCEED (ek-sed′), *v.t.* to go beyond the limit or measure of ; excel.

EXCEL (-sel′), *v.i.* to possess good qualities in a great degree : *v.t.* surpass.

EXCELLENCE (ek′se-lens), *n.* the state of excelling in anything ; superior merit.

EXCELLENCY (-len-si), *n.* a title of honour of various high officials.

EXCELLENT (-lent), *adj.* of great value, merit, or virtue.

EXCELSIOR (ek-sel′si-or), *adj.* yet higher : *n.* wood shavings used for packing.

EXCEPT (-sept′), *v.t.* to omit or leave out ; exclude.

EXCEPTION (-sep′shun), *n.* omission ; exclusion ; objection ; offence taken (with *to*).

EXCEPTIONABLE (-a-bl), *adj.* objectionable.

EXCERPT (-serpt′), *v.t.* to take out or select from, as a book ; quote.

EXCESS (-ses′), *n.* superfluity ; intemperance.

EXCESSIVE (′iv), *adj.* extreme.

EXCHANGE (eks-chanj′), *v.t.* to give in return for an equivalent ; barter : *n.* a place where merchants meet (often change).

EXCHANGEABLE (′a-bl), *adj.* that which may be exchanged ; ratable.

EXCHEQUER (-chek′er), *n.* a treasury.

EXCISABLE (ek-siz′a-bl), *adj.* dutiable.

EXCISE (-siz′), *v.t.* to levy an excise duty upon.

EXCISION (-sizh′un), *n.* destruction ; ruin ; amputation.

EXCITABILITY (-sit-ta-bil′i-ti), *n.* sensitiveness to irritation.

EXCITANT (-sit′ant), *n.* a stimulant.

EXCITATION (-ta′shun), *n.* the act of exciting.

EXCITE (-sit′), *v.t.* to animate ; rouse.

EXCITEMENT (′ment), *n.* commotion ; sensation ; stimulation.

EXCLAIM (eks-klam′), *v.i.* & *v.t.* to cry out abruptly.

EXCLAMATION (-kla-ma′shun), *n.* an abrupt or clamorous outcry ; a mark (!) in writing or printing.

EXCLAMATORY (-klam′a-to-ri), *adj.* expressing exclamation.

EXCLUDE (-klud′), *v.t.* to shut out ; prohibit.

EXCLUSION (-klu′zhun), *n.* the act of excluding.

EXCLUSIVE (′siv), *adj.* shutting out from limits fixed by law.

EXCOMMUNICATE (′ni-kat), *v.t.* ᴏ punish by cutting off from membership and communication.

EXCREMENT (′kre-ment), *n.* matter

discharged from an animal after digestion.

EXCRESCENCE (-kres'ens), *n.* an unnatural or disfiguring outgrowth.

EXCRETA (-kre'ta), *n.pl.* useless matter eliminated from the body.

EXCRETORY ('to-ri), *n.* a duct or vessel that transmits excreted matter.

EXCRUCIATE (-kroo'shi-at), *v.t.* to inflict severe pains upon.

EXCULPATE (-kul'pat), *v.t.* to exonerate.

EXCULPATORY ('pa-to-ri), *adj.* vindicatory.

EXCURSION (-ker'shun), *n.* a pleasure trip ; a short or rapid tour.

EXCUSABLE (-kuz'a-bl), *adv.* pardonable.

EXCUSE (-kuz'), *v.t.* to pardon : (-kus'), *n.* apology ; pretext.

EXECRATE (ek'se-krat), *v.t.* to imprecate ; detest.

EXECRATION (-kra'shun), *n.* imprecation ; detestation.

EXECUTE ('se-kut), *v.t.* to perform ; carry into effect ; put to death.

EXECUTION (-ku'shun), *n.* performance ; completion ; capital punishment.

EXECUTIVE (egs-ek'u-tiv), *adj.* administrative ; active : *n.* an official or body ; the administrative branch of a government.

EXECUTOR ('u-ter), *n.* a person appointed by a testator to see that the terms of his will are carried out.

EXECUTORY ('u-to-ri), *adj.* pertaining to the execution of laws.

EXECUTRIX ('u-triks), *n.* a woman who serves as an executor.

EXEGESIS (ek-se-je'sis), *n.* explanation or interpretation of a text or passage, especially of the Bible.

EXEMPLAR (egz-em'plar), *n.* something serving as a model ; example.

EXEMPLARY (-em'pla-ri), *adj.* serving as a copy or model.

EXEMPLIFY ('pli-fi), *v.t.* to illustrate by example ; transcribe.

EXEMPT (-empt'), *v.t.* grant immunity to : *adj.* free from some duty or obligation (with *from*).

EXEMPTION (-zemp'shun), *n.* state of being exempt.

EXERCISE (ek'ser-siz), *v.t.* to exert ; practise ; employ actively ; make anxious : *v.i.* to undergo training : *n.* bodily exertion.

EXERT (-ert'), *v.t.* to put forth ; use with an effort.

EXEUNT (ek'se-unt), *n.* they go out ; a common direction in plays.

EXFOLIATION (-fo-li-a'shun), *n.* the act of scaling or peeling off.

EXHALATION (eks-ha-la'shun), *n.* the act of exhaling ; emanation.

EXHALE (-hal'), *v.t.* to breathe forth ; cause to evaporate.

EXHAUST (egz-awst'), *v.t.* to drain ; weaken ; wear out by exertion ; discuss.

EXHAUSTIBLE ('ti-bl), *adj.* capable of being exhausted.

EXHAUSTION (-awst'chun), *n.* lack of strength or energy.

EXHIBIT (egz-ib'it, eks-hib'it), *v.t.* to present to view ; display ; show.

EXHIBITION (ex-hi-bish'un), *n.* the act of exhibiting ; a public show.

EXHILARATE (egz-il'a-rat, eks-hil'a-rat), *v.t.* to make joyous ; enliven.

EXHORT (egz-ort', eks-hort'), *v.t.* to incite by appeal ; caution ; admonish.

EXHORTATORY ('ta-to-ri), *adj.* tending to exhort.

EXHUME (eks-hum'), *v.t.* to disinter.

EXIGENCY (ek'si-jen-si), *n.* pressing necessity ; urgency.

EXILE (ek'sil), *v.t.* to banish from one's native country.

EXIST (eg-zist'), *v.i.* to have existence.

EXISTENCE ('tens), *n.* life ; duration ; occurrence.

EXISTENT ('tent), *adj.* having being.

EXIT (ek'sit), *n.* the act of going out ; egress.

EXO-, a prefix denoting *out of, outside.*

EX OFFICIO (o-fish'i-o), by virtue of office.

EXONERATE (egz-on'er-at), *v.t.* to free from the imputation of a fault ; acquit ; justify.

EXORBITANCE (egz-or'bi-tans), *n.* going beyond due limits ; excess.

EXORBITANT (-tant), *adj.* excessive.

EXORCISE (eks'or-siz), *v.t.* to expel (an evil spirit), by incantations

EXORCISM (-sizm), *n.* the act of expelling evil spirits.

EXOTERIC (so-ter′ik), *adj.* external; public; opposed to *esoteric*.

EXOTIC (egz-ot′ik), *adj.* foreign.

EXPAND (eks-pand′), *v.t.* to distend; dilate.

EXPANSE (-pans′), *n.* a continuous area; the firmament; extent.

EXPANSIBLE (-pan′si-bl), *adj.* capable of, or permitting, expansion.

EXPANSION (-pan′shun), *n.* the state of being expanded.

EXPANSIVE (′siv), *adj.* widely extended; large.

EX PARTE (par′te), one-sided.

EXPATIATE (eks-pa′shi-at), *v.i.* to enlarge in statement or language.

EXPATRIATE (-pat′ri-at), *v.t.* to drive from one's native country.

EXPECT (-pekt′), *v.t.* to wait for; look for with an apprehension.

EXPECTANCE (′tans), *n.* the act or state of expecting.

EXPECTANT (′tant), *adj.* waiting in expectation; presumptive.

EXPECTATION (-ta′shun), *n.* the act of looking forward to; anticipation.

EXPECTORANT (′to-rant), *n.* a medicine that promotes expectoration.

EXPECTORATE (′to-rat), *v.t.* to eject from the lungs by coughing, etc.; spit.

EXPEDIENCY (eks-pe′di-en-si), *n.* fitness; propriety.

EXPEDIENT (′di-ent), *adj.* fit; convenient; suitable: *n.* device.

EXPEDITE (′pe-dit), *v.t.* to hasten; facilitate.

EXPEDITION (-dish′un), *n.* haste; despatch; a march, voyage, etc.

EXPEDITIONARY (-a-ri), *adj.* pertaining to, or constituting, an expedition.

EXPEDITIOUS (′us), *adj.* quick; speedy.

EXPEL (-pel′), *v.t.* to drive away; force out; exclude.

EXPEND (-pend′), *v.t.* to lay out; spend.

EXPENDITURE (′di-tur), *n.* a laying out, as money, time, labour, etc.

EXPENSE (-pens′), *n.* expenditure; drain on resources; cost.

EXPENSIVE (-pen′siv), *adj.* causing expense; high-priced.

EXPERIENCE (-pe′ri-ens), *n.* knowledge gained by trial and practice; test.

EXPERIMENT (-per′i-ment), *n.* a trial or operation to discover something.

EXPERIMENTAL (′tal), *adj.* pertaining to experiment; learned by experience.

EXPERT (-pert′), *adj.* skilful; adroit.

EXPERT (eks′pert), *n.* a specialist.

EXPIATE (′pi-at), *v.t.* to atone for.

EXPIATORY (-a-to-ri), *adj.* having the nature of atonement.

EXPIRATION (-pi-ra′shun), *n.* termination.

EXPIRE (-pir′), *v.t.* to breathe out from the lungs: *v.i.* to die.

EXPLAIN (-plan′), *v.t.* to make intelligible or clear.

EXPLANATION (-pla-na′shun), *n.* elucidation; interpretation.

EXPLANATORY (-plan′a-to-ri), *adj.* serving to explain.

EXPLETIVE (′ple-tiv), *n.* a word not necessary for the sense inserted in a sentence for ornament.

EXPLICABLE (′pli-ka-bl), *adj.* that may be explained or interpreted.

EXPLICIT (-plis′it), *adj.* plain; definite.

EXPLODE (-plod′), *v.i.* to burst forth with sudden noise and violence; collapse; refute.

EXPLOIT (-ploit′), *v.t.* to make use of for one's own profit; put to use: *n.* a remarkable deed.

EXPLOITATION (-ploi-ta′shun), *n.* the improvement of lands, working of mines, etc.; selfish utilization.

EXPLORATION (-plo-ra′shun), *n.* the act of exploring; careful investigation or search.

EXPLORE (-plor′), *v.t.* to search into or examine thoroughly.

EXPLOSION (-plo′zhun), *n.* a sudden bursting with a loud report.

EXPLOSIVE (′siv), *n.* any substance that causes an explosion.

EXPONENT (-po′nent), *n.* the index

of an algebraical power; one who explains or interprets.

EXPONENTIAL (-nen'shal), *adj.* pertaining to an exponent.

EXPORT (-port'), *v.t.* to send or carry out of a country, as merchandise : *v.i.* to send goods to a foreign country ; (eks'port), *n.* a commodity exported.

EXPOSE (-poz'), *v.t.* to lay open ; put forward for sale ; disclose ; lay open to censure or ridicule.

EXPOSITION (-zish'un), *n.* an explanation ; an exhibition.

EXPOSITOR (-poz'i-ter), *n.* one who expounds or interprets.

EXPOSITORY ('i-to-ri), *adj.* serving to elucidate or explain.

EX POST FACTO (post fak'to), [Latin, from an after act], by virtue of something done afterwards.

EXPOSTULATE (-pos'tu-lat), *v.i.* to reason earnestly or remonstrate (followed by *with*, *on* or *upon*).

EXPOSURE (-po'zhur), *n.* the act of exposing ; situation.

EXPOUND (-pound'), *v.t.* to set forth ; make clear.

EXPRESS (-pres'), *v.t.* to utter ; show ; represent ; squeeze out ; despatch by express : *adj.* exact ; resembling precisely : *n.* an express-train.

EXPRESSIBLE ('i-bl), *adj.* capable of being expressed.

EXPRESSION (-presh'un), *n.* a saying ; mode of speech ; transient change of the countenance.

EXPRESSIVE (-pres'iv), *adj.* serving to express forcibly.

EXPRESSMAN ('man), *n.* the person who takes charge of express matter.

EXPULSION (-pul'shun), *n.* forcible ejection.

EXPUNGE (-punj'), *v.t.* to erase.

EXPURGATE ('per-gat), *v.t.* to remove whatever is offensive to good taste or morality from.

EXPURGATOR (eks'per-ga-ter), *n.* one who expurgates books, etc.

EXQUISITE ('kwi-zit), *adj.* refined ; delicate ; nice : *n.* a dandy.

EXTANT ('tant), *adj.* still existing.

EXTEMPORANEOUS (-tem-po-ra'-ne-us), *adj.* unpremeditated ; without previous study.

EXTEMPORE (-tem'po-re), *adv.* without study or premeditation.

EXTEMPORIZE ('po-riz), *v.t.* to compose on the spur of the moment.

EXTEND (-tend'), *v.t.* to enlarge ; amplify ; continue ; diffuse.

EXTENSION ('shun), *n.* the act of extending ; a branch line of railway, etc. ; space regarded as having dimensions.

EXTENSIVE ('siv), *adj.* having great extent ; wide.

EXTENSIVELY (-li), *adv.* widely ; largely.

EXTENT (-tent'), *n.* size ; compass ; reach.

EXTENUATE (-ten'u-at), *v.t.* to offer excuses for ; mitigate.

EXTENUATORY (-to-ri), *adj.* palliative.

EXTERIOR (-te'ri-er), *adj.* outward ; external : *n.* outer surface.

EXTERMINATE (-ter'mi-nat), *v.t.* to annihilate ; root out.

EXTERMINATION (-na'shun), *n.* total destruction.

EXTERMINATOR (-na-ter), *n.* one who, or that which, exterminates.

EXTERN (-tern'), *n.* a non-resident scholar.

EXTERNAL (-ter'nal), *adj.* outside ; exterior ; superficial.

EXTINCT (-tingkt'), *adj.* extinguished; no longer existing.

EXTINGUISH (-ting'gwish), *v.t.* to put out ; render legally dead.

EXTINGUISHER (-er), *n.* one who, or that which, extinguishes.

EXTIRPATE ('ter-pat), *v.t.* to eradicate ; destroy ; exterminate.

EXTIRPATIVE (-tiv), *adj.* capable of, or tending to, extirpate.

EXTOL (tol'), *v.t.* to praise highly ; magnify.

EXTORT (-tort'), *v.t.* to obtain by threats, violence, or injustice.

EXTORTION (-tor'shun), *n.* oppressive or unjust exaction.

EXTORTIONATE ('shun-at), *adj.* characterized by extortion ; unjust.

EXTORTIONER ('shun-er), *n.* one who practises extortion.

EXTRA ('tra), *adj.* additional : *n.* an edition of a newspaper issued for some particular object.

EXTRACT (-trakt'), *v.t.* to draw out of : *n.* (eks'trakt), a substance extracted by distillation, solution, etc. ; an abstract or excerpt from a book ; quotation.

EXTRACTION (-trak'shun), *n.* the act of extracting ; lineage, birth, or descent.

EXTRADITE ('tra-dit), *v.t.* to surrender (a person), to another government under the terms of a treaty of extradition.

EXTRADITION (-dish'un), *n.* the surrender by the government of one nation to another of a person guilty of a crime, in accordance with the terms of a treaty existing between the two nations.

EXTRANEOUS (-tra'ne-us), *adj.* external ; not essential.

EXTRAORDINARY (-tror'di-na-ri, -tra-or'di-na-ri), *adj.* uncommon ; unusual ; remarkable ; rare ; eminent ; special.

EXTRAVAGANCE (-trav'a-gans), *n.* excess in anything, especially expenditure.

EXTRAVAGANT ('a-gant), *adj.* wasteful ; prodigal ; irregular ; visionary.

EXTREME (-trem'), *adj.* of the highest degree ; last ; utmost ; furthest ; final : *pl.* points at the greatest distance from each other.

EXTREMIST (-trem'ist), *n.* a supporter of extreme views or practice.

EXTREMITY (-trem'i-ti), *n.* the utmost point or degree ; remotest part ; utmost violence, vigour, or necessity ; end : *pl.* the limbs.

EXTRICATE ('tri-kat), *v.t.* to free from difficulties ; disembarrass.

EXTRINSIC (-trin'sik), *adj.* external ; not essential ; foreign.

EXTROVERSION (-tro-ver'shun), *n.* the turning of an inner part outward.

EXTRUDE (-trood'), *v.t.* to thrust out.

EXUBERANCE (egz-u'ber-ans), *n.* superabundance.

EXUBERANT (-ant), *adj.* copious.

EXUDE (eks-ud'), *v.t.* to discharge gradually through pores.

EXULT (egz-ult'), *v.i.* to rejoice in triumph ; be glad above measure.

EXULTANT ('tant), *adj.* rejoicing triumphantly.

EXULTATION (-ta'shun), *n.* joy over a victory ; rapturous delight.

EYE (i), *n.* the organ of sight ; the eyeball ; sight ; a small perforation ; bud.

EYEWITNESS ('wit-nes), *n.* one who testifies to what he has seen.

F

F, f (ef), *n.* the sixth letter in the English alphabet.

F, f, *n.* an abbreviation.

F, *n.* a medieval Roman numeral denoting 40 ; with a bar (F̄), 40,000.

F MAJOR (ma'jer), a major key or scale indicated by one flat.

F MINOR (mi-ner), a minor key or scale indicated by four flats.

F PANEL (pan'el), a panel formed like capital F.

F SHARP (sharp), a tone half a step above that of F.

F SHARP MAJOR, a major key or scale indicated by six sharps.

F SHARP MINOR, a minor key or scale indicated by three sharps.

FA (fa), *n.* the fourth note in the sol-fa musical notation ; the subdominant of any major key.

FABLE (fa'bl), *n.* a short fictitious narrative intended to convey some moral ; an idle story.

FABRIC (fab'rik), *n.* a building ; a woven, felted, or knitted material.

FABRICATE ('ri-kat), *v.t.* to construct ; invent falsely.

FABRICATOR (-ka-ter), *n.* one who fabricates.

FABULIST ('u-list), *n.* a writer of fables.

FABULOUS ('u-lus), *adj.* fictitious ; mythical.

FACADE (fa-sad'), *n.* [French], a face or front ; front elevation.

FACE (fas), *n.* the countenance ; front ; visage ; surface : *v.t.* to meet in front.

FACET (fas'et), *n.* a small surface or face.

FACETIOUS (fa-se'shus), *adj.* humorous ; jocular.

FACIAL (fa'shal), *adj.* pertaining to the face.

FACIES ('shi-ez), *n.* the face ; the general aspect of any group of organisms or of rocks.

FACILE (fas'il), *adj.* yielding ; affable.

FACILITATE (fa-sil'i-tat), *v.t.* to make easy or less difficult.

FACILITY ('i-ti), *n.* dexterity ; ease ; pliancy ; ready compliance.

FACING (fas'ing), *n.* a covering in front for ornamental or other purposes.

FACSIMILE (fak-sim'i-le), *n.* an exact reproduction of an original.

FACT (fakt), *n.* reality ; event ; truth.

FACTION (fak'shun), *n.* a party in disloyal opposition ; dissension.

FACTIOUS ('shus), *adj.* given to, or characterized by, faction ; turbulent.

FACTITIOUS (-tish'us), *adj.* artificial ; sham.

FACTOR ('ter), *n.* an agent who transacts business for another ; one of two or more quantities (multiplier and multiplicand) which, multiplied together, give a product ; any circumstances, etc., which produces a result.

FACTORY ('to-ri), *n.* a manufactory ; a trading settlement.

FACTOTUM (-to'tum), *n.* a man of all work.

FACULTY ('ul-ti), *n.* any mental or physical power ; mental capacity ; ability ; ease ; the members collectively of any one of the learned professions.

FAD (fad), *n.* a pet idea or hobby.

FADE (fad), *v.i.* to lose colour or distinctness ; languish ; wither.

FAG (fag), *v.i.* to work hard ; grow weary ; drudge for another.

FAG-END ('end), *n.* the latter or meaner part of anything.

FAGOT, FAGGOT ('ot), *n.* a bundle of sticks, twigs, or branches.

FAHRENHEIT (fa'ren-hit), *n.* a thermometer scale, having 32° as the freezing point and 212° as the boiling point of water.

FAIL (fal), *v.i.* to fall short ; decline ; turn out badly ; become bankrupt : *v.t.* to be wanting, or insufficient for.

FAILING ('ing), *n.* a fault ; weakness ; infirmity.

FAILURE (fal'ur), *n.* the act of failing ; omission ; want of success ; lapse.

FAIN (fan), *adv.* willingly, gladly.

FAINT (fant), *v.i.* to become feeble ; lose consciousness ; swoon ; lose courage and hope : *adj.* feeble ; languid.

FAIR (far), *adj.* beautiful ; handsome ; pleasing to the eye or mind ; not cloudy ; fine ; favourable ; just ; a market held at particular times.

FAIRY (far'i), *n.* an elf ; fay ; sprite ; brownie.

FAIRYLAND (-land), *n.* supposed abode of fairies.

FAITH (fath), *n.* belief ; trust ; fidelity ; honesty ; a system of doctrines or tenets.

FAITHFUL (fool'), *adj.* trustworthy ; truthful ; loyal : *n.* Christians in full communion (with *the*).

FAKE (fak), *v.t.* to cover up imperfections with the view to deception : *n.* canard ; hoax ; a swindler.

FAKER ('er), *n.* one who fakes ; a swindler ; pickpocket.

FALCON (fawl'kn, faw'kn), *n.* a predatory bird trained for hunting.

FALL (fawl), *v.i.* to drop from a higher to a lower place ; descend ; sink ; flow into ; perish.

FALLACIOUS (fal-la'shus), *adj.* deceptive.

FALLACY ('a-si), *n.* a mistake ; an unsound method of reasoning ; sophism.

FALLEN (fawl'n), *p.adj.* degraded ; ruined ; outcast ; overthrown ; dead.

FALLIBILITY (fal-i-bil'i-ti), *n.* the state of being fallible ; liability to err.

FALLIBLE ('i-bl), *adj.* liable to be

deceived, or mislead ; prone to err, or fail.

FALLING (fawl'ing), *p.adj.* moving or hanging downwards ; sinking.

FALLOW (fal'o), *adj.* ploughed but not sown for the season ; untilled.

FALLOW-DEER (-der), *n.* a deer of yellowish-brown colour.

FALSE (fawls), *adj.* untrue ; dishonest ; disloyal.

FALSEHOOD ('hood), *n.* a lie.

FALSETTO (fawl-set'o), *n.* an artificial tone higher in key than the natural compass of the voice.

FALSIFICATION (-si-fi-ka'shun), *n.* wilful misrepresentation.

FALSIFY ('si-fi), *v.t.* to counterfeit ; forge : *v.i.* to lie.

FALSITY ('si-ti), *n.* an untruth ; false statement.

FALTER ('ter), *v.t.* to utter in a weak, trembling manner (with *out*).

FAME (fam), *n.* public report ; celebrity ; renown.

FAMILIAR (fa-mil'yer), *adj.* well acquainted, or intimate, with ; domestic ; affable ; easy.

FAMILIARITY (-i-ar'i-ti), *n.* intimacy ; freedom from conventionality.

FAMILIARIZE ('yer-iz), *v.t.* make familiar ; habituate.

FAMILY (fam'i-li), *n.* a household ; a body of persons descended from a common ancestor ; tribe ; race ; genealogy ; noble lineage ; class ; a group of animals larger than a genus.

FAMINE (fam'in), *n.* extreme dearth ; great scarcity.

FAMISH ('ish), *v.t.* & *v.i.* to starve.

FAMOUS (fa'mus), *adj.* renowned ; conspicuous ; noted.

FAN (fan), *v.t.* to cool with a fan ; ventilate ; winnow : *n.* an enthusiastic lover of any sport ; an instrument used for exciting a current of air.

FANATIC (fa-nat'ik), *n.* one who is intemperately zealous : *adj.* visionary.

FANATICISM ('i-sizm), *n.* extravagant or frenzied zeal.

FANCIED (fan'sid), *adj.* imaginary.

FANCIER ('si-er), *n.* one who breeds or sells animals and birds.

FANCIFUL ('si-fool), *adj.* unreal ; whimsical ; wild.

FANCY ('si), *v.t.* to imagine ; take liking to : *adj.* ornamental ; elegant.

FANE (fan), *n.* a temple ; church.

FANFARE (fan'far), *n.* a flourish of trumpets ; noise.

FANG (fang), *n.* the poison-tooth of a serpent ; a tusk.

FANTAIL (fan'tal), *n.* a variety of pigeon.

FANTAN ('tan), *n.* a Chinese gambling game.

FANTASIA ('ta, ta'zhi-a), *n.* a medley of familiar airs.

FANTASTIC (-tas'tik), *adj.* odd ; whimsical ; grotesque ; also fantastical.

FANTASY, see phantasy.

FAR (far), *adj.* remote ; distant ; extending widely or at length.

FARAD (far'ad), *n.* a unit of electric capacity.

FARCE (fars), *n.* a short comedy.

FARCICAL (far'si-kal), *adj.* ludicrous.

FARE (far), *v.i.* to be in any state, either good or ill ; live ; succeed ; result : *n.* the sum paid for transportation ; provisions of a table ; entertainment.

FARINA (fa-re', fa-ri'na), *n.* starch, flour or meal.

FARINACEOUS (-na'shus), *adj.* like meal.

FARINOSE (far'i-nos), *adj.* mealy.

FARM (farm), *n.* a portion of land, cultivated.

FARMER ('mer), *n.* one who cultivates a farm ; agriculturist.

FARMERETTE ('ette), *n.* a girl or woman engaged in farm work.

FARO (fa'ro), *n.* a game of chance, played with cards.

FARRAGO (fa-ra'go), *n.* a medley.

FARRIER (far'i-er), *n.* one who shoes horses ; a veterinary.

FARTHER (far'*th*er), *adj.* more distant or remote.

FARTHING ('*th*ing), *n.* ¼ of an English penny.

FASCINATE (fas'i-nat), *v.t.* to bewitch ; captivate.

FASCINATION (-na'shun), *n.* any invisible influence that overpowers the mind or will.

FASCISTI (fa-she'sta, fas-kes'ti), *n.*

Italian reform party organized in 1919 to oppose all radical and revolutionary movements in Italy. Benito Mussolini became premier (1922).

FASHION (fash'un), *n.* the shape or form of anything; conventional custom.

FASHIONABLE (-a-bl), *adj.* according to the prevailing mode.

FASHION-PLATE (fash'un-plat), *n.* a drawing representing the current fashions in dress.

FAST (fast), *v.i.* to abstain from food.

FAST (fast), *adj.* quick; speedy in motion; expeditious; firm; immovable; dissipated.

FASTENING (fas'n-ing), *n.* a bolt or clasp.

FASTIDIOUS (-tid'i-us), *adj.* overnice; hard to please.

FASTING (fast'ing), *n.* abstinence from food.

FASTNESS ('nes), *n.* a fortress or natural stronghold.

FAT (fat), *adj.* corpulent; fleshy; adipose; greasy.

FATAL (fa'tal), *adj.* causing death; mortal; fateful.

FATALISM (-izm), *n.* the doctrine that all things happen by irresistible necessity.

FATALIST (-ist), *n.* a believer in fatalism.

FATALITY ('i-ti), *n.* predetermined order or series of events; destiny; a calamity.

FATE (fat), *n.* destiny: *pl.* [F-], the three classic goddesses, Clotho, Lachesis, and Atropos.

FATED (fa'ted), *p.adj.* decreed by fate; destined.

FATHER (fa'ther), *n.* a male parent.

FATHERLY (-li), *adv.* like a father.

FATHOM (farh'um), *n.* a measure of length=6 ft.: *v.t.* to reach; ascertain depth of.

FATIGUE (fa-teg'), *n.* weariness.

FATIGUE DUTY (du'ti), any labour assigned to a soldier.

FATLING ('ling), *n.* a young animal fattened for slaughter.

FATTEN ('n), *v.t.* to make fat, plump, or stout; feed for the table; make fertile or abundant.

FATUITY (fa-tu'i-ti), *n.* weakness of intellect; obstinate folly.

FATUOUS (fat'u-us), *adj.* silly; obstinately foolish; illusory.

FAUCES (faw'sez), *n.pl.* the upper part of the throat.

FAUCET ('set), *n.* a short pipe with a valve.

FAUGH (faw), *interj.* an exclamation expressive of disgust.

FAULT (fawlt), *n.* a slight crime or offence; blemish; defect.

FAULTFINDER ('fin-der), *n.* one given to finding fault.

FAULTY ('ti), *adj.* imperfect.

FAUN (fawn), *n.* a classic woodland deity, resembling a satyr.

FAUNA (faw'na), *n.* [*pl.* faunæ ('ne)], the animals characteristic of any particular region.

FAUX PAS (fo pa'), [French], an error or slip in respect of good manners.

FAVOUR (fa'ver), *n.* kindness; support; patronage; good will; facility: *v.t.* to befriend.

FAVOURABLE (-a-bl), *adj.* advantageous; friendly; partial.

FAVOURITE (-it), *n.* one who, or that which, is particularly esteemed; one regarded with undue preference: *adj.* preferred; esteemed.

FAWN (fawn), *n.* a young deer: *v.i. & v.t.* to court servilely (with *on* or *upon*).

FAWNING ('ing), *n.* gross flattery.

FAY (fa), *n.* an elf; fairy.

FAZE (faz), *v.i.* to worry; annoy.

FEALTY (fe'al-ti), *n.* loyalty; fidelity.

FEAR (fer), *n.* apprehension of evil or danger; dread; anxiety: *v.i.* to be in fear.

FEARFUL ('fool), *adj.* timorous; apprehensive; inspiring fear.

FEARLESS ('les), *adj.* intrepid.

FEARSOME (fer'sum), *adj.* fearful; terrible.

FEASIBILITY (fe-zi-bil'i-ti), *n.* practicability.

FEASIBLE (fe'zi-bl), *adj.* practicable.

FEAST (fest), *n.* a sumptuous repast.

FEAT (fet), *n.* a notable achievement or performance.

FEATHER (feth'er), *n.* part of the

exterior covering of a bird ; a plume.

FEATHERY (-i), *adj.* resembling feathers ; very light.

FEATURE (fe'tur), *n.* lineament ; outline ; characteristic ; appearance.

FEAZE (fez), *v.t.* to disturb.

FEBRIFUGE (feb'ri-fuj), *n.* a medicine that lessens or dispels fever.

FEBRILE (feb', fe'bril), *adj.* pertaining to fever.

FEBRUARY (feb'roo-a-ri), *n.* the second month of the year.

FECKLESS (fek'less), *adj.* trifling ; shiftless.

FECULA (fek'u-la), *n.* farina.

FECULENCE ('lens), *n.* dregs.

FECULENT ('lent), *adj.* turbid.

FECUND (fek', fe'kund), *adj.* fruitful ; prolific.

FECUNDATE (fek'un-dat), *v.t.* to make prolific ; fertilize.

FECUNDITY (fe-kun'di-ti), *n.* fruitfulness ; prolificness ; germination.

FEDERAL (fed'er-al), *adj.* pertaining to a league or treaty.

FEDERAL, *adj.* supporting the cause of the Union in the American civil war (1861-'65).

FEDERALISM (-izm), *n.* the doctrine of federal union.

FEDERALIZE (-iz), *v.i.* to bring together in a political federacy.

FEDERATE (-at), *adj.* united by compact.

FEDERATION (-a'shun), *n.* a league.

FEE (fe), *n.* a compensat on ; a gratuity.

FEEBLE (fe'bl), *adj.* weak ; infirm.

FEED (fed), *v.t.* to give food to ; graze or pasture : *v.i.* to eat ; subsist (with *on* or *upon*).

FEEL (fel), *v.t.* to be conscious of ; test : *n.* touch ; sensation.

FEELING ('ing), *p.adj.* easily affected ; sympathetic : *n.* sense of touch.

FEE SIMPLE (fe sim'pl), an estate held by a person in his own right.

FEIGN (fan), *v.t.* to pretend ; invent.

FEINT (fant), *n.* a pretence ; mock attack.

FELICITATE (fe-lis'i-tat), *v.t.* to congratulate.

FELICITATION (fe-lis'i-ta'shun), *n.* congratulation.

FELICITOUS ('i-tus), *adj.* happiness ;

appropriate.

FELICITOUSLY (-li), *adv.* suitably.

FELICITY ('i-ti), *n.* a condition of happiness ; prosperity ; appropriateness.

FELINE (fe'lin), *adj.* resembling a cat ; stealthy ; treacherous.

FELL (fel), *v.t.* to hew, cut, or knock down ; turn down (a seam) : *adj.* cruel ; savage ; hideous.

FELLOE ('o), *n.* one of the curved pieces of wood which form the rim of a wheel.

FELLOW ('o), *n.* a companion or associate ; an individual.

FELLOWSHIP (-ship), *n.* association ; communion ; intimacy ; society.

FELON (fel'un), *n.* one guilty of felony ; a whitlow.

FELONIOUS (fe-lo'ni-us), *adj.* malignant.

FELONY (fel'o-ni), *n.* a crime punishable by death or imprisonment.

FELT (felt), *n.* fabric compacted by pressure or heat.

FELTING ('ing), *n.* the material of felt.

FEMALE (fe'mal), *adj.* pertaining to that sex which produces young ; feminine ; womanly.

FEME COVERTE (fem kuv'ert), *n.* a married woman.

FEME SOL (sol), *n.* an unmarried woman.

FEMININE (fem'i-nin), *adj.* pertaining to, or characteristic of, women ; delicate.

FEMININITY ('i-ti), *n.* the state of being feminine ; womankind.

FEMINISM (fem'in-izm), *n.* a movement of women towards equality with man.

FEMME DE CHAMBRE (fam' de shang'br), *n.* a lady's-maid.

FEMORAL (fem'o-ral), *adj.* pertaining to the thigh.

FEMUR (fe'mur), *n.* the thigh-bone.

FEN (fen), *n.* low, flat, marsh land.

FENCE (fens), *n.* defence ; guard ; a boundary consisting of posts, wire, etc. ; enclosure ; a receiver of stolen goods.

FENCING ('sing), *n.* the art of skilfully using a foil or sword.

FEND (fend), *v.t.* to ward off.

FENDER ('der), *n.* any protecting device.

FENNEL (fen'el), *n.* an aromatic herb.

FENNY ('i), *adj.* marshy.

FER-DE-LANCE (fer-de-langs'), *n.* a poisonous snake of the West Indies and South America.

FERIAL ('ri-al), *adj.* pertaining to weekdays and holidays.

FERMENT (fer'ment), *n.* internal commotion; tumult : *v.t.* (fer-ment'), to produce fermentation in; excite.

FERMENTATION (-men-ta'shun), *n.* the chemical decomposition which takes place in an organic substance.

FERN (fern), *n.* a cryptogamous or flowerless plant.

FERNERY ('er-i), *n.* a place for ferns.

FEROCIOUS (fe-ro'shus), *adj.* savage; fierce; rapacious; of cruel nature.

FEROCITY (-ros'i-ti), *n.* savageness; inhuman cruelty.

FERRATE (fer'at), *n.* a salt of ferric acid.

FERRET (fer'et), *n.* a domesticated variety of weasel : *v.t.* to search minutely.

FERRO BRONZE (fer'o-bronz), *n.* an alloy composed of iron, copper and zinc.

FERROUS (fer'us), *adj.* pertaining to, or obtained from, iron.

FERRULE (fer'ool), *n.* a metal cap placed at the end of a stick, etc.

FERRY ('i), *n.* a passage across a river, etc.; a ferry-boat : *v.t.* to convey across a river, etc., in a boat.

FERTILE (fer'til), *adj.* fruitful; reproductive; rich in resources or invention.

FERTILITY (-til'i-ti), *n.* abundance; fecundity; richness of resources or invention.

FERTILIZATION (-i-za'shun), *n.* the act or process of making fertile.

FERTILIZE ('ti-liz), *v.t.* to make fertile; impregnate.

FERTILIZER (-er), *n.* any material used as a manure for the land.

FERULE (fer'ool), *n.* a rod or flat stick.

FERVENCY (fer'ven-si), *n.* earnestness; ardour.

FERVENT ('vent), *adj.* zealous.

FERVENTLY ('li), *adv.* with fervour.

FERVID ('vid), *adj.* burning; ardent; fiery; intense; eager.

FERVOUR ('ver), *n.* zeal; warmth.

FESTAL (fes'tal), *adj.* joyous; festive; hilarious.

FESTER ('ter), *v.i.* to become ulcerated; suppurate; rankle.

FESTIVAL ('ti-val), *n.* a joyful celebration.

FESTIVE ('tiv), *adj.* gay; joyous; merry.

FESTIVITY (-tiv'i-ti), *n.* social gaiety.

FESTOON (-toon'), *n.* a wreath or garland suspended in a curve : *v.t.* to decorate with.

FETCH (fech), *v.t.* to go after and bring; obtain as its price.

FETE (fat), *n.* a festival or holiday : *v.t.* to entertain.

FETE DAY (da), a birthday celebration.

FETID (fe'tid, fet'id), *adj.* giving forth an offensive smell.

FETISH (fe'tish, fet'ish), *n.* any material object supposed to give to its possessor power over a deity.

FETISHISM (-izm), *n.* belief in fetishes; superstitious devotions.

FETLOCK ('lok), *n.* a tuft of hair behind a horse's pastern joint.

FETTER ('er), *n.* a chain or shackle for the feet (usually *pl.*).

FEUD (fud), *n.* a vindictive quarrel between clans or families.

FEUILLETON (foo-i-tong'), *n.* a newspaper serial.

FEVER (fe'ver), *n.* a disease characterized by marked increase of heat of the skin.

FEW (fu), *adj.* not many; limited.

FEZ (fez), *n.* a brimless, felt hat worn by Turks, Egyptians, etc.

FIANCE (fe-ang-sa'), *n.* [French], one betrothed for marriage. *Fem.* fiancée.

FIASCO (fe-as'ko), *n.* a complete or ludicrous failure.

FIAT (fi'at), *n.* a peremptory decree.

FIB (fib), *n.* a falsehood.

FIBBER ('er), *n.* one who fibs.

FIBRIL (fi'bril), *n.* a small fibre.

FICHU (fe-shoo'), *n.* [French], a light three-cornered article of ladies' dress.

FICKLE (fik′l), *adj.* capricious.

FICTILE (fik′til), *adj.* readily moulded.

FICTION (′shun), *n.* the act of feigning or inventing ; a literary production of the imagination.

FICTITIOUS (-tish′us), *adj.* pertaining to fiction ; false ; unreal.

FIDDLE (fid′l), *n.* a violin.

FIDDLER (fid′ler), *n.* a violinist.

FIDELITY (fi-del′i-ti), *n.* integrity ; honesty ; loyalty ; reliability.

FIDGET (fij′et), *n.* one who is fidgety ; nervous restlessness ; often in *pl.*

FIDGETY (′et-i), *adj.* restless.

FIDUCIAL (fi-du′shal), *adj.* of the nature of a trust ; confident.

FIDUCIARY (′shi-a-ri), *n.* a trustee : *adj.* confident ; unwavering.

FIE (fi), *interj.* for shame !

FIELD (feld), *n.* a piece of land for tillage or pasture ; sphere of action ; a wide expanse.

FIELD DAY (da), *n.* a military review ; a day of unusual excitement.

FIELD MARSHAL (mar′shal), *n.* highest rank in the British army.

FIEND (fend), *n.* one who is intensely wicked ; a monomaniac.

FIENDISH (′ish), *adj.* like a fiend.

FIERCE (fers), *adj.* savage ; violent ; ferocious.

FIERCELY (′li), *adv.* in a fierce manner.

FIERINESS (fi′e-ri-nes), *n.* the quality of being fiery.

FIERY (fi′er-i), *adj.* pertaining to fire ; passionate ; easily roused.

FIFE (fif), *n.* a shrill-toned musical instrument of the flute class.

FIFTEEN (fif′ten), *adj.* consisting of 5 and 10.

FIFTEENTH (′tenth), *n.* one of 15 equal parts.

FIFTH (fifth), *n.* one of 5 equal parts.

FIFTIETH (fif′ti-eth), *n.* one of 50 equal parts.

FIFTY (′ti), *adj.* consisting of five times 10.

FIG (fig), *n.* the fruit of the fig-tree.

FIGHT (fit), *v.i.* contend in battle ; offer resistance : *n.* a combat ; contest.

FIGMENT (′ment), *n.* something feigned or imagined.

FIGURATIVE (′ur-a-tiv), *adj.* representing by figure ; symbolical.

FIGURE (′ur), *n.* the outline or shape of a person or object ; appearance ; idea ; pattern ; type ; sign or character denoting a number : *v.i.* to be conspicuous ; cipher.

FIGUREHEAD (-hed), *n.* a carved figure placed at the prow of a ship.

FIGWORT (fig′wert), *n.* a plant.

FILAMENT (fil′a-ment), *n.* a fine thread.

FILBERT (fil′bert), *n.* the edible nut of the cultivated hazel.

FILCH (filch), *v.t.* to pilfer ; rob.

FILE (fil), *n.* an orderly record of papers ; a line of soldiers ; a tool of hard steel with small grooves : *v.t.* to cut or smooth with a file ; place papers on a file.

FILIAL (fil′i-al), *adj.* pertaining to a son or daughter ; due to a father.

FILIATION (-a′shun), *n.* affiliation.

FILIBUSTER (-i-bus′ter), *n.* a freebooter ; buccaneer ; to delay legislation by obstructive tactics.

FILIGREE (′i-gre), *adj.* made of, or relating to, work in filigree : *n.* delicate ornamental work.

FILING (fil′ing), *n.* the act of using a file : *pl.* fine fragments rubbed off by the action of a file.

FILIPINO (fil-i-pe′no), *n.* a native of the Philippine Islands.

FILL (fil), *v.t.* to make full ; satisfy ; engage ; employ ; supply : *v.i.* to become full or replete ; pour a glass or vessel full.

FILLER (′er), *n.* one who, or that which, fills ; composition for stopping up holes.

FILLET (′et), *n.* a narrow band worn around the forehead ; the fleshy part of the thigh ; said of meats.

FILLIP (′ip), *n.* a sudden sharp jerk or stroke with the finger.

FILLY (′i), *n.* a young mare.

FILM (film), *n.* a thin skin or filament ; the flexible strip used in making moving pictures.

FILMY (′i), *adj.* composed of, or resembling, films.

FILOSE (fi′los), *adj.* thread-like.

FILTER (fil′ter), *n.* any material or

apparatus by which water or any other liquid is purified.

FILTH (filth), *n.* foul matter ; dirt.

FILTHINESS (fil'thi-nes), *n.* uncleanness ; impurity.

FILTHY ('thi), *adj.* foul ; dirty ; obscene.

FILTRATE (fil'trat), *v.t.* to filter.

FIN (fin), *n.* one of the organs of locomotion of a fish.

FINABLE (fin'a-bl), *adj.* liable to a fine.

FINAL (fin'al), *adj.* pertaining to the end ; ultimate ; decisive.

FINAL CAUSE (kawz), the end for which a thing is done.

FINALE (fe-na'la), *n.* the last passage in a musical composition ; the final act, etc.

FINALITY (fi-nal'i-ti), *n.* completeness.

FINANCE (fi-nans'), *n.* the public revenue of a government ; the science of management of monetary affairs ; usually in *pl.*

FINANCIAL (-nan'shal), *adj.* pertaining to finance.

FINANCIER (fin-an-ser'), *n.* one skilled in the principles of banking.

FIND (find), *v.t.* to discover ; ascertain by experiment ; regain, as something lost.

FINDER ('der), *n.* one who, or that which, finds.

FIN DE SIECLE (fang de sye'kl), [French], at the end of the century ; modern.

FINDING (fin'ding), *n.* discovery ; the verdict of a jury, or court.

FINE (fin), *v.t.* to impose a monetary penalty upon.

FINE (fin), *adj.* slender ; thin ; keen ; pure ; refined ; delicate ; elegant ; noble ; showy ; admirable ; splendid.

FINERY (fin'er-i), *n.* personal adornment.

FINESSE (fi-nes'), *n.* artifice or stratagem ; skill ; dexterity.

FINGER (fing'ger), *n.* one of the five divisions of the hand.

FINGERING (-ing), *n.* the act of manipulating the fingers on a fingered instrument.

FINGERLING ('ling), *n.* a young trout.

FINGER-PRINT (-print), *n.* an impression of a finger or thumb used to identify criminals.

FINICAL ('i-kal), *adj.* fastidious ; over particular.

FINICALITY ('i-ti), *n.* the characteristic of being finical.

FINING (fin'ing), *n.* clarification.

FINIS (fi'nis), *n.* the end.

FINISH (fin'ish), *v.t.* to complete ; conclude ; make perfect ; polish.

FINITE (fi'nit), *adj.* having limits : *n.* that which is finite (with *the*).

FINNAN HADDIE (fin'an had'i), a smoked haddock.

FINNY ('i), *adj.* having fins.

FINSEN LAMP (fin'sen lamp), *n.* a light for developing rays of ultraviolet light.

FIORD (fyord), *n.* a long narrow inlet or arm of the sea between high rocks or banks.

FIR (fer), *n.* any of various conebearing, evergreen trees.

FIRE (fir), *n.* heat and light evolved by ignition and combustion ; intensity of feeling ; ardour.

FIREARMS ('armz), *n.pl.* rifles, guns, etc.

FIRE-BALLOON (-ba-loon'), *n.* a balloon inflated by hot air.

FIREBRAND ('brand), *n.* a piece of burning wood ; an incendiary ; one who excites mischief.

FIRE-BRIGADE (fir'bri-gad), *n.* the members of a fire department.

FIREBUG ('bug), *n.* an incendiary.

FIRECRACKER ('krak-er), *n.* a small explosive firework.

FIRE-DAMP ('damp), *n.* carburetted hydrogen.

FIRE-ENGINE ('en-jin), *n.* a hand, steam or motor engine to extinguish a fire.

FIREFLY ('fli), *n.* a winged insect which emits light at night.

FIREMAN ('man), *n.* one trained to extinguish fires ; a stoker.

FIRESIDE ('sid), *n.* the hearth.

FIREWORK ('werk), *n.pl.* a pyrotechnic display.

FIRKIN (fer'kin), *n.* a small wooden vessel for holding butter, etc. ; a

measure of capacity, ¼ of a barrel ;
9 gals.

FIRM (ferm), *adj.* hard ; compact ;
solid, steadfast : *n.* a commercial
partnership.

FIRMAMENT (fer'ma-ment), *n.* the
sky.

FIRST (ferst), *adj.* the ordinal of one ;
foremost in place, rank, dignity,
time, excellence, etc.

FIRST-AID (-ad), *n.* treatment given
by a layman while waiting for a
physician.

FIRST-CLASS ('klas), *adj.* of the
highest excellence, rank, or quality.

FIRST-MATE ('mat), *n.* in the
merchant marine, the officer next in
rank to the captain.

FIRST-RATE ('rat), *adj.* of the highest
excellence : *adv.* excellently.

FISCAL (fis'kal), *adj.* pertaining to the
exchequer or public revenues ;
financial.

FISH (fish), *n.* a vetebrate, aquatic
animal furnished with permanent
gills.

FISHERMAN ('er-man), *n.* one whose
occupation it is to catch fish ; a
fishing-smack.

FISHERY ('er-i), *n.* the business of
catching fish ; a fishing-ground.

FISH-GLUE ('gloo), *n.* glue prepared
from fishbones.

FISHING ('ing), *n.* the sport, or business of taking fish.

FISH-JOINT ('joint), *n.* a pair of iron
plates for fastening the ends of two
rails together.

FISHMONGER ('mung-ger), *n.* one
who sells fish.

FISH-SOUND ('sound), *n.* the
swimming or air-bladder of a fish.

FISH-WEIR ('wer), *n.* a dam for
stopping or preserving fish.

FISHY ('i), *adj.* like fish ; dull ;
questionable.

FISSI-, prefix meaning *cleft*, or indicating *fission*.

FISSILE (fis'il), *adj.* capable of being
split ; said of rocks.

FISSURE (fish'ur), *n.* a cleft or crack ;
a narrow opening.

FISTIC (fis'tik), *adj.* pertaining to
pugilism.

FISTICUFFS ('ti-kufs), *n.* a combat
with the fists ; boxing.

FISTULA ('tu-la), *n.* a deep pipe-like
ulcer.

FIT (fit), *v.t.* adapt ; qualify ; adjust ;
equip ; benefit : *v.i.* to be proper or
suitable : *adj.* suitable ; qualified.

FIT (fit), *n.* a sudden attack of disease
attended with convulsions.

FITTER ('er), *n.* one who adjusts
pipes, or puts the parts of a machine
together ; one who fits on clothing.

FITTING ('ing), *p.adj.* suitable.

FIVE (fiv), *adj.* consisting of 4 and 1.

FIX (fiks), *v.t.* to make fast, secure ;
direct steadily ; set or place permanently ; adjust.

FIXATION (fik-sa'shun), *n.* stability.

FIXED (fikst), *p.adj.* firm ; lasting ;
settled ; permanent.

FIXED STAR (star), a star which
retains relatively the same position
in the heavens.

FIXITY ('i-ti), *n.* stability.

FIXTURE (fiks'tur), *n.* that which is
firmly fixed.

FIZZ (fiz), *n.* a hissing noise.

FIZZLE (fiz'l), *v.i.* to burn with a fizz
and soon go out.

FLABBERGAST (flab'er-gast), *v.t.*
to astonish, astound.

FLABBY ('i), *adj.* easily shaking
or yielding to the touch.

FLABELLATE (fla-bel'at), *adj.* fan-
shaped.

FLACCID (flak'sid), *adj.* flabby ;
weak.

FLAG (flag), *n.* a piece of cloth or
bunting used as a standard, ensign,
signal, etc. : *v.i.* to become weary.

FLAGELLANT (flaj'e-lant), *adj.* using
a whip or scourge.

FLAGELLATE ('e-lat), *v.t.* to whip.

FLAGEOLET (flaj-o-let'), *n.* a musical
instrument of the flute class.

FLAGGING (flag'ing), *n.* pavement of
flagstones : *adj.* growing weak.

FLAG-OFFICER (-of'i-ser), *n.* an
admiral.

FLAGON (flag'un), *n.* a large drinking
vessel.

FLAGRANT (fla'grant), *adj.* openly
wicked ; glaring ; notorious.

FLAGRANTE DELICTO (-gran'te de-lik'to), [Latin], in the very act.

FLAIL (flal), *n.* a wooden instrument for threshing wheat, etc.

FLAKE (flak), *n.* a small film of anything loosely held together, as snow.

FLAKY ('i), *adj.* consisting of flakes.

FLAM (flam), *n.* a falsehood; freak.

FLAMBEAU ('bo), *n.* [*pl.* flambeaux ('boz)], a lighted torch.

FLAMBOYANT (-boi'ant), *adj.* denoting a florid or showy style.

FLAME (flam), *n.* fire; ardour of temper or passion : *v.i.* to burst into flame; blaze.

FLAMINGO (fla-ming'go), *n.* a long-legged, web-footed bird.

FLANGE (flanj), *n.* a raised or projecting rim for preventing a wheel slipping.

FLANK (flangk), *n.* the fleshy part of an animal between the ribs and hip; the side of an army, regiment, etc. : *v.t.* to attack or turn the flank or side of (an army).

FLANNEL (flan'el), *n.* a soft-textured cloth.

FLANNEL-CAKE (flan'el-cake), *n.* a griddle cake of flour, raised with baking powder.

FLANNELET (-et'), *n.* a soft cotton material resembling flannel.

FLAP (flap), *n.* anything broad and flexible, hanging loosely.

FLAPJACK (flap'jak), *n.* a pancake.

FLARE (flar), *n.* a large, unsteady, glaring light.

FLASH (flash), *n.* a sudden, quick light.

FLASHLIGHT (-lit), *n.* a momentary brilliant light for taking photographs.

FLASHY ('i), *adj.* empty; gaudy.

FLASK (flask), *n.* a small bottle.

FLAT (flat), *adj.* level; even; smooth; insipid; dull; *n.* a set of rooms on one floor; an apartment.

FLATTEN ('n), *v.t.* to lay flat; make level or even; beat down.

FLATTER ('er), *v.t.* to gain over or please by complimentary speech.

FLATTERY ('er-i), *n.* adulation; false praise.

FLATULENCE ('u-lens), *n.* distension of the stomach, caused by gases generated within it; emptiness; conceit.

FLAUNT (flant), *v.i.* to make an ostentatious display in dress; a boast; brag.

FLAVOUR ('ver), *n.* a particular smell or taste : *v.t.* to impart a flavour to.

FLAW (flaw), *n.* a blemish.

FLAX (flaks), *n.* a plant.

FLAXSEED ('sed), *n.* linseed.

FLAY (fla), *v.t.* to strip off; skin; torture.

FLEA (fle), *n.* a small blood-sucking insect.

FLECK (flek), *n.* a streak or spot : *v.t.* to streak or spot.

FLEDGE (flej), *v.i.* to acquire the full plumage or feathers.

FLEDGLING ('ling), *n.* young bird just fledged.

FLEE (fle), *v.t.* to run away from; avoid.

FLEECE (flees), *n.* the whole wool shorn from a sheep at one time : *v.t.* to strip; plunder by injustice or fraud.

FLEECE-WOOL ('wool), *n.* wool cut from a living animal.

FLEER (fler), *v.i.* to mock or sneer.

FLEET (flet), *adj.* swift; rapid : *n.* a company of warships or merchant vessels.

FLESH (flesh), *n.* that part of an animal body underlying the skin; animal food; pulp of fruit, etc.; carnal state or appetites.

FLESHINGS ('ingz), *n.pl.* flesh-coloured tights; scrapings from hides.

FLESHLINESS ('li-nes), *n.* carnality.

FLESHLY ('li), *adj.* corporeal; carnal : *adv.* carnally.

FLEUR-DE-LIS (floor-de-le'), *n.* [*pl.* fleurs-de-lis], the royal emblem of France; name for various irises.

FLEXIBILITY (flek-si-bil'i-ti), *n.* the state or quality of being flexible.

FLEXIBLE ('si-bl), *adj.* easily bent; pliant; yielding to persuasion.

FLEXOR (flek'ser), *n.* a muscle that acts in bending the joints.

FLEXURE ('shur), *n.* a curve or fold; joint.

FLICK (flik), *n.* **a light, quick stroke**

FLICKER ('er), *v.i.* to move with an unsteady and quick motion : *n.* a bird of North America.

FLIER (fli'er), *n.* one who flies, or flees ; a fugitive.

FLIES, *pl.* of fly.

FLIGHT (flit), *n.* the act, process, manner, or power of flying ; hasty departure ; a series of steps.

FLIGHTILY (i-li), *adv.* capriciously.

FLIGHTY ('i), *adj.* changeful ; capricious ; wild ; giddy.

FLIMSILY (flim'zi-li), *adv.* in a flimsy manner.

FLIMSINESS ('zi-nes), *n.* being flimsy.

FLIMSY ('zi), *adj.* unsubstantial ; thin ; weak ; ineffective.

FLINCH (flinch), *v.t.* to shrink or draw back, as from pain, danger.

FLINDER (flin'der), *n.* a splinter.

FLING (fling), *v.t.* to throw or hurl ; scatter.

FLINT (flint), *n.* a variety of quartz.

FLINTY ('ti), *adj.* hard ; obdurate.

FLIPPANCY (flip'an-si), *n.* pertness ; thoughtless fluency of speech.

FLIPPANT ('ant), *adj.* characterized by thoughtless levity of speech.

FLIPPER ('er), *n.* a broad fin used in swimming, as that of the whale, seal, or turtle.

FLIRT (flert), *v.t.* move to and fro with a rapid action : *v.i.* make love from mere amusement : *n.* a coquette.

FLIRTATION (fler-ta'shun), *n.* the act of flirting.

FLIRTATIOUS ('shus), *adj.* inclined to flirt.

FLIRTING ('ting), *n.* coquetry.

FLIT (flit), *v.i.* to pass lightly and swiftly along ; fly away ; skim ; migrate.

FLITTING (flit'ing), *n.* the act of flying or moving swiftly.

FLOAT (flot), *v.t.* to cause to rest or be conveyed on the surface of a liquid ; to start, sell, or dispose of ; put in circulation.

FLOCCULENCE ('u-lens), *n.* the state of being flocculent.

FLOCCULUS ('u-lus), *n.* [*pl.* flocculi (-li)], a small flake ; a small tuft of down or wool-like hair.

FLOCK (flok), *n.* a company or collec-tion of sheep or birds ; a congrega-tion.

FLOE (flo), *n.* a large mass of floating ice.

FLOG (flog), *v.t.* to whip ; chastise.

FLOOD (flud), *n.* a great flow of water ; inundation ; high tide ; [F-], the Deluge.

FLOOR (flor), *n.* the part of a house, room, etc., on which one treads ; storey.

FLOP (flop), *v.i.* to plump down ; fall loosely and flatly.

FLORA (flo'ra), *n.* the wild plants of a particular region.

FLORAL ('ral), *adj.* pertaining to flowers.

FLOREATED ('re-a-ted), *adj.* with floral decorations.

FLORESCENCE (flo-res'ens), *n.* the flowering of a plant.

FLORET ('ret), *n.* a little flower.

FLORICAN (flo'ri-kan), *n.* an Indian bustard.

FLORICULTURE ('ri-kul-tur), *n.* the culture of flowers.

FLORICULTURIST ('tur-ist), *n.* one who is skilled in floriculture.

FLORID (flor'id), *adj.* bright in colour ; profusely embellished.

FLORIN (flor'in), *n.* an English silver coin. Value 2s.

FLORIST (flo'rist), *n.* one who culti-vates or sells flowers.

FLOSS (flos), *n.* floss-silk ; the soft, downy, silken substance in the husks of certain plants.

FLOSSY ('i), *adj.* like floss ; downy.

FLOTATION (flo-ta'shun), *n.* act of financing an enterprise ; the science of floating bodies.

FLOTILLA (-til'a), *n.* a fleet of small vessels.

FLOTSAM (flot'sam), *n.* goods lost in shipwreck, and found floating upon the sea.

FLOUNCE (flouns), *n.* a narrow piece of cloth sewed to the skirt of a dress or petticoat ; indicative of impatience.

FLOUNDER (floun'der), *v.i.* to struggle, as an animal in the mire : *n.* a flat sea-fish.

FLOUR (flour), *n.* the fine meal of ground wheat ; a fine soft powder.

FLOURISH (flur'ish), *v.i.* to prosper or thrive ; be vigorous ; embellish.

FLOURY (flour'i), *adj.* resembling, or covered with, flour.

FLOUT (flout), *v.t.* to insult ; jeer : *v.i.* to scoff.

FLOW (flo), *v.i.* to run or spread, as water ; circulate.

FLOWER (flou'er), *n.* that part of a plant which contains the reproductive organs ; blossom.

FLOWERET (-et), *n.* a little flower.

FLOWING (flo'ing), *p.adj.* moving, or pouring forth ; fluent.

FLUCTUATE (fluk'tu-at), *v.i.* to roll to and fro ; undulate ; be irresolute.

FLUE (flu), *n.* a pipe or passage to convey away smoke, hot air, etc.

FLUENCY (flu'en-si), *n.* the quality of being fluent.

FLUENT ('ent), *adj.* possessing readiness and ease of speech ; voluble ; eloquent.

FLUFF (fluf), *n.* light down or fur nap.

FLUFFINESS ('i-nes), *n.* the quality of being fluffy.

FLUID (flu'id), *adj.* liquid or gaseous.

FLUIDITY (-id'i-ti), *n.* the state or quality of being fluid.

FLUKE (flook), *n.* the broad part of an anchor ; a flounder ; a lucky stroke.

FLUKY ('i), *adj.* obtained by chance.

FLUME (floom), *n.* a channel for the conveyance of water.

FLUMMERY (flum'er-i), *n.* blanc-mange ; insipidity ; humbug.

FLUNK (flungk), *n.* a complete failure.

FLUNKY, FLUNKEY ('i), *n.* a liveried servant ; a toady.

FLUORESCE (floo-o-res'), *v.i.* to exhibit fluorescence.

FLUORESCENCE ('ens), *n.* the property possessed by certain substances of becoming luminous when exposed to X-rays or other forms of radiant energy.

FLUORESCENT ('ent), *adj.* pertaining to fluorescence.

FLURRIED (flur'id), *adj.* excited ; worried.

FLURRY (flur'i), *v.t.* to agitate, confuse.

FLUSH (flush), *v.t.* to cause to blush ; clean out with a rush of water : *n.* abundance.

FLUSTER (flus'ter), *v.t.* to confuse or agitate.

FLUTE (floot), *n.* a tubular wind-instrument furnished with finger-holes and keys.

FLUTING (floot'ing), *n.* a channel or groove ; a flute-shaped crimp.

FLUTTER (flut'er), *v.i.* to move or flap the wings rapidly.

FLUVIAL (floo'vi-al), *adj.* pertaining to rivers.

FLUX (fluks), *n.* any flow of matter ; a substance added to assist in the reduction of a metal by fusion.

FLY (fli), *v.i.* to move through the air with wings ; pass swiftly ; run away : *n.* a two-winged insect of many species.

FLYER, FLIER (fli'er), *n.* one or that which flies ; a flying-machine.

FLYING SQUIRREL (skwer'el), a squirrel having elastic folds of skin attached to the legs and body, permitting it to make long, flying leaps.

FLY-WHEEL (-hwel), *n.* a heavy wheel in a machine which regulates its motion.

FOAL (fol), *n.* the young of a horse, ass, or camel.

FOAM (fom), *n.* the white substance formed on a liquid by violent agitation or fermentation ; froth ; spume.

FOB (fob), *n.* a small pocket.

FOCAL (fo'kal), *adj.* pertaining to a focus.

FOCUS (fo'kus), *n.* [*pl.* foci ('si)], the point where a system of rays of light or heat meet after being reflected or refracted ; any central point : *v.t.* to bring to a focus or centre.

FODDER (fod'er), *n.* food for horses, cattle, or sheep.

FOE (fo), *n.* a personal enemy.

FOEMAN (fo'man), *n.* an adversary in war.

FŒTAL (fe'tal), *adj.* pertaining to the fœtus.

FŒTICIDE ('ti-sid), *n.* the destruction of a fœtus in the womb ; criminal abortion.

FOG (fog), *n.* watery vapour near the

surface of the sea or land ; bewilderment : *v.i.* to become foggy.

FOG-BANK ('bangk), *n.* a dense mass of fog.

FOGGILY (fog'i-li), *adv.* dimly.

FOGGY ('i), *adj.* abounding in fog ; bewildered ; obscure.

FOGY (fo'gi), *n.* a person of old-fashioned or eccentric habits.

FOIBLE (foi'bl), *n.* a failing or imperfection in character.

FOIL (foil), *v.t.* to baffle or frustrate : *n.* a long thin fencing weapon.

FOIST (foist), *v.t.* to palm off slyly (with *in, into, upon*).

FOKKER (fok'er), *n.* a high-powered monoplane.

FOLD (fold), *v.t.* to bend one part over another ; enclose : *n.* a pen, as for sheep.

FOLDEROL (fol'de-rol), *n.* mere nonsense ; a silly trifle.

FOLIACEOUS (fo'li-a'shus), *adj.* resembling, or having, leaves.

FOLIAGE ('li-aj), *n.* leaves collectively.

FOLIATED ('li-at-ed), *p.adj.* splitting into laminæ.

FOLIATION (-a'shun), *n.* lamination ; said of a mineral ; the number of the leaves of a book.

FOLIO (fo'li-o), *n.* a sheet of paper folded once ; a page of MS. or printed matter.

FOLIOSE ('li-os), *adj.* resembling a leaf.

FOLK (fok), *n.* people in general ; nation or race ; one's relatives.

FOLKLORE ('lor), *n.* popular traditions, customs, beliefs, etc.

FOLK-SONG ('song), *n.* a song illustrative of the common life of the people.

FOLLICLE (fol'i-kl), *n.* a seed-vessel ; a very small tube or cavity.

FOLLOW (fol'o), *v.t.* to go or come after ; pursue ; succeed in order.

FOLLY (fol'i), *n.* want of understanding ; foolishness.

FOMENT (fo-ment'), *v.t.* to excite ; stir up or instigate.

FOMENTATION (-men-ta'shun), *n.* the act of fomenting.

FOND (fond), *adj.* affectionate ; loving ; indulgent (with *of*).

FONDLE (fon'dl), *v.t.* to caress ; treat with tenderness.

FONT (font), *n.* a stone receptacle to hold the water used in baptizing ; an assortment of type.

FOOD (food), *n.* nutriment ; nourishment ; that which sustains.

FOOL (fool), *n.* a person devoid of reason.

FOOLHARDINESS ('har-di-nes), *n.* a courage without sense.

FOOLHARDY ('har-di), *adj.* foolishly bold.

FOOLING ('ing), *n.* foolish speech or conduct.

FOOLISH ('ish), *adj.* acting without reason or judgment.

FOOLSCAP (foolz'kap), *n.* a size of paper about 17 in. by 14 in.

FOOT (foot), *n.* that part of the leg on which an animal walks or stands ; the lower part of anything ; a measure equal to 12 in. ; infantry soldiers : *v.t.* to add figures in a column, and place the total at the bottom.

FOOTAGE (foot'aj), *n.* a standard of measurement in mining ; sum paid for work ; in motion pictures, length of reel.

FOOTBALL ('bawl), *n.* a large rubber bag encased in leather, used in the game of football ; a field game.

FOOTING ('ing), *n.* ground or support for the feet ; tread ; the adding of a colum of figures ; the sum of same.

FOOTMAN ('man), *n.* a livery servant.

FOOTPAD ('pad), *n.* a highwayman.

FOOT-POUND ('pound), *n.* the unit of energy equal to work required to raise 1 lb. through a space of 1 ft.

FOP (fop), *n.* a dandy.

FOPPERY ('er-i), *n.* dandyism.

FOR (for), *prep.* in place of ; on account of ; for the sake of ; notwithstanding ; to the number or amount of : *conj.* because ; since.

FOR-, a prefix meaning *thoroughly, before, greatly.*

FORAGE (for'aj), *n.* food for horses and cattle ; a search for provisions.

FORAY (for'a), *n.* a predatory expedition.

FORBADE, *p.t.* of forbid.

FORBEAR (-bar′), *v.t.* to abstain from ; excuse ; spare : *n.* an ancestor.

FORBEARANCE (′ans), *n.* patience ; indulgence ; self-command.

FORBID (-bid′), *v.t.* to prohibit ; command not to do ; oppose.

FORCE (fors), *n.* active power ; vigour ; strength ; energy ; violence ; power to persuade or convince ; troops ; armament ; a trained or organized body : *v.t.* to compel ; impel ; push ; press ; strain ; cause to grow or ripen by artificial means.

FORCEMEAT (fors′met), *n.* meat chopped fine and seasoned.

FORCEPS (for′seps), *n.* pincers or pliers for seizing and extracting.

FORCIBLE (for′si-bl), *adj.* characterized by mental or physical power ; vigorous.

FORCIBLY (′si-bli), *adv.* in a forcible manner.

FORD (ford), *n.* a shallow part of a stream, etc. : *v.t.* to wade through.

FORE (for), *n.* the foremost or leading place.

FORE-, a prefix meaning *before, in front*.

FOREBODE (for-bod′), *v.t.* to presage.

FORECAST (′kast), *n.* foresight ; prediction of the weather : *v.t.* (for-kast′), to plan or calculate beforehand ; predict.

FORECASTLE (fok′sl), *n.* the part of a vessel forward of the foremast.

FORECLOSE (for-kloz′), *v.t.* to cut off from the right of redemption, said of a mortgage.

FOREFATHER (′fa-*th*er), *n.* a male ancestor.

FOREHEAD (for′ed), *n.* that part of the face between the eyes and the hair ; brow.

FOREIGN (for′in), *adj.* belonging to another nation ; remote.

FORELAND (for′land), *n.* a headland.

FORELOCK (′lok), *n.* a lock of hair growing on the forehead.

FOREMAN (′man), *n.* the spokesman of a jury ; an overseer.

FOREMOST (′most), *adj.* chief ; first.

FORENSIC (fo-ren′sik), *adj.* pertaining to, or used in, courts of justice or public debate.

FORESIGHT (′sit), *n.* prescience.

FOREST (for′est), *n.* a large extent of ground covered with trees ; woodland : *adj.* rustic ; sylvan.

FORESTALL (for-stawl′), *v.t.* anticipate.

FORESTER (for′est-er), *n.* one skilled in forestry.

FORESTRY (′est-ri), *n.* the art of cultivating forests.

FORETELL (for-tel′), *v.t.* to predict.

FOREVER (for-ev′er), *adv.* endless ; for eternity.

FORFEIT (for′fit), *n.* a fine or penalty.

FORFEITURE (′fi-tur), *n.* penalty.

FORFEND (-fend′), *v.t.* to ward off.

FORGATHER (-ga*th*′er), *v.i.* to assemble ; associate (with *with*).

FORGE (forj), *v.t.* to fashion (a piece of metal) by heating and hammering ; counterfeit, with intent to defraud.

FORGEABLE (′a-bl), *adj.* capable of being forged.

FORGER (′jer), *n.* one who commits the crime of forgery ; a fabricator.

FORGERY (-i), *n.* the act of counterfeiting the handwriting of another with intent to defraud ; the act of counterfeiting.

FORGET (for-get′), *v.t.* to lose the remembrance of ; overlook or neglect.

FORGETABLE (′a-bl), *adj.* liable to be forgotten.

FORGET-ME-NOT (′me-not), *n.* a perennial plant with small sky-blue flowers.

FORGIVABLE (-giv′a-bl), *adj.* that may be forgiven.

FORGIVE (-giv′), *v.t.* to pardon ; remit, as a sin, offence, debt, etc.

FORGO (-go′), *v.t.* to renounce or refrain from ; give up : *v.t.* precede.

FORK (fork), *n.* an instrument with two or more prongs ; the branch or space caused by the junction of two roads or rivers.

FORLORN (-lorn′), *adj.* abandoned ; deserted ; destitute ; bereft.

FORM (form), *n.* the external appearance or shape of anything ; image ; likeness ; orderly arrangement ; types, plates, etc., imposed in a chase ready for printing : v.t. to give shape to ; create.

FORMAL ('mal), adj. according to form or established rules ; precise.

FORMALDEHYDE (for-mal'de-hid), n. a disinfectant and antiseptic.

FORMALITY ('i-ti), n. strict adherence to external or customary forms.

FORMAT (for-mat'), n. general style of a book printed and bound.

FORMATION (-ma'shun), n. structure ; figure ; productions.

FORMATIVE ('ma-tiv), adj. plastic ; germinal : n. a word formed by adding a prefix, or suffix.

FORMER ('mer), adj. first mentioned : n. a maker of formes (in printing).

FORMICANT ('mi-kant), adj. weak : said of the pulse.

FORMIDABLE ('mi-da-bl), adj. fearful ; powerful.

FORMULA ('mu-la), n. [pl. formulas (-laz), formulæ (-le)], a prescribed form, rule, or model ; a group of symbols ; a prescription.

FORMULATE ('mu-lat), v.t. fix or state, in definite terms.

FORNICATION (-ni-ka'shun), n. the incontinence of unmarried persons, male or female.

FORSAKE (-sak'), v.t. desert ; abandon ; depart from.

FORSOOTH (-sooth'), adv. verily ; in truth.

FORSWEAR (-swar'), v.i. to swear falsely ; commit perjury.

FORT (fort), n. a castle ; fortress.

FORTE (fort), n. one's strong point, or special talent.

FORTH (forth), adv. onward in time, place, or order ; forward ; abroad.

FORTIFICATION (-ti-fi-ka'shun), n. a military defensive work.

FORTIFY ('ti-fi), v.t. to strengthen ; make strong ; encourage or confirm.

FORTITUDE (for'ti-tud), n. mental strength to endure suffering or adversity with courage.

FORTNIGHT (fort'nit), n. 14 days.

FORTRESS (for'tres), n. a large permanent fortified place for defence or security.

FORTUITOUS (for-tu'i-tus), adj.

happening by chance ; accidental.

FORTUITY ('i-ti), n. an accidental occurrence.

FORTUNATE (for'tu-nat), adj. happening by good fortune ; auspicious ; successful.

FORTUNE ('tun), n. the good or ill that happens to mankind ; fate ; estate ; wealth.

FORTUNE-HUNTER (-hun'ter), n. one who seeks to marry an heiress.

FORUM (for'um), n. [pl. fora ('a), forums ('umz)], a place of public resort, or court of law.

FORWARD (for'werd), adj. situated near the front ; ready ; prompt ; presumptuous.

FORWARDER (-er), n. one who forwards or promotes.

FOSSIL (fos'il), n. any organic body which by burial in the earth's strata has become petrified.

FOSSILIFEROUS (-if'er-us), adj. containing fossils.

FOSSILIZE (-iz), v.t. to petrify : v.i. to become antiquated.

FOSTER ('ter), v.t. to nourish ; nurse.

FOSTER-BROTHER (bruh'er), n. a brother by nursing, but not by birth.

FOSTER-CHILD (-child), n. a child nursed or reared by one who is not its parent.

FOUGHT, imp. & p.p. of fight.

FOUL (foul), adj. offensive ; dirty ; impure ; scurrilous ; filthy ; hateful ; loathsome ; disgraceful ; unfair.

FOUND (found), v.t. to lay the basis of ; build ; fix firmly ; establish.

FOUNDATION (foun-da'shun), n. the basis or lowest part of a structure ; ground-work ; the principles or origin of anything.

FOUNDER (foun'der), n. one who founds or originates ; builder ; one who casts metal : v.i. to fill and sink ; go lame.

FOUNDLING (foun'dling), n. a child of unknown parentage.

FOUNDRY ('dri), n. the place where metal casting is carried on.

FOUNT (fount), n. a fountain or spring ; original source.

FOUNTAIN (foun'tin), n. a natural

or artificial spring of water; a jet or spout of water.

FOUNTAIN-PEN (-pen), *n.* a pen having a reservoir of ink in the holder.

FOUR-IN-HAND (for'in-hand), *n.* a coach drawn by four horses; a necktie.

FOUR-O'CLOCK ('o-klok), *n.* common garden plant.

FOURSCORE ('skor), *adj.* eighty units.

FOURTH (forth), *n.* one of 4 equal parts; a musical interval of two tones and one semitone.

FOWL (foul), *n.* a gallinaceous bird, especially the domestic cock or hen; poultry.

FOWLER ('er), *n.* one who catches or kills wild birds for sport or food.

FOX (foks), *n.* a vulpine mammal with a long bushy tail, noted for its cunning.

FOXED (fokst), *p.adj.* stained, as timber, or spotted, as prints, books, etc.

FOXGLOVE ('gluv), *n.* a plant of the figwort family.

FOX-GRAPE ('grap), *n.* a variety of grape.

FOXHOUND ('hound), *n.* one of a breed of dogs used for fox-hunting.

FOXINESS ('i-nes), *n.* sly cunning, or shrewdness.

FOX-TERRIER (-ter'i-er), *n.* one of a wiry, muscular breed of dogs.

FOXY ('i), *adj.* pertaining to, or resembling, a fox; cunning.

FOYER (fwa-ya'), *n.* [French], the lobby of a theatre.

FRACAS (fra'kas), *n.* a noisy quarrel.

FRACTION (frak'shun), *n.* a part broken off; act of breaking; a part of a unit, as ¼.

FRACTIONAL (-al), *adj.* pertaining to, or constituting, a fraction; very small.

FRACTIOUS ('shus), *adj.* unruly; cross.

FRACTURE ('tur), *n.* act, or result of breaking; a part broken: separation: *v.t.* to break, or crack, as a bone, etc.

FRAGILE (fraj'il), *adj.* easily broken; weak; delicate.

FRAGMENT (frag'ment), *n.* a part broken off from a whole.

FRAGRANCE (fra'grans), *n.* the state or quality of being fragrant.

FRAGRANT ('grant) *adj.* sweet-smelling.

FRAIL (fral), *adj.* fragile; infirm.

FRAME (fram), *n.* something constructed or composed of parts fitted and joined together; a compositor's stand; shape; temper; state; invent; adapt.

FRAMEWORK ('werk), *n.* that which encloses or supports something else.

FRANC (frangk), *n.* a French coin, the unit of monetary value.

FRANCHISE (fran'chiz), *n.* the constitutional right of suffrage.

FRANCO- (frang'ko), a combining form denoting *France*.

FRANGIBLE (fran'ji-bl), *adj.* easily broken.

FRANK (frangk), *adj.* open; candid; outspoken; unreserved: *v.t.* to send or have conveyed free of charge.

FRANKFURTER (frangk'fur-ter), *n.* a sausage of mixed meats.

FRANKINCENSE ('in-sens), *n.* a fragrant incense.

FRANKLY ('li), *adv.* candidly.

FRANKNESS ('nes), *n.* candour.

FRANTIC (fran'tik), *adj.* violently mad or distracted; outrageous.

FRAPPE (fra-pa'), *adj.* [French], chilled with ice: *n.* an iced beverage.

FRATERNAL (fra-ter'nal), *adj.* pertaining to, becoming, or like, brothers.

FRATERNITY (fra-ter'ni-ti), *n.* brotherly relationship; associated together by a common bond of interest.

FRATERNIZE (frat'er-niz), *v.i.* to associate or hold fellowship as brothers.

FRATRICIDE (frat'ri-sid), *n.* one who kills a brother.

FRAUD (frawd), *n.* deceit; artifice; trick; a humbug.

FRAUDULENCE ('u-lens), *n.* deceitfulness; trickery; unfairness.

FRAUDULENT ('u-lent), *adj.* characterized by fraud.

FRAUGHT (frawt), *adj.* laden; charged.

FRAY (fra), *n.* a riot ; quarrel ; a chafe.

FRAYING ('ing), *n.* the act of wearing away by friction.

FRAZZLE (fraz'l), *n.* worn-out woven stuff, rope, etc.

FREAK (frek), *n.* sudden or capricious change of mind, or whim ; a prank ; an abnormal animal or plant.

FRECKLE (frek'l), *n.* a brownish spot in the skin.

FREE (fre), *adj.* without restraint ; at liberty ; permitted ; liberal ; generous.

FREEBOOTER ('boot-er), *n.* one who roves about for plunder.

FREE CITY (sit'i), *n.* a city having an independent government.

FREEDOM (fre'dum), *n.* the state of being free ; liberty ; independence.

FREE-HAND ('hand), *adj.* drawn by hand without instruments.

FREE-HANDED (-ed), *adj.* generous ; liberal.

FREEHOLD ('hold), *n.* an estate or tenement held by fee-simple, fee-tail, or for life.

FREE-LANCE ('lans), *n.* one who acts, speaks, or writes irrespective of any party ; in journalism one not attached to the regular staff, but paid for special work.

FREEMAN ('man), *n.* one in the enjoyment of liberty.

FREEMASON ('ma-sn), *n.* a member of a social association whose principles are brotherly love, charity, and mutual aid.

FREESTONE ('ston), *n.* a sandstone suitable for working.

FREE TRADE (trad), *n.* trade with other countries unrestricted by tariffs or customs duties.

FREEWILL ('wil), *n.* the power to act freely ; *adj.* voluntary.

FREEZE (frez), *v.t.* to congeal or harden into ice ; kill by cold : *v.i.* be at or below the temperature of 32° F.

FREEZING-POINT ('ing-point), *n.* the temperature at which water freezes, which is 32° above zero.

FREIGHT (frat), *n.* the goods with which a vessel is loaded ; cargo ; goods carried by rail.

FRENCH (french), *adj.* pertaining to France, its inhabitants or language.

FRENCH LEAVE (lev), departure without ceremony or notice.

FRENZIED (fren'zid), *p.adj.* affected with frenzy ; delirious.

FRENZY ('zi), *n.* violent agitation ; temporary madness.

FREQUENCE (fre'kwens), **FREQUENCY** ('kwen-si), *n.* the repeated occurence of a thing at short intervals.

FREQUENT ('kwent), *adj.* recurring often.

FREQUENTLY (-li), *adv.* often ; repeatedly.

FRESCO (fres'ko), *n.* a method of wall-painting in water colours.

FRESH (fresh), *adj.* new ; recent ; in good condition ; lively ; brisk ; pure and cool.

FRESHET ('et), *n.* a flood caused by melting snow or heavy rain.

FRESHMAN ('man), *n.* a college student in his first year.

FRET (fret), *v.t.* to corrode ; agitate ; vex ; irritate.

FRETFUL ('fool), *adj.* peevish.

FRET-SAW ('saw), *n.* a saw with fine teeth, used for cutting scrolls.

FREUDIAN (froi'di-an), *adj.* according to the practices of Dr. Sigmund Freud.

FRIABILITY (fri-a-bil'i-ti), *n.* the state or quality of being friable.

FRIABLE ('a-bl), *adj.* readily crumbled, or reduced to powder.

FRIAR ('er), *n.* one of an order of monks in R.C. Church ; a monk.

FRICASSE (frik-a-se'), *n.* a dish of chicken, etc., cut into small pieces, stewed and fried with a sauce.

FRICTION ('shun), *n.* resistance to the motion of a body, caused by contact with the surface upon which it moves.

FRICTIONAL (-al), *adj.* pertaining to, or produced by, friction.

FRIDAY (fri'da), *n.* the sixth day of the week.

FRIEND (frend), *n.* one attached to another by affection, regard, or esteem.

FRIEND, *n.* a member of the Society of Friends ; called *Quakers*.

FRIENDSHIP ('ship), *n.* intimacy ; mutual attachment ; good will.

FRIEZE (frez), *n.* the middle part of the entablature of a column ; a coarse woollen cloth.

FRIGATE (frig'at), *n.* formerly a war-ship with an upper flush deck.

FRIGHT (frit), *n.* a sudden and violent fear ; alarm.

FRIGHTEN ('n), *v.t.* to terrify.

FRIGHTFUL ('fool), *adj.* terrible ; dreadful.

FRIGID (frij'id), *adj.* wintry ; cold in temperament ; stiff ; formal ; dull.

FRIGIDITY (fri-jid'i-ti), *n.* the state of being frigid ; coldness.

FRILL (fril), *n.* a ruffle : *pl.* affectation of manner.

FRINGE (frinj), *n.* an ornamental border of hanging cords, etc. ; margin ; extremity.

FRIPPERY (frip'er-i), *adj.* trumpery ; contemptible.

FRISK (frisk), *v.i.* to gambol or dance in frolic.

FRISKY ('ki), *adj.* lively in action ; gay.

FRITTER (frit'er), *v.t.* to waste by degrees : *n.* a small cake with meat or fruit in it.

FRIVOLITY (fri-vol'i-ti), *n.* levity ; a trifling act.

FRIVOLOUS (friv'o-lus), *adj.* trifling ; trivial.

FRIZETTE (fri-zet'), *n.* a small piece of hair worn as a bang.

FRIZZ (friz), *v.t.* to curl or crisp.

FRIZZLE (friz'l), *v.t.* to curl on hot coals ; curl or frizz.

FRO (fro), *adv.* away from ; backward.

FROCK (frok), *n.* a loose upper garment ; dress ; a monk's habit.

FROG (frog), *n.* a small tailless web-footed amphibian.

FROLIC (frol'ik), *n.* a scene of gaiety ; a sportive outburst.

FROLICSOME (-sum), *adj.* full of frolic.

FROM (from), *prep.* out of, away ; since.

FROND (frond), *n.* the leaf of a fern, palm, seaweed.

FRONT (frunt), *n.* the forehead ; the forepart or foremost of anything.

FRONTAGE ('aj), *n.* the front part of a building or area.

FRONTAL (fron'tal), *adj.* pertaining to the front or forehead.

FRONTIER (fron'ter), *n.* the boundary or limits of a country.

FRONTISPIECE (fron'tis-pes), *n.* an illustration facing the front page of a book.

FROST (frost), *n.* minute frozen particles of moisture.

FROSTBITE ('bit), *v.t.* a state of deadness with arrested circulation in any part of the body occasioned by exposure to severe frost.

FROSTING ('ting), *n.* a preparation of fine sugar and white of egg for covering cakes.

FROTH (froth), *n.* the mass of bubbles formed on the surface of a liquid by fermentation ; superficial knowledge.

FROTHY ('i), *adj.* full of froth ; empty ; frivolous.

FROW (frou), *n.* a German or Dutch woman.

FROWARD (fro'werd), *adj.* perverse ; wayward.

FROWN (froun), *n.* a contraction of the brow indicative of displeasure, etc. : *v.i.* to scowl ; lower.

FROZEN (froz'en), *p.adj.* congealed, killed with cold ; icy.

FRUCTIFY (fruk'ti-fi), *v.t.* to make productive ; fertilize.

FRUGAL (froo'gal), *adj.* thrifty.

FRUGALITY ('i-ti), *n.* thrift ; economy.

FRUIT (froot), *n.* the product of a tree or plant containing the seed ; product.

FRUITAGE ('aj), *n.* fruit collectively ; product.

FRUITERER ('er-er), *n.* one who deals in fruit.

FRUITFUL ('fool), *adj.* prolific.

FRUITION (froo-ish'un), *n.* the bearing of fruit ; realization.

FRUITY (froot'i), *adj.* full-flavoured ; rich.

FRUSTRATE (frus'trat), *v.t.* to defeat or thwart ; nullify.

FRY (fri), *v.t.* to cook with fat : *n.* young fish.

FUCHSIA (fu'shi-a), *n.* a garden plant with handsome flowers.

FUDDLE (fud'l), *v.t.* to stupefy with drink ; intoxicate.

FUDGE (fuj), *n.* a made-up story ; a candy : *interj.* nonsense.

FUEL (fu'el), *n.* combustible material for supplying a fire.

FUGITIVE (fu'ji-tiv), *adj.* unstable ; volatile ; fleeting ; not permanent ; fleeing from danger, or duty.

FUGUE (fug), *n.* a musical composition.

FULCRUM (ful'krum), *n.* [*pl.* fulcra ('kra)], that part of a lever on which it rests.

FULFILL, FULFIL (fool-fil'), *v.t.* to complete or accomplish ; execute.

FULGENCY (ful'jen-si), *n.* brightness splendour.

FULL (fool), *adj.* filled ; having no empty space.

FULL-DRESS ('dres), *n.* dress for formal occasions.

FULLER'S-EARTH ('erz-erth), *n.* a soft clay used for fulling cloth and the removal of grease.

FULLY (fool'i), *adv.* completely.

FULMINATE (ful'mi-nat), *v.t.* to cause to explode : *v.i.* to detonate.

FULSOME (ful'sum), *adj.* offensive ; gross.

FULVOUS (ful'vus), *adj.* tawny.

FUMBLE (fum'bl), *v.i.* to grope or feel about ; handle awkwardly.

FUME (fum), *n.* vapour or exhalation.

FUMIGATE ('i-gat), *v.t.* smoke ; perfume ; disinfect.

FUN (fun), *n.* mirth ; drollery ; sport.

FUNCTION (fungk'shun), *n.* the discharge or performance of any duty, office or business ; faculty ; power ; the office of any organ, animal or vegetable.

FUNCTIONARY (-a-ri), *n.* one who holds an office or trust.

FUND (fund), *n.* established stock of capital : *pl.* money.

FUNDAMENTAL ('da-men'tal), *adj.* pertaining to a foundation or basis.

FUNDAMENTAL BASS (bas), that part in musical harmony which contains the fundamental notes of chords.

FUNDED (fun'ded), *p.adj.* converted into a permanent loan.

FUNERAL (fu'ner-al), *n.* the ceremony of burying a dead human body.

FUNEREAL (-ne're-al), *adj.* pertaining to, or suitable for, a funeral ; mournful ; sad.

FUNGOUS (fung'gus), *adj.* pertaining to the nature of fungi.

FUNGUS ('gus), *n.* [*pl.* fungi (fun'ji)] a cryptogamous plant, as mildew, mushroom, etc.

FUNK (fungk), *n.* a coward ; cowardice ; fright : *v.i.* to shrink, or back out.

FUNNEL (fun'el), *n.* a wide-mouthed, conical vessel terminating in a spout for pouring liquids into close vessels.

FUNNY ('i), *adj.* comical ; droll ; provoking laughter.

FUNNY-BONE (-bon), *n.* the lower part of the elbow over which the nerve of the ulna passes.

FUR (fer), *n.* the coat of certain animals.

FURBELOW ('be-lo), *n.* an ornament of feminine attire.

FURBISH ('bish), *v.t.* to make bright by rubbing ; renovate.

FURIOUS (fu'ri-us), *adj.* full of fury ; frenzied ; mad.

FURL (ferl), *v.t.* to roll up.

FURLONG (fer'long), *n.* ⅛th of a mile.

FURLOUGH ('lo), *n.* leave of absence.

FURNACE ('nas), *n.* a chamber for producing a violent heat.

FURNISH ('nish), *v.i.* to supply with what is requisite ; fit out.

FURNITURE ('ni-tur), *n.* the necessary equipments of a house, etc.

FUROR, FURORE (fu'ror, fu-ro're), *n.* a great outburst of excitement.

FURRIER (fur'i-er), *n.* one who prepares or sells furs ; fur-dresser.

FURROW (fur'o), *n.* a trench made in the ground by a plough.

FURRY (fer'i), *adj.* covered with, or consisting of, fur.

FURTHER (fer'ther), *adj.* more distant ; additional.

FURTHERANCE (-ans), *n.* advancement.

FURTHERMORE (-mor), *adv.* moreover.

FURTHERMOST (-most), *adj.* most remote.

FURTHEST ('*th*est), *adj.* most distant.

FURTIVE (fer'tiv), *adj.* sly ; secret ; stealthy.

FURY (fu'ri), *n.* violent or uncontrollable rage ; madness.

FUSE (fuz), *v.t.* to liquefy by heat ; melt : *n.* a small tube filled with an inflammable material used for exploding gunpowder, etc.

FUSELAGE (fu'ze-laj), *n.* the framework of an airplane ; the cockpit.

FUSIBLE (fu'si-bl), *adj.* capable of being fused.

FUSILEER, FUSILIER (-zi-ler'), *n.* a soldier of one of several British regiments.

FUSILLADE (-zi-lad'), *n.* a simultaneous discharge of firearms.

FUSION ('zhun), *n.* melting by heat ; union by, or as by, melting.

FUSS (fus), *n.* irritating activity ; disorderly bustling about ; confusion ; stir : *v.i.* to worry.

FUSTIAN ('chan), *n.* a kind of coarse twilled cotton cloth, as corduroy, velveteen, etc. ; bombast.

FUSTY ('ti), *adj.* ill-smelling ; mouldy ; meddlesome ; officious.

FUTILE (fu'til), *adj.* vain ; useless.

FUTILITY (-til'i-ti), *n.* the quality of being futile.

FUTURE ('tur), *n.* time to come yet ; a tense in grammar ; a commodity, etc.

FUTURIST (fu'tur-ist), *n.* one of a new school of painters which seeks to present the individuality of the artist without considering naturalism.

FUTURITY (fu-tu'ri-ti), *n.* time to come ; future events.

FUZZ (fuz), *n.* fine, minute articles of down, wool, etc.

FYKE (fik), *n.* a kind of fishtrap.

G

G, g (je), *n.* a letter ; the seventh letter of the English alphabet.

G, g, *n.* an abbreviation.

G, *n.* a Roman numeral denoting 400 ; with a bar (Ḡ), 40,000.

G FLAT (flat), the tone half a step below G.

G FLAT MAJOR (ma'jer), a major scale having a signature of six flats.

G MAJOR, a major scale having a signature of one sharp.

G MINOR (mi'ner), a minor scale having a signature of two sharps.

G SHARP (sharp), the tone half a step above G.

G SHARP MINOR, a minor scale having a signature of five sharps.

G STRING (string), a string tuned to G.

GABARDINE, GABERDINE (gaber-den'), *n.* a coarse smock frock.

GABBLE (gab'l), *n.* rapid, incoherent talk.

GABLE (ga'bl), *n.* the triangular end of a building.

GAD (gad), *v.i.* to roam about in a purposeless manner : *n.* mining tool.

GADABOUT (gad'a-bout), *n.* an idler.

GADFLY ('fli), *n.* a fly that stings cattle.

GAEL (gal), *n.* one of the Celtic or Keltic race.

GAELIC ('ik), *adj.* pertaining to, or belonging to, the Celtic or Keltic inhabitants of the Scottish Highlands, or to their language.

GAFF (gaf), *n.* a hook for landing salmon, etc. ; a boom or yard.

GAG (gag), *n.* something placed in the mouth to hinder speech : *v.i.* to choke.

GAGE, GAUGE (gaj), *n.* a standard of measure : *v.t.* to ascertain the capacity of ; estimate.

GAGER (gaj'er), *n.* see gauger.

GAIETY (ga'e-ti), *n.* being gay ; merriment ; pleasure ; finery.

GAILY (ga'li), *adv.* merrily ; finely.

GAIN (gan), *n.* advantage ; profit : *v.i.* to obtain ; earn ; win.

GAINSAY ('sa), *v.t.* to contradict ; oppose.

GAIRISH, same as garish.

GAIT (gat), *n.* manner of walking; way or course.

GAITER ('er), *n.* a covering of cloth for the ankle.

GALA (ga'la), *n.* a festive show; pomp.

GALACTO- (ga-lak'to), a combining form from Greek *gala*, milk.

GALANTINE (gal'an-tin), *n.* a dish served cold in its own jelly.

GALATEA (-a-te'a), *n.* cotton fabric with blue and red stripes.

GALAXY (gal'ak-si), *n.* the Milky Way: *n.* [g-], an assemblage of splendid persons or things.

GALE (gal), *n.* a strong wind.

GALENA (ga-le'na), *n.* sulphide of lead.

GALL (gawl), *n.* the bile; malignant feeling; rancour; a wound caused by friction: *v.i.* to fret; be vexed, etc.

GALL-BLADDER (-blad'er), *n.* a membranous sac in vertebrates.

GALLANT (gal'ant), *adj.* brave; chivalrous: *n.* a beau.

GALLANT (gal-ant'), *adj.* showing courtesy and respectful deference to women.

GALLANTLY (gal'ant-li), *adv.* bravely; (gal-ant'li), politely.

GALLANTRY ('an-tri), *n.* bravery; heroism; polite and deferential attention to women.

GALLEON ('e-on), *n.* a large Spanish three-decked vessel.

GALLERY ('er-i), *n.* a corridor; the upper seats of a theatre, church, assembly-room, etc.

GALLEY (gal'i), *n.* a low, flat, one-decked vessel propelled by oars; the cook-house of a ship; frame for composed type.

GALLIC ('ik), *adj.* pertaining to ancient Gaul, or modern France.

GALLING (gawl'ing), *p.adj.* chafing; irritating.

GALLIVANT (gal'i-vant), *v.i.* to idle or gad about with women.

GALLNUT (gawl'nut), a round excrescence on a species of oak.

GALLON (gal'un), *n.* a liquid measure = 4 quarts; a dry measure = ⅛th of a bushel.

GALLOP (gal'up), *n.* the rapid for-ward springing movement of a horse.

GALLOWS ('oz), *n.* a structure used for hanging criminals.

GALLSTONE (gawl'ston), *n.* a calculus formed in the gall bladder or biliary duct.

GALORE (ga-lor'), *adv.* in great plenty.

GALOSH (ga-losh'), *n.* an overshoe.

GALVANIC (gal-van'ik), *adj.* pertaining to galvanism; voltaic; spasmodic.

GALVANIZE (-iz), *v.t.* to subject to the action of an electric current; hence, to stimulate; excite.

GALVANOMETER (-va-nom'e-ter), *n.* an instrument for measuring the presence, extent, and direction of an electric current.

GAMBLE (gam'bl), *v.i.* play for money: *v.t.* to squander in gaming (with *away*).

GAMBLER (gam'bler), *n.* one who gambles.

GAMBOL ('bol), *n.* a dancing or skipping about for joy or sport; frolic.

GAMBREL-ROOF ('brel-roof), *n.* a roof the upper part of which slopes off from the lower.

GAME (gam), *n.* a sport or diversion; birds or mammals hunted for their flesh.

GAMELY ('li), *adv.* pluckily.

GAMING (gam'ing), *n.* playing stakes; gambling.

GAMMON ('un), *n.* a hoax; imposition: *interj.* nonsense.

GAMUT (gam'ut), *n.* the lines and spaces upon which musical notes are written or printed.

GANDER (gan'der), *n.* a male goose.

GANG (gang), *n.* a number of persons associated together for a particular purpose.

GANGRENE ('gren), *n.* the first state of mortification.

GANGSTER (gang'ster), *n.* one of a gang of desperate characters.

GANGWAY (gang'wa), *n.* a temporary passageway.

GAOL, same as jail.

GAP (gap), *n.* an opening; passage.

GAPE (gap), *v.i.* to open the mouth wide, as from wonder, etc.; yawn.

GAR (gar), *n.* a garfish.

GARAGE (ga-razh′, gar′aj), *n.* an enclosed place for automobiles; a hangar.

GARB (garb), *n.* a dress: *v.t.* to clothe.

GARBAGE (′baj), *n.* offal; refuse.

GARBLE (gar′bl), *v.t.* select such parts of as are wanted or may serve some particular purpose: *n.pl.* siftings.

GARCON (-song′), *n.* [French], a boy; waiter.

GARDEN (′dn), *n.* a piece of ground set apart for the cultivation of flowers, fruit, vegetables, etc.

GARFISH (gar′fish), *n.* a marine fish with a long body and spear-like snout.

GARGLE (′gl), *n.* a medicinal liquid applied to the throat and mouth.

GARGOYLE (′goil), *n.* in Gothic architecture, a projecting stone water-spout, in the form of a grotesquely shaped man or animal.

GARISH (gar′ish), *adj.* gaudy; dazzling.

GARLAND (gar′land), *n.* a chaplet or wreath made of flowers, etc.; a collection of choice extracts of prose or poetry.

GARLIC (′lik), *n.* a bulbous-rooted plant.

GARMENT (′ment), *n.* any article of clothing; a vestment.

GARNER (′ner), *n.* a granary: *v.t.* to gather up.

GARNET (′net), *n.* a precious stone.

GARNISH (′nish), *n.* an ornament or decoration; something laid round a dish as an embellishment.

GARNISHEE (-e′), *n.* the person in whose hands the property of another is attached pending the claims of a third party.

GARNISHMENT (-ment), *n.* an embellishment; a warning or summons.

GARNITURE (′ni-tur), *n.* embellishment.

GARRET (gar′et), *n.* the uppermost room of a house.

GARRISON (′i-sn), *n.* a body of troops stationed in a fort or fortified place.

GARROTE (ga-rot′), *n.* strangulation: *v.t.* to execute with a garrote.

GARRULITY (ga-roo′li-ti), *n.* incessant and inconsequent loquacity.

GARRULOUS (gar′oo-lus), *adj.* characterized by garrulity; verbose.

GARTER (gar′ter), *n.* an elastic band, etc., by which a stocking is held up.

GARTER-SNAKE (-snak), *n.* an innocuous yellow-striped snake.

GAS (gas), *n.* matter in an aeriform state; nitrous oxide used as an anæsthetic.

GASCONADE (-kun-ad′), *n.* boastful or blustering talk: *v.i.* to bluster; boast.

GASEOUS (′e-us), *adj.* having the nature or form of gas.

GASH (gash), *n.* a gaping wound.

GASKET (′ket), *n.* a thin round piece of rubber, metal, etc., to make a tight joint.

GASLOG (gas′log), *n.* a fireplace, made of hollow, perforated metal and lighted by gas.

GAS-MASK (-mask), *n.* a head-piece to prevent inhaling poisonous gases.

GASOLINE (′o-len), *n.* a volatile inflammable product of petroleum.

GASP (gasp), *v.i.* to catch the breath with difficulty; crave earnestly.

GASSY (′i), *adj.* impregnated with gas.

GASTERO-, GASTRO-, combining forms from the Greek *gaster*, stomach, or belly.

GASTRALGIA (-tral′ji-a), *n.* neuralgia of the stomach.

GASTRIC (′trik), *adj.* pertaining to the stomach.

GASTRIC JUICE (jus), *n.* acid fluid secreted in the mucous membrane of the stomach.

GASTRITIS (-tri′tis), *n.* inflammation of the stomach.

GASTRONOMIC (-tro-nom′ik), *adj.* pertaining to gastronomy.

GASTRONOMY (-tron′o-mi), *n.* the art of good eating, or the preparation of food.

GATE (gat), *n.* a frame of wood, iron, etc., closing an entrance or passage.

GATHER (gath′er), *v.t.* to assemble; collect; bring into one place; pick up.

GATHERING (-ing), *n.* the act of assembling together.

GAUDILY ('i-li), *adv.* in a gaudy manner.

GAUDY ('i), *adj.* showy; vulgar.

GAUGE (gaj), same as gage.

GAUGER ('er), *n.* one who gauges.

GAUGING ('ing), *n.* the art of measuring the contents of vessels of capacity.

GAUL (gawl), *n.* an inhabitant of ancient Gaul or France.

GAUNT (gawnt), *adj.* pinched and lean.

GAUNTLET (gawnt'let), *n.* a long, stout glove.

GAUZE (gawz), *n.* a very thin light, transparent material.

GAUZY ('i), *adj.* thin and semi-transparent, like gauze.

GAVEL (gav'el), *n.* a small mallet.

GAWKY (gawk'i), *adj.* awkward; ungainly.

GAY (ga), *adj.* lively; merry; cheerful.

GAZE (gaz), *v.i.* to look earnestly and fixedly : *n.* a steady, fixed look.

GAZELLE (ga-zel'), *n.* a small, elegant, swift-footed antelope.

GAZETTEER (gaz-et-ter'), *n.* a dictionary of geographical names.

GEAR (ger), *n.* accoutrements; apparatus; tackle; harness.

GEARING ('ing), *n.* ropes and tackle; working parts collectively.

GEAR-WHEEL ('hwel), *n.* a cogwheel.

GELATIN, GELATINE (jel'a-tin), *n.* animal jelly.

GELATINATE (je-lat'i-nat), *v.t.* to convert into gelatine or a jelly-like substance.

GELD (geld), *v.t.* to castrate : said of horses.

GELDING ('ing), *n.* a young castrated horse.

GELIDITY (je-lid'i-ti), *n.* intense cold; iciness.

GELOSE (jel'os), *n.* a vegetable gummy carbohydrate.

GEM (jem), *n.* a precious stone; any perfect or rare object.

GEMINI ('i-ni), *n.pl.* one of the signs in the zodiac (Castor and Pollux), known as the twins.

GENDARME (zhang-darm'), *n.* [*pl.* gendarmes], in France and Belgium, an armed policeman.

GENDER (jen'der), *n.* the grammatical distinction of sex.

GENEALOGICAL (je-ne-, jen-e-a-loj'i-kal), *adj.* exhibiting descent.

GENEALOGIST (-al'o-jist), *n.* one skilled in tracing pedigrees.

GENEALOGY ('o-ji), *n.* the science that treats of tracing pedigrees.

GENERA, *pl.* of genus.

GENERAL (jen'er-al), *adj.* relating to a whole genus, kind, class, order, or race; usual; ordinary; common : *n.* the commander of an army division.

GENERALISSIMO (-is'i-mo), *n.* a commander-in-chief.

GENERALITY ('i-ti), *n.* the state of being general; bulk; majority.

GENERALIZATION (-i-za'shun), *n.* result of generalizing; an induction.

GENERALIZE ('er-al-iz), *v.t.* infer inductively, as a general principle from particular instances.

GENERATE ('er-at), *v.t.* to produce; procreate; originate.

GENERATION (-a'shun), *n.* the act or process of generating; people of the same period; progeny.

GENERATIVE ('er-a-tiv), *adj.* having the power to generate.

GENERATOR ('er-a-ter), *n.* one who, or that which, generates; a machine in which steam or gas is produced.

GENERIC (je-ner'ik), *adj.* pertaining to a genus, kind, or class; opposed to *specific*; comprehensive.

GENEROSITY (jen-er-os'i-ti), *n.* liberality; magnanimity; munificent.

GENEROUS ('er-us), *adj.* characterized by liberality; munificent; bountiful; high-minded; honourable; strong.

GENESIS ('e-sis), *n.* originating; beginning.

GENIAL (jen'yal), *adj.* kindly and sympathetic; cordial.

GENIALITY ('i-ti), *n.* the quality of being genial.

GENITAL (jen'i-tal), *adj.* pertaining to generation.

GENITIVE ('i-tiv), *n.* a grammatical case, indicating origin, possession, or relation.

GENIUS (jen'yus), *n.* innate bent of mind or disposition ; remarkable aptitude for some special pursuit, etc.

GENRE (zhang'r), *n.* [French], a style of art representing some scene of common life.

GENTEEL (jen-tel'), *adj.* graceful or elegant ; polite ; well bred.

GENTIAN ('shan), *n.* a bitter herb with tonic roots.

GENTILE ('til, *n.* to the Jews, one outside their race or faith.

GENTILITY (-til'i-ti), *n.* good breeding ; social status and refinement.

GENTLE ('tl), *adj.* mild and refined ; kindly ; peaceful ; docile.

GENTLEMAN (-man), *n.* a well-bred and honourable man.

GENTLEWOMAN (-woom'an), *n.* a woman of good birth and breeding ; lady.

GENTRY ('tri), *n.* the upper class of society.

GENUINE ('u-in), *adj.* real ; unadulterated ; not hypocritical ; open.

GENUS (je'nus), *n.* [*pl.* genera (jen'er-a)], a classification ranking above a species and next below a subfamily ; a group of related species ; an order ; a class.

GEO-, a combining form signifying *earth, ground.*

GEOCENTRIC (je-o-sen'trik), *adj.* pertaining to the centre of the earth.

GEODETIC SURVEY (je-o-det'ik ser'va), *n.* a determination of the figure, etc., of portions of the earth by geodetic processes.

GEOGRAPHER (-og'ra-fer), *n.* one who is versed in, or a writer on, geography.

GEOGRAPHIC (je-o-graf'ik), **GEOGRAPHICAL** (-graf'i-kal), *adj.* pertaining to geography.

GEOGRAPHY (je-og'ra-fi), *n.* the science that describes the surface of the earth, and its division into continents, kingdoms, etc.

GEOLOGIC (loj'ik), **GEOLOGICAL** (-o-loj'i-kal), *adj.* pertaining to geology.

GEOLOGIST (-ol'o-jist), *n.* one versed in geology.

GEOLOGY ('o-ji), *n.* the science that investigates the structure of the earth, the successive physical changes it has undergone, and the causes which have operated in producing such alterations in the crust of the globe.

GEOMETRIC (-o-met'rik), **GEOMETRICAL** (-ri-kal), *adj.* pertaining to, or done by geometry.

GEOMETRICIAN (-om-e-trish'an), *n.* one who is skilled in geometry.

GEOMETRY (-om'e-tri), *n.* the measurements of lines, angles, surfaces, and solids, with their various relations.

GERANIUM (-ra'ni-um), *n.* a plant cultivated for its handsome flowers.

GERM (jerm), *n.* the rudimentary form of an organism.

GERMANE (jer-man'), *adj.* related ; relevant.

GERMICIDE (jer'mi-sid), *n.* a substance to destroy germs.

GERMINAL ('mi-nal), *adj.* pertaining to a germ or seedbud.

GERMINATE ('mi-nat), *v.i.* to begin to develop into a higher form.

GERMINATION (-na'shun), *n.* the first act of growth in a seed, bud, or germ.

GERMULE (jer'mul), *n.* a small or incipient germ.

GERRYMANDER (ger-i-man'der), *v.t.* to divide, as a state, voting district, etc., so as to give an unfair advantage to a particular political party.

GERUND (jer'und), *n.* a kind of verbal noun.

GESTATION (jes-ta'shun), *n.* pregnancy.

GESTICULATE (-tik'u-lat), *v.i.* to make gestures or motions.

GESTURE ('tur), *n.* a movement of the face, body or limbs, to express ideas, emotions, etc.

GET (get), *v.t.* to obtain ; procure ; gain ; acquire ; deserve.

GEYSER (ge'ser), *n.* an intermittent hot or boiling spring from which water or mud is ejected.

GHASTLINESS (gast'li-nes), *n.* the quality or state of being ghastly.

GHASTLY ('li), *adj.* death-like ; pale ; haggard ; cadaverous.

GHERKIN (ger'kin), *n.* a small cucumber for pickling.

GHETTO (get'o), *n.* the Jewish quarter.

GHOST (gost), *n.* the spirit of a deceased person ; apparition.

GHOUL (gool), *n.* one who robs graves or the dead.

GIANT (ji'ant), *n.* a man of extraordinary bulk or stature.

GIBBERISH (gib'er-ish), *n.* rapid incoherent talk.

GIBBET (jib'et), *n.* a gallows : *v.t.* expose to public scorn.

GIBBON (gib'un), *n.* an anthropoid ape of southern Asia.

GIBE (jib), *n.* a scoff ; taunt.

GIBLET (jib'let), *n.* one of the edible internal parts of a fowl.

GIDDINESS (gid'i-nes), *n.* the state of being giddy.

GIDDY ('i), *adj.* having a confused whirling sensation in the head ; frivolous.

GIFT (gift), *n.* present ; donation ; natural talent.

GIFTED ('ed), *adj.* talented.

GIGANTIC (ji-gan'tik), *adj.* huge ; colossal.

GIGGLE (gig'l), *v.i.* to laugh in a nervous, foolish manner.

GILD (gild), *v.t.* to overlay or wash with gold ; illuminate.

GILDING ('ing), *n.* the art or process of overlaying or covering with gold leaf, powder, etc.

GILL (gil), *n.* the respiratory organ of aquatic animals, especially fishes.

GILL (jil), *n.* ¼ of a pint.

GILLYFLOWER (jil'i-flou-er), *n.* a plant of the mustard family.

GILT (gilt), *adj.* covered with, or yellow like, gold : *n.* gilding.

GIMCRACK (jim'krak), *adj.* showy, but of no value ; trumpery.

GIMLET (gim'let), *n.* a small boring-tool with a pointed screw.

GIMP (gimp), *n.* a kind of interlaced silk trimming.

GIN (jin), *n.* an aromatic alcoholic liquid ; a machine for clearing cotton fibres from the seed.

GINGER ('jer), *n.* the dried root of a pungent aromatic plant.

GINGERBREAD (-bred), *n.* a cake made of flour, ginger, molasses, sugar, etc.

GINGERLY (-li), *adv.* cautiously.

GINGHAM (ging'am), *n.* a cotton dress-cloth.

GINSENG (jin'seng), *n.* an herb with an aromatic root.

GIPSY, GYPSY (jip'si), *n.* one of a wandering, dark-skinned, and dark-eyed race, of Eastern origin.

GIRAFFE (ji-raf'), *n.* a large ruminant mammal of Africa.

GIRD (gerd), *v.t.* to bind ; encircle ; brace.

GIRDER ('er), *n.* a main beam in a floor.

GIRDLE (ger'dl), *n.* a belt ; anything that encompasses.

GIRL (gerl), *n.* a female child.

GIRLHOOD ('hood), *n.* girls collectively ; the earlier state of maidenhood.

GIRT (gert), *p.adj.* moored taut by two cables.

GIRTH (gerth), *n.* anything that binds or encircles.

GIST (jist), *n.* the substance of a matter ; main point ; object.

GIVE (giv), *v.t.* to bestow ; confer without reward.

GIVEN (giv'n), *p.adj.* bestowed ; granted.

GIZZARD (giz'ard), *n.* the second stomach of birds.

GLACE (gla-sa'), *adj.* [French], finished with a smooth surface ; iced or cooled.

GLACIAL ('shal), *adj.* pertaining to, consisting of, or caused by, ice.

GLACIER (gla'shi-er, glas'i-er), *n.* a vast accumulation of ice and snow, found in the valleys and ravines of lofty mountains.

GLAD (glad), *adj.* joyous ; pleased ; cheerful.

GLADE (glad), *n.* an open space or passage in a wood or forest.

GLADIATOR (glad'i-a-ter), *n.* in ancient Rome a professional swordsman.

GLADIATORIAL (-a-to'ri-al), *adj.* pertaining to gladiators.

GLADIOLUS (glad-i-o'lus), *n.* a plant of the iris family.

GLADSOME (glad'sum), *adj.* joyous; gay; cheerful.

GLAIR (glar), *n.* the white of egg.

GLAMOUR (glam'er), *n.* fascination; witchery: *v.t.* to fascinate.

GLANCE (glans), *n.* a quick passing look of the eye; a momentary view.

GLAND (gland), *n.* a bodily organ by which secretion is carried on.

GLANDULAR ('du-lar), *adj.* pertaining to glands.

GLANDULE ('dul), *n.* a small gland.

GLARE (glar), *n.* a bright, dazzling light; a fierce, piercing look.

GLARING ('ing), *p.adj.* emitting or reflecting a dazzling light.

GLASS (glas), *n.* a hard, brittle, transparent substance; a drinking glass; a mirror.

GLAZE (glaz), *v.t.* to furnish with glass: *n.* the vitreous or glassy coating on potter's ware.

GLAZIER ('zher), *n.* one who sets glass in windows, etc.

GLEAM (glem), *n.* a stream of light: *v.i.* to emit brightness.

GLEAN (glen), *v.t.* to gather, as grain; collect little by little; infer.

GLEBE (gleb), *n.* land belonging to a parish church.

GLEE (gle), *n.* gaiety; mirth.

GLEN (glen), *n.* a narrow valley.

GLIB (glib), *adj.* voluble; flippant.

GLIDE (glid), *v.i.* flow or move along smoothly and noiselessly.

GLIDER (glid'er), *n.* an aeroplane without motor power; a power boat of very shallow draft and high speed.

GLIM (glim), *n.* a faint light.

GLIMMER ('er), *v.i.* to shine faintly and intermittently.

GLIMPSE (glimps), *n.* a weak, faint light; transient view.

GLINT (glint), *n.* a gleam of light.

GLISTEN (glis'n), *v.i.* to sparkle with light; shine: *n.* a glitter.

GLITTER (glit'er), *v.i.* to sparkle with light; gleam; be showy, or specious.

GLOAMING (glom'ing), *n.* twilight.

GLOAT (glot), *v.i.* to stare steadfastly; exult with feelings of lust or cruelty.

GLOBE (glob), *n.* a spherical body; ball; the terraqueous earth (with *the*).

GLOBE-TROTTER ('trot-er), *n.* an extensive traveller.

GLOBI, a *prefix* in various scientific words, meaning a *ball*, or *ball-shaped*. Globo.

GLOBULAR (glob'u-lar), *adj.* globe-like; spherical. Also globose.

GLOBULE (glob'ul), *n.* a small spherical particle.

GLOMERATE (glom'er-at), *adj.* gathered into a roundish head or mass.

GLOOM (gloom), *n.* partial darkness; obscurity; melancholy; depression; sadness; sullenness.

GLOOMINESS ('i-nes), *n.* the state of being gloomy.

GLOOMY ('i), *adj.* dismal; melancholy; dispirited; cheerless; morose.

GLORIA (glo'ri-a), *n.* an ascription of praise, especially the *Gloria in Excelsis* and *Gloria Patri*.

GLORIFICATION (-ri-fi-ka'shun), *n.* exaltation to honour and dignity.

GLORIFY ('ri-fi), *v.t.* to raise in honour and dignity.

GLORIOUS ('ri-us), *adj.* illustrious; celebrated; magnificent.

GLORY ('ri), *n.* splendour; magnificence; distinction; honour; the Divine perfection or presence.

GLOSS (glos), *n.* lustre from a polished surface; specious show.

GLOSSARY ('a-ri), *n.* a dictionary of obsolete, obscure, or technical words; an explanatory vocabulary.

GLOSSINESS ('i-nes), *n.* superficial lustre.

GLOSSO-, a combining form from the Greek *glossa*, tongue.

GLOSSY ('i), *adj.* having a lustrous smooth surface; smooth and plausible.

GLOTTIC ('ik), *adj.* pertaining to a language.

GLOVE (gluv), *n.* a hand-covering.

GLOW (glo), *v.i.* to shine with intense heat; radiate heat and light: *n.* ardour; emotion.

GLOWER (glou'er), *v.i.* to stare with a threatening or angry countenance.

GLOWWORM (glo'werm), *n.* a beetle, the wingless female of which emits a shining green light at night.

GLOZE (gloz), *v.t.* to gloss over.

GLUCOSE (gloo'kos), *n.* the particular form of sugar existing in many animal and vegetable organisms.

GLUE (gloo), *n.* a tenacious, viscid cement.

GLUM (glum), *adj.* gloomy ; sullen.

GLUT (glut), *n.* a superabundance ; a surfeit.

GLUTEN (gloo'ten), *n.* a tough grey albuminous substance obtained from wheat and other grains.

GLUTINOUS ('ti-nus), *adj.* viscid ; gluey.

GLUTTON (glut'n), *n.* one who eats to excess.

GLUTTONOUS (-us), *adj.* pertaining to, or characterized by, gluttony.

GLUTTONY (-i), *n.* eating to excess.

GLYCERIN, GLYCERINE (glis'er-in), *n.* a sweet, colourless, viscid liquid obtained from oils, fat, etc.

GNARL (narl), *n.* a knot on the trunk or branch of a tree.

GNARLED ('d), *adj.* full of knots ; distorted.

GNASH (nash), *v.t.* to strike together, as the teeth.

GNAT (nat), *n.* a small stinging winged insect, allied to the mosquito.

GNAW (naw), *v.t.* to bite off, or eat away, by degrees ; corrode.

GNEISS (nis), *n.* a crystallized rock composed of quartz, mica, and feldspar.

GNOME (nom), *n.* a fabulous goblin.

GNOSIS (no'sis), *adj.* higher knowledge or insight.

GNOSTIC (nos'tik), *adj.* pertaining to the Gnostics.

GNOSTICISM ('ti-sizm), *n.* a system of religion mixed with Greek and Oriental philosophy (1st-6th century A.D.).

GNU (noo), *n.* a ruminant horned animal.

GO (go), *v.i.* to depart ; proceed ; move on.

GOAD (god), *n.* a pointed stick to urge on cattle: *v.t.* to urge forward.

GOAL (gol), *n.* the winning post at a race, etc. ; hence, the end aimed at.

GOAT (got), *n.* a ruminating horned quadruped.

GOATEE (go-te'), *n.* a tuft of hair on the chin.

GOB (gob), *n.* a lump, piece or chunk ; [Slang], a sailor of the U.S. navy.

GOBBLE (gob'l), *v.t.* to swallow hastily or greedily : *v.i.* to utter a cry like a turkey.

GOBELIN (gob'e-lin), *adj.* a superior kind of French tapestry.

GOBLET (gob'let), *n.* a drinking-vessel.

GOBLIN ('lin), *n.* an evil spirit.

GO-CART ('kart), *n.* a child's cart.

GOD (god), *n.* the Supreme Deity and self-existent Creator and Upholder of the universe.

GODCHILD ('child), *n.* one for whom one is sponsor at baptism.

GODDESS ('es), *n.* a female deity.

GODFATHER ('fa-ther), *n.* one who acts as sponsor to another at baptism.

GODHEAD ('hed), *n.* the Divine essence, nature, and attributes ; the Supreme Deity.

GODLINESS ('li-nes), *n.* piety.

GODLY ('li), *adj.* devout ; pious.

GODMOTHER ('muth-er), *n.* a female sponsor at baptism.

GOD'S ACRE (godz'a-ker), *n.* a church-yard.

GODSEND (god'send), *n.* unexpected assistance.

GODSPEED ('sped), *n.* success; prosperity; a prosperous journey.

GOING (go'ing), *n.* the act of departing.

GOITRE (goi'ter), *n.* a swelling of the glands in the front part and side of the neck.

GOLD (gold), *n.* a metallic element, soft, ductile, and a bright yellow when pure ; money.

GOLDEN (gold'n), *adj.* formed of, or resembling, gold ; bright ; most valuable ; excellent.

GOLDEN AGE (aj), the fabled primeval age of perfect human happiness and innocency.

GOLDEN PHEASANT (fez'ant), *n.* a handsome Chinese pheasant.

GOLDEN PLOVER (pluv'er), *n.* a game bird.

GOLDENROD (-rod), *n.* a tall plant of the aster family with yellow flowers.

GOLDEN RULE (rool), the rule to treat others as we ourselves wish to be treated.

GOLDFINCH ('finch), *n.* a beautiful singing bird.

GOLDFISH ('fish), *n.* an orange-coloured fresh-water fish.

GOLDSMITH ('smith), *n.* a worker in gold, or dealer in gold-plate.

GOLF (golf), *n.* a game played with a small gutta-percha ball and club-headed sticks.

GOLGOTHA (gol'go-tha), *n.* [Hebrew], the place where Jesus Christ was crucified.

GONDOLA (gon'do-la), *n.* a long narrow Venetian pleasure boat propelled by one oar; car used for carrying coal, etc.

GONDOLIER (-do-ler'), *n.* rower of a gondola.

GONE (gon), *p.adj.* passed; lost.

GONG (gong), *n.* a tambourine-shaped musical instrument.

GONO, a *prefix* in many scientific words, meaning *generation, reproduction*, as *gono*-blast, a reproductive cell.

GOOBER (goo'ber), *n.* a peanut.

GOOD (good), *adj.* having excellent qualities; proper, fit for, adapted to, any particular object; moral; kind.

GOOD-BYE (good-bi'), *n.* salutation at parting; contraction of " God be with you."

GOOD FRIDAY (fri'da), *n.* a day of fasting in commemoration of the crucifixion of Jesus Christ.

GOODLY ('li), *adj.* good-looking; noble; considerable.

GOODS AND CHATTELS (chat'lz), personal property.

GOODWILL (-wil'), *n.* benevolence; kindly feeling; the value a business has over and above stock-in-trade, etc.

GOOSE (goos), *n.* a web-footed domesticated bird; a tailor's smoothing iron.

GOOSEBERRY (gooz'ber-i), *n.* the acid fruit of a barbed garden-shrub.

GOOSE-FLESH (goos'flesh), *n.* a pimpled condition of the skin, caused by terror or cold.

GOOSENECK (goos'nek), *n.* a bent iron fitted to a boom.

GOOSESTEP ('step), *n.* the stiff parade step of the German soldiers.

GOPHER (go'fer), *v.i.* to mine unsystematically: *n.* a North American burrowing, rat-like rodent.

GORE (gor), *n.* congealed or clotted blood; a triangular piece sewn into a dress, sail, etc.

GORGE (gorj), *n.* the throat; gullet; a narrow passage between mountains or hills: *v.t.* to swallow with greediness; satiate.

GORGEOUS ('jus), *adj.* splendid; showy; inclined to magnificence.

GORILLA (go-ril'a), *n.* an African anthropoid ape some 5 ft. in height, with powerful limbs.

GORMAND (gor'mand), **GOURMAND** (goor'mand), *n.* a greedy or ravenous eater; glutton.

GORMANDIZE ('man-diz), *v.i.* to eat greedily or voraciously.

GORY (gor'i), *adj.* covered or stained with blood.

GOSLING (goz'ling), *n.* a young goose; a catkin.

GOSPEL (gos'pel), *n.* the announcement of the salvation of mankind by Jesus Christ; the history of the life and doctrines of Jesus Christ, contained in the New Testament.

GOSPELLER (-er), *n.* an evangelist.

GOSSAMER ('a-mer), *n.* a very thin, soft, filmy, strong gauze.

GOSSIP ('ip), *n.* scandal; a babbler: *v.i.* to tell idle tales about others; tattle.

GOSSOON (go-soon'), *n.* a young lad.

GOTH (goth), *n.* one of the Teutonic tribe that overran the Roman Empire (3rd and 4th centuries A.D.).

GOTHIC ('ik), *adj.* pertaining to the Goths: *n.* the Gothic or pointed style of architecture.

GOUGE (gouj), *n.* a rounded hollow chisel for cutting grooves or holes ; a swindle.

GOULASH (goo'lash), *n.* a meat stew, richly seasoned.

GOURD (gord), *n.* a fruit, the hard shell of which is used for holding liquids.

GOURMAND (goor'mand, Fr. 'mang), *n.* a glutton ; an epicure. *Also* gourmet.

GOUT (gout), *n.* a painful inflammatory disease of the joints, especially of the great toe.

GOVERN (guv'ern), *v.t.* to control by authority ; regulate ; direct ; manage ; restrain.

GOVERNANCE (-nans), *n.* government ; control.

GOVERNESS (-nes), *n.* a lady who trains and instructs children.

GOVERNMENT (-ment), *n.* administration of public affairs ; established state of legal authority ; executive power.

GOVERNOR ('er-ner), *n.* one who is invested with supreme authority ; chief ruler ; tutor ; a device for regulating an engine, etc.

GOWN (goun), *n.* a woman's outer garment ; a long loose robe worn by professional men.

GRAB (grab), *v.t.* to seize suddenly and forcibly ; snatch.

GRABBLE ('l), *v.i.* to feel about ; grope.

GRACE (gras), *n.* any excellence ; elegance ; beauty ; embellishment ; the unmerited favour and love of God toward man in Christ ; virtue ; a brief prayer before or after meals.

GRACEFUL ('fool), *adj.* full of grace or beauty.

GRACIOUS (gra'shus), *adj.* kindly ; affable ; polite.

GRADATE (gra'dat), *v.t.* to produce in grades.

GRADATION (gra-da'shun), *n.* a regular advance or progress.

GRADATORY (grad'a-to-ri), *n.* a series of steps leading from a cloister into a church.

GRADE (grad), *n.* a step or degree in rank, dignity, quality, order, etc. ; the rise or descent of a railroad, etc.

GRADIENT (gra'di-ent), *adj.* advancing by steps : *n.* the part of a road which slopes.

GRADUAL (grad'u-al), *adj.* proceeding by degrees ; step by step.

GRADUATE ('u-at), *n.* one on whom an academical degree has been conferred : *v.t.* to mark with degrees.

GRADUATION (-a'shun), *n.* the conferring or reception of an academical degree.

GRADUATOR ('u-a-ter), *n.* an electromagnet for making and breaking a telegraphic circuit.

GRAFT (graft), *n.* a small shoot of a tree inserted into another tree ; an unlawful or irregular perquisite ; a bribe.

GRAFTER (graf'ter), *n.* an office holder, employee, or any person under pay who acquires perquisites dishonestly.

GRAIL (gral), *n.* the Holy Grail, the cup used by Jesus when He instituted the Sacrament ; a cup ; a chalice.

GRAIN (gran), *n.* any minute hard mass ; a single seed of corn ; the seeds of cereals collectively ; a unit of weight = 1-20th of a scruple, 1-24th of a pennyweight ; texture.

GRAINING ('ing), *n.* painting in imitation of the grain or texture of wood.

GRAM, see gramme.

GRAMERCY (gra-mer'si), *interj.* expressing thankfulness.

GRAMMAR (gram'er), *n.* the art of speaking or writing a language correctly ; an elementary treatise on language.

GRAMMARIAN (gra-ma'ri-an), *n.* one who is versed in grammar.

GRAMMATICAL (-mat'ik-al), *adj.* pertaining to grammar, or its rules.

GRAMME (gram), *n.* the unit of weight in the metric system, 15.43 grains troy.

GRAMOPHONE ('o-fon), *n.* an instrument for recording and reproducing speech or music.

GRAMPUS ('pus), *n.* a large cetacean ; a corpulent person.

GRANARY (gran'a-ri), *n.* a storehouse for grain.

GRAND (grand), *adj.* illustrious ; chief ; great ; magnificent ; splendid ; sublime ; noble ; implying the second degree of parentage or descent.

GRANDCHILD (grand'child), *n.* the child of one's son or daughter.

GRANDEE (gran-de'), *n.* a Spanish nobleman of the highest rank.

GRANDEUR ('jur), *n.* greatness ; vastness ; sublimity.

GRANDFATHER (grand'father), *n.* the father of one's father or mother.

GRANDILOQUENT (gran-dil'o-kwent), *adj.* speaking in bombastic style.

GRANDIOSE ('di-os), *adj.* really or affectedly grand or impressive.

GRANDMA (gran'ma), *n.* a grand-mother.

GRANDMOTHER (grand'muth-er), *n.* a father's or mother's mother.

GRANDPARENT ('par-ent), *n.* the parent of one's parents.

GRANGE (granj), *n.* a farm with its dwelling-house, appurtenances, etc. ; a powerful agricultural association in the U.S.

GRANITE (gran'it), *n.* a massive crystalline rock composed of quartz, feldspar, and mica.

GRANNY (gran'i), *n.* abbr. of grand-mother.

GRANT (grant), *v.t.* to give or confer, especially in response to a request ; admit as true (what has not been proved) ; concede.

GRANTEE (-te'), *n.* the person to whom property is transferred by deed, etc.

GRANTOR ('er), *n.* one who transfers property by deed, etc.

GRANULAR (gran'u-lar), *adj.* com-posed of, or resembling, grains or granules.

GRANULATE ('u-lat), *v.t.* to form into grains or small masses.

GRANULE ('ul), *n.* a small grain.

GRAPE (grap), *n.* the fruit of the grapevine.

GRAPEFRUIT (-frut), *n.* a large, round, citrous tropical fruit.

GRAPHIC (graf'ik), **GRAPHICAL** (-i-kal), *adj.* pertaining to the art of writing or delineating ; vividly described.

GRAPHITE ('it), *n.* a metallic variety of carbon.

GRAPHO-, a combining form from the Greek *graphein*, to write.

GRAPHOLOGY (graf-ol'o-ji), *n.* the art of describing character by the handwriting.

GRAPHOPHONE ('o-fon), *n.* a form of the phonograph.

GRAPPLE (grap'l), *v.t.* to lay fast hold of : *n.* a close fight.

GRASP (grasp), *v.t.* to seize or catch at.

GRASPING ('ing), *p.adj.* avaricious.

GRASS (gras), *n.* field or hill pasture ; herbage.

GRASSHOPPER ('hop-er), *n.* a large nimble insect of the locust kind.

GRASS-WIDOW ('wid-o), *n.* a woman not living with her husband.

GRASSY ('i), *adj.* abounding in, covered with, grass.

GRATE (grat), *n.* a framework to hold fuel ; a set of bars : *v.t.* to rub or wear away by friction : *v.i.* make a harsh noise.

GRATEFUL ('fool), *adj.* thankful ; pleasurable.

GRATER (-er), *n.* a device with a rough surface for grating.

GRATIFICATION (grat-i-fi-ka'shun), *n.* satisfaction ; pleasure ; reward or recompense.

GRATIFY ('i-fi), *v.t.* to indulge ; delight ; humour.

GRATING (grat'ing), *n.* an open frame-work : *p.adj.* harsh ; irritating.

GRATIS (gra'tis), *adv.* gratuitously.

GRATITUDE (grat'i-tud), *n.* appre-ciation of favours received ; thank-fulness.

GRATUITOUS (gra-tu'i-tus), *adj.* freely bestowed ; voluntary.

GRATUITY ('i-ti), *n.* a donation or gift.

GRAVE (grav), *adj.* serious ; solemn ; thoughtful ; sedate : *n.* an excavation for a dead body.

GRAVEL (grav'l), *n.* fragments of

rock coarser than sand; disease occasioned by the presence of calculi in the bladder and kidneys.

GRAVELY (grav'li), *adv.* in a grave manner.

GRAVER ('er), *n.* a cutting tool; an engraver.

GRAVESTONE (grav'ston), *n.* a stone placed at a grave.

GRAVEYARD (grav'yard), *n.* a cemetery.

GRAVIMETER (gra-vim'e-ter), *n.* an instrument for measuring the specific gravity of liquid or solid bodies.

GRAVITATE (grav'i-tat), *v.i.* to be acted upon by the force of gravity.

GRAVITATION (-i-ta'shun), *n.* the force which attracts material bodies to each other.

GRAVITY ('i-ti), *n.* that force which tends to draw all bodies toward the centre of the earth; weight; importance; solemnity.

GRAVY (gra'vi), *n.* the fatty juice from roasting flesh.

GRAY, GREY (gra), *adj.* of a dull white colour; dull: *n.* a dull white colour; something dull.

GRAYLING (gra'ling), *n.* a fresh-water fish of the salmon family.

GRAZE (graz), *v.t.* to touch or rub lightly: *v.i.* to eat grass.

GREASE (gres), *n.* soft animal fat; oily matter.

GREASER ('er), *n.* one who, or that which, greases.

GREASY ('i), *adj.* oily; unctuous; foggy; muddy.

GREAT (grat), *adj.* large; chief; principal; weighty; marvellous; eminent; illustrious; noble; able; accomplished.

GREAT BRITAIN (brit'n), England, Scotland and Wales combined.

GREAT DANE (dan), one of a breed of dogs.

GREAT LAKES (laks), the large lakes: Superior, Michigan, Erie, Huron and Ontario in North America.

GREAT PRIMER (prim'er), a size of type.

GREAT PYRAMID (pir'a-mid), the pyramid of Cheops, near Cairo.

GREAT SEAL (sel), the chief official seal of a kingdom, state, etc.

GRECIAN (gre'shan), *adj.* pertaining to Greece.

GRECO (gre'ko), a *prefix* meaning *Greek.*

GREED (gred), *n.* avarice; greediness.

GREEDY ('i), *adj.* voracious; gluttonous; eagerly desirous; covetous.

GREEK (grek), *adj.* pertaining to, or resembling, Greece or the Greeks; Hellenic: *n.* the people of Greece; the language of Greece.

GREEK CHURCH (cherch), *n.* the Eastern or Oriental Church.

GREEK ORDERS (or'derz), in architecture, the Doric, Ionic, and Corinthian orders.

GREEN (gren), *adj.* having the colour of growing plants; a colour composed of blue and yellow; fresh; flourishing; unripe.

GREENBACK ('bak), *n.* a paper money (U.S. legal-tender note) with a green back.

GREENGAGE (-gaj), *n.* a plum.

GREEN GOODS (goodz), counterfeit paper money.

GREENHORN ('horn), *n.* a simpleton; novice.

GREENHOUSE ('hous), *n.* a conservatory.

GREENROOM ('room), *n.* the actors' retiring-room in a theatre.

GREENSICKNESS ('sik-nes), *n.* chlorosis.

GREET (gret), *v.t.* salute in kindness or respect; congratulate.

GREETING ('ing), *n.* a salutation.

GREGARIAN (gre-ga'ri-an), *adj.* living in herds.

GREGARIOUS (gre-ga'ri-us), *adj.* associating together in herds.

GREGORIAN CALENDAR (gre-go'ri-an kal'en-der), the reformed calendar introduced, 1582, by Pope Gregory XIII.

GRENADE (gre-nad'), *n.* an explosive shell fired by a fuse and thrown by hand.

GRENADIER (gren-a-der'), *n.* originally a foot soldier who threw grenades.

GRENADINE (-a-den'), *n.* a dress fabric of thin gauzy silk or wool.

GREYHOUND ('hound), *n.* a slender, swift hound.

GRID (grid), *n.* a perforated plate, used in a storage battery; a part in a radio tube.

GRIDDLE (grid'l), *n.* broad, shallow pan, for cooking griddle cakes.

GRIDE (grid), *v.t.* to scrape with a rasping sound.

GRIDIRON ('i-ern), *n.* a grated iron utensil for broiling meat, etc.; a football field. (Slang.)

GRIEF (gref), *n.* mental pain on account of present or past trouble.

GRIEVANCE (grev'ans), *n.* a sense of wrong or oppression.

GRIEVE (grev), *v.t.* to cause to experience grief; afflict mentally.

GRIEVOUS ('us), *adj.* causing grief or sorrow; oppressive; pitiable.

GRILL (grill), *v.t.* to broil; torment: *n.* a gridiron; grilled meat.

GRILLE (gril), *n.* an open grating or screen of wood or metal.

GRIM (grim), *adj.* of a forbidding aspect; stern and surly; hideous.

GRIMACE (gri-mas'), *n.* a distortion of the countenance; smirk.

GRIME (grim), *n.* foul matter.

GRIMY ('i), *adj.* full of grime.

GRIN (grin), *n.* a broad smile: *v.i.* to show the teeth in laughter, scorn, or pain.

GRIND (grind), *v.t.* to pulverize, sharpen or smooth by friction; oppress; harass.

GRINDER ('der), *n.* one who, or that which, grinds; a molar tooth.

GRINDSTONE ('ston), *n.* a flat, circular stone for sharpening tools, etc.

GRINGO (gring'go), *n.* in Spanish America, a foreigner.

GRIP (grip), *n.* a grasp with the hand held firmly; a hilt or handle: *v.i.* to take fast hold.

GRIPE (grip), *n.* a squeeze; pressure; pinching distress: *pl.* colic.

GRIPING ('ing), *adj.* avaricious; purgative.

GRIPPE (grip, grep), *n.* influenza.

GRIPPER (grip'er), *n.* a mechanical device for seizing and holding.

GRISETTE (gre-zet'), *n.* [French], a Parisian shopgirl.

GRISLY (griz'li), *adj.* terrible; savage-looking.

GRIST (grist), *n.* grain for grinding.

GRISTLE (gris'l), *n.* cartilage.

GRISTLY ('li), *adj.* cartilaginous.

GRIT (grit), *n.* rough, hard particles, as sand, etc.; firmness; courage.

GRIZZLY (griz'li), *adj.* somewhat gray: *n.* a large, fierce bear of North America.

GROAN (gron), *n.* a low, deep sound uttered in pain or sorrow.

GROAT (grot), *n.* formerly a silver coin current in England, value 4d.; a trifling sum.

GROCER (gro'ser), *n.* one who sells groceries.

GROCERY (-i), *n.* tea, coffee, sugar, spices, etc. (usually *pl.*); a grocer's shop.

GROG (grog), *n.* a mixture of spirits and water.

GROGGERY ('er-i), *n.* a grogshop.

GROGGY ('i), *adj.* tipsy; staggering as if dazed.

GROIN (groin), *n.* the depressed part of the human body between the thigh and the abdomen.

GROMMET (grom'et), *n.* an eyelet of metal.

GROOM (groom), *n.* a man or boy who has charge of horses; a bridegroom.

GROOMSMAN (groomz'man), *n.* one who attends a bridegroom; best man.

GROOVE (groov), *n.* a channel or furrow, especially as cut by a tool; settled habit or routine.

GROPE (grop), *v.i.* to feel one's way with the hands, as in the dark; seek blindly.

GROSBEAK (gros'bek), *n.* one of various warblers with a large stout beak.

GROSGRAIN (gro'gran), *n.* a stout double-corded silk.

GROSS (gros), *adj.* bulky; thick; coarse; rude; indelicate; flagrant; dull; heavy; corpulent; dense: *n.* 12 dozen; entire amount.

GROTESQUE (gro-tesk'), *adj.* extravagant ; whimsical ; ridiculous.

GROTTO (grot'o), *n.* a natural or artificial cavern in the earth.

GROUCH (grouch), *n.* a sulky mood.

GROUCHY ('i), *adj.* sullen ; ill-tempered.

GROUND (ground), *n.* the earth or soil ; foundation ; cause or reason ; origin ; connection of an electric current with the earth : *pl.* dregs or sediment : *v.t.* to place or set on, or in, the ground.

GROUND-HOG ('hog), *n.* the wood-chuck ; the aardvark.

GROUND-HOG DAY (da), *n.* February 2.

GROUND-SWELL ('swel), *n.* a broad, deep, heavy, rolling sea.

GROUP (groop), *n.* a small crowd or assemblage ; a cluster.

GROUSE (grous), *n.* a moor-fowl ; prairie-hen : *v.i.* grumble.

GROUT (grout), *n.* a semi-liquid mortar.

GROUTY (grout'i), *adj.* cross ; sulky.

GROVE (grov), *n.* a small wood.

GROVEL (grov'el), *v.i.* to move with the body prostrate on the ground ; be mean or debased.

GROVELLING (-ing), *p.adj.* mean ; undignified.

GROW (gro), *v.t.* to cultivate : *v.i.* to increase in stature or size by natural organic development.

GROWL (groul), *n.* a deep angry snarl or murmur.

GROWTH (groth), *n.* advancement ; increase ; progress.

GRUB (grub), *v.t.* to dig up ; root out of the ground ; provide with food : *n.* the larva of a beetle, moth or other insect ; food.

GRUBSTAKE (grub'stak), *n.* outfit given to a miner for exploration.

GRUDGE (gruj), *v.t.* to regard with envy or discontent : *n.* secret malice.

GRUEL (groo'el), *n.* a light, semi-liquid food made of oatmeal, etc., for invalids.

GRUESOME (groo'sum), *adj.* horrible of aspect ; inspiring gloom or horror.

GRUFF (gruf), *adj.* harsh ; hoarse.

GRUMBLE (grum'bl), *v.i.* to murmur discontentedly ; find fault.

GRUMPILY (grump'i-li), *adv.* in a grumpy manner.

GRUMPY ('pi), *adj.* surly ; cross.

GRUNT (grunt), *n.* the guttural noise of a hog.

GUANO ('no), *n.* the dung of sea-birds used as a fertilizer.

GUARANTEE (gar-an-te'), *n.* an engagement to secure the fulfillment of an agreement ; one who becomes surety : *v.t.* be responsible for.

GUARANTY (gar'an-ti), *n.* a guarantee ; a security.

GUARD (gard), *v.t.* to watch over or protect : *v.i.* be cautious (with *against*) : *n.* any contrivance or device for security ; an official in charge of a train.

GUARDIAN ('i-an), *n.* one who has the care of the person or property of another.

GUARD-SHIP ('ship), *n.* a warship stationed at a port or harbour for its protection.

GUARDSMAN (gardz'man), *n.* an officer or soldier of the guards.

GUAVA (gwa'va), *n.* a tree of tropical America yielding a pear-shaped fruit, from which a jelly is made.

GUBERNATORIAL (gu-ber-na-to'-ri-al), *adj.* pertaining to a governor or to his office.

GUDGEON (guj'un), *n.* a small edible fresh-water fish ; a person who is easily imposed upon.

GUERDON (ger'dun), *n.* a reward.

GUERILLA (ge-ril'a), *n.* one of an irregular force engaged in harassing an enemy in small bands ; petty warfare.

GUESS (ges), *n.* a conjecture.

GUEST (gest), *n.* one who is entertained at the house or table of another.

GUIDABLE (gid'a-bl), *adj.* that may be guided.

GUIDANCE ('ans), *n.* direction; leading.

GUIDE (gid), *n.* one who leads or directs ; conductor ; director : *v.t.* regulate.

GUIDON (gi'dun), *n.* the forked flag of a troop of light cavalry.

GUILD (gild), *n.* a fraternity; corporation; association.

GUILE (gil), *n.* deceit; cunning; duplicity.

GUILEFUL ('fool), *adj.* full of guile.

GUILLOTINE ('o-ten), *n.* an apparatus, used in France, for beheading a criminal.

GUILT (gilt), *n.* liable to a penalty; criminality.

GUILTILY ('ti-li), *adv.* in a guilty manner.

GUILTY ('ti), *adj.* justly chargeable with a crime; wicked; criminal.

GUIMPE (gamp), *n.* chemisette used with low-necked gown.

GUINEA (gin'i), *n.* formerly a gold coin in England, now a price value of 21s.

GUINEA-FOWL (-foul), *n.* a greyish-blue African bird.

GUINEA-PIG (-pig), *n.* a small domesticated South American rodent, allied to the cavy.

GUISE (giz), *n.* external appearance; dress; mien.

GUITAR (gi-tar'), *n.* a six-stringed instrument on the principle of the violin, played with the fingers.

GULCH (gulch), *n.* a rocky or rough narrow valley.

GULF (gulf), *n.* an arm of the sea extending into the land; an abyss.

GULF STREAM (strem), *n.* a vast warm ocean-current flowing from the Gulf of Mexico northward to Nantucket Island and Eastward across the Atlantic.

GULL (gul), *n.* a web-footed sea-fowl; one who is easily cheated: *v.t.* to cheat; deceive.

GULLET ('et), *n.* the throat; œsophagus.

GULLIBILITY (gul-i-bil'i-ti), *n.* capacity for being gulled.

GULLIBLE (gul'i-bl), *adj.* capable of being easily deceived.

GULLY ('i), *n.* a channel or hollow worn by water; narrow ravine.

GULP (gulp), *v.t.* to swallow eagerly or in large drafts.

GUM (gum), *n.* the soft, fleshy part of the jaws; a substance that exudes from certain trees.

GUM-ARABIC (ar'a-bik), *n.* a gum obtained from various species of acacia.

GUMBO ('bo), *n.* soup made from the gummy pods of the okra.

GUMMY ('i), *adj.* like gum.

GUMPTION (gump'shun), *n.* quickness of perception; common sense.

GUMPTIOUS ('shus), *adj.* shrewd; smart.

GUN (gun), *n.* an instrument for discharging shot; a portable fire-arm; a pistol.

GUNCOTTON ('kot-n), *n.* a highly explosive substance.

GUN-METAL ('met-al), *n.* an alloy of copper and tin.

GUNNER ('er), *n.* one who works a gun; an artilleryman; a warrant-officer in the navy.

GUNNY ('i), *n.* a coarse heavy sack-cloth of jute or hemp.

GUNPOWDER ('pou-der), *n.* an explosive substance composed of sulphur, nitre and charcoal; a kind of tea.

GUNWALE (gun'l), *n.* the upper edge of the side of a ship next to the bulwarks.

GURGLE (ger'gl), *v.i.* to flow or run with a purling, bubbling sound.

GUSH (gush), *v.i.* to issue with violence; flow copiously; be extravagantly sentimental.

GUSHER ('er), *n.* one who, or that which, gushes; an oil well that discharges without the aid of machinery.

GUSSET (gus'et), *n.* a small triangular piece of cloth inserted in a garment to strengthen or enlarge a part.

GUST (gust), *n.* a sudden squall; taste; relish.

GUSTATORY ('ta-to-ri), *adj.* pertaining to the taste.

GUSTFUL ('fool). *adj.* full of gusto.

GUSTO ('to), *n.* zest; relish.

GUSTY ('ti), *adj.* characterized by gusts.

GUT (gut), *n.* an intestine; catgut: *v.t.* to extract the entrails of; to plunder.

GUTTA-PERCHA (gut'a-per'cha), *n.* the inspissated juice extracted from an evergreen tree of various tropical regions.

GUTTER ('er), *n.* a channel for carrying away water.

GUTTERAL (gut'ur-al), *adj.* pertaining to the throat.

GUY (gi), *n.* a rope, chain, etc., to swing and keep steady a heavy body ; [Slang], a person oddly or dowdily dressed : *v.i.* to ridicule ; delude.

GUZZLE (guz'l), *v.i.* to drink greedily and immoderately.

GYMN-, GYMNO, a combining form from the Greek *gymnos,* naked.

GYMNASIUM (jim-na'zi-um), *n.* a building where gymnastic exercises are practised.

GYMNAST ('nast), *n.* one who practises, or is expert in, gymnastics.

GYMNASTICS ('tiks), *n.pl.* athletic exercises.

GYNE-, GYNECO-, combining forms from the Greek *gyne,* woman, female·

GYNECOLOGY (jin-e-kol'o-ji), *n.* that branch of medical science which treats of the functions and diseases of women.

GYPSUM (jip'sum), *n.* sulphate of lime ; plaster of Paris.

GYPSY, same as Gipsy.

GYRATE (ji'rate), *v.i.* to revolve round a central point ; rotate.

GYRATORY ('ra-to-ri), *adj.* revolving in circle.

GYRE (jir), *n.* the circular motion of a moving body : *v.i.* to gyrate.

GYROPLANE (ji'ro-plan), *n.* flying machine able to ascend and descend vertically.

GYROCOMPASS (ji'ro-kom'pas), *n.* a compass operated by a gyroscope and uninfluenced by the earth's magnetism.

GYROSCOPE (ji'ro-skop), *n.* an instrument for demonstrating the laws of rotation.

H

H, h (ach), *n.* the eighth letter of the English alphabet.

H, h, *n.* an abbreviation.

H, *n.* a Roman numeral denoting 200 ; with a bar (H̄), 200,000.

HA (ha), *interj.* an expression of wonder, joy, etc.

HABEAS CORPUS (ha'be-as kor'-pus), [Latin, you have the body], a writ to produce a prisoner.

HABERDASHER (hab'er-dash-er), *n.* a dealer in men's furnishings and small wares.

HABILIMENT (ha-bil'i-ment), *n.* an article of clothing : *pl.* dress.

HABILITATE ('i-tat), *v.i.* to become qualified.

HABIT (hab'it), *n.* ordinary course of conduct ; disposition ; established custom ; dress.

HABITABLE ('it-abl), *adj.* fit to be dwelt in.

HABITANT ('i-tant), *n.* a dweller.

HABITAT ('i-tat), *n.* the natural locality of animals, plants, etc., in their wild state.

HABITATION (-i-ta'shun), *n.* residence or place of abode.

HABITUAL (ha-bit'u-al), *adj.* formed or acquired by use ; customary ; inveterate.

HABITUATE ('u-at), *v.t.* to make familiar by use or custom.

HABITUDE (hab'i-tud), *n.* habit ; customary manner or mode.

HABITUE (ha-bit'u-a), *n.* one who habitually frequents a place.

HACIENDA (ha-si-en'da), *n.* [Spanish], in Spanish America, a large plantation.

HACK (hak), *v.t.* to cut irregularly and into small pieces ; notch : *n.* a horse or carriage let out for hire ; literary drudge.

HACK SAW (saw), *n.* a fine-toothed saw for cutting metals.

HACKBERRY ('ber-ri), *n.* a large North American forest tree, with an edible fruit.

HACKLE (hak'l), *v.t.* to dress or comb, as flax or hemp ; tear into pieces.

HACKMAN (hak'man), *n.* the driver of a hack for hire.

HACKMATACK ('ma-tak), *n.* the red American larch or tamarack.

HACKNEY ('ni), *v.t.* to wear out by constant use; to make common or trite.

HACKNEYED ('nid), *p.adj.* worn out; commonplace.

HADDOCK (had'ok), *n.* seafish of the cod family.

HADES (ha'dez), *n.* the abode and state of the dead.

HÆMA-, HÆMAT-, HÆMATO-, HÆMO-, combining forms from the Greek *haima*, blood.

HÆMACHROME (hem'a-krom), *n.* the colouring matter of the blood.

HÆMATIC (he-mat'ik), *adj.* pertaining to the blood; full of blood.

HAFT (haft), *n.* a handle of a tool or knife.

HAG (hag), *n.* a witch; a parasite on fishes.

HAGGARD ('ard), *adj.* worn and anxious in appearance.

HAGGLE ('l), *v.i.* to contend over trifles.

HAIL (hal), *n.* frozen raindrops; a call or salutation.

HAIR (har), *n.* the filaments growing out of the skin of a mammal.

HAIRSPLITTING ('split-ing), *adj.* making oversubtle or very minute distinctions, in reasoning or statement.

HAIRSPRING ('spring), *n.* a very fine spring to regulate the balance wheel of a watch.

HAIR-TRIGGER (har'trig-er), *n.* a delicately adjusted secondary trigger.

HAKE (hak), *n.* edible seafish allied to cod.

HALBERD (hal'berd), **HALBERT** ('bert), *n.* a mediæval weapon.

HALCYON ('si-un), *adj.* peaceful; happy; calm : *n.* the kingfisher.

HALCYON DAYS (daz), days of peace, contentment, or happiness.

HALE (hal), *adj.* healthy; hearty.

HALF (haf), *n.* [*pl.* halves (havz)], one of two equal parts

HALF-BLOOD ('blud) *n.* one whose parents are of different races.

HALF-BREED ('bred) *n.* a person of mixed blood.

HALF-CASTE ('kast) *n.* a person of European and Asiatic blood; a half-breed.

HALF-MAST (-mast), *n.* the position of a flag half-way up its pole, as a mark of respect to the dead.

HALF-TONE (half'ton), *n.* a plate obtained by taking a photograph of an object through a net or screen.

HALIBUT (hal'i-but), *n.* a large edible flat-fish.

HALITOSIS (hal-i-to'sis), *n.* foul breath.

HALL (hawl), *n.* a large room; a court of justice; a passageway; a room for lectures, etc.

HALLELUJAH (hal-e-loo'ya), *n.* an ascription of praise to God.

HALL-MARK (hawl'mark), *n.* official mark attesting the quality of gold and silver articles.

HALLO (ha-lo'), *halloo* (-loo'), *interj.* an exclamation to call attention.

HALLOW (hal'o), *v.t.* to consecrate; revere.

HALLOWEEN (-en'), *n.* the Eve of All Saints, Oct. 31.

HALLUCINATION (ha-lu-si-na'-shun), *n.* belief in something imaginary; error.

HALO (ha'lo), *n.* a circle of light round the sun or moon; in art, the representation of light, usually around the head of a saint.

HALT (hawlt), *n.* a stop in marching : *v.i.* to be lame; limp.

HALTER ('er), *n.* a rope for leading or holding a horse.

HALVE (hav), *v.t.* to divide into two equal parts.

HALVED (havd), *adj.* in golf, having equal scores.

HALYARD (hal'yard), *n.* a rope or tackle for hoisting a sail, flag, etc.

HAM (ham), *n.* a thigh of a pig, salted and smoked.

HAMAMELIS (-a-me'lis), *n.* a genus of shrubs, to which the witch-hazel belongs.

HAME (ham), *n.* one of the curved bars on a horse collar.

HAMLET ('let), *n.* a small village.

HAMMER ('er), *n.* an instrument with a handle and iron head for driving nails, beating metals, etc.: *v.t.* to forge, beat.

HAMMOCK ('ok), *n.* a swinging bed usually of network or canvas.

HAMPER ('per), *n.* a basket for carrying food, etc.; the rigging of a ship: *v.t.* embarrass; impede.

HAMSHACKLE ('shak'l), *v.t.* fasten the head of an animal to one of its forelegs, as a horse.

HAMSTRING ('string), *v.t.* to lame by cutting the tendons of the ham; hence, to cripple; disable.

HAND (hand), *n.* the extremity of the arm connected with the wrist; a measure of 4 in.; style of writing; an employee.

HANDCUFF (hand'kuf), *n.* a manacle.

HAND GRENADE (gre-nad'), *n.* an explosive for hand-throwing.

HANDICAP (hand'di-kap), *n.* certain conditions imposed on contestants in races or other contests in order to bring about equality.

HANDICAPPER (-kap-er), *n.* the official who assigns the weights in a handicap race.

HANDICRAFT ('di-kraft), *n.* skill in working with the hands.

HANDIWORK (-werk), *n.* work produced by the hands.

HANDKERCHIEF (hang'ker-chif), *n.* a piece of linen, silk or other fabric to wipe the face or nose.

HANDLE (han'd'l), *n.* that part of a tool, vessel, etc., grasped by the hand: *v.t.* to manage; manipulate; buy, sell, or invest in: *v.i.* to work with the hands.

HANDMADE ('mad), *adj.* made by hand.

HANDSCREW ('skroo), *n.* a lifting-jack.

HANDSOME (han'sum), *adj.* pleasing to look upon; graceful; liberal.

HANDWRITING (hand'rit-ing), *n.* personal penmanship.

HANDY ('di), *adj.* dexterous; skilful; convenient.

HANG (hang), *v.t.* to suspend; suspend by the neck.

HANGAR (hang'gar), *n.* a shed or shelter for aeroplanes, and other aircraft.

HANGER ('er), *n.* that by which something is suspended.

HANGMAN ('man), *n.* a public executioner.

HANGNAIL ('nal), *n.* a small piece of skin hanging from the root of a finger-nail.

HANK (hangk), *n.* a skein of yarn.

HANKER ('er), *v.i.* to desire eagerly (with *after*).

HANKY-PANKY (hang'ki-pang'ki), *n.* jugglery; trickery.

HANSOM (han'sum), *n.* a two-wheeled cab.

HAP (hap), *v.i.* to happen; befall casually.

HAPHAZARD ('haz-ard), *n.* chance; accident: *adj.* casual.

HAPLESS (hap'less), *adj.* unfortunate; unhappy.

HAPLY ('li), *adv.* by chance; perhaps.

HAPPEN ('n), *v.i.* to chance; occur.

HAPPILY ('i-li), *adv.* successfully; felicitously.

HAPPINESS ('i-nes), *n.* the state of being happy; felicitousness.

HAPPY ('i), *adj.* enjoying pleasure or good; successful; prosperous; propitious.

HARA-KIRI (ha'ra-ke-ri), *n.* in Japan a method of suicide.

HARANGUE (ha-rang'), *n.* a violent or passionate public address or oration.

HARASS (har'as), *v.t.* to annoy or vex.

HARBINGER (har'bin-jer), *n.* a precursor; forerunner.

HARBOUR ('ber), *n.* a port or haven for ships; any place of refuge.

HARD (hard), *adj.* compact and solid; firm; unyielding; laborious; fatiguing; cruel; severe.

HARD-BY (hard-bi'), *adv.* near by.

HARDEN (har'd'n), *v.t.* to make hard or harder.

HARDIHOOD ('di-hood), *n.* effrontery; physical endurance.

HARDLY ('li), *adv.* with difficulty; scarcely; vigorously; severely; without delicacy; unfavourably.

HARDSHIP ('ship), *n.* oppression; severe labour or want.

HARD-TACK ('tak), *n.* large, hard biscuit.

HARDWARE ('war), *n.* manufactured articles of metal, etc.

HARDY ('di), *adj.* robust; strong; bold.

HARE (har), *n.* a rodent, with long ears, larger than a rabbit.

HAREBELL ('bel), *n.* a perennial herb producing blue flowers.

HAREBRAINED ('brand), *adj.* volatile; wild.

HARELIP ('lip), *n.* an upper lip, which is divided in the middle.

HAREM (ha'rem), *n.* the apartments of the women and children in a Mohammedan house.

HARK (hark), *v.i.* to listen.

HARLEQUIN (har'le-kwin), *n.* a performer in a pantomime: *adj.* fantastic; particoloured.

HARLOT ('lot), *n.* a prostitute.

HARM (harm), *n.* injury; hurt; damage.

HARMFUL (harm'fool), *adj.* hurtful; injurious.

HARMLESS ('les), *adj.* free from harm; innocent; mild.

HARMONIC (har-mon'ik), *adj.* musical; concordant; harmonious.

HARMONICA (-mon'i-ka), *n.* a musical instrument.

HARMONIOUS (-mo'ni-us), *adj.* concordant; musical; symmetrical.

HARMONIZE ('mo-niz), *v.t.* to render harmonious; cause to agree; reconcile.

HARMONIST ('mo-nist), *n.* one who is skilled in harmony; an expounder of the harmony of the Scriptures.

HARMONY ('mo-ni), *n.* unison; just adaptation of parts to one another; accord in feeling, sentiment, etc.

HARNESS ('nes), *n.* the working gear of a horse.

HARP (harp), *n.* a musical stringed instrument of triangular shape.

HARPOON (har-poon'), *n.* a long barb-headed spear.

HARPSICHORD (harp'si-kord), *n.* the precursor of the pianoforte.

HARROW (har'o), *n.* an agricultural instrument for breaking up clods: *v.t.* to lacerate or torment.

HARRY (har'i), *v.t.* to annoy or vex; tease; harass.

HARSH (harsh), *adj.* discordant; jarring; austere.

HART (hart), *n.* the male of the red deer.

HARTSHORN (harts'horn), *n.* a volatile preparation of ammonia.

HARUM-SCARUM (har'um-skar'-um), *adj.* giddy; wild; reckless.

HARVEST (har'vest), *n.* the season of gathering: *v.t.* to gather in, as corn; reap.

HARVEST HOME (hom), *n.* harvest festival.

HARVEST MOON (moon), *n.* the full moon near the time of the autumnal equinox, about Sept. 23.

HASH (hash), *n.* meat cut and cooked with vegetables; a mixture: *v.t.* to chop small and mix.

HASLET (has'let), *n.* the liver, heart, and lungs of a sheep, or pig.

HASP (hasp), *n.* a clasp folded over a staple and secured with a padlock.

HASSOCK (has'ok), *n.* a padded mat for kneeling upon; a small tuft of grass.

HASTE (hast), *n.* celerity; speed; urgency.

HASTEN (has'sn), *v.t.* to hurry; urge forward.

HASTY ('ti), *adj.* precipitate; quick; speedy; rash.

HASTY PUDDING (pud'ing), *n.* a batter of meal, or flour, cooked by stirring it in boiling water.

HAT (hat), *n.* a covering for the head, with a crown and brim.

HATBAND ('band), *n.* a band worn round the hat.

HATCH (hach), *v.t.* to produce (young) from eggs; plot or contrive: *n.* brood; plot; trapdoor: *pl.* doors or openings by which a descent is made from one deck of a ship to another.

HATCHERY ('er-i), *n.* a place where eggs are artificially hatched, especially those of fish.

HATCHET ('et), *n.* a small axe.

HATCHWAY ('wa), *n.* an opening in the deck of a vessel for passage below.

HATE (hat), *v.t.* to dislike intensely ; detest.

HATEFUL ('fool), *adj.* causing hate.

HATRED (ha'tred), *n.* bitter aversion.

HATTER (hat'er), *n.* a maker of hats.

HAUGHTILY (haw'ti-li), *adv.* in a haughty manner.

HAUGHTY ('ti), *adj.* proud and disdainful ; contemptuous.

HAUL (hawl), *v.t.* to pull or draw : *n.* draught of a net ; a single catch.

HAUNCH (hawnch), *n.* the fleshy part of the hip and buttock.

HAUNT (hawnt), *n.* a place of accustomed resort.

HAUTEUR (ho-tur'), *n.* [French], haughty bearing or spirit.

HAVE (hav), *v.t.* to possess ; take, hold or bear ; enjoy.

HAVEN (ha'v'n), *n.* a place of shelter and safety.

HAVERSACK (hav'er-sak), *n.* a strong coarse linen bag in which soldiers carry their rations when marching.

HAVOC ('ok), *n.* wide and general destruction ; devastation.

HAW (haw), *n.* the hawthorn, or its fruit ; a hesitation in speech.

HAWK (hawk), *n.* a name for various raptorial birds of the falcon family : *v.t.* to cry, or carry about, for sale.

HAWKER ('er), *n.* a pedlar ; falconer.

HAWKWEED ('wed), *n.* a plant of the aster family with yellow flowers.

HAWSE-HOLE (hawz'hol), *n.* one of the two holes under a ship's bow through which the cable passes.

HAWSER (haw'ser), *n.* a thick rope or cable.

HAWTHORN (haw'thorn), *n.* a prickly shrub or tree of the rose family.

HAY (ha), *n.* dried grass, clover, etc.

HAYCOCK ('kok), *n.* a conical pile of hay.

HAY-FEVER ('fe-ver), *n.* a catarrh, accompanied by itching, sneezing, slight fever, and pains in the head.

HAYMOW ('mow), *n.* a mass of hay laid up in a barn.

HAZARD (haz'ard), *n.* chance ; risk ; peril ; accident ; casualty ; a gambling game ; in golf, an obstacle that renders the game more difficult : *v.t.* risk ; venture ; imperil.

HAZARDOUS ('ar-dus), *adj.* risky ; perilous.

HAZE (haz), *n.* a slight fog or mist ; dimness of sight or knowledge : *v.t.* to play practical jokes.

HAZEL ('l), *n.* a bushy tree or shrub producing edible nuts.

HAZINESS ('i-nes), *n.* the state of being hazy.

HAZY ('i), *adj.* misty ; obscure.

HE (he), *pron.* the male personified. Sometimes used as a noun, and often prefixed as *he-goat.*

HEAD (hed), *n.* the uppermost part of the body of an animal that contains the face, brain, etc. ; chief or principal part of anything.

HEADACHE (hed'ak), *n.* pain in the head.

HEADER ('er), *n.* a plunge or fall foremost.

HEADLAND ('land), *n.* a promontory.

HEADLIGHT (-'lit), *n.* a light, with a strong reflector for locomotives, automobiles, etc.

HEADLINE ('lin), *n.* a line of type displayed conspicuously at the top of a newspaper, etc.

HEADLONG ('long), *adj.* precipitate ; violent ; thoughtless.

HEADMAN (hed'man), *n.* a leader in a community ; a chief.

HEADSTONE (-ston), *n.* a stone erected over a grave in memory of the dead.

HEADSTRONG ('strong), *adj.* self-willed.

HEADWIND ('wind), *n.* a contrary wind.

HEAL (hel), *v.t.* to restore to health ; reconcile.

HEALING ('ing), *p.adj.* curative.

HEALTH (helth), *n.* freedom from bodily pain or disease; vigour of mind; moral purity; a toast or pledge.

HEALTHFUL ('fool), *adj.* promoting health; salubrious.

HEALTHY ('thi), *adj.* noting a sound condition of body.

HEAP (hep), *n.* a pile or collection of things thrown together.

HEAR (her), *v.t.* to perceive by the ear; attend or listen to.

HEARING ('ing), *n.* the sense by which sound is perceived; judicial investigation.

HEARKEN (har'k'n), *v.i.* to listen; attend to what is uttered.

HEARSAY ('sa), *n.* rumour.

HEARSE (hers), *n.* a vehicle for the conveyance of dead bodies to the grave.

HEART (hart), *n.* the organ in animals by which the blood is circulated through the arteries, etc.; emotion; tenderness; affection; courage; spirit; energy.

HEARTACHE ('ak), *n.* sorrow; grief.

HEART-BROKEN ('bro-ken), *adj.* overwhelmingly grieved.

HEARTBURN ('bern), *n.* a burning affection of the esophagus.

HEARTED ('ed), *adj.* having a heart: used in compounds, denoting generally affections, qualities, etc., as good-*hearted*, etc.

HEARTEN ('n), *v.t.* to give courage to; inspirit.

HEARTFELT ('felt), *adj.* sincere.

HEARTH (harth), *n.* that part of a room where the fire is made.

HEARTILY ('ti-li), *adv.* cordially.

HEARTINESS ('ti-ness), *n.* cordiality.

HEART-RENDING (-rend'ing), *adj.* causing distressing grief.

HEARTSORE (-sor), *adj.* intensely grieved.

HEARTY (har'ti), *adj.* cordial; sincere; open; warm; strong; vigorous; kind; healthy.

HEAT (het), *n.* a form of energy made manifest by the effects of fire, the sun's rays, etc.; the state of being hot; effervescence; ardour; vehe-

mence; a course at a race; hot weather: *v.t.* to make hot.

HEATH (heth), *n.* a small evergreen flowering shrub with rose-coloured flowers; heather; moorland.

HEATHEN (he'*th*n), *n.* one who does not believe in God of the Bible; a pagan.

HEATHER (heth'er), same as heath.

HEAVE (hev), *v.t.* to hoist or lift up; throw.

HEAVEN (hev'n), *n.* the abode of God and the blessed; the firmament or sky; blessed.

HEAVEN, *n.* used as an equivalent to God or Providence.

HEAVINESS (hev'i-nes), *n.* the quality of being heavy.

HEAVY ('i), *adj.* ponderous; weighty; oppressive; dull; dense; powerful; loud; indigestible.

HEBRAIC (he-bra'ik), *adj.* pertaining to the Hebrews.

HEBREW ('broo), *adj.* Jewish: *n.* the Hebrew language; a Jew.

HECATO, a *prefix* meaning a *hundred*: also hecaton, hect, hecto.

HECATOMB ('a-toom), *n.* any large sacrifice or slaughter.

HECK (hek), *n.* a rack for fodder.

HECKLE (hek'l), *v.t.* to badger; torment.

HECTARE ('tar), *n.* a French land measure = 100 ares, or 2.47 acres.

HECTIC ('tik), *adj.* constitutional; denoting a wasting away of the body; consumptive; feverish.

HECTOGRAM ('to-gram), *n.* a French weight = 100 grammes, or 3.53 ounces.

HECTOGRAPH ('to-graf), *n.* an apparatus for multiplying copies of a letter or drawing.

HECTOLITRE ('to-le-tr), *n.* a French liquid measure = 100 litres or 26.42 gallons.

HECTOMETRE ('to-me-tr), *n.* a French measure of length = 100 metres, or 328 feet, 1 inch.

HECTOR ('ter), *v.t.* to bully or bluster.

HEDGE (hej), *n.* a fence of bushes or shrubs: *v.t.* to encircle; invest.

HEDGEHOG ('hog), *n.* an insectivorous mammal covered on the back with spines or prickles.

HEED (hed), *v.t.* to regard with care : *n.* careful attention ; regard.

HEEDFUL ('fool), *adj.* cautious ; attentive.

HEEDLESS ('les), *adj.* careless.

HEEL (hel), *n.* the hinder part of the foot ; anything shaped like a heel.

HEELER ('er), *n.* [Slang], a political hanger-on.

HEFT (heft), *n.* handle ; an effort ; weight.

HEGEMONY (he-jem'o-ni), *n.* leadership ; applied to a state predominating over another.

HEGIRA (he-ji'ra), *n.* the flight of Mohammed from Mecca to Medina (622 A.D.) ; any exodus.

HEIFER (hef'er), *n.* a young cow.

HEIGH-HO ! (hi'ho), *interj.* an expression of languor.

HEIGHT (hit), *n.* altitude ; elevation.

HEIGHTEN ('en), *v.t.* to make high or higher ; elevate ; aggravate ; improve.

HEINOUS (ha'nus), *adj.* atrocious ; flagrant.

HEIR (ar), *n.* one who succeeds another in the possession of property, title, office, mental gifts, etc.

HEIR-APPARENT (-ap-pa'rent), *n.* one whose right to succeed is indefeasible at law if he outlives his ancestor.

HEIRESS ('es), *n.* a female heir.

HEIRLOOM ('loom), *n.* any movable or personal chattel, which by its connection with an estate descends to the heir.

HEIR-PRESUMPTIVE (-pre-sump'tiv), *n.* one who will succeed as heir if his right is not barred by the birth of one nearer in succession than himself.

HELIAC (he'li-ak), **HELIACAL** ('ak-al), *adj.* pertaining to the sun.

HELIANTHUS (he-li-an'thus), *n.* a genus of plants of the aster family ; [h-], the sunflowers.

HELIC, a *prefix* meaning *spiral* : also helico.

HELIO-, a combining form from the Greek *helios*, the sun.

HELIOTROPE (he'li-o-trop), *n.* a plant or shrub with small white, or purple, flowers.

HELIUM ('li-um), *n.* a light non-explosive gas used for inflating balloons, airships, etc.

HELIX ('liks), *n.* [*pl.* helices (hel'i-sez)], a spiral ; a circumvolution ; the margin of the external ear.

HELL (hel), *n.* see *Hades:* the place of punishment for the wicked after death ; hence, any place or condition of extreme misery or evil.

HELLAS (hel'as), *n.* ancient Greece.

HELLEBORE ('e-bor), *n.* a perennial herb : a vermin destroyer.

HELLENE ('en), *n.* a Greek.

HELLENIC (he-len'ik), *adj.* pertaining to the ancient Greeks.

HELLO (he-lo'), **HULLO** (hul-o'), *interj.* common exclamation of greetings.

HELM (helm), *n.* the apparatus for steering a ship ; tiller.

HELMET (hel'met), *n.* metal or leather armour for the head.

HELO, a *prefix* meaning *nail*, occurring in various scientific words, as *helo*-dont, having nail-like teeth ; *helo*-derm, a Mexican poisonous lizard.

HELP (help), *v.t.* to give assistance to ; add ; support ; sustain ; succour ; relieve : *v.i.* to lend aid.

HELPFUL ('fool), *adj.* affording help.

HELPLESS (-'les), *adj.* feeble ; unable to assist oneself.

HELTER-SKELTER (hel'ter-skel'ter), *adv.* in hurry and confusion.

HELVE (helv), *n.* the handle of an axe, etc.

HEM (hem), *n.* the edge of a garment ; an ejaculatory sound : *v.t.* to form a hem ; shut in.

HEMATIN (hem'a-tin), *n.* a dark-brown or black pigment.

HEMI-, a Greek prefix signifying *half*.

HEMISPHERE (hem'i-sfer), *n.* a half sphere ; half of the terrestrial or celestial globe.

HEMLOCK (hem'lok), *n.* a wild poisonous plant of the parsley family ; an evergreen tree of the pine family.

HEMORRHAGE (hem'o-raj), *n.*

bleeding from the lungs, arteries, veins, etc.

HEMORRHOIDS ('o-roidz), *n. pl.* bleeding piles.

HEMP (hemp), *n.* a plant of the nettle family.

HEMPEN ('p'n), *adj.* pertaining to, or made of, hemp.

HEN (hen), *n.* the female bird.

HENCE (hens), *adv.* from this place, source, or time: *interj.* away! begone!

HENCEFORTH (-forth') **HENCE-FORWARD** (-for'werd), *adv.* from this time forward.

HENCHMAN (hench'man), *n.* one who serves in a political campaign under another for pay.

HENDECA, a *prefix* meaning eleven, as *hendeca*hedron, a solid figure having eleven plane faces.

HENNA (hen'a), *n.* a tropical shrub from the powdered leaves of which a cosmetic is made; a reddish-orange colour.

HENRY (hen'ri), *n.* the unit of inductance in electricity.

HEPAT, a *prefix* meaning *the liver*: also hepato, as *hepato*cele, hernia of the liver.

HEPATIC (he-pat'ik), *adj.* pertaining to the liver.

HEPATICA ('i-ka), *n.* a genus of vernal herbs; the common liver-wort.

HEPT, a *prefix* meaning *seven*: also hepta, as *hepta*chord, a series of seven notes.

HEPTARCHY ('tar-ki), *n.* a government by seven rulers.

HER (her), *pron.* the objective and possessive case of the personal pronoun *she*.

HERALD (her'ald), *n.* a precursor: *v.i.* to introduce; proclaim; usher in.

HERALDRY (her'ald-ri), *n.* the science that treats of armorial bearings, and of determining pedigrees, etc.

HERB (erb, herb), *n.* a plant with a soft and succulent stem that, after flowering, withers away.

HERBACEOUS (her-ba'shus), *adj.* pertaining to herbs.

HERBAGE ('baj), *n.* herbs collectively; grass; pasturage.

HERCULEAN (ku'le-an), *adj.* pertaining to Hercules, the hero of Grecian mythology; huge; powerful; difficult.

HERD (herd), *n.* a collection of beasts or cattle; crowd; a rabble.

HERE (her), *adv.* in, or to, this place; at this point.

HEREAFTER (her-af'ter), *n.* a future state or condition.

HEREBY (-bi), *adv.* by virtue of this; near.

HEREDITABLE (he-red'it-a-bl), *adj.* that may be inherited.

HEREDITAMENT (her-e-dit'a-ment), *n.* property inherited.

HEREDITARY (he-red'i-ta-ri), *adj.* passing from an ancestor to a descendant.

HEREDITY ('i-di), *n.* the transmission of physical or mental characteristics or qualities from parent to offspring.

HEREIN (her-in'), *adv.* in this.

HERESY (her'e-si), *n.* an opinion or doctrine at variance with the tenets of a church or party considered as orthodox.

HERETIC ('e-tik), *n.* one who holds, or maintains heretical opinions.

HERETICAL (he-ret'i-kal), *adj.* pertaining to, or having the character of, heresy.

HERETOFORE (her-too-for'), *adv.* previously; hitherto.

HERITAGE (her'i-taj), *n.* an estate that passes from an ancestor to a descendant; a birthright.

HERMETIC (her-met'ik), *adj.* perfectly closed and airtight.

HERMETICALLY ('i-kal-i), *adv.* in an airtight manner.

HERMIT ('mit), *n.* one who retires from society and lives in solitude.

HERMITAGE ('mi-taj), *n.* the abode of a hermit.

HERMITICAL ('i-kal), *adj.* solitary.

HERNIA ('ni-a), *n.* a protrusion of some part of the intestine, or other internal organ; rupture.

HERNIAL ('ni-al), *adj.* pertaining to, or resembling, hernia.

HERO (he'ro), *n.* a man of distinguished courage ; chief character in a play, novel, etc.

HEROIC (he-ro'ik), *adj.* having the qualities of a hero ; venturesome ; drastic.

HEROIC VERSE (vers), epic poetry.

HEROIN (he-ro'in), *n.* a white crystalline acetyl derivative of morphine.

HEROINE (her'o-in), *n. fem.* of hero.

HEROISM (her'o-izm), *n.* qualities of a hero.

HERON ('un), *n.* a wading bird with a long neck and long legs.

HERPES (her'pez), *n.* a skin disease.

HERRING ('ing), *n.* an edible sea-fish.

HERRING-BONE (-bon), *n.* a kind of cross-stitch.

HERTZIAN WAVES (hert'si-an wavz), ether waves.

HESITANCE (hez'i-tans), **HESITANCY** (-tan-si), *n.* hesitation ; suspense.

HESITATE ('i-tat), *v.i.* to be in suspense or uncertainty ; pause ; vacillate ; stammer.

HESPER (hes'per), *n.* the evening star.

HESPERIDES (-per'i-dez), *n. pl.* in Grecian mythology, the four sisters who guarded the golden apples.

HESSIAN FLY (fli), *n.* a small fly the larvæ of which are very destructive to corn crops.

HETERO-, a combining form from the Greek *heteros*, other, different.

HETERODOX (het'er-o-doks), *adj.* deviating from an accepted doctrine.

HETERODOXY (-dok-si), *n.* an unorthodox doctrine or opinion ; heresy.

HETEROGENEOUS (-je'ne-us), *adj.* opposite or dissimilar in character, quality, structure, etc.

HETEROSCOPY (het-er-os'ko-pi), *n.* difference of vision in the two eyes.

HEW (hu), *v.t.* to cut or shape, as with an axe ; hack ; chop.

HEXA, a *prefix* meaning *six* : also hex, as *hexa*chord, a six-stringed musical instrument.

HEXAMETER (hex-am'e-ter), *n.* a verse of six feet.

HEXICOLOGY (hek-si-kol'o-ji), *n.*

that branch of biology which treats of the relation of organisms to their environment.

HIATUS (hi-a'tus), *n.* a break ; vacancy ; gap ; the concurrence of two vowels, words or syllables.

HIBERNATE ('ber-nat), *v.i.* to pass the winter in a state of torpor, as certain animals.

HIBERNIA (hi-ber'ni-a), *n.* the name given by the Romans to Ireland.

HICCUP, HICCOUGH (hik'up), *n.* a short convulsive cough.

HIC JACET (ja'set), [Latin, here lies], an inscription on tombstones.

HICKORY ('o-ri), *n.* an American nut-bearing tree of the walnut family.

HID (hid), **HIDDEN** (hid'n), *p.adj.* concealed ; not known ; secret.

HIDE (hid), *v.t.* to conceal ; secrets ; disguise ; whip : *n.* an animal's skin.

HIDEBOUND ('bound), *adj.* prejudiced ; bigoted.

HIDEOUS (hid'e-us), *adj.* shocking ; dreadful ; horrible.

HIDING (hid'ing), *n.* concealment ; a beating.

HIE (hi), *v.t.* to excite ; speed *v.i.* to hasten.

HIERARCH ('er-ark), *n.* the chief ruler of an ecclesiastical body.

HIERARCHY (-ar-ki), *n.* the higher and lower clergy of a church ; priesthood.

HIERO, a *prefix* meaning *sacred*, as *hiero*phant, a priest in ancient Greece.

HIEROGLYPH (hi'er-o-glif), *n.* a word or character presumed to contain some hidden meaning.

HIEROGLYPHIC (hi-er-o-glif'ik), *n.* a character in the picture writings of ancient Egyptians.

HIGGLE (hig'l), *v.i.* to chaffer ; dispute about trifles.

HIGH (hi), *adj.* lofty ; exalted in degree or quality ; chief ; head ; honourable ; noble ; intense ; tempestuous ; shrill.

HIGHBOY (-boi), *n.* a tall chest of drawers mounted on legs.

HIGH CHURCH (cherch), in Anglican Communion attaching great importance to ritual, ceremonies and symbols.

HIGH-COLOURED ('kul-erd), *adj.* flushed ; vivid ; exaggerated.

HIGHFALUTIN (-fa-lu'tin), *adj.* bombastic.

HIGH-FLOWN ('flon), *adj.* elevated ; proud ; inflated.

HIGH-HANDED ('han'ded), *adj.* violent ; arbitrary.

HIGH HAT (hat), [Slang], a person of importance ; an aristocrat.

HIGH-HATTING *n.* effort to impress with undue importance.

HIGH JINKS (jingks), a sportive jollification.

HIGHLAND ('land), *n.* a mountainous region.

HIGHLY ('li), *adv.* in a high manner ; in a great degree.

HIGH-MINDED (-min-ded), *adj.* possessing elevated feelings.

HIGHROAD ('rod), *n.* a highway.

HIGH-ROLLER (hi-rol'er), *n.* one who lives extravagantly.

HIGHSTRUNG ('strung), *adj.* extremely sensitive.

HIGH-TONED ('tond), *adj.* principled ; fashionable.

HIGHWAY ('wa), *n.* a public road.

HIGHWAYMAN (-man), *n.* one who robs on the public road.

HIKE (hik), *v.i.* to tramp or march over a given course.

HILARIOUS (hi-la'ri-us), *adj.* merry ; exhilarated.

HILARITY (-lar'i-ti), *n.* noisy merriment.

HILL (hil), *n.* an elevation less than a mountain ; a small mound or heap.

HILLOCK ('ok), *n.* a small hill.

HILT (hilt), *n.* a handle, especially of a sword.

HIM (him), *pron.* the objective case of he.

HIND (hind), *n.* the female of deer : *adj.* backward.

HINDER (hind'er), *adj.* belonging to the rear of anything.

HINDER (hin'der), *v.t.* to obstruct or impede.

HINDERMOST, *adj.* same as hindmost.

HINDMOST (hind'most), *adj.* in the extreme rear.

HINDRANCE (hin'drans), *n.* obstruction.

HINDU, HINDOO ('doo), *n.* a native of Hindustan belonging to the Aryan race.

HINGE (hinj), *n.* the joint or hook on which a door, etc., turns or swings.

HINT (hint), *v.t.* to suggest : *n.* a distant allusion.

HIP (hip), *n.* the upper fleshy part of the thigh ; fruit of the wild-briar.

HIPPO-, a combining form from the Greek *hippos*, horse.

HIPPODROME ('o-drom), *n.* an ancient Greek racecourse for equestrian games and chariots ; a circus.

HIPPOPOTAMUS (-pot'a-mus), *n.* [*pl.* hippopotami (-mi)], a large pachydermatous aquatic animal of Africa.

HIRE (hir), *v.t.* to engage for temporary service at a certain price ; let or lease.

HIRELING (hir'ling), *n.* one who serves for hire : *adj.* mercenary.

HIRSUTE (her'sut), *adj.* hairy ; shaggy.

HIS (hiz), *adj.* belonging to him : *pron.* possessive case of *he* and *it*.

HISS (his), *n.* a noise resembling that of a serpent or goose.

HIST (hist), *interj.* silence ! hark !

HISTO, a *prefix* meaning *tissue*, as *histo*graphy, a description of organic tissues.

HISTOLOGY (-tol'o-ji), *n.* microscopic anatomy.

HISTORIAN (-to'ri-an), *n.* a writer or student of history.

HISTORIC (-tor'ik), *adj.* pertaining to, contained in, or celebrated in, history.

HISTORY ('to-ri), *n.* a narration of facts and events arranged chronologically with their causes and effects.

HISTRIONIC (-tri-on'ik), *adj.* pertaining to actors or the stage ; theatrical.

HIT (hit), *v.t.* to strike ; give a blow to ; touch (the mark) ; attain to.

HITCH (hich), *n.* a catch ; that which acts like a catch ; impediment.

HITHER (hith'er), *adv.* to this place.

HIVE (hiv), *n.* an artificial receptacle for bees ; a swarm of bees.

HIVES (hivz), *n.pl.* a cutaneous affection ; nettle rash.

HOAR (hor), *adj.* white ; ancient.

HOARD (hord), *n.* a store or treasure laid up secretly.

HOARFROST (hor'frost), *n.* white particles of frozen dew or moisture.

HOARHOUND ('hound), *n.* a white, bitter, perennial herb.

HOARSE (hors), *adj.* rough and harsh in sound, as the voice when affected by a cold.

HOAX (hoks), *n.* a practical joke.

HOBBLE (hob'l), *v.i.* to walk with a limp or awkward step.

HOBBLE-DE-HOY (-de-hoi'), *n.* a lad between boyhood and manhood ; an awkward youth.

HOBBY (hob'i), *n.* a favourite pursuit or object ; a hobby-horse.

HOBBY-HORSE (-hors), *n.* a wooden rocking-horse.

HOBGOBLIN (-gob'lin), *n.* a goblin, sprite, or elf ; an apparition.

HOBNAIL ('nal), *n.* a short thick nail with a large head.

HOBNOB ('nob), *v.i.* to associate intimately together.

HOBO (ho'bo), *n.* a tramp.

HOCK (hok), *n.* the joint between the knee and the fetlock ; [U.S. Slang], pawn.

HOCKEY ('i), *n.* an outdoor game played with a ball and curved clubs.

HOCUS-POCUS (ho'kus-po'kus), *n.* a juggler's trick ; a juggler.

HOD (hod), *n.* a wooden trough, affixed to a long handle.

HODGE-PODGE (hoj'poj), *n.* a medley of ingredients.

HOE (ho), *n.* an agricultural tool.

HOG (hog), *n.* a swine ; the domestic pig, sow, or boar.

HOGGISH ('ish), *adj.* acting like a hog.

HOGSHEAD (hogs'hed), *n.* a measure of capacity = 52½ imperial gals. or 63 wine gals. ; a large barrel or cask.

HOIDEN, HOYDEN (hoi'dn), *n.* a rude, rustic girl ; romp.

HOIST (hoist), *v.t.* to lift or raise with tackle ; heave.

HOITY-TOITY (hoi'ti-toi'ti), *interj.* an exclamation of surprise, rebuke, etc.

HOKY-POKY (ho'ki-po'ki), *n.* ice-cream peddled on the streets.

HOKUM (ho'kum), *n.* [Slang], non-sense.

HOLD (hold), *v.t.* to grasp and keep in the hand ; clutch ; retain ; keep : *n.* that part of a vessel where the cargo is stored.

HOLDING ('ing), *n.* anything held ; tenure or right of possession.

HOLD-UP (hold'up), *n.* an assault for the purpose of robbery.

HOLE (hol), *n.* a cavity ; hollow place ; a difficulty or dilemma.

HOLIDAY (hol'i-da), *n.* a day of gaiety and joy in celebration of some event, etc.

HOLINESS (ho'li-nes), *n.* freedom from sin ; moral and spiritual purity ; sacredness ; [H-], a title of the Pope.

HOLLAND (hol'and), *n.* fine un-bleached linen, glazed or unglazed.

HOLLO (hol'o), *v.i.* to shout to one at a distance : *n.* a greeting.

HOLLOW ('o), *adj.* having a void space within ; opposed to *solid ;* unreal ; insincere.

HOLLY ('li), *n.* an evergreen tree or shrub with glossy, prickly leaves and red berries.

HOLO-, a combining form from the Greek *holos*, whole.

HOLOCAUST (hol'o-kawst), *n.* wholly consumed by fire with great loss of lives.

HOLSTER (hol'ster), *n.* a leather pistol-case.

HOLT (holt), *n.* a wooded hill ; a burrow or hiding place.

HOLY (ho'li), *adj.* pure ; sinless ; pious ; sacred ; consecrated.

HOLY GHOST, same as Holy Spirit.

HOLY LAND (land), Palestine.

HOLY OF HOLIES (ho'liz), inner-most and most sacred shrine of the Jewish tabernacle containing the ark of the covenant.

HOLY SPIRIT (spir′it), God ; the third person of the Trinity.

HOLYSTONE (-ston), *n.* a large flat piece of sandstone used for scouring decks.

HOLY WRIT (rit), the Sacred Scriptures.

HOMAGE (hom′aj), *n.* deference ; reverence.

HOMALO, a *prefix*, meaning *even*, *plane*, as *homaloi*dal, flat plane.

HOME (hom), *n.* one's abode or residence.

HOMELY (′li), *adj.* plain-featured ; unpretending ; simple.

HOMEO-, a combining form from the Greek *homoios*, like.

HOMEOPATH (ho′me-o-path), *n.* one who practises homeopathy.

HOMEOPATHIC (ho-me-o-path′ik), *adj.* of or pertaining to homeopathy.

HOMEOPATHY (op′a-thi), *n.* the medical system introduced by Hahnemann (1755-1843).

HOME RULE (hom rool), local self-government.

HOMESPUN (hom′spun), *n.* a coarse woollen cloth.

HOMESTEAD (′sted), *n.* a dwelling-house with the adjacent land.

HOMICIDAL (hom′i-si-dal), *adj.* pertaining to homicide.

HOMICIDE (′i-sid), *n.* the killing of a human being ; one who kills another.

HOMILETICS (let′iks), *n.* that branch of theology which treats of sermons.

HOMILIST (′i-list), *n.* a preacher ; a writer of homilies.

HOMILY (′i-li), *n.* a plain religious discourse or sermon.

HOMING (hom′ing), *adj.* returning home ; said of carrier pigeons.

HOMINY (hom′i-ni), *n.* Indian corn soaked so as to remove the hull.

HOMO (ho′mo), *n.* Man ; the genus of mammals consisting of mankind.

HOMO-, a combining form from the Greek *homos*, the same.

HOMŒOPATHY, same as homeopathy.

HOMOGAMY (ho-mog′a-mi), *n.* the assortive mating of animals or human beings in the widest sense.

HOMOGENEOUS (-je′ne-us), *adj.* uniform ; composed of similar parts or elements.

HOMOGENOUS (-moj′e-nus), *adj.* of the same origin.

HOMOLOGOUS (-mol′o-gus), *adj.* identical.

HOMOLOGY (ho-mol′o-ji), *n.* affinity of structure.

HOMONYM (hom′o-nim, ho′mo-nim), *n.* a word alike in sound, but differing in meaning, as *pair*, *pare*, *pear*.

HONE (hon), *n.* a whetstone : *v.t.* to sharpen on a hone.

HONEST (on′est), *adj.* upright ; just ; sincere ; honourable ; equitable ; fair ; righteous ; chaste.

HONESTY (′es-ti), *n.* the quality of being honest.

HONEY (hun′i), *n.* a sweet, viscid, syrupy substance collected by bees from flowers.

HONEY-BEE (-be), *n.* the hive-bee.

HONEYCOMB (-kom), *n.* the waxen cells made by bees to contain their honey, eggs, etc.

HONEYDEW (-du), *n.* a saccharine secretion from the leaves of certain plants.

HONEY LOCUST (lo′kust), a large American tree of the bean family.

HONEYMOON (-moon), *n.* the first month after marriage.

HONEYSUCKLE (-suk′l), *n.* a climbing vine with fragrant flowers.

HONK (honk), *n.* the cry of wild geese ; the sound of an automobile horn.

HONOUR (on′er), *n.* respectful regard ; esteem ; worship ; reputation ; exalted rank ; fame ; magnanimity ; self-respect ; chastity ; glory : *v.t.* to treat with respect.

HONOURABLE (-a-bl), *adj.* high-minded ; illustrious ; upright.

HONORARIUM (on-o-ra′ri-um), *n.* a fee paid to a professional man.

HONORARY (′er-a-ri), *adj.* done, or conferred, as an honour.

HOOD (hood), *n.* a soft wrapper or covering for the head ; cover for the motor of an automobile.

HOODLUM (hood'lum), *n.* a rough or bully ; a rowdy.

HOODOO (hoo'doo), *n.* a person or thing that causes ill-luck.

HOODWINK (hood'wingk), *v.t.* to deceive.

HOOF (hoof), *n.* the horny substance covering the feet of certain mammals, as horses, etc.

HOOK (hook), *n.* a curved piece of metal, bone, etc. ; a hold or catch ; a fish-hook ; a cape or headland.

HOOK-WORM (-werm), *n.* a parasite which enters the human body by the feet and produces inanition.

HOOLIGAN (hoo'li-gan), *n.* [Slang], a rowdy ; a tough.

HOOP (hoop), *n.* a metal or wooden band to hold together the staves of a cask, etc. : *v.t.* to encircle.

HOOPING-COUGH, same as whooping-cough.

HOOSEGOW (hoos'gou), *n.* [Slang], a lockup ; guard-house.

HOP (hop), *v.i.* to proceed by short leaps ; to limp ; to dance.

HOPE (hop), *n.* the desire of good accompanied by expectation ; anticipation ; confidence : *v.t.* to expect with confidence or desire.

HOPEFUL ('fool), *adj.* full of hope ; promising success.

HOPELESS (-'les), *adj.* without hope.

HOPPER (hop'er), *n.* a name for various leaping insects ; a wooden trough or funnel through which grain passes into a mill.

HOPSCOTCH ('skoch), *n.* a children's game.

HORDE (hord), *n.* a nomadic tribe ; a vast multitude ; pack or swarm.

HOREHOUND, same as hoarhound.

HORIZON (ho-ri'zun), *n.* the circular line where the sky and earth, or sea, appear to meet.

HORIZONTAL (hor-i-zon'tal), *adj.* parallel to the horizon ; level ; opposed to vertical.

HORNET (hor'net), *n.* a large species of wasp which inflicts a severe sting.

HORNPIPE (horn'pip), *n.* a lively dance, especially by sailors.

HOROLOGE (hor'o-loj), *n.* a mechan-

ism, as a clock, etc., for marking the hours.

HOROLOGY (ho-rol'o-ji), *n.* the art of measuring time, or of constructing time-pieces.

HOROSCOPE (hor'o-skop), *n.* a representation of the heavens at any time, especially at one's birth.

HORRIBLE ('i-bl), *adj.* terrible ; dreadful.

HORRID ('id), *adj.* dreadful ; hideous ; most obnoxious.

HORRIFIC (ho-rif'ik), *adj.* causing horror.

HORRIFY ('i-fi), *v.t.* to fill or strike with horror.

HORROR ('er), *n.* excessive fear ; extreme dread ; great disgust.

HORS DE COMBAT (or de cong-ba'), [French], out of the fight ; disabled.

HORS-D'ŒUVRE (-doov'r), *n.* [French], special dishes served as appetizers.

HORSE (hors), *n.* a hoofed animal, used for riding on or drawing burdens ; a frame-work.

HORSE-CHESTNUT ('ches'nut), *n.* an umbrageous tree of the buckeye family.

HORSEFLY ('fli), *n.* a large fly that stings horses ; a gadfly.

HORSE-POWER ('pou-er), *n.* the theoretical unit of work of a steam-engine = 33,000 lbs. raised 1 ft. in 1 minute.

HORSE-RADISH ('rad-ish), *n.* a plant of the mustard family.

HORSE-SENSE (-sens), *n.* practical common sense.

HORSESHOE ('shoo), *n.* a U-shaped metal shoe to protect the hoof of a horse.

HORTICULTURE (hor-ti-kul'tur), *n.* the art of cultivating gardens.

HORTICULTURIST (-ist), *n.* one who is skilled in horticulture.

HOSANNA (ho-zan'a), *n.* an exclamation of praise and glory to God.

HOSE (hoz), *n.pl.* stockings ; flexible tubing for conveying water, etc.

HOSIERY (ho'zher-i), *n.* stockings, underclothing, etc.

HOSPITABLE (hos'pit-a-bl), *adj.* entertaining friends or strangers.

HOSPITAL ('pi-tal), *n.* an institution for the medical treatment and care of the sick.

HOSPITALITY ('-ti), *n.* the practice of entertaining friends and strangers with kindness and liberality.

HOST (host), *n.* a crowd; multitude; one who entertains another; a landlord of a hotel; [H-], the consecrated bread or wafer of the Eucharist.

HOSTAGE (hos'taj), *n.* a person who remains in the hands of another as a pledge for the fulfilment of certain conditions.

HOSTELRY ('tel-ri), *n.* an inn.

HOSTESS (host'es), *n.* a female host.

HOSTILE (hos'til), *adj.* showing animosity; inimical; adverse.

HOSTILITY (-til'i-ti), *n.* the state of being hostile; antagonism *pl.* acts of warfare.

HOSTLER (os'ler), *n.* one who takes charge of horses at an inn.

HOT (hot), *adj.* having much heat; burning; fiery; furious; pungent.

HOTCHPOTCH (hoch'poch), *n.* a mixture of various ingredients.

HOTEL (ho-tel'), *n.* a superior inn.

HOTHEAD (hot'hed), *n.* one easily aroused to anger.

HOTHOUSE (hot'hous), *n.* a glazed building heated for rearing plants.

HOTPRESS ('pres), *v.t.* to gloss paper or linen by passing it between heated rollers.

HOTSPUR (hot'sper), *n.* a man of hasty and precipitate valour.

HOUND (hound), *n.* a particular breed of hunting dog.

HOUR (our), *n.* the $\frac{1}{24}$th part of a day; 60 minutes; particular time.

HOUR-GLASS (our'glas), *n.* a device for measuring time by running sand through a narrow opening between two apartments of a glass vessel.

HOURI (hou', hoo'ri), *n.* one of the nymphs of the Mohammedan paradise.

HOUSE (hous), *n.* a building for residence; family or race; one of the

divisions of a legislative or ecclesiastical body; a mercantile firm.

HOUSE-BOAT ('bot), *n.* a covered beamy boat fitted up as a residence.

HOUSEHOLD ('hold), *n.* a family living together: *adj.* domestic.

HOUSING (hous'ing), *n.* the act of providing with, or bringing into, a house; a shelter; a part of machinery formed to receive another part.

HOVEL (hov'l), *n.* a mean habitation; hut or cabin.

HOVER (huv'er), *v.i.* to flutter over or about.

HOW (hou), *adv.* in what manner; to what degree or extent; for what reason.

HOWDAH (hou'da), *n.* a protected seat for riding on an elephant or camel.

HOWEVER (-ev'er), *adv.* in whatever manner or degree; at all events: *conj.* notwithstanding; yet.

HOWITZER ('it-ser), *n.* a short cannon for throwing shells.

HOWL (houl), *n.* the prolonged cry of a dog or wolf; roar, like the wind.

HOWLING ('ing), *p.adj.* dreary; dismal; extreme; wild; piercing; dreadful; also, great, as a *howling* success.

HUB (hub), *n.* the nave of a wheel; anything central.

HUBBUB (hub'ub), *n.* uproar.

HUCKABACK (huk'a-bak), *n.* a rough kind of linen or cotton cloth.

HUCKLEBERRY ('l-ber-i), *n.* a dark-blue, palatable berry which grows on a shrub of the heath family.

HUCKSTER ('ster), *n.* one who retails small articles on the streets.

HUDDLE (hud'l), *v.t.* to crowd together; collect closely: *n.* confusion; crowd.

HUE (hu), *n.* colour tint; a shouting; clamour.

HUE AND CRY (kri), the loud outcry raised in the pursuit of felons.

HUFF (huf), *v.t.* to puff or blow up; treat with insolence: *n.* fit of petulence.

HUG (hug), *n.* a close embrace.

HUGE (huj), *adj.* vast; very large.

HUGELY ('li), *adv.* immensely.

HUGENESS ('nes), *n.* enormous bulk.

HUGUENOT (hu'ge-not), *n.* one of the French Protestants of the 16th and 17th centuries.

HULK (hulk), *n.* the body of a ship, especially if old or dismantled.

HULKING ('ing), *n.* unwieldy; bulky.

HULL (hul), *n.* outer covering; the body or frame of a vessel.

HULLABALOO (-a-ba-loo'), *n.* uproar; noisy contention.

HUM (hum), *n.* the noise of bees and other insects in flight; a low, monotonous sound.

HUMAN (hu'man), *adj.* pertaining to, or characteristic of, man or mankind.

HUMANE (-man'), *adj.* benevolent; kind; compassionate.

HUMANENESS ('nes), *n.* the quality of being humane.

HUMANITARIAN (-i-ta'ri-an), *n.* one who believes that the duty of man consists of acting rightly to others.

HUMANITY ('i-ti), *n.* mankind; philanthropy; kindness; benevolence.

HUMBLE (hum'bl), *adj.* having a low estimate of one's self; modest; meek; submissive.

HUMBUG ('bug), *n.* a fraud; sham; a plausible deceiver: *v.t.* impose upon; hoax.

HUMDINGER (hum-ding'er), *n.* [Slang], something that excels.

HUMDRUM ('drum), *adj.* dull; monotonous; commonplace.

HUMERAL (hu'mer-al), *adj.* pertaining to the shoulder.

HUMERO, a *prefix* meaning *shoulder*.

HUMID (hu'mid), *adj.* damp; moist.

HUMIDITY ('i-ti), *n.* dampness; moisture.

HUMIDOR (hu'mi-dor), *n.* a chest or jar to keep cigars or tobacco in a moist condition.

HUMILIATE (-mil'i-at), *v.t.* to humble; abase.

HUMILIATION (-a'shun), *n.* mortification; abasement.

HUMILITY (-mil'i-ti), *n.* modesty; self-abasement.

HUMMING BIRD (hum'ing berd), *n.* a very small and beautiful bird, allied to the swift.

HUMMOCK ('ok), *n.* a large mass of floating ice; a hillock or mound.

HUMOUR (u'mer), *n.* wit; merriment; caprice; proud conceit; temper; petulance; peevishness.

HUMORIST (ist), *n.* a droll person; one whose writing or conversation is humorous.

HUMOROUS ('us), *adj.* comical; laughable.

HUMP (hump), *n.* a protuberance on the back.

HUMPTY-DUMPTY ('ti-dump'ti), *adj.* characterized by short limbs and a round body.

HUMUS ('mus), *n.* vegetable mould.

HUNCH (hunch), *n.* a hump; lump; a thrust with the fist or elbow; an intuition.

HUNCH-BACK (hunch'bak), *n.* one with a hump on his back.

HUNDRED (hun'dred), *n.* the number of 10 times 10; the symbol C, denoting 100.

HUNDREDWEIGHT ('dred-wat), *n.* the 1-20th part of a ton.

HUNGER (hung'ger), *n.* keenness of appetite.

HUNGER-STRIKE (hung'ger-strik), *n.* refusing food in order to excite sympathy.

HUNGRILY ('gri-li), *adj.* in a hungry manner.

HUNGRY ('gri), *adj.* having a keen appetite; emaciated.

HUNK (hungk), *n.* [Slang], a lump.

HUNKY ('i), *adj.* [Slang], well done: also *hunky-dory*.

HUNT (hunt), *v.t.* to pursue, or chase; follow closely; search after: *v.i.* to follow the chase: *n.* pursuit of game or wild animals.

HUNTER ('er), *n.* a huntsman.

HUNTRESS ('res), *n.* a female hunter.

HUNTSMAN (huntz'man), *n.* a hunter

HURDLE (her'dl), *n.* a fence to be leaped over in steeplechasing.

HURDY-GURDY ('di-ger'di), *n.* a street hand-organ.

HURL (herl), *v.t.* to throw with violence; drive forcibly.

HURLY-BURLY (her'li-ber'li), *n.* tumult; great commotion.

HURRAH (hoo-ra′), *n.* a shout of joy, triumph, applause, etc.

HURRICANE (hur′i-kan), *n.* a gale of extreme violence.

HURRICANE-DECK (-dek), *n.* the bridge-deck of a steamship.

HURRIED (′d), *p.adj.* hasty.

HURRY (′i), *v.t.* to impel to greater speed; hasten on; accelerate: *n.* haste.

HURRY-SCURRY (-skur′i), *n.* confused bustle.

HURT (hert), *v.t.* to grieve; injure; impair or damage: *n.* a wound; injury.

HURTLE (hert′l), *v.t.* to move violently.

HUSBAND (huz′band), *n.* a married man: *v.t.* to use with economy.

HUSBANDMAN (-man), *n.* a farmer.

HUSBANDRY (-ri), *n.* agriculture.

HUSH (hush), *interj.* be still! silence! *n.* silence.

HUSK (husk), *n.* the dry outer covering of certain fruits or seeds.

HUSKILY (′ki-li), *adj.* hoarsely.

HUSKING-BEE (′ing-be), *n.* a social gathering to assist in husking corn.

HUSKY (′ki), *adj.* consisting of husks; worthless; rough or hoarse: said of the voice: *n.* a northern sledge dog.

HUSSY (huz′i), *n.* a worthless woman.

HUSTLE (hus′l), *v.t.* to jostle; mob.

HUT (hut), *n.* a small cabin.

HUTCH (huch), *n.* a bin, box, or chest; a coop or pen.

HUZZAH, same as hurrah.

HYACINTH (hi′a-sinth), *n.* a bulbous plant of the lily family.

HYÆNA (hi-e′na), *n.* same as hyena.

HYAL, a *prefix* meaning *glass*, as *hyaline*, like glass. Also hyalo: *hyalography*, the art of writing or engraving upon glass.

HYALINE (hi′a-lin), *adj.* glassy; transparent.

HYBRID (hi′brid), *n.* an animal or plant produced by interbreeding different species or varieties.

HYBRIDIZE (-iz), *v.t.* to interbreed and thus produce hybrids.

HYDR, a *prefix* meaning water, also the *presence* of *hydrogen*. Also

hydro, as *hydr*acid, an acid containing hydrogen, but no oxygen.

HYDRANGEA (-dran′je-a), *n.* a genus of shrubs of the saxifrage family.

HYDRANT (′drant), *n.* a plug with a valve connected with a water main.

HYDRAULIC (-draw′lik), *adj.* pertaining to fluids in motion; denoting force exerted by waters: *n.pl.* the science of liquids in motion.

HYDRIC (′drik), *adj.* pertaining to hydrogen in combination.

HYDRO. See hydr.

HYDRO-AEROPLANE (-a′er-o-plan), **HYDRO-AIRPLANE** (-ar′-plan), *n.* an aeroplane with floats enabling it to alight on the water; a seaplane.

HYDROCHLORIC ACID (-klo′rik as′id), a colourless, pungent, gaseous compound emitting strong fumes.

HYDROGEN (′dro-jen), *n.* a colourless, gaseous, inflammable substance, which liquefies under great pressure: when combined with oxygen it produces water.

HYDROMETER (-drom′e-ter), *n.* an instrument for determining the specific gravity, strength, etc., of fluids.

HYDROPHOBIA (-fo′bi-a), *n.* a morbid dread of water; a violent infection attacking certain carnivores, especially the dog and wolf; rabies.

HYDROPLANE (′dro-plan), *n.* a fast light motorboat so constructed as to lessen friction by partially rising from the water at speed.

HYENA (hi-e′na), *n.* a bristly-maned, wolflike, carnivorous quadruped.

HYGEIAN (-je′an), *adj.* pertaining to Hygeia, the goddess of health.

HYGIENE (′jen), *n.* the science of health, its preservation.

HYGIENIC (-ji-en′ik), *adj.* pertaining to hygiene.

HYGRO-, a combining form from the Greek *hygros*, wet.

HYMEN (hi′men), *n.* the god of marriage; [h-], the wedded state.

HYMENEAL (-e′al), *p.adj.* pertaining to marriage; nuptial.

HYMN (him), *n.* a sacred song or ode.

HYMNAL ('nal), *n.* a collection of hymns.

HYPER-, a *prefix* signifying *over, above.*

HYPERBOLE ('bo-le), *n.* a figure of speech which expresses more or less than the truth ; exaggeration.

HYPERCRITICAL (-krit'i-kal), *adj.* over-critical ; given to fault-finding.

HYPHEN (hi'fen), *n.* a mark (-) joining two words or syllables.

HYPNO-, a combining form from the Greek *hypnos*, sleep.

HYPNOTISM (hip'no-tizm), *n.* a state effected artificially, in which the mind becomes passive and responsive to the will of another.

HYPNOTIZE ('no-tiz), *v.t.* to produce, or subject to, hypnotism.

HYPO-, a *prefix* signifying *under, beneath.*

HYPOCHONDRIA (hip-o-kon'dria), *n.* a mental disorder characterized by extreme melancholy.

HYPOCRISY (hi-pok'ri-si), *n.* a feigning to be what one is not ; dissimulation ; false profession.

HYPOCRITE (hip'o-krit), *n.* one who practices hypocrisy.

HYPODERMIC (hi-po-der'mik), *adj.* pertaining to the parts under the skin, or to the hypodermis : *n.* an injection into the subcutaneous tissues.

HYPOGASTRIUM (-gas'tri-um), *n.*

[*pl.* hypogastria (-a)], the middle part of the lower region of the abdomen.

HYPOSTYLE (hi'po-stil), *n.* a roof supported by columns.

HYPOSULPHITE (-sul'fit), *n.* a salt of hyposulphurous acid.

HYPOTENUSE (-pot'e-nus), *n.* the side of a right-angled triangle opposite the right angle.

HYPOTHECATE (hi-poth'e-kat), *v.t.* to assign something for security.

HYPOTHESIS (-poth'e-sis), *n.* [*pl.* hypotheses (-sez)], something assumed for the purpose of argument.

HYPOTHETIC (-po-thet'ik), **HYPO-THETICAL** ('i-kal), *adj.* based on hypothesis ; conjectural.

HYPSI-, a combining form from the Greek *hypsi*, on high.

HYSON (hi'son), *n.* a grade of green tea.

HYSSOP (his'up), *n.* an aromatic herb of the mint family with clusters of blue flowers.

HYSTERIA (his-te'ri-a), *n.* a nervous affection, characterized by choking sensations, paroxysms of laughter or weeping.

HYSTERICAL (-ter'i-kal), *adj.* affected by hysterics ; violently emotional.

HYSTERICS (his-ter'iks), *n.pl.* hysteria.

HYZONE (hi'zon), *n.* an unstable gaseous form of hydrogen.

I

I, i, (i), *n.* the ninth letter of the English alphabet.

I, i, *n.* an abbreviation.

I, i, *n.* a Roman numeral denoting 1, written in either form : when repeated, a unit is to be added, when placed before *v, x, l,* etc., a unit is to be taken away.

I, *pron.,* the pronoun by which a speaker or writer designates himself ; the pronoun of the first person, singular, nominative case.

IAMBIC (i-am'bik), *n.* an iambus ; a satirical poem in iambic verse.

IAMBUS ('bus), *n.* a metrical foot

of two syllables, the first short, the second long.

IBEX ('beks), *n.* a species of mountain wild goat.

IBIS ('bis), *n.* one of a sub-family of large wading birds.

ICE (is), *n.* frozen water ; a frozen confection.

ICEBERG ('berg), *n.* a large mass of ice detached from a glacier, and floating in the sea.

ICE BOAT (bot), *n.* a boat mounted on runners and propelled by sails on ice.

ICE CREAM (krem'), *n.* cream, etc., sweetened, flavoured and frozen.

ICE HOCKEY (hok'i), *n.* a game played on ice.

ICE PACK (pak), *n.* a field of drifting ice, packed together.

ICHTHYO-, a combining form from the Greek *ichthys*, a fish.

ICHTHYOLOGY (-o'o-ji), *n.* branch of zoology which treats of fishes.

ICICLE (i'si-kl), *n.* a pendant of ice formed by the freezing of dripping water.

ICILY ('si-li), *adv.* in an icy manner.

ICINESS ('si-nes), *n.* coldness.

ICING ('sing), *n.* a coating, as of liquid sugar, etc. ; frosting.

ICON (i'kon), *n.* in the Greek Church, a sacred image or picture. Also *ikon.*

ICONO-, a combining form from the Greek *eikon*, an image.

ICONOCLASM (i-kon'o-klazm), *n.* the breaking of images.

ICONOCLAST (i-kon'o-klast), *n.* an image breaker ; one who attacks superstitions or shams.

ICTUS (ik'tus), *n.* a blow or stroke ; in prosody and music, rhythmical or metrical accent.

ICY (i'si), *adj.* cold ; chilling.

IDEA (-de'a), *n.* a mental image or picture ; a conception of what ought to be ; an abstract principle ; opinion ; belief ; plan.

IDEAL (de'al), *adj.* existing in imagination only ; visionary ; conforming to a standard of perfection ; perfect : *n.* a mental conception, or an individual regarded as the standard of perfection.

IDEALISM (-izm), *n.* in art, the effort to realize, by elimination and combination, the highest type of any natural object ; the doctrine that all our knowledge of objects is a knowledge of ideas.

IDEALIST (-ist), *n.* one who holds the doctrine of idealism ; a visionary.

IDEALITY ('i-ti), *n.* the quality of being ideal ; the faculty to form ideals.

IDEALIZE (-iz), *v.t.* to make ideal.

IDEM (i'dem), *adj.* or *pron.* [Latin], the same.

IDENTICAL (-den'ti-kal), *adj.* expressing sameness.

IDENTIFY (-den'ti-fi), *v.t.* to make, prove to be, or consider as, the same.

IDENTITY ('ti-ti), *n.* essential or practical sameness.

IDEOLOGY (i-de-ol'o-ji), *n.* the science of ideas.

IDES (idz), *n.pl.* in the ancient Roman calendar, the eighth day after the nones—the 15th of March, May, July, October, and the 13th of the other months.

IDIO-, a combining form from the Greek *idios*, one's own, personal.

IDIOCY (id'i-o-si), **IDIOTCY** (-ot-si), *n.* the state of being an idiot ; mental imbecility.

IDIOM ('i-um), *n.* a turn of expression peculiar to a language.

IDIOMATIC (-o-mat'ik), *adj.* peculiar to a language.

IDIOSYNCRASY (-sin'kra-si), *n.* a characteristic peculiar to an individual.

IDIOT ('i-ot), *n.* one of weak intellect.

IDIOTIC (-ot'ik), *adj.* foolish ; fatuous.

IDLE (i'dl), *adj.* unoccupied ; unemployed ; unused ; vain ; irrelevant ; futile ; lazy.

IDLENESS (-nes), *n.* inactivity ; laziness.

IDLER (i'dler), *n.* one who idles ; a gearing-wheel.

IDOL (i'dol), *n.* an image as an object of worship.

IDOLATER ('a-ter), *n.* an idol-worshipper.

IDOLATRY ('a-tri), *n.* the paying of Divine honours to idols, images ; excessive admiration.

IDOLIZE ('dol-iz), *v.t.* love or admire to excess.

IDYL (i'dil), *n.* a short, highly-wrought pastoral poem.

IDYLIST (i'dil-ist), *n.* a composer of idyls.

IDYLLIC ('ik), *adj.* pastoral.

IF (if), *conj.* on the condition ; supposing that ; whether ; although : *n.* a condition, or supposition.

IGLOO (ig'loo), *n.* an Eskimo house.

IGNEOUS ('ne-us), *adj.* pertaining to fire.

IGNI-, a combining form from the Latin *ignis*, fire.

IGNIS FATUUS ('nis fat'u-us), *n.* a light appearing in the night on swamps and marshes; popularly called *will-o'-the-wisp* and *jack-o-lantern*; a delusion.

IGNITE ('nit), *v.t.* to set on fire.

IGNITION (-nish'un), *n.* the act of igniting.

IGNITION-BOX (-boks), *n.* the explosion-chamber of an internal combustion engine.

IGNOBLE (-no'bl), *adj.* of mean character or quality.

IGNOMINIOUS (-no-min'i-us), *adj.* deserving disgrace; despicable.

IGNOMINY (ig'no-min-i), *n.* public disgrace or dishonour; cause or source of disgrace.

IGNORAMUS (-ra'mus), *n.* an ignorant person.

IGNORANCE (-rans), *n.* the state of being ignorant; want of knowledge.

IGNORANT (-rant), *adj.* uninstructed; illiterate.

IGNORE (ig-nor'), *v.t.* to treat as unknown; disregard.

IGUANA (i-gwa'na), *n.* a large tropical American lizard, having a sac under the throat.

IL, a *prefix,* another form of *in* when followed by *l,* meaning *not,* as *il*literate, uneducated.

ILIAD (il'i-ad), *n.* the celebrated Greek poem in 24 books, ascribed to Homer.

ILIUM (il'i-um), *n.* the dorsal or upper part of the hipbone.

ILK (ilk), *adj.* & *n.* same; rarely used, except in phrase, *of that ilk.*

ILL (il), *adj.* bad or evil; sick; diseased; unfriendly; not proper.

ILLAPSE (-laps'), *v.i.* to fall, pass or glide; to lapse.

ILLATION (i-la'shun), *n.* an inference.

ILL-BRED -(bred), *adj.* rude; impolite.

ILL-DISPOSED (-dis-pozd'), *adj.* unfriendly.

ILLEGAL (il-le'gal), *adj.* contrary to law.

ILLEGIBLE (il-lej'i-bl), *adj.* hard to read; not plain or clear.

ILLEGITIMATE (il-le-jit'i-mat), *adj.* irregular; born out of wedlock.

ILLICIT (-lis'it), *adj.* unlicensed; unlawful.

ILLIMITABLE (-lim'it-a-bl), *adj.* immeasurable; vast; infinite.

ILLITERACY (-lit'er-a-si), *n.* inability to read and write.

ILLITERATE (-at), *adj.* ignorant.

ILL-NATURED (-na'cher'd), *adj.* cross; surly.

ILLNESS ('nes), *n.* disease; sickness.

ILLOGICAL (-loj'i-kal), *adj.* contrary to the rules of logic.

ILL-TEMPERED (-tem'perd), *adj.* crabbed; quarrelsome.

ILLUDE (-lud'), *v.t.* to mock; deceive; delude.

ILLUME (i-lum'), *v.t.* enlighten.

ILLUMINANT (-lum'i-nant), *n.* anything which illuminates or affords light.

ILLUMINATE ('i-nat), *v.t.* to give light to; enlighten.

ILLUMINATOR ('mi-na-ter), *n.* a condenser or reflector; an illuminant.

ILLUSION ('zhun), *n.* false perception; hallucination.

ILLUSIONIST (-ist), *n.* a sleight-of-hand performer.

ILLUSIVE (il-lu'siv), *adj.* deceptive.

ILLUSTRATE (-us'trat), *v.t.* to make clear or intelligible; elucidate by means of pictures, etc.

ILLUSTRATION (-tra'shun), *n.* a comparison or example which explains or corroborates; a picture designed to elucidate.

ILLUSTRATOR ('us-tra-ter), *n.* one who illustrates.

ILLUSTRIOUS ('tri-us), *adj.* distinguished; eminent; renowned; glorious; famous.

IMAGE (im'aj), *n.* an imitation of any person or thing; a statue; an idol; a counterpart.

IMAGERY ('aj-ri), *n.* vivid description in speaking, or writing; forms of the fancy.

IMAGINABLE (aj'i-na-bl), *adj.* that may be imagined.

IMAGINARY ('i-na-ri), *adj.* existing only in imagination; unreal.

IMAGINATION (-na'shun), *n.* the image-forming power of the mind; a mental conception.

IMAGINATIVE ('i-na-tiv), *adj.* proceeding from imagination ; fanciful.

IMAGINE (aj'in), *v.t.* to form a mental picture of ; conceive ; conjecture ; think ; suppose : *v.i.* to fancy ; surmise.

IMAGIST (im'aj-ist), *n.* one of an advanced school of artists and poets.

IMBECILE (im'be-sil), *adj.* feebleminded ; idiotic.

IMBECILITY (-sil'i-ti), *n.* mental weakness.

IMBIBE (-bib'), *v.t.* to drink in.

IMBROGLIO (-bro'lyo), *n.* misunderstanding ; entanglement ; strife ; perplexity.

IMBRUE (-broo'), *v.t.* to wet or moisten ; soak ; drench.

IMBUE (-bu'), *v.t.* to absorb ; impress, as on the mind.

IMITABLE ('i-ta-bl), *adj.* capable of, or worthy of, imitation.

IMITATE ('i-tat), *v.t.* to use as a model or pattern ; to counterfeit ; copy.

IMITATION (-ta'shun), *n.* the act of imitating ; not genuine.

IMITATIVE ('i-ta-tiv), *adj.* inclined to, or aiming at, imitation.

IMITATOR ('i-ta-ter), *n.* one who imitates.

IMMACULATE (-mak'u-lat), *adj.* without blemish ; undefiled.

IMMATERIAL (-ma-te'ri-al), *adj.* spiritual ; disembodied ; unimportant.

IMMATURE (-ma-tur'), *adj.* not ripe ; crude.

IMMATURELY (-tur'li), *adv.* crudely.

IMMATURITY (-tur'i-ti), *n.* unripeness ; incompleteness.

IMMEASURABILITY (-mezh-ur-a-bil'i-ti), *n.* the quality of not being measurable.

IMMEASURABLE ('ur-a-bl), *adj.* not to be measured ; immense ; vast.

IMMEDIATE (-me'di-at), *adj.* next ; direct ; approximate ; instant.

IMMEMORIAL (-me-mor'i-al), *adj.* extending beyond the reach of memory, record, or tradition.

IMMENSE (-mens'), *adj.* immeasurable ; boundless ; vast : *n.* infinite space ; immensity.

IMMENSITY ('si-ti), *n.* immeasur-

ableness ; infinite space ; vastness in extent or bulk.

IMMERGE (-merj'), *v.t.* to plunge into or under anything, especially a fluid ; immerse.

IMMERSE (-mers'), *v.t.* to plunge into ; sink ; dip ; baptize by immersion.

IMMERSED (-merst'), *p.adj.* deeply occupied, engrossed, or involved.

IMMERSION (mer'shun), *n.* the state of being immersed ; baptism by dipping the whole person into water.

IMMIGRANT ('i-grant), *adj.* passing or coming into, as into a new place of residence : *n.* one who immigrates.

IMMIGRATE ('i-grat), *v.i.* to come into a new place of residence, especially to come into a country to settle.

IMMINENCE ('i-nens), *n.* nearness ; impending evil or danger.

IMMINENT ('i-nent), *adj.* threatening or about to fall or occur immediately.

IMMOBILE (im-mo'bil), *adj.* unmovable.

IMMOBILITY (mo-bil'i-ti), *n.* fixedness in place or state.

IMMODERATE (-mod'er-at), *adj.* extravagant ; intemperate.

IMMODEST (-mod'est), *adj.* forward ; arrogant ; indelicate.

IMMODESTY (-mod'es-ti), *n.* want of modesty.

IMMOLATE ('o-lat), *v.t.* to kill as a sacrificial victim.

IMMORAL (-mor'al), *adj.* vicious ; dissolute ; unprincipled.

IMMORALITY (-mo-ral'i-ti), *n.* the quality of being immoral.

IMMORTAL (-mor'tal), *adj.* not subject to death ; imperishable.

IMMORTALITY (-tal'i-ti), *n.* exemption from death or oblivion ; unending existence.

IMMORTALIZE ('tal-iz), *v.t.* to render immortal.

IMMORTELLE (-mor-tel'), *n.* a plant ; an everlasting.

IMMOVABILITY (-moov-a-bil'i-ti), *n.* fixedness.

IMMOVABLE ('a-bl), *adj.* fixed ;

steadfast ; unchanging ; unfeeling : *n.pl.* land, or things fixed to land, as trees, buildings.

IMMUNE (-mun'), *adj.* exempt, as from a disease.

IMMUNE SERUM (se'rum), serum of an immunized animal that may be used as an antidote to a bacterial poison.

IMMUNITY (-mun'i-ti), *n.* freedom from natural or usual liability ; a physical condition by which the body is able to resist disease.

IMMURE (-mur'), *v.t.* to enclose within walls ; confine.

IMMUTABILITY (-mut-a-bil'i-ti), *n.* unchangeableness.

IMMUTABLE (-mut'a-bl), *adj.* unchangeable ; invariable.

IMP (imp), *n.* an inferior devil ; a hobgoblin.

IMPACT (im'pakt), *n.* collision.

IMPAIR (-par'), *v.t.* to make worse ; deteriorate.

IMPAIRMENT ('ment), *n.* injury.

IMPALE (-pal'), *v.t.* to fix on a stake.

IMPALPABLE (-pal'pa-bl), *adj.* not to be perceived by touch ; not material ; incorporeal ; unreal.

IMPANEL (-pan'el), *v.t.* to summon to serve on a jury ; draw from the panel and swear in.

IMPARITY (-par'i-ti), *n.* inequality ; disproportion.

IMPART (-part'), *v.t.* to give ; to make known.

IMPARTIAL (par'shal), *adj.* free from partiality ; equitable ; fair.

IMPARTIALITY (-shi-al'i-ti), *n.* freedom from bias ; fairness.

IMPARTIALLY (par'shal-li), *adv.* justly ; fairly.

IMPARTIBLE ('ti-bl), *adj.* capable of being communicated ; indivisible.

IMPASSABLE (-pas'a-bl), *adj.* not admitting passage.

IMPASSIONED (-pash'und), *p.adj.* moved to strong feeling.

IMPASSIVE (-pas'iv), *adj.* apathetic ; insusceptible.

IMPATIENCE (-pa'shens), *n.* the state of being impatient.

IMPATIENT ('shent), *adj.* exhibiting

or expressing strong feeling (with *at*) ; eager (with *for*).

IMPAWN (-pawn'), *v.t.* to put in pawn ; deposit as security.

IMPEACH (-pech'), *v.t.* to call in question ; accuse before a tribunal of official misconduct.

IMPEACHMENT ('ment), *n.* the arraignment of a public officer for malfeasance in office.

IMPECCABILITY (-pek-a-bil'i-ti), *n.* exemption from sin, error, or wrongdoing.

IMPECCABLE (-pek'a-bl), *adj.* not liable to sin ; faultless.

IMPECUNIOSITY (-pe-ku-ni-os'i-ti), *n.* want of money ; poverty.

IMPECUNIOUS ('ni-us), *adj.* without money ; poor.

IMPEDE (-ped'), *v.t.* to obstruct ; hinder.

IMPEDIMENT (-ped'i-ment), *n.* obstruction ; obstacle ; hindrance.

IMPEDIMENTA (-ped-i-men'ta), *n.pl.* encumbrances ; travelling equipage ; military supplies.

IMPEL (-pel'), *v.t.* constrain to any kind of motion or action.

IMPELLENT ('ent), *n.* a motive or impelling power.

IMPEND (-pend'), *v.i.* to hang over ; be at hand.

IMPENDENT ('dent), *adj.* impending.

IMPENDING ('ing), *p.adj.* overhanging ; close at hand.

IMPENETRABILITY (-pen-e-tra-bil'i-ti), *n.* that property of matter in virtue of which no two bodies can occupy the same space at the same time.

IMPENETRABLE ('e-tra-bl), *adj.* not penetrable ; impervious.

IMPENITENCE (-pen'i-tens), *n.* hardness of heart ; stubborn wickedness.

IMPENITENT ('i-tent), *adj.* not contrite ; obdurate.

IMPERATIVE (-per'a-tiv), *n.* that mood of a verb that expresses command, entreaty or exhortation.

IMPERATIVELY (-li), *adv.* peremptorily.

IMPERCEPTIBLE (-sep'ti-bl), *adj.* that cannot be immediately perceived by the senses, or easily apprehended by the mind.

IMPERFECT ('fekt), *adj.* wanting in completeness or excellence; defective.

IMPERFECTION (-fek'shun), *n* a defect or blemish, physical, mental, or moral.

IMPERIAL (-pe'ri-al), *adj.* pertaining to an empire or emperor.

IMPERIALISM (-izm), *n.* the policy of imperial federation; policy of territorial expansion.

IMPERIALIST (-ist), *n.* one who favours imperialism.

IMPERIL (per'il), *v.t.* to put in peril; endanger; jeopardize.

IMPERIOUS (-pe'ri-us), *adj.* domineering; overbearing.

IMPERISHABLE (-per'ish-a-bl), *adj.* indestructible; permanently enduring.

IMPERMANENT (-per'ma-nent), *adj.* not permanent.

IMPERMEABLE ('me-a-bl), *adj.* impervious; impenetrable.

IMPERSONAL ('sun-al), *adj.* not referring to a particular person: *n.* an impersonal verb.

IMPERSONATE ('sun-at), *v.t.* to invest with personality; to represent the person or character of another.

IMPERSONATOR (-a-ter), *n.* one who impersonates; an actor.

IMPERTINENCE ('ti-nens), *n.* lack of respect for others; forwardness; rudeness.

IMPERTINENT ('ti-nent), *adj.* inapposite; inapplicable; rude, or offensive in behaviour.

IMPERTURBABLE ('ba-bl), *adj.* not easily disturbed, agitated, or disconcerted; cool; calm.

IMPERVIOUS ('vi-ous), *adj.* not to be passed through or penetrated; impenetrable.

IMPETUOSITY (-pet-u-os'i-ti), *n.* vehemence; violence; force.

IMPETUOUS ('u-us), *adj.* rushing with force and violence; vehement in feeling.

IMPETUS ('pe-tus), *n.* the force with which any body is driven or impelled.

IMPIETY (-pi'e-ti), *n.* want of piety; disregard of the Supreme Being.

IMPINGE (-pinj'), *v.i.* strike or dash; clash; come in collision (with *on*, *upon*, or *against*).

IMPIOUS ('pi-us), *adj.* irreligious; wicked.

IMPLACABILITY (-pla-ka-bil'i-ti), *n.* a state of irreconcilable enmity.

IMPLACABLE (-pla'ka-bl), *adj.* not to be pacified or appeased.

IMPLANT (-plant'), *v.t.* to fix for growth; ingraft.

IMPLEAD (-pled'), *v.t.* to accuse; impeach.

IMPLEMENT ('ple-ment), *n.* an instrument, tool, or utensil.

IMPLICATE ('pli-kat), *v.t.* to infold; involve; entangle.

IMPLICATION (-ka'shun), *n.* entanglement; deduction.

IMPLICIT (-plis'it), *adj.* implied; trusting in the word or authority of another; submissive.

IMPLORE (-plor'), *v.t.* to entreat earnestly: *v.i.* pray; supplicate.

IMPLY (-pli'), *v.t.* to contain by implication; signify by inference; insinuate.

IMPOLICY (-pol'i-si), *n.* want of policy; inexpediency.

IMPOLITE (-po-lit'), *adj.* wanting in good manners; coarse.

IMPOLITELY ('li), *adv.* ill-manneredly.

IMPOLITENESS (-lit'nes), *n.* rudeness.

IMPOLITIC (-pol'i-tik), *adj.* unwise; injudicious; indiscreet.

IMPONDERABLE (-pon'der-a-bl), *adj.* not capable of being weighed; without (sensible) weight.

IMPOROUS (-po'rus), *adj.* without pores; solid.

IMPORT (-port'), *v.t.* to bring into a country from abroad; imply; signify.

IMPORTANCE (-por'tans), *n.* high place in public estimation; high self-esteem.

IMPORTANT ('tant), *adj.* of much significance; momentous; of high standing; pompous.

IMPORTATION (-ta'shun), *n.* bringing merchandise into a country from abroad.

IMPORTER (-por'ter), *n.* a merchant who imports goods, etc.

IMPORTUNATE (-por'tu-nat), *adj.* persistent; urgent.

IMPORTUNE (-por-tun'), *v.t.* to harass with perpetual demands.

IMPORTUNITY (-tu'ni-ti), *n.* persistent solicitation.

IMPOSE (-poz'), *v.t.* to place upon : as, to *impose* the hands in confirmation or ordination; lay upon, as a burden, punishment, or charge; to palm off.

IMPOSING ('ing), *p.adj.* stately; grand; impressive.

IMPOSITION (-po-zish'un), *n.* that which is imposed, levied, or enjoined; a trick, fraud, or deception.

IMPOSSIBILITY (-pos-i-bil'i-ti), *n.* character of being impossible.

IMPOSSIBLE (-pos'i-bl), *adj.* that which cannot be done; inconceivable; hopeless.

IMPOST ('post), *n.* that which is imposed or levied; a tax.

IMPOSTOR (pos'ter), *n.* one who imposes upon others by an assumed character or false pretensions.

IMPOSTURE (-pos'tur), *n.* deception.

IMPOTENCE ('po-tens), *n.* the state of being impotent in body or mind; want of capacity.

IMPOTENT ('po-tent), *adj.* wanting in physical, intellectual, or moral power; weak.

IMPOUND (-pound'), *v.t.* to shut up in a pound or pen as stray cattle.

IMPOVERISH (-pov'er-ish), *v.t.* to make poor; reduce to poverty.

IMPRACTICABLE ('ti-ka-bl), *adj.* not easily dealt with; unmanageable; impossible.

IMPRECATE ('pre-kat), *v.t.* to invoke, especially an evil or curse, upon.

IMPREGNABLE ('na-bl), *adj.* not to be captured, as a fortress; not to be overcome.

IMPREGNABLY (-bli), *adv.* so as to defy attack.

IMPREGNATE (-preg'nat), *v.t.* to fecundate; fertilize; imbue.

IMPRESARIO (-pra-sa're-o), *n.* the manager of an opera or concert company.

IMPRESS (-pres'), *v.t.* to mark, stamp, or print by pressure; to affect the mind; inculcate.

IMPRESSION (-presh'un), *n.* the mark made by a stamp or mould; style of character formed by external force or influence; remembrance, or belief.

IMPRESSIONABLE (-a-bl), *adj.* susceptible.

IMPRESSIONISM ('un-izm), *n.* the doctrine that natural objects should be painted—in literature described— so as to reproduce only their larger and more immediate effect or impressions, without elaboration of details but with due regard for colour and light.

IMPRESSIVE (-pres'iv), *adj.* having the power of affecting and gaining attention and feeling.

IMPRESSMENT (-pres'ment), *n.* the act of seizing for public use.

IMPRIMATUR (im-pri-ma'ter), *n.* approval given to print and publish certain books.

IMPRIMIS (-pri'mis), *adv.* in the first place; first of a series.

IMPRINT (-print'), *v.t.* to mark by pressure; to stamp, as letters and words on paper, by means of inked types; print; impress deeply, as on the mind or memory : *n.* (im'print), an impression; the publisher's or printer's name on a book, etc.

IMPRISON (-priz'n), *v.t.* to put into a prison; detain in custody.

IMPROBABILITY (-prob-a-bil'i-ti), *n.* unlikelihood; an improbable event.

IMPROBABLE ('a-bl), *adj.* unlikely.

IMPROBITY (-prob'i-ti), *n.* want of rectitude; dishonesty.

IMPROMPTU (-promp'tu), *adv.* without preparation; extempore.

IMPROPER (-pro'er), *adj.* not well adapted; unseemly.

IMPROPERLY (-prop'er-li), *adv.* wrongly; indecently.

IMPROPRIETY (-pri'e-ti), *n.* the quality of being improper.

IMPROVABLE (-proov'a-bl), *adj.* capable of being improved.

IMPROVE (-proov´), *v.t.* to make better ; turn to account.

IMPROVEMENT (´ment), *n.* advancement of anything from good to better : *pl.* betterments.

IMPROVIDENCE (-prov´i-dens), *n.* want of foresight or thrift.

IMPROVIDENT (´i-dent), *adj.* lacking foresight or thrift ; careless.

IMPROVISATION (-i-sa´shun), *n.* the act of improvising ; an impromptu.

IMPROVISE (-pro-viz´), *v.t.* to compose extemporaneously, especially verse or music.

IMPRUDENCE (-proo´dens), *n.* want of prudence ; carelessness of consequences.

IMPRUDENT (´dent), *adj.* indiscreet ; injudicious.

IMPUDENCE (´pu-dens), *n.* shamelessness ; rudeness ; forwardness.

IMPUDENT (´pu-dent), *adj.* shameless ; offensively forward.

IMPUGN (-pun´), *v.t.* to attack by arguments ; contradict.

IMPULSE (´puls), *n.* force communicated suddenly ; a mental force directly urging to action.

IMPULSION (-pul´shun), *n.* the act of impelling ; instigation.

IMPULSIVE (´siv), *adj.* actuated by, or resulting from, impulse ; passionate.

IMPUNITY (-pu´ni-ti), *n.* freedom from punishment, injury.

IMPURE (-pur´), *adj.* unchaste ; unclean ; dirty.

IMPURITY (-pu´ri-ti), *n.* state of being impure.

IMPUTABLE (-put´a-bl), *adj.* that may be imputed, charged, or ascribed.

IMPUTATION (-ta´shun), *n.* censure ; reproach ; insinuation.

IMPUTE (-put´), *v.t.* to charge, attribute, or ascribe, especially a fault.

IN (in), *adj.* inward ; internal : *v.t.* to put in ; store : *adv.* close by ; into, or enclosed, in a place : *prep.* among ; amidst ; into ; enclosed ; presence in one's home or office ; nature or state of.

IN-, a prefix from the English preposition and adverb, *in,* and, also,

from the Latin preposition, *in,* meaning *in, into, on, within, towards.*

IN-, an inseparable particle meaning *not*, and used instead of *non-, un-* : for the sake of euphony, the *n.* in this particle or prefix, becomes *m* before *b* and *p*, *l* before *l*, and *r* before *r*.

INABILITY (in-a-bil´i-ti), *n.* want of power, strength, or resource.

INACCESSIBLE (-ak-ses´i-bl), *adj.* denoting that which cannot be attained, or reached.

INACCURACY (-ak´u-ra-si), *n.* state of being inaccurate ; error.

INACCURATE (-rat), *adj.* not accurate ; incorrect ; wrong.

INACTION (-ak´shun), *n.* lack of activity ; idleness.

INACTIVE (´tiv), *adj.* not active.

INACTIVITY (-tiv´i-ti), *n.* inaction.

INADEQUATE (ad´e-kwat), *adj.* deficient ; insufficient.

INADMISSIBLE (-mis´i-bl), *adj.* not admissible.

INADVERTENCE (-ad-vert´ens), *n.* oversight ; mistake.

INADVERTENT (´ent), *adj.* inattentive ; heedless ; careless.

INADVISABLE (viz´a-bl), *adj.* inexpedient ; not advisable.

INALIENABLE (-al´yen-a-bl), *adj.* that cannot, or should not, be alienated.

INALIENABLENESS (-nes), *n.* inalienability.

INALIENABLY (-bli), *adv.* so as to be inalienable.

INAMORATA (in-am-o-ra´ta), *n.* [Italian], a sweetheart.

INANE (-an´), *adj.* empty ; void ; senseless ; silly ; pointless.

INANIMATE (-an´i-mat), *adj.* dead ; spiritless ; lifeless.

INANITION (-a-nish´un), *n.* emptiness ; exhaustion.

INANITY (-an´i-ti), *n.* emptiness ; mental vacuity ; frivolity : *pl.* vanities.

INAPPLICABLE (-ap´li-ka-bl), *adj.* unsuitable ; not adapted to.

INAPPRECIABLE (-pre´shi-a-bl), *adj.* not to be appreciated or estimated.

INAPPROPRIATE (-pro´pri-at), *adj.* unbecoming ; unsuitable.

INAPT (in-apt'), *adj*. unsuitable.

INARTICULATE (in-ar'tik'u-lat), *adj*. not uttered with intelligible distinctness; incapable of speech.

INARTISTIC (-ar-tis'tik), *adj*. not conforming to the ethics of art.

INASMUCH (-az-much'), *adv*. in a like degree; because.

INATTENTION (in-a-ten'shun), *n*. heedlessness; neglect.

INAUDIBLE (-aw'di-bl), *adj*. not audible.

INAUGURAL ('gu-ral), *adj*. pertaining to an inauguration : *n*. an inaugural address.

INAUGURATE ('gu-rat), *v.t*. to induct into office with appropriate ceremonies; consecrate.

INAUSPICIOUS (-spish'us), *adj*. ill-omened; unlucky; unfavourable.

INBEING ('be-ing), *n*. inherent existence; essence.

INBREED (-bred'), *v.t*. to breed from animals closely related.

INCALCULABLE (in-kal'ku-la-bl), *adj*. beyond calculation.

INCANDESCE (-kan-des'), *v.t*. to glow with heat.

INCANDESCENCE ('ens), *n*. white heat.

INCANDESCENT ('ent), *adj*. glowing.

INCANDESCENT LAMP (lamp), a bulb heated to incandescence by an electric current.

INCANTATION (-kan-ta'shun), *n*. a magical charm said or sung.

INCAPABLE (-ka'pa-bl), *adj*. not capable; lacking in power.

INCAPACITATE (-ka-pas'i-tat), *v.t*. to render incapable or unfit.

INCAPACITY (-ti), *n*. lack of power, physical or mental.

INCARCERATE (-kar'ser-at), *v.t*. to imprison; confine.

INCARCERATION (-ra'shun), *n*. imprisonment; confinement.

INCARNATE ('nat), *v.t*. to clothe with flesh; embody in flesh.

INCARNATION (-na'shun), *n*. embodiment in human form.

INCAUTIOUS (kaw'shus), *adj*. wanting in caution; not circumspect.

INCENDIARISM (-sen'di-a-rizm), *n*. the act of an incendiary; arson.

INCENDIARY ('di-a-ri), *adj*. the malicious burning of property; tending to excite passion or violence; inflammatory; seditious.

INCENSE (in-sens'), *v.t*. to fire; inflame with anger; provoke; irritate: *n*. (in'sens), any aromatic material which emits a perfume when burned, as spices, etc.

INCENTIVE (sen'tiv), *adj*. inciting; encouraging: *n*. motive; spur, stimulus.

INCEPTION (-sep'shun), *n*. reception; beginning.

INCEPTIVE (-sep'tiv), *adj*. beginning; denoting beginning: *n*. an inceptive word or phrase.

INCESSANT (ses'ant), *adj*. unceasing; ceaseless; continuous.

INCH (inch), *n*. $\frac{1}{12}$th of a foot: *v.i*. move slowly.

INCHOATE (in'ko-at), *adj*. just begun; incipient; elementary; incomplete.

INCIDENCE ('si-dens), *n*. the direction in which a ray of light or heat falls upon a surface.

INCIDENT ('si-dent), *adj*. falling upon; apt to occur; appertaining; casual; subordinate.

INCIDENTAL ('tal), *adj*. casual; subordinate: *pl*. minor expenses.

INCINERATE (-sin'er-at), *v.t*. to burn to ashes.

INCIPIENCE (-sip'i-ens), *n*. beginning; commencement.

INCIPIENT ('i-ent), *adj*. initial.

INCISION (-sizh'un), *n*. a cut.

INCISIVE (-si'siv), *adj*. having the quality of cutting into; sharp.

INCISIVELY (-li), *adv*. with incision.

INCISOR (-si'zer), *n*. a cutting tooth.

INCITE (-sit'), *v.t*. spur on; encourage; impel.

INCITEMENT ('ment), *n*. incentive; impulse; encouragement.

INCIVIC (in-siv'ik), *adj*. deficient in good citizenship.

INCIVILITY (-si-vil'i-ti), *n*. lack of civility; impoliteness.

INCLEMENCY (-klem'en-si), *n*. severity of temper; storminess.

INCLEMENT ('ent), *adj*. unmerciful; tempestuous.

INCLINATION (-kli-na'shun), *n.* a leaning; deviation from normal direction or position; disposition; slant; propensity.

INCLINE (-klin'), *v.i.* to lean; bow; be disposed: *v.t.* to direct; turn; dispose: *n.* (in-klin', in'klin), a slope; gradient.

INCLINED (-klind'), *p.adj.* having a tendency; sloping; disposed.

INCLOSE (-kloz'), *v.t.* to encompass; surround; put into an envelope.

INCLOSURE (-klo'zhur), *n.* the act of inclosing.

INCLUDE (-klood'), *v.t.* to inclose; comprise or comprehend.

INCLUSION (-kloo'zhun), *n.* the act of including; that which is included.

INCLUSIVE ('siv), *adj.* inclosing; including.

INCOERCIBLE (in-ko-er'si-bl), *adj.* incapable of being forced or coerced.

INCOGNITO (-kog'ni-to), *adj.* unknown or disguised: *n.* assumed name: *Fem.* incognita.

INCOGNIZANT (-kog'ni-zant), *adj.* unaware.

INCOHERENCE (-ko-her'ens), *n.* want of cohesion; looseness; want of connection; incongruity; inconsequence.

INCOHERENT ('ent), *a.* incongruous; inconsecutive.

INCOHESION (-he'zhun), *n.* want of cohesion.

INCOMBUSTIBLE (-kom-bus'ti-bl), *adj.* that cannot be consumed by fire.

INCOME ('kum), *n.* the gain from labour, business, property, or capital.

INCOME TAX (tax), *n.* the tax levied by a government on the income of an individual or corporation, with allowances for specified exemptions.

INCOMMENSURABLE ('shoo-ra-bl), *adj.* having no common measure.

INCOMMENSURATE (-rat), *adj.* incommensurable; inadequate.

INCOMMODE (-ko-mod'), *v.t.* to give inconvenience to; disturb.

INCOMMUNICABLE (-mu'ni-ka-bl), *adj.* that cannot be communicated or told.

INCOMPARABLE (-kom'pa-ra-bl),

adj. unequalled; transcendent; peerless.

INCOMPATIBILITY (-pat-i-bil'i-ti), *n.* irreconcilableness.

INCOMPATIBLE ('i-bl), *adj.* inconsistent; incongruous: *n. pl.* persons or things irreconcilably disagreeing with each other.

INCOMPETENCE (-kom'pe-tens), *n.* inability; insufficiency; inadequacy.

INCOMPETENCY (-si), *n.* lack of capacity; inability.

INCOMPETENT ('pe-tent), *adj.* wanting ability; inadequate.

INCOMPLETE (-plet'), *adj.* imperfect; defective.

INCOMPREHENSIBLE (-pre-hen'-si-bl), *adj.* illimitable; inconceivable.

INCONCEIVABLE (-sev'a-bl), *adj.* incapable of being conceived or imagined; incredible.

INCONCLUSIVE (kloo'siv), *adj.* unconvincing; ineffective; inefficient.

INCONDENSIBLE (-den'si-bl), *adj.* incapable of being made more dense or compact.

INCONGRUITY (groo'i-ti), *n.* want of mutual fitness; unsuitableness.

INCONGRUOUS (-kong'groo-us), *adj.* reciprocally disagreeing; inharmonious; inappropriate.

INCONSEQUENCE ('se-kwens), *n.* want of logical sequence; inconclusiveness.

INCONSEQUENT (-kwent), *adj.* illogical; irrelevant.

INCONSIDERABLE (-sid'er-a-bl), *adj.* unimportant.

INCONSIDERATE (-sid'er-at), *adj.* without consideration; thoughtless.

INCONSIDERATELY (-li), *adv.* thoughtlessly.

INCONSISTENCY (-sis'ten-si), *n.* incongruity.

INCONSISTENT ('tent), *adj.* discrepant; lacking uniformity.

INCONSOLABLE (-sol'a-bl), *adj.* not to be consoled or comforted.

INCONSPICUOUS (-spik'u-us), *adj.* not easily perceived.

INCONSTANCY ('stan-si), *n.* changeableness.

INCONSTANT ('stant), *adj.* unstable; variable; capricious.

INCONTESTABLE (-test'a-bl), *adj.* incontrovertible.

INCONTINENCE ('ti-nens), *n.* lack of restraint.

INCONTINENT ('ti-nent), *adj.* unrestrained ; unchaste.

INCONTROVERTIBLE (-tro-ver'ti-bl), *adj.* not admitting of controversy ; indisputable.

INCONVENIENCE (-ven'yens), *n.* unfitness ; troublesomeness ; disadvantage.

INCONVENIENT ('yent), *adj.* inexpedient.

INCONVERTIBLE (-ver'ti-bl), *adj.* incapable of being converted into, or exchanged for, something else.

INCORPORATE (-kor'po-rat), *v.t.* to embody ; unite ; associate ; assimilate ; blend ; form into a corporation.

INCORPORATION (-po-ra'shun), *n.* combination ; assimilation ; mixture ; a corporation.

INCORPORATOR (-ra-ter), *n.* one who incorporates.

INCORPOREAL (-kor-po're-al), *adj.* not corporeal ; immaterial ; intangible.

INCORRECT (-ko-rekt'), *adj.* faulty ; inaccurate ; improper.

INCORRIGIBLE (-kor'i-ji-bl), *adj.* bad beyond correction ; irreclaimable.

INCORRUPT (-ko-rupt'), *adj.* unimpaired ; upright ; honest.

INCORRUPTIBLE (-rup'ti-bl), *adj.* incapable of physical corruption.

INCREASE (-kres'), *v.i.* to augment ; multiply ; grow ; wax : *v.t.* to enhance ; aggravate ; enlarge : *n.* (in'-kres), increment ; produce ; issue.

INCREDIBILITY (-kred-i-bil'i-ti), *n.* the quality of being incredible.

INCREDIBLE ('i-bl), *adj.* unimaginable ; inconceivable.

INCREDIBLY (-bli), *adv.* in an incredible manner.

INCREDULITY (kre-du'li-ti), *n.* scepticism ; disbelief.

INCREDULOUS (-kred'u-lus), *adj.* hard of belief ; sceptical.

INCREMENT ('kre-ment), *n.* increase; augmentation ; produce.

INCRESCENT (-kres'ent), *p.adj.* increasing.

INCRIMINATE (-krim'i-nat), *v.t.* to charge with a crime ; accuse.

INCRUST (in-krust'), *v.t.* to coat ; overlay ; to inlay, as mosaic.

INCUBATE ('ku-bat), *v.t.* to develop germs, eggs, etc., by warmth.

INCUBATOR ('ku-ba-ter), *n.* an apparatus for hatching eggs.

INCUBUS ('ku-bus), *n.* [*pl.* incubi (-bi)], a nightmare.

INCULCATE (-kul'kat), *v.t.* to impress upon the mind.

INCULPATE (in-kul-pat), *v.t.* to blame ; incriminate.

INCUMBENCY (-kum'ben-si), *n.* full possession and exercise of any office.

INCUMBENT ('bent), *adj.* lying upon ; imposed as a duty : *n.* the holder of an office.

INCUR (-ker), *v.t.* to become liable to, by one's own action.

INCURABLE (-kur'a-bl), *adj.* irremediable ; incorrigible.

INCURSION (in-ker'shun), *n.* an inroad ; raid ; invasion.

INCURVATE ('vat), *adj.* bent inward ; curved.

INDEBTED (in-det'ed), *adj.* being in debt.

INDECENCY (-de'sen-si), *n.* want of decency, modesty, or good manners.

INDECENT ('sent), *adj.* immodest ; indelicate ; obscene.

INDECISION (-de-sizh'un), *n.* want of decision ; irresolution.

INDECISIVE (-si'siv), *adj.* not bringing to a final issue ; inconclusive.

INDECOROUS (-de-ko'rus, -dek'o-rus), *adj.* violating any accepted rule of conduct.

INDEED (-ded'), *adv.* in fact ; in truth.

INDEFATIGABLE (-fat'i-ga-bl), *adj.* not to be wearied out.

INDEFENSIBLE (-fen'si-bl), *adj.* that cannot be defended, or justified.

INDEFINABLE (-fi'na-bl), *adj.* that which cannot be defined.

INDEFINITE (-def'i-nit), *adj.* not defined ; not precise ; vague.

INDEFINITELY (-li), *adv.* to an indefinite degree.

INDELIBLE (-del'i-bl), *adj.* not to

be blotted out, effaced, or obliterated.

INDELICACY (-del'i-ka-si), *n.* that which is offensive to modesty or refined taste.

INDELICATE ('i-kat), *adj.* coarse; indecent.

INDEMNIFICATION (dem-ni-fi-ka'-shun), *n.* reimbursement of loss.

INDEMNIFY ('ni-fi), *v.t.* to secure or insure against loss; reimburse.

INDEMNITY ('ni-ti), *n.* compensation for loss.

INDENT (-dent'), *v.t.* to make a dent in; dent; notch: *n.* an order for goods.

INDENTATION (den-ta'shun), *n.* a dent or dint.

INDENTURE ('tur), *n.* a covenant or deed.

INDEPENDENCE (-de-pen'dens), *n.* freedom from support or governance by others; a competency; self-reliance.

INDEPENDENCE DAY (da), July 4, the anniversary of the (U.S.) Declaration of Independence (1776).

INDEPENDENT ('dent), *adj.* not dependent, supported by, or governed by, another; having a competency; free.

INDESCRIBABLE (-skrib'a-bl), *adj.* beyond description.

INDESTRUCTIBLE (-struk'ti-bl), *adj.* everlasting.

INDETERMINATE (-ter'mi-nat), *adj.* not settled, or fixed; indefinite; not precise.

INDEX ('deks), *n.* that which points out or indicates; a table of contents.

INDEX FINGER (fing'ger), *n.* the fore-finger.

INDIA (in'di-a), *n.* the central peninsula (1,581,410 sq. miles) in Southern Asia. Pop. over 389 millions.

INDIAN CORN (-an korn), a native American cereal.

INDIAN SUMMER (sum'er), a period of mild weather late in autumn.

INDIA-RUBBER ('di-a-rub'er), *n.* the inspissated sap of various tropical trees; caoutchouc.

INDICATE ('di-kat), *v.t.* to point out; show; suggest; hint.

INDICATION (-ka'shun), *n.* information; token; evidence; sign.

INDICATIVE (-dik'a-tiv), *adj.* pointing out; bringing to notice.

INDICATOR ('di-ka-ter), *n.* one who, or that which, indicates.

INDICT (dit'), *v.t.* to charge with a crime.

INDICTABLE ('a-bl), *adj.* punishable.

INDICTMENT ('ment), *n.* a written accusation against a prisoner presented by a grand jury to a court.

INDIFFERENCE (-dif'er-ens), *n.* unconcernedness; unimportance; mediocrity.

INDIFFERENT ('er-ent), *adj.* unconcerned; unimportant.

INDIGENCE ('di-jens), *n.* poverty; want.

INDIGENOUS (-dij'e-nus), *adj.* not exotic; not imported; innate; inherent; native.

INDIGENT ('di-jent), *adj.* destitute; needy.

INDIGESTIBLE (-jest'i-bl), *adj.* not digestible.

INDIGESTION (-jes'chun), *n.* difficulty in digesting food; dyspepsia.

INDIGNANT (-dig'nant), *adj.* inflamed with mingled anger and disdain.

INDIGNATION (-na'shun), *n.* anger at what is unworthy, unjust dishonourable, or base.

INDIGNITY (-dig'ni-ti), *n.* an action intended to lower the dignity of another; insult.

INDIGO ('di-go), *n.* a blue dye-stuff.

INDIRECT (-di-rekt'), *adj.* not straight or rectilinear; not straightforward.

INDISCREET (-dis-kret'), *adj.* wanting in discretion; imprudent.

INDISCRETION (-dis-kresh'un), *n.* imprudence; an imprudent act.

INDISCRIMINATE (-krim'i-nat), *adj.* promiscuous; confused.

INDISPENSABLE (-pen'sa-bl), *adj.* absolutely necessary.

INDISPOSE (-dis-poz'), *v.t.* to disincline; unfit.

INDISPOSITION (po-zish'un), *n.* slight illness; disinclination.

INDISPUTABLE (-dis'pu-ta-bl), *adj.* too evident to admit of dispute.

INDISSOLUBLE ('o-lu-bl), *adj.* not dissoluble or dissolvable.

INDISTINCT (-dis-tingkt'), *adj.* undefined ; indefinite ; confused.

INDISTINGUISHABLE (-ting'-gwish-a-bl), *adj.* incapable of being distinguished.

INDITE (-dit'), *v.t.* to compose ; write.

INDIVIDUAL (-di-vij'u-al, -vid'u-al), *adj.* existing as a single indivisible entity : *n.* a single person, animal, or thing.

INDIVIDUALISM (-izm), *n.* a social system in which each individual works for himself alone.

INDIVIDUALIST (-ist), *n.* one who holds the theory of individualism.

INDIVIDUALITY (-al'i-ti), *n.* separate or distinct existence ; distinctive character.

INDIVISIBILITY (-viz-bil'i-ti), *n.* the property of being indivisible.

INDIVISABLE ('i-bl), *adj.* not separable into parts.

INDOCILE (in-dos'il), *adj.* unteachable ; intractable.

INDOCILITY (-do-sil'i-ti), *n.* the quality of being indocile.

INDOCTRINATE (-dok'tri-nat), *v.t.* to imbue with learning.

INDOLENCE ('do-lens), *n.* laziness ; supineness.

INDOLENT (-lent), *adj.* indulging in ease.

INDOMITABLE (-dom'i-ta-bl), *adj.* untamable ; invincible.

INDOOR (in'dor), *adj.* pertaining to that in a house or building.

INDORSE (-dors'), *v.t.* to write on the back of, as a cheque, etc. ; sanction ; approve.

INDORSEE (-se'), *n.* a person to whom a cheque, etc., is indorsed.

INDORSEMENT ('ment), *n.* the act of writing on the back of a cheque, etc. ; approval ; sanction.

INDORSER ('ser), *n.* one who indorses.

INDUBITABLE (-du'bi-ta-bl), *adj.* too evident to be doubted.

INDUCE (dus'), *v.t.* to influence ; prevail upon ; effect ; cause ; to infer by induction.

INDUCEMENT (-dus'ment), *n.* that which induces ; motive.

INDUCIBLE ('i-bl), *adj.* capable of being induced, or inferred.

INDUCT (-dukt'), *v.t.* to introduce ; install into an office.

INDUCTANCE ('tans), *n.* the capacity for induction by an active electric circuit.

INDUCTION (-duk'shun), *n.* the introduction of a person into an office ; the process of discovering and proving general propositions from particular cases ; electrical or magnetic influence without direct contact.

INDUCTION COIL (koil), an apparatus for generating an electric current by electro-magnetic induction.

INDUCTIVE PHILOSOPHY (fil-os'o-fi), the name given by Bacon to experimental science.

INDUCTIVITY (-tiv'i-ti), *n.* specific inductive capacity.

INDUCTOR ('ter), *n.* that part of an electric apparatus which acts inductively.

INDICATOR COMPASS, see Earth Inductor Compass.

INDULGE (-dulj'), *v.t.* to be kind or complaisant to ; humour.

INDULGENT ('jent), *adj.* showing favour ; kind.

INDURATE (-'du-rat), *v.i.* to grow hard : *v.t.* render obdurate.

INDUSTRIAL (-dus'tri-al), *adj.* pertaining to productive industry.

INDUSTRIALISM ('tri-al-izm), *n.* a state of society marked by the predominance of industrial pursuits.

INDUSTRIALLY (-li), *adv.* with reference to industry or industrialism.

INDUSTRIOUS ('tri-us), *adj.* characterized by diligence ; hard-working.

INDUSTRY ('dus-tri), *n.* steady application to business or labour ; a particular branch of work or trade.

INEBRIATE (-e'bri-at), *v.t.* to make drunk ; intoxicate.

INEBRIETY (-bri'e-ti), *n.* intoxication.

INEDIBLE (-ed'i-bl), *adj.* not fit for food.

INEFFABLE (ef'a-bl), *adj.* unspeakable ; inexpressible.

INEFFACEABLE (-e-fas'a-bl), *adv.*

that which cannot be erased or obliterated.

INEFFECTIVE (-e-fek'tiv), *adj.* not producing the desired effect.

INEFFECTUAL (-fek'tu-al), *adj.* unavailing.

INEFFICACIOUS (-ef-i-ka'shus), *adj.* inefficient ; powerless.

INEFFICACY (-ef'i-ka-si), *n.* lack of efficacy ; failure of effect.

INEFFICIENCY (in-e-fish'en-si), *n.* incompetency.

INEFFICIENT ('ent), *adj.* incapable.

INELEGANCE (-el'e-gans), *n.* want of good taste.

INELEGANT ('e-gant), *adj.* offensive to good taste.

INELIGIBLE ('i-ji-bl), *adj.* unworthy of choice ; unsuitable.

INEPT (in-ept'), *adj.* unsuitable ; unfit.

INEPTITUDE (-ep'ti-tud), *n.* unsuitableness.

INEPTLY (-ept'li), *adv.* foolishly.

INEQUALITY (-e-kwal'i-ti), *n.* difference ; unevenness ; inadequacy.

INEQUITABLE (-ek'wi-ta-bl), *adj.* not according to equity ; unjust.

INEQUITY ('wi-ti), *n.* injustice.

INERT (-ert'), *adj.* lifeless ; sluggish.

INERTIA (-er'shi-a), *n.* inertness ; sluggishness ; that property of matter by virtue of which it tends to remain at rest, or, if in motion, to continue in the same direction unless acted upon by an external force.

INESTIMABLE (-es'ti-ma-bl), *adj.* incalculable ; invaluable.

INEVITABLE (-ev'i-ta-bl), *adj.* not to be evaded ; unavoidable.

INEVITABLY (-bli), *adv.* unavoidably.

INEXACT (-egz-akt'), *adj.* not precise or correct.

INEXCUSABLE (-eks-ku'za-bl), *adj.* unpardonable.

INEXHAUSTIBLE (-egs-awst'i-bl), *adj.* unfailing ; unwearied.

INEXORABILITY (-eks-o-ra-bil'i-ti), *n.* incapability of being moved by entreaty.

INEXORABLE ('o-ra-bl), *adj.* unyielding ; unrelenting.

INEXPEDIENCE (-pe'di-ens), **INEXPEDIENCY** (-pe'di-en-si), *n.* unsuitableness ; inadvisability.

INEXPEDIENT ('di-ent), *adj.* unsuitable to circumstances.

INEXPENSIVE (-pen'siv), *adj.* cheap.

INEXPERIENCE (-pe'ri-ens), *n.* want of experience.

INEXPERT (-pert'), *adj.* unskilled.

INEXPIABLE ('pi-a-bl), *adj.* that which cannot be atoned for.

INEXPLICABLE ('pli-ka-bl), *adj.* not to be explained.

INEXPLICIT (-eks-plis'it), *adj.* not clear.

INEXPRESSIBLE (-pres'i-bl), *adj.* incapable of being described.

INEXTINGUISHABLE (-ting'-gwish-a-bl), *adj.* unquenchable.

INEXTRICABLE ('tri-ka-bl), *adj.* not extricable ; intricate ; involved.

INFALLIBILITY (-fal-i-bil'i-ti), *n.* the quality of being infallible.

INFALLIBLE (-fal'i-bl), *adj.* incapable of erring.

INFAMOUS ('fa-mus), *adj.* odious ; scandalous.

INFAMY ('fa-mi), *n.* ignominy.

INFANCY ('fan-si), *n.* early childhood ; in law, the period of life from birth to the age of twenty-one.

INFANT ('fant), *n.* a young child.

INFANTICIDE ('ti-sid), *n.* the murder of an infant.

INFANTILE ('fan-til), *adj.* childish.

INFANTILE PARALYSIS (pa-ral'i-sis), an acute disease, attacking young children, and sometimes adults ; poliomyelitis.

INFANTRY ('fan-tri), *n.* foot soldiers.

INFARE ('far), *n.* a house-warming.

INFATUATE (-fat'u-at), *v.t.* to inspire with fatuous passion.

INFATUATION (-u-a'shun), *n.* extravagant folly ; fatuous passion.

INFECT (-fekt'), *v.t.* to taint, especially with disease, physical or moral.

INFECTION (-fek'shun), *n.* contamination ; an infectious disease.

INFECTIOUS ('shus), *adj.* communicate by infection ; demoralizing.

INFECUNDITY (-fe-kun'di-ti), *n.* barrenness.

INFELICITOUS (-fe-lis'i-tus), *adj.* unfortunate ; inappropriate.

INFELICITY (-lis'i-ti), *n.* misfortune ; unhappiness.

INFER (-fer'), *v.t.* to derive by induction or deduction.

INFERABLE ('a-bl), *adj.* capable of being inferred.

INFERENCE ('fer-ens), *n.* the conclusion ; deduction ; induction.

INFERENTIAL (-en'shal), *adj.* deduced by inference.

INFERIOR (-fe'ri-er), *adj.* lower in place, rank, or quality ; subordinate.

INFERIORITY (-ri-or'i-ti), *n.* lower state or quality.

INFERNAL (-fer'nal), *adj.* hellish ; diabolical ; fiendish.

INFERNO ('no), *n.* a place or position of torment ; hell.

INFEST (-fest), *v.t.* to attack ; overrun.

INFIDEL ('fi-del), *adj.* rejecting all religion ; a sceptic.

INFIDELITY (-del'i-ti), *n.* disbelief in all religion ; violation of the marriage contract by adultery.

INFIELD ('feld), *n.* a field near a farmhouse ; a baseball diamond, 30 x 30 yds.

INFILTRATE (-fil'trat), *v.t.* to pass through, as in filtering.

INFINITE (in'fin-it), *adj.* immeasurable ; endless : *n.* [I-], God ; the Creator ; the Infinite.

INFINITELY (-li), *adv.* vastly.

INFINITESIMAL (-fin-i-tes'i-mal), *adj.* infinitely small.

INFINITIVE (in-fin'i-tiv), *adj.* in grammar, undefined : *n.* that form of the verb which merely expresses action without any reference to person or number.

INFINITUDE ('i-tud), *n.* unlimited extent, infinity.

INFINITY ('i-ti), *n.* unlimited extent of time, space, or quantity.

INFIRM (-ferm'), *adj.* weak-minded ; vacillating ; insecure.

INFIRMARY ('ma-ri), *n.* a hospital for the sick.

INFIRMITY ('mi-ti), *n.* debility ; imbecility ; malady ; failing ; foible.

INFIX (-fiks'), *v.t.* to fix or fasten in ; implant ; insert.

INFLAME (-flam'), *v.t.* to set on fire ; excite ; provoke ; irritate.

INFLAMMABLE (-flam'a-bl), *adj.* combustible ; excitable.

INFLAMMATION (-ma'shun), *n.* a morbid process, characterized by pain, redness, heat, and swelling.

INFLAMMATORY ('a-to-ri), *adj.* tending to excite passion, tumult, or sedition.

INFLATABLE (-flat'a-bl), *adj.* capable of being inflated.

INFLATE (-flat'), *v.t.* to swell, or distend ; puff up ; elate.

INFLATION (-fla'shun), *n.* distention ; pomposity ; bombast.

INFLECT (-flekt'), *v.t.* bend ; modulate ; vary the terminations of ; decline ; conjugate.

INFLECTION (-flek'shun), *n.* a bend or bending ; modulation of the voice ; variation of nouns, verbs, etc., by declension and conjugation.

INFLEX (fleks'), *v.t.* to inflect ; curve inward.

INFLEXIBILITY (-flek-si-bil'i-ti), *n.* stiffness ; obstinacy.

INFLEXIBLE ('si-bl), *adj.* rigid ; stiff ; inexorable ; unalterable.

INFLEXIBLY (-bli), *adv.* rigidly ; inexorably.

INFLICT (-flikt'), *v.t.* cause to suffer pain ; impose as a punishment.

INFLUENCE ('floo-ens), *n.* energy or potency tending to produce effects insensibly and invisibly : *v.t.* to exercise influence on, physically or morally.

INFLUENTIAL (-en'shal), *adj.* having or exerting influence.

INFLUENZA (en'za), *n.* an epidemic catarrh accompanied by fever, pains, and nervous prostration.

INFLUX ('fluks), *n.* an inflow ; infusion.

INFORM (-form'), *v.t.* to impart information to ; apprise of facts in the way of warning ; instruct.

INFORMAL (-for'mal), *adj.* not according to form, custom, or rule ; irregular ; unceremonious.

INFORMALLY (-li), *adv.* in an informal manner.

INFORMANT (-for'mant), *n.* one who gives information.

INFORMATION (-for-ma′shun), *n*. communicated knowledge.

INFORMER (-for′mer), *n*. one who informs.

INFRA- (in′fra), a prefix denoting *below, beneath, on the lower side.*

INFRACTION (-frak′shun), *n*. a violation of law ; infringement.

INFRANGIBLE (-fran′ji-bl), *adj*. that which cannot be broken.

INFREQUENCE (-fre′kwens), *n*. rareness.

INFREQUENT (′kwent), *adj*. seldom occurring.

INFRINGE (-frinj′), *v.i*. to encroach : followed by *on* or *upon*.

INFRINGEMENT (′ment), *n*. violation or breach, as of a law, patent, trade-mark, copyright, etc.

INFURIATE (-fu′ri-at), *v.t*. to enrage, madden.

INFUSE (-fuz′), *v.t*. to instil.

INFUSIBLE (-fu′zi-bl), *adj*. not capable of being fused.

INFUSION (-fu′zhun), *n*. a pouring in, or something poured in.

INGENIOUS (-je′ni-us), *adj*. inventive ; clever.

INGENUITY (in-je-nu′i-ti), *n*. cleverness in contriving or inventing ; skill.

INGENUOUS (in-jen′u-us), *adj*. frank ; open ; sincere ; candid.

INGLORIOUS (-glo′ri-us), *adj*. without glory ; disgraceful ; shameful.

INGOT (′got), *n*. a cast mass of metal.

INGRAIN (-gran′), *v.t*. to dye with any deep, lasting colour.

INGRATE (in′grat), *n*. an ungrateful person.

INGRATIATE (-gra′shi-at), *v.t*. to insinuate (one's self), into the favour of another.

INGRATITUDE (-grat′i-tud), *n*. insensibility to kindness.

INGREDIENT (-gre′di-ent), *n*. a component part of a compound body.

INGRESS (′gres), *n*. entrance.

INHABIT (-hab′it), *v.t*. to dwell in.

INHABITABLE (-hab′i-ta-bl), *adj*. fit for habitation.

INHABITANT (′i-tant), *n*. a permanent resident.

INHABITATION (-i-ta′shun), *n*. continued residence.

INHALATION (-la′shun), *n*. the act of inhaling.

INHALE (-hal′), *v.t*. to draw into the lungs ; breathe in.

INHARMONIOUS (-har-mo′ni-us), *adj*. unmusical ; discordant.

INHERE (-her′), *v.i*. to be an essential part of.

INHERENT (′ent), *adj*. innate.

INHERIT (-her′it), *v.t*. to possess from an ancestor by succession.

INHERITANCE (′i-tans), *n*. the act of inheriting ; a possession.

INHIBIT (-hib′it), *v.t*. to restrain ; prohibit ; interdict.

INHIBITION (-hi-bish′un), *n*. prohibition ; restriction.

INHOSPITABLE (-hos′pi-ta-bl), *adj*. affording no shelter ; barren.

INHUMAN (-hu′man), *adj*. cruel ; unfeeling.

INHUMANITY (-man′i-ti), *n*. cruelty.

INIMICAL (-im′i-kal), *adj*. hostile.

INIMITABLE (′i-ta-bl), *adj*. matchless ; unrivalled.

INIQUITOUS (-ik′kwi-tus), *adj*. wicked ; unjust.

INIQUITY (′kwi-ti), *n*. wickedness ; injustice ; crime ; evil.

INITIAL (-ish′al), *adj*. incipient : *n*. a letter placed at the beginning of a word, etc. : *pl*. the first letters of a person's name placed separately.

INITIATE (′i-at), *v.t*. to instruct in the first principles of anything.

INITIATION (-i-a′shun), *n*. the act of initiating.

INITIATIVE (′i-a-tiv), *adj*. introductory.

INJECT (-jekt′), *v.t*. to throw in.

INJECTION (in-jek′shun), *n*. an enema.

INJECTOR (′ter), *n*. one who, or that which, injects.

INJUDICIOUS (-joo-dish′us), *adj*. not judicious ; indiscreet.

INJUNCTION (-jungk′shun), *n*. command, order, or precept ; a writ of equity or prohibition.

INJURE (′jocr), *v.t*. to hurt ; harm.

INJURIOUS (-joo′ri-us), *adj*. hurtful.

INJURY (′joo-ri), *n*. detriment ; loss ; damage.

INJUSTICE (-jus′tis), *n*. violation of another's rights ; injury.

INK (ingk), *n.* a fluid used for writing, printing, etc.

INKLING ('ling), *n.* an intimation; hint.

INLAID (-in-lad'), *p.adj.* decorated by the insertion of ivory, wood, metal, etc.

INLAND (in'land), *adj.* situated in the interior of a country; remote from the sea.

INLAY (-la'), *v.t.* to ornament (a surface) by laying in pieces of ivory, wood, metal, etc.

INLET (-let'), *v.t.* to inlay; insert: *n.* (in'let), an entrance.

INLY ('li), *adv.* inwardly; secretly.

INMATE (in'mat), *n.* one who inhabits a house with others.

INMOST ('most), *adj.* deepest within.

INN (in), *n.* a small hotel; a hostelry.

INNATE ('nat), *adj.* inborn; native.

INNER ('er), *adj.* internal; interior.

INNERVATE (-ner'vat), *v.t.* to stimulate.

INNERVATION (-er-va'shun), *n.* special activity or stimulus in any part of the nervous system.

INNINGS ('ings), *n.pl.* the turn of a side or player to bat.

INNOCENCE ('o-sens), *n.* purity; harmlessness; mental imbecility.

INNOCENT ('o-sent), *adj.* blameless; pure in heart and life.

INNOCUOUS (i-nok'us), *adj.* harmless.

INNOVATE ('o-vat), *v.i.* to introduce new things.

INNOVATION (-va'shun), *n.* the introduction of something new.

INNOVATOR ('o-va-ter), *n.* one who introduces new things.

INNOXIOUS (i-nok'shus), *n.* harmless.

INNUENDO (in-u-en'do), *n.* an oblique hint; insinuation.

INNUMERABLE (i-nu'mer-a-bl), *adj.* that cannot be counted; very numerous.

INNUTRITIOUS (in-u-trish'us), *adj.* not affording nutrition.

INOCULATE (in-ok'u-lat), *v.t.* to communicate (a disease) by the insertion of infectious matter with the object of protecting or curing.

INODOROUS (in-o'do-rus), *adj.* lacking odour.

INOFFENSIVE (in-o-fen'siv), *adj.* harmless; not objectionable.

INOPERATIVE (in-op'er-a-tiv), *adj.* without effect.

INOPPORTUNE (in-op-or-tun'), *adj.* untimely; not appropriate.

INORDINATE (or'di-nat), *adj.* immoderate; excessive.

INORGANIC (-gan'ik), *adj.* designating, or composed of, matter other than vegetable or animal.

INQUEST ('kwest), *n.* a coroner's inquiry with a jury into the cause of a sudden death.

INQUIRE (-kwir'), *v.i.* to seek for or ask by questions.

INQUIRY (-kwir'i), *n.* search by question; investigation; research.

INQUISITION (-kwi-zish'un), *n.* inquiry; examination.

INQUISITIVE (-kwis'i-tiv), *adj.* prying; curious.

INQUISITOR ('i-ter), *n.* one who makes inquiries or investigates.

INROAD ('rod), *n.* a hostile incursion.

INSALUBRIOUS (in-sa-lu'bri-us), *adj.* unhealthful.

INSANE (-san'), *adj.* mentally deranged; irrational.

INSANITY (-san'i-ti), *n.* derangement of mind or intellect; madness.

INSATIABLE (-sa'shi-a-bl), *adj.* that cannot be satisfied or appeased.

INSCRIBE (-skrib'), *v.t.* to write or engrave upon.

INSCRIPTION (-skrip'shun), *n.* that which is inscribed; a dedicatory address.

INSCRUTABLE ('ta-bl), *adj.* incomprehensible.

INSECT ('sekt), *n.* one of a numerous class of articulate animals, the *Insecta.*

INSECTICIDE ('ti-sid), *n.* a powder for destroying insects.

INSECURE (in-se-kur'), *adj.* unsafe.

INSENSATE (-sen'sat), *adj.* soulless; mad; brutish.

INSENSIBLE ('si-bl), *adj.* heedless; callous; senseless.

INSENSITIVE (-sen'si-tiv), *adj.* without feeling.

INSEPARABLE 262 INSTINCT

INSEPARABLE (-sep'a-ra-bl), *adj.* incapable of being separated.

INSERT (-sert'), *v.t.* to place in.

INSERTION (-ser'shun), *n.* that which is inserted.

INSET ('set), *n.* a leaf or leaves inserted in a newspaper, magazine, etc. : *v.t.* (in-set'), to set in.

INSIDE ('sid), *adj.* interior ; being within : *adv.* & *prep.* within.

INSIDIOUS (-sid'i-us), *adj.* treacherous ; deceitful.

INSIGHT ('sit), *n.* intuition ; discernment.

INSIGNIA (-sig'ni-a), *n.pl.* badges of honour or office.

INSIGNIFICANCE (-nif'i-kans), *n.* unimportance.

INSIGNIFICANT ('i-kant), *adj.* trivial ; contemptible.

INSINCERE (in-sin-ser'), *adj.* hypocritical ; untrustworthy.

INSINUATE ('u-at), *v.t.* to ingratiate, suggest or hint indirectly.

INSINUATION (-u-a'shun), *n.* the act of insinuating.

INSIPID (-sip'id), *adj.* tasteless.

INSIPIDITY (-si-pid'i-ti), *n.* vapidity ; tastelessness.

INSIST (-sist'), *v.i.* to be persistent or peremptory.

INSISTENCE ('tens), *n.* the act of insisting ; persistence.

INSNARE (in-snar'), *v.t.* to entrap.

INSOBRIETY (-so-bri'e-ti), *n.* drunkenness.

INSOLENCE ('so-lens), *n.* offensive impertinence.

INSOLENT ('so-lent), *adj.* insulting ; grossly rude.

INSOLUBLE (-sol'u-bl), *adj.* that cannot be dissolved ; inexplicable.

INSOLVENCY ('ven-si), *n.* the state of being insolvent ; bankruptcy.

INSOLVENT ('vent), *adj.* unable to pay all debts ; bankrupt.

INSOMNIA (in-som'ni-a), *n.* sleeplessness.

INSOUCIANCE (ang-soo'si-angs), *n.* [French], heedlessness ; indifference.

INSOUCIANT (ang-soo'si-ang), *adj.* [French], indifferent ; careless.

INSPECT (-spekt'), *v.t.* to examine critically ; test officially.

INSPECTION (-spek'shun), *n.* careful or critical scrutiny.

INSPECTOR ('ter), *n.* one who inspects or oversees ; an official.

INSPIRATION (-spi-ra'shun), *n.* the act of drawing air into the lungs ; creative influence of genius.

INSPIRATIONAL (-spi-ra'shun-al), *adj.* pertaining to inspiration.

INSPIRATORY (-spir'a-to-ri), *adj.* pertaining to inspiration.

INSPIRE (-spir'), *v.t.* to draw (air), into the lungs ; breathe into ; imbue with ideas ; infuse into the mind ; exhilarate or enliven.

INSPIRIT (-spir'it), *v.t.* to infuse spirit into ; animate ; exhilarate ; cheer.

INSTABILITY (-sta-bil'i-ti), *n.* inconstancy ; fickleness.

INSTABLE (-sta'bl), *adj.* inconstant ; fickle.

INSTALL (-stawl'), *v.t.* to instate in an office or rank.

INSTALLATION (-la'shun), *n.* the act of installing.

INSTALMENT ('ment), *n.* payment of part of money due.

INSTANCE ('stans), *v.t.* to refer to, or offer as an example : *n.* something offered as an illustration.

INSTANT ('stant), *adj.* urgent ; immediate ; passing ; current : *n.* a particular moment of time.

INSTANTANEOUS (-tan-ta'ne-us), *adj.* at a particular moment ; done in an instant.

INSTANTER (-stan'ter), *adv.* immediately.

INSTANTLY (-stant'li), *adv.* at once.

INSTEAD (-sted'), *adv.* in room or place (with *of*).

INSTEP ('step), *n.* the arched forepart of the human foot.

INSTIGATE ('sti-gat), *v.t.* to provoke ; urge ; incite ; goad.

INSTIGATION (-ga'shun), *n.* incitement to evil.

INSTIGATOR (-ga'ter), *n.* one who instigates.

INSTIL (-stil'), *v.t.* to insinuate gradually, as if by drops.

INSTINCT ('stingkt), *n.* natural impulse ; natural aptitude ; sagacity.

INSTINCTIVE (-stingk'tiv), *adj.* acting or prompted by instinct; spontaneous.

INSTITUTE ('sti-tut), *v.t.* to establish; fix; originate; ordain.

INSTITUTION (-tu'shun), *n.* a corporate body or society for promoting a particular object.

INSTITUTOR ('sti-tu-ter), *n.* a founder.

INSTRUCT (-strukt'), *v.t.* to teach; educate.

INSTRUCTION (-struk'shun), *n.* education; knowledge acquired by education: *pl.* directions; an order, etc.

INSTRUCTIVE (-struk'tiv), *adj.* conveying instruction.

INSTRUCTOR ('ter), *n.* one who instructs.

INSTRUMENT ('stroo-ment), *n.* that by which anything is effected; a tool or implement; agent; a writing containing the terms of a contract, etc.

INSTRUMENTAL (-men'tal), *adj.* conducive to some end; helpful.

INSTRUMENTATION (ta'shun), *n.* the arrangement of music for a combination of instruments.

INSUBORDINATE (-sub-or'di-nat), *adj.* not submitting to authority.

INSUBORDINATION (di-na'shun), *n.* the state of being insubordinate.

INSUFFERABLE (suf'er-a-bl), *adj.* intolerable; unendurable.

INSUFFERABLY (-bli), *adv.* intolerably.

INSULAR ('su-lar), *adj.* pertaining to an island; narrow.

INSULATE ('su-lat), *v.t.* to place alone; separate by a non-conductor from other conducting bodies.

INSULATION (-la'shun), *n.* the act of insulating.

INSULATOR ('ter), *n.* a non-conductor of electricity, heat, or sound.

INSULIN (in'sul-in), *n.* a drug which reduces sugar in the blood, used as a diabetic remedy.

INSULT ('sult), *n.* an affront or indignity: *v.t.* (in-sult'), to treat with gross indignity, with contempt, or abuse.

INSUPERABLE (-su'per-a-bl), *adj.* not to be overcome; invincible.

INSURABLE (-shur'a-bl), *adj.* capable of being insured.

INSURANCE ('ans), *n.* a contract entered into to secure against loss by fire, etc.

INSURE (-shoor'), *v.t.* to contract on certain conditions; secure against loss or damage by fire, etc.

INSURGENT (-ser'jent), *adj.* rising against constituted authority: *n.* a rebel.

INSURRECTION (-su-rek'shun), *n.* hostility to constituted authority; rebellion.

INSUSCEPTIBLE (-sep'ti-bl), *adj.* obdurate; apathetic.

INTACT (-takt'), *adj.* entire; uninjured.

INTAKE (in'tak), *n,* that which is taken in; opposed to outgo.

INTANGIBLE (-tan'ji-bl), *adj.* incapable of being touched.

INTEGER (in'te-jer), *n.* the whole; opposed to *fraction.*

INTEGRAL ('te-gral), *adj.* complete.

INTEGRATE ('te-grat), *v.t.* to bring together the parts of.

INTEGRITY (-teg'ri-ti), *n.* uprightness; virtue; honesty; soundness.

INTEGUMENT (-teg'u-ment), *n.* an external covering or skin.

INTELLECT ('te-lekt), *n.* the mind or understanding.

INTELLECTUAL (-lek'tu-al), *adj.* pertaining to the intellect; mental; ideal.

INTELLIGENCE (-tel'i-jens), *n.* intellectual capacity; understanding; mind; news.

INTELLIGENT ('i-jent), *adj.* exhibiting knowledge; clever; acute; discerning.

INTELLIGENTSIA (si-a), *n.* the educated class as distinguished from the ignorant.

INTELLIGIBLE ('i-ji-bl), *adj.* capable of being understood; clear.

INTEMPERANCE (-tem'per-ans), *n.* want of moderation or self-restraint; excess, especially in the use of alcoholic liquors.

INTEMPERATE ('per-at), *adj.* want

of moderation or self-restraint; excessive.

INTEND (-tend'), *v.t.* to purpose; mean.

INTENDED ('ded), *n.* an affianced lover.

INTENSE (-tens'), *adj.* strained; forced; ardent; vehement.

INTENSIFY (-ten'si-fi), *v.t.* to render more intense; heighten.

INTENSITY ('si-ti), *n.* the state or quality of being intense.

INTENSIVE ('siv), *adj.* serving to intensify.

INTENT (-tent'), *adj.* anxiously diligent; constantly or assiduously directed (with *on*): *n.* purpose; aim.

INTENTION (-ten'shun), *n.* purpose; fixed design.

INTER (-ter'), *v.t.* to bury.

INTER- (in'ter), a prefix signifying *among*, *between*, *amid*, *mutually*.

INTERBOROUGH (-bur'o), *adj.* existing or carried on between boroughs.

INTERCEDE (-sed'), *v.i.* to mediate as a friend between persons.

INTERCEPT (-sept'), *v.t.* to stop and seize in the way; cut off.

INTERCESSION (-sesh'un), *n.* the act of interceding; mediation.

INTERCESSOR (-ses'er), *n.* a mediator.

INTERCOURSE ('ter-kors), *n.* connection; mutual exchange; fellowship.

INTERDICT (-dikt'), *v.t.* to restrain or forbid.

INTEREST ('ter-est), *v.t.* to engage the attention; cause to take a share in: *n.* advantage; influence; profit; premium paid for the use of money.

INTERESTING (-ing), *p.adj.* engaging the attention; inviting curiosity.

INTERFERE (-fer'), *v.i.* to interpose or meddle in the affairs of others; oppose.

INTERFERENCE ('ens), *n.* the act of interfering.

INTERIM ('ter-im), *n.* intervening time or period.

INTERIOR (-te'ri-or), *adj.* not exterior; inner; internal.

INTERJECT (in-ter-jekt'), *v.t.* to interpose.

INTERJECTION (-ter-jek'shun), *n.* an exclamation.

INTERLARD (in-ter-lard'), *v.t.* to insert or inject matter in a discourse not exactly germane.

INTERLINEAR (-lin'e-ar), *adj.* written or printed between other lines, as a translation.

INTERLOCK (-lok'), *v.t.* to unite with; interlace.

INTERLOCUTORY (-lok'u-to-ri), *adj.* conversational; not final.

INTERLOPER ('ter-lo-per), *n.* an intruder.

INTERLUDE ('ter-lud), *n.* a short entertainment; a short instrumental passage played between the acts of an opera, etc.

INTERMEDIARY (-me'di-a-ri), *adj.* intervening: *n.* an agent.

INTERMEDIATE ('di-at), *adj.* existing or lying in the middle; intervening.

INTERMENT ('ment), *n.* burial.

INTERMEZZO (-med'zo), *n.* [Italian], an interlude.

INTERMINABLE (-ter'mi-na-bl), *adj.* having no limit.

INTERMINGLE (in-ter-ming'gl), *v.t.* to mix together.

INTERMISSION (-mish'un), *n.* interruption; pause; recess.

INTERMIT (-mit'), *v.t.* to interrupt; suspend.

INTERMITTENT (-mit'ent), *adj.* alternating; recurrent.

INTERN (-tern'), *v.t.* to confine; place under arrest.

INTERNAL (-ter'nal), *adj.* interior; inward; domestic.

INTERNALLY (-li), *adv.* inwardly.

INTERNATIONAL (-nash'un-al), *adj.* pertaining to two or more nations in common.

INTERNE (ang-tarn'), *n.* [French], a physician; who assists in a hospital to gain experience.

INTERNECINE (-ne'sin) *adj.* mutually destructive; deadly.

INTERPELLATE (-ter-pel'at), *v.t.* to question.

INTERPLEADER (-pled'er), *n.* a legal proceeding to determine who has the prior right to press a claim.

INTERPOLATE ('po-lat), *v.t.* to insert in a book or writing new or spurious matter.

INTERPOSE (-poz'), *v.t.* to place between ; thrust in ; interrupt.

INTERPRET ('pret), *v.t.* to explain the meaning of ; construe.

INTERPRETATION (-ta'shun), *n.* the act of interpreting ; explanation.

INTERPRETER (-pre-ter), *n.* one who interprets.

INTERREGNUM (-reg'num), *n.* time of abeyance.

INTERROGATE ('o-gat), *v.t.* to question : *v.i.* to ask questions.

INTERROGATION (-ga'shun), *n.* a question ; inquiry ; a mark (?) denoting a question.

INTERROGATIVE (-ter-og'a-tiv), *adj.* denoting a question.

INTERROGATOR (-ter'o-ga-ter), *n.* one who interrogates.

INTERROGATORY (-te'rog'a-to-ri), *adj.* pertaining to a question.

INTERRUPT (-rupt'), *v.t.* to stop or hinder by breaking in upon : *v.i.* interpolate.

INTERRUPTION ('shun), *n.* hindrance ; obstruction.

INTERSECT (-sekt'), *v.t.* to cut or divide mutually.

INTERSECTION (-sek'shun), *n.* place of crossing.

INTERSPERSE (in-ter-spers), *v.t.* to scatter between or among.

INTERSTATE ('ter-stat), *adj.* between the states.

INTERSTELLAR (-stel'ar), *adj.* pertaining to space between the stars.

INTERSTICE ('ter-stis, -ter'stis), *n.* a narrow space between things ; crevice.

INTERURBAN (in-ter-er'ban), *adj.* between two or more towns or cities.

INTERVAL ('ter-val), *n.* time between periods, events, states, or conditions.

INTERVALE ('ter-val), *n.* low ground between hills.

INTERVENE (-ven'), *v.i.* to come between ; interpose ; interfere.

INTERVENTION (-ven'shun), *n.* the act of intervening ; mediation.

INTERVIEW ('ter-vu), *v.t.* to visit, to obtain particulars : *n.* a personal conference or meeting.

INTESTATE ('tat), *adj.* dying without having made a valid will.

INTESTINAL ('ti-nal), *adj.* pertaining to the intestines.

INTESTINE ('tin), *adj.* internal ; not foreign : *n.pl.* the bowels ; entrails.

INTIMACY ('ti-ma-si), *n.* confidential friendship.

INTIMATE ('ti-mat), *adj.* well acquainted ; familiar ; confidential ; complete : *v.t.* to indicate.

INTIMATION (-ma'shun), *n.* an indirect suggestion ; announcement.

INTIMIDATE (-tim'i-dat), *v.t.* to make afraid.

INTIMIDATION (-da'shun), *n.* the use of threats or violence to influence the actions of another.

INTO ('too), *prep.* expressing entrance upon, occupation of, passing from one state or condition to another, motion toward, etc. ; within ; to the inside of.

INTOLERABLE (-tol'er-a-bl), *adj.* unbearable.

INTOLERANCE ('er-ans), *n.* want of toleration of the opinions or beliefs of others.

INTOLERANT ('er-ant), *adj.* bigoted ; unable to bear or endure (with *of*).

INTONATION (-to-na'shun), *n.* modulation of the voice.

INTONE (-ton'), *v.t.* to recite in monotone.

IN TOTO (in to'to), [Latin], entirely.

INTOXICANT (-tok'si-kant), *n.* that which intoxicates.

INTOXICATE ('si-kat), *v.t.* to make drunk by spirituous liquors.

INTOXICATION (-ka'shun), *n.* act of intoxicating.

INTRA-, a prefix signifying *within*.

INTRACELLULAR (in-tra-sel'u-lar), *adj.* within and around a cell.

INTRACTABLE (-trak'ta-bl), *adj.* unmanageable.

INTRACTILE ('til), *adj.* incapable of being drawn out.

INTRAMURAL (-mu'ral), *adj.* within the walls, as of a town or city.

INTRANSITIVE ('si-tiv), *adj.* not requiring an object : said of certain verbs.

INTRENCH (in-trench'), *v.t.* to protect by means of ditches.

INTREPID (-trep'id), *adj.* bold ; fearless.

INTRICACY ('tri-ka-si), *n.* being intricate ; perplexity.

INTRICATE ('tri-kat), *adj.* entangled or involved.

INTRIGANT (in'tri-gant), *n.* one who intrigues or plots.

INTRIGUE (in-treg'), *v.i.* to carry on a secret plot.

INTRINSIC (-trin'sik), *adj.* pertaining to that which is inherent ; real ; genuine.

INTRINSICALLY (-kal-li), *adv.* inherently.

INTRO-, a prefix meaning *within, into.*

INTRODUCE (-tro-dus'), *v.t.* to bring into use, notice, or acquaintance ; insert.

INTRODUCTION (-duk'shun), *n.* the act of introducing ; presentation ; a preface.

INTRODUCTORY ('to-ri), *adj.* serving to introduce.

INTROMISSION (-tro-mish'un), *n.* insertion ; introduction.

INTROSPECTION (in-tro-spek' shun), *n.* examination of one's thoughts or motives.

INTRUDE (-trood'), *v.i.* to thrust one's self in without invitation or welcome.

INTRUDER ('der), *n.* a trespasser.

INTRUSION ('zhun), *n.* encroachment ; unlawful entry.

INTUITION (-tu-ish'un), *n.* instinctive perception.

INTUITIVE ('-tiv), *adj.* perceived immediately by the mind.

INUNDATE (in'un-dat), un'dat), *v.t.* to fill with an overflowing abundance ; flood.

INUNDATION (-da'shun), *n.* overflow ; flood.

INURE (ur), *v.t.* to habituate.

INVADE (-vad'), *v.t.* to infringe upon ; violate.

INVALID (-val'id), *adj.* of no force or authority ; null and void : *n.* (in'va-lid), one who is weak or infirm in health.

INVALIDATE (-val'i-dat), *v.t.* to weaken the validity of.

INVALIDITY (-va-lid'i-ti), *n.* want of legal force or argument.

INVALUABLE (-val'u-a-bl), *adj.* priceless.

INVARIABLE (-va'ri-a-bl), *adj.* constant.

INVARIABLY (-bli), *adv.* constantly.

INVASION (-va'zhun), *n.* hostile incursion ; encroachment.

INVASIVE (-va'siv), *adj.* aggressive.

INVECTIVE (-vek'tiv), *n.* violent censure, sarcasm, or abuse.

INVEIGH (-va'), *v.i.* to rail against ; utter censure.

INVEIGLE (-ve'gl), *v.t.* to entice ; seduce.

INVENT (-vent), *v.t.* to find out by original study ; devise or contrive.

INVENTION (-ven'shun), *n.* discovery ; creative faculty ; concoction ; fabrication.

INVENTIVE ('tiv), *adj.* quick at contriving ; ready in expedients.

INVENTOR ('ter), *n.* one who invents.

INVENTORY ('ven-to-ri), *n.* a catalogue or list of goods, furniture, etc.

INVERSE (-vers'), *adj.* contrary in tendency, direction, or effect.

INVERSION (-ver'shun), *n.* contrary change of order or position.

INVERT (-vert'), *v.t.* to turn upside down.

INVERTEBRATE ('te-brat), *n.* one of the Invertebrata : *adj.* having no backbone ; having no force of character ; weak.

INVERTED (-ver'ted), *adj.* turned upside down.

INVEST (-vest'), *v.t.* to place or lay out, as money ; clothe, as with authority, or dignity ; surround.

INVESTIGATE (-ves'ti-gat), *v.t.* to ascertain by careful inquiry ; examine.

INVESTIGATION (-ga'shun), *n.* the act of investigating ; search.

INVESTIGATOR ('ter), *n.* one who investigates.

INVESTITURE ('ti-tur), *n.* the act of giving legal possession.

INVESTMENT (-vest'ment), *n.* laying out money productively.

INVESTOR (-ves'ter), *n.* one who invests.

INVETERACY (-vet'er-a-si), *n.* the state of being inveterate; spitefulness; malignity; obstinacy.

INVETERATE ('er-at), *adj.* habitual; malignant; spiteful.

INVIDIOUS (-vid'i-us), *adj.* likely to provoke ill-will or envy.

INVIGORATE (-vig'o-rat), *v.t.* to give vigour to; animate.

INVINCIBLE (vin'si-bl), *adj.* unconquerable.

INVIOLABILITY (-vi-o-la-bil'i-ti), *n.* the quality of being inviolable.

INVIOLABLE ('o-la-bl), *adj.* that cannot be profaned or injured.

INVISIBLE ('i-bl), *adj.* that cannot be seen; not in sight.

INVITATION (-vi-ta'shun), *n.* the act of inviting; polite solicitation.

INVITE (-vit'), *v.t.* to ask, solicit, or summon; persuade; allure.

INVITING ('ing), *p.adj.* tempting.

INVOCATION (-vo-ka'shun), *n.* the act or form of invoking.

INVOICE ('vois), *n.* a document announcing the despatch of goods with their prices, quantity, etc.

INVOKE (-vok'), *v.t.* to address in prayer or supplication.

INVOLUNTARY (-vol'un-ta-ri), *adj.* without will of choice.

INVOLUTION (-lu'shun), *n.* the act of involving or infolding; the process of raising an arithmetical or algebraical quantity to a higher power.

INVOLVE (-volv'), *v.t.* to complicate; entangle; embroil.

INVULNERABILITY (-vul-ner-a-bil'-i-ti), *n.* the quality of being invulnerable.

INVULNERABLE (-vul'ner-a-bl), *adj.* that cannot be wounded or injured.

INWARD ('werd), *adj.* situated within; in the mind.

INWARDLY (-li), *adv.* in an inward manner; secretly.

INWROUGHT (-rawt'), *p.adj.* worked in.

IODINE (i'o-din), *n.* a non-metallic element of the halogen group; powerful antiseptic.

ION (i'on), *n.* an atom bearing an electric charge.

IOTA (i-o'ta), *n.* a very small quantity.

IPECAC (ip'e-kak), *n.* ipecacuanha.

IPECACUANHA (ip-e-kak-u-an'a), *n.* the root of a South American plant.

IPSO FACTO (ip'so fak'to), [Latin], by the fact itself.

IR, *prefix* meaning *not.*

IRASCIBILITY (i-ras-i-bil'i-ti), *n.* quality of being irascible.

IRASCIBLE ('i-bl), *n.* easily excited to anger.

IRATE (-rat'), *adj.* angry; enraged.

IRE (ir), *n.* anger; wrath; passion.

IRIDESCENCE (ir-i-des'ens), *n.* colours like those of the rainbow.

IRIDESCENT ('ent), *adj.* exhibiting iridescence.

IRIDIUM (i-rid'i-um), *n.* a metallic element.

IRIS ('ris), *n.* the coloured circular curtain in the aqueous humour in front of the eye lens; the rainbow, [I-], a genus of plants.

IRISH ('rish), *adj.* pertaining to Ireland.

IRISH FREE STATE (fre stat), a state formed by the three provinces of Ireland (Munster, Leinster and Connaught), which was granted independent parliamentary powers by Great Britain, through a treaty, signed Dec. 6, 1921.

IRK (erk), *v.t.* to weary : *v.i.* to become tired.

IRKSOME ('sum), *adj.* tedious; wearisome.

IRON (i'ern), *n.* the most common and useful of the metals.

IRONICAL (i-ron'i-kal), *adj.* expressing one thing and meaning another.

IRONY ('ron-i), *n.* subtle sarcasm.

IRRADIANCE (-ra'di-ans), *n.* sending forth luminous rays; lustre.

IRRADIANT (-ant), *adj.* emiting rays of light.

IRRADIATE ('di-at), *v.t.* to illuminate ; brighten.

IRRATIONAL (i-rash'un-al), *adj.* without reason ; absurd.

IRRECLAIMABLE (ir-e-klam'a-bl), *adj.* that which cannot be reclaimed.

IRRECONCILABLE (i-rek-un-sil'a-bl), *adj.* not reconcilable.

IRREDEEMABLE (ir-e-dem'a-bl), *adj.* impossible of redemption.

IRREGULAR (i-reg'u-lar), *adj.* not conforming to rule.

IRRELEVANT (ir-rel'e-vant), *adj.* not pertaining to ; unrelated to the subject discussed.

IRREPARABLE (i-rep'a-ra-bl), *adj.* not capable of repair.

IRREPRESSIBLE (ir-e-pres'i-bl), *adj.* unrestrainable.

IRREPROACHABLE (ir-e-proch'a-bl), *adj.* without blame or reproach.

IRRESISTIBLE (ir-e-sist'i-bl), *adj.* not to be resisted.

IRRESOLUTE (i-rez'o-lut), *adj.* undecided ; vacillating.

IRRESPECTIVE (ir-e-spek'tiv), *adj.* regardless (with *of*).

IRRESPONSIBLE (ir-e-spon'si-bl), *adj.* with no responsibility.

IRREVERENT (i-rev'er-ent), *adj.* wanting in reverence.

IRREVOCABLE (i-rev'o-ka-bl), *adj.* not to be recalled ; final.

IRRIGABLE (ir'i-ga-bl), *adj.* capable of being irrigated.

IRRIGATE ('i-gat), *v.t.* to moisten (land), by causing water to flow over.

IRRITABILITY (-i-ta-bil'i-ti), *n.* the quality or state of being irritable.

IRRITABLE ('i-ta-bl), *adj.* easily provoked to anger ; easily stimulated to perform some physical function.

IRRITANT ('i-tant), *adj.* causing irritation : *n.* anything which causes irritation.

IRRITATE ('i-tat), *v.t.* to provoke or make angry ; excite heat and redness in.

IRRITATION (-ta'shun), *n.* exasperation ; vexation ; impatience.

IRRUPTION (-rup'shun), *n.* a bursting or rushing in ; sudden invasion.

IS (iz), 3rd per. sing. of the substantive verb *be*.

ISHMAELITE (ish'ma-el-it), *n.* a descendant of Ishmael ; hence, a social outcast.

ISINGLASS (i'zing-glas), *n.* a white semi-transparent substance prepared from the sounds or air-bladders of the sturgeon, cod, etc.

ISLAND (i'land), *n.* a tract of land surrounded by water.

ISLE (il), *n.* an island.

ISLET (i'let), *n.* a small island.

ISM (izm), *n.* a system or theory.

ISO-, a combining form from the Greek *isos*, equal.

ISOCHROMATIC (i'so-kro-mat'ik), *adj.* having the same colour.

ISODYNAMIC (-di-nam'ik), *adj.* having equal force.

ISOLATE (is'o-lat), *v.t.* to place alone ; insulate.

ISOLATION (-la'shun), *n.* the state of being isolated.

ISOSCELES (i-sos'e-lez), *adj.* a triangle having two equal sides.

ISRAEL (iz'ra-el), *n.* Jacob ; Jacob's descendants ; the Hebrews.

ISRAELITE (iz'ra-el-it), *n.* a descendant of Israel ; a Jew.

ISSUE (ish'u), *n.* the egress ; that which flows or passes out ; discharge ; flux ; publication ; offspring ; lineal descendants.

ISTHMUS (is'mus, ist'mus), *n.* a neck of land connecting two larger portions.

IT (it), *pron.* the neuter pronoun of the third person and having the same plural as (*they, their, theirs, them*).

ITALIC (i-tal'ik), *n.* a slender, sloping kind of type (*italic*) : used for emphasis, etc. : *n.pl.* italic type.

ITALICIZE ('i-siz), *v.t.* to write or print in italics.

ITCH (ich), *n.* a parasitic cutaneous disease causing great irritation.

ITEM (i'tem), *n.* a separate article or particular : *adv.* also.

ITEMIZE (i'tem-iz), *v.t.* to set forth in detail ; to give the items.

ITERATE (it'er-at), *v.t.* to repeat.

ITERATION (-a'shun), *n.* repetition.

ITERATIVE ('er-a-tiv), *adj.* repeating.

ITINERACY (i-tin′er-a-si), *n.* the practice of itinerating.

ITINERANCY (′er-an-si), *n.* a passing from place to place.

ITINERANT (′er-ant), *adj.* passing from place to place : *n.* one who travels from place to place.

ITINERARY (′er-a-ri), *adj.* pertaining to, or done on, a journey ; travelling from place to place : *n.* a traveller's guide book.

ITINERATE (′er-at), *v.i.* to travel from place to place.

ITINERATION (-a′shun), *n.* a preaching, or lecturing, tour.

IVORY (i′vo-ri), *n.* the hard, bony, white dentine which forms the tusks of the elephant, walrus, etc. : *adj.* made of, or like, ivory.

IVY (i′vi), *n.* a clinging evergreen shrub of the ginseng family.

IZTLE (is′tli), *n.* a variety of volcanic rock, very hard and adapted for polish.

IZZARD (iz′ard), *n.* ancient term for the letter z; the ibex.

J

J, j (ja), *n.* the tenth letter in the English alphabet.

J, j, *n.* an abbreviation.

JAB (jab), *n.* a poke ; punch : *v.t.* to poke rudely.

JABBER (′er), *v.i.* to talk rapidly ; chatter.

JABOT (zha-bo′), *n.* the lace frill on a woman's bodice.

JACK (jak), *n.* any of various mechanical devices, as a spit, a lever, a wedge, a bench hook, etc. ; a device for lifting heavy bodies.

JACKAL (′awl), *n.* a dog-like carnivorous animal which hunts in packs.

JACKASS (′as), *n.* the male ass ; donkey.

JACKDAW (′daw), *n.* a small species of crow.

JACKET (′et), *n.* a short tailless coat ; a covering to prevent radiation of heat ; a wrapper.

JACKKNIFE (′nif), *n.* a large pocket knife.

JACK-SNIPE (′snip), *n.* a shore bird, called sandpiper.

JADE (jad), *n.* a silicate of magnesia and lime of green colour.

JAG (jag), *n.* a notch ; projecting point ; a small load : *v.t.* to cut into notches.

JAGUAR (ja-gwar′), *n.* a fierce animal of South America, resembling the leopard.

JAIL (jal), *n.* a prison ; a bridewell.

JAM (jam), *n.* a conserve ; a squeeze ; block ; crush : *v.t.* to squeeze or crush.

JAMB (jam), *n.* one of the upright sides of a doorway, window-opening, or fireplace.

JANGLE (jang′gl), *v.i.* to quarrel or wrangle : *n.* a discordant sound.

JANITOR (′i-ter), *n.* a doorkeeper ; one who takes care of a building.

JANUARY (jan′u-a-ri), *n.* the first month in the year ; from the Latin god, Janus.

JAPAN (ja-pan′), *n.* an empire comprising several large islands off the coast of Asia.

JAPAN (ja-pan′), *n.* a kind of varnish made up of shellac, linseed oil, and turpentine : *v.t.* to make black and glossy.

JAR (jar), *n.* an earthenware or glass vessel ; a jolt ; harsh sound.

JARDINIERE (zhar-din-yar′), *n.* [French], an ornamental flower-pot of porcelain or metal.

JARGON (jar′gon), *n.* confused, unintelligible talk.

JASMINE (jas′min), *n.* a garden plant with fragrant, white flowers.

JASPER (′per), **JASPERITE** (-it), *n.* an opaque, many-shaded variety of quartz.

JAUNDICE (jan′dis), *n.* a disease characterized by yellowishness of the eye-balls, skin, etc.

JAUNT (jant, jont), *n.* a short excursion or ramble.

JAUNTY (′i), *adj.* gay ; showy.

JAVA (ja′va), *n.* the largest island of the Dutch East Indies.

JAVELIN (jav′lin), *n.* a light spear.

JAW (jaw), *n.* the bones of the mouth in which the teeth are placed.

JAY (ja), *n.* a crow-like, chattering bird.

JAYWALKER (ja'wawk-er), *n.* one who crosses a street or highway carelessly without the protection of right of way.

JAZZ (jaz), *n.* a negro term for syncopated music or ragtime.

JAZZ BAND (band), a band which plays ragtime.

JEALOUS (jel'us), *adj.* characterized by jealousy.

JEALOUSY (-i), *n.* suspicious fear or watchfulness, especially the fear of being supplanted by a rival.

JEER (jer), *v.t.* to scoff at; ridicule.

JEHOVAH (je-ho'va), *n.* Lord God of the Hebrews.

JEHU (je'hu), *n.* a king of Israel; [j-], a cab driver.

JELLY (i), *n.* the stiffened gelatinous juice of fruit, meat, etc., after boiling.

JEMMY (jem'i), **JIMMY** (jim'i), *n.* a short crowbar used by burglars.

JENNY (i), *n.* a machine for spinning: used adjectively as *jenny*-wren, etc.

JEOPARD (jep'ard), **JEOPARDIZE** (ar-diz), *v.t.* to expose to loss or injury; hazard.

JEOPARDY (-di), *n.* hazard; peril.

JEREMIAD (jer-e-mi'ad), *n.* lamentation, especially over modern degeneracy; from the Book of Lamentations of Jeremiah.

JERK (jerk), *v.t.* to give a sudden pull, twist, or push to.

JERKIN (jer'kin), *n.* a short coat or jacket.

JERRY (jer'i), *adj.* constructed hastily, as a *jerry*-built house; flimsy.

JESSE (jes'e), *n.* a large branched candlestick used in churches.

JEST (jest), *n.* humorous pleasantry; fun: *v.i.* to joke.

JESTER (-ter), *n.* a joker; a buffoon.

JESUIT (jez'u-it), *n.* a member of the R.C. Society of Jesus, founded by Ignatius of Loyola, 1534.

JESUS (je'zus), *n.* the Founder of the Christian religion, believed by His followers to be the incarnate Son of God. See *Luke* 1-31; *Matt.* 16-16.

JET (jet), *n.* a stream of water suddenly emitted; a variety of lignite; a gas spray.

JETSAM (sam), *n.* that part of a ship's cargo which is thrown into the sea to lighten the vessel in case of peril: opposed to *flotsam*.

JETTY (i), *n.* a structure extending into the water, used as a pier, mole, or wall, to restrain or direct currents.

JEW (joo), *n.* an Israelite; Hebrew: *Fem.* Jewess.

JEWEL (el), *n.* a valuable ornament; gem; precious stone.

JEWELLER (-er), *n.* one who makes or deals in jewels.

JEWELRY (-ri), *n.* jewels collectively.

JEWISH (ish), *adj.* pertaining to the Jews, their language, customs, etc.

JEWRY (ri), *n.* Judæa; the Jewish race or Jews collectively.

JEW'S-HARP (harp), *n.* a small musical instrument.

JIB (jib), *n.* a triangular sail projecting beyond the bow.

JIBE, another form of gibe.

JIFFY (jif'i), *n.* an instant.

JIG (jig), *n.* a quick, lively dance.

JIGGER (er), *n.* one who jigs; name for various mechanical devices.

JILT (jilt), *n.* a coquette or flirt.

JINGLE (jing'gl), *n.* a sharp tinkling metallic sound; meaningless rhyme.

JINRIKISHA (jin-rik'i-sha), *n.* a small Japanese two-wheeled carriage.

JINX (jingks), *n.* [Slang], a hoodoo.

JITNEY, *n.* [Slang], a nickel.

JITNEY-BUS, *n.* an automobile conveying passengers for a low fare.

JIUJITSU, JUJUTSU (ju-jit'soo), *n.* a Japanese system of wrestling.

JOBBER (job'er), *n.* a middleman.

JOBBERY (er-i), *n.* low intriguing for private advantage or political ends.

JOCKEY (jok'i), *n.* one who rides a horse in a race; groom.

JOCOSE (jo-kos'), *adj.* humorous.

JOCULAR (jok'u-lar), *adj.* making jokes.

JOCULARITY (i-ti), *n.* merriment.

JOCUND (und), *adj.* jovial; gay.

JOG (jog), *v.t.* to push or shake slightly; stimulate.

JOHN BULL (jon bool'), the English nation personified.

JOHN DOE (do), a term used in law when the true name is unknown. *Fem.* "Jane Doe."

JOHNNY-CAKE (-kak), *n.* a flat cake of Indian meal.

JOIN (join), *v.t.* to unite; connect; associate.

JOINDER ('der), *n.* in law, the coupling of two or more causes of action into the same declaration.

JOINER ('er), *n.* one who, or that which, joins; a carpenter.

JOINT (joint), *n.* the place where two or more things join; articulation of limbs.

JOIST (joist), *n.* a horizontal timber to which the boards of a floor or laths of a ceiling are fastened.

JOKE (jok), *n.* something said or done to excite mirth; jest.

JOKER ('er), *n.* a jester.

JOLLIFICATION (jol-i-fi-ka'shun), *n.* merrymaking.

JOLLITY ('i-ti), *n.* being jolly.

JOLLY ('i), *adj.* full of life and mirth; gay; companionable.

JOLT (jolt), *v.t.* to shake by sudden jerks : *n.* a sudden jerk.

JONQUIL (jon'kwil), *n.* a species of narcissus.

JOSS (jos), *n.* a Chinese god or idol.

JOSTLE (jos'l), *v.t.* to push against; elbow.

JOT (jot), *v.t.* to make a memorandum of (with *down*).

JOURNAL (jer'nal), *n.* a record of news or events; diary; the part of a machine which rotates against the bearing.

JOURNALISM (-izm), *n.* the profession of a journalist.

JOURNALIST (-ist), *n.* an editor or contributor to a journal.

JOURNEY (jer'ni), *n.* passage from one place to another.

JOURNEYMAN (-man), *n.* a mechanic who has served his apprenticeship.

JOUST (joost), *n.* a mediæval mock combat.

JOVIAL (jo'vi-al), *adj.* merry.

JOVIALITY ('i-ti), *n.* conviviality; mirth.

JOWL (joul), *n.* the jaw or cheek.

JOY (joi), *n.* gaiety; gladness.

JOYFUL ('fool), *adj.* full of joy.

JOY-RIDE ('rid), *n.* [Slang], a reckless ride in a motor-car.

JUBILANT (joo'bi-lant), *adj.* expressing exultation; triumphant.

JUBILATION (-la'shun), *n.* a shouting for joy; declaration of triumph.

JUBILEE ('bi-le), *n.* a Jewish festival; the 50th anniversary of any event.

JUDAISM ('da-izm), *n.* the religious rites and doctrines of the Jews.

JUDGE (juj), *n.* the presiding official in a court of law; arbitrator; connoisseur.

JUDGMENT ('ment), *n.* the act of judging; a judicial decision; mental faculty of deciding correctly by the comparison of facts and ideas; penetration.

JUDICATURE (joo'di-ka-tur), *n.* power of dispensing justice by legal trial.

JUDICIAL (-dish'al), *adj.* pertaining to the administration of justice.

JUDICIARY ('i-a-ri), *adj.* pertaining to courts of justice.

JUDICIOUS ('us), *adj.* prudent; discreet.

JUG (jug), *n.* an earthenware vessel.

JUGGERNAUT (jug'er-nawt), *n.* a name of Krishna, a god of the Hindus, whose image was borne on a car underneath the wheels of which his devotees threw themselves to be crushed; hence, ruthless sacrifice.

JUGGLE (jug'l), *v.t.* to cheat by artifice : *v.i.* to conjure.

JUGOSLAVIAN (ju-go-sla-vi-an), *n.* a native of Jugoslavia.

JUGULAR (joo'gu-lar), *adj.* pertaining to the neck, or throat, or jugular vein.

JUICE (joos), *n.* a sap; the fluid part of plants and fruits; a term for electricity.

JULY (joo-li'), *n.* seventh calendar month : named from Julius Cæsar's birth in that month.

JUMBLE (jum'bl), *n.* a confused mass; a kind of thin cake : *v.i.* to mix or unite confusedly.

JUMBLE SALE (sal), *n*. a charity sale of second-hand articles; a rummage sale.

JUMBO ('bo), *n*. anything unusually large.

JUMP (jump), *n*. a spring or bound.

JUNCTION (jungk'shun), *n*. union.

JUNCTURE (jung'tur), *n*. articulation; particular or critical occasion.

JUNE (jun), *n*. the sixth calendar month.

JUNGLE (jung'gl), *n*. a dense tropical thicket of forest trees, tall grasses, etc.

JUNIOR (joon'yer), *adj*. younger.

JUNIPER (joo'ni-per), *n*. an evergreen shrub of the pine family.

JUNK (jungk), *n*. scraps of metal, glass, etc.; materials of little value.

JUNKER (yung'ker), *n*. a German military enthusiast.

JUNKET (jung'ket), *n*. a preparation of curds and cream; excursion; picnic.

JUNTA (jun'ta), *n*. a Central or South American legislative assembly or council.

JUPON (joo'pon), *n*. a petticoat.

JURIDICAL (-rid'i-kal), *adj*. pertaining to law.

JURISDICTION (-ris-dik'shun), *n*. legal authority; extent of power; district.

JURISPRUDENCE (-proo'dens), *n*. legal science; system of laws of a country.

JURIST ('rist), *n*. one skilled in legal science.

JUROR ('rer), *n*. a juryman.

JURY ('ri), *n*. a body of men, usually twelve, selected by law and sworn to inquire into or decide on the evidence.

JURY-MAST (-mast), *n*. a temporary mast.

JUS (jus), *n*. [*pl*. jures (joo'rez)], [Latin], a right that may be legally enforced.

JUST (just), *adj*. conformable to divine or human laws; upright; impartial.

JUSTICE (jus'tis), *n*. rectitude in dealing with others; impartiality; a judge or magistrate.

JUSTICE OF THE PEACE (pes), a local magistrate.

JUSTICIARY (-tish'i-a-ri), *n*. a judge.

JUSTIFIABLE ('ti-fi'a-bl), *adj*. defensible.

JUSTIFICATION (-ka'shun), *n*. vindication or defence.

JUSTIFY ('ti-fi), *v.t*. to show or prove to be just or right; vindicate.

JUT (jut), *v.i*. to project beyond the main body : *n*. a protection.

JUTE (joot), *n*. the fibre of an East Indian plant used for ropes, bagging, mats, etc.

JUVENILE (joo've-nil), *adj*. youthful : *n*. a young person.

JUXTA-, a prefix signifying *near, close proximity*.

JUXTAPOSITION (juks-ta-po-zish'-un), *n*. a placing of a person or thing near to, or side by side with, another person or thing; contiguity.

K

K, k (ka), *n*. the eleventh letter of the English alphabet.

K, k, *n*. an abbreviation.

K, *n*. a Roman numeral denoting 250 ; with a bar ($\bar{\mathrm{K}}$), 250,000.

KAIAK (ki'ak), *n*. an Arctic canoe.

KAISER (ki'zer), *n*. the title of the former emperors of Germany and Austria.

KALE (kal), *n*. a cabbage with open curled leaves : sea-kale.

KALEIDOSCOPE (ka-li'do-skop), *n*. an optical instrument which causes designs in it to appear in a variety of colours.

KANGAROO (kang-ga-roo'), *n*. a mammal of Australia.

KAOLIN (ka'o-lin), *n*. a hydrous silicate for china or porcelain.

KARYO, a prefix meaning *nucleus*, occurring in various scientific words.

KATYDID (ka'ti-did), *n*. a green, arboreal insect.

KEDGE (kej), *n*. a light anchor.

KEDS (keds), *n*. a canvas shoe with rubber soles.

KEEL (kel), *n*. the chief and lowest

timber of a vessel extending from stem to stern and supporting the whole frame.

KEEN (ken), *adj.* sharp ; eager ; piercing ; bitter ; acute.

KEEP (kep), *v.t.* to have the care of ; guard ; preserve ; maintain ; do ; observe ; fulfil.

KEEPING ('ing), *n.* care ; custody ; harmony, congruity.

KEEPSAKE ('sak), *n.* something kept as a souvenir of the giver.

KEG (keg), *n.* a small barrel.

KELEP (kel'ep), *n.* a Guatemalan ant now imported into southern U.S. to prey on the cotton boll-weevil.

KELP (kelp), *n.* the calcined ashes of sea-weeds, from which iodine is obtained.

KELPIE (kel'pi), *n.* a malevolent water-sprite, supposed to take the form of a horse.

KEMP (kemp), *n.* coarse, rough hair or wool ; refuse of fur.

KEN (ken), *n.* view ; knowledge.

KENNEL ('el), *n.* a house for a dog.

KENO (ke'no), *n.* a game of chance.

KERMESS (ker'mes), *n.* an indoor or outdoor festival.

KERNEL ('nel), *n.* a grain or seed ; the edible substance of a nut.

KEROSENE ('o-sen), *n.* refined petroleum.

KERSEY ('zi), *n.* a coarse, smooth-faced cloth.

KETCHUP ('up), *n.* a sauce prepared from tomatoes, etc., also *catsup* and *catchup.*

KETTLE (ket'l), *n.* a utensil for boiling liquids.

KEY (ke), *n.* a portable metal instrument for operating a lock ; clef ; solution ; the tonality of a music scale ; pitch of the voice ; a coral islet.

KEYNOTE ('not), *n.* the fundamental note ; ruling principle.

KEYSTONE ('ston), *n.* central stone of arch.

KHAKI (ka'ki), *n.* a light drab-coloured cloth.

KICK (kik), *n.* a blow with the foot ; a recoil.

KID (kid), *n.* the young of the goat, or its soft skin.

KIDNAP ('nap), *v.t.* to carry off by unlawful force, or by fraud.

KIDNEY ('ni), *n.* one of two oblong organs which separate the urine from the blood.

KILL (kil), *v.t.* to deprive of life.

KILN (kiln), *n.* a furnace, oven or pile for burning or drying.

KILO-, a prefix meaning a *thousand*: used in units of measurement.

KILOGRAM, KILOGRAMME ('o-gram), *n.* 1,000 grammes = 2.2046 lb. : usually abbreviated to kilo.

KILOLITRE (-le'tr), *n.* 1,000 litres = 220 imperial gals. (about).

KILOMETRE (-me'tr), *n.* 1,000 metres = 3,280.8 feet.

KILOWATT (kil'o-wot), *n.* unit of electric power ; one thousand watts.

KILT (kilt), *n.* a short, plaited, tartan petticoat worn by Scotchmen.

KIMONO (ki-mo'no), *n.* the loose outer robe of the Japanese.

KIN (kin), *n.* relationship.

KIND (kind), *adj.* benevolent ; affectionate : *n.* quality ; variety ; sort.

KINDERGARTEN (kin'der-gar-ten), *n.* a school for young children in which they are taught by diverting object lessons, etc.

KINDLE (kind'l), *v.t.* to set fire to.

KINDLINESS (kind'li-nes), *n.* kindly disposition.

KINDLY ('li), *adj.* benevolent ; sympathetic ; beneficial.

KINDRED (kin'dred), *adj.* of like nature or character ; cognate : *n.* relationship.

KINEMACOLOUR (kin'e-ma-kul-er), *n.* a moving picture in natural colours.

KINETIC (ki-net'ik), *adj.* pertaining to, or imparting, motion ; active.

KINETOPHONE (o-fon), *n.* machine for synchronizing films with sound.

KING (king), *n.* a male sovereign.

KINGDOM ('dum), *n.* the territory ruled by a king or queen.

KINGFISHER ('fish-er), *n.* a fish-eating bird.

KINK (kingk), *n.* a twist in a rope or thread when doubled ; whim.

KINNIKINIC (kin-i-ki-nik'), *n.* a kind of tobacco smoked by the American Indians.

KINSFOLK (kinz'fok), *n.pl.* relatives.

KIOSK (ki-osk'), *n.* a Turkish open pavilion or summer house.

KIP (kip), *n.* the skin of a calf or small cattle.

KIRK (kerk), *n.* [Scotch], a church; the Church of Scotland (with *the*).

KISMET (kis'met, kis'ma), *n.* [Mohammedan], fate; destiny.

KISS (kis), *n.* a salute or caress with the lips.

KIT (kit), *n.* travelling necessaries, outfit, etc.

KITCHEN (kich'en), *n.* a room set apart for cooking.

KITCHENETTE (kich-en-et'), *n.* a small kitchen in apartment houses or studios.

KITE (kit), *n.* a rapacious bird of prey; a light frame covered with paper or linen for flying in the air; an accommodation bill.

KITH (kith), *n.* used in phrase *kith and kin*, meaning family relations.

KITTEN (kit'n), *n.* a young cat.

KLEPTOMANIA (klep-to-ma'ni-a), *n.* a form of insanity; an irresistible propensity to steal.

KNACK (nak), *n.* adroitness; dexterity.

KNAPSACK (nap'sak), *n.* a travelling case carried on the back.

KNAVE (nav), *n.* a dishonest or deceitful person.

KNAVERY ('er-i), *n.* dishonesty; fraud.

KNEAD (ned), *v.t.* to work into a mass, as dough.

KNEE (ne), *n.* the articulation of the leg and thigh bones.

KNEECAP ('kap), *n.* a flattened oval bone on the forepart of the knee-joint; patella.

KNEEL (nel), *v.i.* to bend, or fall upon, the knees.

KNELL (nel), *n.* the sound of a bell when struck, especially a funeral bell; an ill omen.

KNICKERBOCKER (nik'er-bok-er), *n.* a descendant of one of the early Dutch of Manhattan, New York.

KNICK-KNACK ('nak), *n.* a little ornamental trifle.

KNIFE (nif), *n.* a cutting instrument with sharp-edged blade set in a handle; edged blade of a machine.

KNIGHT (nit), *n.* one who holds non-hereditary rank next below a baronet, entitling him to the prefix *Sir*.

KNIGHT-ERRANT (-er'ant), *n.* a mediæval gentleman who went forth armed to redress wrongs.

KNIGHT TEMPLAR (tem'plar), one of a military order established in the 12th century; one belonging to a certain rank or degree in Masonry.

KNIT (nit), *v.t.* to tie, unite, or draw together; weave together by needles.

KNOB (nob), *n.* the rounded handle of a door, etc.; round protuberance.

KNOCK (nok), *n.* a blow or stroke with something hard or heavy; rap.

KNOLL (nol), *n.* a rounded hillock; hilltop.

KNOT (not), *n.* an interweaving or tying of thread or cord, etc.; anything resembling a knot; entanglement; difficulty; a hard part in a piece of wood; a division of a log-line (47.42 ft.); a nautical mile = 2,025 yds.; group.

KNOTTY ('i), *adj.* full of knots; rugged; difficult.

KNOW (no), *v.t.* to perceive with the mind; understand clearly.

KNOWING ('ing), *p.adj.* having knowledge.

KNOWLEDGE (nol'ej), *n.* clear perception of a truth or fact; erudition; acquaintance; information.

KNOWN (non), *adj.* recognized; understood.

KNUCKLE (nuk'l), *n.* the projecting joint of the fingers.

KODAK (ko'adk), *n.* a portable camera for taking instantaneous photographs. The name is a registered trade-mark.

KOHINOOR (ko'hi-noor), *n.* the large Indian diamond, weighing originally 792 carats, reduced by cutting to 106¼.

KOHLRABI ('ra-bi, -ra'bi), *n.* a variety of cabbage.

KOPJE (kop'i), *n.* a hillock.

KORAN (ko'ran), *n.* the book of scriptures of the Mohammedans.

KOSHER (ko'sher), *adj.* applied to

meat prepared according to the Hebrew ordinances.

KOUMISS, KUMISS (koo′mis), *n.* a spirituous beverage made by the Tartars from fermented mare's milk.

KREMLIN (krem′lin), *n.* a Russian citadel, especially [K-] that of Moscow.

L

L, 1 (el), *n.* the twelfth letter of the English alphabet.

L, l, *n.* an abbreviation.

L, *n.* a numeral in the Roman notation denoting 50; with a bar (L̄), 50,000.

LABEL (la′bel), *n.* a small slip or tag, attached to anything to indicate its destination, ownership, etc.

LABIATE (′bi-at), *adj.* like a lip.

LABOUR (′ber), *n.* toil or exertion, physical or mental; effort; difficulty; pain; parturition.

LABORATORY (lab′o-ra-to-ri), *n.* a place where scientific experiments and operations are carried on.

LABORIOUS (la-bo′ri-us), *adj.* difficult; toilsome.

LABRADOR (lab′ra-dor), *n.* the name of a great peninsula north of the Gulf of St. Lawrence between Hudson Bay and the Atlantic Ocean: area, 510,000 sq. m.

LABYRINTH (lab′i-rinth), *n.* a series of intricate winding passages; a maze.

LACE (las), *n.* an ornamental fabric: *v.t.* to fasten with a lace; adorn with lace; beat.

LACERATE (las′er-at), *v.t.* to rend; harrow; wound.

LACERATION (-a′shun), *n.* a harrowing of the feelings; a rent.

LACHRYMAL (lak′ri-mal), *adj.* pertaining to tears.

LACHRYMOSE (′ri-mos), *adj.* tearful; sad.

LACK (lak), *v.i.* to be in need; to be deficient: *n.* want.

LACKADAISICAL (-a-da′zi-kal), *adj.* pensive or sentimental.

LACKEY (′i), *n.* a menial attendant.

LACONIC (la-kon′ik), *adj.* expressing much in few words.

LACONICALLY (-kal-li), *adv.* briefly.

LACQUER (lak′er), *n.* a varnish: *v.t.* to varnish with lacquer.

LACROSSE (la-kros′), *n.* a Canadian ball game, played with netted hooked sticks for each of 12 players.

LACTEAL (lak′te-al), *adj.* pertaining to, or like, milk; conveying chyle: *n.pl.* the lymphatic vessels.

LACTI-, LACTO-, combining forms from the Latin *lac*, milk.

LACTOSE (-tos), *n.* a crystalline sugar present in milk.

LACUNA (la-ku′na), *n.* [*pl.* lacunæ (′ne)], a blank space; hiatus.

LAD (lad), *n.* a boy or youth.

LADDER (′er), *n.* framework consisting of two parallel side pieces connected by bars or steps.

LADDIE (′i), *n.* [Scotch], a lad.

LADE (lad), *v.t.* to load; burden.

LADING (′ing), *n.* the act of loading.

LADLE (′l), *n.* a deep spoon.

LADRONE (la-dron′), *n.* a robber; bandit.

LADY (la′di), *n.* a well-bred woman.

LAG (lag), *v.i.* to move slowly; loiter.

LAGGARD (lag′ard), *n.* a slow person; loiterer.

LAGOON (la-goon′), *n.* a shallow lake formed at the mouth of a river or near the sea.

LAID (lad), *p.adj.* marked with fine parallel ribbed lines: said of paper, & *p.p.* of lay.

LAIN, *p.p.* of lie.

LAIR (lar), *n.* the covert of a wild beast.

LAITY (la′i-ti), *n.* the people, as distinguished from the clergy.

LAKE (lak), *n.* a large body of water surrounded by land.

LAMA (la′ma), *n.* a Tibetan Buddhist priest or monk.

LAMB (lam), *n.* young of a sheep.

LAMBENT (′bent), *adj.* flickering.

LAMBKIN (′kin), *n.* a little lamb.

LAMBREQUIN (′bre-kin), *n.* a festooned drapery.

LAMBSKIN ('skin), *n.* the skin of a lamb.

LAME (lam), *adj.* crippled or disabled.

LAMENESS ('nes), *n.* state of being lame.

LAMENT (la-ment'), *v.t.* to mourn for.

LAMENTABLE (lam'en-ta-bl), *adj.* to be lamented ; mournful.

LAMENTATION (-ta'shun), *n.* grief audibly expressed ; outcry.

LAMINA ('i-na), *n.* [*pl.* laminæ (-ne)], a thin plate or scale.

LAMINAL (-nal), **LAMINAR** (-nar), *adj.* composed of thin plates.

LAMINATION (-i-na'shun), *n.* division into thin plates.

LAMP (lamp), *n.* any device for producing artificial light.

LAMPBLACK ('black), *n.* finely divided charcoal.

LAMPOON (lam-poon'), *n.* satire designed to bring subject of it into contempt.

LANCE (lans), *n.* a long shaft of wood with a spear head.

LANCET ('set), *n.* a surgeon's knife.

LAND (land), *n.* the solid portion of the surface of the globe ; the earth : *v.t.* to set on shore.

LANDAU (lan-daw), *n.* a kind of covered carriage.

LANDLORD (land'lord), *n.* one who owns and leases real estate ; keeper of hotel or inn.

LANDLUBBER ('lub-er), *n.* one not a sailor.

LANDSCAPE ('skap), *n.* the general aspect of a country, or a picture representing it.

LANE (lan), *n.* a narrow path.

LANGUAGE (lang'gwej), *n.* human speech ; style or expression.

LANGUID ('gwid), *adj.* wanting energy ; weak.

LANGUISH ('gwish), *v.i.* weak or spiritless ; pine away.

LANGUOR (lang-gwer), *n.* listlessness.

LANK (langk), *adj.* lean ; slender.

LANKY ('i), *adj.* tall and thin.

LANTERN (lan'tern), *n.* a transparent case for holding or carrying a light.

LANTERN-JAWED (-jawd), *adj.* having a long, thin face.

LANYARD ('yard), *n.* a piece of rope, cord, etc., for fastening marine tackle.

LAPEL (la-pel'), *n.* the part of a coat-collar folded in the front.

LAPID, a prefix meaning *stone.*

LAPIDARIST (lap'i-da-rist), *n.* one versed in the knowledge of gems and precious stones.

LAPIDARY (lap'i-da-ri), *n.* an artificer who cuts and sets precious stones.

LAPSABLE (lap'sa-bl), *adj.* capable of lapsing.

LAPSE (laps), *v.i.* fall by degrees ; fail in duty.

LAPSUS ('sus), *n.* a slip or mistake.

LARBOARD (lar'bord), *n.* the left-hand side of a ship.

LARCENOUS ('se-nus), *adj.* thievish.

LARCENY ('se-ni), *n.* theft.

LARCH (larch), *n.* a deciduous tree of the pine family.

LARD (lard), *n.* the fat of swine melted down.

LARDER ('der), *n.* a pantry.

LARGE (larj), *adj.* great in size; bulky ; comprehensive.

LARGESS (lar'jes), *n.* a gift or bounty.

LARGO (lar'go), *n.* a slow movement in music.

LARIAT (lar'i-at), *n.* a rope for lassoing.

LARK (lark), *n.* a well-known song-bird ; a frolic.

LARKSPUR ('sper), *n.* a plant with blue, spurred flowers.

LARRUP (lar'up), *v.t.* to beat or flog.

LARVA (lar'va), *n.* [*pl.* larvæ ('ve)], an insect in the first stage of its metamorphosis after leaving the egg.

LARVAL ('val), *adj.* pertaining to a larva.

LARYNGITIS (lar-in-ji'tis), *n.* inflammation of the larynx.

LARYNGO- (la-ring'go), a combining form indicating *relation to the larynx.*

LARYNX (lar'ingks), *n.* the upper part of the trachea or windpipe.

LASCIVIOUS (la-siv'i-us), *adj.* lustful.

LASH (lash), *v.t.* fasten or bind with a cord or rope : *v.i.* to apply the whip ; flog.

LASS (las), *n.* a young girl.

LASSIE (las'i), *n.* [Scotch], a lass.

LASSITUDE ('i-tud), *n.* weariness; languor.

LASSO ('o), *n.* a rope, usually of hide, with a noose.

LAST (last), *adj.* coming after all others in time, place, or order : *adv.* finally.

LASTLY ('li), *adv.* in the last place.

LATCH (lach), *n.* a door catch.

LATCHET ('et), *n.* a shoe string.

LATE (lat), *adj.* tardy; long delayed; recent.

LATELY (lat'li), *adv.* not long ago.

LATENT (la'tent), *n.* concealed; invisible.

LATERAL (lat'er-al), *adj.* pertaining to the side.

LATERO, a prefix meaning *side*.

LATH (lath), *n.* a strip of wood.

LATHE (la*th*), *n.* a machine for turning and polishing articles of wood, metal, etc.

LATHER (la*th*'er), *n.* froth made by moistened soap.

LATIN (lat'in), *adj.* pertaining to Latin; pertaining to Latium, ancient Rome.

LATITUDE ('i-tud), *n.* distance on the earth's surface as measured by degrees north or south from the equator; breadth; extent; laxity.

LATITUDINAL ('di-nal), *adj.* pertaining to latitude.

LATITUDINARIAN (-di-na'ri-an), *adj.* wide in range or scope : *n.* one who holds broad views.

LATTER ('er), *adj.* the second of two things; recent; modern.

LATTICE ('is), *n.* crossed open work of metal or wood.

LAUD (lawd), *v.t.* to praise highly; extol.

LAUDABLE ('a-bl), *adj.* commendable.

LAUDANUM ('a-num), *n.* a preparation of opium.

LAUDATORY (lawd'a-to-ri), *adj.* expressing praise.

LAUGH (laf), *n.* a convulsive sound caused by merriment.

LAUGHTER ('ter), *n.* a movement of the facial muscles and the eyes caused by a feeling of merriment or pleasure.

LAUNCH (lanch), *v.t.* to move or cause to slide into the water, as a vessel; hurl; dart; send forth : *n.* open motor-boat.

LAUNDER (lan'der), *v.t.* to wash and iron, as clothes.

LAUNDRESS ('dres), *n.* a woman who washes and irons clothes.

LAUNDRY ('dri), *n.* a place where clothes are washed and ironed.

LAUREATE (law're-at), *n.* one crowned with laurel; poet-laureate.

LAUREL ('rel), *n.* evergreen shrub.

LAVA (la'va), *n.* molten volcanic matter.

LAVALLIERE (lav'a-ler'), *n.* a necklace with pendant.

LAVATORY (lav'a-to-ri), *n.* a toilet room.

LAVE (lav), *v.t. & v.i.* to bathe or wash.

LAVENDER (lav'en-der), *n.* an aromatic shrub.

LAVISH (lav'ish), *adj.* profuse; extravagant.

LAW (law), *n.* a rule of action established by authority.

LAWFUL ('fool), *adj.* just; legal.

LAWLESS (les), *adj.* not according to law; unruly.

LAWN (lawn), *n.* a plot of grass kept closely mown; fine cambric.

LAWN MOWER (mo'er), *n.* a machine with revolving blades, used to clip grass.

LAWN TENNIS (ten'is), *n.* an outdoor game played with balls and rackets over a net.

LAWSUIT ('sut), *n.* an action at law.

LAWYER ('yer), *n.* one authorized to practise law.

LAX (laks), *adj.* loose; vague; weak.

LAXATIVE ('a-tiv), *adj.* purgative.

LAXITY ('i-ti), *n.* quality of being lax.

LAY (la), *v.t.* to put or place; spread over; cause to lie down; settle; calm.

LAYER ('er), *n.* a stratum, row, or bed.

LAYMAN ('man), *n.* one of the people, as distinguished from a professional man.

LAYOUT (la'out), *n.* an outfit, as of tools.

LAZY (la'zi), *adj.* idle; indolent.

LEA (le), *n.* a meadow.

LEACH (lech), *v.t.* to wash by draining : *v.i.* to cause a liquid to percolate through a mass, as of coffee, ashes, etc.

LEAD (led), *n.* a soft, heavy, ductile, bluish-grey metal ; a plummet for sounding depths at sea.

LEAD (led), *v.t.* to conduct ; precede ; allure ; induce.

LEADED (led'ed), *p.adj.* separated by leads ; set in, or covered with, lead.

LEADEN ('en), *adj.* made of, or coloured like, lead ; heavy ; sluggish.

LEADER (led'er), *n.* one who leads ; the chief editorial of a newspaper.

LEAF (lef), *n.* one of the thin, flat parts of a plant ; something resembling a leaf ; part of a book ; part of a table.

LEAFAGE ('aj), *n.* leaves collectively.

LEAFLET ('let), *n.* a small leaf ; a circular.

LEAGUE (leg), *n.* an alliance for mutual interests ; 3 miles.

LEAGUE OF NATIONS (na'shunz), an association of nations which came into existence January 10, 1920.

LEAK (lek), *v.i.* to let water in or out through a hole, etc.

LEAL (lel), *adj.* true-hearted.

LEAN (len), *v.i.* to incline or deviate from an upright position.

LEAP (lep), *v.t.* to jump or spring over.

LEAP YEAR (yer), *n.* a year of 366 days, when February has 29 days ; every year divisible by 4, except those divisible by 100 but not by 400.

LEARN (lern), *v.i.* to gain or receive knowledge or skill.

LEARNED ('ed), *p.adj.* erudite ; well educated.

LEASE (les), *n.* a written contract for the letting of land or tenements for a specified time.

LEASEHOLD ('hold), *n.* property held by lease : *adj.* held on lease.

LEASH (lesh), *n.* a thong or cord for holding in restraint, as a dog.

LEAST (lest), *adj.* smallest in degree, size, etc.

LEATHER (le*th*'er), *n.* the tanned skin of an animal.

LEATHERETTE (-et'), *n.* imitation leather.

LEAVE (lev), *n.* permission granted ; departure ; farewell : *v.t.* to depart from ; for sake ; abandon.

LEAVEN (lev'n), *v.t.* to produce fermentation in ; taint ; imbue.

LECHERY ('er-i), *n.* lustfulness.

LECTERN (lek'tern), *n.* the reading desk of a church.

LECTION ('shun), *n.* a portion of the Scriptures to be read in church service.

LECTURE ('tur), *n.* a formal discourse on any subject ; reprimand.

LEDGE (lej), *n.* a shelf ; ridge ; layer ; edge.

LEDGER ('er), *n.* the principal account book of a business.

LEE (le), *n.* the side or quarter opposite that from which the wind blows.

LEECH (lech), *n.* an aquatic worm furnished with a sucker.

LEEK (lek), *n.* a biennial plant of the onion family with a bulbous root.

LEER (ler), *n.* a sly, sidelong look indicative of malice or triumph.

LEEWARD (le'werd), *n.* the direction toward which the wind blows.

LEEWAY (le'wa), *n.* the lateral drift of a vessel to leeward of her course ; time or room for action.

LEFT (left), *adj.* opposite to the *right*.

LEG (leg), *n.* one of the limbs by which men and animals walk.

LEGACY ('a-si), *n.* a gift by will of money or property ; bequest.

LEGAL (le'gal), *adj.* permitted by law ; legitimate.

LEGALITY ('i-ti), *n.* conformity to law.

LEGALIZE ('iz), *v.t.* to make lawful.

LEGALLY ('li), *adv.* lawfully.

LEGATE (leg'at), *n.* Papal ambassador ; envoy.

LEGATEE (-a-te'), *n.* a person to whom a legacy is bequeathed.

LEGATION (le-ga'shun), *n.* an embassy ; a diplomatic mission.

LEGEND (lej'end), *n.* a romantic or non-historical story ; myth.

LEGENDARY ('en-da-ri), *adj.* fabulous ; mythical.

LEGERDEMAIN (-er-de-man'), *n.* sleight of hand.

LEGGINGS (leg'ingz), *n.pl.* long gaiters.

LEGIBILITY (lej-i-bil'i-ti), *n.* the state of being legible.

LEGIBLE ('i-bl), *adj.* clear; distinct; apparent.

LEGIBLY ('i-bli), *adv.* clearly; distinctly.

LEGION (le'jun), *n.* a division of the ancient Roman army; a great number.

LEGION OF HONOUR (on'er), an order of merit instituted by Napoleon in 1802.

LEGIONARY ('jun-a-ri), *adj.* pertaining to legions; innumerable.

LEGISLATE (lej'is-lat), *v.i.* to make or enact a law.

LEGISLATION (-la'shun), *n.* the act of making laws.

LEGISLATIVE ('is-la-tiv), *adj.* pertaining to legislation.

LEGISLATOR (-la-ter), *n.* a lawgiver.

LEGISLATURE (-la-tur), *n.* that body in a state which is invested with the power of enacting and repealing laws.

LEGITIMACY (le-jit'i-ma-si), *n.* the state of being legitimate.

LEGITIMATE ('i-mat), *adj.* lawful; real; logically correct.

LEISURE (le'zhur), *n.* spare time.

LEMON (lem'un), *n.* a fruit of *Citrus Limonum.*

LEMONADE (-ad), *n.* a beverage of water flavoured with lemon juice.

LEMUR (le'mer), *n.* a small animal allied to the monkeys.

LEND (lend), *v.t.* to grant to another for temporary use: *v.i.* to make a loan.

LENGTH (length), *n.* the measure of anything from end to end; extent; duration.

LENGTHY ('thi), *adj.* long and tiresome.

LENIENCY (le'ni-en-si, len'yen-si), *n.* clemency.

LENIENT ('ni-ent), len'yent), *adj.* mild; merciful.

LENITIVE (len'i-tiv), *adj.* assuaging; emollient.

LENITY (len'i-ti), *n.* mildness; humanity.

LENS (lenz), *n.* a convex, or concave, glass adapted for changing the direction of rays of light and thus magnifying or diminishing the apparent size of objects.

LENT (lent), *n.* an annual season of fasting, consisting of 40 days, in preparation for Easter Day.

LENTIL ('til), *n.* a leguminous plant.

LEONINE (le'o-nin), *adj.* like a lion.

LEOPARD (lep'erd), *n.* a large, cat-like beast of prey.

LEPER ('er), *n.* one affected with leprosy.

LEPROSY ('ro-si), *n.* a chronic skin disease.

LEPROUS ('rus), *adj.* infected with leprosy.

LEPTO, a prefix meaning *small, slender, delicate*: also lept.

LESE MAJESTY (lez maj'es-ti), *n.* a crime against royalty or the sovereign power; treason.

LESION (le'zhun), *n.* injury.

LESS (les), *adj.* not so much; smaller.

LESSEE (-e'), *n.* one to whom lease is granted.

LESSEN ('en), *v.t.* to make less; reduce.

LESSER ('er), *adj.* a double comparative of *less.*

LESSON (les'n), *n.* that which a pupil learns or repeats; exercise; precept.

LESSOR ('or), *n.* the grantor of a lease.

LEST (lest), *conj.* that not; for fear that.

LET (let), *v.t.* to permit; grant to a tenant; lease; give out on contract.

LETHAL (le'thal), *adj.* deadly; fatal.

LETHARGY (leth'ar-ji), *n.* morbid drowsiness; apathy.

LETTER (let'er), *n.* a mark or character used to represent a sound; written or printed communication.

LETTER OF CREDIT (kred'it), a letter from a banker authorizing the person who holds it to draw upon him up to a specified amount.

LETTERS PATENT ('erz pat'ent), a

written document of the government, authorizing a person to do some act.

LETTUCE (let'is), *n.* a common garden herb.

LEUC-, LEUCO-, combining forms from the Greek *leukos*, white.

LEUCOCYTE (lu'ko-sit), *n.* one of the white blood corpuscles which prey upon bacteria in the blood.

LEVANT (le-vant)', *n.* the eastern coasts of the Mediterranean.

LEVEE (lev'e), *n.* a morning reception ; a river embankment : *v.i.* to embank.

LEVEL ('el), *n.* a horizontal plane or line ; surface without inequalities ; state of equality ; standard ; an instrument for indicating a horizontal line or plane : *adj.* even ; smooth.

LEVER (lev'er, le'ver), *n.* a bar of metal, etc., turning on a support (fulcrum) for raising a weight.

LEVERAGE (-aj), *n.* the mechanical power gained by using a lever.

LEVIABLE (lev'i-a-bl), *adj.* that may be levied upon or seized.

LEVIATHAN (le-vi'a-than), *n.* a large whale ; anything huge.

LEVITATION (lev-i-ta'shun), *n.* lightness ; buoyancy.

LEVITY (lev'i-ti), *n.* lightness of disposition, conduct, etc.

LEVY ('i), *v.t.* to raise or collect, as an army or tax ; seize in execution.

LEWD (lud), *adj.* licentious.

LEXICOGRAPHER (lek-si-kog'ra-fer), *n.* editor or compiler of a dictionary.

LEXICON (lek'si-kon), *n.* vocabulary ; dictionary of words.

LIABILITY (-a-bil'i-ti), *n.* the state of being liable : *pl.* debts.

LIABLE ('a-bl), *adj.* exposed to damage, danger, expense, etc.

LIAISON (le-a-zong'), *n.* [French], illicit relations between a man and a woman.

LIAR (li'er), *n.* one who is untruthful.

LIBATION (-ba'shun), *n.* pouring wine or oil on the ground, as a sacrifice to some deity.

LIBEL ('bel), *n.* any writing, print, publication, or picture calculated to injure reputation or character of anyone : *v.t.* to file a libel, as against a ship or goods.

LIBELLOUS (-us), *adj.* containing, or of the nature of, a libel.

LIBERAL (lib'er-al), *adj.* generous ; munificent ; plentiful.

LIBERALITY (-al'i-ti), *n.* generosity ; magnanimity ; mental breadth.

LIBERATE ('er-at), *v.t.* to set free.

LIBERATOR (-a-ter), *n.* one who liberates.

LIBERTINE ('er-tin), *n.* a debauchee : *adj.* licentious.

LIBERTY ('er-ti), *n.* freedom ; immunity.

LIBIDINOUS (li-bid'i-nus), *adj.* lustful.

LIBRARIAN (-bra'ri-an), *n.* the custodian of a library.

LIBRARY ('bra-ri), *n.* an arranged collection of books.

LIBRATION (-bra'shun), *n.* balancing ; equipoise.

LIBRETTIST (li-bret'ist), *n.* the writer of a libretto.

LIBRETTO ('o), *n.* a book containing the words of an opera, oratorio, etc.

LICE (lis), *pl.* of louse.

LICENCE (li'sens), *n.* permission ; leave ; unrestrained liberty.

LICENTIOUS ('shus), *adj.* lascivious ; dissolute.

LICHEN (li'ken, lich'en), *n.* a cellular flowerless plant.

LICIT (lis'it), *adj.* lawful.

LICK (lik), *v.t.* to pass the tongue over ; lap up ; vanquish ; chastise.

LICORICE (lik'o-ris), *n.* the root of inspissated juice of the licorice-plant.

LID (lid), *n.* a cover closing an aperture ; top ; eyelid.

LIE (li), *v.i.* to rest in a recumbent position.

LIE (li), *v.i.* to utter a falsehood : *n.* falsehood.

LIEF (lef), *adv.* willingly ; rather.

LIEGE (leg), *adj.* bound by feudal service or tenure.

LIEN (le'en, li'en, len), *n.* a legal claim upon property ; security for payment.

LIEU (lu), *n.* place ; stead: preceded by *in*.

LIEUTENANT (-ten'ant), *n*. an officer ranking next below a captain in the army and a commander in the navy ; a deputy.

LIFE (lif), *n*. animate existence ; vitality ; the story of a life.

LIFEGUARD (-gard), *n*. a bodyguard ; an expert swimmer employed at a bathing resort.

LIFE NET (net), *n*. a net used by firemen.

LIFT (lift), *v.t*. to raise from the ground ; elevate ; *n*. elevator

LIGAMENT (lig'a-ment), *n*. a strong elastic tissue connecting the extremities of movable bones ; bond or tie.

LIGATURE (lig'a-tur), *n*. a narrow bandage or tie.

LIGHT (lit), *n*. the imponderable agent by which objects are rendered visible by its action on the retina ; day ; an illuminating or enlightening agent ; aspect : *adj*. clear ; bright ; not heavy.

LIGHTEN ('en), *v.t*. to make light.

LIGHTER ('er), *n*. a large open barge for loading and unloading vessels.

LIGHTHOUSE ('hous), *n*. a structure furnished with a brilliant light to indicate points of danger to mariners at night.

LIGHTNING ('ning), *n*. discharge of atmospheric electricity.

LIGHT YEAR *n*. (yer), the space traversed by a beam of light at the speed of 186,330 miles a second in a year.

LIGNITE ('nit), *n*. wood converted into an imperfect kind of coal.

LIGNUM-VITÆ ('num-vi'te), *n*. the very heavy hard wood of a South American tree.

LIKE (lik), *adj*. similar ; resembling ; equal or nearly equal ; disposed : *v.t*. enjoy.

LIKELY ('li), *adj*. probable ; suitable.

LIKEN (lik'n), *v.t*. to compare.

LIKENESS ('nes), *n*. similarity ; portrait.

LIKING ('ing), *n*. preference ; fondness.

LILAC (li'lak), *n*. an ornamental shrub with pale purple or white flowers.

LILLIPUTIAN (lil-i-pu'shan), *n*. a dwarf.

LILY (lil'i), *n*. a plant with bulbous roots and handsome, white, wax-like flowers.

LIMB (lim), *n*. a jointed or articulated part of an animal body ; branch of a tree.

LIME (lim), *n*. a calcareous earth obtained by the action of heat upon limestone ; an edible, juicy fruit.

LIMELIGHT ('lit), *n*. a brilliant light produced by the action of lighted hydrogen and oxygen upon lime.

LIMERICK (lim'er-ik), *n*. a nonsense stanza of five lines.

LIMIT ('it), *n*. a border or boundary ; utmost extent.

LIMITATION (-i-ta'shun), *n*. restriction.

LIMITED (-ed), *adj*. confined within limits.

LIMN (lim), *v.t*. to paint or draw.

LIMOUSINE (le-moo-zen'), *n*. a type of automobile with a closed body.

LIMP (limp), *adj*. flexible ; flaccid : *n*. a halt in one's gait.

LINCHPIN (linch'pin), *n*. the pin which goes through the end of the axle of a wheel.

LINDBERGH, CHARLES A., 1903- (lind'burg), an American aviator. Flew from New York to Paris, May 20-21, 1927, 3,600 miles in 33½ hours. On his return made a tour of U.S. cities and Latin American countries in the monoplane, " Spirit of St. Louis."

LINDEN (lin'den), *n*. a tree with heart-shaped leaves.

LINE (lin), *n*. length without breadth ; a string or cord ; extended row ; occupation ; particular class of goods ; descent.

LINEAGE (lin'e-aj), *n*. ancestral line of descent.

LINEAL ('e-al), *adj*. composed of lines ; in direct line from an ancestor.

LINEAMENT ('e-a-ment), *n*. feature ; outline.

LINEAR ('e-ar), *adj*. pertaining to lines ; a straight direction.

LINEN (lin'en), *n*. a cloth made of flax ; underclothing.

LINER (li'ner), *n.* a steamship belonging to a S.S. company.

LINGER ('ger), *v.i.* to delay ; loiter.

LINGERIE (lang-zhe-re'), *n.* [French], woman's underclothing.

LINGO (ling'go), *n.* [Slang], language.

LINGUAL (gwal), *adj.* pertaining to, or formed by, the tongue.

LINGUIST ('gwist), *n.* one skilled in languages.

LINIMENT (lin'i-ment), *n.* a medicated liquid for the skin.

LINING (lin'ing), *n.* inside covering.

LINK (lingk), *n.* a single ring or division of a chain ; a land measure 7.92 inches ; connection : *pl.* golfing grounds.

LINOLEUM (li-no'le-um), *n.* a floor cloth.

LINOTYPE (lin'o-tip), *n.* a machine for composing and casting words or lines for printing.

LINSEED (lin'sed), *n.* the seed of flax.

LINSEED OIL (oil), *n.* oil from flaxseed.

LINT (lint), *n.* scraped linen used for dressing wounds.

LINTEL (lin'tel), *n.* the horizontal top piece of a door or window.

LION (li'un), *n.* a large, powerful carnivorous mammal of the cat family.

LIONESS (li'un-es), *n.* a female lion.

LIONIZE (-iz), *v.t.* to treat as an object of peculiar interest.

LIP (lip), *n.* one of the two borders of the mouth.

LIPPED (lipt'), *adj.* having lips or rounded edges.

LIQUEFY (lik'wi-fi), *v.t.* to melt or make liquid : *v.i.* to become liquid.

LIQUEUR (li-kur'), *n.* an aromatic alcoholic cordial.

LIQUID (lik'wid), *adj.* not solid ; readily flowing ; devoid of harshness : *n.* one of the consonants *l, m, n, r*.

LIQUID AIR (ar), air brought to a liquid condition by great pressure.

LIQUIDATE ('wi-date), *v.t.* to pay off, as a debt.

LIQUIDATION (-da'shun), *n.* settlement of the affairs of a bankrupt's estate.

LIQUOR (lik'er), *n.* an alcoholic beverage ; a liquid.

LIRA (le'ra), *n.* [*pl.* lire (le're)], an Italian coin equivalent to a franc.

LISLE (lil), *n.* a fine thread or lace.

LISP (lisp), *v.i.* to pronounce *s and z* nearly like *th*.

LISSOM (lis'um), *n.* supple.

LIST (list), *n.* a catalogue or register ; inclination to one side : *v.t.* catalogue.

LISTEN (lis'n), *v.i.* to hear ; hearken.

LISTING ('ing), *n.* act of making a schedule.

LISTLESS ('les), *adj.* languid.

LIT, *p.t.* & *p.p.* of light.

LITANY (lit'a-ni), *n.* a solemn responsive form of supplication.

LITRE (le'tr), *n.* in the metric system, a measure of capacity =61,026 cubic inches, or a little more than 1 quart.

LITERACY (lit'er-a-si), *n.* the state of being able to read and write.

LITERAL ('er-al), *adj.* following exact words.

LITERARY ('er-a-ri), *adj.* pertaining to literature.

LITERATE ('er-at), *adj.* instructed ; learned : *n.* a literary man.

LITERATI (-e-ra'ti), *n.pl.* the learned.

LITERATIM (-ra'tim), *adv.* literally.

LITERATURE ('er-a-tur), *n.* the written or printed literary productions of a country or period.

LITHE (lith), *adj.* supple ; pliant.

LITHESOME ('sum), *adj.* nimble.

LITHOGRAPH (lith'o-graf), *n.* a print reproduced from a drawing on stone.

LITHOGRAPHY (li-thog'ra-fi), *n.* the art of making a design on stone so that ink-impressions can be taken from it.

LITIGANT (lit'i-gant), *n.* one who contends in law.

LITIGATION (-ga'shun), *n.* the act or process of carrying on a lawsuit.

LITIGIOUS (li-ti'jus), *adj.* given to carrying on lawsuits.

LITTER (lit'er), *n.* a framework with a bed, for carrying a person in a recumbent position ; state of confusion or untidiness ; number of young produced at one birth, as pigs, etc.

LITTERATEUR (le-ta-ra-ter'), *n.* [French], a literary man.

LITTLE (lit'l), *adj.* small in size, quantity, duration, or importance.

LITTORAL ('o-ral), *adj.* pertaining to, near, or living on, the shore.

LITURGY (lit'er-ji), *n.* the prescribed forms or ritual for worship.

LIVE (liv), *v.i.* to exist or have life; reside; endure; subsist.

LIVELIHOOD (liv'li-hood), *n.* means of living.

LIVELY ('li), *adj.* active; brisk.

LIVER (liv'er), *n.* one who lives; a glandular organ.

LIVERY ('er-i), *n.* a costume worn by servants; being kept, as horses.

I IVERYMAN (-man), *n.* the keeper of a livery stable.

LIVERY STABLE (sta'bl), *n.* a stable where horses are kept and let for hire.

LIVID ('id), *adj.* black and blue; discoloured.

LIVING ('ing), *p.adj.* having life; flowing; vigorous; active.

LIZARD (liz'ard), *n.* a saurian reptile.

LLAMA (la'ma), *n.* a South American woolly-haired ruminant.

LO (lo), *interj.* behold! see!

LOAD (lod), *v.t.* to burden; weigh down; embarrass; freight: *v.i.* to take on a load.

LOADED ('ed), *p.adj.* laden.

LOADSTAR ('star), *n.* the pole-star.

LOADSTONE, LODESTONE ('ston), *n.* magnetic oxide of iron; magnet.

LOAF (lof), *v.i.* to idle away time: *n.* cake of bread.

LOAFER ('er), *n.* an idler.

LOAM (lom), *n.* rich, vegetable mould, with clay and sand.

LOAN (lon), *n.* a sum of money lent for a period.

LOATH (loth), *adj.* unwilling.

LOATHE (loth), *v.t.* to regard with abhorrence or disgust.

LOBBY (lob'i), *n.* a small hall or waiting room; passage opening.

LOBBYIST (-ist), *n.* a person, not a member, who tries to influence the votes of members of a legislative body.

LOBE (lob), *n.* any rounded and projecting part.

LOBELIA (lo-be'-le-ya), *n.* agenus of herbaceous plants.

LOBSTER (lob'ster), *n.* an edible marine decapod crustacean.

LOCAL (lo'kal), *adj.* restricted to a particular place.

LOCALISM ('kal-izm), *n.* a word, idiom, or custom restricted to a particular locality.

LOCALITY (-kal'i-ti), *n.* limitation to a place; position.

LOCALIZE ('kal-iz), *v.t.* to limit to a particular place.

LOCALLY (-li), *adv.* with respect to place.

LOCATE (lo'kat), *v.t.* to place.

LOCATION (-ka'shun), *n.* place.

LOCH (lokh), *n.* [Scotch], a lake.

LOCK (lok), *n.* a device for fastening a door, etc.; anything that fastens; enclosure for raising and lowering the water within.

LOCKER ('er), *n.* a receptacle secured by a lock.

LOCKET ('et), *n.* a small gold or silver case attached to a necklace or chain.

LOCKJAW ('jaw), *n.* tetanus.

LOCKOUT ('out), *n.* the exclusion of workmen from a factory by an employer to compel them to accept his terms.

LOCKUP ('up), *n.* a jail.

LOCO (lo'ko), *n.* various poisonous herbs or weeds of the U.S.

LOCOMOTION (-mo'shun), *n.* moving from place to place.

LOCOMOTIVE ('tiv), *adj.* not stationary: *n.* a steam engine for drawing railway cars.

LOCOMOTOR ATAXIA (-tor-a-tak'-si-a), *n* an affection of the spinal cord characterized by want of co-ordination of the movements of the legs.

LOCUST (lo'kust), *n.* a migratory and destructive winged insect; a tree.

LOCUTION (lo-ku'shun), *n.* a mode of speech; phrase.

LODE (lod), *n.* a vein containing metallic ore.

LODGE (loj), *v.t.* to furnish with a temporary dwelling; deposit for safe keeping: *n.* a small house in a park; place where members of an association meet.

LODGING ('ing), *n.* a place of temporary residence.

LOFT (loft), *n.* a room directly beneath a roof.

LOFTILY ('ti-li), *adv.* in a lofty manner.

LOFTY ('ti), *adj.* very high; proud; stately; sublime.

LOG (log), *n.* an undressed piece of timber; a log-book; a daily record of a ship's speed.

LOGARITHM ('a-rithm), *n.* the exponent of the power to which a fixed number (the base) must be raised in order to produce a given number.

LOG-BOOK ('book), *n.* a ship's diary.

LOGE (lozh), *n.* box in a theatre.

LOGGERHEAD ('er-hed), *n.* a blockhead; a large turtle.

LOGGIA (loj'a), *n.* a covered gallery or portico.

LOGGING (log'ing), *n.* the business of cutting down timber.

LOGIC (loj'ik), *n.* the science of correct reasoning.

LOGICAL (-ikal), *adj.* according to the rules of logic.

LOGICIAN (lo-jish'an), *n.* one skilled in logic.

LOGO-, a combining form from the Greek *logos*, speech.

LOGROLLING (log'rol-ing), *n.* the act of rolling logs; united action for mutual benefit.

LOGWOOD ('wood), *n.* a wood of a deep-red colour, used in dyeing.

LOIN (loin), *n.* the lower part of the back.

LOITER (loi'ter) *v.t.* to idle (with *away*): *v.i.* to spend time idly.

LOLL (lol), *v.i.* to lounge at ease.

LONE (lon), *adj.* solitary; retired.

LONELINESS ('li-nes), *n.* state of being lonely.

LONELY ('li), *adj.* deserted; solitary.

LONESOME ('sum), *adj.* secluded from society; depressed.

LONG (long) *adj.* not short; extended in time, or length; drawn out; slow; tedious.

LONG DOZEN (duz'n), thirteen.

LONG-DRAWN (-drawn), *adj.* protracted.

LONGEVITY (lon-jev'i-ti), *n.* extended age.

LONGHAND ('hand), *n.* ordinary handwriting, as distinguished from *shorthand*.

LONGI-, a prefix signifying *long*.

LONGING (long'ing), *n.* earnest desire.

LONGITUDE (long'ji-tud), *n.* distance east and west on the earth's surface measured from a certain meridian or place, estimated in degrees.

LONG-PRIMER ('prim-er), *n.* a size of type between small pica and bourgeois.

LONGSHOREMAN (long'shor-man), *n.* a wharf labourer.

LOOK (look), *v.i.* to direct the eye to anything; direct the mind or attention to; examine; expect; watch.

LOOM (loom), *n.* a frame or machine for weaving cloth: *v.i.* to appear larger than the real dimensions and indistinctly.

LOON (loon), *n.* the northern water diver; a foolish person.

LOONY ('i), *adj.* [Slang], crazed.

LOOP (loop), *n.* a folding or doubling of string, rope, etc.; an aerial manœuvre with an airplane.

LOOPHOLE ('hol), *n.* a narrow aperture for observation or defence.

LOOSE (loos), *adj.* not fast; unbound vague; unconnected.

LOOSEN (loos'n), *v.t.* free from tightness, restraint, or tension.

LOOT (loot), *v.t.* to pillage or plunder.

LOPSIDED (lop'sid-ed), *adj.* heavier on one side.

LOQUACIOUS (lo-kwa'shus), *adj.* talkative.

LORE (lor), *n.* learning; instruction.

LORGNETTE (lor-nyet'), *n.* [French], a long-handled opera glass.

LORN (lorn), *adj.* forsaken; forlorn.

LOSE (looz), *v..* to be deprived of; cease to have in possession; mislay.

LOSS (los), *n.* detriment; injury; privation; failure; defeat.

LOST (lost), *p.adj.* missing; destroyed.

LOT (lot), *n.* destiny; portion or parcel; great quantity.

LOTION ('shun), *n.* a medicated fluid for outward application.

LOTTERY (lot'er-i), *n.* a distribution of prizes by chance.

LOTUS (lo'tus), *n.* a genus of the water lily family.

LOUD (loud), *adj*. noisy; ostentatious; showy.

LOUD-SPEAKER (-spek′er), *n*. in radio, a device for reproducing sounds.

LOUNGE (lounj), *v.i*. to saunter about in a lazy manner; loll : *n*. a couch.

LOUSE (lous), *n*. any parasitic insect.

LOUT (lout), *n*. an awkward fellow.

LOUVRE (loo′vr), *n*. the famous art museum in Paris.

LOVABLE (luv′a-bl), *adj*. worthy of love.

LOVE (luv), *n*. a strong feeling of affection; parental care.

LOVELY (′li), *adj*. amiable; beautiful.

LOVING (′ing), *p.adj*. affectionate.

LOW (lo), *adj*. not high; depressed; shallow; subdued; moderate; vulgar.

LOWER (′er), *v.t*. to lessen or bring down.

LOWERING (lou′er-ing), *p.adj*. overcast with clouds; gloomy.

LOWING (′ing), *n*. the bellow of cattle.

LOWLAND (′land), *adj*. pertaining to a low or level country.

LOWLINESS (′li-nes), *n*. the state of being lowly.

LOWLY (′li), *adj*. humble; modest.

LOYAL (loi′al), *adj*. faithful in allegiance.

LOYALIST (-ist), *n*. one who adheres to and supports the authority of his sovereign or country.

LOZENGE (loz′enj), *n*. a rhomb; a sweet-meat.

LUBRICANT (lu′bri-kant), *n*. a substance for lubricating, as grease, oil, etc.

LUBRICATE (-kat), *v.t*. to make smooth or slippery.

LUCERNE (-sern′), *n*. a clover-like plant; alfalfa.

LUCID (′sid), *adj*. clear; readily understood; transparent.

LUCIFER (′si-fer), *n*. the morning star; Satan; a match.

LUCIFERIN (lu-si-fer-in), *n*. a substance which produces the glow in fireflies.

LUCKY (′i), *adj*. having good fortune; successful.

LUCRATIVE (lu′kra-tiv), *adj*. profitable.

LUCRE (loo′ker), *n*. money.

LUDICROUS (lu′di-krus), *adj*. exciting mirth; comical.

LUFF (luf), *n*. that part of a ship toward the wind : *v.i*. to steer nearer to the wind.

LUGGAGE (lug′aj), *n*. baggage.

LUGUBRIOUS (lu-gu′bri-us), *adj*. mournful; doleful.

LUKEWARM (luk′warm), *adj*. moderately warm.

LULL (lul), *v.t*. to soothe to sleep; quiet : *n*. abatement.

LULLABY (′a-bi), *n*. a cradle-song.

LUMBAGO (lum-ba′go), *n*. rheumatism of the muscles of the loins.

LUMBER (′ber), *n*. rubbish; forest timber sawed for market.

LUMBERMAN (′ber-man), *n*. one who is engaged in the lumber trade.

LUMINARY (lu′mi-na-ri), *n*. a body emitting light; a heavenly body.

LUMINIFEROUS (-nif′er-us), *adj*. emitting, or transmitting, light.

LUMINOSITY (-nos′it-i), *n*. state of being luminous.

LUMINOUS (′mi-nus), *adj*. bright; clear; perspicuous.

LUMP (lump), *n*. a small mass; aggregate; gross; a swelling.

LUNACY (lu′na-si), *n*. mental unsoundness.

LUNAR (′nar), *adj*. pertaining to, measured by, or influenced by, the moon.

LUNATE (′nat), *adj*. crescent-shaped.

LUNATIC (′na-tik), *n*. one who is insane.

LUNCH (lunch), *n*. a light midday meal.

LUNETTE (lu-net′), *n*. anything shaped like a half-moon.

LUNG (lung), *n*. one of two organs of respiration.

LUNGE (lunj), *n*. a sudden thrust; sudden lurch.

LUPINE (lu′pin), *n*. a plant : *adj*. (lu′pin), pertaining to a wolf.

LURCH (lerch), *n*. a sudden roll to one side, as of a ship; tendency; a difficult position.

LURE (lur), *v.t*. to allure : *n*. bait.

LURID (lu′rid), *adj*. ghastly; pale; gloomy; sensational.

LURK (lerk), *v.i.* to lie in wait.

LUSCIOUS (lush'us), *adj.* delightful to the taste or sense.

LUSH (lush), *adj.* rich and juicy.

LUSTFUL (lust'fool), *adj.* sensual; robust.

LUSTILY (lus'ti-li), *adv.* in a lusty manner.

LUSTRE (lus'ter), *n.* brightness; splendour; renown.

LUSTROUS ('trus), *adj.* having a lustre.

LUSTY (lus'ti), *adj.* robust and vigorous; healthy.

LUTE (lut), *n.* a stringed musical instrument of the guitar family.

LUTHERAN (lu'ther-an), *adj.* pertaining to Luther.

LUTHERANISM (-iz), *n.* the teaching of the Lutheran Church.

LUXE (luks), *n.* superior quality; usually with *de* (of).

LUXURIANCE (lug-zhu'ri-ans), *n.* excessive abundance.

LUXURIANT ('ri-ant), *adj.* superabundant; superfluous.

LUXURIATE ('ri-at), *v.i.* to live luxuriously.

LUXURIOUS ('ri-us), *adj.* pertaining to luxury; indulging in luxury.

LUXURY (luk'shu-ri), *n.* extravagant indulgence in the pleasures of the senses, dress, etc.; a dainty.

LY, a suffix meaning *like*, or *pertaining to*, as woman*ly*, etc.

LYCEUM (li-se'um), *n.* a literary seminary, association or academy.

LYE (li), *n.* an alkaline wood ash solution.

LYNCH (linch), *v.t.* to judge and punish by lynch-law.

LYNCH-LAW ('law), *n.* summary punishment by individuals without legal rights.

LYNX (lingks), *n.* a fierce cat-like animal noted for its keen sight.

LYRE (lir), *n.* a musical instrument of the harp kind.

LYRIC POETRY (po'et-ri), poetry expressive of the emotions.

LYSSA (lis'a), *n.* hydrophobia.

M

M, m (em), *n.* the thirteenth letter of the English alphabet.

M, m, *n.* an abbreviation.

M, *n.* a Roman numeral denoting 1,000; with a bar (M̄), 1,000,000.

M.A. *abbr.* Master of Arts degree.

MA (mah), *abbr.* for mamma.

MACADAMIZE (mak-ad'am-iz), *v.t.* to cover (a road) with small broken stone, to form a smooth hard surface.

MACARONI (-a-ro'ni), *n.* a paste composed chiefly of fine flour and made into long, thin tubes.

MACAROON (-roon'), *n.* a small cake made of flour, eggs, almonds, sugar.

MACE (mas), *n.* a massive staff; second covering of nutmeg.

MACERATE (mas'er-at), *v.t.* to soften the parts by steeping in a fluid.

MACHINATION (mak-i-n'shun), *n.* a plot; artifice.

MACHINE (ma-shen'), *n.* any contrivance to increase and regulate motive power; an engine; a political organization.

MACHINERY ('er-i), *n.* machines collectively; parts of a machine.

MACHINIST ('ist), *n.* one skilled in the principles of machinery.

MACKEREL (mak'er-el), *n.* an edible marine fish.

MACKINTOSH (mak'in-tosh), *n.* an india-rubber waterproof overcoat.

MACROCOSM (mak'ro-kozm), *n.* the universe.

MAD (mad), *adj.* insane; furious with rage.

MADAM ('am), *n.* a complimentary title for a lady.

MADCAP ('kap), *n.* a wild, thoughtless, eccentric person.

MADDEN ('n), *v.t.* to make mad or furious.

MADE (mad), *adj.* artificially produced or formed.

MADEMOISELLE (mad-mwa-zel'), *n.* in France, a title of courtesy given to a young lady.

MADRIGAL ('ri-gal), *n.* a pastoral

poem ; a part song unaccompanied by music.

MAELSTROM (mal'strom), *n.* a celebrated whirlpool on the Norwegian coast ; hence [m-], a destructive influence.

MAFIA (ma'fi-a), *n.* a secret order in Sicily.

MAGAZINE (mag-a-zen'), *n.* a warehouse ; chamber in a gun ; a literary periodical.

MAGENTA (ma-jen'ta), *n.* a red dye.

MAGGOT (mag'ot), *n.* the footless larva of a fly.

MAGIC (maj'ik), *n.* the pretended art of working by the power or assistance of the supernatural.

MAGICIAN (ma-jish'an), *n.* one skilled in magic.

MAGISTERIAL (maj-is-te'ri-al), *adj.* pertaining to a master or magistrate.

MAGISTRATE ('is-trat), *n.* a civil officer with certain judicial and executive power.

MAGNA CARTA (mag'na kar'ta), *n.* the Great Charter, forming the basis of civil liberty, granted by King John of England, 1215.

MAGNANIMITY (-na-nim'i-ti), *n.* greatness of mind ; nobility.

MAGNANIMOUS (-nan'i-mus), *adj.* generous ; courageous ; heroic.

MAGNATE ('nat), *n.* a person of distinction ; nobleman.

MAGNET ('net), *n.* the lode-stone ; a magnetized steel bar.

MAGNETIC ('ik), *adj.* pertaining to magnetism ; possessing personal attractive power.

MAGNETISM ('net-izm), *n.* that property possessed by various bodies. as iron or steel, of attracting or repelling similar substances according to certain physical laws.

MAGNETIZE ('net-iz), *v.t.* to communicate magnetic properties to.

MAGNETO-, a prefix meaning pertaining to, or caused by, *magnetism.*

MAGNIFICENCE (-nif'i-sens), *n.* grandeur ; splendour ; pomp.

MAGNIFICENT ('i-sent), *adj.* splendid ; sublime.

MAGNIFY ('ni-fi), *v.t.* to make great or greater.

MAGNILOQUENT (-nil'o-kwent), *adj.* pompous in style or speech ; bombastic.

MAGNITUDE ('ni-tud), *n.* comparative size or bulk ; importance.

MAGNOLIA (-no'li-a), *n.* a genus of trees producing beautiful pink flowers.

MAGPIE ('pi), *n.* a chattering bird of the crow family.

MAGUEY ('wa, ma-ga'e), *n.* the century plant.

MAHOGANY (ma-hog'a-ni), *n.* a tree of tropical America yielding a dark reddish-brown wood.

MAHOUT (ma-hout'), *n.* an elephant driver or keeper.

MAID (mad), *n.* a young unmarried woman ; virgin ; a servant.

MAIDEN ('en), *n.* a virgin ; girl : *adj.* pure ; innocent ; unsullied.

MAIL (mal), *n.* defensive body armour ; government system for conveying letters, etc.

MAILABLE ('a-bl), *adj.* admissible by post.

MAILED (mald), *adj.* clad in mail ; posted.

MAIL-CHUTE (mal'shoot), *n.* a vertical mail tube.

MAIL-ORDER (mal'or'der), *n.* a purchase-order received by mail.

MAIM (mam), *v.t.* to cripple or mutilate.

MAIN (man), *adj.* chief ; principal.

MAINTAIN (-tan'), *v.t.* to support ; sustain ; defend ; vindicate.

MAINTENANCE ('te-nans), *n.* sustenance ; support ; indication ; champerty.

MAIZE (maz), *n.* Indian corn.

MAJESTIC (ma-jes'tik), *adj.* having dignity of person or mien ; stately ; noble.

MAJESTY (maj'es-ti), *n.* sovereignty ; grandeur ; nobility.

MAJOLICA (ma-jol'i-ka), *n.* a fine soft enamelled kind of pottery.

MAJOR (ma'jer), *adj.* greater ; greater by a semitone : *n.* a military officer next in rank above a captain.

MAJOR-GENERAL (-jen'er-al), *n.* an officer next in rank below a lieutenant-general.

MAJORITY (ma-jor'i-ti), *n.* greater number ; full legal age (21).

MAKE (mak), *v.t.* to create ; fashion ; fabricate ; compose ; produce or effect ; acquire ; incur.

MAKESHIFT (mak'shift), *n.* a temporary expedient.

MAKE-UP ('up), *n.* the general composition of anything ; artificial preparation.

MAL-, a prefix signifying *ill, evil.*

MALADY (mal'a-di), *n.* a disease, mental or physical.

MALAPROPISM ('a-prop-izm), *n.* a grotesque misuse of fine words : from Mrs. Malaprop in Sheridan's " The Rivals."

MALAPROPOS (-ap-ro-po'), *adj.* unseasonable ; inopportune ; inartistic.

MALARIA (ma-la'ri-a), *n.* noxious exhalation from marshy land, producing fevers, etc.

MALCONTENT (mal'kon-tent), *adj.* discontented.

MALE (mal), *adj.* pertaining to the sex that begets young ; not female ; a man or boy.

MALEDICTION (mal-e-dik'shun), *n.* denunciation ; execration ; curse.

MALEFACTOR ('e-fak-ter), *n.* an evil doer ; criminal.

MALEVOLENCE (mal-ev'o-lens), *n.* spitefulness ; ill-will.

MALFEASANCE (mal-fe'zans), *n.* an illegal act or deed.

MALFORMATION (-for-ma'shun), *n.* faulty or abnormal structure of an organism.

MALICE (mal'is), *n.* evil intention to injure others ; deliberate mischief.

MALICIOUS (ma-lish'us), *adj.* ill-will or spite ; prompted by hatred.

MALIGN (-lin), *v.t.* to speak evil of ; slander : *adj.* hurtful.

MALIGNANT ('nant), *adj.* malicious ; pernicious ; virulent.

MALIGNER (-lin'er), *n.* one who maligns.

MALIGNITY (-lig'ni-ti), *n.* malignant ; malice ; virulence.

MALL (mawl), *n.* a large heavy wooden mallet or beetle ; a public walk.

MALLARD (mal'ard), *n.* a wild duck.

MALLEABLE ('e-a-bl), *adj.* capable of being extended by hammering or rolling.

MALLET ('et), *n.* a wooden hammer.

MALLEUS ('e-us), *n.* one of the three small auditory bones of the ear.

MALNUTRITION (mal-nu-trish'un), *n.* a state of health in which the food is not properly assimilated.

MALPRACTICE (mal-prak'tis), *n.* professional misconduct ; illegal or immoral practice.

MALT (mawlt), *n.* barley, or other grain, steeped in water, fermented, and kiln dried for brewing.

MALTREAT (mal-tret'), *v.t.* to treat ill or roughly.

MAMMA (ma'ma), *n.* children's name for mother.

MAMMAL (mam'al), *n.* one of the Mammalia.

MAMMALIA (ma-ma'li-a), *n. pl.* the highest class of the Vertebrata.

MAMMON (mam'un), *n.* riches ; worldly gain.

MAMMOTH ('oth), *n.* one of an extinct species of huge elephants : *adj.* gigantic.

MAN (man), *n.* an adult male of the human species ; mankind.

MANACLE ('a-kl), *n.* a handcuff.

MANAGE ('aj), *v.t.* to conduct or carry on ; govern ; wield.

MANAGEABLE ('aj-a-bl), *adj.* easy to be managed ; docile.

MANAGEMENT ('aj-ment), *n.* the act of managing ; skill in directing.

MANAGER ('a-jer), *n.* one who directs or conducts anything.

MANAKIN ('a-kin), *n.* species of bird.

MANATEE (-a-te'), *n.* the sea-cow.

MANDAMUS (-da'mus), *n.* [Latin, we command], writ issued by superior court.

MANDARIN (-da-ren'), *n.* in China, an official or magistrate.

MANDATARY ('da-ta-ri), **MANDATORY** (-to-ri), *n.* a person to whom a mandate is given.

MANDATE ('dat), *n.* an order ; command.

MANDATORY ('da-to-ri), *adj.* containing a mandate ; obligatory.

MANDIBLE ('di-bl), *n.* the jaw.

MANDOLIN ('do-lin), *n.* a musical instrument.

MANDRAKE ('drak), *n.* a plant of the night-shade family.

MANDRILL ('dril), *n.* the blue-faced baboon of West Africa.

MANE (man), *n.* the long hair on the neck of certain quadrupeds.

MANEGE (ma-nazh'), *n.* the art of horsemanship.

MANES (ma'nez), *n.pl.* the shades of the departed.

MANŒUVRE (ma-noo'ver), *n.* adroit management or operation in military or naval affairs ; stratagem.

MANFUL (man'fool), *adj.* courageous.

MANGE (manj), *n.* a cutaneous disease of dogs, cattle, etc.

MANGER (man'jer), *n.* a feeding trough for horses or cattle.

MANGLE (mang'gl), *v.t.* to lacerate ; mutilate ; hack : *n.* a machine for smoothing cloth.

MANGLER (mang'gler), *n.* a meat-chopping machine.

MANGROVE (mang'grov), *n.* one of a family of trees and shrubs.

MANGY (man'ji), *adj.* affected with the mange.

MANIA (ma'ni-a), *n.* violent insanity ; excessive desire for anything.

MANIAC ('ni-ak), *adj.* affected with mania : *n.* a madman.

MANICURE (man'i-kur), *n.* the care of hands, nails, etc.

MANIFEST ('i-fest), *adj.* clear ; plain ; apparent : *n.* the invoice of a cargo.

MANIFESTATION (-ta'shun), *n.* exhibition ; revelation.

MANIFESTO (-fes'to), *n.* a public declaration.

MANIFOLD ('i-fold), *adj.* numerous ; multiplied ; complicated.

MANIKIN ('i-kin), *n.* a dwarf ; an artist's or dressmaker's model.

MANILA, MANILLA (ma-nil'a), *n.* a kind of cigar ; a hemp used for ropes, matting, paper, etc.

MANIPULATE (ma-nip'u-lat), *v.t.* to operate or work by means of the hands ; treat ; control the action of by management ; falsify.

MANIPULATION (-la'shun), *n.* manual dexterity ; falsification.

MANIPULATOR ('u-la-ter), *n.* one who manipulates.

MANLINESS ('li-nes), *n.* the state or quality of being manly.

MANLY ('li), *adj.* courageous ; noble ; dignified ; resolute.

MANNA ('a), *n.* food miraculously supplied to the Israelites in the wilderness.

MANNER ('er), *n.* method ; habit ; custom ; sort ; mien ; aspect.

MANNERLY (-li), *adj.* polite ; respectful.

MANNISH ('ish), *adj.* masculine.

MANOR (man'er), *n.* the district over which a feudal lord held authority.

MANSION (man'shun), *n.* a large dwelling-house.

MANSLAUGHTER ('slaw-ter), *n.* the unlawful killing of a human being, without malice or premeditation.

MANTEL ('tel), *n.* a narrow ornamental slab above a fireplace.

MANTLE (man'tl), *n.* a loose cloak or cape ; a sheath.

MANUAL ('u-al), *adj.* pertaining to the hands : *n.* a handy compendium.

MANUFACTORY (-fak'to-ri), *n.* the place where goods are manufactured.

MANUFACTURE ('tur), *v.t.* to produce artificially.

MANURE (ma-nur'), *n.* any fertilizing substance.

MANUS (ma'nus), *n.* the hand.

MANUSCRIPT (man'u-skript), *n.* a book or paper written by hand, or typewriter.

MANY (men'i), *adj.* numerous.

MAP (map), *n.* a representation of the earth or some portion of it on a plane surface.

MAPLE (ma'pl), *n.* a deciduous tree of many varieties.

MAR (mar), *v.t.* to disfigure ; injure ; damage.

MARATHON (mar'a-thon), *n.* in athletics, a long distance race of 26 miles, 385 yards.

MARAUD (ma-rawd'), *v.i.* to rove in search of plunder.

MARBLE (mar'bl), *n.* a hard limestone of various colours, capable of taking a fine polish.

MARCH (march), *n.* third month of the year.

MARCH (march), *n.* a regular, measured walk, especially of soldiers; steady onward movement; a musical composition.

MARCONIGRAM (mar-ko'ni-gram), *n.* a message sent by Marconi's system of wireless telegraphy.

MARE (mar), *n.* the female horse.

MARE'S-NEST (marz'nest), *n.* some fancied discovery which proves to be false.

MARGARINE (mar'ga-ren), *n.* artificial, or imitation, butter.

MARGIN (jin), *n.* border; the part of a page at the edge; latitude.

MARGINALIA (-ji-na'li-a), *n. pl.* marginal notes.

MARIGOLD (mar'i-gold), *n.* a plant of the aster family.

MARINE (ma-ren'), *adj.* pertaining to, living in, or formed by, the sea; naval : *n.* collective shipping of a country.

MARINER (mar'i-ner), *n.* a sailor.

MARIONETTE (mar-i-o-net'), *n.* a puppet moved by strings.

MARITAL ('i-tal), *adj.* pertaining to marriage.

MARITIME ('i-tim), *adj.* pertaining to the sea; naval.

MARK (mark), *n.* a visible sign by which anything is known.

MARKEDLY ('ed-li), *adv.* distinctly.

MARKET (mar'ket), *n.* a public place for the sale or purchase of commodities; rate or price.

MARKSMAN (marks'man), *n.* one skilful in shooting.

MARL (marl), *n.* calcareous earth.

MARLINE (mar'lin), *n.* light tarred cord for binding the ends of ropes.

MARLINE-SPIKE (mar'lin-spik), *n.* a pointed piece of iron used for splicing ropes.

MARMALADE ('ma-lad), *n.* a preserve made of oranges, etc.

MARMOSET ('mo-zet), *n.* one of a species of small S.A. monkeys.

MARMOT ('mot), *n.* a thick-bodied, short-legged rodent with coarse fur and bushy tail.

MAROON (ma-roon'), *n.* formerly a fugitive slave in the West Indies; one who is marooned; dull red colour : *v.t.* to abandon on a desert island.

MARPLOT (mar'plot), *n.* one who frustrates some plan by his officious interference.

MARQUETRY (mar'ket-ri), *n.* inlaid work.

MARRIAGE (mar'ij), *n.* the act of legally uniting a man and woman in wedlock.

MARRIAGEABLE ('ij-a-bl), *adj.* fit, or of an age, to be married.

MARRIED ('id), *p.adj.* united in wedlock; conjugal.

MARROW ('o), *n.* the medulla or oily tissue which fills the cavities of bones.

MARRY ('i), *v.t.* to wed; to join in wedlock.

MARS (marz), *n.* the Roman god of war; one of the planets.

MARSEILLAISE (mar-sa-yaz'), *n.* national anthem of France.

MARSH (marsh), *n.* swampy land.

MARSHAL (mar'shal), *n.* an official of high rank who superintends and regulates state ceremonies; in the French army, the highest military officer; a sheriff : *v.t.* to arrange or dispose in order.

MARSHMALLOW (-mal'o), *n.* a plant; a confection.

MARSHY ('shi), *adj.* swampy.

MART (mart), *n.* a market.

MARTEN ('ten), *n.* a small animal of the weasel kind.

MARTIAL ('shal), *adj.* pertaining to war; military.

MARTIAL LAW (law), a code of regulations enforced by the military power and applicable to civilians in time of war, insurrection, etc.

MARTIAN (mar'shan), *n.* a supposititious inhabitant of Mars.

MARTIN ('tin), *n.* a bird allied to the swallow.

MARTINET (-ti-net'), *n.* a strict disciplinarian.

MARTINGALE ('tin-gal), *n.* a broad strap passing from the nose-band to the girth of a horse.

MARTYR ('ter), *n.* one who testifies

by his death to his faith or principles ; one who suffers acutely.

MARVEL ('vel), *n.* something extraordinary ; a prodigy.

MARVELLOUS (-us), *adj.* exciting wonder ; incredible.

MASCOT (mas'kot), *n.* a person or thing supposed to bring good fortune.

MASCULINE ('ku-lin), *adj.* pertaining to, having the qualities of, or suitable for, a man ; manly ; powerful ; robust.

MASH (mash), *n.* a soft or pulpy mass.

MASK (mask), *n.* a cover or partial cover to conceal the face ; a masquerade.

MASON (ma'sn), *n.* a builder in stone ; [M-], a Freemason.

MASONIC (-son'ik), *adj.* pertaining to Freemasons.

MASONRY ('sn-ri), *n.* the art or occupation of a mason ; that which is built by masons ; [M-], Freemasonry.

MASQUERADE (mas-ker-ad'), *n.* a ball or festive gathering where masks are worn ; a disguise.

MASS (mas), *n.* a large quantity ; lump ; body of things collectively ; ponderance ; density : *pl.* common people (with *the*).

MASS (mas), *n.* in the R.C. Church, the celebration of the Eucharist.

MASSACRE (mas'a-ker), *n.* indiscriminate slaughter.

MASSAGE (ma-sazh'), *n.* [French], a method of treatment by rubbing or kneading the body.

MASSIVE (mas'iv), *adj.* weighty ; heavy ; bulky.

MASSY ('i), *adj.* massive.

MASTER (mas'ter), *n.* one who rules or commands others ; an expert commander of a merchant vessel.

MASTERY (-i), *n.* dominion.

MASTICATE ('ti-kat), *v.t.* to grind with the teeth ; chew.

MASTICATION (-ka'shun), *n.* masticating ; chewing.

MASTIFF (mas'tif), *n.* a large, powerful variety of dogs.

MASTODON (mas'to-don), *n.* one of an extinct genus of mammals.

MASTOID ('toid), *adj.* breast-like.

MATCH (mach), *n.* anything that readily ignites ; a lucifer ; an equal ; game or contest ; marriage.

MATCHMAKER ('mak'er), *n.* one who seeks to arrange marriages ; one who makes matches for igniting.

MATE (mat), *n.* a companion ; an equal ; an officer in the merchant service ranking below the captain.

MATER (ma'ter), *n.* [Latin], a mother ; one of the two membranes covering the brain.

MATERIAL (ma-te'ri-al), *adj.* consisting of matter ; not spiritual ; corporeal ; essential.

MATERIALISM (-izm), *n.* the doctrine that all spiritual phenomena are the result of organized matter.

MATERIALIZE (-iz), *v.t.* to invest with material characteristics.

MATERIA MEDICA *n.* (ma-te'ri-a med'i-ka), the science which treats of the substances used in medicine.

MATERNAL (-ter'nal), *adj.* motherly.

MATERNITY ('ni-ti), *n.* the character or relationship of a mother.

MATHEMATICAL (math-e-mat'i-)kal), *adj.* pertaining to mathematics ; theoretically precise.

MATHEMATICIAN (-ma-tish'an), *n.* one skilled in mathematics.

MATHEMATICS (-mat'iks), *n.* the science of numbers and space.

MATIN (mat'in), *adj.* pertaining to the morning or to matins : *n.* morning prayer.

MATINEE (-i-na'), *n.* a reception, or musical or dramatic performance held in the daytime.

MATRICIDAL (mat'ri-si-dal), *adj.* pertaining to matricide.

MATRICIDE ('ri-sid), *n.* the murder of a mother by a son or daughter.

MATRICULATE (ma-trik'u-lat), *v.t.* to admit to the membership of a college or university.

MATRIMONIAL (mat-ri-mo'ni-al), *adj.* pertaining to marriage ; nuptial.

MATRIMONY ('ri-mo-ni), *n.* marriage.

MATRIX (ma'triks), *n.* [*pl.* matrices (mat'ri-sez)], the womb ; a mould ; a copper plate for moulding type : *pl.*

(in dyeing) the 5 colours, black, white, blue, red and yellow, from which all other colours are formed.

MATRON (ma'tron), *n.* a married woman; lady superintendent of an institution.

MATTED ('ed), *adj.* covered with a mat; closely tangled together.

MATTER ('er), *n.* that which occupies space, and is perceptible by the senses; body; substance; thing of importance.

MATTRESS ('res), *n.* a quilted bed stuffed with hair, etc.

MATURE (ma-tur'), *adj.* ripe; full-grown: *v.i.* to become ripe.

MATURITY ('i-ti), *n.* ripeness; full development.

MATUTINAL (mat-u-ti'nal), *adj.* pertaining to the morning.

MATZOTH (mat'soth), *n.pl.* unleavened bread eaten by the Jews.

MAUDLIN ('lin), *adj.* weakly and foolishly sentimental.

MAUL (mawl), *n.* a large wooden hammer; to maltreat severely.

MAUSOLEUM (maw-so-le'um), *n.* a stately tomb or monument.

MAUVE (mov), *n.* a soft lilac or purple colour.

MAVERICK (mav'er-ik), *n.* in western U.S. an unbranded animal.

MAVIS (ma'vis), *n.* the song-thrush.

MAW (maw), *n.* the stomach of animals; the craw of a bird.

MAWKISH (mawk'ish), *adj.* loathsome; affectedly sentimental.

MAXILLARY (mak'si-la-ri), *adj.* pertaining to the jaw or jaw-bone.

MAXIM ('sim), *n.* an established principle or truth; proverb.

MAXIMUM ('si-mum), *n.* the greatest number, quantity, or degree, attainable.

MAY (ma), *n.* the fifth month of the year; springtime.

MAYBE (ma'be), *adv.* perhaps.

MAYHEM (ma'hem), *n.* an unlawful attack on a person which results in mutilation or maiming.

MAYONNAISE (ma-o-naz'), *n.* [French], a condiment or salad dressing.

MAYOR (ma'er), *n.* the chief magistrate of a city or borough.

MAYORALTY (-al-ti), *n.* the office, or term of office, of a mayor.

MAYPOLE ('pol), *n.* a pole around which May festivities are held.

MAZE (maz), *n.* bewilderment.

ME (me), *pron.* myself; the person speaking; objective case of *I*.

MEAD (med), *n.* a fermented liquor; a meadow.

MEADOW (med'o), *n.* a tract of rich pasture land.

MEAGRE (me'ger), *adj.* thin; scanty; poor; barren; lean.

MEAL (mel), *n.* edible ground grain; a repast.

MEALY-MOUTHED (mel'i-mouthd), *adj.* unwilling to tell the truth in plain words.

MEAN (men), *adj.* wanting in dignity or honour; vulgar; inferior; sordid; stingy; middle; not excessive: *pl.* resources: *v.t.* to have in the mind or intention.

MEANDER (me-an'der), *v.t.* to wind or flow round.

MEANING (men'ing), *n.* intention; sense.

MEASLES (me'zlz), *n.* an infectious disease characterized by fever and small red spots on the skin.

MEASURABLE (mezh'er-a-bl), *adj.* capable of being measured.

MEASURE ('er), *n.* the standard by which the volume or extent of anything is compared; an instrument for measuring; musical time; metre.

MEAT (met), *n.* animal food; victuals; that which nourishes.

MECHANIC (me-kan'ik), *n.* a skilled workman: *pl.* the science of the laws of matter and motion.

MECHANICAL ('i-kal), *adj.* pertaining to the principles of mechanics.

MECHANICIAN (mek-a-nish'an), *n.* one skilled in mechanics.

MECHANICS ('iks), *n.* the science which treats of the actions of forces upon bodies in producing either motion or rest.

MECHANISM (mek'a-nizm), *n.* parts of a machine.

MEDAL (med'al), *n.* a coin-shaped piece of metal impressed with a device or inscription to commemor- ate some event, distinguished person, etc.

MEDDLE (med'l), *v.i.* to interpose or interfere officiously.

MEDDLER ('ler), *n.* an officious person ; busybody.

MEDIÆVAL, same as medieval.

MEDIAN (me'di-an), *adj.* pertaining to the middle of anything.

MEDIATE (-at), *v.i.* to interpose as a mutual friend.

MEDIATOR (di-a-ter), *n.* one who mediates ; an intercessor.

MEDICAL (med'i-kal), *adj.* pertaining to, or connected with, medicine.

MEDICAMENT (me-dik'a-ment), *n.* a medicine or healing application.

MEDICATE (med'i-kat), *v.t.* to impregnate or tincture with anything medicinal.

MEDICINAL (me-dis'i-nal), *adj.* having the properties of, or used in, medicine.

MEDICINE (med'i-sin), *n.* the science which relates to treatment and alleviation of disease.

MEDIEVAL (me-di-e'val), *adj.* pertaining to, or characteristic of, the Middle Ages (8th-15th centuries A.D.).

MEDIOCRE (me'di-o-ker), *adj.* of medium quality ; ordinary ability.

MEDIOCRITY (-ok'ri-ti), *adj.* of moderate degrees ; a person of ordinary ability.

MEDITATE (med'i-tat), *v.i.* to muse or ponder.

MEDITATION (-ta'shun), *n.* deep thought.

MEDIUM (me'di-um), *n.* [*pl.* media (-a)], a mean ; anything intervening ; agency ; ordinary quality.

MEDLEY (med'li), *n.* mixture or confused mass of different ingredients ; a musical performance of several pieces abruptly changing from one to the other.

MEED (med), *n.* recompense ; reward.

MEEK (mek), *adj.* gentle ; submissive.

MEER (mer), *n.* a boundary.

MEERSCHAUM ('shum), *n.* a clay-like silicate of magnesia ; a tobacco pipe of this material.

MEET (met), *v.t.* to come up to ; confront ; encounter ; receive ; satisfy ; come upon ; answer.

MEETING ('ing), *n.* an assembling or coming together ; junction.

MEGAPHONE (meg'a-fon), *n.* a device for magnifying the volume of sound.

MEGRIM (me'grim), *n.* a sick or neuralgic headache.

MELANCHOLIA (mel-an-ko'li-a), *n.* a form of insanity characterized by great depression of spirits.

MELANCHOLY ('an-kol-i), *n.* great depression of spirits.

MELEE (ma-la'), *n.* a hand-to-hand conflict ; scuffle ; affray.

MELIORATE (mel'yo-rat), *v.t.* to improve or make better ; ameliorate.

MELLIFLUENT (me-lif'lu-ent), *adj.* smooth ; sweetly flowing.

MELLOW ('o), *adj.* fully ripe.

MELODEON (me-lo'de-on), *n.* a small reed organ.

MELODIOUS ('di-us), *adj.* full of melody ; musical.

MELODRAMA (mel-o-dra'ma), *n.* a play characterized by highly sensational incidents.

MELODY ('o-di), *n.* the arrangements of different musical sounds for a single voice or instrument.

MELON ('un), *n.* the juicy fruit of a plant of the cucumber family.

MELT (melt), *v.t.* & *v.i.* to change from a solid to a liquid state ; dissolve.

MEMBER (mem'ber), *n.* a limb or organ ; essential part of anything.

MEMBRANE ('bran), *n.* a thin fold or layer of tissue forming the covering of some part or organ.

MEMBRANOUS ('bra-nus), *adj.* pertaining to membranes.

MEMENTO (me-men'to), *n.* a souvenir ; memorial.

MEMOIR (mem'war), *n.* a history written from personal experience and knowledge ; a biography or autobiography.

MEMORABLE ('o-ra-bl), *adj.* worthy of remembrance ; remarkable ; notable.

MEMORANDUM (-o-ran'dum), *n.*

[*pl.* memoranda ('da)], a note to assist the memory ; summary or outline.

MEMORIAL (me-mo'ri-al), *adj.* commemorative : *n.* an informal diplomatic paper.

MEMORIAL DAY (da), in the U.S. Decoration Day, May 30.

MEMORIALIZE (-iz), *v.t.* to petition by means of a memorial.

MEMORY (mem'o-ri), *n.* that faculty of the mind by which it retains the knowledge of previous occurrences, facts, thoughts, etc., and recalls them.

MENACE (men'as), *n.* a threat.

MENACINGLY ('as-ing-li), *adv.* in a threatening manner.

MENAGERIE (me-naj'er-i), *n.* a place where wild animals are kept for exhibition.

MEND (mend), *v.i.* to repair (that which is broken or worn) ; make good or better ; reform.

MENDACIOUS (men-da'shus), *adj.* given to falsehood ; false.

MENDACITY (-das'i-ti), *n.* falsehood ; habitual lying.

MENDICANCY ('di-kan-si), *n.* begging ; also mendicity.

MENDICANT (-kant), *adj.* practising begging : *n.* a beggar.

MENHADEN (-ha'dn), *n.* a marine fish.

MENIAL (me'ni-al), men'yal), *adj.* mean ; servile.

MENSTRUAL (men'stroo-al), *adj.* occurring monthly.

MENSURABLE ('shu-ra-bl), *adj.* measurable.

MENSURATION (-ra'shun), *n.* the act or process of taking the measure or dimensions of anything.

MENTAL ('tal), *adj.* pertaining to the mind ; intellectual.

MENTION ('shun), *n.* a brief notice ; casual remark ; hint.

MENTOR ('ter), *n.* a wise and faithful counsellor.

MENU ('u), *n.* a bill of fare.

MERCANTILE (mer'kan-til), *adj.* commercial.

MERCENARY ('se-na-ri), *n.* a soldier hired into foreign service.

MERCHANDISE ('chan-diz), *n.* goods bought and sold.

MERCHANT ('chant), *n.* one who traffics or carries on trade.

MERCIFUL ('si-fool), *adj.* tenderhearted ; compassionate.

MERCILESS (-les), *adj.* unfeeling ; cruel.

MERCURIAL (-ke'ri-al), *adj.* active ; volatile ; fickle.

MERCURY ('ku-ri), *n.* the nearest known planet to the son ; quicksilver.

MERCY ('si), *n.* clemency ; forbearance ; compassion ; beneficence.

MERE (mer), *adj.* such and no more ; simple ; entire ; absolute: *n.* a lake.

MERETRICIOUS (mer-e-trish'us), *adj.* lustful ; tawdry.

MERGE (merj), *v.t.* to absorb or swallow up.

MERGER (mer'jer), *n.* the placing of the operations of two or more competing interests under the control of a single body.

MERIDIAN (me-rid'i-an), *n.* midday ; noon.

MERINGUE (me-rang'), *n.* whites of eggs and powdered sugar beaten to a froth and used for icing on cakes, puddings, pies, etc.

MERINO (me-re'no), *n.* one of a breed of sheep with a fine wool.

MERIT (mer'it), *n.* excellence ; worth : *pl.* essential circumstances.

MERITORIOUS (-i-to'ri-us), *adj.* having merit ; deserving of reward or praise.

MERMAID (mer'mad), *n.* a fabled marine creature.

MERRIMENT ('i-ment), *n.* mirth ; fun ; frolic ; gaiety.

MERRY ('i), *adj.* full of mirth ; gay ; sportive ; jovial ; pleasant.

MERRY-ANDREW (-an'droo), *n.* a buffoon.

MESA (ma'sa), *n.* elevated table-land.

MESALLIANCE (ma-sal-yangs'), *n.* [French], marriage with one of lower social position.

MESH (mesh), *n.* an opening or interstice of a net : *v.t.* to ensnare.

MESMERISM ('mer-izm), *n.* the act of inducing an abnormal state of the mental and nervous system in which the thoughts and actions of the patient are controlled by the will of the experimenter.

MESS (mes), *n.* a state of dirt, or confusion : *v.i.* to eat together : *v.t.* to furnish with food ; to soil ; befoul.

MESSAGE ('aj), *n.* a communication ; an official communication.

MESSENGER ('en-jer), *n.* one who conveys a message.

MESSIAH (me-si'a), **MESIAS** (-si'as), *n.* Christ, the Anointed One.

MESSIEURS (mes'yerz), *n. pl.* [French], Sirs : abbreviated to Messrs.

MESTIZO (-te'zo), *n.* a Mexican of mixed blood.

MET-, META-, METH-, combining forms signifying *between, over, after, duplicate, resembling, change.*

METABOLISM (me-tab'o-lizm), *n.* the continuous process by which living cells or tissues undergo chemical changes.

METAL (met'al), *n.* an elementary substance having certain physical characteristics.

METALLIC (me-tal'ik), *adj.* pertaining to, or like, metal.

METALLURGIST (met'al-er-jist), *n.* one who is skilled in metallurgy.

METALLURGY (-ji), *n.* the art or process of working metals and of separating them from their ores.

METAMORPHOSE (-mor'foz), *v.t.* to change into a different form.

METAPHOR ('a-for), *n.* a figure of speech by which one word is employed for another of which it is the image.

METAPHORICALLY (-for'i-kal-i), *adv.* in metaphors.

METAPHYSICAL (-fiz'i-kal), *adj.* pertaining to metaphysics.

METAPHYSICIAN (-fi-zish'an), *n.* one who is skilled in metaphisics.

METAPHYSICS (-fiz'iks), *n.* mental philosophy ; the science of first principles.

METE (met), *v.t.* to allot ; distribute.

METEOR (me'te-or), *n.* a transient luminous body in the sky.

METEORIC (or'ik), *adj.* transitorily brilliant.

METEORITE ('te-or-it), *n.* a stone or metallic body which has fallen from space.

METEOROLOGY (-ol'o-ji), *n.* the science of the atmosphere, especially weather and climate.

METER (me'ter), *n.* an instrument for registering automatically ; the amount measured by it.

METRE (me'ter), *n.* a rhythmic arrangement of syllables in verse ; unit of length in decimal system = 39.37 inches.

METHINKS (me-thinks'), *v.i.* it appears or seems to me.

METHOD (meth'od), *n.* system ; order ; classification.

METHODICAL ('i-kal), *adj.* characterized by method ; systematic.

METHODICALLY (-li), *adv.* in a methodical manner.

METHODIST ('o-dist), *n.* one of a sect of Protestant Christians founded by John Wesley.

METHODIZE ('o-diz), *v.t.* to reduce to method ; systematize.

METHYL (meth'il), *n.* the hydrocarbon radical of methyl alcohol.

METHYL ALCOHOL (al'ko-hol), a colourless liquid commonly known as *wood alcohol :* it is highly poisonous.

METICULOUS (me-tik'u-lus), *adj.* unduly cautious ; excessively timid.

METIER (ma-tya'), *n.* [French], calling, profession, or trade.

METONYMY (me-ton'i-mi), *n.* a figure of speech in which one word is used for another that it suggests.

METRIC (met'rik), *adj.* pertaining to the decimal system of weights and measures.

METROLOGY (me-trol'o-ji), *n.* the science of weights and measures.

METRONOME ('ro-nom), *n.* an instrument which beats musical time.

METROPOLIS (me-trop'o-lis), *n.* the capital or chief city of a kingdom or country.

METROPOLITAN (-tro-pol'i-tan), *adj.* pertaining to a capital city : *n.* a bishop ; an archbishop.

METTLE (met'l), *n.* spirit ; fortitude ; temperament.

MEW (mu), *n.* the cry of a cat.

MEZZANINE (mez'a-nen), *n.* a low intermediate story between two higher ones.

MEZZO (med'zo), *adj.* [Italian], moderate.

MEZZO-SOPRANO (-so-pra'no), *n.* a voice between a soprano and contralto.

MICA (mi'ka), *n.* a mineral divisible into thin transparent plates.

MICE, *pl.* of mouse.

MICROBE (mi-krob), *n.* a minute microscopical organism found in the blood of animals, especially those suffering from disease.

MICROMETER (-krom'e-ter), *n.* an instrument for measuring minute distances, or apparent diameters.

MICROMILLIMETRE (-kro-mil'i-me-ter), *n.* the 1,000,000th part of a metre.

MICROPHONE ('kro-fon), *n.* an instrument for intensifying very minute sounds.

MICROSCOPE ('kro-skop), *n.* an optical instrument for magnifying minute objects.

MICROSCOPIC (-skop'ik), *adj.* very small or minute.

MICROVOLT ('kro-volt), *n.* the 1,000,000th part of a volt.

MID (mid), *adj.* middle : *n.* a midshipman.

MIDDLE ('l), *adj.* equally distant from the extreme : *n.* central part; the waist.

MIDDLE AGES (aj'ez), the period between the 8th and 15th centuries A.D.

MIDDLEMAN (-man), *n.* a broker.

MIDDLING ('ling), *adj.* of middle rank, size, or quality; moderate : *n.pl.* the coarser part of flour.

MIDGE (mij), *n.* a gnat.

MIDNIGHT (mid'nit), *n.* 12 o'clock at night.

MIDRIFF ('rif), *n.* the diaphragm separating the cavity of the chest from the stomach.

MIDSHIPMAN ('ship-man), *n.* a junior naval officer.

MIDST (midst), *n.* the middle.

MIDWIFE (mid'wif), *n.* a woman who assists at childbirth.

MIEN (men), *n.* external appearance; air; look.

MIGHT (mit), *n.* power; strength.

MIGHTILY ('i-li), *adv.* with great power; vehemently.

MIGHTY ('i), *adj.* powerful; momentous; wonderful; huge.

MIGNONETTE (min-yun-et'), *n.* a fragrant annual with greenish-white flowers.

MIGRATORY (mi'gra-to-ri), *adj.* removing or passing from one place of abode or resort to another; roving; nomad.

MIKADO (mi-ka'do), *n.* the Japanese emperor.

MILCH (milch), *adj.* yielding milk.

MILD (mild), *adj.* gentle in temper and disposition.

MILDEW (mil'du), *n.* a disease of plants produced by fungi.

MILE (mil), *n.* the English statute mile contains 1,760 yds., the geographical or nautical mile $\frac{1}{60}$th of a degree of latitude or almost 2,026 yds.

MILEAGE ('aj), *n.* an allowance for expenses per mile; length in miles.

MILITANCY (mil'i-tan-si), *n.* warfare; militarism.

MILITANT ('i-tant), *adj.* war-like.

MILITARISM ('i-ta-rizm), *n.* military spirit or policy.

MILITARY ('i-ta-ri), *adj.* pertaining to soldiers or to arms.

MILITIA (mi-lish'a), *n.* citizens enrolled and trained for internal defence.

MILK (milk), *n.* a white fluid secreted by the mammary glands of female mammals.

MILKSOP ('sop), *n.* an effeminate weak person.

MILKY WAY (wa), *n.* a broad luminous band across the heavens, consisting of innumerable stars and nebulæ.

MILLENNIUM (mi-len'i-um), *n.* the space of 1,000 years, especially that period during which Satan will be bound and Christ will reign on earth. *Rev.* xx. 1-5.

MILLER (mil'er), *n.* one who keeps or works a flour mill; a moth.

MILLET ('et), *n.* a grass cultivated as a forage.

MILLI-, a combining form from the Latin *mille*, a thousand.

MILLIARD ('i-ard), *n.* one thousand millions ; a billion.

MILLIER (me-lya'), *n.* [French], in the metric system, a ton = 1,000,000 grams.

MILLIGRAM (mil'i-gram), *n.* the 1,000th part of a gram.

MILLILITRE ('i-le-ter), *n.* the 1,000th part of a litre.

MILLIMETRE ('li-me-ter), *n.* the 1,000th part of a metre.

MILLINER ('i-ner), *n.* one who makes women's hats, headdresses, etc.

MILLION ('yun), *n.* the number of ten hundred thousand.

MILLIONAIRE (-ar'), *n.* a person who is worth a million.

MILL POND (pond), *n.* a reservoir of water for driving a mill.

MILL RACE (ras), *n.* a current of water that drives a mill.

MILLSTONE ('ston), *n.* one of two flat cylindrical stones for grinding grain.

MILT (milt), *n.* the spleen.

MIMEOGRAPH (mim'e-o-graf), *n.* a machine for making copies of letters, etc.

MIMIC ('ik), *adj.* inclined to imitate ; imitative.

MIMICRY (-ik-ri), *n.* ludicrous imitation for sport or ridicule.

MIMOSA (mi-mo'sa), *n.* a genus of tropical trees and shrubs.

MINARET (mina-ret), *n.* a tall slender turret attached to a mosque.

MINATORY ('a-to-ri), *adj.* threatening.

MINCE (mins), *v.t.* to cut or chop into minute pieces ; extenuate or suppress.

MINCING ('sing), *adj.* affectedly elegant.

MIND (mind), *n.* the intellectual or rational faculty in man ; consciousness ; intelligence ; soul ; memory ; intention ; opinion.

MINDFUL ('fool), *adj.* bearing in mind ; observant ; attentive.

MINE (min), *pron.* belonging to me ; possessive case of *I*.

MINE (min), *n.* an excavation in the earth from which minerals, precious stones, etc., are extracted.

MINERAL (min'er-al), *n.* any inorganic body of definite chemical composition found on the surface of, or in, the earth.

MINERALOGY (-al'o-ji), *n.* the science of minerals.

MINGLE (ming'gl), *v.t.* to intermix ; join or combine ; blend.

MINIATURE (min'i-a-tur), *n.* a very small painting ; *adj.* minute.

MINIM ('im), *n.* the smallest liquid measure ; a single drop; a note in music.

MINIMIZE (-iz), *v.t.* reduce to a minimum.

MINIMUM ('i-mum), *n.* [*pl.* minima (ma)], the least quantity ; trifle.

MINING (min'ing), *p.adj.* burrowing in the earth.

MINION (min'yun), *n.* a size of type, 7 point.

MINISTER ('is-ter), *n.* ambassador ; a clergyman ; a servant : *v.t.* to supply ; administer clerical or lay service ; supply things necessary.

MINISTERIAL (-te'ri-al), *adj.* pertaining to ministry, or service.

MINISTRY ('is-tri), *n.* the service of a minister of religion ; the functions of a minister of state.

MINK (mingk), *n.* a carnivorous mammal allied to the weasel.

MINNOW (min'o), *n.* a freshwater fish of small size.

MINOR (mi'ner), *adj.* smaller ; less ; less by a semitone [music] : *n.* one of either sex who is under the age of 21.

MINORITY (mi-nor'i-ti), *n.* the smallest number ; opposed to *majority*.

MINSTREL (min'strel), *n.* in medieval times, men who travelled from place to place singing their musical compositions to the accompaniment of a harp.

MINT (mint), *n.* the place where money is coined by a government ; a plant.

MINTAGE (min'taj), *n.* coin produced in a mint ; duty paid for coining gold or silver.

MINUET ('u-et), *n.* a graceful dance ; music for such a dance.

MINUS (mi'nus), *n.* the sign (—) of subtraction.

MINUTE (-nut'), *adj.* very small ; precise : *n.* (min'it), ₆₀th part of an hour or of a degree ; an official record.

MINUTIÆ (mi-nu'shi-e), *n. pl.* smaller or minor details or particulars.

MINX (mingks), *n.* a pert girl.

MIRACLE (mir'a-kl), *n.* a supernatural occurrence or act.

MIRACULOUS (mi-rak'u-lus), *adj.* performed supernaturally ; wonderful.

MIRAGE (mi-razh'), *n.* [Fr.] an optical illusion, as of ships, land, etc., apparently seen in the air, generally inverted.

MIRE (mir), *n.* deep mud.

MIRROR (mir'er), *n.* a looking-glass.

MIRTH (merth), *n.* gaiety ; social merriment ; hilarity ; jollity.

MIRY (mir'i), *adj.* abounding in, or covered with mire.

MIS-, a prefix indicating wrong, *wrongly :* it is placed before *nouns,* verbs, and participles, and generally makes the meaning of the word obvious, hence, most of the words to which it is prefixed are omitted from the list of definitions.

MISADVENTURE (mis-ad-ven'tur), *n.* an unlucky accident ; misfortune.

MISALLIANCE (-a-li'ans), *n.* an improper alliance by marriage.

MISANTHROPE ('an-throp), *n.* a hater of mankind.

MISAPPREHEND (-ap-re-hend'), *v.t.* to misunderstand.

MISCARRY (-kar'i), *v.i.* to go wrong.

MISCELLANEOUS (-e-la'ne-us), *adj.* mixed together ; promiscuous.

MISCELLANY ('e-la-ni), *n.* a mixture of various kinds.

MISCHANCE (-chans'), *n.* misfortune ; mishap.

MISCHIEF ('chif), *n.* harm ; injury ; hurt ; damage.

MISCHIEVOUS ('chi-vus), *adj.* hurtful ; inclined to mischief.

MISCONCEIVE (-kon-sev'), *v.t.* to conceive wrongly ; misjudge.

MISCONDUCT (-kon-dukt'), *v.t.* to mismanage : (mis-kon'dukt), *n.* bad behaviour.

MISCREANT ('kre-ant), *n.* an unscrupulous villain ; vile wretch.

MISDEMEANOUR (-de-men'er), *n.* evil conduct.

MISER (mi'zer), *n.* a covetous man who denies himself the comforts of life.

MISERABLE (miz'er-a-bl), *adj.* wretched ; very unhappy.

MISERY ('er-i), *n.* extreme misfortune.

MISFEASANCE (-fe'zans), *n.* legal trespass.

MISFORTUNE (mis-for'tun), *n.* calamity ; disaster.

MISGIVING (-giv'ing), *n.* a presentiment or premonition of evil.

MISLAY (-la'), *v.t.* to misplace.

MISNOMER (-no'mer), *n.* a name wrongly applied.

MISREPRESENT (-rep-re-zent'), *v.t.* to represent falsely.

MISS, *n.* a young unmarried girl ; failure to hit, reach, perceive, or obtain.

MISSILE (mis'il), *n.* a weapon or thing thrown to injure.

MISSION (mish'un), *n.* embassy ; delegation ; commission.

MISSIONARY (-a-ri), *n.* a person who is sent to teach religion.

MISSIVE (mis'iv), *n.* a letter or message.

MIST (mist), *n.* visible watery vapour.

MISTAKABLE (mis-tak'a-bl), *adj.* liable to be mistaken.

MISTAKE (-tak), *v.t.* to misunderstand ; misconceive ; misjudge.

MISTER ('ter), *n.* a title of address prefixed to a man's name : abbreviated *Mr.*

MISTILY ('ti-li), *adv.* obscurely ; darkly.

MISTLETOE (miz'l-to), *n.* an evergreen parasitic shrub growing on trees.

MISTRESS (mis'tres), *n.* a woman who exercises authority or governs.

MISTRESS (mi'stres), *n.* a title of address prefixed to the name of a married woman : abbreviated *Mrs.*

MISTY ('ti), *adj.* dim ; clouded.

MISUNDERSTAND (-un-der-stand'), *v.t.* to take in a wrong sense.

MITE (mit), *n.* a minute insect ; an arachnid.

MITIGATE (mit'i-gat), *v.t.* to render less severe or rigorous ; soften ; alleviate.

MITIGATION (-ga'shun), *n.* the act of mitigating.

MITIGATOR ('i-ga-ter), *n.* one who, or that which, mitigates.

MITTEN (mit'n), *n.* a fingerless winter glove.

MIX (miks), *v.t.* to unite or blend into one mass or compound ; join : *v.i.* associate ; mingle.

MIXER (mik'ser), *n.* one who mixes ; an apparatus for mixing.

MIXTURE ('tur), *n.* a compound formed by mixing.

MIZZEN (miz'n), *n.* the hindmost of the fore-and-aft sails of a vessel.

MIZZLE ('l), *n.* fine rain.

MNEMONICS (ne-mon'iks), *n. pl.* the art of developing and improving the memory.

MOAN (mon), *v.i.* to utter a low sound as from pain or sorrow.

MOAT (mot), *n.* a ditch round a fortress, etc.

MOB (mob), *n.* a rude, disorderly crowd.

MOBILE (mo'bil), *adj.* easily moved.

MOBILITY (-bil'i-ti), *n.* susceptibility of motion.

MOBILIZATION (-i-za'shun), *n.* the act of mobilizing.

MOBILIZE (-iz), *v.t.* to make ready for active service, as soldiers.

MOBOCRACY (mob-ok'ra-si), *n.* the rule, or ascendency, of the mob.

MOCCASIN (mok'a-sin), *n.* a deerskin shoe worn by the N.A. Indians ; a poisonous snake of U.S.

MOCK (mok), *v.t.* to ridicule ; mimic.

MOCKERY ('er-i), *n.* derision ; ridicule ; delusion.

MOCKING BIRD (berd), *n.* an American thrush noted for mimicry of other birds.

MODAL (mo'dal), *adj.* pertaining to mode or form.

MODE (mod), *n.* form ; custom ; fashion ; manner ; style.

MODEL (mod'el), *n.* a pattern of something to be made, or reproduced; example for imitation.

MODERATE (mod'er-at), *v.t.* to keep within bounds ; lessen ; qualify : *v.i.* preside as a moderator : *adj.* restrained ; frugal ; calm ; reasonable; mild.

MODERATION (-a'shun), *n.* freedom from excess ; equanimity.

MODERATOR (mod'er-a-ter), *n.* that which moderates or restrains ; the presiding officer at a meeting or discussion.

MODERN ('ern), *adj.* pertaining to the present ; recent.

MODERNIZE (mod'er-niz), *v.t.* to render modern in usage or taste.

MODEST ('est), *adj.* restrained by propriety ; decent ; chaste.

MODESTY ('es-ti), *n.* propriety of behaviour or manner ; chastity ; diffidence ; moderation.

MODICUM ('i-kum), *n.* a little.

MODIFICATION (-i-fi-ka'shun), *n.* slight change in form.

MODIFY ('i-fi), *v.t.* to vary ; qualify ; reduce.

MODISTE (mo-dest'), *n.* [Fr.], a fashionable dressmaker.

MODULATE (mod'u-lat), *v.t.* to vary the sound of.

MOHAMMED (mo-ham'ed), **MAHOMET** (ma-ham'ed), *n.* an Arabian prophet (A.D. 569-632), founder of Islam.

MOIETY (moi'e-ti), *n.* one of two equal parts or shares ; half ; a very small quantity.

MOIL (moil), *v.i.* to toil ; drudge.

MOIRE (mor), *n.* [French], watered silk and other fabrics so processed.

MOIST (moist), *adj.* humid ; damp.

MOISTURE ('tur), *n.* a moderate degree of dampness ; slight wetness.

MOLAR (mo'lar), *n.* a double tooth or grinder.

MOLASSES (-las'ez), *n.* treacle.

MOULD (mold), *n.* fine, soft earth ; a fungoid growth, on decaying or damp vegetable matter ; a matrix, in which something is cast or shaped.

MOULDER ('er), *v.t.* to turn into dust by natural decay : *n.* one who moulds.

MOULDINESS ('i-nes), *n.* the state of being mouldy.

MOLE (mol), *n.* a dark-coloured mark or small protuberance on the skin ; a small soft-furred, burrowing animal ; a breakwater.

MOLECULE (mol'e-kul), *n.* until recently the smallest known quantity of an element which can exist separately.

MOLEST (mo-lest'), *v.t.* to annoy, or interfere with ; trouble ; vex.

MOLESTATION (mol-es-ta'shun), *n.* interference ; annoyance.

MOLLIFY ('i-fi), *v.t.* to calm ; soften ; assuage.

MOLLUSCA (mo-lus'ka), *n.pl.* a division of the Invertebrata : the shellfish.

MOLLYCODDLE (mol'i-kod'l), *n.* an effeminate person.

MOLOCH (mo'lok), *n.* the firegod of the ancient Phœnicians and Ammonites.

MOLT, MOULT (molt), *v.i.* to cast the feathers, hair, skin, etc.

MOLTEN (molt'en), *adj.* melted.

MOMENT (mo'ment), *n.* an instant ; importance ; value.

MOMENTARY ('men-ta-ri), *adj.* lasting only for, or done in, a moment.

MOMENTOUS (-men'tus), *adj.* very important.

MOMENTUM (-men'tum), *n.* impetus.

MONACHISM (mon'a-kizm), *n.* monastic life or system.

MONAD ('ad), *n.* an ultimate atom ; an elementary organism.

MONARCH ('ark), *n.* a supreme ruler : *adj.* supreme.

MONARCHY ('ar-ki), *n.* government in which the supreme power, either absolute or limited, is vested in a monarch.

MONASTERY ('as-ter-i), *n.* a home for religious retirement for men.

MONDAY (mun'da), *n.* the second day of the week.

MONETARY (mon'e-ta-ri), *adj.* per-

taining to money.

MONETIZE ('e-tiz), *v.t.* give standard or current value to.

MONEY ('i), *n.* coin ; specie ; gold, silver, or other metal stamped (or printed notes) by legal authority and used as money.

MONGER (mun'ger), *n.* a dealer.

MONGOL (mong'gol), **MONGOLIAN** (-go'li-an), *adj.* pertaining to Mongolia.

MONGREL (mung'grel), *adj.* of a mixed breed or kind.

MONISM (mon'izm), *n.* the doctrine of the unity of substance.

MONITION (mo-nish'un), *n.* admonition ; warning ; notice.

MONITOR (mon'i-ter), *n.* one who warns or admonishes ; armed, turreted iron-clad ; a lizard.

MONK (mungk), *n.* a man who devotes himself exclusively to a religious life.

MONKEY (mung'ki), *n.* a quadrumanous mammal of the species *Simiidæ.*

MONKSHOOD (mungks'hood), *n.* aconite.

MONO-, a prefix signifying *one, single, alone.*

MONOGAMOUS (mo-nog'a-mus), *adj.* mating with but one of the opposite sex.

MONOGAMY (-nog'a-mi), *n.* marriage of one wife only.

MONOGRAM (mon'o-gram), *n.* a cipher or character formed by the interweaving of two or more letters.

MONOGRAPH ('o-graf), *n.* a paper or treatise written on one particular subject.

MONOLITH ('o-lith), *n.* a pillar or column formed of a single stone.

MONOLOGUE ('o-log), *n.* a dramatic scene spoken by one person.

MONOMANIA (-ma'ni-a), *n.* mental derangement in regard to one subject only.

MONOPLANE (mon'o-plan), *n.* an aeroplane supported by a single sustaining surface.

MONOPOLIST (mo-nop'o-list), *n.* one who has a monopoly, or monopolizes.

MONOPOLIZE ('o-liz), *v.t.* to engross the whole of.

MONOSYLLABLE (mon'o-sil-a-bl), *n.* a word of one syllable.

MONOTHEISM (-the-izm), *n.* the doctrine of, or belief in, one God.

MONOTONE (-ton), *n.* recitation on a single note or key.

MONOTONOUS (mo-not'o-nus), *adj.* continued in the same unvarying tone ; wearisome.

MONOTONY ('o-ni), *n.* unvarying or irksome sameness.

MONOTYPE ('o-tip), *n.* a machine that sets type by casting single letters instead of lines of words as in the *linotype*.

MONSIEUR (me-syu'), *n.* [*pl.* messieurs (ma-syu')], a French title of courtesy, equivalent to *Sir* or *Mr.*

MONSOON (mon-soon'), *n.* a periodical wind in the Indian Ocean blowing from the southwest from April to October, and from the north-east during the other part of the year.

MONSTER ('ster), *n.* anything out of the usual course of nature ; prodigy ; deformed.

MONSTROSITY (-stros'i-ti), *n.* being monstrous ; an unnatural production.

MONSTROUS ('strus), *adj.* huge ; horrible ; enormous.

MONTH (munth), *n.* one of the twelve divisions of the year, either calendar or lunar.

MONUMENT (mon'u-ment), *n.* anything that perpetuates the memory of a person or event.

MOOD (mood), *n.* style ; manner ; variation in the form of a verb to express the manner of action or being.

MOODY ('i), *adj.* abstracted and pensive ; sad ; gloomy.

MOON (moon), *n.* the satellite that revolves round the earth.

MOONSHINE ('shin), *n.* moonlight ; show without reality.

MOONSHINER (-er), *n.* a distiller or smuggler of illicit liquor.

MOONSTONE ('ston), *n.* a translucent stone of yellow-white colour.

MOONY ('i), *adj.* crescent-shaped ; weakly sentimental.

MOOR (moor), *n.* an extensive tract of waste land covered with heather, etc. : *v.t.* to anchor.

MOORING ('ing), *n.* the act of securing a vessel to a particular place : *pl.* the place where a vessel is moored.

MOOSE (moos), *n.* a large North American deer resembling the European elk.

MOOT (moot), *n.* a meeting for discussion on a supposed case : *adj.* subject for debate.

MOOT COURT (cort), a mock court in which law students try imaginary cases for practice.

MOPE (mop), *v.i.* to be silent, dull or dispirited.

MOQUETTE (mo-ket), *n.* [French], a kind of carpet.

MORAINE (mo-ran'), *n.* a line of rocks and gravel at the edges and base of glaciers.

MORAL (mor'al), *adj.* conformed to right ; virtuous : *n.* inner meaning : *pl.* moral philosophy or ethics ; behaviour.

MORALE (mo-ral'), *n.* moral condition.

MORALITY (mo-ral'i-ti), *n.* the doctrine or practice of the duties of life.

MORALIZE (mor'al-iz), *v.t.* to apply or explain in a moral sense ; render moral.

MORAL PHILOSOPHY (fil-os'o-fi), ethics.

MORASS (mo-ras'), *n.* a swamp.

MORATORIUM (mor-a-to'ri-um), *n.* legalized right to postpone payment of a debt after it, otherwise, would fall due.

MORBID (mor'bid), *adj.* pertaining to disease ; sickly ; unhealthy.

MORDANT ('dant), *adj.* biting into or fixing colours ; sarcastic.

MORE (mor), *adj.* greater number, quality, extent ; additional ; longer.

MOREOVER (-o'ver), *adv.* besides.

MORGANATIC (mor-ga-nat'ik), *adj.* noting the marriage of a man of royal rank with a woman of inferior degree, whose children are legitimate but cannot inherit their father's rank or possessions.

MORGUE (morg), *n.* a place where the bodies of persons unknown found dead are exposed for identification.

MORIBUND (mor'i-bund), *adj.* dying; at the point of death.

MORMON ('mun), *n.* one of a sect organized April 6, 1830, as the Church of Jesus Christ of Latter-day Saints; called *Mormons*.

MORNING ('ning), *n.* the early part of the day.

MORNING WATCH (woch), watch on shipboard from 4 a.m. to 8 a.m.

MOROCCO (mo-rok'o), *n.* a fine kind of grained leather of goatskin or sheepskin.

MORON ('ron), *n.* a mentally defective person.

MOROSE (-ros'), *adj.* sullen; austere; gloomy.

MORPHIA (mor'fi-a), *n.* the narcotic principle of opium; also *morphine*.

MORPHOLOGICAL (-fo-loj'i-kal), *adj.* pertaining to morphology.

MORPHOLOGY (-fol'o-ji), *n.* the science of the forms of the organs of animals and plants.

MORRIS CHAIR (char), an easy chair, with adjustable back.

MORROW (mor'o), *n.* the next day.

MORSEL (mor'sel), *n.* a small piece.

MORSE TELEGRAPH (tel'e-graf), the telegraph using the dot-and-dash system invented by S. B. Morse, 1835.

MORTAL (mor'tal), *adj.* subject to death; fatal; violent; extreme; tedious; human.

MORTALITY (-tal'i-ti), *n.* the condition of being mortal; mankind.

MORTAR ('ter), *n.* a vessel in which substances are pounded with a pestle; short cannon used for throwing shells at high angles; a building cement of lime, sand, and water.

MORTGAGE ('gaj), *n.* a deed conveying property to a creditor as security for the payment of a debt.

MORTGAGEE (-ga-je'), *n.* the person to whom a mortgage is made or given.

MORTGAGOR ('ga-jer), *n.* the person who grants a mortgage.

MORTICIAN (mor-tish'an), *n.* an undertaker; funeral director.

MORTIFICATION (-ti-fi-ka'shun), *n.* gangrene; subjugation of the passions and appetites by abstinence; humiliation; vexation; chagrin.

MORTIFY ('ti-fi), *v.t.* to destroy the vital functions of; humble; depress; chagrin.

MORTIFYING (-ing), *adj.* humiliating; vexatious.

MORTISE ('tis), *n.* a hole or space made in wood to receive a tenon.

MORTUARY (mor'tu-a-ri), *n.* a building for the dead pending burial.

MOSAIC (mo-za'ik), *adj.* pertaining to Moses and his writings.

MOSAIC (-za'ik), *n.* a design formed by the union of very minute pieces of glass, stone, etc., of various colours, inlaid in a ground of cement or metal.

MOSQUE (mosk), *n.* a Mohammedan temple.

MOSQUITO (mus-ke'to), *n.* a two-winged insect, the female of which has a long proboscis with which it punctures the skin and extracts blood.

MOSS (mos), *n.* a natural order of cryptogamous bog plants.

MOSS-ROSE ('roz), *n.* a variety of rose with a moss-like calyx.

MOST (most), *adj.* greatest in number, quantity, or degree.

MOT (mo), *n.* [French], a witty saying.

MOTE (mot), *n.* a very small particle.

MOTH (moth), *n.* a lepidopterous insect or its larvæ, which feed upon cloth, fur, etc.

MOTHER (muth'er), *n.* one who has given birth to a child; an elderly woman; a matron; origin or source.

MOTHER-IN-LAW (-in-law), *n.* the mother of one's husband or wife.

MOTHER-OF-PEARL (-perl), *n.* the hard, silvery internal layer of various kinds of shells.

MOTHERS' DAY (muth'erz day), the second Sunday in May, when mothers are specially honoured.

MOTION (mo'shun), *n.* animal life and action; impulse, desire, or passion; internal activity.

MOTION PICTURE (pik'tur), see moving picture.

MOTIVE ('tiv), *adj.* causing motion; able or tending to move: *n.* that which excites to action; inducement; reason; stimulus; in art, leading idea, or conception.

MOTIVE POWER (pou'er), *n.* any natural agent.

MOTLEY (mot'li), *adj.* covered with parts of various colours; heterogeneous.

MOTOR (mo'ter), *n.* that which produces motion, or power.

MOTORCYCLE (-si-kl), *n.* a bicycle propelled by a motor.

MOTORDROME (-drom), *n.* a field for automobile and motorcycle races.

MOTORMAN (mo'ter-man), *n.* the operator of an electric passenger car.

MOTTLE (mot'l), *v.t.* to mark with spots of various colours.

MOTTO ('o), *n.* a concise sentence added to a device, suggesting some guiding principle, etc.

MOUNT (mount), *n.* a hill or mountain: *v.t.* to climb; ascend; bestride; furnish with horses.

MOUNTAIN (moun'tin), *n.* a large mass of rock or earth rising above the level of the adjacent country; usually over 2,000 feet.

MOUNTAINEER (-er'), *n.* one who dwells among mountains.

MOUNTAINOUS (-ti-nus), *adj.* full of, or resembling, mountains.

MOUNTAIN SHEEP (shep), *n.* the bighorn of the Rocky Mountains.

MOUNTEBANK (moun'te-bangk), *n.* a quack-doctor; boastful pretender.

MOURN (morn), *v.i.* to grieve; be sorrowful; lament.

MOURNFUL ('fool), *adj.* expressing sorrow; sad.

MOUSE (mous), *n.* a small rodent.

MOUSTACHE (mus-tash'), *n.* hair worn on a man's upper lip.

MOUTH (mouth), *n.* the opening in the head of an animal by which it receives food and utters sounds.

MOUTHFUL ('fool), *n.* as much as can be put into the mouth at one time.

MOVABILITY (moov-a-bil'i-ti), *n.* the state or quality of being movable.

MOVABLE ('a-bl), *adj.* capable of being moved or conveyed: *n.pl.* goods, wares or furniture.

MOVE (moov), *v.t.* to cause to change place or position; impel; set in motion; influence; propose formally.

MOVEMENT ('ment), *n.* the act or manner of moving; motion; excitement; emotion; agitation.

MOVING ('ing), *p.adj.* causing motion; change of position; stirring the passions or affections; pathetic.

MOVING PICTURE (pik'tur), popular term for all animated screen pictures; also the *Movies.*

MOW (mo), *v.t.* to cut down with, or as with, a scythe.

MOW (mou), *n.* a heap of hay, etc., stowed in a barn.

MOWN, *p.p.* of mow.

MUCH (much), *adj.* great in quantity or amount; number.

MUCILAGE (mu'si-laj), *n.* a gummy or gelatinous substance; gum of plants.

MUCILAGINOUS (-laj'i-nus), *adj.* pertaining to mucilage or gum.

MUCKRAKER (muk'ra-ker), *n.* one who rakes muck; a censorious and abusive writer or speaker.

MUCOUS (mu'kus), *adj.* pertaining to mucus; viscous.

MUCOUS MEMBRANE (mem'-bran), the moist, glandular lining of the cavities and canals of the human body.

MUCUS ('kus), *n.* the viscid fluid secreted by the mucous membrane.

MUD (mud), *n.* soft, wet earth; mire.

MUDDLE ('l), *v.t.* to make a mess of or confuse; cloud or stupefy.

MUFF (muf), *n.* a warm, soft cylindrical cover of fur, etc., to keep the hands warm: *v.t.* to handle awkwardly; fail to hold (a ball), when catching it.

MUFFIN ('in), *n.* a soft, light, spongy, round cake.

MUFFLE ('l), *v.t.* to wrap up warmly; cover up so as to deaden sound.

MUFFLER ('ler), *n.* a scarf worn around the throat; a device for deadening the noise of escaping gases, as on an automobile.

MUFTI ('ti), *n.* a doctor of Mohammedan law; civilian dress worn by a naval or military officer when off duty.

MUG (mug), *n.* an eathenware or metallic drinking vessel.

MUGGY ('i), *adj.* warm, damp, and close; mouldy.

MULATTO (mu-lat'o), *n.* the offspring of negro and white parents.

MULBERRY (mul'ber-i), *n.* a tree with dentate or lobed leaves upon which silkworms feed.

MULCH (mulch), *n.* half rotten straw, litter, etc., used to protect the roots of trees, plants, etc.

MULCT (mulkt), *n.* a fine, especially for some misdemeanour.

MULE (mul), *n.* the offspring of a male ass and a mare.

MULETEER (-e-ter'), *n.* a mule driver.

MULLEIN (mul'in), *n.* a tall herb with coarse, woolly leaves.

MULLET ('et), *n.* an edible spiny-rayed fish.

MULTI-, a prefix signifying *more than one, many, much, several.*

MULTIFARIOUS (-fa'risus), *adj.* having great diversity or variety.

MULTIPLE (mul'ti-pl), *adj.* consisting of many parts; repeated many times.

MULTIPLEX ('ti-pleks), *adj.* manifold.

MULTIPLICATION (-ka'shun), *n.* the act or process of multiplying.

MULTIPLICITY (-plis'i-ti), *n.* the state of being manifold; a great number.

MULTIPLY ('ti-pli), *v.t.* to cause to increase in number.

MULTITUDE ('ti-tud), *n.* a great number; crowd; assembly; populace (with *the*).

MULTITUDINOUS (-tu'di-nus), *adj.* pertaining to, or consisting of, a multitude; numerous.

MULTUM IN PARVO (par'vo), [Latin], much in little.

MUM (mum), *adj.* silent.

MUMBLE ('bl), *v.t.* & *v.i.* to mutter or speak indistinctly.

MUMMER ('er), *n.* one who makes sport in disguise; a masker.

MUMMERY ('er-i), *n.* masquerading.

MUMMY ('i), *n.* a dead body embalmed after the manner of ancient Egyptians.

MUMP (mump), *v.i.* & *v.t.* to nibble; cheat; whine or sulk.

MUMPS (mumps), *n.* a contagious febrile disease, characterized by the swelling of the glands of the neck.

MUNCH (munch), *v.t.* & *v.i.* to chew with an audible crunching noise.

MUNDANE (mun'dan), *adj.* pertaining to the world.

MUNICIPAL (mu-nis'i-pal), *adj.* pertaining to a city or local self-government.

MUNICIPALITY ('i-ti), *n.* a corporate town or city.

MUNIFICENCE (-nif'i-sens), *n.* liberality.

MUNIFICENT ('i-sent), *adj.* bountiful.

MUNITIONS (-nish'unz), *n.pl.* military stores or material.

MURAL (mu'ral), *adj.* pertaining to, growing on, or resembling, a wall.

MURDER (mer'der), *n.* the intentional killing of one human being by another; mangle; mar or ruin.

MURDERER (-er), *n.* one guilty of murder.

MURDERESS (-es), *n.* a woman who intentionally kills a human being.

MURDEROUS ('der-us), *adj.* pertaining to, guilty of, or attended with, murder.

MURINE (mu'rin), *adj.* pertaining to mice and rats.

MURK (merk), *n.* gloom.

MURKY ('ki), *adj.* dark; gloomy.

MURMUR (mer'mur), *n.* a low, indistinct sound; a complaint in a low muttering tone.

MUSCATEL (mus-ka-tel'), *n.* a variety of rich wine; the grapes which produce it; a sweet fragrant pear.

MUSCLE ('i), *n.* a highly contractile organ of fibrous tissue by which movement in an animal body is effected; muscular strength.

MUSCULAR ('ku-lar), *adj.* pertaining to muscles; strong; vigorous; brawny.

MUSE (muz), *n.* any one of the nine classical goddesses who preside over poetry, history, arts, etc.

MUSE (muz), *v.i.* to study in silence ; meditate.

MUSEUM (mu-ze'um), *n.* a collection of natural, scientific or literary curiosities, or of works of art.

MUSH (mush), *n.* boiled Indian maize meal.

MUSHROOM ('room), *n.* an edible fungus.

MUSIC (mu'zik), *n.* the art or science of harmonic sounds ; harmony or melody.

MUSICAL ('zi-kal), *adj.* pertaining to music ; melodious.

MUSICALE (-zi-kal'), *n.* a social musical party.

MUSICIAN (-zish'an), *n.* one skilled in the science of music.

MUSING (muz'ing), *n.* meditation.

MUSK (musk), *n.* a strong-scented substance obtained from the male musk deer.

MUSK DEER (der), *n.* a small hornless deer of Central Asia, the male of which yields the musk of commerce.

MUSKET (mus'ket), *n.* the firearm formerly used by infantry.

MUSKETEER (-er'), *n.* a soldier armed with a musket.

MUSKETRY (-ri), *n.* firearm practice.

MUSKMELON ('mel-un), *n.* an edible fruit ; a cantaloupe.

MUSK OX (oks), *n.* an Arctic bovine animal.

MUSK RAT (musk'rat), *n.* an aquatic rodent of North America valuable for its fur.

MUSLIN (muz'lin), *n.* a fine, thin, cotton cloth or fabric.

MUSS (mus), *n.* disorder.

MUSSEL ('l), *n.* a marine edible bivalve.

MUSSY (mus'i), *adj.* disordered.

MUST (must), *n.* unfermented expressed grape juice ; mustiness : *v.i.* to be obliged morally or physically ; defective verb.

MUSTANG ('tang), *n.* the small, hardy, semi-wild horse of the prairies.

MUSTARD ('tard), *n.* an annual herb and its seed ; the condiment prepared from the powder of the seeds.

MUSTER ('ter), *n.* an assembly of troops for review or active service ; assemblage ; collection.

MUSTY ('ti), *adj.* spoiled with damp, mould, or age ; spiritless ; antiquated.

MUTABILITY (mu-ta-bil'i-ti), *n.* being subject to change ; instability.

MUTABLE ('ta-bl), *adj.* susceptible of change.

MUTATION (mu-ta'shun), *n.* alteration ; change.

MUTE (mut), *adj.* silent ; dumb ; not pronounced or sounded.

MUTILATE (mu'ti-lat), *v.t.* to render imperfect ; maim.

MUTINEER (-ti-ner'), *n.* one who is guilty of mutiny : *v.i.* to mutiny.

MUTINOUS ('ti-nus), *adj.* disposed to, or guilty of, mutiny ; seditious.

MUTINY ('ti-ni), *n.* insurrection against constituted authority.

MUTTER (mut'er), *v.i.* to utter words in a low voice with compressed lips ; murmur.

MUTTON ('n), *n.* the flesh of sheep as a food ; a sheep.

MUTUAL (mu'tu-al), *adj.* reciprocal.

MUTUALITY (-al'i-ti), *n.* reciprocation.

MUZZLE (muz'l), *n.* the projecting mouth, lips, and nose of an animal ; snout ; the mouth of a gun, etc., a fastening or cover for the mouth of a dog, etc.

MUZZY ('i), *adj.* muddled.

MY (mi), *poss. pron.* belonging to me ; the possessive case of *I*, denoting simple possession.

MYO-, a combining form from the Greek *mys*, muscle.

MYOPIA (mi-o'pi-a), *n.* shortsightedness.

MYRIAD (mir'i-ad), *n.* the number of 10,000 ; a very large number : *adj.* innumerable.

MYRIAGRAMME ('i-a-gram), *n.* in the metric system, 10,000 grams.

MYRIALITRE (-le-tr), *n.* in the metric system, 10,000 litres.

MYRIAMETRE (-me-tr), *n.* in the metric system, 10,000 metres.

MYRIARE ('-ar), *n.* in the metric system, 10,000 ares.

MYRRH (mer), *n.* the aromatic gummy, resin which exudes from several trees, or shrubs, growing in Arabia and Abyssinia.

MYRTLE (mer'tl), *n.* a small tree with glossy evergreen leaves, white, or pale-pink, flowers, and black berries, all of which are used in perfumes.

MYSELF (mi-self'), *pron.* I, or me, in person.

MYSTERIOUS (mys-te'ri-us), *adj.* not clear to the understanding ; obscure ; incomprehensible.

MYSTERY ('ter-i), *n.* something secret, obscure, or unexplained.

MYSTICISM ('ti-sizm), *n.* [M], the teachings or doctrines of the Mystics.

MYSTIFICATION (-fi-ka'shun), *n.* the act of mystifying.

MYSTIFY ('ti-fi), *v.t.* to obscure ; bewilder ; puzzle.

MYTH (mith), *n.* a legend ; poetic fiction ; a fabulous narrative.

MYTHOLOGICAL (-o-loj'i-kal), *adj.* pertaining to mythology ; mythical.

MYTHOLOGY ('o-ji), *n.* the collected body or system of the traditions or legends of a people in which are embodied their beliefs concerning their origin, gods, heroes, etc.

N

N, n (en), the fourteenth letter of the English alphabet.

N, n, *n.* an abbreviation.

N, n, *n.* a Roman numeral denoting 90 or 900 ; with a bar (N̄), 9,000 or 90,000.

NAB (nab), *v.t.* to seize unexpectedly.

NABOB (na'bob), *n.* in India, a deputy under the Mogul Empire ; a very wealthy man.

NACRE (na'ker), *n.* mother-of-pearl.

NACREOUS ('kre-us), *adj.* having an iridescent lustre.

NADIR (na'der), *n.* that part of the heavens directly under our feet ; or directly opposite to the zenith.

NÆVOSE ('vos), *adj.* freckled.

NÆVUS (ne'vus), *n.* a birthmark.

NAG (nag), *n.* a small horse : *v.t.* to find fault with continually.

NAGGY (nag'i), *adj.* disposed to nag.

NAGGLE (nag'l), *v.i.* to haggle over petty matters.

NAIAD (na'yad), *n.* a water-nymph.

NAIL (nal), *n.* the horny substance at the ends of the human fingers and toes ; 2¼ inches ; a pointed piece of metal usually with a head.

NAINSOOK (nan'sook), *n.* a thick kind of muslin.

NAÏVE (na-ev'), *adj.* [Fr.], artless.

NAÏVETÉ (na-ev-ta'), *n.* [Fr.], natural, unaffected simplicity or ingenuousness.

NAKED (na'ked), *adj.* unclothed ; bare ; exposed to view ; plain.

NAMBY-PAMBY (nam'bi-pam'bi), *adj.* weakly sentimental : *v.t.* to coddle.

NAME (nam), *n.* that by which a person or thing is called ; designation ; character ; reputation ; fame.

NAMELY ('li), *adv.* that is to say.

NANKEEN (nan-ken'), *n.* a buff-coloured cotton cloth.

NAP (nap), *n.* a short slumber ; doze ; the woolly substance on cloth.

NAPE (nap), *n.* the back of the neck.

NAPERY (na'per-i), *n.* table-linen.

NAPTHA (naf'tha), *n.* a clear, volatile, inflammable liquid distilled from petroleum, etc.

NAPKIN (nap'kin), *n.* small cloth, specifically one used at table for wiping hands, etc.

NARCISSUS (nar-sis'us), *n.* a genus of ornamental bulbous plants.

NARCOSIS (-ko'sis), *n.* stupefaction from the effects of a narcotic.

NARCOTIC (-kot'ik), *adj.* producing coma or torpor.

NARRATE (na-rat'), *v.t.* to tell ; recite ; write, as a story.

NARRATION (-ra'shun), *n.* statement, written or verbal.

NARRATIVE (nar'a-tiv), *n.* recital of a story or event ; tale.

NARRATOR (na-ra'ter), *n.* one who narrates.

NARROW (nar'o), *adj.* of little breadth or extent; limited; straitened; contracted in mind; bigoted; ungenerous.

NARROW-MINDEDNESS (-min-'ded-ness), *n.* illiberal; bigoted.

NARWHAL (nar'hwal), *n.* a cetaceous mammal allied to the whale.

NASAL (na'zal), *adj.* pertaining to the nose.

NASCENT (nas'ent), *adj.* beginning to exist, or to grow.

NASTILY (nas'ti-li), *adv.* filthily; disagreeably.

NASTURTIUM (nas-ter'shi-um), *n.* a garden herb of the geranium family.

NASTY (nas'ti), *adj.* dirty; nauseous; filthy; obscene; foul.

NATAL (na'tal), *adj.* pertaining to one's birth or birthday; indigenous.

NATANT ('tant), *adj.* floating on water, as lily pads.

NATATORIAL (na-ta-to'ri-al), *adj.* swimming.

NATION (na'shun), *n.* the inhabitants of one country under the same government.

NATIONAL (nash'un-al), *adj.* pertaining to a nation; public; general.

NATIONALITY ('i-ti), *n.* national character; patriotism; nation.

NATIONALLY (-li), *adv.* as a nation.

NATIVE (na'tiv), *adj.* pertaining to the time and place of birth; produced by nature.

NATIVITY, *n.* the birth of Christ (with *the*).

NATTILY (nat'i-li), *adv.* tidily; neatly.

NATTY ('i), *adj.* tidy; neat; smart.

NATURAL ('u-ral), *adj.* pertaining to nature; inborn; not artificial; unassumed; music, according to the scale of C major.

NATURAL HISTORY (his'to-ri), the scientific description of the earth and its various productions, especially the animal kingdom.

NATURALISM (-izm), *n.* mere state of nature; realism.

NATURALIST (-ist), *n.* one skilled in natural history.

NATURALISTIC (-is'tik), *adj.* realistic.

NATURALIZATION (-i-za'shun), *n.* the act of investing a foreigner with the rights and privileges of a natural-born citizen.

NATURALIZE (-iz), *v.t.* to make natural; acclimate; invest (a foreigner) with the privileges of citizenship.

NATURE (na'cher, nat'ur), *n.* the universe; essential qualities; species; natural order of things; personal character.

NAUGHT (nawt), *n.* nothing.

NAUGHTY ('ti), *adj.* bad; perverse or mischievous.

NAUSEA (naw'she-a), *n.* a strong sensation of sickness; loathing or disgust.

NAUSEATE ('she-at), *v.t.* to affect with nausea; loathe.

NAUSEOUS ('shus), *adj.* loathsome; abhorent.

NAUTICAL (naw'ti-kal), *adj.* pertaining to ships, sailors, or navigation.

NAUTILUS ('ti-lus), *n.* [*pl.* nautili], any member of a genus of cephalopods.

NAVAHO, NAVAJO (nav'a-ho), *n.* one of a tribe of Indians inhabiting New Mexico and Arizona.

NAVAL (na'val), *adj.* pertaining to ships or a navy; maritime.

NAVE (nav), *n.* the middle or body of a church, extending from the chancel to the principal entrance.

NAVEL (na'v'l), *n.* the depression in the centre of the lower part of the abdomen, indicating where the umbilical cord was joined.

NAVIGABLE (nav'i-ga-bl), *adj.* capable of being navigated.

NAVIGATE ('i-gat), *v.i.* to pass on the water by a ship or vessel; sail.

NAVIGATION (-ga'shun), *n.* the science of navigating ships.

NAVIGATOR ('i-ga-ter), *n.* one skilled in navigation.

NAVVY (nav'i), *n.* a labourer employed in constructing railways, canals, etc.

NAVY (na'vi), *n.* the ships of war including men, stores, etc., belonging to a nation.

NAY (na), *adv.* no : *n.* a refusal or denial.

NAZARENE (naz-a-ren'), *n.* a native of Nazareth : applied to Jesus Christ.

NEAP (nep), *adj.* low ; applied to tides.

NEAR (ner), *adj.* not far distant in time, place, or degree ; close ; intimate.

NEAT (net), *n.* bovine cattle collectively : *adj.* tidy ; trim and clean ; simple and elegant ; chaste.

NEATSFOOT (netz'foot), *n.* the foot of an ox or cow.

NEB (neb), *n.* a bird's beak ; mouth ; tip ; point.

NEBULA ('u-la), *n.* [*pl.* nebulæ (-le)], a faint, misty patch of light in the heavens produced by groups of stars too remote to be seen singly.

NEBULAR ('u-lar), *adj.* pertaining to nebulæ.

NEBULOUS ('u-lus), *adj.* pertaining to a nebula ; cloudy ; hazy.

NECESSARILY (nes'e-sa-ri-li), *adv.* by necessity.

NECESSARY ('e-sa-ri), *adj.* that which cannot be otherwise ; essential ; indispensable : *pl.* things requisite.

NECESSITATE (ne-ses'i-tat), *v.t.* to make necessary ; compel.

NECESSITOUS ('i-tus), *adj.* very poor ; needy.

NECESSITY ('i-ti), *n.* compulsion ; extreme poverty : *pl.* things necessary for human life.

NECK (nek), *n.* that part of the body between the head and trunk ; something shaped like a neck.

NECKLACE ('las), *n.* a string of beads or ornaments, as pearls, etc., worn round the neck.

NECRO- (nek'ro), a combining form from the Greek *nekras*, dead, a dead body.

NECROLOGY (-rol'o-ji), *n.* a register, or account, of the dead.

NECROMANCER ('ro-man-ser), *n.* a conjurer.

NECROMANCY (-si), *n.* the pretended art of predicting future events by communication with the dead.

NECROPOLIS (-rop'o-lis), *n.* a cemetery.

NECROSIS (-ro'sis), *n.* mortification and death of a bone.

NECTAR (nek'tar), *n.* in classic mythology, the wine of the gods ; any delicious beverage.

NECTARINE ('tar-in), *n.* a variety of peach.

NÉE (na), *p.adj.* born : sometimes placed with the name of a married woman (to show her family name before marriage), as Madame Jones née Smith.

NEED (ned), *n.* necessity ; urgent want ; poverty.

NEEDFUL ('fool), *adj.* necessary.

NEEDLE (ne'd'l), *n.* a small sharp; pointed steel instrument furnished with an eye to hold thread.

NEEDS (nedz), *adv.* necessarily ; indispensably.

NEEDY (ned'i), *adj.* very poor.

NE'ER (nar), *adv.* contraction of never.

NEFARIOUS (ne-far'i-us), *adj.* extremely wicked ; vile.

NEGATION (ne-ga'shun), *n.* denial ; absence of certain qualities.

NEGATIVE (neg'a-tiv), *adj.* denying, refusing ; having the power of veto ; noting a quantity to be subtracted : *n.* a proposition by which something is denied ; right of veto ; a photograph in which the lights and shades of the object are the opposite of those in nature.

NEGLECT (-lekt'), *n.* omission ; habitual negligence ; disregard.

NEGLECTFUL ('fool), *adj.* careless.

NEGLIGEE (-li-zha'), *n.* a loosely fitting dress or gown.

NEGLIGENCE (li-jens) *n.* carelessness.

NEGLIGENT ('li-jent), *adj.* careless.

NEGLIGIBLE ('li-ji-bl), *adj.* that which may be neglected ; of little account or value.

NEGOTIABLE ('shi-a-bl), *adj.* capable of being negotiated, transferred, or exchanged.

NEGOTIATE (ne-go'shi-at), *v.i.* to treat with others in business, private or state affairs.

NEGOTIATION (-a'shun), *n.* the

act of negotiating or transacting business ; treaty.

NEGOTIATOR ('shi-a-ter), *n.* one who negotiates.

NEGRESS (ne'gres), *n.* the female of the negro.

NEGRO (gro), *n.* a black man of African blood ; one of the black and woolly-haired type of mankind.

NEGROID ('groid), *adj.* of the negro type.

NEIGH (na), *v.i.* to utter the cry, or whinny, of a horse.

NEIGHBOUR (na'ber), *n.* one who dwells near to another.

NEIGHBOURHOOD (-hood), *n.* adjacent district ; vicinity.

NEIGHBOURLY (-li), *adj.* like a neighbour ; social ; civil ; friendly.

NEIGHING ('ing) *n.* a whinnying.

NEITHER (ne', ni'ther), *adj. & pron.* not the one or the other : *conj.* not either.

NEMESIS (nem'e-sis), *n.* retributive vengeance : from Nemesis, the avenging deity of the Greeks.

NEO-, a combining form from the Greek *neos*, new, recent, young.

NEOLITH (ne'o-lith), *n.* a neolithic stone implement.

NEOLITHIC (-lith'ik), *adj.* pertaining to the polished stone age.

NEOLOGISM (-ol'o-jizm), *n.* a new word or phrase introduced into a language.

NEOLOGIST ('o-jist), *n.* an innovator in language or religion.

NEON (ne'on), *n.* a recently discovered gaseous element existing in the air.

NEOPHYTE ('o-fit), *n.* a novice of a religious order ; a beginner.

NEOPLASTIC (-plas'tik), **NEOPLASTY** (ne'o-plas-ti), *n.* the restoration of tissues by granulation.

NEPHEW (nev'u), *n.* son of a brother or sister.

NEPHRITIC (-frit'ik), *adj.* pertaining to the kidneys.

NEPHRITIS (ne-fri'tis), *n.* inflammation of the kidneys.

NEPOTISM (nep'o-tizm), *n.* favouritism shown to relatives in conferring favours, etc.

NEPOTIST (-tist), *n.* one who favours relatives.

NERVE (nerv), *n.* one of the grey fibres which convey sensation from all parts of the body to the brain and originate motion ; tendon ; sinew ; strength ; manliness.

NERVOUS ('vus), *adj.* pertaining to nerves ; easily agitated ; vigorous in style.

NERVOUS SYSTEM (sis'tem), the nerves considered collectively.

NERVY (ner'vi), *adj.* nervous ; sinewy ; cheeky.

NESCIENCE (nesh'i-ens), *n.* state of not knowing ; ignorance.

NEST (nest), *n.* the bed or dwelling prepared by a bird.

NESTLE (nes'l), *v.i.* to lie close and snug ; take shelter.

NET (net), *n.* a fabric knotted into meshes for catching birds, fish, etc. anything resembling or made like a net ; a snare : *adj.* clear of all charges or deductions ; opposed to *gross*.

NETHER (neth'er), *adj.* lying beneath ; lower.

NETTLE (net'l), *n.* a herb that emits a stinging juice when broken : *v.t.* to provoke or irritate.

NETWORK (-werk), *n.* open crochet work ; netting ; a number of radio stations broadcasting the same event simultaneously.

NEURAL (nu'ral), *adj.* pertaining to the nerves.

NEURALGIA (-ral'ji-a), *n.* acute pain in a nerve.

NEURASTHENIA (nu-ras-the'ni-a), *n.* brain and nerve exhaustion ; depression of the vital forces.

NEURITIS (-ri'tis), *n.* inflammation of a nerve.

NEUROPATH (nu'ro-path), **NEUROPATHIST** (-rop'a-thist), *n.* a specialist in nervous diseases.

NEUROPATHIC (-path'ik), *adj.* pertaining to nervous disease.

NEUROSIS (-ro'sis), *n.* nervous disease.

NEUROTIC (-rot'ik), *adj.* pertaining to, or affecting, the nerves.

NEUTER ('ter), *adj.* of neither sex; sexless; intransitive; neutral.

NEUTRAL ('tral), *adj.* unbiased; indifferent; taking no part on either side in a contest.

NEUTRALITY ('i-ti), *n.* the state of being neutral.

NEUTRALIZE ('tral-iz), *v.t.* to make neutral; render inactive.

NEUTRAL TINT (tint), a dull gray.

NEUTRODYNE (nu'tro-din), *n.* a radio receiver in which the circuit is designed for rapid frequency amplification, with the neutralization of capacity coupling.

NÉVÉ (na-va'), *n.* [French], the granular compressed snow which forms glacier ice.

NEVER (nev'er), *adv.* not at any time.

NEVERTHELESS (-*the*-les'), *adv.* notwithstanding; in spite of that.

NEW (nu), *adj.* recent in origin; modern; novel; modern; fresh.

NEWEL ('el), *n.* the post at the foot, or turn, of any stairway.

NEW-FANGLED (-fang'gld), *adj.* new-fashioned.

NEWS (nuz), *n.* recent intelligence; tidings.

NEWSPAPER ('pa-per), *n.* a paper published periodically, usually daily or weekly, containing the most recent news.

NEW STYLE (stil), the Gregorian or present style of computing the calendar; opposed to the former or Julian method.

NEW TESTAMENT (tes'ta-ment), that portion of the Bible made up of the covenant of God with man, as is embodied in the teachings of Jesus Christ.

NEW THOUGHT (thawt), advanced views or progressiveness in all departments of human knowledge.

NEXT (nekst), *adj.* nearest in time, place, degree, or rank.

NEXUS (nek'sus), *n.* a connection or tie between the members of a group, or series.

NIB (nib), *n.* the point of anything, especially a pen.

NIBBLE ('l), *v.t.* & *v.i.* to bite by little at a time.

NIBLICK (nib'lik), *n.* a heavy, iron, round-headed golf club.

NICE (nis), *adj.* fastidious; precise; delicate; refined; socially agreeable; pleasing to the palate.

NICETY ('e-ti), *n.* fastidious delicacy; precision; minute accuracy.

NICHE (nich), *n.* a recess in a wall for a statue, etc.

NICK (nik), *n.* a small cut or indentation; the critical moment.

NICKEL ('l), *n.* a greyish-white ductile metal; a five-cent coin.

NICOTINE ('o-ten), *n.* an acrid, poisonous alkaloid, extracted from tobacco.

NIDIFICATION (nid-i-fi-ka'shun), *n.* the act of building a nest; rearing young, etc.

NIECE (nes), *n.* the daughter of a brother or sister.

NIGGARD (nig'ard), *adj.* parsimonious; miserly.

NIGGARDLY (-li), *adv.* like a niggard.

NIGGLE (nig'l), *v.i.* to trifle.

NIGH (ni), *adj.* near in time or place; adjacent.

NIGHT (nit), *n.* the time from sunset to sunrise; darkness.

NIGHTINGALE (in-gal), *n.* bird of the thrush family, noted for its melodious song at night.

NIGHTMARE ('mar), *n.* a dreadful dream; an incubus.

NIGHTSHADE (-shad), *n.* a poisonous weed with white flowers and black berries.

NIHIL (ni'hil), *n.* nothing.

NIHILISM (ni'hil-izm), *n.* scepticism which denies that anything, even existence, can be known; [N-], the doctrine of a former extreme party in Russia, who aimed to destroy the then existing institutions.

NIHILIST (-ist), *n.* a supporter of Nihilism.

NIL (nil), *n.* nothing.

NIMBLE (nim'bl), *adj.* quick and active; alert; lively.

NIMBUS (nim'bus), *n.* in art, the

halo surrounding the heads of divinities and saints ; a rain-cloud.

NINNY (nin'i), *n.* a simpleton.

NIP (nip), *n.* a pinch ; a blast as by cold.

NIPPLE (nip'l), *n.* a teat.

NIT (nit), *n.* the egg of any small insect.

NITRIC ACID (ni'trik as'id), a powerful acid ; aquafortis.

NITROGELATIN (-jel'a-tin), *n.* a powerful explosive.

NITROGEN (ni'tro-jen), *n.* a gaseous element, colourless, odourless, tasteless, constituting about ⅘ of the atmosphere.

NITROGLYCERIN, NITRO-GLYCERINE (-glis'er-in), *n.* a highly explosive oily liquid made of nitric and sulphuric acid.

NO (no), *adv.* a word of denial or refusal ; opposed to *yes.*

NOBBY ('bli), *adj.* capital ; stylish.

NOBEL PRIZE (no-bel' priz), one of the annual prizes, amounting to nearly $40,000, given by the Nobel Foundation for distinction in various departments of science, in literature, or in the promotion of peace.

NOBILITY (no-bil'i-ti), *n.* noble birth ; grandeur ; dignity.

NOBLE (no'bl), *adj.* illustrious ; magnanimous ; generous ; exalted in rank.

NOBLY ('bli), *adv.* in a noble manner.

NOBODY ('bod-i), *n.* no one ; a person of no importance.

NOCENT ('sent), *adj.* harmful.

NOCTURNAL (nok-ter'nal), *adj.* pertaining to, done, or happening at, night.

NOCTURNE ('tern), *n.* a night scene ; a musical composition appropriate to the night ; a lullaby.

NOD (nod), *n.* a quick inclination of the head as a token of assent.

NODATED (no'dat-ed), *adj.* knotted.

NODE (nod), *n.* a knot ; knob.

NODULE ('ul), *n.* a little knot.

NOGGIN (nog'in), *n.* a small mug ; a liquid measure = 1 gill.

NOISE (noiz), *n.* sound ; clamour ; outcry.

NOISOME (noi'sum), *adj.* injurious to health ; noxious ; disgusting.

NOISY (noiz'i), *adj.* turbulent.

NOMAD (nom'ad, no'mad), *n.* one of a tribe that wanders in search of game, etc.

NOMENCLATURE (no'men-kla-tur), *n.* the words, terms, or language used in any art or science.

NOMINAL (nom'i-nal), *adj.* existing only in name ; inconsiderable.

NOMINATE ('i-nat), *v.t.* to propose for an office ; appoint.

NOMINATIVE ('i-na-tiv), *adj.* noting in grammar the case of the subject.

NOMINATOR ('i-na-ter), *n.* one who nominates.

NOMINEE (-i-ne'), *n.* one who is proposed for an office.

NON-, a prefix signifying *not.*

NONAGE (non'aj), *n.* minority.

NONAGENARIAN (-a-je-na'ri-an), *n.* a person ninety years old.

NONCE (nons), *n.* the present time.

NONCHALANCE (nong-sha-langs'), *n.* [French], coolness ; indifference.

NONCHALANT (-lang'), *adj.* cool ; indifferent.

NONCONDUCTOR (non-kon-duk'ter), *n.* an insulator for sound, heat, electricity, etc.

NONDESCRIPT (non'de-skript), *n.* a person or thing that cannot be easily described.

NONE (nun), *adj.* not any ; not one : *pron.* no one ; nothing : *adv.* not at all.

NONENTITY (non-en'ti-ti), *n.* a thing not existing ; a person of no importance.

NONPAREIL (non-pa-rel'), *adj.* without an equal ; a 6 point size of type.

NONPLUS ('plus), *v.t.* to throw into complete perplexity ; puzzle.

NONSENSE ('sens), *n.* language without meaning ; absurd talk.

NONSUIT ('sut), *n.* the withdrawal of a suit during trial either voluntarily or by judgment of the court on the discovery of error or defect in the pleadings.

NOOK (nook), *n.* a small recess or secluded retreat.

NOON (noon), *n.* the middle of the day, 12 o'clock ; height.

NOOSE (noos), *n.* a running knot.

NOR (nor), *conj.* and not ; likewise

not ; a negative particle correlative to *neither* or *not*.

NORMAL ('mal), *adj*. according to rule ; regular ; perpendicular.

NORMALCY (nor'mal-si), **NORMALITY** (-mal'i-ti), *n*. state of being normal.

NORMAN ('man), *adj*. pertaining to the Normans, Normandy, or to their style of architecture.

NORTH (north), *n*. one of the four cardinal points ; the point opposite to the south.

NORTHERN ('*th*ern), *adj*. in, from, or toward, the north.

NORTHERN LIGHTS (lits), *n.pl*. the aurora borealis.

NORTH STAR (star), *n*. the pole-star.

NOSE (noz), *n*. the organ of smell ; scent ; nozzle.

NOSE DIVE (div), the downward plunge of an airplane.

NOSEGAY ('ga), *n*. a bouquet.

NOSTALGIA (nos-tal'ji-a), *n*. homesickness.

NOSTRIL ('tril), *n*. one of the two openings in the nose.

NOSTRUM ('trum), *n*. a quack medicine.

NOT (not), *adv*. in no way ; to no extent ; a word expressive of denial or refusal.

NOTABILITY (-ta-bil'i-ti), *n*. a person of note.

NOTABLE (no'ta-bl), *adj*. worthy of notice ; memorable ; notorious ; remarkable ; industrious ; thrifty.

NOTARIAL (no-ta'ri-al), *adj*. pertaining to, or done by, a notary.

NOTARY (no'ta-ri), *n*. an official authorized to attest deeds, etc.

NOTATION (-ta'shun), *n*. the act of recording by marks or symbols ; a system of signs or symbols.

NOTCH (noch), *n*. a small cut.

NOTE (not), *n*. a memorandum ; reputation ; brief explanation ; short letter ; a mark or sign representing a musical sound ; a paper acknowledging a debt and promising payment ; a bank or government note.

NOTED ('ed), *p.adj*. celebrated.

NOTEWORTHY (-wer'*th*i), *adj*. remarkable.

NOTHING (nuth'ing), *n*. not anything ; a cipher.

NOTHINGNESS (-nes), *n*. non-existence.

NOTICE (no'tis), *n*. attention ; remark ; advice ; information ; warning ; public intimation.

NOTICEABLE (a-bl), *adj*. worthy of observation ; remarkable.

NOTIFICATION (-ti-fi-ka'shun), *n*. giving notice ; notice given.

NOTIFY ('ti-fi), *v.t*. to give notice to.

NOTION ('shun), *n*. opinion ; belief ; inclination : *pl*. small wares. [American.]

NOTORIETY (-to-ri'e-ti), *n*. the state of being notorious.

NOTORIOUS (-to'ri-us), *adj*. publicly known ; usually in a bad sense.

NOTWITHSTANDING (not-*with*-stand'ing), *prep*. in spite of : *conj*. although : *adv*. however ; yet.

NOUGAT (noo-ga'), *n*. a confection of almonds, etc.

NOUGHT, see naught.

NOUN (noun), *n*. in grammar, the name of any person, place or thing ; a substantive.

NOURISH (nur'ish), *v.t*. to feed or bring up ; support ; maintain ; educate.

NOURISHING (-ing), *p.adj*. nutritious.

NOURISHMENT (-ment), *n*. that which nourishes.

NOVEL (nov'el), *adj*. of recent origin or introduction ; new : *n*. a fictitious tale or romance.

NOVELETTE (-et'), *n*. a short novel.

NOVELIST ('el-ist), *n*. a writer of novels.

NOVELTY ('el-ti), *n*. newness ; something new.

NOVEMBER (no-vem'ber), *n*. the eleventh month of the year.

NOVICE (nov'is), *n*. a beginner.

NOVITIATE (no-vish'i-at), *n*. the state of a novice.

NOW (nou), *adv*. at the present time ; quite recently.

NOWISE (no'wiz), *adv.* not in any manner or degree.

NOXIOUS (nok'shus), *adj.* harmful ; pernicious ; deadly.

NOZZLE (noz'l), *n.* a projecting tube forming the vent of a hose, or pipe.

NUANCE (nu-angs'), *n.* [French], a shade of difference.

NUB (nub), *n.* a nob ; lump.

NUCLEUS ('kle-us), *n.* the central mass around which matter accretes or grows ; the head of a comet.

NUDATION (-da'shun), *n.* act of making bare.

NUDE (nud), *adj.* bare ; naked ; void.

NUDGE (nuj), *v.t.* to touch gently, as with the elbow.

NUDITY (nu'di-ti), *n.* nakedness.

NUGATORY (nu'ga-to-ri), *adj.* trifling ; useless.

NUGGET (nug'et), *n.* a lump or mass of metal, especially of gold.

NUISANCE (nu'sans), *n.* anything offensive or annoying.

NULL (nul), *adj.* of no legal force ; void.

NULLIFICATION (-i-fi-ka'shun), *n.* the act of nullifying.

NULLIFY ('i-fi), *v.t.* to annul or render void.

NULLITY (nul'i-ty), *n.* want of existence, force, or validity.

NUMB (num), *adj.* deprived of sensation or motion ; torpid.

NUMBER ('ber), *n.* a unit ; one, or more than one ; multitude ; one, of a series ; a collection of things ; poetry ; metre, or verse.

NUMERAL (nu'mer-al), *adj.* pertaining to number : *n.* a symbol or word expressing a number.

NUMERATE (-at), *v.t.* to reckon or enumerate ; point or read, as figures.

NUMERATOR ('mer-a-ter), *n.* one who numbers ; the figure or figures above the line in fractions which indicate how many parts of a unit are taken.

NUMERICAL (-mer'i-kal), *adj.* represented by numbers.

NUMEROUS ('mer-us), *adj.* consisting of a great number.

NUMISMATIC (-miz-mat'ik), *adj.* pertaining to coins or medals.

NUMSKULL ('skul), *n.* a blockhead.

NUN (nun), *n.* a female devoted to a religious life and seclusion.

NUNCIO ('shi-o), *n.* a papal ambassador ; a messenger.

NUNNERY (nun'er-i), *n.* a convent in which nuns reside.

NUPTIAL (nup'shal), *adj.* pertaining to marriage : *n.pl.* a marriage.

NURSE (ners), *n.* a woman who has the care of infants ; one who tends the sick or infirm : *v.t.* to bring up ; tend in sickness ; promote ; economize.

NURSERY ('er-i), *n.* an appartment for young children ; a place or garden for rearing plants.

NURSLING ('ling), *n.* an infant.

NURTURE (ner'tur), *n.* that which nourishes ; diet ; food ; education.

NUT (nut), *n.* the fruit of certain trees, containing a kernel inclosed in a shell ; a piece of metal grooved for screwing on to the end of a bolt.

NUTHATCH (nut'hach), *n.* a small bird.

NUTMEG (nut'meg), *n.* the aromatic kernel of the fruit of an East Indian tree.

NUTRIA (nu'tri-a), *n.* the fur of a South American rodent called the coypu.

NUTRIENT ('tri-ent), *adj.* promoting growth.

NUTRIMENT ('tri-ment), *n.* nourishment.

NUTRITION (-trish'un), *n.* that which nourishes ; food.

NUTRITIOUS ('us), *adj.* affording nutrition.

NUTRITIVE ('tri-tiv), *adj.* pertaining to, or having the quality of, nutrition.

NUTTY (nut'i), *adj.* abounding in, or tasting like, nuts.

NUX VOMICA (nuks vom'i-ka), *n.* the flat, poisonous seed of an East Indian tree.

NYMPH (nimf), *n.* in classic mythology, a goddess of nature inhabiting the mountains, woods, streams, etc.

O

O, o (o), *n.* the fifteenth letter of the English alphabet.

O, *o. n.* an abbreviation.

O, *n.* a Roman numeral denoting 11; with a bar (ō), 11,000.

OAK (ok), *n.* a valuable forest tree, the timber of which is used extensively for building purposes and for furniture.

OAKUM ('um), *n.* old ropes untwisted and pulled into loose hemp.

OAR (or), *n.* a light pole with a broad blade, for rowing a boat.

OASIS (o-a'sis), *n.* [*pl.* oases ('sez)], a fertile spot in a barren, sandy desert.

OAT (ot), *n.* an edible grain or seed of a cereal grass; the plant itself.

OATH (oth), *n.* a solemn declaration of truth-telling with an appeal to God as witness; a blasphemous use of the name of God.

OATMEAL (ot'mel), *n.* ground oats.

OB-, a prefix signifying *before, against, toward, in front of, reversed.*

OBDURACY ('du-ra-si), *n.* obdurate conduct or quality.

OBDURATE ('du-rat), *adj.* hardened in heart or feelings, especially against moral influence.

OBEDIENCE (o-be'di-ens), *n.* submission to authority; dutifulness.

OBEDIENT ('di-ent), *adj.* dutiful.

OBEISANCE (-ba'sans), *n.* a bow or curtsey; act of reverence.

OBELISK (ob'e-lisk), *n.* a lofty, four-sided stone pillar gradually tapering as it rises.

OBESE (o-bes'), *adj.* corpulent.

OBESITY (-bes'i-ti), *n.* excessive corpulence, especially of an unhealthy kind.

OBEY (-ba'), *v.t.* to submit to the rule or authority of.

OBFUSCATE (ob-fus'kat), *v.t.* to bewilder.

OBITUARY (o-bit'u-a-ri), *n.* a register of deaths; an account of a deceased person.

OBJECT (ob-jekt'), *v.t.* to urge against; oppose : *n.* (ob'jekt), anything placed before the mind or senses; motive; end.

OBJECTION (-jek'shun), *n.* adverse reason; difficulty raised.

OBJECTIONABLE (-a-bl), *adj.* liable or open to objection; reprehensible.

OBJECTIVE ('tiv), *adj.* pertaining to an object; external to the mind : *n.* the accusative case; an objective point.

OBJECTIVITY (-tiv'i-ti), *n.* the state or quality of being objective.

OBJURGATE (-jer'gat), *v.t.* to chide or reprove.

OBJURGATION (-ga'shun), *n.* strong reproof.

OBJURGATORY ('ga-to-ri), *adj.* expressing sharp rebuke.

OBLATE (-lat'), *adj.* depressed or flattened at the poles; consecrated.

OBLATION (-la'shun), *n.* an offering or sacrifice in religious worship.

OBLIGATE (ob'li-gat), *v.t.* to bind by law; oblige.

OBLIGATION (-li-ga'shun), *n.* the binding power of a vow, promise, or contract; in law, a bond to which a penalty is annexed.

OBLIGATORY (ob-lig'a-to-ri, ob'li-ga-to-ri), *adj.* morally or legally binding.

OBLIGE (o-blij'), *v.t.* to constrain by force, morally, legally, or physically; bind by some favour or kindness rendered.

OBLIGEE (ob-li-je'), *n.* one to whom a bond is given.

OBLIQUE (-lek'), *adj.* deviating from a right line; not parallel.

OBLIQUITY (ob-lik'wi-ti), *n.* being oblique; moral error.

OBLITERATE (-lit'er-at), *v.t.* to efface or wear out; destroy.

OBLIVION (-liv'i-un), *n.* forgetfulness; state of being forgotten.

OBLIVIOUS ('i-us), *adj.* forgetful; mentally absent.

OBLONG ('long), *adj.* longer than broad.

OBLOQUY ('lo-kwi), *n.* reproachful language; calumny; slander; reproach; infamy.

OBNOXIOUS (nok'shus), *adj.* hateful; offensive; unpopular.

OBOE (o'boi, o'bo-e), *n.* a musical wind instrument of the reed class.

OBOVATE (-o'vat); *adj.* inversely ovate.

OBSCENE (ob-sen'), *adj.* offensive to chastity; indecent.

OBSCENELY ('li), *adv.* in an obscene manner.

OBSCURE (-skur'), *adj.* without light or distinctness; dark; not easily understood; secluded; humble.

OBSEQUIES ('se-kwiz), *n.pl.* funeral rites.

OBSEQUIOUS (-se'kwi-us), *adj.* servile; compliant to excess.

OBSERVABLE (-zer'va-bl), *adj.* capable of being observed; remarkable.

OBSERVANCE ('vans), *n.* the act of observing; rule of practice.

OBSERVANT ('vant), *adj.* attentive; mindful.

OBSERVATION (-va'shun), *n.* the act of observing; attention; remark; note.

OBSERVATORY ('va-to-ri), *n.* a building fitted up for astronomical research.

OBSERVE (-zerv'), *v.t.* to keep in view; celebrate; mention.

OBSESS (ob-ses'), *v.t.* to influence to an unreasonable degree.

OBSESSION (ob-sesh'un), *n.* the state of being possessed by one idea to the exclusion of others.

OBSOLESCENCE (so-les'ens), *n.* the state of becoming obsolete.

OBSOLETE ('so-let), *adj.* out of date; disused.

OBSTETRIC (-stet'rik), **OBSTETRICAL** ('ri-kal), *adj.* pertaining to midwifery.

OBSTETRICIAN (-ste-trish'an), *n.* an accoucheur.

OBSTETRICS (ob-stet'riks), *n.* the science of midwifery.

OBSTINACY ('sti-na-si), *n.* stubbornness.

OBSTINATE ('sti-nat), *adj.* pertinaciously adhering to one's opinion or purpose; stubborn.

OBSTREPEROUS (-strep'er-us), *adj.* clamorously noisy; turbulent.

OBSTRUCT (-strukt'), *v.t.* to block up or impede; interrupt.

OBSTRUCTION (-struk'shun), *n.* an impediment.

OBTAIN (-tan'), *v.t.* to get possession of; gain; acquire; win; procure.

OBTRUDE (-trood'), *v.t.* to thrust in or upon; urge or offer with unreasonable importunity.

OBTRUSIVE (troo'siv), *adj.* inclined or apt to intrude.

OBTUSE (-tus'), *adj.* not pointed or acute; dull.

OBTUSENESS ('nes), *n.* bluntness; mental dullness.

OBVERSE (-vers'), *adj.* facing one; opposed to *reverse*; bearing the head; said of a coin or medal; narrower at the base than the top.

OBVERT (-vert), *v.t.* to turn toward; face.

OBVIATE ('vi-at), *v.t.* to remove, as difficulties or objections.

OBVIOUS ('vi-us), *adj.* evident; manifest; plain.

OBVOLUTE ('vo-lut), *adj.* arranged to overlap.

OCCASION (o-ka'shun), *n.* occurrence; state of affairs; opportunity; incidental cause or need; exigence.

OCCASIONAL (-al), *adj.* incidental or casual.

OCCIDENT (ok'si-dent), *n.* the West; the countries west of Asia Minor; Western Hemisphere.

OCCULT (o-kult'), *adj.* hidden; secret; invisible.

OCCULTISM ('tizm), *n.* investigation of mysterious and supernatural things, occurrences, and phenomena.

OCCUPANCY (ok'u-pan-si), *n.* the act of taking and holding in possession.

OCCUPANT (-pant), *n.* one who has possession.

OCCUPATION (-pa'shun), *n.* business, employment, or calling.

OCCUPY ('u-pi), *v.t.* to take possession of; fill or cover; employ: *v.i.* to traffic.

OCCUR (o-ker'), *v.i.* to happen or take place; come to mind.

OCCURRENCE (-kur'ens), *n.* an accident, event, or incident.

OCEAN (o'shan), *n.* the vast expanse of salt water covering about ¾ of the globe.

OCEANIC (-she-an'ik), *adj.* pertaining to the ocean.

OCHRE (o'ker), *n.* a fine yellow- or brown-coloured clay.

O'CLOCK (o-klok'), a contraction for *of the clock.*

OCTA-, OCTO-, a prefix signifying *eight.*

OCTAGON (ok'ta-gon), *n.* a plane figure of 8 sides and 8 angles.

OCTAGONAL (-tag'o-nal), *adj.* having 8 sides and 8 angles.

OCTAVE ('tav), *n.* an eighth; an interval of 12 semitones; the eighth tone in a scale; the 8th day after a church festival.

OCTAVO (-ta'vo), *n.* a sheet of printing paper folded in 8 leaves or 16 pages (8vo).

OCTOBER (-to'ber), *n.* the tenth month of the year.

OCTODECIMO (-to-des'i-mo), *adj.* consisting of 18 leaves or 36 pages to a sheet: *n.* a book of such size (18mo).

OCTOGENARIAN (-to-je-na'ri-an), one who is 80 years old.

OCTOPUS ('to-pus), *n.* the type genus of the Octopoda; the eight-armed cuttle-fish.

OCTOROON (-to-roon'), *n.* the offspring of a white person and a quadroon.

OCTUPLE ('tu-pl), *adj.* eightfold.

OCULAR ('u-lar), *adj.* pertaining to the eye; known from actual sight.

OCULIST ('u-list), *n.* one who is skilled in the treatment of eye diseases.

ODD (od), *adj.* not even; not divisible by 2; unusual; eccentric.

ODD FELLOW ('fel-o), *n.* a member of the Independent Order of Odd Fellows (I.O.O.F.).

ODDITY ('i-ti), *n.* a person or thing that is peculiar; eccentricity; strangeness.

ODDS (odz), *n.pl.* inequality; advantage; superiority; quarrel; dispute.

ODE (od), *n.* a short song; lyric poem.

ODIOUS (o'di-us), *adj.* offensive.

ODIUM ('di-um), *n.* hatred; stigma; dislike.

ODONTO-, a combining form from the Greek *odous*, a tooth.

ODONTOID (-don'toid), *adj.* tooth-like.

ODOUR (o'der), *n.* a scent; estimation.

ODORIFEROUS (-der-if'er-us), *adj.* diffusing fragrance.

ODOROUS ('der-us), *adj.* emitting an odour; fragrant.

ODYSSEY (od'i-si), *n.* the great epic poem of Homer.

O'ER, same as over; poetical.

OF (ov), *prep.* from; out of; belonging to; according to; proceeding from.

OFFAL (of'al), *n.* refuse; waste meat.

OFFENCE (-fens'), *n.* any cause of anger or displeasure; insult; injury.

OFFEND (o-fend'), *v.t.* to displease or make angry; molest or annoy; pain.

OFFENSIVE (-fen'siv), *adj.* annoying; disagreeable; disgusting; used in attack.

OFFER (off'er), *v.t.* to present for acceptance or refusal; proffer.

OFFICE (of'is), *n.* public or private business; employment; function; act of worship; apartment for business.

OFFICER ('is-er), *n.* a person commissioned to perform a certain public duty.

OFFICIAL (o-fish'al), *adj.* pertaining to an office or public duty; from the proper authority.

OFFICIATE ('i-at), *v.i.* to perform the duties of an office.

OFFICIOUS ('us), *adj.* too forward in offering services; meddling.

OFFING (of'ing), *n.* that part of the sea with deep water off the shore.

OFFSCOURING ('skour-ing), *n.* refuse.

OFFSCUM ('skum), *n.* dregs; filth.

OFFSET ('set), *n.* a sum set aside as an equivalent for another; a branch that touches the soil and takes root.

OFFSPRING ('spring), *n.* that which is produced by an animal or plant; child; children; descendants.

OFTEN (of''n), *adv.* many times; frequently.

OGLE (o'gl), *v.t.* to look fondly at with a side glance.

OGRE (o'ger), *n.* an imaginary man-eating monster or giant.

OH (o), *interj.* an exclamation of wonder, pain, or anxiety.

OHM (om), *n.* the unit of electrical resistance.

OIL (oil), *n.* an unctuous, inflammable substance obtained from animal, vegetable, and mineral matter.

OILINESS ('i-nes), *n.* oily quality; greasiness.

OINTMENT (oint'ment), *n.* an unctuous substance applied to a wound or injured part.

OKAPI (o-ka'pi), *n.* animal resembling a giraffe.

OKRA (ok'ra), *n.* a plant of southern U.S. and the West Indies, used as pickles, and a basis for soups, stews, etc.; gumbo.

OLD (old), *adj.* aged; decayed by time; ancient; out of date.

OLDEN (ol'den), *adj.* ancient; bygone.

OLD GLORY (glo'ri), the Flag of the U.S., the Stars and Stripes.

OLDISH (old'ish), *adj.* somewhat old.

OLD TESTAMENT (tes'ta-ment), the covenant of God with the Hebrews as set forth in the Bible.

OLEAGINOUS (o-le-aj'i-nus), *adj.* oily; unctuous.

OLEANDER (-an'der), *n.* an evergreen shrub with fragrant flowers.

OLEO-, a combining form from the Latin *oleum*, oil.

OLEOMARGARINE (-o-mar'ga-ren), *n.* imitation butter.

OLFACTORY (ol-fak'to-ri), *adj.* pertaining to the sense of smell.

OLIGARCHAL (ol'i-gar'kal), **OLIGARCHIC** ('kik), **OLIGARCHICAL** ('ki-kal), *adj.* pertaining to an oligarchy.

OLIGARCHY ('i-gar-ki), *n.* government in which the supreme power is in the hands of a few.

OLIVE (ol'iv), *n.* a tree cultivated from the earliest times in southern Europe and the Near East for its fruit and wood.

OLIVE-BRANCH (-branch), *n.* branch of olive; emblem of peace.

OLIVE OIL (oil), *n.* an edible oil expressed from olives.

OLYMPIC (o-lim'pik), *adj.* pertaining to Mt. Olympus; referring to the games of ancient Greece or to the modern games patterned after the ancient sports.

OLYMPIC GAMES (gamz), a modern revival of the ancient contests held on Mt. Olympus; they occur every four years and are held in various capitals of the world.

OMEGA (o-me'ga), *n.* the last letter of the Greek alphabet; hence, the last; end.

OMELET (om'e-let), *n.* eggs beaten in milk and fried.

OMEN (o'men), *n.* a sign of some future event.

OMINOUS (om'i-nus), *adj.* foreboding evil; inauspicious.

OMISSION (o-mish'un), *n.* neglect or failure to do something required.

OMIT (-mit'), *v.t.* to leave out; neglect.

OMNI-, a prefix signifying *all, entirely.*

OMNIBUS (om'ni-bus), *n.* a public four-wheeled vehicle for passengers.

OMNINESCIENCE (-nes'shi-ens), *n.* ignorance of everything.

OMNIPOTENCE (-nip'o-tens), *n.* unlimited power.

OMNIPOTENT ('o-tent), *adj.* having unlimited power.

OMNIPOTENT, *n.* God (with *the*).

OMNIPRESENCE (-ni-prez'ens), *n.* universal presence.

OMNISCIENT (-nish'ent), *adj.* knowing all things; infinitely wise.

OMNIVOROUS (-niv'er-us), *adj.* feeding upon animal and vegetable food.

ON (on), *prep.* upon; in contact with the upper part; at; near: *adv.* forward; onward.

ONCE (wuns), *adv.* at one time; formerly.

ONE (wun), *adj.* single in number; individual.

ONEROUS (on'er-us), *adj.* burden-some; weighty; oppressive.

ONE-STEP (wun'step), *n.* a very simple and popular modern dance.

ONION (un'yun), *n.* the well-known, common, garden vegetable plant.

ONLY (on'li), *adj.* single : *adv.* singly; merely.

ONSET ('set), *n.* an assault; attack.

ONSLAUGHT ('slawt), *n.* a furious attack.

ONTOLOGY (on-tol'o-ji), *n.* the logic of pure being; the science that investigates the nature of being.

ONUS (o'nus), *n.* a burden; duty.

ONWARD (on'werd), *adj.* advancing; progressing : *adv.* in advance.

ONYX (on'iks), *n.* a variety of agate.

OOLONG (oo'long), *n.* a Chinese black tea.

OOZE (ooz), *n.* soft mud or slime; gentle flow.

OPACITY (o-pas'i-ti), *n.* opaqueness.

OPAL ('pal), *n.* a precious stone, exhibiting a play of various colours.

OPALINE ('pal-in), *adj.* pertaining to, or resembling, the opal.

OPAQUE (-pak'), *adj.* not transparent.

OPAQUENESS (-nes), *n.* the quality or state of being opaque.

OPEN (o'p'n), *adj.* not shut; un-fastened; clear of trees; expanded; uncovered; unsealed; clear; un-reserved; generous; frank; sincere.

OPENING (-ing), *n.* an aperture; beginning; opportunity.

OPERA (op'er-a), *n.* a musical drama.

OPERA BOUFFE (o-pa-ra'boof), [French], a comic opera.

OPERATE ('er-at), *v.i.* to work; produce a certain effect; perform a surgical operation.

OPERATIC (-at'ik), *adj.* pertaining to the opera.

OPERATION (-a'shun), *n.* agency; effect; manipulation; surgical per-formance with instruments.

OPERATIVE ('er-a-tiv), *adj.* effica-cious; vigorous : *n.* a workman.

OPERATOR ('er-a-ter), *n.* one who, or that which, operates.

OPHTHALMIA (of-thal'mi-a), *n.* inflammation of the eye or eyeball.

OPHTHALMOLOGIST (-mol'o-jist), *n.* one who is skilled in diseases of the eye.

OPIATE (o'pi-at), *n.* a medicine compounded with opium to induce sleep or rest; narcotic.

OPINE (o-pin'), *v.i.* to think; be of opinion.

OPINION (-pin'yun), *n.* belief or judgment; estimation of the value, or importance, of a thing.

OPINIONATED (-a-ted), *adj.* firm or obstinate in one's opinions.

OPIUM (o'pi-um), *n.* a drug prepared from the inspissated juice of a poppy.

OPOSSUM (o-pos'um), *n.* an American marsupial mammal.

OPPONENT (o-po'nent), *adj.* oppo-site; adverse; antagonistic : *n.* one who opposes; adversary.

OPPORTUNE (op'or-tun, -tun'), *adj.* well-timed; seasonable.

OPPORTUNITY (-tu'ni-ti), *n.* con-venient time or occasion.

OPPOSE (-poz'), *v.t.* to act against; resist; check.

OPPOSITE (op'o-zit), *adj.* placed in front; contrary; adverse.

OPPOSITION (-zish'un), *n.* hostile resistance; contrariety.

OPPRESS (o-pres'), *v.t.* to burden; lie heavily upon.

OPPRESSION (-presh'un), *n.* hard-ship; calamity; injustice; lassitude; dullness.

OPPRESSIVE (-pres'iv), *adj.* un-justly severe; tyrannical.

OPPRESSOR ('er), *n.* one who oppresses.

OPPROBRIOUS (-pro'bri-us), *adj.* expressive of opprobrium.

OPPROBRIUM ('bri-um), *n.* re-proach with disdain or contempt.

OPTIC (op'tik), *adj.* pertaining to vision : also *optical*.

OPTICIAN (-tish'an), *n.* one skilled in optics.

OPTIMISM ('ti-mizm), *n.* the doc-trine that everything in the present existence is for the best.

OPTIMIST ('ti-mist), *n.* one who holds the doctrine of optimism.

OPTIMISTIC (-mis'tik), *adj.* sanguine.

OPTION ('shun), *n.* power or right of choice ; wish ; selection.

OPTIONAL (-al), *adj.* left to one's wish or choice.

OPTOLOGIST (-tol'o-jist), *n.* a sight-testing optician.

OPTOMETER (-tom'e-ter), *n.* an optical instrument for measuring the range of vision.

OPTOMETRY (-tri), *n.* measurement of the range of vision by means of an optometer.

OPULENCE ('u-lens), *n.* wealth ; riches ; plenty.

OPULENT ('u-lent), *adj.* wealthy ; rich.

OPUS (o'pus), *n.* [*pl.* opera (op'er-a)], a work ; musical composition.

OR (or), *conj.* the correlative of *either*.

ORACLE ('a-kl), *n.* a prophetic declaration ; a prophet of reputed wisdom.

ORACULAR (o-rak'u-lar), *adj.* dogmatically magisterial ; ambiguous ; venerable.

ORAL (o'ral), *adj.* verbal.

ORALLY (-li), *adv.* verbally.

ORANGE (or'enj), *n.* a round, juicy fruit with a reddish-yellow rind ; the tree that produces this fruit.

ORANGEMAN (-man), *n.* a member of a political society of Irish Protestants.

ORANG-OUTANG (o-rang'oo-tang), *n.* the great anthropoid ape.

ORATION (-ra'shun), *n.* a formal public speech.

ORATOR (or'a-ter), *n.* one who makes an oration ; an eloquent speaker.

ORATORIO (-to'ri-o), *n.* a musical composition having a sacred theme as its subject.

ORATORY ('a-to-ri), *n.* the art of an orator ; eloquence.

ORB (orb), *n.* a circular body ; sphere ; the eye.

ORBIT (or'bit), *n.* the bony cavity of the eye ; the path described by a heavenly body during its periodical revolution.

ORCHARD ('cherd), *n.* an inclosure of fruit trees.

ORCHESTRA (or'kes-tra), *n.* in a theatre or music hall, the place occupied by the musicians ; the body of musicians.

ORCHID ('kid), *n.* a plant with a handsome flower, often of fantastic shape, of the genus Orchis.

ORDAIN (-dan'), *v.t.* to appoint ; institute ; invest with ministerial functions.

ORDEAL ('del), *n.* a medieval trial by fire, water, combat, etc., to determine the guilt or innocence of an accused person ; hence, a severe trial or test.

ORDER ('der), *n.* rule ; regulation ; command ; class ; rank ; degree ; a religious fraternity.

ORDERLY ('der-li), *adj.* well regulated ; methodical ; peaceable : *n.* a soldier who attends upon an officer.

ORDINANCE ('di-nans), *n.* an established rule, rite, or law.

ORDINARILY ('di-na-ri-li), *adj.* according to established rule ; usually.

ORDINARY ('di-na-ri), *adj.* usual ; customary ; commonplace ; mediocre.

ORDINATION (-na'shun), *n.* the act of conferring holy orders.

ORDNANCE (ord'nans), *n.* artillery ; military supplies.

ORE (or), *n.* metal as extracted from the earth.

ORGAN (or'gan), *n.* a musical instrument ; means of communication ; that part of living structure by means of which some function is performed.

ORGANDIE ('gan-di), *n.* thin muslin.

ORGANIC (gan'ik), **ORGANICAL** (-i-kal), *adj.* pertaining to organs ; instrumental.

ORGANISM ('gan-izm), *n.* organical structure.

ORGANIST (-ist), *n.* a performer on the organ.

ORGANIZATION (-i-za'shun), *n.* organic structure ; the act of organizing.

ORGANIZE ('gan-iz), *v.t.* to carry out a scheme efficiently ; systematize.

ORGANISER (-er), *n.* one who organizes.

ORGY ('ji), *n.* a drunken revel.

ORIENT (o'ri-ent), *adj.* Oriental : *n.* the East.

ORIENT ('ri-ent), *adj.* bright ; lustrous ; rising : *v.t.* to define.

ORIENTAL (-en'tal), *adj.* pertaining to the East.

ORIENTATION (-ta'shun), *n.* the determination of the position of the east ; eastward position.

ORIFICE (or'i-fis), *n.* a mouth or aperture.

ORIGIN ('i-jin), *n.* beginning ; first existence ; source ; cause.

ORIGINAL (o-rij'i-nal), *adj.* first in order ; having power to originate ; not copied.

ORIGINALLY (-li), *adv.* at first.

ORIGINATE (-rij'i-nat), *v.t.* to bring into existence.

ORIGINATION (-na'shun), *n.* first production ; source.

ORIGINATOR ('i-na-ter), *n.* one who originates.

ORIOLE (o'ri-ol), *n.* one of a family of birds ; the *golden oriole*, the *Baltimore oriole*, the *orchard oriole*.

ORMOLU (or'mo-loo), *n.* bronze or copper gilt in imitation of gold.

ORNAMENT ('na-ment), *n.* anything that adorns or beautifies.

ORNAMENTATION (-ta'shun), *n.* decoration.

ORNATE (-nat'), *adj.* ornamented.

ORNATELY ('li), *adv.* in an ornate manner.

ORNITHOLOGY ('ni-thol'o-ji), *n.* the scientific study of the structure, habits, etc., of birds.

OROIDE (o'ro-id), *n.* an alloy of tin and copper resembling gold in colour.

OROTUND (o'ro-tund), *adj.* characterized by fullness, clearness, strength, and smoothness.

ORPHAN (or'fan), *n.* a child bereft of one or both parents.

ORPHANAGE (-aj), *n.* the state of an orphan ; an institution for orphans.

ORRIS ('is), *n.* gold or silver lace ; the iris.

ORRIS-ROOT (-root), *n.* the dried roots of the Florentine orris : used in perfumery.

ORTHO-, a combining form from the Greek *orthos*, straight, right, direct.

ORTHODOX (or'tho-doks), *adj.* holding, or in accordance with, the received or established belief or doctrine.

ORTHODOXY (-dok-si), *n.* conformity to orthodox belief or opinion.

ORTHOGRAPHER (-thog'ra-fer), **ORTHOGRAPHIST** (-fist), *n.* one skilled in orthography.

ORTHOGRAPHIC (-tho-graf'ik), **ORTHOGRAPHICAL** (-i-kal), *adj.* pertaining to orthography ; correctly spelt.

ORTHOGRAPHY (-thog'ra-fi), *n.* the art of spelling and writing words correctly.

ORTHOLOGY (-thol'o-ji), *n.* art of using words correctly.

ORTHOPHONY (or-thof'o-ni), *n.* art of correct speaking.

ORTOLAN ('to-lan), *n.* a small bird, allied to the bunting.

ORYX (o'riks), *n.* a genus of large, African antelopes.

OS (os), *n.* [Latin], [*pl.* ossa ('a)], a bone.

OS (os), *n.* [Latin], [*pl.* ora (o'ra)], a mouth ; opening.

OSCILLATE ('i-lat), *v.i.* & *v.t.* to swing backwards and forwards ; vibrate.

OSCILLATOR (os'i-la-ter), *n.* that which oscillates ; a device for producing electric current.

OSCULANT (os'ku-lant), *adj.* kissing ; clinging.

OSCULATE ('ku-lat), *v.t.* & *v.i.* to kiss.

OSCULATION (-la'shun), *n.* kissing.

OSSEOUS ('e-us), *adj.* pertaining to, consisting of, or like, bone.

OSSIFICATION (os-i-fi-ka'shun), *n.* conversion of soft animal tissue into bone.

OSSIFORM ('i-form), *adj.* like bone.

OSSIFY ('i-fi), *v.t.* to convert into bone or into a bone-like substance.

OSTENSIBLE (-ten'si-bl), *adj.* apparent ; plausible.

OSTENSIVE ('ten-siv), *adj.* showing ; exhibiting.

OSTENTATION (-ta'shun), *n.* ambitious or vain display.

OSTENTATIOUS ('shus), *adj.* fond of show ; intended for vain display ; gaudy.

OSTEOPATH (os'te-o-path), *n.* a practitioner of osteopathy.

OSTEOPATHY (-op'a-thi), *n.* a system of therapeutics in which the treatment is by manipulation of the bones, muscles, and nerve centres.

OSTLER (os'ler), *n.* a man who attends to horses at an inn.

OSTRACISM ('tra-sizm), *n.* banishment by ostracizing.

OSTRACIZE ('tra-siz), *v.t.* to banish by popular vote ; exclude from public or private favour.

OSTRICH ('trich), *n.* the largest of all birds ; valued for its plumes.

OTHER (uth'er), *adj.* noting something besides ; different ; contrary : *pron.* one remaining, or part remaining ; a different one : *adv.* otherwise : *conj.* or ; either : *n.* that which is an opposite of something else.

OTHERWISE (-wiz), *adv.* in another manner ; in other respects : *conj.* else.

OTIOSE (o'shi-os), *adj.* idle ; useless ; functionless.

OTIOSITY (-os'i-ti), *n.* state of idleness.

OTTOMAN (ot'o-man), *adj.* pertaining to the Turks.

OTTOMAN ('o-man), *n.* a cushioned seat ; a corded silk fabric.

OUGHT (awt), *v.i.* to be under obligation ; be fit, necessary, or proper : *n.* a cipher ; naught.

OUNCE (ouns), *n.* a weight $\frac{1}{16}$th of a pound avoirdupois ; $\frac{1}{12}$th of a pound troy ; a carnivorous animal.

OUR (our), *pron.* pertaining to, or belonging to, us.

OURSELVES (-selvz'), *pron. pl.* we or us, not others.

OUST (oust), *v.t.* to eject ; put out ; bar ; remove.

OUSTER (ous'ter), *n.* in law, dispossession.

OUT (out), *adj.* outside ; external ; not engaged.

OUT-, used as a combining form and as a separable and inseparable prefix in many compounds, and as the meaning of most is obvious, such do not find a place in the list of definitions.

OUTCAST ('kast), *adj.* cast out ; rejected : *n.* an exile.

OUTCRY ('kri), *n.* clamour ; tumult.

OUTFIT ('fit), *n.* equipment.

OUTLANDER (out'lan-der), *n.* a foreigner.

OUTLAW ('law), *n.* one who is deprived of legal benefits and protection.

OUTLINE ('lin), *n.* a line bounding or defining a figure ; first sketch : *v.t.* to sketch out ; to give principal facts.

OUTPUT (out'poot), *n.* the total quantity of any product manufactured or produced.

OUTRAGE ('raj), *n.* open and excessive violence ; wanton abuse.

OUTRE (oo-tra'), *adj.* [Fr.], overstrained ; exaggerated.

OUTRIGHT ('rit), *adj.* positive ; downright : *adv.* completely.

OUTSIDE ('sid), *n.* the external part of anything ; utmost.

OUTSPOKEN (spo-kn), *adj.* candid ; frank.

OUTWARD ('werd), *adj.* external ; visible ; extrinsic.

OUTWARD-BOUND (-bound), *adj.* sailing to foreign parts.

OUTWIT (-wit), *v.t.* to overreach, or defeat, by superior skill or cunning.

OVAL (o'val), *adj.* shaped like an egg ; elliptical.

OVARY ('va-ri), *n.* the organ in a female animal in which the ova or first germs of future life are formed.

OVATION (o-va'shun), *n.* an enthusiastic demonstration of public esteem.

OVEN (uv'n), *n.* a place or apparatus for baking or heating.

OVERBEARING (-bar'ing), *adj.* arrogant ; tyrannical.

OVERCAST (-kast), *n.* a covering, especially of clouds ; a calculation in excess : *adj.* cloudy.

OVERCOME (-kum), *v.t.* to conquer ; subdue ; vanquish.

OVERHAUL (-hawl), *v.t.* to examine thoroughly ; overtake ; gain upon.

OVERPLUS (-plus), *n.* excess.

OVERPOWER (-pou'er), *v.t.* to vanquish.

OVERPRODUCTION (-pro-duk'-shun), *n.* supply in excess of the demand.

OVERSEER (-se'er), *n.* a superintendent.

OVERT ('vert), *adj.* open ; public.

OVERTAKE (o-ver-tak'), *v.t.* to catch by pursuit ; take by surprise.

OVERTHROW (-thro'), *v.t.* to demolish ; vanquish ; destroy : *n.* ('ver-thro), ruin ; defeat.

OVERTONES (-tonz), *n.pl.* harmonics.

OVERTURE (-tur), *n.* an offer or proposal ; opening ; a musical introduction.

OVERWHELM (-hwelm'), *v.t.* to crush or destroy utterly.

OVIPAROUS (o-vip'a-rus), *adj.* denoting reproduction by eggs that hatch outside the body.

OVOVIVIPAROUS (o-vo-vi-vip'a-rus), *adj.* denoting the production of eggs that are hatched within the body, as is the case with certain reptiles and fishes.

OWE (o), *v.t.* to be indebted, or under obligation to ; be obliged to pay.

OWING ('ing), *p.adj.* due as a debt ; ascribable to.

OWL (oul), *n.* a raptorial, nocturnal bird.

OWN (on), *adj.* belonging to ; peculiar or proper to.

OWNER ('er), *n.* lawful proprietor.

OWNERSHIP ('er-ship), *n.* rightful possession.

OXALIC ACID (ok-sal'ik as'id), a diabasic acid.

OXEYE (oks'i), *n.* the yellow daisy ; the field camomile.

OXIDIZE ('si-diz), *v.t.* to convert into an oxide : *v.i.* to be converted into an oxide.

OXY-, a combining form from the Greek *oxys*, indicating the presence of *oxygen* or its compounds.

OXYGEN (ok'si-jen), *n.* a colourless, inodorous gas, which, with nitrogen and argon, constitutes ⅕th by volume of the atmosphere and, in combination with hydrogen, forms water.

OXYGENATE (-si-jen-at), **OXYGENIZE** (-jen-iz), *v.t.* to combine with oxygen.

OXYHYDROGEN (-si-hi'dro-jen), *adj.* consisting of a mixture of oxygen and hydrogen.

OYER (o'yer), *n.* a hearing or trial of legal causes.

OYER AND TERMINER (ter'mi-ner), a court constituted by commission to hear and determine special causes.

OYSTER (ois'ter), *n.* a marine bivalve mollusk.

OZONE (o'zon), *n.* an allotropic form of oxygen present in the atmosphere, especially after electrical disturbance.

OZONIZER (-niz-er), *n.* an apparatus for converting oxygen into ozone.

P

P, p (pe), *n.* the sixteenth letter of the English alphabet.

P, p, *n.* an abbreviation.

P, *n.* a Roman numeral denoting 400 ; with a bar (P̄), 400,000.

PA (pa), *n.* abbreviation of papa.

PABULUM (pab'u-lum), *n.* food ; nourishment.

PACE (pas), *n.* a step ; manner of walking ; length of stride.

PACHY- (pak'i), a combining form from the Greek *pachys*, thick.

PACHYDERM (-derm), *n.* one of the Pachydermata ; an elephant.

PACIFIC (pa-sif'ik), *adj.* peace-making ; conciliatory ; peaceful : *n.* [P.-], the Pacific Ocean.

PACIFICATION (-i-ka'shun), *n.* the act of peace-making ; conciliation.

PACIFICATOR (-sif'i-ka-ter), *n.* a peacemaker.

PACIFIST (pas'i-fist), *n.* one who opposes war.

PACIFY ('i-fi), *v.i.* to calm or appease; assuage.

PACK (pak), *n.* a large bundle; load; burden.

PACKAGE ('aj), *n.* a bundle of goods.

PACKER (pak'er), *n.* one who packs.

PACKET ('et), *n.* a small pack, or parcel; a vessel sailing between two or more ports.

PACT (pakt), *n.* a compact.

PAD (pad), *n.* a cushion; a tablet of writing paper; the leaf of an aquatic plant.

PADDING ('ing), *n.* material used for stuffing.

PADDLE ('l), *v.i.* play in the water: *v.t.* to propel by paddle.

PADDOCK ('uk), *n.* a small field adjacent to a stable.

PADLOCK (pad'lok), *n.* a lock with a link to pass through a staple or eye.

PADRONE (pa-dro'na), *n.* [Italian], an Italian employer of labour.

PÆAN (pe'an), *n.* a triumphal song.

PÆONY, same as peony.

PAGAN (pa'gan), *n.* a heathen.

PAGANISM (-izm), *n.* idolatry.

PAGE (paj), *n.* a boy in livery; a male attendant on a legislative body; one side of the leaf of a book.

PAGEANT (paj'ent), *n.* a spectacle.

PAGEANTRY (-ri), *n.* ostentatious display.

PAGINATION (-na'shun), *n.* the making into pages.

PAGODA (pa-go'da), *n.* a Buddhist temple; a Hindu idol temple.

PAIL (pal), *n.* an open vessel of wood or metal for carrying water, etc.

PAIN (pan), *n.* physical or mental suffering; penalty.

PAINFUL ('fool), *adj.* full of, or causing pain.

PAINT (pant), *v.t.* to represent by delineation and colours; depict; cover with colour: *n.* a colouring substance or pigment.

PAINTER (pan'ter), *n.* one whose occupation is to paint; an artist; a rope for fastening a boat.

PAIR (par), *n.* two things of a kind.

PAJAMAS (pa-ja'maz), *n.pl.* a sleeping costume.

PAL (pal), *n.* an intimate friend; accomplice.

PALACE (pal'as), *n.* the residence of a sovereign or bishop.

PALÆO-, PALEO- (pal'e-o), a combining form from the Greek *palaios*, ancient.

PALÆOETHNOLOGY (-eth-nol'o-ji), *n.* the science which treats of the earliest races of mankind.

PALÆOLITH (-o-lith), *n.* a rude stone object or implement of the early Stone Age.

PALATABLE (pal'at-a-bl), *adj.* agreeable to the taste; savoury.

PALATE ('at), *n.* the roof of the mouth; taste or relish.

PALATIAL (pa-la'shal), *adj.* pertaining to a palace; royal.

PALAVER (pa-la'ver), *n.* a public conference; superfluous or idle talk; chatter.

PALE (pal), *adj.* wan; wanting in colour; of a faint lustre.

PALETTE (pal'et), *n.* a thin oval wood, or porcelain plate, for mixing and holding colours.

PALFREY (pawl'fri), *n.* a small saddle-horse for a lady's use.

PALINDROME (pal'in-drom), *n.* a word, verse, or sentence which reads the same backward or forward, as " Able was I ere I saw Elba."

PALING ('ing), *n.* a fence constructed of pales.

PALINGENESIS (pal-in-jen'-e-sis), *n.* new birth or regeneration.

PALISADE (-i-sad'), *n.* a fence or fortification formed of stakes driven into the ground; a line of rocks jutting up in bold relief.

PALISH (pal'ish), *adj.* somewhat pale.

PALL (pawl), *n.* a cloak or mantle; something that produces a gloomy effect; a coffin covering: *v.i.* to become insipid; lose strength.

PALLADIUM (pa-la'di-um), *n.* any safeguard of a liberty, or privilege.

PALLBEARER (pawl'bar-er), *n.* one at a funeral who attends to the coffin.

PALLET (pal'et), *n.* a palette; a name for various tools; a small, rough bed.

PALLIATE ('i-at), *v.t.* to excuse or cover over ; extenuate.

PALLIATION (-a'shun), *n.* extenuation ; mitigation.

PALLIATIVE ('i-a-tiv), *adj.* tending to lessen or mitigate.

PALLID ('id), *adj.* pale ; wan.

PALLOR (pal'er), *n.* paleness.

PALM (pam), *n.* a tree or shrub of the palm family ; the inner part of the hand.

PALMETTO (pal-met'o), *n.* a species of palm tree.

PALMISTRY (pam'is-tri), *n.* the pretended art of foretelling the future by examination of the lines and marks of a person's hand.

PALM SUNDAY (pam sun'da), *n.* the Sunday next before Easter.

PALMY (pam'i), *adj.* flourishing.

PALPABILITY (pal-pa-bil'i-ti), *n.* the state or quality of being palpable.

PALPABLE ('pa-bl), *adj.* easily perceived ; obvious.

PALPABLY ('pa-bli), *adv.* obviously.

PALPITATE ('po-tat), *v.i.* to beat or throb.

PALPITATION (-ta'shun), *n.* abnormal beating or throbbing of the heart.

PALSIED (pawl'zid), *p.adj.* having palsy.

PALSY ('zi), *n.* paralysis : *v.t.* to paralyze.

PALTER ('ter), *v.i.* to trifle.

PALTRY ('tri), *adj.* worthless.

PAMPAS (pam'paz), *n.pl.* in South America, vast plains covered with luxuriant pasture.

PAMPER ('per), *v.t.* to satiate.

PAMPHLET (pam'flet), *n.* a small unbound book.

PAMPHLETEER (-er'), *n.* a writer of pamphlets.

PAN-, a *prefix* meaning all, universal.

PAN (pan), *n.* a shallow, metallic or earthenware dish ; any similar vessel ; a hard subsoil.

PANACEA (pan-a-se'a), *n.* a universal remedy or medicine.

PAN-AMERICA (pan-a-mer'i-ka), *n.* a political term for the American republics.

PANCRATIC (-krat'ik), *adj.* excelling in gymnastic exercises.

PANCREAS (pang'kre-as), *n.* a large fleshy gland (the sweetbread) secreting a fluid that assists in the process of digestion.

PANDEMONIUM (-de-mo'ni-um), *n.* a place of general disorder.

PANDER ('der), *v.i.* to act as an agent for the gratification of the passions or prejudices of o'hers.

PANE (pan), *n.* a plate of glass.

PANEGYRIC (-e-jir'ik), *n.* ovation or encomium.

PANEGYRIZE ('e-ji-riz), *v.t.* to praise or commend highly.

PANEL (el), *n.* a piece of board, the edges of which are inserted in a frame ; a schedule containing the names of persons summoned to serve as jurors ; the jury.

PANG (pang), *n.* a violent pain ; agony, mental or physical.

PANIC ('ik), *n.* a sudden fright ; a kind of millet : *adj.* suddenly and violently alarming ; said of fear.

PANNIER (pan'yer, 'ni-er), *n.* one of two baskets suspended across the back of a horse, mule, or ass, for carrying produce.

PANNIKIN ('i-kin), *n.* a small tin cup.

PANOPLY ('o-pli), *n.* any magnificent covering ; gorgeous surroundings or environment.

PANORAMA (pan-o-ra'ma), *n.* a picture of objects observed from a central point ; a landscape unfolding of scenery from all sides.

PANPATHY (pan'pa-thi), *n.* a feeling or sentiment shared by all people.

PANSY ('zi), *n.* a flower ; the heart's-ease.

PANT (pant), *v.i.* to breathe rapidly ; desire ardently.

PANTAGRAPH, same as pantograph.

PANTALETTES (pan-ta-lets'), *n.pl.* loose drawers for women or children.

PANTALOON (-ta-loon'), *n.* a buffoon in a pantomine : *pl.* a pair of trousers.

PANTHEISM ('the-izm), *n.* the doctrine that the universe in its totality is God.

PANTHER ('ther), *n.* a fierce, feline, carnivorous animal.

PANTOGRAPH ('to-graf), *n.* an instrument for copying drawings, designs, etc., on an enlarged or reduced scale.

PANTOLOGY (-tol'o-ji), *n.* a system of universal knowledge.

PANTOMIME ('to-mim), *n.* a representation in dumb show.

PANTRY ('tri), *n.* a provision closet.

PANTS (pantz), *n.pl.* drawers worn by males.

PAP (pap), *n.* soft food for infants ; a nipple, or breast.

PAPA (pa-pa', pa'pa), *n.* a word of endearment for father.

PAPACY (pa'pa-si), *n.* the office, dignity, or authority, of the Pope.

PAPAL ('pal), *adj.* pertaining to the Pope, or the Church of Rome.

PAPAW (pa-paw'), *n.* a fruit-bearing tree of tropical America.

PAPER (pa'per), *n.* a thin flexible substance made of various materials, as rags, wood pulp, used for writing or printing upon ; a piece of paper ; newspaper ; an essay or literary contribution.

PAPIER-MACHE (pa-pya'ma-sha'), *n.* [French], paper pulp moulded into various shapes for ornament and use.

PAPRIKA (pa'pre-ka), *n.* the dried ripe fruit of a plant of the Capsicum genus.

PAPYRUS (pa-pi'rus), *n.* [*pl.* papyri ('ri)], a species of Egyptian reed, from the pith of which the ancients made paper ; a manuscript on papyrus.

PAR (par), *n.* state of equality ; nominal and market value.

PARA-, a prefix meaning *beyond, beside, divergence.*

PARABLE (par'a-bl), *n.* an allegorical method of conveying instruction by means of a fable from which a moral is drawn.

PARACHUTE ('a-shoot), *n.* a life-saving umbrella-shaped apparatus for descending from a balloon, airship, or airplane.

PARADE (pa-rad'), *n.* ostentatious display ; show ; military display.

PARADOX (par'a-doks), *n.* something apparently absurd or incredible, yet may be true in fact ; a tenet contrary to received opinions.

PARAFFIN, PARAFFINE ('a-fin), *n.* a white crystalline substance ; a constituent of petroleum.

PARAGON ('a-gon), *n.* something of extraordinary excellence.

PARAGRAPH ('a-graf), *n.* a short passage ; a reference mark (¶) ; an item of newspaper intelligence.

PARALLEL ('a-lel), *adj.* extended in the same direction and equidistant at all points ; having the same direction or tendency ; corresponding.

PARALLELOGRAM ('o-gram), *n.* a plane 4-sided figure whose opposite sides are parallel and equal.

PARALYSIS (pa-ral'i-sis), *n.* loss of the power of sensation of one or parts of the body.

PARALYTIC (par-a-lit'ik), *n.* one who is affected with paralysis.

PARALYZE ('a-liz), *v.t.* to affect with paralysis ; unnerve.

PARAMOUNT (par'a-mount), *adj.* superior to all others.

PARAMOUR (par'a-moor), *n.* an illicit lover.

PARANOIA (par-a-noi'a), *n.* a kind of monomania.

PARAPET ('a-pet), *n.* a wall breast-high.

PARAPHERNALIA (-fer-na'li-a), *n.pl.* ornaments of dress generally ; equipment ; trappings.

PARAPHRASE ('a-fraz), *n.* a free translation or explanation.

PARASITE ('a-sit), *n.* a hanger-on ; an animal or plant nourished by another to which it attaches itself.

PARASITIC (-sit'ik), *adj.* meanly servile or fawning ; living at expense of another animal or plant.

PARASOL ('a-sol), *n.* a lady's sun-shade.

PARAVANE (par'a-van), *n.* a water-plane, with projecting fins : used for clearing the course of vessels from mines, etc. ; an otter.

PARBOIL (par'boil), *v.t.* to boil partially.

PARCEL ('sel), *n.* a small bundle or package ; little part.

PARCEL POST (par'sel post), a government mailing system for parcels in which the postal charge is regulated according to distance and weight.

PARCENARY (par'se-na-ri), *n.* co-heirship.

PARCENER (-ner), *n.* a co-heir.

PARCH (parch), *v.t.* to scorch; dry to excess.

PARCHMENT ('ment), *n.* the skin of a sheep, goat, etc., dressed and prepared for writing upon; a deed.

PARD (pard), *n.* a leopard; [Slang] boon companion.

PARDON (par'dn), *v.t.* to forgive : *n.* official remission of a penalty.

PARDONABLE (-a-bl),*adj.* excusable.

PARE (par), *v.t.* to cut away little by little; reduce.

PAREGORIC (par-e-gor'ik), *n.* a camphorated tincture of opium to assuage pain.

PARENT (par'ent), *n.* a father or mother; origin.

PARENTAGE (-aj), *n.* extraction; birth.

PARENTHESIS (pa-ren'the-sis), *n.* [*pl.* parentheses (-sez)], an explanatory word or clause inserted in a sentence, which is grammatically complete without it : indicated by the marks ( ).

PARESIS (par-re'sis),*n.* partial paralysis; softening of the brain.

PARHELION (par-he'li-on), *n.* a bright light seen near the sun.

PARI-, a prefix signifying *equal*.

PARIAH (pa-ri'a), *n.* one of the lowest class of Hindus without caste; hence, an outcast.

PARIAN (pa'ri-an), *n.* a fine porcelain used for statuettes, etc.

PARISH (par'ish), *n.* an ecclesiastical district; a congregation.

PARISHIONER ('on-er), *n.* one who belongs to a parish.

PARISIAN (pa-riz'i-an, -rizh'an), *n.* a native or inhabitant of Paris.

PARIS GREEN (par'is gren), copper aceto-arsenite.

PARITY ('i-ti), *n.* equality; likeness.

PARK (park), *n.* a large inclosed piece of ground : *v.t.* mass together; place automobiles, etc., in a space for the purpose.

PARKEE (par'ke), *n.* an outer coat worn by Eskimos.

PARLANCE (par'lans), *n.* conversation; idiom of conversation.

PARLEY ('li), *n.* a conference.

PARLIAMENT ('li-ment), *n.* the supreme legislative assembly of Great Britain, consisting of the House of Lords, and the House of Commons; a legislative assembly in British colonies.

PARLIAMENTARY ('ta-ri), *adj.* in accordance with the usages of Parliament.

PARLOUR ('ler), *n.* reception room; drawing room.

PARLOUS (par'lus), *adj.* risky; uncertain.

PAROCHIAL (pa-ro'ki-al), *adj.* pertaining to a parish; limited; narrow.

PARODY ('o-di), *n.* a burlesque imitation of a serious poem.

PAROLE (pa-rol'), *n.* one released on word of honour.

PAROXYSM ('ok-sizm), *n.* a sudden spasm, or a fit of acute pain.

PARQUET, PARQUETTE (par-ket'), *n.* a flooring of parquetry; the floor space of a theatre back of the orchestra rail.

PARRAKEET (par'a-ket), *n.* a small long-tailed parrot.

PARRICIDE ('i-sid), *n.* the murderer of a father or mother.

PARROT (par'ot), *n.* a tropical bird capable of being trained to imitate the human voice.

PARRY ('i), *v.t.* to ward off, as a blow.

PARSE (pars), *v.t.* to resolve by grammatical rules a sentence into its component parts.

PARSEC (par'sek), *n.* a unit of space in astronomy, equivalent to almost 19 trillions of miles.

PARSIMONIOUS (-si-mo'ni-us), *adj.* frugal to excess; miserly.

PARSIMONY ('si-mon-i), *n.* closeness in expenditure; niggardliness.

PARSLEY (pars'li), *n.* a common garden herb.

PARSNIP ('nip), *n.* an edible herb with a carrot-like root.

PARSON (par'sn), *n.* a clergyman.

PARSONAGE (-aj), *n.* the residence of an incumbent.

PART (part), *n.* something less than the whole; piece; portion; ingredient; share; member or organ.

PARTAKE (par-tak'), *v.i.* to take part or share in common with others.

PARTED (par'ted), *adj.* separated.

PARTERRE (-tar'), *n.* a series of flower beds arranged in formal designs; floor of a theatre under the gallery.

PARTIAL ('shal), *adj.* inclined to favour one side or party; biased.

PARTICIPANT (-tis'i-pant), *adj.* sharing : *n.* one who shares or partakes.

PARTICIPATE ('i-pat), *v.i.* to partake : *v.t.* to have part of; share.

PARTICIPATION (-pa'shun), *n.* division into shares; companionship.

PARTICIPLE ('ti-si-pl), *n.* a word which partakes of the nature of a verb and of an adjective.

PARTICLE ('ti-kl), *n.* an atom; a very small portion of matter; a word non-inflected, or not used alone.

PARTICULAR (-tik'u-lar), *adj.* individual peculiar or special; characteristic; exclusive; exact; minute.

PARTICULARIZE ('u-lar-iz), *v.t.* to give the particulars of.

PARTICULARLY ('u-lar-li), *adv.* especially.

PARTING ('ting), *p.adj.* separating; given when separating.

PARTISAN (par'ti-zan), *n.* an adherent of a party or faction.

PARTITION (-tish'un), *n.* the act or state of being divided; separation; a dividing wall.

PARTITIVE ('ti-tiv), *adj.* noting a part.

PARTLY (part'li), *adv.* in part.

PARTNER ('ner), *n.* one who is associated with another.

PARTNERSHIP (-ship), *n.* union of two or more persons in the same business or profession.

PARTRIDGE (par'trij), *n.* a gallinaceous game bird.

PARTURITION (-tu-rish'un), *n.* the act of bringing forth young.

PARTY ('ti), *n.* a number of persons united for a particular purpose; faction; single individual spoken of.

PARVENU (par've-nu), *n.* one who on acquiring sudden wealth endeavours to take a place in society to which he is not fitted; an upstart.

PASCHAL (pas'kal), *adj.* pertaining to the feast of the Passover or Easter.

PASHA, PACHA (pash'a), *n.* a Turkish title given to high officials.

PASS (pas), *v.i.* to move from one place or state to another; be progressive; disappear; be enacted; be current : *v.t.* omit; disregard; give authority to; transfer; void : *n.* a narrow passage; a narrow way between two mountains.

PASSABLE ('a-bl), *adj.* that may be passed, travelled, or navigated; tolerable.

PASSAGE (pas'aj), *n.* entrance or exit; legal enactment; single clause or portion of a book; migratory habits.

PASSE (pa-sa'), *adj.* [French], worn out; out of style.

PASSENGER (pas'en-jer), *n.* one who travels in or on a conveyance.

PASSING (pas'ing), *p.adj.* departing; the conveyance of something from one to another : *adv.* exceedingly.

PASSION (pash'un), *n.* violent agitation of mind in anger; love; ardour; intense desire.

PASSION, *n.* the sufferings of Christ in His last agonies.

PASSION PLAY (pla), *n.* a dramatic representation of the Passion of the Saviour.

PASSION SUNDAY (sun'da), *n.* the 5th Sunday in Lent.

PASSIVE (pas'iv), *adj.* submissive.

PASSIVENESS (-nes), *n.* state of non-resistance.

PASSOVER (pas'o-ver), *n.* a Jewish feast commemorative of the passing of the destroying angel over the houses of the Israelites when he slew the first-born of the Egyptians.

PASSPORT ('port), *n.* an official permit to travel in a foreign country.

PASSWORD ('werd), *n.* a word by which friends are distinguished from strangers or enemies.

PAST (past), *p.adj.* having been ; gone by ; completed.

PASTE (past), *n.* a mixture of flour, starch, or the like, with water, used as a cement ; dough prepared for pies, etc.

PASTEBOARD ('bord), *n.* thick stiff paper.

PASTEL (pas'tel), *n.* a coloured crayon ; a picture drawn with such crayon.

PASTIL (pas'til), **PASTILLE** ('tel), *n.* a small cone of aromatic paste used for fumigating a room ; a medicated lozenge.

PASTIME (pas'tim), *n.* diversion ; sport.

PASTOR ('ter), *n.* a clergyman or minister having spiritual charge of a church and congregation.

PASTORAL (al), *adj.* pertaining to shepherds ; hence, rural ; relating to a pastor.

PASTORATE ('ter-at), *n.* the office or jurisdiction of a pastor.

PASTRY (pas'tri), *n.* pies, etc., made of light puffy dough.

PASTURAGE ('tur-aj), *n.* pasture.

PASTURE ('tur), *n.* land under grass for grazing cattle.

PAT (pat), *n.* a light, quick touch with the hand ; a small lump of butter from a mould : *adj.* apt ; exact.

PATCH (pach), *n.* a piece applied to cover a hole or rent ; a plot of ground.

PATCHOULI (pa-choo'li), *n.* an East Indian mint shrub from which is prepared a strong perfume.

PATE (pat), *n.* crown of the head.

PATENT (pat'ent, pa'tent), *adj.* apparent ; open to the perusal of all ; a sole right secured by letters patent.

PATENTEE (-te'), *n.* one who has secured a patent.

PATENT LEATHER (leth'er), *n.* a varnished or japanned leather.

PATERFAMILIAS (pa-ter-fa-mil'i-as), *n.* the father of a family.

PATERNAL (pa-ter'nal), *adj.* pertaining to a father ; hereditary.

PATERNITY (-ter'ni-ti), *n.* paternal relations ; authorship.

PATERNOSTER (pa'ter-nos-ter), *n.* the Lord's Prayer ; a rosary.

PATH (path), *n.* a road ; footway.

PATHETIC (pa-thet'ik), *adj.* affecting the emotions ; sad.

PATHOLOGY (-thol'o-ji), *n.* the science that treats of diseases, their causes, symptoms, progress, and results.

PATHOS (pa'thos), *n.* expression of deep feeling ; mental emotions.

PATIENCE ('shens), *n.* the quality of being patient or calmly enduring.

PATIENT ('shent), *adj.* suffering pain, hardship, affliction, etc., with calmness ; persevering : *n.* person under medical treatment.

PATNESS (pat'nes), *n.* appropriateness.

PATOIS (pa-twa'), *n.* provincial dialect.

PATRIARCH (pa'tri-ark), *n.* the founder or head of a family ; an aged man.

PATRICIAN (pa-trish'an), *n.* one of the senators of ancient Rome ; a nobleman.

PATRICIDE (pat'ri-sid), *n.* one who slays his or her father.

PATRIMONY ('ri-mo-ni), *n.* an estate or right inherited from a father or one's ancestors.

PATRIOT (pat'ri-, pa'tri-ot), *n.* one who loves, and is devoted to, his native country.

PATRIOTIC (-ri-ot'ik), *adj.* characterized by patriotism.

PATRIOTISM ('ri-ot-izm), *n.* love of one's country.

PATROL (pa-trol'), *n.* a guard of soldiers for a district to preserve order.

PATRON (pa'tron), *n.* a guardian or supporter.

PATRONAGE (-aj), *n.* special support.

PATRONESS (-es), *n.* a woman who promotes social functions.

PATRONIZE (-iz), *v.t.* to act as a patron toward ; support or protect.

PATRONYMIC (pat-ro-nim'ik), *adj.* derived from the name of an ancestor.

PATTER ('er), *v.i.* to strike with a

quick succession of light sounds; mumble; mutter; talk foolishly: *n.* idle chatter.

PATTERN ('ern), *n.* a model, sample, or specimen; anything cut out to be copied.

PATTY ('i), *n.* a small pie.

PAUCITY (paw'si-ti), *n.* smallness of number or quantity.

PAUNCH (panch, pawnch), *n.* the abdomen; the first stomach of a ruminant.

PAUPER (paw'per), *n.* a person without means of support; one who is supported by the poor rates.

PAUPERIZE (-iz), *v.t.* to reduce to pauperism.

PAUSE (pawz), *n.* cessation; temporary stop; a break in writing indicated by the mark [——]; a mark of cessation in speaking; a mark [⌢] in music, indicating the continuance of a note or rest.

PAVE (pav), *v.t.* to cover or lay with stones, bricks, etc.

PAVEMENT (pav'ment), *n.* a paved roadway or floor.

PAVILION (pa-vil'yun), *n.* a large tent; a temporary, movable habitation; summer-house.

PAVING (pa'ving), *n.* pavement.

PAW (paw), *n.* the foot of an animal with claws.

PAWN (pawn), *n.* something given as security for the redemption of a pledge; a common piece at chess.

PAWNBROKER ('bro-ker), *n.* one who lends money on the security of valuables deposited with him.

PAWPAW, see papaw.

PAX (paks), *n.* a small crucifix

PAY (pa), *v.t.* to discharge a debt to; compensate; reward; fulfill.

PAYEE (-e'), *n.* one to whom money is paid.

PEA (pe), *n.* a leguminous, climbing, garden herb.

PEACE (pes), *n.* a state of rest or tranquility; calm.

PEACEFUL ('fool), *adj.* full of peace; pacific; quiet; calm.

PEACH (pech), *n.* a low, many-branched tree; the sweet, juicy fruit of this tree: *v.i.* [Slang], to turn informer; betray accomplices.

PEACOCK (pe'kok), *n.* a gallinaceous bird with handsome plumage.

PEA-JACKET ('jak-et), *n.* a seaman's heavy jacket.

PEAK (pek), *n.* the sharp-pointed summit or jutting part of a mountain or hill; pointed end; greatest height.

PEAKED (pekt), *adj.* pointed; ending in a point.

PEAKISH (pek'ish), *adj.* having pale, thin features.

PEAL (pel), *n.* a loud sound, as of thunder, bells, etc.

PEAN, same as pæan.

PEANUT (pe'nut), *n.* a trailing plant of the bean family; the edible nut-like fruit.

PEAR (par), *n.* a small fruit tree; the fleshy, edible fruit.

PEARL (perl), *n.* a hard, smooth, grayish-white, iridescent substance (nacre), found within the shell of certain mollusks; a small size of type.

PEARLINESS (per'li-nes), *n.* the quality of being pearly.

PEARLING (per'ling), *n.* fishing for pearls.

PEARLY ('li), *adj.* resembling pearls; clear; transparent.

PEART (pert), *adj.* brisk; saucy.

PEASANT (pez'ant), *n.* a countryman; rustic labourer: *adj.* rural; rustic.

PEASANTRY (-ri), *n.* peasants collectively.

PEASE (pez), *n.pl.* peas collectively.

PEAT (pet), *n.* decayed vegetable matter, used as fuel.

PEAT BOG (bog), a marsh abounding in peat.

PEAVY (pe'vi), *n.* a hand lever with an iron point and movable iron hook, used in logging.

PEBBLE (peb'l), *n.* a roundish stone; rock crystal.

PECAN (pe-kan'), *n.* a species of North American hickory, or the nut it produces.

PECCABLE (pek'a-bl), *adj.* liable to sin.

PECCADILLO (-dil'o), *n.* a trifling fault.

PECCARY ('a-ri), *n.* a South American mammal, allied to the hog.

PECK (peck), *n.* ¼ of a bushel ; quick, sharp stroke with the beak.

PECTORAL ('to-ral), *adj.* pertaining to, good for, or worn on, the chest.

PECULATE (u'lat), *v.i.* to embezzle.

PECULATOR ('u-la-ter), *n.* one who peculates.

PECULIAR (pe-kul'yar), *adj.* exclusively individual ; appropriate ; strange.

PECULIARLY ('lyar-li), *adv.* in a peculiar manner.

PECULIARITY (-ku-li-ar'i-ti), *n.* something peculiar or characteristic.

PECUNIARY ('ni-ar-i), *adj.* pertaining to or consisting of, money ; monetary.

PEDAGOGIC (ped-a-goj'ik), **PEDAGOGICAL** ('i-kal), *adj.* pertaining to a pedagogue or to science of teaching.

PEDAGOGUE ('a-gog), *n.* a schoolmaster ; pedant.

PEDAL (ped'al), *adj.* pertaining to a foot.

PEDANT ('ant), *n.* one who makes an ostentatious display of his learning.

PEDANTIC (pe-dan'tik), *adj.* pertaining to, or characterized by, pedantry.

PEDANTRY (ped'ant-ri), *n.* ostentatious display of learning.

PEDATE ('at), *adj.* palmate, with the two lateral sections lengthened and lobed.

PEDDLE ('l), *v.i.* to travel about selling small wares.

PEDDLER, PEDLER, PEDLAR ('ler), *n.* one who peddles.

PEDDLING ('ling), *adj.* trifling.

PEDESTAL (ped'es-tal), *n.* the base of a column, statue, etc.

PEDESTRIAN (pe-des'tri-an), *adj.* going on foot ; walking.

PEDICEL (ped'i-sel), *n.* a short footstalk.

PEDICURE (ped'i-kur), *n.* the care of the feet ; a chiropodist.

PEDIFORM ('i-form), *adj.* footshaped.

PEDIGREE ('i-gre), *n.* lineage ; genealogy.

PEDOLOGY (pe-dol'o-ji), *n.* pediatrics ; child study.

PEDOMETER (pe-dom'e-ter), *n.* instrument recording paces and distances in walking.

PEEK (pek), *n.* a glance ; a peep.

PEEL (pel), *v.t.* to strip the skin, bark, or rind from : *n.* a baker's oven shovel.

PEEP (pep), *v.i.* to chirp or cry, as young birds ; look slyly.

PEER (per), *n.* one of the same rank ; an equal ; associate ; a nobleman.

PEERAGE ('aj), *n.* the rank or dignity of a peer.

PEERESS ('es), *n.* a peer's wife.

PEERLESS ('les), *adj.* without an equal.

PEEVISH (pev'ish), *adj.* fretful.

PEG (peg), *n.* a small, pointed wooden pin.

PEIGNOIR (pen-war'), *n.* [French], a woman's loose morning gown.

PELAGIC (pe-laj'ik), *adj.* pertaining to the ocean.

PELF (pelf), *n.* money ; wealth.

PELICAN (pel'i-kan), *n.* a large fish-eating, web-footed bird.

PELL (pel), *n.* a skin or hide.

PELLET (pel'et), *n.* a little ball ; one of the globules of small shot.

PELLICLE ('i-kl), *n.* a thin skin or film.

PELL-MELL ('mel), *adj.* denoting a state of confusion :*n.* confusion.

PELLUCID (pe-lu'sid), *adj.* perfectly clear ; transparent.

PELT (pelt), *n.* a raw hide ; a blow from something thrown : *v.i.* to fall heavily as rain.

PELTRY (pel'tri), *n.* skins of furred animals collectively.

PELVIC (pel'vik), *adj.* pertaining to the pelvis.

PELVIS ('vis), *n.* the bony cavity in the lower part of the abdomen.

PEMMICAN (pem'i-kan), *n.* lean meat, dried, pounded, and pressed into cakes.

PEN (pen), *n.* a small inclosure ; coop ; an instrument for writing.

PENAL (pe'nal), *adj.* enacting, inflicting, or incurring punishment for crime ; punitive.

PENALIZE (pe'nal-iz), *v.t.* to render subject to penalty or punishment.

PENALTY (pen'al-ti), *n.* legal punishment either on the person or by a fine.

PENANCE (pen'ans), *n.* self-imposed suffering, as an expression of contrition for sin ; repentance.

PENATES (pe-na'tez), *n.pl.* the household gods of the ancient Romans.

PENCE, *pl.* of penny.

PENCHANT (pang-shang', pen'-chant), *n.* [French], a strong inclination or taste.

PENCIL (pen'sil), *n.* a cylinder containing graphite, carbon, lead, chalk etc., for writing.

PENDANT ('dant), *n.* anything hanging for ornamentation.

PENDENCY ('den-si), *n.* suspense ; indecision.

PENDENT ('dent), *adj.* hanging ; projecting ; swinging.

PENDING ('ding), *adj.* undecided ; in suspense.

PENDULUM ('du-lum), *n.* a body suspended so that it may vibrate backwards and forwards about a fixed point by the force of gravity and momentum.

PENETRABILITY (pen-e-tra-bil'i-ti) *n.* the susceptibility of being entered or passed through by another body.

PENETRABLE ('e-tra-bl), *adj.* that may be penetrated.

PENETRALIA (-tra'li-a), *n.pl.* the inner part of a temple, house, etc. ; mysteries.

PENETRANT ('e-trant), *adj.* penetrating ; subtle ; acute.

PENETRATE ('e-trat), *v.t.* to pierce into ; enter ; bore or perforate ; affect deeply.

PENGUIN ('gwin), *n.* a large sea-fowl with rudimentary wings.

PENINSULA (pen-in'su-la), *n.* a portion of jutting land nearly surrounded by water.

PENINSULAR ('su-lar), *adj.* pertaining to, or shaped like, a peninsula.

PENITENCE (pen'i-tens), *n.* sorrow for sin ; state of being penitent.

PENITENT ('i-tent), *adj.* repentant.

PENITENTIARY (-ten'sha-ri), *adj.*

pertaining to penance : *n.* a state prison.

PENNANT ('ant), *n.* a long narrow strip of bunting at the mast-heads of certain ships.

PENNILESS (pen'i-les), *adj.* without money ; destitute.

PENNY (-i), *n.* a bronze coin of Gt. Britain, of which there are twelve to the shilling.

PENNYROYAL (-roi'al), *n.* an aromatic herb of the mint family.

PENNYWEIGHT (-wat), *n.* a weight = 24 grains troy.

PENOLOGIST (pe-no'o-jist), *n.* a student of penology.

PENOLOGY (pe-nol'o-ji), *n.* scientific study of punishments, prison management, etc.

PENSION (pen'shun), *n.* a subsidy or allowance.

PENSIONER (-er), *n.* one who receives a pension.

PENSIVE ('siv), *adj.* thoughtful ; sad.

PENTA-, a combining form from the Greek *pente*, five.

PENTAGON (pen'ta-gon), *n.* a figure of 5 sides and 5 angles.

PENTATEUCH ('ta-tuk), *n.* the first 5 books of the Old Testament.

PENTECOST ('te-kost), *n.* a Jewish festival kept on the 50th day after the second day of the Passover ; a festival of the Christian Church.

PENULT (pe'nult, pe-nult), *n.* the last syllable of a word but one.

PENULTIMATE ('ti-mat), *adj.* last but one.

PENUMBRA (-num'bra), *n.* a partial shadow on the exterior of the perfect shadow of an eclipse.

PENURIOUS (-nu'ri-us), *adj.* miserly ; sordid.

PENURY (pen'u-ri), *n.* poverty.

PEONY (pe'o-ni), *n.* a perennial plant of the crowfoot family.

PEOPLE (pe'pl), *n.* persons generally ; human beings.

PEP (pep), *n.* [Slang], energy ; snap ; vigour ; vim.

PEPPER (pep'er), *n.* a hot, pungent spice prepared from the ground seeds of an East Indian plant.

PEPPERMINT (-mint), *n.* an aromatic herb; the cordial prepared from it.

PEPPERWORT (-wert), *n.* a cress.

PEPPERY (-i), *adj.* like pepper; fiery pungent.

PEPSIN ('sin), *n.* a nitrogenous ferment contained in gastric juice.

PEPTIC ('tik), *adj.* pertaining to, or promoting, digestion.

PER (per), *prep.* through; by means of; used in Latin phrases, as *per annum*.

PER-, a prefix signifying *through, by means of, very, exceedingly*; also, denoting a higher degree of valence in two similar compounds, and the highest degree of combination among similar compounds.

PERADVENTURE (per-ad-ven'tur), *adv.* by chance.

PERAMBULATE (-am'bu-lat), *v.t.* to walk over; traverse.

PERAMBULATOR ('bu-la-ter), *n.* one who perambulates; a baby carriage.

PERCALE (-kal'), *n.* a cotton fabric with a linen finish.

PERCEIVABLE (-se'va-bl), *adj.* discernible by the mind.

PERCEIVE (-sev'), *v.t.* to obtain knowledge by the senses; discern.

PER CENT (sent), the rate of allowance or interest by the hundred.

PERCENTAGE (-sent'aj), *n.* proportional allowance per hundred.

PERCEPT (per'sept), *n.* a knowledge of things derived through the senses.

PERCEPTIBLE ('ti-bl), *adj.* that may be perceived.

PERCEPTIBLY (-bli), *adv.* so as to be perceived.

PERCEPTION (-sep'shun), *n.* receiving knowledge of external things by the medium of the senses; idea; conception.

PERCH (perch), *n.* a freshwater fish; a measure of length = 5½ yards; also 30¼ sq. yds.; a pole, branch, or framework on which birds sit or roost.

PERCHANCE (per-chans'), *adv.* perhaps.

PERCIPIENT (-sip'i-ent), *adj.* perceiving.

PERCOLATE ('ko-lat), *v.i.* to pass through small spaces; filter.

PERCOLATOR ('ko-la-ter), *n.* a filtering machine or vessel; a coffee-pot fitted with a filter.

PERCUSSION (-kush'un), *n.* violent collision.

PERCUSSIVE (-kus'iv), *adj.* striking against.

PER DIEM (di'em), [Latin], by the day.

PERDITION (-dish'un), *n.* total destruction; ruin.

PERDU (-du'), *adj.* forlorn; hidden.

PEREGRINATION (-e-gri-na'shun), *n.* the act of travelling about.

PEREMPTORILY ('emp-to-ri-li), *adv.* in a peremptory manner.

PEREMPTORY ('emp-to-ri), *adj.* positive; final; decisive.

PERENNIAL (-en'i-al), *adj.* lasting through the year; perpetual; plants that continue more than 2 years.

PERFECT ('fekt), *adj.* complete; without defect or blemish; blameless; pure : *n.* in grammar, the tense that expresses completed action.

PERFECTIBILITY (-fek-ti-bil'i-ti), *n.* the capacity for becoming perfect.

PERFECTION ('shun), *n.* the state of being perfect; supreme excellence.

PERFIDIOUS (-fid'i-us), *adj.* treacherous; faithless.

PERFIDY ('fi-di), *n.* violation of a trust reposed.

PERFORATE ('fo-rat), *v.t.* to pierce or bore through.

PERFORATION (-ra'shun), *n.* a hole bored through.

PERFORCE (-fors'), *adv.* by force or necessity; compel.

PERFORM (-form'), *v.t.* to do or carry out; execute; achieve; fulfil.

PERFORMANCE (-for'mans), *n.* execution; completion; deed; an entertainment.

PERFUME (-fum'), *v.t.* to impregnate with a pleasant odour; scent : *n.* (per'fum), a sweet-smelling scent.

PERFUNCTORILY (-fungk'to-ri-li), *adv.* carelessly.

PERFUNCTORY ('to-ri), *adj.* done carelessly or negligently.

PERGOLA (per'go-la), *n.* an arbour passageway.

PERHAPS (-haps'), *adv.* possibly.

PERI (pe'ri), *n.* in Persian mythology, a descendant of a fallen spirit excluded from paradise ; a fairy.

PERI (per-i), a prefix, meaning *around,* as peribolos.

PERIANTH ('i-anth), *n.* a floral envelope.

PERIASTRON (-as'tron), *adj.* among, or around, the stars.

PERICARDIUM (-kar'di-um), *n.* the membrane that surrounds the heart.

PERICARP ('i-karp), *n.* seed-vessel of a plant.

PERIGEE (-je), *n.* that point in the orbit of the moon, or of a planet, nearest the earth.

PERIHELION (-he'li-on), *n.* that point in the orbit of a planet, or a comet, nearest the sun.

PERIL (per'il), *n.* exposure to injury ; danger ; risk.

PERILOUS (per'i-lus), *adj.* hazardous.

PERIMETER (pe-rim'e-ter), *n.* the outer boundary of a plane surface.

PERIOD (pe'ri-od), *n.* a circuit or cycle ; interval of time ; a division of geological time ; an epoch ; conclusion ; a dot [.] to mark the end of a sentence.

PERIODIC (-od'ik), *adj.* occurring at regular intervals.

PERIODICAL ('i-kal), *adj.* recurring at intervals : *n.* a magazine or other publication published at stated intervals.

PERIODICITY (-o-dis'i-ti), *n.* the state or quality of being periodic ; electric frequency.

PERIPHERY (-rif'er-i), *n.* the circumference of a circle, ellipse, or similar figure.

PERIPHRASIS (-rif'ra-sis), *n.* circumlocution ; the using of many words to express but little.

PERIQUE (pe-rek'), *n.* strong black tobacco.

PERISCOPE (per'i-skop), *n.* an optical instrument used on submarines.

PERISH ('ish), *v.i.* to lose life or vitality ; decay or die.

PERISHABLE ('per-ish-a-bl), *adj.* liable to decay ; mortal.

PERISTALTIC (per-i-stal'tik), *adj.* pertaining to the peculiar worm-like movement of the intestines by which their contents are forced onward.

PERISTYLE ('i-stil), *n.* an open court in or near a building surrounded by a row of columns.

PERIWINKLE (-wing'kl), *n.* a perennial creeping plant ; a small univalve mollusk.

PERJURE (per'jur), *v.t.* to violate the oath of ; cause to swear falsely.

PERJURY ('ju-ri), *n.* the act of swearing falsely.

PERK (perk), *v.t.* to make trim or smart.

PERKY ('ki), *adj.* jaunty ; smart.

PERMANENCE ('ma-nens), *n.* the state or quality of being permanent ; duration.

PERMANENT (-nent), *adj.* lasting ; durable.

PERMEABLE ('me-a-bl), *adj.* that may be passed through.

PERMEATE ('me-at), *v.t.* to penetrate and pass through.

PERMISSIBLE (-mis'i-bl), *adj.* that may be permitted.

PERMISSION (-mish'un), *n.* the act of permitting ; leave.

PERMIT (-mit'), *v.t.* to consent to ; grant liberty to do something ; tolerate.

PERMUTATION (-mu-ta'shun), *n.* the exchange of one thing for another.

PERNICIOUS (-nish'us), *adj.* highly injurious or hurtful ; destructive.

PERNICKETY (-nik'et-i), *adj.* attentive to trifles ; fussy.

PERORATE (per'o-rat), *v.t.* to declaim : *v.i.* to speak at length.

PERORATION (-o-ra'shun), *n.* the concluding part of an oration.

PERPENDICULAR (-pen-dik'ular), *adj.* standing at right angles to a given line or surface ; perfectly upright.

PERPETRATE ('pe-trat), *v.t.* to commit ; perform (in a bad sense), as to perpetrate a crime.

PERPETRATOR ('pe-tra-ter), *n.* one who perpetrates.

PERPETUAL (-pet'u-al), *adj.* never ceasing ; not temporary.

PERPETUATE ('u-at), *v.t.* to make perpetual.

PERPETUATION (-a'shun), *n.* the act of perpetuating.

PERPETUITY (-pe-tu'i-ti), *n.* the state of being perpetual ; endless duration.

PERPLEX (-pleks'), *v.t.* to make difficult to be understood.

PERPLEXITY (-plek'si-ti), *n.* embarrassment ; doubt.

PERQUISITE (-kwi-zit), *n.* a gift or allowance in addition to regular wages or salary.

PERRY ('i), *n.* the fermented juice of pears.

PERSECUTE (per'se-kut), *v.t.* to harass or ill-treat.

PERSECUTION (-ku'shun), *n.* the act of persecuting.

PERSECUTOR (-ter), *n.* one who persecutes.

PERSEVERANCE (-ver'ans), *n.* the act or state of persevering.

PERSEVERE (-se-ver'), *v.i.* to persist in any undertaking.

PERSIFLAGE (per'si-flazh), *n.* sarcastic talk ; flippant chatter.

PERSIMMON (-sim'un), *n.* an American plum-like fruit.

PERSIST (-sist'), *v.i.* to continue steadily in any course commenced ; persevere.

PERSISTENCE (-sis'tens), **PERSISTENCY** ('ten-si), *n.* being persistent ; obstinacy.

PERSISTENT ('tent), *adj.* continuing, constant ; persevering.

PERSON ('sn), *n.* a human being ; one's self.

PERSONAL (-al), *adj.* pertaining to men or women ; relating, or peculiar, to a person and his private affairs.

PERSONALITY (-al'i-ti), *n.* that which constitutes distinction of person.

PERSONALTY (-al-ti), *n.* personal estate, or all kinds of movable property.

PERSONATE (-at), *v.t.* to represent by an assumed character ; counterfeit.

PERSONATOR (-ter), *n.* one who assumes the character of another.

PERSONIFICATION (-son-i-fi-ka'-shun), *n.* the act of personifying.

PERSONIFY ('i-fi), *v.t.* to represent as endowed with personal qualities.

PERSONNEL (per-so-nel'), *n.* [French], the body of persons employed in any public or private service.

PERSPECTIVE (per-spek'tiv), *adj.* pertaining to, or in accordance with, the art of perspective : *n.* a vista or view.

PERSPICACIOUS (-spi-ka'shus), *adj.* mentally acute ; quick-sighted.

PERSPICACITY (-kas'i-ti), *n.* acuteness of sight or discernment.

PERSPICUITY (-ku'i-ti), *n.* mental clearness ; lucidity.

PERSPICUOUS (-spik'u-us), *adj.* easily understood ; evident ; clear.

PERSPIRATION (-spi-ra'shun), *n.* excretion by the pores of the skin ; sweat.

PERSPIRE (-spir'), *v.i.* to excrete by the pores of the skin ; sweat.

PERSUADE (-swad'), *v.t.* to influence by argument, advice, entreaty, etc.

PERSUASION ('zhun), *n.* the act or art of persuading ; the state of being persuaded ; settled belief.

PERSUASIVE ('siv), *adj.* having the power to persuade.

PERT (pert), *adj.* saucy ; forward.

PERTAIN (per-tan'), *v.i.* to belong ; have relation or reference to something.

PERTINACIOUS (-ti-na'shus), *adj.* unyielding ; obstinate.

PERTINACITY (-nas'i-ti), *n.* the quality of being pertinacious.

PERTINENCE ('ti-nens), *n.* suitableness ; fitness.

PERTINENT ('ti-nent), *adj.* fitting or appropriate ; relevant.

PERTURB (-terb'), *v.t.* to agitate ; disturb ; disquiet.

PERTURBATION (-tur-ba'shun), *n.* mental agitation or disquietude.

PERUSAL (pe-rooz'al), *n.* study or examination.

PERUSE (-rooz'), *v.t.* to read with attention ; examine.

PERUVIAN BARK (-roo'vi-an bark), *n.* cinchona.

PERVADE (per-vad'), *v.t.* to penetrate ; extend ; be diffused all over.

PERVASION (-va'shun), *n.* the act of pervading.

PERVERSE (-vers'), *adj.* obstinate ; untractable.

PERVERSENESS ('nes), *n.* disposition to thwart or annoy.

PERVERSION (-ver'shun), *n.* a turning from truth or propriety ; misapplication.

PERVERT (-vert), *v.t.* to turn from the true end or proper purpose ; misapply ; distort.

PERVERTED ('ted), *p.adj.* turned from the right ; corrupted.

PERVIOUS ('vi-us), *adj.* permeable ; open.

PESKY (pes'ki), *adj.* troublesome ; annoying.

PESO (pa'so), *n.* a dollar ; a term used in the Spanish states of South America.

PESSIMISM (pes'i-mizm), *n.* the doctrine that the present state of existence is essentially evil.

PESSIMIST (-mist), *n.* one who looks on the worst side of everything.

PESSIMISTIC (-mis'tik), *adj.* gloomy.

PEST (pest), *n.* a fatal epidemic disease ; plague ; anything very annoying.

PESTER (pes'ter), *v.t.* to annoy.

PESTIFEROUS (-tif'er-us), *adj.* physically or morally noxious.

PESTILENCE ('ti-lens), *n.* an infectious or contagious disease.

PESTILENT ('ti-lent), *adj.* noxious to health, morals, or society.

PESTILENTIAL (-len'shal), *adj.* pernicious ; destructive.

PESTLE (pes'l), *n.* an instrument for pounding substances in a mortar.

PET (pet), *n.* a sudden fit of peevishness : *adj.* favourite : *v.t.* to fondle or indulge.

PETAL ('al), *n.* a flower-leaf.

PETITION (pe-tish'un), *n.* an earnest supplication or prayer ; a paper or document containing a written request.

PETITIONER (-er), *n.* one who asks or supplicates.

PETIT JURY (pet'i joo'ri), a trial jury.

PETREL ('rel), *n.* a web-footed oceanic bird : sometimes called Mother Carey's chicken.

PETRIFICATION (pet-ri-fak'shun), *n.* the process of changing animal or vegetable substance into stone ; a fossil.

PETRIFY ('ri-fi), *v.t.* to change into stone ; fix in silent amazement or fear.

PETROGRAD ('ro-grad), *n.* new name of St. Petersburg, Russia (1914), now called Leningrad.

PETROL ('rol), *n.* a variety of naphtha.

PETROLEUM (pe-tro'le-um), *n.* an inflammable, dark, yellowish-brown bituminous liquid issuing from the earth ; mineral oil ; rock oil : it yields several valuable volatile distillates, as paraffin, kerosene, benzine, naphtha, gasoline, petroleum, ether, etc.

PETROLOGY (pe-trol'o-ji), *n.* the scientific study of rocks.

PETTICOAT (pet'i-kot), *n.* a woman's loose underskirt.

PETTIFOGGER ('i-fog-er), *n.* a lawyer who practices in petty cases.

PETTINESS ('i-nes), *n.* smallness ; unimportance.

PETTY ('i), *adj.* trifling ; inconsiderable ; unimportant ; contemptible.

PETTY JURY, same as petit jury.

PETULANCE ('u-lans), **PETULANCY** (-lan-si), *n.* peevishness ; caprice.

PETULANT ('u-lant), *adj.* peevish ; capricious.

PETUNIA (pe-tu'ni-a), *n.* a genus of ornamental plants of the nightshade family with handsome flowers.

PEW (pu), *n.* an inclosed seat in a church for several persons.

PEWTER (pu'ter), *n.* an alloy of tin, lead, antimony, etc.: *adj.* made of pewter.

PHAETON (fa'e-ton), *n.* an open four-wheeled carriage.

PHALANGE (fa-lanj'), *n.* one of the bones of a finger or toe.

PHALANX (fa'langks), *n.* [*pl.* phalanges (-lan'jez)], any close compact body : *pl.* the small bones of the fingers and toes.

PHANTASM (fan′tazm), *n.* a vision or spectre.

PHANTASY (fan′ta-si), *n.* a fancied image, or representation.

PHANTOM (′tom), *n.* an apparition ; a vision.

PHARMACEUTIC (far-ma-su′tik), **PHARMACEUTICAL** (-su′ti-kal), *adj.* pertaining to pharmaceutics.

PHARMACIST (far′ma-sist), *n.* a druggist.

PHARMACY (′ma-si), *n.* the art of preparing and compounding medicines ; a drug-store.

PHAROS (fa′ros), *n.* a lighthouse ; a beacon.

PHARYNX (far′ingks), *n.* the muscular or membranous sac at the upper part of the esophagus.

PHASE (faz), *n.* a recurring change in illumination of the moon, or a planet ; aspect ; appearance.

PHEASANT (fez′ant), *n.* a gallinaceous bird with brilliant plumage.

PHENIX (fe′niks), *n.* a sacred bird of Egyptian mythology.

PHENOL (fe′nol), *n.* a derivative of coal tar known as *carbolic acid.*

PHENOMENAL (-nom′en-al), *adj.* pertaining to phenomena ; unusual.

PHENOMENON (′e-non), *n.* [*pl.* phenomena (′e-na)], something marvellous or wonderful; something beyond ordinary conception.

PHIAL (fi′al), *n.* a small glass bottle or vessel.

PHILANDER (-lan′der), *v.i.* to make silly love.

PHILANTHROPIC (fil-an-throp′ik), *adj.* loving mankind ; benevolent.

PHILANTHROPIST (fi-lan′thro-pist), *n.* one who loves and seeks to benefit mankind.

PHILANTHROPY (-pi), *n.* love of mankind ; benevolence.

PHILATELIST (-lat′e-list), *n.* a collector of postage stamps.

PHILATELY (′e-li), *n.* the systematic collection of postage stamps.

PHILHARMONIC (fil-har-mon′ik), *adj.* loving harmony ; noting a musical society.

PHILIPPIC (fi-lip′ik), *n.* a speech of vehement invective.

PHILO-, a combining form from the Greek *philos,* loving.

PHILOLOGICAL (fil-o-loj′i-kal), *adj.* pertaining to philology.

PHILOLOGIST (-ol′o-jist), *n.* one skilled in philology.

PHILOLOGY (-ji), *n.* the scientific study of languages and their structure and mutual relation.

PHILOSOPHER (fi-los′o-fer), *n.* a student of philosophy ; one noted for calm judgment and practical wisdom.

PHILOSOPHIC (fil-o-sof′ik), *adj.* rational ; wise ; calm.

PHILOSOPHY (fi-los′o-fi), *n.* the knowledge of the causes of phenomenia both of mind and matter ; reasoned science ; practical wisdom.

PHLEGM (flem), *n.* mucus secreted in the air passages of the throat.

PHLEGMATIC (fleg-mat′ik), *adj.* pertaining to phlegm ; sluggish ; dull.

PHLOX (floks), *n.* a large genus of American herbs with handsome flowers.

PHŒNIX, same as phenix.

PHONE (fon), *n.* abbreviation of telephone ; an element of speech.

PHONETIC (fo-net′ik), *adj.* pertaining to the voice or sounds.

PHONETICALLY (′i-kal-i), *adv.* by sounds.

PHONOGRAPH (′no-graf), *n.* an instrument to record or reproduce articulate speech or sounds.

PHOSPHATE (fos′fat), *n.* a salt of phosphoric acid.

PHOSPHORESCENCE (-for-es′-ens), *n.* emission of light under certain conditions by substances at common temperatures.

PHOSPHORESCENT (′ent), *adj.* luminous.

PHOSPHORUS (-us), *n.* a yellowish, wax-like, inflammable, non-metallic element, luminous in the dark.

PHOTO (fo′to), *n.* a photograph.

PHOTOGRAPH (′to-graf), *n.* a photographic picture.

PHOTOGRAPHY (-tog′ra-fi), *n.* the art or process of producing pictures by the action of light on certain substances sensitized by various chemical processes.

PHOTOPLAY ('to-pla), *n.* a moving-picture play.

PHOTORADIOGRAM (-to-ra'di-o-gram), *n.* a photograph or picture transmitted by radio.

PHRASE (fraz), *n.* a part of a sentence; brief, pithy expression ; idiom ; style or manner : *v.t.* to style ; express in appropriate words.

PHRASEOLOGY (-e-ol'o-ji), *n.* style, manner, or peculiarity of expression ; a collection of phrases.

PHRENOLOGIST (fre-nol'o-jist), *n.* one who is skilled in phrenology.

PHRENOLOGY ('o-ji), *n.* the theory that the human mind or brain, as connected with the moral, intellectual, and sensual dispositions of the individual, can be indicated by the undulations or " bumps," on the head.

PHYSIC (fiz'ik), *n.* the science of medicine, or art of healing ; medicine; a cathartic.

PHYSICAL ('i-kal), *adj.* pertaining to nature, or to material things ; perceptible to the senses ; pertaining to physics ; medicinal.

PHYSICIAN (fi-zish'an), *n.* one legally qualified to prescribe remedies for diseases.

PHYSICS (fiz'iks), *n.* physical science or natural philosophy.

PHYSIOGNOMIST (-i-og'no-mist), *n.* one who is skilled in physiognomy.

PHYSIOGNOMY (-mi), *n.* the science of discerning the character of the mind from the features of the countenance ; the face ; outward appearance.

PHYSIOLOGICAL (-i-o-loj'i-kal), *adj.* pertaining to physiology.

PHYSIOLOGIST (-i-ol'o-jist), *n.* one who is skilled in physiology.

PHYSIOLOGY (-ol'o-ji), *n.* the science that treats of the vital functions performed by the organs of animals and plants.

PHYSIQUE (fi-zek'), *n.* physical or bodily structure or constitution.

PIANISSIMO (pe-a-nis'i-mo), *adj.* in music, soft.

PIANIST (pi-an'ist), *n.* a performer on piano.

PIANO (pi-an'o), *n.* a pianoforte.

PIANOFORTE (-for'ta), *n.* a stringed musical instrument, the notes of which are produced by hammers acted upon by keys.

PIAZZA (-as'a), *n.* an open square surrounded by buildings or colonnades ; a walk under a roof supported by pillars.

PICA (pi'ka), *n.* a size of type in printing, now known as 12 point.

PICAROON (pik-a-roon'), *n.* a robber.

PICAYUNE (-yoon'), *n.* a small silver coin ; a trifle.

PICCANINNY (pik'a-nin-i), *n.* a negro baby or child.

PICCOLO ('o-lo), *n.* small flute having notes an octave higher than the ordinary flute.

PICK (pik), *n.* a sharp-pointed iron tool ; choice or selection : *v.t.* to pluck or gather ; separate with the fingers ; choose or select.

PICKAXE ('aks), *n.* an excavating tool, pointed at one end and broad at the other.

PICKEREL ('er-el), *n.* a fish of the pike family.

PICKET ('et), *n.* a pointed stake used in fortification ; pale of a fence ; a military guard to give notice of the approach of an enemy.

PICKLE ('l), *n.* a mixture of brine and water, etc., for preserving food ; vegetables, etc. ; embarrassment or difficulty.

PICKLOCK ('lok), *n.* an instrument for picking locks ; a thief.

PICKPOCKET (pik'pok-et), *n.* a thief.

PICNIC ('nik), *n.* a short excursion into the country by a pleasure party carrying their own provisions.

PICTORIAL (pik-to'ri-al), *adj.* pertaining to, or illustrated by, pictures.

PICTURE ('tur, 'chur), *n.* a painting or drawing.

PICTURESQUE (-esk'), *adj.* giving vivid impression of nature or reality ;

graphic; abounding with vivid and striking imagery.

PIE (pi), *n.* printer's type confusedly mixed; meat or fruit covered with paste and baked.

PIEBALD ('bawld), *adj.* having patches of colours, as a piebald pony.

PIECE (pes), *n.* a part of anything; literary or artistic composition; separate performance; coin.

PIECEMEAL ('mel), *adv.* made of pieces or parts; by little and little in succession.

PIED (pid), *adj.* variegated.

PIER (per), *n.* a mass of masonry supporting an arch, bridge, etc.; mole or jetty; wharf.

PIERCE (pers), *v.t.* to penetrate; affect deeply; explore.

PIER GLASS (per glas), *n.* an ornamental mirror.

PIETY (pi'e-ti), *n.* reverence for, and duty toward God.

PIFFLE (pif'l), *n.* nonsense: *interj.* a contemptuous exclamation.

PIG (pig), *n.* the young of swine; a swine; pork; an oblong mass of unforged metal.

PIGEON (pij'un), *n.* a bird of a widely distributed family.

PIGEON-HOLE (-hol), *n.* a compartment in a desk or cabinet for papers, etc.

PIGEON-TOED (-tod), *adj.* having the toes turned inwards.

PIGGERY (pig'er-i), *n.* a place for pigs.

PIG-HEADED (-hed'ed), *adj.* stubborn; stupid.

PIG IRON (i'ern), *n.* iron cast in pigs.

PIGMENT ('ment), *n.* paint; colouring matter in plants, or animals.

PIGNUT (pig'nut), *n.* the bitter nut of a species of hickory.

PIGSKIN (-skin), *n.* skin of a hog; leather made from it.

PIGSTY ('sti), *n.* a pen for pigs.

PIKE (pik), *n.* a weapon with a shaft and spearhead; a fresh-water fish; a road; a turnpike.

PIKER (pi'ker), *n.* [Slang], a person who acts timidly and in a small way.

PILASTER (pi-las'ter), *n.* a square column or pillar inserted partly in a wall.

PILE (pil), *n.* a beam driven into the ground to make a firm foundation; mass or heap; accumulation; large building; nap of cloth; a fortune: *pl.* hemorrhoids.

PILFER (pil'fer), *v.t.* to steal.

PILFERER (-er), *n.* a petty thief.

PILGRIM ('grim), *n.* a traveller; one who travels from a distance to visit some sacred place.

PILGRIMAGE (-aj), *n.* a journey especially to some sacred place.

PILL (pil), *n.* a small ball of some medicinal substance.

PILLAGE ('aj), *n.* the act of plundering; spoil.

PILLAR ('ar), *n.* a column to support a structure; monument.

PILLOW ('o), *n.* a cloth case filled with feathers, etc.

PILLOW-CASE (-kas), *n.* a covering for a pillow, usually of linen.

PILOT (pi'lot), *n.* one who conducts a vessel in or out of a harbour or where navigation is difficult or dangerous; one qualified to operate a flying machine; a guide.

PIMENTO (-men'to), *n.* berry of a West Indian tree of the myrtle family; allspice.

PIMIENTO (-myen'to), *n.* the Spanish sweet pepper.

PIMPLE ('pl), *n.* a small pustule.

PIN (pin), *n.* a short piece of wire sharpened at one end and having a head at the other.

PINAFORE (pin'a-for), *n.* a loose apron to protect children's dresses.

PINCERS, same as pinchers.

PINCH (pinch), *v.t.* to squeeze or nip; oppress or distress.

PINCHERS (pinch'erz), *n.* an instrument for drawing out nails, etc.; nippers.

PINE (pin), *n.* a cone-bearing tree with needle-shaped, evergreen leaves: *v.i.* to waste away from distress, anxiety, worry, etc.

PINEAPPLE (pin'ap-l), *n.* the juicy edible fruit of a tropical plant.

PINION ('yun), *n.* the last joint of a bird's wing; a wing; the smaller of two geared wheels; a shackle.

PINK (pingk), *n.* a shade of light-red

colour ; a garden plant with fragrant flowers.

PINNACE (pin′as), *n.* a small, light, schooner-rigged boat with oars.

PINNACLE (′a-kl), *n.* a high point like a spire.

PINOCHLE (pe′nuk-l), *n.* a German game at cards.

PINT (pint), *n.* one-eighth of a gallon.

PINTO (pen′to), *adj.* piebald.

PIONEER (pi-o-ner′), *n.* one who goes before to prepare the way for another.

PIOUS (′us), *adj.* dutiful to God, or to parents ; religious ; devout.

PIP (pip), *n.* the seed of certain fruit : a disease in fowls.

PIPE (pip), *n.* any long hollow tube ; a tube with a bowl for smoking tobacco ; a wine measure equal to 2 hogsheads, or 105 imperial gallons, or 126 wine-gallons.

PIPPIN (′in), *n.* a variety of apple.

PIQUANCY (pe′kan-si), *n.* the quality of being piquant.

PIQUANT (′kant), *adj.* pungent ; racy.

PIQUE (pek), *n.* slight anger or resentment ; wounded pride.

PIQUET (pik′et), *n.* a card game.

PIRACY (pi′ra-si), *n.* the act or crime of a pirate ; infringement of copyright.

PIRATE (′rat), *n.* a robber on the high seas ; one who infringes the law of copyright.

PIROUETTE (pir-oo-et′),*n.* a whirling or turning about on the toes.

PISCICULTURE (pis′i-kul-tur), *n.* the artificial breeding and rearing of fishes.

PISTACHIO (pis-ta′shi-o), *n.* a small tree of southern Europe ; the seed of this tree used in flavouring.

PISTIL (′til), *n.* the seed-bearing organ in the centre of a flower.

PISTOL (′tol), *n.* a small hand-gun.

PISTON (′tun), *n.* a solid disk of metal or wood, fitting exactly and moving up and down the barrel of a pump, or in the cylinder of an engine.

PISTON-ROD (-rod), *n.* the rod that connects the piston with the crank-shaft.

PIT (pit), *n.* a deep hole in the earth.

PITCH (pich), *n.* the solid black resinous substance obtained from boiled tar ; resinous sap of pines ; a casting forward or down ; degree of rate ; slope ; the degree of acuteness or graveness of a musical note.

PITCHBLENDE (′blend), *n.* a black oxide of uranium ; it is the chief source of radium.

PITCHER (′er), *n.* one who pitches, especially, in baseball ; a vessel for holding water.

PITCHFORK (′fork), *n.* a long-handled fork for pitching hay, straw, etc.

PITEOUS (pit′e-us), *adj.* exciting pity ; sorrowful ; sad.

PITFALL (′fawl), *n.* a pit ; a trap.

PITH (pith), *n.* the soft spongy substance in the centre of plants ; marrow ; quintessence.

PITHILY (pith′i-li), *adv.* in a pithy manner.

PITHY (′i), *adj.* of the nature of pith ; forcible ; terse.

PITIFUL (′i-fool), *adj.* moving compassion ; insignificant.

PITILESS (′i-les), *adj.* without pity or compassion ; merciless.

PITTANCE (′ans), *n.* a small allowance, especially of money.

PITTED (′ed), *p.adj.* marked with indentations or small hollows.

PITY (pit′i), *n.* sympathy with distress ; compassion.

PIVOT (piv′ot), *n.* the short shaft on which some related part, or mechanism, revolves or rotates ; turns.

PIXY (pik′si), *n.* a fairy.

PLACABLE (′ka-bl), *adj.* that may be appeased or pacified ; forgiving.

PLACARD (plak′ard), *n.* a printed card placed on a wall, etc., as a notice.

PLACATE (pla′kat, plak′at), *v.t.* to appease ; satisfy ; conciliate.

PLACE (plas), *n.* a special spot or locality ; situation ; position ; site ; residence ; office ; city or town ; room ; existence ; duty.

PLACENTA (pla-sen′ta), *n.* the vascular organ attached to the fetus in the womb ; the afterbirth.

PLACER (plas′er), *n.* a mineral deposit near the surface which is not a vein; the place where such deposits are washed.

PLACID (plas'id), *adj.* calm; peaceful; mild.

PLACIDITY (pla-sid'i-ti), *n.* the state or quality of being placid.

PLACKET (plak'et), *n.* a slit in a skirt; a woman's pocket.

PLAGIARISM (pla'ji-a-rizm), *n.* the act of plagiarizing.

PLAGIARIST (-rist), *n.* one who steals from the writings of another and passes them off as his own production.

PLAGIARIZE (-riz), *v.t.* to steal from the writings of another.

PLAGUE (plag), *n.* a malignant epidemic; anything very troublesome or annoying.

PLAGUY ('gi), *adj.* vexatious.

PLAICE (plas), *n.* an edible flatfish.

PLAID (plad), *n.* a checkered woollen cloth.

PLAIN (plan), *adj.* level; flat; even; smooth; clear; evident; easily understood; homely.

PLAINT (plant), *n.* lamentation.

PLAINTIFF (plan'tif), *n.* one who begins a suit at law.

PLAINTIVE ('tiv), *adj.* expressing grief or sorrow; sad.

PLAIT (plat), *n.* a flat fold; braid.

PLAN (plan), *n.* a drawing as of a building, etc.; scheme or project.

PLANE (plan), *adj.* flat; level; even: *n.* in geometry, an even superfices; an airplane; a carpenter's tool.

PLANET (plan'et), *n.* a heavenly body revolving round the sun.

PLANK (plangk), *n.* a piece of sawn timber thicker than a board; an item in a political programme or policy: *v.t.* to pay (with *down*).

PLANT (plant), *n.* any vegetable organism; sprout or sapling; the tools, machinery, or fixtures of any trade or business.

PLANTATION (-ta'shun), *n.* a cultivated estate for cotton, sugar, etc.

PLANTER ('ter), *n.* one who plants; the owner of a plantation.

PLAQUE (plak), *n.* a metal or terracotta plate upon which flowers,

figures, etc., are enamelled or painted.

PLASH (plash), *n.* a puddle; pond: *v.t.* to splash with water.

PLASM (plazm), *n.* a mould or matrix.

PLASMA (plaz'ma), *n.* the colourless fluid of the blood in which the red corpuscles float; protoplasm.

PLASTER (plas'ter), *n.* a composition of lime, sand, and water, for coating walls; a medicinal application for external use; used for casts, mouldings, etc.

PLASTIC (plas'tik), *adj.* capable of being formed or moulded.

PLATE (plat), *n.* a thin piece of metal; a small shallow vessel used at table; an engraved piece of metal; an electrotype; a book illustration; household articles, of gold or silver.

PLATEAU (pla-to'), *n.* [*pl.* plateaux (-toz')], elevated, broad, flat land.

PLATE GLASS (plat glas), *n.* a fine kind of glass cast in thick plates.

PLATFORM ('form), *n.* a flat floor of wood, stone, etc., raised above the level of the ground; political programme or policy, of which each item is called a *plank*.

PLATING (plat'ing), *n.* the art of overlaying or covering anything with a metallic plate.

PLATINUM (-num), *n.* a grayish-white metal, very hard and ductile; one of the most valuable metals.

PLATITUDE ('i-tud), *n.* insipidity; dullness; a weak, empty remark.

PLATOON (pla-toon'), *n.* two files of soldiers forming a subdivision of a military unit.

PLATTER (plat'er), *n.* a large, flat dish.

PLATY-, a combining form from the Greek *platys*, broad, wide, flat.

PLATYPUS (plat'i-pus), *n.* the Australian duckbill.

PLAUDIT (plaw'dit), *n.* applause.

PLAUSIBILITY (-zi-bil'i-ti), *n.* the state or quality of being plausible; speciousness.

PLAUSIBLE ('zi-bl), *adj.* specious; superficially pleasing.

PLAY (pla), *n.* any exercise or occupation for amusement; exertion of powers ; diversion ; pastime ; drama, tragedy, or comedy ; scope ; practice.

PLAYFUL (pla'fool), *adj.* sportive ; lively.

PLAZA (pla'za), *n.* an open square or market place.

PLEA (ple), *n.* an excuse or apology ; urgent entreaty.

PLEAD (pled), *v.i.* to argue or reason in support of a cause.

PLEASANT (plez'ant), *adj.* delightful ; agreeable ; cheerful.

PLEASANTRY (ri), *n.* merriment ; lively talk ; gaiety.

PLEASE (plez), *v.t.* to gratify ; give pleasure to.

PLEASURE ('ur), *n.* gratification ; agreeable emotions.

PLEAT, see plait.

PLEBEIAN (ple-be'yan), *adj.* pertaining to the plebs or Roman commonalty ; pertaining to the common people.

PLEBISCITE (pleb'i-sit), *n.* a vote taken of the entire community by universal suffrage on some special matter submitted.

PLEDGE (plej), *n.* anything placed as a security or guarantee ; pawn ; hostage ; a health in drinking.

PLEDGET ('et), *n.* a flat piece of lint placed over a wound.

PLENARY (ple'na-ri), *adj.* full ; complete.

PLENIPOTENTIARY (plen-i-po-ten'shi-a-ri), *adj.* having full power : *n.* an ambassador invested with full powers.

PLENITUDE (plen'i-tud), *n.* fullness.

PLENTEOUS ('te-us), *adj.* abundant.

PLENTIFUL ('ti-fool), *adj.* yielding abundance ; copious.

PLENTY ('ti), *n.* abundance.

PLETHORA (pleth'o-ra), *n.* abnormal fullness of blood ; overabundance.

PLETHORIC (ple-thor'ik), *adj.* having excess of blood.

PLEURA (ploo'ra), *n.* [*pl.* pleuræ ('re)], a delicate serous membrane covering the interior of the thorax and each lung.

PLEURISY ('ri-si), *n.* inflammation of the pleura.

PLEXUS (plek'sus), *n.* a network of veins, nerves, etc.

PLIABILITY (pli-a-bil'i-ti), *n.* the state of being pliable.

PLIABLE ('a-bl), *adj.* easily bent ; flexible ; easy to be persuaded.

PLIANCY ('an-si), *n.* pliant quality.

PLIANT ('ant), *adj.* flexible ; easily bent ; yielding to moral suasion.

PLICATE ('kat), *adj.* plaited ; folded in the form of a fan.

PLIERS ('erz), *n.* a kind of small pinchers.

PLIGHT (plit), *n.* a dangerous or distressed condition ; predicament.

PLOD (plod), *v.i.* to travel laboriously ; drudge or toil.

PLOT (plot), *n.* a scheme, conspiracy, or plan ; intrigue ; chain of incidents in a play, novel, etc., gradually developed ; a small area of ground : *v.t.* to devise ; make a plan of : *v.i.* to conspire ; conspire against another.

PLOVER (pluv'er), *n.* a shore-bird.

PLOUGH (plou), *n.* an agricultural implement.

PLOUGHSHARE ('shar), *n.* the iron part of a plough that cuts the soil.

PLUCK (pluk), *v.t.* to pull off, out, or up ; snatch ; pick or gather : *n.* courage.

PLUCKY ('i) *adj.* having courage.

PLUG (plug), *n.* a piece of wood, etc., used for stopping a hole.

PLUM (plum), *n.* the edible stone-fruit, of any one of various trees of the genus *Prunus* : the tree.

PLUMAGE (ploom'aj), *n.* a bird's feathers.

PLUMB (plum), *n.* a heavy bob, suspended at the extremity of a line to indicate the perpendicularity of work done, as a wall, etc.

PLUMBAGO (-ba'go), *n.* a mineral of carbon and iron, used for lead pencils ; a form of carbon.

PLUMBER ('er), *n.* one engaged in plumbing.

PLUMBING ('ing), *n.* the occupation of putting into buildings the pipes, traps, etc., for the conveyance of water, gas, and sewage.

PLUMCOT (plum´kot), *n.* a hybrid fruit produced by Luther Burbank (1849-1926), American horticulturist, by crossing the plum and the apricot.

PLUME (ploom), *n.* a feather ; crest : *v.t.* to pick and adjust the feathers of ; boast ; pride (used reflectively).

PLUMMET (plum´et), *n.* a leaden weight attached to a stout cord, used for sounding depths, etc.

PLUMP (plump), *adj.* round and sleek with fullness of flesh ; in good condition ; downright ; a knot or cluster of individuals.

PLUNDER (plun´der), *n.* booty ; pillage : *v.t.* to spoil ; rob.

PLUNGE (plunj), *v.t.* to put suddenly into water or any other liquid.

PLURAL (´ral), *adj.* consisting of more than one.

PLURALITY (ploo-ral´i-ti), *n.* the majority ; the excess of votes cast for any one candidate over the candidate who receives the next largest number of votes at an election where there are three or more candidates for the same office.

PLUS (plus), *n.* the sign (+) used to denote addition ; the sign to denote positive in electricity ; above zero.

PLUSH (plush), *n.* a shaggy cloth with a pile ; woollen velvet.

PLUTOCRACY (ploo-tok´ra-si), *n.* rule or government by the rich.

PLUTOCRAT (ploo´to-krat), *n.* one who exercises political power or influence by virtue of his wealth.

PLUVIAL (´vi-al), *adj.* rainy.

PLY (pli), *v.t.* to work on closely ; practise diligently ; urge or solicit : *v.i.* to run regularly between ports.

PNEUMATIC (nu-mat´ik), *adj.* pertaining to air.

PNEUMATIC TYRE (tir), a tyre made of rubber and inflated with air.

PNEUMONIA (-mo´ni-a), *n.* acute inflammation of the lungs.

POACH (poch), *v.i.* to trespass upon preserves to shoot or steal game : *v.t.* to cook (eggs) by breaking them into boiling water.

POCKET (pok´et), *n.* a small bag inserted in a garment for carrying small articles.

POD (pod), *n.* pericarp of the covering of the seed of certain plants, as the pea, etc.

POEM (po´em), *n.* a metrical or poetical composition ; a poetic conception.

POET (´et), *n.* one gifted in writing poetry.

POET LAUREATE (law´re-at), *n.* a court poet.

POETRY (´et-ri), *n.* a metrical composition produced by creative imagination.

POGROM (po´grom), *n.* in Russia, an outburst against Jews.

POIGNANCY (poin´an-si), *n.* state of being poignant.

POIGNANT (´ant), *adj.* stimulating to the palate ; irritating.

POINSETTIA (-set´i-a), *n.* a South American shrub with deep green foliage and scarlet flowers.

POINT (point), *n.* the sharp end of any instrument ; mark or dot ; mark in punctuation ; a spot ; exact place ; aim ; small promontory ; unit of measurement for type-bodies = .0138 inch, or one-twelfth of a pica.

POINT-BLANK (´blangk), *adj.* horizontal ; straight to the mark ; direct.

POISE (poiz), *n.* weight ; balance ; equilibrium.

POISON (poi´zm), *n.* anything noxious or destructive to life, health, or morality ; venom.

POISON IVY (i´vi), a species of sumac.

POKE (pok), *n.* a thrust or push ; a bag or sack.

POKER (´er), *n.* a metal bar for stirring fires ; a card game.

POKY (po´ki), *adj.* lacking spirit or interest ; show ; stupid ; stuffy.

POLAR (´lar), *adj.* pertaining to the poles.

POLE (pol), *n.* a long staff ; a measure = 5½ yards ; a square measure = 30¼ yards ; a measuring instrument ; one of the extremities of the imaginary axis of the earth.

POLECAT (´kat), *n.* a small carnivorous animal ; a skunk.

POLEMIC (po-lem´ik), *n.* a controversialist : *pl.* the art of controversy.

POLE-STAR (pol'star), *n.* the north star (Polaris) situated in Ursa Minor, within 1½ degrees of the true pole; a guide.

POLICE (po-les'), *n.* an organized force of civil officers for preserving order.

POLICY (pol'i-si), *n.* the art or method of government; system of regulative measures; course of conduct; a contract of insurance.

POLIOMYELITIS (pol-i-o-mi-e-li'-tis), *n.* inflammation of the spinal cord; infantile paralysis.

POLISH ('ish), *v.t.* to make smooth or glossy by friction; make polite or refined.

POLITE (po-lit'), *adj.* well-bred; refined in manner; courteous.

POLITIC ('i-tik), *adj.* shrewd; specious; sagacious; especially in policy: *n.pl.* the administration of public affairs; political opinions.

POLITICAL (po-lit'i-kal), *adj.* pertaining to politics.

POLITICAL ECONOMY (e-kon'o-mi), the science that treats of wealth, its nature, production, distribution, and consumption, and the laws which regulate and govern these.

POLITICIAN ('i-tish'an), *n.* one who is skilled in politics.

POLITY ('i-ti), *n.* form of constitution of civil government of a state.

POLKA (pol'ka), *n.* a dance of Bohemian origin.

POLL (pol), *n.* the head; a register of persons; number of votes recorded at an election.

POLLEN ('en), *n.* the fertilizing powder in the cells of the anthers of flowers.

POLLINATE (pol'i-nat), *v.t.* to convey pollen to (a pistil).

POLL-TAX (pol'taks), *n.* a capitation tax.

POLLUTE (po-lut'), *v.t.* to defile; render unclean; taint with guilt.

POLLUTION (po-lu'shun), *n.* defilement.

POLO (po'lo), *n.* a game played while on horseback.

POLTROON (pol-troon'), *n.* a coward.

POLYGAMY (pol-ig'a-mi), *n.* the possession, by a man, with more than one wife at the same time.

POLYGLOT (pol'i-glot), *adj.* containing many languages.

POLYSCOPE (-skop), *n.* a multiplying lens.

POLYSYLLABLE (-sil'a-bil), *n.* a word consisting of three or more syllables.

POLYTECHNIC (-tek'nik), *adj.* noting, including, or giving instruction in, the arts and sciences.

POLYTHEISM ('i-the-izm), *n.* the doctrine of a plurality of gods.

POMADE (po-mad'), *n.* a perfumed ointment for dressing the hair.

POMEGRANATE (pom'gran-at), *n.* the fruit of a tropical Asiatic tree.

POMOLOGY (po-mol'o-ji), *n.* the science of cultivating fruit and trees, especially apples.

POMP (pomp), *n.* ostentatious display; grandeur; parade.

POMPANO (pom'pa-no), *n.* a valuable food fish.

POMPON (pom'pon), *n.* a tufted ornament; a variety of chrysanthemum.

POMPOSITY (-pos'i-ti), *n.* the state of being pompous.

POMPOUS (pom'pus), *adj.* stately; grand; self-important.

POND (pond), *n.* a pool of water.

PONDER (pon'der), *v.t.* to weigh mentally : *v.i.* to deliberate.

PONDERABLE ('der-a-bl), *adj.* capable of being weighed.

PONDEROUS ('der-us), *adj.* very heavy; weighty; important; dull.

PONE (pon), *n.* bread made of maize meal and milk.

PONGEE (pon-je'), *n.* a kind of silk.

PONTIFF ('tif), *n.* a high priest; bishop; the Pope.

PONTOON (pon-toon'), *n.* a buoyant, flat-bottomed structure; a bridge of boats; the float of a sea-plane.

PONY (po'ni), *n.* a small horse.

POOL (pool), *n.* a small body of water.

POOR (poor), *adj.* necessitous; destitute of riches; dejected; insignificant; lean.

POPE (pop), *n.* the head of the R.C. Church.

POPINJAY ('in-ja), *n.* a parrot; a coxcomb; a fop.

POPLAR (pop'lar), *n.* a tree of rapid growth, with a white soft wood.

POPPY ('i), *n.* a plant with bright flowers of various shades.

POPULACE ('u-las), *n.* the people.

POPULAR ('u-lar), *adj.* pertaining to, suitable for, or pleasing to, the people; well liked.

POPULARIZE (-iz), *v.t.* to render popular.

POPULATION (-la'shun), *n.* the habitants of a place, etc., collectively.

POPULOUS ('u-lus), *adj.* thickly peopled.

PORCELAIN (pors'lan), *n.* a fine, white, thin, semi-transparent kind of earthenware.

PORCH (porch), *n.* a vestibule supported by pillars; portico.

PORCUPINE (por'ku-pin), *n.* a rodent, about two feet long, having strong, sharp spines.

PORE (por), *n.* a minute hole in the skin through which perspiration passes to the surface: *v.i.* to look with steady continued attention or application.

PORGY ('ji), *n.* a food fish.

PORK (pork), *n.* the flesh of swine.

PORKER ('ker), *n.* a pig.

POROUS ('rus), *adj.* having pores; permeable by water or other liquid.

PORPOISE (por'pus), *n.* a gregarious cetacean.

PORRIDGE (por'ij), *n.* oatmeal boiled slowly in water until it thickens.

PORT (port), *n.* a harbour; harem; the left side of a ship; porthole; gate; a dark-coloured wine.

PORTABLE ('ta-bl), *adj.* that may be easily carried by hand or about the person.

PORTAL ('tal), *n.* an arch over a gateway or door.

PORTEND (por-tend'), *v.t.* to indicate advance; presage; forebode.

PORTENT (por'tent), *n.* an omen.

PORTENTOUS ('tus), *adj.* ominous; foreshadowing evil.

PORTER (por'ter), *n.* a door- or gate-keeper; one who carries parcels, etc., for hire.

PORTFOLIO (-fo'li-o), *n.* a portable case for papers, drawings, etc.; the office and functions of a minister of state.

PORTHOLE ('hol), *n.* a window-shaped hole in the side of a ship.

PORTIERE (por-tyar'), *n.* [French] a door-curtain.

PORTION (por'shun), *n.* a piece or part; allotment; dividend.

PORTLY ('li), *adj.* stately of mien; corpulent.

PORTRAIT (por'trat), *n.* a picture of an individual or face drawn from life.

PORTRAY (-tra'), *v.t.* to paint or draw the likeness of; describe in words.

PORTRAYAL ('al), *n.* description.

POSE (poz), *n.* attitude or position: *v.i.* to assume an attitude.

POSER (poz'er), *n.* one who, or that which, poses or puzzles.

POSITION (po-zish'un), *n.* situation; attitude; office; social status; sphere of influence.

POSITIVE (pos'i-tiv), *adj.* actual; direct; explicit; over confident; incontestable; noting one of two opposed qualities, etc., with the sign +: *n.* reality; a word which affirms or asserts existence; a photograph with the natural lights and shades restored.

POSITIVELY (-li), *adv.* absolutely.

POSSE (pos'e), *n.* an improvised force for police duties; a small body of men.

POSSESS (po-zes'), *v.t.* to have as an owner; occupy; seize.

POSSESSION (-zesh'un), *n.* the having, holding, or detention of property; property or estate.

POSSIBILITY (-i-bil'i-ti), *n.* being possible; contingency.

POSSIBLE ('i-bl), *adj.* that may happen or exist.

POST (post), *n.* a piece of timber, etc., set erect, as a support; established system of conveying and delivering letters; the mail; military station; a trading post.

POSTAGE (pos'taj), *n.* the fee for conveyance by post.

POSTAL (pos'tal), *adj.* pertaining to the post office or mail service.

POSTER (pos'ter), *n.* a large advertising bill.

POSTERITY (-ter'i-ti), *n.* succeeding generations ; descendants.

POST FACTO (post fak'to), done after the act ; retrospective.

POSTFIX ('fiks), *v.t.* to affix : *n.* an affix.

POST-GRADUATE (-grad'u-at), *adj.* denoting studies pursued after graduation.

POSTHUMOUS (post'hu-mus), *adj.* born after the death of the father ; published after the death of an author.

POSTMASTER (post'mas-ter), *n.* the superintendent of a post office.

POSTMASTER-GENERAL, (-jen'-er-al), *n.* the chief officer of the Post Office department.

POST MERIDIAN (-me-rid'i-an), *n.* afternoon : abbreviated P.M.

POST OFFICE (of'is), *n.* an office where mail is received and distributed.

POSTPONE (pon'), *v.t.* to delay ; defer.

POSTSCRIPT ('skript), *n.* a paragraph added to a letter after the writer's signature.

POSTULATE (pos'tu-lat), *v.t.* to assume without proof ; solicit ; demand ; claim ; affirm ; assert.

POSTURE ('tur), *n.* attitude : *v.i.* to assume a particular position.

POT (pot), *n.* a metallic or earthenware vessel of a round shape, used for various purposes.

POTASH (pot'ash), *n.* a powerful alkali obtained from the ashes of certain plants.

POTATION (po-ta'shun), *n.* drinking bout ; a beverage.

POTATO (-ta'to), *n.* the edible tuber, widely cultivated ; the plant itself.

POTENCY (po'ten-si), *n.* power, physical or mental.

POTENT ('tent), *adj.* powerful.

POTENTIAL (po-ten'shal), *adj.* existing in possibility, not in reality ; latent in grammar, a mood expressing power, possibility.

POTHER (poth'er), *n.* confusion.

POTION (po'shun), *n.* a dose.

POTPOURRI (po-poo-re'),*n.* [French], a medley, especially of musical airs ; a dish similar to a beef stew.

POTTERY ('er-i), *n.* earthenware of all kinds; the place where it is made.

POTTLE (pot'l), *n.* a liquid measure = 4 pints.

POUCH (pouch), *n.* a small bag.

POULTERER (pol'ter-er), *n.* a dealer in poultry.

POULTICE ('tis), *n.* a soft preparation applied to a sore part of the body ; a cataplasm.

POULTRY ('tri), *n.* domestic fowls.

POUND (pound), *n.* a standard weight = 16 ounces avoirdupois, or 12 ounces troy ; a monetary unit of Great Britain = 20 shillings ; an inclosure for confining stray animals.

POUR (por), *v.t.* to empty ; send forth ; give vent to ; utter.

POUT (pout), *n.* a thrusting out of the lips ; fit of sullenness.

POUTER ('er), *n.* one who pouts ; one of a breed of pigeons.

POVERTY (pov'er-ti), *n.* indigence ; necessity ; penury ; deficiency or defect.

POWDER ('der), *n.* any dry substance in fine particles.

POWER (pou'er), *n.* ability ; energy ; force ; strength ; rule or authority.

POWERFUL (-fool), *adj.* mighty ; forcible ; strong.

PRACTICABILITY (prak-ti-ka-bil'i-ti), *n.* the state of being practicable.

PRACTICABLE ('ti-ka-bl), *adj.* that may be done, or used; feasible ; possible.

PRACTICAL ('ti-kal), *adj.* pertaining to action or use ; useful.

PRACTICE (prak'tis), *n.* frequent or customary action ; exercise of any profession.

PRACTITIONER (-tish'un-er), *n.* one who is engaged in the exercise of any profession.

PRÆ-, a prefix from the Latin *prae*, before.

PRAGMATIC (prag-mat'ik), **PRAG-MATICAL** (-mat'i-kal), *adj.* meddling; officious.

PRAIRIE (pra'ri), *n.* an extensive, treeless tract of level or undulating land covered with tall grass.

PRAIRIE DOG (dog), *n.* a small burrowing rodent.

PRAISE (praz), *n.* approbation; commendation; tribute of gratitude; worship of God.

PRAISEWORTHY (praz'wer-*thi*), *adj.* worthy of praise.

PRANCE (prans), *n.* a spring or bound.

PRANK (prangk), *n.* a frolic; mischievous trick.

PRATE (prat), *v.i.* to talk idly; be loquacious.

PRATTLE (prat'l), *n.* childish talk.

PRAXIS (prak'sis), *n.* an example or series of examples for exercise.

PRAY (pra), *v.t.* to ask earnestly; address or petition.

PRAYER (prar), *n.* a solemn address to the Supreme Being.

PREACH (prech), *v.i.* to pronounce a public discourse on a sacred subject.

PREADAMITE (pre-ad'am-it), *adj.* existing before Adam.

PREAMBLE (pre'am-bl), *n.* an introduction or preface.

PREBEND (preb'end), *n.* the stipend granted to a canon.

PRECARIOUS (pre-ka'ri-us), *adj.* uncertain; held by a doubtful tenure.

PRECAUTION (pre-kaw'shun), *n.* caution taken beforehand; preventive measure.

PRECEDE (pre-sed'), *v.t.* to go before in time, place, rank, or importance.

PRECEDENCE (-sed'ens), **PRECEDENCY** (-sed'en-si), *n.* priority; relative rank in social etiquette.

PRECEDENT (pre-sed'ent), *adj.* going before; anterior: *n.* (pres'e-dent), something previously said or done; a parallel case in the past.

PRECEDING (pre-sed'ing), *p.adj.* going before; antecedent.

PRECEPT (pre'sept), *n.* an authoritative command; maxim.

PRECEPTOR ('ter), *n.* an instructor or teacher.

PRECEPTRESS (-tres), *n.* a female teacher.

PRECINCT (pre'singkt), *n.* an outward limit or boundary; a division of a city, as for police control.

PRECIOUS (presh'us), *adj.* of great price or value; costly; highly esteemed.

PRECIPICE (pres'i-pis), *n.* a steep descent, nearly or quite perpendicular.

PRECIPITANCE (pre-sip'i-tans), **PRECIPITANCY** (-sip'i-tan-si), *n.* haste in resolving or carrying out a purpose.

PRECIPITANT ('i-tant), *adj.* falling headlong; hasty.

PRECIPITATE (-sip'i-tat), *v.t.* to throw headlong; urge on violently: *adj.* headlong; overhasty: *n.* a substance precipitated.

PRECIPITATION (-ta'shun), *n.* rash haste; that which is precipitated.

PRECIPITOUS ('i-tus), *adj.* very steep; headlong; rash; hasty.

PRECIS (pra-se'), *n.* [French], an abstract; summary.

PRECISE (pre'sis), *adj.* exact; strict; accurate; definite; punctilious.

PRECISELY ('li), *adv.* in a precise manner.

PRECISIAN (-sizh'an), *n.* a punctilious person.

PRECLUDE (-klood'), *v.t.* to shut out; obviate; prevent.

PRECLUSION (-kloo'zhun), *n.* the act of precluding; being precluded.

PRECOCIOUS (-ko'shus), *adj.* prematurely ripe or developed; pertly forward.

PRECONCEIVE (-kon-sev'), *v.t.* to form an opinion beforehand.

PRECURSOR (pre-ker'ser), *n.* that which precedes; forerunner; omen.

PRECURSORY ('so-ri), *adj.* indicating something that is to happen or follow.

PREDATORY (pred'a-to-ri), *adj.* rapacious; plundering; pillaging.

PREDECESSOR (pre-de-ses'er), *n.* one who has preceded another in the same office, business, position, etc.; an ancestor.

PREDESTINATION (-na′shun), *n.* foreordaining ; the doctrine that God has from all eternity decreed whatever comes to pass, especially, by an unchangeable purpose, the eternal life or death of man.

PREDICABLE (′i-ka-bl), *adj.* capable of being predicated.

PREDICAMENT (pre-dik′a-ment), *n.* in logic, that which is predicated or asserted ; a category ; a peculiar situation ; critical condition or state.

PREDICATE (pred′i-kat), *v.t.* to affirm one thing of another ; found : *n.* in logic, that which is affirmed or denied of the subject ; in grammar, the word or words which express what is said of the subject.

PREDICATION (-ka′shun), *n.* affirmation.

PREDICT (pre-dikt′), *v.t.* to foretell ; prophesy.

PREDICTION (pre-dik′shun), *n.* the declaration of a future event ; prophecy.

PREDIGESTION (pre-di-jes′chun), *n.* the peptonizing of food.

PREDILECTION (pre-di-lek′shun), *n.* preference beforehand ; partiality.

PREDISPOSE (-dis-poz′), *v.t.* to incline beforehand.

PREDISPOSITION (pre-dis-po-zish′un), *n.* previous inclination or propensity ; prejudice.

PREDOMINANCE (-dom′i-nans), **PREDOMINANCY** (-dom′i-nan-si), *n.* prevalence over others ; superiority in power, authority, etc.

PREDOMINANT (′i-nant), *adj.* superior ; controlling.

PREDOMINATE (′i-nat), *v.i.* to be superior in strength, power, authority, etc.

PRE-EMINENCE (pre-em′i-nens), *n.* superiority in rank, order, quality, condition, etc.

PRE-EMINENT (-nent), *adj.* distinguished above others ; surpassing in quality, rank, etc.

PRE-EMPT (pre-empt′), *v.t.* establish a right or claim to, before others.

PRE-EMPTION (-emp′shun), *n.* the act or right of purchasing before others.

PREEN (pren), *v.t.* to cleanse, trim and compose with the beak, as birds.

PREFACE (pref′as), *n.* the introduction to a book, etc.

PREFATORY (′a-to-ri), *adj.* introductory.

PREFECT (pre′fekt), *n.* a civil magistrate or governor ; monitor.

PREFECTURE (′fek-tur), *n.* the office, jurisdiction, or official residence of a prefect.

PREFER (pre-fer′), *v.t.* to regard or esteem more than something else.

PREFERENCE (pref′er-ens), *n.* act of preferring ; the thing preferred.

PREFERENTIAL (-en′shal), *adj.* having a preference.

PREFERMENT (pre-fer′ment), *n.* promotion, especially in the church ; in law, priority of right.

PREFIX (pre′fiks), *n.* a particle or syllable placed before a word to modify its signification : *v.t.* (pre-fiks′), to place before or at the beginning of.

PREGNANCY (preg′nan-si), *n.* the state of being pregnant ; quickness of apprehension.

PREGNANT (′nant), *adj.* being with young ; fruitful ; full of importance or significance.

PREHENSIBLE (pre-hen′si-bl), *adj.* that may be seized.

PREHENSION (′shun), *n.* a taking hold.

PREJUDGE (pre-juj′), *v.t.* to condemn beforehand, or hastily.

PREJUDICE (prej′u-dis), *n.* previous and unfavourable bias ; detriment ; injury.

PREJUDICIAL (-dish′al), *adj.* disadvantageous ; biased.

PRELACY (prel′a-si), *n.* episcopacy ; bishops collectively.

PRELATE (′at), *n.* an ecclesiastical dignitary.

PRELIMINARY (-lim′i-na-ri), *adj.* preceding main discourse or business ; introductory.

PRELUDE (prel′ud, pre′lud), *n.* a short piece of music played as an introduction ; preface.

PRELUSIVE (pre-lu′siv), **PRELUSORY** (-so-ri), *adj.* introductory.

PREMATURE (pre-ma-tur′), *adj.* arriving, occurring, or done, before the proper time.

PREMEDITATE (pre-med′i-tat), *v.t.* to design, conceive, or deliberate, beforehand.

PREMIER (pre′mi-er, prem′yer), *adj.* first ; chief : *n.* the prime minister.

PREMIERE (pre-mi-yer′), *n.* [French], the first performance of a play.

PREMISE (pre-miz′), *v.t.* to explain previously ; lay down as propositions to reason from : *n.* (prem′us), a proposition antecedently assumed and laid down : *pl.* a building and its adjuncts.

PREMIUM (pre′mi-um), *n.* a recompense or reward ; bonus ; payment for insurance.

PREMONITION (pre-mo-nish′un), *n.* previous warning ; forewarning.

PREMONITORY (-mon′i-to-ri), *adj.* giving warning beforehand.

PREOCCUPY (pre-ok′u-pi), *v.t.* to take prior possession of.

PREPARATION (pre-a-ra′shun), *n.* the act of preparing or fitting for a particular purpose ; readiness ; that which is prepared.

PREPARATORY (-par′a-to-ri), *adj.* previously necessary ; introductory.

PREPARE (pre-par′), *v.t.* to make ready for ; to arrange.

PREPENSE (-pens′), *adj.* premeditated.

PREPONDERANCE (pon′der-ans), *n.* superiority of weight, power, force, or influence.

PREPONDERANT (-ant), *adj.* outweighing.

PREPONDERATE (′der-at), *v.t.* to outweigh.

PREPOSITION (prep-o-zish′un), *n.* a word placed before a noun or pronoun to indicate its relation to some other word in the sentence.

PREPOSSESS (pre-po-zes′), *v.t.* to occupy beforehand ; bias.

PREPOSSESSING (′ing), *p.adj.* tending to win or secure favour ; attractive.

PREPOSTEROUS (pre-pos′ter-us),

adj. contrary to nature or reason, ridiculous ; absurd.

PREREQUISITE (pre-rek′wi-zit), *n.* something necessary to accomplish an end or object.

PREROGATIVE (-rog′a-tiv), *n.* an exclusive or peculiar privilege.

PRESAGE (pres′aj), *n.* a foreboding or presentiment : *v.t.* (pre-saj′), to forebode ; predict.

PRESBYTER (pres′bi-ter), *n.* an elder, minister, or priest ; in the Presbyterian Church, a member of the presbytery.

PRESBYTERIAN (-bi-te′ri-an), *n.* one of a Protestant body governed by presbyters.

PRESCIENCE (pre′shi-ens), *n.* foreknowledge.

PRESCIENT (′shi-ent), *adj.* foreknowing.

PRESCRIBE (pre-skrib′), *v.t.* to set down authoritatively ; direct medically ; appoint.

PRESCRIPTION (-skrip′shun), *n.* a written direction for the preparation of a medicine ; recipe.

PRESENCE (prez′ens), *n.* the state or quality of being present ; quickness at expedients ; approach face to face ; society ; mien ; bearing.

PRESENT (′ent), *adj.* being in a certain place ; at hand or in sight ; at this time ; instant or immediate : *n.* the present time ; a gift.

PRESENTIENT (-sen′shent), *adj.* having previous perception.

PRESENTIMENT (′ti-ment), *n.* previous apprehension of something about to come or happen (usually of impending evil).

PRESENTMENT (pre-zent′ment), *n.* the thing presented.

PRESERVABLE (-zer′va-bl), *adj.* that may be preserved.

PRESERVATION (prez-er-va′shun), *n.* being preserved from injury or decay.

PRESERVE (-zerv′), *v.t.* to defend ; uphold ; save ; keep in a sound state.

PRESIDE (pre-zid′), *v.i.* to direct or control ; superintend.

PRESIDENCY (prez′i-den-si), *n.* the

office, dignity, term, jurisdiction, or residence of a president.

PRESIDENT ('i-dent), *n.* one who presides over a corporation or assembly ; [P-], the highest officer of a republic.

Presidents of U.S.	Inaugurated year	age
George Washington	1789	57
John Adams	1797	62
Thomas Jefferson	1801	58
James Madison	1809	58
James Monroe	1817	59
John Quincy Adams	1825	58
Andrew Jackson	1829	62
Martin Van Buren	1837	55
Wm. H. Harrison	1841	68
John Tyler	1841	51
James K. Polk	1845	50
Zachary Taylor	1849	65
Millard Fillmore	1850	50
Franklin Pierce	1853	49
James Buchanan	1857	66
Abraham Lincoln	1861	52
Andrew Johnson	1865	57
Ulysses S. Grant	1869	47
Rutherford B. Hayes	1877	54
James A. Garfield	1881	49
Chester A. Arthur	1881	51
Grover Cleveland	1885	48
Benjamin Harrison	1889	55
Grover Cleveland	1893	56
William McKinley	1897	54
Theodore Roosevelt	1901	43
William H. Taft	1909	52
Woodrow Wilson	1913	56
Warren G. Harding	1921	56
Calvin Coolidge	1923	51
Herbert Clark Hoover	1929	55
Franklin Delano Roosevelt	1932	50
,, ,, ,,	1936	54
,, ,, ,,	1940	58
,, ,, ,,	1944	62
Harry Shippe Truman	1945	61

PRESIDENTIAL (-den'shal), *adj.* pertaining to a president.

PRESS (pres), *v.t.* to urge ; squeeze or crush ; compel ; crowd upon ; distress ; hurry ; make smooth, as cloth, etc. : *n.* an instrument or machine for compressing anything ; a printing machine ; newspaper and periodical literature.

PRESSING ('ing), *p.adj.* urgent.

PRESTIDIGITATOR (-ti-dij'i-ta⁻ter), *n.* an expert juggler.

PRESTIGE ('tij, -tezh'), *n.* moral influence due to past reputation, achievements, etc.

PRESTO (pres'to), *adv.* quickly.

PRESUME (pre-zum'), *v.t.* to take for granted on probable grounds ; suppose.

PRESUMPTION (-zump'shun), *n.* strong probability ; arrogance or overconfidence.

PRESUMPTUOUS ('tu-us), *adj.* bold ; arrogant ; willful ; rash.

PRESUPPOSE (pre-su-poz'), *v.t.* to take for granted ; imply as antecedent.

PRETEND (pre-tend'), *v.t.* to allege or put forward falsely ; simulate ; counterfeit ; assert.

PRETENDER (-ten'der), *n.* one who lays claim to anything under the guise of a right ; one who pretends.

PRETENCE (-tens'), *n.* false or hypocritical profession ; unfounded claim ; pretext.

PRETENSION (-ten'shun), *n.* a claim, true or false ; assumed right.

PRETER-, prefix signifying *beyond, past, more than.*

PRETERIT, PRETERITE (pret'er-it, -it), *adj.* past : *n.* the past tense.

PRETEXT (pre'tekst), *n.* a pretence or excuse.

PRETTILY (prit'i-li), *adv.* in a pretty manner.

PRETTY ('i), *adj.* pleasing ; attractive ; moderately large or excellent ; fine : *adv.* fairly ; tolerably.

PRETZEL (pret'zel), *n.* a hard wheaten biscuit, made in the form of a knot and salted on the surface.

PREVAIL (pre-val'), *v.i.* to overcome ; operate effectually.

PREVALENCE (prev-a'lens), *n.* superior strength, influence, or efficacy.

PREVALENT ('lent), *adj.* predominant ; victorious ; most general.

PREVARICATE (pre-var'i-kat), *v.i.* to evade the truth ; quibble.

PREVARICATOR (-var'i-ka-ter), *n.* one who prevaricates.

PREVENT (-vent'), *v.t.* to hinder ; thwart ; check ; frustrate.

PREVENTION (-ven'shun), *n.* hindrance or obstruction.

PREVENTIVE ('tiv), *n.* that which prevents.

PREVIOUS (pre'vi-us), *adj.* going before ; anterior.

PREVISION (-vizh'un), *n.* foreknowledge.

PREY (pra), *n.* plunder ; booty ; that which may be, or is, seized by a wild beast for food : *v.i.* to take booty or plunder ; weigh heavily (with *on* or *upon*).

PRICE (pris), *n.* the current value of a commodity ; cost ; reward.

PRICELESS ('les), *adj.* invaluable.

PRICK (prik), *n.* a puncture ; dot or point ; thorn ; goad ; remorse.

PRIDE (prid), *n.* inordinate self-esteem ; arrogance ; honourable self-respect ; personal dignity.

PRIEST (prest), *n.* an ecclesiastic.

PRIGGISH (prig'ish), *adj.* conceited.

PRIM (prim), *adj.* precise ; formally neat.

PRIMACY (pri'ma-si), *n.* the office or dignity of a primate.

PRIMA DONNA (pre'ma don'a), the principal female singer in an opera.

PRIMAL (pri'mal), *adj.* first.

PRIMARILY (pri'ma-ri-li), *adv.* in the first place ; originally.

PRIMARY ('ma-ri), *adj.* in the first order of time, place, or rank ; chief ; original ; principal ; preparatory ; denoting the inducing current in an electric circuit : *n.* a meeting of voters of an election district for the purpose of selecting a candidate.

PRIMATE ('mat), *n.* an archbishop.

PRIME (prim), *adj.* first in order of rank, time, or importance ; excellent.

PRIME NUMBER (num'ber), a number not divisible without remainder.

PRIMER (prim'er), *n.* an elementary text book.

PRIMEVAL (pri-me'val), *adj.* of the earliest age or time ; original.

PRIMITIVE (prim'i-tiv), *adj.* original ; not derivative ; old-fashioned.

PRIMOGENITURE (pri-mo-jen'i-tur), *n.* seniority of birth.

PRIMORDIAL (-mor'di-al), *adj.* existing from the beginning.

PRIMP (primp), *v.i.* to deck (one's self), in a prim or affected manner ; prink.

PRIMROSE (prim'roz), *n.* a spring flower of a pale yellow colour.

PRIMULA (prim'u-la), *n.* a genus of perennial herbs typifying Primulaceæ.

PRIMULACÆ (-la'se-e), *n. pl.* the primrose family of perennial herbs.

PRINCE (prins), *n.* a ruler or sovereign ; the son of a king or sovereign.

PRINCESS (prin'ses), *n.* the daughter of a sovereign ; the wife of a prince.

PRINCIPAL (prin'si-pal), *adj.* occupying the first place or rank ; chief in character, degree, or importance : *n.* a head of a firm, school, or college ; a capital sum lent at interest.

PRINCIPALITY (-si-pal'i-ti), *n.* the territory of a prince.

PRINCIPALLY ('si-pal-li), *adv.* chiefly.

PRINCIPLE ('si-pl), *n.* source of origin ; element ; fundamental truth or doctrine ; reason ; foundation of morality or religion.

PRINK (pringk), *v.t.* to deck out in a showy or ostentatious fashion.

PRINT (print), *n.* a mark or character made by impression ; anything produced by printing : *pl.* engravings ; printed cotton.

PRINTER ('er), *n.* one engaged in the business of printing.

PRINTING ('ing), *n.* the art or act of impressing figures or characters on paper, etc. ; typography.

PRIOR (pri'er), *adj.* coming before, in time ; former : *adv.* previously : *n.* the head of a priory or monastery.

PRIORITY (or'i-ti), *n.* the state of being first in rank, time, or place ; first claim.

PRISM (prizm), *n.* a solid whose bases are similar, equal, and parallel, and whose sides are parallelograms ; an optical instrument.

PRISMATIC (priz-mat'ik), *adj.* resembling the spectrum ; showing vari-coloured tints.

PRISMATIC COLOURS (kul'erz), the seven colours into which a ray of light is decomposed when re-fracted from a prism.

PRISON (priz'n), *n.* a building for the confinement of criminals, etc.; jail.

PRISONER (-er), *n.* a captive; a person confined against his will.

PRISTINE (pris'tin), *adj.* first; original; primitive.

PRIVACY (pri'va-si, priv'a-si), *n.* place of seclusion; secrecy.

PRIVATE (pri'vat), *adj.* personal; alone; secret; not public; secluded; unofficial : *n.* a common soldier.

PRIVATEER (-va-ter'), *n.* a private vessel formerly licensed by the government to seize and plunder the ships of an enemy.

PRIVATION (-va'shun), *n.* destitution; hardship; absence.

PRIVET (priv'et), *n.* an ornamental, bushy, evergreen shrub.

PRIVILEGE ('i-lej), *n.* peculiar advantage, right, or immunity; prerogative.

PRIZE (priz), *n.* a reward gained in a competition, etc. : *v.t.* to value; esteem.

PRO-, a prefix signifying *before, forward, in front,* and the like.

PRO AND CON (pro, kon), for and against.

PROBABILITY (prob-a-bil'i-ti), *n.* appearance of truth; likelihood.

PROBABLE ('a-bl), *adj.* specious; likely to occur.

PROBATE (pro'bat), *n.* the official proof of wills.

PROBATION (-ba'shun), *n.* evidence; proof; moral trial; novitiate.

PROBE (prob), *n.* a surgical instrument for examining a wound : *v.t.* to examine with a probe; scrutinize.

PROBITY (prob'i-ti), *n.* integrity; sincerity.

PROBLEM ('lem), *n.* a question for solution.

PROBLEMATICAL (-at'i-kal), *adj.* questionable; doubtful.

PROBOSCIS (pro-bos'is), *n.* the trunk of an elephant.

PROCEDURE (pro-se'dur), *n.* manner of proceeding; process.

PROCEED (-sed), *v.i.* to advance; issue; make progress; carry on a legal process : *n. pl.* money resulting from a commercial transaction.

PROCEEDING ('ing), *n.* advancement; transaction; operation : *pl.* legal process; transactions of a society.

PROCESS (pros'es), *n.* progressive course; series of measures or changes; proceedings in a legal action.

PROCESSION (pro-sesh'un), *n.* a train of persons in a formal march.

PROCESSIONAL (-al), *adj.* pertaining to a procession.

PROCLAIM (-klam), *v.t.* to announce officially; publish.

PROCLAMATION (prok-la-ma'-shun), *n.* an official announcement; edict.

PROCLIVITY (pro-kliv'i-ti), *n.* an inclination; tendency.

PROCRASTINATE (-kras'ti-nat), *v.t.* to put off to a future time : *v.i.* to be dilatory.

PROCRASTINATION (-na'shun), *n.* delay.

PROCRASTINATOR ('ti-na-ter), *n.* one who delays.

PROCREATE ('kre-at), *v.t.* to generate and produce; beget.

PROCREATIVE ('kre-a-tiv), *adj.* generative.

PROCREATOR (-ter), *n.* one who begets.

PROCUMBENT (-kum'bent), *adj.* lying down; prostrate; trailing.

PROCURABLE (-kur'a-bl), *adj.* obtainable.

PROCURATOR (prok'u-ra-ter), *n.* one who manages another's affairs, especially legal interests.

PROCURE (pro-kur'), *v.t.* to get or obtain : cause.

PROD (prod), *n.* a goad : *v.t.* to goad.

PRODIGAL ('-gal), *adj.* extravagant in expenditure; lavish; wasteful : *n.* a spendthrift.

PRODICALITY ('i-ti), *n.* the state or quality of being prodigal; extravagance; lavishness.

PRODIGIOUS (pro-dij'us), *adj.* enormous; adapted to excite wonder.

PRODIGY (prod'i-ji), *n.* anything wonderful or extraordinary; a miracle.

PRODUCE (pro-dus'), *v.t.* to exhibit or bring to view; manufacture; extend: *n.* (prod'us), that which is yielded or brought forth; result.

PRODUCT (prod'ukt), *n.* that which is produced by nature, or made by art; work; result.

PRODUCTION (pro-duk'shun), *n.* that which is produced.

PRODUCTIVE ('tiv), *adj.* generative; fertile.

PROEM (pro'em), *n.* a preface or introduction.

PROFANATION (prof'a-na'shun), *n.* desecration.

PROFANE (pro-fan'), *adj.* secular; irreverent; irreligious; blasphemous.

PROFANITY (-fan'i-ti), *n.* that which is profane; profane language or action.

PROFESS (-fes), *v.t.* to make open declaration of; acknowledge.

PROFESSION (-fesh'un), *n.* open declaration or avowal; calling or vocation; collective body of persons in a profession.

PROFESSIONAL (-al), *n.* one who makes his living by his art.

PROFESSOR ('er), *n.* one who makes an outward profession of religion; one who publicly teaches any branch of knowledge.

PROFFER (prof-er), *v.t.* to offer for acceptance; tender.

PROFICIENCY (pro-fish'en-si), *n.* degree of advancement in any branch of knowledge, science, or art.

PROFICIENT ('ent), *adj.* thoroughly qualified, or skilled.

PROFILE (pro'fil), *n.* a head or portrait in a side view; outline.

PROFIT (prof'it), *n.* pecuniary gain; emolument.

PROFITABLE (-a-bl), *adj.* yielding or bringing profit; lucrative.

PROFITABLY (-bli), *adv.* with profit.

PROFITEER (prof'i-ter), *n.* a mercenary speculator, especially in public necessities.

PROFLIGACY ('li-ga-si), *n.* vicious conduct; corruption of morals.

PROFLIGATE ('li-gat), *adj.* abandoned to vice; dissolute: *n.* a blackguard.

PROFOUND (pro-found'), *adj.* abstruse; deep; intense.

PROFUNDITY (-fun'di-ti), *n.* depth of place, knowledge, skill, etc.

PROFUSE (-fus'), *adj.* liberal to excess.

PROFUSION (-fu'zhun), *n.* lavishness; excess; abundance.

PROGENITOR (-jen'i-ter), *n.* an ancestor; forefather.

PROGENITURE ('i-tur), *n.* a birth or begetting.

PROGENY (proj'en-i), *n.* offspring; descendants.

PROGNOSIS (prog-no'sis), *n.* knowledge of the probable result of a disease from its symptoms.

PROGNOSTICATE ('ti-kat), *v.t.* to foretell.

PROGRAMME (pro'gram), *n.* an outline of a public entertainment, ceremony, etc.

PROGRESS (prog'res), *n.* a moving or going forward; proficiency: *v.i.* (pro-gres'), to increase in proficiency.

PROGRESSIVE ('iv), *adj.* making progress; improving.

PROHIBIT (-hib'it), *v.t.* to forbid; interdict by authority.

PROHIBITIVE (-hib'i-tiv), *adj.* tending to prohibit.

PROJECT (proj'ekt), *n.* a design or scheme: *v.t.* (pro-jekt'), to throw or cast forward; plan or scheme: *v.i.* to jut out.

PROJECTILE (pro-jek'til), *n.* a body thrown forward, especially through the air; a bullet, shot, etc.

PROJECTION (-jek'shun), *n.* that which juts out; a plan represented on a plane.

PROJECTOR ('ter), *n.* one who projects; an optical instrument.

PROJECTURE ('tur), *n.* a jutting out.

PROLETARIAN (-le-ta'ri-an), *adj.* pertaining to the common people.

PROLETARIAT ('ri-at), *n.* wage-earning class; the workers.

PROLIFIC (-lif'ik), *adj.* productive; fertile.

PROLIX (pro-liks'), *adj.* tedious and verbose ; not concise.

PROLIXITY (-lik'si-ti), *n.* verbosity ; minute detail.

PROLOGUE (pro'log), *n.* an introduction or preface.

PROLONG (pro-long'), *v.t.* to lengthen.

PROMENADE (prom-e-nad'), *n.* a walk for pleasure, show or exercise.

PROMINENCE (prom'i-nens), *n.* the state or quality of being prominent ; a projection.

PROMINENT ('i-nent), *adj.* conspicuous ; chief ; protuberant.

PROMISCUOUS (pro-mis'ku-us), *adj.* confused ; mingled ; indiscriminate.

PROMISE (prom'is), *n.* an engagement to do or not to do something.

PROMISSORY ('i-so-ri), *adj.* containing a promise or covenant to do, or not to do, something.

PROMISORY NOTE (not), *n.* a written promise to pay a certain sum at a specified date in consideration of value received.

PROMONTORY ('on-to-ri), *n.* a high cape, a point of land jutting into the sea.

PROMOTE (pro-mot'), *v.t.* to advance, forward, or elevate.

PROMOTION (-mo'shun), *n.* advancement ; preferment.

PROMPT (prompt), *adj.* ready and quick to act, immediate.

PROMPTITUDE (promp'ti-tud), *n.* readiness ; alacrity.

PROMULGATE (pro-mul'gat), *v.t.* to publish.

PROMULGATOR ('mul-ga-ter), *n.* one who promulgates.

PRONE (pron), *adj.* lying with face downwards ; not erect.

PRONG (prong), *n.* the spike of a fork.

PRONOMINAL (pro-nom'i-nal), *adj.* pertaining to a pronoun.

PRONOUN (pro'noun), *n.* a word which refers to, or is used in the place of, a noun.

PRONOUNCE (pro-nouns'), *v.t.* to speak or utter distinctly ; articulate ; affirm.

PRONOUNCEMENT (-nouns'ment), *n.* an emphatic declaration.

PRONUNCIATION (-nun-si-a'shun), *n.* the act or manner of articulating words or syllables.

PROOF (proof), *n.* convincing evidence ; test or experiment ; reason ; argument ; demonstration ; impenetrability ; an impression taken from type.

PROP (prop), *n.* a support or stay.

PROPAGANDA (-gan'da), *n.* any methods for the propagation of doctrines, principles, etc., religious or secular.

PROPAGATE ('a-gat), *v.t.* to continue or spread by generation or successive production ; extend.

PROPAGATION (-ga'shun), *n.* spreading or extension.

PROPEL (pro-pel'), *v.t.* to drive forward ; urge onward by force.

PROPELLER ('er), *n.* a screw-propeller ; vessel so propelled.

PROPENSITY (-pen'si-ti), *n.* natural tendency ; bias.

PROPER (prop'er), *adj.* fit or suitable ; correct ; appropriate ; respectable ; chaste.

PROPERTY ('er-ti), *n.* a peculiar attribute, quality, or disposition ; exclusive right of possession ; the thing owned ; estate ; goods.

PROPHECY (prof'e-si), *n.* prediction of something to take place in the future.

PROPHESY ('e-si), *v.t.* to foretell future events.

PROPHET ('et), *n.* one who foretells future events, especially one inspired by God.

PROPHETIC (pro-fet'ik), *adj.* predictive.

PROPHYLACTIC (prof-i-lak'tik), *adj.* guarding, or preserving, against disease.

PROPINQUITY (pro-ping'kwi-ti), *n.* nearness of place, time, or relationship.

PROPITIATE (-pish'i-at), *v.t.* to conciliate ; make propitious : *v.i.* to atone.

PROPITIOUS (-pish'us), *adj.* favourable.

PROPONENT (-po'nent), *n.* one who makes a proposal.

PROPORTION (pro-por'shun), *n.* comparative relation of one thing to another; ratio; rate; symmetrical relation.

PROPOSAL (-poz'al), *n.* that which is offered for consideration; offer of marriage.

PROPOSE (-poz'), *v.t.* to bring forward or offer for consideration : *v.i.* to make an offer of marriage.

PROPOSITION (prop-o-zish'un), *n.* an offer of terms; proposal; a theorem or problem for solution.

PROPOUND (pro-pound'), *v.t.* put or set as a question.

PROPRIETOR (-pri'e-ter), *n.* one who has a legal right to anything; owner.

PROPRIETY ('e-ti), *n.* conformity to established rules or custom; decorum; fitness.

PROPULSION (-pul'shun), *n.* act of propelling.

PRO RATA (pro ra'ta), [Latin], according to share or liability; in proportion.

PRORATE ('rat), *v.t.* to distribute in equal shares.

PROROGUE (pro-rog'), *v.t.* to terminate a session of; to postpone.

PROSAIC (-za'ik), *adj.* commonplace; uninteresting.

PROSCENIUM (-se'ni-um), *n.* that part of the stage from the curtain to the orchestra.

PROSCRIBE (-skrib'), *v.t.* outlaw; interdict; reject.

PROSCRIPTION (-skrip'shun), *n.* outlawry; interdiction.

PROSE (proz), *n.* ordinary spoken or written language.

PROSECUTE (pros'e-kut), *v.t.* to follow or pursue with the view to reach or accomplish; accuse of a crime before a legal tribunal.

PROSECUTION (-ku'shun), *n.* pursuit; the institution and carrying on of a legal suit.

PROSECUTOR ('e-ku-ter), *n.* one who carries on a legal suit with another.

PROSECUTRIX (-ku'triks), *n.* a female prosecutor.

PROSELYTE ('e-lit), *n.* a convert to some religion, belief, or party.

PROSODY (pros'o-di), *n.* that part of grammar that treats of quantity, accent, and the laws of versification.

PROSPECT ('pekt), *n.* a view of something distant; scene; object of view; expectation : *v.t.* (pro-spekt'), to search or explore.

PROSPECTIVE (pro-spek'tiv), *adj.* looking forward; in prospect.

PROSPECTOR (pros'pek-ter), *n.* one who searches for valuable minerals.

PROSPECTUS (pro-spek'tus), *n.* an outline of a proposed undertaking; sketch, or plan.

PROSPER (pros'per), *v.t.* to render successful; favour.

PROSPERITY ('i-ti), *n.* successful progress in any business or enterprise.

PROSPEROUS ('us), *adj.* successful.

PROSTITUTE ('ti-tut), *v.t.* to offer to hire for lewd use or base ends.

PROSTRATE ('trat), *adj.* lying at full length; extended on the ground.

PROSTRATION (-tra'shun), *n.* great depression; exhaustion of the vital powers.

PROSY (proz'i), *adv.* tedious; dull.

PROTEAN (pro'te-an), *adj.* readily assuming different shapes.

PROTECT (pro-tekt'), *v.t.* to cover over; defend; shield; shelter; support.

PROTECTION (-tek'shun), *n.* defence; shelter; security.

PROTECTIONISM (-izm), *n.* the doctrine that certain home industries and produce should be encouraged by the imposition of duties on foreign imports.

PROTECTOR ('ter), *n.* one who protects; guardian.

PROTECTORATE (-at), *n.* government or defence by a protector.

PROTEGE (-ta-zha), *n.* one who is under protection or guardianship of another : *fem.* protegée.

PROTEIDS (pro'te-idz), *n.pl.* a class of nitrogenous compounds, as albumen, fibrin, casein, etc., which form animal tissue.

PROTEST (pro-test'), *v.i.* to affirm with solemnity; remonstrate: *n.* (pro'test), a solemn declaration of opinion against something.

PROTESTANT (prot'es-tant), *n.* a member of any of those bodies of Christians that do not belong to the Roman Catholic or Greek church.

PROTESTANTISM (-izm), *n.* the doctrines or religion of Protestants, the chief principle of which is strict conformity to the letter and spirit of the Bible.

PROTESTATION (-ta'shun), *n.* a formal declaration of dissent.

PROTOCOL (pro'to-kol), *n.* the rough draft of a treaty, diplomatic despatch, etc.

PROTON (pro'ton), *n.* an electrically charged particle, a component of the atom, smaller than the electron.

PROTOPLASM ('to-plazm), *n.* semi-fluid albuminous substance, regarded as the ultimate basis of physical life.

PROTOTYPE ('to-tip), *n.* the original from which others are copied; an ancestral form.

PROTOZOA (-zo'a), *n.pl.* lowest division of the animal kingdom.

PROTRACT (-trakt'), *v.t.* to draw out in time; prolong.

PROTRUDE (-trood'), *v.t.* thrust out or push forward.

PROTUBERANCE (-tu'ber-ans), *n.* a swelling; a prominence; tumour.

PROUD (proud), *adj.* arrogant; ostentatious; haughty; pleased; grand; gratified.

PROVABLE (proov'a-bl), *adj.* capable of being proved.

PROVE (proov), *v.t.* establish or ascertain by argument or other evidence; experience; endure.

PROVENDER (prov'en-der), *n.* dry food for beasts, as hay, etc.

PROVERB ('erb), *n.* a short, familiar, pithy saying, expressing some well-known truth or common fact of experience; adage.

PROVERBIAL (pro-ver'bi-al), *adj.* pertaining to proverbs; widely spoken of, or well known.

PROVIDE (pro-vid'), *v.t.* to make ready beforehand; furnish.

PROVIDENCE (prov'i-dens), *n.* timely care or preparation; economy; prudence; care of God for his creatures.

PROVIDENT ('i-dent), *adj.* careful for the future; prudent.

PROVIDENTIAL (-den'shal), *adj.* proceeding from divine providence.

PROVIDENTIALLY (-li), *adv.* in a providential manner.

PROVINCE ('ins), *n.* a division of an empire, state, or region; proper office.

PROVISION (-vizh'un), *n.* measures taken beforehand; accumulation of stores.

PROVISO (-vi'zo), *n.* a conditional clause or stipulation in a deed.

PROVISORY ('zo-ri), *adj.* conditional.

PROVOCATION (prov'o-ka'shun), *n.* that which excites to anger.

PROVOCATIVE (pro-vok'a-tiv), *n.* anything that tends to provoke; incitement.

PROVOKE (-vok'), *v.t.* enrage or irritate; exasperate.

PROVOKING ('ing), *p.adj.* vexatious.

PROVOST (prov'ust, pro'vo, pro-vo'), *n.* superintendent or president; chief magistrate.

PROW (prou), *n.* the bow of a ship.

PROWESS ('es), *n.* bravery; valour.

PROWL (proul), *v.i.* to wander stealthily, as for prey or plunder.

PROXIMATE (prok'si-mat), *adj.* immediate.

PROXIMITY (-sim'i-ti), *n.* immediate nearness in place, time, or alliance.

PROXIMO ('si-mo), *adv.* in, or of, the next or coming month.

PROXY ('si), *n.* the agency of a substitute.

PRUDE (prood), *n.* a woman who affects great reserve, coyness, and excessive virtue.

PRUDENCE (proo'dens), *n.* wisdom applied to practice.

PRUDENT ('dent), *adj.* judicious; cautious; circumspect.

PRUDENTIAL (-den'shal), *adj.* proceeding from prudence.

PRUDERY ('der-i), *n.* affected niceness or scrupulousness in conduct.

PRUDISH (proo'dish), *adj.* like a prude; affectedly precise, nice.

PRUNE (proon), *n.* a dried plum : *v.t.* to cut superfluous twigs or branches from (a vine, bush or tree) ; trim.

PRUSSIC ACID (prus'ik as'id), *n.* a hydrocyanic acid ; a deadly poison.

PRY (pri), *n.* a sly inspection ; a lever.

PSALM (sam), *n.* a sacred song.

PSALTER (sawl'ter), *n.* the Book of Psalms.

PSEUDONYM (su'do-nim), *n.* fictitous name.

PSHAW (shaw), *interj.* an expression of contempt, etc.

PSORIASIS (so-ri'a-sis), *n.* itch.

PSYCHIATRY (si-ki'a-tri), *n.* treatment of diseases of the mind.

PSYCHICAL (si'ki-kal), *adj.* pertaining to, or connected with, the human soul, spirit, or mind ; psychological.

PSYCHOANALYSIS (si-ko-a-nal'i-sis), *n.* a diagnosis of mental and nervous afflictions by analysing the emotions and investigating the history of the patient.

PSYCHOLOGICAL (-loj'i-kal), *adj.* pertaining to psychology.

PSYCHOLOGIST ('o-jist), *n.* one skilled in psychology.

PSYCHOLOGY (-kol'o-ji), *n.* the science that treats of mental phenomena ; mental philosophy ; metaphysics.

PSYCHOTHERAPY (si-ko-ther'api), *n.* a system for treating functional nervous disorders by mental suggestion.

PTOMAINES (to'manz), *n.pl.* a class of alkaloids of a highly poisonous nature, originating in decaying or dead matter.

PUBERTY ('ber-ti), *n.* the age at which a person of either sex is capable of generation.

PUBLIC (pub'lik), *adj.* belonging to the people ; open ; generally known : *n.* people in general.

PUBLICAN ('li-kan), *n.* one who keeps a public house.

PUBLICATION (-li-ka'shun), *n.* the act of publishing or making public ; any printed work.

PUBLICIST ('li-sist), *n.* a writer on current events.

PUBLICITY (-lis'i-ti), *n.* public notoriety.

PUBLIC SCHOOL (skool), a school controlled and maintained by civil authority.

PUBLISH ('lish), *v.t.* to make known ; announce or proclaim ; divulge.

PUCKER (puk'er), *v.t.* & *v.i.* to gather into small folds ; wrinkle.

PUDDING (pood'ing), *n.* a soft kind of food made of flour and various ingredients.

PUDDLE (pud'l), *n.* small pool of dirty water : *v.t.* convert (pig-iron) into wrought-iron.

PUDGY (puj'i), *adj.* short and fat.

PUEBLO (pweb'lo), *n.* building of adobe or sun-dried brick built by Indians of south-western U.S.

PUERILE (pu'er-il), *adj.* juvenile ; boyish ; trifling.

PUFFING (puf'ing), *n.* exaggerated praise, quick and hard breathing.

PUGILISM (pu'ji-lizm), *n.* boxing or prize-fighting.

PUGILIST (-list), *n.* a boxer or prize-fighter.

PUGNACIOUS (pug-na'shus), *adj.* quarrelsome.

PUGNACITY (-nas'i-ti), *n.* inclination to fight ; quarrelsomeness.

PUISSANCE (pu'is-ans), *n.* power.

PUISSANT (-ant), *adj.* powerful, strong.

PULCHRITUDE (pul'kri-tud), *n.* beauty ; comeliness.

PULING (pul'ing), *adj.* whining.

PULL (pool), *v.t.* to draw toward one.

PULLET ('et), *n.* a young hen.

PULLEY ('i), *n.* a small wheel turning about an axis, and having a groove in which a rope works.

PULMONARY (pul'mo-na-ri), *adj.* pertaining to, or affecting, the lungs.

PULMOTOR (pul-mo'ter), *n.* an apparatus for artificial respiration.

PULP (pulp), *n.* soft, fleshy part of bodies : *v.t.* to reduce to pulp.

PULPIT (pool'pit), *n.* an elevated or inclosed desk in a church from which the sermon is delivered.

PULSATE (pul'sat), *v.i.* to throb.

PULSE (puls), *n.* the rhythmic beating of the heart or arteries ; vibration ; public or private opinion ; leguminous plants.

PULVERIZATION (pul-ver-i-za´shun), *n.* the act of pulverizing.

PULVERIZE (´ver-iz), *v.t.* to reduce to powder.

PUMICE (pum´is), *n.* a porous, light, volcanic lava.

PUMP (pump), *n.* a machine for raising liquids ; a light low shoe : *v.t.* extract (information) by questions.

PUMPKIN (pump´kin), *n.* a large, trailing, hairy vine ; the round, large fruit of this vine.

PUN (pun), *n.* a play upon words : *v.i.* to play upon words similar in sound, but having a different meaning.

PUNCH (punch), *n.* a tool for stamping or perforating ; a beverage ; a blow or thrust.

PUNCHINELLO (pun-chi-nel´o), *n.* the thick-set, hump-backed figure in a puppet-show ; a grotesque person.

PUNCTATE (pungk´tat), *adj.* dotted with small spots ; pointed.

PUNCTILIO (-til´i-o), *n.* a nice point in conduct or ceremony.

PUNCTILIOUS (´i-us, -til´yus), *adj.* very nice or precise in conduct or ceremony ; exact to excess.

PUNCTUAL (´tu-al), *adj.* observing, or done at, the exact time.

PUNCTUALITY (-al´i-ti), *n.* the quality of being punctual.

PUNCTUATE (´tu-at), *v.t.* to mark with points.

PUNCTUATION (-a´shun), *n.* the act or art of dividing sentences by points.

PUNDIT (pun´dit), *n.* a solemn pretender to learning.

PUNGENT (pun´jent), *adj.* piercing ; biting ; sarcastic ; caustic.

PUNISH (pun´ish), *v.t.* to cause loss or pain to ; chastise ; correct.

PUNISHMENT (-ment), *n.* pain, loss, or penalty.

PUNITIVE (pun´i-tiv), *adj.* inflicting punishment.

PUNK (pungk), *n.* decayed wood ; a foolish argument ; nonsense.

PUNSTER (pun´ster), *n.* one addicted to punning.

PUNT (punt), *n.* a flat-bottomed boat.

PUNY (pu´ni), *adj.* weak ; feeble ; petty.

PUPIL (´pil), *n.* a person receiving instruction ; the opening in the iris of the eye.

PUPPET (pup´et), *n.* a marionette ; one who is under the influence and control of another.

PUPPY (´i), *n.* a young dog.

PURBLIND (per´blind), *adj.* seeing obscurely.

PURCHASE (per´chas), *v.t.* to obtain by paying an equivalent ; acquire ; buy : *n.* value ; worth.

PURE (pur), *adj.* free from moral or physical defilement ; chaste ; unadulterated ; clean ; holy ; real.

PURGATION (per-ga´shun), *n.* clearing from imputed guilt.

PURGATORY (per´ga-to-ri), *n.* an intermediate state or condition in the after life, according to R.C. doctrine ; a state of temporary misery.

PURGE (perj), *v.t.* to cleanse or free from impurities or guilt : *n.* a cathartic medicine.

PURGING (per´jing), *n.* diarrhoea or dysentery.

PURIFICATION (pu-ri-fi-ka´shun), *n.* purifying ; state of being purified.

PURIFY (´ri-fi), *v.t.* to render pure ; free from impurities.

PURISM (pur´izm), *n.* affectation in the precise use of words in literary style.

PURIST (pur´ist), *n.* one who is scrupulously precise in literary style.

PURITAN (pu´ri-tan), *n.* [P-], one of a body of Nonconformists in the 16th and 17th centuries who insisted on rigid adherence to the letter of Scripture in points of doctrine and of practice.

PURITY (´ri-ti), *n.* chastity ; cleanness ; freedom from adulteration.

PURL (perl), *v.i.* to ripple or flow with a gentle murmur.

PURLIEUS (per´luz), *n.pl.* environs.

PURLOIN (per-loin´), *v.t.* to steal.

PURPLE ('pl), *adj.* of the colour of blended blue and red; regal; livid.

PURPORT ('port), *n.* meaning; design; signification.

PURPOSE ('pus), *n.* design; end or aim desired.

PURR (per), *n.* the low murmuring of a cat.

PURSE (pers), *n.* a small bag for money: sum of money: *v.t.* to pucker or wrinkle.

PURSER ('er), *n.* an officer having charge of the provisions, clothing, and money of a ship; paymaster.

PURSUANT (pur-su'ant), *adj.* done in consequence of.

PURSUE (-su'), *v.t.* to follow for some end; prosecute; chase; seek.

PURSUIT (-sut'), *n.* prosecution; chase; occupation; attainment.

PURSUIVANT (per'swi-vant), *n.* an attendant or follower of.

PURULENCE (pu'roo-lens), **PURULENCY** (-len-si), *n.* generation of pus.

PURVEY (pur-va'), *v.i.* to make provision for.

PURVEYANCE ('ans), *n.* the procuring of provisions.

PURVEYOR ('er), *n.* one who provides provisions.

PURVIEW (per'vu), *n.* extent; proviso; body of a statute.

PUS (pus), *n.* the matter in sores, etc.

PUSH (poosh), *v.t.* to press against with force; urge forward: *n.* a thrust; effort; assault; exigency; extremity; persistent endeavour.

PUSHER (-er), *n.* a very energetic person.

PUSHING ('ing), *adj.* enterprising; energetic.

PUSILLANIMITY (pu-sil-a-nim'i-ti), *n.* cowardliness; weakness of spirit.

PUSILLANIMOUS (-an'i-mus), *adj.* cowardly; faint-hearted.

PUSTULE ('tul), *n.* a small elevation of the skin, or pimple containing pus.

PUT (poot), *v.t.* to place in, or bring into, any state or condition; cause; drive into action; incite; propose; apply; lay or deposit; throw in; state in language.

PUTATIVE (pu'ta-tiv), *adj.* reputed; supposed.

PUTREFACTION (pu-tre-fak'shun), *n.* decomposition; rottenness.

PUTREFY ('tre-fi), *v.t.* to cause to rot or decay.

PUTRESCENT ('ent), *adj.* rotten.

PUTRIDITY (-trid'i-ti), *n.* putrid state.

PUTT (put), *n.* in golf, a stroke made on a putting green.

PUTTER (put'er), *n.* in golf, a club used for playing a short stroke.

PUTTY ('i), *n.* a compound of whiting and linseed-oil used in glazing: *v.t.* to cement with putty.

PUZZLE (puz'l), *n.* something that tries the ingenuity, perplexes, or causes embarrassment.

PYEMIA, PYÆMIA (pi-e'mi-a), *n.* blood-poisoning.

PYGMEAN (pig-me'an), *adj.* dwarfish.

PYGMY ('mi), *n.* one of a race of Negritos inhabiting Central Africa; a dwarf.

PYJAMAS, same as pajamas.

PYRAMID (pir'a-mid), *n.* a solid body standing on a triangular, square, or polygonal base, having its triangular sides terminating in a point at the apex.

PYRAMID OF CHEOPS (ke'ops), the largest of the three great pyramids at Gizeh, Egypt.

PYRE (pir), *n.* a funeral pile.

PYRITE (pi'rit), *n.* a metallic, isometric disulphide of iron.

PYROTECHNIC (pi-ro-tek'nik), *adj.* pertaining to fireworks.

PYROTECHNICS ('niks), *n.* fireworks.

PYRRHIC (pir'ik), *n.* a metrical foot of two syllables.

PYRRHIC VICTORY (vik'to-ri), a victory gained at enormous cost or loss.

PYXIS (pik'sis), *n.* a small box; a jewel-case; socket of the hip-bone.

Q

Q, q (ku), *n.* a letter; the seventeenth letter of the English alphabet.

Q, q, *n.* an abbreviation.

Q, *n.* a medieval Roman numeral denoting 500; with a bar (Q̄), 500,000; also stands for 90.

QUACK (kwak), *n.* the cry of the duck; pretender to medical skill.

QUAD (kwod), *n.* the court of a college, prison, etc.

QUADRA ('ra), *n.* a square border or fillet of an Ionian column; a plinth.

QUADRANGLE ('rang-gl), *n.* a plane figure with four angles and four sides.

QUADRANT ('rant), *n.* the fourth part of a circle, an arc of 90°; an instrument for taking elevations.

QUADRENNIAL (-ren'i-al), *adj.* comprising, or occurring, every four years.

QUADRI- (kwod'ri), a combining form from the Latin *quattuor* four.

QUADRILLE (kwa-dril'), *n.* a dance by four sets of couples.

QUADROON (-roon'), *n.* the offspring of a mulatto and a white.

QUADRUPED ('roo-ped), *n.* a four-footed animal : *adj.* four-footed.

QUADRUPLE ('roo-p'l), *adj.* four-fold.

QUAFF (kwaf), *v.t.* to drink or swallow in large quantities.

QUAGMIRE (kwag'mir), *n.* wet, boggy ground.

QUAHOG (kwa-hog'), *n.* a species of clam.

QUAIL (kwal), *v.i.* to sink in spirit; lose heart; cower : *n.* a gallinaceous bird; the bobwhite.

QUAINT (kwant), *adj.* singular and antique; odd; neat.

QUAKE (kwak), *v.i.* to tremble or shake; be agitated.

QUAKER ('er), *n.* one of a religious sect, the Society of Friends, founded by Geo. Fox, about 1650.

QUALIFICATION (kwol'i-fi-ka'shun), *n.* any quality which fits a person for any occupation; legal power or ability; limitation.

QUALIFIED (-fid), *p.adj.* fit; competent; adequate.

QUALIFY ('i-fi), *v.t.* to render fit or capable for any office, occupation, etc.; render legally capable; make fit; limit.

QUALITY ('i-ti), *n.* attribute; disposition; rank; superior birth.

QUALM (kwam), *n.* a sudden fit of sickness; nausea; scruple.

QUANDARY (kwon'da-ri), *n.* a state of difficulty or perplexity.

QUANTITATIVE ('ti-ta-tiv), *adj.* pertaining to quantity.

QUANTITY ('ti-ti), *n.* that property of anything that may be increased or diminished.

QUARANTINE (kwor'an-ten), *n.* the time during which a vessel suspected of carrying infectious disease is prohibited from intercourse with shore.

QUARREL ('el), *n.* an angry dispute; altercation.

QUARRELSOME (-sum), *adj.* inclined to quarrel.

QUARRY ('i), *n.* a place where stone is excavated for building purposes, etc.; object of chase.

QUART (kwort), *n.* 2 pints or ¼ of a gallon.

QUARTER (kwor'ter), *n.* the 4th part; 28 pounds avoirdupois; 8 bushels; the 4th part of an hour, or of a year; a phase of the moon.

QUARTERMASTER ('ter-mas-ter), *n.* an officer whose duty it is to assign quarters and provide food, clothing, forage, ammunition, etc., for a regiment : in the navy, a petty officer who attends to the steerage, signals, stowage, etc., of ships.

QUARTET, QUARTETTE (-tet'), *n.* anything in fours.

QUARTO ('to), *n.* a book about 9½ by 12 inches, abbreviated 4to : *adj.* having four leaves to the sheet.

QUARTZ (kworts), *n.* a mineral compound of pure silica.

QUASH (kwosh), *v.t.* to crush; subdue suddenly or completely.

QUASI (kwa'si), *adv.* as if; as it were; seemingly.

QUATRAIN (kwot'ran), *n.* stanza of four lines.

QUAVER (kwa'ver), *v.t.* to shake or tremble; vibrate.

QUAY (ke), *n.* a wharf.

QUEASY (kwe'zi), *adj.* affected with, or causing, nausea.

QUEEN (kwen), *n.* a female sovereign.

QUEEN CONSORT (kon'sort), the wife of a reigning king.

QUEEN DOWAGER (dou'a-jer), the widow of a king.

QUEEN'S WARE (war), cream-coloured earthenware.

QUEER (kwer), *adj.* odd; singular; droll; strange.

QUELL (kwel), *v.t.* to crush or subdue.

QUENCH (kwench), *v.t.* to extinguish; check; allay.

QUERIST (kwe'rist), *n.* one who asks questions.

QUERULOUS (kwer'oo-lus), *adj.* complaining; discontented.

QUERY (kwe'ri), *n.* a question; an inquiry to be resolved.

QUEST (kwest), *n.* search; inquiry.

QUESTION (kwes'chun), *n.* an inquiry; interrogation; doubt.

QUESTIONNAIRE (ar'), *n.* series of questions submitted to obtain information.

QUEUE (ku), *n.* a plait of hair worn behind; the tail of a wig; a line of persons.

QUIBBLE (kwib'l), *n.* a petty evasion or cavil; play on words.

QUIBBLING ('ling), *n.* evasion.

QUICK (kwik), *adj.* rapid; hasty; active; nimble; ready; sharp in discernment; sprightly.

QUICKEN ('n), *v.i.* to vivify.

QUICKLIME ('lim), *n.* lime burnt and unslaked.

QUICKLY ('li), *adv.* soon; swiftly.

QUICKSAND ('sand), *n.* sand saturated with water and readily yielding to pressure.

QUICKSILVER ('sil-ver), *n.* fluid mercury.

QUICK-WITTED (-wit'ed), *adj.* keen.

QUIDDITY ('i-ti), *n.* the essence of anything; a trifling nicety.

QUIDNUNC ('nungk), *n.* one who is curious to know everything that passes.

QUIESCE (kwi-es'), *v.i.* to be silent.

QUIESCENCE ('ens), *n.* repose or rest; mental quietude.

QUIESCENT ('ent), *adj.* reposing or resting; calm; silent.

QUIET (kwi'et), *adj.* still; calm; peaceable; gentle; secluded; subdued and modest; not showy.

QUIETLY ('et-li), *adv.* peaceably; silently.

QUIETUDE ('e-tud), *n.* tranquility.

QUIETUS (-e'tus), *n.* rest; death; knockout blow.

QUILL (kwil), *n.* the large, strong feather of a bird's wing.

QUILT (kwilt), *n.* a kind of heavy coverlet or counterpane.

QUINARY (kwi'na-ri), *adj.* consisting of, or arranged in, fives.

QUINCE (kwins), *n.* the fruit of a small tree of the apple family.

QUININE (kwi'nin), *n.* an alkaline bitter substance obtained from the bark of the cinchona tree.

QUINQUAGESIMA SUNDAY (kwin-kwa-ges'i-ma sun'da), *n.* the Sunday next before Lent.

QUINSY ('zi), *n.* inflammation of the tonsils of the throat.

QUINTAL (kwin'tal), *n.* a weight of 100 or 112 lb.

QUINTESSENCE (kwin-tes'ens), *n.* the pure concentrated essence of anything; vital or essential part.

QUINTET, QUINTETTE (-tet'), *n.* a musical composition in five obligato parts.

QUINTUPLE ('tu-pl), *v.t.* to make fivefold: *adj.* fivefold.

QUIP (kwip), *n.* a gibe; jest; a droll saying; quibble.

QUIRE (kwir), *n.* 24 sheets of paper.

QUIRK (kwerk), *n.* an artful evasion; subterfuge; quibble.

QUIRT (kwert), *n.* in S.A. a rawhide riding whip.

QUIT (kwit), *v.t.* to depart from; discharge (an obligation); give up; forsake.

QUITE (kwit), *adj.* wholly; completely.

QUITTANCE (kwit'ans), *n.* discharge from a debt, or obligation.

QUIVER (kwiv'er), *n.* a case for arrows; a trembling or shivering.

QUIXOTIC (kwik-sot'ik), **QUIXOTICAL** ('i-kal), *adj.* chivalrous or romantic to extravagance.

QUIZ (kwiz), *n.* a question designed to puzzle anyone : *v.t.* to puzzle; banter; hoax.

QUIZZICAL ('i-kal), *adj.* given to, or of the nature of, quizzing; comical.

QUOD (kwod), *n.* a quadrangle; prison.

QUOD VIDE (ve'da), [Latin], which see; see that word elsewhere. (Abbr. q. v.)

QUOIN (koin), *n.* external angle of a building; wedge-shaped block to tighten pages of type for printing.

QUOIT (kwoit, koit), *n.* a circular ring of iron to be pitched at a fixed object.

QUORUM (kwo'rum), *n.* number of members of a body or corporation necessary to transact business.

QUOTA (kwo'ta), *n.* part or share assigned to each.

QUOTATION (-ta'shun), *n.* that which is quoted; current price.

QUOTATION MARK (mark), the mark (" ") used to denote the beginning and end of a quotation.

QUOTE (kwot), *v.t.* to adduce (a passage) from some author or speaker; give the current price of.

QUOTIENT (kwo'shent), *n.* the number resulting from the division of one number by another.

QUOTUM ('tum), *n.* share; proportion.

R

R, r, (ar), *n.* a letter; the eighteenth letter of the English alphabet.

R, r, *n.* an abbreviation.

R, r, *n.* a medieval Roman numeral denoting 80; with a bar ($\bar{\text{R}}$), 80,000.

RABBET (rab'et), *n.* a groove cut in the edge of a plank, etc.

RABBI ('i), *n.* a Jewish doctor or interpreter of the law.

RABBIT ('it), *n.* a burrowing rodent animal.

RABBLE (T), *n.* a noisy crowd or mob.

RABID ('id), *adj.* mad; enthusiastic to excess.

RABIES (ra'bi-ez), *n.* hydrophobia.

RACCOON (ra-koon'), *n.* an animal of North America, with a valuable fur.

RACE (ras), *n.* contest of speed; career; descent or lineage; breed or variety.

RACEME (ra-sem'), *n.* a flower cluster.

RACIAL (ra'shal), *adj.* pertaining to race or lineage.

RACK (rak), *n.* a frame in which articles are arranged; a grating above a manger; entire ruin.

RACKET ('et), *n.* a clattering noise; a hilarious merrymaking; a network bat used in tennis.

RACONTEUR (ra-kong-ter'), *n.* an expert teller of anecdotes.

RACQUET, another form of racket.

RACY (ra'si), *adj.* having a strong flavour; mentally exciting; piquant.

RADIAL (ra'di-al), *adj.* pertaining to a ray; pertaining to the radius of the forearm : *n.* a radiating part.

RADIANCE ('di-ans), **RADIANCY** (-an-si), *n.* brilliant brightness; splendour.

RADIANT ('di-ant), *adj.* emitting rays of light or heat; shining; brilliant.

RADIATE ('di-at), *v.t.* to send out as rays.

RADIATION (-a'shun), *n.* the emission or diffusion of rays of light or heat from a luminous or heated body.

RADIATOR ('di-a-ter), *n.* the body from which rays radiate; a chamber, coil, drum, etc., in an apartment, heated by steam, or hot water; a water-cooling device used with gasoline motors.

RADICAL (rad'i-kal), *adj.* pertaining to the root or origin ; fundamental ; original ; underived ; extreme ; [R-], one of the ultra-liberal party in politics.

RADICALLY ('i-kal-i), *adv.* essentially ; entirely.

RADICATE ('i-kat), *v.t.* to plant deeply and firmly.

RADICEL ('i-sel), *n.* a rootlet.

RADICLE ('l-kl), *n.* that part in the embryo in the seed of a plant which becomes the root.

RADIO (ra'di-o), *n.* anything transmitted or received by electric waves.

RADIOACTIVE (ra'di-o-ak'tiv), *adj.* emitting rays ; exhibiting the properties possessed by radium.

RADIOAMPLIFIER (-am'pli-fi-er) *n.* a vacuum tube which increases the intensity of any sound received by radio.

RADIOBROADCASTING, see broadcast.

RADIODETECTOR (de-tect'or), *n.* an electric tube used to discover the presence of electric waves.

RADIOFREQUENCY (-fre'kwen-si), *n.* the frequency of electric waves in radio.

RADIOGRAM (gram), *n.* a message by wireless electrical waves.

RADIOGRAPH (-graf), *n.* a negative picture obtained by radioactivity.

RADIOSCOPY (-os'ko-pi), *n.* the examination of bodies by X-rays.

RADISH (rad'ish), *n.* a plant with an edible root.

RADIUM (ra'di-um), *n.* a radioactive element discovered in pitchblende, possessing the property of giving off luminous and actinic rays, accompanied by heat, without apparent loss of energy, bulk or weight.

RADIUS (ra'di-us), *n.* [*pl.* radii (-i)], a straight line from the centre to the circumference of a circle ; exterior bone of the forearm.

RAFF (raf), *n.* a jumble ; refuse.

RAFFIA (raf'i-a), *n.* a fibre much used in basketry and for mats and cordage.

RAFFLE ('l), *n.* a kind of lottery.

RAFT (raft), *n.* a float of logs.

RAFTER ('ter), *n.* an inclined beam supporting the roof of a house.

RAG (rag), *n.* a fragment of cloth.

RAGAMUFFIN ('a-muf-in), *n.* a disreputable fellow.

RAGE (raj), *n.* excessive and uncontrolled anger ; vehemence ; extreme desire.

RAGGED (rag'ed), *adj.* worn into rags ; destitute ; rough ; jagged.

RAGING (raj'ing), *p.adj.* acting with fury ; violent ; frantic.

RAGOUT (ra-goo'), *n.* a dish of stewed meats, etc.

RAGTIME (rag'tim), *n.* in music, syncopated time.

RAID (rad), *n.* a hostile or predatory incursion.

RAIL (ral), *n.* a bar of timber or metal extending from one support to another ; a railway : *v.i.* to brawl ; scoff.

RAILLERY ('er-i), *n.* good-humoured irony or satire ; banter.

RAILWAY ('wa), *n.* a way or road laid with two parallel iron or steel rails along which cars are drawn by steam power or electricity.

RAIMENT (ra'ment), *n.* clothing.

RAIN (ran), *n.* water in drops from the clouds : *v.t.* to pour down like rain.

RAINBOW ('bo), *n.* the bright-coloured arc formed in the heavens by the refraction and reflection of the sun's rays falling upon watery particles.

RAISE (raz), *v.t.* to cause to rise ; life up ; elevate ; originate or produce ; promote ; rouse ; increase ; construct ; levy ; collect.

RAISIN (ra'zn), *n.* a dried grape.

RAKE (rak), *n.* a toothed gathering tool ; inclination or slope ; a roué.

RALLY (ral'i), *v.t.* to collect and arrange, as troops in confusion ; reunite : *v.i.* to return to order ; recover strength : *n.* a mass meeting.

RAM (ram), *n.* the male of a sheep ; a hydraulic engine : *v.t.* to push or press with force.

RAMBLE ('bl), *v.i.* to wander or rove about ; visit many places.

RAMEE, RAMIE (ram'e), *n.* an

Asiatic plant, the fibre of which is woven into many fabrics.

RAMIFICATION (ram-i-fi-ka'shun), *n.* a division or separation into branches ; sub-division.

RAMPAGE (ram-paj'), *v.i.* to prance about furiously.

RAMPANT ('pant), *adj.* over-leaping restraint or natural bounds ; in heraldry, standing upright on the hind legs.

RAMPART ('part), *n.* a mound or wall surrounding a fortified place.

RAMSHACKLE ('shak-l), *adj.* loose ; out of repair.

RANCH (ranch), *n.* a large farm, for the raising of horses and cattle.

RANCHER (ran'cher), *n.* the owner of a ranch, or one who helps to run it.

RANCID (ran'sid), *adj.* having a rank, unpleasant smell ; musty.

RANCOUR (rang'ker), *n.* implacable enmity ; deep spite or malice.

RANCOROUS (-us), *adj.* malignant.

RAND (rand), *n.* an edge, or border ; [R-], a gold-bearing district in South Africa (with *the*).

RANDOM (ran'dum). *adj.* done haphazard ; left to chance.

RANGE (ranj), *v.t.* to set or arrange in a row ; place in proper order ; rove over : *n.* extent of discourse or roaming ; power ; a kitchen stove ; a tract of land for grazing ; a mountain chain ; a class or series.

RANGER ('er), *n.* a rover ; the official of a park or forest.

RANK (rangk), *n.* a row or line ; station or position ; grade ; dignity ; eminence : *adj.* excessive ; coarse ; rancid.

RANKLE ('l), *v.i.* to grow more rank or strong ; fester ; become mentally irritated.

RANSACK (ran'sak), *v.t.* to search minutely ; rummage ; plunder.

RANSOM ('sum), *v.t.* to free from captivity, slavery, or punishment, by a payment ; atone for.

RANT (rant), *v.i.* to bluster or be noisily wordy.

RAP (rap), *v.i.* to strike a quick, sharp blow ; knock.

RAPACIOUS (ra-pa'shus), *adj.* given to plunder, seizing forcibly ; greedy.

RAPACITY (-pas'i-ti), *n.* the quality of being rapacious.

RAPE (rap), *n.* a seizing and carrying away by force : *v.t.* to ravish.

RAPID (rap'id), *adj.* very quick or swift : *n.pl.* a swift current in a river.

RAPIER (ra'pi-er), *n.* a long thin sword used for thrusting.

RAPINE (rap'in, 'in), *n.* plundering or seizing forcibly ; pillage.

RAPPROCHEMENT (ra-prosh-mang'), *n.* [French] ; an understanding.

RAPSCALLION (rap-skal'yun), *n.* a rascal.

RAPT (rapt), *p.adj.* enraptured.

RAPTURE ('tur), *n.* ecstasy ; enthusiasm.

RARE (rar), *adj.* scarce ; uncommon ; unusual ; incomparable ; almost raw.

RAREBIT ('bit), *n.* a dainty morsel ; a Welsh rabbit.

RAREFACTION (rar-e-fak'shun), *n.* the act of rarefying or rendering less dense.

RAREFY (rar'e-fi), *v.t.* to make rare, thin, or less dense ; expand.

RARELY ('li), *adv.* seldom.

RARITY ('i-ti), *n.* a rare article ; exceptional excellence.

RASCAL (ras'kal), *n.* a mean fellow.

RASCALITY ('i-ti), *n.* petty villainy or dishonesty.

RASH (rash), *adj.* hasty ; incautious ; precipitate.

RASHER ('er), *n.* a slice of bacon.

RASP (rasp), *v.t.* to rub with, or as with, a rough instrument : *n.* a rough file.

RASPBERRY (raz'ber-i), *n.* a thimble-shaped fruit ; shrub of the same name.

RAT (rat), *n.* a destructive rodent.

RATABLE (rat'a-bl), *adj.* assessed at a certain value.

RATCH (rach), *n.* a ratchet-wheel.

RATCHET (-et), *n.* a pawl, or detent, for holding a ratchet-wheel.

RATCHET-WHEEL (-hwel), *n.* notched wheel into a tooth of which a pawl fits which keeps it from reversing.

RATE (rat), *n.* ratio or proportion, price fixed or stated.

RATHER (rath'er), *adv.* sooner; more willingly; on the contrary.

RATIFICATION (rat-i-fi-ka'shun), *n.* the act of ratifying.

RATIFY ('i-fi), *v.t.* to sanction; settle or confirm.

RATING (rat'ing), *n.* classification according to standard.

RATIO (ra'shi-o), *n.* the relation or proportion of one thing or quantity to another.

RATIOCINATE (rash-i-os'i-nat), *v.i.* to reason deductively; argue.

RATION (ra'shun), *n.* an allowance.

RATIONAL (rash'un-al), *adj.* agreeable to reason; wise; judicious.

RATIONALE (rash-un-a'le), *n.* a series of reasons assigned for any opinion, action, etc.

RATIONALITY (-al'i-ti), *n.* power of reasoning; reasonableness; mental sanity.

RATTAN (ra-tan'), *n.* stems of several species of palms used in furniture.

RATTLE (rat'l), *v.i.* to produce rapidly sharp noises; speak rapidly or noisily; a child's toy.

RATTLED (rat'ld), *p.adj.* confused; bewildered.

RATTLESNAKE (-snak), *n.* a venomous snake with hard bony rings on the tail, producing a rattling sound.

RATTLING ('ling), *adj.* a rapid succession of sharp, noisy sounds.

RAUCOUS (raw'kus), *adj.* hoarse; harsh.

RAVAGE (rav'aj), *v.t.* to lay waste; pillage; plunder or sack.

RAVE (rav), *v.i.* to rage as a madman.

RAVEL (rav'l), *v.t.* to unweave or untwist; involve or entangle.

RAVEN (ra'vn), *n.* a large bird of the crow family.

RAVEN (rav'n), *v.t.* to devour with greediness: *n.* violence; plunder.

RAVENOUS ('n-us), *adj.* devouring with rapacity.

RAVINE (ra-ven'), *n.* a mountain gorge.

RAVISH (rav'ish), *v.t.* to seize and to carry away by force.

RAW (raw), *adj.* uncooked; crude; inexperienced; cold and damp.

RAY (ra), *n.* a line or pencil of light proceeding from a radiant point; light; beam of intellectual light; perception of apprehension.

RAZE (raz), *v.t.* to level to the ground; blot out; efface.

RAZOR ('zer), *n.* a sharp-edged cutting instrument used for shaving.

REACH (rech), *v.t.* to touch with the extended hand; stretch forth; arrive at; include.

READ (red), *v.t.* to observe and apprehend the meaning of (something written, printed or inscribed); peruse.

READABLE (red'a-bl), *adj.* worth reading; legible.

READER ('er), *n.* one who reads; a reading-book.

READILY (red'i-li), *adv.* quickly; easily; willingly.

READINESS ('i-nes), *n.* promptness; cheerfulness.

READING (red'ing), *adj.* addicted to reading: *n.* perusal of books; lecture; matter to be read.

READJUST (re-a-just'), *v.t.* to rearrange.

READY (red'i), *adj.* prepared; quick; prompt; willing; near.

REAL (re'al), *adj.* actually existing; not fictious; genuine; true.

REAL ESTATE (es-tat'), lands and all appertaining to them.

REALISM (re'al-izm), *n.* the representation of nature or social life as it actually appears.

REALITY ('i-ti), *n.* actual existence; fact; truth.

REALIZATION (-i-za'shun), *n.* the act of realizing fulfilment of one's expectations.

REALIZE ('al-iz), *v.t.* to bring into being; make real; achieve; complete.

REALLY ('al-i), *adv.* with actual existence; in truth.

REALM (relm), *n.* royal jurisdiction or territory; kingdom; empire; state.

REALITY (re'al-ti), *n.* real estate.

REAM (rem), *n.* 20 quires, or 480 sheets of paper.

REAP (rep), *v.t.* to cut with a scythe, etc.; gather in: *v.i.* to receive as a reward.

REAPER (-er), *n.* one who reaps; a reaping-machine.

REAR (rer), *n.* the part behind the rest; last in order: *v.t.* to raise or lift up; exalt; build; educate; bring to maturity.

REAR-ADMIRAL (-ad'mir-al), *n.* in the U.S. Navy, an officer ranking next below the admiral; in some navies, an officer ranking next below a vice-admiral.

REASON (re'zn), *n.* that mental faculty in man which enables him to deduce inferences from facts, and to distinguish between right and wrong.

REASONABLE (-a-bl), *adj.* rational; equitable; moderate; fair.

REASSURE (re-a-shoor'), *v.t.* to restore to confidence; comfort.

REBATE (re-bat'), *n.* a deduction; discount: *v.t.* to abate or diminish.

REBEL (reb'el), *n.* one who revolts from his allegiance or defies constituted authority.

REBELLION (-bel'yun), *n.* insurrection against constituted authority; revolt.

REBOUND (re-bound'), *v.i.* to start or leap back; to reverberate.

REBUFF (-buf'), *n.* a beating back; sudden check or resistance; defeat; refusal.

REBUKE (-buk'), *n.* reprimand or reproof; chiding, chastisement.

REBUS (re'bus), *n.* an enigmatical representation by pictures instead of words.

REBUT (re-but'), *v.t.* to beat back; oppose by argument or proof; repel.

REBUTTAL ('al), *n.* the act of rebutting.

RECALCITRANT (-kal'si-trant), *adj.* refractory.

RECALL (re-kawl'), *v.t.* to call back; remember; revoke; withdraw.

RECANT (-kant'), *v.t.* to withdraw or retract; abjure.

RECANTATION (re-kan-ta'shun), *n.* a declaration recalling and contradicting a former one.

RECAPITULATE (-ka-pit'u-lat), *v.t.* to go over, or summarize (the chief points).

RECEDE (-sed'), *v.i.* to fall back or retrograde; retreat.

RECEIPT (-set'), *n.* reception; a recipe: *v.t.* to sign in acknowledgment of.

RECEIVABLE (-sev'a-bl), *adj.* capable of being received.

RECEIVE (-sev'), *v.t.* to accept; obtain; entertain; suffer; take in.

RECEIVER (-er'), *n.* one who, or that which, receives; a person appointed by a court to manage property in bankruptcy; a radio receiver.

RECENCY (re'sen-si), *n.* lateness of time; newness.

RECENT (re'sent), *adj.* of late origin or occurrence; new.

RECEPTACLE (re-sep'ta-kl), *n.* a vessel or place into which anything is received.

RECEPTIBILITY (-ti-bil'i-ti), *n.* the quality of being receivable.

RECEPTION ('shun), *n.* welcome; social entertainment; admission.

RECESS (re-ses'), *n.* withdrawal; seclusion; remission of business; a niche.

RECESSION (-sesh'un), *n.* the act of receding or withdrawal.

RECESSIONAL (-sesh'un-al), *n.* the hymn or chant sung in church at the end of the services.

RECHERCHE (re-sher-sha'), *adj.* [French], uncommon; exquisite; choice.

RECIPE (res'i-pe), *n.* a medical prescription; formula for compounding anything.

RECIPIENT (re-sip'i-ent), *n.* one who receives.

RECIPROCAL ('ro-kal), *adj.* mutual; alternating; mutually agreeing.

RECIPROCATE ('ro-kat), *v.t.* to give and receive mutually.

RECIPROCITY (res-i-pros'i-ti), *n.* equal mutual rights or benefits to be yielded or enjoyed.

RECITAL (re-si'tal), *n.* rehearsal; narrative.

RECITATION (res-i-ta'shun), *n.* delivery of a composition committed to memory.

RECITE (re-sit'), *v.t.* to repeat aloud from memory; enumerate.

RECKLESS ('les), *adj.* heedless; careless; thoughtless.

RECKON ('n), *v.i.* to count or compute; number : *v.i.* to pay a penalty.

RECLAIM (re-klam'), *v.t.* to call back; demand the return of; reform.

RECLINE (-klin'), *v.i.* to rest or repose.

RECLUSE (-kloos'), *n.* one who lives in retirement; hermit.

RECOGNITION (rek'og-nish'un), *n.* recognizing; being recognized; remembrance.

RECOGNIZANCE (re-kog'ni-zans, -kon'i-zans), *n.* avowal; acknowledgment.

RECOGNIZE (rek'og-niz), *v.t.* to know again; acknowledge; avow; admit.

RECOIL (re-koil'), *v.i.* to retreat; draw back; rebound.

RECOLLECT (rek-o-lekt'), *v.t. & v.i.* to recall to mind.

RECOLLECTION (rek-o-lek'shun), *n.* memory; that which is remembered.

RECOMMEND (-mend'), *v.t.* to commend to another; advise.

RECOMMENDATION (-men-da'-shun), *n.* favourable introduction.

RECOMMIT (re-ko-mit'), *v.t.* to commit anew.

RECOMPENSE (rek'om-pens), *n.* an equivalent given in return; reward.

RECONCILE ('on-sil), *v.t.* to restore to friendship after estrangement; harmonize.

RECONCILIATION (-sil-i-a'shun), *n.* renewal of friendship; expiation or atonement.

RECONDITE ('on-dit), *adj.* deep; secret.

RECONNAISSANCE (re-kon'a-sans), *n.* the act of reconnoitering; a survey.

RECONNOITRE (rek-o-noi'ter), *v.t.* to make a survey of; examine for scientific purposes.

RECONSTRUCT (re-kon-strukt'), *v.t.* to construct again.

RECORD (re-kord'), *v.t.* to remember; register or enrol; celebrate : *n.* (rek'ord), an authentic memorial; register : *pl.* public documents.

RECOUNT (re-kount'), *v.t.* to go over or narrate in detail : *n.* (re'count), counting again, as of ballots.

RECOUP (re-koop'), *v.t.* to indemnify or make good.

RECOURSE (re-kors'), *n.* a going to for aid or protection.

RECOVER (-kuv'er), *v.t.* to regain; retrieve; cure; cover again.

RECOVERY ('er-i), *n.* restoration to health; legal right to something.

RECREANT (rek're-ant), *adj.* cowardly; mean-spirited; false.

RECREATION (-re-a'shun), *n.* refreshment after toil, etc. : *n.* (re-kre-a'shun), a new creation.

RECRIMINATE (re-krim'i-nat), *v.i.* to return one accusation with another.

RECRIMINATION (-na'shun), *n.* the act of recriminating.

RECRUDESCE (re-kroo-des'), *v.i.* to come into renewed vigour.

RECRUDESCENCE (-kroo-des'ens), *n.* the breaking out afresh or anew.

RECRUIT (-kroot'), *v.t.* to supply with new soldiers; restore to health : *v.i.* to obtain fresh supplies : *n.* a sailor, or soldier, newly-enlisted.

RECTANGLE (rck'tang-gl), *n.* a 4-sided figure with 4 right angles.

RECTANGULAR ('gu-lar), *adj.* right-angled.

RECTIFICATION (-fi-ka'shun), *n.* the act of setting right; repeated distillation.

RECTIFY ('ti-fi), *v.t.* to set right; refine by distillation.

RECTILINEAL (-ti-lin'e-al), **RECTILINEAR** (-ar), *adj.* bounded by straight lines.

RECTITUDE ('ti-tud), *n.* rightness of principles and practice; honesty; moral integrity.

RECTOR ('ter), *n.* a clergyman.

RECTORY ('to-ri), *n.* the house of a rector.

RECTUM ('tum), *n.* the lowest part of the great intestine.

RECUMBENCY (re-kum'ben-si), *n.* leaning or reclining.

RECUMBENT ('bent), *adj.* reclining.

RECUPERATE (-ku'per-at), *v.t.* & *v.i.* to recover.

RECUPERATION (-a'shun), *n.* recovery.

RECUR (ker'), *v.i.* to return to the mind ; happen at a stated interval.

RECURRENCE (-kur'ens), *n.* return ; resort.

RED (red), *n.* one of the primary colours.

RED CROSS (kros), a society for the relief of victims of war, calamity and disease.

REDDEN ('n), *v.t.* to make red.

REDEEM (re-dem'), *v.t.* to ransom from bondage ; rescue ; perform ; recover.

REDEEMER ('er), *n.* Jesus Christ,the Saviour.

REDEMPTION (-demp'shun), *n.* repurchase ; release ; ransom ; salvation of mankind by Jesus Christ.

REDIVIVUS (red-i-viv'us), *adj.* come to life again ; revived.

REDOLENCE ('o-lens), *n.* fragrance.

REDOLENT ('o-lent), *adj.* emitting a sweet smell ; fragrant.

REDOUBTABLE (re-dout'a-bl), *adj.* formidable ; valiant.

REDOUND (-dound'), *v.i.* to tend or contribute ; be in excess.

REDRESS (re-dres'), *v.t.* to amend or set right ; compensate.

RED SQUIRREL (skwer'el), a small, reddish-coloured rodent with a bushy tail, of the species *sciurus*.

RED TAPE (tap), tape used for tying official documents ; excessive formality.

REDUCE (re-dus'), *v.t.* to bring into a lower state ; degrade ; diminish ; conquer ; shorten.

REDUCTION (-duk'shun), *n.* the act of reducing ; diminution ; conquest or subjugation.

REDUNDANCE (dun'dans), **RE-DUNDANCY** (-si), *n.* superfluity ; excess.

REDUNDANT ('dant), *adj.* superfluous.

REDUPLICATE (-du'pli-kat), *v.t.* to double again ; repeat ; multiply.

REED (red), *n.* a large, coarse grass, with jointed hollow stems ; tube of a musical instrument.

REEF (ref), *n.* that part of a sail which can be reduced by small ropes ; a chain of rock lying at or near the surface of the water.

REEK (rek), *n.* smoke ; steam ; exhalation.

REEL (rel), *n.* a thousand feet of picture film ; bobbin ; a fish line holder ; a dance.

RE-ENFORCE (re-en-fors'), *v.t.* to strengthen by addition.

REFECTORY (fek'to-ri), *n.* an eating room or hall.

REFER (-fer'), *v.t.* to submit to another for information, or decision : *v.i.* to allude ; appeal ; hint.

REFERABLE (ref'er-a-bl), *adj.* that may be referred ; ascribable.

REFEREE (ref-er-e'), *n.* an umpire.

REFERENCE ('er-ens), *n.* the act of referring ; allusion ; a recommendation.

REFERENDUM (ref-er-en'dum), *n.* the referring of a bill or act of the legislature to the people for decision by vote.

REFERENTIAL (-en'shal), *adj.* pertaining to something else.

REFINE (-fin'), *v.t.* to separate from impurities ; polish ; educate or improve.

REFINEMENT ('ment), *n.* elegance ; polish ; purity of taste, mind, morals, etc.

REFIT (re-fit'), *v.t.* to make fit for use again.

REFLECT (-flekt'), *v.t.* to throw back : *v.i.* to be thrown back, as rays of light, etc. ; consider in the mind ; cast reproach or censure (with *upon*).

REFLECTING ('ting), *p.adj.* making reflection ; thoughtful ; casting reproach or censure.

REFLECTION, REFLEXION (-flek'shun), *n.* the turning of thought back upon past experiences ; attentive consideration ; reproach or censure ; reflected heat, light, colour, image in mirror.

REFLECTOR ('ter), *n.* a polished surface reflecting rays of light or heat.

REFLEX ('fleks), *adj.* bent or turned back ; directed backwards ; reflective.

REFORM (re-form'), *v.t.* to make better ; change, or return to a former good state ; introduce improvement in ; amend ; correct.

REFORMATION (ref-or-ma'shun), *n.* amendment ; political redress ; the act of forming again or anew ; [R-], the great religious movement of the 16th century which resulted in Protestantism.

REFORMATORY (re-for'ma-to-ri), *adj.* tending to reform : *n.* an institution for the reformation of juvenile offenders.

REFORMER (-for'mer), *n.* one who effects, or endeavours to effect, reformation, religious, moral, or political.

REFRACTION (-frak'shun), *n.* change from a straight line, which a ray of light or heat assumes when passing through a smooth surface into a medium of greater density.

REFRACTORY ('to-ri), *adj.* sullenly or perversely obstinate.

REFRAGABLE (ref'ra-ga-bl), *adj.* that which may be refuted.

REFRAIN (re-fran'), *v.t.* to restrain : *v.i.* to forbear.

REFRESH (-fresh'), *v.t.* to revive ; restore.

REFRESHMENT ('ment), *n.* that which refreshes, as food or rest.

REFRIGERATOR (-frij'er-a-ter), *n.* a cabinet or vessel for preserving or cooling things by means of ice.

REFUGE (ref'uj), *n.* protection from danger or distress ; shelter or asylum.

REFUGEE (-u-je'), *n.* one who flees for protection.

REFULGENCE (re-ful'jens), *n.* brightness ; splendour.

REFULGENT ('jent), *adj.* brilliant ; splendid.

REFUND (-fund'), *v.t.* to pay back ; reimburse.

REFUSAL (-fuz'al), *n.* the act of refusing ; rejection ; option.

REFUSE (-fuz'), *v.a.* to deny or reject :

v.i. to decline to accept : *n.* (ref'us), worthless matter.

REFUTABLE (re-fut'a-bl), *adj.* capable of being refuted.

REFUTE (re-fut'), *v.t.* to prove to be false or erroneous ; disprove.

REGAIN (-gan'), *v.t.* to get back ; reach again.

REGAL (re'gal), *adj.* kingly ; royal.

REGALE (re-gal'), *v.t.* to entertain with something to delight the senses : *v.i.* to feast.

REGALIA (-ga'li-a), *n.pl.* the ensigns of sovereignty ; decorations of an order or office.

REGARD (re-gard'), *v.t.* to heed ; esteem ; consider ; respect ; value : *pl.* good wishes.

REGATTA (-gat'a), *n.* a sailing or rowing race.

REGENCY (re'jen-si), *n.* the office or jurisdiction of a regent.

REGENERATE ('er-at), *v.t.* to renew the heart of ; produce anew : *adj.* reformed.

REGENT (re'jent), *adj.* exercising vicarious authority : *n.* in the U.S. a member of the governing board of a State university.

REGICIDE ('i-sid), *n.* the murder, or murderer, of a king.

REGIME (ra-zhem'), *n.* mode ; system or rule of government.

REGIMEN (rej'i-men), *n.* systematic regulation of diet or habit ; rule.

REGIMENT (rej'i-ment), *n.* a number of companies of soldiers under the command of a colonel.

REGION (re'jun), *n.* a tract of land ; country.

REGISTER (rej'is-ter), *n.* an official written record ; an official recorder ; the book containing such record ; that which registers, records, or regulates ; an organ stop ; musical compass or range.

REGISTRAR (-trar), *n.* an official who keeps a register or record.

REGISTRATION (-tra'shun), *n.* the act of inserting in a register ; enrolment, as of voters.

REGISTRY ('is-tri), *n.* the place where a register is kept ; an official book.

REGNANT ('nant), *adj.* reigning; prevalent.

REGRESS (re-gres'), *v.i.* to go back; return.

REGRESSION (re-gresh'un), *n.* a backward movement.

REGRET (-gret'), *n.* mental sorrow or concern for anything; remorse.

REGRETTABLE ('a-bl), *adj.* admitting of, or causing regret.

REGULAR (reg'u-lar), *adj.* according to rule, order, or established usage; consistent; uniform; methodical; exact.

REGULARITY (-lar'i-ti), *n.* conformity to rule; uniformity.

REGULATE ('u-lat), *v.t.* put in good order; adjust by rule.

REGULATION (-la'shun), *n.* order; method; rule.

REGULATOR (-la-ter), *n.* one who, or that which, regulates.

REGURGITATE (re-ger'ji-tat), *v.t.* to throw or surge back.

REHABILITATE (re-ha-bil'i-tat), *v.t.* to restore to former condition or status.

REHEARSAL (re-her'sal), *n.* a recital in private prior to a public performance.

REHEARSE (-hers'), *v.t.* to repeat; recite before public performance.

REIGN (ran), *v.i.* to exercise sovereign authority; rule.

REIMBURSE (re-im-bers'), *v.t.* to refund.

REIMBURSEMENT ('ment), *n.* refunding.

REIN (ran), *n.* the strap of a bridle; an instrument for curbing, restraining, or governing: *v.t.* restrain; control.

REINDEER (ran'der), *n.* a large Arctic deer.

REINFORCE, see re-enforce.

REINS (ranz), *n.* the kidneys; inner parts; loins.

REINSTATE (re-in-stat'), *v.t.* to restore to a former state.

REITERATE (re-it'er-at), *v.t.* to repeat; say over again.

REITERATION (-it-er-a'shun), *n.* repetition.

REJECT (re-jekt'), *v.t.* to refuse renounce; discard.

REJOICE (-jois'), *v.i.* to feel or express joy or gladness; exult.

REJOICING ('ing), *n.* expression of joy or gladness.

REJOIN (-join'), *v.t.* to unite again: *v.i.* to answer a reply.

REJOINDER ('der), *n.* an answer to a reply.

REJUVENATE (re-ju'ven-at), *v.t.* to make youthful again.

RELAPSE (-laps'), *v.i.* to return to a former bad state or habit.

RELATE (-lat), *v.t.* to tell; describe; recite; narrate.

RELATION (-la'shun), *n.* mutual connection between two or more things; kinsman or kinswoman.

RELATIONSHIP (-ship), *n.* the state of being related by kindred, affinity, or other alliance.

RELATIVE (rel'a-tiv), *adj.* having, or expressing, relation; pertinent: *n.* a relative pronoun or a word relating to its antecedent; a person connected by kinship.

RELATIVITY (-tiv'i-ti), *n.* the quality of being relative; the theory that all knowledge of velocity is relative.

RELAX (re-laks'), *v.i.* to slacken; render less tense, rigorous, or severe.

RELEASE (-les'), *v.t.* to set free; discharge.

RELEGATE (rel'e-gat), *v.t.* to banish; consign.

RELENT (re-lent'), *v.i.* to grow less hard or severe; yield.

RELENTLESS ('les), *adj.* pitiless; lacking sympathy.

RELEVANCE (rel'e-vans), **RELEVANCY** (-van'si), *n.* applicability; pertinence.

RELEVANT ('e-vant), *adj.* applicable; related; pertinent.

RELIABILITY (re-li-a-bil'i-ti), *n.* the state of being reliable.

RELIABLE ('a-bl), *adj.* trustworthy.

RELIANCE ('ans), *n.* confidence; trust.

RELIC (rel'ik), *n.* that which is left after the loss or decay of the rest; memorial or souvenir.

RELICT ('ikt), *n.* a widow, or widower.

RELIEF (re-lef'), *n.* that which mitigates pain, grief, etc.; aid; redress.

RELIEVE (-lev'), *v.t.* to free from pain; suffering, grief, etc.

RELIGION (re-lij'un), *n.* any system of faith or worship; piety; devotion; fidelity.

RELIGIOUS (-lij'us), *adj.* godly; pious; devotional.

RELINQUISH (-ling'kwish), *v.t.* to forsake or abandon; quit.

RELISH (rel'ish), *v.t.* to like the taste of; use with pleasure; enjoy.

RELUCTANCE (re-luk'tans), *n.* unwillingness.

RELUCTANT ('tant), *adj.* unwilling.

RELY (-li'), *v.i.* to trust or have confidence in.

REMAIN (-man'), *v.i.* to continue; stay; last; endure: *n.pl.* a dead body.

REMAINDER (re-man'der), *n.* that which is left after a part has been taken away.

REMAND (-mand'), *v.t.* to recommit or send back.

REMARK (-mark'), *v.t.* to note or observe; express; say.

REMARKABLE (-mar'ka-bl), *adj.* worthy of notice or remark.

REMEDIABLE (re-me'di-a-bl), *adj.* admitting remedy.

REMEDIAL ('di-al), *adj.* affording, or intended for, a remedy.

REMEDY (rem'e-di), *n.* that which cures a disease, or counteracts an evil; a restorative.

REMEMBER (re-mem'ber), *v.t.* to recall to mind; attend to.

REMEMBRANCE ('brans), *n.* memory; recollection.

REMIND (re-mind'), *v.t.* to bring to the remembrance of.

REMINISCENCE (rem-i-nis'ens), *n.* recovery of ideas; memory.

REMINISCENT ('ent), *adj.* dwelling upon the past.

REMISE (re-miz'), *v.t.* to resign or surrender by deed.

REMISS (-mis'), *adj.* careless; heedless; dilatory.

REMISSION (-mish'un), *n.* pardon; abatement.

REMIT (-mit'), *v.t.* to pardon; transmit, as money, etc.

REMITTANCE ('ans), *n.* that which is remitted; the sending of money, bills, etc., in payment.

REMNANT (rem'nant), *n.* a small cutting, of cloth; remainder.

REMONETIZE (re-mon'e-tiz), *v.t.* to restore to circulation as legal tender.

REMONSTRANCE (-mon'strans), *n.* strong representation against something complained of; expostulation.

REMONSTRATE ('strat), *v.t. & v.i.* strong reasons against some act or course complained of; expostulate.

REMORSE (re-mors'), *n.* anguish of mind caused by the sense of guilt.

REMORSELESS ('les), *adj.* cruel; merciless.

REMOTE (-mot'), *adj.* distant in time or space; alien; foreign.

REMOVABLE (-moov'a-bl), *adj.* capable of being removed.

REMOVAL ('al), *n.* change of place; dismissal.

REMOVE (-moov'), *v.t.* to put from its place; withdraw; cut off: *n.* change of place.

REMUNERATE (-mu'ner-at), *v.t.* to reward; recompense.

REMUNERATION (-a'shun), *n.* recompense; reward.

REMUNERATIVE ('mer-a-tiv), *adj.* lucrative; profitable.

RENASCENCE (re-nas'ens), *n.* new birth, life, or form.

RENASCENT (re-nas'ent), *adj.* denoting new birth.

RENCONTRE (rank-kong'tr), *n.* [French], a casual meeting in opposition or contest; collision.

REND (rend), *v.t.* to tear apart with violence; split; lacerate.

RENDER (ren'der), *v.t.* to return; pay back; make up; deliver; afford; yield; furnish; reproduce.

RENDEZVOUS (rang'da-voo, ren'de-voo), *n.* [French], appointed place of meeting.

RENDITION (ren-dish'un), *n.* a dramatic, or musical interpretation; surrender; translation.

RENEGADE (ren'e-gad), *n.* one who renounces his faith; apostate; traitor; deserter.

RENEGE (re-neg'), *v.i.* to fail to comply with one's promise or obligation.

RENEW (re-nu'), *v.t.* to restore; renovate; reinvigorate.

RENEWAL ('al), *n.* renovation; revival.

RENNET (ren'et), *n.* the membrane lining the fourth stomach of a young ruminant.

RENOUNCE (re-nouns'), *v.t.* to disown; repudiate; reject.

RENOVATE (ren'o-vat), *v.t.* to restore to a previous condition, or to a good state; repair.

RENOVATION (-va'shun), *n.* renewal.

RENOWN (re-noun'), *n.* celebrity; fame; distinction.

RENOWNED (-nound'), *p.adj.* celebrated famous; distinguished.

RENT (rent), *n.* a tear; fissure; periodical payment for the use of property.

RENUNCIATION (re-nun-si-a'shun), *n.* disavowal; rejection.

REORGANIZATION (re-or-gan-i-za'shun), *n.* being arranged or formed anew.

REPAIR (re-par'), *v.i.* to go to a (specified) place; betake one's self: *v.t.* to restore after injury; mend.

REPARABLE (rep'a-ra-bl), *adj.* capable of being repaired.

REPARATION (-a-ra'shun), *n.* restoration to a good condition; restitution.

REPARTEE (rep-ar-te'), *n.* a ready, witty reply.

REPAST (re-past'), *n.* a meal; victuals.

REPATRIATE (re-pa'tri-at), *v.t.* to return a person to his own country; restore citizenship.

REPAY (re-pa'), *v.t.* to pay back; refund.

REPEAL (re-pel'), *v.t.* to revoke or abrogate; annul : *n.* revocation.

REPEAT (-pet'), *v.t.* to do or speak a second time; iterate; recite.

REPEL (-pel'), *v.t.* to drive back; resist.

REPELLENT ('ent), *adj.* driving back; repulsive.

REPENT (-pent'), *v.i.* to feel pain or sorrow on account of something done or left undone.

REPENTANCE (-pen'tans), *n.* contrition; sorrow for sin.

REPERTOIRE (rep'er-twar), *n.* [French], a repository; stock of dramas, songs, etc.

REPERTORY (-to-ri), *n.* a storehouse; treasury.

REPETITION (-e-tish'un), *n.* the act of repeating.

REPINE (re-pin'), *v.i.* to fret one's self; murmur; complaint.

REPLACE (re-plas'), *v.t.* to restore to a former place; furnish an equivalent.

REPLENISH (-plen'ish), *v.t.* to fill up again; re-stock.

REPLETE (-plet'), *adj.* completely filled; full.

REPLETION (-ple'shun), *n.* a state of extreme fullness; plethora.

REPLEVIN (-plev'in), *n.* an action to recover goods wrongfully seized.

REPLICA (rep'li-ka), *n.* a copy of an original picture or statue.

REPLY (re-pli'), *v.i.* to answer; respond.

REPORT (-port'), *v.t.* to give an account of; relate; tell from one to another; rumour; hearsay; noise.

REPORTER (-por'ter), *n.* one who reports news items, etc., for a newspaper.

REPOSE (re-poz'), *v.t.* to lay to rest; place confidence or trust (with *in* or *on*).

REPOSITORY (-poz'i-to-ri), *n.* a warehouse for the storing of goods.

REPREHEND (rep-re-hend'), *v.t.* to censure.

REPREHENSIBLE (-hen'si-bl), *adj.* deserving censure; culpable.

REPREHENSION ('shun), *n.* censure; reproof.

REPREHENSIVE ('siv), *adj.* given to, or containing, reproof.

REPRESENT (rep-re-zent'), *v.t.* to exhibit the image of; show; describe; give an account of; (re-pre-zent'), to reproduce; to present again.

REPRESENTATION (-zen-ta'shun), *n.* portrayal; description; likeness; image or picture.

REPRESENTATIVE ('ta-tiv), *adj.* having the power or character of another ; typical : *n.* a member of Congress or of a State Legislature.

REPRESS (re-pres'), *v.t.* to restrain.

REPRESSIVE (-pres'iv), *adj.* serving to repress.

REPRIEVE (-prev'), *v.t.* to grant a respite to ; delay the execution of.

REPRIMAND (rep'ri-mand), *v.t.* to reprove severely.

REPRISAL (re-priz'al), *n.* something done or seized by way of retaliation.

REPROACH (-proch'), *v.t.* to censure severely ; upbraid.

REPROBATE (rep'ro-bat), *v.t.* to condemn strongly or with detestation : *n.* a profligate person.

REPRODUCE (re-pro-dus'), *v.t.* to cause to exist ; anew : *v.i.* to produce offspring.

REPROOF (re-proof'), *n.* censure ; rebuke.

REPROVE (-proov'), *v.t.* to censure ; reprimand ; rebuke.

REPTILE (rep'til), *n.* a cold-blooded vertebrate, as a snake.

REPTILIAN (til'i-an), *adj.* pertaining to, or like, a reptile.

REPUBLIC (re-pub'lik), *n.* a state or country in which the supreme power is vested in representatives elected by popular vote ; commonwealth.

REPUBLICAN ('li-kan), *adj.* [R-], a member of the Republican party.

REPUDIATE (-pu'di-at), *v.t.* to disown or disclaim ; disavow.

REPUDIATION (-a'shun), *n.* disavowal ; rejection.

REPUDIATOR ('di-a-ter), *n.* one who repudiates.

REPUGNANCE (-pug'nans), *n.* aversion ; reluctance ; dislike.

REPUGNANT ('nant), *adj.* highly offensive.

REPULSE (puls'), *v.t.* to drive back ; repel.

REPULSION (-pul'shun), *n.* the act of driving back ; being repelled ; aversion.

REPULSIVE ('siv), *adj.* forbidding ; disgusting.

REPUTABLE (rep'u-ta-bl), *adj.* esteemed ; honourable ; respectable.

REPUTATION (-ta'shun), *n.* good name or character ; honour.

REPUTE (re-put'), *n.* estimation ; character ; reputation.

REQUEST (-kwest'), *n.* desire expressed ; petition ; prayer ; demand.

REQUIEM (re'kwi-em), *n.* a Mass, for the repose of the soul of a person deceased.

REQUIRE (re-kwir'), *v.t.* to demand ; exact ; need.

REQUIREMENT ('ment), *n.* that which is required.

REQUISITE (rek'wi-zit), *adj.* needful ; indispensable.

REQUISITION (-wi-zish'un), *n.* demand, especially a written one.

REQUITAL (-kwit'al), *n.* retaliation.

REQUITE (-kwit'), *v.t.* to recompense ; retaliate ; revenge.

RESCIND (re-sind'), *v.t.* to annul.

RESCISSION (-sizh'un), *n.* act of annulling.

RESCUE (res'ku), *v.t.* to set free from danger, restraint, or violence ; liberate.

RESEARCH (re-serch'), *n.* laborious, careful inquiry or investigation.

RESEMBLANCE (-zem'blans), *n.* likeness.

RESEMBLE (-zem'bl), *v.t.* to have similarity to.

RESENT (-zent'), *v.t.* to consider as an injury or affront.

RESENTMENT ('ment), *n.* deep sense of injury.

RESERVATION (rez-er-va'shun), *n.* anything kept back ; public land reserved for some particular use.

RESERVE (re-zerv'), *v.t.* to keep in store ; hold back for future use ; retain : *n.* caution in speaking or acting.

RESERVOIR (rez'er-vwar), *n.* a place where anything (usually fluids and liquids) is collected and stored for use.

RESET (re-set'), *v.t.* to set again.

RESIDE (re-zid'), *v.i.* to dwell or inhabit ; live in.

RESIDENCE (rez'i-dens), *n.* place of abode ; domicile.

RESIDENT (rez'i-dent), *n.* one who dwells in a place.

RESIDUAL (re-zid'u-al), *adj.* remaining after a part has been taken away.

RESIDUE (rez'i-du), *n.* remainder.

RESIDUUM (re-zid'u-um), *n.* that which is left after a chemical process.

RESIGN (-zin'), *v.t.* to withdraw from ; submit calmly.

RESIGNATION (res-ig-na'shun), *n.* the act of resigning ; patience.

RESILIENCY (re-zil'i-en-si), *n.* power of recovery, elasticity.

RESILIENT (re-zil'i-ent), *adj.* springing back.

RESIN (rez'in), *n.* an organic vegetable substance which exudes from trees in the form of gum.

RESIST (re-zist), *v.t.* to oppose.

RESISTANCE (-zis'tans), *n.* opposition.

RESISTLESS ('les), *adj.* irresistible.

RESOLUTE (rez'o-lut), *adj.* determined ; decided.

RESOLUTION (-lu'shun), *n.* analysis ; fixed determination ; formal proposal.

RESOLVABLE ('va-bl), *adj.* capable of being resolved.

RESOLVE (-zolv'), *v.t.* to reduce to constituent parts ; analyze ; solve ; decide ; determine by vote: *n.* a determination.

RESOLVED (-zolvd'), *p.adj.* firm.

RESOLVENT (-zol'vent), *adj.* causing solution : *n.* any solvent.

RESONANCE (rez'o-nans), *n.* the quality of being resonant.

RESONANT ('o-nant), *adj.* returning sound.

RESORT (re-zort'), *v.i.* to betake one's self ; go often ; have recourse ; apply : *n.* place much frequented.

RESOUND (-zound'), *v.i. & v.t.* to reverberate ; spread the renown of ; sound again.

RESOURCE (-sors'), *n.* source of help or supply ; means of any kind.

RESOURCEFUL ('fool), *adj.* quick in planning ; rich in expedients.

RESPECT (re-spekt'), *n.* regard ; expression of esteem ; deference ; manner of treating others.

RESPECTABLE ('ta-bl), *adj.* worthy of respect.

RESPECTIVE (-spek'tiv), *adj.* not absolute ; relative.

RESPECTIVELY (-li), *adv.* singly considered.

RESPIRABLE (-spir'a-bl), *adj.* that may be, or is fit to be, breathed.

RESPIRATION (res-pi-ra'shun), *n.* the act or process of breathing.

RESPIRATOR ('pi-ra-ter), *n.* a network contrivance for protecting the lungs from cold, fog, etc.

RESPITE (res'pit), *n.* pause or temporary cessation of anything ; delay ; reprieve.

RESPLENDENCE (re-splen'dens), *n.* brilliant lustre.

RESPLENDENT ('dent), *adj.* intensely bright.

RESPOND (-spond'), *v.i.* to answer or reply ; be liable for payment.

RESPONSE (-spons'), *n.* reply.

RESPONSIBLE (-spon'si-bl), *adj.* answerable ; liable.

RESPONSIBILITY (-si-bil'i-ti), *n.* that for which one is accountable.

REST (rest), *n.* cessation from motion or disturbance ; quiet ; peace ; repose; sleep ; remainder.

RESTAURANT (res'to-rant, -to-rang'), *n.* an eating-house.

RESTFUL ('fool), *adj.* quiet.

RESTITUTION (-ti-tu'shun), *n.* compensation ; amends.

RESTIVE (res'tiv), *adj.* impatient of control ; obstinate ; uneasy.

RESTLESS ('les), *adj.* fidgety ; disturbed.

RESTORATION (res-to-ra'shun), *n.* the act of restoring ; renewal ; repair.

RESTORE (-stor'), *v.t.* to bring back to its former strength ; repair ; rebuild ; heal or cure ; renew.

RESTRAIN (-stran'), *v.t.* to check ; repress.

RESTRAINT (-strant'), *n.* being restrained ; limitation.

RESTRICT (-strikt'), *v.t.* to confine.

RESTRICTION (-strik'shun), *n.* limitation ; confinement.

RESULT (-zult'), *v.i.* to follow as a consequence ; to come to a decision ; ensue ; decree.

RESULTANT (-zul'tant), *n.* a single

force compounded of two or more forces.

RESUME (re-zum), *v.t.* to begin again ; continue.

RESUMPTION (re-zump'shun), *n.* the act of resuming.

RESURRECT (rez-u-rekt'), *v.t.* to disinter ; restore to life.

RESURRECTION (-rek'shun), *n.* a rising again from the dead ; [R], the rising of Christ from the dead.

RESUSCITATE (re-sus'i-tat), *v.t.* to revive from apparent death ; revivify.

RETAIL (re-tal'), *v.t.* to sell in small quantities : *n.* (re'tal), sale of goods in small quantities.

RETAIN (-tan'), *v.t.* to hold or keep in possession ; detain.

RETALIATE (-tal'i-at), *v.t.* to return by giving like for like.

RETARD (-tard'), *v.t.* to delay ; keep back.

RETARDATION (-tar-da'shun), *n.* hindrance ; postponement.

RETARDATIVE ('da-tiv), *adj.* tending to retard.

RETENTION (re-ten'shun), *n.* act of holding back.

RETENTIVE ('tiv), *adj.* having power to retain.

RETICENCE (ret'i-sens), *n.* silence ; reserve.

RETICENT ('i-sent), *adj.* silent ; reserved.

RETICULE (ret'i-kul), *n.* a lady's handbag or workbag.

RETINA (ret'i-na), *n.* the inner coat of the eye, containing the ends of the sensory nerves which receive the impressions which give rise to vision.

RETINUE ('i-nu), *n.* the attendants of a person of distinction.

RETIRE (-tir'), *v.i.* to go to a place of privacy ; withdraw ; retreat ; to go to bed.

RETORT (-tort'), *n.* censure ; incivility, etc., returned ; sharp reply ; a vessel used in laboratory experiments.

RETRACT (re-trakt'), *v.t.* to draw, or take back ; recall ; rescind.

RETRACTION (trak'shun), *n.* withdrawal ; revocation.

RETRACTOR ('ter), *n.* one who retracts.

RETREAT (re-tret'), *n.* the act of withdrawing or retiring ; shelter.

RETRENCH (-trench'), *v.t.* to furnish with a retrenchment : *v.i.* cut down expenses.

RETRIBUTION (ret-ri-bu'shun), *n.* reward or punishment suitable to the action.

RETRIEVABLE (-trev'a-bl), *adj.* capable of being retrieved.

RETRIEVE (-trev'), *v.t.* to recover.

RETRO-, a prefix signifying *back*, *backward*.

RETROACTIVE (-tro-ak'tiv), *adj.* tending to operate backward ; retrospective.

RETROCEDE (re-tro-sed', ret'ro-sed), *v.t.* to cede or grant back.

RETROGRADE (ret'ro-grad), *adj.* going or moving backwards ; going from a better to a worse moral condition.

RETROGRESSION (-gresh'un), *n.* the act of going backward.

RETROSPECTION (ret-ro-spek' shun), *n.* looking back on the past.

RETROSPECTIVE ('tiv), *adj.* looking back on things past.

RETROVERSION (-ver'shun), *n.* a turning or falling backward.

RETURN (re-tern'), *v.i.* to come back : *v.t.* to repay ; restore ; requite ; elect : *n.* retrogression ; repayment.

REUNION (re-un'yun), *n.* a festive gathering of familiar friends.

REVEAL (re-vel'), *v.t.* to make known ; disclose.

REVEILLE (rev-el-e', re-val'ye), *n.* the beat of a drum, or bugle call, at daybreak.

REVEL (rev'el), *n.* a riotous feast.

REVELATION (rev-e-la'shun), *n.* making known ; that which is revealed.

REVENGE (re-venj'), *v.t.* to avenge : *n.* retaliation ; malice.

REVENUE (re'e-nu), *n.* the general income of a state, derived from the annual taxes, excise, customs, etc. ; annual profits from lands, etc.

REVERBERATE (re-ver'ber-at), *v.t.* to send back, as sound ; re-echo.

REVERE (-ver'), *v.t.* to reverence.

REVERENCE (rev'er-ens), *n.* veneration ; honour ; respect ; a title given to clergy (with *his*, *your*).

REVEREND (-end), *adj.* worthy of reverence ; applied to priests and ministers.

REVERIE ('er-i), *n.* deep musing.

REVERSAL (re-ver'sal), *n.* overthrow or annulling ; repeal.

REVERSE (vers'), *adj.* turned backward ; made or declared void : *n.* change ; vicissitude ; defeat.

REVERT (-vert'), *v.t.* to turn back ; change ; reverse.

REVEST (-vest'), *v.i.* to vest again, as with rank or authority.

REVIEW (-vu'), *v.t.* to consider over again ; re examine ; look back ; revise ; inspect (troops, etc.).

REVIEWER ('er), *n.* a book critic ; one who writes reviews.

REVILE (-vil'), *v.t.* to address with opprobrious language.

REVISE (-viz'), *v.t.* to review and amend ; examine for correction.

REVISION (-vizh'un), *n.* examining for correction.

REVIVAL (-vi'val), *n.* the act of reviving ; recovery ; renewal of life ; spiritual awakening.

REVIVE (-viv'), *v.t.* to restore to life again ; renovate ; reproduce.

REVIVIFY (-viv'i-fi), *v.t.* to re-animate ; quicken.

REVOCABLE (rev'o-ka-bl), *adj.* denoting that may be revoked.

REVOCATION (-ka'shun), *n.* recall repeal ; reversal.

REVOKE (re-vok'), *v.t.* to recall ; repeal ; annul.

REVOLT (-volt'), *n.* rebellion ; insurrection.

REVOLTING ('ting), *p.adj.* disgusting ; repellent.

REVOLUTE (rev'o-lut), *adj.* rolled backwards.

REVOLUTION (-lu'shun), *n.* rotation ; change or alteration of system ; sudden change in the government of a country ; the means adopted to bring about such change.

REVOLUTIONIST ('shun-ist), *n.* one who organizes or takes part in a revolution.

REVOLUTIONIZE ('shun-iz), *v.t.* to cause a revolution or entire change of government, or of any system.

REVOLVE (re-volv'), *v.i.* to turn round ; roll in a circle ; to rotate.

REVUE (re-vu'), *n.* a burlesque musical comedy.

REVULSION (re-vul'shun), *n.* sudden and violent change, especially of feeling.

REWARD (re-wawrd', -ward'), *n.* recompense ; retribution ; punishment ; gift in token of merit.

REYNARD (ren'ard), *n.* the fox.

RHAPSODY (rap'so-di), *n.* any unconnected or rambling composition.

RHEOSTAT (re'o-stat), *n.* an apparatus for regulating an electric current.

RHETORIC (ret'o-rik), *n.* the art of speaking, or writing, with elegance and force.

RHETORICAL (re-tor'i-kal), *adj.* figurative ; declamatory.

RHEUMATISM (roo'ma-tizm), *n.* a painful disease of the muscles and joints.

RHINOCEROS (ri-nos'er-os), *n.* a large pachydermatous animal.

RHIZOME (ri'zom), *n.* a thick stem running along or under the ground, producing roots below and shoots above.

RHODODENDRON (ro-do den' dron), *n.* a genus of ornamental, evergreen shrubs.

RHUBARB (roo'barb), *n.* a plant used for culinary purposes : roots used as a purgative.

RHUMKORFF COIL (rum-korf-coil), *n.* an induction coil.

RHYME (rim), *n.* harmonical succession of sounds ; poetry : *v.i.* to make verses or rhymes.

RHYTHM (rithm, ri*th*m), *n.* the harmonious recurrence of sound, accent, and movement.

RIBALD (rib'ald), *adj.* low ; filthy.

RIBBON ('un), *n.* a fillet or strip of silk, etc. ; narrow strip.

RICE (ris), *n.* a valuable food grain.

RICH (rich), *adj.* wealthy ; opulent ;

sumptuous; valuable; splendid; fertile; fruitful.

RICK (rik), *n.* a pile of hay or corn, and usually sheltered.

RICKETS ('ets), *n.* a disease affecting children.

RICKETY ('et-i), *adj.* feeble in the joints; unsteady.

RICHOCHET (-o-sha', -o-shet'), *n.* the rebounding of a shot or shell, etc., along the ground or water.

RID (rid), *v.t.* to set free; deliver; clear or destroy.

RIDDANCE ('ans), *n.* ridding or clearing away; deliverance.

RIDDLE ('l), *n.* an enigma; puzzling question: *v.t.* to perforate, as with shot.

RIDE (rid), *v.i. & v.t.* to be borne along, as on horseback or in a vehicle; sit, float or rest on.

RIDGE (rij), *n.* anything formed like an animal's back; a continuous range of hills, etc.

RIDICULE (rid'i-kul), *n.* words or action designed to bring the subject of it into contempt; banter.

RIDICULOUS (ri-dik'u-lus), *adj.* exciting ridicule; preposterous; absurd; ludicrous; droll.

RIFE (rif), *adj.* prevalent; common.

RIFFRAFF (rif'raf), *n.* refuse; the rabble.

RIFLE (ri'fl), *n.* a gun with the barrel spirally grooved: *v.t.* to pillage.

RIFT (rift), *n.* an opening or split in anything; fissure.

RIGGER (rig'er), *n.* one who rigs ships.

RIGGING ('ing), *n.* the ropes by which the masts of a vessel are supported, and the sails extended, furled and controlled.

RIGHT (rit), *adj.* correct; fit; true; exact; most direct; noting the side opposed to the left; well performed: *n.* uprightness; truth; justice; rectitude.

RIGHT ANGLE (ang'gl), an angle of 90 degrees.

RIGHTEOUS ('yus), *adj.* just; equitable; honest; holy.

RIGHTEOUSNESS (nes), *n.* holiness; justice; moral integrity.

RIGHTFUL ('fool), *adj.* having a just claim.

RIGID (rij'id), *adj.* stiff; inflexible; strict; stern; severely just.

RIGIDITY (ri-jid'i-ti), *n.* stiffness; resistance to change.

RIGMAROLE (rig'ma-rol), *n.* foolish, disconnected talk.

RIGOROUS (rig'er-us), *adj.* stern; inflexible; scrupulously accurate.

RIGOUR ('er), *n.* stiffness or severity; exactitude; strictness.

RILE (ril), *v.t.* to irritate; annoy; stir up.

RIM (rim), *n.* a border or margin.

RIME (rim), *n.* hoar-frost; another spelling for rhyme.

RIMPLE (rim'pl), *n.* a wrinkle: *v.t.* to become wrinkled.

RIND (rind), *n.* the outer covering of fruit, etc.; bark.

RING (ring), *n.* a circle; anything circular in form; combination for private ends: *v.t.* to cause to sound, as metal when struck.

RINGING ('ing), *p.adj.* sounding like a bell; resonant.

RINGWORM ('werm), *n.* a contagious cutaneous disease.

RINK (ringk), *n.* ice field for skating upon.

RINSE (rins), *v.t.* to cleanse lightly with clean water.

RIOT (ri'ot), *n.* uproar; tumult; noisy revelry.

RIP (rip), *v.t.* divide by tearing or cutting.

RIPARIAN (ri-pa'ri-an), *adj.* pertaining to the banks of a river, bay or inlet.

RIPE (rip), *adj.* brought to maturity or perfection.

RIPPLE (rip'l), *n.* a small curling wave on the surface of water.

RISE (riz), *v.i.* to ascend; get up; swell in quantity or extent; come in view or existence; be promoted; thrive.

RISIBILITY (riz-i-bil'i-ti), *n.* inclination to laughter.

RISK (risk), *n.* hazard; peril; danger.

RITE (rit), *n.* a solemn religious act.

RIVAL (ri'val), *n.* competitor.

RIVALRY (-ri), *n.* competition.

RIVE (riv), *v.t.* to rend asunder.

RIVER (riv'er), *n.* a large running stream.

RIVET (riv'et), *n.* a short metal bolt clinched by hammering.

RIVULET (riv'u-let), *n.* a little stream.

ROAD (rod), *n.* a public way; path; a roadstead.

ROAM (rom), *v.i.* to wander about; ramble.

ROAR (ror), *n.* the deep full cry of a large animal; sound of wind or sea, etc.

ROAST (rost), *v.t.* to cook before a fire, or in an oven; to banter or ridicule; criticise severely.

ROB (rob), *v.t.* to steal; plunder.

ROBBER ('er), *n.* a thief.

ROBIN (rob'in), *n.* a bird of the thrush family.

ROBUST (ro-bust'), *adj.* hardy; strong; vigorous; muscular.

ROCK (rok), *n.* a large mass of stone; a movement to and fro.

ROCKET ('et), *n.* a firework fastened to a stick.

ROCK OIL (oil), petroleum.

ROCKY ('i), *adj.* full of rocks; stony; inflexible.

ROD (rod), *n.* a wand; 5½ yards.

RODENT (ro'dent), *adj.* gnawing : *n.* any animal of the Rodentia.

RODENTIA (ro-den'shi-a), *n.* the order consisting of the gnawing mammals, as rats, mice, rabbits, squirrels, beavers, porcupines, etc.

RODEO (ro-da'o), *n.* an exhibition of riding and buck-jumping on bronchos, bulls, etc., by cowboys and women riders.

ROE (ro), *n.* the female of the hart; the spawn of fishes.

ROENTGEN or **RÖNTGEN RAYS** (rent'gen raz), a form of radiant energy, more commonly known as X-rays.

ROGUE (rog), *n.* a dishonest person; knave.

ROGUERY ('er-i), *n.* knavish or dishonest practices.

ROIL (roil), *v.t.* to render turbid; vex or irritate; rile.

ROLE (rol), *n.* a part or character in a play, etc.; function or part.

ROLLER ('er), *n.* a cylinder used for grinding, smoothing, flattening, etc.; long heavy wave.

ROLLICKING (rol'ik-ing), *adj.* jovial; careless; swaggering.

ROLLING (rol'ing), *adj.* moving on, or as on, wheels; undulating.

ROMAN CATHOLIC (kath'o-lik), pertaining to the Church of Rome; a member of the Church of Rome.

ROMANCE (-mans'), *n.* a work of fiction or adventure.

ROMAN NUMERAL (nu'mer-al), a letter representing a number in the Roman system of notation, as I, 1; V, 5; X, 10; L, 50; C, 100; D, 500, etc.

ROMANTIC (-man'tik), *adj.* pertaining to romance; fanciful.

ROMP (romp), *n.* an unrestrained, boisterous girl; play or frolic.

RONDEAU (ron'do), *n.* a little poem.

RONDEL ('del), *n.* a form of French verse in two stanzas.

ROOD (rood), *n.* 40 square poles or perches; a cross or crucifix.

ROOF (roof), *n.* the top covering of a house or other building; canopy.

ROOK (rook), *n.* a bird of the crow family.

ROOKERY ('er-i), *n.* a group of nests on trees where rooks resort; place of low resort.

ROOKIE, ROOKY (-i), *n.* a new recruit.

ROOM (room), *n.* unoccupied place or space; apartment of a house; freedom to act.

ROORBACK (roor'bak), *n.* a lie.

ROOST (roost), *n.* the perch, etc., upon which a bird rests at night.

ROOSTER ('er), *n.* the domestic cock.

ROOT (root), *n.* that part of a plant that descends and fixes itself in the earth; edible root; foundation; basis, or origin.

ROPE (rop), *n.* a thick cord of several strands.

ROPY ('i), *adj.* like a rope; viscous.

ROQUEFORT (rok'fort), *n.* a French mould-streaked cheese.

ROSARY (ro'za-ri), *n.* a garland or chaplet; a string of beads by which prayers are counted.

ROSE (roz), *n.* a hardy shrub of many varieties; the showy, handsome flower of such shrub.

ROSEATE (ro'ze-at), *adj.* rose-coloured; rose-like.

ROSEMARY (roz'ma-ri), *n.* a sweet-smelling evergreen shrub.

ROSETTE (et'), *n.* a cluster of ribbons arranged like a rose.

ROSEWOOD (roz'wood), *n.* a very hard cabinet wood.

ROSILY ('i-li), *adv.* with a rosy glow.

ROSIN (roz'in), *n.* the amber residue left after the distillation of oil of turpentine.

ROSTER (ros'ter), *n.* the list or muster-roll.

ROSTRUM ('trum), *n.* a pulpit or platform.

ROSY (roz'i), *adj.* like a rose; charming; very favourable.

ROT (rot), *v.i.* to putrefy or become decomposed; decay.

ROTARIAN (ro-ta'ri-an), *n.* a member of a Rotary Club.

ROTARY (ro'ta-ri), *adj.* turning on an axis.

ROTARY CLUB (klub), one of an association of the clubs in the U.S. the object of which is to improve civic service.

ROTATE ('tat), *v.t.* to revolve on, or as on, an axis; cause to turn.

ROTATION (-ta'shun), *n.* turning round on an axis; regular succession.

ROTATOR ('ter), *n.* that which imparts a circular motion.

ROTATORY (ro'ta-to-ri), same as rotary.

ROTE (rot), *n.* mechanical repetition, or learning without understanding.

ROTISSERIE (ro-tis-re'), *n.* [French], place where fowls and meats are roasted to order; a restaurant.

ROTTEN (rot'n), *adj.* putrefied; unsound.

ROTUND (ro-tund'), *adj.* spherical.

ROTUNDA (-tun'da), *n.* a circular domed building; a large circular room.

ROUGE (roozh), *n.* a cosmetic for imparting a red tint to cheeks and lips.

ROUGH (ruf), *adj.* rugged; uneven; uncut; unpolished; uncivil; austere; cruel; unfeeling; violent; hard featured; shaggy.

ROUGH HOUSE (house), *v.i.* to create a disturbance; rough play or violence.

ROULETTE (roo-let'), *n.* [French], game of chance.

ROUND (round), *adj.* circular; spherical; globular.

ROUNDABOUT ('a-bout), *adj.* indirect; encompassing.

ROUNDELAY ('de-la), *n.* an ancient song or dance.

ROUND-ROBIN ('rob-bin), *n.* a petition having the signatures written in a circle so as not to show who signed it first.

ROUNDSMAN (roundz'man), *n.* a police officer.

ROUSE (rouz), *v.t.* to awaken; stir to thought or action.

ROUSING ('ing), *p.adj.* stirring; exciting; startling.

ROUST (roust), *v.t.* to disturb.

ROUSTABOUT ('a-bout), *n.* a wharf labourer.

ROUT (rout), *n.* total defeat and flight of an army.

ROUTE (root), *n.* way or road travelled; course; journey.

ROUTINE (roo-ten'), *n.* regular habit or practice.

ROVE (rov), *v.i.* to wander or ramble: *v.t.* draw through an eye.

ROVER ('er), *n.* a wanderer.

ROVING ('ing), *p.adj.* rambling.

ROW (ro), *n.* line; file, or rank: *v.t.* to impel by means of oars.

ROW (rou), *n.* a brawl; noisy disturbance.

ROWDY (rou'di), *adj.* rough *n.* a riotous fellow.

ROWEL ('el), *n.* the small sharp-pointed wheel of a spur.

ROWEN ('en), *n.* aftermath.

ROWLOCK (ro'lok), *n.* the crutch or hollow in the gunwale of a boat which acts as a fulcrum for an oar.

ROYAL (roi'al), *adj.* majestic; kingly; noble; magnificent; excellent of its kind.

ROYALTY ('al-ti), *n.* the character, or status, of a king; a percentage for the use of a patent or copyright work.

RUB (rub), *v.t.* to apply pressure with motion to the surface of.

RUBBER ('er), *n.* one who, or that which, rubs ; caoutchouc or india-rubber.

RUBBISH ('ish), *n.* anything of no value ; nonsense.

RUBBLE ('l), *n.* rough undressed stone.

RUBESCENT (roo-bes'ent), *adj.* becoming red ; flushing.

RUBICUND ('bi-kind), *adj.* inclined to redness ; ruddy.

RUBRICATE ('bri-kat), *v.t.* to mark, or distinguish, with red.

RUBY ('bi), *n.* a precious stone, a size of type.

RUCHE (roosh), *n.* frilled plaited lace, silk, etc.

RUCK (ruk), *v.t.* to wrinkle or crease.

RUCTION ('shun), *n.* a row.

RUDDER (rud'er), *n.* the frame by which a vessel is steered.

RUDDINESS ('i-nes), *n.* redness of complexion.

RUDDY ('i), *adj.* approaching to redness ; florid ; fresh-coloured.

RUDE (rood), *adj.* rough ; barbarous ; uncultivated ; harsh ; unpolite ; crude.

RUDIMENT (roo'di-ment), *n.* first principle ; anything in its first or undeveloped state.

RUDIMENTARY (-men'ta-ri), *adj.* pertaining to, or containing, first principles.

RUE (roo), *v.t.* to lament or be sorry for ; repent of.

RUEFUL ('fool), *adj.* mournful ; sad.

RUFFIAN (ruf'yan), *n.* a brutal, boisterous fellow.

RUFFLE ('l), *v.t.* to wrinkle, pucker, or disarrange ; annoy or vex.

RUG (rug), *n.* a floor covering ; a nappy, woollen cloth, used as a coverlet.

RUGATE (roo'gat), *adj.* wrinkled ; ridged.

RUGGED (rug'ed), *adj.* rough ; shaggy ; brutal ; uncouth.

RUIN (roo'in), *n.* overthrow ; destruction ; downfall ; loss of happiness ; cause of destruction or decay ; ruined building, etc.

RUINOUS ('us), *adj.* decayed ; destructive ; hurtful.

RULE (rool), *n.* standard or guide ; maxim or precept ; law or regulation ; an instrument for drawing lines ; method of performing an operation : *v.t.* to govern or control ; manage or restrain.

RULER ('er), *n.* one who rules or governs ; an instrument.

RUMBLE (rum'bl), *v.i.* to make a low, heavy, continued sound : *n.* an open seat in the back of an automobile.

RUMINANT (roo'mi-nant), *n.* an animal that chews its cud.

RUMINATE ('mi-nat), *v.i.* to chew the cud ; meditate or muse ; ponder.

RUMMAGE (rum'aj), *v.t.* to search carefully for ; ransack.

RUMOUR (roo'mer), *n.* popular report ; current story.

RUMPLE (rum'pl), *v.t.* to fold or plait ; make uneven.

RUMPUS ('pus), *n.* great disturbance.

RUN (run), *v.i.* to pass quickly over the ground ; extend ; move swiftly ; flee for escape ; contend in a race.

RUNABOUT (run'a-bout), *n.* a light, uncovered wagon ; a kind of automobile ; a small, swift motor boat.

RUNG (rung), *n.* step of a ladder.

RUNIC (roo'nik), *n.* the alphabet of the earliest Teutonic nations.

RUNNER (run'er), *n.* one who runs ; racer ; messenger ; support of a sleigh ; roller ; shooting sprig.

RUNNING ('ing), *adj.* moving swiftly ; continuous.

RUNT (runt), *n.* a dwarf animal.

RUPTURE (rup'tur), *n.* the act of bursting or breaking ; state of being broken or violently burst asunder ; breach or interruption of friendly relations ; hernia.

RURAL (roo'ral), *adj.* pertaining to the country.

RUSE (rooz), *n.* a trick ; stratagem.

RUSH (rush), *v.i.* to move or press forward with impetuosity.

RUSK (rusk), *n.* a kind of light, crisp biscuit.

RUSSET (rus'et), *adj.* reddish-brown : *n.* a variety of apple.

RUST (rust), *n.* the reddish matter formed on iron and steel ; mildew on cereals.

RUSTIC (rus'tik), *adj.* pertaining to the country ; rural.

RUSTICATE ('ti-kat), *v.i.* to reside in the country.

RUSTICITY (-tis'i-ti), *n.* rural manners or simplicity.

RUSTLE (rus'l), *v.i.* to make a soft whispering sound, as the rubbing together of silk or dry leaves ; to bestir one's self.

RUSTLER ('ler), *n.* one who rustles ; an enterprising person.

RUSTY (rus'ti), *adj.* covered with rust ; impaired by inactivity.

RUTABAGA (roo-ta-ba'ga), *n.* a variety of turnip.

RUTHFUL (rooth'fool), *adj.* full of sorrow ; causing sorrow.

RUTHLESS ('les), *adj.* cruel ; pitiless.

RYE (ri), *n.* a hardy cereal, closely allied to wheat.

S

S, s (es), *n.* the nineteenth letter of the English alphabet.

S, s, *n.* an abbreviation.

S, *n.* a medieval Roman numeral denoting 7 or 70 ; (with a bar s̄), 70,000.

SABBATH (sab'ath), *n.* the seventh day of the week ; the Christian Sunday.

SABLE (sa'bl), *n.* a kind of weasel valued for its handsome fur.

SABOT (sa-bo'), *n.* a wooden shoe.

SABOTAGE (sa-bo-tazh'), *n.* [French], wanton destruction of employers' property.

SABRE (sa'ber), *n.* a sword having a curved blade.

SAC (sak), *n.* a membranous pouch ; cyst.

SACCHARIN ('a-rin), **SACCHARINE** (-ren), *adj.* pertaining to sugar : *n.* the uncrystallized sugar.

SACCHAROSE ('a-ros), *n.* cane sugar ; any of the group of sugar compounds or carbohydrates.

SACHEM (sa'chem), *n.* a North American Indian chief.

SACHET (sa-sha'), *n.* [French], a small bag filled with a perfume.

SACK (sak), *n.* a bag or pouch, especially a large coarse bag for holding grain, etc. ; loose garment or cloak ; plunder or pillage.

SACKING ('ing), *n.* coarse material used for making sacks ; plundering.

SACRAMENT (sak'ra-ment), *n.* a sign or pledge of grace ; an outward and visible sign of an inward and spiritual grace, instituted by Jesus Christ ; specifically applied to the Lord's Supper.

SACRED (sa'kred), *adj.* pertaining to religion ; consecrated ; inviolable.

SACRIFICE (sak'ri-fis), *n.* destruction or giving up one thing for another ; goods sold at a loss.

SACRILEGE ('ri-lej), *n.* desecration, profanation, or prostitution of something holy.

SACRILEGIOUS (-le'jus), *adj.* violating sacred things ; profane.

SACROSANCT ('ro-sangkt), *adj.* pre-eminently sacred or inviolable.

SAD (sad), *adj.* full of grief.

SADDLE ('l), *n.* a seat for riding on horseback.

SADLY ('li), *adv.* sorrowfully ; miserably.

SADNESS ('nes), *n.* quiet grief ; melancholy.

SAFE (saf), *adj.* free from danger, injury, or damage ; secure from harm; sound ; sure : *n.* a fire- or burglar-proof chest.

SAFEGUARD ('gard), *n.* that which guards or protects.

SAFETY PIN (pin), *n.* a wire clasp-pin.

SAFETY RAZOR (ra'zer), *n.* a razor with a guard.

SAFETY VALVE (valv), *n.* an automatic valve in a boiler set to open under a certain pressure.

SAFFRON (saf'run), *n.* a bulbous plant of the crocus group ; a deep, yellow dye.

SAG (sag), *v.i.* to sink or yield.

SAGA (sa'ga), *n.* a Scandinavian legend, tale, or story.

SAGACIOUS (sa-ga'shus), *adj.* mentally quick; judicious; wise; acute.

SAGACITY (-gas'-i-ti), *n.* discriminative intelligence; acute, practical judgment.

SAGE (saj), *adj.* wise; discerning : *n.* an aromatic herb; a grave philosopher.

SAGE HEN (hen), the female of the sage grouse.

SAGO (sa'go), *n.* a kind of granulated food-starch.

SAIL (sal), *n.* a sheet of canvas spread to catch the wind by means of which a vessel is driven forward in the water : *v.i.* commence a voyage; glide through the air; pass smoothly along.

SAILOR ('er), *n.* a mariner; seaman.

SAINT (sant), *n.* a holy or sanctified person.

ST. NICHOLAS (nik'o-las), Santa Claus.

SAKE (sak), *n.* end; purpose; cause; regard; reason.

SAL (sal), *n.* salt, in chemistry and pharmacy.

SALAAM (sa-lam'), *n.* an Oriental form of salutation.

SALAD (sal'ad), *n.* raw herbs cut up and dressed with vinegar, oil, etc.

SALAMANDER ('a-man-der), *n.* an amphibious animal resembling a lizard.

SAL AMMONIAC (a-mo'ni-ak), a white, crystalline, soluble, ammonium chloride.

SALARIED (sal'a-rid), *p.adj.* having, or receiving, a salary.

SALARY ('a-ri), *n.* recompense; stipend.

SALE (sal), *n.* the act of selling; market; auction; demand.

SALERATUS (sal-e-ra'tus), *n.* sodium bicarbonate.

SALIENT ('li-ent), *adj.* leaping; prominent; conspicuous; projecting : *n.* advanced position in a battle line.

SALIFEROUS (sa-lif'er-us), *adj.* yielding salt; impregnated with salt.

SALINE (sa'lin), *adj.* consisting of, containing, or like, salt.

SALIVA (sa-li'va), *n.* the watery fluid or spittle secreted in the mouth.

SALLOW (sal'o), *adj.* of a pale, sickly, yellow colour.

SALLY ('i), *n.* a sudden rushing forth of troops to attack the besiegers; sudden outburst of wit or fancy.

SALMON (sam'un), *n.* a marine fish which ascends fresh-water rivers to spawn.

SALMON TROUT (trout), *n.* a sea trout.

SALOL (sal'ol), *n.* a colourless crystalline compound prepared from salicylic acid.

SALON (sa-long'), *n.* [French], an apartment for a formal reception; hence, a fashionable assembly; a room or gallery where pictures and objects of art are exhibited.

SALOON (sa-loon'), *n.* a hall or state apartment; large reception room; fine art exhibition; bar-room.

SALPINX (sal'pingks), *n.* a Eustachian tube.

SALSIFY (sal'si-fi), *n.* plant of aster family.

SALT (sawlt), *n.* chloride of sodium, obtained from the earth, or by the evaporation of sea water.

SALTPETRE (-pe'ter), *n.* potassium nitrate; nitre.

SALUBRIOUS (sa-lu'bri-us), *adj.* healthy.

SALUTARY (sal'u-ta-ri), *adj.* healthful; wholesome; beneficent.

SALUTATION (-u-ta'shun), *n.* act or manner of saluting; greeting, or paying respect.

SALUTATORY (sa-lu'ta-to-ri), *adj.* saluting; greeting.

SALUTE (sa-lut'), *n.* a mark of military respect shown by raising the hand to the helmet, etc.; a kiss; greeting; salvo of artillery, lowering of a flag, etc.

SALVABLE (sal'va-bl), *adj.* capable of being saved.

SALVAGE ('vaj), *n.* compensation given to those who assist at saving a vessel or cargo at sea; the goods or vessel saved.

SALVATION (-va'shun), *n.* rescue; spiritual deliverance from sin and death.

SALVATION ARMY (ar'mi), *n.* a religious and charitable organization founded by William Booth.

SALVE (sav), *n.* a healing ointment : *v.t.* to smoothen ; palliate.

SALVER (sal'ver), *n.* a tray on which anything is presented or served.

SALVO ('vo), *n.* a discharge of a number of guns intended as a salute.

SAMARITAN (sa-mar'i-tan), *n.* a native of Samaria : a kind, charitable person.

SAM BROWNE BELT, *n.* belt worn by commissioned officers in World War and later adopted as part of regular uniform.

SAME (sam), *adj.* identical in kind or degree ; exactly alike ; before-mentioned.

SAMOVAR (sam'o-var), *n.* a Russian tea-urn.

SAMPLE ('pl), *n.* a specimen ; model ; pattern.

SANATIVE (san'a-tiv), *adj.* tending to heal or cure.

SANATORIUM (-to'ri-um), *n.* a health retreat.

SANCTIFICATION (sangk-ti-fi-ka'-shun), *n.* state of being sanctified ; consecration.

SANCTIMONIOUS (-ti-mo'ni-us), *adj.* having the appearance of, or affecting, sanctity.

SANCTION ('shun), *n.* the act of giving authority to ; authority ; custom.

SANCTITY ('ti-ti), *n.* purity ; inviolability ; sacredness ; solemnity.

SANCTUARY ('tu-a-ri), *n.* consecrated place ; temple ; part of a church around the altar ; inviolable asylum ; shelter ; refuge.

SANCTUM ('tum), *n.* a sacred or private place ; a room for personal use.

SAND (sand), *n.* fine particles of crushed or worn rock.

SANDAL (san'dal), *n.* a kind of shoe fastened by straps to the foot.

SAND BLAST (blast), *n.* a current of air or steam carrying sand at high velocity, used in etching glass and in cleaning the surfaces of metals, stone buildings, etc.

SANDWICH ('wich), *n.* two thin slices of bread with ham, etc., between ; anything like a sandwich.

SANDY (san'di), *adj.* composed of, abounding in, of the colour of, or covered with sand.

SANE (san), *adj.* mentally sound or healthy.

SANGUINARY ('gwi-na-ri), *adj.* attended with much bloodshed ; murderous.

SANGUINE ('gwin), *adj.* warm and ardent in temper ; hopeful ; confident.

SANITARIUM (-ta'ri-um), *n.* a retreat where the treatment is prophylactic instead of therapeutic.

SANITARY (san'i-ta-ri), *adj.* connected with, or tending to promote, health.

SANITATION (-ta'shun), *n.* practice of making sanitary ; hygiene.

SANITY ('i-ti), *n.* saneness.

SAP (sap), *n.* the watery circulating juice of a plant ; the sap of the Maple : *v.t.* to undermine ; to wear away.

SAPIENCE (sa'pi-ens), *n.* knowledge ; wisdom.

SAPIENT ('pi-ent), *adj.* wise.

SAPLING (sap'ling), *n.* a young tree.

SAPONACEOUS (-o-na'shus), *adj.* resembling, or having the qualities of, soap ; unctuous.

SAPORIFIC (sap-o-rif'ik), *adj.* producing taste or relish.

SAPOROUS ('o-rus), *adj.* having, or stimulating, taste ; savoury.

SAPPER ('er), *n.* a soldier employed in digging tunnels for explosive mines.

SAPPHIRE (saf'ir), *n.* a precious stone of a blue colour.

SAPPY ('i), *adj.* full of sap.

SARCASM (sar'kazm), *n.* a bitter, cutting, satirical expression.

SARCASTIC (-kas'tik), *adj.* bitterly satirical.

SARCOPHAGUS (-kof'a-gus), *n.* a limestone coffin used by the Greeks.

SARDINE (sar-den'), *n.* a species of pilchard (Mediterranean) and preserved in oil for export.

SARDONIC (-don'ik), *adj.* forced,

bitter, or heartless : said of a laugh or smile.

SARDONYX ('do-niks), *n.* a variety of onyx made up of alternate layers of chalcedony and cornelian.

SARSAPARILLA (sar-sa-pa-ril'a), *n.* a tropical American climbing plant.

SASH (sash), *n.* a band, ribbon, or scarf, worn round the waist or over the shoulder ; a frame for holding panes of glass.

SASSAFRAS (sas'a-fras), *n.* a tree allied to the laurel.

SATAN (sa'tan), *n.* the Devil.

SATANIC (-tan'ik), *adj.* diabolical ; very malicious.

SATCHEL (sach'el), *n.* a small bag for carrying small articles.

SATE (sat), *v.t.* to satisfy the appetites or desires of.

SATEEN (sa-ten'), *n.* a fabric in imitation of satin.

SATELITE (sat'e-lit), *n.* a small planet revolving round a larger one ; an obsequious attendant.

SATIABLE (sa'shi-a-bl), *adj.* capable of being gratified or satiated.

SATIATE ('shi-at), *v.t.* to fill ; surfeit ; glut ; *adj.* glutted.

SATIN (sat'in), *n.* a closely woven ; glossy silk.

SATIRE (sat'ir), *n.* sarcasm ; ridicule.

SATIRIST (sat'i-rist), *n.* a writer of satire ; one who satirizes.

SATISFACTION (sat-is-fak'shun), *n.* contentment ; gratification ; payment ; redress ; conviction.

SATISFACTORY ('to-ri), *adj.* giving satisfaction or content ; making redress.

SATISFY ('is-fi), *v.t.* to gratify to the fullest degree ; free from doubt or uncertainty ; pay in full ; discharge.

SATURATE ('u-rat), *v.t.* to soak or imbue.

SATURATION (-ra'shun), *n.* impregnation of one substance by another until the latter can contain no more.

SATURDAY ('er-da), *n.* the seventh day of the week ; the Jewish sabbath.

SATURN (sat'ern), *n.* the planet next in magnitude to Jupiter.

SATURNINE (sat'er-nin), *adj.* dull ; morose ; gloomy.

SAUCE (saws), *n.* a liquid condiment or seasoning for food ; any mixtures used as a relish ; pertness.

SAUCEPAN (-pan), *n.* a small metal pot used in cooking.

SAUCER (saw'ser), *n.* shallow piece of china, etc., in which tea- or coffee-cup is placed.

SAUCY ('si), *adj.* pert ; impudent.

SAUNTER (san'ter, sawn'ter), *v.i.* to wander about idly ; loiter ; linger.

SAUSAGE (saw'saj), *n.* the gut of an animal stuffed with seasoned minced meat.

SAUTERNE (-tern'), *n.* a French white wine.

SAVABLE (sav'a-bl), *adj.* capable of being saved.

SAVAGE (sav'aj), *adj.* uncivilized ; wild ; cruel ; fierce ; pitiless.

SAVAGERY ('aj-ri), *n.* state of being wild or uncivilized.

SAVANNA (sa-van'a), *n.* an extensive open plain ; also *Savannah*.

SAVANT (-vang'), *n.* [French], a man of learning or science.

SAVE (sav), *v.t.* to bring out of danger ; preserve from evil ; rescue ; deliver from spiritual death ; prevent ; lay by.

SAVING (sav'ing), *adj.* preserving ; frugal ; reserving : *pl.* money, etc., saved.

SAVIOUR (sav'yer), *n.* Jesus Christ, the Redeemer (with *the*).

SAVOIR-FAIRE (sa-vwar-far'), *n.* [French], an intuitive knowledge of what is the right thing ; tact.

SAVOR, SAVOUR (sa'ver), *n.* flavour ; taste ; relish ; scent.

SAVORY, SAVOURY ('ver-i), *n.* an aromatic culinary, garden herb ; mint : *adj.* pleasing to the taste, or smell.

SAW (saw), *n.* a cutting steel instrument with a toothed edge ; a proverb or wise saying.

SAXOPHONE (sak'so-fon), *n.* a brass musical, finger-key instrument with a single reed and clarinet mouthpiece.

SAY (sa), *v.t.* to utter in words ; declare ; speak ; decide ; allege ; pronounce.

SAYING ('ing), *n.* the act of speaking; expression; adage.

SCABBARD (skab'ard), *n.* the sheath in which the blade of a sword is kept.

SCAFFOLD (skaf'old), *n.* a temporary timber stage or structure.

SCALAWAG (skal'a-wag), *n.* a scamp; scapegrace.

SCALD (skawld), *v.t.* to burn with hot liquid or steam; expose to violent heat or hot liquid.

SCALE (skal), *n.* the dish of a balance; a balance; the small bony or horny plate of a fish, reptile, or insect; any thin plate or layer; series of musical tones; basis for a numerical system.

SCALLOP (skol'op), *n.* a marine bivalve; an oyster dish: *v.t.* to cut the edge or border of in scallops or curves; bake in a scallop dish.

SCALP (skalp), *n.* the skin on the top of the head.

SCALPER ('per), *n.* one who scalps; a milling machine; a surgeon's instrument; an unofficial dealer in tickets.

SCALY (skal'i), *adj.* covered with, or like, scales; mean; caddish.

SCAMP (skamp), *n.* a rascal; worthless fellow; rogue.

SCAMPER (skam'per), *v.i.* to run with speed; hasten away.

SCAN (skan), *v.t.* to distinguish the metrical structure of a poem; examine by counting the metrical feet or syllables; scrutinize.

SCANDAL ('dal), *n.* offence occasioned by the faults of another; opprobrium; defamation; disgrace.

SCANDALOUS (-us), *adj.* giving offence to the conscience or moral sense.

SCANT (skant), *adj.* not full or abundant; scarcely sufficient.

SCANTLING (skant'ling), *n.* a piece of timber cut or sawn of small size.

SCANTY (skan'ti), *adj.* narrow; barely sufficient; scant.

SCAPE (skap), *n.* the shaft of a column where it leaves the base.

SCAPEGOAT ('got), *n.* one who bears the blame for others.

SCAPEGRACE ('gras), *n.* a graceless, unprincipled fellow.

SCAPULA (skap'u-la), *n.* the shoulder-blade.

SCAR (skar), *n.* a mark caused by a wound; mark or blemish.

SCARAB (skar'ab), *n.* a gem or seal cut in the form of a beetle worn as a charm by the ancient Egyptians.

SCARAMOUCH (skar'a-mouch), *n.* a boastful coward.

SCARCE (skars), *adj.* not common; not plentiful.

SCARCELY ('li), *adv.* seldom.

SCARE (skar), *v.t.* to strike with sudden terror; frighten.

SCARF (skarf), *n.* a light handkerchief or tie; sash.

SCARLATINA (skar-la-te'na), *n.* scarlet fever of a mild form.

SCARLET ('let), *n.* a bright red colour; cloth of such a colour: *adj.* of a scarlet colour.

SCARLET FEVER (fe'ver), contagious febrile disease.

SCARP (skarp), *n.* slope or declivity.

SCARY (ska'ri), *adj.* causing, or subject to, sudden fright.

SCATHE (ska*th*), *v.t.* to injure or hurt.

SCATHING ('ing), *adj.* injurious; hurtful; very severe or bitter.

SCATTER (skat'er), *v.t.* to strew or throw loosely about.

SCAVENGER (skav'enj-er), *n.* a man employed to collect refuse.

SCENARIO (sha-na'ri-o), *n.* [*pl.* scenari (-nar'e)], [Italian], the sketch of a plot or chief incidents of a libretto, moving picture, or play.

SCENE (sen), *n.* part of a play or photoplay; spectacle; exhibition; display of feeling or passion.

SCENERY ('er-i), *n.* the appearance of anything presented to the vision; general aspect.

SCENIC (sen'ik), *adj.* pertaining to scenery; dramatic.

SCENT (sent), *n.* odour; sense of smell.

SCEPTIC (skep'tik), *n.* one who doubts the truth of any doctrine or system.

SCEPTICISM ('ti-sizm), *n.* incredulity; the doctrine that no facts can be known with certainty beyond the range of experience.

SCEPTRE (sep'ter), *n.* a staff borne by a sovereign as the emblem of authority ; royal mace.

SCHEDULE (shed'ul), *n.* a written or printed paper containing a list, or inventory.

SCHEME (skem), *n.* a plan ; contrivance ; purpose ; plot.

SCHISM (sizm), *n.* a split or division, especially permanent division or separation in the Christian Church ; offence of causing such a division.

SCHIST (shist), *n.* any rock that splits into slates or slabs.

SCHOLAR (skol'er), *n.* a student ; disciple ; man of letters ; a person of much learning.

SCHOLARSHIP ('er-ship), *n.* high attainments in literature or science ; learning ; erudition.

SCHOLASTIC (sko-las'tik), *adj.* pertaining to a scholar or schools.

SCHOOL (skool), *n.* a place where instruction is given ; scholars or pupils collectively ; any means of knowledge.

SCHOONER (skoon'er), *n.* a vessel with 2 masts, sometimes more, rigged fore and aft.

SCHOTTISCHE (shot'ish), *n.* a kind of polka.

SCIATIC (si-at'ik), *adj.* pertaining to, or affecting, the hip.

SCIATICA (-at'i-ka), *n.* neuralgia of the sciatic nerve.

SCIENCE ('ens), *n.* systematized knowledge of any one department of mind or matter.

SCIENTIFIC (en-tif'ik), *adj.* pertaining to science ; skilful.

SCIENTIST ('en-tist), *n.* one skilled in, or devoted to, science.

SCIMITAR (sim'i-ter), *n.* an Oriental sword with a curved blade.

SCINTILLA (sin-til'a), *n.* a spark ; the least trace.

SCINTILLATE (sin'til-at), *v.i.* to emit sparks, fire, or igneous particles ; twinkle.

SCION (si'on), *n.* the sprout or shoot of a plant ; a descendant ; heir.

SCISSORS (siz'erz), *n.pl.* a cutting instrument resembling shears, but smaller.

SCOFF (skof), *n.* an expression of scorn or contempt ; ridicule; derision.

SCOLD (skold), *v.i.* to chide sharply or rudely ; rail in a loud or violent manner.

SCOOP (skoop), *n.* a large ladle ; deep shovel ; kind of scuttle ; a big gain in speculation ; a newspaper beat.

SCOOT (skoot), *v.i.* to walk or run hastily.

SCOPE (skop), *n.* room or opportunity for free outlook or action ; aim or intention.

SCORCH (skorch), *v.t.* to burn or roast slightly ; parch, shrivel, or affect painfully with heat.

SCORCHER ('er), *n.* something that scorches ; a hot, blistering day ; one who travels at a high rate of speed.

SCORE (skor), *n.* a notch or incision, especially one made as a reckoning ; the number 20 ; bill ; account ; behalf ; sake ; reason ; copy of a small musical work showing the component parts.

SCORN (skorn), *n.* extreme and lofty contempt ; haughty disdain.

SCORPION (skor'pi-un), *n.* an arachnid or arthropod with a poisonous sting.

SCOTCH (skoch), *n.* the people of Scotland ; their dialects.

SCOTCH (skoch), *n.* a wedge, etc., to prevent slipping or rolling : *v.t.* to cut or wound superficially.

SCOUNDREL (skoun'drel), *n.* a man without honour or virtue.

SCOUR (skour), *v.t.* to clean by friction ; cleanse from grease, etc. ; pass swiftly along ; search thoroughly.

SCOURGE (skerj), *n.* a whip with thongs used as a punishment.

SCOUT (skout), *n.* a person sent out to obtain and bring in information, especially of the movements, etc., of an enemy ; a boy scout, or a girl scout.

SCOW (skou), *n.* a large flat-bottomed boat.

SCOWL (skoul), *v.i.* to wrinkle the brows in frowning or displeasure ; look sullen or angry.

SCRAG (skrag), *n.* anything thin, lean, or rough.

SCRAGGY ('i), *adj.* lean ; thin ; unkempt ; rough.

SCRAMBLE (skram'bl), *v.i.* to clamber with the hands and feet ; seize or catch hold of anything with eagerness ; mix and cook in a confused mass as, to *scramble* eggs ; *n.* a rude, eager struggle.

SCRANCH (skranch), *v.t.* to grind with the teeth ; crunch.

SCRAP (skrap), *n.* a small or detached piece ; fragment.

SCRAPE (skrap), *v.t.* to rub with something sharp ; clean by rubbing ; remove by scraping.

SCRATCH (skrach), *v.t.* to mark or tear the surface of, with something pointed ; wound slightly ; tear or dig with the claws ; erase.

SCRAWL (skrawl), *v.t. & v.i.* to write or draw irregularly or hastily ; scribble.

SCRAWNY (skraw'ni), *adj.* thin ; lean ; raw-boned ; skinny.

SCREAK (skrek), *n.* a shriek ; screech.

SCREAM (skrem), *n.* a sharp, shrill cry, as of fear or pain.

SCREECH (skrech), *n.* a harsh, shrill cry.

SCREED (skred), *n.* a loud, shrill sound ; a fragment or piece ; a harangue ; a piece of poor prose or verse.

SCREEN (skren), *n.* a light movable partition for protection ; coarse sieve ; the sheet upon which moving pictures are thrown.

SCREW (skroo), *n.* a cylinder of metal or wood grooved spirally ; one of the six mechanical powers ; screw-propeller ; an extortioner; a skinflint.

SCRIBBLE (skrib'l), *v.t.* to write hastily and carelessly.

SCRIBE (skrib), *n.* a writer ; clerk ; amanuensis.

SCRIM (skrim), *n.* a kind of fabric of cotton or linen for making blinds, etc.

SCRIMMAGE ('aj), *n.* a general row or tussle.

SCRIMP (skrimp), *v.t.* to make small, narrow, or short ; limit or straiten : *v.i.* to be parsimonious.

SCRIP (skrip), *n.* a satchel ; schedule ; certificate ; writing.

SCRIPT (skript), *n.* a piece of writing ; style of writing ; type if imitation of writing.

SCRIPTURAL (skrip'tur-al), *adj.* pertaining to, contained in, or according to, the Scriptures ; Biblical.

SCRIPTURE ('tur), *n.* sacred writing ; biblical text : *pl.* [S-], the books of the Old and New Testaments : the Bible.

SCRIVENER (skriv'ner), *n.* one who draws up contracts, prepares writings, etc.

SCROFULA (skrof'u-la), *n.* a disease caused by the formation and deposition of tubercles in the organs and tissues of the body.

SCROLL (skrol), *n.* a roll of paper or parchment.

SCRUB (skrub), *v.t.* to rub hard ; wash with rubbing or a wet brush.

SCRUBBY ('i), *adj.* stunted in growth.

SCRUFF (skruf), *n.* the back of the neck.

SCRUPLE (skroo'pl), *n.* $\frac{1}{3}$ of a dram, or 20 grains ; hesitation, especially from conscientious motives.

SCRUPULOUS ('pu-lus), *adj.* full of scruples ; conscientious ; exact ; careful ; strict.

SCRUTINIZE ('ti-niz), *v.t.* to inspect or examine closely.

SCRUTINY ('ti-ni), *n.* close inspection or examination.

SCUD (skud), *v.i.* to run quickly ; run before a gale of wind with little or no sail spread.

SCUFF (skuf), *v.t.* to soil by wear ; mar.

SCUFFLE (skuf'l), *v.i.* to fight or struggle confusedly.

SCULL (skul), *n.* one of a pair of short oars ; an oar used at the stern of a boat to propel it.

SCULLERY ('er-i), *n.* a place where culinary utensils, etc., are kept.

SCULPTOR (skulp'ter), *n.* one who practices the art of sculpture. *Fem.* sculptress.

SCULPTURAL ('tu-ral), *adj.* pertaining to sculpture.

SCULPTURE ('tur), *n.* the art of carving, cutting, or hewing stone or other material into images, etc.

SCUM (skum), *n.* impurities which rise to the surface of liquid when boiled or fermented.

SCUP (skup), *n.* a marine food fish.

SCUPPER (skup'er), *n.* a hole or drain in the side of a ship to carry off deck water.

SCURF (skerf), *n.* minute, white, flaky scales formed on the skin; dandruff.

SCURRILE (skur'il), *adj.* grossly opprobrious.

SCURRILOUS (skur'i-lus), *adj.* mean; foul-mouthed; vile : containing low indency or abuse.

SCURRY (skur'i), *v.i.* to hasten or move rapidly along.

SCURVY ('vi), *adj.* scabby; vile; contemptible; mean; paltry: *n.* a disease.

SCUTCHEON (skuch'un), *n.* an escutcheon; shield for a keyhole.

SCUTTLE (skut'l), *v.i.* to hasten or hurry: *v.t.* to cut a hole or holes in (a ship) to sink it: *n.* a pail for holding coals; lid or door in a roof, etc., hatchway.

SCYTHE (sith), *n.* a curved cutting instrument, used for mowing grass, etc.

SEA (se), *n.* an expanse of salt water, less in extent than an ocean; a billow or large wave.

SEABOARD (-bord), *n.* the country bordering the sea-coast.

SEAFARER ('fa-rer), *n.* a mariner.

SEAL (sel), *n.* a carnivorous marine mammal; a stamp or die.

SEA LION (li'un), *n.* one of various large-eared seals.

SEALSKIN (-skin), *n.* the skin of the fur seal; a jacket or cape of this material.

SEAM (sem), *n.* the line formed by the sewing of two pieces of material together; thin layer.

SEAMAN (se'man), *n.* a sailor.

SEAMANSHIP (-ship), *n.* skill in navigation.

SEAMSTRESS (sem'stres), *n.* a needle-woman.

SEANCE (sa'ans; Fr. sa-angs'), *n.* [French], a session as of some deliberate body; a meeting of spiritualists.

SEAR, SERE (ser), *adj.* withered; dried up: *v.t.* to wither; dry up; scorch; cauterize.

SEARCH (serch), *v.t.* to seek for; go over and examine; explore.

SEARCHLIGHT ('lit), *n.* a strong electric arclight with reflector, set in a swivel.

SEARED (serd), *adj.* callous; cauterized.

SEASON (se'zn), *n.* any particular time as distinguished from others; one of the four divisions of the year: *v.t.* to mature; render palatable.

SEASONABLE (-a-bl), *adj.* occurring or done in good, or proper time; opportune.

SEASONING (-ing), *n.* that which is added to give relish to food.

SEAT (set), *n.* that on which anyone sits; chair; post of authority; residence.

SEAWEED (-wed), *n.* any plant growing in the sea.

SECEDE (se-sed'), *v.i.* to withdraw from fellowship, communion, or association.

SECESSION (-sesh'un), *n.* the act of seceding.

SECESSIONIST (-ist), *n.* an upholder of secession; one who took part with the Southern States of America in the Civil War, 1861-65.

SECKEL (sek'l), *n.* a small pear of a reddish-brown colour.

SECLUDE (se-klood'), *v.t.* to keep apart from the society of others; exclude.

SECLUSION (-kloo'zhun), *n.* privacy.

SECOND (sek'und), *adj.* next to the first in order of place, or time; next in value, excellence, merit, dignity, or importance; inferior: *n.* the 60th part of a minute of time, or of a degree: *pl.* not of 1st quality.

SECONDARY ('un-da-ri), *adj.* succeeding; next in order to the first.

SECONDHAND (-hand), *adj.* not new; received after being used.

SECRECY (se'kre-si), *n.* concealment ; retirement ; solitude ; discretion.

SECRET ('kret), *adj.* hidden or concealed silent ; private.

SECRETARIAL (sek-re-ta'ri-al), *adj.* pertaining to, or befitting, a secretary.

SECRETARY ('re-ta-ri), *n.* a confidential person employed to assist another in business, etc. ; one who transacts the business of a government department, company, etc. ; an escritoire.

SECRETE (se-kret'), *v.t.* to hide, or conceal.

SECRETION (-kre'shun), *n.* any substance or fluid secreted.

SECRETIVE ('tiv), *adj.* given to secrecy.

SECT (sekt), *n.* persons united by a common attachment to some particular doctrine.

SECTARIAN (sek-ta'ri-an), *adj.* pertaining to a sect.

SECTION ('shun), *n.* part or division ; slice ; division or subdivision of a chapter or statute ; distinct part of a country, people, community, or class ; one of the squares (640 acres) into which public lands are divided.

SECTOR ('ter), *n.* that part of a circle included between two radii and the arc.

SECULAR ('u-lar), *adj.* pertaining to this present world, or to things not sacred ; worldly ; temporal.

SECUND (se'kund), *adj.* unilateral.

SECURE (se-kur'), *v.t.* to make safe ; protect ; guarantee ; make fast ; confine effectually ; gain possession of ; put beyond hazard of losing or not receiving (with *against* or *from*).

SECURITY ('i-ti), *n.* freedom from fear or danger ; assurance ; certainty ; something given to secure the fulfilment of a contract ; pledge ; evidence of debt.

SEDAN (-dan), *n.* a covered chair ; a style of inclosed automobile.

SEDATE (-dat'), *adj.* calm ; composed ; quiet ; serious ; unruffled.

SEDATIVE (sed'a-tiv), *adj.* allaying nervous irritation and irritability : *n.* medicine having such an effect.

SEDENTARY ('en-ta-ri), *adj.* accustomed to pass much time in a sitting posture ; inactive.

SEDGE (sej), *n.* a coarse grass growing in swamps and on the banks of rivers.

SEDIMENT (sed'i-ment), *n.* the matter which settles at the bottom of a liquid ; dregs.

SEDITION (se-dish'un), *n.* any offence against the state less grave than insurrection or treason.

SEDITIOUS ('us), *adj.* pertaining to sedition.

SEDUCE (-dus'), *v.t.* to entice from the paths of rectitude, duty, or virtue, etc.

SEDUCTION (-duk'shun), *n.* the act of seducing.

SEDULOUS (sed'u-lus), *adj.* steadily industrious and persevering in business, or endeavour ; diligent ; untiring.

SEED (sed), *n.* that part of a plant that contains the embryo of the future plant : *v.i.* to sow, as with seed.

SEEDY ('i), *adj.* abounding with, or run to, seeds ; having the flavour of weeds ; shabby ; exhausted and miserable.

SEEING (se'ing), *n.* the act of power of sight : *conj.* inasmuch as ; considering ; since.

SEEK (sek), *v.t.* to go in search of ; look for ; resort to ; inquire for.

SEEM (sem), *v.i.* to appear ; look ; have the resemblance of truth or fact ; pretend.

SEEMLINESS ('li-nes), *n.* propriety ; decency ; comeliness.

SEEMLY ('li), *adj.* fit or becoming ; decent ; proper ; comely.

SEEP (sep), *v.i.* to ooze out slowly.

SEER (ser), *n.* one who foresees future events.

SEETHE (seth), *v.t.* to boil.

SEGMENT (seg'ment), *n.* a part divided or set off ; section.

SEGREGATE (seg're-gat), *v.t.* to separate from others.

SEIDLITZ (sed'lits), *adj.* designating the alkaline waters of Seidlitz, Bohemia.

SEINE (san), *n.* a large fishing-net.

SEISMIC (sis'mik), **SEISMICAL** (-mi-kal), *adj.* pertaining to, or produced by, an earthquake.

SEISMOGRAPH ('mo-graf), *n.* an instrument for recording the undulatory motions, durations, and direction of earthquakes.

SEISMOLOGY (-mol'o-ji), *n.* the scientific study of earthquakes.

SEIZABLE (sez'a-bl), *adj.* capable of being seized.

SEIZE (sez), *v.t.* to take possession of forcibly or suddenly; grasp; snatch; comprehend.

SEIZURE ('zhur), *n.* the act of seizing; sudden attack, as of a disease.

SELDOM (sel'dum), *adv.* rarely; not often.

SELECT (se-lekt'), *adj.* more valuable or excellent than others; choice; superior.

SELF (self), *n.* one's own person; personal interest; personality.

SELFISH (sel'fish), *adj.* attentive only to one's own interests; egotistical.

SELFISHNESS (-nes), *n.* regardless of the interests of others.

SELL (sel), *v.t.* to transfer to another for an equivalent, as property, goods, etc.; vend.

SELTZER (selt'zer), *n.* an effervescing mineral water.

SELVAGE (sel'vaj), *n.* the edge of cloth so closed by weaving as to prevent ravelling.

SEMAPHORE (sem'a-for), *n.* a mechanical apparatus for signalling by means of arms, lanterns, flags, etc.

SEMBLANCE (sem'blans), *n.* likeness; resemblance.

SEMESTER (se-mes'ter), *n.* a period or term of six months; a college term.

SEMICOLON (sem'i-ko'lon), *n.* a mark in punctuation (;).

SEMINAL ('i-nal), *adj.* pertaining to seed; primary; radical; original.

SEMINARY (sem'i-na-ri), *n.* a place of education; school, academy.

SENATE (sen'at), *n.* the upper house of Congress, or of a State legislature.

SENATOR ('a-ter), *n.* a member of a senate.

SEND (send), *v.t.* to throw, cast, or impel; cause to go in any manner; dispatch.

SENDER ('der), *n.* a telephonic or telegraphic transmitter; one who sends.

SENILE (se'nil), *adj.* pertaining to old age.

SENIOR (sen'yer), *adj.* prior in age, dignity, rank or office; elder: *n.* a student in the fourth year of his college.

SENSATE (sen'sat), *adj.* perceived by, or through, the senses.

SENSATION (-sa'shun), *n.* perception by the senses.

SENSE (sens), *n.* discernment; understanding; conviction; correct judgment; opinion; meaning; signification; moral perception.

SENSELESS (les), *adj.* incapable of sensation; unconscious; foolish; stupid.

SENSIBILITY (sen-si-bil'i-ti), *n.* acuteness of perception or emotion; delicacy of feeling.

SENSIBLE ('si-bl), *adj.* capable of being perceived by the senses or the mind; judicious; reasonable; intelligent.

SENSITIVE (-tiv), *adj.* having keen sense or feeling; easily affected or moved.

SENSUAL ('shu-al), *adj.* pertaining to the senses; not spiritual or intellectual; carnal.

SENTENCE ('tens), *n.* judgment, opinion, or decision; series of words so arranged as to convey a determinate sense or meaning.

SENTENTIOUS (-ten'shus), *adj.* short and energetic; terse; abounding in maxims.

SENTIENT ('shi-ent), *adj.* having faculties of sensation and perception.

SENTIMENT ('ti-ment), *n.* a thought; feeling; sensibility; emotion; regard; opinion.

SENTINEL ('ti-nel), *n.* one who watches or guards.

SENTRY ('tri), *n.* a sentinel.

SEPARABLE (sep'a-ra-bl), *adj.* capable of being separated or divided.

SEPARATE ('a-rat), *v.t.* to part or

divide; disunite; disconnect; distinct.

SEPARATION (-ra'shun), *n.* disconnection; legal disunion of married persons.

SEPARATOR (-ter), *n.* one who, or that which, separates.

SEPTEMBER (sep-tem'ber), *n.* ninth month of the year.

SEPTENNIAL (ten'i-al), *adj.* occurring once in, or containing, seven years.

SEPTET, SEPTETTE (-tet'), *n.* a musical composition for seven voices; a group of seven persons.

SEPTIC ('tik), *adj.* having the power to promote putrefaction.

SEPTILLION (-til'yun) *n.* in France and U.S. a number expressed by unity with 24 ciphers; in England, a number expressed by unity with 42 ciphers.

SEPTUAGENARIAN (-tu-a-je-na'ri-an), *n.* a person seventy years old.

SEPTUAGESIMA (-a-jes'i-ma), *n.* the third Sunday before Lent.

SEPTUAGINT ('tu-a-jint), *n.* the Greek version of the Old Testament.

SEPULCHRE ('ul-ker), *n.* a grave or tomb; place of burial.

SEQUEL (se'kwel) *n.* succeeding part or result; continuation; consequence.

SEQUENCE (se'kwens), *n.* order of succession; series; result.

SEQUESTER (-kwes'ter), *v.t.* to separate from the owner for a time.

SEQUESTERED ('terd), *adj.* secluded; retired.

SERAPHIC (-raf'ik), *adj.* sublime; angelic.

SERE (ser), *adj.* dry; withered.

SERENADE ('e-nad), *n.* evening music in the open air: *v.t.* to entertain with a serenade.

SERENE (se-ren'), *adj.* clear and calm; placid; unruffled.

SERENITY (-ren'i-ti), *n.* calmness of mind; equanimity of temper; coolness; composure.

SERF (serf), *n.* a slave of the soil, in the Middle Ages.

SERGE (serj), *n.* a twilled woollen stuff.

SERGEANT (sar'jent), *n.* a non-commissioned officer ranking next above a corporal; a police officer of superior rank.

SERGEANT AT ARMS (armz), an official of an assembly who preserves order.

SERIAL (se-ri-al), *adj.* pertaining to a series.

SERIATIM (-a'tim), *adv.* in regular order.

SERIES ('rez), *n.* a number of things or events standing or succeeding in order; sequence.

SERIO-COMIC (-ri-o-kom'ik), *adj.* having a mixture of seriousness and comicality.

SERIOUS ('ri-us), *adj.* grave in manner or disposition; in earnest.

SERMON (ser'mun), *n.* a discourse on a text of Scripture; homily.

SERPENT (ser'pent), *n.* a large snake.

SERRATE ('at), *adj.* notched on the edge like a saw.

SERRIED ('id), *adj.* crowded.

SERUM (se'rum), *n.* the thin, yellowish, watery fluid secreted of the serous membranes.

SERVANT (ser'vant), *n.* one who serves; a domestic.

SERVE (serv), *v.t.* to work for; perform duties for; worship; supply with, as food, etc.

SERVICE (ser'vis), *n.* duty required or performed in any office; spiritual obedience and reverence; course of dishes at table; assistance, or kindness to another.

SERVILE ('vil), *adj.* meanly submissive or obsequious.

SERVILITY (-vil'i-ti), *n.* obsequiousness; baseness.

SESQUI- (ses'kwi-), a combining form signifying *one and a half times.*

SESQUICENTENNIAL (sen-ten'i-al), *adj.* of, or pertaining to, a century and a half.

SESSION (sesh'un), *n.* the actual sitting or assembling of a court, council, or legislative body.

SETTEE (se-te'), *n.* a long seat with a back for several persons.

SETTLE (set'l), *v.t.* to place or set in a fixed state; establish; cause to sink or subdue; free from uncertainty ; compose ; fix by a legal act ; liquidate ; pay ; clear of dregs ; colonize.

SETTLEMENT (-ment), *n.* establishment in life or business ; condition ; jointure granted to a wife ; liquidation ; a colony newly settled.

SETTLER ('ler), *n.* a colonist.

SEVER (sev'er), *v.t.* to divide or separate with violence ; keep distinct or apart.

SEVERAL ('er-al), *adj.* distinct ; separate ; consisting of a number, but not many ; various.

SEVERANCE (-ans), *n.* separation ; partition.

SEVERE (se-ver'), *adj.* strict ; austere ; rigid ; harsh ; grave ; serious ; inclement ; inflexible ; painful ; critical.

SEVERITY ('i-ti), *n.* the quality of being severe ; harshness ; rigour ; inclemency.

SEW (so), *v.t.* to unite or fasten together with a needle and thread.

SEWAGE (su'aj), *n.* the wastage carried off by a sewer.

SEX (seks), *n.* the physical distinction between male and female.

SEXAGENARIAN (-sa-je-na'ri-an),*n.* one who is sixty years old.

SEX HYGIENE (hi-jen'), the conservation of functions peculiar to each sex, especially those concerning the birth of children.

SEXTANT ('tant), *n.* the sixth part of a circle ; an instrument for measuring angular distances between objects.

SEXTON ('tun), *n.* an under official of a church whose duty is to attend to the building, funerals, etc.

SEXTUPLE ('tu-pl), *adj.* sixfold : *v.t.* to multiply by six.

SEXUAL (sek'shu-al), *adj.* pertaining to sex.

SHABBY (shab'i), *adj.* threadbare or worn, as clothes.

SHACK (shak), *n.* a hut ; log cabin ; a tramp.

SHACKLE (shak'l), *n.* anything that confines the hands or legs ; fetters.

SHADE (shad), *n.* graduation of light ; screen or cover.

SHADOW ('o), *n.* shade within defined limits ; dark part of a picture.

SHADOWY ('o-i), *adj.* full of shadows; dim ; unreal ; typical.

SHADY (shad'i), *adj.* sheltered from the glare of light or heat.

SHAFT (shaft), *n.* an arrow ; entrance to a mine ; carriage-pole ; handle.

SHAGGY (shag'i), *adj.* rough with long hair or wool ; rugged.

SHAKE (shak), *v.t.* to cause to shiver ; move with a quick, short motion ; agitate ; vibrate.

SHAKESPEARIAN (shak-sper'i-an), *adj.* pertaining to Shakespeare.

SHAKY (shak'i), *adj.* in a shaking condition ; feeble ; unsound.

SHALE (shal), *n.* a husk ; a laminated, argillaceous rock.

SHALL (shal), *v.i.* aim to ; are to ; denoting simple futurity ; are, or art, to ; is to ; denoting obedience to a command or promise.

SHALLOW ('o), *adj.* having little depth ; superficial ; trifling.

SHAM (sham), *n.* a fraud, or make-believe ; imposture.

SHAMBLE (sham'bl), *v.i.* to walk awkwardly and unsteadily : *n.pl.* a slaughter-house.

SHAME (sham), *n.* a painful sensation caused by the sense of guilt, impropriety ; reproach incurred or suffered.

SHAMEFUL ('fool), *adj.* disgraceful ; indecent.

SHAMPOO (-poo'), *v.t.* to wash and rub scalp and hair with soap, etc.

SHAMROCK ('rok), *n.* a trefoil clover plant ; the Irish emblem.

SHANGHAI (shang'hi), *n.* one of a breed of poultry : *v.t.* to drug a person so as to ship him as a sailor.

SHANK (shangk), *n.* the leg from the knee to the ankle.

SHANTY (shan'ti), *n.* a rude hut.

SHAPE (shap), *n.* the form of anything.

SHAPELY ('li), *adj.* symmetrical.

SHARE (shar), *n.* a portion or part.

SHARK (shark), *n.* a large, voracious fish.

SHARP (sharp), *adj.* having a very thin edge or fine point ; keen ; acute ; subtle : *n.* a character in music which raises a note a semitone.

SHATTER (shat'er), *v.t.* to break into many pieces at once.

SHAVE (shav), *v.t.* to cut or pare off with a razor or other sharp-edged instrument ; cut in thin slices.

SHAWL (shawl), *n.* a square cloth of various materials used as a loose outer covering.

SHE (she), *pron.* an object personified as feminine ; a female.

SHEAF (shef), *n.* a quantity of grain bound together ; a bundle.

SHEAR (sher), *v.t.* to cut or clip ; reap : *n.pl.* a cutting instrument.

SHEATH (sheth), *n.* a scabbard.

SHEATHE (she*th*), *v.t.* encase with a protecting covering.

SHED (shed), *v.t.* to pour off or diffuse : *n.* a building with front or sides open.

SHEEN (shen), *n.* brightness ; splendour.

SHEEP (shep), *n., s. & pl.* a ruminant animal.

SHEER (sher), *adj.* pure ; unmixed ; precipitous.

SHEET (shet), *n.* a large thin slice of anything ; bedcovering ; broad piece of paper ; letter ; newspaper.

SHEIK (shek, shak), *n.* an Arabian chief ; a beau Brummel.

SHEKEL (shek'el), *n.* an ancient Jewish coin, or weight.

SHELF (shelf), *n.* a flat ledge or board for holding anything.

SHELL (shel), *n.* a hard outside covering ; a hollow projectile.

SHELLAC (she-lak'), *n.* crude resin lac.

SHELTER (shel'ter), *n.* security ; asylum ; harbour ; defence.

SHELVE (shelv), *v.t.* to place on a shelf ; dismiss from service; postpone.

SHEPHERD (shep'erd), *n.* one who tends sheep.

SHERIFF (sher'if), *n.* the chief court officer of a county.

SHEW. Same as show.

SHIBBOLETH (ship'o-leth), *n.* the test-word of a party ; a watchword.

SHIELD (sheld), *n.* a broad piece of defensive armour ; defence or protection.

SHIFT (shift), *n.* a change ; substitution ; a chemise.

SHIFTLESS ('les), *adj.* improvident.

SHILLING (shil'ing), *n.* a British coin equal in value to twelve pennies.

SHIMMER (shim'er), *v.t.* to shine unsteadily or tremulously.

SHIMMY (shimmy), *n.* a chemise ; a dance.

SHIN (shin), *n.* the forepart of the leg below the knee.

SHINDY ('di), *n.* [Slang], an uproar.

SHINE (shin), *v.i.* to emit rays of light ; be bright or beautiful.

SHINGLE (shing'gl), *n.* a thin piece of wood used for roofing ; gravel : *pl.* a cutaneous disease.

SHINY (shin'i), *adj.* diffusing light ; glossy.

SHIP (ship), *n.* any large marine vessel.

SHIPPING ('ing), *n.* act of sending or conveying ; ships collectively.

SHIPSHAPE ('shap), *adj.* in good order : *adv.* neatly.

SHIPWRECK (-rek), *n.* total, or partial, loss of a ship at sea.

SHIRK (sherk), *v.t.* to avoid.

SHIVER (shiv'er), *n.* a tremor or quivering from fear, cold, etc.

SHOCK (shok), *n.* violent agitation of feeling ; impact ; collision ; disturbance of mind ; grain, in cocks.

SHOCKING ('ing), *adj.* extremely offensive or horrifying.

SHODDY (shod'i), *n.* any goods of inferior material : *adj.* not genuine.

SHOE (shoo), *n.* a low covering for the foot.

SHOOT (shoot), *v.t.* to discharge a firearm : *n.* a young branch.

SHOP (shop), *n.* a building where goods are sold ; place where mechanics work.

SHORE (shor), *n.* the land bordering the sea or waterway ; a prop or support.

SHORT (short), *adj.* not long ; inadequate ; defective ; deficient ; abrupt ; petulant ; brief.

SHORTHAND ('hand), *n.* a system of writing by abbreviated symbols.

SHOULD, preterit tense of *shall*.

SHOULDER (shol'der), *n.* the joint connecting the human arm, or the foreleg of a quadruped, to the body.

SHOUT (shout), *n.* a loud and sudden

cry of joy, triumph, encouragement, warning, etc.

SHOVE (shuv), n. forcible push.

SHOVEL (′l), n. an implement for lifting and throwing coal, etc.

SHOW (sho), v.t. to present to view; display; disclose; make clear; guide; direct; teach : v.i. to appear; manifest one's self : n. exhibition or spectacle.

SHOWER (shou′er), n. a fall of rain or hail of short duration.

SHRAPNEL (shrap′nel), n. a projectile filled with bullets and a bursting charge.

SHRED (shred), n. a long narrow piece torn or cut off; piece or fragment.

SHREW (shroo), n. a vexatious woman; a small, burrowing animal, resembling a mouse.

SHREWD (shrood), adj. sharp-witted or clever in practical affairs; sagacious; sly; astute.

SHREWISH (shroo′ish), adj. like a shrew.

SHRIEK (shrek), n. a sharp, shrill cry.

SHRILL (shril), adj. sharp and piercing in tone.

SHRIMP (shrimp), n. a small shell-fish allied to the lobster; anything very small of its kind; a dwarf.

SHRINE (shrin), n. a case in which sacred relics are deposited; any sacred place.

SHRINK (shringk), v.i. to contract spontaneously; become wrinkled; withdraw; recoil.

SHRIVEL (shriv′l), v.i. to be drawn into wrinkles; contract.

SHROUD (shroud), n. a winding sheet or covering for the dead : pl. a set of large ropes supporting the masts.

SHROVE, p.t. of shrive.

SHRUB (shrub), n. a woody plant of less size than a tree.

SHRUBBERY (′er-i), n. a collection of shrubs.

SHRUG (shrug), v.t. to contract or draw up (the shoulders) to express doubt, contempt, dislike, etc.

SHUCK (shuck), n. a shell or husk.

SHUDDER (shud′er), n. a trembling with fear or horror; cold shivering.

SHUFFLE (shuf′l), v.t. to push from one to another; change the relative positions of; prevaricate : n. artifice or evasion; slovenly, irregular gait.

SHUN (shun), v.t. to avoid; keep clear of; escape from; neglect; decline.

SHUNT (shunt), n. a turning off to a side rail: v.t. to turn off a train.

SHUT (shut), v.t. to close so as to prevent entrance or exit; exclude.

SHUTTER (′er), n. a movable screen for a window.

SHUTTLE (′l), n. an instrument used in weaving; sliding thread-holder in a sewing machine.

SHY (shi), adj. timid; cautious; reserved; suspicious; modest.

SHYSTER (′ster), n. one of a profession who conducts business in a mean and tricky manner.

SIBYL (′il), n. a seeress.

SICK (sik), adj. ill in health; affected with nausea; indisposed.

SICKLE (′l), n. a reaping hook.

SIDEREAL (si-de′re-al), adj. pertaining to the stars; astral.

SIDEREAL YEAR (yer), the time occupied by the earth in completing its revolution round the sun.

SIDING (sid′ing), n. a railroad track by the side of the main track.

SIEGE (sej), n. the investing of a place by an army to compel its surrender.

SIERRA (si-er′a), n. a chain of mountains with serrated ridges.

SIESTA (-es′ta), n. midday nap.

SIEVE (siv), n. a utensil for separating the finer from the coarser parts of a substance.

SIFT (sift), v.t. to separate with, or as with, a sieve.

SIGH (si), v.i. to inhale and respire with a deep, audible breathing; grieve; lament.

SIGHT (sit), n. the act of seeing; perception; judgment; spectacle; view.

SIGN (sin), n. mark, token, or symbol; indication; omen; wonder; sign-board.

SIGNAL (sig′nal), n. a sign for giving notice at a distance : adj. memorable; distinguished; remarkable.

SIGNALIZE (-iz), *v.t.* to make especially conspicuous.

SIGNATORY ('na-to-ri), *adj.* signing : *n.* one who signs or subscribes.

SIGNATURE ('na-tur), *n.* name of a person written by himself.

SIGNET (sig'net), *n.* a seal.

SIGNIFICANCE (-nif'i-kans), *n.* meaning or import ; consequence.

SIGNIFY ('ni-fi), *v.t.* to show by a sign, mark, or token ; denote ; make known ; manifest.

SILAGE, same as ensilage.

SILENCE (si'lens), *n.* entire absence of sound ; taciturnity ; obscurity ; oblivion.

SILENT ('lent), *adj.* noiseless ; quiet.

SILEX (si'leks), *n.* flint.

SILHOUETTE (sil-oo-et'), *n.* the outline or profile filled in with black.

SILICON ('i-kon), *n.* a non-metallic element.

SILK (silk), *n.* a fine, soft, tenacious thread, spun by certain caterpillars.

SILKINESS (sil'ki-nes), *n.* the quality of being silky.

SILL (sil), *n.* the foundation of anything in timber or stone, especially the piece at the bottom of a door or window.

SILLILY ('i-li), *adv.* foolishly.

SILLY ('i), *adj.* weak in intellect ; foolish ; indiscreet.

SILO (si'lo), *n.* a store pit, for packing green fodder, etc.

SILT (silt), *n.* mud or sand deposited by running or standing water.

SILVER (sil'ver), *n.* a metallic element, used for coins and articles of plate, etc ; money.

SIMIAN (sim'i-an), *adj.* pertaining to, characteristic of, or like an ape.

SIMILAR ('i-lar), *adj.* having a general likeness ; alike.

SIMILARITY (-lar'i-ti), *n.* resemblance.

SIMILE ('i-le), *n.* a likening by comparison to illustrate something.

SIMMER ('er), *v.t. & v.i.* to boil gently.

SIMONY (sim'o-ni), *n.* buying or selling ecclesiastical preferment ; traffic in anything sacred.

SIMPER (sim'per), *v.i.* to smile in an affected or silly manner.

SIMPLE (sim'pl), *adj.* single ; not complex ; undivided ; pure ; plain ; unadorned ; sincere ; natural ; unaffected ; clear ; humble ; plain.

SIMPLETON (-tun), *n.* one who is foolish or of weak intellect.

SIMPLICITY (-plis'i-ti), *n.* artlessness of mind ; clearness ; innocence.

SIMPLIFY ('pli-fi), *v.t.* make plain or easy.

SIMPLY ('pli), *adv.* in a simple manner.

SIMULATE ('u-lat), *v.t.* to pretend or counterfeit.

SIMULTANEOUS (si-mul-ta'ne-us), *adj.* happening at the same time.

SIN (sin), *n.* willful transgression of the divine law ; neglect of the laws of morality and religion ; transgression ; iniquity : *v.i.* to commit sin.

SINCE (sins), *adv.* from that time ; before this or now.

SINCERE (sin-ser'), *adj.* true ; honest ; genuine ; frank.

SINCERELY (-li), *adj.* in a sincere manner.

SINCERITY (-ser'i-ti), *n.* freedom from hypocrisy or pretence.

SINE (si'ne), *prep.* [Latin], without.

SINECURE (si'ne-kur), *n.* an office with compensation and little work to do.

SINE DIE (si'ne di'e), [Latin], literally without a day ; an adjournment *sine die* without setting a day for next meeting.

SINEW (sin'u), *n.* a tendon.

SINFUL ('fool), *adj.* wicked ; impious.

SING (sing), *v.i.* to utter melodious sounds.

SINGE (sinj), *v.t.* to burn slightly.

SINGLE (sing'gl), *adj.* consisting of one only ; alone ; separate.

SINGLY (sing'gli), *adv.* individually.

SINGULAR ('gu-lar), *adj.* alone ; uncommon ; unusual ; strange ; extraordinary.

SINGULARITY (-lar'i-ti), *n.* peculiarity ; oddity.

SINISTER (sin'is-ter), *adj.* inauspicious ; evil ; ill-omened ; corrupt.

SINNER (sin'er), *n.* one who sins.

SINN FEIN (shin fan), literally, we ourselves ; an Irish political society, organized in 1905.

SINUATE (sin'u-at), *adi.* having the margin alternately curved inward and outward.

SINUOSITY (-os'i-ti), *n.* a wavy line.

SINUOUS ('u-us), *adj.* winding ; crooked.

SIP (sip), *v.t.* to imbibe in small quantities ; taste.

SIPHON, SYPHON (si'fon), *n.* a bent pipe or tube having one end longer than the other, used for drawing off liquids.

SIR (ser), *n.* the title of a baronet or knight ; a term of respect.

SIREN (si'ren), *n.* one of certain fabulous nymphs that lured mariners to destruction ; hence, a woman dangerous from her fascinations ; a foghorn.

SIRLOIN (ser'loin), *n.* the upper part of the loin, of beef.

SISAL (si-sal'), *n.* an agave, the fibre which is used as hemp.

SISS (sis), *n.* a hissing noise.

SISTER (sis'ter), *n.* a female born of the same parents as another person.

SISTER-IN-LAW (-in-law), *n.* sister of one's husband or wife ; wife of one's brother.

SITE (sit), *n.* local position ; ground-plot.

SITTING (sit'ing), *adj.* resting on the haunches ; incubating : *n.* a session.

SITUATE ('u-at), *adj.* placed.

SITUATED ('u-a-ted), *adj.* having a position ; placed with respect to any other object.

SITUATION (-a'shun), *n.* position ; locality ; circumstances ; office ; employment.

SITZ BATH (sits bath), a bath for bathing in a sitting posture.

SIXPENCE (siks'pens), *n.* a British silver coin, equal in value to six pennies.

SIX SCORE ('skor), *n. & adj.* six times twenty.

SIXTEENTH ('tenth), *adj.* next in order after the fifteenth.

SIXTIETH ('ti-eth), *adj.* next in order after the fifty-ninth.

SIXTY ('ti), *n.* the product of six and ten : *adj.* ten times six.

SIZABLE (siz'a-bl), *adj.* of considerable or suitable size.

SIZE (siz), *n.* thin glue ; magnitude or bulk.

SIZZLE (siz'l), *v.i.* to make a hissing sound ; to fry.

SKATE (skat), *n.* kind of flat fish of the ray family ; a metallic runner to slide over ice ; a roller shoe.

SKEDADDLE (ske-dad'l), *v.i.* to run away, especially in terror.

SKEIN (skan), *n.* quantity of thread, silk, etc., in coils.

SKELETON (skel'e-tun), *n.* the bones of an animal separated from the flesh ; framework of anything ; outline.

SKETCH (skech), *n.* an outline ; first rough draft.

SKEW (sku), *n.* distortion ; perversion ; an oblique movement.

SKEWER ('er), *n.* a pin of wood or metal for securing meat, etc.

SKI (ske), *n.* a wooden runner attached to the foot for sliding on snow.

SKID (skid), *n.* a sliding wedge or drag to retard the motion of a vehicle ; a fender to protect the side of a ship.

SKIDOO (ski-doo'), *v.i.* [U.S. Slang], to vamose ; beat it.

SKIFF (skif), *n.* a small light boat.

SKILFUL (skil'fool), *adj.* expert in any art or science ; clever.

SKILL (skil), *n.* aptitude.

SKILLED (skild), *adj.* possessing skill.

SKILLET (skil'et), *n.* a small culinary vessel.

SKIM (skim), *v.t.* to remove the scum from : *v.i.* to pass lightly over.

SKIMMER ('er), *n.* a perforated ladle.

SKIMP (skimp), *v.t.* to do carelessly : *v.i.* to be parsimonious.

SKIN (skin), *n.* the external covering of an animal body.

SKINFLINT ('flint), *n.* a niggard.

SKIP (skip), *v.t.* to leap lightly over ; omit : *v.i.* to pass over unnoticed.

SKIPPER ('er), *n.* one who, or that which, skips ; a sea-captain.

SKIRMISH (sker'mish), *n.* a slight

combat or irregular fight between two small parties.

SKIRT (skert), *n.* part of a dress below the waist ; margin or border.

SKIT (skit), *n.* brief satire ; burlesque.

SKITTISH ('ish), *adj.* shy ; easily frightened ; volatile ; vivacious.

SKIVER (skiv'er), *n.* a leather of sheepskin tanned and split.

SKULK (skulk), *v.i.* lurk ; avoid work : *n.* a skulker.

SKULL (skul), *n.* the bony case inclosing the brain of a vertebrate animal.

SKUNK (skungk), *n.* an American, nocturnal animal allied to the weasel.

SKY (ski), *n.* the region of clouds surrounding the earth.

SKYLARK ('lark), *n.* a species of lark.

SKYLARKING (-ing), *n.* frolicking.

SKYSCRAPER ('skra-per), *n.* a lofty building.

SLAB (slab), *n.* a flat piece of marble or stone ; the first cut of a log.

SLACK (slak), *adj.* loose ; not busy ; backward.

SLACKEN ('n), *v.i.* to become slack or less firm, tense, or rigid ; languish.

SLACKER ('er), *n.* a person who tries to avoid work or duty, especially military duty.

SLAG (slag), *n.* the dross of a metal ; vitrified cinders.

SLAKE (slak), *v.t.* quench ; extinguish.

SLAM (slam), *v.t.* to shut violently ; put down with force and noise.

SLANDER (slan'der), *n.* a false or malicious report ; verbal defamation.

SLANDEROUS (-us), *adj.* uttering slanders.

SLANG (slang), *n.* a colloquial language or expression current at any particular period.

SLANT (slant), *n.* an inclined plane ; a passing.

SLAP (slap), *n.* a blow given with the open hand.

SLAPDASH ('dash), *n.* rough, careless work : *adj.* unthinking.

SLASH (slash), *n.* a random cut ; slit in costume.

SLATE (slat), *n.* rock that splits into thin plates ; thin stone for roofing ; tablet of stone for writing upon.

SLAUGHTER (slaw'ter), *n.* great destruction of life by violence ; carnage ; killing of oxen, etc.

SLAVE (slav), *n.* a human being held in bondage.

SLAW (slaw), *n.* sliced cabbage served as a salad.

SLAY (sla), *v.t.* to kill suddenly or with violence.

SLED (sled), *n.* a vehicle for snow or ice travelling.

SLEDGE (slej), *n.* a large, heavy hammer ; a large sled.

SLEEK (slek), *adj.* smooth ; glossy.

SLEEP (slep), *n.* slumber ; rest.

SLEEPER ('er), *n.* one who sleeps ; a piece of timber supporting a railway track ; a sleeping car.

SLEET (slet), *n.* frozen rain mingled with snow.

SLEEVE (slev), *n.* the part of a garment that covers the arm.

SLEIGH (sla), *n.* a vehicle, with runners, for use on snow or ice.

SLEIGHT (slit), *n.* dexterity ; cunning ; artful trick.

SLENDER (slen'der), *adj.* feeble ; slim ; moderate.

SLEUTHHOUND ('hound), *n.* a bloodhound.

SLEW (sloo), *n.* a boggy place ; *p.t.* of slay.

SLICE (slis), *n.* a thin broad piece of anything : *v.t.* to cut into thin pieces.

SLICK (slik), *adj.* smooth ; slippery.

SLICKER ('er), *n.* a waterproof overcoat.

SLIDE (slid), *v.i.* to pass smoothly over a surface ; glide ; slip.

SLIGHT (slit), *adj.* feeble ; inconsiderable ; unimportant ; not severe ; trifling ; slender.

SLIM (slim), *adj.* of small diameter ; slender.

SLIME (slim), *n.* any viscous substance.

SLIMSY (slim'zi), *adj.* frail.

SLING (sling), *n.* an instrument for throwing stones ; a throw ; hanging bandage for an injured arm.

SLINK (slingk), *v.i.* to sneak off.

SLIP (slip), *v.i.* to glide or slide ; miss one's foothold ; fall down ; depart or escape.

SLIPPER ('er), *n.* a kind of loose shoe

SLIPPERY ('er-i), *adj.* non-adhesive ; unstable ; smooth.

SLIPPY (i), *adj.* slippery.

SLIPSHOD ('shod), *adj.* slovenly.

SLITHER (sli*th*'er), *v.i.* to slide.

SLIVER (sliv'er), *v.t.* to cut into thin pieces : *n.* a splinter.

SLOGAN (slo'gan), *n.* a warcry ; an identifying trade word or phrase.

SLOOP (sloop), *n.* a one-masted vessel with fore-and-aft sails.

SLOPE (slop), *n.* surface inclining gradually downwards : *v.t.* to incline or slant ; direct obliquely.

SLOPPY ('i), *adj.* wet ; muddy.

SLOT (slot), *n.* a narrow aperture ; groove ; opening for coin in an automatic machine.

SLOTH (sloth), *n.* idleness.

SLOTHFUL ('fool), *adj.* lazy.

SLOUCH (slouch), *n.* ungainly, clown-ish gait.

SLOUGH (slou), *n.* a deep muddy place ; a bog.

SLOVEN (sluv'en), *n.* one who is negligent of order and neatness and appearance.

SLOVENLY (-li), *adj.* lacking neatness or order.

SLOW (slo), *adj.* dilatory ; not prompt or quick ; dull.

SLUDGE (sluj), *n.* slush ; mire.

SLUE (sloo), *v.t.* to twist round : *v.i.* to turn about (with *round*).

SLUG (slug), *n.* a shell-less mollusk allied to the common snail ; a strip of metal for spacing type.

SLUGGARD ('ard), *n.* one who is habitually lazy and idle.

SLUICE (sloos), *n.* a gate for excluding or regulating the flow of water in a canal, etc.

SLUM (slum), *n.* the poor district of a city or town.

SLUMBER ('ber), *v.i.* to sleep lightly ; doze.

SLUMP (slump), *n.* a bog ; a sudden fall in prices, etc.

SLUR (sler), *v.t.* to sully ; soil ; con-taminate ; pass over superficially ; disparage : *n.* a stain ; stigma ; innuendo.

SLUSH (slush), *n.* half-melted snow.

SLY (sli), *adj.* artfully cunning.

SMACK (smak), *n.* a quick, smart blow ; loud kiss ; flavour ; taste ; a fishing vessel.

SMALL (smawl), *adj.* little in quantity or degree ; inconsiderable ; narrow-minded ; mean.

SMALLPOX ('poks), *n.* a contagious, feverish disease.

SMART (smart), *adj.* causing a quick, sharp pain ; poignant ; sharp ; clever ; brilliant ; witty ; vivacious.

SMASH (smash), *v.t.* to break in pieces by violence ; crush.

SMATTER (smat'er), *v.i.* to talk superficially or ignorantly.

SMATTERING (-ing), *n.* superficial knowledge.

SMEAR (smer), *v.t.* to daub ; pollute.

SMELL (smel), *v.t.* to perceive by the nose.

SMELT (smelt), *n.* a small coast fish : *v.t.* to fuse, as an ore.

SMILAX (smi'laks), *n.* a climbing plant of the lily family.

SMILE (smil), *v.i.* to express pleasure, joy, love or kindness by the coun-tenance.

SMIRCH (smerch), *v.t.* to smear, disparage.

SMIRK (smerk), *v.i.* to smile affectedly or conceitedly.

SMITE (smit), *v.t.* to strike ; kill ; blast ; chasten.

SMITHY (smith'i), *n.* a blacksmith's workshop.

SMOCK (smok), *n.* a chemise ; smock frock.

SMOKE (smok), *n.* the vapour that escapes when a substance is burned.

SMOKY ('i), *adj.* filled with smoke.

SMOOTH (smoo*th*), *adj.* even sur-faced ; glossy ; bland ; soothing.

SMOTHER (smu*th*'er), *v.t.* to destroy the life of by suffocation ; stifle.

SMOULDER (smol'der), *v.i.* to burn slowly or smoke without vent.

SMUDGE (smuj), *n.* a smear or stain : *v.t.* to blacken with smoke.

SMUG (smug), *adj.* affectedly precise or prim ; spruce ; neat.

SMUGGLE ('l), *v.t.* to import secretly without paying custom-house duties.

SMUT (smut), *n.* a spot or stain made by soot or similar dirty matter.

SNACK (snak), *n.* a slight, hasty repast.

SNAFFLE (snaf'l), *n.* a bit for a bridle jointed in the middle and rings at the ends.

SNAG (snag), *n.* a short rough branch ; knot.

SNAIL (snal), *n.* a slow-creeping mollusk with a spiral shell.

SNAKE (snak), *n.* a reptile or serpent.

SNAKY ('i), *adj.* like a snake ; deceitful; sly.

SNAP (snap), *v.t.* to break at once ; crack ; bite suddenly and unexpectedly.

SNAPPISH ('ish), *adj.* apt to snap, or eager to bite ; peevish ; caustic.

SNAPSHOT (snap'shot), *n.* instantaneous photograph.

SNARE (snar), *n.* a running noose of cord or wire for catching an animal.

SNARL (snarl), *v.i.* to growl like an angry dog ; speak surlily.

SNATCH (snach), *v.i.* seize anything suddenly.

SNEAK (snek), *v.i.* to creep or steal away meanly : *n.* a mean, servile fellow ; petty thief.

SNEER (sner), *v.i.* to show contempt by some facial expression ; scoff.

SNEEZE (snez), *v.i.* a sudden and violent rush of air through the mouth and nostrils.

SNICKER (snik'er), *n.* half-suppressed laugh ; a giggle.

SNIFF (snif), *v.t.* to smell or scent : *n.* the act of sniffing.

SNIGGER, same as snicker.

SNIP (snip), *n.* a single cut with scissors ; small piece.

SNIPE (snip), *n.* a long-billed, slender shore bird.

SNIPER (snip'er), *n.* one who fires on an enemy from concealment.

SNIVEL (sniv'el), *v.i.* to run at the nose ; snuff audibly ; cry, as a child.

SNOB (snob), *n.* a vulgar person who apes gentility ; vulgar upstart.

SNOBBISH ('ish), *adj.* characteristic of, or like, a snob.

SNOOP (snoop), *v.i.* to pry where one has no business : *n.* a sneak ; spy.

SNOOPER ('er), *n.* a low sneak.

SNOOZE (snooz), *v.i.* to doze ; take a nap.

SNORE (snor), *n.* a noisy breathing in sleep.

SNOUT (snout), *n.* the muzzle of a beast.

SNOW (sno), *n.* frozen particles of vapour in the atmosphere.

SNOWDROP ('drop), *n.* a bulbous plant with white flowers.

SNOWFALL ('fawl), *n.* the quantity of snow which falls during a given time.

SNOWFLAKE (-flak), *n.* a particle of snow.

SNOWSHOE (-shoo), *n.* a wooden frame with catgut netting for walking on snow.

SNOWY ('i), *adj.* white like snow ; covered with snow.

SNUB (snub), *n.* an intended slight ; reprimand.

SNUFF (snuf), *v.t.* to draw in through the nose ; smell or scent : *n.* powdered tobacco inhaled through the nose.

SNUG (snug), *adj.* lying close and warm ; compact.

SNUGGERY ('er-i), *n.* a warm, cosy place.

SNUGGLE ('l), *v.i.* to lie close for warmth and comfort.

SO (so), *adv.* in a like manner or degree ; in high degree ; as has been stated ; for this reason ; therefore.

SOAK (sok), *v.t.* steep in a fluid ; wet thoroughly.

SOAP (sop), *n.* a compound of oils or fats and an alkali.

SOAR (sor), *v.i.* to fly aloft ; mount upwards ; rise in thought or imagination.

SOB (sob), *v.i.* to sigh in a convulsive manner with tears.

SOBER (so'ber), *adj.* temperate ; self-possessed ; calm ; steady ; sedate.

SOBRIETY (-bri'e-ti), *n.* temperance ; calmness ; seriousness.

SOBRIQUET (so'bri-ka ; Fr. so-bre-ka'), *n.* an assumed name ; a nick-name.

SOCCER (sok'er), *n.* a kind of football game.

SOCIABILITY (so-sha-bil'i-ti), *n.* disposition to associate and converse with others.

SOCIABLE ('sha-bl), *adj.* social; companionable; affable.

SOCIAL ('shal), *adj.* pertaining to men as living in society; convivial.

SOCIALISM (-izm), *n.* an economic theory or system of the reconstruction of society on the basis of co-operation of labour and community of property.

SOCIALIST (-ist), *n.* an advocate of socialism.

SOCIALIZE ('shal-iz), *v.t.* to render social.

SOCIETY (so-si'e-ti), *n.* a number of persons united for a common interest; more cultivated portion of any community in its social relations, etc.

SOCIOLOGICAL (-shi-o-loj'ik-al), *adj.* pertaining to sociology.

SOCIOLOGY ('o-ji), *n.* the science of the constitution, evolution, and phenomena of human society.

SOCK (sok), *n.* a short stocking; a blow with the fist.

SOCKDOLAGER (-dol'a-jer), *n.* a conclusive argument; a decisive blow; a whopper.

SOCKET ('et), *n.* a hollow into which something is fitted.

SOD (sod), *n.* turf; sward.

SODA (so'da), *n.* the decahydrate of sodium carbonate, called *washing soda;* sodium bicarbonate, called *baking soda,* or *saleratus;* sodium hydroxide, called *caustic soda;* soda water.

SODALITY (so-dal'i-ti), *n.* a brotherhood for social, or religious, service.

SODDEN (sod'n), *adj.* heavy with moisture; imperfectly cooked; saturated.

SODDY ('i), *adj.* turfy.

SOFA (so'fa), *n.* a long seat with stuffed bottom, back, and arms.

SOFT (soft), *adj.* easily yielding to pressure; malleable.

SOFTEN (sof'n), *v.t.* to make soft or softer; tone down; palliate; assuage; render less rude or offensive.

SOGGY (sog'i), *adj.* soaked; wet; heavy.

SOIL (soil), *n.* the top stratum of the earth's surface; land; dirt.

SOIREE (swa-ra'), *n.* [French], an evening party.

SOJOURN (so'jern, so-jern'), *v.i.* to dwell for a time.

SOL (sol), *n.* the sun.

SOL (sol), *n.* the fifth note of the diatonic scale.

SOLACE (sol'as), *n.* comfort in sorrow; consolation.

SOLAR (so'lar), *adj.* pertaining to, measured by, or proceeding from, the sun.

SOLAR SYSTEM (sis'tem), the sun, with the heavenly bodies that revolve about it as the centre of their orbits.

SOLDER (saw'der), *n.* a metallic alloy for uniting metals.

SOLDIER (sol'jer), *n.* a person engaged in military service.

SOLE (sol), *n.* the underside of the foot; bottom of a boot or shoe, etc.; a flat fish.

SOLECISM (sol'e-sizm), *n.* a breach of the rules of syntax; impropriety; absurdity.

SOLEMN (sol'em), *adj.* characterized by religious rites or ceremonies; inspiring awe; serious; devout.

SOLEMNITY ('ni-ti), *n.* a religious rite or ceremony; gravity; impressiveness.

SOLICIT (so-lis'it), *v.t.* to ask for with earnestness; entreat.

SOLICITOR ('i-ter), *n.* an attorney; a canvasser.

SOLICITIOUS ('i-tus), *adj.* eager; anxious.

SOLICITUDE ('i-tud), *n.* concern; anxiety; carefulness.

SOLID (sol'id), *adj.* compact; cubic; not hollow; dense; heavy; weighty.

SOLIDARITY (-i-dar'i-ti), *n.* community of interests and responsibilities.

SOLIDIFY (-lid'i-fi), *v.t.* to make solid : *v.i.* to harden.

SOLIDITY (so-lid'i-ti), *n.* density; compactness; stability; truth.

SOLILOQUIZE (so-lil'o-kwiz), *v.i.* to utter as soliloquy.

SOLILOQUY ('o-kwi), *n.* a talking or discourse to one's self.

SOLITAIRE (sol-i-tar'), *n.* a game played by one person; hermit.

SOLITARY ('i-ta-ri), *adj.* lonely; single; remote; unoccupied; gloomy.

SOLITUDE ('i-tud), *n.* loneliness; seclusion; desert.

SOLO (so'lo), *n.* an air, or musical piece, performed by a single instrument or by one vocalist.

SOLOIST (-ist), *n.* one who performs or sings a solo.

SOLUBILITY (-u-bil'i-ti), *n.* being soluble or dissolvable.

SOLUBLE ('u-bl), *adj.* capable of solution.

SOLUTION (-lu'shun), *n.* a liquid formed by the action of a solvent upon a substance; disintegration; explanation.

SOLVABLE ('va-bl), *adj.* capable of being solved.

SOLVE (solv), *v.t.* to explain; clear up; dissolve.

SOLVENCY (sol-ven'si), *n.* the state or quality of being solvent.

SOLVENT (sol'vent), *n.* any liquid or agent, that dissolves another substance: *adj.* able to discharge just claims or debts.

SOMBRE (som'ber), *adj.* dull; melancholy; dark; gloomy.

SOMBRERO (-bra'ro), *n.* a kind of broad-brimmed hat.

SOMBROUS ('brus), *adj.* gloomy; dull.

SOME (sum), *adj.* denoting an indeterminate number, or quantity; limited in degree; not exactly known; indicating a part: *pron.* a number not definitely known: *adv.* approximately.

SOMEHOW ('hou), *adv.* in one way or another; by some means.

SOMERSAULT ('er-sawlt), *n.* a leap in which a person turns with his heels over his head.

SOMETHING ('thing), *n.* a thing unknown; part or portion; indefinite quantity or degree.

SOMETIME ('tim), *adv.* formerly; once.

SOMEWHAT ('hwot), *n.* more or less: *adv.* in some degree or extent.

SOMEWHERE ('hwar), *adv.* in one place or another.

SOMNAMBULISM (som-nam'bu-lizm), *n.* walking in sleep.

SOMNOLENCE ('no-lens), **SOMNOLENCY** (-len-si), *n.* sleepiness; drowsiness.

SON (sun), *n.* male issue of a parent.

SONG (song), *n.* a lyrical poem or ballad; notes of birds.

SONGSTER ('ster), *n.* one skilled in singing; a singing bird.

SON-IN-LAW (-law), *n.* the husband of one's daughter.

SONNET (son'et), *n.* a lyric poem.

SONOROUS (so-no'rus), *adj.* giving a clear sound when struck; resonant.

SOON (soon), *adv.* in a short time; without delay.

SOOT (soot), *n.* minute particles of carbon.

SOOTH (sooth), *n.* truth.

SOOTHE (sooth), *v.t.* to comfort; allay; pacify; assuage.

SOOTY (soot'i), *adj.* pertaining to, producing, or like, soot; dusky.

SOPHISM (sof'izm), *n.* a specious but fallacious argument; fallacy.

SOPHIST ('ist), *n.* a fallacious or captious reasoner.

SOPHISTICAL (so-fis'ti-kal), *adj.* fallaciously subtle; quibbling.

SOPHISTICATE ('ti-kat), *v.t.* to render worthless by adulteration; pervert; alter a text to deceive.

SOPHISTICATED (-kat-ed), *adj.* worldly-wise.

SOPHISTRY (sof'is-tri), *n.* unsound argument.

SOPHOMORE ('o-mor), *n.* a student in his second academic year.

SOPORIFIC (so-po-rif'ik), *n.* an opiate or anodyne.

SOPPY (sop'i), *adj.* soaked or saturated with a liquid.

SOPRANO (so-pra'no), *n.* the highest kind of female voice.

SORBONNE (sor-bon'), *n.* a famous seat of learning in Paris.

SORCERER ('ser-er), *n.* a magician or enchanter.

SORCERY (-i), *n.* witchcraft; magic; enchantment.

SORDID ('did), *adj.* mean; vile; base; niggardly; meanly avaricious.

SORE (sor), *adj.* inflamed; painful; sensitive; susceptible of irritation.

SORGHUM (sor'gum), *n.* a cane-like grass, yielding sugar.

SORORITY (so-ror'i-ti), *n.* a secret organization of women only; an association of college girls.

SOROSIS (so-ro'sis), *n.* a woman's club or association.

SORREL (sor'el), *n.* one of several low perennial herbs.

SORROW ('o), *n.* mental pain; sadness; woe; grief.

SORRY ('i), *adj.* feeling regret for loss; sympathetic; pained.

SORT (sort), *n.* a kind or species; class, rank, or order.

SORTIE (sor'te), *n.* issuing of a body of troops from a besieged place to attack the besiegers.

S.O.S., *n.* a wireless call for help from a ship in peril.

SOT (sot), *n.* a habitual drunkard.

SOTTISH (sot'ish), *adj.* like a sot.

SOTTO VOCE (sot'o vo'cha), *adv.* [Italian], in an undertone.

SOUBRETTE (-bret'), *n.* an actress who plays a frivolous part.

SOUGH (sou, suf), *n.* a hollow murmur or whistling, as of the wind.

SOUGHT, *p.t.* & *p.p.* of seek.

SOUL (sol), *n.* the spiritual and immortal part in man; reason or intellect; conscience.

SOUND (sound), *adj.* whole; entire; unbroken; healthy; founded on truth or right: *n.* the impression made on the ear by the vibrations of the air; noise.

SOUP (soop), *n.* a liquid food prepared by boiling.

SOUR (sour), *adj.* tart; acid; rancid; not sweet; cross; morose.

SOURCE (sors), *n.* that from which anything arises or originates.

SOUSE (sous), *n.* anything steeped or preserved in pickle.

SOUTH (south), *n.* that one of the four cardinal points, opposite the north.

SOUVENIR (soo-ve-ner'), *n.* a memento or keepsake.

SOVEREIGN (suv'er-in), *adj.* royal; supreme in power: *n.* a king, emperor, or queen; a British gold coin=20s.

SOVEREIGNTY (-ti), *n.* supreme power or dominion.

SOVIET (so've-yet), *n.* the governing body in Russia, established by the revolution of 1917.

SOW (sou), *n.* a female pig.

SOW (so), *v.t.* to scatter, as seed.

SPA (spa), *n.* a spring of mineral water.

SPACE (spas), *n.* extension; room; interval between lines; time.

SPACIOUS (spa'shus), *adj.* extending far and wide; roomy.

SPAGHETTI (spa-get'i), *n.* macaroni in long thin strips.

SPANGLE (span'gl), *n.* any glittering ornament, especially for a dress.

SPANIEL ('yel), *n.* any of several breeds of dogs with long wavy hair and drooping ears.

SPAR (spar), *n.* a lustrous crystalline mineral; a mast, yard, boom, etc.: *v.i.* to box; contest in words.

SPARE (spar), *v.t.* to part with without inconvenience; omit; treat tenderly; permit to exist.

SPARING (spar'ing), *adj.* frugal; abstemious.

SPARK (spark), *n.* a small particle of fire.

SPARKLE (spark'kl), *v.i.* to emit sparks; glisten; scintillate.

SPARK-PLUG (spark'plug), *n.* a contrivance for exploding the gas in a motor or internal-combustion engine, by means of an electric spark.

SPARROW (spar'o), *n.* a small bird of the passerine family.

SPARSE (spars), *adj.* thinly scattered.

SPARTAN (spar'tan), *adj.* hardy; undaunted; severe.

SPASM (spazm), *n.* a sudden, violent, involuntary contraction of the muscles.

SPASMODIC (spaz-mod'ik), *adj.* pertaining to spasms.

SPAT (spat), *n.* the spawn of shellfish; a petty quarrel: *pl.* gaiters.

SPATTER (spat'er), *v.t.* to sprinkle with liquid; defame.

SPATULA (spat'u-la), *n.* a broad flat, thin, flexible knife.

SPAVIN (spav'in), *n.* a disease of horses, characterized by a swelling in the hock joint.

SPAWN (spawn), *n.* the ova of fishes, etc.

SPEAK (spek), *v.i.* to utter articulate sounds ; said of human beings.

SPEAR (sper), *n.* a lance with barbed prongs for spearing.

SPECIAL (spesh'al), *adj.* designed for a particular purpose ; distinctive ; uncommon.

SPECIALIST (-ist), *n.* one who devotes himself to a particular branch of a profession, etc.

SPECIALITY (-i-al'i-ti), *n.* the special or distinctive mark of a person or thing ; special department, etc.

SPECIALIZE ('al-iz), *v.i.* to concentrate on some special branch of knowledge.

SPECIALTY ('al-ti), *n.* that for which a person is noted or distinguished.

SPECIE (spe'shi), *n.* coined money.

SPECIES ('shez), *n.* a group of individuals agreeing in common attributes and called by a common name ; a subdivision of a genus ; kind ; sort.

SPECIFIC (spe-sif'ik), *adj.* definite or particular ; precise.

SPECIFICATION (spes-i-fi-ka'shun), *n.* detailed statement of particulars.

SPECIFIC GRAVITY (grav'i-ti), the ratio of the weight of a body to another body of equal volume.

SPECIFY ('i-fi), *v.t.* to mention or name particularly.

SPECIMEN ('i-men), *n.* a sample.

SPECIOUS (spe'shus), *adj.* plausible ; ostensible ; fair.

SPECK (spek), *n.* a spot ; flaw ; blemish ; small particle.

SPECKLE ('l), *v.t.* to variegate with spots of a different colour.

SPECTACLE ('ta-kl), *n.* pageant ; exhibition : *pl.* an optical instrument to assist the vision.

SPECTACULAR (-tak'u-lar), *adj.* adapted to excite wonder or admiration by scenic effect.

SPECTATOR (-ta'ter), *n.* a beholder.

SPECTRE (spek'tr), *n.* a ghost or apparition.

SPECTRAL ('tral), *adj.* ghostly ; per-taining to, or produced by, the spectrum.

SPECULATE ('u-lat), *v.i.* to consider or meditate upon ; purchase stock, etc., with expectation of profit.

SPECULATION (-la'shun), *n.* intellectual examination ; theory ; purchase with expectation of quick profit.

SPECULATOR (-ter), *n.* one who speculates.

SPEECH (spech), *n.* the faculty of uttering articulate sounds or words.

SPEED (sped), *n.* velocity ; swiftness ; quickness.

SPEEDING ('ing), *n.* the act of driving an automobile faster than legal limit.

SPEEDOMETER (-om'e-ter) *n.* an instrument showing the velocity of a moving vehicle.

SPEEDY ('i), *adj.* prompt ; quick ; hasty.

SPELL (spel), *n.* arrangement of letters in a word ; a charm or incantation : *v.t.* to write, repeat, or point out the proper letters of.

SPELLBOUND (-bound), *adj.* fascinated ; enraptured.

SPELLING ('ing), *n.* proper arrangement of letters in a word ; orthography.

SPEND (spend), *v.t.* to lay out, as money ; give for any purpose.

SPENDTHRIFT ('thrift), *adj.* prodigal ; extravagant.

SPERM (sperm), *n.* spermaceti ; spawn.

SPERMACETI (sper-ma-se'ti), *n.* a waxy substance obtained from the head of the sperm-whale.

SPEW (spu), *v.i.* to vomit.

SPHERE (sfer), *n.* a globe or globular body ; circuit or range of knowledge.

SPHERICAL (sfer'i-kal), *adj.* globular.

SPHINX (sfingks), *n.* a fabled monster having the head of a woman and the body of a lioness.

SPICE (spis), *n.* any of various aromatic and pungent herbs, or vegetables used for seasoning food ; relish.

SPICK-AND-SPAN (spik, span), *adj.* new ; fresh.

SPICULAR (spik′u-lar), *adj.* dart-like.

SPICY (spi′si), *adj.* aromatic ; fragrant ; pungent ; racy.

SPIDER (′der), *n.* an insect that spins webs to ensnare its prey.

SPIDER WEB (web), a silken web woven by a spider.

SPIGOT (spig′ot), *n.* a plug of wood to stop the venthole of a cask.

SPIKE (spik), *n.* a large kind of nail ; ear of grain.

SPILL (spil), *v.t.* to fall or run over.

SPIN (spin), *v.t.* to draw out and twist into threads ; protract ; cause to whirl rapidly.

SPINACH (′aj), *n.* a common garden pot-herb.

SPINAL (spi′nal), *adj.* pertaining to the spine.

SPINAL COLUMN (kol′um), the backbone ; the spine.

SPINDLE (spin′dl), *n.* the long thin rod used in spinning wheels for twisting the thread.

SPINDRIFT (′drift), *n.* spray blown from the waves of the sea.

SPINE (spin), *n.* in vertebrates, the backbone.

SPINNAKER (spin′a-ker), *n.* a large jib-like sail on the mainmast of a racing vessel.

SPINSTER (spin′ster), *n.* an un-married woman.

SPINY (spin′i), *adj.* full of spines.

SPIRAL (spi′ral), *adj.* winding around a centre like the thread of a screw : *n.* the spiral path described by an airplane.

SPIRE (spir), *n.* a slender stalk or blade ; steeple top.

SPIRIT (spir′it), *n.* the soul ; 'ife ; courage ; energy ; vivacity ; power of mind, moral and intellectual ; genius ; real meaning ; essence ; any liquid produced by distillation.

SPIRIT OF ST. LOUIS (sant′loo-is), the name of the airplane made world-famous by Col. Charles A. Lindbergh; *See Lindbergh.*

SPIRITUAL (spir′it-u-al), *adj.* in-corporeal ; pure ; holy ; ecclesiastical.

SPIRITUALISM (-izm), *n.* the state of being spiritual ; the philosophical

doctrine that nothing is real except soul or spirit.

SPIRITUALITY (-al′i-ti), *n.* spiritual nature.

SPIRITUALIZE (-iz), *v.t.* to free from sensuality ; make spiritual.

SPIRITUEL (spe-re-tu-el′), *adj.* [French], refined ; ethereal ; bright ; pure : *fem.* spirituelle.

SPIROCHETTE (spi′ro-keet), *n.* one of group of micro-organisms.

SPIT (spit), *n.* a long pointed rod on which meat is roasted ; saliva.

SPITE (spit), *n.* petty malice.

SPITEFUL (′fool), *adj.* malicious ; malignant.

SPITTLE (′l), *n.* saliva.

SPLASH (splash), *v.t.* to spatter with water, mud, etc.

SPLATTER (splat′er), *v.t.* to splash.

SPLAY (spla), *n.* spread ; expansion ; bevel ; slope : *v.t.* to dislocate.

SPLEEN (splen), *n.* a soft, vascular organ near the large extremity of the stomach ; ill-humour.

SPLENDENT (splen′dent), *adj.* brilliant ; illustrious ; shining.

SPLENLID (′did), *adj.* magnificent ; brilliant ; famous ; heroic.

SPLENDOUR (′der), *n.* magnificence ; pomp.

SPLENETIC (sple-net′ik), *adj.* fret-ful , peevish ; melancholy.

SPLICE (splis), *v.t.* to unite, as two ropes, by interweaving the strands.

SPLINT (splint), *n.* a thin piece of wood to keep a broken bone, etc., in position.

SPLINTER (splin′ter), *n.* a thin piece of wood, etc., fragment.

SPLIT (split), *v.t.* to divide length-wise ; tear asunder violently ; cleave ; rupture ; disunite.

SPLOTCH (sploch), *n.* a stain ; daub.

SPLURGE (splerj), *n.* a great display.

SPLUTTER (splut′er), *v.i.* to speak hastily and confusedly.

SPOIL (spoil), *v.t.* to plunder ; cor-rupt ; ruin.

SPOKEN (spok′n), *adj.* oral ; speaking.

SPOLIATE (spo′li-at), *v.t.* to plunder ; rob ; ruin.

SPOLIATION (spo-li-a′shun), *n.* the act of plundering.

SPONGE (spunj), *n.* the porous, elastic, fibrous framework of a fixed marine animal.

SPONGY ('ji), *adj.* flexible and full of small cavities ; like a sponge.

SPONSOR ('ser), *n.* a surety ; a godfather or godmother.

SPONTANEITY (-ta-ne'i-ti), *n.* tendency in animal and vegetable organisms to undergo changes irrespective of environment.

SPONTANEOUS (-ta'ne-us), *adj.* proceeding from natural disposition or impulses ; acting by internal impulse or natural law.

SPOON (spoon), *n.* a small implement for dipping in liquids.

SPOONY ('i), *n.* a simpleton.

SPOOR (spoor), *n.* the track or trail of any wild animal.

SPORADIC (spo-rad'ik), *adj.* occurring separately or apart from others of the same kind ; single.

SPORE (spor), *n.* a minute grain in cryptogamous plants which performs the function of a seed.

SPORT (sport), *n.* diversion ; jest ; mirth ; play ; outdoor recreation ; an animal or plant which deviates in its organism from the normal condition.

SPORTIVE ('tiv), *adj.* frolicsome.

SPORTSMAN (sports'man), *n.* one who pursues sports, as hunting, sailing, etc.

SPOT (spot), *n.* a blot or mark ; discoloured place or stain ; blemish ; locality.

SPOTLIGHT ('lit), *n.* an adjustable calcium light for throwing a shifting light on a stage.

SPOTTED ('ed), *adj.* tarnished ; sullied.

SPOUSE (spouz), *n.* a married person.

SPOUT (spout), *n.* the projecting mouth of a vessel ; pipe for conducting a liquid.

SPRAIN (spran), *n.* an excessive strain of the muscles.

SPRAT (sprat), *n.* a small fish ; a kind of herring.

SPRAWL (sprawl), *v.i.* to stretch the body carelessly when in a horizontal position ; lie.

SPRAY (spra), *n.* a branch with its smaller branches ; small particles of water, etc. ; dashed in the air from a hose or atomizer, etc.

SPREAD (spred), *v.t.* to extend in all directions ; unfurl ; open ; scatter.

SPREE (spre), *n.* a merry frolic; carousal.

SPRIG (sprig), *n.* a small twig.

SPRIGHTLY (sprit'li), *adj.* vivacious; brisk ; animated.

SPRING (spring), *v.i.* to arise ; originate ; appear ; shoot up ; leap ; bound ; start or rise up suddenly ; fly back : *n.* a leap or bound ; an elastic body used for various mechanical purposes ; source ; a fountain of water ; one of the four seasons of the year.

SPRINGTIDE ('tid), *n.* the tide which happens at or near the new and full moon ; springtime.

SPRINGY ('i), *adj.* elastic ; light.

SPRINKLE (spring'kl), *v.t.* to scatter in small drops.

SPRINT (sprint), *n.* a run for a short distance at full speed.

SPROUT (sprout), *v.i.* to germinate : *n.* a shoot ; bud.

SPRUCE (sproos), *n.* a handsome evergreen tree of the pine family : *adj.* smart ; trim ; neat.

SPRY (spri), *adj.* nimble ; sharp.

SPUD (spud), *n.* a potato.

SPUME (spum), *n.* froth ; foam.

SPUNK (spungk), *n.* mettle ; courage ; spirit.

SPUR (sper), *n.* a rowel with sharp points worn on the heel of a boot for urging on a horse ; any incentive to action.

SPURIOUS (spu'ri-us), *adj.* not genuine ; counterfeit ; false.

SPURN (spern), *v.t.* to drive away, as with the foot ; reject with contempt.

SPURT (spert), *v.i.* to issue forth suddenly or violently : *n.* a brief, sudden effort.

SPUTTER (sput'er), *v.i.* to throw out moisture in scattered drops ; speak rapidly and indistinctly.

SPY (spi), *v.t.* to discover, especially at a distance ; gain sight of ; detect ; explore ; examine secretly : *n.* a secret agent.

SQUAB (skwob), *n.* a young pigeon.

SQUABBLE ('i), *v.i.* to wrangle or dispute in a noisy manner.

SQUAD (skwod), *n.* any small party.

SQUADRON ('run), *n.* a division of a regiment of cavalry, comprising two troops ; a detachment of war vessels ; a number of military aeroplanes engaged in special service.

SQUALID (skwol'id), *adj.* dirty ; foul ; poverty-stricken.

SQUALL (skwawl), *n.* a sudden and violent gust of wind ; a loud scream.

SQUALOR (skwol'er, skwa'lor), *n.* foulness ; dirt.

SQUANDER (skwon'der), *v.t.* to spend lavishly or wastefully.

SQUARE (skwar), *n.* a parallelogram having 4 equal sides and 4 right angles ; a mathematical instrument for measuring right angles ; true ; upright ; honest.

SQUARE-ROOT ('root), *n.* that number or quantity which, multiplied by itself, produces the given number or quantity, as 2 is the square root of 4.

SQUASH (skwosh), *v.t.* to crush ; mash : *n.* the edible fruit of a trailing vine.

SQUATTER (skwot'er), *n.* one who settles on land without a title.

SQUAW (skwaw), *n.* a North American Indian woman.

SQUAWK (skwawk), *v.i.* a loud, harsh noise.

SQUEAL (skwel), *v.i.* to cry with a sharp, shrill, prolonged sound.

SQUEAMISH (skwem'ish), *adj.* sickish at stomach ; fastidious.

SQUEEZE (skwez), *v.t.* to press between two bodies ; crush ; embrace forcibly.

SQUELCH (skwelch), *v.t.* to crush ; silence.

SQUIB (skwib), *n.* a kind of firework ; petty lampoon.

SQUID (skwid), *n.* a name for various ten-armed cephalopods ; cuttlefish.

SQUILL (skwil), *n.* a bulbous plant of the lily family.

SQUINT (skwint), *adj.* looking obliquely ; said of the eyes.

SQUIRE (skwir), *n.* title of a justice of the peace.

SQUIRM (skwerm), *v.i.* to wriggle ; writhe.

SQUIRREL (skwer'el), *n.* an arboreal rodent.

SQUIRT (skwert), *v.t.* to eject in a stream from a small orifice.

STAB (stab), *v.t.* to pierce with, or as with, a pointed weapon.

STABILITY (sta-bil'i-ti), *n.* firmness of character ; fixedness : also, stableness.

STABILIZE (stab'i-liz), *v.t.* to make stable.

STABLE (stab'bl), *adj.* fixed ; firm ; constant : *n.* a building in which animals, especially horses, are cared for.

STACK (stak), *n.* a large quantity of hay, corn, wood, etc., piled up in regular form.

STADIUM (sta'di-um), *n.* a Greek linear measure = 606¾ ft. ; the course for foot-races at the Olympic games ; a place for athletic contests.

STAFF (staf), *n.* a support ; prop ; pole, handle, or bar ; wand as a badge of office ; the lines and spaces on which music is written ; number of persons engaged in any undertaking.

STAGE (staj), *n.* an elevated platform ; the theatrical profession ; coach.

STAGGER (stag'er), *v.i.* to totter or reel ; hesitate.

STAGING (staj'ing), *n.* a temporary structure of boards and posts ; play production.

STAGNANT (stag'nant), *adj.* not flowing ; motionless ; torpid ; dull.

STAGNATE ('nat), *v.i.* to be motionless ; become torpid, inactive, or dull.

STAGY (sta'ji), *adj.* characteristic of the stage ; unreal.

STAID (stad), *adj.* sober ; sedate.

STAIN (stan), *v.t.* to blot ; spot ; tinge with colour ; dye ; tarnish.

STAIR (star), *n.* a step : *pl.* a flight of steps.

STAIRCASE ('kas), *n.* a set of steps with railings, etc.

STAKE (stak), *n.* a post or strong stick fixed in the ground ; palisade.

STALACTITE (sta-lak'tit), *n.* an icicle-like incrustation of carbonate of lime, etc., formed by percolation in caverns, etc.

STALE (stal), *adj.* not fresh or new; vapid.

STALK (stawk), *v.t.* to hunt game with stealth : *n.* the stem of a plant.

STALL (stawl), *n.* that part of a stable where horses, etc., are cared for.

STALLION (stal′yun), *n.* an unaltered male horse.

STALWART (stawl′wert), *adj.* sturdy ; strong ; brave ; daring.

STAMEN (sta′men), *n.* [*pl.* stamina (stam′i-na)], the pollen-bearing organ of a flower.

STAMINA (stam′i-na), *n.pl.* tone and vigour of the animal system ; backbone.

STAMMER (stam′er), *v.i.* to hesitate or falter in speaking ; stutter.

STAMP (stamp), *v.i.* to strike or beat the foot forcibly on the ground : *n.* the act of stamping ; die ; the impression made ; official mark ; small piece of paper having value impressed upon it by government, required to be affixed to a letter, etc. ; character or reputation.

STAMPEDE (stam-ped′), *n.* a sudden panic seizing a herd of animals.

STANCH (stanch), **STAUNCH** (stanch), *adj.* firm ; constant ; trustworthy.

STANCHION (stan′shun), *n.* a support or post of iron or wood.

STANDARD (stan′dard), *n.* an ensign or flag ; established rule or model ; criterion.

STANDARDIZE (stan′dar-diz), *v.t.* to cause to conform to a standard.

STANDING (′ing), *n.* duration ; reputation ; rank or status.

STAND-PATTER (-pat′er), *n.* a politician who sticks to his party under all circumstances.

STANZA (stan′za), *n.* metrical division of a poem.

STAPES (sta′pez), *n.* a stirrup bone of the ear.

STAPLE (sta′pl), *n.* the chief production or industry of a country or district ; loop of metal for holding a bolt, etc.

STAR (star), *n.* any celestial body ; anything resembling a star ; an asterisk (*).

STARBOARD (′bord), *n.* the right-hand side of a vessel looking toward the bow.

STARCH (starch), *n.* an element of most of the foodstuffs.

STARE (star), *n.* a fixed look with wide-open eyes : *v.t.* to gaze at.

STARK (stark), *adj.* stiff ; strong ; pure ; utter.

STARRY (star′i), *adj.* abounding in stars ; star-shaped.

START (start), *v.i.* to be moved or twitched suddenly ; shrink ; move abruptly ; set out ; begin ; loosen.

STARTLE (star′t′l), *v.t.* to frighten suddenly ; shock.

STARVATION (star-va′shun), *n.* the state of being starved ; a lack of food.

STARVE (starv), *v.i.* to suffer extreme hunger.

STATE (stat), *n.* circumstances or condition.

STATE, *n.* one of the federated commonwealths composing the United States of America : *pl.* the United States of America (with *the*) ; abbreviated U.S. in this Dictionary.

STATECRAFT (′kraft), *n.* statesmanship.

STATED (′ed), *adj.* fixed ; regular.

STATEDLY (-ed-li), *adv.* at fixed times.

STATELY (′li), *adj.* grand ; majestic ; dignified.

STATEMENT (′ment), *n.* narrative or recital.

STATESMAN (stats′man), *n.* one who is skilled in public affairs.

STATIC (stat′ik), *adj.* pertaining to bodies at rest or in equilibrium ; in radio, denoting disturbances in reception due to atmospheric electricity.

STATION (sta′shun), *n.* position ; rank or condition of life ; class or order ; place on a railway for passengers or goods ; sphere of duty ; place in society.

STATIONARY (-a-ri), *adj.* fixed.

STATIONER (′shun-er), *n.* one who sells writing materials, blank books, etc.

STATIONERY (-er-i), *n.* stationer's articles.

STATISTIC (sta-tis'tik), **STATISTICAL** ('ti-kal), *adj.* pertaining to statistics.

STATISTICIAN (stat-is-tish'an), *n.* one skilled in statistics.

STATISTICS (sta-tis'tiks), *n.* the science of the classification and arrangement of facts relating to the condition of a people or class.

STATUARY (stat'u-a-ri), *n.* the art of carving statues; statues collectively.

STATUE ('u), *n.* the representation of a person, animal, or any being sculptured or modelled.

STATUESQUE (-u-esk'), *adj.* having the characteristics of a statue; well shaped; dignified in appearance.

STATUETTE (-u-et'), *n.* a little statue.

STATURE ('ur), *n.* the natural height; growth.

STATUS (sta'tus), *n.* condition; social standing or place; rank.

STATUTE ('ut), *n.* written law.

STATUTORY ('u-to-ri), *adj.* depending on statute for its authority.

STAVE (stav), *n.* one of the thin narrow strips of wood forming the sides of a cask; a music staff.

STEADFAST (sted'fast), *adj.* steady; constant; uniform.

STEADY ('i), *adj.* fixed; regular; firm; constant; resolute; undeviating; unwavering.

STEAK (stak), *n.* a slice of beef, etc., for broiling, or frying.

STEAL (stel), *v.t.* to take without leave or right.

STEALTH (stelth), *n.* secret means employed to accomplish an object.

STEALTHILY ('i-li), *adv.* in a stealthy manner.

STEALTHY ('i), *adj.* done or performed by stealth; sly.

STEAM (stem), *n.* vapour into which water is changed when heated to boiling-point; vapour.

STEED (sted), *n.* a mettlesome horse.

STEEL (stel), *n.* iron refined and combined with carbon; anything made of steel.

STEEP (step), *adj.* rising or descending with abrupt inclination.

STEEPLE (ste'pl), *n.* a tower or turret tapering to a point; spire.

STEER (ster), *n.* a young male of the ox kind; bullock: *v.t.* control; guide.

STEERAGE ('aj), *n.* the act or practice of steering; that part of a ship allotted to passengers paying the lowest fares.

STEIN (stin), *n.* a mug.

STELLAR (stel'ar), *adj.* pertaining to stars; astral; starry.

STEM (stem), *n.* the principal axis of a tree or plant; anything resembling a stem; a stalk; branch of a family: *v.t.* to resist or check.

STENCH (stench), *n.* a strong, offensive odour.

STENCIL (sten'sil), *n.* a thin plate of metal with a pattern, etc., cut out, used for marking, etc.

STENOGRAPHER (ste-nog'ra-fer), *n.* a shorthand writer.

STENOGRAPHY (ste-nog'ra-fi), *n.* the art of writing in shorthand.

STEP (step), *n.* the distance measured by the foot in walking or running; pace; measure; procedure; stair.

STEREOPTICON (-op'ti-kon, ti-kon), *n.* a magic-lantern.

STERILE ('il), *adj.* barren; destitute of ideas.

STERILITY (ste-ril'i-ti), *n.* barrenness.

STERILIZATION (ster-i-li-za'shun), *n.* rendering sterile; state of being sterile.

STERILIZE (-liz), *v.t.* to make sterile; free from germs.

STERLING ('ling), *adj.* pure; genuine; of high merit: *n.* the standard of fineness of legal English coin, for gold, .916, for silver, .925.

STERN (stern), *adj.* harsh or severe in countenance or manners; austere; steadfast; being in the stern.

STERNUM (ster'num), *n.* the breast bone.

STERNWAY (stern'wa), *n.* movement of a vessel backwards.

STET (stet), *v.t.* to mark with the word *stet* (let it stand) on a proof, indicating that something marked for omission is to remain.

STETHOSCOPE (steth'o-skop), *n.* an instrument for examining the chest.

STEVEDORE (stev'e-dor), *n.* one who loads or unloads a vessel.

STEW (stu), *v.t.* to boil slowly or with simmering heat : *n.* a dish prepared by stewing ; state of heat, worry, confusion.

STEWARD ('erd), *n.* one who manages the domestic concerns of a family or institution ; person employed at a hotel, club, or on board ship to superintend culinary affairs ; staterooms, etc. : *fem.* stewardess.

STEWARDSHIP (-ship), *n.* management.

STICKY (stik'i), *adj.* adhesive ; glutinous ; viscous.

STIFF (stif), *adj.* not easily bent ; rigid ; inflexible ; stubborn ; strong ; violent ; not natural or easy ; constrained.

STIFFEN ('n), *v.t.* to make stiff ; make more thick or viscous.

STIFLE (sti'f'l), *v.t.* to suffocate ; smother ; extinguish ; suppress or conceal.

STIGMA (stig'ma), *n.* [*pl.* stigmas, stigmata ('maz, 'ma-ta)], a mark made with a branding-iron ; mark of infamy or disgrace ; the receptive upper part of the pistil of a flower on which the pollen which fertilizes it falls.

STIGMATIZE ('ma-tiz), *v.t.* to mark with a stigma or brand ; hold up to reproach, or infamy.

STILE (stil), *n.* a set of steps to pass from one side of a fence or wall, etc., to the other.

STILETTO (stil-let'o), *n.* a small dagger with a thin, rounded, pointed blade.

STILL (stil), *adj.* at rest ; without motion ; quiet ; calm ; silent : *adv.* nevertheless ; always ; after that : *n.* an apparatus for distilling.

STILLNESS ('nes), *n.* silence.

STIMULANT (stim'u-lant), *adj.* producing transient increase of vital energy.

STIMULATE ('u-lat), *v.t.* to excite or rouse ; animate ; goad ; encourage.

STIMULUS (-lus), *n.* [*pl.* stimuli (li)] a spur ; incentive ; stimulant.

STING (sting), *n.* the poisonous weapon with which certain animals, plants and insects are furnished : *v.t.* to cause acute pain to ; goad.

STINGING ('ing), *p.adj.* acutely painful.

STINGY (stin'ji), *adj.* close and covetous.

STINT (stint), *v.t.* to restrain : *v.i.* to be sparing.

STINTED ('ted), *p.adj.* restricted.

STIPEND (sti'pend), *n.* a salary.

STIPPLE (stip'l), *v.t.* to engrave by means of dots.

STIPULATE ('u-lat), *v.t.* to arrange by special mention.

STIPULATION (-u-la'shun), *n.* a special condition in a contract.

STIR (ster), *v.t.* to put into motion ; move ; incite ; agitate.

STIRPS (sterps), *n.* family ; race ; stem ; root.

STIRRING ('ing), *adj.* busy ; bustling.

STIRRUP (stir'up, ster'up), *n.* an iron hoop suspended from a saddle.

STITCH (stich), *v.t.* to sew.

STOCK (stok), *n.* family, or lineage ; fund ; capital ; store cattle ; foundation of soups, etc. ; a kind of flower : *pl.* public funds ; shares of capital : *v.t.* to store up ; fill ; supply.

STOCKADE (-ad'), *n.* a line of posts used as a barrier for defence, or enclosure for cattle.

STOCKBROKER, (-bro'ker), *n.* one who buys, or sells, stocks for others.

STOCK COMPANY (kum'pa-ni), an incorporated company which issues stock ; a theatrical company playing a special repertoire.

STOCK EXCHANGE (eks-chanj'), where stocks are bought and sold ; an association of stockbrokers.

STOCKHOLDER (-hol-der), *n.* one who owns shares in a corporation.

STOCKING ('ing), *n.* a close-fitting covering for the foot and leg.

STOCKJOBBER ('job-er), *n.* one who speculates in stocks and shares.

STOCKSTILL ('stil), *adj.* motionless.

STOCKY (-i), *adj.* thickset.

STOCKYARD (-yard), *n.* an extensive

inclosure with stalls, pens, etc., convenient to a railway, into which cattle, sheep and swine are kept.

STODGY (stoj), *adj.* miry; sticky; dull.

STOKE (stok), *v.t.* maintain and tend the fire in, as to *stoke* a furnace.

STOKER ('er), *n.* one who attends to the furnace; a fireman.

STOLID (stol'id), *adj.* stupid; dull.

STOLIDITY ('i-ti), *n.* intellectual dullness.

STOMACH (stum'ak), *n.* the principal organ of digestion in the body; appetite; inclination; haughtiness.

STONE (ston), *n.* a hard mass of mineral matter; gem; material used for building; hard seed of certain fruits; a weight, usually 14 lb. avoirdupois; hardness.

STONE-BLIND ('blind), *adj.* quite blind.

STONECROP ('krop), *n.* a mosslike plant with fleshy, pungent leaves and yellow flowers; grows in interstices of rocks.

STONEWARE ('war), *n.* a coarse kind of pottery baked hard and glazed.

STONY ('i), *adj.* pertaining to, of the nature of, or like, stone; rocky; hard; cruel; inflexible; pitiless.

STOOL (stool), *n.* a seat without a back for one person.

STOOP (stoop), *v.i.* to bend the body downward and forward; descend from rank or dignity; submit; condescend: *n.* outside stairway, veranda, or porch.

STOP (stop), *v.t.* to hinder, check, or impede; intercept; cessation.

STOPPLE ('i), *n.* a cork or plug.

STORAGE (stor'aj), *n.* safekeeping of goods in a warehouse, etc.

STORAGE BATTERY (bat'er-i), a battery, with a store of electrical energy.

STORE (stor), *n.* a large number; stock accumulated; abundance or plenty; warehouse; shop.

STORK (stork), *n.* a large wading bird, with long legs and large pointed bill.

STORM (storm), *n.* a violent atmo-

spheric disturbance; tempest; heavy fall of rain, snow, or hail.

STORY (sto'ri), *n.* a fictious narrative; short romance; history; division of the height of a building.

STOUT (stout), *adj.* corpulent; thickset; lusty; resolute; strong.

STOVE (stov), *n.* an apparatus for cooking or heating.

STOW (sto), *v.t.* lay up; pack.

STOWAWAY ('a-wa), *n.* one who conceals himself on a vessel leaving port to obtain a free passage.

STRADDLE (strad'l), *v.i.* to stand or walk with the legs wide apart.

STRAGGLE (strag'l), *v.i.* to wander from the direct course or way; ramble; rove; occur at intervals.

STRAIGHT (strat), *adj.* not crooked; right; direct; upright.

STRAIGHTEN ("n), *v.t.* to make straight.

STRAIGHTFORWARD (-for'werd), *adj.* not deviating; honest; open.

STRAIGHTWAY ('wa), *adv.* at once.

STRAIN (stran), *n.* stock; lineage; descent; tune or melody; a violent effort; injury by over-exertion: *v.t.* to filter.

STRAINER ('er), *n.* one who, or that which, strains.

STRAIT (strat), *adj.* narrow; not broad; confined; distressful; difficult: *n.* a narrow passage of water connecting two seas; difficulty; poverty.

STRAIT-JACKET ('jak-et), *n.* a kind of garment for confining mad or delirious persons.

STRAIT-LACED ('last), *adj.* laced tightly; strict in manners or morals.

STRAND (strand), *n.* the shore of a sea, ocean, or large lake; twists of a rope: *v.t.* run aground.

STRANDED (-ed), *adj.* without funds; moneyless; helpless; grounded.

STRANGE (stranj), *adj.* not domestic; novel; unusual; reserved; inexperienced; unfamiliar.

STRANGER (stran'jer), *n.* a foreigner; guest or visitor.

STRANGLE (strang'gl), *v.t.* to choke; suppress or stifle.

STRANGULATION (-gu-la'shun), *n.* suffocation ; close constriction.

STRAPPING ('ing), *adj.* tall ; strong ; well-made ; handsome.

STRATAGEM (strat'a-jem), *n.* an artifice or plan for deception of any kind.

STRATEGIC (stra-te'jik), *adj.* strategy or artifice : *n.pl.* military warfare ; direction of a campaign.

STRATEGY (strat'e-ji), *n.* use of artifice or stratagem in carrying out some design.

STRATIFICATION (-i-fi-ka'shun), *n.* the process of being arranged or deposited in layers.

STRATUM (stra'tum), *n.* [*pl.* strata ('ta)], a bed of earth or rock, consisting generally of layers.

STRAW (straw), *n.* the dried stalks of grain.

STRAWBERRY ('ber-i), *n.* a sweet, luscious berry.

STRAY (stra), *v.i.* to wander ; deviate ; err : *n.* a person or thing that strays.

STREAK (strek), *n.* a line of colour.

STREAKY ('i), *adj.* having streaks.

STREAM (strem), *n.* anything flowing out of a source ; river, rivulet, or brook.

STREAMER ('er), *n.* a long narrow flag or pennon.

STREAMLET ('let), *n.* a rivulet ; a rill.

STREET (stret), *n.* a public road in a city or town.

STRENGTH (strength), *n.* active or passive power ; muscular force ; vigour ; power of endurance or resistance ; toughness.

STRENGTHEN ('n), *v.t.* to make strong ; confirm.

STRENUOUS (stren'u-us), *adj.* ardent ; zealous ; strong ; vigorous ; bold.

STRESS (stres), *n.* urgency ; strain ; pressure ; force.

STRETCH (strech), *v.t.* to draw out ; extend or expand ; strain ; exaggerate.

STRETCHER ('er), *n.* a frame or litter for carrying the sick or dead.

STREW (stroo), *v.t.* to spread by scattering ; scatter loosely.

STRICKEN (strik'en), *p.adj.* affected by weakness or disease ; smitten ; wounded.

STRICT (strikt), *adj.* vigorous ; exact ; severe ; enforcing discipline.

STRIDE (strid), *n.* a long step.

STRIFE (strif), *n.* discord ; conflict ; quarrel ; enmity ; war.

STRIKE (strik), *v.t.* to hit with a blow or with force ; dash ; collide ; affect strongly or sensibly : *v.i.* cease from work.

STRIKING ('ing), *adj.* impressive ; forcible ; wonderful.

STRING (string), *n.* a small cord or line ; cord of a musical instrument.

STRINGENCY (strin'jen-si), *n.* the state or quality of being stringent.

STRINGENT (strin'jent), *adj.* severe ; rigid ; strict ; binding ; tense.

STRINGER (string'er), *n.* a tie-beam ; a string-piece.

STRINGY (-i), *adj.* ropy ; viscid ; sticky.

STRIP (strip), *v.t.* deprive of a covering ; skin or peel ; pillage ; bereave ; take away.

STRIPE (strip), *v.t.* to variegate with lines of different colours ; lash or whip.

STRIPLING (strip'ling), *n.* a youth.

STRIVE (striv), *v.i.* to labour hard or earnestly ; aim ; struggle.

STROKE (strok), *n.* a knock or blow ; calamity or affliction ; sudden paralysis ; gentle touch.

STROLL (strol), *v.i.* to wander ; ramble.

STROLLER ('er), *n.* one who strolls ; an itinerant player.

STRONG (strong), *adj.* robust ; healthy ; vigorous ; having power of endurance ; powerful ; violent ; muscular.

STRONGHOLD ('hold), *n.* a fortress.

STRONG-MINDED (-min'ded), *adj.* having a strong, vigorous mind or intellect.

STROP (strop), *n.* strip of leather for sharpening razors.

STRUCTURAL (struk'tur-ral), *adj.* pertaining to structure.

STRUCTURE ('tur), *n.* an edifice or building ; form.

STRUGGLE (strug'l), *v.i.* to use

violent efforts with contortions of the body ; strive with efforts ; contend.

STRUM (strum), *v.t.* & *v.i.* to play badly and noisily on a stringed instrument.

STRUT (strut), *v.i.* to walk with affected dignity : *n.* a support of timber.

STRYCHNINE ('nin), *n.* a highly poisonous alkaloid.

STUBBORN (stub'ern), *adj.* inflexibly headstrong ; obstinate.

STUBBY (stub'i), *adj.* short, thick and bristly.

STUCCO (stuk'o), *n.* kind of plaster used as a coating for walls.

STUCK-UP (stuk'up), *adj.* conceited.

STUD (stud), *n.* an ornamental knob ; a collar button ; an upright beam or scantling ; collection of breeding horses ; a stallion.

STUDDING ('ing), *n.* studs or joists collectively.

STUDENT (stu'dent), *n.* a scholar ; one devoted to books or learning ; systematic observer.

STUDIED ('id), *adj.* well-read ; precise or formal ; premeditated.

STUDIO (stu'di-o), *n.* an artist's workroom.

STUDIOUS ('di-us), *adj.* devoted to study ; diligent ; deliberate ; careful (with *of*).

STUDY (stud'i), *n.* the application of the mind to acquisition of knowledge ; any particular branch of learning.

STUFF (stuf), *n.* materials out of which anything is made ; textile fabrics ; goods ; refuse matter ; nonsense.

STUFFING ('ing), *n.* the material with which anything is stuffed, especially bread, seasoning, etc., put into fowl for roasting.

STUFFY ('i),*adj.* close or ill-ventilated.

STULTIFY ('ti-fi), *v.t.* to make nugatory.

STUMBLE (stum'bl), *v.i.* to trip up or fall in walking ; light (with *on* or *upon*) ; to err.

STUMP (stump), *n.* part remaining after amputation, etc.

STUN (stun), *v.t.* to render senseless ;

surprise completely ; astonish.

STUNNING ('ing), *adj.* overpowering ; [slang], remarkably fine or large.

STUNT (stunt), *v.t.* to check in growth or progress : *n.* an allotted task.

STUPEFACTION (-fak'shun), *n.* insensibility ; torpor ; stupidity.

STUPEFY ('pe-fi), *v.t.* to deprive of sensibility ; make stupid ; dull.

STUPENDOUS (stu-pen'dus), *adj.* overcoming the senses by its vastness ; astonishing.

STUPID (stu'pid), *adj.* insensible ; dull ; silly ; nonsensical.

STUPIDITY ('i-ti), *n.* extreme dullness ; crass ignorance ; folly.

STUPOR ('per), *n.* numbness ; lethargy.

STURDILY (ster'di-li), *adv.* in a sturdy manner.

STURDY ('di), *adj.* hardy ; robust ; strong ; vigorous.

STUTTER (stut'er), *v.i.* to speak with hesitation or stammering.

STY (sti), *n.* a pen or enclosure for swine ; a boil upon the eyelid.

STYLE (stil), *n.* a sharp-pointed engraving tool ; appellation or title ; distinctive manner of writing with regard to the choice of words, etc. ; manner of speaking ; fashion ; manner.

STYLISH (stil'ish), *adj.* fashionable ; modish.

STYLIST ('ist), *n.* a master of literary style.

STYLUS (sti'lus), *n.* a sharp-pointed instrument for manifolding with carbon paper.

STYPTIC (stip'tik), *adj.* stopping bleeding.

SUABLE (su'a-bl), *adj.* capable of being, or liable to be, sued.

SUASION ('zhun), *n.* persuasion.

SUAVE (swav, swav), *adj.* pleasant in manner.

SUAVITY (swav'i-ti), *n.* urbanity.

SUB-, a prefix ordinarily signifying *under*, *from under* ; for the sake of euphony, *sub* becomes *suc*, *suf*, *sug*, *sum*, *sup*, *sur*, before *c*, *f*, *g*, *m*, *p*, *v*, respectively ; in some cases it becomes *subs*, *sus*, or *su* : as many words carrying this prefix are self-explanatory, they are omitted from the list of definitions.

SUBACID (-as'id), *adj.* slightly acid.

SUBALTERNATE (-ter'nat), *adj.* successive.

SUBCONSCIOUS (-kon'shus), *adj.* dimly conscious.

SUBDUE (-du'), *v.t.* to overcome or conquer ; vanquish ; reduce ; lower ; tone down.

SUBJECT ('jekt), *adj.* under the power or control of another ; subordinate ; disposed ; liable : *n.* theme ; topic ; design : *v.t.* (subjekt'), to render subordinate ; subjugate ; expose.

SUBJECTION (-jek'shun), *n.* the act of subjecting.

SUBJECTIVE ('tiv), *adj.* derived from one's own consciousness.

SUBJOIN (-join'), *v.t.* to affix.

SUBJUGATE ('ju-gat), *v.t.* to conquer by force.

SUBJUNCTIVE (-jungk'tiv), *adj.* noting a form of the verb expressive of contingency, condition, or hypothesis.

SUBLIMATE ('li-mat), *v.t.* to convert (a solid) by heat into vapour, which on cooling returns to the solid state ; refine ; purify ; exalt.

SUBLIME (-lim'), *adj.* awakening feelings of awe and reverence ; exalted.

SUBMARINE (sub-ma-ren'), *adj.* located or found under the sea : *n.* a boat that may be submerged and propelled under water.

SUBMERGE (-merj'), *v.t.* place under water ; overwhelm.

SUBMERSION (-mer'shun), **SUBMERGENCE** (-mer'jens), *n.* the act of submerging ; state of being submerged.

SUBMISSION (-mish'un), *n.* obedience.

SUBMISSIVE (-mis'iv), *adj.* yielding to authority ; obedient.

SUBMIT (-mit'), *v.t.* to yield to the authority of another ; surrender.

SUBORDINATE (-or'di-nat), *adj.* inferior in rank, value, power, or importance.

SUBORNATION (-or-na'shun), *n.*

inducing a person to commit perjury.

SUBPŒNA (-pe'na), *n.* a writ commanding the attendance of a person in court.

SUBROGATE ('ro-gat), *v.t.* substitute.

SUBSCRIBE (-skrib'), *v.t.* to write or annex (one's name), to a paper or document : *v.i.* to give consent.

SUBSCRIPTION (-skrip'shun), *n.* name subscribed ; signature ; sum of money subscribed.

SUBSEQUENT ('se-kwent), *adj.* following or coming after in time or order.

SUBSERVE (-serv'), *v.t.* to be subservient to ; promote.

SUBSIDE (-sid'), *v.i.* tend downwards ; settle ; abate ; become calm.

SUBSIDENCE ('ens), *n.* the act of subsiding or sinking down.

SUBSIDIARY (-sid'i-a-ri), *adj.* auxiliary ; tributary.

SUBSIDIZE ('si-diz), *v.t.* to furnish with a subsidy.

SUBSIDY ('si-di), *n.* public grant to aid an enterprise.

SUBSIST (-sist'), *v.i.* to have existence ; have the means of livelihood.

SUBSISTENCE (-sis'tens), *n.* maintenance ; livelihood.

SUBSTANCE ('stans), *n.* essential part of anything.

SUBSTANTIAL (-stan'shal), *adj.* containing the essential parts ; solid ; material ; corporeal.

SUBSTANTIATE ('shi-at), *v.t.* to establish the truth of by proof or competent evidence.

SUBSTANTIATION (-shi-a'shun), *n.* proof ; incontrovertible evidence.

SUBSTANTIVE ('stan-tiv), *adj.* real ; essential : *n.* that part of speech which expresses the existence of anything material, or immaterial ; a noun.

SUBSTITUTE ('sti-tut), *v.t.* to put in the place of another ; change.

SUBSTITUTION (-tu'shun), *n.* the act of substituting.

SUBTERFUGE ('ter-fuj), *n.* an evasion or artifice ; trick ; shift.

SUBTERRANEAN (-a'ne-an), *adj.* below the surface ; beneath the earth.

SUBTILE (sub'til, sut'l), *adj.* delicately constructed; fine; rarefied.

SUBTLE (sut'l), *adj.* artful; insinuating; crafty.

SUBTLETY (-ti), *n.* acuteness of intellect; cunning; shrewdness.

SUBTRACT (-trakt'), *v.t.* to withdraw or take away; deduct.

SUBTRACTION (-trak'shun), *n.* the act of subtracting.

SUBTREASURY (sub-trezh'ur-i), *n.* a branch of the U.S. treasury.

SUBULATE (su'bu-lat), *adj.* awl-shaped.

SUBURB (sub'erb), *n.* an outlying district of a city or town : *pl.* environs.

SUBURBAN (-er'ban), *adj.* pertaining to the suburbs.

SUBVENTION (-ven'shun), *n.* a government grant or subsidy.

SUBVERSION (-ver'shun), *n.* overthrow; ruin.

SUBVERSIVE ('siv), *adj.* tending to subvert.

SUBVERT (-vert'), *v.t.* to ruin; overthrow; corrupt.

SUBVERTIBLE (-ver'ti-bl), *adj.* capable of being subverted.

SUBWAY ('wa), *n.* an underground passage or railroad.

SUCCEED (suk-sed'), *v.i.* to follow in order; obtain one's wishes; be successful.

SUCCESS (-ses'), *n.* prosperity; a person, or thing, which achieves favour or gain.

SUCCESSFUL (-fool), *adj.* prosperous; fortunate.

SUCCESSFULLY (-li), *adv.* in a successful manner.

SUCCESSION ('shun), *n.* the act of following in order; lineage; rotation, as of crops.

SUCCESSIVE ('iv), *adj.* following in uninterrupted order; consecutive.

SUCCESSOR ('er), *n.* one who succeeds or follows another.

SUCCINCT (-singkt'), *adj.* tersely expressed.

SUCCOTASH (suk'o-tash), *n.* a dish of green corn and beans boiled together.

SUCCOUR (suk'er), *v.t.* to help or relieve when in difficulty or distress; aid.

SUCCULENCE ('u-lens), *n.* juiciness.

SUCCULENT ('u-lent), *adj.* juicy.

SUCCUMB (su-kum'), *v.i.* to yield; submit; sink; die.

SUCH (such), *adj.* the same that, or as referred to; denoting a particular person or thing : *adv.* so as.

SUCK (suk), *v.t.* to draw in.

SUCKER ('er), *n.* animal; piston of a pump; a tube through which anything is drawn; shoot of a plant from the lower part of the stem.

SUCKLE ('l), *v.t.* to nurse at the breast.

SUCKLING ('ling), *n.* an unweaned child or animal.

SUCTION (suk'shun), *n.* drawing fluids by the removal of the atmospheric pressure.

SUDDEN (sud'n), *adj.* instantaneous; without notice; quick.

SUDS (sudz), *n.pl.* soapy water.

SUE (su), *v.t.* to prosecute at law : *v.i.* to entreat; beg; petition.

SUEDE (swad), *n.* undressed kid or lamb skin, tanned and used for gloves, etc.

SUET (su'et), *n.* the hard fat around the kidneys and loins of sheep, etc.

SUFFER (suf'er), *v.t.* to feel with a sense of pain; undergo; bear.

SUFFERABLE (-a-bl), *adj.* that may be tolerated; permissible.

SUFFERANCE ('er-ans), *n.* patience under pain; toleration.

SUFFERING ('ing), *n.* physical or mental pain; distress; loss or injury endured.

SUFFICE (su-fiz'), *v.i.* to be sufficient; *v.t.* to satisfy.

SUFFICIENCY (fish'en-si), *n.* competence; self-confidence; conceit.

SUFFICIENT ('ent), *adj.* equal to any end or purpose; adequate; competent.

SUFFIX (suf'iks), *n.* a letter or syllable added at the end of a word; affix : *v.t.* (suf-iks'), to add, as a letter or syllable at the end of a word.

SUFFOCATE ('o-kat), *v.t.* to choke; smother; stifle.

SUFFOCATION (-ka'shun), *n.* the act of suffocating.

SUFFRAGE ('raj), *n.* vote, or right to vote ; franchise ; voice or vote given on a controverted subject.

SUFFRAGETTE (-ra-jet'), *n.* a woman who seeks equal suffrage.

SUFFRAGIST ('ra-jist), *n.* one who advocates general suffrage.

SUFFUSE (su-fuz'), *v.t.* to spread over, as with a fluid or a colour.

SUGAR (shoog'er), *n.* a sweet crystalline substance obtained from the sugar-cane, beets, etc.

SUGAR MAPLE (ma'pl), *n.* the hard maple, from the sap of which maple-sugar is made.

SUGGEST (sug-jest'), *v.t.* to introduce indirectly to the mind ; hint ; insinuate.

SUGGESTION (-jes'chun), *n.* the act of suggesting ; thing suggested ; hint.

SUGGESTIVE ('tiv), *adj.* containing, or full of, suggestion.

SUICIDAL (su'i-sid-al), *adj.* pertaining to, or partaking of, suicide.

SUICIDE ('i-sid), *n.* a person who kills himself ; ruin of one's own interests.

SUIT (sut), *n.* a set of things that correspond each to each ; personal outfit, the seeking of a favour ; petition or prayer ; an action or process at law.

SUITABILITY (-a-bil'i-ti), *n.* being suitable.

SUITABLE ('a-bl), *adj.* fitting ; appropriate.

SUITE (swet), *n.* a retinue or company ; series ; set, as of rooms, etc.

SUITOR (sut'er), *n.* a petitioner ; supplicant ; lover.

SULK (sulk), *v.i.* to be sulky.

SULKY (sul'ki), *adj.* silently sullen : *n.* a kind of two-wheeled vehicle.

SULLEN (sul'en), *adj.* morosely silent ; dismal ; heavy.

SULLY ('i), *v.t.* to tarnish or soil ; dirty ; stain.

SULPHATE ('fat), *n.* a salt of sulphuric acid.

SULPHIDE ('fid), *n.* a combination of sulphur with an element or radical.

SULPHUR ('fur, 'fer), *n.* a non-metallic element brittle and of a yellow colour, insoluble in water, but fusible by heat.

SULPHUR-BOTTOM (-bot'um), *n.* the finback or blue whale or rorqual which reaches a length of 90 feet ; largest of all mammals.

SULPHUREOUS (-fu're-us), *adj.* consisting of, impregnated with, or having the qualities of, sulphur.

SULPHURIC (-fu'rik), *adj.* obtained from, or containing, sulphur.

SULPHURIC-ACID (as'id), *n.* a heavy, corrosive liquid, composed of sulphur, oxygen, and water ; oil of vitriol.

SULTRY ('tri), *adj.* very hot, close, and oppressive.

SUM (sum), *n.* the aggregate of two or more things taken together ; whole ; total.

SUMAC (su'mak), *n.* a plant or shrub, used in tanning, dyeing, and medicine.

SUMMARILY (sum'a-ril-i), *adv.* in a short way or method ; concisely.

SUMMARIZE ('a-riz), *v.t.* to state concisely.

SUMMARY ('a-ri), *adj.* brief ; laconic ; compendious : *n.* an abridgment.

SUMMER ('er), *n.* that part of the year which comprises June, July, and August ; a happy period.

SUMMIT ('it), *n.* the top or highest point.

SUMMON ('un), *v.t.* to cite or call by authority.

SUMPTUARY (sump'tu-a-ri), *adj.* pertaining to, or regulating, expenses.

SUMPTUOUS ('tu-us), *adj.* expensive ; costly ; luxurious ; magnificent.

SUN (sun), *n.* the luminous body around which the earth, and other planets of the solar system revolve.

SUNDAE (sun'da), *n.* ice cream and fresh fruit or fruit syrup.

SUNDAY ('da), *n.* the first day of the week ; the Lord's Day.

SUNDAY SCHOOL (skool), *n.* a school for religious instruction.

SUNDER ('der), *v.t.* to divide or rend.

SUNDIAL (sun'di-al), *n.* a contrivance for measuring time by the shadow of the sun.

SUNDRIES ('driz), *n.pl.* numerous

small or miscellaneous articles or matters.

SUNDRY ('dri), *adj.* various; several.

SUNKEN (sungk"n), *adj.* lying on the bottom of the sea; fallen or pressed down.

SUNNINESS (sun'i-nes), *n.* brightness; cheerfulness; warmth from the sun.

SUNNY (sun'i), *adj.* exposed to the sun; bright; warm; cheerful.

SUNRISE (sun'riz), *n.* the rising of the sun above the eastern horizon; early morning; the east.

SUNSET (sun'set), *n.* the setting of the sun above the western horizon; twilight; the west.

SUNSHINE ('shin), *n.* the light or rays of the sun; warmth; brightness.

SUNSTROKE ('strok), *n.* a kind of apoplexy, caused by the intense heat of the sun's rays.

SUN-UP ('up), *n.* sunrise.

SUP (sup), *v.i.* to take supper: *n.* a small mouthful; sip.

SUPER (su'per), *n.* anything of large size, good quality, fine degree, etc.

SUPER-, a prefix signifying *above*, *over*, *beyond*, *in excess;* also, in chemistry, to denote that the ingredient to which it is prefixed is present in *large* degree.

SUPERABUNDANCE (-a-bun'dans), *n.* excess.

SUPERANNUATE (su-per-an'u-at), *v.t.* to pension on account of old age.

SUPERB (su-perb'), *adj.* grand; proud; stately; elegant; first-rate; sumptuous.

SUPERCILIOUS (su-per-sil'i-us), *adj.* haughty; proud; disdainful; dictatorial; overbearing.

SUPERDREADNOUGHT (-dred'-nawt), *n.* the most gigantic type of modern battleship.

SUPEREROGATION (-er-o-ga'-shun), *n.* the performance of more than is required by duty.

SUPERFICIAL (-fish'a), *adj.* pertaining to the surface; slight; not deep; unlearned.

SUPERFICIALITY (-i-al'i-ti), *n.* being superficial; slight knowledge.

SUPERFINE ('per-fin), *adj.* very fine

or excellent; of the best quality.

SUPERFLUITY (-floo'i-ti), *n.* superabundance; excess.

SUPERFLUOUS ('floo-us), *adj.* more than enough or necessary; excessive.

SUPERHEAT (-het'), *v.t.* to heat to an extreme degree.

SUPERIMPOSE (-im-poz'), *v.t.* to lay or impose on something else.

SUPERINDUCE (-in-dus'), *v.t.* to bring in or upon, as an addition.

SUPERINTEND (-in-tend'), *v.t.* to have charge of; direct or control.

SUPERINTENDENCE (-ten'dens), *n.* supervision; oversight; control.

SUPERINTENDENT ('dent), *n.* one who superintends.

SUPERIOR (su-pe'ri-er), *adj.* stronger; surpassing others; unconquered; preferable; beyond the power or influence of: *n.* one who is superior to others.

SUPERIORITY (-or'i-ti), *n.* being superior; pre-eminence; advantage.

SUPERLATIVE (-per'la-tiv), *adj.* superior to all others; highest in degree.

SUPERNAL ('nal), *adj.* celestial.

SUPERNATURAL (-nat'u-ral), *adj.* beyond the powers or laws of nature.

SUPERNUMERARY (-nu'mer-a-ri), *n.* a person or thing beyond the stated or required number.

SUPERSCRIBE (-skrib'), *v.t.* to write, inscribe, or engrave, on the outside or top.

SUPERSCRIPTION (-skrip'shun), *n.* the address or direction.

SUPERSEDE (-sed'), *v.t.* to set aside or render null and void; take the place of.

SUPERSTITION (-stish'un), *n.* belief in the supernatural; false worship; extreme observance of religious rites.

SUPERSTITIOUS ('us), *adj.* pertaining to superstition.

SUPERSTRUCTURE (-struk'-tur), *n.* anything built or founded on something else.

SUPERTAX (-taks), *n.* any tax above normal; also *surtax*.

SUPERVENE (-ven'), *v.i.* to come

upon as something extraneous; occur; happen.

SUPERVISE (-viz'), *v.t.* to oversee.

SUPERVISION (-vizh'un), *n.* the act of supervising.

SUPERVISOR (-vi'zer), *n.* an overseer.

SUPINE (su-pin'), *adj.* lying on the back; indolent; careless; inattentive; negligent.

SUPINELY ('li), *adv.* in a supine manner.

SUPPER (sup'er), *n.* the evening meal; an evening banquet.

SUPPLANT (su-plant'), *v.t.* to displace; supersede.

SUPPLE (sup'l), *adj.* flexible; yielding.

SUPPLEMENT ('le-ment), *v.t.* to add something to; fill up or supply: *n.* addition to a newspaper or magazine; appendix.

SUPPLEMENTAL (-men'tal), *adj.* additional.

SUPPLEMENTARY (-men'ta-ri), *adj.* additional.

SUPPLENESS (sup'l-nes), *n.* being supple; pliancy.

SUPPLIANT (sup'li-ant), *adj.* beseeching; entreating; suing.

SUPPLICANT (-kant), *adj.* asking with humility.

SUPPLICATE (-kat), *v.t.* to ask or beg humbly and earnestly.

SUPPLICATION (-ka'shun), *n.* humble and earnest prayer or entreaty.

SUPPLICATORY ('li-ka-to-ri), *adj.* pertaining to, supplication.

SUPPLIER (su-pli'er), *n.* one who, or that which, supplies.

SUPPLY (su-pli'), *v.t.* to furnish with what is required; provide; serve; fill.

SUPPORT (-port'), *v.t.* to sustain; bear up; endure; uphold; favour; second; incur; carry on.

SUPPORTER (-por'ter), *n.* one who supports; an advocate; adherent of a party.

SUPPOSE (-poz'), *v.t.* to imagine; assume as true; think.

SUPPOSITION (sup-o-zish'un), *n.* the act of assumption.

SUPPOSITITIOUS (su-poz-i-tish'-us), *adj.* supposed or imaginary; not genuine.

SUPPRESS (-pres'), *v.t.* to subdue; crush; quell; conceal; restrain.

SUPPURATION (-ra'shun), *n.* pus generated in a sore.

SUPREMACY (su-prem'a-si), *n.* highest authority; supreme power.

SUPREME (-prem'), *adj.* highest in power or authority; most excellent.

SURCEASE (sur-ses'), *v.i.* to stop entirely: *n.* the end.

SURCHARGE (sur-charj'), *v.t.* to give an excessive load: *n.* an excessive charge.

SURCINGLE (ser'sing-gl), *n.* a girth, belt, or girdle for passing around the body of an animal and securing the saddle or some burden, etc.

SURCOAT ('kot), *n.* a coat worn over another coat or garment.

SURE (shoor), *adj.* certain; reliable; firm; safe.

SURELY ('li), *adv.* certainly; without doubt.

SURENESS ('nes), *n.* certainty.

SURETY ('ti), *n.* certainty; guarantee; hostage.

SURF (serf), *n.* swell of the sea that breaks upon the shore.

SURFACE (ser'fas), *n.* exterior part of anything; outside.

SURFBOAT (serf-bot), *n.* a strong, light boat for going through the surf.

SURFEIT (ser'fit), *n.* excess in eating or drinking.

SURGE (serj), *n.* a large wave or billow; great roll; swell.

SURGEON (ser'jun), *n.* one who practises surgery.

SURGERY ('jer-i), *n.* act and art of treating injuries or diseases by manual operations.

SURLY ('li), *adj.* gloomily morose; rough; uncivil.

SURMISE (sur-miz'), *n.* guess or conjecture; suspicion.

SURMOUNT (sur-mount'), *v.t.* to overcome; conquer; vanquish; exceed.

SURNAME (ser'nam), *n.* a name added to a given name.

SURPASS (sur-pas'), *v.t.* to exceed; excel.

SURPLUS ('plus), *n.* that which remains over and above what is required; excess.

SURPRISE (-priz'), *n.* astonishment; sudden emotion.

SURPRISING (-priz'ing), *adj.* extraordinary.

SURRENDER (su-ren'der), *v.t.* to yield or give up on compulsion.

SURREPTITIOUS (sur-ep-tish'us), *adj.* done by stealth or fraud; unauthorized.

SURROGATE ('o-gat), *n.* a probate judge.

SURROUND (su-round'), *v.t.* to encompass; environ; invest.

SURVEILLANCE (sur-val'yans), *n.* watch; oversight; supervision.

SURVEY (-va'), *v.t.* to inspect; overlook; examine; measure and estimate, as land.

SURVEYOR ('er), *n.* one who surveys.

SURVIVAL (sur-viv'al), *n.* continuance beyond the life of another.

SURVIVE (-viv'), *v.t.* to live longer than; outlive.

SURVIVOR ('er), *n.* one who outlives another.

SUSCEPTIBILITY (su-sep-ti-bil'i-ti), *n.* being susceptible.

SUSCEPTIBLE ('ti-bl), *adj.* capable of admitting something additional, or any change, influence, affection, etc.; impressible.

SUSPECT (-pekt'), *v.t.* to have a suspicion of; imagine to exist; mistrust.

SUSPEND (-pend'), *v.t.* to make to hang by anything; delay; interrupt; debar temporarily.

SUSPENDER (-pen'der), *n.* one who, or that which, suspends: *pl.* braces.

SUSPENSE (-pens'), *n.* a state of uncertainty, doubt, or anxiety; indecision.

SUSPENSION (-pen'shun), *n.* a floating, as of minute particles, in a liquid; a keeping in doubt; uncertainty; delay; interruption.

SUSPICION (-pish'un), *n.* distrust; want of confidence; imagination of something wrong.

SUSTAIN (-tan), *v.t.* to maintain; keep; support; nourish; bear; endure, strengthen.

SUSTENANCE ('te-nans), *n.* that which supports life; food; support.

SUSTENTATION (-ten-ta'shun), *n.* support or maintenance.

SUTLER (sut'ler), *n.* a person who follows an army and sells provisions, etc.

SUZERAINTY (su'ze-ran-ti), *n.* paramount authority.

SWAB (swob), *n.* a mop.

SWADDLE (swod'l), *v.t.* to swathe or bind tightly, especially infants.

SWAG (swag), *v.i.* to hang heavily; sag: *n.* thieves' booty.

SWAGGER ('er), *v.i.* to bully or bluster; strut haughtily.

SWAIN (swan), *n.* a peasant; sweetheart.

SWALLOW (swol'o), *n.* a migratory passerine bird: *v.t.* to take into the stomach; absorb; engulf; put up with.

SWAMP (swomp), *n.* wet or boggy land: *v.t.* overset or sink in water; ruin.

SWAN (swon), *n.* a web-footed, heavy-bodied aquatic bird.

SWAP (swop), *v.t.* to barter.

SWARD (swawrd), *n.* the grassy surface of land.

SWARM (swawrm), *v.i.* to throng together in a crowd: *n.* a cluster of bees.

SWARTHY (swor'thi), *adj.* of a dark or tawny hue; dark-skinned.

SWASH (swosh), *n.* a dashing or splashing of water.

SWASHY ('i), *adj.* soft, like fruit too ripe.

SWATH (swoth), *n.* a line or ridge of grass or grain as cut down by the mower.

SWATHE (swath), *v.t.* to bind with a bandage; wrap.

SWAY (swa), *v.t.* to move backwards and forwards; influence; bias; govern: *n.* rule; authority.

SWEAR (swar), *v.i.* to make a solemn declaration on oath; use profane language.

SWEAT (swet) *n.* perspiration.

SWEATER (swet'er), *n.* a heavy, knitted, woollen garment.

SWEATING SYSTEM ('ing sis'tem), the system by which middlemen employ people to work in their homes for very low wages.

SWEATSHOP (swet'shop), *n.* a place where the employees are overworked and paid low wages.

SWEET (swet), *adj.* pleasing to the senses, as smell, taste, etc.

SWEETBREAD ('bred), *n.* a calf's pancreas.

SWEETBRIER ('bri-er), *n.* the dog rose.

SWEET CORN (korn), *n.* a kind of maize.

SWEET-FLAG ('flag), *n.* an aromatic plant with sword-shaped leaves ; calamus.

SWEET OIL (oil), *n.* olive oil.

SWEET PEA (pe), *n.* a well-known climbing garden plant.

SWEET WILLIAM (wil'yam), *n.* a beautiful flowering plant of the pink kind.

SWELL (swel), *v.i.* to expand or enlarge ; be inflated ; be puffed up.

SWELTER ('ter), *v.t.* to perspire profusely : *n.* haste.

SWERVE (swerv), *v.i.* to turn aside ; deviate ; incline.

SWIFT (swift), *adj.* fleet ; rapid ; quick.

SWILL (swil), *v.t.* to drink greedily : *n.* refuse of the kitchen.

SWIM (swim), *v.i.* move in the water by the hands and feet.

SWIMMINGLY ('ing-li), *adv.* with great success.

SWINDLE (swin'dl), *v.t.* to cheat : *n.* a gross fraud.

SWINE (swin), *n.* pigs and hogs collectively

SWINISH (swin'ish), *adj.* pertaining to swine ; bestial.

SWIPE (swip), *n.* a vigorous blow.

SWIRL (swerl), *v.i.* to rush along in, or form, eddies.

SWISH (swish), *v.t.* to lash ; flog : *n.* a rustling sound.

SWITCH (swich), *n.* a thin, flexible rod ; a movable rail for transferring a railway carriage, etc., from one track to another ; a device for connecting one electric circuit with another.

SWIVEL (swiv'l), *n.* something fixed in another body so as to turn round in it ; twisting link in a chain.

SWOON (swoon), *v.i.* to sink into a fainting fit : *n.* syncope.

SWOOP (swoop), *v.t.* to fall upon and seize at once, as prey.

SWORD (sord), *n.* a keen-edged weapon.

SWORN (sworn), *p.adj.* oath-bound ; pledged.

SYCAMORE (sik'a-mor), *n.* a tree of the maple family.

SYCOPHANT ('o-fant), *n.* a mean or servile flatterer.

SYLLABLE (sil'a-bl), *n.* that part of a word which can be uttered distinctly by a single effort of the voice.

SYLLABUS ('a-bus), *n.* a table of contents ; abstract.

SYLLOGISM ('o-jizm), *n.* an argument stated in logical form.

SYLVAN ('van), *adj.* rustic ; woody ; shady.

SYMBOL (sim'bol), *n.* an emblem or sign representing something else ; type.

SYMBOLIZE (-iz), *v.t.* to represent by symbols.

SYMMETRIC (si-met'rik), **SYMMETRICAL** (-met'ri-kal), *adj.* harmonious ; proportionate.

SYMMETRY ('-tri), *n.* harmony of parts to each other.

SYMPATHETIC (-pa-thet'ik), **SYMPATHETICAL** (-pa-thet'i-kal), *adj.* compassionate.

SYMPATHIZE ('pa-thiz), *v.i.* to have a mutual feeling with another ; be compassionate.

SYMPATHY ('pa-thi), *n.* mutual feeling ; compassion.

SYMPHONIC (-fon'ik), *adj.* agreeing in sound.

SYMPHONY ('fo-ni), *n.* harmony of sound ; a musical composition for a full band of instruments.

SYMPOSIUM (-po'zi-um), *n.* [*pl.* symposia (-a)], an article in a magazine in which various writers express their views on some given topic.

SYMPTOM (simp'tom), *n.* that which indicates the existence of something else of which it is the effect.

SYN-, a prefix signifying *with, together, at the same time :* it becomes *sym* before *p, b,* and *m,* and *syl* before *l.*

SYNAGOGUE ('a-gog), *n.* Jewish place of worship.

SYNCHRONIZE ('kro-niz), *v.i.* to happen simultaneously.

SYNCHRONOUS ('kro-nus), *adj.* happening at the same time.

SYNCOPATE (sing'ko-pat), *v.t.* to contract by omitting a letter or letters from the middle of (a word).

SYNCOPATION (-pa'shun), *n.* the act of syncopating ; the welding of the second half of a beat with the first half of the following into one tone.

SYNCOPE ('ko-pe), *n.* the omission of a letter or letters from the middle of a word ; sudden faintness or swoon.

SYNDICALISM (sin'di-ka-lizm), *n.* an economic movement which aims at the federation of all workers, and the abolition of all non-producers.

SYNDICATE ('di-kat), *n.* a combination of capitalists to promote some special undertaking.

SYNOD ('od), *n.* a church council.

SYNONYM ('o-nim), *n.* a word having nearly the same signification as another.

SYNONYMOUS (si-non'i-mus), *adj.* expressing the same, or nearly the same, meaning or idea.

SYNOPSIS (si-nop'sis), *n.* a general or collective view of any subject ; summary.

SYNTAX ('taks), *n.* that part of grammar which teaches of the proper construction and the arrangement of words in a sentence.

SYNTHESIS ('the-sis), *n.* [*pl.* syntheses (-sez)], composition, or putting of two or more things together ; combination of separate elements : opposed to *analysis.*

SYNTHETIC (-thet'ik), **SYNTHETICAL** (-i-kal), *adj.* pertaining to synthesis.

SYRINGA (si-ring'ga), *n.* a small genus of ornamental shrubs of the olive family.

SYRINGE (sir'inj), *n.* a tube operated by a piston, as a small pump.

SYRUP (sir'up), *n.* a solution of sugar in water ; the boiled juice of fruits.

SYSTEM (sis'tem), *n.* combination of parts, orderly arrangement according to some common law ; method of transacting business.

SYSTEMATIC (-at'ik), *adj.* methodical.

SYSTEMATIZE ('tem-a-tiz), *v.t.* to reduce to a system.

T

T, t, (te), the twentieth letter in the English alphabet.

T, t, an abbreviation.

T, a Roman numeral denoting 160 ; with a bar (T̄), 160,000.

TABASCO (ta-bas'ko), *n.* a pungent and biting sauce ; extract of peppers.

TABERNACLE (tab'er-na-kl), *n.* a temple ; a place of worship ; the human body as the temporary dwelling of the soul.

TABLE (ta'bl), *n.* a flat, smooth board, furnished with legs ; figures methodically arranged.

TABLEAU (tab'lo), *n.* [*pl.* tableaux ('loz)], a striking and vivid representation.

TABLE D'HOTE (tab'l' dot) a meal at a fixed price.

TABLE-LAND (ta'bl-land), *n.* a plateau.

TABLET (tab'let), *n.* a small table ; medicine in the form of a flat disc ; monument.

TABLOID (tab'loid), *n.* used to denote something condensed, as in tabloid newspapers.

TABOO, TABU (ta-boo'), *n.* ban ; prohibition.

TABULAR (tab'u-lar), *adj.* computed, or arranged in, tables or schedules.

TABULATE ('u-lat), *v.t.* to reduce to tables or synopses.

TACIT (tas'it), *adj.* implied, but not expressed verbally.

TACITURN ('i-tern), *adj.* habitually silent.

TACKLE (tak'l), *n.* the ropes, rigging, etc., of a vessel; apparatus for raising or lowering heavy weights; implements or gear.

TACT (takt), *n.* nice discernment and delicate skill in saying and doing exactly what is expedient or suitable in given circumstances.

TACTICIAN (-tish'an), *n.* one skilled in tactics.

TACTICS ('tiks), *n.* science of disposing and manœuvring naval and military forces for battle.

TACTUAL (tak'tu-al), *adj.* pertaining to the organs of touch.

TADPOLE (tad'pol), *n.* the larva of a frog.

TAFFETA (taf'e-ta), *n.* a fine, thin, glossy, silken fabric.

TAFFRAIL ('ral), *n.* rail round a ship's stern.

TAILOR (ta'ler), *n.* one who makes clothing.

TAINT (tant), *n.* corruption; infection; spot or stain; disgrace.

TAKE (tak), *v.t.* to lay or seize hold of; obtain; receive mentally.

TALC (talk), *n.* a hydrous silicate of magnesia.

TALE (tal), *n.* a narrative or story.

TALENT (tal'ent), *n.* among the ancients, a weight, coin, or sum of money of varying value; mental capacity; eminent ability; skill.

TALISMAN ('is-man), *n.* an amulet; charm.

TALK (tawk), *v.i.* to utter words; converse.

TALKATIVE ('a-tiv), *adj.* loquacious.

TALLOW (tal'o), *n.* melted fat; candle-grease.

TALLY ('i), *n.* one thing made to suit another; a record.

TALLY-HO (-ho), *interj. & n.* the huntman's cry to incite his hounds; a four-in-hand coach.

TALMI-GOLD (tal'mi gold), *n.* cheap imitation of gold; brass.

TALMUD (tal'mud), *n.* the book which contains the whole body of the Jewish civil and canonical laws and traditions.

TALON ('on), *n.* the claw of a bird of prey.

TAMABLE (tam'a-bl), *adj.* capable of being tamed.

TAMARACK (tam'a-rak), *n.* the American black larch.

TAMBOURINE ('ber-en'), *n.* a small hand-drum with little cymbals inserted in the hoop.

TAME (tam), *adj.* domesticated; spiritless; insipid : *v.t.* to subdue.

TAMP (tamp), *v.t.* to block up with clay, or similar material, the blast-hole in a rock to direct the course of the explosion; drive in or down by repeated strokes.

TAMPER ('per), *v.i.* to meddle; use bribery.

TAN (tan), *v.t.* to convert (a hide) into leather; make brown by exposure to the sun.

TANDEM ('dem), *n.* with two horses harnessed one before the other; a bicycle for two.

TANG (tang), *n.* a strong taste or flavour; sound or tone.

TANGENT ('jent), *adj.* touching : *n.* a straight line that meets or touches a circle or curve, but when produced, does not cut it.

TANGERINE (-jer-en'), *n.* a kind of orange.

TANGIBLE ('ji-bl), *adj.* perceptible to the touch; evident; real.

TANGLE (tang'gl), *v.t.* difficult to unravel; implicate; embarrass.

TANGO (tang'go), *n.* a form of Spanish dance.

TANK (tangk), *n.* a large cistern for storing water or other liquid; an armoured tractor.

TANNER (tan'er), *n.* one who tans hides.

TANNERY (-i), *n.* a place where hides are tanned.

TANNIC ('ik), *adj.* obtained from bark.

TANNIC-ACID (as'id), *n.* an astringent principle in oak-bark and gall-nuts.

TANTALIZE ('ta-liz), *v.t.* to tease or torment by exciting false hopes or fears; provoke.

TANTAMOUNT ('ta-mount), *adj.* equivalent in value or signification.

TANTRUM ('trum), *n.* a sudden outburst of temper.

TAP (tap), *v.t.* to strike or touch lightly.

TAPE (tap), *n.* a narrow band of linen, cotton or paper.

TAPER (ta'per), *n.* a small wax candle : *v.i.* to become gradually more slender.

TAPESTRY (tap'es-tri), *n.* a textile fabric of wool or silk ornamented with a raised design, figures, etc.

TAPEWORM (tap'werm), *n.* a flat ribbon-like intestinal worm.

TAPIOCA (tap-i-o'ka), *n.* a farinaceous food obtained from the root of the cassava.

TAPIS (ta-pe'), *n.* [French], tapestry formerly used to cover a council table; now used only in the expression *on the tapis*, that is, up for consideration.

TAPPING ('ing), *n.* a tap; a surgical operation for dropsy.

TAPROOT ('root), *n.* main root of a plant.

TAPS (taps), *n.* the bugle call, signifying "lights out"; also sounded at a military burial (*colloq.*).

TAR (tar), *n.* a thick, dark-brown, oily, viscous substance.

TARANTULA (ta-ran'tu-la), *n.* a large, venomous, hairy spider.

TARDILY ('di-li), *adv.* slowly.

TARDY ('di), *adj.* moving with a slow pace or motion; dilatory.

TARE (tar), *n.* an allowance made for the weight of the container.

TARGET (tar'get), *n.* butt or mark set up for marksmanship.

TARIFF (tar'if), *n.* a schedule of dutiable goods, specifying the customs, rates, etc., to be paid or allowed; a duty levied.

TARNISH (tar'nish), *n.* blemish : *v.t.* to diminish the luster of; sully.

TARPAULIN (-paw'lin), *n.* stout waterproof canvas.

TARRY (tar'i), *v.i.* to stay behind; linger.

TART (tart), *adj.* sharp to the taste; acid; severe : *n.* small open pie.

TARTAR ('tar), *n.* a deposit from the juice of grapes; a phosphate concretion which gathers on the teeth.

TASK (task), *n.* business or study imposed by another; duty.

TASSEL (tas'l), *n.* pendent ornament of silk, wool, etc.

TASTE (tast), *v.t.* to perceive by the tongue and palate; participate in; experience : *n.* discernment of the sublime or beautiful.

TASTEFUL ('fool), *adj.* savoury; showing good taste.

TASTY ('ti), *adj.* showing taste; savoury.

TATTER (tat'er), *n.* a loose hanging rag : *pl.* rags.

TATTERDEMALION (-ter-de-mal'-yun), *n.* a ragged fellow.

TATTLE ('l), *v.i.* to talk idly; tell tales or secrets.

TATTOO (ta-too'), *n.* a beat of drum; mark or figure made by puncturing the skin with a needle and rubbing a stain or dye into the wounds.

TAUNT (tant), *adj.* lofty : *n.* bitter or sarcastic reproach : *v.t.* to provoke.

TAUT (tawt), *adj.* tight; stretched; snug; secure.

TAUTOLOGY (-tol'o-ji), *n.* repetition of the same thing or idea in different words.

TAVERN (tav'ern), *n.* an inn or hotel.

TAWDRY ('dri), *adj.* showy without elegance; gaudily dressed.

TAX (taks), *n.* a rate or duty on income or property, etc., to defray government expenses : *v.t.* burden or oppress; accuse.

TAXATION (-a'shun), *n.* the system of raising revenues.

TAXICAB (tak'si-kab), *n.* an automobile for rent, having a device that records the time and cost of trip.

TAXIDERMIST ('si-der-mist), *n.* one skilled in taxidermy.

TAXIDERMY ('si-der-mi), *n.* the

art of stuffing and arranging speci-
mens of natural history.

TAXIMETER (tak-sim'e-ter), *n.* the
recording device used on a taxicab.

TEA (te), *n.* an evergreen shrub grown
in the orient ; a beverage made
from the dried leaves.

TEACH (tech), *v.t.* to impart knowledge to ; instruct ; inform.

TEAM (tem), *n.* two or more animals,
harnessed to the same vehicle for
drawing ; number of persons to
form a side in a game.

TEAR (ter), *n.* a small drop of moisture
from the eye.

TEAR (tar), *n.* a rent : *v.t.* to rend ;
disrupt ; lacerate.

TEARFUL (ter'fool), *adj.* shedding
tears.

TEASE (tez), *v.t.* to irritate or annoy.

TEAT (tet), *n.* nipple of the female
breast.

TECHNIQUE (tek-nek'), *n.* artistic
execution.

TECHNOLOGY (tech-nol'o-ji), *n.* the
science of the industrial arts.

TE DEUM (te de'um), an ancient
hymn of the Christian Church.

TEDIOUS (te'di-us, ted'yus), *adj.*
wearisome ; tiresome.

TEDIUM ('di-um), *n.* wearisomeness.

TEE (te), *n.* the mark aimed at in
quoits and curling ; nodule of earth,
from which the ball is struck at golf ;
a pipe connection.

TEEM (tem), *v.i.* to be prolific ; be full.

TEEN (ten), *n.* sorrow : *pl.* years of
one's age ending in *-teen.*

TEETOTALER (te-to-tal-er), *n.* a
total abstainer from intoxicating
liquors.

TEGUMENT (teg'u-ment), *n.* natural
covering or envelope ; skin.

TE-HEE (te-he'), *n.* a titter.

TELAUTOGRAPH (tel-aw'to-graf),
n. a telegraphic instrument for
reproducing writings or drawings at
a distance.

TELEGRAM ('e-gram), *n.* a telegraphic communication.

TELEGRAPH ('e-graf), *n.* an instrument for communicating intelligence
rapidly between certain points, by
means of electricity.

TELEPATHY (te-lep'a-thi), *n.* the
supposed transference of thought
from one person to another by the
exercise of the will.

TELEPHONE (tel'e-fon), *n.* an instrument for reproducing sound at a
distance by means of electricity.

TELESCOPE (tel'e-skop), *n.* an
optical instrument for viewing
objects at a distance.

TELL (tel), *v.t.* to express or make
known by words ; narrate ; communicate.

TELLER ('er), *n.* one who tells ; a
bank clerk who receives, or pays out ;
one who counts ballots.

TEMPERITY (te-mer'i-ti), *n.* foolhardiness ; rashness.

TEMPER (tem'per), *v.t.* to modify
or regulate ; qualify ; assuage ; calm ;
bring to a proper degree of hardness ;
n. mental disposition.

TEMPERAMENT ('per-a-ment), *n.*
natural constitution or organization.

TEMPERANCE ('per-ans), *n.* moderation ; patience ; sobriety ; total
abstinence.

TEMPERATE ('per-at), *adj.* moderate ; abstemious ; calm.

TEMPERATURE ('per-a-tur), *n.*
degree of heat or cold.

TEMPEST ('pest), *n.* wind rushing
with great violence ; hurricane ;
tumult.

TEMPESTUOUS (-pes'tu-us), *adj.*
very stormy ; violent.

TEMPLE ('pl), *n.* place of public
worship ; the flat part of either
side of the head above the cheek-
bones.

TEMPORAL ('po-ral), *adj.* secular ;
measured or restricted by time ;
civil or political.

TEMPORARY (-po-ra-ri), *adj.* existing or continuing for a limited time.

TEMPT (tempt), *v.t.* to test ; persuade ; defy ; allure ; entice.

TEMPTATION (temp-ta'shun), *n.*
enticement, especially to evil.

TEMPTER (temp'ter), *n.* one who
tempts ; [T-], the Devil. *Fem.*
temptress.

TEMPTING ('ting), *adj.* alluring.

TENABLE (ten'a-bl), *adj*. capable of being held ; maintained, or defended.

TENACIOUS (te-na'shus), *adj*. cohesive ; tough ; obstinate.

TENACITY (-nas'i-ti), *n*. cohesiveness ; adhesiveness.

TENANCY (ten'an-si), *n*. the holding of land or tenements on certain conditions ; tenure.

TENANT ('ant), *n*. one who holds lands or tenements on certain conditions.

TENDENCY (ten'den-si), *n*. inclination ; aim ; direction.

TENDER ('der), *adj*. sensitive ; soft ; not hard ; weak and feeble ; easily influenced by love, pity, etc. ; compassionate ; pathetic ; gentle : *n*. vehicle attached to a locomotive containing coal and water ; an offer or proposal.

TENDERFOOT ('der-foot), *n*. one who is new to a frontier district.

TENDERLOIN (ten'der-loin), *n*. a choice cut of beef, pork, etc.

TENDON ('dun), *n*. the fibres which connect the muscles to the bones.

TENDRIL ('dril), *n*. the slender, twining part of a plant.

TENEMENT ('e-ment), *n*. a house, shop, land, etc., held by a tenant ; any kind of permanent property, as land, etc.

TENET (ten'et), *n*. a doctrine, dogma, opinion, or belief held or maintained as true.

TENNIS ('is), *n*. a game played with rackets ; a ball, a net and marked square called a court.

TENOR ('er), *n*. manner of continuity ; general tendency or drift ; purport or substance ; the highest of adult male voices between bass and alto.

TENSE (tens), *adj*. drawn tightly ; rigid ; not lax : *n*. a modification in the inflection of a verb, expressing time of action.

TENSILE (ten'sil), *adj*. ductile.

TENSION ('shun), *n*. mental strain ; expansive or elastic force.

TENT (tent), *n*. a temporary shelter or canvas.

TENTACLE (ten'ta-kl), *n*. an organ in certain invertebrate animals used for feeling, prehension, or locomotion.

TENTATIVE ('ta-tiv), *adj*. experimental ; conjectural ; based on trial.

TENUOUS (ten'u-us), *adj*. slender ; not dense.

TENURE ('ur), *n*. manner of holding real estate ; term of holding.

TEPEFY (tep'e-fi), *v.t.* to make tepid : *v.i.* to become tepid.

TEPID ('id), *adj*. moderately warm ; lukewarm.

TEPIDITY (te-pid'i-ti), *n*. moderate warmth.

TERCENTENARY (ter-sen'te-na-ri), *adj*. comprising 300 years.

TERM (term), *n*. a limited time : *pl*. conditions.

TERMAGANT (ter'ma-gant), *adj*. noisy and violent : *n*. a virago.

TERMINABLE ('mi-na-bl), *adj*. that which may be discontinued.

TERMINAL ('mi-nal), *adj*. pertaining to the end or extremity.

TERMINATE ('mi-nat), *v.t.* to limit or end.

TERMINATION (-na'shun), *n*. a bound or limit ; end ; conclusion or result.

TERMINOLOGY (-mi-mol'o-ji), *n*. the technical terms used in any trade, profession, etc.

TERMINUS ('mi-nus), *n*. [*pl*. termini (-ni)], a limit or boundary.

TERN (tern), *n*. an aquatic bird allied to the gull : *adj*. arranged in threes.

TERRA (ter'a), *n*. the earth.

TERRACE ('as), *n*. a raised level space or platform of earth with sloping sides usually laid with turf ; row of houses.

TERRA COTTA (kot'a), *n*. a composition of fine clay and sand used for statues, etc. ; a reddish-brown tint.

TERRA FIRMA (fer'ma), *n*. the solid earth.

TERRAIN (ter'an), *n*. tract of land.

TERRESTRIAL (-es'tri-al), *adj*. pertaining to the earth.

TERRIBLE ('i-bl), *adj*. exciting or causing fear or awe ; dreadful.

TERRIER ('i-er), *n.* one of a breed of small dogs.

TERRIFY ('i-fi), *v.t.* to frighten or alarm exceedingly.

TERRITORIAL (-i-to'ri-al), *adj.* pertaining to a territory.

TERRITORY ('i-to-ri), *n.* the extent of land within a jurisdiction; large tract of land.

TERROR ('er), *n.* extreme fear; fright.

TERRORIZE (-iz), *v.t.* to intimidate or coerce by terror.

TERSE (ters), *adj.* elegantly and forcibly concise.

TERTIAN (ter'shan), *adj.* occurring, or recurring, every third day.

TERTIARY ('shi-a-ri), *adj.* of the third order, rank, or formation.

TESSELLATE (tes'el-at), *v.t.* to lay, as pavement, with squares or checkered work.

TEST (test), *n.* an examination; a standard; a trial; proof.

TESTAMENT ('ta-ment), *n.* an instrument in writing disposing of the estate of a person; will; [T-], one of the two great divisions of the Bible.

TESTAMENTARY (-men'ta-ri), *adj.* pertaining to a will.

TESTATE ('tat), *adj.* having left a will.

TESTATOR (-ta'ter), *n.* one who makes and leaves a will. *Fem. testatrix.*

TESTIFY ('ti-fi), *v.i.* to bear witness; give evidence.

TESTIMONIAL (-ti-mo'ni-al), *n.* a writing or certificate bearing testimony to character proficiency, etc.; a present.

TESTIMONY ('ti-mo-ni), *n.* evidence; proof.

TESTINESS ('ti-nes), *n.* peevishness.

TESTING ('ting), *n.* assay; proof; trial.

TESTY ('ti), *adj.* peevish; morose; irritable.

TETANUS (tet'a-nus), *n.* a disease called *lockjaw.*

TETHER (teth'er), *n.* a rope for confining an animal within certain limits.

TETTER (tet'er), *n.* a cutaneous disease.

TEXT (tekst), *n.* that on which a comment is written; original words of an author; verse, etc., of Scripture forming the subject of a sermon; topic.

TEXTBOOK (-book), *n.* a standard book of instruction.

TEXTILE ('til), *adj.* pertaining to weaving; capable of being woven : *n.* a woven fabric.

TEXTURE ('tur), *n.* manner of weaving; web; filaments or fibres interwoven; tissue.

THANK (thangk), *v.t.* to express gratitude or obligation to.

THANKSGIVING (thangks-giving), *n.* act of expressing gratitude for favours and mercies.

THANKSGIVING DAY (da), *n.* a day set apart annually in the U.S., usually the last Thursday in November, for thanksgiving to God.

THATCH (thach), *n.* straw, reeds, etc., used for covering the roofs of cottages, stacks, etc.

THAW (thaw), *v.i.* to melt or become liquid, as ice or snow.

THEATRE (the'a-ter), *n.* a public building where dramatic representations, etc., are given; scene or sphere of action.

THEFT (theft), *n.* act of stealing; robbery.

THEISM (the'izm), *n.* the belief in the existence of a God; opposed to *atheism.*

THEME (them), *n.* the subject or topic of a discourse or dissertation.

THEODOLITE (the-od'o-lit), *n.* an instrument for measuring horizontal and vertical angles and ascertaining distances and heights.

THEOLOGIAN (-o-lo'ji-an), *n.* one versed in theology.

THEOLOGY (-ol'o-ji), *n.* the science that treats of the existence, nature, and attributes of God, especially of man's relations to God; divinity.

THEOREM ('o-rem), *n.* a proposition to be proved; an established principle.

THEORETICAL (o-ret'i-kal), *adj.* pertaining to theory ; not practical ; speculative.

THEORIZE ('o-riz), *v.i.* to form a theory ; speculate.

THEORY ('o-ri), *n.* an exposition of the abstract principles of a science or art considered apart from practice ; hypothesis.

THEOSOPHY (-os'o-fi), *n.* a system of philosophy which professes to investigate the unexplained laws of nature ; it teaches a sort of pantheistic evolution by reincarnation.

THERAPEUTIC (ther-a-pu'tik), *adj.* curative ; pertaining to the healing art.

THEREFORE (ther'for), *adv. & conj.* for that or this reason.

THERM (therm), *n.* a thermal- or heat-unit.

THERMAL (ther'mal), *adj.* pertaining to heat ; warm.

THERMOMETER (-mom'e-ter), *n.* an instrument for measuring temperature.

THERMOSTAT ('mo-stat), *n.* an automatic apparatus for regulating temperature.

THESAURUS (the-saw'rus), *n.* a storehouse or treasury of words and phrases.

THESIS (the'sis), *n.* [*pl.* theses ('sez)], an essay or dissertation on some particular subject.

THEWS (thuz), *n.pl.* muscles ; strength.

THICK (thik), *adj.* not thin ; compact ; dense ; misty ; indistinct ; dull ; closely set ; crowded.

THICKEN ('n), *v.t.* to make thick or thicker ; render dense.

THICKET ('et), *n.* a close wood.

THICKSET ('set), *adj.* closely planted ; having a thick body.

THIEF (thef), *n.* a robber.

THIEVE (thev), *v.t. & v.i.* to steal.

THIGH (thi), *n.* the thick muscular part of the leg.

THIMBLE (thim'bl), *n.* a cup-shaped metallic protective cover for the finger in sewing ; an iron sail-ring fitted to receive a rope.

THIMBLERIG (-rig), *n.* a sleight-of-hand trick in which a pea is pre-

tended to be hidden under one of three thimbles.

THIN (thin), *adj.* having little thickness ; slim ; slender ; poor ; slight ; meagre.

THINK (thingk), *v.i.* to have the mind occupied on some subject ; form an opinion by reasoning ; believe ; imagine ; recollect.

THIRST (therst), *n.* a great desire for drink ; craving for anything.

THISTLE (this'l), *n.* a strong, prickly plant.

THITHER (thith'er), *adv.* to that place or end.

THONG (thong), *n.* a thin leather strap or string for fastening something.

THORAX (tho'raks), *n.* the chest.

THORN (thorn), *n.* a prickle or spine growing on a tree or shrub.

THOROUGH (thur'o), *adj.* perfect ; finished ; complete ; methodical.

THOROUGHBRED (-bred), *adj.* of pure and unmixed breed ; high-spirited.

THOROUGHFARE (-far), *n.* a passage from one street opening to another.

THOUGH (tho), *conj.* granting or, supposing that ; notwithstanding that ; if : *adv.* nevertheless ; however.

THOUGHT (thawt), *n.* meditation ; study ; care or anxiety.

THRALDOM (thrawl'dom), *n.* serfdom ; slavery.

THRASH (thrash), *v.t.* to beat out (grain) from the husk ; beat or flog soundly.

THRASHING ('ing), *n.* the operation of separating grain from the husk ; a sound flogging.

THREAT (thret), *n.* a menace ; a declaration of an intention to injure

THREATEN ('n), *v.i.* to use threats.

THRESH, same as thrash.

THRESHOLD (thresh'old), *n.* sill of a door ; entrance ; door.

THRIFT (thrift), *n.* frugality ; economical management.

THRILL (thril), *v.t.* to pierce ; cause to have a shivering, tingling, or exquisite sensation.

THRIVE (thriv), *v.i.* to prosper by industry, economy, and good management.

THROAT (throt), *n.* the forepart of the neck of an animal.

THROATY ('i), *adj.* guttural; deep; full.

THROB (throb), *v.i.* to palpitate.

THROE (thro), *n.* agony; extreme pain.

THRONE (thron), *n.* a chair of state; sovereign power.

THRONG (throng), *n.* a multitude; crowd.

THROSTLE (throsˈl), *n.* the song-thrush.

THROTTLE (throtˈl), *v.t.* to strangle or choke; a throttle-valve.

THROUGH (throo), *prep.* from end to end of; in the midst of; among.

THROW (thro), *v.t.* to fling or hurl; cast to a distance; cast in any manner.

THROWN (thron), *p.adj.* hurled; pitched aside.

THRUM (thrum), play idly or unskillfully on (a stringed instrument).

THRUSH (thrush), *n.* a migratory songbird.

THRUST (thrust), *v.t.* to push or drive with force; urge or impel.

THUD (thud), *n.* a dull sound produced by a body falling on a comparatively soft substance.

THUG (thug), *n.* a ruffian; assassin.

THUMB (thum), *n.* the short, thick digit of the human hand.

THUMP (thump), *n.* a heavy blow.

THUNDER (thunˈder), *n.* the noise accompanying lightning.

THUNDERBOLT (-bolt), *n.* a shaft of lightning accompanied with thunder; something resembling lightning in suddenness and terror.

THUNDERSTRUCK (-struk), *p.adj.* astonished by sudden amazement, etc.

THURIBLE (thuˈri-bl), *n.* a censer.

THURSDAY (therzˈda), *n.* the fifth day of the week.

THWACK (thwak), *v.t.* to strike with something flat and heavy; thump.

THWART (thwawrt), *adj.* crosswise; oblique: *v.t.* to oppose; frustrate.

THYME (tim), *n.* a common aromatic, garden mint.

THYROID (thiˈroid), *adj.* pertaining to the principal cartilage of the larynx; shield-shaped.

TIARA (ti-aˈra), *n.* the triple crown worn by the Pope; a diadem.

TICK (tik), *n.* a name for various parasites; a case for holding feathers, etc., for bedding; small mark; small, quick, distinct sound or beat.

TICKET ('et), *n.* a label or card giving its possessor some specific right; label specifying price, etc.

TICKLE ('l), *v.t.* to touch lightly so as to produce a laughing sensation; gratify; amuse.

TIDAL (tidˈal), *adj.* pertaining to the tides.

TIDE (tid), *n.* the regular rising and falling of the sea, rivers, etc.; stream; time; season; turning point.

TIDILY (tiˈdi-li), *adv.* in a neat manner.

TIDINGS ('dingz), *n.pl.* news.

TIDY (tiˈdi), *adj.* kept or dressed in proper neatness; trim; neat.

TIE (ti), *n.* knot or fastening; bond; obligation; beam or rod for holding two parts together; equality in numbers.

TIER (ter), *n.* a row or rank.

TIERCE (ters), *n.* a cask of 42 gallons.

TIFF (tif), *n.* a slight quarrel.

TIFFIN (tifˈin), *n.* midday lunch in India.

TIGER (tiˈger), *n.* a large, fierce, rapacious quadruped of Asia.

TIGHT (tit), *adj.* not loose; close; tenacious; compactly built; not leaky; taut; snug; parsimonious.

TILE (til), *n.* a thin slab of baked clay.

TILL (til), *n.* a money drawer: *prep.* to the time of; to the time when: *conj.* to the degree that; until: *v.t.* to prepare (land) for seed, etc.; cultivate.

TILLAGE ('aj), *n.* husbandry; agriculture.

TILLER ('er), *n.* a husbandman; handle or lever for the rudder of a vessel.

TILTH (tilth), *n.* cultivated land.

TIMBER (tim'ber), *n.* the body or stem of a tree; wood suitable for construction, etc.; wooded land.

TIMBRE ('ber), *n.* tone or character of musical sound.

TIME (tim), *n.* measure of duration, whether past, present, or future; particular period of duration; age or period during which anything occurred or a person lived; present life or existence; season; era; epoch; repetition; leisure; musical measure or duration of sounds.

TIMELOCK (tim'lok), *n.* a lock with clockwork attachment set to open at a certain time.

TIMELY ('li), *adj.* opportune.

TIMEPIECE (-pes), *n.* a clock or watch.

TIME-TABLE ('ta'bl), *n.* a schedule of events; a statement of the time of departure and arrival of trains.

TIMID (tim'id), *adj.* wanting in courage; faint-hearted; fearful.

TIMIDITY ('i-ti), *n.* want of courage.

TIMOROUS (tim'er-us), *adj.* fearful of danger.

TIMOTHY ('o-thi), *n.* a valuable grass; hay fodder.

TIN (tin), *n.* a silvery-white, soft, malleable and fusible metal.

TINCTURE (tingk'tur), *n.* a tinge or shade of colour; slight taste or quality; solution.

TINDER (tin'der), *n.* any inflammable material used to kindle a fire from a spark, as rotten wood.

TINE (tin), *n.* a tooth or spike.

TINFOIL (tin'foil), *n.* tin beaten into thin leaf.

TING (ting), *n.* a sharp, bell-like sound.

TINGE (tinj), *v.i.* to stain or colour; impregnate; dye.

TINGLE (tin'gl), *v.i.* to feel a thrilling sensation, or pain.

TINKER (ting'ker), *n.* a mender of metal pots, kettles, etc.; an unskilled workman.

TINKLE ('kl), *n.* a small, quick, sharp, ringing sound.

TINSEL (tin'sel), *n.* a strip of cloth overlaid or interwoven with lustrous metallic material.

TINT (tint), *n.* a slight colouring distinct from the principal colour; hue or shade.

TINTINNABULATION (tin-ti-nab-u-la'shun), *n.* a tinkling sound, as of bells.

TINY (ti'ni), *adj.* very small.

TIP (tip), *n.* a point or top of anything small; end; ferrule or nozzle; gentle stroke; a gratuity; private hint.

TIPPLE ('i), *v.t.* to sip frequently : *n.* liquor.

TIPSY ('si), *adj.* intoxicated.

TIRADE (ti-rad'), *n.* a long, violent, declamatory speech; strain of censure.

TIRE (tir), *n.* a hoop of iron or rubber for a wheel : *v.t.* to weary or fatigue; exhaust the patience of.

TIRESOME ('sum), *adj.* wearisome; tedious; fatiguing.

TISSUE (tish'u), *n.* any thin or delicate texture or fabric; cell formation; connected series.

TISSUED ('ud), *adj.* variegated.

TITANIC (ti-tan'ik), *adj.* huge; immense; of great strength.

TITBIT (tit'bit), *n.* a choice morsel.

TIT FOR TAT (tat), *colloq.* exact or fair retaliation.

TITHE (ti*th*), *n.* the tenth part of anything; a small part.

TITILLATE (tit'i-lat), *v.t.* to tickle.

TITLE (ti'tl), *n.* an inscription over, or at the beginning of something; name; appellation of dignity, rank, distinction, or pre-eminence; claim of right.

TITLE-DEED (-ded), *n.* the written evidence of right of ownership of property.

TITTER (tit'er), *v.t.* to giggle; see-saw : *n.* a restrained laugh.

TITTLE (tit'l), *n.* a small particle; iota.

TITULAR ('u-lar), *adj.* existing in name or title only; nominal.

T.N.T., abbreviation and symbol of trinitrotoluol (*q.v.*).

TOAD (tod), *n.* a jumping, tailless reptile, resembling the frog.

TOADSTOOL ('stool), *n.* a name of numerous species of fungi.

TOAST (tost), *n.* bread scorched or

browned; the act of drinking to some sentiment.

TOASTMASTER ('mas-ter), *n.* one who presides at a public dinner.

TOBACCO (to-bak'o), *n.* an annual plant of the nightshade family; the leaves are prepared for smoking, etc.

TOBOGGAN (-bog'an), *n.* a kind of flat sledge made of thin strips of hard wood turned up at the front.

TOCOLOGY (to-kol'o-ji), *n.* the science of midwifery; obstetrics.

TOCSIN (tok'sin), *n.* an alarm bell.

TODDLE (tod'l), *v.i.* to walk with short, tottering steps like a child.

TOE (to), *n.* one of the five digits of the foot.

TOGETHER (too-geth'er), *adv.* mutually; in union; uninterruptedly.

TOGGERY (tog'er-i), *n.* clothes; articles.

TOGGLE-IRON (i'ern), *n.* a harpoon with a crosspiece working on a pivot near the point.

TOIL (toil), *n.* labour; fatiguing exertion; snare; net.

TOILET ('et), *n.* a dressing-table; attire; a toilet room.

TOILSOME ('sum), *adj.* laborious.

TOKEN ('kn), *n.* a mark or sign.

TOLERABLE (tol'er-a-bl), *adj.* endurable; supportable; fairly good.

TOLERABLY (-bli), *adv.* passably.

TOLERANCE ('er-ans), *n.* endurance; toleration.

TOLERATE ('er-at), *v.t.* to endure; permit.

TOLERATION (-a'shun), *n.* allowance of that which is not wholly approved; freedom from bigotry.

TOLL (tol), *n.* the sound of a bell slowly repeated at short intervals; a duty or tax.

TOMAHAWK (tom'a-hawk), *n.* a hatchet used by the N.A. Indians.

TOMATO (to-ma'to), *n.* the pulpy, edible fruit of a well-known plant.

TOMB (toom), *n.* a grave, or vault; monument.

TOMBOY ('bol), *n.* a wild, romping girl.

TOME (tom), *n.* a large book.

TOMFOOLERY (tom-fool'er-i), *n.* nonsense.

TO-MORROW (too-mor'o), *n.* the day after the present.

TOMTIT ('tit), *n.* the titmouse.

TON (tun), *n.* 20 hundred-weight; 2,240 lb. avoirdupois, the *long ton;* 2,000 lb. the *short ton;* a unit of capacity for ship freight equivalent to 40 cubic feet.

TONALITY (to-nal'i-ti), *n.* key relationship; accuracy of pitch.

TONE (ton), *n.* character of sound; note; accent; quality of the voice; prevailing style or character; harmony of the colours of a painting : *v.i.* to harmonize or agree in tone or shade.

TONG (tong), *n.* a Chinese secret society.

TONGS (tongz), *n.pl.* an instrument consisting of a pair of levers acting on a swivel for grasping objects.

TONGUE (tung), *n.* the chief organ of speech and taste; dialect; clapper of a bell.

TONIC (ton'ik), *adj.* pertaining to, or based on, the keynote; increasing tension; strengthening.

TONNAGE (tun'aj), *n.* the weight of goods carried; carrying capacity, of a vessel.

TONSILS (ton'silz), *n.pl.* two glands situated at the sides of the throat.

TONSILITIS, TONSILLITIS (-sil-i'tis), *n.* inflammation of the tonsils.

TONSORIAL (ton-so'ri-al), *adj.* pertaining to shaving or to a barber.

TONTINE (-ten'), *adj.* a system of life insurance.

TOO (too), *adv.* more than enough; likewise; in addition; over and above; also.

TOOL (tool), *n.* an instrument of manual operation; an accomplice.

TOOT (toot), *v.t.* to sound, as a horn.

TOOTH (tooth), *n.* [*pl.* teeth (teth)], one of the hard bony processes growing in the jaws, which serve for biting and chewing, any projection resembling a tooth.

TOOTHACHE (-ak), *n.* neuralgic pain in a tooth or in the teeth.

TOOTHSOME ('sum), *adj.* palatable.

TOP (top), *n.* the highest part; summit ; upper side or surface ; a child's toy.

TOPIC (top'ik), *n.* a subject of discourse, or argument.

TOPOGRAPHY (to-pog'ra-fi), *n.* the features of a region or locality.

TOPPING ('top'ing), *adj.* rising above ; surpassing.

TOPPLE ('l), *v.i.* to fall forward ; tumble down.

TOPSY-TURVY ('si-ter'vi), *adv.* in an inverted position ; in confusion.

TOQUE (tok), *n.* a kind of bonnet ; a hat without brim.

TORAH (to'ra), *n.* the Mosaic law.

TORCH (torch), *n.* a large light from resinous wood, flax, etc. ; flambeau.

TORMENT (tor'ment), *n.* extreme pain ; torture ; anguish : *v.t.* (tor-ment'), to put to extreme pain ; torture ; harass.

TORNADO (tor-na'do), *n.* a violent tempest or whirlwind.

TORPEDO (tor-pe'do), *n.* a cigar-shaped metal case, containing explosives, fired from a torpedo boat or submarine, for destroying ships, at sea ; a submarine mine ; kind of firework.

TORPEDO-BOAT (bot), *n.* a swift vessel of the navy for firing torpedoes.

TORPID ('pid), *adj.* numb ; inactive ; dormant.

TORPIDITY ('i-ti), *n.* inactivity.

TORPOR ('per), *n.* numbness.

TORRENT ('ent), *n.* a violent and rapid stream ; heavy fall, as of rain.

TORRENTIAL (to-ren'shal), *adj.* of the nature of a torrent.

TORRID (tor'id), *adj.* dried with heat ; extremely hot.

TORSION (tor'shun), *n.* the act of turning or twisting.

TORSO ('so), *n.* the trunk of a human body.

TORT (tort), *n.* in law, any wrong, injury, or damage.

TORTOISE (tor'tis), *n.* a land or fresh-water turtle.

TORTUOUS ('tu-us), *adj.* crooked ; twisted ; underhand.

TORTURE ('tur), *n.* agony of mind or body ; excruciating pain.

2 E

TOSS (tos), *v.t.* to throw with the hand ; throw upward ; jerk.

TOT (tot), *n.* anything small ; a little child.

TOTAL (to'tal), *adj.* whole ; complete ; full.

TOTALITY (-tal'i-ti), *n.* entire quantity, amount, or sum.

TOTE (tot), *v.t.* to carry.

TOTEM (to'tem), *n.* an animal, plant, or object adopted as a symbol, by certain tribes of Alaska.

TOTTER (tot'er), *v.i.* to shake as if about to fall ; be unsteady ; stagger ; reel.

TOUCH (tuch), *v.t.* to come in contact with ; perceive by feeling ; handle slightly ; meddle with ; give a light stroke to ; affect the senses or sensibility of.

TOUCHDOWN ('doun), *n.* a point scored in football by carrying the ball across opponents' goal line.

TOUCHILY ('i-li), *adv.* fretfully.

TOUCHINESS ('i-nes), *n.* irritability.

TOUCHING ('ing), *adj.* pathetic : *n.* the act of coming in contact with : *prep.* with respect to ; concerning.

TOUCHY ('i), *adj.* irritable.

TOUGH (tuf), *adj.* not easily broken ; able to endure hardship ; strong ; firm ; tenacious.

TOUPEE (too-pe'), *n.* a small wig.

TOUR (toor), *n.* a circuitous journey ; excursion ; trip.

TOURING CAR ('ing kar), *n.* an open automobile.

TOURIST ('ist), *n.* excursionist.

TOURNAMENT ('na-ment), *n.* contest of skill.

TOURNEY ('ni), *n.* a sporting contest.

TOURNIQUET ('ni-ket), *n.* a band twisted for compressing an artery and arresting hæmorrhage.

TOUSLE, TOUZLE (touz'l), *v.t.* to pull or tear ; worry.

TOUT (tout), *n.* one who secretly watches race horses in training, in order to give private information to bettors ; a hotel runner : *v.i.* solicit patronage.

TOUT-ENSEMBLE (too-tan-sang'-bl), *n.* [French], the general effect of a work of art, costume, etc., regarded as a whole.

TOW (to), *v.t.* to pull through the water by means of a rope : *n.* the fibrous part of flax or hemp.

TOWARD (to'ard), **TOWARDS** ('ardz), *prep.* in the direction of ; with respect to.

TOWEL (tou'el), *n.* a cloth for wiping the hands, etc.

TOWER (tou'er), *n.* a lofty building, square or circular ; fortress.

TOWN (toun), *n.* any collection of buildings larger than a village.

TOWNSHIP ('ship), *n.* in the U.S. a territorial subdivision of a county.

TOXEMIA, TOXÆMIA (tok-se'mi-a), *n.* blood poisoning.

TOXIC ('sik), *adj.* poisonous.

TOXICOLOGY (si-kol'o-ji), *n.* the science that treats of poisons, their effects, antidotes, etc.

TOXIN (tok'sin), *n.* a poison produced by the action of bacteria upon organic matter.

TRACE (tras), *n.* a mark left by anything passing ; small quantity : *v.t.* follow exactly.

TRACER ('er), *n.* one who traces drawings ; an inquiry agent.

TRACHEA (tra'ke'a), *n.* the windpipe.

TRACK (trak), *n.* a mark or impression left by the foot ; beaten path ; course or way ; permanent way of a railroad.

TRACKAGE ('aj), *n.* towage ; railroad-tracks collectively.

TRACKLESS ('les), *adj.* unmarked by footprints ; untrodden.

TRACT (trakt), *n.* a short treatise ; region of indefinite extent ; expanse.

TRACTABILITY (-ta-bil'i-ti), *n.* docility.

TRACTABLE ('ta-bl), *adj.* docile ; easily instructed.

TRACTATE (trak'tat), *n.* a small book or treatise.

TRACTILE ('til), *adj.* ductile.

TRACTION ('shun), *n.* being drawn ; attraction ; rolling ; friction.

TRACTIVE ('tiv), *adj.* pulling.

TRACTOR (ter), *n.* that which draws ; an automobile used for drawing or pulling.

TRADE (trad), *n.* commerce ; business,

buying and selling ; traffic.

TRADE-MARK ('mark), *n.* a distinguishing device affixed by a merchant to his goods as a guarantee of genuineness.

TRADE-PRICE ('pris), *n.* price paid by the retailer.

TRADER ('er), *n.* one engaged in trade or commerce.

TRADESMAN (tradz'man), *n.* a shopkeeper ; a mechanic engaged in some special branch of labour.

TRADES-UNION ('un-yun), *n.* an organized combination of workmen for the protection of their interests.

TRADITION (tra-dish'un), *n.* that which is so handed down ; ancient custom.

TRADUCE (tra-dus'), *v.t.* to slander.

TRAFFIC (traf'ik), *n.* business or trade ; commerce ; transportation.

TRAGEDIAN (tra-je'di-an), *n.* an actor, or writer of tragedies.

TRAGEDIENNE (-je'di-en), *n.* an actress of tragedy.

TRAGEDY (traj'e-di), *n.* a dramatic poem representing some event, or series of events, in the life of a person, or persons ; a melancholy and fatal event.

TRAGIC ('ik), **TRAGICAL** (-i-kal), *adj.* calamitous ; fatal ; terrible.

TRAIL (tral), *v.t.* to draw along the ground ; hunt or follow by tracking : a path through a wilderness.

TRAIN (tran), *n.* railway carriages or trucks coupled together ; retinue ; connected series ; suite : *v.t.* to instruct.

TRAINER ('er), *n.* an instructor.

TRAIT (trat *or* tra), *n.* a peculiar feature or characteristic ; touch.

TRAITOR (tra'ter), *n.* one who betrays any confidence ; a deceiver.

TRAITOROUS ('ter-us), *adj.* guilty of treason ; perfidious.

TRAJECTORY (tra-jek'to-ri), *n.* the curve described by a body in space, under the action of certain forces.

TRAM (tram), *n.* one of the rails of a tramway ; a tramway ; tramcar.

TRAMCAR (-kar), *n.* a street car.

TRAMMEL ('el), *n.* anything that impedes progress, action, or freedom.

TRAMP (tramp), *v.t.* to tread upon forcibly : *v.i.* to wander : *n.* a vagrant traveller.

TRAMPLE ('pl), *v.t.* to tread under the feet ; treat with insult or contempt.

TRAMWAY ('wa), *n.* a street railway ; a tram road.

TRANCE (trans), *n.* temporary suspension of sensation and volition ; swoon ; catalepsy.

TRANQUIL (trang'kwil), *adj.* calm ; quiet ; undisturbed.

TRANQUILLITY ('i-ti), *n.* calmness ; quiet.

TRANSACT (trans-akt'), *v.t.* to carry through ; negotiate.

TRANSACTION (-ak'shun), *n.* that which is done or performed ; a proceeding ; affair : *pl.* report of a scientific or learned society.

TRANSATLANTIC (-at-lan'tik), *adj.* lying beyond the Atlantic Ocean.

TRANSCEND (tran-send'), *v.t.* to surpass ; surmount ; excel.

TRANSCENDENCE (-sen'dens), **TRANSCENDENCY** ('den-si), *n.* being transcendent ; supereminence.

TRANSCENDENT ('dent), *adj.* surpassing others in excellence.

TRANSCRIBE (-skrib'), *v.t.* to copy.

TRANSCRIPT ('skript), *n.* a written copy from an original.

TRANSFER (trans'fer), *v.t.* to convey from one person or place to another ; convey : *n.* (trans'fer), conveyance of a right, title, property, etc., from one person to another.

TRANSFERABLE ('a-bl), *adj.* capable of being transferred.

TRANSFIGURATION (-fig-u-ra'-shun), *n.* a change of form or appearance, especially the supernatural change in the personal appearance of Jesus Christ on the mount.

TRANSFIGURE (-fig'ur), *v.t.* to change the outward form or appearance of.

TRANSFIX (fiks'), *v.t.* to pierce through.

TRANSFORM (-form'), *v.t.* to change the shape or appearance of ; convert or change the character of ; transmute.

TRANSFORMATION (-for-ma'-shun), *n.* transmutation ; metamorphosis ; conversion.

TRANSFORMER ('mer), *n.* a device for raising or lowering electric pressure.

TRANSFUSE (-fuz'), *v.t.* to pour out of one vessel into another ; instil.

TRANSGRESS (-gres'), *v.i.* to offend by the violation or infraction of any law, rule, etc. ; sin.

TRANSGRESSOR (-gres'er), *n.* an offender ; a sinner.

TRANSIENT (tran'shent), *adj.* fleeting ; brief : *n.* a transient guest.

TRANSIT ('sit), *n.* a passage through or over ; mode of travel.

TRANSITION (-sish'un), *n.* the passage from one place or state to another.

TRANSITIVE ('si-tiv), *adj.* noting an action passing from a subject to an object.

TRANSITORILY (-to-ri-li), *adv.* with a short continuance.

TRANSITORY (-ri), *adj.* evanescent ; fleeting ; unstable.

TRANSLATE (trans-lat'), *v.t.* to render from one language into another ; interpret.

TRANSLATION (-la'shun), *n.* that which is translated ; removal ; version.

TRANSLATOR ('ter), *n.* one who translates.

TRANSLUCENT (-lu'sent), *adj.* partially transparent.

TRANSMIGRATE (trans'mi-grat), *v.i.* to migrate from one country to another.

TRANSMIGRATION (-gra'shun), *n.* the passing of the soul from one body to another after death.

TRANSMISSIBLE ('i-bl), *adj.* denoting that may be passed from one to another, or through a body or substance.

TRANSMIT (-mit'), *v.t.* to send from one place or person to another.

TRANSMITTER ('er), *n.* one who, or that which, transmits ; an electrical sending instrument.

TRANSMUTATION (-mu-ta'shun), *n.* change from one form, nature, substance, or species, into another.

TRANSOM (tran'som, *n.* a crossbeam over a door; a window above a door.

TRANSPARENCE (-par'ens), **TRANSPARENCY** (-par'en-si), *n.* the state or quality of being transparent.

TRANSPARENT ('ent), *adj.* having the property of transmitting rays of light; clear.

TRANSPIRE (-spir'), *v.i.* to be excreted through the pores of the skin; be exhaled; become known; come to pass; occur.

TRANSPLANT (trans-plant'), *v.t.* to remove and establish elsewhere.

TRANSPORT (-port'), *v.t.* to carry across or from one place to another: *n.* (trans'port), conveyance for baggage or stores; manifestation of anger; rapture; ecstasy.

TRANSPOSE (-poz'), *v.t.* to change the place or order of, by putting each in the place of the other.

TRANSUBSTANTIATION (transub-stan-shi-a'shun), *n.* the doctrine of the R.C. and Eastern Churches that, at consecration, the elements in the Eucharist are converted into the veritable body and blood of Christ.

TRANSUDE (-sud'), *v.i.* to pass or ooze through the pores or interstices of a substance.

TRANSVERSE (trans-vers'), *adj.* crosswise; broader than long.

TRAP (trap), *n.* an instrument for snaring; ambush; stratagem; a valve in a pipe to prevent a return flow; heavy igneous rock, etc.

TRAPEZE (tra-pez'), *n.* a swinging horizontal bar suspended by ropes.

TRAPPER (trap'er), *n.* one who traps animals.

TRASH (trash), *n.* refuse; rubbish.

TRASHY ('i), *adj.* worthless; useless.

TRAVAIL (trav'il, 'al), *n.* labour with pain; severe toil.

TRAVEL (trav'el), *v.i.* to journey, especially to foreign or distant places; proceed; move.

TRAVELOGUE (trav'e-log), *n.* illustrated talk on travel.

TRAVERSE ('ers), *adj.* lying or being across; athwart; crosswise.

TRAVESTY ('es-ti), *n.* a burlesque or parody.

TRAWL (trawl), *n.* a large net of peculiar construction used in deepsea fishing.

TRAWLER ('er), *n.* one who trawls; a fishing vessel used in trawling.

TRAY (tra), *n.* a broad, flat vessel for holding or carrying dishes, etc.

TREACHEROUS (trech'er-us), *adj.* perfidious; faithless.

TREACHERY ('er-i), *n.* treasonable or perfidious conduct; perfidy.

TREACLE (tre'kl), *n.* a syrup drained from sugar in the process of refining.

TREAD (tred), *v.i.* to step or walk: *v.t.* to walk on: *n.* a step; part of a wheel that comes in contact with the ground.

TREADLE ('l), *n.* that part of a loom or other machine moved by the foot; a lever.

TREASON (tre'zn), *n.* the offence of betraying the state or subverting the government of the state to which the offender belongs; rebellion.

TREASURE (trezh'ur), *n.* wealth; abundance; plenty; something highly valued.

TREASURER (-er), *n.* one who has the charge of receipts and disbursements of money.

TREASURY ('ur-i), *n.* a place or building where the public revenues are deposited and the public debts discharged.

TREASURY NOTE (not), *n.* a demand note issued by the U.S. treasury.

TREAT (tret), *v.t.* to handle in a particular manner; behave toward; entertain; discourse on; apply remedies to; test.

TREATISE ('is), *n.* a written composition on some particular subject, in which its principles are discussed or explained.

TREATMENT ('ment), *n.* usage; management; manipulation.

TREATY (tre'ti), *n.* league or agree-

ment between two or more states,
etc. ; negotiation.

TREBLE (treb'l), *adj.* threefold ;
triple ; in music, pertaining to the
highest vocal, or instrumental part.

TREE (tre), *n.* any woody plant having
a single trunk and branches.

TREFOIL ('foil), *n.* clover ; any of
various trifoliate plants.

TRELLIS (trel'is), *n.* a frame for
supporting vines, etc.

TREMBLE (trem'bl), *v.i.* to shake
involuntarily ; shudder.

TREMENDOUS (tre-men'dus), *adj.*
dreadful ; terrible ; enormous ;
marvellous.

TREMOR (tre'mor, trem'er), *n.*
trembling ; quivering motion.

TREMULOUS ('u-lus), *adj.* trembling ; quivering ; shaking.

TRENCH (trench), *n.* a long, narrow
cut or ditch.

TRENCHANT (tren'chant), *adj.*
sharp ; keen ; severe.

TREND (trend), *n.* inclination in a
particular direction ; general tendency.

TREPANNING (tre-pan'ing), *n.* the
surgical operation of taking out a
piece of the skull to remove pressure
on the brain.

TREPIDATION (trep-i-da'shun), *n.*
an involuntary trembling ; confused
haste.

TRESPASS (tres'pas), *v.i.* to commit
any offence ; sin ; intrude.

TRESS (tres), *n.* a lock of hair.

TRESTLE (tres'l), *n.* a movable form
for supporting anything ; a framework for supporting a railroad over
a hollow.

TREY (tra), *n.* a three at cards or dice.

TRI, a prefix signifying *three, thrice,
threefold*.

TRIABLE (tri'a-bl), *adj.* capable of
being tried or subjected to test.

TRIAD (tri'ad), *n.* a union of three.

TRIAL ('al), *n.* an attempt or endeavour ; examination by test or
experience ; test of virtue, etc. ;
judicial examination.

TRIANGLE ('ang-gl), *n.* a plane
bounded by three lines, and having
three angles ; a musical instrument.

TRIANGULAR (-ang'gu-lar), *adj.*
having three angles ; shaped like a
triangle.

TRIBE (trib), *n.* a group ; clan.

TRIBULATION (trib-u-la'shun), *n.*
severe affliction ; deep sorrow.

TRIBUNAL (tri-bu'nal), *n.* the seat
of a judge ; court of justice.

TRIBUNE (trib'un), *n.* raised stand
or rostrum from which speeches are
delivered.

TRIBUTARY ('u-ta-ri), *adj.* paying
tribute ; yielding supplies : *n.* a stream
which distributes water to another
stream.

TRIBUTE ('ut), *n.* personal contribution made in token of services
rendered or acknowledgment due.

TRICE (tris), *n.* an instant : *v.t.* to haul.

TRICK (trik), *n.* a strategem or artifice ;
deception ; legerdemain.

TRICKERY ('er-i), *n.* deception ;
fraud ; imposture.

TRICKLE ('l), *v.i.* to flow gently
down ; run down in drops.

TRICKSTER ('ster), *n.* a cheat.

TRICOLOUR (tri'kul-er), *n.* a flag of
three colours ; French national ensign.

TRICUSPID (-kus'pid), *adj.* threepointed.

TRICYCLE ('si-kl), *n.* a three-wheeled
modernized form of velocipede.

TRIDENT ('dent), *n.* a sceptre or
spear with three prongs, especially
the sceptre of Neptune.

TRIED (trid), *p.adj.* trustworthy ;
faithful.

TRIENNIAL (tri-en'i-al), *adj.* occurring in, or continuing for, three years.

TRIFLE ('fl), *n.* nothing of importance ;
v.t. to waste or fritter away.

TRIFLING ('fling), *adj.* of small value
or importance.

TRIG (trig), *adj.* trim ; neat.

TRIGGER (trig'er), *n.* a catch which,
when pulled, releases the hammer of
a gun.

TRIGONOMETRY ('o-nom'e-tri), *n.*
the science of measuring the sides
and angles of triangles, and ascertain-
in the relations between them by
certain parts which are given.

TRILL (tril), *n.* a shake or quaver of
the voice.

TRILLION ('yun), *n.* in England, a unit followed by eighteen ciphers; in the U.S. and France, a unit followed by twelve ciphers.

TRILOGY ('o-ji), *n.* a series of three dramas, but forming one poetical and historical picture.

TRIM (trim), *adj.* neat; compact; in good order or service : *v.t.* to decorate or adorn.

TRINITROTOLUOL (tri-ni'tro-tol'-u-ol), **TRINITROTOLUENE** (-en), *n.* a very high-powered blasting explosive; also, used for filling " high explosive " shells : abbr. T.N.T.

TRINITY (trin'i-ti), *n.* the union of the Father, the Son, and the Holy Ghost in one Godhead.

TRINKET (tring'ket), *n.* a small ornament or jewel.

TRIO (tre'o), *n.* a set of three; composition for three voices or instruments.

TRIP (trip), *v.i.* to run or step lightly or nimbly; stumble; err; take an excursion.

TRIPE (trip), *n.* the large stomach of a ruminating animal prepared for food.

TRIPLANE (tri'plan), *n.* an aeroplane of three planes or sustaining surfaces.

TRIPLE (trip'l), *adj.* threefold.

TRIPLET ('let), *n.* a combination of three; one of three children born at a birth.

TRIPLICATE ('li-kat), *adj.* threefold.

TRIPOD (tri'pod), *n.* a three-legged stand for a camera, etc.

TRISECTION (-sek'shun), *n.* division into three parts.

TRITE (trit), *adj.* worn out; stale; hackneyed.

TRIUMPH (tri'umf), *n.* state of joy at success; victory.

TRIUMPHAL (-um'fal), *adj.* a triumph.

TRIUMPHANT ('fant), *adj.* rejoicing for victory; victorious.

TRIUMVIR (-um'ver), *n.* [*pl.* triumviri ('vi-ri)], one of three men united in office.

TRIUMVIRATE ('vi-rat), *n.* a coalition of three men in office or authority.

TRIVIAL (triv'i-al), *adj.* trifling; commonplace.

TRIVIALITY (-al'i-ti), *n.* being trivial; a trifle.

TROCHE (tro'ke), *n.* a medicinal lozenge.

TROCHEE ('ke), *n.* a metrical foot of two syllables, the first long, the second short.

TROGLODYTE (trog'lo-dit), *n.* a cave dweller; said of certain tribes; an anthropoid ape.

TROLL (trol), *n.* a giant; sorceress; a kind of song; reel on a fishing-rod.

TROLLEY ('i), *n.* a hand truck; a grooved metal wheel travelling in contact with an electric wire.

TROLLEY CAR (kar), *n.* a car with trolley and an electric motor.

TROMBONE (trom'bon), *n.* a brass instrument of the trumpet kind.

TROOP (troop), *n.* a herd or flock; a unit of cavalry; a company of Boy Scouts : *pl.* a large body of soldiers.

TROPHY (tro'fi), *n.* a memorial of a victory; memento.

TROPIC (trop'ik), *n.* of the two small circles of the celestial sphere, situated at each side of the equator, at a distance of 23° 28' and parallel to it, within the limits of which the sun moves in his yearly course.

TROT (trot), *v.i.* to move faster than a walk.

TROTH (troth), *n.* betrothal; fidelity; truth.

TROTTER (trot'er), *n.* a trotting horse; sheep's foot.

TROUBLE (trub'l), *n.* mental agitation, distress, or worry.

TROUBLOUS ('lus), *adj.* full of trouble.

TROUGH (trof), *n.* a long, hollow vessel for holding a liquid, food, etc.

TROUNCE (trouns), *v.t.* to beat soundly.

TROUPE (troop), *n.* a company of performers.

TROUSERS (trou'zerz), *n.pl.* a garment worn by men and boys.

TROUSSEAU (troo-so), *n.* [*pl.* trousseaux (-soz')] [Fr.], a bride's outfit.

TROUT (trout), *n.* a fresh-water fish allied to the salmon.

TROVE (trov), *n.* that which is found unexpectedly : used generally with " treasure."

TROVER (tro'ver), *n.* an action at law to recover goods wrongfully withheld.

TROW (tro), *v.i.* to think or suppose.

TROWEL (trou'el), *n.* a flat, triangular tool used for spreading mortar ; a gardener's tool.

TROY WEIGHT (troi wat), a system of weights in which the pound contains twelve ounces, the ounce twenty pennyweights, and the pennyweight twenty-four grains : used by jewellers.

TRUANT (tru'ant), *n.* one who absents himself from school without leave ; loiterer.

TRUCE (troos), *n.* a temporary peace or cessation of hostilities.

TRUCK (truk), *n.* a heavy automobile built to carry a load of from one to ten tons ; a wheeled vehicle for carrying goods ; garden vegetables.

TRUCKLE (ʼl), *v.i.* to yield obsequiously to another's will.

TRUCULENCE (ʼu-lens), **TRUCULENCY** (-len-si), *n.* ferocity ; rudeness.

TRUCULENT (ʼu-lent), *adj.* ferocious; rude ; coarse.

TRUDGE (truj), *v.i.* to travel on foot, especially with labour or fatigue.

TRUE (troo), *adj.* faithful or loyal ; genuine ; correct.

TRUE-BLUE (ʼbloo), *adj.* of inflexible honesty and fidelity.

TRUISM (ʼizm), *n.* a self-evident truth.

TRULY (ʼli), *adv.* in agreement with truth or fact ; precisely ; sincerely.

TRUMP (trump), *n.* a trumpet ; a winning card.

TRUMPERY (ʼper-i), *n.* worthless finery ; rubbish.

TRUMPET (trumpʼet), *n.* a metal wind instrument formed of a single curved tube.

TRUNCATE (trungʼkat), *adj.* appearing as if cut off at the top.

TRUNCHEON (trunʼchun), *n.* a short staff or cudgel.

TRUNDLE (ʼdl), *v.t.* to roll along.

TRUNDLE-BED (ʼbed), *n.* a low, small bed.

TRUNK (trungk), *n.* the stem of a tree ; main body of anything ; elephant's proboscis ; large travelling box.

TRUSS (trus), *n.* a surgical apparatus for the relief of hernia ; timbers fastened together for the support of a roof.

TRUST (trust), *n.* confidence ; faith ; credit ; reliance ; combination of capitalists ; an estate held for the benefit of another.

TRUSTEE (trus-teʼ), *n.* a person who manages property for the benefit of others.

TRUSTY (ʼti), *adj.* faithful.

TRUTH (trooth), *n.* agreement with reality ; eternal principle of right, or law of order ; veracity ; fact ; righteousness.

TRY (tri), *v.t.* to prove by experiment ; test or prove ; examine ; subject to severe trial ; examine judicially.

TRYING (ʼing), *adj.* afflictive ; difficult.

TRYST (trist,), *n.* a place of meeting.

TUBE (tub), *n.* a hollow cylinder for conveying fluids ; pipe ; subway.

TUBER (tuʼber), *n.* a thickened, roundish, underground stem.

TUBERCULAR (ʼku-lar), *adj.* affected with tuberculosis.

TUBERCULOSIS (-loʼsis), *n.* a disease ; consumption.

TUBEROSE (ʼber-os), *n.* an odoriferous plant with liliaceous flowers.

TUBEROUS (tuʼber-us), *adj.* covered with knobs or warts.

TUBING (tubʼing), *n.* tubes collectively.

TUCK (tuk), *n.* a fold in a garment.

TUCKER (ʼer), *n.* an instrument for making tucks ; a state of weariness.

TUESDAY (tuzʼda), *n.* the third day of the week.

TUFT (tuft), *n.* a small bunch.

TUG (tug), *n.* a pull with great effort ; a towing vessel.

TUITION (tu-ish'un), *n.* instruction ; fee for instruction.

TULIP ('lip), *n.* a bulbous plant with bell-shaped flowers.

TULLE (tool), *n.* [French], a delicate silk lace or netting.

TUMBLE (tum'bl), *v.i.* to fall suddenly ; roll about : *v.t.* to throw down.

TUMBLER ('bler), *n.* one who tumbles ; a kind of drinking-glass.

TUMID (tu'mid), *adj.* swollen ; distended ; bombastic ; pompous.

TUMIDITY ('i-ti), *n.* the state of being tumid.

TUMOUR ('mer), *n.* a morbid swelling or enlargement of any part of the body.

TUMULT (tu'mult), *n.* noisy confusion ; riot.

TUMULTUOUS (-mul'tu-us), *adj.* characterized by tumult.

TUN (tun), *n.* a large cask ; measure of 252 gallons.

TUNABLE (tun'a-bl), *adj.* capable of being tuned ; harmonious.

TUNE (tun), *n.* a series of musical notes with unity of keynote ; melody ; short musical composition.

TUNE IN, *colloq.* in radio, to adjust the frequency of a receiving set to make it correspond to the wave length of the sending station.

TUNIC (tu'nik), *n.* loose kind of frock worn by women and boys ; military coat.

TUNNEL (tun'el), *n.* an underground passage cut through a hill or under a river ; funnel.

TURBID (ter'bid), *adj.* muddy ; thick ; confused.

TURBINE ('bin), *n.* a wheel turning on a vertical axis and driven by water ; a steam engine on turbine principles.

TURBULENCE ('bu-lens), *n.* disorder ; agitation.

TUREEN (tu-ren'), *n.* a deep table-vessel for holding soup.

TURF (terf), *n.* the grassy surface of untilled land ; horse-racing ; race-course.

TURGESCENCE (ter-jes'ens), *n.* inflation.

TURGID ('jid), *adj.* distended beyond the natural size ; inflated.

TURKEY ('ki), *n.* a large American fowl of the pheasant family.

TURMOIL ('moil), *n.* a harassing labour ; worrying confusion ; noise.

TURN (tern), *v.t.* to cause or make to go round ; change the direction of ; reverse.

TURNCOAT (tern'kot), *n.* a deserter ; a renegade.

TURNER (ter'ner), *n.* one who turns articles in a lathe.

TURNIP ('nip), *n.* a plant with a solid bulbous root.

TURNKEY (tern'ke), *n.* a prison warder.

TURNPIKE ('pik), *n.* a gate or bar to stop vehicles, and sometimes foot passengers, etc., until toll is paid.

TURPENTINE (ter'pen-tin), *n.* the resinous or viscid juice of pine and fir trees.

TURPITUDE ('p' tud), *n.* moral depravity.

TURQUOISE ('kwoiz), *n.* a precious bluish-green stone.

TURRET (tur'et), *n.* a small tower ; iron tower on a man-of-war.

TURTLE (ter'tl), *n.* a large edible sea-tortoise.

TUSH (tush), *interj.* an expression of contempt or rebuke.

TUSK (tusk), *n.* the long, pointed tooth on each side of the upper jaw of certain mammals.

TUSSLE (tus'l), *n.* a scuffle.

TUTELAGE (tu'te-laj), *n.* guardianship.

TUTOR ('ter), *n.* a teacher ; guardian.

TUXEDO (tuk-se'do), *n.* a sack coat used in lieu of a full-dress coat on semiformal occasions.

TWADDLE (twod'l), *n.* silly talk.

TWAIN (twan), *n. & adj.* two.

TWANG (twang), *n.* a sharp, quick, vibrating sound ; a nasal tone.

TWEED (twed), *n.* a soft, woolly cloth material.

TWEEZERS (twe'zerz), *n.pl.* small pincers for pulling out hairs, type, etc.

TWELFTH DAY (da), *n.* Epiphany.

TWELVEMO (twelv'mo), *n. & adj.* same as duodecimo.

TWICE (twis), *adv.* two times.

TWIDDLE (twid'l), *v.t.* to twirl in a light manner.

TWILIGHT (twi'lit), *n.* the faint light after sunset.

TWIN (twin), *adj.* double; closely resembling : *n.* one of two born at a birth.

TWINE (twin), *v.t.* to twist; wind round; unite closely : *n.* a strong cord.

TWINGE (twinj), *v.t.* to affect with a sudden sharp pain.

TWINKLE (twing'kl), *n.* a quick motion of the eye; short, tremulous light; an instant.

TWIRL (twerl), *v.t.* to move or turn round rapidly; to whirl.

TWIST (twist), *v.t.* to unite or form by winding together; interlace.

TWISTER (twis'ter), *n.* one who twists; a cyclone.

TWIT (twit), *v.t.* to annoy by reminding of a fault, etc.

TWITCH (twich), *v.t.* to pull with a sudden jerk.

TWITTER (twit'er), *v.i.* to make a succession of small, tremulous sounds, as a bird.

TYMPAN (tim'pan), *n.* a thickness of paper, cloth or other material, placed on the impression-surface (platen) of a printing-press.

TYPE (tip), *v.t.* to typify; reproduce by a typewriter : *n.* an emblem, sign, or symbol; figure or design; distinguishing mark; general form or structure; original design; a letter in metal or wood for printing from. Different sizes of printing types based on the point system.

TYPEWRITER ('ri-ter), *n.* a machine for producing letters by means of an inked ribbon and types.

TYPHOID (ti-foid), *adj.* pertaining to typhus : *n.* an enteric fever, occasioned by a bacillus occurring in the system.

TYPHOON (-foon'), *n.* a violent whirlwind occurring in the seas of the Far East.

TYPHUS ('fus), *n.* a contagious fever, often occurring as an epidemic.

TYPICAL (tip'i-kal), *adj.* figurative; characteristic.

TYPIFY ('i-fi), *v.t.* to represent by an image or emblem; foreshadow.

TYPIST (tip'ist), *n.* one who operates a typewriter.

TYPOGRAPHER (ti-pog'ra-fer), *n.* a printer.

TYPOGRAPHY (-pog'ra-fi), *n.* the art of printing.

TYPOTHETÆ (ti-poth'e-te), *n.pl.* printers collectively; [T-], the association of master printers of the U.S. and Canada.

TYRANNICAL (-ran'i-kal), *adj.* pertaining to, or characteristic of, a tyrant; despotic; cruel.

TYRANNIZE (tir'a-niz), *v.i.* to oppress.

TYRANNOUS ('a-nus), *adj.* despotic; tyrannical.

TYRANNY ('a-ni), *n.* the government or conduct of a tyrant; severity; absolute power imperiously administered.

TYRANT (ti-rant), *n.* an oppressor; despot.

TYRO (ti'ro), *n.* a beginner; novice.

U

U, u (u), the twenty-first letter in the English alphabet.

U, u, an abbreviation.

UBIQUITOUS (u-bik'wi-tus), *adj.* existing everywhere.

UBIQUITY ('wi-ti), *n.* omnipresence.

UDDER (ud'er), *n.* the organ of a mammal which secretes the milk.

UGLY (ug'li), *adj.* unsightly.

UKULELE (oo-koo-la'la), *n.* a musical instrument.

ULCER (ul'ser), *n.* a sore, with a secretion of pus.

ULSTER (ul'ster), *n.* a loose overcoat.

ULTERIOR (-te'ri-er), *adj.* lying beyond or on the further side; more distant.

ULTIMA ('ti-ma), *adj.* farthest; *n.* the last syllable of a word.

ULTIMATE ('ti-mat), *adj.* utmost ; final.

ULTIMATUM (-ti-ma'tum), *n.* [*pl.* ultimata, ('ta)], final conditions offered prior to the declaration of war or legal action.

ULTIMO ('ti-mo), *adv.* in the month preceding the present.

ULTRA ('tra), *adj.* extreme.

ULTRAMARINE (-ma-ren'), *n.* a beautiful, permanent, blue pigment.

ULTRAMONTANISM (-mon'-ta-nizm), *n.* extreme views of the Pope's authority and infallibility.

UMBER (um'ber), *n.* a brown pigment.

UMBILICAL (-bil'i-kal), *adj.* pertaining to, or formed like, the navel.

UMBILICUS (-bil'i-kus), *n.* the navel.

UMBRA ('bra), *n.* the dark cone of a shadow projected from a planet or satellite on the side opposite to the sun.

UMBRAGE ('braj), *n.* screen of trees or foliage ; resentment.

UMBRAGEOUS (-bra'jus), *adj.* shady ; resentful.

UMBRELLA (-brel'a), *n.* a covered sliding frame carried in the hand as a screen against rain or sun.

UMPIRE (um'pir), *n.* a third party to whom a dispute is referred for settlement ; one chosen to see that the rules of games, etc., are observed.

UNABRIDGED (un-a-brijd), *adj.* not shortened or condensed.

UNANIMOUS (u-nan'i-mus), agreeing in opinion.

UNASSUMING (un-a-sum'ing), *adj.* without pretence ; modest.

UNCANNY (-kan'i), *adj.* weird ; mysterious.

UNCHASTE (-chast'), *adj.* immodest.

UNCLE (ung'kl), *n.* the brother of one's father or mother.

UNCOMFORTABLE (un-kum'fer-ta-bl), *adj.* without comfort ; uneasy.

UNCONSCIONABLE (-kon'shun-a-bl), *adj.* out of all reason or expectation.

UNCONSCIOUS (-kon'shus), *adj.* without consciousness.

UNCONSTITUTIONAL (-kon-sti-tu'shun-al), *adj.* in conflict with a constitution ; unlawful.

UNCONVENTIONAL (-kon-ven'shun-al), *adj.* not according to form or custom.

UNCOUTH (-kooth'), *adj.* clumsy ; awkward.

UNCTION (ungk'shun), *n.* the act of anointing as a symbol of consecration.

UNCTUOUS ('tu-us), *adj.* oily ; soothing ; lenitive.

UNDAUNTED (un-dan'ted), *adj.* bold ; fearless ; unafraid.

UNDEMONSTRATIVE (-de-mon'stra-tiv), *adj.* not showing one's feelings ; phlegmatic.

UNDER ('der), *prep.* beneath ; subordinate to ; less than.

UNDERGO (-go'), *v.t.* to pass through or experience ; suffer.

UNDERGRADUATE (-grad'u-at), *n.* a student who has not taken his first degree.

UNDERHAND (-hand), *adj.* done by meanness or fraud.

UNDERLING (-ling), *n.* a servant.

UNDERMINE (-min'), *v.t.* to dig under.

UNDERNEATH (-neth'), *adv.* beneath.

UNDERPIN (-pin), *v.t.* to prop by placing supports underneath.

UNDERSTAND (-stand), *v.t.* to perceive by the mind ; assume or imply ; know by experience.

UNDERSTUDY (-stud-i), *n.* an actor who learns a part to be played by him in the absence of another actor.

UNDERTAKE (-tak), *v.t.* to take under one's management ; assume ; attempt.

UNDERTAKER ('der-tak-er), *n.* one who prepares the dead for burial ; a mortician.

UNDERTAKING ('ing), *n.* any business or project a person engages to perform.

UNDERTOW (-to), *n.* a current under the surface flowing in opposite direction to the surface, current, or tide.

UNDERWORLD (-werld), *n.* the criminal classes.

UNDERWRITE (-rit'), *v.t.* to subscribe one's name to (a policy of marine insurance).

UNDINE (-den'), *n.* a water-nymph.

UNDO (-doo'), *v.t.* to loosen; to do away with that which has been done.

UNDUE (-du'), *adj.* improper; excessive; not legal.

UNDULATE ('du-lat), *v.t. & v.i.* to wave, or move like waves; vibrate.

UNEARNED INCREMENT (in'krement, the increase of the value of land or property without labour or expenditure on the part of the owner.

UNEQUIVOCAL (-e-kwiv'o-kal), *adj.* clear; not ambiguous.

UNGUAL (ung'gwal), *adj.* pertaining to, or having, a nail, claw, or hoof.

UNGUENT ('gwent), *n.* an ointment; lubricating substance.

UNICORN (u'ni-korn), *n.* a fabled animal resembling a horse, but with a horn.

UNIFORM ('ni-form), *adj.* having only one form; consistent with itself: *n.* an official or regulation dress.

UNIFORMITY ('mi-ti), *n.* resemblance; conformity to one pattern; accord.

UNIFY ('ni-fi). *v.t.* to form into one; make a unit of.

UNILATERAL (-lat'er-a!), *adj.* one-sided.

UNINURED (-in-urd'), *adj.* not inured; not accustomed.

UNION (un'yun), *n.* combination; coalition; concord; conjunction.

UNIONISM (-izm), *n.* doctrine of trades unionism.

UNIPED (u'ni-ped), *adj.* one-footed.

UNIQUE (-nek'), *adj.* without another of the same kind; unparalleled.

UNISON ('ni-sun), *n.* concord.

UNIT ('nit), *n.* one; a single person or thing; standard amount or quantity.

UNITE (u-nit'), *v.t.* to incorporate into one; make to agree or adhere; join by a legal or moral bond.

UNITY ('ni-ti), *n.* concord; uniformity; agreement; harmony.

UNIVERSAL (-ni-ver'sal), *adj.* all-prevading; embracing or comprehending the whole; general.

UNIVERSE ('ni-vers), *n.* the whole system of created things; world.

UNIVERSITY (-ver'si-ti), *n.* an assemblage of colleges or incorporated institutions for instruction in the higher branches of art, science, etc.

UNKEMPT (un-kempt'), *adj.* uncombed; rough.

UNLAWFUL (-law'fool), *adj.* in violation of law.

UNLESS (-les'), *conj.* except; if not.

UNMANAGEABLE (-man'aj-a-bl), *adj.* beyond control.

UNNERVE (-nerv'), *v.t.* to deprive of strength or power; weaken.

UNOBTRUSIVE (-ob-troo'siv), *adj.* not obtrusive; modest.

UNPARALLELED (-par'a-leld), *adj.* without parallel.

UNPRECEDENTED (-pres'e-dented), *adj.* without precedent.

UNPREMEDITATED (-pre-med'ita-ted), *adj.* not arranged or thought of beforehand.

UNPRETENTIOUS (-pre-ten'shus), *adj.* modest in action or demeanour.

UNPRINCIPLED (-prin'si-pld), *adj.* with no principles.

UNPROPITIOUS (-pro-pish'us), *adj.* not propitious.

UNREGENERATE (-re-jen'er-at), **UNREGENERATED** (-at-ed), *adj.* not converted.

UNRULY (-roo'li), *adj.* ungovernable.

UNSAVOURY (-sa'ver-i), *adj.* displeasing to taste or smell.

UNSCATHED (-skathd'), *adj.* uninjured; without harm.

UNSCRUPULOUS (-skroo'pu-lus), *adj.* without principle.

UNSEEMLY (-sem'li), *adj.* not seemly; unbecoming.

UNSEEN (-sen'), *adj.* invisible.

UNSOPHISTICATED (-so-fis'ti-ka-ted), *adj.* without experience.

UNSPEAKABLE (-spek'a-bl), *adj.* not to be mentioned or spoken of.

UNSTABLE (-sta'bl), *adj.* not firm; not reliable.

UNTENABLE (-ten'a-bl), *adj.* not tenable; incapable of defence.

UNTIL (-til'), *prep.* till; as long as.

UNTO ('too), *prep.* to.

UNTOWARD (-to'ard), *adj.* obstinate; ungraceful; unlucky.

UNTRUTH (-trooth′), *n.* a falsehood.

UNTUTORED (-tu′terd), *adj.* untaught ; ignorant.

UNUTTERABLE (-ut′er-a-bl), *adj.* ineffable ; vile.

UNWARY (-wa′ri), *adj.* incautious ; careless.

UNWIELDY (-wel′di), *adj.* difficult to move ; awkward.

UNWITTING (-wit′ing), *adj.* not aware ; without knowledge of.

UNWORLDLY (-werld′li), *adj.* not influenced by worldly or sordid motives.

UPBRAID (-up-brad′), *v.t.* to reproach.

UPBRINGING (′bring-ing), *n.* bringing up ; raising ; rearing.

UPHEAVAL (-hev′al), *n.* a lifting from below ; a lifting of strata by some internal force.

UPHEAVE (-hev′), *v.t.* to lift up from beneath.

UPHOLSTER (-hol′ster), *v.t.* to furnish furniture, etc., with covers, cushions, hangings, etc. ; stuff or pad and cover cushions, mattresses, etc.

UPHOLSTERY (′ster-i), *n.* the business of an upholsterer.

UPPISH (′ish), *adj.* arrogant ; assuming.

UPRIGHT (′rit), *adj.* erect ; just ; honest ; equitable.

UPRISING (-riz′ing), *n.* rebellion.

UPROAR (′ror), *n.* noisy disturbance ; clamour.

UPROARIOUS (′i-us), *adj.* making great noise and tumult.

UPWARD, UPWARDS (′werdz), *adv.* toward a higher place or source.

URBAN (er′ban), *adj.* pertaining to a city or town.

URBANE (-ban′), *adj.* polite ; refined.

URBANITY (-ban′i-ti), *n.* politeness ; refinement.

URCHIN (′chin), *n.* a small boy.

UREMIA (u-re′mi-a), *n.* poisoning of the blood by hurtful substances.

URGE (erj), *v.t.* to incite ; impel ; insist upon.

URGENCY (er′jen-si), *n.* importunity.

URGENT (′jent), *adj.* pressing ; calling for immediate attention.

URIC ACID (u′rik as′id), *n.* an almost insoluble compound found in urine.

URINE (′rin), *n.* a fluid excretion from the kidneys.

URN (ern), *n.* a roundish vessel of various materials.

US (us), *pron.* objective case plural of the pronoun of the 1st person.

USABLE (uz′a-bl), *adj.* denoting that can be used.

USAGE (′aj), *n.* mode of using.

USEFUL (us′fool), *adj.* full of use ; beneficial.

USELESS (′les), *adj.* of no use.

USHER (ush′er), *n.* a doorkeeper ; an officer who introduces strangers.

USUAL (u′zhu-al), *adj.* customary.

USUFRUCT (′zu-frukt), *n.* the temporary use of lands and tenements belonging to another.

USURER (′zhu-rer), *n.* a person who lends money at an exorbitant rate of interest.

USURP (-zerp′), *v.t.* to take possession of by force, or without right.

USURY (′zhu-ri), *n.* interest on money beyond the legal rate of interest.

UTENSIL (-ten′sil), *n.* an implement, especially one used for domestic or culinary purposes.

UTILITY (-til′i-ti), *n.* usefulness ; intrinsic value.

UTILIZE (′til-iz), *v.t.* to make useful or profitable.

UTMOST (ut′most), *adj.* in the greatest degree ; most distant.

UTOPIAN (u-to′pi-an), *adj.* pertaining to the imaginary island described by Sir Thomas More in his "Utopia," where the most perfect system of laws and institutions existed ; hence, ideal.

UTTER (ut′er), *adj.* entire ; absolute ; unqualified ; total : *v.t.* to speak ; pronounce.

UTTERANCE (-ans), *n.* vocal expression ; speech ; style of speaking.

UTTERMOST (′er-most), *adj.* extreme ; in the furthest, greatest, or highest degree.

UVULA (′vu-la), *n.* the fleshy, conical body, attached to the soft palate, at the back part of the tongue.

V

V, v (ve), the twenty-second letter in the English alphabet.

V, v, an abbreviation.

V, a numeral in the Roman notation denoting 5; with a bar (V̄), 5,000.

VACANCY (va'kan-si), *n.* state of being vacant or empty; listlessness.

VACANT ('kant), *adj.* empty.

VACATE ('kat), *v.t.* to make vacant.

VACATION (-ka'shun), *n.* intermission of a stated employment, or judicial proceedings; holidays.

VACCINATE (vak'si-nat), *v.t.* inoculate with vaccine.

VACCINE ('sin), *n.* the virus of cowpox, as used in vaccination.

VACILLATE (vas'i-lat), *v.i.* to fluctuate in mind or opinion.

VACUOUS (vak'u-us), *adj.* empty; vacant.

VACUUM ('u-um), *n.* a space devoid of all matter; void.

VACUUM TUBE (tub), *n.* highly exhausted glass tube containing elements used in radio; an electric lamp.

VAGABOND (vag'a-bond), *adj.* without fixed habitation: *n.* a vagrant.

VAGARY (va-ga'ri), *n.* a wild freak; whim.

VAGUE (vag), *adj.* indefinite.

VAGUELY ('li), *adv.* in a vague manner.

VAIN (van), *adj.* empty; deceitful; conceited.

VAINGLORIOUS (-glo'ri-us), *adj.* boastful.

VALE (val), *n.* a valley.

VALEDICTORY (-e-dik'to-ri), *adj.* bidding farewell: *n.* a farewell oration.

VALENTINE ('en-tin), *n.* love missive sent on February 14th.

VALET ('et), *n.* a gentleman's servant.

VALIANT ('yant), *adj.* brave; heroic.

VALID ('id), *adj.* having legal force; not defective; sound.

VALIDITY (va-lid'i-ti), *n.* legal force; soundness; strength; justness.

VALISE (va-les'), *n.* small portmanteau.

VALLEY (val'i), *n.* tract of land situated between ranges of hills.

VALOUR (val'er), *n.* bravery; intrepidity.

VALOROUS ('er-us), *adj.* brave; intrepid.

VALUABLE ('u-a-bl), *adj.* possessing useful qualities; costly.

VALUATION (-u-a'shun), *n.* estimated worth or price.

VALUE ('u), *n.* that which renders anything useful or estimable; price.

VALVE (valv), *n.* a lid or cover opening in one direction and shutting in another.

VAMOSE (va-mos'), *v.i.* to depart quickly; decamp.

VAMP (vamp), *n.* the upper leather of a boot or shoe; [Slang], to inveigle; entice.

VAMPIRE (vam'pir), *n.* a fabled demon; a large bat of South America.

VAN (van), *n.* the front of an army or fleet; a large covered wagon.

VANDAL ('dal), *n.* [v-], one hostile to art or literature; one who ruthlessly destroys.

VANE (van), *n.* a weathercock.

VANGUARD ('gard), *n.* the advance guard of an army.

VANILLA (van-nil'a), *n.* a flavouring extract made from the seeds of a tropical plant.

VANISH (van'ish), *v.i.* to disappear; pass away; be lost.

VANITY ('i-ti), *n.* love of indiscriminate admiration; idle show; emptiness.

VANQUISH (vang'kwish), *v.t.* to conquer; subdue; refute.

VANTAGE (van'taj), *n.* advantage.

VAPID (vap'id), *adj.* dull; insipid.

VAPOUR (va'per), *n.* the gas into which most liquids and solids are converted by heat; steam; mist.

VAPORIZE ('iz), *v.t.* to convert into vapour.

VAPOROUS (-us), *adj.* full of, or like, vapour; unreal; vain.

VAPORY (-i), *adj.* full of vapours.

VARIABILITY (va-ri-a-bil'i-ti), *n.* the state or quality of being variable; changeableness.

VARIABLE ('ri-a-bl), *adj.* changeable; inconstant; fickle.

VARIANCE (-ans), *n.* difference; quarrel.

VARIANT (-ant), *adj.* variable; different.

VARIATE (-at), *v.t.* to diversify.

VARIATION (-ri-a'shun), *n.* modification; diversity; extent to which a thing changes.

VARICELLA (var-i-sel'a), *n.* chicken-pox.

VARICOSE ('i-kos), *adj.* abnormally swollen or enlarged; said of veins.

VARIED (va'rid), *adj.* altered.

VARIEGATE ('ri-e-gat), *v.t.* to mark with different colours or tints.

VARIETY (-ri'e-ti), *n.* inter-mixture, or succession of different things.

VARIOLA ('o-la), *n.* smallpox.

VARIOUS ('ri-us), *adj.* several.

VARNISH (var'nish), *n.* a viscid, resinous liquid, used for giving a gloss to wood or metal work.

VARY (va'ri), *v.t.* to change.

VASCULAR (vas'ku-lar), *adj.* consisting of, or containing, vessels as part of a structure of animal and vegetable organisms.

VASE (vas, vaz), *n.* an ornamental vessel resembling an urn.

VASSAL ('al), *n.* a bondman.

VAST (vast), *adj.* immense.

VAT (vat), *n.* a very large tub.

VATICAN ('i-kan), *n.* the palace of the Pope at Rome.

VAUDEVILLE (vod'vil), *n.* miscellaneous theatricals.

VAULT (vawlt), *n.* cellar; prison.

VAUNT (vant, vaunt), *v.i.* to boast.

VEAL (vel), *n.* calf's flesh.

VEDETTE (ve-det'), *n.* a mounted sentinel.

VEER (ver), *v.i.* change direction.

VEGETABLE (vej'e-ta-bl), *adj.* plant or root cultivated for the table, etc.

VEGETARIAN (-ta'ri-an), *n.* one who abstains from a meat diet and lives on fruit, vegetables, etc.

VEGETABLE ('e-tat), *v.i.* to grow as a plant; live indolently.

VEHEMENCE (ve'he-mens), **VEHEMENCY** (-men-si), *n.* impetuosity; animated fervour.

VEHEMENT ('he-ment), *adj.* passionate; energetic.

VEHICLE ('hi-kl), *n.* any kind of carriage or conveyance; anything by means of which something else is transmitted.

VEIL (val), *n.* a covering more or less transparent for the face; a screen.

VEIN (van), *n.* one of the vessels which convey blood from the arteries to the heart; seam of rock filled with metallic or mineral matter.

VELDT (velt), *n.* open country in South Africa.

VELLUM (vel'um), *n.* fine parchment.

VELOCIPEDE (ve-los'i-ped), *n.* the original form of the bicycle.

VELOCITY ('i-ti), *n.* speed.

VELOURS (ve-loor'), *n.* a dress fabric similar to plush.

VELVET (vel'vet), *n.* a silk fabric with short, close, soft nap.

VELVETEEN (-ve-ten'), *n.* imitation velvet.

VENAL (ve'nal), *adj.* that may be bought, or bribed; mercenary.

VENALITY (-nal'i-ti), *n.* prostitution of talents or services for money or reward.

VENATION (-na'shun), *n.* arrangement of veins in a leaf.

VEND (vend), *v.t.* to sell; offer for sale.

VENDEE (ven-de'), *n.* the buyer.

VENDETTA (-det'a), *n.* a kind of feud.

VENDIBLE ('di-bl), *a.* saleable.

VENDOR ('dor), *n.* the seller.

VENEER (ve-ner'), *v.t.* to overlay with a thin slice of ornamental or more valuable wood; hence, give a gloss to.

VENENIFIC (ven-e-nif'ik), *adj.* relating to, or producing, poison.

VENERABLE ('er-a-bl), *adj.* worthy or being venerated or reverenced.

VENERATE ('er-at), *v.t.* to esteem as sacred; revere.

VENERATION (-a'shun), *n.* the highest degree of respect and reverence.

VENESECTION (ve-ne-sek'shun), *n.* opening a vein ; phlebotomy.

VENGEANCE (ven'jans), *n.* the infliction of pain on another for an injury received.

VENGEFUL (venj'fool), *adj.* vindictive ; retributive.

VENIAL (ve'ni-al), *adj.* pardonable.

VENIRE (ve-ni're), *n.* a judicial writ issued to a sheriff or a coroner for summoning a jury.

VENISON (ven'i-zn), *n.* deer's flesh.

VENOM ('um), *n.* poison introduced into the system.

VENOMOUS (-us), *adj.* poisonous.

VENOUS (ve'nus), *adj.* pertaining to, contained in, or consisting of, veins.

VENT (vent), *n.* a small opening for the escape of air, etc. ; outlet.

VENTILATE (ven'ti-lat), *v.t.* to open to the free passage of air.

VENTILATOR ('ti-la-ter), *n.* a contrivance for regulating the free admission of air.

VENTRILOQUISM (-tril'o-kwizm), *n.* the act or art of speaking as from another source than the voice.

VENTURE ('tur), *n.* an undertaking of chance or danger.

VENTURESOME ('sum), *adj.* intrepid ; rash.

VENUE (ven'u), *n.* the place where an action in law is laid.

VERACIOUS (ve-ra'shus), *adj.* truthful ; true.

VERACITY (-ras'i-ti), *n.* truthfulness ; truth.

VERANDA (ran'da), *n.* a covered balcony or open portico supported by light pillars.

VERB (verb), *n.* that part of speech which signifies to be, to do, or to suffer.

VERBAL (ver'bal), *adj.* expressed in words ; oral.

VERBALLY (-i), *adv.* orally ; verbatim.

VERBENA (-be'na), *n.* a genus of ornamental fragrant plants.

VERBIAGE ('bi-aj), *n.* verbosity.

VERBOSE (-bos'), *adj.* wordy.

VERBOSITY (-bos'i-ti), *n.* the use of more words than are necessary.

VERDANT ('dant), *adj.* green ; fresh ; inexperienced.

VERDICT ('dikt), *n.* the finding of a jury on a trial ; judgment.

VERDIGRIS ('di-gres), *n.* the blue-green substance which forms on copper or brass.

VERDITER ('di-ter), *n.* a blue, or green, pigment from carbonate of copper.

VERDURE ('dur), *n.* freshness of vegetation.

VERGE (verj), *n.* border or limit.

VERIFIABLE (ver'i-fi-a-bl), *adj.* capable of being verified.

VERIFICATION (-i-fi-ka'shun), *n.* proving to be true.

VERIFY ('i-fi), *v.t.* to prove to be true ; fulfil.

VERILY ('i-li), *adv.* in truth ; certainly.

VERISIMILITUDE (-i-si-mil'i-tud), *n.* the appearance of truth ; probability.

VERITABLE ('i-ta-bl), *adj.* true ; genuine.

VERITY ('i-ti), *n.* agreement with fact ; truth ; reality.

VERJUICE ('joos), *n.* an acid liquor expressed from unripe grapes, apples, etc. ; tartness.

VERMICELLI (-mi-sel'i), *n.* the stiff paste or dough of a certain flour dried in long slender sticks.

VERMIFUGE ('mi-fuj), *n.* a medicine to expel worms from the body.

VERMILION (-mil'yun), *n.* a brilliant red pigment.

VERMIN ('min), *n.* noxious small animals or insects, as rats, fleas, etc.

VERMUTH, VERMOUTH ('mooth), *n.* a liqueur flavoured with aromatic herbs.

VERNACULAR (-mak'u-lar), *adj.* pertaining to one's native language.

VERNAL ('nal), *adj.* pertaining to, or appearing in, the spring.

VERSATILE ('sa-til), *adj.* turning with ease from one thing, subject, or opinion to another.

VERSE (vers), *n.* a stanza ; poetry ; short division of any composition.

VERSED (verst), *adj.* skilled.

VERSIFICATION (ver-si-fi-ka'shun),

n. the art or practice of composing metrical verses.

VERSION ('shun), *n.* a translation from one language into another ; an account of some incident from an individual's point of view.

VERSUS ('sus), *prep.* against ; chiefly used in legal forms.

VERTEBRA ('te-bra), *n.* [*pl.* vertebræ (-bre)], a single bone of the spinal column.

VERTEBRAL ('te-bral), *adj.* pertaining to the vertebræ.

VERTEX ('teks), *n.* [*pl.* vertices ('ti-sez)], the top, summit, or crown ; apex ; zenith.

VERTICAL ('ti-kal), *adj.* pertaining to the vertex.

VERTICALLY (-i), *adv.* perpendicularly.

VERTICIL ('ti-sil), *n.* a whorl.

VERTIGO ('ti-go), *n.* dizziness.

VERTU, VIRTU ('too), *n.* objects of art ; artistic quality.

VERVE (verv), *n.* the enthusiasm which animates a poet or artist ; spirit ; energy.

VERY (ver'i), *adj.* identical ; the same : *adv.* extremely.

VESICATION (ves-i-ka'shun), *n.* the process of raising blisters on the skin.

VESICLE ('l-kl), *n.* a cyst ; sac.

VESPER (ves'per), *n.* the evening ; an evening hymn : *n.pl.* the sixth hour of the R.C. Breviary.

VESSEL ('el), *n.* a utensil for holding something ; a boat or ship.

VEST (vest), *n.* waistcoat : *v.t.* invest closely ; give fixed right.

VESTAL (ves'tal), *adj.* pertaining to, or sacred to, the Roman goddess Vesta ; chaste ; pure.

VESTED ('ted), *adj.* clothed ; fixed.

VESTIBULE ('ti-bul), *n.* porch or entrance into a house.

VESTMENT (vest'ment), *n.* a garment.

VESTRY (ves'tri), *n.* a room in a church for ecclesiastical vestments, etc.

VESTURE ('tur), *n.* clothing ; covering.

VETERAN (vet'er-an), *adj.* long exercised or experienced.

VETERINARY ('er-i-na-ri), *adj.* pertaining to the art of healing the diseases of domestic animals, as horses, etc.

VETO (ve'to), *n.* authoritative prohibition ; refuse assent to.

VEX (veks), *v.t.* to irritate ; tease.

VEXATION (vek-sa'shun), *n.* annoyance ; worry.

VEXATIOUS ('shus), *adj.* annoying ; troublesome.

VIA (vi'a), *n.* a Roman highway : *prep.* by way of.

VIADUCT ('a-dukt), *n.* an arched structure for conveying a railway, road, etc.

VIAL ('al), *n.* a small glass bottle.

VIANDS ('andz), *n.pl.* dressed meat ; food.

VIBRATE ('brat), *v.i.* to oscillate ; shake ; quiver ; swing ; waver.

VIBRATION (-bra'shun), *n.* oscillation ; resonance.

VICAR (vik'er), *n.* a deputy ; a parish priest.

VICE (vis), *n.* a fault, or blemish ; depravity ; immorality ; a substitute.

VICE-PRESIDENT (-prez'i-dent), *n.* one who acts in the absence of a president.

VICEROY ('roi), *n.* a governor of a country ruling in the name, and by the authority, of the sovereign.

VICE VERSA (vi'se ver'sa), [Latin], conversely ; the order or relations being reversed.

VICINAGE (vis'i-naj), *n.* an adjoining place.

VICINITY (vi-sin'i-ti), *n.* nearness in place ; proximity.

VICIOUS (vish'us), *adj.* faulty ; corrupt ; unruly ; spiteful.

VICISSITUDE (vi-sis'i-tud), *n.* change ; alternation.

VICTIM (vik'tim), *n.* one who suffers from a wrong or injury ; dupe.

VICTIMIZE (-iz), *v.t.* to swindle ; deceive.

VICTOR ('ter), *n.* conqueror.

VICTORIOUS (-to'ri-us), *adj.* having conquered in battle or contest ; triumphant.

VICTORY ('to-ri), *n.* the defeat of an enemy, or an antagonist.

VICTUAL (vit'l), *v.t.* to supply or store with provisions for food.

VIDE (vi'de), *v.t.* see [Latin].

VIEW (vu), *v.t.* to look upon; see; regard attentively.

VIGIL (vij'il), *n.* a watching.

VIGILANCE ('i-lans), *n.* watchfulness; caution.

VIGILANT ('i-lant), *adj.* alert; cautious.

VIGNETTE (vin-yet'), *n.* a small engraving without a definite border.

VIGOUR (vig'er), *n.* physical or mental strength and energy.

VIGOROUS ('er-us), *adj.* robust; forcible.

VILE (vil), *adj.* worthless; despicable; morally base.

VILIFIER ('i-fi-er), *n.* a defamer.

VILIFY ('i-fi), *v.t.* to defame.

VILLA ('a), *n.* a country seat.

VILLAGE ('aj), *n.* a small assemblage of houses, less than a town.

VILLAIN ('in), *n.* a criminal; rogue; rascal; scoundrel.

VILLAINOUS (-us), *adj.* vile.

VILLAINY (-i), *n.* extreme depravity.

VIM (vim), *n.* force; vigour; energy; spirit.

VINACEOUS (vi-na'shus), *adj.* pertaining to grapes or wine.

VINCIBLE (vin'si-bl), *adj.* capable of being conquered.

VINDICATE ('di-kat), *v.t.* to prove to be valid; defend successfully.

VINDICATION (-ka'shun), *n.* justification against; defence; support by proof.

VINDICATOR ('di-ka-ter), *n.* one who vindicates.

VINDICATORY (-to-ri), *adj.* serving to vindicate, justify, or punish.

VINDICTIVE (-dik'tiv), *adj.* given to, or prompted by, revenge.

VINE (vin), *n.* a plant that climbs or twines around; the grape-vine.

VINEGAR ('e-ger), *n.* an acid obtained by fermentation.

VINEYARD (vin'yard), *n.* a plantation of vines producing grapes.

VINOUS (vi'nus), *adj.* pertaining to, having the qualities of, or like, wine.

VINTAGE (vin'taj), *n.* the yearly crop or produce of the grape.

VIOL (vi'ol), *n.* a four-stringed musical instrument played with a bow.

VIOLA (ve-o'la), *n.* the tenor violin.

VIOLABLE (vi'o-la-bl), *adj.* capable of being violated or broken.

VIOLATE ('o-lat), *v.t.* to break forcibly; injure; ravish; outrage; desecrate.

VIOLATION (-la'shun), *n.* rape; outrage; act of irreverence or profanation.

VIOLATER ('o-la-ter), *n.* one who violates.

VIOLENCE ('o-lens), *n.* physical or moral force; vehemence.

VIOLENT ('o-lent), *adj.* vehement; impetuous; furious; severe.

VIOLET ('o-let), *n.* a low plant with drooping head-stalk; bearing beautiful purplish-blue flowers; the colour of violet.

VIOLIN (-o-lin'), *n.* a four-stringed musical instrument, played with a bow.

VIOLINIST ('ist), *n.* a performer on the violin.

VIOLONCELLO (-chel'o), *n.* [Italian] a large four-stringed instrument of the viol class.

VIPER (vi'per), *n.* a name of certain poisonous serpents; in Britain the common adder.

VIRGIN (ver'jin), *n.* a maiden: *adj.* chaste; modest; pure.

VIRGINAL (-al), *adj.* maidenly; chaste.

VIRGINITY ('i-ti), *n.* maidenhood.

VIRILE (vir'il), *adj.* masculine.

VIRILITY (vi-ril'i-ti), *n.* manhood.

VIRTU, see vertu.

VIRTUAL (ver'tu-al), *adj.* in essence or affect, though not in fact.

VIRTUE ('tu), *n.* rectitude; strength; efficacy; valour.

VIRTUOSO (-tu-o'so), *n.* [*pl.* virtuosi ('se)], one skilled in the fine arts, antiquities, etc.

VIRTUOUS ('tu-us), *adj.* moral.

VIRULENT ('u-lent), *adj.* very poisonous or venomous.

VIS (vis), *n.* power; force.

VISAGE (viz'aj), *n.* the countenance.

VIS-A-VIS (ve-za-ve'), *n.* one who is face to face with another.

VISCERA (vis'er-a), *n.pl.* the heart, lungs, liver and intestines.

VISCID ('id), *adj.* sticky; glutinous.

VISCOUNT (vi'kount), *n.* a nobleman next in rank below an earl.

VISCOUS (vis'kus), *adj.* adhesive or glutinous.

VISE, VICE (vis), *n.* a device with two jaws for holding articles in filing, or the like.

VISE (ve-za'), *n.* [French], an official indorsement on a passport.

VISIBILITY (viz-i-bil'i-ti), *n.* perceptibility.

VISIBLE ('bl), *adj.* perceptible by the eye; in view; obvious; apparent.

VISION (vizh'un), *n.* sight; divine revelation; apparition; creation of the imagination.

VISIONARY (-a-ri), *adj.* existing only in the imagination.

VISITANT ('i-tant), *n.* a visitor.

VISITATION (vis-i-ta'shun), *n.* official visit; infliction of good or evil.

VISITOR (viz'i-ter), *n.* one who calls upon any one.

VISUAL (vizh'u-al), *adj.* pertaining to, or used to, sight.

VISUALIZE (-iz), *v.t.* to make visable; see in fancy.

VITAGRAPH (vit'a-graf), *n.* a form of cinematograph.

VITAL (vi'tal), *adj.* mortal; essential.

VITALITY ('i-ti), *n.* vital force.

VITALIZE ('tal-iz), *v.t.* to endow with life; animate.

VITALLY (-i), *adv.* essentially.

VITALS ('talz), *n.pl.* the organs of the body essential to life.

VITASCOPE (vi'ta-skop), *n.* an apparatus for projecting kinetographic pictures in life size upon a canvas.

VITELLUS ('us), *n.* the yolk of an egg.

VITIATE (vish'i-at), *v.t.* to render faulty or defective; taint; deprave; annul.

VITICULTURE (vit'i-kul-tur), *n.* vine culture.

VITRIC (vit'rik), *adj.* glass-like.

VITRIFY ('ri-fi), *v.t.* to convert by heat and fusion into glass.

VITRIOL ('ri-ol), *n.* sulphuric acid.

VITRIOLIC (-ol'ik), *adj.* pertaining to vitriol; corrosive; caustic; sarcastic.

VITUPERATE (vi-tu'per-at), *v.t.* to censure abusively.

VITUPERATION (-a'shun), *n.* abusive censure.

VIVACIOUS (vi-va'shus), *adj.* lively; gay.

VIVACITY (-vas'i-ti), *n.* liveliness; animation.

VIVA VOCE ('va vo'se), [Latin], orally; by word of mouth.

VIVID (viv'id), *adj.* life-like; realistic.

VIVIFY (viv'i-fi), *v.t.* to endue with life; quicken.

VIVIPAROUS (vi-vip'a-rus), *adj.* producing young alive from the body.

VIVISECT (viv-i-sekt'), *v.t.* to dissect the living body of.

VIVISECTION (-sek'shun), *n.* the dissection of a living animal for scientific study.

VIXEN (vik's'n), *n.* a female fox; ill-tempered woman.

VIZ. (viz), *adv.* namely; to wit.

VIZIER (vi-zer'), *n.* a high officer or councillor of state in Mohammedan countries.

VOCABULARY (vo-kab'u-la-ri), *n.* a collection of words of a language, science, etc.; number of words a person uses in speech or writing.

VOCAL (vo'kal), *adj.* pertaining to voice or speech.

VOCALIST (-ist), *n.* a singer.

VOCALIZE (-iz), *v.t.* to form into voice.

VOCATION (-ka'shun), *n.* calling; occupation.

VOCIFERATE (vo-sif'er-at), *v.i.* to clamour; bawl.

VOCIFEROUS ('er-us), *adj.* clamorous; noisy.

VOGUE (vog), *n.* fashion; custom.

VOICE (vois), *n.* faculty of speech; language.

VOID (void), *adj.* empty; wanting.

VOLATILE (vol'a-til), *adj.* easily passing into the aeriform state.

VOLCANIC (-kan'ik), *adj.* pertaining to a volcano.

VOLCANO (-ka'no), *n.* a vent in the

earth's crust through which rocks, earth, etc., are ejected with violent force.

VOLITION (vo-lish'un), *n.* the act or power of willing or exerting choice.

VOLITIVE (vol'i-tiv), *adj.* pertaining to, or having the power of, will.

VOLLEY ('i), *n.* the simultaneous discharge of a number of small-arms.

VOLPLANE (vol'plan), *v.i.* to descend in an aeroplane from a great height without motor power.

VOLT (volt), *n.* the circular tread of a horse; a unit of electromotive force.

VOLTMETER (volt'me-ter), *n.* an instrument for measuring voltage.

VOLUBILITY (-u-bil'i-ti), *n.* excessive fluency of speech.

VOLUBLE ('u-bl), *adj.* fluent in speech.

VOLUME ('yum), *n.* a single book; mass or bulk.

VOLUMINOUS (vo-lu'mi-nus), *adj.* extensive; copious.

VOLUNTARILY (vol'un-ta-ri-li), *adv.* spontaneously.

VOLUNTARY ('un-ta-ri), *adj.* acting from choice or free will.

VOLUNTEER (-un-ter'), *n.* one who enters into any service of his own free will.

VOLUPTUARY (vo-lup'tu-a-ri), *n.* one given to sensuality or luxury.

VOLUTED (lut'ed), *adj.* having a spiral scroll.

VOMIT (vom'it), *v.i.* to eject the contents of the stomach by the mouth.

VORACIOUS (vo-ra'shus), *adj.* greedy in eating; ravenous.

VORACITY (-ras'i-ti), *n.* the quality of being voracious.

VORTEX (vor'teks), *n.* [*pl.* vortices ('ti-sez)], the hollow and circular form assumed by a liquid when set in rotation; whirlpool.

VOTARY (vo'ta-ri), *n.* one addicted to some particular pursuit.

VOTE (vot), *n.* an expression of choice for some particular candidate for an office, etc., by ballot.

VOTER ('er), *n.* an elector.

VOTING ('ing), *v.i.* expression of opinion or preference by suffrage.

VOTING MACHINE (ma-shen'), *n.* a machine which counts and registers the votes at an election.

VOTIVE (vo'tiv), *adj.* given, consecrated, or promised by vow.

VOUCH (vouch), *v.t.* to attest; guarantee.

VOUCHER ('er), *n.* one who gives attestation or witness; a document guaranteeing the accuracy of accounts.

VOUCHSAFE (-saf'), *v.t.* to concede.

VOW (vou), *n.* a solemn promise.

VOWEL ('el), *n.* a single open sound uttered without any constriction of the vocal organs.

VOYAGE (voi'aj), *n.* a journey by water from one place to another.

VULCANITE (vul'kan-it), *n.* vulcanized india-rubber.

VULGAR ('gar), *adj.* common; general; vernacular; plebeian; unrefined; coarse; mean.

VULGARIAN (-ga'ri-an), *n.* any person with vulgar ideas.

VULGARITY (-gar'i-ti), *n.* coarseness of manners or language.

VULNERABLE ('ner-a-bl), *adj.* capable of being wounded.

VULPINE ('pin), *adj.* pertaining to a fox; cunning.

VULTURE ('tur), *n.* a large, carnivorous, voracious bird of prey.

VYING (vi'ing), *p.adj.* competing; emulating.

W

W, w (dub'l-u), the twenty-third letter in the English alphabet.

W, w, an abbreviation.

WABBLE, WOBBLE (wob'l), *n.* an unsteady motion or gait.

WADDING (wod'ing), *n.* a soft stuff of loose texture used for stuffing garments, etc.

WADDLE ('l), *v.i.* to move from side to side in walking.

WADDLER ('ler), *n.* one who waddles.

WADE (wad), *v.i.* to walk through

any substance that yields to the feet, as water, snow, etc.

WAFER (wa'fer), *n.* a small paste disk for securing letters, etc.

WAFFLE (wof'l), *n.* soft indented cake, baked in a waffle-iron.

WAFT (waft), *n.* a puff of wind.

WAG (wag), *v.i.* to move backwards and forwards : *n.* a joker.

WAGE (waj), *v.t.* to engage in : *n.* payment for service rendered : *pl.* hire paid.

WAGER (wa'jer), *n.* that which is risked on an uncertainty or contingency ; a bet.

WAGGISH (wag'ish), *adj.* humorous.

WAGON ('un), *n.* a four-wheeled heavy vehicle.

WAIF (waf), *n.* a homeless wanderer.

WAIL (wal), *v.t.* to lament : *v.i.* to express sorrow audibly.

WAINSCOT (wan'skot), *n.* panelled wooden lining on walls.

WAINWRIGHT ('rit), *n.* a maker of wagons.

WAIST (wast), *n.* the narrowest part of the body just below the ribs ; bodice of a dress.

WAISTCOAT ('kot), *n.* a short, sleeveless garment worn by men.

WAIT (wat), *v.i.* to watch ; remain quiet.

WAITER ('er), *n.* a servant in attendance at table ; tray.

WAITRESS (wat'res), *n.* girl who attends table.

WAIVE (wav), *v.t.* to give up a claim to ; to forego.

WAKE (wak), *v.i.* to be awake ; cease to sleep.

WAKEFUL ('fool), *adj.* watchful.

WALK (wawk), *v.i.* to advance by alternate steps ; go at a moderate pace ; take exercise.

WALL (wawl), *n.* a structure of stone, brick, etc.

WALLET (wol'et), *n.* a bag or knapsack ; a pocketbook.

WALLFLOWER ('flour-er), *n.* a hardy garden perennial.

WALLOP (wol'up), *v.t.* to beat soundly : *n.* a blow.

WALLOW ('o), *v.i.* to live in vice or filth : *n.* a place where an animal wallows.

WALNUT ('nut), *n.* valuable timber tree.

WALRUS (wol'rus), *n.* a large, carnivorous, marine mammal.

WALTZ (wawltz), *n.* a kind of dance.

WAMPUM (wom'pum), *n.* beads made of shells, used by the North American Indians as money and for ornament.

WAN (won), *adj.* pale ; sickly.

WAND (wond), *n.* a long, slender rod.

WANDER (won'der), *v.i.* to ramble about aimlessly ; stroll.

WANDERLUST (won'der-lust), *n.* love of constant travel.

WANE (wan), *v.i.* to become less ; diminish ; decrease.

WANNESS (won'nes), *n.* wan condition.

WANT (wawnt), *n.* the thing that is lacking ; deficiency ; necessity ; penury.

WANTING ('ting), *p.adj.* lacking ; absent.

WANTON (won'tun), *adj.* licentious ; unrestrained.

WAPITI (wop'i-ti), *n.* a large North American deer.

WAR (wawr), *n.* a contest between states carried on by force ; armed conflict.

WARBLE (wawr'bl), *v.t. & v.i.* to sing in a trilling manner.

WARBLER ('bler), *n.* a singing-bird.

WARD (wawrd), *v.t.* to guard : *n.* division of a city or town ; person entrusted to the care of a guardian.

WARDEN ('"n), *n.* a guardian.

WARDROBE ('rob), *n.* portable closet for clothes ; wearing apparel.

WAREHOUSE (war'hous), *n.* a building for storing goods.

WARES (warz), *n.* merchandise.

WARFARE (wawr'far), *n.* hostilities.

WARILY (war'i-li), *adv.* cautiously.

WARINESS ('i-nes), *n.* caution.

WARM (wawrm), *adj.* having heat.

WARMTH (wawrmth), *n.* moderate heat.

WARN (wawrn), *v.t.* to caution.

WARP (wawrp), *n.* the threads which extend lengthwise in the loom, and

are crossed by the woof ; a twist out of shape.

WARRANT (wor'ant), *v.t.* to guarantee ; authorize ; maintain : *n.* a writ.

WARRANTY ('ti), *n.* guarantee ; security ; authorization.

WARREN ('en), *n.* an enclosure for rabbits, etc.

WARRIOR (wawr'i-er), *n.* a soldier.

WART (wawrt), *n.* a dry excrescence on the human skin.

WARY (wa'ri), *adj.* cautious.

WASH (wosh), *v.t.* to cleanse.

WASHOUT (wosh'out), *n.* a ditch or chasm caused by a violent current of water.

WASP (wosp), *n.* a winged insect with a sharp sting.

WASTE (wast), *v.t.* to destroy wantonly ; diminish ; squander : *adj.* unproductive : *n.* a desolate region ; refuse.

WASTREL (was'trel), *n.* a spendthrift ; a vagabond.

WATCH (woch), *n.* close observation ; guard ; vigilance ; sentry ; watchman ; pocket timepiece.

WATCHFUL (fool), *adj.* vigilant.

WATCHWORD ('werd), *n.* a password ; a rallying cry.

WATER (waw'ter), *n.* a colourless, inodorous, transparent fluid, consisting of two volumes of hydrogen to one of oxygen.

WATERCOURSE (-kors), *n.* a channel or bed for running water.

WATERED STOCKS (stoks), shares of stock added to the capital of a corporation without cash or property value.

WATERFALL (waw'ter-fawl), *n.* a cascade ; a cataract.

WATER-LINE (lin), *n.* a line to which the water rises on the hull of a ship.

WATER-LOGGED (waw'ter-logd), *adj.* saturated with water so as to be unmanageable.

WATERPROOF (-proof), *adv.* impervious to water : *n.* a rain-coat.

WATT (wot), *n.* an electrical unit of power.

WATTLE ('l), *n.* fleshy lobe under the throat of a fowl ; wands interwoven.

WAVE (wav), *n.* the alternate rising and falling of water above its natural level ; undulation ; signal made by waving.

WAVE-LENGTH (-length), *n.* in radio, the distance between the crests of the undulating electric wave.

WAVELET ('let), *n.* a little wave; a ripple.

WAVY ('i), *adj.* undulating.

WAX (waks), *n.* beeswax ; any tenacious substance like beeswax.

WAXY (wak'si), *adj.* adhesive ; angry.

WAYWARD ('werd), *adj.* perverse, froward.

WE (we), *pron.*, the personal pronoun, 1st person plural, nominative case ; plural of *I*.

WEAK (wek), *adj.* feeble ; soft ; pliant ; unfortified ; vacillating.

WEAKEN ('n), *v.t.* to reduce in quality or strength.

WEAKLING (wek'ling), *n.* a person weak in moral or physical strength.

WEAL (wel), *n.* welfare.

WEALTH (welth), *n.* riches ; affluence ; worldly possessions.

WEALTHY ('thi), *adj.* rich.

WEAN (wen), *v.t.* to accustom and reconcile to a want or deprivation of the breast ; alienate.

WEAPON (wep'n), *n.* any instrument of offence or defence.

WEAR (war), *v.t.* to impair or waste by time, usage, friction, etc. ; carry as covering on the body.

WEARILY (we'ri-li), *adv.* in a weary manner.

WEARISOME ('ri-sum), *adj.* fatiguing ; tedious.

WEARY ('ri), *adj.* worn out physically or mentally.

WEASEL (we'z'l), *n.* a small carnivorous animal.

WEASEL WORDS (wurdz), words used to deceive.

WEATHER (weth'er), *n.* the state of the atmosphere with respect to cold, heat, wet, dryness, etc. : *v.t.* endure or resist bravely.

WEAVE (wev), *v.t.* to twist or interlace, as threads, together ; form, as cloth, in a loom.

WEAZEN (we'zn), *n.* sharp and thin ; withered.

WEB (web), *n.* texture of threads, or threadlike materials ; tissue or texture.

WEBBING ('ing), *n.* a narrow woven fabric of cotton or flax.

WED (wed), *v.t.* to marry ; unite.

WEDDING ('ing), *n.* marriage.

WEDGE (wej), *n.* a piece of wood or metal, used for rending or compressing, etc.

WEDLOCK ('lok), *n.* matrimony.

WEDNESDAY (wenz'da), *n.* the fourth day of the week.

WEE (we), *adj.* very small.

WEED (wed), *n.* any plant growing uncultivated, or noxious to cultivated crops.

WEEDY ('i), *adj.* pertaining to weeds ; thin and lank.

WEEK (wek), *n.* a period of seven days.

WEEK-DAY ('da), *n.* any day of the week except Sunday.

WEEN (wen), *v.i.* to think ; fancy.

WEEP (wep), *v.i.* to shed tears : *v.i.* to lament.

WEEPING ('ing), *n.* the act of shedding tears.

WEEPING OAK (ok), *n.* the valley oak.

WEEPING WILLOW (wil'o), *n.* a willow, the branches of which droop.

WEEVIL (we'vl), *n.* a small beetle, the larvæ of which are very destructive to grain.

WEFT (weft), *n.* the woof or piling of cloth ; the threads crossing the warp.

WEIGH (wa), *v.t.* to ascertain the weight of ; reflect on carefully.

WEIGHT (wat), *n.* the quality of being heavy ; gravity ; mass ; something oppressive ; pressure ; power ; importance.

WEIGHTINESS ('i-nes), *n.* heaviness ; importance ; force.

WEIGHTY ('i), *adj.* heavy ; ponderous ; momentous.

WEIR (wer), *n.* a dam across a stream to raise the level of the water ; enclosure for catching fish.

WEIRD (werd), *adj.* pertaining to fate or destiny ; supernatural.

WELCOME (wel'kum), *adj.* received with gladness or hospitality : *n.* kind reception to a guest or newcomer.

WELD (weld), *v.t.* to unite by hammering or fusion.

WELFARE (wel'far), *n.* prosperity ; happiness.

WELKIN ('kin), *n.* the sky.

WELL (wel), *n.* shaft sunk to reach a supply of water or other liquid : *v.i.* to flow or issue forth : *adv.* right ; justly ; suitably ; adequately ; favourably ; far ; not a little : *adj.* fortunate ; sound ; healthy ; safe.

WELL-BRED ('bred), *adj.* refined in manners ; cultivated.

WELSH (welsh), *v.t.* & *v.i.* to avoid payment of a debt.

WELSHER (wel'sher), *n.* one who bets or receives money as bets, and absconds without paying.

WELSH-RABBIT (-rab'it), *n.* melted cheese, spread upon toast.

WELT (welt), *n.* a narrow strip of leather around a shoe between the upper leather and sole ; a blow.

WELTER ('ter), *v.t.* to roll in mud or foul matter ; wallow.

WEN (wen), *n.* a fleshy and movable tumor ; a cyst.

WEND (wend), *v.i.* to go ; pass : *v.t.* to direct (one's way or course).

WEST (west), *n.* one of the four cardinal points, exactly opposite the east ; point where the sun appears to set.

WESTERN HEMISPHERE (hem'i-sfer), the terrestrial division of the world which includes North and South America.

WET (wet), *v.t.* to make wet ; saturate or moisten with water or some other liquid.

WET-NURSE (ners), *n.* a nurse who suckles the child of another.

WHACK (hwak), *n.* a smart, resounding blow ; large piece.

WHALE (hwal), *n.* any of several large aquatic mammals : *v.t.* to beat soundly.

WHARF (hwawrf), *n.* quay or dock on the shore of a harbour, river, etc.

WHAT (hwot), *pron.* that which ; the thing that ; something : *adj.* how great ; of what sort, character, etc.

WHEAT (hwet), *n.* an annual cereal grain from which flour is extracted by a milling process.

WHEATEN ('n), *adj.* made of wheat.

WHEEDLE (hwe'dl), *v.t.* to entice with flattering words; cajole; coax.

WHEEL (hwel), *n.* a circular frame or solid piece of wood or metal turning on its own axis; any wheel-shaped mechanical contrivance.

WHEELBARROW (hwel'bar-o), *n.* a barrow, usually with one wheel and two handles.

WHEELWRIGHT ('rit), *n.* a maker of wheels and wheeled carriages.

WHEEZE (hwez), *v.i.* to breathe hard and audibly.

WHEEZY ('i), *adj.* affected with wheezing.

WHELM (hwelm), *v.t.* to overwhelm.

WHELP (hwelp), *n.* the young of a dog, lion, fox, etc., cub.

WHEN (hwen), *adv.* at, or after, the time that; at what time; although.

WHERE (hwar), *adv.* at which place or places; whither.

WHEREAS (az'), *conj.* when in fact or truth; since; seeing that.

WHEREBY (-bi'), *adj.* by which or what.

WHEREFORE ('for), *n.* cause or reason: *adv.* for which or what reason; why.

WHET (hwet), *v.t.* to sharpen; stimulate.

WHETHER (hwe*th*'er), *pron.* which of two: *conj.* which of two alter-natives (followed by *or*).

WHETSTONE (hwet'ston), *n.* a stone for sharpening edged tools, etc.

WHEY (hwa), *n.* the thin, sweet, watery part of milk, after separation from the curd.

WHICH (hwich), *pron.* an interroga-tive, used to ask of a person or thing of a group or class: as a relative, it is used in place of *who*, and refers to inanimate things and the lower animals without distinction of gender.

WHIFF (hwif), *n.* a sudden breath of air, smoke, etc.; light puff.

WHIFFLE ('l), *v.i.* to be fickle or unsteady; prevaricate.

WHIFFLETREE, same as swingle-tree.

WHILE (hwil), *n.* space of time; duration: *conj.* during the time that: *v.t.* to pass the time pleasantly; usually followed by *away*.

WHILST (hwilst), *adv.* while.

WHIM (hwim), *n.* a capricious fancy; freak; notion.

WHIMPER ('per), *v.t.* to utter in a low, whining or crying tone.

WHIMSICAL ('zi-kal), *adj.* fantas-tical; odd in appearance.

WHIP (hwip), *v.t.* to strike or punish; surpass in competition; beat into a froth; beat out; sew lightly.

WHIPPING ('ing), *n.* the act of punishing with the lash or rod.

WHIPPOORWILL ('poor-wil), *n.* a small nocturnal bird.

WHIR (hwer), *v.i.* to revolve quickly with a whizzing noise.

WHIRL (hwerl), *v.t.* to turn round rapidly: *v.i.* to turn or move along swiftly.

WHIRLPOOL (-pool), *n.* a body of water moving with a circular motion forming a vortex or gulf.

WHIRLWIND ('wind), *n.* a violent wind moving spirally.

WHISK (hwisk), *v.t.* to sweep or stir rapidly.

WHISKERS ('kerz), *n.pl.* the hair on a man's face.

WHISKEY, WHISKY (hwis'ki), *n.* an intoxicant distilled from barley, rye, etc.

WHISPER ('per), *v.i.* to speak in a low voice.

WHIST (hwist), *n.* a card game: *interj.* hush!

WHISTLE (hwis'l), *v.i.* to make a shrill sound: *v.t.* to call or signal by a whistle.

WHITECAP (hwit'kap), *n.* the foamy crest of a wave.

WHITE FEATHER (feth'er), *colloq.* cowardice.

WHITE HOUSE (hous), the official residence at Washington, D.C., of the President.

WHITE-LIVERED ('liv-erd), *adj.* cowardly; pusillanimous.

WHITEN ('n), *v.t.* to make white.

WHITEWASH ('wosh), *n.* a composition of lime, whiting, size, water, etc.

WHITHER (whith'er), *adv.* to what place ; to what ; how far.

WHITING (hwit'ing), *n.* pulverized chalk cleansed from impurities.

WHITTLE (hwit'l), *v.t.* to cut, dress, or sharpen with a knife.

WHIZ (hwiz), *v.i.* to make a humming or hissing noise.

WHOA (hwo), *interj.* stop ! stand ! hold ! a word used by drivers.

WHOLE (hol), *adj.* containing all ; complete ; hale and sound : *n.* the sum of all its parts ; the total.

WHOLESALE ('sal), *n.* sale of goods in large quantity.

WHOLESOME ('sum), *adj.* sound ; promoting or favouring morals, religion, or prosperity.

WHOLLY (ho'li), *adv.* entirely ; exclusively.

WHOOPING-COUGH (hoop'ing-kof), *n.* a disease of children accompanied by a convulsive cough.

WHOPPER ('er), *n.* something unusually large ; a monstrous lie.

WHORL (hwerl, hworl), *n.* any set of organs or appendages arranged in a circle round an axis, as flowers or leaves.

WHORTLEBERRY (hwer'tl-ber-i), *n.* the huckleberry ; often called blueberry.

WICK (wik), *n.* the cotton or substance of a candle or lamp.

WICKED ('ed), *adj.* evil in principle or practice ; sinful.

WICKET ('et), *n.* a small gate.

WIDE (wid), *adj.* broad ; vast ; very capacious.

WIDOW (wid'o), *n.* a woman bereaved of her husband and remaining unmarried.

WIDOWER (-er), *n.* a man bereaved of his wife and remaining unmarried.

WIDTH (width), *n.* extent of a thing from side to side.

WIELD (weld), *v.t.* control or sway ; handle.

WIFE (wif), *n.* a woman united in lawful wedlock.

WIG (wir), *n.* false hair worn on the head.

WIGGING (wig'ing), *n.* a scolding.

WIGGLE, same as wriggle.

WIGWAG (wig'wag), *n.* a signalling flag : *v.i.* to wave to and fro.

WIGWAM (wig'wawm), *n.* an Indian tent.

WILDERNESS (wil'der-nes), *n.* a region or tract of land uncultivated and uninhabited.

WILE (wil), *n.* a sly artifice : *v.t.* to cause to pass pleasantly (with *away*) ; lure ; beguile.

WILL (wil), *n.* the faculty of the mind by which one chooses or determines.

WILFUL (wil'fool), *adj.* stubborn ; inflexible.

WILLING ('ing), *adj.* inclined to do or grant.

WILL-O'-THE-WISP (wil'o-*the*-wisp'), *n.* an ignis fatuus; a vain pursuit.

WILLOW ('o), *n.* a tree of genus *Salix*.

WILLOWY (wil'o-i), *adj.* slender ; graceful.

WILY (wi-li), *adj.* cunning ; crafty.

WINCE (wins), *v.i.* to twist or turn as in pain ; shrink.

WINCH (winch), *n.* a device on which to coil a rope.

WIND (wind), *n.* air in perceptible motion ; breath ; flatulence ; idle words : *v.i.* (wind), to turn round something ; twist ; meander.

WINDER (win'der), *n.* a trailing plant ; a key for turning a mechanism.

WINDFALL (wind'fawl), *n.* fruit blown down by the wind ; unexpected good fortune.

WINDING (wind'ing), *n.* a bend, turn or twist.

WINDLASS (wind'las), *n.* a horizontal cylinder, with rope, or chain, by means of which heavy weights, etc., are raised.

WINDMILL (wind'mill), *n.* a structure containing sails or contrivances to be revolved by the wind.

WINDPIPE (wind'pip), *n.* the trachea.

WIND-SHIELD (wind'sheld), *n.* framed glass in front of an automobile.

WINDWARD (wind'werd), *n.* the direction from which the wind blows.

WINE (win), *n.* the fermented juice of grapes.

WINK (wingk), *v.i.* to close and open the eyelids with a quick motion

WINKING ('ing), *n.* act of shutting and opening the eyes rapidly.

WINNER (win'er), *n.* one who wins.

WINNING ('ing), *adj.* attractive; charming: *n.pl.* money gained in any contest.

WINNOW ('o), *v.t.* to separate the chaff from (grain), fan; sift or examine.

WINSOME ('sum), *adj.* pretty.

WINTER ('ter), *n.* the cold season of the year.

WINTER SOLSTICE (sol'stis), in northern regions, the first point in the ecliptic at which the sun is farthest south (about Dec. 21) from the equator.

WINY (win'i), *adj.* vinous.

WIRELESS (wir'les), *adj.* designating a method whereby speech in general and other sounds are transmitted through the air without wires, by means of electric waves, now known as radio broadcasting.

WIRELESS TELEGRAPHY (te-leg'ra-fi), any form of telegraphic communication effected by means of electricity without the use of wire circuits.

WIRELESS TELEPHONY (te-lef'o-ni), a system of telephoning without wires.

WIREPULLING ('pool-ing), *n.* secret influence or intrigue.

WIRE-TAPPER (wir-tap'er), *n.* one who illicitly intercepts telegraph or telephone messages by tapping the wire.

WIRY (wir'i), *adj.* made of, or like, wire; strong and flexible.

WISDOM (wiz'dom), *n.* knowledge practically applied to the best ends; natural sagacity.

WISE (wiz), *adj.* judging correctly from experience; possessing wisdom; skilful; learned; discreet.

WISEACRE ('a-ker), *n.* pretender to learning.

WISELY ('li), *adv.* in a wise manner.

WISHING (wish'ing), *n.* a wish.

WISP (wisp), *n.* a handful, as of straw or hay.

WISTFUL (wist'fool), *adj.* sadly longing; pensive.

WITCH (wich), *n.* a sorceress.

WITCHCRAFT ('kraft), *n.* supernatural or magical powers.

WITCHERY ('er-i), *n.* fascination.

WITCH-HAZEL ('ha-zel), *n.* a shrub of the genus *Hamamelis*; an extract of the bark is used for bruises, sprains, etc.

WITCHING, same as bewitching.

WITH (with), *prep.* denoting nearness or connection.

WITHAL (with-awl'), *adv.* also; likewise.

WITHE (with), *n.* a tough, flexible twig; twisted band of twigs.

WITHER (with'er), *v.t.* to cause to fade and become dry; decay.

WITLESS (wit'les), *adj.* stupid.

WITNESS (wit'nes), *n.* attestation of a fact or event; testimony; one who attests.

WITTICISM ('i-sizm), *n.* a witty remark.

WITTINESS ('i-nes), *n.* the quality of being witty.

WITTY ('i), *adj.* smartly or cleverly facetious; satirical.

WIZARD (wiz'ard), *n.* enchanter; sorcerer; conjurer.

WIZEN ("n), *adj.* dried up; shrivelled.

WOE (wo), *n.* sorrow; grief; misery.

WOFUL ('fool), *adj.* sad; mean; also woeful.

WOLD (wold), *n.* a district without woods.

WOLF (woolf), *n.* a fierce carnivorous animal of the dog kind.

WOMAN (woom'an), *n.* an adult person of the female sex.

WOMAN SUFFRAGE (suf'raj), women's right to vote.

WOMB (woom), *n.* the uterus.

WONDER (wun'der), *n.* astonishment; cause of wonder; marvel; miracle; prodigy.

WONDERFUL (-fool), *adj.* exciting wonder; strange.

WONT (wunt), *n.* habit; custom; usage.

WONTED ('ed), *adj.* habitual; usual.

WOO (woo), *v.t.* to solicit in love.

WOOD (wood), *n.* collection of growing trees; solid part of trees.

WOODCOCK ('kok), *n.* wild bird allied to snipe.

WOODEN ('n), *adj.* produced as from wood; stiff; awkward.

WOODMAN ('man), *n.* a forester; one who fells timber.

WOODPECKER ('pek-er), *n.* a bird that taps the trunks of trees to discover insects.

WOOD PULP (pulp), *n.* pulp for paper-making, prepared by special treatment of spruce, poplar, hemlock, and other pines.

WOOD SPIRIT (spir'it), *n.* a very poisonous form of alcohol; wood alcohol.

WOOER (woo'er), *n.* one who woos.

WOOF (woof), *n.* the weft or cross-threads in weaving; texture.

WOOING (woo'ing), *adj.* courting.

WOOL (wool), *n.* the soft, fine hair which covers sheep, etc.

WOOLGATHERING (-gath'er-ing), *n.* indulgence of idle fancies: *adj.* dreamy.

WOOLPACK ('pak), *n.* a bale of wool, 240 lb.

WORD (werd), *n.* an articulate sound, or combination of sounds expressing an idea.

WORDINESS ('di-nes), *n.* verbosity.

WORDY ('di), *adj.* verbose.

WORK (werk), *n.* physical or intellectual effort directed to some end.

WORLD (werld), *n.* the earth and its inhabitants; universe.

WORLDLY ('li), *adj.* pertaining to this life and its enjoyments.

WORMWOOD (werm'wood), *n.* bitter plant, Absinthium.

WORRIED (wur'id), *adj.* harassed; tired.

WORRIMENT ('i-ment), *n.* anxiety.

WORRY ('i), *v.t.* to tear or mangle with the teeth; harass with anxiety or care.

WORSE (wers), *adj.* [*comp.* of bad] : *n.* loss; defeat.

WORSHIP (wer'ship), *n.* act of paying divine honour to God.

WORST (werst), *adj.* bad or evil in the highest degree.

WORSTED (woos'ted), *n.* twisted thread spun out of woollen yarn; (wurst'ed), defeated in a contest.

WORTH (werth), *n.* value; price; moral excellence.

WORTHILY (wer'thi-li), *adv.* in a worthy manner; justly.

WORTHLESS (werth'les), *adj.* having no value, virtue, or excellence.

WORTHY (wer'thi); *adj.* having worth or excellence; estimable.

WOUND (woond, wound), *n.* a hurt; injury.

WRACK (rak), *n.* seaweed; ruin; destruction.

WRAITH (rath), *n.* [Scotch], the supposed ghost of a person seen immediately before, or at the time of his death.

WRANGLE (rang'g'l), *v.i.* to dispute angrily or noisily.

WRANGLER ('gler), *n.* an angry or noisy disputant.

WRAP (rap), *v.t.* to roll or wind together; cover with something rolled around; involve : *n.* a wrapper, shawl, or rug.

WRAPPER ('er), *n.* one who, or that which, wraps; that in which anything is inclosed or wrapped; loose garment.

WRATH (rath), *n.* violent anger; indignation.

WRATHFUL ('fool), *adj.* violently angry.

WREAK (rek), *v.t.* to execute in vengeance or passion.

WREATH (reth), *n.* anything curled or twisted; garland.

WREATHE (reth), *v.t.* to twist into a wreath; intertwine.

WRECK (rek), *n.* the destruction of a ship; remains of anything ruined; destruction.

WRECKAGE ('aj), *n.* remains of anything resulting from violent destruction.

WRECKER ('er), *n.* one who plunders, or causes, wrecks.

WREN (ren), *n.* a small insessoid bird.

WRENCH (rench), *v.t.* to wring or pull with a twist; strain: *n.* instrument for turning or unloosening nuts, bolts, etc.

WREST (rest), *v.t.* to twist, wrench, or force from by violence; distort.

WRESTLE (res'l), *v.i.* to contend by grappling with another.

WRESTLER ('ler), *n.* one who wrestles.

WRETCH (rech), *n.* a despicable or worthless person.

WRIGGLE (rig'l), *v.i.* to twist to and fro.

WRIGHT (rit), *n.* one occupied in some mechanical operation; artificer.

WRING (ring), *v.t.* to twist; force or compress; extort.

WRINKLE ('kl), *n.* a small ridge or furrow on a smooth surface; crease; useful hint or idea.

WRITE (rit), *v.i.* to form letters with the pen; send letters; compose books.

WRITER ('er), *n.* clerk or amanuensis; author; journalist.

WRITHE (rith), *v.i.* to twist with violence; pervert.

WRITING (rit'ing), *n.* process of forming characters or letters on paper, etc., in such arrangement as to convey a determinate meaning; any literary production.

WRONG (rong), *adj.* not morally right; false; unjust; mistaken; not fit or suitable; incorrect.

WRONGDOER (-doo-er), *n.* one who does wrong.

WROTH (rawth), *adj.* much exasperated; angry; incensed.

WROUGHT-IRON (rawt'i-ern), *n.* iron made malleable and capable of being welded.

WRY (ri), *adj.* distorted; twisted.

WRYLY ('li), *adv.* in a wry manner.

WRYNESS ('nes), *n.* the state or quality of being wry or distorted.

X

X, x (eks), the twenty-fourth letter in the English alphabet.

X, x, an abbreviation.

X, a numeral in the Roman notation denoting 10; with a bar ($\bar{X}$), 10,000; horizontally placed (×), 1,000.

XANTHIC (zan'thik), *adj.* tending to a yellow colour.

XANTHO-, a combining form from the Greek *xanthos*, yellow.

XANTHOCHROOUS (zan-thok'ro-us), *adj.* yellow-skinned.

XANTHOS ('thus), *adj.* yellow; designating peoples of yellow complexion, as the Mongolians.

XENIA (ze'ni-a), *adj.* the direct influence of pollen on the seed.

XENI-, a combining form from the Greek *xenos*, strange, foreign.

XENOPARASITE (zen-o-par'a-sit), *n.* parasitic fungus that can grow on its host plant only when the latter is injured or diseased.

XERASIA (ze-ra'si-a), *n.* a disease of the scalp, characterized by dryness.

XERO-, a combining form from the Greek *xeros*, dry.

XERODERMA (ze-ro-der'ma), *n.* a disease of the skin characterized by dryness.

XEROFORM (ze'ro-form), *n.* a yellowish-green powder, used as an antiseptic in treating wounds.

XEROPHIL (-fil), *n.* a plant adapted to drought.

XEROPHILUS (-rof'i-lus), *adj.* able to withstand the absence of moisture; drought-loving.

XEROPHYTE ('ro-fit), *n.* xerophilous plant.

XEROSTATIC (-ro-stat'ik), *adj.* growing under practically uniform conditions of dryness of soil and climate.

XEROTIC (-rot'ik), *adj.* dry.

XEROTRIPSIS (-ro-trip'sis), *n.* dry friction.

XEROTROPISM (-trop'izm), *n.* the tendency of plants to change their position so as to escape drought and keep from withering.

XIPHOID (zi'foid), *adj.* sword-shaped.

X-RAYS (raz), *n.pl.* the Roentgen rays, a form of radiant energy.

XYLAN (zi'lan), *n.* a gummy substance in wood tissue; tree gum.

XYLENE ('len), *n.* a colourless oily liquid found in coal and wood tar.

XYLENOL ('le-nol), *n.* a phenol derivative of xylene.

XYLIC ('lik), *adj.* pertaining to, or derived from, xylene.

XYLITE ('lit), *n.* a syrupy liquid obtained through the reduction of xylose ; a kind of asbestos.

XYLO-, a combining form from the Greek *xylon*, wood.

XYLOCARP (zi'lo-karp), *n.* a hard fruit.

XYLOGEN ('lo-jen), *n.* woody tissue.

XYLOGLYPHY (-log'li-fi), *n.* fancy wood carving.

XYLOGRAPH ('lo-graf), *n.* an engraving on wood ; an impression from such an engraving.

XYLOGRAPHY (-log'ra-fi), *n.* art or process of engraving on wood and taking impressions from the engravings thus made.

XYLOID ('loid), *adj.* like wood.

XYLOIDIN (-loid'in), *n.* an explosive compound produced by the action of nitric acid on starch.

XYLOL, same as xylene.

XYLOLOGY (zi-loi'o-ji), *n.* a study of the structure of wood.

XYLOMETER (-lom'e-ter), *n.* an instrument for determining the specific gravity of wood.

XYLONITE (-lon'it), *n.* a kind of compressed gun-cotton, resembling ivory, used for making various articles, as combs, ornaments, etc. ; celluloid.

XYLOPHAGIDÆ (-lo-faj'i-de), *n.pl.* a family of dipterous insects the larvæ of which live in old or decayed wood.

XYLOPHAGOUS (-lof'a-gus), *adj.* denoting the boring, destroying, or eating of wood ; applied to certain crustaceans, mollusks and larvæ.

XYLOPHONE ('lo-fon), *n.* a musical instrument consisting of a graduated series of wooden bars, and sounded by means of small wooden hammers ; also, an instrument for determining the vibratory properties of different woods.

XYLOPLASTIC (-plas'tik), *adj.* relating to casts made from wood pulp.

XYLOPYROGRAPHY (-pi-rog'ra-fi), *n.* pyrography upon wood.

XYLOSE ('los), *n.* wood sugar.

XYLOSTEIN (-los'te-in), *n.* a bitter crystalline glucoside found in the poisonous berries of the honeysuckle.

XYLOTILE ('lo-til), *n.* a hydrous silicate of magnesium and iron from altered asbestos.

XYLOTOMY (-lot'o-mi), *n.* the preparation of minute pieces of wood for microscopic purposes.

XYRIS ('ris), *n.* a genus of tropical sedge-like plants with yellow flowers.

XYST (zist), *n.* in ancient Greece and Rome, a long portico built for athletic games and exercises in stormy weather.

XYSTER (zis'ter), *n.* a surgical instrument for scraping bones.

XYSTUS ('tus), *n.* same as xyst.

Y

Y, y (wi), *n.* the twenty-fifth letter of the English alphabet.

Y, y, *n.* an abbreviation.

Y, *n.* a numeral in the Roman notation denoting 150 ; with a bar (Ȳ), 150,000.

YACHT (yot), *n.* a quick-sailing or power vessel used for pleasure or racing.

YACHTING ('ing), *adj.* pertaining to a yacht.

YACHTSMAN (yots'man), *n.* the owner or sailer of a yacht.

YAK (yak), *n.* large wild ox of Tibet and Central Asia.

YAK-LACE ('las), *n.* pillow lace made from the long, silky hair of the yak.

YAKUI (ya'ke), one of a tribe of belligerent Indians along the Yakui River in Mexico.

YAM (yam), *n.* a large edible tuber of various climbing plants : it much resembles the sweet potato.

YANK (yangk), *v.t.* to jerk or twist.

YANKEE (yang'ke), *n.* a popular

name of a New England American : used generally for a citizen of the U.S.

YANKEE-DOODLE (-doo'dl), *n.* a popular melody of the U.S.

YANKING (yangk'ing), *adj.* active ; pushing.

YANOLITE (yan'o-lit), *n.* a kind of garnet.

YAP (yap), *v.i.* to yelp or bark, as a dog ; [Slang], to jabber ; talk nonsensically : *n.* a yelp or bark ; [Slang], a silly person ; a worthless fellow.

YARD (yard), *n.* a standard measure of length = 3 ft. ; a long piece of timber on a mast for spreading square sails ; an enclosure adjoining a house.

YARDARM (yard'arm), *n.* one of the two ends of a ship's yard.

YARDSTICK ('stik), *n.* a measuring stick of three feet in length.

YARN (yarn), *n.* spun wool ; one of the threads of a rope ; a sailor's story.

YAWN (yawn), *n.* an involuntary opening of the jaws through drowsiness.

YAWNING ('ing), *adj.* gaping ; drowsy.

YAWP (yawp), same as yelp.

YEA (ya), *adv.* yes ; truly.

YEAR (yer), *n.* period during which the earth makes one complete revolution round the sun (365¼ days) : *pl.* age ; old age.

YEARBOOK ('book), *n.* a book published at the end of the year, with statistics and information regarding various interests.

YEARLING (-ling), *n.* an animal one year old, or in its second year.

YEARLY (li), *adj.* occurring once a year ; annual.

YEARN (yern), *v.i.* to feel an earnest desire.

YEARNING ('ing), *n.* strong desire.

YEAST (yest), *n.* an aggregation of minute cells of fungi that form a yellowish froth which when brought in contact with saccharine matter develops alcoholic fermentation ; any substance for raising dough.

YEASTINESS (yes'ti-nes), *n.* the state or quality of being yeasty.

YEASTY ('ti), *adj.* pertaining to, like or containing, yeast ; frothy.

YEGGMAN (yeg'man), *n.* [Slang], a burglar ; a safe-blower.

YELK, same as yolk.

YELL (yel), *n.* a sharp, discordant cry, as of agony : *v.t.* to scream.

YELLOW ('o), *adj.* of a bright, pure colour resembling gold.

YELLOW FEVER (fe'ver), *n.* an acute infectious fever.

YELLOW-HAMMER (-ham-er), *n.* a woodpecker commonly called the *flicker.*

YELLOW-LEGS (legz), *n.* a shorebird with long, yellow legs.

YELP (yelp), *n.* a sharp bark.

YEN (yen), *n.* the monetary unit of Japan, equal to 100 sen and worth about half-a-dollar in U.S. currency.

YEOMAN (yo'man), *n.* a farmer ; in the U.S. navy, a petty officer in charge of stores.

YEOMANRY (-ri), *n.* yeomen collectively ; volunteer cavalry.

YES (yes), *adv.* yea ; opposed to *no* : *n.* an affirmative reply.

YESTERDAY ('ter-da), *n.* the day last past ; recent time.

YET (yet), *adv.* in addition ; still ; moreover : *conj.* nevertheless ; however.

YEW (yoo), *n.* a large evergreen coniferous tree.

YIELD (yeld), *v.t.* to submit ; produce ; concede.

YIELDING ('ing), *adj.* inclined to give way or comply ; accommodating.

YOGA (yo'ga), *n.* a form of Hindu ascetic philosophy which inculcates abandonment of all worldly interests and objects.

YOGI (yo'ge), *n.* one of a religious order in India.

YOKE (yok), *n.* bond, tie, or link ; pair or couple ; service ; mark of slavery : *v.t.* couple ; enslave ; confine.

YOLK (yok), *n.* yellow part of an egg.

YOM KIPPUR (kip'er), *n.* the Jewish Day of Atonement.

YONDER (yon'der), *adj.* at a distance, but in view.

YORE (yor), *adv.* in old time ; long ago (poetical).

YOU (u, yoo), *pron.* the personal pronoun of the 2nd person, plural; the person, place, or thing addressed; used in the singular for *thou* and *thee*.

YOUNG (yung), *adj.* inexperienced; not matured; raw; vigorous; fresh; pertaining to youth; of youthful appearance : *n.* offspring collectively.

YOUNGSTER ('ster), *n.* a young person; lad.

YOUNKER (yun'ker), *n.* a young fellow; stripling.

YOUR (yoor), *adj.* belonging to you : used in *sing.* and *pl.*

YOURS (yoorz), *pron.* the possessive case of *you* : used in *sing.* and *pl.*

YOURSELF (-self'), *pron.* emphatic form of you; you in your own person.

YOUTH (yooth), *n.* early life; a young person; young persons collectively; condition of being young.

YOUTHFUL ('fool), *adj.* pertaining to youth; fresh; vigorous.

YOWL (youl), *n.* a howl.

YUCCA (yuk'a), *n.* a sub-tropical American plant.

YULE (yool), *n.* Christmas.

YULETIDE ('tid), *n.* Christmastide.

Z

Z, z (ze), the twenty-sixth and last letter in the English alphabet.

Z, z, an abbreviation.

Z, a numeral in the Roman notation denoting 2,000; with a bar ($\bar{z}$), 2,000,000.

ZANY (za'ni), *n.* a buffoon.

ZEAL (zel), *n.* eager attention; active interest.

ZEALOT (zel'ut), *n.* an enthusiast; one fanatically devoted to a cause.

ZEALOUS ('us), *adj.* enthusiastic.

ZEBRA (ze'bra), *n.* a wild equine animal of Africa, with black and white stripes.

ZEBU ('bu), *n.* the Indian ox or cow.

ZENANA (-na'na), *n.* in India, that part of a house reserved exclusively for women.

ZENITH (nith), *n.* the point in the heavens directly over the head of the spectator; greatest height.

ZEOLITE ('o-lit), *n.* any of an extensive group of minerals, consisting of hydrated silicates.

ZEPHYR (zef'er), *n.* soft, gentle breeze.

ZEPPELIN (zep'e-lin), *n.* one of several types of rigid dirigible airships.

ZERO (ze'ro), *n.* nothing; a cipher; the numeral 0; point on a scale from which measures or degrees are counted; lowest point in a standard of comparison.

ZERO HOUR (our), *colloq.* in military tactics, the hour in which an attack, which has been previously planned, is begun.

ZEST (zest), *n.* relish; keen enjoyment : *v.t.* to give relish to; cut into slips; peel.

ZEUS (zus), *n.* father of the gods, in Greek mythology.

ZIGZAG (zig'zag), *adj.* having short, sharp turns.

ZINC (zingk), *n.* a bluish-white metal

ZION (zi'un), *n.* a hill in Jerusalem the royal residence of King David and his successors, seat of the temple, and place of Hebrew worship.

ZIONISM (-izm), *n.* a project for the reëstablishment of the Jews as a nation in Palestine.

ZIP (zip), *n.* a hissing or sibilant sound.

ZITHER (zith'er), *n.* a stringed musical instrument consisting of a sounding board over which are stretched from 30 to 40 strings.

ZODIAC (zo'di-ak), *n.* an imaginary broad belt in the heavens, containing twelve constellations or signs which the sun traverses annually.

ZODIACAL LIGHT ('a-kal lit), a luminous tract of the sky of triangular shape, its base being on the horizon; seen in the evening at twilight, and before dawn.

ZONE (zon), *n.* one of the 5 great belts into which the surface of the earth is divided with respect to latitude and temperature ; that belt or district within which certain animal or plant forms of life are confined ; a girdle or belt ; one of the areas covered by the U.S. parcel-post system.

ZOO (zoo), *n.* a park or other large inclosure in which live animals are kept for public exhibition ; zoölogical garden.

ZOÖ (zo'o), a combining form from the Greek *zoon,* an animal.

ZOOGENE ('o-jen), *adj.* of animal origin, as coral islands, or beds of limestone.

ZOOGENIC ('ik), *adj.* of animal, as distinguished from vegetable, origin.

ZOOGENOUS (-oj'e-nus), *adj.* of animal origin ; acquired by man from the lower animals, as in case of certain diseases.

ZOOGEOGRAPHY (-o-je-og'ra-fi), *n.* faunal geography ; a description of the distribution of animals throughout the world.

ZOOGLŒA (-gle'a), *n.* a mass of bacteria inclosed in a viscous or gelatinous substance.

ZOOGRAPHY (-og'ra-fi), *n.* the description of animals, their forms and habits.

ZOOID ('oid), *adj.* having the nature of an animal.

ZOOLATRY (-ol'a-tri), *n.* animal worship.

ZOOLITE ('o-lit), *n.* a fossil animal.

ZOOLOGICAL (-o-loj'i-kal), *adj.* pertaining to zoölogy.

ZOOLOGIST (-ol'o-jist), *n.* one skilled in zoölogy.

ZOOLOGY ('i-ji), *n.* that part of biology that treats of animals, their structure, classification, habits, and distribution.

ZOOMELANIN (-o-mel'a-nin), *n.* a black pigment found in the feathers of many kinds of birds.

ZOOMETRY (-om'e-tri), *n.* the scientific measurement of animals.

ZOOMORPHISM ('o-mor'fizm), *n.* the representation of a deity in the form, or with the attributes, of an animal ; use of animal forms for ornamentation.

ZOOPHILIST (-of'i-list), *n.* a lover of animals.

ZOOPHOBIA (-o-fo'bi-a), *n.* a morbid fear or dread of animals.

ZOOPHYSICS (-fiz'iks), *n.* branch of zoology which treats of the physical structure and functions of the organs of animals.

ZOOPHYTE (-fit), *n.* an animal of low organization bearing some external resemblance to a plant.

ZOOSPERM ('o-sperm), *n.* a spermatozoon ; a spermatic particle.

ZOUAVE (zoo-av'), *n.* a soldier of a light infantry corps of the French army, wearing an Arab dress.

ZOUNDS (zounde), *interj.* expression of anger.

ZWIEBACK (tsve'bak), *n.* [German], bread toasted in crisp slices.

ZYGO- (zig'o), a combining form from the Greek *zygon,* a yoke.

ZYMASE (zimas), *n.* the transforming substance in yeast cells which effects alcoholic fermentation.

ZYMIC (zim'ik), *adj.* produced by fermentation.

ZYMO- (zi'mo), a combining form from the Greek *zyme,* leaven, denoting *fermentation.*

ZYMOCYTE (-sit), *n.* a microorganism that produces fermentation.

ZYMOGEN (-jen), *n.* any substance that by internal changes gives rise to a ferment.

ZYMOLOGY (-mol'o-ji), *n.* the doctrine of fermentation ; a treatise on fermentation of liquids.

ZYMOMETER (-mom'e-ter), *n.* an instrument for ascertaining the degree of fermentation in different liquids.

ZYMOPHORE ('mo-for), *adj.* poisonous.

ZYMOPHYTE (-fit), *n.* a bacterial ferment that frees fatty acids from neutral fats.

ZYMOSCOPE (-skop), *n.* an instrument for determining the amount of carbonic acid developed by sugar in fermentation.

ZYMOSIS ('sis), *n.* a fermentation ; the process by which an infectious disease is believed to be developed.

ZYMOTIC (-mot'ik), *adj.* relating to, or produced by, fermentation; pertaining to contagious diseases.

ZYMOTIC DISEASE (di-zez'), a contagious or epidemic disease, supposed to be produced by a virus or organism which acts like a ferment.

ZYMURGY (zi'mer-ji), *n.* that branch of industrial chemistry which deals with the processes of fermentation in brewing, wine-making, etc.

ZYRIAN (zir'i-an), *n.* member of a tribe of people living in north-eastern Russia.

ZYTHEM (zi'them), **ZYTHUM** (zi'thum), *n.* an ancient beverage made from malted wheat.

ZYZZLE (ziz'l), *v.i.* to make a spluttering or hissing sound; sizzle.

COMMERCIAL TERMS

A1. Of first quality. Used technically in shipping, but applied to other matters. The mark originated with the English Lloyds, who rate vessels A1, A2, and so down. In the American system the registry descends from A by fractions, A1, A1¼, A1½, A1¾, A2.

ACCEPTANCE. Agreement by the *drawee* of negotiable paper to pay the same. Agreement to terms offered.

ACCEPTOR. He who by his signature makes acceptance.

ACCOMMODATION PAPER. Notes or bills not representing an actual sale or trade transaction, but merely drawn to be discounted for the benefit of drawer, acceptor or indorsers, or all combined.

ACCOUNT. A statement of sums and amounts due from one person to another.

ACCOUNT CURRENT. A running account for a certain period, showing what is due at the present time.

ACCOUNT SALES. The account of a broker or commission agent, showing amount and rate of sales, expenses of freight, commission, etc., and *net* amount due the principal.

ACQUITTANCE. A written receipt in full, or discharge from all claims.

ADJUSTMENT. Settlement of claims in marine or fire insurance. Determining amount of loss and liability. In accounts, the settling of a disputed account.

AD VALOREM [Lat.]. According to the value.

AD VALOREM DUTIES. Duties levied on goods according to value; not by quantity, weight or measure. Opposed to *Specific Duties*.

AGENT. One who acts for another.

ALLOWANCE. Deduction from gross weight or amount. Sailor's rations.

AMOUNT GROSS. The total sum or aggregate.

AMOUNT NET. Total sum less proper deduction for expenses, discount, or charges.

ANTEDATE. To date beforehand.

APPRAISEMENT. Ascertaining the value of goods or property.

APPRAISER. He who appraises. In particular, an officer of government who ascertains the value of dutiable goods.

APPROPRIATION. Setting apart for a specific purpose. Government grant of money.

ARBITRATION OF EXCHANGES. Comparison of currency of intermediate places, to discover whether it is more profitable to forward money directly or indirectly.

ASSAY. To test the purity of precious metals.

ASSETS. Funds of an individual, firm, or corporation; resources; opposed to liabilities.

ASSIGNEE. A person to whom an assignment is made; trustee for the creditors of a bankrupt estate.

ASSIGNMENT. Transfer of property for safe keeping, adjustment, or benefit of creditors.

ASSIGNOR. One who transfers his property to assignees for the benefit of creditors or for other reasons.

ATTORNEY, POWER OF. Written authority for one person to act for another.

AUDIT. To scrutinize accounts and vouchers.

AUDITOR. One authorized to examine accounts; an officer of the United States Treasury.

AVERAGE. The mean value; medium quality; a fair sample.

BALANCE SHEET. A paper giving a summary and state of a business as to assets, liabilities and to show surplus or loss.

BALANCE OF TRADE. Difference in value between total exports and imports of a country.

BANKRUPT. One unable to meet his liabilities; the word literally means *broken up.*

BARREL BULK. In freight measurement, 5 cubic feet.

BEAR. A Stock Exchange term for one who strives to depress the price of stocks.

BILL, FOREIGN. A bill of exchange payable in a foreign country; usually drawn in duplicate or triplicate.

BILL OF ENTRY. A bill of goods entered at the custom-house.

BILL OF EXCHANGE. A written order from one person to another, ordering or requesting him to pay a certain sum of money to a third person on a given date.

BILL OF LADING. A receipt given for goods shipped.

BILL OF SALE. A contract under seal for the sale of goods.

BILL OF SIGHT. A form of Custom House entry, allowing consignee to see goods before paying duty.

BONA FIDE [Lat.] in good faith.

BOND. A legal document by which a person binds himself to pay money or do something under penalty of paying a sum fixed.

BOND CREDITOR. A creditor whose debt is secured by a bond.

BOND DEBT. A debt contracted under obligation of a bond.

BONDED GOODS. Goods on which bonds instead of cash have been given for import duties.

BONDED WAREHOUSE. Buildings owned by persons approved of by the Secretary of the Treasury, and who have given bonds for the strict observance of the revenue laws; used for storing imported merchandise until the duties are paid or the goods reshipped without entry.

BONDSMAN. One who gives security for the payment of money, performance of an act, or integrity of another.

BONUS. Additional money paid beyond interest; extra profits.

BREAKAGE. Allowance made by a shipper for loss by the destruction of fragile wares.

BREAKING BULK. Opening packages of goods in transit.

BROKER. An agent or factor; a middleman paid by commission; the most common are *Bill, Exchange, Insurance, Produce, Ship,* and *Stock Brokers.*

BULL. A Stock Exchange term for one who believes that the value of stocks will rise and speculates for a rise, "goes long" on a stock.

BULLION. Uncoined gold or silver.

CALL. Demand for payment of instalments due on stock.

CALL. A Stock Exchange term for a privilege given to another to "call" for delivery of stock at a time and price fixed.

CAPITAL. Money invested in business; amount of assets.

CAPITAL STOCK. The aggregate amount invested in a stock company; total value of stock at par.

CARRIER. One who carries goods for another.

CARTE BLANCHE. [Fr.] Literally white paper; full power to decide.

CERTIFICATE. A written voucher, as, a certificate of deposit, a stock-certificate.

CERTIFIED CHEQUE. One accepted by the bank on which it is drawn and certified as good.

CHARTER. A grant by a State empowering a corporated association to do business.

CHEQUE. An order on a bank for payment of money to bearer or the order of some person.

C.I.F. Cost of insurance and freight, used of importers and exporters.

CLEARANCE. A Custom House certificate that a ship is free to leave.

CLEARING. 1. Entering a ship at the Custom House and obtaining clearance. 2. In banking, exchange of cheques and settling balances at the Clearing House.

CLEARING HOUSE. A banking exchange for daily settlements of balances.

C.O.D. Collect on delivery.

COLLATERAL SECURITY. A secondary security to be available if the chief security is not sufficient.

COMMISSION. An agent's percentage for transacting business.

COMMISSION BROKER. One who buys or sells on commission.

COMPOSITION. A payment by a debtor of a percentage of his debts as settlement in full.

COMPOUND INTEREST. Interest on both principal and interest.

CONSIGNEE. One to whom goods are sent.

CONSIGNMENT. Goods sent to an agent to be sold.

CONVEYANCE. A written instrument by which property is transferred; a deed.

CORNER. In stock and grain broker's slang, the buying up of a large quantity of stock or grain to raise the price.

COUPON. [Fr.] A certificate of interest attached to bonds or stock, to be cut off when due.

CREDIT. In bookkeeping, value received or transferred from the party; opposite of *debit;* financial standing; power to obtain loans.

CREDITOR. One to whom money or value is due.

CURRENCY. The circulating medium of a country.

CURRENT. Passing freely; now running, as, *current accounts.*

CUSTOMS. Taxes on goods exported or imported.

DEBIT. To make debtor; opposite of credit; a charge entered.

DEBTOR. One who owes; opposite of creditor.

DEFICIT. A lack of funds to balance accounts.

DEMURRAGE. Forfeit money for detention of vessels beyond the time allowed by a charter-party.

DERELICT. Ship abandoned at sea.

DISCHARGE. To pay a debt; to unload a ship.

DISCOUNT. A sum thrown off the amount of a note or bill; a deduction;

to discount is to lend money on bills after deducting the interest.

DISSOLUTION. Breaking up of a partnership.

DIVIDEND. Payment of the profits of a stock concern, *pro rata,* proportional payment to creditors out of a bankrupt estate.

DOCKAGE OR DOCK DUES. Charges for the use of a dock.

DRAFT. An order to pay money; a rough copy of a writing; a deduction from gross weight of goods; number of feet which a ship sinks in the water.

DRAW. To make a draft; to call for funds.

DRAWEE. The one on whom a draft or bill is drawn.

DRAWER. The maker of a draft or bill of exchange.

DUE BILL. A written acknowledgment of debt.

DUN. To demand payment repeatedly.

DUTIES. Taxes levied by a government on exports or imports.

EAGLE. A gold coin of the United States, value ten dollars.

E. E. Abbreviation for *errors excepted.*

EMBARGO. Order of a government forbidding ships to leave its ports.

ENDORSE. To transfer notes, bills, or cheques by writing one's name on the back; to guarantee payment.

ENDORSEE. He in whose favour endorsement is made.

ENDORSER. One who endorses.

ENTRY. In bookkeeping, any record made; depositing a ship's papers with the Custom House.

E. O. M. End of the month.

EXAMINER. A Custom House officer who compares goods with invoices.

EXCHANGE. Place where merchants meet to transact business; percentage on sale of bills; difference of value between different currencies.

EXPORT. To send goods to a foreign country.

EXPORTER. One who exports.

EXPORTS. The goods of merchandise exported.

EXTENSION. Allowance of time for payment to a debtor; carrying out items of a bill or account.

E. & O. E. "Errors and Omissions Excepted."

FACTOR. An agent appointed to sell goods on commission; a consignee.

FAIR. Of average quality; above middling.

FINANCE. Funds; public money; revenue.

FINANCIER. One skilled in money matters.

FIRM. Name, style or title of a business concern; the partners taken collectively.

FLAT. Inactive; depressed; dull; *flat value* of stock and bonds is the value without interest.

FLOTSAM. Goods thrown into the sea which float.

F. O. B. "Free on board"; cartage and shipping expenses included to point of departure of railroad or ship.

FOREIGN BILL. A bill of exchange drawn in one country upon a citizen of another.

FREIGHT. Sums paid for transportation of merchandise or hire of a ship.

FUNDED. Made into a long time loan on which interest is paid.

GAUGE. To measure the contents of a cask; measure or standard.

GOODWILL. The value of an established business in the way of trade and custom.

GROSS. Twelve dozen; total amount; opposed to *net.*

GROSS TON. Twenty-two hundred and forty pounds.

GUARANTEE. The one to whom security is given or guaranty made.

GUARANTOR. One making a guaranty.

GUARANTY. Security; an undertaking that one person will pay money to another or fulfill a contract.

HOGSHEAD. A measure of capacity; 2 barrels, or 63 gallons; a large cask.

HONOUR. To accept and pay a note, draft or bill.

HYPOTHECATE. To pledge as security; to mortgage chattels.

IMPORTER. A merchant who imports goods.

IMPORTS. Goods brought from a foreign country.

IMPOST. Government tax on imported goods.

INDEMNIFICATION. Making good a loss; securing one against damages.

INDEMNITY. Guarantee against loss; freedom; compensation for damages suffered.

INDULGENCE. Extension of time for payment.

INSOLVENT. Unable to pay outstanding liabilities; bankrupt.

INSTALMENT. A part payment or part delivery of goods.

INSURANCE. A contract in which one party, the *insurer,* agrees in consideration of the *premium,* to pay a certain sum on the death of the *insured* or to indemnify him for loss to property by fire or marine risks.

INSURANCE BROKER. One who negotiates insurance contracts.

INTEREST. Money paid for use of money; share in a business or venture.

INVENTORY. A list of goods and merchandise on hand; any enumeration of articles; a schedule.

INVESTMENT. Placing of money in business or securities.

INVOICE. Account of merchandise shipped, with prices and charges annexed.

JETSAM. Goods thrown into the sea which sink.

JETTISON. Throwing goods overboard or cutting away masts and sails to save a vessel.

JOBBER. One who buys from importers or manufacturers and sells to retailers; a middleman.

JOB LOT. Goods left over; an odd assortment.

LAME DUCK. Stock-brokers' term for one unable to meet his liabilities.

LAY DOWN. Cost of merchandise

including charges and freight to destination.

LEAKAGE. An allowance made for waste by leaking of casks.

LETTER OF CREDIT. One authorizing credit to a certain amount to be given to the bearer.

LICENSE. Permission to trade or act.

LIEN. A hold or claim on property to secure a debt.

LIGHTERAGE. Payment for unloading ships by lighters or boats.

LIQUIDATION. Settlement or adjustment of liabilities.

LLOYD'S An association of English marine underwriters (insurers). The company possesses complete records of everything pertaining to marine matters and has a vast correspondence. To rate on Lloyd's books as A1 is accepted as conclusive evidence of excellence.

LLOYD'S REGISTER. A yearly register of tonnage, age, character, and condition of ships, issued by Lloyd's.

MANIFEST. A list or invoice of a ship's cargo and passengers to be exhibited at Custom Houses.

MARKET. A public place of sale for provisions or other wares. Stocks and bonds collectively.

MATURITY. Time fixed for payment ; becoming due.

MERCANTILE PAPER. Notes or bills issued by merchants for goods bought or consigned.

MERCHANTABLE. Fit for market ; in sound condition.

MINIMUM. Lowest price ; least quantity possible.

MINT. A place for coining money.

NEGOTIABLE PAPER. Notes, bills, and drafts which may be transferred with all their rights by indorsement or assignment.

NET. The clear amount ; what remains after deducting charges and expenses.

NET WEIGHT. Weight of merchandise without bag, box, or covering.

NOTE OF HAND. A written undertaking to pay money at a certain time.

ON SALE. Goods left with another to be accounted for as sold.

OPEN ACCOUNT. A running or unsettled account.

OPTION. Permission to choose ; in stock-broking, privilege of taking or delivering stock at a given day and price.

OVERDUE. Applied to a note or draft, the specified time for payment of which has passed.

PAR VALUE. The face or nominal value.

PAYABLE. Justly due ; capable of payment.

PAYEE. The person to whose order a note, bill, or draft is to be paid.

PER CENT. [Lat.] By the hundred ; rates of interest, discount, etc.

PER CENTAGE. [Lat.] An allowance reckoned by hundredth parts ; commission.

PER CONTRA. [Lat.] To the opposite side of an account.

PORT. A harbour for vessels ; a commercial city.

PORT OF ENTRY. A port where a Custom House is established for the entry of imports.

POST-DATE. To date after the real time.

PREMIUM. A sum beyond par value ; the amount paid annually in insurance contracts.

PRIME. Of first quality ; superior.

PRINCIPAL. The sum on which interest is paid.

PRO RATA. [Lat.] A proportional distribution.

PROTEST. Notice to the sureties of a note that it was not paid at maturity or to the drawer of a draft that acceptance was refused.

REBATE. Deduction ; abatement ; discount ; giving back part of sum already paid.

REINSURANCE. Transfer of part of the contract of insurance from one insurer to another.

RESPONDENTIA BOND. A bond

for a loan secured by the cargo of a ship.

SALVAGE. Compensation given those who rescue ship or cargo from loss.

SET-OFF. A counterclaim or cross debt arising from a different matter from the one in question.

SHORT. To " sell short " is to sell for future delivery what one has not got, in hopes that prices will fall.

SIGHT. The time when a bill is presented to the drawee.

SIGHT DRAFT. One payable at *sight*, i.e., when presented.

SPECIE. Any kind of coined money.

STAPLE. Principal commodity of a country or district.

STERLING. Lawful or standard money of Great Britain.

STOCK. Shares in the capital of corporations ; goods on hand.

STOCK BROKER. One who buys and sells stock on commission.

STOCK EXCHANGE. Place where shares of stock are bought and sold.

STOCK JOBBER. One who speculates in stocks.

SUPERCARGO. An agent who accompanies cargo to care for and sell it.

SURETY. One who binds himself to pay money in case another person fails to pay, to fill a contract, or to serve with integrity.

SURVEYOR. Agent of an insurance company to examine and report on applications for marine or fire insurance.

SUSPEND. To fail ; to stop payment.

SUSPENSE ACCOUNT. An account made of doubtful balances to ascertain probable profit or loss.

TARE. Allowance in weight or quantity on account of cask, bag, or covering.

TRADE DISCOUNT. An allowance made to dealers from the list price.

TRADE PRICE. That allowed by wholesalers to retailers.

ULLAGE. What a cask lacks of being full.

VENDEE. One to whom something is sold.

VENDOR. A seller.

VOUCHER. A book, receipt, entry, or other document which establishes the truth of accounts.

WAY BILL. List of goods given to a carrier.

WHARFAGE. Fees paid for use of a wharf.

ABBREVIATIONS

abbr.	.	.	.	.	abbreviation
adj.	.	.	.	.	adjective
adv.	.	.	.	.	adverb
colloq.	.	.	.	.	colloquial
conj.	.	.	.	.	conjunction
fem.	.	.	.	.	feminine
Fr.	.	.	.	.	French
interj.	.	.	.	.	interjection
n.	.	.	.	.	noun
N.A.	.	.	.	.	North American
pl.	.	.	.	.	plural
p.p.	.	.	.	.	past participle
prep.	.	.	.	.	preposition
p.t. & pret.	.	.	.	.	preterite
pres.	.	.	.	.	present
pron.	.	.	.	.	pronoun
R.C.	.	.	.	.	Roman Catholic
sing.	.	.	.	.	singular
S.A.	.	.	.	.	South American
U.S.	.	.	.	.	United States of America
v.	.	.	.	.	verb
v.i.	.	.	.	.	verb intransitive
v.t.	.	.	.	.	verb transitive